Library of
Davidson College

DE-COL-ONIZ-ATION

THE ADMINISTRATION AND FUTURE OF THE COLONIES, 1919-1960

RUDOLF VON ALBERTINI
WITH A NEW PREFACE TO THIS EDITION

DECOLONIZATION

DECOLONIZATION

The Administration
and Future of the Colonies,
1919–1960

WITH A NEW PREFACE TO THIS EDITION

Rudolf von Albertini

Translated from the German by Francisca Garvie

AFRICANA PUBLISHING COMPANY

A division of Holmes & Meier Publishers, Inc.
New York   London

Reprinted in 1982 by
Africana Publishing Company, a division of
Holmes & Meier Publishers, Inc.
30 Irving Place
New York, N. Y. 10003

Great Britain
Holmes & Meier Publishers, Ltd.
131 Trafalgar Road
Greenwich, London SE10 9TX

Published in Germany under the title
*Dekolonisation: Die Diskussion über
Verwaltung und Zukunft der Kolonien*
1919–1960, Copyright © 1966 by Westdeutscher
Verlag, Köln und Opladen.

Original translation copyright © 1971 by
Doubleday & Company, Inc.

Preface to the 1982 edition copyright © 1982 by
Holmes & Meier Publishers, Inc.

Published by arrangement with
Doubleday & Company, Inc.

All rights reserved

Library of Congress Cataloging in Publication Data

Albertini, Rudolf von.
   Decolonization: the administration and future of
the colonies, 1919–1960.

   Translation of: Dekolonisation.
   Reprint. Originally published: Garden City, N.Y.:
Doubleday, 1971.
   Bibliography: p.
   Includes index.
   1. Decolonization—History. 2. Colonies—
Administration—History. I. Title.
JV308.A6513   1981   325′.31′09   81-13998
ISBN 0-8419-0603-3   AACR2
ISBN 0-8419-0654-8 (pbk.)

Manufactured in the United States of America

For Hajo Holborn

I believe that there is one subject of enquiry which is of fundamental interest. It is the study of the conceptions which have from time to time determined the outlook of a European Power in its relations with the indigenous peoples of Asia or Africa over whom it exercises political control.

Lord Hailey

CONTENTS

PREFACE TO THE 1982 EDITION	xi
PREFACE TO THE AMERICAN EDITION	xxvii
PREFACE TO THE FIRST EDITION	xxix
INTRODUCTION: International Aspects	1

I. Great Britain

The Third British Empire	33
The British Commonwealth of Nations	48
The Question of Dominion Status for India (1917–1939)	59
Trusteeship and Self-government in the Colonies	78
Colonial Development, 1929–1940	99
The Colonial Doctrine of the Labour Party	115
Indirect Rule in West Africa	124
East Africa: Kenya and Closer Union	142
The Discussion during the Second World War	158
The Labour Party during and after the Second World War	175
India on the Road to Independence, 1939–1947	184
Burma and Ceylon	196
From Legislative Council to Independence: The Gold Coast and Nigeria	212
Partnership in the Rhodesian Federation?	230
From the British Commonwealth of Nations to the Multi-racial Commonwealth	250

II. France

La plus grande France and Economic Development	265
Assimilation or Association?	278
The Socialist Party	309
Assimilation in Algeria (1919–1939)	319
Direct Administration in West Africa	336
Lyautey and the Protectorate in Morocco	347
Colonial Politics during the Second World War	358
The Union française	382
Indochina, Tunisia and Morocco	396
The Revision of the Union française and the Post-war Discussion, 1946–1955	406
Black Africa and the *Loi Cadre* (1946–1956)	425
The Communauté	443
From Algérie française to the République Algérienne	452

III. Towards a Comparison

The Decolonization of an Anti-colonial Power: The United States in the Philippines	473
The Unsuccessful Commonwealth: The Netherlands in Indonesia	487
Belgian Paternalism in the Congo	499
Doctrine vs. Reality of Assimilation: Portugal in Africa	514
CONCLUSION	523
NOTES	527
BIBLIOGRAPHY	643
INDEX	665

PREFACE
TO THE 1982 EDITION

This book, the German-language edition of which appeared in 1966, had not been originally envisioned as a history of decolonization. When I began my preliminary work on it around 1960, the Algerian War was having a great impact on me. As an historian focusing on the modern history of France, I was following that war with special interest. The bloody war in Indochina had already dealt a heavy blow to the Fourth Republic. The conflict in and over Algeria sounded its death knell and enabled General De Gaulle to seize power. He gradually came to accept an independent Algeria, while at the same time using the vague concept of a "Community" in an effort to reconcile the African colonies' demands for autonomy with France's claims to a leadership role. The year 1960 turned into "Africa Year" as numerous colonies became independent nations. A year later I came face-to-face with the problems of one of those new nations in the course of a rather lengthy trip through Nigeria.

The questions that interested me as an historian at that time were: Had the colonial powers faced up to the matter of the coming emancipation of the colonies? If so, when and to what extent? What plans for the future did they consider in the process? Did they gear their colonial administration to the impending break, and if so, how? What sort of target dates had they envisioned? What differences were there between Great Britain and France? As the two most important colonial powers, they would have to occupy center stage in all such inquiries. Great Britain liquidated her world empire without much bloodshed. By contrast, France had engaged in unremitting warfare since 1946 in an attempt to maintain her claims to overseas rule. Was there some difference in the imperial conception of those two powers that accounted for this fact?

The subtitle of the original German edition of my book was: *"Die Diskussion über Verwaltung und Zukunft der Kolonien 1919–1960"* [*The Discussion of the Administration and Future of the Colonies*]. But in the course of my work it became increasingly clear that the whole discussion in the press, the media, parties, and parliaments would have to be tied in with the international scene on the one hand and with the concrete situation in the individual spheres of jurisdiction on the other.

Now the situation in the colonies themselves bore the strong imprint of national movements. Usually this meant parties made up of indigenous elites. Their demands for codetermination, self-determination, and eventual independence brought pressure to bear on the colonial authorities—hence on the governments of the metropolises as well. There were demonstrations and riotous outbreaks. In some areas these turned into real revolts whose goal was national revolution. The colonial authorities had to react with repressive measures and/or reforms, adapt to the new circumstances, revise their timetables, and ultimately accept the independence of their colonies.

The result of this more or less lengthy process was the same everywhere: i.e., the independence of former colonies. However, there were differences in the reaction to the challenge of anticolonial nationalism, in the shifts in direction towards repression or reform. These differences were influenced by hitherto existing factors: the practices and conceptions of rulership, and the way in which the future of the colonial regime had been perceived. So it was that my book gradually broadened into a history of decolonization, even though my original plan had been simply to trace the thought processes at work—not on some lofty philosophical plane but on the "nitty-gritty" level of political debate—and thus make a contribution to the history of Europe's self-understanding.

There were reservations and limitations, of course. Some of them were brought up and briefly defended in my Preface to the German edition, but it was here that criticism was entitled to step into the picture. My book did not purport to offer textbook coverage of every region and territory. Nevertheless any discussion of decolonization in the British Empire should have brought in the naval bases (to cite one example): e.g., Gibraltar, Malta, Cyprus, Suez, Aden, and Singapore. In the nineteenth and early twentieth centuries they had been vital for the maintenance of the sea lanes to India, the Pacific dominions, and China. Even after World War II, they still seemed vital to England if she was to remain a Great Power and meet her "obligations" in Asiatic areas. Those obligations included such things as defending Australia and New Zealand, holding China in check, and stemming the inroads of communism. In the whole debate over the future of the colonies, the bases were seldom brought up. The reason was that the very idea of giving them up was unthinkable, and was categorically rejected right into the decade of the 1950s.

Take the case of Malta. For a brief period, some people toyed with the possibility of integration, of a deputy from Malta sitting in the British Parliament. Then Malta took the "normal" road to independence. To some extent NATO took England's place, meeting Mintoff's demands for payments that would cover the maintenance of the naval base.

British policy was less successful on Cyprus. Only after a protracted conflict did Cyprus achieve independence in the year 1960. The attempt to maintain a position of power on the Suez Canal ended in a debacle in 1956, and Great Britain was effectively eliminated from Near East politics. England withdrew from Aden in 1967 after bloody clashes in the city. Operating from Singapore, Britain intervened in the civil war in Malaya (the 1948–1957 "Emergency") and in the "Confrontation" with Indonesia. Then in 1967, as a result of domestic political pressure in England and dwindling monetary reserves, it abruptly announced that it was withdrawing the fleet and giving up the base. This led to an unprecedented situation: the native regime under Lee Kuan Yen condemned these moves; for mainly economic reasons it would have preferred to see the one-time colonial power stay on.

The loss of British positions of strength in its "Informal Empire" also should have been studied. That would include the withdrawal of British investments from Latin America and the growing influence of the United States there; the abolition of treaty ports and extraterritorial rights in China as early as the period between the wars; and, in particular, Britain's whole Middle East policy.[1] Indeed one could propound the thesis that it was precisely in areas not under direct colonial rule that England was most opposed to nationalist strivings, or at the very least had greater reservations and demanded more security guarantees. Baldly formulated, then, the thesis would be that Britain provoked the conflict with Nasser, the Mossadegh Affair in Iran, and the bloody 1958 overthrow in Iran.

Despite the aforementioned limitations, I must confess to a feeling of satisfaction with my book as it was published in 1966. It still remains, I believe, the only broadly based treatment of decolonization. In French we now have Henri Grimal's *La Décolonisation 1919–1963*.[2] In German we also have Franz Ansprenger's treatment: *Die Auflösung der Kolonialreiche*.[3] These two books go more deeply into nationalist movements than I did, but they are overviews rather than products of personal research.

More recent studies of the behavior of the metropolises are sparse. Adopting a political-science approach, David Goldsworthy has examined the relative evaluation of colonial issues in the two British parties between 1945 and 1961.[4] He explores the influence of divergent factions within the parties, but he also seeks to pinpoint such things as the reasons for the end of the earlier "bipartisan approach" towards the end of the 1950s. He points to a "wind of change," a changed attitude among Conservatives after the 1959 election as new leaders emerged (Macleod, Butler). For many years the basic work on the attitude of the Labour Party will be the one by an Indian historian, Partha Sarathi Gupta, who sifts through a treasure trove of published and unpublished materials and very skillfully links opinions on imperial matters with associated political, economic, and strategic problems facing Great Britain.[5] The result is a rich store of new insights, and the fairness of his judgment deserves special mention. Consider, for example, the suspicion that England opened the way for the Moslem League to form Pakistan in order to weaken the two Indian succession states for the sake of its own strategic and economic interests. Gupta explicitly rejects this notion, at least for 1946.

For France there is Bruce Marshall's book on the 1945–1946 constitutional debate.[6] He starts off from the republican idea of human rights and popular sovereignty, and the myth of an indivisible republic uniting metropolises, to which the politicians appealed. He points up the significance that the overseas territories had for De Gaulle, and then he describes in detail the debate over the constitution of the Fourth Republic. It ended in a compromise which

> made it highly probable that colonial nationalists would resort to extralegal channels in order to gain their objectives. These actions could only provoke repression by metropolitan authorities dedicated to preserving the unity of the republic and preventing secession. Thus, the failure to comprehend the power of native nationalism in the colonies and to fashion institutions capable of encouraging an orderly process of decolonization in accord with the explicit desires of the native deputies led directly to the tragic colonial wars that dominated French politics until the 1960s.

Since 1966 countless books and articles have appeared that deal with the history of specific regions and colonies in the period between the wars and during the phase of decolonization. I cannot mention even the most important ones here, but I should point out that a few basic publications were already available to me at that time. Moreover, in recent years historians have not shown any special interest in the war years and the postwar period. Either they have concentrated on the period between the wars or else they have approached the problems of the independent states from the standpoint of political science or the economics of development. One important reason for this surprising lack of interest in the decolonization process must surely be the fact that the archives for those years still remain closed to some extent. Hence we must look to the future for detailed studies of the decision-making processes in both the metropolises and the colonies.

That new and interesting pieces of information are to be expected may be seen from two articles that deal with the activity of Sir Andrew Cohen in the Colonial Office.[7] On the basis of unpublished material it is evident that postwar planning for West Africa during the war itself did not produce any really new approaches. American pressure was being exerted, an intensification of economic and social development was deemed necessary, and differences with the Western-trained elite were reckoned with. But the supposed reform of local government was only meant to aid and abet socioeconomic activity and serve as a check on the agitation of the new elites. The talk was of "progress towards self-government," but that did not mean that a transfer of power was clearly

PREFACE TO THE 1982 EDITION

envisioned. A real change came only when Creech Jones took over the Colonial Office in the fall of 1946. He established a commission in which Cohen played a significant role. In the spring of 1947 the commission proposed a four-stage plan whereby the government of the colonies would gradually pass to African ministers responsible to Parliament. Twenty or more years were envisioned for the transition. This new concept was not made public, due to pressure from the governor, who opposed it, but it found expression in diluted form in official declarations. It was undoubtedly because of this that the transfer of power was set in motion after the Accra Riots of 1948 and that the projected time period was shortened.

In recent years the whole discussion of imperialism has been reactivated. Do we find anything similar with regard to decolonization? Have new theories been developed, or new concepts formulated, to give us a better understanding of decolonization and show us how it is to be integrated into the broader context of modern history? The fact is that expansion has attracted much greater interest among historians than has decolonization. Let me mention only a few items relating to imperial expansion. There is Robinson and Gallagher's concept of the imperialism of free trade, and the debate it has triggered.[8] There is the theory of social imperialism, which the German historian H. U. Wehler elaborated to interpret Bismarck's colonial policy; its validity for other powers has been examined and tested.[9] There is Fieldhouse's theory of peripheral imperialism.[10] There is the reactivated debate over the scope and significance of the Marxist theory of imperialism, with the answers varying greatly even within Marxist circles. There is also a plethora of studies on the role of resistance and collaboration during the phase of colonial conquest. The reopened discussion of imperialism has found its way into large tomes and into countless readers.

By comparison, the theoretical debate over decolonization is on the wane. In a new and brilliant paper Robinson discusses the phenomenon of collaboration between the colonial power and Asian-African elites.[11] In the Europe-centered vision of imperialism and colonialism, this phenomenon has been paid much too little attention. With whom was there collaboration, and in what way? The answer varied with time and place. A readiness for collaboration could render the imposition of rulership unnecessary, or on the other hand facilitate it. By the same token, the absence of elements ready and willing to collaborate might provoke military expansion. On the other hand, collaboration with groups within the subject society was also necessary to maintain rule. Hence it was also necessary for the colonial government, which might change its "partner" over the years: "The permutations of collaboration shifted whenever a collaborating element, whether of the modern or neotraditional elite, grew too powerful or too dissatisfied, and above all, whenever a major element in colonial politics, whether cooperating or in opposition, threatened to unite an urban elite with a mass, rural following."

What the nationalists had to do, in fact, was this. They had to bring old and new elites, and also regional, ethnic, and religious groups, into the parties which they headed. In that way they could choke off the ruling alliance that had been in operation. When that happened, the time for the withdrawal of the colonial power had come:

> When the colonial rulers had run out of indigenous collaborators, they either chose to leave or were compelled to go. Their national opponents in the modern elite sooner or later succeeded in detaching the indigenous political elements from the colonial regime until they eventually formed a united front of non-collaboration against it. Hence the inversion of collaboration into non-cooperation largely determines the timing of decolonization.

This "theory of collaboration" certainly opens up new perspectives for a systematic-comparative history of imperialist expansion, and for a more nuanced understanding of the structures and techniques of colonial rule. But I, for one, doubt that the same is true for the history and interpretation of decolonization. The notion that the colonial powers withdrew on the basis of their own free decision and a plan drawn up in the metropolises has not found any serious advocates among historians. It has not been advocated by me, for example, even though my interest has been focused on the whole debate in the metropolises and the decolonization strategies elaborated there. One simply does not get anywhere unless one takes anticolonial nationalism into account. Every portrayal of the process of decolonization shows clearly that to the very end, both the metropolises and the colonial regimes tried to satisfy the "moderate nationalists" with promises or real but partial reforms. In this way they hoped to retard or block the development of "radical nationalism" on a broad front.

This raises the question: Can the development of nationalism in Asia and Africa be schematized and, if so, to what extent? Did it, in other words, proceed in clearly definable phases: e.g., from the association stage and the first parties of urban elites and notables to the formation of real mass parties which then, at some point, actually confronted the colonial power with the alternative of repression or withdrawal? In any case, historical research would do well to pose the questions raised by the concept of collaboration when it comes to detailing, on the basis of opened archives, the discussion in the colonial ministries of the metropolises and the conflict with the national movement in the colonies.

Future research will also have to pay much greater attention to the economic factors and aspects than I did in my book. Before 1966 there were few studies in economic history for the colonial period. In recent years there has been marked progress in this area. Still, to cite but one example, we are only now beginning to get thematic treatments of the consequences of the economic crisis of the early 1930s.[12] Detailed findings for specific regions are still lacking for the most part.

From the standpoint of the history of decolonization, one might ask whether the effects of the crisis accelerated or retarded the decolonization process. The price collapse of tropical exports is well known. There was a correspondingly rapid deterioration in the terms of trade for the colonies. The earnings of the colonial regimes decreased, compelling them to adopt economy measures. Mining companies and European planters had to curtail production or face bankruptcy. Asian and African peasants cultivating export products on native farms achieved earnings that hardly covered their production costs. Indebtedness rose sharply; farmers lost their land to creditors.

By the same token it was precisely during this crisis that the colonial powers took increased interest in their colonies. The decline in exports and the shift to defensive, protectionist measures fanned the hope that they might obtain increased raw materials and markets in their own colonial empire, which was protected by tariff policy against imports from third-party countries. The share of the colonies in the foreign trade of the metropolises rose correspondingly, particularly in the case of France. In British India, on the other hand, tariffs were raised during the 1930s—mainly due to budgetary considerations. The rise was particularly noticeable on textiles, sugar, cement, and paper. This gave a strong boost to industrialization. Between 1929 and 1931 the sale of British textiles in India dropped from 1248 million yards to 376 million yards. All efforts by London to obtain a preferential tariff favoring Lancashire ran aground on the resistance of the Indian government, which wanted to forestall the expected storm of indignation. In negotiations over the constitution, however, Tomlinson has shown that New Delhi stubbornly stuck to imperial control over finances—in the interest of the large British credit vis-a-vis India.[13] In the Dutch East Indies the government promoted industrialization to compensate somewhat for the collapse of the sugar industry on Java.[14]

What needs to be explored is how the economic crisis and the subsequent recovery affected nationalist movements. One assumes that there is a close connection with the trend towards radicalization around 1934.

In his economic history of West Africa, Hopkins introduces a paradigm to explain the trend towards radicalization.[15] He does not see it simply as the result of pauperization, the incipient flight to the cities, and the lack of jobs for young Western-educated people. He also sees it rooted in the shift from an open economy to a closed economy. Hopkins views the colonial economy of the nineteenth and early twentieth centuries as an open economy. Its characteristics were: an outward orientation, increasing exportation of staple products and importation of consumer goods, dependence on world-market prices, lower tariffs, and a laissez-faire administration policy.

The economic crisis was a crisis for the open economy. Government had to intervene with market regulations, tariffs, currency controls, and promotion of the domestic market. It was also pressed by demands for industrialization and a national currency of its own. The colonial government, however, was incapable of meeting these demands because, among other things, they were opposed by concrete imperial interests. The governments of the independent states then made the shift to a closed economy, though with conflicting results.

Tomlinson feels that this paradigm is also applicable to India. The destructive impact of world economic forces on the Indian domestic economy between the wars was exacerbated by the government of India's continuing need, for its own purposes, to maintain an open economy in India. The strains that resulted from this, especially during the early 1930s, helped to increase opposition to British rule both among the masses and among opinion formers.

One consequence of the government of India's failure to implement policies to mitigate the impact of the Great Depression on the Indian economy had been to strengthen the tendency among Indian businessmen to regard the Congress, rather than the government, as the body best able and most willing to secure for them the place in the domestic economy and polity that they desired.[16]

In any case, as a result of the crisis the metropolises began to reexamine their policy of colonial development. To put it more accurately, they gradually became aware of the fact that a colonial development policy had to be formulated. This meant giving up the hitherto prevailing principle that the colonies had to meet their expenses out of their own income (plus loans). It meant accepting the new principle that the metropolises would have to dig into their own budgets and make funds available for investments in the economic and social sectors. In the chapter entitled "Colonial Development, 1929–1940," I examined the incipient discussion, which found embodiment in the Colonial Development Fund.

But here a broad and important field opens up for research.[17] The debate in the ministries of the metropolises must be delineated on the basis of unpublished official documents and carried through into the post–World War II period. What must be made clear, in particular, is exactly what sort of colonial economic policy was envisioned and planned. Were the colonies still regarded as economic appendages of the metropolises? Was there a willingness to promote industrialization in the colonies, even if that would entail competition with the metropolis?

Further questions suggest themselves. What was the relationship between the economy of the metropolises after World War II and the decolonization then setting in? During and after the war, the dependent regions had taken on enormous importance for the colonial powers. The British colonies, for example, had shipped large quantities of raw materials and foodstuffs to England and the United States. Since these exports were not counterbalanced by imports, the colonies had amassed large credits in pounds and dollars. In the period of the dollar shortage after the war, it was Malaya, Nigeria, and the Gold Coast especially that were the big dollar-earners for Great Britain. Implementing big investment schemes, such as the "Ground Nuts Scheme" in Tanganyika, London also hoped to be able to reduce imports from the dollar realm.

The same point applies to France. With FIDES *(Fonds d'Investissement pour le Développement Economique et Social)* in 1946, France introduced an investment policy expressly backed by the government. Cathérine Coquéry-Vidrovitsch, the Marxist historian of Africa, goes so far as to describe the years 1946–1952 as "the great years of French colonial imperialism."[18] That would be all the more true for the Belgian Congo.

One would naturally have tended to assume that this new, intensified interest in the colonies significantly reduced the readiness of people in the metropolises to accept the national demands of colonized peoples and to proceed with decolonization. Indeed the renewed interest presumably threatened to block such a policy altogether. This certainly was the case in France. The stance of colonial interest groups in and outside Parliament are well known, and I dealt with them. But only future investigations will prove to what extent they actually did influence the decision-making process in the metropolis.

In the case of Great Britain it will be even more difficult to amass such proof. The transfer of power in India, for example, seems to have evoked surprisingly little interest in British business circles. Perhaps it was because the Indian market had been lost to Lancashire even before the war; or because there were more pressing problems between 1945 and 1947, such as reconstruction, the future of German industry, and economic relations with the United States. Or perhaps the reason was that the independence of India simply had to be accepted; and it was assumed that British business interests in India were not directly threatened, that intensive trade relations would continue in one form or another.

A study of the Gold Coast has shown that contacts between commercial firms and the colonial regime were closer during and after the war than they had been before it.[19] Nevertheless, the business world scarcely said a word about the constitutional reforms of 1946–1951, and the United Africa Company began to africanize its ranks. Obviously the UAC was far-sighted enough to realize the value of good relations with nationalist leaders. It assumed, of course, that the latter would not be able to push forward with economic development without the UAC. In eastern and central Africa, and especially in Rhodesia, business first sided with the white settlers and oriented itself around the autonomy of the white man's countries. Later, around 1960, it shifted course in a short period of time as the transition to African administrations loomed.

How are we to explain this relatively meager opposition of business to decolonization? It is possible that we historians overestimate the direct influence of business groups on political decision making and underestimate the independence of governments and bureaucracies vis-a-vis pressure groups. Perhaps the structural change in the capitalist system also plays a role here. Traditional firms engaged in business with the colonies—and also such businesses as textile and shipping firms—have shown a relative loss in importance in comparison with the automobile, electrical, and chemical industries. Today's giant concerns, which operate as multinationals, have not been dependent on colonial rule; moreover, their investment activity has been geared primarily to industrial countries.

Another unanswered question is whether the decline in the price of raw materials and the renewed worsening of the terms of trade after 1952 had any decisive impact on the behavior of the business sector. Coquéry-Vidrovitsch talks about a "pivotal year," which resulted in "the first manifestations in favor of disengagement in business circles."[20] People recognized that colonial rule was beginning to cost the metropolis dearly. So gradually there was a shift to new ways of exploiting the former colonies—now as independent nations still firmly integrated into the capitalist world economy. Immanuel Wallerstein argues similarly:

> Once these movements began to link up with mass protest, the potential cost of colonial administration rose drastically, both the direct costs resulting from the need to expand the bureaucracy for purposes of control and the indirect costs of investment in infrastructure required for purposes of political appeasement. This provided the major impetus for decolonization.[21]

Can such considerations of profitability really be proven, however? Or are we dealing with an interpretation of decolonization, a Marxist interpretation, which is designed to explain it in primarily economic terms and thus minimize it? With regard to the Belgian Congo, for example, Jean Stengers expressly rejects the thesis that the reins of government were dropped in 1959 because of financial considerations. Stengers acknowledges that around 1957 the budget dropped from a sound state and showed increasing deficits; as a result, there were sharply increased expenses for government administration and education. At the same time, however, people in government fully realized that the independence of the Congo would cost Belgium dearly. "Thus there had been no room in Belgian policy for an actuarial reckoning."[22]

What is suggested, therefore, is that we do comparative studies; and that we make an effort to systematize the decolonization undertaken by various colonial powers, as well as the decolonization process in individual lands and regions, in accordance with specific criteria and approaches to the issues. But this is easier said than done.[23] There has been a similar demand for a comparative approach to other major themes—e.g., nationalism, imperialism, and fascism—but the results have fallen far short of expectations.

In my book I tried to adopt a comparative perspective. In both the regional sections and the all too brief synopsis I pointed up the two, basically opposed, conceptions of decolonization: a gradual granting of self-government in the case of Great Britain, and a gradual process of integration and assimilation into the national territory in the case of France. Then I tried to explain the policies of other powers as variants of one or the other conception. My initial framing of the question itself, therefore, met the demand for a comparative approach to some extent. But Tony Smith is certainly correct in the criticism he levels at me.[24] He points out that the course of events in specific regions dominates in my book; that I considered only one aspect, not the multiplicity and variety of the variables that come into play in the process of decolonization. In my Introduction I did bring up such things as the international dimension, strategic and economic considerations and interests; later in the book, however, I alluded to them only casually in my interpretations, and I did not dwell on them at all in a comparative sense.

In a noteworthy contribution Tony Smith himself has tried to show what the sought-after comparative approach might look like.[25] He starts off from the situation in 1945. The anticolonialism of the United States and the Soviet Union, combined with the nationalist movement in the colonies, had rendered obsolete the question whether the colonies were to be freed. Now it was only a question of "how" this was to take place. With formulations that come close to my own explanations and results, Smith first stresses the difference in the "legacy of colonial traditions." On the one hand Great Britain had the Legislative Councils in the colonies, the Balfour Declaration of 1926, and the Indian Constitution of 1935. Thanks to them, Great Britain had elaborated procedures acknowledging representative groups and "tending towards independence." France, by contrast, had strictly rejected self-government in the Brazzaville Declaration of 1944. Even in the Constitution of the Fourth Republic, with its *Union française,* France was not ready to grant that.

That does not suffice, however, to give us an understanding of the postwar policy of the two colonial powers. So Smith calls our attention to the fact that the relationship of Great Britain to the United States was basically different from that of France. The close cooperation of the two English-speaking countries in and after the war made it easier for London to accept its loss of power. By contrast Roosevelt's overt antipathy to De Gaulle enabled France to see anti-French intrigues by the United States everywhere, and hence to uphold its own prestige as a great power. This is, in fact, a valuable insight.

Smith then compares the political systems and the way they functioned in the decolonization process. His thesis is that the decisive factor was not the difference between a functioning two-party system and an impotent coalition-system but rather the attitude of the socialists. In 1946–1947 the Labour government lined up behind the withdrawal from India; the French government under Ramadier, on the other hand, got involved in the Indochina War. Hence "it is aggregate national characteristics which emerge as the most decisive." This result of a comparison is also worthwhile. However, the appeal to national characteristics is unsatisfactory. The difference in the attitude of the two socialist parties lies precisely in the fact that the Labour Party had for decades been calling for the gradual granting of self-government, whereas the SFIO had internalized the republican tradition of integration and assimilation. If so, that would underline once more the importance of the two differing imperial conceptions.

In the second part of his paper Smith stresses the necessity of including the nationalist movements in any analysis of the decolonization process. For example, he alludes to the fact that in 1946–1947, France shifted to a policy of repression in Indochina, Algeria, Madagascar, and Black Africa, but that the results differed from place to place: war in Indochina, and later in Algeria; but with Houphouët-Boigny on the Ivory Coast, a course shift to collaboration. Concludes Smith: "The local power position of the predominant nationalists is the key variable to analyze for an understanding of the colonial response to metropolitan policy."

Smith discusses the role of traditional and modern elites, their relationship to the rural masses, the situation of the Communist parties in Southeast Asia, and the Japanese policy of occupation.[26] But he also acknowledges that the way in which the colonial powers reacted to the challenge contributed significantly to the outcome of the conflict. A military conflict in India, which might well have been possible if the Conservative party under Churchill had won the 1945 election, would probably have bolstered the radical factions in and outside the Congress party. An arrangement could have been worked out with Ho Chi Minh in 1946. And the manipulation of the Algerian elections in 1947 was an important precondition for the 1954 uprising. To that extent, then, the stance of the metropolises, which occupied center stage in my book, again comes into play. Smith rightly stresses the multiplicity and complexity of the nationalist movements, showing, for example, that there were significant underlying differences between the settler colony of Kenya and the settler colony of Algeria. In the last analysis, his paper offers more incentives for a comparison of the nationalist movements in

PREFACE TO THE 1982 EDITION

Asia and Africa during the decolonization phase than for "a comparative study of French and British decolonization."

In contrast to the decade of the 1960s when my book was written, it is now the tendency, indeed the fashion, to play down the historical significance of decolonization. Perhaps this is less true among historians than among social scientists and journalists who deal with the problems of developing countries. One reason may be that the latter have little or no interest in the history of the Third World, often contenting themselves with cliché-ridden comments about economic exploitation and the alleged destruction of non-European cultures. Another reason may be the generation gap, insofar as many people writing about the problems of underdeveloped countries today did not live through the decolonization years themselves. But surely the most important reason is the fact that the winning of political independence has not brought to the nations and peoples of the Third World what the nationalists promised and expected: rapid economic growth, social progress, and political freedom both at home and in foreign relations.

What decolonization brought—so the argument runs today—was a merely formal independence that effected little change in the power structures prevailing at home and in the international system. Economic independence—interpreted not as self-sufficiency but as the ability to make free decisions about one's own course of development and one's own resources—must still be fought for and won. The former colonies still export raw materials and tropical foodstuffs for the most part, without being able to set the price, and they are dependent more than ever on foreign capital and know-how. The white colonial government has disappeared, only to be replaced by a small indigenous bourgeoisie. In its interests, values, and consumption patterns, this bourgeoisie models itself on the old colonial powers and, like them, exploits the masses. In the best of cases, direct dependence on the former colonial power has been relaxed and "diversified"; but dependence on the industrial countries, the multinationals, and the capitalist world economy continues. The concept of "neocolonialism" has taken root. It is now bandied about, mainly but not exclusively by leftist journalists.

Is such a line of argument justified? Is it true that the independence won by the former colonies is a merely formal one, that it has no real relevance for them? Was decolonization merely a convenient alibi, camouflaging the shift to new (or even old) forms of informal rule? I think not. I would certainly not deny the present-day forms of structural dependence existing between underdeveloped lands and the industrialized nations. They certainly are different from, and more irritating than, those existing between small and large industrialized nations. But one is pushing the notion of dependence too far when one denies the considerable scope for free decision making that is at the disposal of not only the larger but even most of the smaller one-time colonies—not only in the realm of foreign policy but also in the realm of economic, social, and cultural policy. As far back as 1959 the socialist John Strachey was right when he wrote:

> Once an even nominally sovereign local government is established, forces are inevitably set in motion which tend in the direction of genuine independence. Imperialist control can go on, often for some time, but it becomes more and more precarious. To say that the advent of even partial political independence makes no difference is a grotesque oversimplification.[27]

In recent years this scope for free decision making has certainly increased rather than diminished. Zaïre, whose economy is still foreign controlled despite nationalization and whose ruler, Mobutu, would have been toppled long ago except for French and American backing, is not typical. Even in Chad, where French troops intervened in the civil war for many years, the influence of the former colonial power has markedly diminished. Dependence on the world market does exist. The new nations do have to cope with pressure from the great powers, demands from, for example, the International Monetary Fund, and possible ultimatums from multinational corporations. But that does not justify denigrating the national independence they won through tough negotiations or armed conflict, or calling it merely "formal."

Nationalism in the new states may often seem shrill, compensating for a lack of cohesion at home and a lack of clout abroad. But it is also an expression of pride over having become masters of their own destiny. It may well be true that in many former colonies the one-time nationalists have made nice deals with their old white masters and are exercising power to their own advantage. But I think it is unfair to jump in and pin the label of "neocolonial bourgeoisie" on the Western-trained leadership, alleging that they have no interest in the fate of their own nation and no sense of responsibility towards the masses.

One can say that the historical function of colonialism was to integrate Asian and African peoples into the world economic system controlled by Europe. It is even true that the former colonies are still peripheral areas within that system, even though they have achieved the status of independent states. But it is not right to minimize the process of decolonization as if it were an ephemeral phenomenon, to downplay the achievement of the former colonies in getting the colonial powers to retreat and eventually depart. It is not fair to suggest that some sort of indirect rule has merely returned to replace direct rule. Viewing it from an historical perspective, we are faced with a process of the utmost significance; and we will feel its effects and consequences more and more in the future.

Rudolf von Albertini
October 1980

NOTES

1. Elizabeth Monroe, *Britain's Moment in the Middle East, 1914–1956* (1963); M. A. Fitzsimons, *Empire by Treaty: Britain and the Middle East in the Twentieth Century* (1965).
2. Henri Grimal, *La Décolonisation 1919–1963* (1963).
3. Franz Ansprenger, *Auflösung der Kolonialreiche* (dtv-Weltgeschichte des 20. Jahrhunderts, vol. 13) (1966).
4. David Goldsworthy, *Colonial Issues in British Politics, 1945–1961* (1971).
5. Partha Sarathi Gupta, *Imperialism and the British Labour Movement, 1914–1964* (1975).
6. D. Bruce Marshall, *The French Constitutional Myth and Constitution-Making in the Fourth Republic* (1973).
7. John W. Cell, "On the Eve of Decolonizaton: The Colonial Office's Plans for the Transfer of Power in Africa, 1947," in: *Journal of Imperial and Commonwealth History* 8 (May 1980); and Ronald Robinson, "Andrew Cohen and the Transfer of Power in Tropical Africa, 1940–1951," in: W. H. Morris-Jones and Georges Fischer, eds., *Decolonisation and After: The British and French Experience* (1980).
8. Wm. Roger Louis, ed., *Imperialism: The Robinson and Gallagher Controversy* (1976).
9. H.-U. Wehler, *Bismarck und der Imperialismus*, 2nd edition (1970), and Wolfgang J. Mommsen, ed., *Der Moderne Imperialismus* (1971).
10. D. K. Fieldhouse, *Economics and Empire, 1830–1914* (1973).
11. Ronald Robinson, "Non-European Foundations of European Imperialism: Sketch for a Theory of Collaboration," in: Roger Owen, Bob Sutcliffe, eds., *The Theory of Imperialism* (1972).
12. "L'Afrique et la crise de 1930 (1924–1938)," in: *Revue française d'histoire d'outre-mer* 63, Nos. 232–233 (1976).
13. B. R. Tomlinson, *The Political Economy of the Raj, 1914–1947: The Economics of Decolonization in India* (1979), pp. 122seq.
14. Rudolf von Albertini, *Europäische Kolonialherrschaft, 1880–1940* (1976), p. 146.
15. A. G. Hopkins, *An Economic History of West Africa* (1973), pp. 168–9.
16. Tomlinson, *op. cit.*, pp. 161, 163.
17. J. M. Lee, *Colonial Development and Good Government. A Study of the Ideas Expressed by the British Official Classes in Planning Decolonization, 1939–1964* (1967), is exclusively based on published source materials but touches on economic questions.
18. Cathérine Coquéry-Vidrovitch, "La mise en dépendance de l'Afrique noire: Essai de périodisation, 1880–1970," in: *Cahiers d'études africaines* 16 (1976).
19. Josephine Milburn, *British Business and Ghanaian Independence* (1977). See also Hopkins, *op. cit.*, p. 278: "The decision to make room for aspiring Africans was also an astute political move. By the close of the 1940's it was apparent that the long term interests of the expatriate firms lay in securing a stake for themselves in an Africa ruled by Africans rather than by Europeans. By providing more opportunities for indigenous traders, the expatriate firms advanced their own interests and also improved their image in the eyes of their most vociferous critics."
20. Milburn, *op. cit.*, pp. 39, 42.
21. Immanuel Wallerstein, "Three Stages of African Involvement in the World Economy," in: Peter C. W. Gutkind, Immanuel Wallerstein, eds., *The Political Economy of Contemporary Africa* (1976), p. 48.

22. Jean Stengers, "La Belgique et le Congo," in: *Histoire de la Belgique contemporaine* (1974).

23. In 1976 British and French scholars met in Paris "for the purpose of comparing their countries' experiences in the process of decolonisation and continuing relations with their former colonial territories." Even a common catalogue of questions to be dealt with had been prepared. The scholars made important contributions. Nonetheless, one looks in vain for any real comparisons in the papers as published by Morris-Jones and Fischer, *op. cit.*

24. Tony Smith, ed. *The End of the European Empire: Decolonization after World War II* (1975), p. 257.

25. Tony Smith, "A Comparative Study of French and British Decolonization," in: *Comparative Studies in Society and History* 20 (1978).

26. I myself have strongly stressed the importance of the Japanese occupation. India and Ceylon never fell under Japanese occupation. Consequently, the leadership of the nationalist movements remained in the hands of the bourgeois elite. In Burma, Dutch India, and Vietnam the occupation resulted in a sort of power vacuum. This enabled formerly not very influential radical groups to come to the fore in 1945 and to prevent any comeback of the colonial rulers expelled by the Japanese in 1941–1942. See p. 208 but also my essay "The Impact of the Two World Wars on the Decline of Colonialism," in: *Journal of Contemporary History* (1969), reprinted in: *The End of the European Empire, loc. cit.*

27. John Strachey, *The End of Empire* (1959), p. 233.

PREFACE
TO THE AMERICAN EDITION

The American edition of my book, which was completed as a manuscript in 1965 and first published in German in 1966, has not been revised. Today I would probably re-word some sentences as well as differentiate or supplement some statements. The large monographical literature that appeared in the meantime has not been worked up nor included in the notes. Besides, my bibliography did not claim any completeness and contained only books and articles that I made direct use of.

Some inaccuracies have been set right owing to the critics—I have no illusion that there are not many more, though I hope of small importance.

I should especially like to thank Francisca Garvie for the great diligence with which she translated the book, as well as Anne Freedgood for her good services.

Zurich
January 1970

PREFACE
TO THE FIRST EDITION

The subtitle indicates the main themes of this inquiry. I do not propose to present a general history of decolonization nor to describe the internal development of a large number of colonial territories in the last decades before their independence. My subject is Europe's attitude toward the future of its colonies, when and how Europe came to accept decolonization, and the concepts and doctrines on which the administration of the colonies and by the same token the process of decolonization were based. This book does not set out to offer a contribution to the history of Asian and African states, which would be beyond my scope, but rather to examine an aspect of European history that I believe to be important. Between 1919 and 1960 European expansion was coming to an end and Europe was withdrawing from its colonial positions. It seemed of interest to trace the outer and inner forces pressing for decolonization and to make an historical survey of the attitudes of the colonial powers during this process.

I have taken a comparative approach in order to give a broader view of the predominantly national perspectives of the time; comparison of the divergent traditions, doctrines, and theories will show the outstanding features of measures taken in the different countries and the various attempts to find a solution. I have concentrated on Great Britain and France and dealt with the lesser colonial powers only in brief. Even so, it was necessary to impose limits:

Important regions (the West Indies, the Middle East) and colonies (e.g. Malaya) have been omitted; others (e.g. Kenya, Tunisia) have been considered during only a certain period. This was not an arbitrary selection; it followed from the theme of the inquiry, in which I wanted to support and clarify general statements by concrete examples.

For certain territories the attitude of the colonial power was the most interesting question, and in these cases their territories' economic, social and political development is outlined but not described as fully as could be desired.

I have taken due note of the "challenge" represented by the national emancipation movements; they do not really form a part of this inquiry, however. Brief outlines would not have done them justice and would have led to oversimplification.

The reader may regret the absence of any discussion on the Russian colonial territories. It would have been extremely interesting to include a comparative study of the Soviet Union's integrationist policy of decolonization and its particular problems. Ignorance of the language and the facts prevented this. The same applies to Japanese colonial policy.

In order to substantiate by direct evidence the picture gained from literary sources, I spent several weeks in Africa—Nigeria, Senegal, Morocco —in 1961. Numerous discussions with politicians, colonial officials and journalists personally involved in their countries' colonial policies provided important information. I would like to extend my sincere thanks to these persons, and above all to Miss Margery Perham (Oxford), James Griffiths (London), John Drysdale (London) and P. O. Lapie (Paris).

The Deutsche Forschungsgemeinschaft put research assistants at my disposal and financed two research visits to Paris and London. I am particularly indebted to the Rockefeller Foundation, which offered a generous research grant that I used to work undisturbed in Yale University Library.

Dusch/Paspels (Switzerland), Heidelberg
Autumn 1965

Introduction:
International Aspects

The First World War was of such obvious historical significance that it seems a natural starting-point for a discussion of the age of decolonization. Yet the history of decolonization, that is, of the movement of dissociation of the colonies, can be traced back much farther—to the struggle for independence of the English colonies in North America and to the secession of the Spanish colonies in the south. True, these events involved a desire for autonomy on the part of immigrant settlers and their descendants, and not a movement of subjugated natives. The people who established new communities and then struggled to free themselves from the mother country were Europeans. Yet the American revolution constituted an example and consequently strongly influenced British imperial outlook in the nineteenth century. After the loss of the American colonies, London sought to prevent a break with the settlers in other parts of the world by preparing the way for self-government and, later, by granting dominion status. Nineteenth-century liberals, who believed in free trade and the free exchange of goods, expected and even welcomed colonists' attempts to emancipate themselves.

France also had to consider the future of its colonies. The eighteenth-century *philosophes* had always assumed that France would eventually give up its colonial territories, but the Revolution produced a new and specifically French idea: that decolonization should lead not to dissociation and independence but to integration into the mother country by means of extended civil rights and parliamentary representation. An important theme of this book will be to show the divergence of the French and British paths—already visible at the end of the eighteenth century—which arose from different concepts of state and nationhood. We will examine the significance of this divergence in relation to both the colonial issue in general and methods of administration after the First World War.

So both the theory and practice of decolonization preceded the new imperialist expansion that, after 1870, led to the "partition of the world". In the British colonies theory and practice ran parallel. But to the continental mind during this period such notions were obscured by the quest for power. Europe arrogantly proclaimed its superiority of race and civilization, saw itself destined to dominate foreign peoples permanently and justified this ideologically as the "white man's burden". By the use of modern technology Europe established a world-wide system of communications, which enabled it to open up and exploit the colonies economically. At the same time the foreign peoples were confronted by modern administration and civilization, brought closer to Europe, and drawn into a process of Europeanization and Westernization. What Hans Freyer has called "European World History" began. Around the turn of the century European expansion reached its apogee and consolidated itself; imperialists became less concerned with acquiring new territory than with developing more practicable, efficient administrations and the regular exchange of goods—allegedly based on community of interests—between areas rich in raw materials and the industrial states. Decolonization was scarcely mentioned any more. European colonial domination was considered secure, at least for the forseeable future, and it was not questioned.

But even before 1914 a reaction set in, both in Europe and in the colonies and semi-colonial territories. After the Boer war colonial administrative practices began to be severely criticized, especially in England. In 1902 J. A. Hobson laid the ground for a socialist interpretation of imperialism. At the same time movements demanding national self-government were appearing in Asia. Japan's victory over Russia seemed to be a signal that must be followed—provided that "Westernization" had first taken place. In China revolution broke out in 1911. In India, Indochina and Indonesia, new organizations were formed that not only called for internal re-organization and gradual emancipation, but also demanded independence and challenged the colonial powers by their very existence as well as by propaganda, sabotage and terrorism. In the Middle East, the significant "Young Turk" revolution of 1908, which aimed at combining a sense of the past with energetic modernization, heralded the birth of an Arab nationalism directed against European dominance.

The First World War accelerated these movements. Asia and Africa were drawn into the "European world war" although, with the exception of Japan, mostly in a passive fashion. Until 1914 the "white man's world" had appeared to constitute a unity, based on a continuous and indisputable technical, cultural and military superiority. But this unity was destroyed in a fratricidal war in which each side used official and unofficial propaganda to weaken the power of the enemy—accusing him of criminal behaviour in his colonies and trying to arouse his subjects to revolution. As a result the prestige of Europe as a whole was undermined. Hundreds of thousands of colonial soldiers and workers sent to fight on European, Middle Eastern and African battlefields were torn from their homes and confronted with new experiences. At the same time, greater demands were made on colonial economies. Forcibly increasing export production in agriculture and mining, together with attempts to industrialize, may have benefitted the new colonial middle class, but it also led to urbanization and created the conditions for the birth of both an agrarian and an industrial proletariat. Recruiting of soldiers, confiscation of property and rising prices for consumer goods resulted in social discontent which could be politically exploited by nationalist leaders. The result was increasing unrest.

The colonial powers found themselves forced to make concessions and sometimes quite far-reaching pledges in order to avoid trouble, encourage the war effort and safeguard their positions. For instance, in 1917 Great Britain declared that the aim of British policy in India was the gradual grant of responsible government. In 1918 the British Government established the Montagu-Chelmsford Commission which led to the reforms of 1919. In the Middle East a protectorate was set up over Egypt in 1914 and Egypt's existing status was "legalized". Mesopotamia was conquered by British-Indian troops. London supported the Arabs in their struggle with the Ottoman Empire and at the same time promised them the creation of "independent Arab states", which suggested that Britain had changed its policy and renounced its previous claim to dominance. France, too, was forced to make concessions to the Muslims in Algeria and in 1916 declared that the Four Communes in Senegal were to be fully integrated and assimilated. The primary aim of these concessions was to stimulate the recruiting of colonial troops.

The world political situation in 1918 was fundamentally different from that of the pre-war period. At first the Allied victory seemed to represent a new peak of imperial expansion, since England and France not only divided up between them the possessions of their rival, Germany, but also gained new territories in the Middle East after the defeat of the Ottoman Empire. This, however, soon proved precarious and deceptive. Europe was exhausted, heavily damaged economically and no longer either able or willing to maintain its position of dominance by any possible means, including large-scale military action. This necessarily led to a more conciliatory attitude in colonial questions. In any case the European system of states and European predominance were shattered. Since the intervention of the United States in 1917, Europe could no longer determine its future alone but had to come to terms with the presence of this great non-European power, which now began to occupy a leading economic position.

The Allies justified the war against the Central Powers ideologically as a war for freedom and democracy, against annexation and aggression.

They saw it as the "war to end war" and asserted that its main aim was to inaugurate a new and just world order, based on the democratic will of the people. Accordingly the "oppressed" peoples were called upon to turn against their rulers and claim their national sovereignty. Under President Woodrow Wilson the United States took the lead in calling for sovereign rights, condemning annexation and proclaiming the League of Nations a supra-national organization; in the Fourteen Points Wilson presented the world with a programme for future peace. The summons was heard in the colonial and semi-colonial territories, and from China to Morocco nationalists claimed their sovereign rights and turned against the colonial powers.

In actual fact, Wilson had intended the Fourteen Points to apply primarily to Europe, particularly Eastern Europe, and had not meant to declare himself against colonialism.[1] In Point Five the interests of native inhabitants were indeed mentioned, but only in connection with an "impartial adjustment of all colonial claims", which was aimed merely against annexations based on secret treaties. Wilson's violent dispute with South Africa and Australia during the Paris peace conferences was anti-colonialist only in a limited sense. His chief concern was the principle of annexation; a simple annexation of South-West Africa and the German Pacific Islands would have compromised the policy of peace he proclaimed, which was being sought in Paris. The alleged objection to annexation, however, and the principle that nations could be subjected only to rulers they had freely chosen were also to find application in the colonies.

The colonial peoples considered the United States an anti-colonial power and hoped that it would support their emancipation, while the colonial powers felt that America's move was a "challenge" and reproached Wilson for undermining their already precarious domination in Asia and Africa with his noisy proclamations of sovereign rights. The new world political situation and the influence of America, added to the striking change in Europe's attitude towards its colonies, manifested itself in the League of Nations' mandate system. This is not the place for a detailed study of its early history and formation,[2] but it is important to remember that the preparatory discussion took place less in America than in Great Britain. The British pacifists, socialists and colonial reformers most concerned with a permanent peace hoped to end the Great Powers' colonial rivalry by putting all colonies under international supervision and at the same time developing new forms of administration for the "backward" peoples not yet advanced enough for independence. By giving a colonial power a mandate under the control of an international authority they hoped to prevent exploitation of native inhabitants and to establish an effective trusteeship.

What did the mandate system in fact achieve? It would be wrong to see Article 22 of the Covenant of the League of Nations as simply a hypocritical attempt on the part of the victorious powers to conceal their annexation of German and Turkish territories; rather it was a painfully worked-out compromise between conflicting ideas and demands —between annexationists and anti-annexationists, between supporters and opponents of the mandate principle, and between Americans and Europeans. But although the mandate system was proclaimed a new principle, in fact it made annexations possible, in particular in Class C (South-West Africa and the Pacific Islands). The mandate powers considered the settlement final and tried to align the administration of the mandates with that of neighbouring territories. In spite of this the League of Nations and the mandate system did have some effect. In the future, colonies were no longer to be treated as booty, which the respective victors could dispose of as they wished. The colonial issue, as well as the more concrete questions of administration, was internationalized and thereby withdrawn from the authority of sovereign national states. Colonial administration was to serve the interests of the inhabitants and to comply with certain regulations laid down by an international authority. Moreover the League of Nations mandate was seen as a temporary trusteeship of the more "advanced" nations in order to prepare their inhabitants for self-government, i.e. independence. Article 22 in fact made no declaration of universal sovereign rights, but it did recognize "certain communities" of the former Ottoman Empire as "independent states" and laid down that the mandated administration should end when they became capable of self-government. This set a limit to colonial rule—a concession rarely made by the colonial powers before 1914 and only reluctantly after the war.

The League of Nations Advisory Council confirmed, on 4 September 1931, that a mandate would lead to independence if the existing conditions justified the assumption that "le peuple est capable de se conduire seul dans les conditions difficiles du monde moderne" (the people are capable of governing themselves in the difficult conditions of the modern world).[3] But "capacity" had to be defined, and the colonial powers easily found "good reasons" for refusing withdrawal as being premature at this stage. Nevertheless Iraq became an independent kingdom and a member of the League of Nations.

The immediate effects of the mandate administration are difficult to calculate and have not yet been studied in any depth. The fact that the legal basis of the administration in mandated territories was different from that of the colonies was not of decisive significance although it did, for instance, give a governor like Donald Cameron in Tanganyika reasonable grounds for opposing the planned federation of East Africa and for consistently pursuing a policy of Indirect Rule (cf. p. 153). The Permanent Mandate Commission of the League of Nations[4] ensured that the covenants would be observed, issued directives and received the annual reports; the petitions of native inhabitants were also sent to it. But the Commission could neither test the accuracy of the reports nor initiate investigations. Moreover, it had to present its reports to the Advisory Council of the League of Nations and could reach government level only through this body. No doubt this resulted in comprehensive documentation and—in principle at least—in public discussion of cases relating to particular administrations. It is possible that the League of Nations' criticism of French policy in Syria was a contributory factor in the recall of Sarrail.[5] In general, however, the League had little influence, largely because, although the colonial powers were not in the majority in the League, no group of states questioned European colonialism or was able to make the League into a platform for anti-colonialism. The importance of the mandate system is chiefly that, as a result of the First World War and under pressure from America, the principle of international control was declared, began to be put into effect, and could be further developed at an opportune moment. Indeed this is what happened during and after the Second World War, again under strong pressure from America.

The "challenge" did not come only from the United States, however; 1917 was also the year of the Russian Revolution. By a strange historical coincidence, the moment when the European state system collapsed and Europe's hitherto unchallenged hegemony was, if not destroyed, at least endangered, coincided with the appearance of ideological anti-colonialism among the Russian Communists, who sought to undermine European colonial authority and hasten decolonization. Wilson and Lenin simultaneously proclaimed the peoples' sovereign rights, sympathised with national efforts at emancipation and attacked prewar imperialism. But the United States' attack on annexations, although not forgotten in the inter-war period, was reflected only slightly in American foreign policy. Lenin and Bolshevik Russia on the other hand saw anti-colonialism as an effective means of hastening the Communist world revolution. Marx had understandably paid little attention to European colonialism,[6] but as a result of the Indian Mutiny he became interested in British rule in India and analyzed the destructive effects of European capitalism on India's traditional, static economic and social structures. He predicted that this modernization, in the form of railways and administration, was an historical necessity that would not only create Indian unity but also produce a bourgeoisie and a proletariat that would one day turn against England.[7]

Lenin was the first to propound the Communist theory of imperialism, which was based on Hobson and Helferding. In his famous *Imperialism* of 1916 he saw colonial imperialism as "the last stage of capitalism" which, by increasing the monopolization of the forces of production by massive capital exports and ruthless exploitation of colonial and semi-colonial territories, could temporarily postpone its imminent collapse. Colonial profits also made it possible to corrupt the proletariat of the mother country, the more so because the social chauvinism of the workers retarded the outbreak of revolution. When the partition of the world had taken place, however, the rivalry of the imperialist powers could lead only to world war. The war or wars would accentuate the revolutionary situation in the capitalist countries while the development of communications and industry in the colonies would produce a class-conscious proletariat which would turn against both the colonial power and its own feudal and bourgeois ruling class, which was allied with the colonial power. The loss of the colonies would thus strike at the heart of European capitalism, precipitate the crisis and intensify class war. In its own interests the revolutionary proletariat should support the struggle for emancipation in the colonial world and call upon the colonial peoples to turn against their exploiters and oppressors. This would necessarily entail the solidarity of the Bolshevik revolution with all nationalist movements in the colonial and semi-colonial territories.

There is no doubt that the Russian Revolution, which came as an unexpected and successful uprising of the "oppressed" against an autocratic régime—in a predominantly agrarian country moreover—and the Bolshevik appeal to the people of the Soviet Union and the European colonies, had a great deal of influence on young bourgeois intellectuals and won many of them to the cause of the Communist world revolution. Nehru, for instance, tells of the strong impression the Russian Revolution made on him, although he was an aristocrat and very conservatively educated.[8]

In the years to come it was to be the Comintern's task to kindle revolution in the colonial world, by coordinated action and by its own activity and organizations. In the Second Comintern of 1920, Lenin's Twelve Points and the Indian delegate M. N. Roy's supplementary theses were mainly responsible for laying down the principles and tactics of Communist procedure[9]; nothing of real importance was added to this in later years.[10] One question always produced special difficulties and profound differences of opinion: What should the attitude of the Comintern or even the Soviet Union be towards national bourgeois parties and movements? Should they be supported or ignored or even attacked? Lenin suggested forming an anti-imperialist front, although only after an exact analysis of the respective "revolutionary forces" (only the parties that really attacked the colonial system counted as objectively revolutionary) and only if the "independence of the proletarian movement" was preserved. As a result Mustapha Kemal, Shah Reza Khan Pahlevi of Persia, the emir of Afghanistan, the Wafd party in Egypt and, later, Abd-el-Krim in Morocco were supported. But tactics changed several times in the inter-war period,[11] particularly under Stalin, since they depended upon both the evaluation of the world revolutionary situation at a given time and Russia's internal situation—i.e. the balance between left and right within Russia. The best known of these changes in tactics took place in China, but this happened as well in other areas.

An important factor in the discussion in the European countries was Lenin's and Stalin's stern call to the Communist parties to propagate their anti-colonialism openly and actively and to give "systematic aid" to nationalist organizations to help them prepare for open revolt against the colonial power.[12] This was also a declaration of war against the "social chauvinism" of the Socialist parties of the Second Comintern. In fact, as we will see, the Social Democrats were caught in a dilemma between their doctrinaire anti-imperialism and anti-colonialism on the one hand, and treasonable conduct and political and electoral considerations on the other. The Socialist parties within the colonial powers declared themselves in favour of reform and reacted quite kindly to emancipation movements in the colonies, but they rejected the use of force and nationalist revolt and therefore, particularly when they were the ruling party, were even forced occasionally to take repressive measures.

In 1920 the Second Comintern organized the "Congress of Peoples of the East" in Baku, which brought together some two thousand delegates, mostly from the Middle East; it called for a "peoples' crusade" and created a "Council of Propaganda and Action" with a branch in Tashkent, an Institute of Oriental Studies, etc. A Communist league against imperialism, the so-called Congress against Colonial Oppression and Imperialism, was organized in Brussels in 1927, in which George Lansbury of the British Labour party and Nehru as Indian representative took part.[13] Communist parties were founded in the colonies and nationalist organizations were infiltrated.

The main emphasis, apart from China, was on the Middle Eastern countries from Egypt to Persia, and later North Africa and South-East Asia; at first Moscow paid little attention to Africa south of the Sahara. Communist subversion and organization in the inter-war period was modest. Although colonial propaganda connected all nationalist opposition with Communist influence, the strong nationalist parties in Egypt, Tunisia, India and Iraq continued to draw their adherents either from the traditional upper class or from the new middle class of businessmen, officials and intellectuals, who were perhaps attracted to socialist theories and propaganda but would not submit to the Communist doctrines originating in Moscow. In Algeria the "Etoile Nordafricaine" was influenced by Communism, but most of its adherents were Algerian workers in the mother country. The Communist parties of Indonesia and Indochina were more important; although they did not themselves cause the civil disturbances of 1926–1927 and 1930–1931, they actively supported and influenced them. Holland and France would not make any concessions, however, and responded by executions, exiles and the destruction of painstakingly built-up organizations.

Yet international Communism did succeed in becoming an effective force in the colonies. It gained a foothold in several organizations and, above all, exerted an ideological and political influence on representatives of the younger generation of nationalist leaders—some of whom were trained in Moscow. This created a basis for the developments after the Second World War.

The "fratricidal war" of 1914–1918, in which Europe lost prestige and forfeited its power and influence, called into question the very foundations of the bourgeois world with its desire for security and belief in progress and revealed the growing significance of the non-European world, particularly Asia. The demonstrations and bloody riots of 1919–1920 and the double challenge of American and Soviet anti-colonialism created a sense of crisis in the European mind which affected future relations with the colonies. Oswald Spengler should also be mentioned, although his *Decline of the West* was primarily concerned with the question of whether Europe would become stagnant in the final stage of its culture and lose its historical greatness, or whether—the only alternative he offers—it would accept the rising Caesarism and be willing to carry out the technical and imperial achievements still possible to a declining civilization. He first considered the non-European countries as a political issue in a 1924 essay,[14] and then, in *The Hour of Decision* in 1933, included them in his pessimistic cultural prognosis. He believed that in the nascent "age of world wars", which was a decisive moment for the *imperium mundi*, Europe was fighting for its very existence; its prestige was weakened and "at present power has been transferred to the border areas of Asia and America"[15]; the coloured races were involved in a mighty awakening and were threatening white dominance from within and without; but the actual source of their attack on the white man was the "collective mass of the coloured population of the earth, which is slowly becoming conscious of its community".[16] The class war and the race war could now join forces. Asia had regained Russia by Communist revolution and was now undermining white domination of the world; Europe had lost the respect of the coloured races in the First World War and forfeited its role of unquestioned master.[17] Spengler looked towards Russia or Japan, but not India or China, as the leading Asian power of the future; he saw the precariousness of European colonial positions, but rather than supporting decolonization he summoned the white races, led by the young, resourceful and "Faustian" Germany, to take up the challenge of this "hour of decision".

In France the counterpart to Spengler and his popularlity within the framework of the crisis-ridden post-war years was Paul Valéry. Valéry, in his much-quoted 1919 essay *La crise de l'esprit*, discovers with tradition:

> As for us and our civilization, we now know that we are mortal. . . . And we now see that the abyss of history is large enough for everyone. We real-

ize that civilization is as frail as life itself. . . . Will Europe keep its pre-eminence in all things? Will Europe become what it in fact is, that is to say a small corner of the Asian continent?[18]

Europe was seeing its scientific and technological achievements uprooted from their native soil, taken over by other races and used against itself. What the rise of Japan had proved, even before 1914, although it had been noted only reluctantly, was now being realized by everyone. The *Reveil de l'Asie*, as the French expert on Asia René Grousset entitled an essay in 1924, demanded consideration in any analysis of the present or prognosis for the future. Would Europe keep its hegemony? he asked. "Can we not guess that this state of privilege threatens to come to an end?" After the "Europeanization of Asia" would come the "revolution of Asia against Europe". Grousset described the many nationalist and reform movements from Egypt to China, the resistance to the European powers and the incipient revolutions taking place; in a characteristic French post-war attitude he attacked British imperialism and what he termed the awkward policy of England, which had squandered the successes of the First World War and called down on itself the hatred of the Asian peoples. By contrast, Maurice Muret in his 1926 book *Le crépuscule des nations blanches,* in which he quoted Valéry and Spengler, objected to Wilson's proclamation of sovereign rights and the financial imperialism of the United States, and to what he called "le dissolvant bolshéviste". Unlike Grousset, Muret appealed to European solidarity, actually to the solidarity of the white race. France was also interested in British rule in India, he said; it was time European statesmen thought in terms of continents, "but in a spirit of defence". The race conflict would begin with "acts of liberation" on the part of the subjected nations, i.e. with movements of dissociation, which would probably give the white race a breathing space. "In any case, the West would not allow itself to be destroyed without defending itself. Rome was not built in a day, nor was it destroyed overnight."[19]

These analyses of the "awakening of Asia" clearly emphasized the race question, the "rising and clashing tides of colour",[20] and predicted racial disputes. The pre-1914 warnings about the "yellow peril"[21] were now sharpened. Between the wars Europe, understandably perhaps, replied to the threatened loss of its hegemony by a racially-inspired call for resistance. In more positive terms, it was also a call for the still predominantly European viewpoint to be extended to embrace both European and colonial problems.

In Britain the well-known diplomat and writer Harold Nicolson in his 1934 book on Curzon pointed out the apparent paradox—which in fact was characteristic of the world situation at the time—that small nations like the Afghans and the Syrians had begun to rebel at precisely the moment of the Allied victory in 1918. Did they, Nicolson asked, instinctively realize that the existing system of great powers had collapsed and that America was the rising nation? Wilson's and Lenin's proclamations of sovereign rights and attacks on annexation had, he thought, compromised European imperialism and a "tribunal had suddenly sprung into existence to which an appeal could be made against the machine guns of the world powers".[22] Nicolson described as a "readjustment of hitherto recognized values" the fact that a Mustapha Kemal could resist a coalition that had just waged a successful war. And how could one explain the fact that the British people, who as recently as 1898 had joyfully greeted Kitchener's success in the Sudan, were no longer willing, twenty years later, to agree to a trifling expedition to Kabul? The war had profoundly altered British national consciousness and sense of empire.

For Arnold Toynbee, as for Spengler, the change post-war world became the basis for wide-scale cultural and social studies. These studies became known only after the Second World War and today their sensational effect seems as characteristic of the mood and outlook of the public as the effect of Spengler's *Decline of the West* in the 1920s. His basic philosophical theses and many individual points of his analyses have been disputed, yet the work as a whole is admired for its boldness of conception. Toynbee, in a mood of fervent optimism, believed in a gradual settlement between Asia and the West; his political prognosis is a world government. This was a welcome contrast to the prevailing, if latent, mood of pessimism. Elements of his later views are evident in his important 1925 essay *The World after the Peace Conference*,[23] in which he argued that, in comparison to 1914, the European political, economic and cultural system had become a world system. Quite apart from Japan and the United States, a number of South American and Asian states were demanding a say in their own affairs; the Arab world, with which Toynbee felt a particular affinity, was in motion. Europe, rather the colonial powers, were economically destroyed and either could or would no longer implement their rule; on the other hand Western civilization was having an increasing influence on all the foreign civilizations, imposing itself upon them. New political structures and measures for ensuring peace were becoming necessary. The League of Nations had taken the place of European domination and also incorporated the British imperial commonwealth with its loose liberal agreements that reached over and beyond the boundaries of continents. Here Toynbee touched on a theme that was pursued and developed further in the Empire and Commonwealth discussions between the wars and after 1945. The conversion of Empire into Commonwealth could be considered a form of decolonization, which made it easier for Great Britain to meet the "challenge" of the new world situation.

One important aspect of the colonial issue in the inter-war discussions was the world economic situation. Unfortunately, economic history thus far has considered world economics only from a European and American standpoint, or else has studied the development of individual colonies without taking much note of the increasing involvements of the colonies in the world economy and the results of their independence on the market.[24]

Much has been said of the economic importance of the First World War for non-European countries. The war upset or destroyed the system of economic exchange in the world, which was largely free in spite of some tendency to tariff protection, and in which Europe, and Great Britain in particular, stood at the centre. The trade of raw materials and food for industrial goods was conducted chiefly by European entrepreneurs who also placed the capital investments. It was a system that functioned smoothly as long as there were stable currencies and a gold standard. At the outbreak of war, old trade agreements were broken and the mother countries adjusted to a war economy; consumer exports had to be reduced and primary production increased. Although difficult for the non-European countries, this offered certain advantages: on the one hand it meant a fitfully growing market for export products and rising prices and on the other, the possibility of industrialization, particularly in the field of consumer goods. Like the United States and Japan, the British dominions and India derived enormous profits from this.

It was impossible to restore the pre-war economy after 1919, and structural problems appeared. Europe was impoverished, had lost a major part of its foreign investments and for the time being could not export much capital. The United States, on the other hand, had developed into the leading industrial power and risen from a traditional state of debt to become a powerful creditor. New York joined London as financial metropolis and trade centre; but it did not play the same role of international clearing-house. The European countries' large debts resulted in an inflationary trend, and scarcity of dollars and transfer problems became typical of the post-war situation. The colonial powers found it necessary to promote economic development. The manufacture of colonial products important to the mother country and trade within colonial territories were stepped up, and the formation of economic and currency blocks at the cost of a free world economy was propounded as a means of overcoming the incipient crisis, which reached its peak in 1929. Economic considerations were closely linked with questions of world politics and prestige: the concentration on the colonial market was designed to counterbalance what seemed like a doubtful reliance on the United States and help Europe maintain its position as a great power. "The development of the Empire is our economic War of Independence against American domination," wrote Leo Amery, and added, in a fitting adaptation of Canning's famous statement: "We have to call a New World of Imperial development into being to redress the wastage of the old".[25]

After the post-war crisis, which caused social unrest, strikes and political radicalization in the industrial countries and in many of the colonies and gave impetus to emancipation movements, a rapid and in part explosive economic boom occurred in Europe and America. The statistics for individual areas and products are striking evidence: cotton in Egypt, Sudan, Uganda and India; nut-oil and palm-oil, cocoa and coffee in West Africa; sisal in East Africa; rice in Burma and Indochina; sugar in the Philippines; tea in Ceylon; petroleum in the Middle East and Indonesia; copper and diamonds in Rhodesia and the Congo; rubber and tin in Malaya and Indonesia. To appreciate this boom one must be aware of the special structure of the colonial economy. Most of the production concentrated on a few branches in which Western capital was invested, which were promoted and developed. Undeniably the colonies profited from this, and their intakes in tariffs, export duties and taxes rose and could be used to develop their administrations, means of communication and cultural services. But equally the economic boom often applied only to particular sectors and a considerable part of the yield and profit was used for reinvestment in the same sector, for developing the transport system, paying the high salaries of European and American officials and for capital amortization. The native inhabitants often gained remarkably little. Production for domestic needs was also neglected and at most received only slight aid from the administration's modest budget. This one-sided concentration on export production, together with the rapid population increase and the considerable indebtedness of the native producers, often resulted in poverty; the cocoa farmers and petroleum or palm-oil producers of West Africa and the cotton farmers of Sudan and Uganda were the exceptions rather than the rule.

Another important factor was the colonies' clear and direct dependence on the world market, that is, on the extent of consumption and the needs of the industrial countries. Until recently colonial history took little notice of the fact that the extension and intensification of agriculture and mining and the founding of new and rival enterprises in other areas caused the production of food and raw materials to rise more rapidly than the need. As a result, the primary producers, i.e. the colonies, suffered from an unfavourable balance of trade[26] and, in spite of growing production and yields, remained relatively behind in the expanding world market. In some cases this led to immediate or incipient crises of overproduction—e.g. sugar in the West Indies—which could not be successfully counteracted by pools, syndicates, restrictions or international agreements. It is well known that Great Britain attempted to halt the falling prices of rubber in Malaya in 1922 by restricting production and in fact only generated a new source in Indonesia and Liberia.

In spite of a slight increase, the processing of raw materials in the colonies and their actual industrialization remained insignificant during the war. The colonial powers showed little interest in this and therefore rarely granted the tariff protection necessary to the development of an industry. This is understandable, since it meant that India, for example, was able to develop its cotton industry to such an extent that it seriously affected Lancashire and played a considerable part in bringing about the crisis in British industry between the wars.[27] This situation in the colonies made the young, nationalist élite, schooled in the West, susceptible to Marxist promises and gave their nationalism a revolutionary accent. The new élite had scarcely any part in the modern, expanding colonial economy and had access only to the lower levels of the administration and technical cadre; the economic development of their country by foreign enterprises, as well as their dependence on the world market and the fact that the manipulations had been taken out of their hands, seemed to them "alienation" and capitalist exploitation, which could be opposed only by national emancipation and social revolution.

The catastrophic condition of the world economy further aggravated the situation. The prices of raw materials collapsed entirely.[28] Exports dwindled, and production had to be suspended. Plantations and mines went bankrupt and workers were discharged; reduced colonial budgets even forced economy measures in education. The formation of blocs and the trend towards autarchy increased: France isolated itself even further in its tariff policy, while England gave up the gold standard and tried, in Ottawa in 1932, to assure itself a part of the colonial imports by a system of imperial preferences. The effects were conflicting. Even if the mother country took over an increasing amount of the colonial exports, it often could not take the entire production, for example, of cocoa in West Africa or tea in Ceylon. Moreover, colonial products could not compete with those of the mother country. France set limits on its wine and wheat imports from North Africa. But when the European and American economies recovered after 1933 and world trade rose again, the terms still remained unfavourable to the colonies. Europe profited from cheap imports, which provided some compensation for the fall in industrial production.[29] When extremely cheap textiles from Japan threatened the exports of the mother country, Japanese imports into French, British and Dutch colonies were drastically reduced. The colonial inhabitants, already seriously injured by the crisis, at a trading disadvantage and in any case scarcely earning a living wage, were now also cheated of the means of directing their modest consumer power to cheap Japanese goods. The colonial powers tried to justify themselves by declaring that Japan imported few colonial products, which posed severe problems for colonial trade and the balance of payments; but this did not remove the psychological and political repercussions of these and similar measures on the nationalist opposition.

The changes in the structure of the world economy inspired M. J. Bonn, a lecturer in economics in Berlin and, after his emigration, at the London School of Economics, to evolve a far-sighted theory of "counter-colonization" which, although almost forgotten today, deserves to be mentioned.[30] Bonn also introduced the term "decolonization".[31] His concept of colonization was very broad; he saw it as the transfer of political, economic and cultural institutions from one society to another and restricted it neither to nineteenth-century expansion nor to expansion overseas but included the Russian advance in Asia, which he considered a form of Communist colonialism.[32] After the partition of the world a counter-movement had taken place which was gaining pace: "For the time being empire-making has come to a standstill, empire-breaking has been going on on an unprecedented scale".[33] Emigration overseas and capital exports had dwindled while the United States had "uncolonized" itself and was in turn pressing outwards; the British dominions demanded protective tariffs, and in Eastern Europe new states had set up further tariff restrictions. The colonial world, from China to North Africa, was resisting economic and political domination and trying to industrialize on its own. Great Britain had been forced to grant fiscal sovereignty to the dominions and even to India and was now withdrawing from Ireland and China. Unrest was the order of the day; debts were unpaid and currencies inflationary. Everyone was calling for sovereign rights and claiming equal status. Europe, which had coined these ideas, would not be able to halt the countercolonization. "This mission implies the ultimate liquidation of domination. It may be a task of decades or centuries."[34]

While economic and currency blocs were forming, non-colonial powers were demanding free and equal access to the raw materials; Japan and Italy had already gone over to open aggression. Would it be possible, asked Bonn, to overcome these trends towards autarchy and disintegration, or would the conflicts and tensions lead to a new world war?

The crisis in the world economy with its tariff and currency blocs provided Fascist Italy, imperialist Japan and the German National Socialists with adequate reasons for asserting that the colonial question was a problem of international politics and using it as a means of applying diplomatic pressure. They used the slogan "have and have-not" powers to differentiate themselves from the colonial powers of Great Britain and France. Belgium, the Netherlands and Portugal, whose territories were underdeveloped and only thinly settled at that time but who nevertheless controlled a large part of colonial raw material production, were also differentiated from the "young and dynamic", closely settled nations with high birth rates who possessed little or no colonial territory, had to pay for their raw materials with foreign bills and were at the mercy of the "monopolies" of the "plutocratic" powers. Japan tried to justify its expansion in Manchuria and China, Italy its attack on Ethiopia, as the acquisition of living space "necessary to survival", since they were overpopulated and lacked basic raw materials. Yet the colonial question did not become an acute diplomatic issue until Germany announced its new colonial claims. The American and Russian challenge was then joined, although briefly, by the German.

The Weimar Republic had never renounced its claim for the return of the German colonies surrendered at Versailles.[35] The "lie of colonial guilt", i.e. the allegation that German colonial administration had been brutal, on which grounds the victors had refused to return German possessions, had understandably inflamed public opinion and led to protests in the national assembly and by the peace delegation. Germany refused, however, to accept the counterproposal to hand back the former colonies as a League of Nations mandate.[36] The colonial propaganda of the Weimar Republic, heatedly pursued in the press, found grounds here for demanding equal colonial rights; it appealed to the need for land for settlement, sources of raw materials and market outlets. This argument was adopted readily and uncritically in Germany although in fact the former colonies could be of little value to the German economy. Even Hjalmar Schacht urged the return of the German colonies before and after 1933.[37] But the colonial issue played a minor role in the parliamentary debates and foreign policy of the Weimar Republic, although the bourgeois parties pressed it as part of the demand for revision of the "Versailles dictate".[38] Apart from the Communists and some left-wing bourgeois intellectuals,[39] the Social Democrats were alone in officially voicing their disinterest[40]; but the Social Democrats participated in the interfactional colonial alliance.[41] Stresemann had sanctioned the colonial claim and, on Germany's entry into the League of Nations, demanded a part in the administration of the mandate (Germany had become a member of the Mandate Commission in 1927 but received no mandate). His programme of revision included the return or redistribution of the colonies, but he did not give the question special urgency.[42]

In *Mein Kampf*, Hitler settled accounts with Kaiser Wilhelm's policy and openly put overseas expansion behind the need for "living space" in Eastern Europe. In the following years he continued to show little interest in the colonies, seeing them only as the final acquisition to be gained after victory over England and Russia.[43] After his success in the West in 1940, Hitler took certain preparatory military and administrative steps with a view to future colonial administration.[44] At the same time, the colonial propaganda of the Weimar Republic was energetically continued; the surviving organizations of the Imperial Colonial League of 1933–1936 were aligned and made directly subordinate to the party leader by the imperial head of the colonial political office, Ritter von Epp. It became clear that the dispute with Versailles and the demands for living space and raw materials were linked with Hitler's alleged defence of the white race.[45] Officially, however, no colonial claims were made before 1936 and then again in 1937.[46] Hitler at first dismissed the colonial issue from his domestic policy, as in his statement of 5 November 1937 (Hossbach-Protokoll), taking into account British resistance. But diplomatically he tried to assert that it was the "only difference between England and Germany",[47] evidently with the intention of using it as a means of exerting pressure on Britain and gaining a free hand in the East.[48]

Hitler's demands in 1936 and 1937 for the return or redistribution of the colonies caused panic in England. The Government was besieged with questions in Parliament and urged to refuse the demands,[49] while lively discussion among the parties and in the press showed a surprising willingness to comply with them in some form. Schacht's theory about the importance of the former colonies to the German economy, which was taken up again in *Foreign Affairs*,[50] was easy to refute, for instance by a League of Nations enquiry.[51] There was also the moral argument that it was unthinkable to deliver African subjects into the hands of race-conscious, National Socialist Germany. On the other hand, Germany's reproach that Britain was in unilateral control of essential raw materials was considered justified. A solution had to be found.[52] As early as 1935 the Foreign Minister Sir John Simon had cautioned the House of Commons to seek an international solution to the problem of raw materials.[53] The Conservative party, under pressure from the diehards and supported by the weighty speeches of Leo Amery, refused to return the colonies, even as a League of Nations mandate; one of their reasons was the strategic importance of the lines of communication with India. Others, like Noel-Buxton and Arnold Toynbee[54] and the press magnates Rothermere and Beaverbrook,[55] did consider the possibility of a German mandate in Tanganyika or an international agreement that would give everyone free access to the raw materials in a large area of Africa set free by several colonial powers. The Labour party once more proposed subordinating all the colonies to the League of Nations.[56] Discussion of the German demands was always connected with the desire to comply with any "legitimate" efforts to ensure peace.

British diplomats, especially Neville Chamberlain, clearly overestimated German colonial interest and were prepared to make concessions. By a policy of appeasement they hoped to persuade Hitler if not openly to renounce his Eastern expansionism, at least to make definite concessions in disarmament or to return to the League of Nations. They were thinking of Tanganyika and of Belgian, Portuguese and French territories.[57] In France, Foreign Minister Delbos showed some interest in reaching a colonial agreement that would perhaps involve conceding Cameroun.[58] But Britain and France considered such concessions only as their contribution within a "general agreement" which presupposed definite pledges from Hitler. Hitler, however, refused to make such statements, either about his demands or what he was prepared to concede; he did not want to commit himself on his activities in the East and was using the colonies only as a means of exerting pressure on the Western powers. In the spring of 1938 Neville Chamberlain and Arthur Henderson realized this.[59] The colonial question was raised again later during the Czechoslovakian crisis and in the months before the outbreak of war.

The German "challenge" remained a diplomatic intermezzo rather than a genuine danger to European colonial dominance. The German attitude was in any case not really anti-colonial. Neither the Weimar diplomats nor the National Socialists tried to use the loss of the colonies in 1919 as a means of gaining economic and political influence in the colonial and semi-colonial territories. Only a few individuals urged this.[60] Germany supported nationalist organizations in the colonies before and during the Second World War and achieved some success in the Arab territories with its anti-semitism; but the revolutions were not very forcefully pursued and had little success, since Germany wanted colonies for itself, and its racial theories were rejected by the coloured nationalists. Gandhi and Nehru, Bourguiba and Ferhat Abbas and Senghor showed no sympathy at all towards National Socialism and openly declared their allegiance to the Allies.

It is difficult to tell whether the German challenge led the colonial powers to make political concessions to the nationalists. Italy's conquest of Ethiopia brought a new agreement between London and Egypt; but for the same reason Egypt accepted Britain's right of intervention. The increasingly sharp criticism of colonial administration in England and occasionally in France around 1930 may have had some connection with Italian and German claims—as is frequently assumed—but its source was different. Discussions of the colonial question did, however, arouse the interest of a wider public and prepare the ground for a future policy of reform.

The Second World War was of decisive importance in speeding up the incipient change in the political scene. Since the conflict had broken out in Europe, non-European countries could not but see it as another "fratricidal war". But this time the war spread to the colonial territories and was connected with Japan's simultaneous claim to hegemony in the Far East. In the First World War, a colonial power (Germany) had been conquered while the real advocates of colonialism (Great Britain and France) managed to assert their strength in spite of their loss of prestige. The Second World War at first brought about an unexpected and total collapse of these same powers. The defeat of France affected Indochina, North and Central Africa. There were no actual insurrections—the French later liked to point out the loyalty of their subjects—and the Vichy Government was able to assert itself as a colonial power and superficially at least ensure its continuity. But the fact that the dominant power had suffered defeat, that the new government was not recognized by its former allies and was attacked by propaganda and, beyond all this, that Free France called for resistance to the Vichy officials, came as a profound shock to the colonials and gave great impetus to opposition movements. When the Japanese installed themselves in Indochina and the Allies landed in North Africa, since the French were so divided, the occasion seemed ripe for creating new organizations and parties, announcing radical claims and playing off the powers one against the other.

Great Britain suffered its most spectacular defeat in its colonies rather than in Europe. The fall of Singapore, that mighty naval base which had become the symbol of Britain's economic interest, military presence and will to dominate in Asia, must be considered an event of the first order in world history and a milestone in the process of decolonization—not only because it entailed the loss of Malaya and Burma and made possible the Japanese conquest of the Dutch Indies, but because the apparently impossible collapse of a system of domination that, if not actually hated, was still considered alien, made a deep impression on the colonial peoples. The noted French expert on Indochina, Paul Mus, made an acute analysis of the "mutation" in the attitude of the Annamite farmers[61]; he said they saw the defeat as the loss of Britain's divine mission of domination, which could not be credibly restored even by the re-establishment of the external apparatus. Religious beliefs may have been different in Burma and Indonesia, but here too there was a psychological collapse. And as though it were not enough that Europe was defeated, the Asian power, Japan, was now asserting itself, taking over administration and exploiting anti-West and anti-colonial feelings by propaganda and skilful subversion. Japan encouraged nationalist opposition, set up "national" governments and finally proclaimed independence, so that when the colonial powers returned, they found themselves faced by a *fait accompli* of newly independent republics. A new generation of nationalists was appearing; the moderate leaders of the pre-war years who were willing to collaborate were being replaced by a younger, radical, at times Marxist-trained élite who had led the emancipation movement in either collaboration with or resistance to the occupying power. After Japan fell and before the Europeans were established again, the new élite was able to break through and confront the colonial powers with its military force and mass organization.

From Egypt to Ceylon, in the countries not conquered by the Axis, the emancipation accelerated by the war pursued its course in a less radical manner. Nevertheless, it too forced the colonial powers to make concessions that would have been unthinkable before 1939 or at best have been relegated to the distant future. France was forced to grant independence to Syria and Lebanon and to announce reforms in North Africa. Britain promised eventual dominion status to India, Burma and Ceylon. The Netherlands wanted to reach an entirely new agreement with Indonesia. Africa south of the Sahara was a new factor; here the class of African manufacturers, middlemen and intellectuals had grown rapidly in size and importance and was making demands. West Africa became an important economic and military terrain for the Allies: the Americans stationed reinforcements for the Middle East there; production was overtaxed, troops were recruited and appointed to various battlefields. Moreover, General de Gaulle had won a territorial base for Free France in Equatorial Africa. In Brazzaville in 1944 a new post-war policy was announced for French Africa; in the British territories constitutions began to be reformed. Although neither the colonial powers nor the African leaders counted on immediate independence, it was apparent that Africa south of the Sahara had now joined the process of emancipation. The Second World War had the same importance for Africa as the first had for the Middle and Far East.

The rapid spread of radical nationalism in the colonies was matched by a growing readiness in the mother countries to counteract the "revolt of the coloured world", if necessary by military force, as well as by concessions and reforms. This was partly a question of necessity, partly because it was difficult to bring the principles according to which they were waging war against the Axis in line with colonial practice. Above all, the colonial powers wanted to break through the stagnant situation of the late 1930s and find a basis for a "collaboration in partnership". Socialist parties were very active; in England and Free France they had already played a major part in the political discussions and decision-making. In 1945 they were given a role in the government. Now the bourgeois parties as well asserted their "anti-imperialist", "anti-colonial" outlook and showed themselves ready to reform. If in the First World War imperial dominance lost its self-assurance and the "white man's burden" became a doubtful concept, these notions disappeared entirely during and after the Second World War, or had to be reinterpreted in such a way that they appeared to be legitimate and convincing forms of preparing for decolonization and eventual independence.

The "international challenge" that had arisen in 1917 and snowballed in the inter-war period reached its peak and further speeded up the process of decolonization. Decisions of world policy were now in the hands of the "external" powers, America and Russia, and their anti-colonialist policies forced the colonial powers onto the defensive, both during the common-front stage and later during the Cold War.

The United States under Franklin Roosevelt made clear its anti-colonial attitude during the war and in the inter-Allied conferences, as well as in official and press statements.[62] This led to differences of opinion over the interpretation of the Atlantic Charter. Prime Minister Winston Churchill, who had proved himself a diehard imperialist, wanted Article Three, which declared the "right of all peoples to choose the form of government under which they will live", to apply only to the European countries freed from the Axis powers; the Atlantic Charter did not "qualify in any way the various statements of policy which have been made from time to time about the development of constitutional government in India, Burma or other parts of the British Empire".[63] Churchill did not support the idea of a universal right to self-government, nor did he want to be dictated to by the reform policy of the interwar years; doubtless he assumed that even in India self-government was not yet an acute issue. Roosevelt, on the other hand, stated emphatically that the right to self-determination declared by the Atlantic Charter applied to all the peoples of the earth and that America would actively support it. With the support of the 1940 Republican presidential candidate, Wendell Willkie, the American press attacked the colonial powers, symphathized with nationalist movements and warned Europe that America did not want to fight for the reconquest of lost territories. Many of these views were superficial, unjust and occasionally hypocritical, not least with respect to America's own colonial and semi-colonial positions; yet it was recognized that national emancipation in Asia had received enormous impetus from the war and that it was in America's interest to win the sympathies of the new states and try to "canalize" the newly released energies: "Unless the forces of nationalism, which are fast growing more and more powerful in all these vast areas of the earth, are canalized into constructive channels, a devastating state of chaos will ensue. The determination of some of these peoples to secure their freedom cannot longer be thwarted."[64]

President Roosevelt accused Churchill of "old-fashioned" imperialism, urged London to make concessions to India and made contact through special envoys with Congress party leaders. But he did not fail to realize that the decision lay in Britain's hands and that America must not offend its most important ally. Such considerations were absent in the case of France where American anti-colonialism could unfold fully. Roosevelt ostentatiously made contact with the sultan in Casablanca, urged the independence of Syria and Lebanon in Cairo, and even tried to prevent the re-establishment of France in Indochina during the great war conferences. Since, even in the American view, most of the colonies were not yet "ripe" for independence, an extended mandate system was to guarantee that the administration was conducted in the interests of the inhabitants and to prepare them for self-government. By this means it was hoped that the colonial question could be withdrawn from the arena of Great Power rivalry.

In 1945 the League of Nations Mandate was replaced by the Trusteeship of the United Nations. Roosevelt and the U. S. Department of State had originally aimed at a system of trusteeship for all the colonies, but they gave in to British resistance and restricted it to the former mandated territories and some of the areas conquered by the Axis powers; this had been agreed in Yalta. The articles of the United Nations Charter referring to the colonies ended as a compromise after lengthy negotiations in San Francisco between the colonial powers and the anti-colonialists, the latter led by China and supported by the Soviet Union.[65] The Mandate Commission of the League of Nations now became the Trusteeship Council of the United Nations, made up of both mandated and non-mandated territories. It received reports and could send out its own research commissions and hear petitions; its task was to prepare the areas concerned for self-government or independence. Article 73 has been called the "Colonial Charter" of the non-self-governing territories, i.e. the colonies in the literal sense: according to it, the colonial powers retained full power of control but pledged themselves to comply with certain conditions and to present an annual report to the United Nations on economic, social and cultural progress. With some difficulty, the colonial powers managed to avoid having to provide political information and to prevent independence from being declared the ultimate aim. The term "self-government" was agreed upon since it seemed wide enough to cover dominion status or—in the case of France—full integration and membership in the Union française.

The Trusteeship Council was very active. It examined hundreds of petitions and sent out special delegations whose often highly critical reports were submitted to the special commission of the General Assembly. Since states without colonies were in the majority, this led to violent anti-colonial polemics. The anti-colonial bloc tried to extend its influence in the non-self-governing territories, and in 1946, by a rather doubtful legal procedure, a Committee on Information from Non-self-governing Territories was formed to force the colonial powers to give political information and to fix "timetables" for independence. These measures aimed at linking the colonies more closely with the trusteeship areas and providing the United Nations with an important say in the decisions. The colonial powers resisted as a matter of principle, although with little success; they also resisted because they were irritated by the often unobjective criticism levelled at them by the Soviet Union and its satellites, as well as by the South American and Arab states who themselves were far from providing the democratic rights and social progress they demanded of the colonial powers.[66]

It is difficult to assess the influence of the United Nations on decolonization, though doubtless it was considerable. The possibility of addressing petitions to the United Nations, the creation of research commissions in the trusteeship territories, the critical reports and the influence of the anti-colonial bloc in United Nations meetings, gave the colonial opposition opportunity to make extensive demands and to force the colonial powers onto the defensive. France had to grant a special status to Togoland and Cameroon and, by this sudden decolonization, created a precedent that pointed the way via autonomy to independence for other parts of French West Africa and Equatorial Africa. The United Nations consented to 1960 as the date for granting independence to Somaliland, which was administered as a trusteeship by Italy and was perhaps the least developed area of Africa. It is said that the reproach to Belgium that it was neglecting higher education for the Africans in

Ruanda-Urundi and allowing them very little say in political and administrative affairs contributed to the formation of universities in the Congo.[67] But the decisive factor was that, apart from the special agencies of the United Nations, the General Assembly and the Security Council concerned themselves to a very large extent with colonial issues and took a more or less stern stand against the colonial powers in their resolutions. The anti-colonialism of the Asian and African states, supported by the Soviet bloc, found in the United Nations a forum before which it could appeal to world opinion. The colonial powers concerned managed to prevent what they considered unsuitable interference in their domestic affairs and often remained absent from the negotiations or warned against doubtful Communist manoeuvres to gain the sympathies of the "coloured world"; but they could not avoid paying heed to U.N. negotiations and resolutions.

The United States found itself in a dilemma.[68] It considered itself an anti-colonial power and was still willing to defend this attitude fervently. The colonial charter and the United Nations Trusteeship Council were essentially its doing and would never have come into being without United States' initiative. On the other hand, it was aware that the colonial powers were its main allies. True, British imperialism, which had been the stumbling-block for Roosevelt, was coming to an end by itself and more rapidly and completely than the Americans had expected: India, Ceylon and Burma were independent as early as 1948. On the Indonesia question, Washington stood back or tried to negotiate at first; it did not openly oppose the Netherlands until 1948. This irritated the Dutch without contenting the Asians, particularly the Indians. Moreover, during the Indochinese war the colonial question had moved into the sphere of the Cold War. In 1945, the United States refused military aid to France and very soon made contact with the Viet Minh; but after Mao's seizure of power and the Korean war, it found itself forced to reinterpret the "colonial war" as a war of defence against Communism and to grant the French massive military and financial aid. In the 1950s, when the Moroccan, Tunisian and finally Algerian questions demanded a definite stand in the United Nations, the United States again found itself caught in a conflict between, on the one hand, anti-colonialism and the desire to maintain the sympathies of the Asian and African world, and on the other, its allegiance to its Atlantic Treaty partner and its own strategic and economic interests. At least it was now possible to support the emancipation of Africa south of the Sahara more openly.

The Netherlands, France and Portugal may tend, with understandable bias, to hold the United States responsible for the loss of their overseas positions and to overestimate American influence; but it is undeniable that the pronounced anti-colonialism of this leading Western power had some obvious or latent effects on European governments and in the colonies and accelerated the process of decolonization after 1945. The value of the acceleration remains an open question; perhaps it had a negative effect on the young states and on Europe; perhaps the reluctantly accepted pressure from America made it easier for the colonial powers to beat a timely retreat from positions that had become untenable and, in most cases at least, to prevent bloody conflicts.

The Soviet Union supported all the colonial emancipation efforts. It made full use of propaganda against the colonial powers and supported the Afro-Asian "revolution" as part of its own global dispute with the "imperialist West". However, the Soviet Union had its own serious ideological and tactical problem, which was the old question of the function of nationalist bourgeois organizations and Communist parties in the struggle for independence. Stalin's dogmatic attitude prevented him from making full use of his opportunity after 1945. A former specialist on the "national and colonial" question, Stalin had stressed the need for an alliance with the colonial opposition in the 1920s, but showed surprisingly little interest in Asia and Africa during and after the Second World War. After the failure in China in 1927, he concentrated on industrial development of the Soviet Union and later on directly extending his own territorial power. The proletariat in the colonies was still weak and badly organized, and even Mao's successes were not taken seriously at first.

Moscow did not issue new directives until late in 1947.[39] During the war, the Communist parties had been forced to join the Allies and fight against Japan. This had allowed the formation of an "antifascist" front in Japanese-occupied territory, in Indochina—where the rate of success was highest—Indonesia and Burma. It also resulted in a conflict with the Indian Congress party which for many years weakened the Communist party in India. In the Allied war conferences, Stalin naturally supported Roosevelt's anti-colonialism and rather half-heartedly approved the system of trusteeship. But although in San Francisco the Soviet Union supported the anti-colonial bloc and styled itself the "true friend of the peoples suffering under the colonial yoke", it did not allow an open rift to develop with the West; in fact it demanded Russian trusteeship for Tripolitania at the end of the war, evidently with the strategic aim of gaining power in the Mediterranean.[70] At Potsdam, Great Britain and the United States had great difficulty in preventing Russia from becoming a colonial power in North Africa! Stalin, however, was chiefly interested in setting up peoples' democracies in Eastern Europe and hoped to come to power "legally" in certain Western European countries by the skillful use of peoples' fronts. Thorez was deputy prime minister of the French Government that in 1945 replied to unrest in Sétif (Algeria) by brutally repressive measures; and even the Union française gained the approval of the French Communist party.⁷¹ Stalin based himself on Lenin's theory that Western imperialism would never give up its colonial positions voluntarily since capitalism would necessarily collapse without colonies, and that consequently independence could be achieved only by revolution. When the British Labour Government granted independence to India, Burma and Ceylon in 1947, which the Soviet Union had clearly not expected, the Soviets had to interpret this independence as "fake" and "illusory". For the same reason, Nehru and U Nu were labelled "tools of British imperialism" and traitors to the nationalist revolution. In Asia, with the exception of Indochina, decolonization took its course with the help of agitators from the Communist parties but not under their leadership. In 1947–1948, after the expulsion of the Communist parties from the French and Italian Governments, when Stalin tried to impose a solution in Europe by means of revolutionary strikes, the Berlin blockade and the Prague putsch, a Communist uprising was sparked off in Asia, particularly in Burma and Malaysia and in somewhat different form in the Philippines and in India, in the name of a change of course. The uprisings failed, after lengthy civil wars, and the Communist parties were outlawed or found themselves isolated.

Khrushchev fundamentally revised Stalin's policy in Asia and Africa.⁷² The "two camp" concept gave way to the notion of a "tripartite" world, in which former and still-existing colonies played the part of a "neutral zone of peace".⁷³ Nationalist bourgeois parties were recognized, wooed by diplomacy and propaganda, and given developmental aid. The broad outlines of the new course were apparent in the Geneva Conference of 1954 and the Bandung Conference of 1955, Khrushchev's visits to Asia, the "rehabilitation" of Gandhi and the wooing of Nasser—despite the fact that the Communist party in Egypt had been prohibited—together with trade agreements to meet momentary difficulties in the developing countries. The independence or striving towards independence of these countries now counted as "genuine" if they pledged themselves to a bloc-free foreign policy without Western support; this of course meant that there was a chance of winning their sympathies, binding them economically or involving them in a "united anti-imperialist front" against the West, above all against the United States.

The change of course had particularly strong effects in Africa, where decolonization was entering the decisive phase. So far the Soviet Union had paid little attention to Africa. Naturally it had tried to gain a foothold there, either directly or by means of European Communist parties, to win over intellectuals, to train young people and infiltrate the trade-unions; but, as in Asia, it had considered the leading nationalist organizations "petit-bourgeois" tools in the service of British or French interests. This still applied to Nkrumah and his Convention People's party in 1954, as it did to the Nigerians Azikiwe and Awolowo, and Houphouet-Boigny, who had put an end to the collaboration of his Rassemblement Démocratique Africain with the Communist party of France in 1950 and had then become a minister in the government of the mother country. From 1955 on, the Soviet Union and its satellite states began to do intensive research on Africa. They abandoned traditional theories and "legitimized" the nationalist bourgeois organizations. But the revision came too late to play a decisive role in the decolonization of Africa. Morocco and Tunisia and the colonies of British and French West Africa became independent between 1955 and 1960 without any major contribution from the Communist parties. In the Algerian war, in spite of military aid and diplomatic coverage of their rear, the National Liberation Front clearly separated itself from the Communists, not least because the memory of Sétif was still rife. In the Congo, after the mutiny of the Force Publique, a political vacuum formed which the Soviet Union tried to penetrate; but United Nations action was temporarily able to prevent the Cold War from spreading. In East Africa, independent nationalist organizations were at work, although Kenyatta too had been under Communist influence between the wars.

It is possible that in the final phase of decolonization, when the problem takes on a radical form, Communist groups will gain the upper hand in Southern Rhodesia or Portuguese Africa, by a policy of infiltration and terrorism. Whether Communism will manage to seize power in individual emergent nations in the post-colonial era remains to be seen. The Communists have had a certain amount of success certainly; but the young states have shown an unexpected inner resilience and, moreover, are determined to go "their own way to socialism" and to defend their newly won independence and neutral foreign policy against the threat of being made satellites of the Soviet Union. What is important here is that Lenin's and Stalin's theory that decolonization in Asia and Africa was possible only under Communist leadership and that the capitalist West would not survive withdrawal from its colonies has not proved accurate.

The East-West conflict shifted the colonial issue into the realm of world-wide discussion, in which both blocs declared their anti-colonialism and at the same time competed for political and economic influence in the "Third World". This made it more difficult, if not impossible, for the colonial powers to maintain their position. Decolonization was speeded up by the East-West conflict, but not released by it. Important as the international aspects outlined here were, the actual source of all decolonization movements lay in the process of colonization itself. The "opening up of the world" by Europeans necessarily set in motion a process of emancipation which destroyed traditional social structures and led to the formation of "new" societies and nations that had, at a given moment, to resist alien European dominance and demand the sovereign rights proclaimed by their teachers.

Europe did not decolonize of its own accord, although many historians and journalists would prefer to take this view. It was challenged to do so by the colonial peoples. Europe had exhausted itself in two great wars, had brought to life counter-movements, and was no longer willing to maintain its domination by any means. Battles during the retreat could only temporarily conceal the fact that ever since the First World War Europe had become increasingly aware that the colonial domination it had justified ideologically as the "white man's burden", trusteeship, or civilizing mission, was reaching its inevitable conclusion.

I. Great Britain

THE THIRD BRITISH EMPIRE

The term "the Third British Empire" was coined by Alfred Zimmern, professor of international relations at Oxford, in 1926, shortly before the Imperial Conference.[1] Zimmern divided the history of the British Empire into three periods. The first spanned the early expansion overseas and lasted until 1776–1783. The second, from the American War of Independence until the First World War, was marked by the construction of a new Empire, based on sea-power and trade, whose components gradually achieved internal autonomy yet remained politically dependent on the mother country. But during and after the First World War, in the third period, the Empire had been transformed into the British Commonwealth of Nations. This, thought Zimmern, was the beginning of a new era.

The Commonwealth, as the largest single political community, could best be described, in the words of General Smuts and Sir Robert Borden, as "a procession. It consists of a large variety of communities at a number of different stages in their advance towards complete self-government". During the war great states had crumbled, and yet the British Empire, founded on free institutions, had maintained itself, although it too had changed. The unity of the Empire had been demonstrated, thought Zimmern, even though the hopes that it could be given new institutions—a reference to the attempts made to form a federation—had proved mistaken; for the concept of Nationhood was gaining a hold throughout the Empire. London must take this new situation into account. But, he added, what was granted to the colonial settlements could not be denied to the "coloured" parts of the Empire. Zimmern describes as a "landmark" the Pronouncement on Indian Policy of 20 August 1917 which promised "responsible government" to the subcontinent, because it entailed "the definite repudiation of the idea that . . . there can be, under the British flag, one form of constitutional evolution for the West, and another for the East; or one for the white races and another for the non-white". And India was no exception;

what was granted to India must, at the proper time, also be granted to the other, non-white British peoples.² This should not be understood as the disintegration of the Empire, for a number of bonds—however tenuous in legal terms—still held firm and were propelling world politics along the road to international co-operation. As an example of this he quoted the naval agreement of 1922, the new international economic situation and, above all, the League of Nations. He saw the Commwealth as a more closely-knit unit within the League of Nations, a world-wide instrument for the preservation of peace. British imperialism must adapt itself to this new situation. Henceforth the word "British" could no longer be taken to denote a particular race, nationality or territorial division and the idea of "white supremacy" could not be upheld, even though the Anglo-Saxons, as opposed to the Latins, might find it difficult to give up their race-consciousness. Dominions were not simply nations that had not obtained sovereignty; membership in the Commonwealth went beyond mere self-determination. Zimmern considered the theory that nation and state were "unhealthy" terms; on the other hand, "the movement for cultural self-determination which we find springing up within the British Empire is perfectly sound, healthy, and indeed inevitable". London was not attempting assimilation; on the contrary it had depoliticized the concept of nationality and particularly the notion of "British" and as a result had made possible an association of "equal self-respecting communities".³

Alfred Zimmern's account of the problems facing British imperialism in the inter-war period recurred in various forms in the discussions of politicians and political writers. It seemed vital to attempt to assimilate the movements set in motion or accelerated by the war and to employ them in a new concept of Empire that would interpret the transition to a Commonwealth not as a loss of power and prestige but as an intentional process of reconstruction.

The question of the dominions took first place, but withdrawal from the colonies also entered the discussion in so far as this seemed an inevitable development once the British Empire and its future unity was no longer based on the proud uninterrupted exercise of power, but instead justified itself by granting self-government. After 1919 the question of whether, when and how the franchises conceded to the dominions would or could also be granted to the colonies—that is, the territories with no European settlement—was raised, although it did not become a political issue until after the Second World War.

The new political self-awareness apparent in British colonial discussion between the wars was accelerated by the First World War; yet the seeds had been planted long before 1914.⁴ The period of imperial expansion and aggression characterized by the policy of such men as Joseph Chamberlain and Cecil Rhodes ended, as we indicated in the introduction, with the Boer War. The effects of the South African war with its military defeats, doubtful methods and enormous costs had been sobering, and the jingoism spread by the new mass publicity media was wearing off. Under pressure from the German navy, Great Britain began to tone down her traditional imperial rivalries, as demonstrated by the colonial agreement with France in 1904 and the treaty with Russia in 1907. In internal policy, after the failure of Chamberlain's campaign for imperial preference and the Liberal victory in the 1905 elections, other problems came into the forefront. Reports of colonial wars in India, the Sudan and Africa continued to interest the reading public, but the great proconsuls like Curzon, Cromer and Milner had already been dislodged from their key positions before 1914; Campbell-Bannerman and Lloyd George belonged to the anti-imperialist wing of Liberals who had opposed the Boer War. And in reaction to the Boer War, colonial imperialism was undergoing a process of demystification, thanks chiefly to Hobson. In 1902, referring to "special" economic interests, Hobson attempted to show that the nation did not profit from expansion and that the capital could be just as well if not better invested at home. Colonial reformers like E. D. Morel and Sydney Olivier described the crude methods of exploitation most common in the colonies; this incensed the British public during the Congo debate and also became a political issue within the dominions. The immigration of Chinese coolies into South Africa met unexpectedly strong opposition in Parliament. Hobson and the colonial reformers exerted their influence in the Fabian Society and consequently also on the young Labour party. Reform seemed in the air—stricter controls, new administrative measures and also political concessions.

At this point it is sufficient to note the Liberals' South Africa policy and the 1909 Morley-Minto reforms in India. The dominions' growing self-assurance also showed the need for a re-examination and prompt modification of the entire structure of the Empire. With their *Round Table* group, Milner and his "kindergarten" had begun to inspire new faith in the Empire; the aim of the proposed federation was not to increase the number of British territories, but to prevent the disintegration of the Empire and to consolidate it. During and after the First World War it was possible to pursue these new objectives.

At first, however, in 1914, Britain found her traditional policies apparently confirmed. The dominions acknowledged the sovereignty of the mother country and took an active part in the war, although their refusal to do so, or even a complete break with London, could not have been prevented. Even India put money and troops at Britain's disposal. Shortly before the outbreak of war, Lord Curzon, the former viceroy and an exponent of pre-war imperialism, declared:

> An Empire like our own, which has overrun the world, which embraces hundreds of races and scores of States, many of which were claiming,

and rightly, to be counted as nations themselves—that such an Empire should voluntarily hold together when there is no force to compel it to do so, when the forces that are working the direction of separation are so strong, when separation itself is so easy—will be an unparalleled and magnificent achievement.[5]

His prediction has proved true, and innumerable speeches in Parliament and in the press in the following years praised this unity of the Empire, which had successfully withstood the burden of war. But the reference was chiefly to the dominions, for it was they who before, during and after the war constituted the focal point of the discussion and determined the nature of the transformation from Empire to Commonwealth. As Curzon indicated, the non-British and non-white territories (that is to say, India and the colonies) were cursorily lumped together with the dominions, although their military aid to the mother country had only in a sense been voluntary. And in fact Curzon himself had refused to take their claim to nationhood as seriously as that of the dominions. But this identification was significant and finally led to Zimmern's reform theses. The white colonial settlements had travelled the road from representative to responsible government and had been granted the status of dominions. The British did not view this as leading to a dangerous and compulsory disintegration of the Empire; in fact it was the only possible policy in keeping with the English tradition of liberty. During the war this granting of self-government was perceived as an expression of the true nature and meaning of the Empire. And this lead to the gradual acceptance of dominion status for India and the "Dependent Empire" too. Initially, however, it was more a matter of promise than practice.

At first sight, the First World War represented both a splendid corroboration of traditional policies and at the same time the end of British imperial expansion. Two powers—Russia and Germany—who had been competing with Britain in the colonial arena had been eliminated. This meant an end to the threat of a Russian advance via Afghanistan into India or via Persia to the Indian Ocean, as well as the end of Germany's naval resources and claim to world power. By incorporating former German colonies into the Empire, Britain managed to establish the much-coveted Cape-Cairo line. At the same time, the destruction of the Ottoman Empire and the British presence in Palestine and Iraq secured British control of the route to India. This policy was, of course, energetically pursued by the exponents of pre-war imperialism, Curzon, Kitchener, Milner and also Winston Churchill—all one-time members of the War Cabinet. In an address to the king on the occasion of the cease fire in 1919 Lord Curzon expressed the proud self-assurance of the imperialists in these pathetic terms:

... at least we may say this—that the British Flag never flew over a more powerful or a more united Empire than now; Britons never had better cause to look the world in the face; never did our voice count for more in the councils of nations, or in determining the future destinies of mankind. That that voice may be raised in the times that now lie before us in the interests of order and liberty, that that power may be wielded to procure a settlement that shall last, that that Flag may be a token of justice to others as well as a pride to ourselves, is our united hope and prayer. . . .[6]

Anti-imperialist opinion had been suppressed during the war, yet it found widespread public support and remained a live issue for the opposition. The anti-imperialists blamed the war on outdated political policies—secret diplomacy, the arms race, spheres of influence, the "balance of power". In effect they were calling into question the entire structure of traditional foreign and imperial policy. More and more voices began to be raised openly against annexation and the extension of imperialist commitments; considerable sympathy was expressed with Wilson's peace proposals. Socialists began to speak of the "imperialists' war".

The British took an active part in the discussion surrounding the formation of the League of Nations,[7] in which the colonial question was incorporated into the fight against nationalism and militarism. An international administration and the application of the mandate principle promised to prevent new rivalries among the powers and to promote the interests of the native inhabitants. The Union of Democratic Control, with E. D. Morel, Hobson, Brailsford, Norman Angell and Bertrand Russell defended these views strongly and with considerable success. But Liberal intellectuals like Gilbert Murray, and Labourites, were not alone; even Conservatives like Lord Cecil took part in the discussion. Even Lloyd George thought it necessary to be conciliatory and in his famous address to the trade-unions on 5 January 1918 he declared his belief in self-determination, which in the future was also to apply to the colonial peoples. The "consent of the governed" must constitute the basis of the peace negotiations.[8] On 28 November 1918 the Imperial War Cabinet accepted the mandate principle[9] and in Paris Lloyd George described British policy as one of non-annexation, accepted the League of Nations mandate for the former Turkish territories and a few German colonies, and—in the interest of solidarity and future relations with the dominions —supported the demands for annexation made by the Union of South Africa and Australia. Amery, Milner's secretary, relates[10] that Lloyd George did not oppose the imperialists' strategic demands, but that he found himself restricted by the idealistic statements made by Wilson and the British government during the war. The prime minister tried to avoid appearing an old-school annexationist and imperialist.

Great Britain was also beginning to realize that in spite of apparent gains, its position in world politics had changed considerably for the worse. War losses, the liquidation of assets abroad, and large internal debts had resulted in severe economic difficulties. The United States had become a major power; British sea-power, particularly in the Pacific, had become ineffectual; and in the Far East Britain was increasingly faced with emancipation movements. In fact emancipation had been encouraged in the Arab states where Britain had opened negotiations with the Arab sheiks, promising them the establishment of independent states. Immediately after the war the Irish question also took on critical proportions, and in India nationalist opposition was rife. There were riots in Egypt and Mesopotamia; in 1919 Afghanistan attacked India; Persia had rejected all prewar treaties and Turkey, hard hit by the war, disrupted British plans by its impressive national revival.

This is the situation Britain had to face around 1919. The traditional measures no longer seemed to apply and British policy in the Middle East in 1919–1920 was a confused web of conflicting agreements and intentions basically imperialist in tone. At first military measures were attempted to quell local unrest. Meanwhile, however, important members of the bourgeoisie, including some imperialists, were beginning to rethink the problems of Empire and attempting to formulate an imperial and colonial policy in keeping with changed conditions and attitudes. It had become clear that the proud self-assurance which—in spite of growing dissent—had identified British domination in the pre-war years with Pax Britannica and civilization, had weakened during the war and the immediate post-war years. Symptomatically, people were reluctant to call themselves imperialists now; imperialism had become shameful, the term an insult. Anyone who still believed in the Empire had to dispense with any ideas of expansion and relegate the concept of "domination" as far into the background as possible; the defense of colonial positions had to be justified in terms of liberty. It is significant that Milner's "kindergarten" was actively involved in this search for a new concept of Empire. This same search was also to play an important if indefinable role in imperial and colonial policy in the inter-war period with men such as Lionel Curtis, L. S. Amery, Geoffrey Dawson (chief editor of *The Times*) and Philip Kerr (the future Lord Lothian).

Philip Kerr, editor of the *Round Table*, exemplified the changing attitudes. As early as 1916 he sought to strike a middle road between imperialist jingoism and a policy of laissez-faire.[11] He considered that the terms "Empire" and "imperial" were being misapplied. Kerr had of course rejected exploitative imperialism; but even more important, he made a stand against the adherents of what he saw as a misconception of Liberalism, who were not interested in the colonial question and were prepared to leave the "backward peoples" to their own devices without taking into account that their confrontation with the destructive powers of modern economics had proved disastrous: "the backward people is unable to resist, not the virtues, but the vices of civilisation". According to Kerr, the justification of a colonial power lay in the duty, or at least the possibility, of "putting an end to intolerable sufferings among backward peoples". The mission of the Empire was the preservation of peace, law and good government; but it was also the preparation of four hundred million people for "eventual self-government".[12] The war had demonstrated both that "autonomy" was not yet "full self-government" and that the dominions must be granted full equal rights; it had also shown the necessity of a corresponding policy for the dependencies, for "things can never be after the war what they were before".[13] The pace had to be stepped up and the "growing demand for full self-government among the peoples who are still under the tutelage of some more civilized power" had to be taken into account.[14] "The desire for self-government is essentially healthy," and this applied alike to the dominions and to India and Egypt. Of course these aims could be achieved only gradually: "The ruling people ought to govern the dependency as trustees for all mankind, having as their ultimate aim the raising of the inhabitants to the level at which they can govern themselves and share in the great responsibilities of the world." This kind of declaration places Kerr among the reformers. His concept of trusteeship, which we shall discuss more fully later, enabled him to oppose the tendency toward indifference on the part of British policy-makers and the desire for a premature withdrawal from the dependencies, and to encourage more intensive imperial and colonial aid in the name of Britain's inexorable responsibility. All the colonial theories of the following years are contained and anticipated in Kerr's thought. Labour politicians, Liberals and Conservatives were to employ the same or similar terms, like "trusteeship" and "gradual granting of self-government"; the only differences were in the tone of voice and attitude of mind, in the practical application, and not least in the time factor. Some politicians were to hold political concessions to be necessary, others considered them premature.

Kerr's essay *Harvest of Victory*, published in 1919, shows how he tried to adapt himself to the new conditions in world politics.[15] He not only gives due warning of the Russian and Japanese aggressive tendencies which, he thought, obliged the West to remain on the alert, but he also describes the desire for emancipation in the Far and Middle East, realizing that although it may have had some Bolshevik support, it must also be recognized as a "genuine grievance". Kerr held the oligarchic rulers in Great Britain before 1914 responsible for this. They had not worked hard enough to establish self-government and had chosen the easier way of "efficiency". The democratization of England that came as a result of the war, and had also found expression in the new voting rights of 1918, would encourage new ideas and help Great Britain to fulfill its duty of fostering self-government and democracy world-wide. For "unless Great Britain learns, and learns soon, what democracy means, so that she may be able to teach self-government to the peoples for whom she is responsible, the creation of that Commonwealth of which we have dreamed may never come into being".[16] To oppose the new nationalist movements, which Kerr considered the product of Britain's mistakes, comprehensive political reforms had to be introduced. This must not, however, be confused with the "imperialist's" willingness to compromise. These proposals of Kerr's correspond to the concept of Empire as understood by the *Round Table* group: if the Empire was to be transformed into a Commonwealth of self-governing associates, federally connected among themselves, and if the decisive step beyond the prevailing type of colonies was to be risked and voluntary co-operation made possible even for non-white territories (India, Burma, Ceylon, perhaps even Egypt), then these potential Commonwealth members must be granted self-government at the right time. Otherwise the growing, and indeed inevitable, desire for self-government would turn these nations against Great Britain and prevent the formation of the new Commonwealth "of which we have dreamed".

Britain's diminished international stature and the rise of the United States as the "potentially most powerful nation in the world" led Kerr to implicate America in Great Britain's future commitments. He pointed out the Bolshevik threat in the "underdeveloped areas"[17] and the "destructive forces" which, he said, the war had unleashed and to which Africa and Asia could offer but little resistance. To tender aid here was an urgent responsibility for the "Western powers", a new "white man's burden", which had to be shared by all the victorious powers, including the United States.[18] Kerr, who ended his career as British ambassador in Washington in 1940, urged close co-operation between the two Anglo-Saxon countries. In spite of his distrust of Wilson's plans for an international colonial administration, he welcomed the League of Nations[19] as "the alternative to the balance of power".[20] The League and the Commonwealth were in no way mutually exclusive, but complemented one another. Instead of a balance of power which had proved ineffective, he proposed the construction of a multilateral system for the preservation of peace. Here, he believed, the British Empire could become a model for the League of Nations because, for example, it linked nations of different races and thereby forestalled eventual conflict among them. Kerr agreed with Lionel Curtis, the most important member of the *Round Table*, on this matter[21] and also with Arnold Toynbee.[22] Milner, however, is said to have observed with some trepidation that his "disciples"—though by no means all of them—were placing their hopes in the League of Nations instead of in the mighty Empire, the Pax Britannica which spanned the world.[23] The difference of opinion between Milner and his "kindergarten" becomes obvious here. While the proconsul still lived in the pre-war era with its uninterrupted exercise of power, the war had shattered this unquestioning power-consciousness among the younger generation. They pinned their hopes on the League of Nations as the instrument for creating and preserving peace.

A brief look at Lord Milner himself might help to clarify this "generation gap" and at the same time demonstrate the surprising adaptability of the pre-war consul. In *Key to My Position*,²⁴ his 1923 "political testament", he wrote: "I am a Nationalist and not a Cosmopolitan." For Milner continued to consider his duty to his own country and its greatness "The Divine Order of the world, the law of Life and Progress". But while he was a "British Nationalist", Milner did not consider himself insular in his outlook. He was, he said, an imperialist whose patriotism had racial rather than geographic borders. "I feel myself a citizen of the Empire. I feel that Canada is my country, Australia my country." His aim was to establish a community of race, language and civilization. To base the Empire and the Commonwealth on this kind of community meant that it was not possible to give India and the colonies the kind of status the dominions had hitherto had. This attitude distinguishes Milner from his "disciples" like Philip Kerr, who had already anticipated "coloured dominions" and considered the future transition to a "multi-racial Commonwealth" the great mission of the United Kingdom. However, Milner did realize that present relations with the governed peoples could not be sustained forever, since, he admitted, "the more important units of the Dependent Empire will not consent, as they grow up, to remain dependent". He was not proposing independence or dominion status, but "a new form of organization" which would not be based on hierarchic structure but rather would be a "Britannic Alliance of nations of equal status" without any "formal bond". It would be held together by various informal ties and by a system of preference, and would form a far-reaching autarchic unit. In practical terms, Milner started by pointing out the immense economic losses Great Britain had incurred during the war: the country had lost the greater part of its foreign investments and had debts totalling some 1000 million pounds; the export situation with Europe was bad, and no rapid improvement was in sight. But "we are living in a new world, and we must learn to accommodate ourselves to the new conditions". Politically, Britain would have to move closer to Europe; economically, it was necessary to exploit the "almost immeasurable . . . potentialities" of the Empire. True, Britain was doing a great administrative job in the colonies, but the economic backwardness in "our undeveloped estate" was sad. Here lay the great task of the future.²⁵ In the tradition of the "constructive imperialism" of Joseph Chamberlain, for example, Milner proposed an "Imperial Development Fund" and anticipated a colonial economic policy which Britain was not to introduce until 1929 and 1940, and only to implement on a large scale after 1945.

And so, in the person of Milner, the Empire-builder and Empire-apologist, we find a remarkable fusion of the proud imperial self-assurance of the pre-war years and, at the same time, a clear recognition of the problems generated by the war. He continued to believe in the mission of the Empire and in the possibility of its unity, but at the same time he also accepted the reality of decolonization; his conduct during the Egyptian crisis, for example, proved that he was not satisfied with mere declarations. His economic proposals recall Chamberlain's campaign for imperial preference and anticipate the 1929 Colonial Development Fund and the Ottawa agreement of 1932. In the inter-war years his "pupil" L. S. Amery carried on his work and tried to impose his ideas in Parliament and in the press.

Immediately after the war Great Britain's most pressing problem, apart from India, was the emancipation movement in Egypt. It is worth drawing a brief sketch here of British policy and public opinion on this issue, for the important practical problem of Egypt clarifies many of the divergent positions which were to remain relevant for the entire inter-war period.

During the war London had scarcely concerned itself with the future of Egypt. In 1914, when the Khedive fled to Constantinople and Turkey joined the Central Powers, Great Britain had annulled Turkish sovereignty and declared Egypt a protectorate. Subsequently Egypt developed into an important military base. Compulsory recruitment, requisitions, rising prices and lack of consumer goods, crowned by the tactless behaviour of officials and servicemen stationed in the country, served to create bitter anti-British sentiment among the population, a result of which was a considerable increase in support for the nationalist opposition.[26] Under Zaghlul Pasha (1906–1912), Cromer's minister of education, the nationalists became more radical, demanded independence and the abolition of the protectorate after war ended. Neither London nor the British administration in Egypt realized the extent of this opposition in time and as a result no substantial steps were ever taken beyond the establishment of the apparently well-tried system of "benevolent autocracy" firmly embedded behind the façade of a sultan and an Egyptian Government—and this in spite of earlier agreements and the promises of independence made to the Arab sheiks during the war.[27] Accordingly, Lord Balfour wrote to High Commissioner Wingate on 27 November 1918: "the stage has not yet been reached at which self-government is possible"; the British Government had no intentions "of abandoning their responsibilities. . . ."[28] The belief that although Egypt had made enormous progress under British domination, it did not yet possess the requirements for self-government seemed beyond further discussion, and by virtue of this any unpleasant demands could be dismissed as "premature". In fact, Britain was primarily concerned with the Suez Canal, the "life-blood of the Empire", and saw little cause to withdraw from Egypt and thereby endanger its position vis-à-vis the canal. London was therefore unprepared when, late in 1918, Zaghlul demanded an interview with the British Government and proposed to send a delegation to the Paris Peace Conference to promote Egyptian demands for independence. Although the prime minister backed Zaghlul and High Commissioner Wingate supported the demand, the officiating foreign minister, Curzon, refused talks in London. Thereupon the Egyptian prime minister resigned and the agitation became bitter, but the administration continued to send reassuring reports to London. Not until serious disturbances—strikes, demonstrations and acts of sabotage—broke out in March 1919 and the nationalist leaders, including Zaghlul, were arrested did the British Government begin to concern itself with Egypt. Wingate was replaced by Lord Allenby, the victor in the Palestine campaign, and while he took a firm stand, Allenby released Zaghlul and declared himself ready to negotiate.

London ordered a commission of experts under the chairmanship of Colonial Minister Lord Milner to investigate the situation and make proposals for constitutional reforms "under the protectorate"; but their departure was delayed and Milner did not arrive in Cairo till December 1919. By then the situation had reached a state of crisis and the commission was sabotaged. Milner realized the violence inherent in the nationalist movement and decided it was necessary to be conciliatory; he arbitrarily reformulated his instructions, omitted the clause "under the protectorate", and declared himself willing to compromise between Egyptian demands and British interests.[29] In his remarkable report[30] he openly admitted British errors during the war and urged an end of the protectorate and the grant of independence. He said that Egypt had never belonged to the British Empire, that London had always pretended the occupation was only temporary and that Egyptian nationalism was legitimate and must be taken into consideration.

And so we find Milner, the pre-war Empire-builder, completing the break with existing policy and demanding that London order a partial withdrawal from Egypt. Obviously he recognized that the nationalist opposition to the protectorate and to British domination had grown so strong during the war that force alone was no answer, and that an agreement had to be reached by bilateral negotiations. Milner did not pass over the question of the Suez Canal; but very clearly stressed the importance of imperial lines of communication; to safeguard them Britain must never permit the influence of a foreign power in Egypt. Yet he was convinced that a treaty of alliance would ensure Britain a privileged position and, as a result, indirect control over Egyptian foreign policy, since the nationalists were primarily concerned with independence and not necessarily with anti-British policy. Milner went even further, negotiated with Zaghlul in London and managed to draw up a memorandum acceptable to both sides in which Great Britain recognized the independence of Egypt and even its right to diplomatic representation; in return Egypt declared that it would renounce any anti-British foreign policy and, among other things, that British troops should remain stationed in Egypt "for the defence of the imperial trade routes".

Milner's course of action and his report made clear both how perilous Great Britain's position in the Middle East had become, and his own astonishing flexibility and comprehension. The Cabinet and a section of the public, however, were shocked by his arbitrary action and rejected his proposals.[31] Unexpected support came from among those who were directly responsible for the Egyptian situation: High Commissioner Lord Allenby, the specialist on Egyptian affairs in the Foreign Office, and even Montagu, secretary of state for India. These men seem to have recognized that the critical situation in Egypt had to be met by making some far-reaching concessions; after Amritsar and the Indian boycott movement and in the face of the difficulties in Persia and Afghanistan, London had to avoid the grave implications of a military engagement which could not be justified either by internal or external politics. Not even Curzon could dismiss these considerations, although he seems to have defended his position very forcefully in the Cabinet.[32] The well-known *Times* India expert Sir Valentine Chirol did not go quite so far as Milner, but he too criticized the prevailing disregard of Egypt and demand a declaration on the lines of the 1917 Pronouncement on India. He proposed an alliance model led on a dyarchy, in which Egypt should be responsible for part of the administration while British ministers remained in charge of foreign affairs, defence and finance.[33] The *Round Table*, with its imperialist attitudes, and the liberal *Economist*, expressed sympathy with Milner's proposals.[34] The main adversary in the Cabinet, apart from Bonar Law, was Winston Churchill who, in his brusque fashion, strongly opposed any form of concession, would not take the Egyptian nationalists seriously and optimistically thought the affair could be settled by a show of force.[35] Within the Conservative party, the weighty figures of Austen Chamberlain, Lord Salisbury, Lord Selborne and the son of Lord Cromer—all members of families who had played a decisive part in British nineteenth-century expansionism—were ranged on Churchill's side. "We feel as if we were approaching a period of disintegration . . . we are not tired of Empire," Lord Salisbury said in typical diehard style.[36] Prime Minister Lloyd George, who in 1918–1920 hedged opportunistically between anti-imperialist declarations and an aggressive stand in the Turkish question, did not commit himself one way or the other but seems to have submitted to the Conservative majority in the Cabinet.

Lord Lloyd, high commissioner in Egypt from 1924 to 1929, was another exponent of conservatism. In retrospect he sharply criticized the British in 1919–1922 for being unprepared and ill-informed and having lost contact with the masses; by vacillating between harshness and concessions they had forfeited all trustworthiness. Negotiations with Egyptian and Asian nationalists were useless in any case and necessarily led to nothing but more capitulation.[37] Lloyd accepted the British presence in Egypt, considering it "good government" and in the interests of the masses. To grant independence and yet to demand rights of reservation was disgraceful, since this amounted to a renunciation of the only justification for British control in Egypt, namely the role of trustee, and was evading responsibilities while at the same time claiming a privilege. Independence, self-government and democracy were Western slogans that had little meaning in

Asia and certainly did not resolve the concrete problems; only a questionable feudalist upper class would make such demands. The masses would not, for "good administration is their only desire and concern—and it is because we have allowed administration to be obscured by political issues that we have brought such heavy troubles upon the shoulders of all concerned".[38]

Even in the inter-war years Lord Lloyd was profoundly convinced of the legitimacy of British domination. He tended to identify the interests of the colonial power with those of the dominated peoples, he did not take the nationalists seriously and, in the conflict between "good government" and the gradual grant of self-government, he openly declared his allegiance to the former on the grounds of the British welfare policy. Lloyd considered British willingness to make concessions a weakness, a doubtful attempt to evade the difficulties of the post-war period, and he regretted that "the days of our strength and beneficence were gone. Cromer and Kitchener, whose word was power, were but dim memories".[39] But the decisive issue was whether this concept of "benevolent despotism" with its conscious depoliticization, which had been justifiable before 1914 as having led to the most positive achievements in imperial policy, could have any relevance or any hope of success now, after the war. Lord Lloyd believed that it could; the more far-sighted Lord Milner denied it. It seems mistaken to me to see Milner merely as an example of the British ruling classes' desire for domination weakened by the world war.[40]

Lord Lloyd's self-assurance, opinions and arguments are typical of the diehard faction within the Conservative party who were to gain prominence, particularly in the Indian question, under the leadership of Churchill. This attitude was shared by members of the Colonial Service, who needed moral justification to confront the emancipation movements; in clear distinction to the intellectuals of the opposition, they still thought it necessary to assume the function of "trustee" for an indefinite period of time. But later it was to be of decisive significance that the opposition to the diehards had not originated only among the Liberals and the Labour party, but had followers even within the Conservative party. Beside Lord Lloyd stood, so to speak, Lord Milner; and, appropriately, most of his "pupils" showed his same remarkable powers of adaptation, and they helped determine colonial policy in the inter-war years.

The 1921 negotiations with moderate Egyptian representatives came to nothing; the British Government did not feel bound to Milner's proposals and did not wish to discuss the Egyptian demands, particularly the demand for the withdrawal of British troops. However, Lord Allenby urged further concessions and finally—paradoxically enough—it was the High Commissioner himself who in February 1922, under threat of resignation, gave London an ultimatum and forced Lloyd George to capitulate.[41] As early as 28 February the government published a declaration stating that it recognized the independence of Egypt and the end of the protectorate, but would retain certain significant reserved powers: assurance of the imperial lines of communication (i.e. the Suez Canal), defence of Egypt against any foreign attack or intervention (i.e. control over Egyptian foreign policy), protection of the European inhabitants and control of the Sudan. Thus, in 1922, London accepted what the Egyptian nationalists had demanded late in 1918 and what Milner had tried to grant in 1919–1920. What London could have granted in 1918 in an agreement with Zaghlul and from a position of some strength appeared in 1922 as an enforced concession to nationalist agitation and therefore could do no more than temporarily calm Anglo-Egyptian relations.

Great Britain attempted to "solve" the Mesopotamian question in a similar fashion. Here, however, opposition within Britain was weaker since strategic interests were less affected. In addition, arabophiles like Sir Percy Cox, Gertrude Bell and T. E. Lawrence had already prepared the way, and their word had to be honoured; then a bloody uprising emphasized the need for an immediate decision, so that in 1921 even Churchill had to give in. In the parliamentary debate another point of view was heard: Great Britain now had enough "responsibilities" and should not take on any more "burdens". The Marquess of Crewe took this view in his speech in the House of Lords:

> I cannot help feeling, that in undertaking the responsibility for the whole of this vast area [Mesopotamia] we are doing too much. After all, the time is passed when the people of this country will be prepared to play the fairy godmother to all undeveloped parts of the world and to hold themselves responsible for introducing a higher standard of administration in uncivilized countries. We simply cannot afford it.[42]

These words, which try to suggest that Great Britain had committed itself overseas in order to provide the inhabitants of underdeveloped areas with good government and help their development, can only be taken as an attempt to throw an ideological veil over a concrete situation of power politics and established interests: England could or would no longer have any effective political and military power in Mesopotamia and was therefore clearing the way for a "liberal" settlement. This attitude was in fact characteristic of one aspect of the British post-war situation: London was beginning to realize that Great Britain had weakened in spite of war-time successes and could have little interest in keeping control of any additional trouble spots. In the inter-war years this insight made it easier to pursue a policy of conciliation, particularly when there were also other means of safeguarding military positions and economic interests. London continued to suppress disturbances severely, at times even brutally, but nevertheless tried to give in at the right moment and to grant a minimum of concessions in order to avoid the unforeseeable consequences of open conflict. By comparison for instance with France, which tried to incorporate the new territories, including Syria and Lebanon, into a conception of *la plus grande France* in spite of these nations' mandate status, and then considered them as indivisible parts of the national territory whose sovereignty had to be defended by every possible means, Great Britain proved to be more flexible and permitted various forms of government, some of which could even hope to obtain eventual independence. Iraq too became "independent" as early as 1922, though until 1932 it remained bound by the League of Nations mandate; but London could still effectively apply its military, economic and political influence. France, on the other hand, constructed an extensive system of direct administration applying even to the mandated territories, and the attempts by a Popular Front government to grant Syria and Lebanon a treaty-bound independence on the British model failed because of the bourgeois Conservative opposition, and remained "out of the question" until 1939.

This brief introductory survey is intended to provide an overall picture of the changes in British imperial attitudes, hastened or generated by the First World War and to point to a few of the problems besetting Britain in the inter-war years. It is also intended to make clear the differences of opinion within Britain and the tensions within the various parties that determined colonial policy during this time. If we adopt Alfred Zimmern's image of a "procession" of various parts of the Empire on the road to self-government, the following themes become clear:

Although decolonization of the white dominions was practically ended, we nevertheless had to devote a chapter to the Commonwealth. The relationship between the dominions and the mother country remained a focal point in the discussion until 1930 and retroactively affected decolonization in India and the Dependent Empire.

India was the central problem of the Empire in the inter-war period; it was no longer just a matter of reforms, but how and when dominion status was to be granted.

In contrast to France, actual colonial policy is of secondary importance. What were Great Britain's aims and what was achieved during the inter-war years? We have already encountered the important terms "trusteeship" and "self-government" and we must now determine their individual meaning and decide to what extent they were implemented. The example of West Africa on the one hand and of Kenya on the other can serve to illustrate important variants in British policy in Africa and at the same time the ambiguities inherent in the terms "trusteeship" and "self-government".

THE BRITISH COMMONWEALTH OF NATIONS

The conversion of Empire into Commonwealth during and after the First World War was one of Great Britain's major political achievements and represents the conclusion of a process of decolonization. It reconstituted relations between the colonies, which had long been pressing for independence, and the mother country, which, with its sense of empire, tried to maintain the comprehensive imperial league. A formula was found that took the diverging interests into account and managed to satisfy both sides.

At first the new measures applied only to the British "daughter states" where the settlers were British subjects who had always observed British law and had already obtained a high degree of local self-government. Remembering the secession of the American colonies, Britain did not let the problem develop into open warfare. When the Canadian settlers began to show signs of discontent with the Legislative Council, their local parliament, and to come into conflict with the London-appointed governor who held executive power, the famous 1839 report of "Radical Jack", Earl of Durham, pointed out the future path: the Canadians were to receive responsible government so that tensions between the settlers and the mother country would not lead to secession. The recognition of the colonies as nascent nations also made it possible—and this must not be overlooked—to put a stop to the annexationist tendencies of the United States. "Responsible government" meant a government responsible to the elected parliament, i.e. autonomous in its own colonial territory but subject to clear limits in the "imperial sphere" (chiefly foreign policy, overseas trade and constitutional power), which remained in the hands of the mother country. What the American colonies had striven for before 1776, namely full autonomy within the Empire, was now granted the Canadians, first to individual Canadian colonies and then in 1867 to the Federation of Canada. New Zealand received responsible government in 1856; the "Commonwealth of Australia" came into being in 1901; and finally the Union of South Africa in 1909–1910. After the 1907 Colonial Conference the term "dominion" was adopted. The unity of the Empire was guaranteed by the "indivisible Crown", represented in the dominions by the governor-general. Above all, this ensured diplomatic unity. Canada, however, had obtained fiscal autonomy and participated in trade agreements very early on, and had become a member of international technical organizations.

At first British imperialists after 1880 were less concerned with extending their domination over new areas of Asia and Africa than with the crucial question of safeguarding the unity of the Empire in the face of the colonial settlements' autonomy, or perhaps reconstituting it. They considered forming an "organic union" with its own federal institutions, a kind of imperial council or parliament, which would stand beside and yet be distinct from the Parliament of Westminster and would decide on foreign policy, defence, etc. Lord Rosebery and the Imperial Federation League urged this, and Joseph Chamberlain fought for it with his imperial tariffs campaign, which aimed at an "Empire Free Trade" or a system of preferences to consolidate the Empire.[1]

These men were self-confessed imperialists who saw the Empire as the instrument of British power and British influence in the world. But the rise of the Wilhelminian Empire raised the question of whether the mother country really could compete and survive in the arms race, particularly in its naval development, without assistance. Surely it was only right to involve the aspiring dominions? But this did not seem possible unless they were given some say in British foreign policy. It was an inescapable dilemma; either the process of dissolution would continue, or a federation must be formed to create a new unity. Common British origins, law, language and customs did not provide sufficient incentive for integration to guarantee the Empire's future position as a leading world power. Led by Lionel Curtis, the most ardent propagandist of federation, and Philip Kerr, the first editor of the *Round Table*, influential study groups were organized in both the mother country and the dominions with the aim, as stated in a memorandum of 23 January 1910, of forming an "organic union . . . by the establishment of an Imperial Government constitutionally responsible to all the electors of the Empire, and with power to act directly on the individual citizens".[2] But they could not ignore the internal differences of opinion, and in any case, for the time being, it seemed pointless to aim at more than a wider co-operation.[3]

Richard Jebb took the opposite side in his highly respected *Studies in Colonial Nationalism* in 1905.[4] During a world tour, he became aware of the growing nationalism in the dominions, but he thought this should be considered an increase in self-confidence, a "national self-respect" which openly opposed British control and authority but was not "disloyal" or "separatist". The dominions were by no means contemplating a break; they were striving for independence, a trend that was natural, healthy and could not be stopped. Great Britain, he said, must abandon its "colonial view" and, on the basis of equality, implicate the dominions more closely in the military engagements and foreign policy of the Empire. Jebb, "the first publicist who thoroughly understood dominion loyalties",[5] objected to federal institutions and asked only for an alliance of partners, supported by an openly negotiated system of preferences.

The two theories existed side by side during and after the war. But they could not be attributed to opposition between the mother country and the dominions, for the boundaries overlapped. For instance, in the Imperial Conference of 1911, the prime minister of New Zealand, Sir Joseph Ward, demanded an elected imperial council that would decide on defence powers and levy its own taxes. But Canada and South Africa with their non-British minorities refused this, as did the British prime minister, Asquith, who did not want to limit London's monopoly of decision in questions of foreign policy, particularly since the main burden of defence costs had to be borne by Britain.[6] In the years before the war, the dominions were more closely involved in military planning and kept better informed on diplomatic affairs, but the power of decision remained in London and the dominions had only the power of deciding whether to supply troops in case of war.

The crucial question arose in 1914. The British declaration of war on 4 August 1914 automatically applied to the whole Empire, since the British king could not be at war and at peace simultaneously in the same country. But the dominions decided independently on their war credits and troop supplies, which they granted generously in spite of the resistance of the non-British inhabitants. The loyalty of the dominions and the unity of the Empire were proven to the world when Sir Wilfrid Laurier, prime minister of Canada, declared in Parliament on 19 August 1914: "We are British subjects, and to-day we are face to face with the consequences which are involved in that proud fact. Long have we enjoyed the benefits of our British citizenship; to-day it is our duty to accept its responsibilities and its sacrifices."[7]

The dominions raised contingents of troops and supplied raw materials, food and even munitions. A change of emphasis was evident in the Empire, and London took it into account in 1917 by forming the Imperial War Cabinet, which had advisory capacity only, but nevertheless became an important political panel of the Empire. Moreover, the South African, Smuts, was a member of the British War Cabinet.

The federalists had found an incentive and now saw an opportunity for the long-desired reconstruction of the Empire; the spontaneously demonstrated unity was to be ensured for the future by means of institutions. The *Round Table* naturally engaged in very lively activity here: they said the declaration of war in 1914 had proved that foreign policy could not be conducted communally by several governments and that the dominions automatically had to enter the war, in spite of their "autonomous national Government in their own and our esteem".[8] The Empire, they said, had acted as "one state" and had continued to do so in the interests of the common cause and world peace. The *Round Table* attempted, on the basis of the "British nationality" of all Crown subjects, to awaken a national sense of Empire and to confront the dominions with this, saying that the Empire, as the embodiment of values common to all its parts, stood above the dominions. But they agreed that the incongruity between the unity of the Empire from the outside and the dominions' justified claim for a voice in internal affairs had to be resolved and that this required an imperial government which would be responsible not to the British Parliament but to an imperial corporation and thus to the peoples of the Empire.

Lionel Curtis introduced the term "Commonwealth" in his 1916 book *Problem of the Commonwealth* to refer to the Empire of the future. In Cromwell's time the term had been used in the sense of *respublica*; it was first applied to the Empire by Rosebery in 1884.[9] Now it was used to demonstrate programmatically the alliance of freedom and unity. Empire meant a domination which imposed on the dominions duties in foreign policy that were incompatible with self-government. The dominions, said Curtis, had a right to participation and control, but they also had the duty to help shoulder the common responsibility. It is impossible to overlook the fear in these words that in the future Great Britain would no longer be able to bear the common burden of defence alone and would have to share it among the members of the Commonwealth.[10] Curtis was consistent—if not doctrinaire—and drafted a federal constitution inspired by that of the United States; its acceptance would have meant that the Parliament of Westminster was debased to a "local" parliament of the "dominion Great Britain", while an imperial parliament would have had to form an imperial cabinet with central offices and the machinery of control and taxation.

Lionel Curtis' ideas found some response during the war in circles interested in the imperial question. In 1916 Lord Milner, a member of the War Cabinet, considered the British Empire to be potentially the most powerful state system in the world, lacking only a united leadership. He thought the Imperial War Cabinet could become the basis for a conversion of the Empire by constitutional law into a kind of federation.[11] Lord Cromer,[12] the *Round Table* and Philip Kerr, who had become Lloyd George's private secretary in 1916,[13] held similar views. Even the prime minister was infected by the enthusiasm and saw in the Imperial War Cabinet the beginning of a new era in imperial history.[14] The Liberal party leader and minister Herbert Samuel made a different suggestion: since Curtis' plans would hardly prove acceptable in the dominions, he proposed an imperial cabinet and an imperial assembly, both appointed by the dominions but with only advisory capacity, as a possible step in the direction of federation.[15] Lord Bryce also supported this idea.[16] But opinion was divided. In the cabinet, Lord Balfour and Bonar Law, as well as Milner's private secretary L. S. Amery, objected to federal institutions because they realized that the dominions would resist and considered that explicitly constitutional plans would be a threat to the unity for which they were striving.[17] Even within the *Round Table* group, Curtis' ideas were successfully disputed by more realistic thinkers.[18] Did the dominions in fact want federation? Did not their self-confidence, which had grown in the war, demand a further loosening of the ties with Britain and press the claim for the extension of their sovereign rights to include foreign policy? Did the alternatives, federation or dissociation, which the federalists had put forward, have any relevance to the Empire at all?

The constitutional lawyer A. B. Keith was representative of the anti-federalists influenced by Jebb.[19] Keith did not contest the necessity for closer collaboration, "but the difficulties of any federal system . . . are both numerous and formidable".[20] The dominions, he said, were still "dependencies of the United Kingdom" according to international law, but this situation was no longer tenable. Their participation in the war must not be misinterpreted; it was caused not only by a spirit of loyalty and sense of union, but just as much by a desire for freedom and full self-government. Great Britain must comply fully with this demand for independence. "All possible steps must be taken to further the national life within the Empire of the self-governing Dominions. Nor is it doubtful that this end is to be obtained in one way only, the encouragement of the greatest autonomy in self-government with the creation of closer bonds of union between the several parts of the Empire as a whole."[21]

Decolonization could not be halted, he believed. In fact it must be supported if the mother country wanted to retain the allegiance of the colonies. He did not think federation a solution, because the political, economic and military differences between England and the dominions were far too great. Neither Canada and Australia nor the mother country were prepared to surrender their jurisdictions to a federation; the protectionist interests of the dominions also ran counter to federation. Instead, Keith proposed a form of union "which has no existing parallel".[22] Keith made practical proposals for the future of the governor-generals, the Privy Council and the legislative supremacy of the Parliament of Westminster, and suggested a better reform in foreign affairs for the dominions. Anticipating future developments, he wrote:

> The natural solution for the position of the Dominions, suggested by the result of the Conference of 1911, is that each Dominion should proceed to attain complete independence as a unit of international law, and that the Empire should be reconstituted on the basis that on the one hand should stand the United Kingdom in political control of the Crown Colonies and of India, and on the other hand the self-governing Dominions, each as an independent state. . . . It is not suggested that this independence need be separation: the Dominion might still under its new status remain a kingdom closely allied with the United Kingdom in sentiment and under the same monarch, but nevertheless as an independent unit in international law, and therefore internationally not responsible for or involved in the blunder of British foreign policy.[23]

Perhaps the creation of the Imperial War Cabinet made effective coordination possible between the mother country and the dominions, but it was only a temporary, war-time measure to counteract an urgent problem, and not a permanent solution. The 1917 Imperial Conference made it clear that the majority of the dominions was not prepared to agree to any federal plans and certainly did not see the Imperial War Cabinet as a step towards imperial government. In an important resolution, in which they postponed the clarification of constitutional questions to a later special conference, they already indicated their bias:

> They [the dominions] deem it their duty, however, to place on record their view that any such readjustment, while thoroughly preserving all existing powers of self-government and complete control of domestic affairs, should be based upon a full recognition of the Dominions as autonomous nations of an Imperial Commonwealth, should recognize their right to an adequate voice in foreign policy and in foreign relations, and should provide effective arrangements for continuous consultation. . . .[24]

This effectively blocked the way to federation; the dominions demanded full control of their domestic affairs and refused to surrender any of their powers. It was still not clear what "adequate voice" meant, for they still recognized the unity of their foreign policy, at least implicitly, with that of Britain and the preponderance of the British Government.

Worth noting in this period of transition is the use of the term "Imperial Commonwealth". Canadian Prime Minister Borden emphatically refused to let himself be outvoted—particularly in regard to the case of the French Canadians—by an imperial council. He thought the future lay in an "increasingly equal status between the Dominions and the Mother Country",[25] and that the alternatives, federation or independence, were not applicable to the complex situation. By contrast, the New Zealander Massey, who called himself an imperialist, considered imperial conferences insufficient and asked that a "representative Imperial Council" be formed. According to him, the Empire had "the freest and most progressive form of government that the world has ever seen".[26] General Smuts skilfully took up this praise of Empire but stressed that the constitutional development of the daughter states must lead from colonial status to that of self-governing dominions and finally to full independence, "setting aside the Federal solution as not applicable to this Empire, which is not merely a State but a system of States".[27] In *The British Commonwealth*, he gave the term introduced by Curtis his own, different definition: the daughter states must achieve full freedom, and even the supplement "British" was no longer really acceptable. The term "Empire" was also inappropriate, he argued (like Curtis), since Germany, Rome or India were "empires", but the dominions constituted a "Commonwealth" which anticipated a universal league of nations.[28] The only unifying elements remained the

Crown and regular conferences at which the dominions could assert their influence on British foreign policy.

In the following years, Smuts was frequently cited in England in vindication of the concept of the Commonwealth. His followers could point with pride to this Boer general who, in a very few years, had become a good friend of Great Britain and a supporter of the Commonwealth. They willingly ignored the fact that Smuts had stubbornly resisted plans for integration of a constitutional kind and had supported full independence, while at the same time managing to use his relations with London directly in the national interests of South Africa.

The dissolution of the Empire as a unit of international law was completed after 1919. The dominions wanted a part in British peace plans and the Paris negotiations, and London had to give in. The result was a compromise: Lloyd George signed for the whole of the British Empire, but the dominions and India signed the Versailles peace treaty separately and themselves became members of the League of Nations. "A diplomatic unity had declared war: a diplomatic multitude proposed to conclude Peace."[29]

The events of the following years need not be described anew.[30] The first consequences of the decision reached in 1917 appeared in 1919. But the dominions were slow to take advantage of their newly won independence in international law. Although Canada obtained British approval for establishing its own embassy in Washington in 1920, it did not post an ambassador until 1926. During the Chanak crisis, some dominions strongly opposed Lloyd George's isolationist attitude and forced him to change his policy. In the 1923 Imperial Conference, the dominions obtained the right to enter into state agreements, and after the Treaty of Locarno, a treaty signed by Great Britain had to be ratified by the dominions in order to be valid for them too. Yet the dominions continued to use the diplomatic services of the mother country, and in 1939 Canada, for example, had ambassadors only in the United States, Japan and France. In foreign policy they were equally reticent and accepted Great Britain as the leading power and "senior partner" in the Commonwealth. They did not feel threatened from overseas, were not interested in Europe and relied on the defence powers of the mother country. In a certain sense the relationship was even reversed: London bore the defence burden, while the dominions assumed a veto right the British Government had to recognize if it did not want to imperil the unity of the Commonwealth. In the Munich crisis in 1938, the dominions strongly encouraged a policy of appeasement, and their position here has been described as "power without responsibility".[31]

Ireland's rise to dominion status in 1921, the debate about the position of the governor-general in Canada in 1924 and the replacement of Smuts by the "nationalist" Hertzog in South Africa in the same year forced Britain to agree to a "legal" definition of dominion status, in spite of violent resistance. At the 1926 Imperial Conference Lord Balfour managed, "in almost Athanasian terms",[32] to concentrate the diverging theories into the famous formula:

> They [the dominions] are autonomous Communities within the British Empire, equal in status, in no way subordinate one to another in any aspect of their domestic or external [!] affairs, though united by a common allegiance to the Crown, and freely associated as members of the British Commonwealth of Nations. . . . The British Empire is not founded upon negations. It depends essentially, if not formally, on positive ideals. Free institutions are its life-blood. Free Cooperation is its instrument, Peace, security, and progress are among its objects. . . . While equality of status is thus the root principle of our Inter-Imperial Relations the principles of equality appropriate to status do not universally extend to function . . . in the sphere of defence the major share of responsibility rests now and must for some time continue to rest with HMG in Great Britain.[33]

The Conference of Westminster in 1930 supplied the rules of execution and removed the last vestiges of ascendancy by the mother country: the governor-generals became "viceroys" and were no longer the representatives of the British Government in the dominions. The dominion parliaments obtained sovereignty and equal status with the Parliament of Westminster. Relations between the governments were in the hands of the high commissioners. The Colonial Laws Validity Act of 1865 was suspended, and the British right of veto in dominion legislation was dropped. The only remaining institutional parenthesis was that the Crown continued to act as constitutional head of each individual dominion as a symbol of unity.[34] Apart from this, the Commonwealth was to be based not on "law" but on loyalty, customs, free institutions, race, religion and language. The conversion of Empire into Commonwealth was thus complete, although in the meantime the term made current by Curtis had completely altered its meaning and was now used in Smuts' sense.

The Statute of Westminster in 1931 was followed by the Ottawa agreements in 1932. Joseph Chamberlain's bold notion of creating an internal Empire Free Trade and at the same time tariff protection in order to secure the unity of the Empire economically from without was, as we have seen, taken up again by Milner during the post-war crisis. In 1930 the press magnate, Lord Beaverbrook, launched another Empire Free Trade campaign. It had little parliamentary success but gained the support of some "imperialists" such as L. S. Amery and the diehard Lord Lloyd. Beaverbrook was trying to solve the economic crisis "nationally", i.e. within the Empire, while also attempting again to reinforce the imperial league. He pointed out once more that the world powers, America, Russia and Japan, as well as a united Europe, were facing Great Britain with the crucial issue of whether to join one or another of the blocs as a secondary power, or whether to remain an independent and considerably autarchic world power by concentrating on the Empire.[35] It was not for nothing that the supporters of Empire Free Trade were suspicious of the League of Nations, showed little interest in Europe and wanted to retire into the "splendid isolation" of the pre-war era. Ottawa did not bring about imperial economic unity on the basis of internal free trade as had been hoped. The painfully negotiated compromise merely resulted in a system of mutual preferences whose immediate economic significance may have been considerable, but which was soon undermined again by rising prices and special treaties like the one between Canada and the United States in 1935. It in no way affected the independence of the partners, but the network of interests it created certainly contributed to the system's stability and later extension to non-white territories. In affect, it bound the dominions to the mother country and strengthened the loosening structure of the Commonwealth, whose ties consisted essentially of imponderables, by concrete economic measures.

Great Britain found it easy to reconcile itself to the conversion from Empire to Commonwealth. Plans for federation were still submitted occasionally, but usually in adulterated form and always with emphasis on the unity of the Empire in foreign policy.[36] Winston Churchill, a diehard in imperial affairs, reacted sharply to Amery's optimistic words in the parliamentary debate on the Westminster Statute on 20 November 1931 and objected to the surrender of the still existing legislative powers, warning against the effects of this on India [!]; however, he did not engage in serious opposition.[37] Sharp criticism of the 1926 Balfour Declaration was made by, among others, Robert Stokes in his 1930 book *New Imperial Ideas*. He argued that without at least a rudimentary imperial executive, the dissolution of the Empire was inevitable. Lord Lloyd agreed with him in the preface. But this sort of opposition was an exception.

Since either the dominions were not very active in foreign policy or their interests coincided to a large extent with those of the mother country, the dissolution of imperial unity in foreign policy was scarcely apparent at first. It still seemed possible to speak of a whole, and Great Britain was able to assert its claim to world power with some justification. Common membership in the League of Nations also facilitated the transition; Alfred Zimmern called the League a *deus ex machina*.[38] Lionel Curtis' and Philip Kerr's attempts to reconcile the League and the Commonwealth have been outlined above.[39] By contrast, L. S. Amery and Sir Edward Grigg, the future governor of Kenya, believed there was a kind of conflict between the two, since matters of defence remained the responsibility of Great Britain but appeared to be furnished by the League of Nations. At the Geneva Conference the dominions managed to get their international status recognized without having to assume any concrete responsibility.[40] The "imperialists" were understandably concerned with informing the dominions of the advantages they enjoyed by virtue of belonging to the Empire—was not their safety still guaranteed by the British navy and not by some international organization like the League of Nations?

Amery was also involved in drafting the Balfour Declaration, and although he was a little anxious about the risks it entailed for the Empire,[41] he saw it as a solution that fit the situation. He therefore tried, like many others, to present it as an intentional and welcome conclusion of British colonial policy, leading "from self-government to full nationhood".[42] We have mentioned Alfred Zimmern's *Third Empire*, with its typical reinterpretation and ideological exaggeration of the terms of the Declaration. According to him, the Commonwealth was to be understood not as the dissolution of the Empire but as the fulfilment of a concept inspired by the secession of the American colonies and leading, via the Durham Report, to a partnership of nations of British origin with equal rights, who were sovereign and independent but united under a common Crown and sharing common ideals; it was a unity in freedom and served as an example to the world! The Commonwealth was not a state, said the noted lawyer Ernest Barker, "nor is it not a State; for it can feel, believe and even act as one [!]. It remains, at bottom, something beyond and above politics. But what a good thing it is that there should be something of that sort in the world—especially in these days!"[43]

The gradual change of terminology here is worth noting. We have already seen how the words "imperialism" and "imperialist" had been debased and were used only pejoratively, in the sense of domination and aggression. Unlike their master, the "pupils" of Milner no longer described themselves as "imperialists", and this change is evidence both of a new generation and of the new situation obtaining after 1919. But the British Government still adhered to the term "Empire" and the corresponding adjective "imperial". In official language, with its rather conservative terminology, "Empire" referred to the comprehensive imperial league, which also included the Commonwealth, India, the Crown Colonies and the protectorates.[44] There was a tendency, however, to juxtapose Commonwealth, India and the colonial, i.e. dependent Empire[45] or to go a step further and use the word "Commonwealth" for the imperial league as a whole, even though India and the colonies had not yet gained dominion status.

The reinterpretation of Empire as Commonwealth and the attempt to justify ideologically the idea of self-government in the anti-imperialist era seemed to imply the development of the Afro-Asian colonies into dominions. We have seen the beginnings of this decisive new attitude in the case of Philip Kerr[46] and Lionel Curtis. The same applies to Duncan Hall, who played an important part in the constitutional questions of the Commonwealth.[47] The trend is even clearer in the case of Zimmern, with his "procession" image including the colonies. John Coatman might also be noted here. In *Magna Carta*—the title is probably an allusion to Dilke's *Greater Britain* of 1868—he tried to establish a philosophic basis for the Commonwealth in terms of the world historical process of transformation from city state via national state to world state. He described the Commonwealth as "the greatest achievement hitherto recorded in human organization". He also introduced the notion of an "expanding Commonwealth", implying that sooner or later India, Ceylon, Burma and "even less familiar" names would obtain dominion status. "We shall, in fact, see Empire continually transforming itself into Commonwealth."[48]

Such statements accepted the possibility of a future extension of dominion status to non-white areas, foretelling and paving the way for a multi-racial Commonwealth. But they were of a rather incidental nature and seemed unusual or misguided to contemporaries. T. E. Lawrence expected this reaction, as shown by his letter to *The Times* in 1920: "I shall be told that the idea of brown Dominions in the British Empire is grotesque. Yet the Montagu scheme [India] and the Milner scheme [Egypt] are approaches to it, and the only alternative seems to be conquest, which the ordinary Englishman does not want and cannot afford."[49] Similarly, Professor Coupland in his important book *Empire in These Days* asked the apt question: "A dominion of Nigeria, for example, why not?"[50] But even these rare supporters of an extension of dominion status counted on such long delays that the question lost all urgency. It was not for nothing that the Commonwealth was called the "British Commonwealth"! On the whole it still seemed self-evident that the status of "self-governing dominion" was applicable only to the colonies by settlement and that it presupposed common origins, race, language and civilization.[51] The resistance of the French Canadians and Boers only confirmed this traditional thesis; the Commonwealth's strongest incentive for integration really did lie in common origins and traditions. Before 1939 some writers accepted the idea of a multi-racial Commonwealth as a far distant objective but it was never precisely formulated nor was it generally accepted.

An exception that came to the fore as early as 1919 was India. The discussion on India's future faced the British public with the prospect of decolonization during the inter-war period, raised the question of whether responsible government and dominion status could or should be applied to the "coloured" territories, and forced a gradual extension and reformulation of the idea of Commonwealth.

THE QUESTION OF DOMINION STATUS FOR INDIA
(1917–1939)

Even before British rule had spread over the whole subcontinent of India, some far-sighted Englishmen had anticipated future developments, believing dissociation to be inevitable.[1] Was it conceivable, they asked, that a country as small as Great Britain could permanently dominate millions of people of an alien race and civilization? Would not the encounter with the colonial power introduce a process of Westernization which would automatically prompt the desire for self-determination and result in India's turning against the British raj one day? Could and should Great Britain prevent this Westernization? Could imperial domination be reconciled with the liberal credo, and would not a "civilized", independent India be Britain's best kind of trade partner? British liberals were so convinced of the superiority and general validity of Western, Christian civilization that they hardly noticed the racial and cultural differences of the foreign peoples and considered them capable of self-government on the British model. This meant that a time-limit was set on European domination. (Similarly, France had believed in the early nineteenth century that the ideas of 1789 were generally valid and could also be applied elsewhere. France tried to reply to the question of the future in its own way, by integration and assimilation.) Admittedly, these were only individual opinions, albeit important ones; but even the imperialist Sir John Seeley presented his readers with a fascinating vision of a potentially independent India. He thought it would be time to withdraw from India as soon as the effects of British rule led to a nationalist movement.[2]

The argument shifted in the imperialist era. The Indian Mutiny shattered the accepted credo; the opening of the Suez Canal created even stronger political and economic ties, but also separated Europeans and Indians more and more. Added to this, race-consciousness and the late nineteenth-century sense of Empire produced a concept of domination that allowed the non-European peoples their cultural and religious achievements but did not think them capable of modern administration, social responsibility or political self-determination. Great Britain's "benevolent despotism" prevented, it was said, the foreign peoples from sinking back into anarchy; it performed positive and constructive tasks, protected the peasant masses from feudal exploitation and thereby fulfilled its civilizing mission in Asia. Gradually to confer self-government seemed inconceivable; at most the imperialists considered giving the Indians a share of local government, appointing Indian members to the legislative councils and allowing them limited entry into the Indian Civil Service. Imperialists like Lord Curzon considered all these restrictions only natural.[3] Even Richard Jebb, who had described the growing self-confidence in the dominions in 1902, steadfastly denied that there was any parallel between the British colonial settlements and India.[4]

The anti-British agitation provoked by Curzon's domestic policy, added to the nationalist emancipation movement led by the Congress party, seemed to make a change of course necessary after the Liberal victory in the 1905 elections. The result was the Morley-Minto Reforms of 1909,[5] which introduced communal representation in the interests of the Muslims, although it was indirect and with a high census; at the same time the existing legislative councils obtained greater authority, including budget advisory capacity. This was the first step towards representative and parliamentary government. But not in the eyes of London. The viceroy, Lord Minto,[6] and the secretary of state for India, John Morley, a pupil of John Stuart Mill and former colleague of Gladstone, stressed that these reforms were not intended to lead to a parliamentary form of government and protested that this could not be the goal of British policy in India.[7] They were convinced that circumstances in India were not suitable for transplanting elements of British representation, even though the old liberal Morley, who had taken great interest in the Irish question, considered the British raj "unnatural" and doubted very much whether it could last.[8] The main aim of the reforms, he thought, should be to prove Britain's readiness to be more conciliatory and to create bodies through which the Indians could voice their wishes and demands and thus prevent nationalist agitation from becoming open and content at least the moderate wing of the Congress party.

But was it possible to call a halt once the first steps had been taken? It was only natural that even a moderate like Gokhale, who considered the Morley-Minto Reforms a stage in the direction of representative government, should appeal to the Durham Report and demand the gradual conferment of "self-government within the Empire".[9] In 1911 the Indian Government and the liberal under-secretary of state, Montagu, deemed it necessary to satisfy Indian claims for "a larger share in the Government of the Country". They said that bureaucratic good government was no longer sufficient and it was time Britain decided on the aims it was pursuing in India.[10] Conservative reaction was sharp, and the secretary of state, Lord Crewe, had to forcefully deny that the government was aiming at Home Rule for India. He declared that any comparison between India and the dominions was irrelevant and that he, Crewe, saw "no future for India on those lines".[11] Self-government in the dominions was based on British domination of the inhabitants, but India, with its innumerable racial and religious groups, did not possess the necessary conditions for this. Dominion status was "as remote as any Atlantis. . . . We believe that the maintenance and perpetual continuance of British rule in India is the best way of securing the happiness of the Indian people".[12]

Officially, Britain adhered to its "benevolent despotism" until the First World War and had no intention of declaring self-government or even full dominion status the aim of British policy in India. London stood by Milner's "Two Empires", i.e. the theory that the constitutional development of the white dominions was not relevant to Asian territories.[13]

The emancipation movements in Asia and the growth of Indian nationalism gave rise to some doubts about this attitude.[14] Surprisingly enough, it was Milner's "young men" from the *Round Table* group who raised the question of whether Europe would have to withdraw gradually from Asia. In 1912 Sir James Meston, a member of the Indian Civil Service, disputed the idea that India should be permanently treated as a "subject country": "Self-government must become one of the ideals at which our rule in India is to aim."[15] Philip Kerr and Lionel Curtis arrived at similar conclusions, pointing out—and this must be noted—that India could be represented in the imperial parliament they were discussing only if it had responsible government like the dominions: "If we manage to create in India a self-governing, responsible Dominion, and if India, when it is responsible and self-governing, elects to remain within the British Empire, we shall have solved the greatest difficulty which presents itself to the world to-day."[16]

This was a bold notion and touched on a problem that occupied Britain in the inter-war period and immediately before Indian independence. The only hope of persuading India to remain within the British sphere of influence, i.e. to enter the Commonwealth, seemed to be by conferring dominion status or even independence before it was too late. The assumption proved correct in 1947. It also shows how India was gradually aligned with the colonial settlements and why Britain was forced to promise it dominion status. No dates were set, and Britain still considered only the dominion status of pre-1914 days, which, in official terms, meant internal autonomy but no control over external affairs. Yet it was clearly a new step, a transition towards the declaration of 1917 and the reforms of 1919.

The First World War speeded up the process and induced London to make concessions which would have hardly seemed possible before. Britain helped India industrialize and recruited some 1.3 million soldiers and workers who were stationed in East Africa, the Middle East and the Western European battlefields. The failure of the Indian troops in Mesopotamia in 1916 weakened Britain's prestige and provoked sharp criticism of its administrative measures. Gandhi, who led the nationalist movement after the war, expected Britain to reward India's aid to the Empire. The Indian Congress party asked for a declaration from the British about self-government; otherwise, it threatened, more radical groups would take over the leadership.¹⁷ Moreover, the Congress party joined the Muslim League in the Lucknow Pact and made its own constitutional proposals.¹⁸

The government could not ignore the new situation. Prime Minister Herbert Henry Asquith had declared as early as 1914 that "henceforth Indian questions would have to be approached from a different angle of vision",¹⁹ and Viceroy Hardinge had set out the need for reforms in a memorandum in August 1915. The civil servants, he said, would have to apply themselves to the task of preparing India for self-government as "the true friend of the Empire and not merely as dependent".²⁰ When the *Round Table* discussed the future of India, Lionel Curtis clearly interpreted self-government as responsible government. The new viceroy, Chelmsford, requested a memorandum from the group, discussed further procedure with the Executive Committee and submitted his proposals to the Secretary of State in November 1916. Among other things, he advised Britain to issue a declaration to the effect that India's future lay in "a form of self-government", which did not exclude the possibility that Indian institutions would differ from those of the dominions. Since the conservative Secretary of State for India, Austen Chamberlain, also realized the need for such a declaration,²¹ the cabinet discussion was limited to its formulation, to the way in which self-government should be circumscribed. Even Curzon agreed to it, not because he thought Britain ought to be grateful to India, but because England was waging war under the banner of freedom and was sounding the call for nationhood and self-determination everywhere. The unrest inspired by the Russian Revolution had also spread to India, he said, where it was threatening to unleash revolutionary movements. In April 1917 the Imperial War Cabinet decided to allow India to join the Imperial Conference; but Secretary of State Montagu was not able to make his famous declaration until 20 August. It stated that the aim of British policy in India, apart from rapidly giving Indians a greater share in the administration, was the "gradual development of self-governing institutions with a view to the progressive realization of responsible government in India as an integral part of the British Empire".²²

The 20 August declaration was the first official statement of the aim of British rule in India and the way to reach this aim. What had seemed quite inconceivable some years before had now been forced upon Britain by the war: since Britain had become weaker militarily and in foreign affairs, it had to comply with the demands for self-government and issue a kind of "uncolonialization" programme for India. London also abandoned the former thesis that parliamentary government on the British model was out of the question for India. What even the liberals Morley and Crewe had considered impossible was now announced as a programme, for in British terminology responsible government could mean only a government responsible to an elected parliament.²³ Paradoxically, it was Lord Curzon who altered the general formula proposed by Montagu, "ultimate self-government", to the more specific "responsible government".[24]

Responsible government also, and above all, meant dominion status. This was not mentioned in the 1917 declaration, and in 1924 the home minister in India, Malcolm Hailey, later Lord Hailey of the *African Survey*, replied to a query by saying that responsible government was to be interpreted only as a preliminary step towards dominion status.[25] This thesis remained unofficial, yet it aroused the suspicions of the Indians. It is difficult to tell how the cabinet in 1917 understood the phrase "responsible government in India as an integral part of the British Empire", but one may assume that it had no intention of giving up its control of foreign policy, defence, currency, etc. In the year 1917 Britain also decided on the future development of dominion status, which led to the Balfour Declaration of 1926. Should this development also apply to India? Was India really on an equal footing with the white dominions?

Formulas like "self-governing within the Empire" and "a sister nation in the British Empire" were used.

In 1919 India signed the Versailles peace treaty as a quasi-dominion; she became an independent member of the League of Nations in 1920. The Secretary for India, Montagu, said in the House of Commons in August 1918:

> Could you say that in every other part of the British Empire Self-Government was right, but that in India you were going to deny opportunity for access to self-government. . . . We cannot devote more than a century to the tilling of the soil and then refuse to plant the seed. . . .[26]

This was a strong reply to conservative critics in the mother country and a challenge to undertake serious reforms. Montagu also tried to refute the most popular argument for a delimitation between the colonial settlements and India, the thesis that dominion status applied only to the inhabitants of British stock, by pointing out that

> the British Empire which includes the French of Canada and the Dutch of South Africa—to go no further—cannot in any case be based on ties of race alone. It must depend on a common realization of the ends for which the Empire exists, the maintenance of peace and order over wide spaces of territory, the maintenance of freedom and the development of the culture of each nation entity of which the Empire is composed. These are aims which appeal to the imagination of India. As self-government develops patriotism in India we may hope to see the growth of a conscious feeling of organic unity with the Empire as a whole.[27]

This led the way, it could be said, to Alfred Zimmern's theses (cf. p. 33) and the multi-racial commonwealth. In retrospect these formulas may seem rather vague and to refer to a far distant future, yet it would be hard to find any parallel in French and Dutch colonial affairs. Future self-government in Indochina or Indonesia was never mentioned in the interwar period! In fact, the British Government was to refuse for a long time yet to speak openly of dominion status, since this would have barred the way to a settlement with the Congress party. Montagu went to India, negotiated with the viceroy and published the "Report on Indian Constitutional Reforms" in the summer of 1918. Lionel Curtis of the *Round Table* advised on the constitutional questions. This report became the basis of the Montagu-Chelmsford Reforms of 1919 which, according to the preamble, were designed to be one of those "progressive steps" in the direction of self-government. The provinces obtained wider franchise and an elected majority of Indian representatives, in addition to responsible ministers in certain fields (education, local government, health services, economic development) while police, finance, press, etc., remained vested in the governor. This curious separation of responsible government and administration by the government was described by Curtis as a "dyarchy". Instead of the former small council, two chambers elected by the majority were in the Centre, and three Indians entered the executive council in addition to four Britons.

The considerations that inspired these reforms are worth noting. The difficulties of a parliamentary régime in and for India were certainly not underestimated, and the report described in detail the "communal" antagonism, the illiteracy of the peasants, the caste problem, etc. Montagu and Curtis hoped to overcome these difficulties gradually too. Curtis spoke of an Indian nation that would one day decide its own destiny and accused the Europeans in India of having lost contact with the general public and of trying to interpret responsible government only in a limited sense.[28] Starting from the experience of the American colonies, he referred to the Durham Report and proposed "dyarchy" as a solution to the unfruitful and inevitable conflict between an elected parliament and an immovable government. He said London must have faith in the Indian élite and give it real responsibility, not just the power of criticism. Naturally, self-government for the whole of India did not come into question in 1918–1919, and the solution was something of a compromise; but it showed early how concepts and attitudes had changed. All the reforms were now meant as a step towards self-government for India. This meant that the discussion with the Indian nationalists and the discussion in England had finally boiled down to a question of "timing" the "progressive steps" towards this goal. It was only to be expected that London postponed the date to a more or less distant future, while the Indians waited and demanded that Britain fulfil its pledges promptly.

At the end of the war, when the Allies spoke so firmly about granting sovereignty and democratic liberties, Gandhi hoped for very extensive concessions in India and a more generous reward for the Indian war effort than London actually offered. But in spite of critical objections, he did not refuse the report of 1918 or the reforms of 1919. The Congress party accepted them as temporary measures and reluctantly agreed to collaborate.[29] However, the Rowlatt Acts, which provided the viceroy with legal means of dealing with agitators after the withdrawal of his war-time powers, the riots this provoked in Punjab, and the bloodbath of Amritsar and the British reaction to it, unleashed a storm of protest in India and set the stage for the rift between the Indian Government and the Congress party. Gandhi reacted by joining the Caliphate Protest movement and calling for non-co-operation, and the Congress party sabotaged the provincial parliaments. Fiscal sovereignty had been granted India in 1919–1921, and this had quickly led to an increase in industrial output in spite of the currency manipulations, and to giving Indians a greater part in the administration and the army; but this was no substitute for the loss of faith in Britain's willingness to reform and negotiate. The atmosphere had been poisoned and the partners were mutually suspicious.

Indeed, the British attitude to India was decidedly ambiguous after the war. The 1919 reforms had been accepted in Parliament without lengthy discussion or being put to the vote, and in the press noted experts on Indian affairs stressed that a wave of nationalism had gripped India and made concessions necessary in the matter of self-government.[30] Both opposition and reaction also had their say. British officials had agreed to the 1917 declaration, but they refused the "dyarchy" of 1919, with not unjustified reference to the difficulties it would produce. Besides, they were disinclined to surrender the powers of administration and decision-making to the Indians. The Anglo-Indian Society, the organ of the non-civil service Europeans in India, even incited opposition to constitutional reforms. The influential Lord Sydenham (Governor of Bombay, 1907–1913) attacked the idea of making concessions to the allegedly representative intelligentsia of the Congress party: "A government which shows weakness is doomed."[31]

General Dyer, who was responsible for Amritsar, was dismissed from his post, but the Europeans in India, a portion of the London press and numerous members of Parliament thought his actions justified and openly expressed their sympathy. This racist and imperialist reaction on the part of the British public may be explained psychologically and was only temporary; yet it profoundly affected a man like Gandhi and fed anti-British feelings. Montagu, the liberal Secretary of State for India, was also forced to resign.[32] A publication by the Anglo-Indian Society contained a number of references to Montagu's Jewish origins and said that Dyer had prevented a general insurrection in India, whereas the government and the viceroy had given in instead of forcefully intervening against Tilak and Gandhi.[33] In the House of Lords Lord Curzon asked for severe repressive measures.[34] An imperialist book, published under the typical title *The Lost Dominion*, brilliantly and sarcastically described the path to the "dissolution" of the Empire: it was a result of liberal principles and the loss of the will to power and dominion; instead of increasing its social efficiency by a policy of "constructive repression", Britain had irresponsibly surrendered its power to the nationalists and betrayed the Indian masses. If the future proved favourable to England and India, "we will be called wise, if not, cowards".[35] Montagu's successor, Birkenhead, referred to this book in the House of Lords:

> I am not able in any foreseeable future to discern a moment when we may safely, either to ourselves or India, abandon our trust. There is, my Lord, no "lost Dominion", there will be no "lost Dominion" until that moment, if ever it comes [!] when the whole British Empire, with all that it means for civilisation, is splintered in doom.[36]

Because of its insurmountable "communal" problems, India, he said, was not capable of self-government. His was the position of a diehard who could not officially disavow the declaration of 1917 but personally considered it ridiculous and, convinced of the inferiority of the Indian race, did not want to surrender the instruments of power.[37]

Paradoxically, it was Lord Birkenhead who appointed Lord Irwin, later Lord Halifax and British foreign minister, viceroy late in 1925. In 1927 he prematurely sent for the commission of enquiry into Indian constitutional problems which had been provided for in the Act of 1919. His Oxford friend, Sir John Simon, was chairman.[38] Birkenhead took this step with the tactical aim of preventing a future Labour government from coming into office by setting up an early commission for India.[39] The Simon Commission, with Clement Attlee representing the Labour party, was sabotaged by the Indians because they were excluded from it.[40] When the commission presented its report in June 1930, it did not mention dominion status or speak of responsible government in the Centre. In the meantime, the Labour party had come into office; for years it had been urging self-government for India, but since it had to count on the support of the Liberals, it renounced independent action in favour of a supra-party Indian policy. The reformer Lord Irwin conformed to Labour's expectations and ideas. Irwin wanted to make contact with the Congress party and Gandhi and to create a basis of trust for negotiating. Backed by the Labour government, he was able to issue a new, important declaration on 31 October 1929: "I am authorized on behalf of HMG to state clearly that in their judgment it is implicit in the declaration of 1917 that the natural issue of India's constitutional progress, as there contemplated, is the attainment of Dominion status."[41]

By this pronouncement London went even further than the 1917 declaration and managed to break the taboo which had hitherto surrounded the notion of dominion status for India. Thenceforth it was no longer possible to interpret responsible government and self-government as meaning anything else. Moreover, since the Balfour Declaration, dominion status had also included control of foreign affairs and defence; in fact it practically meant independence and went beyond what liberals such as Montagu had wanted to concede during and immediately after the First World War. Irwin accepted the idea of granting India equal status with the white dominions because he realized that any attempt to propose a special status for India would fail and render negotiations with the Congress party impossible.[42] The declaration was well received in India; the historian Gopal speaks of a "revival of trust". Even Gandhi seems to have been ready to make concessions.[43] The Indians did, however, make the condition that negotiations on dominion status should begin at once, possibly with the fixing of a time limit. In the Nehru Report, which contained a practical draft for the constitution, the Congress party described dominion status as "the next, immediate step"; then, under pressure from the left wing, it accepted the Independence Resolution of 31 December 1929. *Swaraj* was henceforth to signify not only self-government but independence and a break with the Empire and Commonwealth. In spring 1930 Gandhi opened a new campaign of civil disobedience and was arrested in May.

So the first Round Table conference was not attended by the Congress party. However, Lord Irwin later managed to persuade Gandhi to come to an agreement (5 May 1931). As a result, prisoners were freed and Gandhi called off civil disobedience and took part in the second Round Table conference in September. But no agreement was reached in London. When the Congress began a new campaign in January 1932, Sir Samuel Hoare, minister for India, and the new viceroy, Lord Willingdon, took active steps: tens of thousands of Indians were arrested, including Gandhi and Nehru. Willingdon confirmed the Irwin declaration but added that dominion status lay far in the future. The efforts of Irwin and the Labour government to persuade India to enter into negotiations were no longer seriously pursued by the new coalition government which, under pressure from the Conservatives, hoped to get by with dictated reforms. In August 1932, the government announced the so-called "Communal Award", the painstakingly achieved right of representation for minority groups, and in March 1933 it published the White Paper on planned constitutional reforms, which were then debated by a Joint Select Committee. The Minister for India, Sir Samuel Hoare, supported by R. A. Butler and Malcolm Hailey, had to face a storm of criticism.[44] The committee's report in November 1934 became the basis of India's new constitution and was passed by Parliament on 5 June 1935 by 386 votes against 122, in spite of renewed violent debate and the objections of both the diehards and the Labour party. Its content is known: in the provinces the dyarchy was to be replaced by responsible governments, while in the Centre a federation was to be formed between British India and the princely states, with a government in the manner of a dyarchy. The "reserved" subjects and additional emergency safeguards remained vested in the viceroy. But we are less interested here in these much described events than in the attitudes and arguments of the parties, with particular reference to the question of dominion status.

Irwin's declaration on 31 October 1929 had provoked violent protest on the part of the diehards.[45] They saw it as a disavowal of the Simon Commission and a concession by the Labour government to the Indian nationalists who were being promised, in the name of a new policy, dominion status as a basis for negotiations. This must be prevented. The Labour party speakers thereupon had to assert that the government was not in fact planning a change of policy and that the declaration was merely a repetition of that of 1917 and a preamble to that of 1919. Within the Conservative party, Winston Churchill took over the leadership of the diehards, with the assistance of the former ministers for India, Lords Reading and Birkenhead; the influential party leaders, Lord Salisbury and Austen Chamberlain; the former high commissioner of Egypt, Lord Lloyd, and the former governor of Kenya, Sir Edward Grigg, besides Lloyd George, the press magnates Beaverbrook and Rothermere and, last but not least, the Lancashire cotton industry. As early as mid-1930, an Indian Empire Society came into being, whose members included many former Indian civil servants. The diehards were strongly represented in the Conservative party's India committee and were able to exert pressure on the party leaders (as in the case of the inter-party discussion on the Rhodesian Federation in 1960; cf. p. 230). Stanley Baldwin managed to assert his leadership of the party, but was anxious to make concessions to the right wing and tried to strengthen the "safeguards" in the draft of the constitution.[46]

The conservative Irwin found support among the Labour party, as well as from Baldwin,[47] Geoffrey Dawson, chief editor of *The Times* who was a former member of Milner's "kindergarten" and therefore very interested in India,[48] and L. S. Amery and Philip Kerr,[49] to mention only a few. He also gained the support of the *Economist* and the *Spectator*. They were all convinced that the diehard point of view was an anachronism and they saw the need to reach a settlement in India. The unrest in Asia and the increasingly radical Indian nationalist movement could no longer be dismissed, they thought, especially since Great Britain was very busy with its own economic crisis and could not risk getting involved in a policy of repression which might lead to military engagement. The British public might still have accepted such a policy before 1914, but in the inter-war period it no longer met with approval. These men realized that peace and order also had to be enforced by the police, but at the same time they sought a compromise solution in the form of a constitution which was guaranteed by Britain yet coincided far enough with Indian wishes for the situation to calm itself. "Rightly or wrongly we have done with the old India; there's a new one afoot and we must make the best of it", wrote Baldwin, discussing the general situation.[50] Similarly, the *Spectator* demanded a "new mental outlook"[51] and the *Economist* turned against Churchill to proclaim the end of the Empire in India.[52]

It was not possible to call a sudden halt on the road to paraliamentary institutions. Samuel Hoare said:

> I do maintain that the old system of paternal government, great as have been its achievements on behalf of the Indian masses in the past, is no longer sufficient. However good it has been, it cannot survive a century of Western education, a long period of free speech and of free press and our own deliberate policy of developing Parliamentary Government.[53]

The dyarchy only partly came up to expectation. Since reforms could not consist of retracting concessions, wider responsibility would have to be granted in order to overcome the resistance of the Congress party and persuade it to collaborate.[54] The reforms in the provinces to which the diehards wanted to restrict themselves were not enough; if India was not to fall apart and to obtain self-government one day, active steps had to be taken with a view to federation and responsible government. Perhaps dominion status still lay in the distant future, but any thoughts of giving India a lower status than the white dominions would be unrealistic. Stanley Baldwin put this well:

> Nobody knows what Dominion status will be when India has responsible government, whether that date be near or distant, but surely no one dreams of a self-governing India with an inferior status. No Indian would dream of an India with an inferior status, nor can we wish that India should be content with an inferior status, because that would mean that we had failed in our work in India. . . . Our work must be done in faith but let us build for the generations [!] to come, there are men who will be putting the coping stone upon this building, they may, haply, not be forgetful of those of us who build in faith among the foundations.[55]

Only thus, on the basis of "equality", was there any real hope that India would elect to remain within the Commonwealth. The diehards, by their obstinacy, were destroying the foundations of trust and risking a definitive break:

> If our Empire today is loyal, as it is, it is largely because we have conceded with good judgment and in good time, the reasonable claims of the units of that Empire gradually to become the controllers of their own affairs. The principle applied elsewhere equally applies to India . . . let us welcome into our Commonwealth of Nations the Indian people. [56]

Theoretically at least, this meant the completion and acceptance of the transition to a multi-racial Commonwealth. But the intensity of Indian nationalism and the central position of the Congress party were underestimated, although Lord Irwin had expressly warned against this kind of deception.[57] For instance, people spoke of a mere Hindu reaction,[58] or declared that only a minority supported the radical course and they were not representative of the Indian élite. Gandhi's attitude was hard to understand and several times the non-co-operation movement was declared bankrupt: was Gandhi an anachronistic ascetic, an agitator without substance or perhaps a cunning politician not to be trusted?[59] The Congress members seemed "lawless", conceited and unconcerned with the well-being of the Indian masses, whereas the moderate nationalists and liberals seemed "practical patriots"; of course the dominant power, Britain, was doing the marking here and deciding what counted as genuine Indian patriotism. In this manner it could maintain the illusion of "co-operation" with the Indians and did not have to admit the failure of what was originally intended to be a policy of reform. This also explains the conciliatory attitude of *The Times*.

There were two major queries under discussion at the Round Table conferences: the position of the racial, religious and social minority groups, and the role of the princes. Gandhi and the Congress party, alleging they spoke for the overwhelming majority of Indians, were reluctant to discuss "communal representation". Meanwhile, London referred to its trust for the different communities, feared internal strife and demanded a prior settlement as a *condition sine qua non*. This attitude was understandable in the case of the Muslim League; but the traditional image of a divided India whose bellicose communities had no communal sense of nationhood overemphasized the role of the non-Hindus, particularly the Muslims, and paid overmuch attention to certain social groups such as the untouchables and the property owners, which made it easy to prevent the Congress party from obtaining a majority in future parliaments and to deny their claim for representation. The second Round Table conference came to grief primarily over this question. The Congress naturally accused London of attempting to divide and rule and with dishonesty. The same applied to the question of the princes. London felt responsible on their behalf and tied to old agreements and thought there were but few ways of getting them to enter the federation. For their part the princes promised, in the interests of their autocratic rule, to back London against the Congress party. Conservative opinion therefore expressed considerable sympathy with the princes, and the diehards managed to make use of this. The political department of the British India Government supported the princes,[60] although the minister for India, Hoare, and even King George V, were irritated by the stubbornness with which they defended their special interests.[61] The constitution gave quite a large advantage to the princes and this was one reason for the Congress party's dissatisfaction with it. The Congress aimed at full responsible government in the Centre and objected to the many "safeguards", especially since dominion status was not mentioned and the diehards were obstinately resisting it.

In fact the diehards were thinking in different terms and were not interested in whether or not India believed in Britain's willingness to reform and make concessions. This is evident in Sir Reginald Craddock's *The Dilemma in India* in 1929. Craddock had served in the Indian Civil Service for forty years, been governor of several provinces and a member of the Executive Council and also belonged to the Joint Select Committee. He is typical of the reactionary conservative attitude of retired ICS officials, who exerted a considerable influence within and without the Conservative party. In fact, as early as 1910 the conservative Viceroy Lord Minto had refused to qualify them as "experts"[62] because they were no longer in touch with the realities of life in India and, turned towards the past, still urged "benevolent despotism". Craddock brings up a favourite argument in his foreword: "With whom should we sympathize most? With the millions who are poor and helpless or with the few who have always exploited them?"[63] His "few" are by no means the autocratic princes or the rich landowners; they are the politicians of the Congress party, with whom London was negotiating, although they had no legitimate claim as the voice of the Indian people. The people only wanted peace and the law and order guaranteed by Great Britain. Craddock also attacked, with some right, the parliamentary officials and business circles with their scanty knowledge of India and their tendency to overlook facts and "to worship phrases". It was ridiculous, he said, to speak of an Indian Nation (a favourite argument of the diehards) that had never existed and perhaps never would exist; accordingly he gives a detailed description of the religious antagonism, the caste system, the poverty and illiteracy in India.

Craddock judged British policy since 1917 severely. Since the appointment of Montagu as Minister for India, Great Britain, he thought, had let more and more concessions be drawn from it, which only provoked new demands and would not restore peace in India. The 1919 reforms had proved a complete failure; confusion reigned in the provincial assemblies; the position of the district officers was undermined and the administrative standard was threatened; money was being wasted and the government was "perpetually humiliated". Craddock quoted memorandums of the Indian Board of Trade and the "European Association" that showed the need for reinforcing government control and warned against handing over the police to Indian ministers.[64] It was ridiculous to speak of self-determination,[65] he said, and responsible government in no way meant full dominion status, at least not that of 1926.[66] As an alternative Craddock proposed an "Indo-British Dominion . . . a task committed to our nation by a Divine Providence". He suggested advisory councils and official majorities and governments with European and Indian ministers. In the Centre, there was to be a durbar with princes, former ministers, large landowners, judges and former officials.[67] It is unnecessary to stress the conservative and even reactionary nature of these ideas: they represent the attitude of a retired Indian civil servant who looks back proudly on his own career, convinced of the superiority of Western civilization and British administration and now feels challenged by the anti-British nationalist agitation.[68]

The reluctance of the diehards and old-school imperialists to acknowledge India's right to dominion status explains their protest at Irwin's declaration of October 1929. As Minister for India in 1928, Birkenhead had criticized Viceroy Irwin for treating Motilal Nehru and S. Jyengar as guests of the government on the occasion of a visit to the north-west province:

> Both of these politicians publicly advocate complete separation from Great Britain as India's ultimate goal. To receive advocates of this policy as guests of Government cannot fail to give it a sort of recognition as a legitimate policy to pursue. This, in my opinion, it is not. You will remember that in dealing with the question of the Indianisation of the Indian army, HMG were averse from using the phrase "Dominion status" to describe even the ultimate and remote goal of Indian political development because it has been laid down that Dominion Status means "the right to decide their own destinies". And this right we were not prepared to accord to India at present, or in any way to prejudice the question whether it should ever [!] be accorded.[69]

Birkenhead's statement shows the difference of opinion between the Labour party and the Conservative party, and even within the Conservative party, between the Minister for India and the viceroy. By his conciliatory attitude towards the Congress leaders, as shown in the visit to the border province, by his declaration of October 1929 and by his attempt to reopen negotiations with Gandhi, Lord Irwin wanted to create a basis for negotiations and, if at all possible, a kind of compromise in the constitutional question. The diehard Lord Birkenhead, on the other hand, was distant from if not hostile to the Congress leaders, did not want to anticipate the future, and by the word "ever" intimated that he was not really willing to accept dominion status as the goal of British policy in India. Birkenhead again gave unmistakable expression to this view in the discussion on the Irwin declaration:

> ... I have only this observation to make after considerable study of these problems. No man who has or who ought to retain a character for sanity or responsibility can assign any proximate period to the date at which you can conceive of India becoming of Dominion status. We are not dealing with the case of a daughter nation of our own creed and of our own blood. We are dealing with a case of a vast multiplication of races, of languages, of religions. Even in the case of the younger daughter com-

munities the process of development was a slow and gradual one. No man has a right to indicate to the Indian people that they are likely in any near period to attain to Dominion status who does not believe that within a near period they will be capable of assuming the same degree of control over their Army, Navy, and Civil Service that is assumed by the self-governing Dominions today. What man in this house can say that he can see in a generation, in two generations, in a hundred years any prospect that the people of India will be in position to assume control of the Army, the Navy, the Civil Service, and to have a Governor-General who will be responsible to the Indian Government and not to any authority in this country . . . ?[70]

Opponents of the October declaration continued to stress the alleged vagueness of the term "dominion" and to declare that the conferment of equal status with the white dominions would be impossible. Lord Crewe, for example, believed that the "ultimate stage of things in India" should not go beyond internal autonomy with as little interference as possible from London; one of his arguments, typically, was the existence of the princely states.[71] Winston Churchill tried to establish a subtle distinction between dominion status and dominion rights; he said the former had been granted India in the world war but not the latter; and the leader of the diehards let it be known that he did not intend to grant it in the future either.[72] All the diehards' not unjustified references to the different conditions obtaining in India and the difficulties of transplanting British institutions cannot conceal the fact that they were chiefly concerned with maintaining imperial rule and postponing self-government *ad calendas Graecas*.

Winston Churchill was particularly anxious about Great Britain's imperial positions. During these years he fought an untiring battle in the party, in Parliament and in public against British India policy, exposing with brilliant polemics the difficulties involved in reform and the contradictions in the official statements; he also distorted the facts and did not shrink from personal attacks. Yet he was unable to offer any alternative except a defence of the *status quo*. In his opinion, the Congress party was an extremely dangerous organization of agitators and rebels led by the "half-naked fakir, Gandhi"; they were untrustworthy and one should not negotiate with them. Churchill also declared himself a protector of the Indian masses who, he said, must not be surrendered to economic and political suppression by what he called the non-representative minority. The decision about the date for the institution reforms lay in the hands of the British Parliament alone. Referring to the Simon Report, Churchill wanted to concede no more than extended autonomy in the provinces; federation and responsible government in the Centre seemed "premature". The promises contained in the White Paper and the constitution would in foreseeable time lead to withdrawal and ultimately the end of British rule in India.[73] There was no point in even mentioning dominion status, which since 1926 implicitly meant the right to total secession. Consequently Churchill stuck firmly to "benevolent despotism", citing its paternalistic achievements: "Our rule in India is as it were a sheet of oil spread over and keeping free from storms a vast and profound ocean of humanity"[74]; British rule was "incomparably the best Government that India has ever seen or ever will see".[75] Churchill acknowledged no Indian right to self-government, even as an "ultimate goal", and went so far as to state that the British were no more aliens in India than the Muslims or Hindus and therefore had a legitimate right to keep to their intention of staying.[76]

Many diehards who had been members of the ICS or provincial governors or had held office in the Indian ministry may honestly have been concerned with Britain's constructive efforts. But Churchill was less interested in India and its inhabitants than in not losing or surrendering the "brightest jewel in the British Crown", since India for him was "the touchstone of our fortunes in the present difficult time".[77] Withdrawal from India would mean far more than the end of British prestige in Asia, it "would mark and consummate the downfall of the British Empire. The great organism would pass at a stroke out of life into history. From such a catastrophe there would be no recovery".[78] The question, as he saw it, was whether Britain wanted to remain a world power, or whether by what he considered unnecessary measures it would sanction its own decline into a "minor power". His resistance to the European policy of appeasement was in a sense preceded by his resistance to the policy of appeasement in India! Churchill was an imperialist in the Indian question, but, paradoxically enough, it was in the spirit of "Little England". Unlike Milner and his school, he did not start out from a sense of Empire which reached its fulfilment in the Commonwealth, but from concern for the mother country whose economic and political power resided in its authority over the Empire. He was convinced that Indian nationalism could be held back with repressive measures, "if only England so wished". He refused to admit any internal threat to British rule and made no attempt to make timely concessions in order to avoid the possibility of bloody conflicts or to create the necessary conditions for India to remain within a multi-racial Commonwealth.

The Labour party, on the other hand, declared in a resolution of the 1918 party conference: "Home Rule for India . . . equally along with South Africa, Australia and other British Dominions".[79] In 1920 the party conference demanded recognition of the right to self-determination, expressing the hope, however, that the independent peoples would ask to remain in the Commonwealth; but this was their own affair.[80] In order to distinguish itself from the Liberals and Conservatives the Labour party initially took a definite anti-imperialist stand and seemed to support early liquidation of the Empire. In the following years, however, it changed course; it too now advocated self-government in stages and postponed the grant of dominion status to "the earliest possible moment".[81] Although the Labour party still maintained India's right to self-determination, the new aim was "full responsible government within the Empire", which meant that from 1929 on its proposals lagged behind the Congress party demands.

The Labour party accepted the 1919 reforms as a step in the right direction; but understandably did not hesitate to express its own wishes, urging wider franchise, responsible governments in the provinces and Indian participation in the Centre.[82] Naturally it had rejected the Rowlatt Bill and strongly opposed the conduct of Dyer and the Indian administration in the Amritsar affair.[83] In subsequent years it also opposed all repressive measures and sternly criticized the administration's treatment of the unions, the policy of the press, etc. In fact, however, the India policy of the first Labour government in 1924 hardly differed from that of the Conservatives; the party had little mobility in Parliament and did not consider India capable of self-government yet. Sydney Olivier, Secretary of State for India, privately made mock of the Congress party leaders[84] and even the left-wing Harold Laski decided that "there is nothing near the necessary degree of moral unity in India to enable us to withdraw".[85] The party criticized the Simon Commission because it had no Indian members, yet took part in it with Attlee. In the Commonwealth Labour Conference on 2 July 1928 MacDonald expressed the hope that a new dominion would soon come into being; but as prime minister of the second Labour government, he limited himself to supporting Lord Irwin. This second government thus made possible the declaration of 31 October 1929, backed the Irwin-Gandhi agreement, and tried to create a favourable atmosphere for the first Round Table conference.[86] But it developed no intitiatives of its own.

No wonder then, that the party leadership was criticized by outsiders like Mrs. Besant[87] and Josiah C. Wedgwood, who demanded extensive concessions and definite time limits,[88] and by the Marxist-oriented Independent Labour party, which urged it to recognize the Congress party as the voice of India and recommended forming a constitutional assembly.[89] At the 1930 party congress, Fenner Brockway proposed a resolution stating India's right to independence and welcoming the Indian nationalist movement; he reproached the Labour government with omitting to declare that "full responsible government" was the point of discussion at the Round Table conference, and further accused it of acting as "policemen of Imperialism". The immediate conferment of dominion status would mean withdrawing troops and giving the Indians firm control of their economic affairs.[90] British pragmatism easily managed to survive Brockway's radical opinions, however, and said that the result of a "hasty, ill-considered departure from India" would be civil war and mass murder, quite apart from the fact that if it accepted the proposed resolution the Labour government would lose all chance of winning the next election.⁹¹ Even Laski, who addressed a memorandum to the prime minister in 1930 and worked out a plan for the constitution with Lord Chancellor Sankey in 1931, described the problem of India as "the biggest crisis in our colonial affairs since 1776" and that of Ireland in the next generation as "a ghastly problem of which the real essence is that we can't govern it and it really is not fit to govern itself".⁹²

After the formation of the National Government and the break with MacDonald, the Labour party resumed its opposition. It condemned the repressive measures taken in 1932–1934 and even though it took part in the Joint Select Committee, it rejected the committee report and the Indian constitution of 1935, chiefly because the preamble did not declare India's right to dominion status, but also because the establishment of franchise was far too conservative and prejudicial to the Congress party.⁹³ In the parliamentary debates in February and June 1935 Clement Attlee firmly voiced his party's position: it was a paradox that the government recognized the validity of the Irwin declaration but had not included the term "dominion status" in the text of the constitution, particularly since India was so conscious of this; "the keynote of the Bill is mistrust", he said. The constitution was trying to limit the effectiveness of the Congress party, which meant that "one of the dominating factors of the situation" was being overlooked. The whole thing was evidence of a "one-sided partnership".⁹⁴ In retrospect one cannot deny that there was some truth in this criticism; but it seems disputable whether a Labour government would have managed to enforce its ideas and negotiate a transitional settlement with Gandhi or Nehru that was acceptable to both sides. Attlee nevertheless recognized, in his 1937 book *The Labour Party in Perspective*, that self-government was hard to achieve in a continent as diverse as India and that the slogan "India for the Indians" was not relevant to the problem.⁹⁵

The only part of the Indian constitution of 1935 which was put into effect in 1937 concerned the provinces. Each was allowed to form a responsible government, although there was some initial obstruction by the Congress party. This at least gave the Indians a chance to experiment in administration and to train themselves for parliamentary government. But the resistance of the princes blocked the establishment of federation, and it must remain an open question whether the British Government should have "forced" them to collaborate.

In the inter-war period, India underwent transition from autocratic control on the colonial model to a semi-responsible government modelled on Great Britain. In the declaration of 21 August 1917 Britain had announced decolonization and accepted dominion status for India, however much the diehards resisted. At first, however, this was still only the "ultimate goal", which would still take long to reach. London continued to rely on the old argument of India's internal problems, which prevented progress other than by very slow stages and which therefore seemed to justify the continuation of British rule. The attempt to prevent the predominance of the Congress party giving consideration to the numerous individual "communal" groups and communities in fact aggravated rather than relieved tensions. Yet we must remember here that it was difficult for London to come to grips with this problem precisely because the British were thinking of a unified India and not even contemplating partition.

The reforms of 1919 and the constitution of 1935 were important steps towards self-government and could be interpreted as proof of British liberalism; but the actual transfer of power still lay in the far distance and the British public in the inter-war period would not have been ready for it. Natural pride in what had been achieved in India was joined to economic and political interests and strategy. Would not the loss of India strike a mortal blow at the British economy, which was already in a state of crisis? Could a free India defend itself against an alien power? These questions fueled a convincing argument for the conservative imperialist politicians, who overlooked the fact that a Japanese attack was unlikely, that Australia and New Zealand were not armed either and that in any case a bilateral defence agreement could have ensured India's protection.

Britain's mere willingness to reform, however, could not content Indian nationalists, and Britain did not succeed in mutually establishing the stages for implementation of the constitution until the achievement of dominion status. Indians' suspicions were aroused by the diehards' reaction to Amritsar, their hostility towards Gandhi, their agitation against Lord Irwin, the October declaration and the agreement with Gandhi, and finally their opposition to the Indian constitution, and this gave impetus to radical agitation and slowed down parliamentary decision-making. If Irwin's policy had been sustained, India might have been ruled by a semi-responsible federal-type government before the outbreak of war and perhaps the later division of the country would never have taken place. However, the diehards' resistance is not surprising. The strongly traditional British upper class was naturally reluctant to give up the "pearl of the Empire" unless absolutely necessary. What is more surprising is that the resistance was not more stubborn and that even within the Conservative party and among the politicians and journalists particularly interested in the Empire there was so much willingness to accept reform.[96] The same applied neither to the French judicial circles to the case of Indochina and North Africa nor to the Dutch bourgeoisie in their attitude towards Indonesia.

In retrospect, the inter-war years appear a transitional period in the history of Anglo-Indian relations, marked by mutual distrust, nationalist agitation, repressive measures, and also important reforms. Great Britain recognized the right to self-government, established responsible governments in the provinces and prepared to reinterpret the concept of dominion status in order to set the stage for a multi-racial Commonwealth. The new concept of Commonwealth saw the conferment of self-government on "coloured" colonies not as the dissolution and destruction of imperial ties but the necessary and ideologically consistent conclusion of British imperial policy.[97] This helped Great Britain adjust itself in a relatively short time to the new situation during and after the Second World War and led to granting India independence in 1947.

TRUSTEESHIP AND SELF-GOVERNMENT IN THE COLONIES

With the dominions decolonized and India on the road to responsible government, it began to become apparent that Great Britain would have to re-examine its policies in regard to the colonies proper.

The "Colonial Empire", as subdivision of the British Empire, included very different geographical, cultural and political entities. Besides the Muslim protectorates and mandated territories in the Middle East, there were the Asian colonies Ceylon, Malaya, Borneo, etc.; in West Africa, Nigeria, the Gold Coast, Sierra Leone and Gambia; and then the East African territories Northern Rhodesia (Southern Rhodesia had been granted responsible government in 1923), Nyasaland, Uganda, and Kenya (where the distinct minority groups of British settlers created special problems), the mandated territory Tanganyika, and the Sudan with its special status. Finally the "dependencies" included such important strategic positions as Gibraltar, Malta, Cyprus, Aden and Hong Kong. Of the West Indian possessions in the American hemisphere Jamaica was the most important. British journalists liked to point to the diversity of the colonial Empire as evidence that its special character resided not in territorial compactness nor in any racial or cultural community, but in the world-wide distribution of these millions of peoples who lived under the British Crown. There were no ideas or illusions like *la plus grande France*, for "Empire" was not meant to refer to an extended mother country or a "Great Britain beyond the seas", but to a worldwide entity whose individual parts were subject to British rule and for whom Britain acted as "trustee".

In a debate in the House of Commons on 30 July 1919, L. S. Amery, for many years a conservative colonial minister, praised the great achievements and sacrifices of the colonies during the war which, he said, obliged Britain to ". . . set up a new and more positive standard of our duty and obligation towards the peoples to whom this house is in the position of a trustee".[1]

In the following years this became the standard phrase, and in a sense it is comparable to France's conception of its *mission civilisatrice*. But what actually was this "trusteeship" that was to be undertaken by the British Parliament? The term derived from British private law and was based, according to Ernest Barker, on the common law and equity of English law courts.[2] It was intended to express the right to certain liberties. More important, however, was its significance in constitutional law: in England, since 1688 at the latest, the power of the state has been understood as the power of the people, which means that it also had to be exercised in the interests of the people; "the powers of King and Parliament were held by them in trust for the benefit of the people of England as the beneficiary of the trust".[3] Locke and Burke use the term "trust" to express specifically English ideas on the relations between people, king, Parliament and government.

It was Edmund Burke who first introduced this "legal metaphor" into the discussion of colonial policy. In his famous speech on the Charter of the East India Company in 1783, he reminded Parliament that political power might only be exerted in the interests of the subjects; rights and privileges were untenable if they contradicted the trust. The East India Company, he said, had been set up by Parliament as a trustee and must act accordingly in India.[4] In the colonies, Parliament was therefore the trustee, although it delegated its authority to the governors. The native inhabitants were "backward peoples" who needed protection, so it was said subsequently, in order to develop. They could not, at least not at the present stage of development, know what was good for them. These theories were formed easily at the time the colonies were settled and their moral justification seemed self-evident. They were the product of the common nineteenth-century European sense of superiority—based as it was on Europe's obvious technical and cultural pre-eminence—added to a moral self-righteousness. Quite apart from well-meaning colonial reformers, even a man such as Joseph Chamberlain used the term "trust" to justify British expansion as economically necessary in the competition with other powers. In his critique of imperialism of 1902, J. A. Hobson contrasted the existing situation and its very questionable effects with imperialist ideology. But in the interests of the natives whose social structures, he said, had been destroyed or were undergoing a radical change in the confrontation with Europe, he could not condone a simple withdrawal, and so he too adopted the principle of trusteeship in vindication of a pertinent and morally acceptable colonial administration.[5] This trusteeship was to be set up and controlled by an international authority. If we dismiss the Congo Act, which was a question of circumstances, we might say that Hobson was the first to make the distinction between national and international trusteeship.

It is here that the British discussion took up during the war (cf. pp. 36–37). At first the most important point was the future of the German colonies in Africa; internationalization seemed the obvious way of preventing them from being involved in future rivalry between the powers. Their subordination to the League of Nations was intended to ensure an open-door policy and the protection of the natives from exploitation. Hobson and the colonial reformer Morel, Buxton and Olivier, joined by the Labour party, thought that "trusteeship" together with international supervision could become the basis for a colonial doctrine which, by contrast with the allegedly exploitative imperialism of the pre-war era, would comply with the envisioned civilizing mission. President Wilson and his advisers took their cue from the British discussion and adopted the mandate principle, which was institutionalized in Article 22 of the League of Nations.

After 1919 trustee and trusteeship became the accepted terms for all who spoke of the nature and principles of British colonial policy. By seeing its colonial domination as "trusteeship", Great Britain, they said, demonstrated its sense of moral responsibility, even altruism. What had been formulated by Article 22 as a requirement of the world conscience was nothing new for Great Britain: a British doctrine had become generally valid and now served as a model for the other powers![6]

The former Governor of Nigeria, Sir Frederick (later Lord) Lugard, made a decisive contribution to popularizing the notion of trusteeship in his extensive work *Dual Mandate in Tropical Africa*, which first appeared in 1922 and enjoyed immense authority during the inter-war years among colonial administrators in London and in the West African administrations.[7] Lugard defined the term "dual mandate" as meaning that the colonial powers acted as trustees both in the interests and for the protection of the native population, and in the interests of the whole world. Since the civilized nations, in particular the European ones, could no longer survive without tropical raw materials and food, they had the moral right to exploit this produce where it was available. The primitive inhabitants could not, he said, refuse access to their resources. "Viewed from this standpoint, the tropics are the heritage of mankind, and neither has the suzerain power a right to their exclusive exploitation, nor have the races which inhabit them a right to deny their bounties to those who need them."[8] Lugard stipulated a legitimate right to colonial domination, on condition that the colonial power in its turn did not bar the access it had gained to others or monopolize it. By virtue of this theory, Great Britain was able to reiterate its old demand for an open-door policy and to criticize French colonial economic policy, accusing France of discriminating against foreign powers and continuing to observe the colonial pact.

Lugard's theories were by no means original. His arguments can be traced back to Francisco de Vitoria and they are even closer to the nineteenth-century British Free Trade policy with its belief in Western superiority and demands for the opening up of all the tropical territories. Lugard could recall Chamberlain's words: "We, in our colonial policy, as fast as we acquire new territory and develop it, develop it as trustees of civilization for the commerce of the world."[9] France and other colonial powers also made use of this argument in order to give their actions moral as well as historical justification—which may be understandable, since the industrial countries did need tropical produce. Today, however, this all seems highly questionable, for who is to decide whether a country is making sufficient use of its resources and making them available to the world? Between the wars these theories were put forward principally by colonialists and conservatives,[10] who clearly conceived of the tropical areas primarily as sources of raw materials for a long time to come. Although a certain tariff or export tax was not in contradiction to the open-door principle, as long as the mother country did not enjoy special privileges, scarcely any mention was made of independent economic development for these countries, or even industrialization. The aim was to achieve an allegedly reciprocal relationship between the economy of the mother country and that of the colony, based on the idea of a liberal, international division of work; in fact this only made possible and justified the exploitation of the colony in the interests of the dominating power.

The exploitation of tropical produce, i.e. of the colonial economy, was also meant to benefit the native inhabitants, or at least to do them as little harm as possible.[11] The colonial power was not to have full control over native labour and was obliged to watch over the natives' private interests and to see to it that they had a "fair share" of the profits. But it was the mandate power who determined what this meant and how far it went! Consequently trusteeship had to prove itself in terms of concrete administration, agrarian law, labour law, tariff and education policy. Lugard, an experienced administrator, did not dispute the fact that a colonial power had to be primarily concerned with economic affairs,[12] but like most of his contemporaries he was convinced that there was no fundamental discrepancy between the economic interests of the mother country and the interests of the native inhabitants, and thought that if the principle of a dual mandate were seriously applied, it could satisfy both parties.[13]

It is easy to see the dual mandate as having little relevance to existing facts and to show it up as no more than a cheap masking of colonialist interests. Indeed, one cannot but distrust the self-praise of British publicists who thought it was enough to refer to the principle of trusteeship and tried to justify domination for an indefinite period of time by pointing to the inability of the "backward peoples" to realize their own interests.

But this kind of interpretation does not do justice to the difficulty of the problem. Even the most critical evaluation must not overlook the moral impulse which in a large part determined the course of British imperialism. This moral impulse also governed in a large part the great proconsuls of the pre-war years and many of the governors and innumerable district commissioners and administrative officials after the war. The British administration invented the notions of "service" and of "fairness"—a product of the rich traditions of the English public schools. Trusteeship was based on these notions and legitimized them. The Colonial Service may have been chiefly concerned with ensuring its domination and with the direct or indirect interests of Great Britain, it may have had close relations with the respective "European communities" and have dissociated itself further socially from the "natives" than did France; yet the Service repeatedly tried to avoid identifying itself with private interests and to fulfil its duty of trustee conscientiously and fairly.

Lugard tried, in his *Dual Mandate*, to show how the needs and interests of the native inhabitants in different administrative fields could at least be reconciled to a certain extent with those of the protector power. The prohibition of forced labour, in contrast to French practice, and the renunciation of plantations benefitting the native producers in West Africa, in contrast to the situation in the Belgian Congo, were some results of this trusteeship. In 1943 Lord Hailey felt justified in saying: "Again and again it has exerted its influence when issues have arisen in which native interests have been at stake, and has often done so with decisive effect."[14] During the debate on East Africa policy, the principle of trusteeship led to the famous Devonshire declaration for Kenya in December 1923 in which the British Government proclaimed the "Paramountcy of Native Interests" in the conflict between the white settlers and the Indian minority (cf. p. 148). British publicity liked to call upon this declaration, and to offer it as proof that Britain took seriously the trusteeship policy and intended to enforce it. The critical historian can reply that the declaration of the paramountcy of African interests was mainly an improvised solution to an apparently insoluble conflict, and that it had little influence on the policy towards the natives of Kenya in the following years, yet one cannot object to it on principle. No less a man than the former Communist and friend of Nkrumah, George Padmore, called it the Magna Carta of Africa.[15] During the inter-war years, everyone who criticized the Kenya settlers and demanded a pro-native policy appealed to the 1923 declaration, and since the British Government saw itself as trustee for the African inhabitants, whether voluntarily or under pressure from the reformers to whom Padmore belonged, it refused to grant the white minority self-government or even dominion status.

There is one aspect of this British doctrine that must not be overlooked. The principle of trusteeship as formulated by Lugard and institutionalized in the League of Nations Mandate was primarily defensive. Above all it was protective; its function was to prevent abuse and exploitation and it was not, or only secondarily, designed as a positive step in a policy of development. A royal instruction to the colonial governors in 1922 demonstrates this. It stated that the task of the imperial representative was "to the utmost of his power, to promote religion and education among the native inhabitants [a task that was in fact almost entirely left to the missionaries] and he is to especially take care to *protect* them in their person and the free enjoyment of their possessions and by all lawful means to *prevent* and *restrain* all violence and injustice which may in any manner be practised or attempted against them".[16]

This idea of maintaining law and preventing exploitation stemmed from nineteenth-century liberalism and conformed to both the British concept of state and to the policy of Free Trade which called for leaving political and economic initiative to the individual and limited itself to securing the "framework" for free, individual development. At the most it took measures against open infringements and abuses. "Law and order" were consequently the central ideas on which the British colonial administration was based; it was particularly proud of the fact that it established and ensured just this. Another feature of British rule was that it survived with a small number of personnel, maintained little more than a loose net of control, intervened as little as possible in the existing social structures and shrank at the use of force. In this respect it was less paternalistic than Belgian rule in the Congo or Dutch practice in Indonesia. This does not, of course, mean that the results were always positive or corresponded to the envisaged goal. J. S. Furnivall in his 1948 work *Colonial Policy and Practice* showed very clearly how the policy of law and order, which gave the outside capitalist forces plenty of room for play and even legal sanctions, led Lower Burma to a catastrophic disintegration of its traditional social structure, whereas Dutch paternalism in Java, using some coercion, accomplished its protective task somewhat better and managed to keep social change within bounds. Not until the late 1930s did criticism of this kind of negative liberal attitude begin in Britain, and some attempts were then made to transform the earlier concept of trusteeship into a more positive policy of development.

Yet another feature characterizes the notion of trusteeship: it is only temporary. Any country that, like Great Britain, used the term and considered itself a trustee, also had to accept the fact that a time limit was implied by this relationship of dependency. The colonial power could legitimately act as trustee only until the moment the "backward peoples" became capable of shaping their own destinies and no longer needed a guardian. In 1941 Ernest Barker wrote as follows:

> When the minor grows to manhood, the trust will determine; he will manage his own affairs and provide for his own benefit himself. The like may happen in public affairs and in the sphere of public law; and this analogy, along with the general analogy of the private trust, may thus be applied to the dependency gained by conquest or cession. Such a dependency is, as it were, a minor, living under a trustee power during its minority. When it becomes adult and mature it will enter into an equal responsibility with the trustee who will relinquish his tutelage: it will become self-governing and will stand by the side of other self-governing States in a community of such States.[17]

We will have to complete this. It is part of the duty and task of the trustee to prepare those in its care for the moment when the dependency relationship will be dissolved and to educate them for self-government. The trustee must gradually surrender the power of decision and responsibility to his ward in increasingly wide areas, according to the latter's age, maturity and ability. This analogy stated that British colonial policy provided the preparation for gradual conferment of self-government. It declared that British domination considered self-government its fulfilment. Of course, the trustee, Great Britain, had sole authority and full sovereignty in deciding how this "education" was to be conducted and when the point of "maturity" had been reached!

On the other hand, the analogy with private law trusteeship also implies the following: in the case where the ward is constitutionally impeded and can never reach the status of responsible adulthood, the tutelage must be maintained for life. Were colonies capable of self-government? Of course, the colonies by settlement were not denied this possibility; the British subject, so to speak, carried self-government overseas with him. The dominions had shown proof of their ability to survive and only the smaller units such as Malta and Cyprus, whose inhabitants were white but non-British or multi-racial, were doubtful cases. But what about the "coloured" areas? Quite apart from the real jingoist imperialists and racial fanatics, even the pre-war proconsuls such as Curzon and Cromer denied the ability of the latter to achieve self-government; there was hardly a doubt in their minds that even India and Egypt required permanent British administration or control if they were not to sink back into "chaos". And what applied to these countries, with their great indigenous culture and an educated class already trained in Western ideas, applied much more unequivocally to the "primitive" races. Before the war there was no hesitation in expressing this opinion openly, even in official statements.

But after 1919 it was scarcely ever talked about openly. Imperialism was now on the defensive; Great Britain had waged a war for the protection of freedom and would or could no longer employ the racial argument. The construction of the "Third Empire", as Alfred Zimmern put it, must no longer be tied to race or nationality. Of course, many of the diehards had not changed their minds and a large number of colonial officials may have continued to doubt the capacity of non-white peoples for self-government—quite apart from the question of time limits. But it had obviously become unfashionable to say this openly and certainly to announce it in any kind of official statement: Great Britain had to proclaim self-government as the aim of its policy. Even the reference to "good government" was no longer sufficient. The colonial official could harp on the difference between self-government and good government and justify himself by saying that Great Britain not only guaranteed "law and order" but also cared in other ways for the well-being of the masses, while the old feudal upper class and the young educated class could neither ensure orderly administration nor educate the masses to social responsibility. In public, people had to speak of self-government, however conditionally. For example, in the previously mentioned parliamentary debate of 30 July 1919, Undersecretary of State Amery stressed that the mandate principle led to "self-government . . . in so far as they are capable of it".[18] The 1926 Imperial Conference took only incidental notice of the Dependent Empire, but did describe as a future task "preparing them also, by slow degrees, even for the opportunities of a greater measure of self-government".[19] And in 1938 colonial minister Malcolm MacDonald summarized the official British attitude between the wars:

> The great purpose of the British Empire is the gradual spread of freedom among all His Majesty's subjects in whatever part of the world they live. That spread of freedom is a slow evolutionary process. In some countries it is more rapid than in others. In some parts of the Empire, in the Dominions, that evolutionary process has been completed, it is finished. Inside the Colonial Empire the evolutionary process is going on all the time. In some colonies like Ceylon the gaining of freedom has already gone very far. In others it is necessarily a much slower process. It may take generations, or even centuries [!], for the peoples in some parts of the Colonial Empire to achieve self-government. But it is a major part of our policy, even among the most backward peoples of Africa, to teach them and to encourage them always to be able to stand a little more on their own feet.[20]

The non-official statements were more detailed. We have referred to Lord Milner's assumption, after the war, that the colonial peoples would not always accept dependent status; when the question was raised in a conversation with an American, Shotwell, of the date when self-government should be granted, Milner considered the moment would have come when the natives demanded a constitution and definite institutions.²¹ Philip Kerr was plainer:

> Great Britain is now committed to the development of self-government in all other parts of the Empire as rapidly as the inhabitants can take over responsible control. The process which has been in India is being extended in various ways to Egypt, Palestine and Malta, and its gradual development everywhere is inevitable.²²

The quintessence of Lord Hailey's 1938 *African Survey* lay in the following words:

> The political future which British policy has assigned to the African colonies must be understood to be that of self-government based on representative institutions. The pursuance of this policy has involved the devolution of as large a share of the authority as possible to the executive government of the colony and the recognition of local legislation as the source of law.²³

And finally let us mention Lord Lugard, who, as we shall see, mistrusted the adoption of British representative institutions and described himself as an imperialist but yet, in 1939, saw British domination as in principle only a temporary "tutelage":

> The imperialist [Lugard distinguishes himself from anti-colonialism and disinterest] clings to his belief that the time has not come to abdicate British sovereignty and its policy of tutelage and guidance, but the trust must be so administered that at some distant day even the most backward may take their place in the world as free self-governing nations as the Dominions have done.²⁴

We should stop for a moment to analyse these statements and the many similar ones. Essentially their theme was self-government, or rather the gradual conferment of self-government, although in fact the stress lay on "gradual" and actual self-government was nowhere near yet. This careful reference to the future took the urgency out of some of these questions and at the same time offered sound justification for colonial domination. What is most important in the context of our discussion is that after the First World War at the latest, Great Britain had at its disposal a doctrine of decolonization. It was still scarcely a topical issue in the field of concrete administration, but the eventual end of British control not only was accepted but even set out as the goal of British colonial policy. The policy was already being justified in the name of its results! This thesis was to influence British policy retrospectively as early as the inter-war period, and after the Second World War it facilitated separation and made it more bearable. In this respect Britain occupied a special position among the colonial powers with the exception of the United States. Belgium in the Congo and the Netherlands in Indonesia still considered their domination secure and to a large extent even dismissed the question of the future from consideration. France, on the other hand, did have a doctrine of decolonization, but it was not based on self-government and so France later found it difficult to make the adjustment.

Did the concept of "self-government" mean the same to conservatives, liberal reformers and socialists, and did they think it equally applicable in the different areas of the colonial Empire? The writings of British publicists and historians indicate that the concept was indeed unequivocal and that the colonial doctrine of the inter-war years was clearly formulated. But it was only by failing to examine the concept itself, paying no attention to the various shades of opinion and meaning in the official statements and making it a leitmotiv of British colonial policy after the First World War that these writers could postulate a definite doctrine, allegedly establishing Great Britain's liberalism. Having suggested this, they did not feel the need to engage in any further general explanation and could turn to the political and economic situation of individual territories to show the great progress that had been made.

If one examines the published writings and follows the discussions in Parliament, it becomes clear that this concept of self-government was neither unequivocal nor uniform. Even the statements we have quoted show, on closer inspection, that self-government did not necessarily entail handing over full administrative and political power to the inhabitants and that it could be restricted to granting certain forms of autonomy or simply allowing the colonial inhabitants effective participation in their own affairs. Nor is it at all clear whether self-government was equated with responsible government, i.e. with dominion status, and whether it included adopting a democratic and representative system on the British model. Districts with arbitrary boundaries questioned the area in which self-government was to be granted, and in the East African settlements it had to be decided whether the white minority or the African majority was legitimately entitled to future self-government. We will have to pay close attention to these questions.

First we must consider somewhat more carefully the administrative structure of the Crown Colonies. Some of them were virtually independent, with administrative and even some legislative autonomy. In these colonies, only the "constitution" as such, which determined the position of the governor, his relations with the representative organs and the authority and composition of the latter, was determined by the Colonial Office in London; usually it was passed as an Order in the Council, without special approval by Parliament. The governor and his subordinates took a greater part in the preparation of the constitution than was the case in the French colonies. The initiative often came from the colony itself, which had its own internal legal code and its own legislative power, an advantage the French colonies lacked. London did of course have a right of veto, but seldom exercised it. There were no general colonial laws and the mother country's legislation was not transposed to the colonies. By contrast with France, Britain was not seeking uniformity and each area was to undergo its "development" according to its own traditions, circumstances and potential. The governor, as representative of the Crown, and the administration subordinate to him were sufficient to maintain the mother country's control. While centralist France also administered its colonies centrally, the British Empire reflected the specifically British combination of a traditional, decentralized administration and wide local autonomy with a centralized legislature. While to a large extent the colonies were "autonomous", they were still part of a strict imperial structure. Great Britain was proud of this "pragmatism", which acknowledged the individuality of the different colonies and was even prepared to promote it. At a governors' conference in 1927, the Colonial Minister Amery said:

> The whole system, with its haphazard complexity and lack of coordination on any structural basis, would be fancy, not to be tolerated for a moment by our more logical neighbours across the Channel. For all that, I believe that our system, or lack of system, has certain advantages. Each Colonial Government and each Colonial Service had grown up on the spot by a continual process of local evolution from the days of our first historical connection with the Colony, the days of the first treaty cession, the first conquest, the original peaceful trading penetration, as the case may be. Each Government and each Service, therefore, is autochthonous, racy of the soil, adapted to local conditions and instinctive in its understanding of those conditions and in its sympathy with the population it administers.[25]

But independent as the individual colonies were, there was a definite similarity in their constitutions. On examination there was obviously a principle involved here, an unbroken thread, a particular series of steps which the colonies had to follow in the evolution of their representative institutions; in each case these steps occurred at a different moment in time, conforming as closely as possible to the varied circumstances among the developing colonies, and yet following a common pattern. The pattern was the gradual transfer of legislature and executive power from the king, i.e. the governor, to the colonial legislative council until full parliamentary government—as well as democratization—had been reached, and the executive became responsible to the elected parliament.

We should trace from the beginning the relations between the legislative council and the governor as holder of executive power.[26] In the first stage, when the territory had the status of Crown Colony, there was an "official majority": the Legislative Council consisted of a majority of higher colonial officers who conferred on the governor's proposed laws. The officers were bound to their instruction and could not vote against the governor; their primary function was to ensure a just and legal procedure. So the legislative council was not yet a representative organ, quite apart from the fact that the native inhabitants were very seldom represented in it. Similarly, the Executive Council was only an advisory board and the governor was not bound to observe its decisions; its members could merely put their opposition "on record".

Relatively soon, non-officials were appointed by the governor and entered the legislative council; and apart from the whites—chiefly in their capacity as representatives of major economic groups—there were also "natives". In Ceylon this occurred as early as 1833 (three Europeans and three Ceylonese), in Barbados in 1843, on the Gold Coast in 1889; in Kenya, on the other hand, this step was not taken until 1944. Since he appointed the council members, the governor of course effectively retained all decision-making power. The introduction of elections was the next step: Ceylon, 1910; Nigeria, 1922; Sierra Leone and Northern Rhodesia, 1924; the Gold Coast, 1925. At first the elected non-officials were in the minority and although they could oppose the government and voice their demands, they could exert no direct pressure on the executive council.[27] Under the pressure of the white and non-white elected members, this tended to lead to a "non-official elected majority", meaning that a kind of "semi-representative government" became one of the transitional steps. In this case, the majority consisted neither of official members nor of elected representatives, but of a union between the officials and the appointed non-officials who, although not bound to their instructions, had close relations with the government. Jamaica reached this semi-representative stage as early as 1884, Ceylon in 1920 and Guiana in 1928. A genuine form of representative government which would correspond to our "constitutional", i.e. not yet fully parliamentary, system was granted Cyprus in 1882, Malta in 1887, and Ceylon, the first non-white colony, in 1924. Here the Legislative Council was composed of twelve officials, two appointed members and thirty-four elected members. The government, however, still retained considerable power and could overrule the majority decision in questions of "paramount importance". In formal terms, however, the legislative power was taken over by the parliament while the executive continued to be vested in the governor, even if native inhabitants had been appointed to the executive council. Nevertheless, this represented a step beyond the Crown Colony system.

Compared to the policies of other colonial powers, these steps towards self-government took place very early, although the imperial government did not surrender any real authority and still retained an effective instrument of power in the civil service. At the head of the "procession" towards autonomy stood the white colonies Malta and Cyprus, followed by the old possessions in the West Indies joined by Ceylon in Asia; West Africa, and even more, East Africa, came at the end, and kept Crown Colony status until after the Second World War. Since the Legislative

Council really did legislate and advise and occasionally also passed important resolutions (by contrast with the legislative bodies of the French colonies, which were insignificant or represented only vested interests), it could serve to familiarize the native inhabitants with the functioning of Western-style representative institutions and give them a part in political decision-making. On the other hand, of course, the colonies had no direct representation in the British Parliament.

This form of government revealed numerous inherent problems, so at most it could be only a transitional thing. The elected representatives did have legislative power, budget authority and the instruments of control, but no direct access to power. They could refuse government proposals and introduce their own motions, but they could not force the government to accept the resolutions they passed. The government could not be overthrown and a vote of no-confidence did not lead to a take-over by the opposition. It was impossible to avoid friction between the Legislative Council and the government, which resulted in a tendency to obstruction, distrust and mutual suspicion. In the case of Ceylon this friction even penetrated to the finance committee, where it produced a mixture of legislation and administration which was obviously not workable. This problem, more or less common in constitutional and non-parliamentary governments, was intensified in the colonies. The majority of the members of parliament were colonials, and as such representatives of the non-white élite; they spoke for the nationalist emancipation movement and with their extensive demands called into question the existing constitution and tried to bring the colonial régime to an end. Britain did not achieve its aim of satisfying at least the national élite by giving it political responsibility and establishing a relationship of trust based on common duties. The dangerous conflict that resulted could lead either to blocking government actions or to the capitulation of the government in order to avoid open crisis. This conflict, however, was not new. The tension between a governor appointed by the king as holder of executive power, and a council elected by the people was the mainspring of the American independence movement. The drafting of Canada's constitution in the nineteenth century had inspired a similar movement, but there it was analysed in time by the Durham Report, and Canada was given dominion status.

Even in the non-white colonies the elected parliament naturally directed its efforts to gaining responsible government as soon as the "stage" of representative government had been reached. But responsible government implied the decisive and critical step by which London would surrender its control. The situation had become critical in Asia during the inter-war period and was urgent in India. Although it made promises, the British Government was not willing to honour them in many cases on the pretext that they were "premature". The transition to a multi-racial Commonwealth still seemed like the dissolution of the Empire, so London tried to avoid the issue of representative government by means of the "dyarchy", applying it first in the individual Indian states. A simple extension of the Morley-Minto Reforms, said Lionel Curtis, would necessarily lead to a "deadlock" between the executive and the legislature and drive both to despair. The only alternative he saw was capitulation.[28] The dyarchy could be described as "semi-responsible government," since a section of the exective power was made parliamentary, but this ingenious system had little success in India, nor was it satisfactory in Malta—the constitution of 1921 had to be suspended in 1930 and again in 1933. Cyprus presented a similar case.[29]

When Ceylon was granted representative government after 1923, its situation was similar to India's in 1919. Since Ceylon was one of the first of the Asian and African colonies to be granted autonomy, and since its constitutional development in these years presents aspects of some general significance, we will analyze it in detail.

At first a problem arose from the simple fact that London did not want to grant the Ceylonese responsible government. The island had great economic and strategic importance and London felt very strongly that British presence and British control had to be ensured. But once representative government had been achieved according to the formula we have outlined, the question of further development naturally came up. What would be a possible solution if it were assumed that responsible government and therefore dominion status were out of the question? The internal situation raised further questions. Ceylon was not a "national" entity composed of a body of people of equal race, religion, language and tradition; it was composed of several heterogeneous "communities": Buddhist Singhalese and Hindu Tamils, as well as Muslims and Christians. These communities lived separately, although they could not be clearly localized in geographic terms. This "communal" problem, which can be compared both to that of India and to the problem of nationalities in Eastern Europe, raised the question of whether and to what extent Western constitutional models could be applied to a situation in which there was no "national consensus", in which party fronts proved themselves to be "communal fronts" and the minority continually feared being outvoted and refused to be incorporated into the British representative system. The attempt to take a further step towards responsible government and thereby if not to solve the "communal" problem, at least to take it into account, led to the experimental constitution of 1931.

In the late autumn of 1927 one of the usual parliamentary commissions, under the chairmanship of the Earl of Donoughmore, visited Ceylon with the object of reporting on the functioning of the 1924 constitution and submitting proposals for reforms. The commission presented its report in June 1928.[30] After stressing the transitory nature of the

1924 ruling, it continued with a pregnant critique of the representative government. It said the problem lay, as we have said above, in the "divorce of power from responsibility",³¹ which had led the parliamentary system *ad absurdum* and shifted the power from a "responsible Executive to an irresponsible Legislature", wrongly undermining the position of the governor and the administration, without giving the Ceylonese a share in the responsibility. The colony was the main victim of this situation, since the necessary corrective measures had not been able to be taken. But, the report said, blame must not be placed on the Ceylonese parliament; it lay in the system itself.

Retrogression to the status of Crown Colony was politically intolerable since Britain wanted to take a step forward, "giving responsibility as well as power". The Ceylonese National Congress demanded full responsible government with a view to possible dominion status and London had to substantiate its refusal to concede this. So the report asserted that the Ceylonese did not yet have sufficient experience and that the non-homogeneous population seemed unsuited for talking over responsibility:

> A condition precedent to the grant of full responsible government must be the growth of a public opinion which will make that grant acceptable, not only to one section, but to all sections of the people; such a development will only be possible if under a new constitution the members of the larger communities so conduct themselves in the reformed Council as to inspire universal confidence.³²

It also said that Ceylon did not possess the necessary political parties for a parliamentary régime and that there was danger of an oligarchic minority rule:

> It seems hardly necessary to observe that HMG is the trustee not merely of the wealthier and more highly educated elements in Ceylon but quite as much of the peasant and the coolie, and of all those poorer classes which form the bulk of the population. To hand over the interests of the latter to the unfettered control of the former would be a betrayal of its trust.³³

The commission thus raised three main arguments against granting responsible government: the lack of administrative experience, the lack of national unity, and the fact that London could not surrender its power and responsibility to the "educated" minority because it was a trustee for the uneducated and politically unorganized masses.

These arguments are familiar from the Indian debate and will come up again in the discussion on Africa. Considered in retrospect they reveal their ambivalence. It is easy to dismiss them as "colonialist" and call upon the declared principle of self-determination; in any case the colonial power does not seem to be the right tribunal to judge the "maturity" and "ability" of its subjects. How are the natives to gain administrative experience when the colonial power occupies the key positions, maintains social discrimination and makes decisions based on its own absolute power? One could say that the "communal" problem was consciously played up on the principle of divide and rule, and ask who indeed could be the voice of the people if not the Western-educated élite. And it is obvious that while Great Britain pretended to consider the good and ill of the population, it in fact defended concrete interests. The arguments put forward to justify the behaviour of the colonial power also substantiate its refusal to comply with the demands of the nationalist opposition. It was easy to dismiss responsible government as "premature"; to proclaim liberal attitudes and defend the *status quo*; to stipulate conditions that must be met and then refuse reforms.

On the other hand, the internal justice of these arguments is undeniable. Unless a territory was to be left entirely to its own devices, the question had to be faced whether a country without European civilization possessed the necessary qualifications for Western-style self-government. Trusteeship was taken seriously and the commitment to "good government" was not just an empty phrase. Between the wars, people rightly feared a disruption of law and order and expected a "refeudalization" that threatened to destroy precisely everything in which the colonial power took justified pride. Great Britain wished to give the impression that it was granting voluntary and not compulsory concessions; but as early as the inter-war period this was no longer so. Any concessions or steps towards self-government were directly related to the nationalist movement; they were undertaken in order to avoid open crisis, to win over the opposition, or to split it and temporarily neutralize it. Nevertheless, Britain did attempt to gradually share a part of the administrative and political responsibility with the colonial peoples.

This also applied to the Ceylon Commission. The Conservative government did not want to refuse reforms and certainly did not want to adhere to the *status quo*. The energy with which the Donoughmore Commission tried to find a compromise was remarkable. In 1928 the commission's report suggested transforming the Legislative Council into a State Council which in turn would be divided into committees; the elected chairmen of the committees were to act as heads of the respective administrative departments and form a kind of ministerial council. Each minister would be solely responsible to the State Council and could be forced to resign by a negative vote. In this way the commission hoped to make it possible for the Ceylonese to have responsible power over the executive organs and at the same time to gain experience without the creation of a cabinet system on the British model or a form of dyarchy. The proposal was based on the model of the London County Council and was intended to help relieve "communal" frictions.

The commission made other suggestions too. It criticized the census franchise because it included only 4 percent of the population, and proposed universal suffrage. The traditional social class of the voters and representatives, it said, had resulted, among other things, in Ceylon's lagging behind in labour rights and social welfare; moreover, it was thought that political education would follow from the exercise of the franchise. Even though the extension of the franchise was intended to reduce the power of the oligarchic opposition, the proposal was still remarkable: the colonial power had taken the decisive step towards universal suffrage, which implied democratization!

The commission also wanted to abolish "communal representation". For a long time the British Government had occupied itself with the difficult question of how a "just" representation, i.e. one which satisfied the different communities, was possible within a "Plural Society" (J. S. Furnivall).[34] It was not only in Asia (India, Burma, Ceylon, Malaya, the Fiji Islands) that the problem was acute, but also in the West Indies, East Africa, Malta and Cyprus. Since the minorities definitely refused the usual form of territorial representation, a form of "communal" representation had been introduced in which each community formed its own electoral body from which it chose its representatives in the Legislative Council. This prevented under-representation or even repression of the minority communities. The council itself, however, was not divided into separate advisory councils as in the French colonies, but acted in unison. While the French introduced separate electoral bodies—*collèges*—in order to guarantee representation of the interests of the minority French colonials, in the British colonies, with the exception of East Africa, communal representation meant adequate consideration of the various non-white communities.[35] By this means, Britain hoped to calm racial and religious tensions and to pave the way for a reconciliation or "rationalization" of the various groups. The possibility of playing off the communities against one another or at least supporting the minorities against the majority community may have played an important role in some cases, and then it led not to reconciliation but to maintaining the oppositions (as in the case of Hindu-Muslim relations in India). But it would be wrong to see the communal electoral bodies as no more than an instrument of a divide and rule policy. "Communal vote" was simply becoming an urgent issue: Cyprus (Muslims and non-Muslims) and India (1909) came first, Ceylon followed in 1910; the problem of the Indian minority in Kenya came up in 1919, and in 1924 in the Straits Settlements the Europeans, Malayans, Indians, Chinese and Eurasians were brought into "equilibrium" by means of communal representation.

The expected relaxing of racial and religious tensions was only partial. As early as 1918 the Montagu-Chelmsford Report had approved abolishing communal representation in India. The Ceylon Commission made the same recommendation.[36] It said that the aim of according democratic institutions with the "plural society" and thereby promoting "unity" had not been achieved; mutual suspicion was still rife, and in fact the separate electoral bodies had only made the capsulating of the communities that much plainer. Now that the 1923 constitution allowed for deputies elected on a purely territorial basis apart from creating "communal" mandates, the commission proposed a purely territorial representation. The additional appointment of some members of the State Council was designed to give more consideration in the future to particular communities, among them the Europeans.

The proposals of the Donoughmore Commission were approved by the British Government and Ceylon obtained a constitution based on the report's proposals in 1931. Both the report and the constitution found surprisingly unanimous support. The conservatives could not very well oppose proposals made by a commission appointed by the Conservative government. *The Times* was reticent, speaking of a "courageous attempt" and describing the universal franchise as a "bold step" and the reform as "experimental"; but it did not oppose it either.[37] The *Round Table* actively supported it,[38] and even though one of its articles was sharply critical, expressing doubts about the functioning of the new constitution, this attitude was intended to defend the parliamentary system and not to dispute the need for a new step towards responsible government.[39] The liberal *Manchester Guardian* had already discussed the transition to responsible government in February 1928 and asked the relevant question: "Is there a half-way house between representative government and responsible government?" It said the dyarchy had not proved itself and that a step forward would have to be taken; of the Asian colonies it thought the most suitable for such an experiment was Ceylon.[40] The Labour opposition also welcomed the participation of Ceylonese in the administration, the general franchise and the abolishing of communal representation.[41] By this attitude the Labour government of 1929 was able to avoid taking initiatives of its own and to limit itself to carrying out the conservative proposals.

With the new constitution a decisive step had been taken from representative to responsible government, though not in the parliamentary sense. The Ceylonese took over the government offices and were responsible to elected deputies. Great Britain, it is true, was still in control of foreign policy and the governor with his reserved powers and his subordinate officials continued to control important decisions. Still, Britain had taken the critical step in which it surrendered a part of the executive power and effectively introduced decolonization. Now British domination could be maintained only by agreement with the Ceylonese élite if Britain wanted to avoid conflict and its unforeseeable consequences. That this path led to responsible government was evident, although remarkably little attention was paid to this fact in Great Britain and it continued to be treated as non-topical. Perhaps this was because of British pragmatism which did not want to concern itself with what appeared to be the distant future, perhaps because the Indian question stood in the forefront and the important decisions related to the Empire were being made there. But we must contrast the situation in Ceylon with that in Indochina and Indonesia, where institutional structures had scarcely changed in the inter-war years, where the representative bodies were insignificant and the number of electors small, where very few "natives" could rise to the upper administrative ranks and the colonial power was certainly not prepared to relax its domination. The Donoughmore Report and the Ceylon constitution of 1931 were also an interesting attempt to find a constitutional system that was compatible with a plural society. An important passage of the report reads:

> It must be our aim not slavishly to follow the forms and practice of the British model which was not designed to meet conditions similar to those obtaining in Ceylon, but to devise a scheme in consonance with local circumstances, a scheme which will be concerned not to reflect an alien philosophy but to give free play to the peculiar genius of the Ceylonese themselves and above all a scheme which may bring about a resolute handling of social and economic questions before, as in most Western lands, they have grown too complicated to remedy.[42]

Martin Wight, the outstanding expert on colonial institutions, commented on these words: "There is not a more representative statement of the aims of British colonial policy in the twentieth century!"[43] This may be an exaggeration, but it is worth noting. Wight is saying that this is the first time the general validity of the British system of government has been "officially" doubted; its significance as a model is being questioned and the report is postulating the need to seek other forms of democratic institutions. For the future, self-government or responsible government could not simply be equated with parliamentary government.

The question of the possibility of transplanting the European system of government, which was revived in the post-colonial era, was not new. It would be worth engaging in separate examinations to see how it was answered at different times in Great Britain and in France. We have already pointed out that before 1914 the Asian and African peoples were considered incapable of self-government. By stressing the racial and religious problems of the "coloured" world, the discrepancy between a small élite and the uneducated masses, the absence of a middle class and the alleged absence of a sense of political responsibility, it became easy to expose the liberal "illusion" and to warn against blessing the Asians or even Africans with highly developed, complex and traditional British institutions. The theory that the adoption of the British representative system with its elections, parliaments and responsible government was impossible in non-white areas could be used as an argument against any form of self-government and served to justify continued domination.

After 1919 the arguments became ambivalent and changed character.

Perhaps conservatives still adhered to the old theories, but liberal administrators, publicists and politicians began to raise the question of whether the British representative system could really serve as a model for the constitutional development of the colonies. Experiences in colonial administration and the development of ethnographic research, which examined the structures of non-European societies, described their specific systems of authority and pointed out both the age and the complexity of these systems, raised doubts as to the accuracy of traditionally held opinions. The concept of self-government had to be redefined; Western-style elections and parliamentary systems might not be suitable for societies with different structures and traditions; the task was to develop suitable institutions for these societies—not with any purpose other than self-government, and by appropriate means. Self-government, it was said, must not be an artificially supported representative system of the British type, which functioned unsatisfactorily if at all; rather it should make possible the adoption of government responsibility and forms of decision-making compatible with the traditions and problems of the respective inhabitants without thereby being undemocratic or untimely. The Donoughmore Commission made an attempt in this direction and in West Africa there were similar efforts. "Indirect Rule" helped its protagonists to found an "African" system of government.

However, these were minor aspects rather than characteristics of British colonial policy between the wars. They deserve some mention in our context because they give evidence of the new tendencies, of the pragmatic British attitude and of the autonomy gained by the colonies within the Empire. The same cannot be said for the French colonial situation. But the course was not pursued consistently, nor was it always successful; even the Ceylon experiment soon proved unsatisfactory and was dropped. The English must have found it difficult to accept systems other than their own or even to introduce them into their own domains, since they were still convinced of the excellence of British institutions and had little knowledge of others. Even when they created special arrangements like the dyarchy, indirect elections or federations, these were incorporated into a British parliamentary system. The question of whether the American presidential system or the Swiss Federal Council were perhaps better suited to the colonial situation and would ensure the necessary stability was seldom raised. Later it was pointed out on Britain's behalf, and with some right, that Britain could not act otherwise than according to British institutions. It was easy to theorize and to draft constitutions, it was said; but it was a different thing altogether to put them into practice and enforce them. A colonial administrative service could best introduce those institutions with which each individual official was most familiar. Nor must it be overlooked that the speakers for the emancipation movements demanded British institutions, whether because they wanted to take the mother country at its word, or because they too knew only the theory and practice of the British system and therefore did not question its exemplary nature or effectiveness. A large number of the nationalist leaders had been educated in British universities, often studying law, and often also had practical experience in their own legislative councils. The Nehru Report of 1928, for instance, was based on the British system. If the colonial power tried to suggest or introduce a different kind of system or special institutions, this was considered discrimination and refused. This kind of criticism was levelled at the 1931 Ceylon constitution.

In a curious unanimity of opinion, which perhaps was symptomatic of the colonial occupation, in years to come both the constitutional experts of the Colonial Office and the nationalists in the colonies used the British governmental system as a model. Responsible government as the final aim of constitutional development was understood as parliamentary government. In accordance with the specifically British combination of basically conservative principles with a pragmatic adaptability to the concrete situation, the different colonies at their various stages of development had a great variety of special rulings, whether in the electoral system, the composition of the councils or their powers. Each colony, even if it was geographically a neighbour to the next, such as Nigeria and the Gold Coast, was treated independently and in the course of decades obtained a series of constitutions which in each case were laboriously worked out by the governor and the Colonial Office—often with the assistance of parliamentary research commissions; at a later stage, negotiations would take place in London with deputies of the nationalist parties—even though they were sometimes unsuccessful —so as to reach a compromise solution and at least to obtain temporary collaboration from the nationalist opposition. This occurred in Egypt and India between the wars, in Ceylon during the Second World War, in West Africa in the late 1940s, in East Africa around 1960. But diverse as the different rulings were, and flexible as Great Britain proved itself in dealing with the individual institutional problems of the different colonies, the unbroken thread by which London, the trustee, led the parts of the Empire from Crown Colony status to self-government, remained visible.

COLONIAL DEVELOPMENT, 1929–1940

At first the dominions were also the focus of imperial economic policy after 1919. During the First World War France had become aware of the economic importance of its overseas colonies and in the 1920s Albert Sarraut made the economic development of the colonies into a formal programme; but in England similar considerations concerned the Commonwealth rather than the Dependent Empire.[1] Admittedly, the colonies supplied important raw materials and food, but Britain considered India and the dominions far more important as economic partners than the colonies, since they bought British industrial goods and offered opportunities for investing British capital. Moreover, the dominions had fiscal sovereignty and were beginning to industrialize while Great Britain, economically weakened by the war, was facing a structural crisis.[2] This explains why the dominions came first. We have briefly mentioned Lord Beaverbrook's Empire Free Trade campaign and the Ottawa agreements in 1932 (cf. p. 55). But, characteristically, these efforts towards an imperial economic system primarily concerned the dominions and applied to the colonies only indirectly.

Unlike France, in England the term "development", as the expression of a new imperial and colonial attitude and an answer to the economic difficulties of the mother country, is seldom found applied to the Dependent Empire in the post-war years. During the war, a self-appointed Empire Resources Development Committee was formed which suggested that British war debts abroad could be speedily repaid by ruthlessly stepping up colonial production. Quite apart from its doubtful value in practical terms, this plan was rejected by the British Government and violently criticized by such men as Lord Lugard: they said it implied a plantation system, would lead to unlimited exploitation of native labour and was incompatible with trusteeship.[3] So, by contrast with the situation after 1945, the economic development of the colonies was neither planned nor encouraged by London after the First World War. It remained based on the potentials of the respective territory and on the world market. We referred earlier to the sometimes astonishing increases in individual areas of production: cocoa on the Gold Coast, petroleum and coconut oil in Nigeria, cotton in the Sudan and Uganda, coffee in Kenya, copper in Northern Rhodesia, tin and unrefined rubber in Malaya. The colonies had no economic ties with the mother country, for it neither committed itself to buy nor did it privilege its exports to the colonies by a tariff policy. In contrast to France, Great Britain maintained its old policy of Free Trade: import or export duties were fiscal policies which benefited the colonial budget, and until 1932 they contained few if any preferences for the mother country.

The principle of "financial self-sufficiency"—meaning that the colonies had to finance themselves out of their own resources—applied in the British Empire as it did in the French colonies; the colony paid no dues to the mother country and their contributions to their own defence costs were usually low and were mainly borne by London. On the other hand, they obtained no direct financial aid either. The Colonial Office urged self-sufficiency and contributed to the regular budget in only a few areas.[4] London was proud of having built up this relationship because it seemed to belie any reproach of exploitation and to underline the autonomy of the colony. Consequently the colonial administration had to pay for such services as schools, sanitation and economic development out of its own budget, which limited its potentialities. It had to postpone any "unproductive" expenditures and, apart from some research and assistance in agriculture, chiefly devoted itself to developing the infrastructure. The extension of the railway system, the ports and roads came first; this seemed justified both in the interest of the British economy and with regard to the colonial budget.[5] The economically stronger colonies had the advantage here. On the Gold Coast for instance, Governor Guggisberg was able to introduce a generous development programme in the 1920s and to finance the exemplary Achimota College[6] out of the rapidly rising cocoa profits. But the poorer colonies who most needed special developmental aid lagged behind. A similar kind of vicious circle occurred in the case of the debts incurred in London for specific projects: since the interest and capital repayments burdened the budget, the richer territories could make more use of this method of financing their development than could the poorer ones.

This traditional financial policy forced the colonial administration to pay particular attention to raising its revenues. They could be increased by raising the income tax, which immediately forced the natives to work harder and thus produced a new kind of forced labour; or they could be increased by forcibly increasing export production, which, however, meant that food production for local needs and long-term projects were neglected.[7] Since the colonial firms' private investments were concentrated on staple products, the administration was obliged to take special care to improve traditional agriculture and to promote a more stable economic development.

The effects of the world slump were catastrophic, and in the 1930s they led to strikes and civil disturbances in Northern Rhodesia, on the Gold Coast and in the West Indies. Ottawa did not manage to provide any help. International agreements made preferences impossible in important colonies (e.g. the Gold Coast, Nigeria, Northern Rhodesia, Tanganyika); in any case the production exceeded the British market's capacity to absorb. The producers of sugar, tropical fruits and tobacco— i.e. mainly the West Indies, Mauritius, Nyasaland, Cyprus—profited from the mother country's preferences while the privileges on British imports were rather prejudicial to colonies such as Gambia, Sierra Leone, Ceylon and Malaya. The system of preferences further promoted the tendency to concentrate on certain export products, although it had long been realized that diversification was an urgent task.[8]

Since colonial budgets were reduced, little could be done for the branches of the economy affected by the crisis. Conservative governments were hardly ready to intervene, even in the mother country. So the colonial economies largely relied on free competition, although, in the absence of trade-unions, the term "competition" can be used only in a limited sense; usually a few major firms controlled the market. The administration seldom intervened in matters of price and income. Even when the African cocoa planters on the Gold Coast replied to an agreement among the trade firms to keep prices down by a strike and consumer boycott, the governor tried to remain "neutral" although a commission of enquiry had agreed that there was considerable justice in the African protests. The Cocoa Marketing Board was not set up until 1947.[9]

But although the administration hardly promoted industrialization in the 1930s, it did fix quotas on the import of cheap Japanese goods (cf. p. 16). The Malayans, the Ceylonese and the elected members in the Gold Coast and Nigeria protested in their legislative councils, but without much success. The Empire historian Coupland also found reason to protest against these and similar measures: he said the government speaker Runciman, by referring to "our markets", admitted that he was concerned with protecting Lancashire. Great Britain was asserting that it saw trusteeship as a partnership; Britain had proposed the preference agreements to the legislative councils, but as long as the latter were not really representative and since in the final analysis they had to obey London, this partnership was still highly dubious; Ceylon had had reason to reject it. "To talk of 'co-operation' unless we are sure it is voluntary goes far to justify what is said abroad of our national hypocrisy."[10]

This trade policy derived from nineteenth-century laissez-faire which was intended to be a form of trusteeship that undertook to guarantee protection and order, but not "development". Could the individual colonies survive and be brought closer to self-government in this way? Could areas that were poor in natural resources and burdened by climatic conditions, tropical diseases, primitive living conditions, rudimentary schooling and small capital, areas which since and because of the introduction of the capitalist economic system and Western legislation suffered from social imbalance and in addition were faced with an increasing population problem "develop" on their own and achieve stability?

There was no lack of criticism of this policy. Colonial reformers and the Labour party described the poverty of the native inhabitants, spoke of exploitation, referred to particularly glaring cases and pointed out the utter inadequacy of achievements so far; they said social legislation must be developed, education promoted and the standard of hygiene raised. The question of who was to pay for these measures was scarcely ever answered. The fact that a considerably larger investment, especially in the poorer colonies, would require financial aid from the mother country's budget was either not realized or was passed over. The same applied to the question of industrialization: liberal administrators and missionary reformers preferred to prevent industrialization, perhaps not because they wanted to preserve the traditional social structures but to avoid disrupting them prematurely. The Labour party representatives had to consider their supporters, who understandably enough showed no interest in colonial competition.

This attitude was slow to change. We have mentioned Lord Milner as a forerunner (cf. p. 41); his interest in the colonies did not stem from concern for the natives, rather he wanted to use the "almost immeasurable economic potentialities" of the colonies to overcome the British slump: "What have we to show comparable to the wonderful development of Morocco under the brilliant and energetic guidance of General Lyautey?" In East Africa, he said, the German planters had been driven out and their plantations left to go to ruin, endangering the natives' living conditions. "Do not let us starve Kenya and Tanganyika!" Many territories could supply raw materials, but they needed roads, railways and irrigation. The Colonial Office was the "Cinderella of the great Public Departments"; in the other ministries the electorate and its parliamentary deputies saw to it that credits were granted and cuts in expenditure avoided! It was a paradox, he said, that the dominions were speeding up their economic growth once they had achieved self-government. In the Dependent Empire this was the task of the mother country. Milner proposed an "Imperial Development Fund" to supply the colonies with the necessary credits "which is all they need to start them on the path of progress".[11] This demand was new and anticipated future developments, even though it was primarily concerned with serving the interests of the mother country and aimed at economic expansion rather than an extension of social services.

The report of the 1925 East Africa Commission, headed by Ormsby-Gore, went a step further.[12] It said that at that time only Kenya could obtain loans under the Colonial Stock Act, whereas this was difficult for the mandates and protectorates, which depended on the goodwill of the finance minister. Tanganyika had not yet recovered from its war losses nor regained its pre-war standard of living; actual grants would presumably no longer be necessary, but one way or another the extension of "the necessary services" must not fail owing to lack of funds. Loans must be granted on the best possible terms. Long-term development projects could not be met from the colonies' own resources and made it necessary to introduce new methods. In conclusion the report stated: "The outstanding problem is the finance of such undertakings. It is clear to us that unless the Imperial Government is prepared to assist liberally in this matter, little or nothing can be done."[13] In a supplementary memorandum, the liberal F. C. Linfield even suggested an "Imperial Development Board" (it is not certain whether he was influenced by Milner) which, furnished with three million pounds a year, could undertake the necessary research and plan long-term projects.[14] Since it was hoped that these resources and investments would provide orders for British industry, the new attitude was described as "enlightened self-interest".[15]

It was the advent of the economic crisis that brought these proposals into public discussion. "Development" consequently became an issue in the 1929 elections. In a speech on 18 April, the conservative Stanley Baldwin stated:

> We are not quite satisfied with the progress we have made in the development of the Colonies. We shall provide out of Imperial funds such sums as are required to pay the interest for the initial years of fruitful schemes in the Colonies, which would otherwise be postponed. We propose to establish an independent commission for this purpose.[16]

This meant that loans were to be granted, as before, but in addition direct credits from the budget were to be made available to the colonies. The Conservative party declared in their electoral programme: "A Colonial Development Fund will be created to assist Colonial Government in financing approved projects of development."[17] *The Times* supported the programme and accused Labour and Liberal members of wanting only to combat unemployment at home or of being uninterested in imperial issues, as were Snowden and Lloyd George. It reminded its readers of Joseph Chamberlain, stressed the colonies' consumer power and repeated Leo Amery's formula: "Here indeed is the new economic world which may be called in to redress the balance of the old."[18] The Conservative party had not taken much notice of the development of the colonies in the 1920s; but now, at the moment of crisis, it recalled its imperial past and proposed the Colonial Development Fund as a means of overcoming the crisis.

The Labour government took up the Conservative party proposal and put it into practice. In July 1929 Parliament passed the Colonial Development Act, which provided one million pounds a year from budget funds "for the purpose of aiding and developing agriculture and industry in the colonies and territories and thereby promoting commerce with industry in the United Kingdom".[19] Agriculture, transport and waterworks were mentioned explicitly, as was the "promotion of public health" and agricultural and technical training, but not education in general, such as the building of schools! The special fund was not intended to cover current administrative expenditures, but to help finance productivity. At the same time it was to help the ailing industry in the mother country to obtain orders, thereby implying that the Colonial Development Fund was largely designed to combat British unemployment, both directly and indirectly.[20] This argument was considered very weighty in the parliamentary debate and the government used it to carry through the bill.[21] Although it was supported by both parties, it encountered a certain amount of distrust. The right wing feared state intervention at the cost of private initiative, waste of money and uncontrollable bureaucratic entanglements on the part of the Colonial Office; while the former Liberal and now Labour M.P. Colonel Wedgwood objected that in Africa, as opposed to the situation in the mother country, the problem was not so much unemployment as lack of employment and that the native peoples' labour force was being exploited. This, he thought, would be aggravated if budget funds were spent to build railways and bridges. The export firms and the East African settlers would profit most and only a small part of the money would be spent on the country itself. In addition by exploiting new coalfields with cheap black labour, it was said, England's already heavily struck coal-mining industry would be further damaged.[22] But James Griffiths, the future colonial minister of the Labour party, said: "I understood the whole object of the Bill was to promote work in this country."[23] This was in fact the main reason for granting money in the following years.[24] No doubt numerous projects were financed which benefited the territory itself and directly served the interests of the natives, but the aim largely remained "colonialist" and only partly complied with the idea of trusteeship. Macmillan points out, perhaps over-critically, that the natives did not so much need railways as schools, hospitals and modernization of local food production; the projects being promoted were often a heavy burden on the local and colonial budgets, since only part of the money could be given as a grant, and did not raise the standard of living or increase the purchasing power of the natives.[25]

We must also note that the sum allocated in 1929 was actually very small. What indeed was the use of a million pounds a year for the enormous area of the Dependent Empire? This did not prevent the *Economist*, speakers in Parliament and other publicists from referring to an act "on generous lines" that would permit "a wide range of activities".[26] The Liberal party leader Samuel even asserted that the colonies were "highly prosperous" whereas the British taxpayer was overburdened since the war, and demanded of the government "that the burden ought not to be laid solely [!] upon the shoulders of the British taxpayer of promoting these further developments". The one million pounds should facilitate short-term investments and then be made available again[27]—as though this annual sum could represent a significant burden on the mother country and its tax-payer! Such opinions revealed prejudice against the colonies and their inhabitants and ignorance of their real problems—an attitude which strangely contradicted Britain's proud sense of Empire and hardly complied with its claim to trusteeship. According to general opinion, the colonies were always primarily objects of "exploitation", since the administration saw to law and order but had few economic obligations and left their development to the initiative of private firms. The importance of the Colonial Development Act of 1929 lay less in the granting of credits than in the break from the traditional principle of colonial "self-sufficiency". That the act was a new departure was proved both by the distrust that greeted it and by the praise accorded to it once the project had succeeded. Today this praise seems very exaggerated. In fact it was only a "policy of development", as we would understand it today, in a very limited sense; and yet the bill meant that a new principle was accepted and it paved the way for a new understanding of colonial problems: it was finally realized that the colonies needed direct financial aid. The expectation of future consumer power presupposed investments which the poorer colonies in particular were not able to provide from their own resources. Development demanded increased activity on London's part, a certain amount of planning and long-term projects. The allocations to the Colonial Development Fund of 1929 may have been small, but once the obligation had been accepted, they could gradually be increased, as they were in 1940. But the theoretic preparation began as early as the 1930s.

The Colonial Office gradually extended its field of activity. Higher-grade officials who could rise to the office of governor were still recruited from the English upper class and educated in public schools and Oxford or Cambridge. The universities took little interest in colonial issues, however, and offered only a few special courses. Great Britain did not have any institution comparable to the French École coloniale! In 1937–1938 Margery Perham and Reginald Coupland directed summer courses on colonial administration.[28] The London School of Economics had a leading ethnologist in Malinowski, whose research into native social structures also gained respect outside academic circles. Until the First World War, the Indian Civil Service was better looked upon than the colonial service, but in the inter-war years the two seem to have gained a certain equality of prestige, which made it easier for the Colonial Office to recruit highly qualified young people.

The laissez-faire policy pursued before 1914 had discouraged interest in economic and social questions, planning, systematic analysis of certain problems, or experts' reports. The Colonial Office was organized according to regions and looked after the correspondence between London and the individual territories. Its "General Department" was badly equipped.

Between the wars, Ormsby-Gore, Wilson and Cunliffe-Lister made some adjustments. The General Department was expanded and became more specialized, although no real economic department was formed until 1934.[29] Colonial Office officials travelled to the colonies more frequently than before, advisory experts for education, medicine, agriculture and finance were appointed and "advisory committees" were formed. The Education Commission with Hans Vischer, the former Swiss missionary and first Director for Education in Northern Nigeria as secretary, submitted an important report in 1925 on education in tropical Africa, which referred to the colonial administration the task of giving financial support to the schools and supervising them,[30] formerly the exclusive responsibility of the missionaries. In 1938 this was followed by the appointment of a labour advisor and the creation of a department for economic development; the number of special labour departments in the individual colonies was increased while the colonies for their part prepared labour ordinances which came into force before or during the war.[31] Yet the officials were few and the funds remained modest: for instance, at first the Tropical Diseases Bureau was allowed one thousand pounds a year[32]; the colonies themselves largely had to pay for the special advisors.

The first extensive general report on the colonies was published in 1938 and served as a draft for the parliamentary debate on the colonial budget. It described in detail the problems and demands of the Dependent Empire and was also intended to provide information to a wider public. In the same year Lord Hailey's monumental African Survey appeared. In his Rhodes Lectures in 1929, General Smuts had pointed to the lack of knowledge of the problems of Black Africa; four years later a committee was formed under the chairmanship of Philip Kerr, which appointed Lord Hailey (who was one of the leading experts on India but had no experience of Africa) chairman of a scientific work team.[33] It was significant that little interest was accorded the extensive research and that the Royal Institute of International Affairs and the American Carnegie Institute bore the costs, rather than the Colonial Office. The *African Survey*, which offered detailed information on geographic features, racial and linguistic conditions, agriculture, transport and industry, as well as education, sanitation, administration and legislation, and which took other African powers apart from the British territories into account, was immediately hailed as an original achievement and an incentive to increasing efforts in Black Africa. In the *Contemporary Review* John Harris described the work as "an historic event for the African continent".[34] Professor Coupland mentioned the *Survey* in his journal *Africa*, remarking that since the war Britain had shown interest in the dominions and India, but not in its African colonies. He said the notion of trusteeship was too vague and traditional to make people aware of the real problems of this continent and that the next ten to fifty years would be decisive![35] Hailey for his part stressed that in some African territories the economic and administrative foundations had only just been laid, and that a "spirit of humanity" and a routine administration were no longer enough; there was a need for exact knowledge of all the circumstances, and extension of social services must take precedence from now on.[36] Among other things Hailey criticized the fact that the large commercial enterprises and mining concerns brought considerable sums into the mother country in the form of dividends and taxes which should by rights go into investments in Africa and increase the local budgets. Economic action must now join political action, but this was not possible without direct aid from the mother country:

> The British people must realise that we ought to be more liberal in our attitude to the need for financing colonial development. I do not question that we are serious in speaking, as we so often speak, of our spirit of trusteeship. But I sometimes wish that we could place our hands on our hearts a little less, and set them to explore our pockets a little more. It is all very well for Great Britain to hold out to the African the priceless boon of Self-Government. We had to fight for our liberties ourselves, and perhaps we find it a little difficult to believe that the path to health, happiness, or perhaps even heaven, does not lie in the possession of a vote. But political advance is not enough. Africa needs a great deal of money spent on it before its inhabitants can attain reasonably satisfactory standards of nutrition, of health and of social life. It is clear that in many cases the money for development can only come from Imperial grants.[37]

The new attitude is clearly visible here. It is evident in the shift of emphasis from the administrative and political to the social field. Law and order and a self-righteous but at first not very concrete promise of future self-government could no longer justify the profession of trusteeship. Trusteeship had to be reinterpreted positively in order to apply to the actual situation in Africa. The real future policy was to be one of development, with the help of budget funds, and it must not be based either directly or indirectly on the interests of the mother country, as was still the case in 1929. Colonial development, in the view of Lord Hailey, should no longer serve to alleviate British export worries and to occupy the British unemployed; its aim was to "develop" the individual territories on the basis of their particular circumstances and potentials and to strengthen their economic and social structures.

In 1938 the equally original book *Capital Investment in Africa* by S. H. Frankel appeared. Using comprehensive statistical material, it discussed the problems of a forced economic development, emphasizing Africa's dependence on outside capital investment, and at the same time showed the heavy burden the loans placed on the colonial budget. He objected to the one-sided promotion of industries such as mining and urged paying greater attention to the problem of the labour force and native food production. Margery Perham succeeded in bringing Frankel to Oxford; but she met with much resistance, since many of her colleagues did not want to recognize colonial economic policy as a special field of study![38]

The urgent need to re-examine the laissez-faire attitude and to interpret trusteeship positively, in terms of economic and social aid, was confirmed by the 1939 *Report on Nutrition in the Colonial Empire*. Using statistical data, the report exposed the serious undernourishment—or improper nourishment—of a major part of the native colonial population. The existing tendency to underestimate material distress in the colonies and to exaggerate the progress in certain territories was contrasted with crude reality. At the same time, a wider public became aware of colonial problems through the disturbances in the West Indies.

The West Indian economy, which was essentially based on the sugar industry, had been in a critical state for years. As early as 1929 a parliamentary commission under the chairmanship of Lord Olivier had described the miserable life of the native farmers and sugar labourers. But neither the Labour nor the Conservative governments pursued the commission's proposals for reform, which included higher preferences for West Indian sugar, guaranteed and higher prices and the establishment of an agency for buying the production.[39] From 1934 on, there were strikes and demonstrations, with numerous deaths in Trinidad in 1937; and in May 1938, there was a general strike and serious disturbances broke out. In the Commons on 14 June Malcolm MacDonald, the colonial minister, announced the formation of a commission of enquiry and promised immediate measures to improve the untenable situation. Only now did Parliament and the public begin to concern themselves with the situation in the West Indies. These colonies were not considered very important economically and therefore seldom discussed in public. Moreover, since these old possessions had achieved rather extensive self-government and, although they did not control it, were at least able to keep the executive within bounds by means of majority-elected assemblies, the mother country thought it had performed its duty as trustee. So the strikes and unrest provided a "rude shock to public opinion in England".[40]

The House of Commons discussed the situation.[41] Reports on the West Indian crisis appeared in the newspapers. Lord Olivier, the former governor and an active reformer, wrote an article in *Nineteenth Century* on the "recent outcry about the failure of British Government in the West Indian Colonies", in which he said that in fact the commission of enquiry was quite superfluous, since the Colonial Office had long known about the miserable situation. But since most of the parliamentarians, not to speak of the electorate, were "exceedingly ignorant about West-Indian affairs", and payments by the mother country were inevitable, the report must now provide the necessary backing; it must not just combat Liberal and Conservative opposition, but also fight certain elements within the Labour party who preferred to employ public funds in the slums and areas of unemployment rather than in the colonies! He added that since the main cause of the crisis was low sugar prices, the commission could in any case do little.[42] The *Round Table* attitude is worth nothing: it did not, as was usual in the conservative colonial press between the wars, trace the "serious discontent" back to political or even Communist activity but to the crisis in the sugar industry which, it said, could pay only minimum wages; this could be traced back to the promotion of sugar-beet plantations with state subvention in the mother country. The plight of the cocoa planters in Trinidad was the result, it said, of overproduction in the Empire, which could not even be remedied by preferences. The *Round Table* proposed to resolve the crisis by an extension of the unions and the employment of inspectors![43]

A book by the historian W. M. Macmillan was significant to the colonial discussion before the outbreak of the Second World War. *Warning from the West Indies, A Tract for the Empire*, when it first appeared in 1936, attracted little notice. In 1938, however, interest had so far awakened that the revised edition, furnished with a new preface, was published as a Penguin Handbook. Macmillan gives a detailed description of geographic and climatic conditions, population factors and the economic and social structure of the West Indies. He thought the problem lay in the fact that in the plantation system introduced by the Europeans, export production had been forced while agricultural production for food was neglected. There was an overproduction crisis in sugar, but the islands had to import food—in 1934 Trinidad had to import 80 percent of its food! For years the West Indian situation had been characterized by wages below subsistence level, unemployment, proletarianization in the towns, miserable living conditions and a low standard of hygiene. A partial readjustment to new products had taken place—such as to bananas in Jamaica—but was difficult to carry through since the prices for coffee and cocoa had fallen in the world market. What was to be done? Macmillan proposed land reform, reorganization of the tenant system, improved schooling, extension of the unions and small industries and, above all, active and large-scale improvement of the health service, housing projects and public works. But this was possible only with generous support from the mother country.

Macmillan continued with general considerations aimed at a policy of development; he considered the 1929 Colonial Development Act a step in the right direction. He thought the doctrine of trusteeship needed to be reinterpreted in more modern terms if it was to retain its credibility and not seem merely an excuse for inactivity.

> The doctrine that these backward countries are our sacred trust under tutelage till capable of standing by themselves is comfortably vague. It may be used to justify decent paternalism, where the trustee protects, but by taking all the responsibility stifles real progress. . . . It is that in the first place the executive Government, the "trustee", must show greater courage than has been usual in its exercise of authority on their behalf. The only rational way of preparing these colonies to stand by themselves is to strengthen the lower strata of society by such measures as we have been discussing. The difficulties are many. The cost of health services and education must far exceed the resources of most colonies, in any case till their benefits have had time to take effect. Tenant rights and other disturbances of old tradition must provoke the opposition of powerful minority interests—hitherto dominant—which are likely to oppose also a more equitable distribution of the burden of taxation. But if trusteeship means anything it means development in the interest of the weaker classes and a firm exercise of authority on their behalf—without second thoughts for British industry, for the precarious state of white colonists, or even for the interests of a black upper class. It must not be as in South Africa where Great Britain herself made "the great refusal".[44]

Macmillan, like Lord Hailey, did not want to see trusteeship understood only in "negative" terms of a protection or in the interests of the existing authority and traditional social structures, but more "positively", in the sense of engaging in widespread activity for the benefit of the masses of people. This required a new attitude on the part of the mother country; it must realize that the laissez-faire policy could not "develop backward peoples" or lead them to take over responsibility. The financial costs of the policy of development must be borne by the mother country since colonial budgets alone could never withstand the transitional phases. This economic and financial aid must not be given with a view to creating orders for the industry of the mother country but should be based on the special circumstances of each territory and should be directed to solving its specific problems. Trusteeship, he thought, meant the opposite of a decline in imperial responsibility!

Macmillan also engaged in a critical analysis of the other major point of British colonial doctrine, the granting of self-government, from the point of view of the actual economic and social problems self-government entailed. He said the West Indian territories had long possessed representative bodies with considerable control. For instance, the parliament of Barbados was a kind of copy of Great Britain's, "complete with established Church, two Chambers, a Court of Grand Sessions, etc". The executive, it was true, remained vested in the governor but the assemblies could oppose him successfully in important issues. He thought the results of this extensive self-government were exceedingly doubtful, since the limited franchise gave a voice only to the minority white settlers and to a small native bourgeoisie; experience had shown that this "representation of the people" obstinately defended its own interests and established vetoes against certain expenses which the government had proposed in the specific interests of the population in the lower income groups. Officials were badly paid, health services sabotaged, economic assistance made impossible. And Great Britain was actually proud of such a form of self-government! He exposed a new facet of the notion of self-government: it was not a matter of indifference who obtained it; its purpose could not be the privileging of a minority. Only if the grant of self-government was accompanied by democratization could a conflict with trusteeship be avoided. This meant that the colonial problem was not resolved simply by granting political rights and powers to a minority, whether white or coloured. The West Indies had proved that this kind of liberal creed led to results which were anything but liberal. Political rights had helped a minority to monopolize the economic wealth and to keep the masses in an inferior position. The colonial power must not continue, in the name of self-government, to overlook the regrettable situation of the majority of the population, but must promote democratization by granting aid, social legislation and extension of the franchise. "Colonial democracy must be helped to its birth."[45] This created a new order of priorities: in place of political concessions came a "policy of development" which in certain cases demanded massive pressure from the elected Legislative Council and which must have seemed "colonialist" to the privileged classes!

Macmillan was not only considering the West Indies. In other places too, he thought that sooner or later unrest would reveal the inadequacy of British policy. The West Indies should serve Britain as a warning:

> The tragedy of the West Indies now needs no emphasis as a warning of the dangers of a complacent neglect which threatens the very foundations of the British Empire all over the world. We cannot afford to allow it to continue to be a habit to wait until there is riot and bloodshed before taking notice of the grievances of our fellow subjects in any of these Dependencies.[46]

The frequent self-praise only covered up ignorance and neglect. Great Britain could do justice to its great responsibility only by granting positive aid:

> By nature and definition colonies are colonies just because they are poor and backward; to allow them to remain so reflects no credit on the colonizing power. The few of British origin, the Dominions, which have shown that maturity can be achieved, now stand with us in the Common-

wealth. The majority remain as they were, and are to be brought to self-dependence only by positive work well done. When I went to the West Indies I was told by men of all shades of opinion that I should find everything ideal and I fully expected to. My doubts when I returned were received coldly by many who are strong critics of our policy in Africa. The nominal freedom and supposed independence of the West Indian peoples had blinded those who should have been more watchful. In fact the root of the trouble lies in lack of knowledge and of sympathetic imagination in the British public responsible for imperial policy.[47]

These words are from the preface to the 1938 edition. By comparison with 1936, Macmillan discerned a certain change in the British attitude. The unrest in the West Indies and the crisis in Palestine, besides the challenge of German colonial claims, had produced a stronger interest on the part of the mother country in the hitherto neglected colonies. The *African Survey* contributed to this as well. We may also assume that Macmillan's demands had a part in influencing the West India Royal Commission which submitted its report late in 1939.[48] The report described in detail the severe economic and social crisis which was the result of a forced concentration on export production; in its recommendations it asked for a special West Indies Welfare Fund of one million pounds per year, which was to be used for agrarian reform, to fight unemployment and to promote housing, welfare services and education; a special committee was to administer the fund, work out plans for development and advise on individual projects. The political problem also came under discussion: the existing electoral qualifications had benefited the landowners and must be replaced promptly by a general franchise; unofficial majorities were to take over the legislature and should obtain a part in the responsibility by means of a committee system: "More and not less participation by the people in the work of government is a real necessity for lasting social advancement."[49]

What Lord Hailey and Macmillan had analyzed and postulated was thus "officially" approved by the report on the West Indies. On the one hand, this meant economic aid; on the other, further steps towards self-government, together with democratization. This was Britain's answer to the 1938 disturbances. Compared to the reactions of other colonial powers in similar cases, it can be described as definitely liberal.

The economic aid to the West Indies and the establishment of a special fund from budget resources were explained as follows: "We do not think the interest of the maintenance of British export trade, or unemployment in Great Britain, should be allowed to stand in the way of certain suggested industrial developments in Jamaica."[50] By adding this, London openly diverged from the 1929 Colonial Development Act. Priority was no longer given to the British economy, but to that of the colony; even the possibility of competition with the mother country no longer stopped London from doing whatever was necessary to develop the potentials of the colonial territories.

How far this new attitude took root in British public opinion shortly before the war is demonstrated by an article in the *Economist* in November 1938. In 1929 the influential journal still had described the credit of one million pounds as "generous"; now it considered that making far greater sums available and extending the scope of the reforms was an urgent necessity. The imperial power, it said, must compile information and carry out more intensive research than before, and above all

> furnish generous funds for development and evolve a centrally directed colonial policy. In the British possessions too much has been left to the devoted labours of the man on the spot, and too little has been known or done in London. Troubles in the West Indies have disclosed the dangers of this negligence, and they are implicit in the details of the African Survey. The future of Africa depends, as the survey shows, upon the natives' own enterprise and social development. It is for the Imperial powers to provide the conditions and resources; to see to social welfare and agricultural regeneration; to furnish knowledge, guidance and financial aid. These are Britain's tasks to-day.[51]

From here the road led to the Colonial Development and Welfare Bill of 1940. Although it was prepared by the administration before the actual outbreak of hostilities, it had a certain connection with the Second World War. In a moment of extreme peril, Great Britain still remembered the Empire and showed great interest in its economic development and political stability. Instead of one million pounds, an annual sum of five million was to be made available in the next ten years, besides a special credit for research and the already mentioned credit for the West Indies. The increase in the sum was considerable, if one recalls the resistance in 1929, even though it still seems minimal with respect to actual needs and by comparison with the means provided after 1945. More important for us here is the new concept underlying the 1940 act. The act stated: "The primary aim of Colonial policy is to protect and advance the interests of the inhabitants of the Colonies."[52] The later addition of the words "and welfare" was to imply that the credits could also be used for education and health services, although this would increase the burden on the colonial budgets rather than provide revenues, nor would the British economy profit by it. Current expenses and even debts could in certain cases be taken over by the fund: "Our object under this legislation is to develop the colonies so that as far as possible they become self-supporting units," Macdonald declared in the Commons.[53] But this goal could not be attained by the traditional methods:

> ... if full and balanced development is to be obtained ... some assistance from outside is necessary at this stage. Few of the colonies have

the good fortune to possess substantial mineral wealth, and in comparatively few are there manufacturing industries of any magnitude. The majority are wholly, or almost wholly, dependent on the more limited resources derived from agriculture. The value of agricultural products varies widely from year to year as conditions fluctuate in the world markets, with the result that colonial revenues provide an unreliable basis for a policy of steady development. In some cases the position is aggravated by the heavy burden of indebtedness . . . many colonies cannot finance out of their own resources the research and survey work, the schemes of major capital enterprise, and the expansion of administrative and technical staffs [that] are necessary for their full and vigorous development. Nor can they always afford, in the absence of such development, an adequate standard of health and education services.[54]

This passage shows very clearly how Hailey's and Macmillan's views prevailed in official circles shortly before the outbreak of the war. Even a few years earlier this attitude would have been almost unthinkable. The constitutional weakness of most of the colonies was acknowledged surprisingly openly, which implicitly at least, meant that a merely "negative" view of trusteeship was officially abandoned. The development towards self-sufficiency could not come out of the colonies' own resources in most cases and required a new system of "grants in aid" from the mother country. The administration, which had hitherto been based on law and order, needed active aid in the economic and social field. It was senseless or impractical to assert that self-government was the aim of British policy as long as conditions for it did not exist. The colonial minister wanted the bill to be understood in this sense: "The bill we are discussing this afternoon breaks new ground. It establishes the duty of tax-payers in this country to contribute directly and for its own sake towards the development in the widest sense of the word of the colonial peoples."[55]

This "new policy" did not mean just making available budget resources for "aid to development"; it also meant wide-scale state intervention in the future, including "planning" and research, and the setting up of state or semi-state financial institutions, in addition to building schools and hospitals. Of course this change of attitude had close connections with British economic and social policy. Under the influence of the economic crisis, the Keynesian economy and the Labour party, the traditional policy of laissez-faire was turned into a combination of private initiative and state intervention which conformed more closely to the complexity of modern economic and social life.

Equally important was the shift in priorities which we have already observed. In the future, investments from private and public funds were to be aimed primarily at the needs of the respective territories, at finding new raw-material suppliers and markets and at creating economically viable structures. A kind of self-government in the economic field was becoming urgent. The difference in the attitude and concepts of the years before and after 1919 is clear. Lord Lugard had started out from the theory that the civilized, i.e. industrialized, peoples had a natural right to tropical raw materials as long as they did not take advantage of this right exclusively at the expense of the natives; now the relationship was reversed. The prime consideration was to be the development of the individual territories and their inhabitants although, incidentally, the British and European economy also profited from the increased production and the creation of new consumer markets.

THE COLONIAL DOCTRINE OF THE LABOUR PARTY

The Labour party always considered itself primarily a socialist party and only to a limited extent as Marxist. Its organization and doctrine grew out of the pragmatically oriented British trade-union movement and an old humanitarian Christian reform ideal, which at times entered a phase of social and political radicalism and took over the liberal inheritance. This characteristic tradition of the British working-class movement, which survived in years to come in spite of the adoption of some Marxist theories, also determined the Labour party's colonial doctrine. Before 1914, the party had no anti-colonialist doctrine, distinguishing it from the socialist parties on the continent. In 1900, led by Bernard Shaw and Sidney Webb, the Fabian Society even openly supported imperialism and rejected the pro-Boer attitude of leading liberals.[1] In the following years the influence of the reformers E. D. Morel, Mary Kingsley, C. R. Buxton and Sydney Olivier, who represented the liberal or radical tradition, made itself felt; they were less interested in a theory of imperialism than in the actual situation in the colonies, and instead of the withdrawal of the colonial power demanded more active reforms to improve the lot of the native population. Hobson provided the Labour party with a "doctrine", since he interpreted colonial imperialism in economic terms; however, Hobson was not a socialist nor even a Marxist, but a radical reformer who anticipated the concept of trusteeship in his demand for an "enlightened" colonial policy.

We have already observed that during the First World War the Labour party adopted the mandate principle of the future League of Nations and made international control a focal point of its colonial programme. It had two aims: to prevent a new rivalry for colonial acquisitions among the world powers, and to replace capitalist exploitation by a policy of reform which would "develop" the "backward peoples" and prepare them for self-government. The Labour party did not only want a detailed formulation of the mandate principle and a well-defined system of international control; it was even more concerned with subordinating all the colonies to the League of Nations. After some discussion, however, it abandoned the idea of internationalizing administration, and agreed to granting individual mandates to the respective colonial powers.[2] In subsequent years, the Labour party stood by its desire to extend the mandate principle to all European colonies—even if this was only a postulate.[3] The significance it accorded the international mandate was specifically British and characteristic of Labour party politicians; the SFIO (French Socialist party) showed little interest in it. The object of the mandate was self-government, whereas the French socialists wanted assimilation.

The new party programme of 1918 elaborated by Sidney Webb referred to colonial policy as follows:

> If we repudiate, on the one hand, the Imperialism that seeks to dominate other races, or to impose our own will on other parts of the British Empire, so we disclaim equally any conception of a selfish and insular "non-interventionism" unregarding of our special obligations to our fellow-citizens overseas; of the corporate duties of one nation to another; of the moral claims upon us of the non-adult races; and of our own indebtedness to the world of which we are a part. . . . With regard to that great Commonwealth of all races, all colours, all religions and all degrees of civilization that we call the British Empire, the Labour Party stands for its maintenance and its progressive development on the lines of Local autonomy and "Home Rule All Round"; the fullest respect for the rights of each people, whatever its colour, to all the democratic Self-Government of which it is capable, and to the proceeds of its own toil upon the resources of its own territorial home; and the closest possible co-operation among all the various members of what has become essentially not an Empire in the cold sense, but of Britannic Alliance. . . .[4]

This statement clearly rejected left-wing socialist and Communist theories. The affirmation of Empire was designed to demonstrate Labour's opposition to colonial "isolationism" and its interest in overseas territories. These tendencies were in fact latent in the party, particularly in the unions, but they continued during the inter-war years. The new concept of Commonwealth made it easier for Labourites to take a stand since it implied an imperial structure based on self-government. But in a curious effacement of the real problems, the party arbitrarily placed dominions and colonies on the same plane and directly juxtaposed them; the same applied to its proposal for an Imperial Council, which was to bring the dominions, India, "and eventually other Dependencies" together in communal consultation. For the rest, Labour supported the "gradual grant of self-government" and trusteeship, but without clearly defining its terms.

The party leaders became aware of the need to concern themselves more deeply than before with the practical problems of the Dependent Empire when they had to prepare the colonial policy of a future Labour government. An Advisory Committee on International Affairs, under the chairmanship of Sidney Webb and with Leonard Woolf as secretary, was formed to deal with colonial affairs and in 1920 created a sub-committee "for Crown colonies and dependencies". In 1919–1920 the party published a memorandum entitled *The Empire in Africa: Labour's Policy*, which stressed the urgency of taking a definite stand: "Labour must now have an imperial policy, springing from Labour principles and applicable in each locality." It contrasted East and West Africa: while in West Africa Great Britain was to a certain extent fulfilling its obligations as trustee, in East Africa, meaning above all Kenya, it was permitting exploitation, since there the land, tax and labour policy reflected the interests of the white settlers. The memorandum demanded an end to the special concessions for the settlers, supported "tribal Self-Government" [!] and set as its goal the development of legislative councils of a representative nature, but avoided going into the problems this entailed in a "plural society".

Hobson's influence is perceptible in Leonard Woolf's important *Empire and Commerce in Africa*, published in 1920.[5] Woolf described, in historical retrospect, the annexation of Africa, as it had been pursued by certain interest groups under the pretext of nationalism. The nation as a whole had not profited from this, but only a small group of people. He pointed out the contradictions between talk about civilization and trusteeship in the era of imperialism and its destructive effects: dispossession of African land, forced labour, war and the destruction of traditional social structures—"effects almost wholly evil".[6] The colonial powers could not, however, simply withdraw, since quite apart from the possible intervention of other powers, this would give even more free play to private enterprise.[7] Economic imperialism "has itself created conditions in which the control must inevitably continue". Woolf saw no alternative either to the principle of trusteeship: "The white man must become the trustee for the interest of Africans."[8] In concrete terms this must mean, he said, reserving the land for the natives, gradually expropriating the settlers' land and systematically extending the educational system. Woolf did not, however, expect very much from a reform policy as long as the European economic system remained capitalist; and even if it became socialist, he thought that the European exploitation of Africa would not stop "until the inevitable Nemesis", i.e. until the uprising of the "beneficiaries against their guardians and benefactors".[9]

In spite of several books, memoranda and pamphlets, the Labour party continued to take little interest in colonial affairs. This was apparent in the annual party conferences. The Empire was briefly mentioned in the Chairman's Address in 1920, when it was said that India and Egypt could become members of the Commonwealth should they wish to do so.[10] A conference resolution confirmed sovereign rights, with particular reference to India, Egypt and Ceylon. The resolution also protested a press law and the miserable social conditions in the West Indies. Similar resolutions were put forward in the next party conferences and they were usually accepted without long discussion. Short but intense discussions took place only when the left-wing radicals put forward their thesis of imperialism, forcing the conference to take a stand.[11] The left wing demanded active co-operation between the British working class and the colonial proletariat in order to create a common front in the fight against imperial capitalism; it demanded immediate independence and interpreted trusteeship and the League of Nations mandate as ideological masks for capitalist exploitation.[12] Such proposals were strongly opposed and rejected by a large majority.[13]

Ramsay MacDonald's first Labour government in 1924 could do little to implement its desire for reform. The colonial minister J. H. Thomas was unprepared and was not capable of initiating a new course. Only in the Egyptian question did MacDonald try to make his government's actions consistent with party resolutions. Since 1919 the party had demanded dominion status or independence for Egypt and MacDonald had often sharply criticized the Conservative governments. Now he tried to begin talks with the Egyptian prime minister and to replace the unilateral declaration of 1922 by an agreement; but he found himself faced with far too extensive counter-demands, in particular the renunciation of the Sudan and withdrawal from Egypt. Even a Labour minister had to take into account Britain's interest in maintaining the imperial lines of communication, above all the Suez Canal: " . . . No British Government can divest itself wholly, even in favour of an ally, of its interest in guarding such a vital link in British communications!"[14]

In a rather long resolution the 1925 conference put forth the broad outlines of the Labour party's colonial policy.[15] In the following year, very belatedly, the party officially confirmed the 1919 memorandum,[16] but nothing new was proposed. This was equally true of the 1928 party programme, *Labour and the Empire*, which contained a section on the Commonwealth. The problems of the Empire remained on the periphery of internal party and trade-union discussions. The 1925 Trade Union Congress, in spite of the opposition of colonial minister Thomas, accepted almost unanimously a very anti-imperialist resolution but it was scarcely able to make its views felt in the party conference.[17] In any case, its attitude was not so much intended to support left-wing radicalism as to express its own neutrality. It is striking, in fact, that the Labour party's colonial doctrine was not formulated by the party leaders—with the exception of Sidney Webb—but by outsiders like Buxton, Wood, Wedgwood and Olivier, who stood in the tradition of the pre-war liberal radical movement for reform and were closely linked with the Anti-Slavery and

Aborigines Protection Society; after 1918 they joined the Labour party and managed to influence its attitude in colonial issues.[18]

The party's attitude to practical issues was scarcely original and we need not go into it in detail here. The Labour party demanded self-government and eventual independence for India, Egypt and Iraq, while it refused to grant self-government or even responsible government to the white minority in the "closer union" issue in East Africa (cf. pp. 124 ff.). It was reluctant to define its terms clearly and many other factors of its policy remained equally vague.[19] Apart from questions of land law, labour law and tax law, the party programmes, conference resolutions, memoranda and questions in parliament were primarily concerned with extension of the educational system and health services. But no one said who was to supply the very extensive funds that were obviously necessary to implement these measures. References to the excessively high profits of the entrepreneurs or the realization that more was being spent on the police than on education were no answer. There was also no mention at all of the fact that in the future, apart from loans and private investments, the mother country would also have to provide assistance from its budget if it was pursuing a consistent socialist policy!

The Labour party did not put forward its own policy of "development aid" apart from the demand for the reform of current administrative methods. Instead, there were references to possible competition between home and colonial industries. For example, the Indian jute and textile industry created difficulties for the mother country's industry and made unemployment at home more acute.[20] The party's "colonialist" attitude here was only thinly veiled by its criticism of the extremely low wages of the native labour force, which, it said, resulted in high profits for the capitalists. In any case, the Labour party did not call for industrialization. On the whole, it too treated trusteeship as a "negative" function, although it delegated new social duties to the state. It is not surprising that it was the Conservative party that proposed the Colonial Development Fund.

The colonial policy of the second Labour government in 1929–1931 was not socialist either and was equally unoriginal. Sidney Webb, who became colonial minister as Lord Passfield, belonged to the moderate wing of the party and even managed to assuage *The Times'* suspicions. The party's special adviser for colonial affairs, Charles R. Buxton, had announced that Labour's policy was a "distinct break with the past" and a "new departure",[21] but some months later the parliamentary under-secretary of state, Shiels, assured the assembled governors that the new government had done nothing revolutionary and did not intend to do so. The government did not consider it right that the change of course at home should correspond to a similar change in colonial policy![22] Neither in East Asia, where the Donoughmore Report became the basis of Ceylon's new constitution in 1931, nor in West Africa, were any new departures apparent. Passfield, it is true, set up a special committee for labour questions and instructed the governors to pay more attention to labour legislation and to promoting the unions[23]; but no constitutional changes were introduced. The party did not implement Lord Olivier's West Indies report because it did not want to subject the British consumer—i.e. Labour voters—to higher sugar prices.[24] However, in the important Kenya question, Lord Passfield rejected Amery's and Grigg's attempts at federation and emphatically confirmed the "paramountcy" of 1923. This embittered the conservatives and the settlers in Kenya and Northern Rhodesia, but Passfield was acting with the full consent of the Colonial Service officials and trying to reach a compromise. This again provoked criticism from the left wing, and the Kenya experts Leys, Ross, Buxton and Oldham pressed him to act more forcefully against the settlers and to defend the natives' interests.[25] The *New Statesman* however, was satisfied with his conduct.[26]

So the Labour party's reform policy appears very modest and one cannot speak of a break with the past. We must realize, however, that MacDonald had to take his liberal coalition partner into consideration. Moreover, every socialist government was regarded with suspicion by the colonial administration, which had a great deal of autonomy and could block any Colonial Office policy with which it disagreed. A change of personnel demanded time, so the colonial minister remained dependent on the consent and certainly on the co-operation of the administration and was limited in his movements. Besides, a prime minister had to relegate colonial questions, which were still considered secondary matters, to the background if he did not want to endanger his government. We shall see that the peoples' front in France in 1936–1937, in spite of its decidedly left-wing course, found itself in a similar situation; it too could not avoid an obvious discrepancy between its programme while in opposition and its actual policy while in office.

The 1933 party conference debated and approved the new report, *The Colonial Empire*. Evidently the party had realized that it still paid too little attention to the Empire. The report stated, for instance, that Labour must take forceful action, although this "very big question" aroused no enthusiasm among the voters and would not help Labour gain a parliamentary majority! Charles R. Buxton brought out the significant points of the report: the next fifty years would require important decisions in colonial policy. Nigeria still seemed to be the model colony, although its indirect rule had a decidedly conservative character. Naturally the report outlined the necessary reforms in the economic and social field: "Trusteeship must be a reality." It also said that further concessions with a view to self-government must be accompanied by democratization[27] and demanded the extension of the educational system, including the high schools. "In considering the future of the Colonial Dependencies, Labour's object, therefore, will be to develop the empire into a Commonwealth of self-governing socialist units." But even for the Labour party, this goal still lay far in the future.

The "Socialist League" was doctrinaire in its anti-colonialism. In reaction to the Labour government of 1929–1931 and its defeat in the 1931 elections, it reactivated the left wing and propagated a stricter left-wing course within the Labour party. The League, whose members or supporters included Cripps, Harold Laski, Brailsford and Fenner Brockway, who was particularly interested in colonial affairs, was excluded from the Labour party in 1937 because of its demands for a peoples' front. In the League's programmatic omnibus volume, J. F. Horriban discussed the "break with Imperialism". Like Cripps[28] he saw the British Empire in Marxist terms as "the supreme expression of British capitalism". A socialist government "should admit fully the right of everyone of those peoples not merely to Self-government but to complete Self-determination".[29] Horriban could not deny, however, that certain areas and peoples were not yet capable of independence and still needed British trusteeship. Leonard Barnes reached a similar conclusion in 1939 in his *Empire or Democracy, A Study of the Colonial Question*. He began by discussing the colonial claims of Germany, Italy and Poland, and decided that the situation would not have come to an international conflict if all the colonies had been subordinated in time to a mandated administration. He came to the same conclusion as Hobson on the uses of the colonies. Only individual interest groups, not the economy as a whole, had derived profits from the colonies. Although the colonies needed their own industries, he did not think the mother country would ever permit this; trusteeship was a utopian concept here. He also criticized Indirect Rule as an artificial method of maintaining a society that had already disintegrated. There was little political freedom in the Dependent Empire and disturbances were subdued in bloody battles. India, Ceylon, Burma and the West Indies were ripe for independence and it was up to the Labour party to support the emancipation movements and—with regard to the international situation—to build up a common system of defence with a free India. Tropical Africa was not yet advanced enough for this, however: too few Africans were sufficiently trained to be able to take over the administration and there were no party organizations. "The immediate question for Africa is not independence but the quickest possible progress towards independence."[30] One could reckon on two ten-year periods in order to reach this aim.[31] So even the anti-colonialist Barnes found himself forced, shortly before the Second World War, to accept British rule in Africa.

Barnes' work contained new critical departures which the Labour party gradually adopted. Indirect Rule in West Africa had long been considered a positive measure in the nature of a trusteeship; but Barnes interpreted it as the instrument of a conservative policy by means of which the traditional feudal rulers were barring educated Africans from access to power. Very soon, trusteeship became a questionable term. In 1938 Harold J. Laski, who belonged to the left wing, sharply criticized the Colonial Service in *The Political Quarterly*: that nice word "trusteeship ... is too flattering to the result obtained", and the colonies were still "the slums of Empire".[32] He said the well-meaning but all too "public-school minded Colonial Civil Service" distrusted reforms and was influenced by the colonial entrepreneurs. England had tried "to run the Empire on the cheap" and made positive efforts only after the outbreak of riots. "The only way to justify colonial possessions is to make the principle of trusteeship so plain a living reality that the record is not open to question. No one can read that record today and claim that this in the case."[33] He did not, however, mention that until now the Labour party had entirely agreed with this "running on the cheap" and had made no proposals for a "positive" policy of development. Laski himself failed to draw the conclusion that in the future funds would have to be made available from the mother country. But in the same issue of *The Political Quarterly*, Charles R. Buxton adopted Hailey's and Macmillan's theses:

> First of all, it should endeavour to shorten to the utmost the period of tutelage. The pace of this must vary in each dependency, but in every part of the world the period could be shortened by a more active policy of economic development, especially in the matter of native agriculture. This in its turn would necessitate for the time being, the abandonment of the principle that each colony must "pay its way" year by year. If we are "trustees", as we claim, we should surely be prepared to spend some money on our "wards". The acceptance of this principle would render possible an increased expenditure on "nationbuilding" services, such as health and education. These are cramped by the present lack of taxable capacity which so severely restricts the annual revenue of a colony.[34]

Here again is the new departure we saw in the British colonial discussion shortly before the war. But it would be useless to search for similar statements either in the party discussions or in the special reports; the initiative came not from the Labour party but from outside circles interested in colonial affairs. Even in Clement Attlee's important book *The Labour Party in Perspective* in 1937, there is no evidence yet of a change of attitude.[35] By contrast the trade-union leader Ernest Bevin displayed a growing interest in the Empire, as did the Trade Union Congress (TUC) in general. As early as 1930, Bevin supported Empire Free Trade—not without stressing that the Soviet Union was also an empire. He said the British Empire should contribute toward overcoming its own economic crisis[36]; subsequently the TUC supported "as full a development as possible of the economic relations between the constituent parts of the British Commonwealth". The new course in foreign policy and the armaments question, to which Bevin made a decisive contribution, thus coincided with a new sense of Empire. With reference to Abyssinia and sanctions, Bevin declared to the TUC: "If we go on being merely anti-imperial where does it lead? It leads to a scramble in the world. It will lead to wars all over the world."[37] Comparison of this attitude with the resolutions of 1921 or 1925 reveals an almost complete change of attitude. Incidentally, it meant that Bevin was going against the left wing too.[38] In 1938 the TUC established a "Special Advisory Commission" for colonial affairs, which included Arthur Creech-Jones, the Labour party colonial minister after 1945; so the leaders of the trade-unions began to take an interest in working conditions in the colonies.[39] Bevin was a member of the Colonial Development Advisory Committee where he had to deal with the practical tasks of colonial administration,[40] particularly the problems of the West Indies.[41] The prominent leader of the working classes reached a conclusion that seems surprising for a socialist: "Our crime isn't exploitation, it's neglect."[42]

This formula characterizes the attitude of the Labour party between the wars. The party's interest in colonial affairs was small. A few anti-imperialist resolutions were considered enough to establish Labour's difference from the Conservatives. The urgent problems of the mother country took precedence. Labour members nevertheless exercised an important function of control, in that their criticism exposed concrete grievances, postulated reforms, and also reminded conservative governments and the colonial administration that the simple reference to trusteeship and future self-government was not sufficient to justify the new "white man's burden". The party also forged organizational and personal contacts with emancipation movements from within and without. We need only recall the London School of Economics and Harold J. Laski; or Fenner Brockway, who openly supported the opposition in the colonies and helped form the African Students Union in London, which became an important organization for African nationalists and counted future national leaders among its members. On the whole the Labour party may have been too moderate for the Asian and African nationalists and not have come up to their expectations, but the personal ties it created and the knowledge that within this great opposition party there was some support for rapid decolonization and some sympathy for emancipation efforts did at least help to create a certain basis of trust between the mother country and the nationalist leaders. This was to England's advantage after the Second World War and contributed to some degree towards making the Multi-racial Commonwealth possible.

INDIRECT RULE IN WEST AFRICA

In the inter-war years the principle of Indirect Rule, to a large extent the creation of Sir Frederick (later Lord) Lugard, one of the British representatives of imperial expansionism and proconsular rule, seemed to represent the essence of British colonial policy and it was applied or intended to apply even beyond West Africa to other areas of the Dependent Empire. This is particularly significant in our context. Great Britain was proud of its policy and convinced it had found a system that complied with its own political traditions and with the trusteeship it proclaimed, as well as with the new mandate principle. The policy, it was thought, was proof of the transition from "exploitation" to the protection and improvement of native civilizations.

Indirect Rule was nothing new in colonial history. In the eighteenth century, France accomplished the transition to territorial rule by means of protectorate agreements with the Indian princes. Great Britain followed the French example and the position of the Indian and Malayan princely states within the Empire can be considered a form of indirect rule. The Dutch in Indonesia also tried to maintain feudal rule and put it to good use. In Africa, indirect rule in Lugard's interpretation was not anticipated or set down as a programme, but developed directly out of the existing situation at the time of the colonial settlements. The usual protectorate agreements with African kings and chieftains, however, can be cited as instances of indirect rule only in a limited sense, since these agreements were more or less fictitious and were often abolished by direct administration. Only in Uganda, which Lugard had helped to annex, did the colonial power encounter a fairly large and well-organized system of African rule which was recognized as such and preserved. The situation in Northern Rhodesia was not unlike that in Uganda. Around 1900, when Lugard penetrated to the north from the tropical south, he came upon the great emirates of Sokoto, Kano, Kaduna and Benue in the savannah belt of Western Sudan. The emirates were based on Fulah conquests of fairly recent date; yet they were political organizations on the Muslim pattern with large populations and urban centres, a tax, and law administration which was exercised by the emirs' officials. Lugard managed to conquer them in a short time but he did not have sufficient staff for a direct take-over of the administration in such a large area. So he had to make agreements with the emirs to ensure that he himself held the highest authority and, apart from that, left the administrative and social order as it was in order to use it as the instrument of British rule.

In the following years the "system" of indirect rule developed from these protectorates born of circumstance. In 1914, when Lugard was appointed the first governor-general of Nigeria, the Crown Colony of Lagos, the Southern Nigerian protectorate and the racially and culturally quite different protectorates of the north came under communal administration. Lugard extended indirect rule in the north and also tried to carry it over into the south. But only in the south-west were there fairly large and organized political structures, whereas in the south-east—in the Ibo territory—Lugard found only small village and tribal communities which had to be amalgamated into larger units rather artificially and arbitrarily. In 1918 Lugard laid down the principle of Indirect Rule in memoranda which served as a guide-line for the residents and district commissioners and laid the foundation for his 1922 book *The Dual Mandate*, the most important treatise on British policy in Africa in the inter-war years.[1] In 1919 he had clearly defined the doctrine and methods of indirect rule:

> The system of Native Administration . . . had been based on a recognition of the authority of the Native Chiefs. The policy of the Government was that these Chiefs should govern their people, not as independent but as dependent Rulers. The orders of Government are not conveyed to the people through them, but emanate from them in accordance, where necessary, with instructions received through the Resident. While they themselves are controlled by Government in matters of policy and of importance, their people are controlled in accordance with that policy by themselves. A Political Officer would consider it as irregular to issue direct orders to an individual native, or even to a village head, as a General commanding a division would to a private soldier, except through his commanding officers.[2]

It is not clear here that the originality and significance of indirect rule did not lie just in making use of existing institutions and authorities. Even a "direct" rule aiming at assimilation, as France tried to establish, could not do without these institutions, since the staff of white officials was never large enough to "rule" every last one of the natives in every village. Every colonial administration needed the chiefs, village headmen, tribal leaders, etc. Indirect rule was to mean that these men were not just used as instruments and mouthpieces but actually ruled. The existing society with its institutions, authorities, laws and customs was to be accepted and gradually modernized, so that it could carry out the functions of local administration.[3] The native was not to be alienated from his environment but to find new possibilities of development within it; the intervention of the colonial power should be "along indigenous lines". The aim was not to approximate the territory to the mother country but to develop the population within the framework of its own African civilization. "Our desire is to make the native 'a good African'."[4]

The traditional bearer of authority was the chieftain, who was both the political head of his tribe or village and also an important sociological integrational factor; he incorporated the unity of past and present, the dead and the living, and was therefore sacred. This is why indirect rule stood or fell with the right choice of chief; he could not be forced upon the tribe but had to be appointed by the community, whether by inheritance or election. Only if his subjects acknowledged him could the system function. Otherwise they would see his orders and instructions only as the orders of the colonial power and the latter would then fail to obtain voluntary co-operation.[5] The legalization of the chief by the administration must not be an arbitrary appointment but rather a *de facto* acknowledgement that incorporated him into the system of government and assured him sovereign rights.[6]

The position and authority of the chief had to be ensured; orders must therefore be given in his name and, as far as possible, emanate from him; the chiefs were not just paid officials as in the French territories.[7] This required tact and patience on the part of the British staff, above all the district commissioner; often they had to accept malpractice and irregularities. The temptation to do everything oneself must be withstood, said Lugard, since it would result in passivity on the part of the village community.[8] Direct intervention or deposing the chief should occur as rarely as possible. But the chiefs, who were only appointed on the terms of the protectorate, were not "independent" either. They and their organs were "advised", i.e. supervised, and were issued instructions which were intended to "educate" them in modern methods of administration and responsibility.

The administration reserved to itself certain vital areas of control: apart from the army and armed police, these consisted above all of general legislation, taxation and land distribution. Yet the "native authorities" headed by the chief were not to be fictions. They were to be allowed to make decisions independently in their own administrative sector. This was the difference between indirect rule and the policy in other territories where the chiefs merely served as executive organs of the colonial power.

Let us first consider the native treasuries. The kinds of taxes to be imposed, and the amount required, was determined by the administration, but taxes were collected by the chief, or in larger areas by his agents. Only a portion of the taxes had to be paid to the administration, while a considerable proportion, varying from 25 to 70 percent, remained at the disposal of the chief and served for local expenses such as the wages of the chief and his officials, the police, prisons, religious ceremonies and sometimes schools. The revenue of the native treasuries of Northern Nigeria rose from 197,000 pounds in 1911 to 7,700,000 pounds in 1929.[9] Having his own treasury raised the prestige of the chief and helped modernize traditional institutions; besides, it ensured that the taxes did not seem like obligations imposed from the outside.

Then there were the native courts. The existing jurisdiction was extended and prescriptive law came into use. The chiefs and elders did not simply participate in the administration of justice, as in the French territories; in fact it was left almost entirely to them. But both jurisdiction and accounts were controlled. Death sentences, for instance, had to be confirmed by the British resident. In the south, small native authorities were assembled into native courts, which were often unsatisfactory.

Lugard was aware of the great difficulties and inevitable mistakes inherent in the system, and realized that the "standards of right and wrong", i.e. the colonial power's concepts of morality and legality, had not yet been accepted. But the decisive factor, thought Lugard, was that a direct administration would not benefit the African society and would leave it in its "primitive" state. Moreover, the small Europeanized élite was already beginning to agitate. He considered India a negative example, because the British administration in India, excellent as it may be, had unnecessarily destroyed the traditional order of things and had taught the Indians nothing but obedience. Accordingly, Lugard judged the princely states positively.[10] In retrospect one can see the major problem of indirect rule arising here: the earnest desire to operate within the traditional society and to give the natives a part in the administration went hand in hand with a conservative tendency to rely exclusively on the native rulers, which meant neglecting the new educated élite.

Indirect rule was applied not only in Nigeria. In the Gold Coast, Governor Sir Gordon Guggisberg strengthen the authority of the chiefs and the native councils in 1927 and extended their jurisdiction. But his attempts to persuade the chiefs to set up native treasuries were only partly successful.[11] In 1921 a department of ethnology was set up under R. S. Rattray which carried out extensive investigations into the structure of the Ashanti kingdom, described its "democratic" aspects and explained the significance of the Golden Stool. During the Ashanti wars the British had tried to seize the Golden Stool; however, when it came to light unexpectedly in 1921 they restored it to the Ashanti as the symbol of their "nation". They also allowed the king, who had been exiled in 1896, to return in 1924, and in 1935 the Ashanti kingdom was officially recognized and a Confederacy Council set up.

There was an interesting attempt to incorporate the chiefs into the Legislative Council. In the colony's new constitution in 1925 there were fifteen official members as opposed to fourteen non-officials, of whom nine were elected Africans. Three represented the towns (elected with a high census) while the other six were "paramount chiefs" elected by the chiefs and their councils on a provincial level. These provincial councils had little power and were primarily intended to have an educational function: smaller units were amalgamated into larger ones, the chiefs were familiarized with the problems of modern administration such as education and agricultural methods. At the same time the administration managed to strengthen the chiefs' powers in order to counterbalance the nascent opposition of the Western-educated Africans. The conservative aspects of indirect rule became apparent here, too.[12] The aims Governor Guggisberg had set himself, namely to actively promote economic development and the educational system and to slowly Africanize the administrative cadre, were only partly successful. True, by means of the indirect electoral system, indirect rule was brought closer to the British type of representation and the former system of nominating African representatives was replaced by elections; but neither the native authorities and provincial councils nor the urban administrations functioned satisfactorily. And in the meantime, the tensions between the traditional class and its chiefs and the rising bourgeoisie and intelligentsia became increasingly more acute.[13]

Donald Cameron brought his many years of experience in Nigeria to East Africa when he was governor of Tanganyika from 1925 to 1931.[14] As early as 1926 he refashioned the direct rule, dating from the German occupation and in which Africans of Arab origin had also been appointed (Akidas), into a system of indirect rule on the Nigerian model. He carefully examined the methods of nomination and the powers of the chiefs and introduced native treasuries and native courts. The numerous native authorities were joined into "federations" whose council met annually to debate questions of taxation, soil erosion, afforestation, tsetse plague, the market structure, etc.

There was another significant feature of Cameron's term as governor. The thinly settled and poor land of Tanganyika is suitable for white settlement only in certain areas; during the German occupation and in the first years after the war land was accordingly apportioned to the settlers for sisal and coffee plantations. In this way Tanganyika could have become a second Kenya, but Cameron used the mandate statute to prevent this. In his opinion trusteeship demanded a different land policy. Cameron did not exclude the white settlers—who certainly fulfilled an important function—but he exerted strict control with suitable agrarian laws and tried to prevent expropriation of native lands. His prime concern was to encourage the African producer. The same applied to labour law. Cameron refused the settlers' demands for administrative aid or higher taxation to force the natives to work as day labourers on their farms. Nor did he accept the whites' demand for self-government. He took trusteeship seriously and did not want to use it to prevent the African population from obtaining self-government. No wonder the settlers opposed this energetic and self-willed governor, who owed his appointment to the Labour government. The former governor of Kenya, Sir Edward Grigg, was led to remark scornfully: "The paramountcy of native interest governed everything."[15]

Donald Cameron became governor-general of Nigeria in 1931. In 1934, in his *Principles of Native Administration and Their Application*, he laid down the new guiding principles of Indirect Rule. This seemed necessary since Lugard's concepts were threatening to freeze into dogma, which was evidence of tendencies inconsistent with the original theory of Indirect Rule. In particular this applied to Sir C. L. Temple, chief secretary of Northern Nigeria from 1910 to 1913 and acting governor from 1914 to 1917, and author of *Native Races and Their Rulers* in 1918.[16] Temple, who dealt exclusively with the emirates of the north, treating them as "quasi-independent" states, wanted to reduce administrative intervention as far as possible. Only thus could the "native races" follow their own laws of development. "You must shut your eyes, up to a certain point, to a great many practices which though not absolutely repugnant to humanity, are nevertheless reprehensible to other ideas."[17] Temple was prepared to exert a great deal of restraint and to leave the feudal autocratic structure of the emirates untouched. His ideal was a "thoroughly able, well-meaning, liberal-minded Emir ruling over a unit untouched by foreign influence".[18] Accordingly he was very wary of the educated African, whom he considered alienated from his tribe and who could therefore only be employed as a minor official. Temple objected strongly to European education in Northern Nigeria, criticized the missions, and thought it would be enough to develop the Muslim schools.[19] Characteristically he remarked: "We may even [!] give him, in very limited numbers, the keys of learning, of art, of science. But what are all these things compared to fellowship, companionship, the society of equals, pride of race, patriotism?"[20] So, rather than modern European civilization, he idealized the Northern Nigerian social structure, wanting not only to preserve it, but even to guard it as much as possible against contact with the modern world. He did not ask himself whether this attitude was still tenable now that the construction of roads and railways, the development of trade and export production, were constantly and irrevocably increasing ties with the coast. The Africans' confrontation with modern life could not be avoided nor could their adaptation be made easier by this method. Such attempts to seal them as hermetically as possible against external influences and eventually to give them autonomy within the framework of the native authorities—and above all of the emirates of the north—made indirect rule a reactionary policy lacking the perspective it undoubtedly had in Lugard's day.

In the south, many of the artificially formed native authorities worked badly and attempts to reform them after extensive anthropological studies did not bring the expected results.[21]

In an important speech to the Legislative Council on 6 March 1933[22] and in his *Principles*, Cameron attacked the dogmatization of Indirect Rule. He said an untouched feudal monarchy and a Northern Nigeria closed to external influence could not be the aim of British policy. The time had come to open the curtain! One could not compare the Muslim emirates to the Indian princely states with their official sovereignty. Not less, but more control and influence were needed today. Cameron pointed to the fact that the "more primitive" Ibo tribes had already culturally outstripped the peoples of the north. If the native authority was not already in existence and the chief not propped up from below, he would prefer direct rule, since the native administration was only a means and not an end in itself. "The end to be sought is, in brief, just government according to civilised standards and the moral and material well-being of the people."[23] Everything should be done "to prevent the old native constitutions from becoming frozen in and thus reactionary".[24] Intervention when necessary must not be avoided just because of principles or for reasons of prestige. The economic and social duty of the colonial power was being forgotten[25]; it was very important "to ensure that by the use of proper channels the fabric of native political organization shall not be broken down under the pressure of modern demands, and that, whenever possible, for the sake of the future, development shall be carried out executively by the native organization".[26]

Cameron's concern differed markedly from Temple's. Cameron did not want indirect rule to mean leaving the African people to their own devices nor guarding them from confrontation with the modern world; rather it should prepare them for this confrontation and facilitate adjustment on the basis of the traditional society.

Governor-General Cameron's new interpretation of Indirect Rule, which could be traced directly to Lugard's original theories, was a reply to the frequent criticism levelled at administrative methods in Nigeria in the 1930s.[27] The discussion of Indirect Rule was among the most interesting aspects of British colonial policy between the wars and deserves special mention in our context, particularly since it paved the way to the post-war position.

W. R. Crocker,[28] a practical man, attacked the tendency of men such as Temple and his successors to make indirect rule into a kind of "secret science".[29] Reality, he said was different from theory.[30] Many native authorities had proved incapable—often the chiefs and elders were very old and illiterate. They had allowed too much corruption in tax-collecting and jurisdiction, which made continual intervention by the administration necessary; indirect rule had thus become impracticable. "Indirect Rule worked to bolster up effete and corrupt chiefs at the expense of their people."

The missionaries, for their part, also had a certain interest in pointing to the discrepancy between doctrine and reality, for they had been given little room for expansion in Northern Nigeria. Lugard's principles had become "shibboleths" and "sentimental nonsense", they said.[31] The feudal Muslim emirs had refused modern education in their territories and were being abetted in this by the administration. Britain was supporting economic development but preventing education; this was not development "along indigenous lines" but a dubious attempt to preserve a society by artificial means.

These men exposed the conservative tendencies and dubious results of indirect rule. They said the administration, like the now popular anthropologists and enthnologists, had shown little or no interest in modernizing the old institutions and authorities and adapting them to new circumstances. The native authorities were too "Arcadian for the anthropologists . . . a model for barbaric or medieval sovereignties".[32] Indirect rule had by no means democratized the emirs and chiefs; instead it had further increased their autocracy. Where they used to be controlled by their fellow-tribesmen, and even, in cases of conflict, deposed or exiled, now the colonial power was helping them to exploit their own subjects. "In other words, the Indirect Rule of the British had established the Direct Rule of the Fula Emirs."[33] Countless grievances and crimes were not even known to the administration and so it was not surprising that it was caught off guard by the 1929 uprising.[34] The result was malpractice and corruption in the name of the European power; in spite of the allegedly indirect control, the chiefs were widely considered to be nothing more than the mouthpieces of the administration, which is why they were often obeyed only under compulsion.[35] This contradicted the concept of trusteeship. Naturally this criticism was taken up by the Labour party, although only just before the outbreak of war.[36]

The most important argument against Indirect Rule, in terms of the future, turned on the very real problem of the position of the "educated Africans" within the system. The new generation of Africans educated and trained in European schools, who did not usually come from the upper classes and represented a new intelligentsia, were totally overlooked by the native authorities. This aggravated the already existing tensions between the old tribal order and the young educated class, and each was suspicious of the other. Since the educated Africans were given no responsibility in the administration, they were driven into opposition.

There can be no doubt of the dislike and open contempt on the part of the administration—and of the Europeans in Africa in general—for this supposedly arrogant class, which was in fact fighting for its place in society. "The dislike of many Indirect Rule Administrators for this class of men often passes all bounds, but they cannot be ignored."[37] British colonial officials knew how to treat the traditional leaders and were also aware of their responsibility to the masses; but they kept their distance from the young bourgeoisie intelligentsia and were rarely prepared to acknowledge them as the rising élite. Since this discrimination seemed justified in terms of indirect rule, the system's latent tendency to conservatism now became clearly apparent. Lugard had already demonstrated his preference for Kaduna in the north, which was still almost untouched by European civilization, to the harbour town of Lagos.[38] Since he did not value the educated Africans, he arbitrarily relegated them to the administrative service, the educational, technical and economic spheres, and only allowed them a political voice in the municipalities.[39] Cameron, however, proposed giving the native authorities a mixed council in which the Western-educated Africans should also be represented; but curiously, or perhaps typically, said nothing further about this class.[40]

So a paradoxical situation arose. We have already mentioned that indirect rule was intended to be a form of local government which would leave local affairs in the hands of the African inhabitants within their own traditional order, so as to gradually familiarize them with modern methods of administration. But since these Western-educated Africans were largely excluded, the result was just the opposite. The idea of "education" in local government with a view to forming a democratic, self-governing unit on the Western model did not work in practice. The native authorities seldom proved able to cope with technical problems and social services and had to rely constantly on the help of the administration. In many cases a more direct form of administration might have been a better preparation for the future than a native authority of elders and chiefs.[41] It is not surprising that the emirates of the north, which were originally much better organized, fell behind those of the south. Although Great Britain had insisted that self-government must first be practised in the local sphere, the Second World War so speeded up the political emancipation of West Africa that the local administration could not keep pace. After 1945, therefore, great efforts were needed to catch up before self-government could be granted.

Britain became aware of this problem in the late 1930s. In a sense Indirect Rule had achieved the opposite of what was originally intended and of which it was so proud. Certainly it let the traditional leaders and authorities "rule", but at the same time it effectively neutralized politically the new classes who were so important to the future. These classes more and more clearly became the mouthpieces of the Africans, however much the administration asserted that they were only a small minority who had dissociated themselves from the tribal tradition and order. As early as 1935, Professor Coupland warned Britain: "Already indeed, it appears that some of the West African intelligentsia suspect our motives and imagine that we want to hold them down to their African past, almost to keep them primitive, for fear lest they become like ourselves and challenge our superiority."[42] A book, *British Empire*, published by Chatham House in 1937, pointed out the inherent weakness of Indirect Rule: "Generally spoken, it is impossible for the educated native (unless he is a chief or the son of a chief) to rise to a post in which the initiation of policy is required and expected."[43] Even Margery Perham, who was close to Lugard, conceded: "Indirect rule may indeed stand or fall according to the expression it affords to the political energies of the educated class."[44] However, like Lugard, in 1937 she still considered this class only in terms of the municipalities and the native authority councils.⁴⁵ Lord Hailey was no longer content with this. He thought that the new tasks in local administration could be performed successfully and the new classes be incorporated in time only if the institutions were adjusted:

> Its [Indirect Rule's] real task will come when the traditional native authorities are faced with the necessity of introducing social services on something more than the rudimentary scale to which they are now accustomed. . . . Up to the present time the fact that the system makes little provision for recognizing educated opinion has not resulted in open opposition to it; in the future however it will inevitably have to meet pressure due to this cause. . . . One of the gravest problems will be the development of a legal and administrative system which will provide for the rapidly growing class whose social life is not assimilative to that of the Europeans but which cannot be suitably regulated by tribal institutions.⁴⁶

Hailey rightly stressed that in the future educated Africans would no longer be content with existing administrative methods. He said they opposed indirect rule, because to them it was certainly no praiseworthy attempt to maintain African institutions and traditions but rather a method of administration based on feudal authorities whom it corrupted; moreover it gave no opportunities to the new educated class and actually prevented self-government.⁴⁷ This opposition was apparent in Nigeria as well as in the Gold Coast, although it was in Nigeria that Guggisberg had tried to train Africans for administrative duties at Achimota College and to give them access to the native councils.⁴⁸ It is sufficient here to quote a meaningful passage from the 1938 *Charter of the Nigerian Youth Movement:*

> We are opposed to the term Indirect Rule literally as well as in principle. Honest trusteeship implies direct British Rule with a view to ultimate Self-Government. We shall therefore strive for the complete abolition of the indirect rule system. Native Administration should be a form of local Government, and it is for that reason that we will encourage and support it.⁴⁹

The educated Africans' movement for emancipation called on the trusteeship to justify their demand for direct rule, evidently believing that trusteeship was more likely than indirect rule to lead to self-government. This raises the important question of the ultimate aim of indirect rule; what was Britain's attitude during the inter-war years to the future of the West African colonies?

We will have to start from Lugard again. Like the pre-war proconsuls he thought it was wrong to transplant the European system of government with its elections, representative bodies and parliamentary majority decisions to Africa. Experience, including India, had shown, he said, that the native peoples with their different traditions and their autocratic past would not be ready for this for generations:

> The ultimate goal of our political teaching must be suited to the genius and temperament of the people or it will lead to failure. Must we not admit that history and modern experience alike contradict the assumption that an educated minority with no tradition of rule can successfully govern kingdoms composed of diverse and warlike races, with ancient feuds, and mutually intolerant creeds? In the larger dependencies of Africa more especially, where the great diversity of race and language, no less than the prohibitive distances render effective representation in any case impracticable, it seems open to doubt whether the path which leads to representative government is conditioned by a certain choice of rulers; primitive tribes which have not yet evolved the rudiments of social organization must in any case be subjected to many years or generations of bureaucratic rule before they can be fitted for representative institutions.[50]

Lugard refused the educated Africans' demand for representative institutions or stronger representation within the existing legislative council as the unjustified claim of a non-representative minority. He was scornful of the pre-1914 legislative council of Lagos[51]; the Nigerian council he himself set up in 1913, which included six Africans, merely had the function of accepting his annual reports.[52] Indirect rule did not need such institutions, said Lugard; the system of combining British administration with native authorities complied with the existing situation and the large variety of tribes, and it would continue to be adequate for a long time to come. Education should be the affair of the native authorities and not of Western institutions. Indirect rule had an important advantage in his opinion: "A native ruler can be guided and controlled and if necessary replaced. An oligarchy of so-called representatives which proves itself unfit to govern is much more difficult to deal with, or, once established, to get rid of."[53] These words betray the proconsul who does not want his powers to be curtailed, shows his disdain of the young élite and his preference to rely on the chiefs who can be guided, and if necessary deposed.

Lugard did however realize in 1922 that "the coloured races of the world are awakening to self-consciousness under Western influence. In Africa tribal rule is disintegrating".[54] This Western influence should be checked as efficiently as possible and intercepted by indirect rule. Great Britain must certainly maintain its trusteeship for decades if not generations to come, even if this should gain it no thanks. It was more dangerous to proceed too quickly than too slowly.[55] The future of indirect rule, the problem of Nigerian unity or of an extension of the legislative councils, were not yet topical problems for Lugard.

In the 1930s his position changed noticeably. He still considered the introduction of a representative system premature, yet he found himself forced by the general turn of events to include this more clearly than before in his plans for the future.[56] In 1939 he finally declared that dominion status was the aim of British colonial policy.[57]

Temple gives us some pointers on the concept of Indirect Rule in the 1920s. He rejected the current opinion that a race could for an indefinite time "remain subject to another",[58] and thought it inevitable that "they will some day recapture their liberty".[59] Indirect rule must create the conditions for this. In one or two generations the Northern Nigerian emirates and the Yoruba units would certainly be able to cope with their internal affairs. "I do not see why in due course, if proper use is made of native institutions, those races which are now subject should not take their places in the ranks of that group of allied nations, as they may I think rightly be called, which form the British Empire."[60] It followed from Temple's concept of indirect rule that he considered certain native authorities, particularly the emirates, as capable of governing themselves autonomously. It is worth noting that he places them on the same level as the dominions, evidently under the assumption that the latter determined only their own internal affairs and not their foreign policy. So in the case of Nigeria foreign policy would still be controlled by Britain; of course only the larger units within the country would obtain autonomy. Temple did not propose a separate Northern Nigeria; he did not ask himself whether the Nigerian central administration established by London in 1912-1914 could serve as the basis for a future state and certainly never contemplated representative or even responsible government. He did not have in mind dominion status for Nigeria, but merely an extension of the native authorities into autonomous districts within the British colony. He did not use the term self-government, but he obviously believed—since he spoke of regaining freedom—that this had already been achieved by granting autonomy on the basis of indirect rule, and that it did not entail a parliamentary system or full dominion status.

Governor-General Sir Hugh Clifford propounded similar ideas in his frequently quoted address to the Nigerian Council on 29 December 1920.[61] He attacked the West African National Conference formed in Accra which had sent a delegation to London the previous autumn and handed colonial minister Milner a memorandum with demands that seem quite moderate today. The members of this organization, he said, were "a self-selected and self-appointed congregation of educated African gentlemen" who were evading their duties to the natural rulers and had adopted political theories inconsistent with the level of African civilization. To talk about a West African nation was ridiculous; even the notion of a Nigerian state—in so far as the impossible was at all possible —must be rejected since, said Clifford, it meant the overthrow of the traditional order: the government promoted the tribal organizations which "are to be regarded as the natural expressions of [African] political genius. ... It is the task of the Government of Nigeria to build up and to fortify these natural institutions". "Real national self-government" concerned these "self-contained and mutually independent Native States".

It is true that around 1920 there was no Nigerian nation yet. There were few links between north and south and the membership of the first African nationalist movement hardly reached beyond the harbour towns. But what is more important for us is that the administration had no intention of creating any kind of Nigerian nation. Plans for the future were confined to a certain autonomy for the native authorities, for which Clifford used the terms "national", "self-government" and "independent". Their ambiguity becomes apparent here; certainly the "gradual grant of self-government" did not necessarily have to entail dominion status and was used in the far more limited sense of extended local autonomy.

In 1934 Donald Cameron went a step further. He stressed the need for a clear definition of aims and demanded the unification of north and south; the individual regions of Nigeria could not become "separate self-governing units".[62] With this assertion he opposed Temple, perhaps also Clifford, and certainly went against current opinion. But although Cameron urged Nigerian unity, he made no real efforts in that direction. In 1922 Clifford had constituted a new legislative council and had introduced the principle of elections: in Lagos and Calabar four African members with high census qualifications were elected. This reform, modest as it was, increased the political consciousness of the Africans and produced the first parties with their own press organs.[63] This went a step further than Lugard. But until 1947 this council remained confined to the south, and until then Nigeria had no central "parliament". The racially, religiously and economically very different areas were not brought together but treated as separate units that were held together only by the networks of transportation and communication, trade and the colonial administration—above all by the technical departments. It is significant that Cameron invited both the emirs of the north and the Yoruba chiefs of the south to conferences intended to widen their vision; but he considered a closer connection between north and south unpractical or premature. The same applies to the Gold Coast where the administration tried to foster a certain regional unity in the colony and in the Ashanti territory (where the term "nation" was used), but continued to govern both parts separately. "Nationhood" was to develop via the above-mentioned provincial councils and thus via the native authorities.[64]

This aspect of British West African policy between the wars is very important by comparison with France. The large administrative units of French West Africa and French Equatorial Africa, which granted only limited autonomy, seemed to incline towards strong African units, while the British administration's indirect rule seemed to favor a definite separatism. Until the Second World War, at any rate, the tendency to "Balkanize" Africa was stronger in the British than in the French colonies.

Cameron's view of the future was unclear. He spoke of "free institutions in the dependent countries and ultimate autonomy" as the aim of indirect rule,[65] but without making it clear exactly what he meant. The term "autonomy" was seldom used in the British colonial discussion; "self-government" usually implied a certain amount of autonomy. Cameron was obviously not thinking in terms of dominion status. In the case of Tanganyika, however, eventual dissociation had to be reckoned with, because the mandate demanded it; a mandate is only valid "until the people can stand by themselves".[66] But here, too, this aim was not to be achieved via elections and a parliamentary system but through the native authorities. The preparation would take decades, thought Cameron, until one day Africans and Europeans could stand beside one another with equal rights and rule Tanganyika together. How this was to be done was left to the future. What is important is that Cameron rejected the concept of the white man's country and contemplated a multi-racial community.[67]

The opinions of Margery Perham, a liberal reformer and recognized expert on West Africa who worked with Lord Lugard, are instructive. In 1934 she clearly accepted future self-government for the African territories: since this had been granted to Canada in the nineteenth century, it was also necessary to allow the Africans "to take their place in the world as self-governing nations".[68] "There comes a time when the most liberal rulers can no longer help a dependent people" and it was Britain's duty to prepare Nigeria for its future as "a stable member of the society of nations".[69] Thus, in the 1930s, she demanded a unified Nigeria, a "sound united state",[70] to be achieved by drawing Indirect Rule to its logical conclusion. The native authorities should be given more responsibility and then be joined into federations, regional at first and then inter-regional. The autocratic tendencies of the emirs and chiefs must not be surrendered to; rather an attempt must be made to link up north and south. Since the educated Africans did not get on with the native authorities, but demanded Western representative institutions —which on the whole was quite understandable—they must, she said (as Cameron had already said), be given more opportunity to take part in the administration. By this she meant, however, only the urban administration, the technical departments of the central administration and the native authorities, and not the administrative service as such.[71] Africans must not be appointed district commissioners, residents or governors. These offices would have to be abolished one day, which would be very difficult if they were occupied by Africans. So she took a logical step beyond the theory, or rather fiction, that indirect rule was simply an advisory task of the British administration. The difference from direct administration, as practised by France, becomes very clear here. In French practice, it was logical to include Africans in the higher administrative service in the name of integration and assimilation; the beginnings of this—we may recall Eboué—occurred before 1939.

The same principle should apply to the legislative council. This had fulfilled its function, said Margery Perham, and the elected Africans had proved themselves. Nevertheless she did not think it advisable to develop the legislature into representative and then responsible government. Nigeria could perhaps one day receive "some form of representative parliamentary government"[72] but only in the distant future and as the conclusion of a process of development which for the time being should occur exclusively within the native authorities.[73]

So Margery Perham addressed herself to the question of future British West African policy, which was usually only touched on briefly, and took the concepts of trusteeship and self-government very seriously. She considered liberal paternalism and self-government to be interdependent and not mutually exclusive terms. Two aspects of her thought are especially important for us. For one, Margery Perham believed the system of indirect rule so far capable of change and development that it would be able to cope successfully with future demands on the local government—an optimistic theory which was doubted by other African experts at that time. Secondly she believed that Indirect Rule could hold its own against the growing demands of Western-educated Africans without provoking a conflict between the colonial power and nationalist movements; only on this condition would the path she suggested have any hope of success. This attitude shows that people still thought there was enough time for London to lay down the guide-lines of a policy that did not take African opposition and the new rising classes seriously. A liberal-minded expert such as Margery Perham did indeed discuss responsible government and dominion status, but considered it unthinkable that this could be achieved for decades to come. She makes even clearer what we have already said about Lugard: around 1920 neither national unity nor a British representative system seemed advisable in Nigeria. In the 1930s, there was a change of attitude which laid the foundation for a general British colonial doctrine, though at first it remained "academic" and scarcely affected administration.

In retrospect, Lord Hailey seems to have recognized the limitations of indirect rule and the need for a timely readjustment earlier and more clearly than Lord Lugard or Margery Perham. He was by no means opposed to Indirect Rule and he too welcomed the attempt to prepare Africa for the modern world from within, i.e. on the basis of its own traditions and organizations; nor did he dispute its evident successes. But he objected to overestimating its value and to the "theological fervour" with which the controversy for or against Indirect Rule was being conducted.[74] The main question, he thought, was which method permitted "more gradual adjustment of native life to the requirements of modern civilization . . .". The true testing point had yet to come; the real challenge was the economy with its cash-crop production, hired labour, transport and finance, and the native authorities were already overburdened. Perham had seen these difficulties but believed the traditional system could stand up to them, whereas Hailey pointed out the need to abandon a method once it no longer served its purpose. He thought it dangerous to take a one-sided interest in the "primitive" classes of the population because this distorted one's perspective. Africans must be given access to higher education and political participation. Britain was "unduly slow to realize the necessity of educating Africans not merely to take the routine of administration off the shoulders of the European officer, but to take part, in a more real sense, in the actual work of the administration". In the conflict between traditional authorities and the modern educated class the latter would eventually win. Here Hailey seems diametrically opposed to Margery Perham in encouraging a more rapid inclusion of Africans into the higher administration. He warned against underestimating the time factor and criticized the fact that no one had given serious thought to the future relations of parliamentary institutions and Indirect Rule. The two systems were not necessarily incompatible, yet one had to decide clearly on the ways and means of integrating them. Lord Hailey obviously thought that indirect rule was still very useful in the local sphere and that a system of indirect election, as Guggisberg wanted for the Gold Coast, would have to take the native authorities into account. On the other hand, Britain would have to introduce representative institutions on the Western model in West Africa too, and not in the distant future, but soon. Here Hailey's views coincide with those of Charles R. Buxton of the Labour party and of W. M. Macmillan.[75] They realized that the successful performance of modern administrative tasks on the one hand and inclusion of the educated Africans in the administration and political responsibility on the other, were the two most urgent problems of the immediate future; so they too doubted whether indirect rule was a practicable solution.

Indirect Rule as a policy had many advantages for Great Britain: it complied with the proclaimed trusteeship and in this sense it was an evolutionary theory; it was also evidence of the English dislike of imposing their own institutions on foreign peoples or aiming at integration or assimilation. And it was cheap, since it needed only a small though qualified staff. This aspect was important, for the British upper classes continued to supply personnel for the Colonial Service but urged economy on the government, Parliament and the public. The Indian case had shown the advantages of managing without the problematic class of "small whites". Therefore, in a remarkable agreement between conservative imperialists, colonial reformers and representatives of the Labour party, Indirect Rule was approved; it also gained the respect of foreign specialists on Africa.[76] Some saw it as an advantageous system because it took a long-term view and did not prematurely transfer British institutions to foreign peoples; others welcomed the "paramountcy of native interests", which made it possible to protect the natives from exploitation and expropriation in questions of land, labour and taxes. Its conservative tendencies were welcomed by one party and at least accepted by the other, since a long-term development was in both their interests and they all thought that Africans should not be abandoned to a confrontation with the capitalist system of economics without protection. Indirect Rule seemed an attempt "to hold the ring, to preserve a fair field within which Africans can strike their own balance between conservatism and adaption".[77]

Only a distorted view of the situation in Africa in the 1920s and 1930s, and only a doctrinaire anti-colonialist, could question the achievements of Indirect Rule. Social structures, institutions and religious traditions were not prematurely destroyed; excessively small communities were incorporated into larger ones or at least familiarized with larger organizations; many native authorities proved themselves sufficiently adaptable to be able to cope with the demands of local government and a process of education was set into motion which was important for the future.

On the other hand, the retarding factors of Indirect Rule must be taken into account. The autocratic tendencies of the emirs, their resistance and often impotence in the face of modern ideas, lead to serious problems. The speed at which Africa was drawn into the maelstrom of modern civilization was underestimated. It is enough here to point to urbanization, the creation of a hired labour force, and the rise of the bourgeoisie and intelligentsia. Direct rule often allowed a quicker adaptation to modern problems that indirect rule which did not intervene, did not urge efficiency and left the native authorities to do very much as they liked.

The system of Indirect Rule was based on the assumption that "we had indefinite time ahead", said an experienced colonial official in critical retrospect.[78] We have tried to show this by describing representative attitudes in the inter-war period. Lugard and his successors started from the idea that the process of "civilization" could take place within the traditional order and under the leadership of the chiefs. They had certainly not overlooked external influences and had warned against disintegration; but they hoped that the adaptation could take place over a very long period of time through the medium of the native authorities. This adaptation was to begin on a small scale, indeed could only begin there, and so the new urban classes had to be neglected.

Yet the partisans of indirect rule did not consciously try to prevent the economic and social rise of these classes, as was the case in South and East Africa and the Belgian Congo, even though they did not take positive measures to encourage it. By barring plantations and European settlers, and with the tremendous expansion of African production and export, the way was clear for the rise of the bourgeoisie; and if efforts in the educational field still seem modest by comparison with those after 1945, still the number of Africans with secondary or high-school education continued to grow. At first Britain did not think it had to accept the claims of this educated group. Radical reforms appeared to be in no way urgent and so, on the whole, the institutional order of Nigeria remained that of 1922, except that the number of Africans elected to the legislative council was increased from seven to ten. The franchise, limited to Lagos and Calabar, was not extended. Africans were not appointed to the executive council until after 1943. Similarly, few Nigerians entered the central offices or the numerous special boards.[79] African participation in the administrative and economic staff was low, although qualified Africans were available in the 1930s. The integration of northern and southern territories was not pursued.

Indirect Rule was not solely responsible for this tendency to maintain the *status quo*, although very often it provided a pretext for postponing reforms. Other colonial powers were equally slow to institute reforms, particularly of political institutions. Paternalism was easy to combine with the absolute authority of the dominating power. The administration did not want to be disturbed in its routine; it was afraid that to include Africans would endanger the compactness of its "corps". Racial segregation was considered necessary in a colonial society. Indirect Rule, but also fear of the restless, demanding or even arrogant intelligentsia, made further steps towards self-government seem "premature".

But we have shown that the experts in London were aware of the new problems and tasks. No less than Lord Hailey wrote in March 1939:

> Prudence seems to lie therefore in securing the early association of educated Africans with our administrative institutions. If we do not do so, there will inevitably arise a state of tension, which, sooner or later, we shall have to meet by large-scale political concessions. And in that case, they will not necessarily be made either in the right way, or to the right class, or with the best result for all the people concerned.[80]

EAST AFRICA: KENYA AND CLOSER UNION

Tropical West Africa was not suitable for British settlers because of its climate. Administrative officials, missionaries and businessmen, most of them employed by a few large trading companies, were the only whites in this vast region. Many of them came to Africa when they were young and spent their lives there. But the Europeans were only "guests" of the country and scarcely ever became permanent residents. They sent their children to school in England and they themselves retired very early and spent their old age in Europe. Moreover, the British administration at first made it very difficult for Europeans to buy land, and later to a large extent prevented it entirely. Indirect rule allowed neither plantations nor individual settlers. African farmers produced the cocoa, groundnuts and palm products.

In East Africa, on the other hand, there were a number of white settlers. Settlement was possible on the high plateaux in spite of the tropical latitudes, because the climate was moderate and there was water. Moreover, East Africa seemed particularly suitable for white immigration because it was so sparsely settled. Settlement required continuous residence in Africa, clearing the land in order to create suitable living conditions, and forming a political community. These factors determined the different treatment of the East African inhabitants. In West Africa, the natives were "objects" of the officials and missionaries; the European tradesman considered them only as producers and consumers; they were Crown subjects whom the whites could treat distantly, disdainfully or benevolently, but whose existence seemed to pose no problems. The situation in East Africa, however, produced conflicts (as in the case of the Boers) in that two radically and culturally very different communities claimed the same land. The sparse settlement of much of the country could only temporarily conceal this conflict which ultimately became acute. The two legal systems clashed. According to the African system, tribal claims, even to unpopulated areas, could not expire; the whites, for their part, claimed the uninhabited land they had settled and wanted to demarcate and reserve for themselves all areas suitable for settlement. At the same time they advocated the formation of reservations for the African inhabitants, on the South African model.

There were other difficulties. Since the white settler could not cultivate his land single-handed, he had to rely on native labour if he was to make his extensive farm lands pay at all. The acute scarcity of labour meant that the Africans could not simply be relegated to their reservations, and ways had to be found to persuade the natives to accept working on European farms in the highlands. This determined British policy towards the natives. The administration was to help "recruit" labour, taxes were to be fixed in such a way that the Africans had to earn the necessary cash on the white farms and, in addition, if the labourer left his place of work he was liable to a special penalty. In order to protect the white settlers' interests, the natives were forbidden to cultivate certain products—for instance coffee in Kenya.

A similar problem necessarily developed in the political and cultural sphere. In West Africa indirect rule could be regarded as the preparation for future African self-government; but in East Africa, and particularly Kenya, the British settlers considered themselves the rulers and tried to create a white man's country. It was obviously in their interests to replace the colonial administration by their own government, and they demanded the self-government that had been granted to the colonists in Canada, Australia and New Zealand, and even to the Boers. This presented London with a serious problem. What would happen to the African inhabitants if London gave in to the settlers' demand? What did self-government mean in this case?

The highland regions of Kenya were settled after 1900. One of the most influential settlers was the later Lord Delamere, a well-known pioneer who has been compared to Cecil Rhodes. With his love of adventure, he acquired and opened up large areas, becoming the social and political leader of the settlers' community.[1] As early as 1906–1908 Lord Elgin, the colonial minister, confirmed that the highlands were to be largely reserved for white settlers.[2] In the First World War, owing to the lack of shipping space for imports and exports, livestock diseases and financial losses, the settlers found themselves hard hit economically; in addition, great demands were made on them by the mobilization and the East African campaign. London, therefore, had to come to their aid and in 1916 promised to allow them to elect representatives to the advisory legislative council. In this matter the settlers tried to gain control of the land and labour laws and the educational system.

Apart from the white minority, there was also a large Indian community in Kenya. For generations the Indians had been active traders on the East African coast and Indian workers had come into the country to help in the construction of the Uganda railway and had then stayed and risen in the social scale. They controlled much of the small trade, handicrafts, craftsmanship and lower administrative positions. In 1921 there were ten thousand Europeans, twenty-three thousand Indians and 2.2 million Africans in the country.

In 1919 the Europeans obtained the franchise promised by Lord Milner and elected eleven representatives to the legislative council. Two appointed Indians represented the interests of their community, but the official majority remained British. As soon as the whites obtained elected representation and tried to gain political control of the colony, the Indians naturally began to feel that their future was in danger. They feared the same discrimination that they suffered in South Africa and demanded equal status with the European immigrants.

The situation may be summed up in four major points:

1. Under the Elgin declaration of 1908, the Europeans continued to claim the highlands, to the exclusion of the Indians.

2. The Europeans wanted Indian immigration to be reduced.

3. The Indians opposed racial segregation in the residential and business quarters of the towns, in force since 1913.

4. The Indians demanded proportional, elected representation in the legislative council and a common roll; the same electoral qualifications should apply to the two communities. The Europeans, on the other hand, insisted on a communal electorate, i.e. separate electoral rolls, and proportional under-representation of the Indians in order to avoid being outvoted.

We will not discuss the Indian question in detail. Its main interest to us is the light it sheds on a general problem. As soon as a minority tries to obtain self-government it has to make laws discriminating against other communities. That is to say, after claiming its legal right to representation, it then has to falsify this same right in order to ensure its own domination. This could not be done gradually, because if the principle of "one man, one vote" was accepted at all, it would inevitably cause the minority to be outvoted by the larger community. The question of a separate or common roll thus became one of life and death for both communities.

The arguments on which the white settlers based their claim to domination are self-evident. They pointed to their status as pioneers, to their higher civilization and to their British origins. They said Kenya was an outpost of British-European civilization and stood at the forefront of a great development. They also asserted that they were protecting the Africans from the exploitation and the demoralizing influence of the Indians.[3]

The discrimination against the Indians in Kenya became an imperial problem, since the Indians were not only supported and backed by the Congress party but also, in a curious overlapping of fronts, by the British Government in Kenya, the India Office in London and not least the House of Lords, which included former viceroys, governors and officials of the Indian Civil Service. India, which had in any case been a critical issue since 1919, seemed more important to them than the small white minority in Kenya. The whites, for their part, gained some support from South Africa.

The British Government tried to compromise. In 1920 Lord Milner promised that two Indians would be elected to the legislative council, thereby recognizing the Indian franchise. He declared that immigration should not be restricted; on the other hand, he confirmed reservation of the highlands to the white settlers. Neither the Indians nor the British Government in India were content with this. The settlers sent Lord Delamere to London and in January 1922 colonial minister Winston Churchill made new pledges on the reservation of the highlands and agreed to immigration legislation.[4] The passage on franchise read as follows:

> We shall apply broadly and comprehensively Mr Rhodes' principles of equal rights for all civilised men. That means Natives and Indians alike who reach and conform to a well-marked European standard shall not be denied the fullest exercise and enjoyment of civic and political rights. The standard to be adopted is obviously a matter of the greatest importance, and is certainly a matter in which the European community have a right to be fully consulted.

On a purely superficial level, this was a refusal to legalize racial discrimination; in principle Africans and Indians were to have equal rights with Europeans. This complied with the traditional British imperial policy, recalling the Cape Colony where, unlike in the Boer republics, Africans were also enfranchised. In practice, however, Churchill was favouring the settlers. It was clear that only a small Indian minority fulfilled Churchill's conditions. Moreover, the Europeans were given a voice in the determination of the "European standard"; the example of South Africa had proved that this could be interpreted very arbitrarily and could be turned into a pretext for ensuring white domination, all the more so since the Churchill declaration added that London was not intending to bar the way to dominion status for Kenya and was "looking forward in the full fruition of time to complete Self-Government". Once the settlers had obtained a majority in the legislative council they could take legal measures to prevent Indians and Africans from reaching the "European standard of civilization". Churchill's pledges were an implicit acceptance of Kenya as a white man's country. He had recognized the British settlers' claim for self-government and Kenya seemed on the way to dominion status.

But matters did not rest there. In the same year, these pledges were recalled under pressure from the India Office. An agreement was then reached between the British and the Indian Government allowing for the following: introduction of the common roll; an increase in the number of enfranchised Indians and in their representatives to four members in the legislative council (as opposed to seven Europeans); desegregation of the residential quarters; no change in the immigration regulations; but, on the other hand, reservation of the highlands for the settlers. So within a year London issued two entirely different directives on its Kenya policy, a clear sign of the difficulties inherent in the East African situation. Evidently London found it hard to decide which policy to pursue, and to compromise in such a decisive question was hardly possible. The Conservative government no doubt would have liked to help the settlers, but since it had to consider India and Indian nationalism it was limited in its movements. It did not comply with the demands of the British settlers because it did not want to impose additional burdens on British domination in India. It is tempting here to draw a parallel with the problem of Southern Rhodesia in 1964 and London's difficult position within the multi-racial Commonwealth.

The Wood-Winterton proposals[5] that had been approved by the British Cabinet had naturally provoked great agitation among the settlers. The mood of rebellion in Kenya led to preparations for a *coup d'état*. The situation can be compared to that in Algeria in 1936: the settlers protested against the decision of the metropolis and threatened to take matters into their own hands. Aggressive declarations were issued, delegations were sent to London, and representations were made to the British press. The agitation and subsequent negotiations resulted in the Devonshire declaration in July 1923:

> *Primarily Kenya is an African territory*, and His Majesty's Government think it necessary definitely to record their considered opinion that the *interests of the African natives must be paramount*, and that if, and when, those interests and the *interests of the immigrant races should conflict, the former should prevail.* ... In the administration of Kenya, HMG regard themselves as exercising a trust on behalf of the African population, and they are *unable to delegate or share this trust*, the object of which may be defined as the protection and advancement of the native races. ...
>
> This paramount duty of trusteeship will continue, as in the past, to be carried out under the Secretary of State for the Colonies by the agents of the Imperial Government, and by *them alone*.
>
> HMG cannot but regard the grant of *responsible Self-Government as out of the question* within any period of time which need now be taken into consideration. Nor, indeed, would they contemplate yet the possibility of substituting an unofficial majority in the Council for the Government official majority.[6]

The interests of the other communities—European, Indian and Arab—"must generally be safeguarded". But the declaration did demand a common roll. The Indians were allowed five seats in the legislative council (as against eleven Europeans). The reservation of the highlands remained, but the limitation on the number of Indian immigrants was to be discontinued.

The American historian Robert G. Gregory has tried to reconstruct the sources of this declaration.[7] According to him, the conservative colonial minister Devonshire, who had no colonial experience, had been subjected to a variety of pressures and tried to find a compromise solution. The paramountcy of native interests was first propounded by the Indians and their representatives in London. They wanted to oppose the settlers' demands for control and to bar the way to responsible government under white leadership. Therefore they raised the question of the African population who, they said, must not be placed at the mercy of the white minority. The settlers for their part asserted that they were protecting the natives from exploitation by "dubious Orientals". The missionaries and colonial reformers, who were less concerned with the Indians than with the Africans, took up this argument and pointed to the mother country's duty as trustee for the native population. Their leader was Dr. J. H. Oldham, the energetic and "diplomatic" secretary of the international council of missionaries. In 1919–1920 he had organized the resistance in London to circulars issued by the governor of Kenya, Northey, instructing the district commissioners in the reservations to induce the natives to accept work on white farms.[8] Oldham first developed the principle of paramountcy; it was also outlined in a *Round Table* article.[9] Consideration of British-Indian relations was added to the "missionary factor" which was naturally backed by the Labour party, but also by Lugard. Thus a pressure group was formed, which successfully opposed Delamere's agitation and persuaded the hesitant government to publish a declaration of principles which established British policy in East Africa on a new basis. In its attempts to reject the Europeans' and Indians' demands, London proclaimed a policy of trusteeship for the African natives, trying in this way to evade the embarrassing situation. The Conservative government had no intention of introducing a radical change of policy and primarily wanted to play for time and to mediate between the agitated parties. Naturally this did not prevent Great Britain from later describing the 1923 declaration as an entirely deliberate decision in the name of trusteeship.

Indeed, one cannot doubt the importance of the Devonshire declaration. By describing both Indians and Europeans as "immigrants", London was rejecting the thesis that the British were "natives" in Africa. In cases of conflict, therefore, the Africans were to come first. The settlers could not be granted responsible government, at least not until the majority of Africans had equal social and political rights. In addition, the declaration stressed that only the mother country could carry out the trusteeship and that it could not be transferred to the settlers. This decision can be understood fully only in terms of British imperial history. Since the time of the Durham Report of 1839, it was taken for granted that eventually the British settlers' community would have a claim to self-government, in the sense of responsible government, which the mother country could not deny. Consideration of the natives was not a valid argument for refusing internal autonomy, although the case of New Zealand had already clearly revealed the difficulties this entailed. London's attempt to maintain control of the

Maori administration had soon failed and control had to be handed over to the settlers, as in the Union of South Africa in 1906–1910. Critical objections, such as that London was ceding its control over the African population, had to be ignored if Britain was to make peace with the Boer republics. In years to come Britain's grant of dominion status to the Boers was interpreted as evidence of a liberal and generous attitude, and not without some justice; but the fact that the Africans had to pay the price of this generosity was overlooked or suppressed.[10] London had carried over this policy into Southern Rhodesia. After the settlers refused to join the Union they were granted responsible government and quasi-dominion status. Once again London had reserved its right of intervention in native affairs, but it did not or could not make use of it in the years to come and thus cleared the way for a native policy which increasingly resembled that of the Union.

The Devonshire declaration, therefore, was a break with tradition. Britain no longer recognized the settlers' claims for self-government and the meaning of the term itself was broadened—though only implicitly at first. Not only British citizens overseas, but all subjects of the Crown, had the right to self-government. As long as the population as a whole could not take over the government, London would act as trustee and the Crown Colony system would remain. Nor could the settlers obtain representative government. Experience had shown that this would be unsuitable, for it would limit London's right of intervention and sooner or later lead to responsible government. There was a shift in the arguments which was clear evidence of the differences between East and West Africa. In West Africa London tried to justify the maintenance of British control for an indeterminate period on the thesis that the small minority of educated Africans was not representative of the masses; in Kenya the same argument was applied against the white settlers!

In 1923 two opposite decisions were reached in Southern Rhodesia and in Kenya; in both cases they were certainly measures of expediency. But these decisions were also evidence of two different traditions in nineteenth-century British colonial policy, both of them designed as liberal and reformist. One was the Durham tradition which aimed at dominion status for the settlers; the other was the tradition of the anti-slavery movement, which took the part of the African natives and appealed to the principle of trusteeship.

The immediate purpose of the Devonshire declaration, namely to find a solution to the extremely tense situation in Kenya, was achieved. The two parties calmed down. The Europeans at least had their presence in the highlands and communal representation confirmed and the Indians were relieved of the threat of a white settlers' government in the near future. But neither community abandoned its objectives: for the Indians, access to the highlands, common roll and better representation in the legislative council; for the settlers, self-government, above all the removal of the Colonial Office and control of land and native policy.

Now, however, the Indian problem was replaced by that of the Africans. It seems that the discussion of the Indians' proper position made the British public aware of Kenya for the first time and revealed to it the problematic nature of the former native policy. The 1923 declaration and the official exercise of trusteeship provided an opportunity for the Labour party and humanitarian Christian reformers to criticize the administration.[11] They discussed and analysed the structure of the colonial settlement and two representative works appeared, Norman Leys' *Kenya* in 1924, and W. McGregor Ross' *Kenya from Within*, 1927. The focal point of the discussion was naturally the land question. The most fertile land had been reserved for a small minority of white settlers by annexation or dubious expropriation. Two thousand Europeans owned about half of the cultivated land,[12] and in spite of declarations to the contrary, more and more land was being added to the reservations although only a part of it was cultivated and the Masai tribes' herds had greatly increased, requiring more grazing land. The employment of native labour was producing a new form of slavery, for the Africans received low pay, were subject to special penalties if they broke their contracts and were not sufficiently protected by law. Moreover, the administration was forcing chiefs in the reservations to place their people at the settlers' disposition. High taxation served the same purpose and was particularly unjust since the settlers did not have to pay income tax[13] and only a small portion of the state revenue received from the natives was returned to the reservations.[14] Hardly anything was being done for African education. Production on the African reservations was kept low in order to create the necessary labour force; this could be demonstrated in so many words by the settlers' statements.[15] Great Britain was supporting or covering up a policy of exploitation and racial discrimination which was totally incompatible with "paramountcy" and trusteeship.

The settlers in Kenya and the conservatives in Britain interpreted the statistics somewhat differently and produced counter-arguments. They said the highlands had originally been unpopulated and in any case consisted of only a small part of the total land; the natives had enough land for themselves. The Masai's herds were uneconomic and must be reduced. Even after the war, the British Government had encouraged white settlement and could not now abandon the settlers. The natives found work and money on the European farms; the direct contact this produced was better than mere administration by officials and missionaries. The economic situation in Kenya made it impossible to make large sums available for African education; yet more was being spent on this than in Tanganyika or Uganda. Although London set itself up as an imperial trustee, it was not even paying out the sums promised to African veterans.[16] The white race had the right, even the duty, to open up

Africa and therefore to reserve itself the highlands. The settlers knew more about how to deal with the natives than did the bureaucracy in London. Although they were by no means anti-African, they could not permit themselves to be outvoted by a mass of uncivilized Africans and Indians. It was unjust to label the settlers slave-holders; they were pioneers working hard at a difficult job who deserved the support of the mother country.[17]

Both sides could bring to bear weighty arguments that seemed well-founded in terms of their different outlooks and derived from the complex situation of a colonial settlement and a multi-racial society living side by side. The problem seemed insoluble.[18] For us it is important because Kenya played an important part in the public and parliamentary discussion between the wars and again after 1945. Colonial reformers and the Labour party directed the main force of their criticism at the situation in Kenya. They described the concrete problems of the colonial situation and brought them to the notice of an interested public. The Conservatives, by contrast, were provoked to come to the settlers' defence and sharply attacked "colonialist" theories.

The British Government continued to try to steer a middle course. In 1925 an East Africa Parliamentary Commission under Ormsby-Gore submitted a report[19] that drew a detailed picture of the concrete problems and formulated some rules of conduct. The report recalled the 1923 declaration and said that native agriculture should be intensified; but it gave clear precedence to the pioneering achievements of the settlers and the importance of their economic and civilizing task. "In order to be pro-native it is not necessary to be anti-white", since East Africa could prosper only by collaboration among the different racial communities. For the time being, white European leadership was still necessary, although it must be supplemented by trusteeship for the benefit of the natives. The report reinterpreted paramountcy, saying that it did not only apply to a single group (i.e. the Africans), but to the community as a whole: "The development of the community sense is one of its [the government's] paramount tasks."[20]

From here the road led to the so-called "dual policy" proposed by the colonial minister, Amery, and the governor of Kenya, Sir Edward Grigg, whom he appointed. Amery expounded this policy in the white paper *Future Policy in Regard to Eastern Africa*.[21] His point of departure was the economic structure of East Africa with its "combination of non-native and native production". Whites and natives were dependent on one another and the agrarian production of both communities must be fostered.[22] Political development must correspond to this allegedly reciprocal relationship. A fixed boundary must be drawn between the white highlands and the native reservations. Tribal organizations should be developed according to the policy of Indirect Rule and should later be expanded into native councils, leading eventually to "self-government in local affairs".²³ This reference to Indirect Rule and native authorities had a decidedly paternalistic conservative accent and justified treating the Africans in the reservations differently from the whites in the highlands.²⁴ There should be no delay in establishing an elected majority of whites in the legislative council. In the future, the African reservations should also be represented, but how and when seemed vague—certainly not by a common roll, and certainly only as a minority.²⁵ The imperial government was to be responsible for native policy for the time being, but with the co-operation of the settlers, who could subsequently take it over.²⁶

It is self-evident that this dual policy was not compatible with the notion of paramountcy. Nor did Amery use the term.²⁷ The attempt to present the dual policy as an interpretation of the Devonshire declaration was not convincing. The conservatives either did not accept the new doctrine, or accepted it only reluctantly and tried to tone it down. It was not possible to reject it openly, but they hoped they could evade it by a reference to the separate development of the two communities, which meant meeting the settlers' demands halfway. It is not surprising that Grigg considered it necessary to increase the number of settlers.²⁸ In principle the concept of dual policy made a white man's country impossible, but in fact Amery and Grigg welcomed self-government for the settlers; at best it was a restatement of Rhodes' "equal rights of all civilised men", for this formula contained no legal discrimination, yet it did not threaten white domination either.²⁹

Dual policy was only one aspect of a much broader discussion. The main topic was the question of "Closer Union" in East Africa, i.e. a federation of Kenya, Tanganyika and Uganda. This was Grigg's and Amery's real objective. The economic advantages of such a union were clear. The railway industry demanded coordination between these territories, and production, currency, finances, tariff policy and defence would benefit by a large-scale economic system under a common executive. Until then each territory had gone its own way without special consideration for its neighbours. Certain parallels in their development showed the advantage of coordinated action and of merging some of the technical branches of the administrations.

Amery and Grigg also had a political purpose—both, we may recall, came from Milner's "kindergarten"! The conquest of German East Africa had made Cecil Rhodes' dream of creating a new dominion from Zambezi to the Sudan a tangible possibility.³⁰ Amery had managed to have a clause included in the League of Nations mandate agreement for Tanganyika which made it possible to incorporate Tanganyika into an East African federation.³¹ Since the "grand solution" could not be achieved, they limited themselves to proposing a union of the three territories, which were in fact interdependent in geographic and economic terms. One day they were to develop into a dominion which would be at least predominantly white.

In 1926–1927 Amery and Grigg began to put out feelers, to arrange conferences and make their first proposals. It soon became clear that the Kenyan settlers could be won over to their plans only if London granted them concessions in the question of unofficial majority representation in the legislative council. Amery and Grigg said that because of its trusteeship "for the weaker part of the population"—in particular, we may add, because of parliamentary opposition!—Great Britain could not immediately grant self-government; but

> the day will come when, with the growth of a large settled community [!] no government in this House can ultimately resist the demand for Self-government. What we want to do is to make sure that the white settlers are conscious of the destiny of East Africa as a great country which they are called upon to lead and inspire [!]; that they should be equally conscious of their responsibility towards other communities and should desire to bring these communities, in the fullness of time [!] into association with themselves on every matter affecting the development of the country.[32]

This affirmation was in keeping with the dual policy: by contrast with the 1923 declaration, the settlers now had a right to self-government. The "association" of Indians and Africans, on the other hand, was formulated only in vague terms and relegated to the distant future.

Amery's and Grigg's plans met with resistance from very different camps, as in the case of the 1922 British Kenya policy. Lord Delamere, speaking for the settlers, was not content with vague promises for the future and demanded full self-government. He said that only if Kenya obtained control over the land, labour and native policies could it join a federation,[33] and asked for "safeguards" against another change of course on the part of the British Government. Delamere feared that the hated "west-coast policy" would also be extended to the federation, considering this incompatible with the concept of the white man's country.[34] So Kenya used the issue of its co-operation in the Closer Union as a means of blackmailing London. Donald Cameron, when he was governor of Tanganyika, opposed federation on entirely different grounds.[35] His concern was more personal. In the interests of his own authority he did not want to be subordinated to a governor-general or high commissioner (Grigg was the man in question) and therefore lose his own freedom of action. Even more important was that his policy of indirect rule, which was designed to prepare the native authorities for self-government, was incompatible with Delamere's plans, especially since it was to be expected that the federation would be dominated by Kenya. In the Closer Union issue then, there were two conflicting concepts of East Africa's future:

on the one hand Indirect Rule and African self-government, on the other, the white man's country.

In Great Britain the opponents of Closer Union were the reformers and the Labour party. Once again Oldham initiated the counter-attack. Lord Lugard joined in with his own proposal: the settlers in the highlands should be granted self-government, while the African reservations should be developed separately, and both communities should be subordinated to a co-ordinating commission under imperial control.[36] Lugard tried to solve the dilemma between self-government for the whites and trusteeship and paramountcy for the natives by splitting Kenya into two separate administrative communities. Grigg showed some sympathy with these proposals, but Delamere rejected them.[37]

Cameron's resistance, the divided opinions in the Cabinet and the expected parliamentary opposition induced Amery to appoint a commission under the chairmanship of Edward Hilton-Young. Oldham became one of the four members and played a decisive part in drafting the report issued early in January 1929.[38] The commission praised Cameron's native authorities and demanded more collaboration with the Africans in Kenya. It opposed responsible government and demanded a common roll for Europeans and Indians. Closer Union required a governor-general who should be responsible for the entire native policy and have far-reaching authority. The Hilton-Young Report tried to return the dual policy to its 1923 basis, quite clearly against the settlers.

Lively discussion took place in Britain. The settlers,[39] like Grigg and Amery[40] found their hopes dashed and protested the commission's proposals, while Cameron[41] and Oldham, backed by Lugard, launched a full-scale campaign to support it. In a remarkable speech in the House of Lords, Lugard accepted the Hilton-Young Report as a starting-point and asked for a joint select committee to clarify it further. He said a new concept must be formulated in order to avoid serious racial conflicts in the future.[42] The archbishop of Canterbury, Charles R. Buxton and Lord Olivier, joined by Lords Cecil, Reading and Lugard, sent a declaration to this effect to *The Times*. Reginald Coupland and Ernest Barker reminded people that the "conception of trust" was a corner-stone of the Empire and warned against making any hasty decision since this decision would be extremely important not only for East Africa but for the entire Empire.[43] *The Times*,[44] the *Economist*[45] and the *Round Table*[46] approved the report and at times sharply criticized the settlers. The different fronts could not, therefore, simply be traced to an opposition between the Labour and Conservative parties, for socialists and liberals also had access to the conservative camp, not least through important people in the colonial administration. It is very striking that Lugard, who saw Indirect Rule in conservative terms and thought African self-government still lay in the far future, nevertheless did not want to set up any obstacles to it and felt morally bound by the principle of trusteeship.

The discussion in 1928–1929 showed that Great Britain was far more conscious than before of the special problems of multi-racial communities. The preparation of a new constitution for Ceylon ran parallel to the Closer Union issue. Here, it is true, problems arose from the Asian communities and not, as in Kenya, from the minority of British settlers; but in both cases it had become difficult to introduce and develop a representative system on the British model. People wanted to show their goodwill to the settlers and acknowledged that the still low level of civilization of the African masses made it seem impossible to expose the white minority to the danger of being politically outvoted; but they thought it equally irresponsible to subject the Africans to the settlers' power. New solutions were called for, but whatever happened London was not to surrender the authority it still had. By comparison with the years around 1920 when the East Africans scarcely entered into the question, the discussion of Closer Union meant a decisive change of attitude.

Colonial minister Amery tried to regain the initiative by sending his under-secretary of state, Sir Samuel Wilson, to East Africa. (Whenever London found itself in an embarrassing situation or faced by obstinate resistance, it sent out commissions. This had happened in India, and now the same thing occurred in East Africa!) Wilson was instructed to come up with a compromise to the proposals of the Hilton-Young Report. He said that concessions would have to be made in Kenya, primarily that native affairs should be administered by the individual territories and the official majority should be abandoned.[47]

Meanwhile the second Labour government had come into office. Lord Passfield helped to formulate the Labour party's colonial doctrine, but he had no personal views on the Closer Union issue. Grigg remained governor. The Labour government did not publish its White Paper on Closer Union until June 1930.[48] Based on the Hilton-Young Report, it again transferred native policy to the high commissioner; in addition Kenya was to obtain a common roll for Indians and Europeans based on their degree of civilization.

At the same time Lord Passfield published a *Memorandum on Native Policy in East Africa*.[49] Unlike the pronouncements of the Conservative governments, this memorandum confirmed the 1923 declaration and all its implications, and added a corollary: "All proposals designed to promote the well-being or the interests of any non-native race must be carefully examined, at the outset, from the standpoint of their effect on the native races."[50] So the notion of paramountcy was to mean that in the future all demands made by the Europeans and Indians were to be considered in terms of the Africans' well-being! The memorandum again stressed that the imperial government alone was responsible for the trusteeship. The settlers were described as "immigrant communities", reservation of the highlands was not confirmed, and it was emphasized again that the colonial power's prime task was the active development of the natives. A few additional statements attempting to accord paramountcy with dual policy cannot hide the fact that Passfield clearly wanted to dissociate himself from his predecessor, Amery. With the 1923 Devonshire declaration, the Labour government openly opposed the concept of the white man's country!

The "Black Papers", as the two Labour memoranda were called in East Africa, were naturally greeted with indignation in Kenya.[51] Governor Grigg protested in a dispatch to the colonial minister and attacked the common roll in every possible way.[52] The Kenya question now became a political issue in the mother country. The Conservative party supported Amery, rejected the new memorandum, and even declared that it would not consider itself bound by it in the future. Attacking the Labour government, Neville Chamberlain said:

> You cannot force constitutional changes upon any British colony or dependency unless those changes command the confidence and goodwill of the people who have got to live with them and operate them. And it is for that reason that I so deeply regret what I regard as the unnecessarily pronative character of the papers that have been presented.[53]

The Labour government managed to prevent the conservatives from continuing on the road to federation mapped out by the Wilson report; but it did not have enough political mobility to carry through the proposals of its own memoranda. It suspended the discussion on Closer Union, however, although the Joint Select Committee requested by the opposition went on examining a great many witnesses and presented a comprehensive report.[54] The report ascertained that the efforts to create an East African community had failed. It again watered down and reinterpreted the principles of paramountcy of 1923 and 1930 and again discussed dual policy; it also rejected the common roll. Finally, the report opposed responsible government for the settlers in Kenya, which meant that a decision had been reached in this important question.[55]

We would suggest, as the *Economist* did,[56] that this decision represented the primary result of the lengthy discussion on paramountcy, dual policy and Closer Union. The statement about the "paramountcy of African interests" had been based on expediency and circumstance, and in the following years it was not fully confirmed by any British government—except the Labour government in 1930—nor did it become a guide-line for any of their Kenya policies. People did indeed refer to it, but interpreting it in such a way as to enable them to make numerous concessions to the settlers' demands. New concepts such as dual policy, co-operative policy or partnership were coined but without any further definition. In concrete administrative questions, land law, matters of taxation and finance, labour law and the educational system, London continued to consider the settlers first, and not the paramountcy of the natives. A certain amount may have been done between the wars for the African reservations, but no credit can be given for any active policy of development. London did not have one and in Kenya the settlers saw to it that the governor refrained from any excessively "pro-native" policy.

Reports from British commissions of enquiry revealed that the settlers were privileged in questions of land and taxation—for years the Europeans successfully opposed the introduction of income tax!—and that the old tensions between the colony and the Colonial Office persisted.[57] Moreover, white farmers continued to rely on native labour and the economic crisis had dealt a severe blow to the country. The African population increased, the size of their herds grew and the land issue became acute. The small African middle class extended its base of operation and made claim to the highlands a focal point of their agitation. In 1938, Kenyatta published his famous work, *Facing Mount Kenya*. In addition, the prohibition of circumcision, which was mainly the work of the missionaries, had loosened the complex web of native social structure and was taken as a direct attack on tribal traditions. These factors led directly to the Mau-Mau uprising in 1954.[58]

There were no institutional changes and the Africans obtained no representation of their own in the legislative council. The interests of the African population were merely attended to, with more or less success, by appointed European officials.

Yet one must not overlook the importance of the 1923 Devonshire declaration and the Closer Union discussion within British Africa policy. In 1919 Kenya was considered a potential white man's country and the interests of the whites appeared to come first. The governor of Kenya, Sir Northey, declared to the Indian Association:

> The principle has been accepted at home, that this country is primarily for European development, and whereas the interest of the Indian will not be lost sight of, in all respects the European must predominate. . . . His Excellency believes, that though Indian interest should not be lost sight of, European interest must be paramount throughout the Protectorate.[59]

But once paramountcy had been declared in discussions with the Indian community, London could no longer officially assert that European interests came first, however much the settlers demanded it, and although the conservatives in the mother country would have been prepared to agree.

In 1923, paramountcy was denied the white settlers and instead granted to the African population! This effectively barred the way to the establishment of a white man's country; at least it meant that London could have pursued this path only by ignoring its own declarations. This, as we have seen, is where the opposition within Britain began. Small as the circle of those interested in colonial issues may have been, public opinion became a more serious factor for the administration to contend with. "There is a very live and very critical body of opinion in the country, both in and out of Parliament, which is intensively interested in the native policy of the Kenya administration and which seems to become more so every day."[60] It is worth noting that this critical attitude toward the government and suspicion of its intentions did not spring from African opposition, nor even from uprisings; it was entirely of internal British origin. It was clear that if Britain's imperial sense of domination was not broken, at least it had been weakened. The forces which during and after the war had engaged in active criticism of colonial policy (forces that were not entirely confined to missionary organizations or a few intellectuals, as was the case before 1914) found strong support in the Labour party and appealed to an interested public.

At the same time that Britain was declaring the paramountcy of native interests in Kenya, however, it granted responsible government to the settlers in Southern Rhodesia. In the conflict represented by these two contradictory actions, between the Durham tradition and trusteeship, the latter ultimately proved more in keeping with the times and with the problems of a colonial settlement. This became more apparent in the following years. The Southern Rhodesian decision was never repeated. The Closer Union proposal failed and East Africa began to be clearly distinct from South Africa. The British Government "officially" rejected the South African Union's racist policy[61] and refused to set up reservations in Northern Rhodesia and Nyasaland. It also refused, in spite of the Union's urgent complaints, to surrender the protectorates of Swaziland, Basutoland and Bechuanaland, which were still under British administration. When plans for a Rhodesian federation came to light, the Bledisloe Commission of 1939 called upon Britain's trusteeship and prevented the proposed amalgamation into a large, Central African white dominion.

The declaration of paramountcy and the discussion of Closer Union may have had little influence on actual measures taken by the colonial administration in East Africa, nor did they achieve direct improvements in the situation of the African population, but they did manage to prevent the creation of new white man's countries. By refusing self-government and reserving the rights of decision and control, Britain left the way open for the introduction of other policies in the East African territories. Self-government was reinterpreted and, instead of applying only to the minority of white settlers, it was accepted as the justified claim of the entire African population. What had still seemed "liberal" in the case of Southern Rhodesia was now considered "imperialist" and therefore untenable for Great Britain—whereas the "colonialist" denial of self-government to Southern Rhodesia seemed "liberal"! The grant of responsible government to Southern Rhodesia was part of a policy of decolonization, while Kenya continued to be administered under an imperialist policy in order to make a different form of decolonization possible. This is the clearest proof of how former traditions, concepts and terms had begun to be questioned in the inter-war years and it plainly shows the emergence of a new attitude and entirely new prospects for future policy.

THE DISCUSSION DURING THE SECOND WORLD WAR

The new attitude in colonial policy which had become apparent in the late 1930s did not take effect until the Second World War. In the face of danger, Great Britain once again experienced the "unity" of its Commonwealth and Empire; it was grateful for the generous political, military and economic aid it received and thought its position as an imperial power and a representative of freedom was ensured. But Britain also suffered an epoch-making defeat and loss of prestige in the Far East, which forced it to devote more thought to the colonies, to critically examine the attitudes and policies of the inter-war years and to plan for the future. British composure was shaken by the unexpected Japanese occupation of Hong Kong, Malaya, Borneo and Burma and by the almost unresisting fall of Singapore, that stronghold of British power in the East, and these events "launched through the Empire an impulse of self-questioning and self-reform".[1] What seemed even more shocking was that the defeat was obviously not just a military one. The British press reported that the native population—with the exception of the Chinese—had not openly shown sympathy for the Japanese, yet they had remained passive and had little concern with defending British domination.[2] Tradesmen and colonial officials fled without any active resistance. They were taken by surprise and confused by the events because they had considered British domination an unassailable fact and, in their typical colonial mentality, had indulged in deluded ideas about the attitude of the inhabitants and the security of British domination in Asia.[3]

Some of the reproaches made under the stress of catastrophe were taken back in the following years. The Netherlands and Denmark had also capitulated without a struggle, it was said, the Malayans had been unarmed and they had given the Japanese surprisingly little active aid. The weak British forces were by no means equal to the brutal Japanese aggression. Still, the shock had its effect. The fall of Singapore was seen as the end of an era, an event which would prevent Great Britain from ever resuming its pre-war position of colonial domination. In March 1942, the *Economist* said:

> For the time, the curtain has rung down on Britain's colonial holding in the Far East, and whenever it is rung up again it will certainly be on a radically different scene. . . . There can be no return to the old system once Japan has been defeated. . . . The need is for entirely new principles, or rather, the consistent application of principles to which lip service has long been paid. For the Colonies—Malaya, Indochina and Netherlands-India—there can be only one goal, the creation of independent nations linked economically, socially and culturally with the old mother country, but learning to stand firmly on their own feet.[4]

The Labour party and the colonial reformers took up the criticism they had begun in the years before the war, denouncing the "imperialist and colonialist" attitude of the Conservatives. They had attacked the administration and the discrepancy between principles proclaimed and actual measures taken, between generous promises and minimal concessions, and they urged the rapid grant of self-government. Even a diehard like the Conservative M.P. Gammans realized that the fall of Singapore was a challenge, although the conclusions he drew from it were "imperialist". He said this did not mean the end of the colonial system, but "we cannot go back to Malaya and Borneo as if nothing happened". It was indefensible that the important office of colonial minister had always been treated as a secondary one and, within the Cabinet, as a kind of dumping ground. He thought Britain must regain its moral and political leadership, by instituting, for example, an imperial council for economy and planning, an imperial air force and imperial civil rights.[5] Gammans was something of an outsider and not very representative of the Conservative party, but he provides an example of how the defeat in the East provoked criticism of pre-war policies and turned thoughts to the future.

Then there were the external influences. The United States entered the war, took over leadership within NATO and demanded acceptance of its demands. Even Churchill could not quite deny America's importance. We have described how Roosevelt's anti-colonialism was felt to be a "challenge" to Great Britain. America's programme of liberation was reflected in the Atlantic Charter which also applied to the colonial peoples. It affected the emancipation movements and hastened the revolution which was already under way. Britain won the war, but was weakened. From then on it tried to avoid conflicts and had to agree to concessions. After the war, the United Nations added its pressure to that of America and Britain's internal difficulties—chiefly economic; at the same time the rise of the Soviet Union created a new situation which faced British imperial and colonial politicians with unanticipated problems.

Criticism of past policies, the search for new formulas and the desire to show that Britain was equal to the challenge without having to break entirely with the past were reflected by the political writers. Once again Lord Hailey is to be cited among the authorities. Since the appearance of his *African Survey* he was highly respected and much quoted in parliamentary debates, books and the press. During the war too, he had frequently expressed his opinion on future problems. His influence, particularly in conservative circles, was considerable.[6]

Hailey briefly sketched the history of the Empire and of colonial expansion, which he thought was caused not only by economic factors. He described the counteractions and reform movements, the humanitarian tradition of the early nineteenth century from which the notion of trusteeship had emerged; the economic and at times Marxist theories that had made the public aware of the problem of "exploitation" and of the questions of labour and land law; and the League of Nations mandate system on which Iraq's independence was founded. He said the innumerable declarations in which Great Britain professed trusteeship and spoke of self-government were no longer enough. The colonial peoples could not be satisfied by them any longer and would with some justification point out that the mother country was exaggerating the difficulties of self-government in a utilitarian and one-sided manner. They wanted "something more explicit", and the pronouncements made so far were "not very informative". The notion of trusteeship may have played an increasingly important part in British colonial administration and even gained some respectability, but

> the use of the term is irritating to the Colonial people. It was intensely unpopular in India. It is becoming equally unpopular in the Colonies, for it has implications on which it is unnecessary to enlarge but which, if I were a native of the Colonies, I should equally resent. If we need to express ourselves in a formula at all, let our relations be those of senior and junior partners in the same enterprise, and let it be said that our contract of partnership involves the progressive increase of the share which the junior partners have in the conduct of the undertaking.[7]

Hailey had already expressed rather critical and unconventional opinions on the current doctrines in 1938–1939; yet we believe that his distrust of the concept of "trusteeship", of the very foundation of British colonial doctrine between the wars, was a result of the new outlook not emerged during the war; it would have been inconceivable before 1940, particularly from a conservative! Now at last the paternalistic attitude inherent in trusteeship was analysed critically and the public was asked to understand the position of the natives who felt their self-respect suffered under this arrangement. Until then Britain had paid little attention to such reactions and the discussion had always made it seem as though Great Britain, conscious of its moral obligations, was granting concessions on its own initiative without regard for the opinions of the peoples concerned. The war forced Britain to take more notice of nationalist emancipation movements and to admit that it was doing so. Consequently war-time and post-war reforms were made in a much less "benevolent" spirit than before; they had been rendered necessary by nationalist opposition and the international situation.

The major objective was "a more constructive interpretation of trusteeship",[8] since

> the objective of colonial policy could no longer be viewed merely as the protection of the native people from exploitation; the emphasis now lay on the necessity for the active and systematic promotion of native welfare.[9]

Hailey considered that the colonial state, like the mother country, now had a greater task than before. It must not wait until a certain stage of development had been reached but must intervene actively to promote this development. Within the colonies themselves the discussion paralleled what was happening in Britain, since even the conservatives were becoming concerned with the planning and acceptance of a welfare state instead of the outworn liberalism. Hailey stressed the fact that the policy of development must not just try to improve the natives' standard of living but "must be viewed as an essential preparation for the enjoyment of Self-Government".[10] Institutions must be founded on an economic and social basis and were relevant, he said, only if the natives could take over the administration and if the former almost absolute dependence on the outside world was loosened.

> The objective cannot therefore be merely to increase the cash resources of the natives of the dependencies or to enlarge their power of purchasing imported commodities. Social progress must be directed along lines which will foster the spirit of enterprise and self-reliance. It must seek the substitution of local for imported personnel, not only in the administrative but the technical services. Economic progress involves the growth of local industries and the organization of local marketing with the view to increasing the participation of natives in the major enterprises now under external control. It must seek to preserve the balance between export production and subsistence cultivation, for it is the latter which is the basis of nutrition and therefore of resistance to disease.[11]

Here the conclusions of the *African Survey*, the discussion on the West Indies and the 1939 Nutrition Report were elaborated into a programme for a future colonial policy that would go beyond paternalism and open up new horizons. Serious efforts were now made to prepare the respective territories for economic, social and political independence; there were even demands for industrialization in order to make economic "self-reliance" possible. The same applies to production for local needs, which must not, it was said, be sold as export. Pre-war ideas were put forward again, expanded and turned into concrete demands. Political concessions, Hailey said, were no substitute for a policy of development.[12] By emphasizing the importance of economic and social factors and of a certain amount of economic independence, which he considered the *conditio sine qua non* of political independence, Hailey did not mean to divert attention from political reforms nor to "depoliticize" colonial emancipation—a tendency which cannot be dismissed in certain other British pronouncements or in French post-war policy. Hailey took seriously the notion of the "gradual granting of self-government" and aimed the policy of development, which had begun with the Colonial Development and Welfare Fund, directly at this goal.

This does not mean that he overlooked the difficulty of realizing his programme. In many cases national boundaries that had been drawn were often artificial or the territories too small. Some peoples were still too "primitive". In other cases one had to deal with feudal lords (Buganda, Barotseland, Malaya) who demanded Britain's acceptance of their rights, and could not simply be ignored. How could one solve the problem of the white settlers? Hailey thought it could not be determined in advance when a colony would be ripe for responsible government. He said it was difficult to lay down general valid lines of development and that there was obviously tension between the nationalist opposition, who pressed for "more political independence", and the government, which felt obliged to protect the minorities. The emirs must not remain in power in West Africa; instead the new and indeed still weak ruling class should be relied upon. It was not yet clear whether the necessary conditions for parliamentary government existed in Asia and Africa. "Good administration" must be guaranteed and must not be prematurely endangered by inter-party conflicts and lack of experience.

> The problem of finding an executive which can hold the confidence of the public, while it is at the same time independent of the majority of the Legislature, is admittedly one of extreme difficulty. But if a solution could be found, it might prove of greater assistance to the cause of Self-Government than a dogmatic insistence on the attempt to develop parliamentary institutions of a normal form.[13]

The old problem of representative government again! The most urgent task was to be the inclusion of the natives in the administrative service[14]; Hailey was no doubt right on this account, for far too little attention had been paid to this question before the war. Here too Hailey established a new policy, which was determined in part by the fact that the question of the future had become more urgent—the emancipation movement was growing and the transitional phases would be shorter than had been thought in 1939.

"What then is to be the final issue of the process, which I can best describe as one of decolonization?"[15] asked Hailey. He was one of the first to use this now current term, stressing that future colonial policy had to be more than mere reform. He said an epoch-making trend was under way. Britain must realize this and act accordingly to prove the validity of its policies. This insight shone through a few inter-war pronouncements but only now was recognized as a real problem.

Hailey was also one of the first to realize that the notion of self-government was by no means as clear as was generally believed and could not always be equated with dominion status. Great Britain had promised the latter to India and Ceylon—we add Burma—but in other cases foreign affairs and defence remained controlled by the mother country even when the colony had obtained self-government, so that it meant only internal autonomy. Hailey warned that one could no longer evade this important question if the concessions hitherto granted were to remain valid.

> In the end, however, we must definitely face the question of whether we do in truth contemplate for the dependencies the final stage to which Self-Government points, namely the attainment by them of the equivalent of Dominion status. There are doubtless some who could regard this as a vision, so distant as to be unsubstantial. But it is the logical outcome of Self-Government. It is the goal to which we have allowed and indeed encouraged the people of the dependencies to look forward. It is an ideal which we could not now abandon without a radical departure from all our past tradition.[16]

This plain statement struck at a critical point of the past declarations. Before 1939, self-government was often spoken of as the goal of British colonial policy, but only seldom—except in the case of India—dominion status. The latter was mentioned only incidentally and even then only as a possibility in the far future. Talk of extending the Commonwealth to include the Asian and African peoples was extremely rare. The notion of self-government remained ambivalent, since according to British principles it could mean only responsible government and therefore dominion status, but this was not "officially" confirmed; people deluded themselves that in some cases self-government could be limited to internal autonomy. Hailey broke through a kind of taboo here and was asking Great Britain to accept the consequences of its proclamations.

Hailey also spoke, however, of an "equivalent of Dominion status". On another occasion he said it was by no means certain whether the Asian and African colonies would join the Commonwealth as new dominions. It was possible, he thought, that they would join together as regional organizations with their own foreign policy and would be only loosely linked with the Commonwealth; this solution could prove a "lesser evil" than the inclusion of members who would endanger the solidarity of the Commonwealth.[17] He did not want to preclude their membership,[18] yet asked himself whether it was possible to create a multi-racial Commonwealth without destroying the Commonwealth itself. He did not make this issue the main goal of British post-war policy however!

When the grant of dominion status seemed to become an actual possibility, a question arose that had scarcely been discussed until then: how to deal with the small and economically weak territories? It seemed senseless to grant dominion status to the West Indian islands or to individual African territories.[19] Federation seemed one solution. It was suggested that viable units could be created by amalgamating individual colonies. Before the war the idea of federation had been debated in East and Central Africa and even in the West Indies, and in 1935 India obtained a federal constitution; but London did not actively try to create larger units until after 1945. Here too Hailey was an innovator.

In Britain, as in the United States, there was much talk between 1942 and 1945 of regional organizations. Coordinating centres had been established for military and economic efforts: an Anglo-American council in Central America; the Middle East Supply Centre; a British high commissioner's office for West Africa. These, it was thought, could serve as models. By proposing regional commissions, Great Britain also hoped to counter America's suggestion of internationalizing all the colonies. By declaring itself prepared to form West Indian or Pacific regional authorities, London was supposedly abandoning any "imperialist" demands and showing that it was concerned only with the economic and social progress of the respective regions. These regional councils, it was said (which, however, had only advisory powers), would be more effective than international administration by the United Nations.[20] The South African Smuts had a secondary objective here. In a much noted article in *Life* on 28 December 1942, he attacked American anti-colonialism and at the same time raised the Union's claim to have a part in determining Britain's East Africa policy.[21] A federation on a regional basis would thus have had close links with the Union of South Africa and could serve as the basis for another white dominion! Other views were put forward as well. The Australian W. K. Hancock, whose *Survey of British Commonwealth Affairs* had an importance akin to that of Lord Hailey's *African Survey*, was perhaps the major expert on imperial political and economic problems. Provoked by American criticism of Great Britain, he published a book strikingly entitled *Argument of Empire* in 1943, which was widely read.[22] In it he contrasted America's lack of understanding with the dominions' voluntary assistance. The dominions, he thought, with their combination of full independence and membership in the British Empire (an association which no foreigner could really understand) could help to overcome the purely nationalist idea of independence; this would be the new path for the future.

Like Hailey, Hancock recalled Alfred Zimmern's image of a procession on the road to self-government; he believed that this image gave an overly optimistic and one-sided view of constitutional questions and needed to be corrected and elaborated. There had been setbacks in Malta and Palestine, while the problem of Kenya, i.e. of the white settlers, was a new one. Only when the native population had obtained the representation due it in the legislative council could the white settlers' bower be extended.[23] Many of the grievances in West Africa were justified: the natives must be given more participation in the administration; London was proceeding too slowly; indirect rule must not oppose the new élite that was pressing for power. Between the wars, Britain had been far too passive and had fed on past gains.[24] If the administration had taken more active economic measures, self-government would have made better progress too. Like Hailey, Hancock added that too little rather than too much had been invested in the colonies; yet private initiative needed controlling and should be supplemented by public enterprise with active co-operation from the mother country.

W. M. Macmillan, author of *Warning from the West Indies*,[25] put forward some rather impulsive critical views. He said that neither the liberals nor the Labour party had managed to formulate a positive policy. The Victorian belief in democracy and laissez-faire was not enough to overcome passivity and stagnation; the "anaemic doctrine of trusteeship" had had some value as a "check on naked power", but it had been practised as a "one-sided relationship" which the colonies were already countering by demanding partnership, the West Indies by dominion status.[26] This criticism of trusteeship coincided entirely with that of Hailey. Macmillan also stressed that self-government required a higher social standard and that this in turn depended on the mother country granting aid to development. "The prime need of the Colonies is a whole series of 'Development Commissions', perhaps on the pattern of the Tennessee Valley Authority." Instead, the Colonial Office had applied the brakes because social difficulties had arisen in the field of mining; it was necessary to supervise investments and to formulate a social policy which accepted an established proletariat. It was essential to promote education far more intensively, both at the elementary and the university level. So far only Hong Kong and Ceylon had their own universities.

Macmillan sharply criticized indirect rule, because in spite of some successes it had to all too often served as an alternative to democratic reforms and had thereby forced the emerging middle classes in Lagos, the Gold Coast and Freetown into opposition. Since local administration was no longer effective, higher authorities were necessary. The representatives of indirect rule "have been shy of the larger problem of representation",[27] and the franchise had not been extended for years. "We want in the first place a clearer formulation of the old creed that Self-Government is the eventual and not too distant goal"[28]; Macmillan saw self-government as a partnership within a "democratic Commonwealth".[29]

In December 1942 the *Round Table* published a programmatic article entitled "Future of the Colonies".[30] This "imperial" publication remarked that the Japanese conquest of Malaya had shown how weakly established British domination was and that it met with little sympathy from the inhabitants. The *Round Table* also considered that the notion of trusteeship was inadequate, arguing that it offered no guide-lines for the active intervention that was urgently necessary.[31] So it tried "to find a basis for this new conception by re-defining our relationship in terms of 'partnership' or 'common citizenship'". In the political sphere, said the *Round Table*, the many official pronouncements had given the impression that responsible government could mean only a parliamentary system and that the colonies therefore had to follow the same path as the dominions; but territories like Malaya lacked the necessary conditions for this and in East Africa the only immediate result had been rule by the white settlers. The main question was whether self-government always meant dominion status and therefore equal status within the Commonwealth.[32] One should determine whether "the substance of Self-Government could not be assured by some other method than that which we now pursuing". The Commonwealth was a unity with definite ideals; "the most suitable type of relationship" must be found between the new and the old "self-governing units". The *Round Table* proposed a special ruling that would leave the hard core of the Commonwealth as it was and affiliate rather than integrate the new Asian and African members. Behind these proposals lay the hope, it would seem, of a compromise reserving certain powers to the mother country. At any rate, the publication that played a decisive role in propagating the idea of the Commonwealth joined Lord Hailey in warning against the possible dangers of a multi-racial Commonwealth.

Other writers rejected this kind of differentiation between old and new dominions. Alfred Zimmern returned to the theses of his 1925 book. After the example of India, which was on the brink of dominion status, he thought that the colonies also should "finally attain equal freedom of Dominion Status".[33] Ernest Barker expressed similar views in *The Ideas and Ideals of the British Empire* in 1941, which we quoted earlier. He thought it likely that in the course of time the Commonwealth would include not just India but also parts of the Dependent Empire.[34] But he demonstrated that he wanted to leave this an open question which he evidently did not yet consider urgent. The same applies to the former colonial minister L. S. Amery, who spoke of an "eventual" inclusion of Africa in the Commonwealth.[35] Such pronouncements could have been termed "liberal" before 1939, but now they seemed outdated, if not reactionary. A pamphlet brought out by young conservatives for which the later minister R. A. Butler wrote the preface, was more in line with the current frame of mind.[36] As good Tories they accepted "imperialism" as the essence of liberal ideals. But they abandoned the traditional belief in their own superiority and agreed that India should obtain "full Dominion Status". The colonies were "hopelessly starved of capital", the 1940 Colonial Development Fund was quite inadequate, neglecting education, among other things. "In due time we may hope to see many Colonies enjoying the rights of full Self-Government, and the benefits of full Dominion Status will become available in the form of Colonial Federation in the West Indies, East Africa and elsewhere." The new generation of conservatives was clearly distinct from the inter-war generation; it adopted Lord Hailey's views and tried to adapt to the new world situation.

These responses indicate the new voices raised in the war-time discussion. Criticism of Britain's passive attitude before 1939 was very strong. Neither the government nor the public had shown sufficient interest in the Empire, it was said, or had proven its desire to undertake reforms.[37] It was suspicious, said Hailey, that Parliament had devoted only a few hours per year to the colonies and their sixty million inhabitants.

> If there is a complaint of the apathy of some of the colonial peoples towards our rule it is nothing compared with the British people towards their own Colonial possessions.[38]

In the future the mother country must increase its activity in the colonies and adopt a new attitude: the colonies must no longer be simply outposts designed to relieve the British economy and to help Britain appear to be a great power; they must be accepted as independent territories whose development must be promoted so that they could later stand on their own feet. Colonial policy, potentially at least, had become an instrument of decolonization! The opinions of the 1930s now took root: the colonies could not develop fast enough on their own to become ripe for self-government. The new policy which had started with the Colonial Development and Welfare Fund had to be greatly extended after the war. The central concept of trusteeship now seemed outdated, passive and paternalistic and was to be replaced by the new notion of "partnership". Similarly, indirect rule was to be replaced by local government adapted to modern requirements.

Great Britain recovered fairly rapidly from the shock imposed by the fall of Singapore. By contrast with the pre-war era, it now definitely prepared for decolonization, knowing that India would obtain home rule soon after the war. Yet Britain still did not feel pressed for time and counted on long delays; it did not set timetables, as the Americans did in their Philippines policy.[39] Moreover, decolonization was to proceed "within the British Empire", although there was some hesitation about accepting Asian and African dominions. This formula may have been vague, but it had considerable significance. The strong emphasis on the unity of Empire and Commonwealth made it possible to interpret self-government as a mere change of status within the Empire rather than as dissociation from it. It was not chance that the word "independence" was deliberately avoided or at most used incidentally.

The politics of the war years had a supra-party character, in spite of Churchill's pre-eminent position. Churchill, who had proved a diehard in the Indian question, saw himself as a kind of legal adviser on British power and greatness; he considered the Empire the backbone of British power and thought that Britain's status as a world power was justified by the Empire. We must recall his vehement protest against American anti-colonialism: "I have not become the King's First Minister in order to preside over the liquidation of the British Empire."[40] He refused to recognize the application of sovereignty proclaimed by the Atlantic Charter to members of the Empire.[41] London alone was entitled to determine their future, and not some international organization. However, Churchill had to make some concessions and to promise India dominion status, although he had sternly refused this before. His reluctance had to give way to the pressure of the military situation in South-East Asia, the severe conflicts in India and the insistence of the Colonial Cabinet. In any case, Churchill was not an "imperialist" in the sense that Milner was one; he was a proud and nationalistic Englishman who regarded the Empire question from the point of view of its advantages to the mother country and took little interest in the economic or political problems of the individual colonies. He initiated few reforms in the postwar years and consented to them only if they did not endanger imperial positions.

We do not know how the Cabinet reacted to Churchill's provocative words. We have seen earlier that liberals and reformers also rejected the American demands, which they considered unjustified, and at the same time regarded them as a "challenge".[42] No one in London wanted to "liquidate" the Empire or to transfer control to the United States or to an international authority. On the other hand, the Labour party protested Churchill's interpretation of the Atlantic Charter[43] and followed Roosevelt. The liberal *Economist* also objected to the attitude "to hold our own" and wanted to see Churchill's statement supplemented by evidence of the desire to reform. The *Economist* stressed the need "to recognize and carry out the responsibilities of Empire more largely, more boldly, and more quickly than in the past". New goals were not necessary, but words must be followed by deeds. In the past, Parliament had shown lack of interest, the Treasury had been small, racial prejudice had been accepted and the poverty, undernourishment even, in India, Africa and the West Indies have stirred no popular indignation. . . . If the war does awaken a wide sense of Imperial responsibility among the British people it will have done a great good.[44]

A month later Lord Bledisloe, chairman of the 1938–1939 East Africa commission, confirmed: "It must be admitted that there was very little vitality and constructive progress in our present colonial policy." The liberal Lord Samuel proposed a "standing joint select committee on colonial affairs" because Parliament was not showing enough interest in the colonies.[45]

The government in its declarations tried to live up to the desire for reform evinced by the political writers, but without committing itself in any way. Its first statement came surprisingly late, on 24 June 1942 in a speech by Under-secretary of State Harold Macmillan to the House of Commons. Macmillan found that there had been no debate on colonial issues since June 1939, and ironically described the earlier debates which had, at best, included reports and discussions on a few schools and railways. Now, however, after the loss of most of the colonies, production both for export and for home consumption was being fostered in the remaining territories "on an immense scale" and industrialization was being promoted. He said the Empire must adapt itself, the theory that colonies dropped from trees like ripe fruit was not apt:

> The war has shown us certain inescapable facts, of which we will learn the lesson Self-Government without security means nothing. Independence without defence is vain. The future of the world is in larger organizations and not in breaking up into a large number of small countries. It is in the light of these events that we should think of our future relationship with the Colonies as a permanent and not a transitory thing. The governing principle of the Colonial Empire should, therefore, be the principle of partnership between the various elements composing it. Out of partnership come understanding and friendship. Within the fabric of the Commonwealth lies the future of the Colonial territories. According to different needs and different conditions there will be the greatest divergence of local responsibility, but, however far these may be developed, there were broad Imperial problems which only admit of corporate resolution. Trade, currency, and monetary questions, defense, transport by sea, land and air—all these are Imperial questions. Capital development itself, on which the future of the territories depends, must be thought of as a whole.[46]

This declaration was, of course, aimed at the United States. Macmillan also quoted Churchill's statement and commented on it: "We are not liquidators. We are going on with the job." He said the future of the colonies lay within the fabric of the Commonwealth and not, as the Americans postulated, in granting them independence. The argument that colonial development required the formation of larger units was popular during the Second World War. His reference to the security which he asserted the Commonwealth alone could provide, is not very convincing since, very recently, Britain had been able to save neither Malaya and Borneo nor Burma from Japanese conquest! But the government did want to show its readiness to reform and therefore officially introduced the notion of partnership. To a question by a Labour M.P., Macmillan replied that at first this would be a relationship between a senior and a junior partner, adding: "I never used—I carefully avoid using —the word Trusteeship at any point in my speech."[47] This meant that he was paying attention to Lord Hailey's criticism in the House of Lords! He also accepted the economic demands: "We need large-scale public investment on public needs."[48] But for the most part the declaration remained rather vague. The notion of partnership is unclear and dominion status was never mentioned—no doubt on purpose; "the greatest divergence of local responsibility" could at best mean internal autonomy, but presumably not parliamentary responsibility. The government thought this would be a way of combining reforms and imperial tradition, on the assumption that the colonies would accept such a partnership and be content with it.

Viscount Cranborne went a step further in a declaration on 3 December 1942:

> ... I said the other day in this House that the British Empire is not static but dynamic. That I believe to be profoundly true. The process of development which I have tried to describe has no fixed limits. It is a continuing process. There is no so far and no further in our policy. We have seen how the old Colonies in Canada, Australia, New Zealand and South Africa have grown into great self-governing nations, on an absolute equality with Great Britain and responsible for their own affairs, but linked to her by the enduring bond of loyalty to the Crown. . . . I see the territories of the Colonial Empire moving along the same road, not perhaps in their present isolation but more closely associated in wider groups, playing an ever growing part in the British Commonwealth of free nations. That is a noble conception which will, I hope and believe, in the fullness of time be realized. . . . But this can be said—and I would repeat it—all the British Colonies at the present time are moving in the right direction. In some cases progress is rapid; in some it is inevitably slow, and to attempt to go too fast would upset existing institutions before the population was ready for others. Of one thing I am sure—the British Colonial Empire is not coming to an end. The work that we have to do is only beginning. We, the citizens of the British Empire, whatever our race, religion, or colour, have a mission to perform, and it is a mission that is essential to the welfare of the world. It is to ensure the survival of the way of life for which the United Nations are fighting, a way of life based on freedom, tolerance, justice and mutual understanding, in harmony with the principles of the Atlantic Charter. In that great mission we must not, and we shall not, fail.[49]

This was the first time, as far as one can tell, that the British Government "officially" declared that dominion status was the aim of its colonial policy, by equating the colonies with the existing members of the Commonwealth. However, it still did not use the actual term "dominion status", in fact it carefully and deliberately avoided it. This was presumably because, although it was in the middle of the war, London did not want to commit itself definitively, nor did it want to give the nationalists an opportunity to call on a definite statement of the government's views. Moreover, this aim was still set in the distant future. Probably the government still hoped it would not have to take the final step and would be able to continue speaking of moving "along the road", i.e. it hoped that internal autonomy would be enough. There was an obvious reluctance to comply with Lord Hailey's demands for a clear definition of what was meant by self-government. Macmillan's statement also showed the tendency, resulting from American criticism, to interpret decolonization as a new imperial mission, in order to justify the Empire once again.[50] It is easy to attack this hypocrisy and the assertions that the maintenance of colonial rule was a service to mankind and a fight for freedom. But one can also argue that decolonization could proceed more smoothly and would provoke less social and psychological reaction if it was not interpreted from the start as an attitude of surrender (which it necessarily appeared to be in the French conception of *"la plus grande France"*, but presented as a mission. The concessions forced on the government by circumstances in the following years could thus be presented as the performance of this mission and as keeping the promise of granting freedom.

The last war-time declaration was issued by Colonel Stanley on 13 July 1943:

> The central purpose of our colonial administration has often been proclaimed. It has been called the doctrine of trusteeship, although I think some of us feel now that the word "trusteeship" is rather too static in its connotation and that we should prefer to combine with the status of trustee the position also of partner.[51] But we are pledged to guide colonial people along the road to self-government within the framework of the British Empire. We are pledged to build up their social and economic institutions, and we are pledged to develop their natural resources. It is no part of our policy . . . to grant self-government to those who are not yet trained in its use, but . . . it is up to us to see that circumstances as soon as possible justify political advances and to ensure that as quickly as possible people are trained and equipped for eventual Self-Government. Therefore the real test of sincerity and success of our Colonial policy is twofold: It is not only the actual political advances that we make, but it is also, and I think more important, the steps that we are taking, economic and social as well as political, to prepare the people for further and future responsibilities.[52]

At another point in his speech Stanley also spoke of seeing

> the various peoples of the various territories develop themselves along the lines of their own national aptitude, their own culture, and their own tradition.[53]

This much quoted statement was nothing new. It merely recapitulated what Stanley's predecessors had said and what the political writers had put forward as a demand for the post-war era: namely, replacing the concept of trusteeship by that of partnership[54]; the need for economic and social aid in order to create the preconditions for self-government; dissociation from the American attitude and acknowledgement of the future task of the Empire[55] (so the aim was not independence but self-government within the Empire, without open commitment to dominion status[56]); willingness to undertake reforms—in the political sphere too— and acceptance of decolonization, although with a paternalistic undertone. It is worth noting how the notions of the time factor had changed in comparison with 1938: at that time the colonial minister stressed that decolonization would be a slow process, extending over generations (cf. p. 85); now, in 1943, the process was to be speeded up and to proceed "as quickly as possible"! Britain even felt obliged to create the preconditions, i.e. to take concrete reform measures in order to prepare for the transition from colonial rule to self-government.

The government did not stop at simple statements. During the war it actually tried to provide evidence of the reform policy it had announced.[57] Since we have dealt with certain territories separately, a few examples will suffice here. The West Indian crisis had provoked a discussion during the late 1930s which was followed by very active reform efforts. These efforts were chiefly directed at breaking through the economic, social and political stagnation and liberating the territories' indigenous energies by means of outside aid. The proposals of the 1938 West India Royal Commission served as the point of departure.[58] An annual credit of one million pounds was granted and Sir Frank Stockdale and his colleagues were entrusted with economic planning, improving agricultural and mining methods and developing the health service, housing and the educational system. Special attention was paid to social legislation and setting up labour departments, and the union movement was strongly encouraged. The unions, which had remained weak until the disturbances in the 1930s, developed rapidly and became the basis of new parties; in Jamaica, for instance, their membership rose from 1089 in 1938 to 57,000 in 1947.[59] The democratization of the legislative council was designed to make it less oligarchic and to pave the way to self-government. In 1944 Jamaica obtained general franchise and semi-responsible government of the lines of the 1931 Ceylon constitution (i.e. a committee system whose chairmen became ministers and took over executive responsibility); three British ex officio officials remained in office, but they were in the minority. In the 1944 elections Bustamente, supported by the sugar industry workers, came to power. Reforms followed in Trinidad, Barbados and British Guiana. Dominion status, however, was to be granted not to the individual colonies but to a West Indian federation, which finally came into being in 1958 after protracted negotiations, but broke up again in 1962.[60] London was not able to prevent "Balkanization" of the West Indies.

In Asia, the discussion naturally centred on India, since the Japanese-occupied Malaya and Burma did not seem particularly topical at first. In 1943, however, London promised Ceylon "full responsible government" and asked the Ceylonese ministers to submit their own proposals. Britain had realized that not only India, but Burma and Ceylon too would have to be granted dominion status after the war, although there was still hope of postponing this by a fairly long transitionary period.

In Africa reforms concentrated at first on the local administration; on the Gold Coast, for instance, a number of town councils obtained African majorities. In addition, in September 1942 the colonial minister issued a directive stating that a greater number of Africans should be included in the higher administrative service. For the first two Ghanaians—one of whom was Busia, the well-known sociologist who later led the Ashanti opposition against Nkrumah—were appointed assistant district commissioners; two Ghanaians were admitted into the executive council for the first time. Constitutional changes were prepared for the Gold Coast and Nigeria; labour departments were also set up in Africa and the coalition government, presumably under pressure from the Labour party, sent British trade-unionists to help develop the African organizations. Britain prepared incisive reforms in the educational system[61] where it was obvious from the start that the lower grades would have to be considerably improved and that the mother country would have to grant substantial financial assistance. Secondary education was to be organized for the first time. In 1945 a commission under Judge Asquith published a report on the question of higher education in the colonies which, in the following years, provided the guide-lines for the actions undertaken; at times it was even used in the independent states. A special commission under Elliot studied African universities and proposed founding a number of African high schools.[62] Temporary association with London University was to facilitate their development and ensure an educational standard. With remarkable consistency, the report stressed that the development of universities was inevitable if British policy aimed at self-government. Local high schools were given precedence as being the "focus of the intellectual self-expression of the people". Here again the difference from French concepts becomes clear. Decolonization was not to lead to integration and assimilation but to self-government, i.e. the colonies should become nations on the basis of their own culture and traditions.

The policy that was initiated with the Colonial Development and

Welfare Act of 1940 did not come to fruition during the war because British industry had to adjust itself to war production and shipping space was scarce. The credits granted in 1940 were not all spent. But a dispatch in June 1941 shows how the Colonial Office tried to harmonize the mother country's war requirements with the interests of the colonies.[63] The colonial administrations were asked to limit importation of vital goods as far as possible by restrictions or higher duties. But these measures, above all the higher duties, were aimed at the well-to-do classes, not least the Europeans, and not at the native population. In fact, everything possible was to be done to raise the natives' shockingly low standard of living— even during the war—in spite of these necessary restrictions. Firms that needed few or no imported goods were to be energetically promoted. The administration was to plan and train African personnel; London would try to make the necessary educational facilities available. Also worth noting is the instruction that budget surpluses should not be remitted to London. The ministry preferred that these resources be retained so that they could be used for reconstruction and development as soon as the war ended. And in fact, during the war most of the colonies managed to collect quite substantial reserves with which they could finance rapid development after 1945 and which could even help them towards independence.

London was not merely content with the creation of reserves. It was even prepared to offer a considerably larger credit than what it had supplied in 1940. In February 1945 Parliament set up a new Colonial Development and Welfare Fund of £120 million, distributed over ten years; of this, £23 million were reserved for research and higher education.[64] By these measures the government consented to the proposals of the political writers.

So even during the war the British Government took a number of precautions to help the Dependent Empire economically, socially and even politically on the road to self-government. Some of the measures may seem modest and even heavy-handed today, particularly the Africanization of the administration. Doubtless Britain had realized that in the postwar years it would have to be prepared for certain radical demands from the emancipation movements which had grown very strong during the war. Yet Britain still underestimated the strength of these movements and did not believe that they might one day exert pressure, or that time was growing short. Evidently the promises made so far had to be put into practice and extended if they were to be continued to be believed; yet Britain still hesitated to include the term "dominion status" or even "independence" in its official proclamations. And however much the politicians and publicists pointed out the importance of the Empire for Great Britain, the average voter still took little interest in colonial questions. At any rate neither the Conservative nor the Labour candidates deemed it necessary to make detailed reference to imperial issues in the electoral campaigns.⁶⁵ Yet the basis had been created for a post-war policy that was very different from the passivity of previous years, and the Labour party was able to pursue it directly. It was to become clear, however, that London was very mistaken in assuming that there was still ample time for reforms and that the promises of self-government would not have to be honoured until the distant future. The programmes by which Great Britain gave its consent to decolonization proved valid, but not so the dates and time lapses that were counted on. Yet London proved sufficiently adaptable to deal with this changed situation too. It altered the dates it had fixed and curtailed the time lapses in order to conclude the transition to a multi-racial Commonwealth without bloody conflicts.

THE LABOUR PARTY DURING AND AFTER THE SECOND WORLD WAR

"What is the long-term policy?" asked Captain Macdonald during the debate on the colonies on 24 June 1942.[1]

> For many years I have been trying to find out the long-term policy of the Colonial Office, but so far without success. . . . We want a new conception of Empire. . . . The end of this war leads to demands from the Colonial Empire, or from some parts of it, for greater responsibility and a greater voice in their own affairs.

Arthur Creech-Jones, the Labour party speaker and future colonial minister, added:

> Imperialism of the old order passed, toughest perhaps in its economic grips. . . . The challenge of Russia, the renaissance of China, the demand for independence by India, are all symptomatic of the ferment that is going on in the minds of men the world over. We cannot estimate the effects of the dynamics of new political ideas, economic doctrines and social creeds on the Colonial peoples to-day. . . . Even trusteeship must be transformed into a positive principle of cooperation of equals in the forward march of men . . . the word is certainly beginning to wear, perhaps because, besides achievement, it has been associated with a certain amount of cant and failure to fulfil the hopes of the Colonial peoples. Nor has this word "trusteeship" the same meaning everywhere. It is irritating in some places and it is unpopular in others. Lord Hailey has admirably expressed[2] what

some of us have been saying for a long time on this matter. Indeed some of us want a new relationship with the Colonial peoples which conveys the idea of equality and fellowship, the idea of service and practical assistance and which expresses it in dynamic and constructive terms. . . . We must formulate a positive policy in place of a weak negative one.[3]

We have shown how the government tried to accede to opposition demands. Harold Macmillan was aware of the critical objections to trusteeship, but in his answer to the reformers he did not make any concrete statements nor say anything really new. Now we may ask whether the Labour party actually managed to formulate a suitable "long-term policy" and whether it implemented this policy when it came into office after the war.

Once again the Fabian Society did the preparatory work. On the recommendation of Rita Hinden, a Fabian Colonial Bureau was formed in October 1940 to deal with practical colonial problems and to establish the guide-lines of post-war Labour policy. Its first members included Leonard Woolf, W. M. Macmillan, Margery Perham and Julian Huxley; Arthur Creech-Jones was chairman and Rita Hinden secretary.[4] In the Fabian tradition, the discussion was led and the proposals were presented by experts and reformers and not by party functionaries or even socialist theoreticians.[5] Memoranda and pamphlets issued by the Bureau were intended not only to formulate a Labour party programme but also to assist the parliamentarians, to prepare material for questions in the House of Commons and to promote more interest in imperial problems among the members of Parliament and the parties. The Fabian Society also acted as a kind of pressure group within the Labour party. The Colonial Bureau established contacts with colonial emancipation movements; in addition it tried to make contact with African students in London and formed a Nigerian Committee as early as 1941. The Fabians' concern was focussed primarily on Africa, and their first report was Rita Hinden's *Plan for Africa*.

At first, the colonial question remained peripheral to Labour party discussions. The 1942 report, *The Old World and the New Society*, for which Harold Laski was responsible, merely reiterated old theories and demands without clearly formulating any political aims. During the party conference the M.P. guest requested that the Labour party issue a charter of freedom for the colonial peoples which would, among other things, abolish the status of colony and set up a council of colonial peoples made up of representatives from the dependent areas.[6] A resolution to this effect was eventually accepted during the next year's conference,[7] but it was not taken very seriously by the party executive. The pamphlet *The Colonies*[8] and the more important *Fabian Colonial Essays* published in 1945 concentrated on practical issues and offered no new ideas.

The Fabians pointed out that while the British public was on the whole indifferent to the problems of the colonies, the general attitude was liberal and there was a desire for reform. Still, the few discussions in Parliament usually took place before empty benches. Even the Labour party was pretty indifferent.[9] One heard fewer partisan statements from either side: the Conservatives spoke less frequently of "some providential sacred trust", while the Labour party restricted itself to "uncritical denunciation about the inequities of imperialism".[10] Once again the Labour party dissociated itself from doctrinaire anti-colonialism.

Labour was now inclined to stress the new situation in world politics and the growth, since the war, of emancipation movements. "A world emerges in which areas hitherto treated as 'non-adult' must share in the general life of mankind."[11] They spoke of the dangers inherent in ignoring nationalist sentiments and the increasing feeling of frustration becoming apparent among the emerging nationalist élite,[12] and stressed the dangers of racial discrimination. The party said it would take care to involve representatives of the nationalist opposition in future planning and work out reforms in collaboration with them. "Let them feel that it is a war of liberation, the travail of the world for a new order."[13]

The Atlantic Charter and American anti-colonialism gave new impetus to Labour's demand to internationalize the colonial question. Naturally, the party did not agree with Churchill's views.[14] By contrast with the Conservatives, the Labour party welcomed an extension of the League of Nations mandate system and accepted a resolution to this effect at the 1943 party conference.[15] However, its hopes were dashed in 1953 when former colonial minister Creech-Jones sharply criticized the U.N. Trusteeship Council.[16] In addition to internationalization, the party also suggested proclaiming a specifically British colonial charter to supplement the Atlantic Charter in order to convince world opinion and the colonial peoples of the sincerity of Britain's intention to decolonize and to set down finally the policy that was to be pursued.[17] The Liberal party supported the proposal and Lord Hailey approved it, at least in part.[18] Such a declaration would no doubt have had considerable effect, but critics rightly pointed out that the general outline of the charter had already been included in government statements and that fuller details or even a definite timetable could not be given because of the great differences among the colonies.

India and Ceylon, which, along with Malta, had been considered ready for self-government in 1939, were now joined by Burma and the West Indies and, particularly, Jamaica; in these cases the Labour party defined self-government as dominion status. There were isolated demands that Britain return Hong Kong to China and Cyprus to Greece.[19] In Asia the granting of dominion status seemed to have solved many problems and interest in the area decreased greatly. In India the Labour party, based on Cripps' proposals, demanded new negotiations. In Africa, it said, there would have to be rather long transitional stages[20] and it was Britain's duty to see them through.[21]

Naturally the Labour party joined in the criticism of Indirect Rule, which it interpreted as anti-democratic in its methods. Woolf said it was

> a powerful instrument of policy for those who hold that the African is incapable of democratic Self-Government of the western type.[22]

He said it had prevented the rise of élites capable of government, and had artificially dissociated the native authorities from the central government instead of building up a democratic form of self-government from below. Modern local government was just as necessary as a more rapid transition in the legislative council from appointed and official members to elected members.[23] The Labour government was to follow these principles in 1945.

The Labour party was particularly concerned with the multi-racial colonies—Malaya and Guiana as well as Kenya. It said that both the homogeneity of the people and sympathy with the minorities must be consciously promoted; separate electoral bodies were no solution, even reserved seats in Parliament would be preferable. The Fabian Society sharply criticized the settlers in Kenya and demanded the inclusion of Africans in the legislative and executive councils, transition to the common roll and the abolishment of the highland reservation.[24] The Labour party endorsed the concept of partnership, asserting that democratization would lead to an increasingly greater balance in favour of the Africans; by force of necessity, the party aimed its policies at the African majority, but avoided saying so openly! Its colonial experts knew that Kenya and Rhodesia would be the "test-cases" of British post-war policy, but did not consider it necessary as yet to come to any final decisions; even in 1950 colonial minister Creech-Jones said: "As yet the issues of majority rule or ultimate independence are almost irrelevant."[25]

There was, of course, detailed discussion of economic and social questions as well as renewed attacks on the land policy of the settlers in East Africa and on the enormous profits made by certain mining concerns. Nationalization was considered inevitable; the development of unions and co-operative societies and a rapid extension of the educational system were absolutely necessary, in addition to better planning in all areas. For this, the colonies would require direct financial assistance from the mother country; the 1940 Colonial Development Act would have to be extended. The party's attitude on this question had changed noticeably. It did not even place restrictions on local industry and in the following years it was Conservative parliamentarians rather than Labour who were to warn against industrializing too quickly. This change of position can be explained in part by the disappearance of unemployment in Britain during and after the war.

The Labour party strongly supported the Commonwealth and countered American criticism as vehemently as the Conservatives. In 1943 Herbert Morrison, a minister in the War Cabinet, took a very pointed stand, asserting that the Commonwealth was not just a British concern but served as a stabilizing factor throughout the world.[26]

> The growth of that association is a model for a world long afflicted by problems arising from the unequal development of different lands and peoples.

Each dominion had begun as a dependency and had then moved on to full freedom. Dominion status meant that decolonization had been achieved; "freedom and independence" were a reality and the United States must finally realize this! Addressing himself to America, the socialist Morrison even judged past British colonial policy in a surprisingly positive way:

> On the whole, and with some exceptions, I would credit us with a human, decent, fair-minded attitude towards the less advanced peoples in our charge.

The earlier idea of an autarchic Empire had proved itself an illusion, he said, and, taking the long view, the British system certainly pursued the interests of the international family of man.

The Labour party certainly could not boast of originality in its conception of decolonization, and few new ideas came to light in later years.[27] Doctrinaire theories were less in evidence than in the pre-war years, but there was increasing interest in the practical problems of the individual colonies. During and after the First World War the representatives of proconsular imperialism were clearly set apart from certain socialists with their Marxist-based anti-colonialism; but in the Second World War the positions began to come closer. The difference between Conservatives and Labourites lay less in specific theories and demands than in the divergence of "attitude". Still, these different attitudes led to similar conclusions. While the Conservatives more or less reluctantly agreed to concessions and reforms, the Labour party found itself forced to give up its theoretical positions and to accept gradual decolonization. Labour wanted to demonstrate its eagerness to reform, but it too had underestimated the strength of the emancipation movements and had reckoned with longer transitionary stages than were really possible.

In the final chapter of her book *Empire and After*, published in 1949, Rita Hinden described the dilemma facing the reformers and the Labour party. Even with the best intentions self-government could not be granted at once, she said, because the foundation was still too weak, and because the minorities still had to be protected and national unities to be maintained; and on the other hand, the opposition was pressing its claims and refusing to co-operate. Rita Hinden rejected the determination of fixed time-limits, although her arguments were not very convincing.[28] In the Philippines this policy had proved rather successful and it was obviously worth debating whether it could not prove useful in Africa as well, in that it would calm the suspicions of the nationalist opposition and induce the administration to hasten the inclusion of Africans into its ranks. Rita Hinden proposed mixed councils so the next reforms and constitutional changes could be negotiated in collaboration with African representatives. Around 1948 the Labour government took this step—first in West Africa, later in East Africa.

When the Labour party came into office in 1945 it took an active interest in colonial affairs. The Colonial Office increased its personnel and greatly expanded its technical and economic departments. It promoted education, and students from the colonies were given grants to study in Britain; it also stepped up its social policy and supported the trade-union movement. A conference of African representatives of colonial legislative councils held in September 1948 is evidence of the desire to collaborate; the conference aimed at establishing personal contacts and informing the administration of practical colonial problems. The focal point of the discussion was reform in local government (cf. pp. 215–16). As a result of the conference, a large number of colonial constitutions were revised, and in the years to come the party could point to the reforms it had initiated.[29] Still, it is clear that any decisive steps were not taken on the party's own initiative nor according to a "plan"; rather they were an answer to nationalist demands and a means of avoiding open conflict. This was very apparent in the case of Burma. Here, the Labour government had no ideas of its own and took over the coalition government's White Paper. It was Lord Mountbatten who finally persuaded the prime minister, Attlee, to take action. Similarly, on the Gold Coast, the Labour government enforced the constitution prepared in 1944 and tried to promote local government.[30] But it did not grant responsible government until the disturbances in 1948. In areas where emancipation movements were still weak and unable to pressure the administration, the Labour government's reforms remained modest. In Kenya, for example, Governor Sir Philip Mitchell, a former colleague of Donald Cameron's, managed after difficult negotiations to open a new legislative council in which the unofficial majority of the "coloureds" gave a parity to the Europeans (four appointed Africans represented the natives); but the attempt to bring the racial communities together in this way failed because the whites, with some exceptions, opposed it while Mau Mau terrorism began to take effect on the African side.[31]

There were also some serious miscalculations, such as the deposing of chief Seretse Khama of Bechuanaland in 1950, quite apart from the preparations for a Rhodesian federation. In spite of some worth-while attempts, there was a distinct dichotomy between Labour's pronouncements while it was in opposition and its cautious actions when it came into office! The Conservatives, above all the diehards, accused the Labour government of liquidating the Empire; at the same time the left wing urged more rapid decolonization. Creech-Jones was reproached with the fact that there was small difference between the policies of the Labour government and those of the coalition government during the war.[32] When Herbert Morrison declared early in 1946 that "we are great friends of the jolly old Empire and are going to stick to it", the Fabian Colonial Bureau objected to these "tactless" words.[33] The journal *Empire* published by the Bureau in the summer of 1946 defended the government and did not dispute the Colonial Office's desire for reform. It pointed to no new paths, however, merely stating that the Labour government should declare that all peoples had a right to self-determination and that it should call a constituent assembly.[34] Harold Laski, by contrast, praised Creech-Jones and pointed out to the Americans in 1947 that no African colony was as yet ready for self-government.[35] In the 1950s the left-wing Labour M.P. Fenner Brockway formed the Movement for Colonial Freedom. Many of the unions and local party organizations belonged to it, as well as about a hundred parliamentarians, and it introduced numerous questions in the House of Commons and even organized protest demonstrations.[36] The Communists, predictably, spoke of the Labour party's "colonial imperialism".[37]

The Labour government certainly did not force the process of decolonization. It had no definite plan, nor did it force the transition to a multi-racial Commonwealth against internal British resistance. Instead, its historical importance lies in the fact that it was prepared to accept the colonial emancipation movements and often tried to establish a new basis of trust with the nationalist opposition. At the critical moment it did not hesitate to make important decisions, as in India, Burma and West Africa. It is doubtful whether a Conservative government under Winston Churchill would have been able to avoid bloody conflicts. In the extremely tense situation in India and Burma, and in the Gold Coast and Nigeria after 1948, real unrest would have made "police action" necessary and this could easily have led to further intervention and have prevented a timely withdrawal for reasons of prestige.

In 1951 the Conservative government could not go back on the decisions that had already been made and therefore had to continue along the lines of Labour policy. Although the Conservatives might still have been willing to resist the trend towards dissociation in Asia in 1945–1947, in 1951 they were no longer prepared for military intervention in West Africa. But East Africa was not yet a "topical" area. The diehards did not have an opportunity until the late 1950s to exert their not inconsiderable influence against "over-hasty" decolonization in East Africa. Until then, the world situation and the new problems of a multi-racial

Commonwealth made themselves felt to such an extent that Prime Minister Macmillan was forced to adapt himself to the "wind of change" and to speed up withdrawal from East Africa.

We must mention here briefly the Labour government's economic policy. During the war people became generally aware of the pressing tasks facing Great Britain in the colonies and realized that they could not be accomplished without direct credits from the mother country. The coalition government had already approved an extended Colonial Development and Welfare Fund. Plans for colonial development had been prepared during the war and in 1948 the Colonial Office had consented to seventeen ten-year programmes for the colonies at a probable cost of £180 million; of this, £59 million were to come from the British budget, the rest from loans and the colonies' own resources. Eighty-two million pounds were set aside for developing the social services.[38] At the end of the war, numerous restrictions were suspended and the road seemed clear for the policy of development announced long before.

New and unexpected difficulties arose, however. Britain itself needed time for economic recovery, so there was little money for investment overseas. But even more important, Great Britain was extremely short of dollars, and of raw materials and certain foods. Since it seemed either impossible or impractical to buy the latter from dollar-bloc countries, it was obviously desirable to forcibly increase agriculture and mining within the Empire, i.e. in the sterling zone. Under the Labour government's austerity policy the colonies were turned into "dollar earners" and their production had to be increased as rapidly as possible to overcome the crisis at home. Even Sir Stafford Cripps, who was formerly left-wing and very anti-imperialist, stressed the urgency of developing African resources. At a governors' conference in November 1947 he said:

> The whole future of the sterling group and its ability to survive depends in my view upon a quick and extensive development of our African resources.[39]

British interest in the colonies was concentrated to a striking degree on the colonies' contribution to overcoming the "dollar shortage".[40] The foreign minister Ernest Bevin bluntly declared:

> I am not prepared to sacrifice the British Empire, because I know that if the British Empire fell . . . it would mean that the standard of life of our constituents [!] would fall considerably.[41]

Bevin, a former trade-union leader, was thus adopting Joseph Chamberlain's arguments: without the Empire the standard of living of the British masses would decline! It is not surprising that the conservative press also called for "dollars from Africa",[42] but until then the Labour party had considered this particular call for exploitation of colonial resources in the interests of the mother country as the essence of imperialist capitalist economic policy. "This world's need became the colonial Empire's opportunity"[43] was not an inaccurate formula in itself, however; it applied to the war-time and post-war situation in so far as relatively high prices were being paid and the mother country had declared itself willing to invest large sums in the colonies of its own initiative. But this formula presupposed a complementary relationship between home and colonial needs which certainly did not exist in such a simplified form.[44] This so-called common interest was part of the "imperialist" argument; the reformers and socialists in particular rejected it because it required a one-sided concentration on export production and would result in the colonies being dependent on overseas suppliers for many vital goods. How, they asked, could the economic and social self-sufficiency of the different colonies—the precondition for self-government—which had been promised so often, be achieved if their economic development was based on the dollar balance and the needs of the mother country?

The much cited, so-called groundnut scheme in Tanganyika provides an example. In order to overcome the acute scarcity of fat in Great Britain, the United Africa Company, a branch of Unilever, had produced a large-scale plan: more than two million hectares of land in the Tanganyikan hinterland was to be cleared, freed of tsetse fly, irrigated and protected against soil erosion in order to allow for the extensive cultivation, with the help of machines, of groundnuts. This project was submitted to the state[45] and approved and in 1947 parliamentary resolution created the Overseas Food Corporation, which was to be financed and controlled by the state, in order to put the plan into practice and prepare further enterprises.[46] Immense sums were invested, but the difficulties were much greater than expected and the project failed. In any case, the shortage of fat passed by itself. But even if it had been successful, the project would have benefited the mother country principally. This kind of concentrated investment would also have been in open contradiction to declared Labour party principles. Naturally, the failure of the groundnuts scheme served the Conservatives as proof of the failure of state enterprise.

It would be wrong, however, to judge the Labour party's policy of development and investment according to the groundnut project alone. Although home needs easily took precedence in the critical post-war years, the credits of the Colonial Development and Welfare Fund were used for a variety of projects and gave the colonial economy useful impetus. A substantial portion of the fund was used for "welfare", particularly education. In the February 1945 parliamentary debate Creech-Jones, in sharp reply to American criticism, presented the new plan as an instrument whereby Britain was consciously liquidating the Empire, since it was giving the colonies the opportunity to stand on their own feet.[47] This sounded rather much like self-praise, but to a certain extent it was true. The credits from the mother country's budget, which began rather modestly in 1929, were increased in 1940 and reached a considerable figure after 1945; they certainly paved the way to independence for the colonies and led to a more rapid decolonization.

INDIA ON THE ROAD TO INDEPENDENCE, 1939–1947

The Second World War, like the first, gave great impetus to the decolonization of India, although the change in policy which this entailed was less radical than in Indochina and the Dutch Indies. The 1935 India Act mapped out the road that would eventually lead to dominion status. The combination of Indian administration in the provinces and British administration in the centre led to difficulties which could have ended in new disturbances, arrests, agitation and negotiations, without bringing about a rapid end of the British raj. The war created a new situation. Great Britain did not entirely forefeit its colonial power, as France and the Netherlands had done, nor was India occupied, as Singapore and Burma were, by Japan. But Europe's precarious position and Japan's frightening advance enabled Indian nationalists to press their claims for independence and forced London to make new concessions. British promises during the war did not satisfy the Indians, yet they went further than earlier concessions and had to be observed when the war was over.

The British discussion on India during and immediately after the war is similar to that around 1930. The question of "timing" was still being debated, and the communal question, i.e. the increasingly embittered conflict between the Congress party and the Muslim League, became the focus of the discussion both in India and in England.

Soon after Britain declared war on Germany, on 3 September 1939, Viceroy Linlithgow declared that India was in a state of war. Since India was not yet a full dominion, the king of England's declaration of war automatically applied to India too. The arrogance of the British rulers and their rather "dusty" conviction that the "good people of India" were loyally behind the mother country in its fight for freedom, took precedence over what would have been the more tactful proposal of first consulting with important Indians such as Gandhi and Nehru, and making some attempt to organize a common front "against fascism". In fact the Congress was highly critical of Germany's policy of aggression and certainly did not intend to ruthlessly exploit the mother country's distress; but the viceroy's attitude gave it cause for protesting Britain's actions and making counter-demands. The Congress said that India could take active part in the war only as a fully recognized partner. London must, therefore, immediately proclaim India's independence and replace the viceroy's executive council by a national Indian government responsible to an Indian parliament. The army, however, could remain under British command.[1]

London was not prepared to agree. Both the Conservatives, who dominated the coalition government, and even the Labour party thought it inexpedient to surrender their rule; they did not trust the Indians with actively co-operating in the British war effort and were convinced that control over the Indian army also implied direct control over the administration. So the rather vague and and inconclusive statement issued by the viceroy on 18 October 1939 merely said that the aim of British policy was "that India may attain its due place among our Dominions". After the war, the government would be prepared to discuss constitutional changes "in the hope of contributing to the ordered and harmonious progress of India towards her goal"; the minority groups would receive special attention.[2] The viceroy agreed that the 1935 India Act needed to be revised and promised a kind of round-table, but carefully refrained from stating that the aim of these negotiations was dominion status. There was no mention of a constitutional assembly such as the Indians demanded. But in the following months London went a step further and defined dominion status for India in such a way, using the term "full dominion status", that India was officially equated with the other members of the Commonwealth.[3] A new declaration on 8 August 1940 went further than the one of October 1939 and made the concrete proposal that Indian representatives should join the executive council to form an advisory war council. After the war, the new constitution "should be primarily the responsibility of the Indians themselves" and not, as hitherto, more or less imposed from above. But there could be no question of a transfer of power unless this constitution was supported by the large communities, i.e. the Hindus and Muslims or the Congress party and the Muslim League.[4]

This was the position the British Government took between 1939 and 1941. At this stage it refused to issue any declarations on the independence of India or its sovereign rights and did not want to discuss constitutional changes until after the war or to fix any definite time limits. London replied to Indian demands by saying that the Indians must make their own suggestions and that it was primarily their own business to work out their constitution. The Indians had to agree among themselves before London could hand over its powers to them.[5] This was a "sensible" attitude and it seemed like an acknowledgement of India's sovereignty.

It was, of course, to Britain's advantage, since it transferred the solution of major difficulties to India without Britain losing its own say. Moreover, London was well aware of the tensions existing between the Hindu and Muslim communities and assumed that agreement would not be reached in the near future!

There were some differences of opinion between the Conservatives and Labourites. The latter reproached the government with proceeding too slowly, held it responsible for the "deadlock" and challenged it to win the Indians' trust by showing its readiness to make concessions. But the Labour party made no real new proposals and agreed that it was impossible to hand over effective control before the end of the war. In contrast to the Conservatives, however, the Labour party, particularly the left wing, wanted to accept the Congress party of Gandhi and Nehru as the sole spokesman for the Indian nationalist movement, and not just as the voice of the Hindus. In October 1939 Sir Stafford Cripps demanded new elections, to be followed by the formation of a government of the "majority parties", of the Congress party in effect.[6] In August 1940 Sorensen said the same: the rights of the minority groups must be recognized, but it was undemocratic to give them a kind of veto right. "The majority party must govern," he said, and, characteristically, ascribed feudalist and fascist tendencies to the Muslim League, although he did not mention it by name.[7] At the 1941 party conference, the M.P. Gordon MacDonald played off the Muslims, whom he called "a very small minority in India" [!], against the Congress party which represented the "sentiments of India".[8] Some of the leading Labour members had personal relations with Congress party politicians and naturally more sympathy with Nehru's democratic and socialist pronouncements than with the religious beliefs and conservative tendencies of the Muslim League. Perhaps the left wing suspected the government and the Conservatives of playing for time, but they were oversimplifying matters and underestimating the strength of the "communal" rivalries and the role of the Muslim League. However, party leader Attlee, as a member of the government, was forced to admit Amery's honesty and pointed out the difficulties facing London because of the Congress.[9]

On the other hand the Conservatives' spokesmen pointed to the government's liberal pronouncements and its readiness to start fresh negotiations after the war; they also recalled that it was the traditional duty of an imperialist power to ensure the rights of the minorities and of the princes. As an example we quote the reply of Samuel Hoare, the Lord Privy Seal, to a criticism by Wedgwood Benn:

> It is these divisions that have made so difficult the task of setting up responsible Government at the Centre and achievement of the great ideal of an All-India Federation. The Princes are afraid of domination by British India; Muslims are firmly opposed to a Hindu majority at the

Centre; the Depressed Classes and other minorities genuinely believe that responsible Government dependent upon a Hindu majority, will sacrifice their interests. These anxieties still exist. I wish that they did not. But as long as they exist it is impossible for the Government to accept a demand for immediate and full responsibility at the centre on a particular date.[10]

This sense of imperial responsibility must be taken seriously, despite the underlying tactical motive of laying the blame on the Indians in order to gain time. The Conservatives' old dislike of the Congress also played a certain part, particularly since the Muslim League was more willing to support the British war effort than the Congress party was. The Muslim League opposed the Congress' policy of non-co-operation and, after the exclusion of the Congress from the provincial governments in October 1939, could command a great deal of consideration. Amery also used the argument about Indian unity; if Great Britain wanted to release the subcontinent as a unit from imperial control, a transfer of power before agreement had been reached among the communities would endanger this unity and provoke civil war.[11]

Various concepts of democracy were voiced during this discussion. The Congress party wanted a simple majority system (universal franchise without separate electoral colleges, proportional representation in a constitutional assembly, etc.); the Labour party tended towards the same principle. But Amery, speaking for the government and the Conservatives, tried to establish that consensus was "the foundation of all free government, of all democracy". He said that majority decisions were not the essence but only a practical rule of democratic procedure, which required a generally accepted basis; the agreement demanded by London must not be interpreted as a veto in the usual sense of the term. So he refused the Congress' demands for a constitutional assembly and universal franchise as being "impossible", on the pretext that the better organized Congress party would then outvote the minority groups.[12] For obvious reasons the Muslim League accepted Amery's reasoning.[13] But for the fact that the various interpretations of democracy were based largely on tactical considerations, one could trace the source of the conflict between the Congress and the Muslim League, and the divergences between Conservatives and Labourites, to the ambivalence between majority will and individual rights inherent in the concept of democracy!

Great Britain and India did not manage to agree on a *modus vivendi* during the war. While the Indians spoke of Britain's delaying tactics, London thought it had shown sufficient proof of goodwill and pointed to the obstinate agitation by the Congress which, it said, had no sense of reality. When the Congress party organized a campaign of individual non-co-operation in autumn 1940, a large number of politicians were arrested. The Muslim League, on the other hand, under the leadership of Jinnah, accepted the famous resolution of Lahore on 23 March 1940. This resolution finally dismissed the 1935 plans for federation and proclaimed the Muslim provinces' right to self-determination and national recognition. Jinnah's "two-nations" theory aimed at dividing India into Hindustan and Pakistan. Thenceforth the Muslim League decided it would collaborate with the British Government only on condition that the latter recognized this claim, as well as the principle of parity with the Congress party on all communal boards—especially in any future constitutional assembly—and finally their claim to represent the entire Muslim minority group. Since it could accept neither the demands of the Congress nor those of the Muslim League, Britain was caught in a dilemma.

The war, and particularly the Japanese attack on Pearl Harbor on 7 December 1941, brought the British and the Indians slightly closer together. The Congress party leaders were freed and the campaign of civil disobedience was stopped; Gandhi retired from the party leadership. The moment for new negotiations seemed to have come. But Britain did not re-examine its Indian policy until the fall of Singapore on 15 February 1942. A special cabinet committee, consisting of Attlee, Amery, John Simon and Stafford Cripps, worked out a "Draft Declaration"[14] reaffirming some of the points from previous pronouncements. For instance, "immediately" after the war an elected constitutional assembly, for which an electoral *modus* was proposed for the time being, would work out a new constitution which London pledged itself to accept. The transfer of power would be determined by a contract with Great Britain. The declaration envisaged a united India which included the princely states, but added that any province that objected to "integration" could receive a constitution of its own corresponding to that of the union. This addition was necessary in order to gain the Muslim League's acceptance of the declaration; at the same time it recognized implicitly the rights to partition and secession.[15] The declaration also recognized the rights of a free India to leave the Commonwealth: "HMG will not impose any restriction on the power of the Indian Union to decide in the future its relationship to the other Member states of the British Commonwealth." It had to do this because the Congress had long decided on "independence" and because this right was inherent in the concept of full dominion status. Nevertheless, it was a step beyond earlier declarations. Until now it had been taken for granted that the Indian union would remain "within the Commonwealth".

We know little of the discussion within the committee and in the Cabinet as a whole. For instance, we do not know whether the declaration was a compromise between the embittered demands of Labour and the Conservatives' theories. What is certain is that, apart from American pressure, only the Japanese advance and India's peril can have persuaded Churchill to agree to these new pledges![16] The same applies to the

Cripps mission that Churchill announced in the House of Commons on 11 March, three days after the fall of Rangoon. Since the military situation was so critical, the diehard Churchill actually had to entrust a left-wing Labour member with this important mission. He hoped that Cripps' "anti-Imperialist" record and personal contacts with Congress leaders would convince them of London's willingness to make concessions. This alone proves the extent to which the war forced Britain to be conciliatory. But the Cripps mission was a failure. The British proposals made on the basis of the Draft Declaration were refused by India, above all by the Congress, which took offence at the assurances they gave to the princely states and the Muslims; moreover Congress wanted to appoint the war minister while Britain wanted to reserve itself this right during the war. Whether the attempt to compromise failed because of what in retrospect seems to be Britain's inflexibility, or whether it could not have been expected to succeed in any case in view of the situation at the time, remains an open question.

The Congress and the Muslim League adhered to their radical positions. One side demanded the immediate withdrawal of the British, even if this should lead to anarchy,[17] while the other postulated the acceptance of Pakistan as a *sine qua non*. Under the assumption that the military situation would force Great Britain to give in, the Congress committee accepted the "Quit India" resolution and launched a new campaign of "passive" but consistent civil disobedience. Demonstrations, acts of sabotage and confrontations with the police could no longer be avoided and the government was forced to take repressive action. Sixty thousand arrests were officially confirmed at the end of 1942.

With the failure of the Cripps mission, and the decreasing Japanese military threat to India, Britain's attitude again became more rigid and there were new attacks on the Congress. On 10 September 1942 Churchill declared in the House of Commons:

> The Indian Congress Party does not represent all India. It does not represent the majority of the people of India. It does not even represent the Hindu masses. It is a political organization built around a party machine and sustained by certain manufacturing and financial interests.[18]

The expediency of this reasoning is obvious. The Labour party called Churchill's attacks a provocation and demanded a reopening of negotiations, but was not itself capable of making any new proposals. Not only Amery, but even Attlee spoke of the "totalitarian aspects" of the Congress[19] and approved of the arrests.[20] From then on, the British Government based its policy on the proposals of the Cripps mission and blamed the "deadlock" on the Indians' intransigence. Lord Halifax, then ambassador in Washington, issued a declaration confirming India's right to leave the Commonwealth if it wished. It was accepted by Churchill,[21] but did not lead to much.

Finally, early in the summer of 1945, Britain again attempted to reopen negotiations with India. The war was coming to an end and London prepared a White Paper with the help of the viceroy, Lord Wavell, appointed in October 1943.[22] The White Paper proposed as an interim solution the creation of an executive council of Indians with equal representation of Hindus and Muslims; the foreign office, the home office and the ministry of finance were to be handed over to Indians, and the British would retain only the high command of the armed forces. The Congress leaders Nehru, Patel and Azad were released, and a conference was announced in Simla. This conference was welcomed both in England and in India as an attempt to break the deadlock, but it proved to be unsuccessful because the Muslim League demanded the right to nominate all Muslim representatives in the new government and the Congress could not accept this demand. The Congress considered itself a non-religious party and was afraid that the large number of Muslims in the party and the party leadership would reduce its representation to Hindus only.

Meanwhile Attlee's Labour government came into office. The king's speech, which set out the government's programme, contained the following words: "In accordance with the promises already made to My Indian peoples, My Government will do their utmost to promote in conjunction with the leaders of Indian opinion the early realisation of full Self-Government in India."[23] But although the Labour party had criticized the coalition government and was prepared to make concessions, at the time it had no practical programme of reforms. Like the Conservatives, it could not agree to a transfer of power without careful preparation and before coming to an agreement with its Indian partners. Yet, as we have said, it was more willing than the Conservatives to meet the Congress party halfway and to be flexible in the communal question. It also had a different view of the "timing" and urged a shorter transitional period.[24] Full dominion status should be the very next step.

New elections were announced on 21 August. London wanted to confer with Wavell again and announced the convocation of a new constitutional assembly on 19 September. In addition, the British Government sent out a Cabinet mission consisting of the minister for India, Lord Pethick-Lawrence, and Stafford Cripps. According to a statement made by Attlee on 15 March 1946, this mission was designed to help India "to attain her freedom as speedily and fully as possible". It was India's own affair to determine its form of government, he said, yet Great Britain hoped that "the Indian people may elect to remain within the British Commonwealth . . . if she does so elect, it must be by her own free will".[25] Stress was laid on a rapid decision and on India's "free will". Attlee added: "We cannot allow a minority to place a veto on the advance of the majority"—a clear warning to the Muslim League to be conciliatory and not to sabotage new British efforts to reach an agreement.

On 16 May, after intensive talks with Indian politicians and a new conference in Simla,[26] Cabinet mission's proposals, based on the memorandum by Azad, the Muslim president of the Congress party,[27] were announced.[28] The mission rejected the Muslim League's demand for a separate Pakistan and proposed a loose union with less control at the centre (foreign policy, defense, transport). It said the communal questions needed the consent of both the great religious communities and that the provinces should be allowed to form into groups having their own constitutions and parliaments. It proposed the election of a constitutional assembly as soon as possible and the formation of an interim government. These proposals, which were in fact a compromise between diametrically opposed positions, were reluctantly accepted by both parties.[29] But the attempt to form an Indian government failed as it had in May 1945. Nehru, on 10 July, accepted the proposals of the Cabinet mission as no more than a basis for discussion and in tactless if not provocative words rejected the idea of grouping the provinces.[30] Consequently, on 29 July, the League revoked its consent and announced a policy of "direct action" against the Congress rather than against Britain. The mass murders in Calcutta (16–19 August) were an indirect result. Urged by Attlee, the viceroy formed a government with the Congress party, led by Nehru, on 2 September; in October he managed to persuade the League to join it. But the League refused to take part in the constitutional assembly. The British Government at a conference in London tried again to reach a solution, but failed. Both parties entrenched themselves in their positions and the riots in several provinces continued.

The new "deadlock" and "the growing deterioration of the situation demanded courageous and drastic steps".[31] On 20 February 1947 the prime minister unexpectedly declared in the House of Commons that the British Government had decided to withdraw from India by June 1948 at the latest, i.e. within fourteen months.[32] He said that hopes of accomplishing the transfer of power as originally intended and of being able to hand over power to elected Indian officials on the basis of a new constitution had not been realized. Nor was there any chance of this in the near future. At the same time Attlee announced the appointment of Lord Mountbatten to succeed Wavell.

The declaration caused a sensation. Great Britain had set a definite time-limit and fixed a date for independence before the hoped-for agreement between the conflicting parties had been reached and before it had negotiated with a generally recognized provisional régime on the ways and means of transferring power. So the deadline for independence did not mean the formal conclusion of a successful movement of dissociation—as was to be the case in years to come. Instead, it simply meant the acceptance of a unilaterally proclaimed and arbitrary time-limit which had to be observed regardless of the situation at that time. Neither before nor afterwards did Britain set this kind of time-limit, since it was felt that fixing a date for independence would be tantamount to surrendering the few means of exerting pressure it still had; moreover, it appeared unseemly to grant a colony independence before establishing the conditions for an orderly transfer of power.

Various factors had caused the Labour government to take this exceptional step.[33] London was annoyed by the failure of all negotiations so far. Instead of trying to come to an agreement, the Indian politicians had not only made radical demands for Britain's immediate withdrawal, but even blamed the lack of agreement on the colonial power. They had accepted proposals for a compromise, then refused them again or sabotaged them without proposing any practical alternative. Britain was genuinely trying to maintain Indian unity, but it could obviously not do so by force. By setting a time-limit, therefore, Britain hoped to compel Indian leaders to give up their negative attitudes and to accept responsibility for the future; perhaps this pressure would persuade them to reach agreement![34] The question was whether London could and should wait much longer and further postpone the withdrawal it had promised so long ago. "Communal" tensions were increasing, and the viceroy was losing power and influence. The executive council, i.e. the former head of the administration, no longer existed and the interim government was not an instrument of British rule and, moreover, did not work. Discipline in the administration was becoming noticeably lax since both Indians and Europeans were preparing for the withdrawal. The army was still under the viceroy, but it too was showing the first signs of dissolution and it might well prove untrustworthy in the event of a new campaign of civil disobedience or a "communal" civil war, when repressive action would be required to maintain law and order. The British armed forces wanted to be released at the end of the war. The Labour government did not intend and was not militarily equipped to carry out a major engagement. In any case, the British economic situation was rather grave and the decision to withdraw had not only been made, but had already been welcomed by a wide sector of the British public.[35] Moreover, Lord Mountbatten had accepted this important office only on condition that it was temporary.[36] The Labour government considered Mountbatten particularly well equipped to liquidate British rule in India. As high commander in South-East Asia he had distinguished himself by his energy and skilful dealings with people. He was known for his left-wing tendencies and had already shown great willingness to conciliate the nationalists in Burma. A member of the royal family seemed an even better man than a Labour party official for ensuring the discipline of officers and civil servants during the difficult transitional period; he might also help reduce the expected resistance on the part of the king and the conservatives, particularly Churchill.[37]

The conservative opposition used Attlee's declaration on 20 February 1947 as an opportunity for vigorous protest against the Labour party's India policy. Both Houses moved a vote of non-confidence. The conservative arguments were based on the proposals of the 1942 Cripps mission, i.e. full dominion status after the war. So in a sense the differences between the parties were narrower than in the 1930s. Privately the diehards may have continued to hold the same views, but in Parliament they could no longer question the possibility of self-government for India or openly differentiate between white and coloured dominions. What remained was the tendency to postulate a number of conditions that had to be fulfilled before London began to transfer power. First was agreement between the parties and the protection of the other minority groups, especially the princes. Britain had "obligations" and must take precautions for an "orderly" retreat. Churchill stressed these obligations, as did Lord Salisbury, who reproached the Labour party with placing the fifty million people of the "depressed classes" (those without a caste) at the mercy of the Congress party.

In fact, the conservative opposition was attempting to postpone the withdrawal, which explains their fury at the deadline. Certainly there were striking arguments against setting a time-limit. For instance, without previous agreement between the Congress and the Muslim League and without a recognized transitional government, Britain's withdrawal threatened India with chaos and destroyed all hope of maintaining national unity. Lord Templewood summarized the 20 February declaration as "morally wrong, practically unworkable, politically unwise".[38] It became clear that the imperialists could not reconcile themselves to the dissociation of India and saw the end of the glorious British rule with despondence and indignation. "It is with deep grief I watch the clattering down of the British Empire, with all the glories and all the services it has rendered to mankind," said Churchill.[39] The two-hundred-year-old Pax Britannica was coming to an end and India was being abandoned to "human misery", thought Lord Selborne,[40] while Lord Cranborne described Attlee's declaration as the death-knell of Britain's association with India.[41]

However the Conservative party was not unanimously against the declaration or the Labour government's India policy. Apart from the real diehards, opponents included Lord Templewood (Indian minister in the 1930s as Samuel Hoare), Lord Simon and R. A. Butler, the conservative pro-reform representative of the younger generation. Butler was more moderate in his speeches and obviously did not want to contradict party leader Churchill! But there was also Lord Halifax (the former viceroy Lord Irwin), who refused to obey party directives and supported Labour. In his carefully considered vote, Halifax tried to explain to the diehards that the Labour party could not be held responsible for the present critical situation, and that the crisis was the result of old agreements, the war and internal Indian tensions. Once independence had been promised, the dilemma of whether to continue waiting for an agreement or whether, giving up hope of this, to take the decisive step anyway, obviously became even more acute: "I gain the impression that the position is rapidly becoming intolerable, for the fundamental reason that at the present moment the Government of India . . . is in a most distasteful condition—namely, a position in which its responsibility is greater than its power."[42] Halifax was aware of the dangers, but on the other hand he did not overestimate the value of agreement; for in the end there would still be the question of whether the terms of the agreement would be observed. It was wrong to speak of evacuation, as though one were leaving a hostile country. There were numerous Indians "who, once suspicion and the old order are removed, will be willing to accept a great deal by way of help and general influence that they would never have accepted in the shape and under the guise of controlling power". Here Lord Halifax's ideas coincided with those of Attlee. Since no agreement had been reached and British power in India was increasingly on the wane, a rapid retreat was not only necessary but also advantageous, regardless of the problems it produced, since it might provide a basis for tolerable if not friendly relations in the post-imperial era. Lord Halifax's views made a considerable impression in the House of Lords and Lord Templewood withdrew his vote of non-confidence and did not refuse his consent. In the House of Commons, the motion was defeated by 337 against 185 votes. A few days later, no less than Amery congratulated Prime Minister Attlee on the acceptance of the Indian Independence Act in Parliament![43]

Today it is debatable whether Lord Mountbatten was not over-hasty in accepting the need for partition and thus removing the last hopes of preventing it. It is equally debatable whether postponing the deadline to 15 August, which the viceroy declared unilaterally on 4 June without the knowledge of the Labour party, was expedient, and whether the massacre of August–September 1947 could have been avoided if preparations for the transfer of power had been better or longer. . . .[44] In any case, a few days later Lord Mountbatten realized that Indian unity was impossible and that preparations for partition had to be made. He even managed to gain Nehru's consent for this "solution". Nehru must have taken into account many of the same factors as Mountbatten; he too was tired of the endless negotiations and wanted to achieve his life's aim, the independence of India, at last. Collaboration with the Muslim League within the interim government had proved impossible—but how was India to perform the grave tasks of the future without a strong and effective central government? Mountbatten managed to solve the problem of the princely states too, and found a way out of the problem of dominion status. On 15 August both parts of India were to be declared dominions and would be able to decide independently whether they wanted to remain within the Commonwealth. The mode of withdrawal was to be worked out very soon. Among other things, the Anglo-Indian army had to be disbanded. The Radcliffe Commission determined the boundaries of the partitioned provinces. However, the viceroy proved wrong in his assumption that there would be no serious "communal" unrest.[45]

The British Parliament discussed the Indian Independence Bill from 4 to 12 July and it was granted the Royal Seal on 18 July. On 14 and 15 August 1947 the Union Jack was lowered in India!

On 4 July, speaking in the House of Commons, Prime Minister Attlee described the Independence Act as "not the abdication but the fulfilment of Britain's mission in India, a sign of strength and vitality of the British Commonwealth", and in a message on 15 August the king spoke of "the fulfilment of a great democratic ideal".[46] In historical terms, there was a certain inherent justice in these confident words. Britain's proud rule in India was based on the idea of eventual self-government and Britain gradually pursued this aim. Often it did so reluctantly and in the face of resistance, or under the weight of the world political situation or the nationalist emancipation movements; but it did so with surprising consistency. What early nineteenth-century liberals had postulated, what Seeley had considered, and what had already been begun, although rather reluctantly, with the pre-1914 reforms—in 1917 the British Government announced as the "ultimate goal" of its India policy and granted it in 1947.

Since the end of the First World War Britain had had to adapt itself to the idea of an independent India, although it continued to reckon on long time-limits and was not forced to alter its timetable until the Second World War. One must compare this attitude with that of other colonial powers in the same situation. An independent Indochina or Indonesia was inconceivable to the general public in the mother countries in 1939 and was still so in 1945. Decolonization began suddenly, and naturally met violent resistance. The attempt to bind former colonies to the mother country by means of institutions, which was pursued to the end, failed in spite of military intervention, and made an orderly transfer of power impossible. Great Britain, by contrast, could start from the concept of Commonwealth, since it had long since renounced the idea of creating federal ties. In the inter-war years, Britain may have hoped to differentiate between the colonial settlements and India, but in later years this proved less and less possible. India had to be promised dominion status, and *eo ipso* dissociation from the Commonwealth was possible. From the time of the Cripps proposals in 1942, even a diehard like Winston Churchill had had to come to terms with this legal situation.

The concept and reality of the Commonwealth enabled the Labour party to harmonize its socialist anti-colonialism with British nationalism and the sense of Empire. After the war, when the coalition government under Churchill was forced to make considerable concessions to India, the British public was prepared to "take the big step" and accept the Labour government's policy. If a Conservative party under Churchill had won the elections of May 1945, it would doubtless have postponed the transfer of power, and would perhaps have missed the right moment for withdrawal. But as things were, the socialist government managed to carry the gradual grant of self-government to a happy end, in the not unjustified hope that a free India would be interested in maintaining good relations with Britain and would decide to remain within the Commonwealth. The Indian Independence Act really was, in this sense, "not the abdication but the fulfilment of Britain's mission in India, a sign of strength and vitality of the British Commonwealth".

BURMA AND CEYLON

Burma had always been overshadowed by India in British imperial policy. It was conquered in the nineteenth century to secure India's defense and administered as a part of India. It was also open to Indian immigration and a large number of Indians served in the armed forces and in the British administration. Indian merchants, money-lenders and landowners played a part in Burma's economic development—particularly in Lower Burma—and most of the Burmese rice-farmers became indebted to the Indians and had to hand over their land to them.[1] The British administration, "based on law and individual freedom", abandoned Burma to a capitalist colonial economy in which the Burmese themselves had only a small part. Meanwhile Burmese social structures and the Buddhist civilization disintegrated or froze. Since the educational system was inadequate, the young generation was not equal to confrontation with the modern world.[2] Constitutional development ran parallel to that of India; in 1923 Burma was ruled as a dyarchy and in 1935-1937, after the partition of India, it received semi-responsible government. The governor retained his reserved powers and controlled the administration, but the predominantly Burmese cabinet now became responsible to an elected parliament. Moreover, London instructed the governor to exercise restraint in the appointment of ministers in parliament and to use his powers in a manner consistent with "partnership", "to the end that Burma may attain its due place among our Dominions".[3] Since the plans for Indian federation had come to nothing, Burma—and Ceylon—headed the procession on the road to full self-government after 1937.[4] In the struggle for power, Burma's political parties gathered strength among the different minority groups and the followers of various Burmese leaders, and some progress was made in the attempt to involve Burmese in the administration. But the economy remained almost exclusively under the control of Europeans and Indians.

Meanwhile a new generation of nationalists was taking shape at the University of Rangoon. Organized into the "All Burma Student Movement", they clearly dissociated themselves from upper-class leaders, adopted strong anti-British and anti-capitalist views, and made contact with India, China and Japan. This small group of intellectuals which, under the leadership of Aung San (b. 1915), called for a student strike in February 1936, would have presented no danger to British rule for many years to come had the Second World War and the Japanese occupation not provided it with a great opportunity.

Like the Indian Congress party, Burmese politicians tried to make their active co-operation in the war effort conditional upon far-reaching concessions from Great Britain. On 23 February 1940 the House of Representatives passed a motion calling for the immediate recognition of Burma "as an independent nation entitled to frame her own constitution".[5] In its reply the British Government spoke of dominion status after the war but would not make a definite commitment or fix a timetable. The prime minister, U Saw, a rather dubious character, demanded a definite promise of full dominion status immediately after the war when he visited London in October and November 1941.[6] Governor Dorman-Smith pressed the secretary of state for India and Burma, L. S. Amery, to fix a date and it appears that Amery showed some readiness to consent, but he was prevented from doing so by Winston Churchill's violent refusal.[7] In the Burma issue the British prime minister once again demonstrated his lack of understanding of the nationalist emancipation movements![8] As a result, the government declaration was vague and did not satisfy the Burmese.[9] It is doubtful, however, whether even generous concessions would have been enough to win Burmese support in the struggle against Japan. What is important here is that London—especially the old diehard Churchill—spoke of dominion status, but did not want to grant it before the end of the war and, moreover, laid down conditions. The war did, however, finally force Britain to fix a definite date and to curtail the proposed transitionary period, promising that negotiations would begin, not in the vague future, but "immediately after the end of the war". But the war also gave the nationalists an opportunity to increase their demands so that they were always one step ahead of what London conceded.

The Japanese invasion provided the opportunity for the younger generation of revolutionary nationalists. Adopting the slogan "Asia for the Asians", they followed Japanese successes with growing self-assurance. The young Aung San and his comrades in the student organization joined the Japanese and marched into Burma with a "Burma Independency Army". The Japanese occupation dealt a severe blow and the entire British administration collapsed. Older Burmese politicians withdrew or were dismissed, while the Indian minority fled, leaving the field open to the younger generation. Although the Japanese occupation army soon met with increasing resistance due to its authoritarian character and infringements upon personal liberties such as forced consignments and forced labour, it skilfully played on the Burmese desire for independence, encouraging nationalist organizations and giving the Burmese a part in the administration. Japan recognized Aung San as head of the Burmese national army and even proclaimed Burma's independence in August 1943. But although Aung San and his comrades collaborated with Japan, they were well aware that this independence was not genuine and that if Japan were victorious Burma would become a protectorate power within the Japanese "co-prosperity" sphere. So, in December 1943, they initiated relations with the British secret service and prepared to attack Japan in order to achieve full independence.

How did London react to this? Did it realize that the Japanese occupation with its policy of encouraging Burmese nationalism had created an entirely new situation in the colony? Governor Dorman-Smith and the Burmese government withdrew to Simla in India where he was instructed to prepare plans for the reconstruction of Burma, which had been heavily damaged by the war. There were two very important issues at stake here. Should Burmese nationalists who had collaborated with Japan be brought to justice as collaborators and traitors, or should they simply be treated as nationalists? Their support might be useful in the military reconquest and without it the restoration of British rule would be faced by internal resistance. Moreover, London thought that reconstruction work could be actively pursued only if Burma was directly administered by Britain during a certain period of transition. Dorman-Smith and the British personnel in Simla reproached themselves with having laid Burma open to destruction because they had not taken adequate defensive measures and hoped to receive generous financial aid from the mother country. It seemed better to postpone constitutional questions, elections and the transfer of power to a Burmese government for the time being.

Admittedly there was a real dilemma. On 16 December 1942 Amery wrote to Dorman-Smith:

> The biggest difficulty is where to strike the right mean between the necessities of a perfectly free hand for reconstruction and our general pledges to Burma and the world for the restoration of self-government.[10]

The governor and secretary-of-state reckoned on a transitional period of five to seven years, but Churchill and the Cabinet refused to fix a deadline. Dorman-Smith pressed for a clear statement since this could gain the co-operation of the Burmese, but the British Government would not listen. In the summer of 1943, shortly before his departure for London, the governor declared in New Delhi:

> We must recognize this as an unexampled opportunity to correct abuses and defects which were apparent under our "prewar" administration. . . . Burma belongs to the Burmese and when the time [shall] come for full self-government, we must try to hand over [a] country for which we have done a good job of work.[11]

Apart from this remarkable criticism of the pre-war administration, the declaration also revealed an earnest desire to reconstruct Burma and stressed the need for an interim period of direct rule. But it conceded no more than Burma had possessed since 1939 or than had been promised since the outbreak of war. Yet Churchill considered the formulation of the declaration, particularly the words "hand over", excessive and greeted Dorman-Smith at a lunch at Chequers with the words, "You're the man, I hear, who wants to give away the Empire!"[12] This remark again shows Churchill's stubborn conservative attitude in imperial questions. It also reveals the difference in attitude between the British Government, which was engaged in stern resistance and was not ready for any hasty concessions, and the liberal colonial governor, who felt himself under an obligation to the district he administered and wanted to show as much goodwill as possible to the nationalists.

In spite of the refusal to issue a statement, a certain amount of discussion on Burma did begin in London. For instance, the position of the Burmese Chamber of Commerce, which represented British economic interests, was clearly conservative and colonialist. It believed that all political decisions should be postponed and that the governor's emergency powers should be extended for an indefinite period. Officials who had collaborated with Japan should be punished, while British firms in the country should be paid compensation and given a privileged position during the reconstruction period. In addition, London should recognize Indian claims to land and mortgages and allow Indian labour to immigrate.[13] The Chamber of Commerce resisted all political concessions and tried to re-establish the unlimited freedom of movement of the Anglo-Indian economic groups that had characterized Burmese economy before the war and against which the young Burmese nationalists had protested so strongly! Presumably the excessively reactionary attitude of the Conservative party and especially among those members of Parliament who had financial interests in Burma and were therefore concerned with Burma's future, found widespread approval. Within the Conservative party, however, younger parliamentarians in favour of reforms formed a counter movement and published, late in 1944, *Blue Print for Burma*.[14] This pamphlet demonstrated how the Burmese economy was controlled by foreigners and how none of the profits of expansion went to the Burmese, how the number of leaseholders had grown to a frightening extent and how even imports mainly benefited non-Burmese. This kind of self-criticism and doubts about the much-praised advantages that the colonial régime bestowed upon the native inhabitants would hardly have been conceivable from a conservative before 1941! The authors of the pamphlet declared themselves in favour of fixing a time-limit: Burma should receive dominion status in six years' time at the latest, although with some reservations regarding Britain's strategic and economic interests. Reconstruction work must be the responsibility of the governor, who should be advised by representative Burmese. A new constitution should be prepared and ratified after the transitional period by a popularly elected Burmese assembly. London should actively promote the take-over by the Burmese of the administration and economy, as well as control and if possible check Indian landownership, for instance by redemption by means of a special loan. British firms should receive compensation from the mother country and not the government of Burma.

Perhaps this conservative programme no longer corresponded to the new power structure in Burma, about which London was not well informed, but it reiterated the older nationalists' major demands and offered a surprisingly generously conceived and practicable basis for further discussion. *The Times* went a step further and rejected any kind of interim period, on the grounds that an attempt to grant Burma less than India had received would contradict earlier pledges and fail to persuade the Burmese to give the co-operation that was so essential.[15] *The Times* also stressed the nationalist resistance in Burma "to the restoration of the old economy"[16]—which led interested British economic groups to dissociate themselves both from *The Times* and from the *Blue Print*.[17]

The conservative study group defended its proposals in the parliamentary debate on 12 December 1944. The group declared that Britain, whose prestige had suffered a great blow since the Japanese advance, must honour its numerous pledges. Since the Japanese had promised Burma independence, the British Government must also issue a declaration if the Allied troops were to be greeted on their re-entry as liberators. Formulas like "as soon as possible" were no longer enough and would appear to be a breach of promise to the Burmese.[18] While other conservatives considered six years too short an interim period, Creech-Jones, the Labour party speaker, considered it too long: "The Burmese will ask us, by what right do we assert our sovereignty over them without their consent." Preparations for responsible government should begin at once, and as far as possible should be made by the Burmese themselves.[19]

Although *The Times* also considered time-limits necessary, the government did not give in; nor would it initiate the transition to dominion status immediately after the reconquest.[20] *The New Statesman and Nation* (23 December) and the *Economist* (16 December) were joined by *The Times* (13 December) in expressing disappointment. But reactionary ideas, concrete economic interests, and not least the personal influence of Winston Churchill won the day. The government gave up the attempt to give political support to its military advance by means of generous promises; it was obviously under the impression that it would be easy to deal with the Burmese nationalists and to re-establish British control without fixing time-limits prematurely or anticipating future decisions.

Nether London nor the governor changed course. Paradoxically it was the high commander in South-East Asia, Lord Mountbatten who, moved by military considerations, took the initiative. He wanted the difficult reconquest of Burma to be supported by the Burmese. This meant recognizing Aung San's Burma National Army, perhaps even providing it with arms and giving it a part in Allied operations. Mountbatten carried out these demands in spite of resistance on the part of his own political advisers, the Simla administration and the British Government! He even had a personal interview with Aung San and on 16 May 1945 they agreed that the Burman National Army should be recognized as an Allied force under British high command. Mountbatten was far-sighted enough to take the new nationalist organizations seriously, above all the anti-fascist People's Freedom League, and even to give them a part in the government eventually. He knew this was the only way to ensure a more or less smooth take-over and to perform the reconstruction work without internal strife. It remains an open question whether he also realized that this was the only means of keeping Burma in the Commonwealth; at any rate he perceived the entirely new situation more quickly and judged it more accurately than London or even the liberal governor Dorman-Smith. At the victory parade in Rangoon on 15 June 1945, the Burman National Army marched as independent troops under Burmese flags. Nothing could show more clearly that the pre-1941 administration and policy could not simply be resumed after the Japanese occupation.

One month earlier, on 17 May 1945, the British Government had finally issued its long-overdue Burma White Paper.[21] Its principal points were: for the first three years, the governor should be in control, after which the constitution of 1935–1937 would come into force; the Burmese could then work out a new constitution whose ultimate aim would be dominion status, "complete self-government within the British Commonwealth". But this was conditional on the signing of an agreement assuring certain British interests; the Shan States and tribal areas (Karen, hill peoples) could decide independently whether they wanted to become part of Burma. So in May 1945 London granted what it had refused in December 1944, in addition to shortening the six years stipulated in the *Blue Print* to three. No date was set for the transition to dominion status and it remained an "ultimate objective". This statement, made far too late, already trailed behind actual circumstances as well as behind Mountbatten's actions, and again gave the Burmese nationalists cause to increase their demands and to be even more insistent. The *Economist* (26 May 1945) thought the declaration was "not an inspiring document" and not likely to assuage Burmese or Indian suspicions, but saw no alternative. The *New Statesman and Nation* wanted the interim period shortened to one year, since it foresaw the danger that the British administration alone would determine new economic policy without Burmese participation. Even the left-wing politicians obviously did not consider it right to grant dominion status immediately.

This was proved by the short debate in the House of Commons on 1 June 1945. Secretary of State Amery tried very hard to interpret the statement as "liberal", promised financial aid for reconstruction and indicated that Dorman-Smith would not fail to give the Burmese a part in this.[22] De Chair, speaking for the Blue Print group, agreed, though more cautiously. But even Stafford Cripps and Creech-Jones praised this White Paper. Cripps even called it "a most admirable presentation of the facts as regards Burma . . . all friends of Burma will be satisfied".[23] Only a few Labour party outsiders, such as Sorensen, rejected it. They said it would not content the Burmese and pointed out that the Philippines had also been destroyed by the war but there reconstruction work had not served as a pretext for direct rule. Once again *The Times* showed its far-sightedness and revealed the motives behind British Burma policy: the Allies, i.e. the Americans, were observing Britain's actions in this first formerly British area to be liberated from the Japanese; it was essential

> to convince the people of the Far East that the Western Powers recognize of a new situation created by the national movements now in process of emerging into self-consciousness.

There followed a remarkable description of the new generation of nationalists, who differed from the "older leaders of the parliamentary type" and whose programme was akin to the "agrarian democracy" in Northern China.

> It is essential that Burmese nationalism should be taken into partnership from the earliest possible moment if its cooperation, essential for the success of British policy, is to be secured.[24]

Liberal Burma experts such as Maurice Collis and J. S. Furnivall, both former colonial officials, understood the consequence of this, realizing that more far-reaching pledges were necessary and that the young Burmese nationalists must be given some political responsibility immediately after the reconquest. Collis suggested discussing dominion status at once,[25] while Furnivall considered appointing a Burmese as governor, with a British high commissioner at his side; this, he hoped would create both the necessary strong government and a new basis of trust.[26]

Naturally the Burmese themselves rejected the White Paper, as did the rather conservative Burma Association in London, which demanded a definite and early date for the grant of dominion status and asked for elections in the near future. Aung San's AFPFL distrusted the White Paper's restricting clauses, seeing them as part of a policy of divide and rule, and demanded the election of a national constitutional assembly and a provisional government as a stage towards full independence. The guerrilla fighters, the officers of the national army and the politicians and officials of a Burma that was protected by Japan but theoretically independent, were understandably not now ready to hand back their power to British officials or to the old Burmese politicians at the moment of their victory! The position of the AFPFL became a crucial issue in the following months. The party asserted that it represented the inhabitants of Burma and wanted to be recognized as a provisional government, or at least to appoint the majority of the ministers in the governor's executive council. These ministers, it said, should receive their instructions from the party and be responsible to it. Governor Dorman-Smith neither could nor would accept such radical demands since he felt under obligation to the Simla administration which was bound to observe the White Paper and refused to recognize the Communist-infiltrated AFPFL as sole representative of Burma. Lord Mountbatten attempted to mediate and tried to persuade Aung San to accept dominion status, i.e. to renounce his demand for independence, but in October he had to hand over his power to the civil government. The highly-paid colonial officers of pre-war years showed little sympathy with the young revolutionary nationalists and, understandably, recognized old debts and land claims again. This led to opposition from the farmers. The same applied to the officers and soldiers, who were not given a part in reconstruction and many of whom were dismissed.[27]

At first there was no change in policy when the Labour government came into office. The party had shown little interest in Burma and had given its approval of the White Paper, which it therefore observed as well. Dorman-Smith received instructions accordingly: he was to see to it that the AFPFL did not come to power prematurely and without elections—for the time being, in fact, he was to issue no statements on dominion status![28] In this sense, the Labour government's policy was more conservative than that of Mountbatten.

We cannot go into detail here on the complex situation in Burma during the next months. In spite of the good relations between Dorman-Smith and Aung San, tensions between the administration and the AFPFL became more and more acute. The young nationalist hero of liberated Burma was unable to turn the AFPFL, which until then had been a kind of collective movement composed of various groups, into a modern mass party organization with branches in the provinces and auxiliary organizations (youth movements and unions). Instead he formed a kind of party army, the "People's Volunteer Organization", and with its support he was able to boycott official decisions and threaten insurrection. In the face of this threat, Dorman-Smith requested his government to re-examine the White Paper in April 1946, believing that the situation could be resolved only if the League was given a part in the government, a constitutional assembly elected soon and Burma granted dominion status in 1948.[29] By so doing, the governor recognized the AFPFL as the major Burmese party, representing the majority of the population, and took the stand Mountbatten had already taken months ago. Open conflict must be avoided at all costs, since Britain no longer had enough troops to suppress a rebellion and the Indian army could not be used. . . .

The Times called for action again. It said the tense situation in Burma was a threat to reconstruction and the Burmese were afraid that the new loan of eighty million pounds would be used as a pretext for maintaining British rule. Attlee's 15 March declaration on India had made a great impression, said *The Times*; now Britain should recognize Burma's right to independence and give the younger nationalist leaders a part in the interim government—in fact, defense and foreign policy should be transferred to them![30]

At last the Labour government took the initiative. Dorman-Smith was ordered back to London, dismissed in rather unseemly fashion, and replaced by Sir Rance, a former colleague of Lord Mountbatten. Mountbatten himself had proposed Sir Rance to Attlee and urged Attlee to take action! Decisions now followed in rapid succession. Rance reorganized his executive council and Aung San was made second-in-command and put in charge of defence and foreign policy [!]. Since Aung San also controlled the majority of ministers through the AFPFL, he was practically prime minister. On 10 November the Burmese issued a kind of ultimatum: elections for the constitutional assembly should take place in April, and by 31 January 1947 London must consent to granting Burma full independence within a year.[31] So the British prime minister was obliged to speed up the pace. On 20 December he declared in the House of Commons that he had invited a delegation from the Burmese executive council to London in order to confer with it on constitutional questions. The White Paper must be replaced and, like India, Burma must receive self-government as soon as possible.

> We do not desire to retain within the Commonwealth and Empire any unwilling peoples. It is for the people of Burma to decide their own future, but we are certain that it will be to their interest, as it will be to ours, if they decide to remain within the Commonwealth. . . . it is the desire and

intention of HMG to hasten forward the time when Burma shall realise her independence, either within or without the Commonwealth.[32]

At the time of the Cripps proposals to India in 1942, Britain had already had to abandon the theory, considered self-evident until then, that full self-government could be granted only in the form of dominion status within the Commonwealth. Now Attlee accepted the possibility that Burma too could become independent. He may have hoped that this unexpected willingness to make concessions would assuage the suspicions of Aung San and his comrades who demanded independence and were under Communist pressure, and make it easier for them to remain in the Commonwealth in spite of everything.

It was too late to debate this in the House of Commons, but Churchill took the opportunity to protest, and declared, in characteristically grandiose and polemic words:

> It was said, in the days of the great administration of Lord Chatham, that one had to get up very early in the morning in order not to miss some of the gains and accessions of territory which were then characteristic of our fortunes. The no less memorable administration of the right hon. Gentleman opposite is distinguished for the opposite set of experiences. The British Empire seems to be running off almost as fast as the American loan. The steady and remorseless process of divesting ourselves of what has been gained by so many generations of toil, administration and sacrifice continues. In the case of Burma it is hardly a year since, by the superb exertions of the Fourteenth Army and enormous sacrifices in life and treasure—sacrifices in British blood and in Indian blood—the Japanese were forced to surrender, destroyed or driven out, and the country was liberated. And yet, although barely a year has passed away, there is this extraordinary haste that we should take the necessary measures to get out of Burma finally and forever.

He said Attlee's action was over-hasty; it was not preceded by elections and it sacrificed old friends: "This haste is appalling. 'Scuttle' is the only word that can be applied."[33] The conservative *Daily Telegraph* (21 December) and the *Yorkshire Post* (21 December) agreed with Churchill's criticisms, and prophesied evil consequences; while *The Times* (21 December), the *Manchester Guardian*, and the *Economist* agreed with Attlee's declaration, saying that only far-reaching concessions of this kind could make British policy sound convincing and perhaps lead to some agreement.

It is tempting to take the prime minister's statement and Churchill's polemic as representative attitudes—although they referred to a specific situation. One speaker was an old diehard, conscious of a great tradition, forced to watch the "liquidation of the Empire" and trying to slow down the wheels of history. The other was the leader of what was formerly the opposition; finding himself in a dangerous situation he took decisive action in order to adapt to the precipitate events and to prevent by generous concessions a final and ominous break with the nationalist emancipation movement.

In January 1947, while preparations were under way to deal with rebellion in case negotiations proved unsuccessful, a Burmese delegation flew to London. The delegates came with suspicion, expecting to be met with delaying tactics, but were soon convinced of Attlee's genuine goodwill.[34] The following agreement was reached: the interim government would be recognized as a dominion government, the parliament, which was soon to be elected, was to work out the new constitution and submit it for inspection to the British Parliament. Special agreements were promised for economic questions and the problem of the mountain tribes. Aung San succeeded with difficulty in persuading his followers to accept this agreement. No decisions had been made at the time about Burma's membership in the Commonwealth. It seems, however, that after a struggle the Burmese leader finally established that Burma would remain within the Commonwealth, but he was under great pressure and could not declare himself openly. In May 1947 the AFPFL congress finally decided in favour of full independence, evidently on the assumption that India would also leave the Commonwealth!

The Labour government did not let these developments intimidate it. It successfully resisted the conservative threat to suspend promised financial aid and signed a generous agreement on the transfer of power. In this way it proved its desire to maintain good relations even if Burma decided to leave the Commonwealth. After the tragic assassination of Aung San and a number of his ministers on 19 July, U Nu came into power and signed the actual independence treaty with Attlee on 17 October 1947. On the occasion of the proclamation of independence on 4 January 1948, the Burmese prime minister said:

> We lost our independence without losing our self-respect, we clung to our culture and our traditions and these we now hold to cherish and to develop. . . . We part without rancour and in friendship from the great British nation which held us in fee.[35]

What does this brief summary of events in Burma mean in the context of our discussion? London did not realize in time that Britain's military defeat and the Japanese occupation of South-East Asia had fundamentally altered the situation within Burma. British prestige had suffered and the colonial administration was temporarily out of action. There had been a political, social and psychological landslide; Japanese rule had produced an entirely new class of nationalists who established themselves as the legitimate representatives of the Burmese people. Their claims had to be taken seriously in 1945. Conditions in Burma were entirely different from those in other territories where British rule was perhaps opposed, but had not been interrupted. London did, in fact, take far more notice than before 1941 of the Asian emancipation movements, which had gained impetus through the war and in the fight against Japan. But it still thought Britain could return to Burma as a liberator and that it would be able to eliminate the army organized by the "traitors" Aung San and his followers, as well as the new political organizations, without much difficulty. London imagined that the promise of dominion status would be sufficient proof of Britain's willingness to reform. No doubt the argument that the vital work of reconstruction came first and that constitutional questions could not be discussed until after a transitional period, was well-meant. Perhaps it was even "objectively correct", although the internal disorder in Burma after independence cannot be taken as evidence of this since the assassination of the leaders was hardly foreseeable. But it was not relevant to the internal situation in Burma after the Japanese occupation. Burma did not want a "benevolent administration", it wanted the withdrawal of the colonial power. It did not want good government, but self-government! The young generation of revolutionary nationalists that had emerged during the war was not prepared to wait until London decided to honour its promises "at the proper time". It wanted immediate independence and intended to exploit Britain's weakness to the full and to use the newly formed mass organizations as a means of exerting pressure.

Even if statements giving generous concessions and precise dates had been issued earlier, this might still not have created a solid basis for trust and negotiations. The 1945 White Paper, however, certainly came too late and was far too conservative in tone to have done so. Perhaps Lord Mountbatten's policy would have been more successful in persuading Burma to remain in the Commonwealth if Aung San had been included in an interim government and if his party had been accepted as the most important voice of the Burmese people.

The case of Burma showed that after a certain point the earlier pledges of "ultimate self-government" were no longer enough. London refused to be specific about its promises, or to fix timetables, as the Americans did in the Philippines, so that British declarations lost conviction and became ineffectual. In fact Britain did not simply offer stubborn resistance nor did it allow an open break to occur; but it was overcome by events and, as a result, turned to the defensive and merely "reacted" in the end. London had mistakenly assumed that it still had full control over Burmese policy and need not grant concessions until it seemed advisable. So it was eventually driven into a situation where it was forced to make decisions on very short notice.

The Labour government's policy was not fundamentally different from that of the rather conservative coalition government of the war years. Yet it was the Labour party which, at the last possible moment, changed course and led Aung San to the conference table. It did not manage to persuade Burma to remain in the Commonwealth, yet it did manage to avoid open conflict. Any further delays, such as a conservative government would probably have tried to impose, would have destroyed the last chance of peace and led to serious unrest. It is quite conceivable that left-wing radical elements within the AFPFL would then have seized power. But the departure of the colonial power at the last moment, thanks to Attlee, made it possible for the Burmese Government to ask Britain for military and economic aid in 1947–1948 during the Communist rebellion, and in this way to assert itself successfully in the dangerous struggle.

While Burma demanded and received full independence after the Second World War, Ceylon was content with dominion status. This difference was not coincidental. It was based on the entirely different conditions in the two countries during the final phase of decolonization. By this we do not mean difference of race, language or historical tradition, nor the particular problems of a plural society in either case, but the fact that Ceylon was not directly affected by the war and was not occupied by the Japanese. In this respect, the case of Burma has more in common with that of Indonesia and Indochina than does Ceylon. In Burma, the colonial power collapsed with the Japanese occupation, young social-revolutionary nationalists replaced the old leaders and gained enough popular support to enable them to face the returning colonial power in 1945 with a *fait accompli* and to claim full independence. But developments in Ceylon proceeded along the "prescribed" lines of the constitution. Ceylon was led by an older generation of politicians, recruited from the British-trained élite, who were not supported by the masses, were prepared to compromise, and preferred evolution to revolution.[36]

Ceylon had been granted semi-responsible government in 1931, not on the Westminster model as in the case of Burma in 1937, but in the manner of the London County Council—a council of state with general franchise whose departmental heads formed a kind of cabinet. It is debatable how well this constitution worked and whether it produced positive results. Certainly the Ceylonese gained experience in political decision-making and administrative responsibility, but the main objective of this rather curious special ruling, namely to relieve "communal" frictions, was not successful.[37] Opposition to the constitution did not die, whether because Ceylonese politicians already demanded full dominion status, or whether because the minority groups, especially the Tamils, felt neglected and demanded more representation in the administration and in the cabinet council. Some criticized the departmental system as being a form of discrimination: Great Britain had refused the Ceylonese its own, much-praised parliamentary system! In 1938 the governor, Sir Andrew Caldecott, joined the critics and advised

London to introduce a "cabinet of the normal type", although without restricting the governor's power. The council of state refused this proposal, saying the minorities demanded additional securities.

The Second World War gave Ceylon an opportunity to demand new concessions with a view to full self-government. On 1 September 1941 the colonial minister acknowledged "the urgency and importance of reform of the constitution", but did not want to discuss it until after the war.[38] As in the case of Burma and India, London refused to introduce constitutional reforms during the war, nor would it make any specific promises; it mentioned neither dominion status nor a timetable. At the time of the Cripps mission to India, the state council demanded that Ceylon too should be promised dominion status and that the mission should also visit Ceylon, but neither request was granted.[39]

Finally, in May 1943, the British Government gave in to the demands of Ceylonese leaders, as well as those of the governor and commanders-in-chief, and issued a specific declaration of its Ceylon policy. After the fall of Hong-Kong and Singapore, Ceylon had become a major military base and raw material supplier. According to the declaration, Ceylon was to receive "full responsible Government under the Crown in all matters of internal administration" while Britain reserved itself foreign policy, defense, foreign trade and currency. After the war, said London, it would be prepared to discuss proposals from the Ceylonese ministers.[40] Britain did not promise dominion status but only internal autonomy.

The offer to the ministers to submit their own proposals was a good psychological move. It proved London's willingness to collaborate and meant abandonment of the former stipulation that a new constitution could be imposed only on the basis of a British commission's report. It must remain an open question whether Britain secretly hoped that the Ceylonese, like the Indians, would not be able to solve their "communal" problems and would not manage to submit any proposals which were agreed to by all the rival communities. The addition to the May declaration, namely that the Ceylonese proposals must obtain a two-thirds majority in the state council, could be interpreted in this way. But in itself the demand that the Singhalese majority in the cabinet work out a compromise which would satisfy at least a proportion of the minority groups, was justifiable. In February 1944, the proposals, largely formulated by the notable English constitutional lawyer Sir Ivor Jennings, then rector of the University of Colombo, were submitted to the governor. However, they did not get the necessary two-thirds majority in the state council and were violently criticized by the minority groups.

The British Government took this as a pretext for setting up a commission under Lord Soulbury to examine the Ceylonese proposals and to gauge the opinions of the different communities. Ceylonese politicians naturally interpreted this as a delaying tactic and, officially at least, boycotted the commission. The commission's report in September 1945, however, was on the same lines as the proposals, though it demanded a second parliamentary chamber and said that the governor's position should be strengthened. The majority of politically aware Ceylonese were in favour of a constitution on the British model, the commission said, and were familiar with the language, history and laws of Great Britain. The mass of the population still lacked political maturity, yet "we think it better to devise a Constitution somewhat in advance of the stage already reached rather than behind it".[41] Previously, the motto of the Colonial Office had been: better too slow than too fast. Now, in the war, Britain wished to demonstrate that it was eager for reforms! Thus the report also decided the old question of whether one could and should transfer the British representative system to an Asian people or whether one should try to find a more suitable system of responsible government. India had already shown that London had no option but to gradually introduce the British system of government. As long as the proposals—for instance for a presidential system of the American type—did not come from the nationalists, any other solution seemed to be a delaying tactic or discrimination.

The report was confirmed by the White Paper of 31 October 1945[42] which in turn became the basis of the new constitution of 1946.[43] It is important to note that in spite of cabinet demands and the personal intervention of the prime minister, Senanayake, dominion status had not yet been granted: "It is clearly not possible to reach that goal in a single step." London was very conscious of its strategic interests in Ceylon. The White Paper merely said that the British Government had "sympathy" for the Ceylonese desire to undertake the final step toward full independence, and that this depended on the functioning of the constitution. These words may have contributed to the state council acceptance of the constitution in November 1946 by 51 votes to 3, a result that underlines the special situation that existed in Ceylon and the moderate nationalism of its leaders, in particular the prime minister. Neither India nor Burma would have been prepared to accept anything less than full dominion status by the end of 1945!

Naturally Ceylonese demands exceeded British concessions. In February 1947, in a letter to the colonial minister, Senanayake demanded dominion status. In autumn 1946 there had been strikes. In view of the coming elections, the prime minister had strengthened his party. New disturbances were possible and would have initiated the demand for full independence. Since they had an interest in Senanayake winning the elections, the governor, the colonial minister and the Colonial Office supported his demands, while the government hesitated, wanting to keep Ceylon as a strategic base.[44] Massive pressure from the Ceylonese finally persuaded the Labour government to give in. Further hesitation would have threatened what had already been gained, weakened Britain's prestige in Asia and in addition strengthened the position of the extremists. On 18 June 1947, Creech-Jones declared in the House of Commons that, as soon as the new government came into office, negotiations would begin for Ceylon to receive "fully responsible Government".[45] The agreement of 11 November granted Ceylon dominion status, but allowed Britain to keep its naval and air bases until 1956 and to give military assistance. The Ceylon Independence Bill was passed on 4 February 1948.[46]

Ceylon demonstrated the road to self-government in "exemplary fashion": decolonization proceeded in accordance with the many implicit or explicit British pronouncements. Without breaking with the mother country, after a number of preliminary stages, the colony finally received dominion status, i.e. "Self-Government within the British Empire". In spite of friction and tensions, in spite of nationalist demands and British resistance, both partners always showed themselves ready for negotiation and compromise. This was how England had imagined decolonization! And so, justifiably we think, Britain was very proud that in the case of Ceylon the process of emancipation took place according to mutual agreement, without unrest, boycotts or threats of riots, and also without repression and bloodshed. Accordingly, on 4 December Lord Addison, the former minister for the dominions, declared in the House of Lords:

> This is the first occasion in our history upon which a Colony, developing this system of Self-Government of its own accord, has deliberately sought to become a Dominion State in our Commonwealth . . . but we hope and expect that it will not be the last.[47]

This short survey is also meant to show that London did not really plan the individual steps in decolonizing its territories, but simply granted demands and made concessions as it considered necessary. London had no definite timetables. It had planned on much longer interim stages, which it gradually shortened under pressure. Contributing to this speeding up were the nationalists, who constantly increased their demands and strengthened their party organization, and the general situation in Asia after the war: Singapore, the American pressure, the example of India. A significant change of attitude began to emerge in Britain. Hitherto Britain had hoped that its resistance to emancipation movements and stubborn adherence to its position of power would uphold the power of the Empire and Britain's irrevocable intention to have an important say in Asia. But now Britain wanted to assure its prestige by voluntarily introducing decolonization. The goodwill Britain had won by its withdrawal from India must not be lost by a display of all too stubborn resistance in another country.

Nothing demonstrates the new relationship between Europe and Asia after 1945 better than this hitherto unknown consideration of prestige. Naturally, London had an interest in delaying its withdrawal from colonial positions, and military considerations were probably more important than economic ones; naturally London's concessions always trailed slightly behind actual events. But Britain proved flexible enough to change course on time and to avoid open disagreement. In the case of Ceylon, the adaptation was relatively easy, since London was faced only by moderate nationalists who did not aim at social revolution and wanted to maintain good relations with Britain. But, paradoxically, this only hastened Britain's withdrawal: London had to make concessions in order to support the moderates and prevent worse things from happening. In view of the rapidly increasingly revolutionary movement in Asia, and later in Africa, the colonial power had to be content if it could hand over control to a moderate nationalist movement and create a favourable basis for relations in the post-colonial era!

Finally, by not demanding independence (as the Indians and the Burmese nationalists did after 1945), but merely dominion status, the Ceylonese involuntarily acted in accordance with the British feeling, which made it easier for London to accede to their demands. It is not surprising that the decolonization of Ceylon gave rise to little discussion or even protest in the mother country. The grant of dominion status was not so much a "liquidation of the Empire" as its conversion into an extended Commonwealth.

FROM LEGISLATIVE COUNCIL TO INDEPENDENCE: THE GOLD COAST AND NIGERIA

We are concerned here with depicting the emancipation movement in West Africa which began with the Second World War. As we have seen, the Atlantic Charter and London's twofold reaction to it provoked the West African Students' Union to issue a declaration demanding, among other things, a united Nigeria and a federal constitution. After the fall of Singapore and Malaya, the students specified their immediate aims and demanded "internal self-government", to be followed by full self-government within five years after the war.[1] After the blockade of the Mediterranean and the loss of Malaya, West Africa became an important strategic and economic base for the Allies. At the beginning of the war, London thought it could not purchase the entire West African production of vital crops, cocoa for instance, due to lack of shipping space, and waited for a production crisis to arise. But instead, production increased considerably after 1942. In June, Churchill appointed

Lord Swinton (the former colonial minister Cunliffe) minister-resident for West Africa, thus underlining the great importance of the Gold Coast and Nigeria to the Allies.[2] London imported the entire production of cocoa, palm-oil, palm-nuts, groundnuts, cotton, tin, diamonds and bauxite, and even promoted local industrialization. Very soon, state offices supervised most of the West African economy. The African producers and middlemen profited, more workers were hired and immigration to urban centres reached a critical level. In 1942 London sent a labour adviser to Nigeria, and by July 1942 the unions joined to form the Nigeria Trade Union Congress, which was to gain political power in years to come.[3] A general strike was even proclaimed in 1945. Thus the war gave a great impetus to "social disintegration and social mobilization". Excessive purchasing power, the lack of imported consumer goods and rising prices, added to the many official rulings, created dissatisfaction and provoked political agitation, particularly after the war.

West Africa became a supply centre for the Near and Far East. With the help of African labour, the Allied forces built airports (thirty in Nigeria alone), expanded ports, bought planes and built repair works. Countless Africans of all social classes came into contact with whites for the first time. In addition, Africans were given military training and a number of African divisions fought in North and East Africa and in Burma.

The Second World War acted as a kind of catalyst. National organizations had begun to appear in the inter-war years, but they had been restricted to a rather narrow class. Now economic expansion and its social effects began to arouse political awareness. African soldiers who were released after the war offered political organizations a new field of recruitment. New leaders appeared: Azikiwe and Awolowo in Nigeria, Danquah and Nkrumah in the Gold Coast. Influential figures, educated in England and America, they were no longer mere individuals facing the colonial administration and voicing African demands while loyally collaborating with the councils and committees. Now they had the sympathy of the masses, adopted radical slogans and tried to impose concessions on the mother country through their organizations, parties and demonstrations.

Even during the tenure of the Labour government, the administration at first underestimated the strength of the West African emancipation movements. In spite of its readiness to speed up reforms, Britain still did not see any need to take the "educated Africans" too seriously and continued to think it could relegate them to local government. The unexpectedly rapid transition from legislative council to full independence was largely imposed on the British Government: after 1945, reforms were always answers to resistance or pressure from the nationalist opposition. However, after its initial hesitation, Britain once again showed that it could cope with the challenge and followed the new course to its logical conclusion. The Conservative government continued as the Labour government had begun.

Once again Margery Perham reflected how London saw the immediate future of West Africa during and just after the war. In 1941, in a brochure addressed primarily to African students, she skilfully compared the British attitude with African demands.[4] She defended indirect rule, advised the Africans to study anthropology, and stressed the role of the unions. But:

> One thing is certain: that you must have foreign rulers, and for a long time to come . . . to-day you have more need of the British nation than we have of you.

This was a well-meant but rather paternalistic piece of advice to the young educated élite to come to terms with colonial rule!

In October 1945, Margery Perham turned to American readers in an article in *Foreign Affairs*.[5] She said Africa could not be compared to the Philippines or Puerto Rico as it was "unready for anything approaching independence". Long-standing contact between the colony and the mother country produces a political and intellectual community, she wrote, and "develops close ties of interest and sentiment", thereby also increasing the colony's desire to enter into a free partnership as a dominion in the Commonwealth. These words were aimed at American anti-colonialists and were designed to explain the sense and significance of the Commonwealth. They also showed that this influential expert on Africa not only reckoned on many more years of colonial ties but, in an optimism that seems curious, assumed that Britain's stay in Africa would lead not to a conflict with the emancipation movements but to an ever better understanding between them and the colonial power. Two years later, however, in the preface to Awolowo's book *Path to Nigerian Freedom*, Perham's benevolent paternalism gave way to open discussion with Nigerian nationalists. Britain, she said, must find out what these young people believed and ask itself, "Have we really accepted this change of purpose?" But Margery Perham continued to believe that the only question was that of the intransigence of a few hundred people. Awolowo himself confirmed, she said, that there was not as yet a Nigerian nation. The time when Nigeria would join a federation or even become a nation "is still far away". Dominion status, she admitted, was the aim of British policy, but still lay in the far distance. First came Nigerian political development within the tribal organizations and the individual regions, and "Britain may for long be required to provide the framework which holds these groups together until they are able to fuse into unity or federation".[6] In 1947, the liberal Mrs. Perham, who looked to the masses rather than to the nationalist leaders, still counted on a long period of transition, during which the colonial power would fulfil its civilizing mission more or less undisturbed. This assumpton, based on a comprehensive knowledge of African social structures and traditions and of the problems of Nigerian unity, may be all too understandable; but Margery Perham evidently overlooked the catalyzing effects of the Second World War and the rapidly growing impatience of the urban bourgeois intelligentsia.

Equally noteworthy is the attitude of W. R. Crocker, who aroused interest in 1936 with his criticism of the doctrinaire rigidity of indirect rule.[7] This former colonial official stressed his impartiality and attacked the self-praise and "cant" he had observed in the Empire Day speeches. But he vehemently opposed the "heroic schemes of economic development" which were being discussed at the time. In the next five to ten years, Britain would have to take care lest its one-sided policy of development did not entirely fragment African society. It would be a pity if the African masses marched into the factories and were exposed without protection to the most dubious products of Western civilization. The African economy was far too important to be allowed to founder and efforts should be made to evolve an "organic policy" on the lines of the American TVA. The same applied, he thought, to political reforms. Crocker was in favour of indirect rule only according to Lugard's interpretation; he discussed reforms and—surprisingly—criticized what he considered a one-sided emphasis on the urban minority.

> The colonial powers have indeed pushed too far. Their great duty today is not to "develop" Africa but to slow down the "development" and to safeguard for Africans a way of life. . . .[8]

These theories were not intended to be "colonialist", for Crocker was less concerned with maintaining colonial rule than with working out a form of social and political development conforming to African conditions. He saw the complexity of the problem of "development", and his sociological arguments are worth noting. But in retrospect, it seems strange that he wanted a "slow-down" and thought that concentration on the native authorities and the agricultural production in Africa would solve the critical situation and prevent an all too rapid emancipation. Here he was perhaps expressing the traditional views of the colonial official who had worked "in the bush" and felt he had a duty to the masses, but was unfamiliar with the urban population and suspicious of the educated African.

Compared to Perham and Crocker, Lord Hailey seems much more realistic. Euphemisms about self-government were no longer enough, he thought, and were far too often linked to "mental reservations".[9] The time factor could no longer be neglected: "the time within which we conceive that this future can be, or may be, realized is in fact an all important factor." The pace of development had vastly increased, he said, and might seem anomalous to the colonial powers; but one must take into consideration the effects of world opinion, the United Nations, and events in Asia: "I suggest that we are likely to see in Africa a rapidly growing process of decolonization." Economic development and political education must be promoted actively. It was quite possible that the Africans would not remain in the Commonwealth, yet one should try to show them the advantages of future membership. Hailey did not indulge in any delusions about having sufficient time to plan and direct African emanicipation as a long-term development and warned against the danger of trailing behind events.

One could say that Britain's post-war West Africa policy, including that of the Labour government, tended to be guided by Margery Perham's theories, whereas after 1948 Britain took heed of Lord Hailey's warnings.

The main issue was the reform of native administrations. We have seen that the criticism of indirect rule that began in the 1930s was generally accepted and played an important part in the discussion of post-war policy. The native authorities only partly fulfilled their function as a "training ground" on the local level for self-government. Economic development and the extension of health services and the educational system posed new problems which the chiefs and elders, who often could neither read nor write, could not deal with adequately. The Colonial Development and Welfare Fund, which made special funds available for local government, required an efficient administration conforming to modern conditions. Moreover, the class of young educated Africans had become more and more important and began to organize and to come into conflict with the traditional authorities. The development of effective local government on the European model became an urgent problem.

As early as 1943 the conservative colonial minister Stanley declared in the House of Commons:

> I regard the extension of local government as one of the quickest and certainly the surest methods of making certain of the extension of central government.[10]

The Labour government made special efforts to promote effective native authorities. An important instruction to the governors in 1947 stated as follows:

> I believe that the key to success lies in the development of an efficient and democratic system of local government. The African governments are now beginning to put their ten-years development programs into execution. The stage has been reached when paper plans must be translated into action and it is in the townships and villages among the people themselves that much of this action must take place. There are many development schemes where success in whole, or in part, depends on the active co-operation of the people and that co-operation can best be secured through

the leadership of local authorities. Without an effective sytem of local government the great mass of the African population will derive only partial benefits from the monies granted for development by the Colonial Legislatures.[14]

The generous policy of development announced was closely related to the need for converting the native authorities, with their traditionally modest sphere of influence, into modern local governments, as is clearly evident here. The political aim was similar:

> An efficient and democratic system of local government is in fact essential to the healthy political development of the African territories; it is the foundation on which their progress must be built.[12]

The democratically organized local authorities were not to serve merely as electoral colleges for the representative bodies and to furnish political staff for the central legislature. They were also to have the political and educational function of familiarizing the Africans with the electoral system, parliamentary procedure and administrative responsibility. It was necessary, said the secretary of state for the colonies in 1949, to represent more than just the "traditional elements" in the rural areas, and to include

> the rising middle classes, the farmers, industrial workers and the educated minority all of whom have an important part to play in the growth of these institutions in their home areas.[13]

The plan to democratize and politicize the rural areas may have been connected with the hope of being able to confront the urban organizations and radical nationalists with moderate representatives of African emancipation, thereby at least temporarily blocking the radical elements.[14] The administration called upon British history and reiterated the old theory that democratization and self-government must exist in the local field before one could create a secure basis for representative institutions. Before 1939 London thought this could be achieved by indirect rule through the native authorities and that there was still a great deal of time for adjustment; but after 1945, it saw the urgency of the need for "modernization" and tried hard to catch up. This situation came at an opportune time for the Labour government. The gradual elimination of the traditional classes conformed with its democratic creed and made it possible to "reform" without yet having to intervene decisively in the centre. The British communal constitution served as model, although the institutions of the mother country were not taken over directly. France decolonized locally, by granting African towns and villages the legal status of *communes*. By contrast, London sent commissions of experts to the colonies and tried by experimental means to work out rulings conforming to local structures. It wanted to put an elected council in the place of the chiefs and councils who had been appointed, i.e. confirmed, and who almost exclusively recruited from among the traditional authorities in the tribes and villages. This council would be representative, receive greater administrative power and be only loosely controlled from above. London did not simply want to eliminate the traditional element but to incorporate it, while it transferred the real power to the "educated middle classes".

A few examples will illustrate this. In South-East Nigeria in 1950–1951, after careful preparations, London introduced a "county [!] council" with subordinate village and district councils; the village councils were elected directly by all the tax-payers, the district councils indirectly. Boundaries had to be redrawn and small native authorities were merged; the tax system was reorganized and the local government was put in charge of education. As an interim solution, the chairman of the native authorities was elected.[15] In South-West Nigeria, where London wanted to show respect for the traditional *Obas*, it divided the councils into elected and traditional members; often *Obas* acted as heads of the council. Since the new generation of native rulers had usually received a European education, the traditional authorities and the new educated élite began to come closer. The process was much slower in the north, owing to the resistance of the firmly entrenched feudalist Muslim emirates. The native authorities remained, but were "modernized" by the introduction of councils with elected members. These councils became a kind of cabinet of the emir. But the number of native authorities was greatly reduced, and Kano, for instance, received its own town council.[16]

The first reforms in the Gold Coast took place as early as 1944. Jurisdiction was transferred to the indigenous authorities, while the right of appointment in the native authorities was underlined and used more than before.[17] This reform, which affected the system of indirect rule from within, was not very successful because "destoolments", i.e. the deposition of the chiefs by their own councils, increased and led to open crises. The transition to genuine local government was not completed until 1951, after the electoral victory of Nkrumah's party. Then the elected councils got an elected chairman, while the chief presided only on ceremonial occasions.[18] A special ministry supervised local government.

After the war indirect rule, on which Great Britain had so prided itself, dropped out of favour within a few years, and the native authorities so painstakingly established were replaced by a more modern local government. Characteristically, the reforms were most fundamental in places where indirect rule had not worked efficiently and where the native authorities were rather artificial. The chiefs and elders were dislodged from their pre-eminent positions while "educated Africans" gained access to the elected councils. In spite of a latent conflict between old and young, between the traditional authorities and the rising bourgeoisie and intelligentsia, there was some evidence of co-operation and community of interest in the following years, as also in French West Africa. For the chiefs continued to enjoy a high regard in rural areas and could therefore gain political influence. Some even took an active part in administration and party politics. The best-known example is the Sadauna of Sokoto, party leader of the Northern People's Congress, prime minister of the North and *éminence grise* of independent Nigeria. In their turn, the parties had to win the co-operation and support of the chiefs and traditional dignitaries if they wanted to gain mass support in the bush too.[19]

Meanwhile the Labour government undertook positive reforms at the local level. Of course it could not grant all the nationalists' demands and it was in its interests to support the traditional authorities for reasons of defence and in order to counterbalance the national opposition, and to incorporate them in the new local government. Whether Labour achieved the aims it proclaimed—"efficiency" and education in democracy—is another question.[20] London counted on a fairly long period of transition before handing over the instruments of power to the centre. The Labour government, like the conservatives, thought it could concentrate on local government for the time being and that this would satisfy the Africans and establish a basis for democratic self-government. This assumption proved wrong and decolonization had to be speeded up. As a result, the Africans could reproach Britain in retrospect with having granted self-government at the centre, in spite of all its earlier pronouncements, before local self-government was properly established.[21]

This brings us to the constitutional development of West Africa. After the stagnation of the 1930s, a reform movement began during the Second World War. The Labour government followed up on the preparations made by the coalition government. In 1942, the first two Africans were appointed to the advisory executive council of the Gold Coast, and in October 1944 Governor Burns announced a new constitution which, however, was not enforced until March 1946. The Ashanti were included and the legislative council, which until then had represented only the "Gold Coast Colony", became an institution embracing the entire state, although at first the northern territories remained outside and received only their own council of chiefs. In this way London began to "amalgamate" inside the larger colonial administrative unit. In addition, the Gold Coast obtained an elected majority in the legislative council and thus became the first African territory to complete the transition to representative government. However, the election was indirect, through the intermediary of town and provincial councils on the one hand, and the Ashanti federation on the other. In a sense this spelled the end of indirect rule, for both the chiefs and notables, and the educated Africans obtained a role in the political decision-making. But the executive remained under the governor while a more rapid Africanization of the administration was planned. The Burns constitution, which represented an important step towards self-government and underlined the desire for reform that arose during the war, was generally accepted by the Africans too.[22]

In Nigeria, Governor Richards prepared a new constitution in 1944–1945, which was put into effect a year later. London described its aims as follows:

> The object of the proposed reforms is to set up a framework within which development towards responsible Government can be planned and carried out on practical lines—a purpose for which it has become apparent that the existing political organisation is inadequate. The proposals have been designed to bridge the gulf between the people and the Government by measure of decentralisation and by a widening of the basis of representation which will bring the established native authorities within the legislative machine. At the same time they provide, by a grant of unofficial majorities in the Legislative and Regional Councils, for an immediate advance along the road to responsible Government.[23]

Richards' statement describes the situation and outlines immediate tasks to be undertaken after the war. Responsible government was officially confirmed as the ultimate aim of Britain's Africa policy. Dominion status was not mentioned—as it was in simultaneous declarations in Asia—but in fact there was scarcely any difference now between responsible government and dominion status, or even independence. In a certain sense responsible government meant even more than dominion status, since it implied decolonization without the promise to remain in the Commonwealth and left the way open for independence or a special ruling. The statement shows how the grant of responsible government was gradually extended from the colonial settlements, via India, Burma and Ceylon, and eventually to Africa, almost under compulsion. At the same time London evidently realized that the previous sharp distinction between the native authorities and the colonial administration could not serve as the basis for a representative system. However, London did not want to simply eliminate the native councils, but to give them a part in the legislative council in order to ensure a smooth transition to a modern system of government.

At the same time that London was contemplating self-government for Africa, the question of Nigerian unity arose. We have seen how before 1939 London did not feel it was urgent to amalgamate north and south; there had even been a tendency to promote regional development. But during the war people began to think in terms of larger units. There was much talk of regional co-operation, since this seemed the only economically and politically viable solution. At first, perhaps, administrative questions took precedence, but they influenced the general political plan. In December 1944 Governor Richards described the existing order as "by its nature unsuited for expansion on a Nigerian basis" and some of his constitutional proposals aimed to "promote the unity of Nigeria".[24] There seem to have been differences of opinion as to the ways and means of unifying north and south. The administration of Northern Nigeria urged a federal solution, while Governor Bourdillon and Lord Hailey were in favour of a more unitarian constitution.[25] The result was a gradual transition from "regionalism" to federation, which was the aim of both the self-assured but conservative north as well as the nationalists Azikiwe and Awolowo, who had built up their parties on a regional basis. While the administration wanted a unified state, combined with decentralized government, in order to prevent the still fragile unity of Nigeria from disintegrating, the Nigerians urged federation and finally imposed their will.[26] In 1947–1948 Awolowo, the political leader of the south-west, and Balewa, later prime minister of the federation, still reproached London with having spent years trying to create an artificial Nigerian unity: the people of Nigeria were far too varied and a Nigerian nation did not exist![27] Paradoxically, while in other cases the nationalists were quick to criticize the colonial power for trying to divide and rule, they now opposed London's attempt to create a state of Nigeria. This curious overlapping of fronts clearly shows London's change of course during the Second World War.

The 1946 Richards constitution contained important innovations. Ibadan, Enugu and Kadvan each obtained a regional parliament with unofficial majorities, elected indirectly through the native authorities; these bodies shared in general legislative responsibilities and control over the regional budgets. They also elected the deputies to the legislative council of Nigeria. The executive council, which included two Nigerians, remained unchanged at first, as in the Gold Coast, and continued to have only advisory powers.

In contrast of the Gold Coast, the African nationalists in Nigeria refused the new constitution entirely.[28] They said London had not asked their advice in the council and had simply imposed the new order on them. Nor had London granted their demand to occupy at least one administrative department. They opposed the consideration given the native authorities and rejected the system of indirect elections, saying that it increased the power of the traditional authorities, whom London was playing off against the emancipated urban classes. London may have considered the new constitution an interesting attempt to combine indirect rule with representative institutions; it certainly also hoped to strengthen the influence of the agrarian backlands and to gain a majority of "moderates" in the parliament thanks to the native authorities. This drove the young leaders and their political followers into opposition.[29]

Both in the Gold Coast and in Nigeria the British Government had counted on a fairly long period of transition.[30] It saw the two constitutions of 1946 as a major step towards self-government and evidence of its desire for reform. Even the Labour government considered this satisfactory for the time being. It was only to be expected that the stage of representative government that had now been reached led to the danger of "power without responsibility" and that the new assemblies would become a forum where the African opposition could announce its radical demands and gain political support, although people like Sir Bourdillon still hoped that the system of indirect elections would prevent conflict. The transition to responsible government was the stated aim of British policy, but it still seemed to lie in the far distance.

By 1948 serious distubances broke out in the Gold Coast.[31] War veterans organized a demonstration and clashed with the police. At the same time increasing dissatisfaction over rising prices and the lack of consumer goods broke like a storm over European and Syrian firms. The two-day riots which spread from Accra to other towns resulted in 29 dead and 237 wounded. The administration had to intervene. It arrested six leaders of the United Gold Coast Convention founded in 1947, including Dr. Danquah and Kwame Nkrumah, the recently elected secretary of the party.

The "Gold Coast Disturbances" had taken the administration by surprise. It had been deceived by the apparent acceptance of the Burns constitution and had evidently underestimated the rapidly growing opposition. So the 1948 riots were a shock, particularly to the Labour government, which had wrongly assumed that one could confine reforms to the local area at first and need not hand over any power at the centre. These riots "changed our mood from one of supreme confidence to utter dismay overnight".[32] It was too late to go back and a radical change of course seemed the only way to prevent a vicious circle of repression and growing opposition. The wave of emancipation had flooded West Africa sooner and more violently than expected. Britain had to readjust and to abandon its timetables if it was to remain in control.

The new attitude is illustrated in the report of the commission of enquiry under A. K. Watson.[33] It exposed the causes of the riots with surprising frankness. Many of the African veterans had developed a "political and national [!] consciousness" and were dissatisfied; there existed

> a feeling of political frustration among the educated Africans who saw no prospect of ever experiencing political power under existing conditions and who regarded the 1946 Constitution as mere window-dressing designed to cover but not to advance their natural aspirations. . . .

The report said the administration had misjudged the effects of Western education and underestimated the tensions with the conservative chiefs and the influence of events in India, Burma and Ceylon. It was not enough to "Africanize" and provide educational facilities. Although corruption was widespread it must under no circumstances be used as a pretext for delaying further steps towards self-government. The 1946 constitution related to pre-war conditions and was therefore outdated. "Substantial" reforms were needed, "not only to gain political experience but also to experience political power". The transition to responsible government must begin: the former advisory executive council should be converted into a cabinet council responsible to the legislative council; five of the nine ministers should be Africans. The governor should at least retain the presidency, the vote and "reserved powers".

This was the breakthrough. Challenged by the riots in Accra, London did not stop at repressive measures but accepted "national" emancipation and took the final step to responsible government with an African majority. At the same time the Watson commission severly criticized Nkrumah and his party and described their aims as Communist!

The colonial minister Creech-Jones accepted the report[34] and in January 1949 appointed a commission consisting only of Africans to work out constitutional proposals. Although Nkrumah was in prison and the chiefs defended conservative opinions in the commission, it was an innovation to collaborate with Africans in this way. London wanted to give a say to the moderates and at the same time refute the charge that it was again imposing a new constitution. The Coussey report[35] largely coincided with the Watson proposals, was fairly well received by the government[36] and the British press, and became the basis of the 1951 constitution.

The moderate African press also accepted the proposals. But Nkrumah demanded "full dominion status", i.e. a cabinet consisting exclusively of Africans, and an end to the governor's reserved powers. He broke with his party and founded the Convention People's party, which was no longer "bourgeois" and became a tool in the hands of its leader. It relied chiefly on the rapidly increasing class of Ghanaians who had only a rudimentary education and were in fairly open conflict with traditional authorities.[37] In 1950, when Nkrumah threatened to turn to "positive action", i.e. to boycotts and strikes, he was arrested again. Yet he had achieved an overwhelming victory in the first general elections in February 1951, so the governor had no choice but to release him and entrust him with forming a cabinet. Later Sir Arden-Clarke defended this action:

> I do not know whether it would have been possible to slow things down and still retain that good will; and if that good will had been lost, I wonder whether Ghana would still be a member of the Commonwealth? That is as far as I will go in answering my own question.[38]

By consistently pursuing his new policy and refusing to employ delaying tactics in 1951, the governor did indeed ensure some goodwill and even relieve Nkrumah's suspicions,[39] so that the final stage of decolonization took place without open conflict. In March 1952 Nkrumah officially became prime minister, and in 1954 the official British ministers were replaced by Africans; the Africanization of the administrative cadre followed rapidly. However, there was some delay because of serious internal tensions, particularly between Nkrumah's CPP and the Ashanti opposition. In May 1956 the colonial minister declared himself ready to fix a date for independence as soon as a newly elected parliament passed a motion to this effect. In 1957 the Gold Coast, under its new name of Ghana, became the first African colony to obtain independence.

After 1948 decolonization also proceeded more quickly in Nigeria.[40] Governor Richards, much disliked by the Africans, was replaced by Sir John Macpherson. The administration began to be Africanized. A commission appointed by the governor clarified the situation and stipulated that "no non-Nigerian should be recruited for any Government post except where no suitable and qualified Nigerian is available". Its own lack of new blood made it easier for the colonial office to give in to the Africans' pressure, and the number of Nigerians in the higher administrative service rose from 23 in 1939 to 182 in 1947, 628 (out of 3679) in 1951 and 786 in 1953. The ten-year plan was put into effect and created new posts for Africans. The governor encouraged democratization of the native authorities and conversion to local government, and made more funds available for a rapid development of the educational system from 1948 on.[41] In the same year the University College of Nigeria was opened in Ibadan. The premature revision of the constitution was intended to be preceded by discussion with representatives from the local, provincial and regional areas. Ostensibly this was in order to give a voice to African opinion and to let it evolve from within; in fact it also helped to strengthen the forces of conservatism and to gain support against the urban organizations of the nationalist parties. The 1951 constitution led, as in the Gold Coast, to the conversion of the executive council into a cabinet council consisting of six British and four Africans appointed by the regions. It gave the regions wider control, but adhered to the indirect electoral system. As a result it was sharply criticized by the Africans from the start. The relationship between south and north now became a focal issue. The north, with its fairly large population but rather backward civilization and lack of political emancipation feared the domination of the non-Muslim south and demanded both a longer period of transition to self-government and representation proportional to its large population. The south, on the other hand, thought it was being blocked on the road to freedom and accused the administration of collaborating with the north. In fact, the north had over 50 percent of the representatives in the legislative council and, when joined by the official members of the cabinet, its ministers could outvote the south. The south was angered by the fact that in March 1953 the Sadauna of Sokoto, leader of the Northern People's Congress, opposed a motion from the south to proclaim self-government for Nigeria in 1956 and replaced the precise date by "as soon as practicable". In May there was a serious clash between northerners and southerners in Kano.

The situation was coming to a head, and there was a danger of secession in the north, so a conference was called in London in July and August 1953 to work out a basis for the 1954 constitution. In order to conciliate the north and save Nigerian unity London gave up the concept of "regional" unity in favour of federation. The regions were to receive African governments with their own prime ministers and could demand full autonomy in 1956. In spite of strong pressure from the nationalists of the south, London refused to fix a date for Nigerian independence and agreed only to consider it within the next three years.

These concessions relieved tensions, and relations improved between the colonial power and the nationalists. The nationalists promised loyalty to the Commonwealth and their attitude helped make the British queen's journey to Nigeria a success. In 1957 the eastern and western regions were granted internal autonomy, while Alhaji Abubakar Tafawa Balewa, from the north, replaced the governor and became first prime minister of Nigeria. Two years later the north was also ready to demand full self-government, thereby fulfilling the last condition for the 1960 declaration of independence in Nigeria.

We have briefly outlined the constitutional development of Nigeria and the Gold Coast between 1945 and 1960 and the road which led from weak representation in the legislative council, via representative government, to full dominion status. The pace quickened noticeably, as the transitional periods had to be shortened and far-reaching concessions had to be granted much sooner than planned. In the beginning the Labour government still thought it had enough time to make reforms gradually and continued to rely predominantly on the support of the traditional leaders. But the 1948 riots taught it a lesson. The African emancipation movement was the main force that persuaded London to risk taking the major step to responsible government. Afterwards, the government and the administration were sensible enough to act generously so as not to lose contact with the African parties again and to bring decolonization to a rapid conclusion without further unnecessary delays. However, even after 1948 London counted on fairly long preliminary periods, trusted that the African leaders would behave "sensibly" and underestimated both the impatience and the rapid radicalization of the nationalists.[42]

Margery Perham still believed in 1951 that it would take years to reach the final stage of independence. She agreed that the elections in the Gold Coast and the formation of an African government were historic events and that one must ask if there were still time for Europe to assert its civilizing power effectively, but she thought it was

> not a very bold speculation to believe that they [the African colonies] may become full self-governing nation-states by the end of the century[1]. It almost seems as though future African writers of history books may thus be able very neatly to sum up the first half of the twentieth century as the age of imperialism, and the second as the age of liberation![43]

Naturally Mrs Perham was not trying to maintain British rule as long as possible but rather was convinced that the African colonies were not yet "ripe" for taking over government and administration. She argued that there was a lack of educated African staff, the administration was not very "Africanized" yet, the economic structure was unstable and overdependent on foreign aid, and the rural masses were still untouched by civilization. Could a state that was still so dependent on foreign aid develop its own initiatives? Could one take the responsibility of premature withdrawal? There was a real dilemma![44]

Another important question was that of the internal unity of the colony. There was no hope for colonial development and a smooth process of decolonization while the state that was to obtain independence was still fragmented. It is striking, in fact, that later discussion of the constitution is dominated by a desire to co-ordinate the divergent areas, tribes and groups within the colony, or at least to reconcile them to some extent and not to release them from imperial control until an institutional framework containing them all had been accepted by all the parties concerned; formerly London had been more concerned with the reserved rights of the colonial power and ways of maintaining certain imperial positions in West Africa. London's attempts to solve the Ashanti problem and to ensure that Northern Nigeria joined the federation were not just delaying tactics. The old British theory that London must not hand over its trusteeship prematurely continued for a long time to preclude any understanding of colonial emancipation and led to the tendency to rely on the traditional classes. In the final phase of decolonization in the Gold Coast and Nigeria this theory had some relevance, however. If power had been transferred prematurely to the nationalist representatives, neither of these states might have achieved unity—or only done so under compulsion and temporarily. We have described the changes in British attitude after 1940: London tried to create larger units and managed to prevent the "Balkanization" of West Africa, or at least a further fragmentation of the existing administrative units. The same applied to the functioning of institutions and the Africanization of the administration. By gradually extending their power and franchise, and by letting them occupy government posts, it was possible to familiarize the Africans with political responsibility. No doubt Britain included Africans in the administration too late and reluctantly,[45] yet it was not too late for the transfer of power to take place almost without friction.

To conclude this survey let us note a few other opinions. They are not representative of the official attitude of the two parties (as a whole Creech-Jones' policy was supported by the conservatives in Parliament, who in turn continued the decolonization begun by the Labour government) but they do afford us an insight into the views of certain interested circles. The West Africa policy inaugurated in 1948 was greeted with suspicion and rejected by the diehards. In the parliamentary debate on 29 July 1949, M.P. Cooper criticized the excessive concessions to the Gold Coast and the Coussey Commission.[46] He thought economic problems should be solved first, "and then the political difficulties will start to fall into place". London was giving the impression "too soon and too quickly that Self-Government should come and that it is just around the corner". Only "a few intellectuals" wanted such excessive constitutional reforms; it is ridiculous to speak of colonial exploitation when it was precisely this minority group of intellectuals that was exploiting its compatriots. The intellectuals had not yet "reached the standard of morality and capacity to handle Self-Government effectively". The mass of Africans did not want self-government "at an early date" but "good, effective and thoroughly understanding leadership". Important party speakers liked to underline the development of local government and the importance of the traditional authorities. Lennox-Boyd, for instance, the future conservative colonial minister, praised the Coussey report because, unlike the Watson Commission's report, it paid attention to the chiefs. This could prevent a "paramount duty", i.e. the dominance of an oligarchic minority, as had happened in Liberia for example. This "democratic" argument was intended, of course, to persuade the government to lengthen the transitional periods and to explain the need for continued British rule.[47] There was "no such thing as a Nigerian people", said Selwyn-Lloyd in the same debate, and extremists must not be allowed to overthrow the "time schedule for constitutional development".[48]

In *Round Table* a conservative writer asked whether indirect rule was really out of date and whether Britain really intended to transfer power to a "small group of westernized Africans". He saw the elimination of the chiefs and the premature grant of self-government "on a western constitutional model" as a betrayal of the population. The emirs had become progressive, the 1946 constitution was a success, and "educated Africans" found offices in the native authorities. Political development was proceeding too quickly and the Colonial Office

> seems to have become infected with its African pupils' belief in the ritual of the ballet-box. . . . What then can now be done? It is not too late to indulge in some clear thinking and to refuse to give way before a movement that can only end in a disastrous lowering of the standards of

administration and an abandonment of all hope of those higher standards of life to which all, Africans and European alike, aspire. The trouble is that the West African politician regards democracy as a means to power, not as a means to opportunity. He sees the power that the chiefs used to wield and the immense power and prestige of democratic Britain and America, and he wants to cash in on his Western education by succeeding to that power himself. He conceives power as an end in itself, not as a means to an end. When one reflects upon the complexity of modern national life, the need for true leadership and a high standard of intelligence and integrity in a wide circle of those concerned with the administration, the prospect of too sudden a surrender of the controls into untried and untrained hands is very gloomy. The gloom is not lightened by our knowledge that the blame for any consequent chaos will be attributed to the British Government, and that amongst those claiming power are admirers of the Soviet, who are anxious to found a totalitarian State on the ruins of democracy.[49]

Three years later the *Round Table* took the opposite view and abandoned the "colonialist" argument. The Labour government was even blamed with not having recognized in time the level of development in the Gold Coast; the "modest constitutional advance" of 1946 was no longer relevant. The Watson Commission's report, which it had criticized before, was now praised and it said the Coussey report had created a new basis of trust. Even Nkrumah and his party were judged objectively. It is worth quoting the last paragraph of this article:

In the first instance, it seems that the granting of the very full self-governing powers contained in the present Constitution were necessary, having regard to the state of the Gold Coast in 1948. It is also true that if more had been granted earlier it might not have been necessary to concede so much now. As to the desirability of what has been done, it is obviously desirable that all British colonies should proceed to Dominion status as soon as they are fit, and should be actively encouraged to that end, but it is difficult to avoid the conclusion that to place a country in the position where success and failure are so evenly set in the balance as they are in the Gold Coast is not really desirable having regard to the irreparable psychological damage that would be done should there be a set-back. Success will depend largely on two things, which rest almost wholly in the hands of the Africans. One is whether they can reconcile themselves quickly to accepting European help in order to accomplish the political and material developments which they require, and to make the terms attractive enough for Europeans to accept them. The other is the formation of a properly organized parliamentary opposition—which is now being attempted through the coalition of Dr Danquah's and Mr Ollemhu's groups —which will break the present vicious circle by which political groups outflank each other by going to extremes. What the Gold Coast in fact wants just now more than anything else is a Conservative party.

Only time can bring about these changes. Although the list of outstanding problems requiring solution may seem formidable, there are certain grounds for optimism. One is that in spite of the doubters the experiment has gone up till now far better than many of the doubters prophesied; the other is the view that Gold Coast Africans are by nature among those who have to find things out for themselves the hard way, but that they possess remarkable qualities of sterling common sense which will ultimately see them through.[50]

Not only the argument, but the style too had changed. The 1948 essay we quoted was hardly distinguishable from pre-war writing, but now decolonization is fully accepted and there are no more formulas such as "trusteeship" or "moral standards". The new African leaders are taken seriously and the situation is discussed openly.[51] I believe this change of attitude and style to be symptomatic, for it reveals, in broad lines, the importance of the years 1948–1950. The Gold Coast disturbances, the Watson report and the Coussey report were signs of a change of course in British West Africa policy which even conservative circles in London had to acknowledge, although reluctantly at first. We must not forget the general political state of the world at that time: after 1945, Britain was weak, India, Burma and Ceylon were successfully decolonized and the Afro-Asian emancipation movements could no longer be ignored. Moreover, Britain's internal state made it impossible to embark on a policy of repression that would have required fairly large forces. So the only option was to try, as Governor Arden-Clarke had put it, to ensure the goodwill of the new leaders by making timely policy changes and trying to persuade the emancipated colonies to remain in the Commonwealth. Once Britain had adjusted to this new situation, the conservatives and "imperialists" also showed themselves prepared to take the consequences and "to make the best of it". There was remarkably little resentment or resistance to the Labour government, nor did the political writers reproach Britain with liquidating the Empire over-hastily—as opposed to corresponding reactions in French legal circles. It is, perhaps, not surprising that an essay on the problems of independence appeared in the *Round Table* as early as 1955.[52] It discussed the internal unity of the new states (e.g. the difficulties of the southern tribes in the Sudan), the need for administrative cadres and the danger of Communist infiltration, but the tone was not polemic and it fully acknowledged the new situation.

PARTNERSHIP IN THE RHODESIAN FEDERATION?

It was foreseeable that the East African territories would be the last arrivals in the "procession" towards independence—apart from a few small territories, strategic positions and the oil sheikhdoms of Arabia. In West Africa it had not been difficult to present self-government and dominion status as the goal of British policy, and it was easy to introduce reforms along traditional lines. So the discussion centred on the question of timing. Because of internal and external circumstances, London sometimes altered the timetables, left out some of the stages it had planned and "prematurely" released a colony from imperial control. But in East Africa London had to take the white settlers into consideration, particularly in Kenya and the two Rhodesias. In West Africa, trusteeship and self-government were a conceptual unit and directly related to one another, since the colonial power justified its existence by preparing the colonies for self-government. But in East Africa a grave question arose in the inter-war years: who should receive self-government, the white settlers, who referred back to the Durham tradition, or the native inhabitants, whose interests London felt obliged to protect? Britain did not manage to give a final answer until 1939. Since it was neither prepared to "sacrifice" the settlers—not even in the distant future—nor to accept the South African "solution" and to aim openly at a "white man's country", it had to keep vague its pronouncements on future East Africa policy. When people spoke of a multi-racial community, the meaning of the term varied according to their political and ideological convictions. Either it meant a conservative and imperialist desire to privilege the white settlers, or it meant progressive and "pro-native" rule, based on the principle of trusteeship. In the Closer Union issue, both positions were represented, but the only decision made was to keep to the *status quo* for the time being and to leave the door open for discussion. After the Second World War there was a similar discussion on the question of a Central African federation. This time a decision had to be made.

In a federation composed of Southern Rhodesia, Northern Rhodesia and Nyasaland, Southern Rhodesia would have occupied a position similar to that of Kenya in the closer union of East Africa. London had been forced to grant Southern Rhodesia responsible government in

1923 after the latter had refused by referendum to join the Union of South Africa.[1] Since it had reserved itself a veto right in native issues, London thought it had successfully complied with the terms of trusteeship, particularly as there still seemed some chance that the predominantly British settlers of Southern Rhodesia would reject the racist policy of the Boers in the Union of South Africa. But later London gave up its claim to reserved rights. L. S. Amery, who was prepared to conciliate the settlers in Kenya and did not take the Devonshire declaration very seriously, passed two laws in 1926-1927 that were very prejudicial to the natives. Similarly, in 1936 the Conservative government took no steps to prevent a Registration Act very similar to one in the Union of South Africa.[2] The policy in regard to the Rhodesian natives tended increasingly towards legally determined segregation and, under its ideological trappings, began to resemble that of the Union. For example, the 1931 Land Apportionment Act drew a boundary between the reservations and "native areas" on the one hand, and the white settlers' territory on the other, and forbade Africans to buy land in the towns. That there was racial discrimination in everyday life, in offices and in the administration, is self-evident. Education for the natives remained primitive, and in 1938 there were still no native secondary schools in Southern Rhodesia.

London continued to govern Northern Rhodesia and Nyasaland. There the settlers were represented in the legislative council, but did not have a majority. Segregation was far less strict, either because the small population of whites had to rely on native labour, or because the administration resisted. There were no reservations and in 1936 Nyasaland declared the entire land a Native Trustland: native agriculture soon developed rather well there.[3] In Northern Rhodesia, the Europeans were concentrated in the towns and in the Copperbelt, where the copper mines that opened up in the 1920s offered white technicians and labourers high wages and other advantages, which the unions defended by maintaining a strict colour bar. Africans were barred from access to vocational training or means of rising in the social scale and even jobs like truck, crane or engine driving remained reserved for whites.[4]

The whites in Northern and Southern Rhodesia considered Britain's policy in the Closer Union issue a dangerous threat to white supremacy and started a movement for amalgamation. They argued that this would make it much easier for them to dissociate themselves both from South Africa and the Boer policy, as well as from the allegedly "pro-native" policy of London. From now on "amalgamation" was seen as a good way of "undermining" and destroying the influence of the Colonial Office, and the grant of responsible government, which in any case could only be a preliminary stage towards full dominion status, seemed a means of ensuring Rhodesia's future as a "white man's country". Lord Passfield's 1930 *Memorandum on Native Policy*, which reaffirmed the paramountcy of 1923 and moreover explicitly ordered the government of Northern Rhodesia to take "immediate steps to ensure conformity", provoked violent protest from the settlers.[5] The 1931 Joint Select Committee and the governor of Northern Rhodesia watered this down and reinterpreted it to the advantage of the settlers (saying that the interests of the whites must not be subordinated to those of the natives)[6]; but in 1936 a conference in Victoria Falls accepted "amalgamation" and "complete self-government". So now, it must be noted, the Northern Rhodesians who had hitherto been rather reluctant, were pressing for amalgamation, while the Rhodesia Labour party in the south, which considered the Northern Rhodesian native policy too soft, opposed it.[7] The British Government refused the demand for amalgamation and appointed a commission under Lord Bledisloe to visit the territories in 1938. The commission report, issued in 1939,[8] said that although amalgamation was a good idea on the whole and would be economically profitable, it must be rejected on the grounds that native policy in the north and the south was too different. In the House of Lords, Lord Bledisloe confirmed that segregation and trusteeship were two "inherently different and divergent" concepts.[9] Not even the conservative members of the commission were ready to hand over policy-making in the colonies to the settlers, or at least not until settlers and natives were "partners" and both sides had accepted the implications of this partnership. The commission also found that the African spokesmen in Northern Rhodesia and Nyasaland definitely opposed amalgamation with the south.

The Bledisloe report complied with London's general policy between the wars: abolishment of reserved rights and conciliation towards the settlers (but acceptance of the separate reservations and legal segregation), but strict refusal to grant self-government either to Northern Rhodesia or to a larger unit.[10]

The federation of the two Rhodesias and Nyasaland did not come into being until after the Second World War. A Labour government had prepared it, and the conservatives put it into effect.

The economic advantage of amalgamation were obvious. Northern Rhodesia's enormously expanding mining industry would counterbalance the predominantly agricultural resources of Southern Rhodesia, which was only beginning to industrialize. The two states were interdependent in their system of communications and they would find it easier to gain the necessary funds for investment jointly. During and after the war there was much talk of future large-scale economies, and as early as 1945 a Central African Council for economic co-ordination was formed. Some specialists doubted the economic urgency of amalgamation, but on the whole it was accepted, by the Labour party too. Southern Rhodesia, which had been rather reluctant hitherto, realized that it could expect considerable gain from Northern Rhodesian copper exports, and these would be the greatest source of revenue in a future federation.

These economic hopes were intimately tied to political aims. Sir Roy Welensky, the former trade-unionist and leader of the whites in Northern Rhodesia, and Sir Huggins, the prime minister of Southern Rhodesia, aimed to create an economically strong central African dominion under white leadership. Northern Rhodesia hoped that by amalgamating it would at last be able to get away from Colonial Office rule. In 1946 Welensky warned

> that by 1968, if the present policy continues, there will be an elected African majority in this Chamber. . . . I don't think, and I want to stress that as strongly as I can, that the next 15 to 20 years will see the black man ready for our form of government. I think it will be a tragedy if that should happen, and I want that on record. I say that for 50 or possibly 100 years the African has an important part to play here, but he has to play that part as a junior partner, and I am prepared to accept him as such. I want some form of self-government and only amalgamation gives us that possibility.[11]

Welensky and Huggins thought that self-government meant first and foremost control over native policy and the power to determine and delay the social and political rise of the Africans. For them the 1948 riots in the Gold Coast and the Coussey report merely confirmed that London intended to continue with the West Africa policy they had already prescribed between the wars and was preparing for African governments. Sooner or later, they were sure, the mother country would "betray" the white settlers in East Africa. In Rhodesia itself, the African National Congress had come into being in 1943 and in 1948 it was followed by a similar organization in Northern Rhodesia. In 1945 and 1948, as in 1935, major strikes provoked violent protest from the whites, especially since the trade-union experts sent out by the Labour government had helped create an African Trade Union in the Copperbelt! The electoral success of Dr Malan's Boer party, which proposed association with South Africa rather than amalgamation with the "black north", at least managed to quiet these whites for a time. But Huggins and later Welensky blackmailed negotiations with London by threatening to join the Union.

The arguments of the whites in Rhodesia also served the conservatives in the mother country in a slightly different form. They thought the large investments in the Copperbelt would be more secure in a consolidated Rhodesia and would promise an industrial boom such as the Union of South Africa had experienced. Personal interests in mining and financial enterprises or family relations with settlers in East Africa confirmed their argument. The settlers, as the mainstays of the Empire, were part of the traditional image of British power and influence in the world, an image the conservatives felt obliged to uphold. As pioneers and a minority group, the white settlers needed imperial protection

—a protection that seemed all the more justified as the conservatives also rejected the Boers and their racist policy. The terms of trusteeship seemed satisfied by reserved rights, the renunciation of open apartheid and minimal African representation in the federal parliament.[12] At the moment when Great Britain had to withdraw from Asia and the Near East, and when decolonization seemed about to begin in West Africa too, the conservatives obviously thought it would be some compensation if a new dominion came into being in Central Africa, an area with unprobed economic potential. It was with this in mind that the conservative minister of state Hopkinson (later Lord Colyton) spoke in Salisbury of a "great new bastion of British power in Central Africa".[13]

The Labour party could not entirely reject the economic arguments, especially since, after 1945, it was trying to expand colonial production in an attempt to overcome the dollar crisis and the lack of raw materials and food. Also, a Central African state seemed more "viable" and likely to offer the native population more advantages than three separate, allegedly complementary territories; in any case Nyasaland was a minor country, they thought, too small and too weak for future self-government, although it supplied labour to Rhodesia. If the settlers were not conciliated they threatened to follow the example of South Africa, whereas federation at least held some hope of keeping the milder form of segregation of the north.

After 1945 the settlers, conservative imperialists and the Labour party had to deal with the same factors, although their aims, hopes and expectations were different. The Labour party was aware of the Africans' distrust of federation, but did not want to pin itself down too soon and was willing to compromise. So the discussion centred on the question of how the rights and the political emancipation of the native inhabitants would be guaranteed in the planned federation.

By 1948 Sir Huggins had given up the idea of amalgamation in the narrow sense, accepting federation instead of union on the model of South Africa. Northern Rhodesia and Nyasaland would keep their colonial status at first and London would continue to be responsible for both agrarian and native policy. At the same time, Welensky was given four ministers from among the settlers and the promise that the governor would not go against the unanimous desire of the elected settler deputies, in spite of the continued majority of official members and African spokesmen in the legislative council. This gave the settlers a kind of veto. As a result of lengthy negotiations, a special minister was to be appointed by the governor and an African Affairs Board was planned to represent African interests in the federation and to collaborate in jurisdiction and other issues affecting the Africans: in case of conflict the British Government would have the last word. Huggins declared that such reserved rights, as experiences in South Africa and Southern Rhodesia had shown, had little importance and could not prevent white supremacy.[14] The Labour government had gone far to conciliate the settlers—they were even to determine the franchise in the federal parliament—and was now ready to form the federation. But it wanted to make quite sure of African agreement before making the final decision. However, the Africans did not agree; the chiefs, party organizations and representative councils in Northern Rhodesia and Nyasaland vehemently opposed the plans for federation, calling on old agreements and their status of "protected persons", and claiming the trusteeship of the Colonial Office. They distrusted the "safeguards" and predicted that Southern Rhodesia would dominate the federation. The third conference in Victoria Falls in September and October 1951 came to grief over this issue and Southern Rhodesian delaying tactics.[15]

That same October the conservatives came into office. Apart from the prime minister, Winston Churchill, the diehards in the Cabinet included Lord Salisbury, the minister for Commonwealth affairs, who was also responsible for Southern Rhodesia, and the colonial minister Lyttelton. Lyttelton declared as early as November that he wanted federation in spite of African resistance. The proposals were altered in favour of the settlers: the minister for native affairs—that "cuckoo's egg" (Huggins)—was dropped. After great difficulty, the declaration that Britain would grant dominion status only when the "inhabitants [i.e. the Africans, too] of the Territories so desired"[16] remained in the preamble. The House of Commons passed the bill on 24 March 1953 by 304 votes to 260, and Southern Rhodesia accepted the federation in April by referendum. In a population of 2,000,000 Africans and 150,000 Europeans only 46,355 voted, of whom 380 were natives! The settlers and official members in the legislatures of Northern Rhodesia and Nyasaland accepted the bill, while the Africans and appointed speakers for the Africans refused it.[17]

The diverging views found expression in violent debate in and out of Parliament. The colonial minister, Lyttelton, dismissed the opposition arguments by saying that in the north the colonial régime would remain, and that it was not the federation's business to determine the political development of Northern Rhodesia and Nyasaland. From now on, constitutional changes, as stated in the preamble, would require a majority agreement.[18] He said the Labour party had prepared the federation, and its present opposition to it was simply a form of parliamentary obstruction. Lyttelton did not deny the Africans' resistance to federation, but called on the mother country's duty to carry through any measure it considered right. So he called on trusteeship to sanction federation.[19] As usual, conservative M.P.s attacked the "minority of agitators" who unjustifiably alleged that they represented the Africans. "African opinion does not exist"![20] One must not distrust the settlers, who were responsible for the economic and cultural development of the territories. Racial discrimination and segregation were justified with regard to the difference in the levels of development. London refused the idea of permanent European rule, said the conservatives—but the white Rhodesians were not Boers but British, i.e. "our own people"! Julian Amery, a son of L. S. Amery, said that the aim of British policy was a "new British Dominion founded on a partnership of all the races". On 24 March 1953, Lyttelton also described federation as the "turning-point in the history of Africa . . . it will solve the question of partnership between the races".[21] He said the British Government trusted Huggins and Welensky as "liberal-minded Englishmen" who, on the basis of Cecil Rhodes' formula of "equal rights for all civilized men", would set up "multi-racial communities".[22]

Partnership and multi-racial communities were the new ideological slogans open to anyone who wanted to justify his own position. Partnership took the place not just of trusteeship but also of paramountcy, although this rather negated the demand for white supremacy and implied future "African states". But even the Labour party did not reckon with this possibility in 1945. Since it also knew of the settlers' strong objections to Lord Passfield's 1930 declaration and wanted to neutralize the conservative opposition, it officially gave up "paramountcy" in 1949 and replaced it by "partnership".[23] The important Labour statement of 13 December 1950 accordingly said "that all persons who are concerned with the future of these Territories [East Africa] will work together towards the goal of true partnership".[24] The conservatives and even the white Rhodesians adopted the concept of partnership. In December 1950 Sir Huggins declared:

> We are anxious to build up this country on the basis of a partnership between the various races, not to use colour as a test of a man's ability and culture; we can only develop and hold this country as partners.[25]

It is interesting to examine what they actually meant by partnership and how they intended to achieve it.

The conservatives could use the dual policy of the 1920s as a starting point. Dual policy opposed both South African apartheid and the "West Africa policy", but practically accepted racial segregation and white supremacy, postulating a slow integration of Africans by representation in the legislative council, census franchise and a relaxing of the colour bar, which would one day lead to a multi-racial community. A common roll, together with Cecil Rhodes' formula, seemed the right tool for this, since the gradual extension of franchise complied with Britain's own traditions, sounded liberal, and yet did not endanger white supremacy in the foreseeable future; nor did it force Britain to grant the settlers' demands for official recognition of Rhodesia as a white man's country. This method also served to hide the differences of opinion within the party: while some Conservatives more or less explicitly took the side of the settlers and interpreted partnership accordingly,[26] others were prepared to take into account potential African emancipation and to exert a certain amount of pressure on the whites, or even to go further than their own policy and grant concessions to the northern territories too. Above all the slogan "partnership" promised a way out of the dilemma of being unable to give either self-government to the settlers or full franchise and majority representation in the legislative council to the Africans. Interpreted in a liberal sense, partnership could mean parity representation in the legislative and executive council, and the "equality of the partners" would then refer not to individuals but to the two racial communities. The Northern Rhodesian Government expressed this view in its 1952 "Statement on Partnership", which attacked segregation.[27] The whole problem of the British East Africa policy lay here: even if such a parity government was declared the "ultimate" aim, the settlers would see it as a threat to their privileged position and to white supremacy; the Africans on the other hand would sooner or later claim the democratic principle of "one man one vote" and not be content with mere parity representation. Between the wars and immediately after the war, partnership in this sense, even had it been officially declared the aim of British policy in territories with strong white minorities, would have offered a viable solution, or at least some hope of one. But in the 1950s, when West Africa was approaching independence and Nkrumah had already formed an African government, there was small hope of persuading African nationalists to accept this form of decolonization.

London, including the Labour party, preferred not to specify the term "partnership". In 1953, when it was in opposition, the Labour party had rejected federation, saying that it meant Britain would forefeit the Africans' trust (the liberal John Moffat in Northern Rhodesia issued the same warning[28]), betray trusteeship and open the way to white supremacy. The African nationalists, it said, were a new "challenge" which England must face up to.[29] The Africans had not been included in the conferences and negotiations and it was no wonder that radical groups were increasingly gaining the upper hand. London must maintain its control until the Africans could effectively represent themselves and had obtained equal rights. This could be achieved by undertaking active measures to extend the educational system and the franchise; there was hope that the racial question would become less important then, and that political parties would form on the basis of class interests. "Equal rights for all civilized men" should be taken seriously, Labour said, and should serve as an instrument for partnership. However, it would require very long transitional periods and the co-operation of the settlers. Neither of these conditions was likely to be fulfilled now, and the Labour party's hope that these measures would successfully solve the problem of the settler minorities and make decolonization possible seems in retrospect highly unrealistic.

The opponents of federation in 1953 included Margery Perham, the Scottish mission in Nyasaland, the archbishop of Canterbury and the well-known empire historians Hancock and Harlow. This group was similar to the one that had opposed the Closer Union plans of the Conservative government in 1930. They were prepared to encourage African opposition to federation and accepted the idea of African emancipation. It seemed better to them not to wait for the African masses to reach a standard of civilization comparable to the European but to give Africans some political power relatively soon, in the hope that this evidence of goodwill would create an atmosphere of co-operation in which London could gradually move forward and which would allow the whites to keep their position of economic leadership. Mrs. Perham[30] and the archbishop of Canterbury[31] were already contemplating the idea of African majorities. In any case, federation threatened to prejudice future political development by leaving it in the hands of the white minorities. It seems that the colonial officials of Northern Rhodesia and Nyasaland did not show much enthusiasm for federation either; their distrust of the settlers stemmed from their very paternalistic attitude.[32]

In the years that followed, the discussion of "partnership" concentrated on the question of East Africa's constitutional development and the franchise. Could and should Great Britain accept universal suffrage for the Africans, i.e. one man one vote? Was it prepared to question the supremacy of the settlers? For a long time the conservatives tried to avoid this grave decision by stressing the difference in the levels of civilization and the whites' mission of leadership. They hoped to extend the franchise so slowly that the question of the future would become irrelevent. This meant that they came close to the settlers' position. As a result the concept of partnership became vague and unconvincing. The Labour party found it much easier to take a stand since it was in opposition and indeed was more and more inclined to openly accept universal suffrage, arguing that what was valid for West Africa could not be denied East and Central Africa. Transitional steps were necessary, they agreed, but the ultimate goal must be the establishment of African governments.[33] So the party overcame its earlier hesitation, at least in terms of doctrine, and was willing to "sacrifice" the white minorities whom it had criticized and opposed from the start.

Whether the partnership foreseen in the preamble of the constitution could create a viable basis for decolonization depended primarily on the attitude of the whites in Southern and Northern Rhodesia after 1953; the first step would have to be a relaxation of the colour bar and a liberalization of African franchise. We must content ourselves with a brief outline of the situation. Economically the Federation was no doubt a success. However, the main reason for its growing prosperity was the huge demand for copper; the construction of the great Kariba Dam was a debatable benefit.[34] The Africans' fear that the Federation would be dominated by Southern Rhodesia proved correct. The northern territories obtained new constitutions and wider African representation, but remained far behind the rate of development in West Africa. This fostered discontent among the African nationalists, resulting in election boycotts, strikes and demonstrations.[35] Southern Rhodesia relaxed the colour bar slightly, but by no means lifted it, not even legally. Sir Huggins skilfully took up the new slogan of partnership, but described it as the relationship of "horse and rider"![36] The Rhodesian settlers made the formula "equal rights for all civilized men" serve as a pretext for preventing Africans from having a part in policy-making in "the foreseeable future".[37] The old argument that the mass of Africans was chiefly interested in economic improvement may have convinced some conservative circles in England, but was obviously irrelevant to the present situation. Sir Huggins did not, it is true, abolish the common roll as South Africa had done, but instead he raised the electoral qualifications in 1951.[38] The number of enfranchised voters remained minimal and the Southern Rhodesian Parliament was "all white"! The Capricorn African Society tried to take a more liberal attitude, but in 1958 the prime minister, Todd, was ousted by an internal party rebellion, on the grounds of his allegedly pro-African policy (he had proposed, among other things, a modest extension of the franchise) and replaced by Edgar Whitehead, who in turn was hard pressed by Field's Dominion party. The white Southern Rhodesians stressed the foundation of a multi-racial university in Salisbury in 1957, but this could not hide the fact that they had no intention of accepting partnership. They felt it was a threat to their privileged minority position.[39]

In 1957–1958 a complicated system of two common rolls was set up at Federation level by changes in the franchise and the constitution. Superficially it conformed to the 1953 agreements and made possible African representation in parliament, but in fact it restricted this representation and, moreover, was even likely to exclude the nationalists entirely.[40] Instead of the desired rapprochement between the two races, it resulted in a distinct polarization. The Africans could no longer legally be refused access to the administration, but this access was manipulated and restricted to subordinate positions. In addition, the British Government refused to make use of its reserved powers. Two disputed laws were approved and in 1957, when the African Affairs Board raised objections to the franchise of the Federation, the colonial minister Lennox-Boyd did not intervene in order to support Welensky (prime minister since 1956) against the Dominion party. This completely discredited the African Affairs Board and the Africans lost all hope that London would intervene for them as trustee. Lennox-Boyd even promised

Welensky that London would decree no law in the federation without being requested to do so by the Rhodesian Government. This proved Huggins' prophecy that the reserved rights would be worth only the paper they were written on.

The increased resistance on the part of the Africans first became apparent in Nyasaland, when Dr Banda, after his return from London in July 1958, took over leadership of the nationalist opposition. He favoured leaving the Federation, demanded an African majority in the legislative council and launched a wave of strikes, demonstrations and attacks against the whites, which culminated in the March 1959 riots. The governor declared a state of emergency, called in federal troops (there were no whites among the casualties!) and arrested the leaders of the African opposition. The British prime minister was obliged to send out a commission of experts under Judge Devlin, which presented an excellent report in July. The report confirmed that there was no proof of any plot for mass murders of whites, as the Rhodesians had asserted, described Nyasaland as a "police state" and criticized the arrest of Dr Banda. It said the African Congress had the backing of the people and expressed a universal antipathy to the Federation.[41] The Labour party used the Devlin report, which discredited Welensky and proved untenable several of the British conservatives' theses, as electoral propaganda; the report is also said to have embarrassed the government and to have provoked Macmillan against Welensky and the settlers. Certainly it contributed to the prime minister's policy change in 1960.

Macmillan introduced his new policy immediately after the October elections. The young and active MacLeod, one of the reformers, became colonial minister in place of Lennox-Boyd, governors were summoned to London and the new minister went on a tour of Africa. As early as December 1960 the governor of Tanganyika announced new elections aimed at giving the legislative council an African majority; the same happened in Uganda in 1961. This means that the two East African territories that had no real settler problem took the West African course and began a rapid decolonization. Even more important was MacLeod's Kenya policy. The minister ordered preparations for opening up the white highlands, suspended the seven-year-old state of emergency, amnestied suspected Mau Maus and held a Kenya conference in London in January and February 1960.[42] The subsequent White Paper promised a common roll, much wider franchise, an elected African majority in the legislative council and African participation in the executive council. MacLeod had taken the decisive step: he had recognized Kenya as a potentially African state, renounced both the concept of white supremacy and a parity solution and was steering towards an African majority government! Britain no longer paid heed to the settlers' protests and refused to treat the colonies with white minorities as special cases. This meant in effect that the attempts to give the white ruling class a privileged position had failed. If London wanted to normalize the confused situation caused by the Mau Mau riots and subsequent repression, and to carry decolonization a step further, it had to risk taking the decisive step to representative government and applying the West Africa policy in East Africa too.

The prime minister supported his colonial minister by making an African tour himself in January and February 1960.[43] In Ghana he spoke of the "wind of change blowing through Africa", of the special position of the African dominions within the Commonwealth and of the mother country's willingness to encouraged decolonization. In a press conference in Lagos Macmillan declared that

> the Government of the United Kingdom have made it clear—abundantly clear—that we will not remove the protection of the British Government to either of the northern Territories—Northern Rhodesia or Nyasaland—until it is clear that the expressed wish of these peoples is to enter into a full and independent federation.

This statement, immediately interpreted by the world press as a landmark in British East Africa policy, in fact only reaffirmed the preamble of the 1953 federal constitution. But it also indicated that London was willing to promote the political development of the African protectorates in the direction of self-government and confronted the federal government with the possible secession of the North. In Northern Rhodesia Macmillan talked with African nationalists recently released from prison, and ordered the Southern Rhodesian whites to liberalize their racist policy.[44] Then, on 3 February, he addressed a well-prepared, politely worded, yet very resolute speech to the South African Parliament.[45] He reminded it of the importance of the British market and British capital for South Africa and pointed out that "the strength of this African national consciousness" raised a decisive question in world politics, namely whether the Asian and African peoples would join the West or the East. British decolonization since the war had been in the interests of the Commonwealth, he said, and Great Britain claimed the responsibility for this—in East Africa too. South African apartheid was not reconcilable with British concepts.

What made Macmillan give free rein to MacLeod, in spite of internal party opposition, commit himself personally and clash directly with both the Rhodesian Government and with South Africa? The question of principles was no doubt secondary. What directly influenced the British prime minister, apart from the critical balance of payments which made extensive engagement in East Africa impossible, was the world political situation and the problems of the Commonwealth. London had obviously realized that the process of decolonization, which so far had proved successful, must not be opposed in East Africa, for this would risk

losing the prestige Britain had gained without bringing the process
permanently to a halt. The Eastern bloc and the neutral states in
and outside the U.N. supported the African nationalists, as did the
United States, and with the independence of the Belgian Congo another potential ally was gone. France was at war in Algeria and a
similar open conflict in East Africa was well within the range of possibilities. In this case the well-armed troops of the white Federal Government would be called in, which would have been untenable in terms
of internal politics and would have jeopardized the Commonwealth, for
the black dominions, and Canada too, protested against racial discrimination. Whether South Africa would remain in the Commonwealth
was another point at issue, and one which could be a threat. However
hard it was, the Conservative government's only hope would be to come
out of its former reticence, take the initiative in East Africa and dissociate itself from racist South Africa in order to retain faith in the
Commonwealth, avoid chaos in the Congo and defend British interests
by continuing negotiations, however limited. The longer it delayed,
the stronger the radical forces became in and outside of the nationalist
movement; the present leaders, particularly Kaunda in Northern Rhodesia,
in whom London had some faith, must not be forced to turn to illegal
actions. Similar considerations influenced the great mining concerns
of Northern Rhodesia. It seemed more expedient to dissolve their close
ties with the white minorities, to support a relaxation of the colour bar
and to prepare for future collaboration with African governments.[46]
London may also have hoped that it could use the northern territories
to exert pressure on the white Rhodesians and to persuade both Southern Rhodesia and the Federal Government to change course. Whatever
the case, London was faced with dilemma: either it had to defend the
settlers and endanger the Commonwealth, or obey political necessity
and "sacrifice" the white minorities. Macmillan decided in favour of
considerations of state!

The British Government's decision was confirmed by the Monckton
Commission, which was to report on the state of Rhodesia for the
planned revision of the federal constitution in 1960 and to submit
proposals. This report was issued in October.[47] The colonial minister
released Dr Banda from prison during the summer and negotiated a
draft constitution with him in London which promised elections in
Nyasaland in 1961 and African majority representation in the legislative
council. The Monckton Commission did not hesitate to criticize the
Federation. The report stated that federation did indeed have great
economic value and should therefore not be given up, but that since
an overwhelming majority of Africans opposed it, it must be extensively
revised (the report proposed at least parity representation for Africans
in the federal parliament). London must admit the right to leave the
Commonwealth and take further steps towards full self-government in

Northern Rhodesia. Federation was inadmissible if racial discrimination continued in Southern Rhodesia.

As was to be expected, Macmillan's and MacLeod's 1960–1961 Africa policy was greeted with great enthusiasm by the liberals and the Labour party, but provoked a storm of resentment in Rhodesia and a serious crisis within the Conservative party. However, the 1959 riots in Nyasaland and the change of policy in London did persuade Southern Rhodesia to relax the colour bar. Hotels were opened to Africans, separate post-office counters were abolished and the alcohol law was liberalized; from 1961 on the unions accepted black members, and the government abolished the legal colour bar in the administration. Prime Minister Welensky gave up the idea of dominion status for the Federation. But the settlers organized resistance against London's new policy and issued new laws for the suppression of the nationalists.[48] The high judge of the Federation, Sir Robert Tredgold, resigned in protest.

We can gauge the mood of the whites at this time from the journal *East Africa and Rhodesia*, which appeared in London but was linked with Welensky's party. This was the same journal that had protested so violently against MacLeod's Kenya conference in January and February 1960, alleging that the entirely inexperienced minister had betrayed the whites, gone back on all his promises and made concessions to the Mau Mau leaders.[49] In November 1962 it described MacLeod as "incomparably the worst Secretary of State of living memory" and a "cynical Prime Minister".[50] Universal franchise was untenable, it said; it was nonsensical and treacherous and the expression of a defeatism that had been ruining the Empire for fifteen years and jeopardizing the Commonwealth.

The Tory wing of the Conservative party opposed Macmillan's policy just as openly and resolutely, though somewhat less brusquely. In March 1960 Lord Salisbury warned against the new Kenya constitution, saying that Britain had considered it its duty to prepare the colonies for self-government but Kenya was not yet ready for it. What would happen, he asked, if a Mboya or even Kenyatta ruled? "The first Elizabethan age was one of expansion, of seeking new worlds to conquer, and ours is becoming more and more an age of retreat." When the Romans withdrew from the outposts, the "dark ages" had dawned there. "Do not let that happen to us—do not let us rashly abandon the outworks until we know that we are handing them into safe and dependable hands."[51] Whose these safe and dependable hands were and whether they would appear after a fairly long and patient wait, Lord Salisbury did not say! The government could refute the stereotyped accusation of premature action by the far more valid argument that radical forces were already pressing for power. In 1960, after Britain's withdrawal from Asia and West Africa, East Africa had become the last bastion of the Empire for supporters of imperial tradition and Tory back-benchers, and their main concern was to defend it. Nor was it surprising that personal interests played a part in the Suez rebellion and, to a certain extent, in the opposition to Britain joining the Common Market. In protest against Macmillan's Cyprus policy, Lord Salisbury resigned his chairmanship of the conservatives in the House of Lords to become a central figure in the Rhodesian lobby within the party.[52] One must not underestimate the role of economic interests here, for MacLeod's opponents included former settlers and conservatives with relatives among the East African settlers, but also members of boards of directors of large mining concerns and finance companies in Rhodesia and South Africa, above all Lord Robins, the chairman of the British South Africa Company. These men had to reckon on losing their immense revenues from the license dues of the copper mines if Northern Rhodesia became independent. With the help of an advertising agency, the Rhodesian lobby launched a propaganda campaign for the Federation and for Prime Minister Welensky. The conservative opposition group was well represented in the East and Central Africa Committee and in the party's Commonwealth Council, and was able to assert its interests at the party conference in October 1960. MacLeod compared the advantages of Britain's making concessions with the effects of U.N. action, and defended the new course in the following memorable words:

> I cannot promise you a popular colonial policy. There will certainly be hardship, sweat and tears, but I hope no blood shed and no bitterness. . . . But we must go this way—there is no other.[53]

A Tory group under Lord Colyton, the former secretary of state for the colonies in 1952–1955 (as Henry Hopkinson) and chairman of the Joint East and Central Africa Board, intervened in the internal party discussion with a memorandum.[54] With considerable diplomatic skill he showed that the formation of multi-racial communities without discrimination and without a colour bar was the duty of the Commonwealth; the mother country's function was to "hold the ring until there is assurance that within such communities minority rights will be respected". The memorandum did not repeat the facile and obviously no longer relevant arguments of Lord Malvern (Sir Huggins) and Lord Robins, nor did it accuse the nationalists of being non-representative "saboteurs", but openly demanded a common roll and the gradual abolition of racial segregation. It said Kenya was headed for independence and Nyasaland too must become a "self-governing African State". The opposition against Macmillan and MacLeod was voiced indirectly: it was wrong to grant universal franchise so soon[55]; a colony could not become independent until it had reached a certain level of political maturity and until racism had "vanished" as a political problem.[56] Nyasaland could obtain self-government only within the Federation.

On the surface, then, the opponents did not deny or dismiss the challenge of change; in fact, however, they approved a policy of *status quo*. The formula "equal rights for all civilized men" served as a pretext for describing the extension of the franchise and the transition to African majorities as "premature".[57] It was unrealistic to wait for the racial conflict to vanish. Meanwhile MacLeod, with his policy of generous concessions, had taken the only possible remaining path to calm the Africans' suspicions and to persuade the relatively moderate nationalists to cooperate. Incidentally, it is striking that in the final phase of decolonization the terms "partnership" and "multi-racial communities" changed in meaning; they no longer implied conciliation of the Africans and African collaboration under predominantly white rule, but instead represented the claim of the white minority for equal rights, or at least participation within an African state!

The Tory opposition to Macmillan and MacLeod gave the BOW group of young conservatives the idea of trying to modernize the party, and they intervened in the colonial issue with their own proposals. They described decolonization in Africa as Britain's honourable duty and approved setting a timetable for Kenya: responsible government should be promised for 1965, independence for 1970. They recommended suspending the state of emergency in Nyasaland, the release of Dr Banda, and a new franchise affecting some hundred thousand Africans. The group dissociated itself from the Federation. These proposals from the reform wing of the Conservative party excited notice and provoked some resistance from the Tories, but were adopted in the main by the government—who even shortened the proposed timetables. The BOW group proposals also provoked the Monday Club of young right-wing conservatives under the patronage of Lord Salisbury to publish its own pamphlets defending Welensky's policy. The chiefs and the moderate nationalists, they asserted, represented the African majority while racial nationalists were an insignificant minority who jeopardized the multi-racial unity of the Federation.[58]

The Tory rebellion reached its height in mid-February 1961, during the discussion on constitutional changes in Northern Rhodesia. The Tories thought MacLeod's White Paper was likely to lead to an anti-federation majority in the legislative council and was therefore a danger to the Federation as such. The Rhodesian lobby and the Tory group within the party tried to prevent this by all possible means, to overthrow MacLeod, and to force Macmillan to change his policy, if not to resign. The Turton motion on 11 February 1961, an ostensibly harmless motion "only" against racial representation (i.e. representation that was to some extent proportional to the population) and demanding franchise on the basis of "equal rights for all civilized men", suddenly obtained 102 signatures from the conservative faction, and threatened, apparently at least, to split the party.⁵⁹ How far the split was prevented by the usual factional discipline, by Welensky's awkward intervention in Northern Rhodesian affairs, and by the realization that the government policy was inevitable, or on the other hand how far it was due to the disinterest of conservative members of Parliament, remains an open question. In any case, the rebellion soon lost its virulence, partly because MacLeod gave in a little to the various pressures and decided to make some changes in the constitution.⁶⁰ But the resistance continued to make itself felt in the opposition of individuals, particularly Lord Salisbury, and gained fresh impetus from the new discussion on the constitution of Northern Rhodesia in January and February 1962⁶¹ and the secession of South Africa from the Commonwealth. Doubtless the rejection of MacLeod's candidature as Macmillan's successor was partly due to his Africa policy.

While the Tory rebels, a large number of back-benchers and the Conservative party resisted change and accused the government of an overhasty departure from East Africa, *The Times* supported Macmillan and MacLeod. On 29 January 1960 it stressed the significance of the Congo independence, praised Macmillan's speech in Capetown,⁶² and supported the colonial minister's attempt to win the approval and collaboration of a section of the African nationalists:

> One of the illusions that will have to go is that Europeans can continue to work towards partnership at the same pace as before, without regard to the accelerated speed of events in West Africa, East Africa, the Belgian Congo. . . .⁶³

So *The Times* opposed the Tories' "too much and too fast" by their own "not enough and too slow"! Unlike in 1953, one could no longer ignore African opinion:

> this shift in balances does not alter the basic argument for or against federation. But it marks a radical change in the equilibrium of forces at the conference table.⁶⁴

The Times, in an article on 13 February entitled "No Going Back", approved the Monckton report and actively supported MacLeod's plans in the Northern Rhodesian debate. It promptly received a series of resentful letters of protest, including one from Lord Salisbury.⁶⁵

The liberal *Economist* went even further than the Monckton report. It said the conference for a revision of the Federation constitution must also discuss the central problem, namely Southern Rhodesia. If white supremacy was allowed to remain there, the secession of the north was inevitable. Dr Banda, Kaunda and Nkomo could accept the Federation only if African representation was greatly extended and followed by a gradual transfer of power "into black hands". All earlier arguments against the transfer of power were out of date now. The *Economist* formulated the dilemma facing London in frank and relentless terms, and very strikingly:

> If the settlers cannot govern by consent, the settlers will not be able to go on governing. Fitness or unfitness to govern is ceasing to be relevant. Either the Africans are going to be set now on the road to power, or they are going to reach for power themselves. The white man has no real choice but to accept this and, having done so, to bargain for the best deal he can get.[66]

With these words the *Economist* summarized MacLeod's East Africa policy. The winds of change were blowing so strongly that it was no use at all to try to delay African emancipation or even to slow it down and adapt it to one's own timetable. Earlier formulas such as "partnership" and "multi-racial community" did not prove workable, whether because the whites resisted stubbornly or because the disparate proportions of the different racial groups made impossible any approach to parity representation,[67] or because the Africans in their turn were quickly becoming race-conscious and clamouring for full power. If Britain wanted to avoid open clashes and bloodshed, it had to accept the African territories as "potentially African states" and grant responsible government immediately. There was no other way out of this critical situation. The old question of who should obtain self-government, the European settlers or the African inhabitants, was decided in advance by African emancipation. It forced London to oppose the settlers and to accept the paramountcy of African interests with all its grave implications. The *Economist* rightly said that even the argument of "fitness" had become irrelevant; it stressed that Africans would still need European aid for a long time to come, but that one could no longer refuse them self-government on these grounds. All one could do was "to bargain the best deal", i.e. a certain amount of bilateral negotiation on the interests of the whites in Africa, to enable the settlers to survive within the African states.

This was relatively easy in Uganda, Tanganyika and even in Kenya, where it achieved notable results. But in the case of the Rhodesian Federation it proved extremely difficult. The numerous negotiations, conferences and new constitutions between 1961 and 1964 cannot be described in detail here.[68] Suffice it to say that the British Government tried to prepare the way in fits and starts following a "tightrope policy" and trying to use delaying tactics. For London had to overcome the resistance of Southern Rhodesia and the federal government, while at the same time trying not to deliver Welensky's and Whitehead's United Federal party into the hands of Field's Dominion party. The black dominions and Canada, as well as the U.N. and America, pressed for concessions to the Africans, but London had to take into account the fact that the Federation and Southern Rhodesia had their own troops and could not be pressured very easily. Moreover, the British Government had very few means of persuasion at its disposal and was being watched suspiciously and blocked by the Tory wing of its own party.

The December 1960 conference on revision of the federal constitution was unsuccessful and the revision had to be postponed. Moreover, London changed the Northern Rhodesian constitution announced for February 1961 in favour of the whites. The resulting extremely complicated system of elections and representation, which clearly reflected London's embarrassment, was rejected by the African nationalists led by Kaunda and by the white liberal party of John Moffat. Since riots were countered by arrests, the *Economist* not inaccurately wrote on 1 July 1961: "The most that can now be hoped for is that the political struggle will stay non-violent." At the same time Southern Rhodesia obtained a new constitution. Whitehead, who had begun to accept the idea of African emancipation and wanted to show London that he was liberal, staged a "build-a-nation" campaign and accepted African representation in parliament; fifteen of the sixty-five members were to be Africans. London renounced its reserved rights, which in any case were very small, and Rhodesia was granted a special constitutional council and a Bill of Rights. But there was an emergency clause by which Rhodesia could supersede these legal barriers. This was how Britain drew the final consequences of the policy it had introduced in 1923!

The well-known difference between the territories under colonial administration and the quasi-dominion of Southern Rhodesia emerged clearly again in February 1961 when the decisive elections were held in Kenya. It was also apparent in April when preparations were made for an African government and Kenyatta's release, when Uganda, Zanzibar and Nyasaland obtained African majorities in the legislative council, and at the end of the year when Tanganyika became independent, as well as when Whitehead outlawed the National Democratic party in December and when he strengthened the Unlawful Organization Act in autumn 1962 and used it against the nationalist party. The electoral success of Field's Rhodesian Front (successor to the Dominion party) in December 1962 marked the end of any hope for a timely change of course.

Butler, who was appointed special minister for Central Africa, had to grant Nyasaland internal self-government including the right to leave the Federation from 1 February 1963. In addition, he promised British financial aid. At first he had hoped to be able at least to persuade Northern Rhodesia to remain within the Federation. But after a fact-finding trip there in March 1963, he was forced to accept the African coalition government formed after the autumn 1962 elections. This sealed the fate of the Federation, even though it was not actually dissolved until the end of the year. On 6 July 1964 Nyasaland became independent, and on 24 October 1964 it was Northern Rhodesia's turn.

There remained one unsolved problem: Southern Rhodesia. Here the ambivalence of London's policy again emerged clearly. On 12 April Butler granted the federal territories the right to "the normal process of independence", and in the following months Nyasaland and Northern Rhodesia followed this "normal" process. But what did "normal" mean in the case of Southern Rhodesia? The white settlers who had enjoyed responsible government and semi-dominion status since 1923, naturally demanded full independence now, in the last phase of decolonization—as a white man's country. But London, in a paradoxical reversal, felt obliged to refuse Southern Rhodesia the very independence it had granted the colonies. Now "normal" no longer meant self-government for the settlers, but the gradual establishment of a "one man one vote" system, i.e. the transition to African majorities! Perhaps in 1953 Britain could still dismiss the African spokesmen's opposition to federation, but now, in the era of change, it was no longer possible to sacrifice 3,000,000 natives to 250,000 whites. Such a step would have provoked a storm of resentment from Asians and Africans and weakened Britain's position in the U.N.; in addition it would have destroyed any prestige Britain had gained so far from its policy of decolonization. Above all, such a step would have been a threat to the multi-racial Commonwealth. But how could London "act" in the case of Southern Rhodesia, whom it had long since granted responsible government and even military forces? The situation was all the more complex in that Britain continued to claim "ultimate" responsibility and reserved itself the final decision on independence. In fact, London had the responsibility but not the power to force the Rhodesian Government to take a certain course.

What should London do if Rhodesia unilaterally declared independence without British consent? In April 1964, the right wing of the Rhodesian Front forced the prime minister, Winston Field, to resign, on the grounds that he had not stated his case forcefully enough in London and was afraid to take rash steps. By contrast, his counterpart and successor, Ian Smith, who belonged to the generation of "white Africans" born in Rhodesia, pressed London for a decision and promised "Independence before Christmas". The arrest of the nationalist Nkomo a very few days after Smith came to power gives evidence of his more resolute right-wing course. In September 1964, Smith seems to have obtained the Conservative government's assent on independence, if he could prove the "general consent" of the Rhodesian people. But Smith did no more than announce a referendum on independence on 5 November, which only previously registered voters would be entitled to sign, and pretended that an assembly of six hundred official tribal chiefs who—behind a screen of police—submitted a unanimous resolution in favour of independence, demonstrated the unanimous consent of the Africans. London refused to recognize this spurious method of gauging opinions.

When the Labour party came into office, tensions between London and Salisbury increased. The Labour government wanted to anticipate the expected unilateral declaration of independence and to support the "moderate" elements under Whitehead. On 27 October 1964 it explicitly declared that it would consider the declaration of independence an "open act of provocation and rebellion". London warned against a breach of constitution and threatened economic sanctions, which would hit Rhodesia particularly hard since Britain had granted preferences on the import of Rhodesian tobacco and sugar.[69] London's determined stand had some temporary effect, but in the new elections in May 1965, Smith gained an overwhelming victory. London and Salisbury negotiated and sought a compromise. But since Britain had to stand by its stipulation of a transition to African majorities in the foreseeable future, and since on the other hand the settlers defended their white supremacy, it was difficult to find a basis for compromise. Moreover, the British Government was being pressed by black members of the Commonwealth to take action and had difficulty in prolonging the negotiations. So the dilemma remained acute. Was it enough for Great Britain to impose economic sanctions if Rhodesia declared independence, or should it take military action against the white Rhodesians? Was the latter possible in terms of internal policy?

On 11 November 1965 Southern Rhodesia took the decisive step and unilaterally declared independence. London considered this an act of rebellion and broke off diplomatic relations, but confined its reprisals to economic sanctions.

FROM THE BRITISH COMMONWEALTH OF NATIONS TO THE MULTI-RACIAL COMMONWEALTH

By contrast with 1914, the British declaration of war on Germany in 1939 did not implicitly apply to the dominions. The 1937 imperial conference had explicitly confirmed the dominions' right, in spite of their "common allegiance" to the Crown, to decide independently on war and peace. The prime ministers of Canada and South Africa were particularly eager to reserve themselves the freedom of decision with respect to London's actions.[1] The dominions did not sign the Guarantee declaration for Poland, yet in September 1939 they followed the example of the mother country. Australia and New Zealand felt bound by Britain's declaration of war, and the Canadian Parliament unanimously decided to enter the war on 9 September. In South Africa, General Hertzog was overthrown after his attempt to declare a kind of neutrality, after which the new government under Smuts entered the war. Only Ireland, always a special case, remained neutral. After the fall of France the dominions were Britain's only allies, so Britain's pride in the solidarity and loyalty of the various parts of the Empire which confirmed their "unity in freedom" and its sense of world power was understandable.

As in the First World War, the common war effort strengthened the position of the dominions. The production of war materials was increased; the flow of consumer goods from the mother country was interrupted and new trade agreements, especially with the United States, had to be negotiated. Canada made resources available and became the mother country's creditor! Contingents of troops from the dominions fought on the different battlefields. Within the Allied war effort, which had been centred in Europe throughout the First World War, the United States took over leadership after 1941. The dominions had to adapt to this. Canada signed direct treaties with the U.S. while Australia and New Zealand received information from Washington and obtained American military and political support against the Japanese. The dominions were forced to extend their diplomatic service and tried to formulate their own foreign policy. This began during the war—although Winston Churchill was still fully recognized as the leader of the Commonwealth —and became apparent at the San Francisco Conference in 1945 where the dominions appeared independently and announced the right of the smaller powers to participate. In the following years they developed their own policies instead of following Great Britain. Since these policies were determined by their respective geographic situations, they were necessarily conditioned by the United States.

There was no imperial war council in the Second World War, particularly since the Canadian Government, and Winston Churchill, vehemently objected to the idea.[2] The telephone and telegraph system, the high commissioners and special committees saw to the necessary co-ordination and co-operation. When the prime ministers of the dominions were in London, they took part in sessions of the British War Cabinet. Yet, both in London and in the dominions, as in 1916–1917, the question arose of whether to extend consultation with the dominions in order to achieve a more or less unified foreign policy in the Commonwealth without limiting the independence of the partners. This time the issue was not so much the participation of the dominions in British foreign policy as how to make the power of the Commonwealth serve British interests. The Labour prime minister Curtin of Australia was responsible for starting the discussions with his demand for "some Imperial authority", at least of a consultative kind, and for an independent secretariat.[3] Australia did not feel it had been adequately consulted on the overall strategic and political planning. It wanted to participate independently in the decision-making and, with a view to the post-war era, wanted a more specialized council before which it could announce its claims and gain Commonwealth support. Smuts, on the other hand, in his famous speech in November 1943, spoke of Europe's loss of power and the Russian threat. Although Britain was covered with glory, he said, it would leave the war economically weakened and with diminished power. It was Britain's duty to take up closer contacts with Western Europe and to assert itself as a spokesman for the Commonwealth. A solely Anglo-Saxon alliance was no solution. At the same time Smuts demanded a regional organization of the colonial Empire; here, of course, his main concern was that South Africa should gain a decisive influence in Central and East Africa.[4]

Lord Halifax, the British ambassador in Washington, was also concerned with the position of the Commonwealth within the new balance of power in world politics. In January 1944 he spoke of the desirability of greater co-operation within the Commonwealth.[5] In September 1939, he said, in spite of information and consultation, the dominions had again been faced with a British decision. In the future this dilemma could be avoided only by isolating the different partners or by a new form of common foreign policy, a kind of interdependence.

> Not Great Britain only but the British Commonwealth and Empire must be the fourth power in that group upon which, under Providence, the peace of the world will henceforth depend.

Lord Halifax was primarily interested in Britain maintaining its position as a world power. Britain, he thought, could justify its claim of belonging to the super-powers of the post-war era by establishing a united Commonwealth under British leadership. In effect, to compensate for its loss of power through the Commonwealth and thereby to assert itself once again as a world power was one of Britain's hopes—however deluded during and after the Second World War.

Curtin's and Halifax's proposals met with a great deal of criticism, particularly from the Canadian prime minister, Mackenzie King. Canada, said King, was fulfilling its Commonwealth obligations and was not interested in an imperial council which merely recalled earlier plans for federation. Canada rejected the idea of creating blocs and would oppose this concept of dominant super-powers through the U.N. and its own activity in the struggle for freedom.[6] The British Government remained reticent because it was aware of the opposition against a new institutional order, even if it was only a consultative board, and did not want to provoke conflict with the dominions. King and Smuts managed to impose their views at the conferences of prime ministers in 1944 and 1946.[7]

There was a final attempt in 1948; in the House of Lords on 17 February, Lord Bruce, former prime minister of Australia, proposed a motion for the creation of an imperial council, since the existing methods of information, consultation and co-operation were no longer adequate.[8] Like Lord Halifax he hoped that by tightening the Commonwealth association Great Britain would be able to assert its position as a world power and confront the super-powers with a system of its own. H. V. Hodson, the former editor of *Round Table* and an Oxford professor, held similar views. In *The Twentieth Century Empire*, published in 1948, he wrote:

> No one of the member nations of the British Commonwealth can aspire to be a great power on its own . . . true independence of policy is possible for the British Commonwealth as a whole, but not for its members separately.[9]

Hodson was clearly thinking in terms of a third power between America and Russia when he said that a Commonwealth under British leadership could prevent Europe from becoming "a cockpit of struggle between East and West". This theory gained some support at the time from conservative imperialists and in the Labour party. Hodson suggested a Commonwealth council, in which India and Pakistan would have equal representation with Britain; Canada and South Africa would have slightly less. And he suggested creating the post of permanent secretary-general. This discussion in 1948 was related to the topical issue of whether England should join a European union. Federation in the Commonwealth seemed an alternative to closer ties with Western Europe—a theory that was revived around 1960 in the discussion on Britain's entry into the Common Market.

Even more representative of the Commonwealth concept in the 1940s were Sir Edward Grigg[10] and L. S. Amery.[11] They too were observing the super-powers and their tendency to federalize and create satellites; they distrusted the U.N., as they had distrusted the League of Nations, and saw the Commonwealth as a potential mediating agent between America and Europe, and between the West and the increasingly important countries of Asia. They considered this role Britain's special mission. Both men thought in terms of imperial tradition and warned against closer relations with America and against joining a European federation. Under no circumstances must there be a radical departure from the principle that the British family came first.[12] But federal plans were unrealistic; the Commonwealth rested on the principle of "free and equal co-operation", and no nation was prepared to give up its sovereign rights. Moreover, informal unity was more effective than a "mechanical unity of structure". This was an all too transparent reaction to a situation of crisis, and its moral is reminiscent of the story of the fox and the sour grapes! However, Grigg and Amery also considered it necessary to increase Commonwealth co-operation, although they thought the idea of a secretariat as a centre of information was unfeasible because of the "curious survival of an older anti-Downing Street complex" in the dominions.¹³ Annual imperial conferences, the promotion of technical organizations, economic development and a system of preferences were old demands that they reiterated. While Grigg wanted regional organizations, Amery wanted to replace the traditional concept of dominions circling like planets round the nucleus of the United Kingdom by a truly "imperial" concept, in which the dominions would receive "imperial status" and assume more responsibility, and Britain would at most have the position of senior partner. In any case the Commonwealth was "still only in its first experimental stage".¹⁴ With such formulas England tried to conceal the dissolution of imperial ties and to interpret the dissolution as merely a preliminary step towards an even more effective Commonwealth.

The notion of Commonwealth continued to be restricted to the "old" dominions and was only slowly extended to include peoples of non-British origin. During the war, however, more voices were raised in favour of a multi-racial Commonwealth. Since Britain had to show its willingness to reform and since it declared that responsible government was the aim of British post-war policy, it had to accept, *eo ipso*, "coloured" dominions. Isolated political writers may have hoped that Britain would continue to reserve certain controls, even in the final phase of decolonization, and that dominion status did not actually imply independence. Or some may have thought that dominion status was so closely bound up with British tradition and so closely connected with the idea of self-government for the British settlers, that one should consider a special status for the black dominions. At any rate this issue was not considered very important and was discussed only incidentally. Certainly there was no question of deliberately "planning" the multiracial Commonwealth. It is not surprising that in 1942-1944 L. S. Amery prophesied the coincidence of Empire and Commonwealth,¹⁵ hoping this would avoid racial conflict; yet he did not take up this idea again in *Thoughts on the Constitution* in 1947, although India and Pakistan, Burma and Ceylon were already on the threshold of independence. Lord Hailey expressed similar views in 1946.¹⁶

Yet the transition was smooth and gradual. It was an implicit part of the policies pursued hitherto. India was the vital link and once India had become a dominion the principle could be extended to other members; in 1917 India had been promised responsible government and official dominion status by 1929; at that time it even had a representative in the Imperial War Cabinet. Concrete questions of future foreign policy, economy, defense, immigration, etc., took precedence in the discussion over the structural problem which the acceptance of new and non-white members into the Commonwealth entailed. Moreover the Commonwealth structure was already so "informal" that institutional questions did not seem acute.¹⁷ The concept of Commonwealth even anticipated this development to a certain extent since this concept had gradually replaced that of Empire and the self-governing dominions were no longer so clearly differentiated from the colonial Empire as before. The transformation of the British Commonwealth of Nations into the multi-racial Commonwealth was not planned nor were its implications discussed or defined, although it may seem so in retrospect; in fact it was the concrete answer to a concrete challenge. British pragmatism rapidly succeeded in finding the appropriate new formulas and in adapting to the new situation.

We have outlined the transfer of power in India. India and Pakistan, as well as Burma and Ceylon, were legally released from colonial rule by what was called the "Independence Act". Until then the word "independence" had been carefully avoided—even in the 1926 Balfour declaration. In 1929, when the Congress party was no longer content with dominion status and translated *swaraj* as independence, London had considered this an insult and for the conservative opposition it had been an additional argument against a policy of conciliation. After the war the Indians and Burmese still thought that the concept of dominion status was too closely bound up with the idea of foreign rule, and the national emancipation movement objected to it, even though the leaders were well aware that in practice it implied independence and that London was admitting the possibility of their leaving the Commonwealth. So the recognition of "independence" now became a *sine qua non* for final negotiations on the transfer of power. The Labour government accepted this condition, in order to achieve its real aim i.e. to persuade new states to remain within the Commonwealth. This was a reversal of fronts. Until now "within the Empire" had always been one of the unspoken conditions in the discussion on the future grant of self-government. It was well-known that the former mother country had few means at its disposal for influencing a dominion, yet people were still under the illusion that the transition to dominion status did not mean a break with the Empire but was simply a kind of change of status within the imperial league. Great Britain did not even need to discuss "demands" for independence, they thought, and could trust that the dominions would remain in the Commonwealth; at the same time they liked to point out the voluntary nature of this membership and, implicitly at least, accepted the right to secession, although this was never officially confirmed. This change in British attitude became apparent in 1942 after the Cripps proposals when London admitted the dominions' right to decide against remaining in the Commonwealth. Only in this way could Britain make its promise of self-government for India sound convincing. The change of emphasis became quite clear in Attlee's declaration on 20 December 1946, when he openly admitted Burma's freedom of choice, and in November 1947 when he more or less agreed to release Burma into independence even though it had decided against staying in the Commonwealth. We have seen that the Tories did not miss this opportunity to protest the "liquidation of the Empire".

But the main issue was India and not Burma. Would it follow Burma? At the time most people counted on it doing so, because the Congress party seemed to have made up its mind long since and because the decision was linked to another question: could a republic become a member of the Commonwealth? On 22 January 1947, when the Indian constituent national assembly approved a resolution that India should become a "sovereign, independent republic", the Congress, and Nehru too, seemed to be confessing their desire to leave the Commonwealth. A republican dominion could not be reconciled with the principle of the Crown as an integral element of the dominion constitutions; this was the only remaining institutional element of the Commonwealth and had become very important—particularly to the conservatives. But for the Indians and Burmese the idea of republic was very closely related to the concept of independence, and spelled nationhood, modernization and democratization. By contrast, a monarchy could lead, they thought, to conflicts with the princely states and could be taken to mean that they had not yet obtained independence.[18]

Neither Britain nor India pressed for a decision, and this made it possible for India to remain within the Commonwealth. That the Labour party adjusted its course on time, the British withdrawal was successful, India received British aid during the partition catastrophe and the friendship between Nehru and Lord Mountbatten were important factors. On 19 October 1948 Nehru declared in London:

> A remarkable change occurred in India after a conflict lasting through generations. There is now very little ill-feeling towards Britain.[19]

Even more important factors were India's view of the world situation and the technical and economic advantages likely to result from membership in the Commonwealth. In the summer of 1948, when Moscow instigated disturbances in Malaya, in Burma and in the Philippines and serious clashes also occurred in India, isolation began to seem unprofitable. The first conference of Commonwealth prime ministers in October, in which India, Pakistan and Ceylon took part, also helped to rouse interest in membership in the "club". On his return journey from London, the prime minister of Ceylon declared in Madras on 5 November 1948: "Ceylon has no intention of seceding from the Commonwealth. The conference was a family gathering." Ali Khan, the prime minister of Pakistan, expressed similar sentiments.[20] And in December the Congress party resolved that the "Congress would welcome India's free association with independent nations of the Commonwealth for their common weal and the promotion of world peace".[21] Thus the decision whether India would remain in the Commonwealth—as a republic—lay with Britain and the old dominions; the decision was made at the conference of prime ministers in April 1949. The final communiqué on 29 April took cognizance of India's intention to become a republic, but also determined that

> the Government of India, have, however, declared and affirmed India's desire to continue her full membership of the Commonwealth of Nations and her acceptance of the King as the symbol of the free association of its independent member nations, and as such Head of the Commonwealth.[22]

So the Republic of India became a member of the Commonwealth, recognizing the Crown only as a symbol of free association and as head of the Commonwealth, while the phrase "alliance to the Crown" and the idea of the Crown as an element of the constitution were dropped. Britain managed to adapt itself to the situation and to conclude the transition from British Commonwealth of Nations to the multi-racial Commonwealth. Although this new formula contradicted the earlier interpretation of Commonwealth structure and relaxed its traditional order, it was fully in line with the 1839, 1917 and 1926 declarations; the inclusion of Asian members into the "club" seemed a logical continuation of the policy pursued hitherto.

The 1949 declaration was really meant only for India and, like the concessions to Ireland between the wars, to settle a special case. But in years to come the Asian and African states followed the Indian example and became republics after a period of transition. Northern Rhodesia did so immediately in 1964, without a preliminary stage. On the other hand, a monarchy became a member of the Commonwealth in 1957 when the Federation of Malaya joined. The decisive factor in all this was that India had decided in 1948 to remain within the Commonwealth. Had India left, the other non-white dominions would surely have followed sooner or later. At the risk of exaggeration one could say that it was not London but India that made the multi-racial Commonwealth possible—and it is with some justification that the Indians can point to the great service they did England![23]

The transition to a multi-racial Commonwealth in 1947–1949 was immediately interpreted as a "watershed" in the history of the British Empire: although it had not really been "planned", it was fully accepted and even ideologized. The inclusion of non-British members could be interpreted as a successful attempt to build a bridge between Asia and the West, demonstrate the partnership of the races, and serve as an example to the world. We will take the words of P. O. Gordon-Walker, the minister for Commonwealth relations in the first post-war years and future foreign minister, as representative of many similar comments:

> One possibility is that the nationalism of Asia may range itself against the nations of the West. That, I think, would be the greatest calamity that could befall the world. It would carry in its train very grave problems and difficulties for the next century or two, and I think the Commonwealth, which includes great Asian as well as great Western nations, is the world's best hope that Asia and the West will develop in friendship and co-operation instead of hostility and suspicion. This, as I see it, is a task that history has confided to the British Commonwealth. There is no other force in the world so well fitted to discharge it, no other association of nations in which the best of Asia and the West is equally represented and intimately united.[24]

In 1962, when the association had expanded to include African members, Gordon-Walker added:

> The Commonwealth will complete its fulfilment and maximise the co-operation of its members for its inherent moral ends when it becomes in truth and without inhibition an Europ-Afro-Asian Commonwealth.[25]

These were the words of an influential Labour party politician. The Labour party saw itself confirmed in its traditional anti-imperialism and readily adjusted its course now that the old dilemma of moral claims and the realities of power politics seemed to be resolving itself[26]. The conservatives found it more difficult to adapt; they had been stressing the predominantly British nature of the Commonwealth for a long time and continued to describe the "old" dominions as the nucleus of the imperial league. Yet they too came to terms with the new situation and even accepted the secession of South Africa, which was so closely bound up with the person and personality of the much-praised Smuts. The Beaverbrook press protested, but *The Times* considered the step inevitable if London wanted to avoid a break with the non-white dominions. Reference to the "multi-racialism" of the Commonwealth justified the grave decision.[27] But the clearest proof of the change of balance within the Commonwealth and the defensive position into which the former mother country found itself driven was the fact that the "new" members of the former colonial Empire could force an "old" dominion and one of such importance in the history of the Commonwealth as South Africa to retire from the "club".

The terminology also changed during this process.[28] In 1939 the phrase "Commonwealth within the Empire" was still current, and "Empire" meant the superstructure of imperial unity which clearly distinguished between "self-governing dominions" and the colonial Empire. During the war Winston Churchill used the term "Commonwealth and Empire", juxtaposing and comparing the two organizations: and he openly postulated that Britain should be the ruler within the Empire. "Empire" was gradually replaced by "Commonwealth", however, which now included the protectorates and dependencies. Amery also adopted this new interpretation, not, he said, because he was ashamed of the term Empire, but in order to indicate that the Empire was becoming transformed into a Commonwealth.[29] Even the word "dominion" went out of circulation, at least in official terminology. The Canadian prime minister, Laurier, considered the term "dominion" the remnant of a claim to domination and an indication of inequality between the partners, since the United Kingdom was not described as a dominion. Instead of "dominion", the expressions "realm", "Commonwealth country" or "member" came into use.[30] Accordingly, in 1947 the Dominion Relations Office was renamed the Commonwealth Relations Office. The word "British" also had to be dropped. It had irritated the French Canadians and the Africans for years—in spite of all the pronouncements to the effect that "British" did not mean a racial and national but a supra-national community. Once the Asians and Africans had decided to remain in the Commonwealth, "British" became entirely inapposite. In 1948 the new Nationality Act gave all Commonwealth citizens the status of "Commonwealth subjects", just as they had been "British subjects" until now, with no distinction of race. In the final communiqué of the conference of prime ministers in 1949, only "Commonwealth" was used: the king also used the expression "our Commonwealth".

Professor Hodson described the Commonwealth that came into being during the war as the "Fourth British Empire",[31] referring back to Alfred Zimmern's "Third British Empire". This phrase had first been introduced by the Indian Panikkar in 1943, to apply to the time when Britain would accept a non-European India as an equal partner.[32] The Canadian Underhill has recently spoken of a "Second Commonwealth" in order to stress the new inclusion of Asian and African members.[33] But the accepted term is "Multi-racial Commonwealth". If names are indeed "symbols of aspiration",[34] then this change of title and meaning gives a clear indication of the road which led from "British Commonwealth of Nations" to "Multi-racial Commonwealth".

To what can the cohesion and effectiveness of the present Commonwealth be attributed? Certainly not its institutions. The "British" dominions of Australia and New Zealand have now dissolved the ties that, in spite of the Westminster Statute, still bound them to Britain after the war.[35] Canada too is preparing a similar change of constitution. The Crown may continue to have some symbolic meaning for the peoples of British origin, but scarcely for non-Britons, Asians and Africans. Certainly the heritage of the colonial power is important: the English language, British education, a certain moral standard, administrative methods, common elements in the legal system and British legal traditions. But the former much-emphasized links formed by a common representative and parliamentary system have already proved fragile, even though Westminster served as a model and was superficially copied.

These imponderables, which link Canadians, Australians and New Zealanders, and also Asians and Africans (particularly the older generation), to the former mother country in spite of colonial rule, cannot be dismissed. But more important are the practical interests and advantages in remaining in the Commonwealth, and they carry considerable weight in discussion of eventual departure. The Commonwealth inherited from the Empire countless agreements, councils, committees, co-ordinating and research centres concerned with economics and communications, as well as universities, the press and the radio: London continues to develop and promote them by means of conferences, exchanges of information, technical aid and an extensive system of grants-in-aid. This is where we find common elements in the technical cadre and personal relations whose effects extend beyond the official organizations and contacts. A member of the Commonwealth enjoys the rights of a British citizen in England; these distinguish him from a "foreigner" and give him several advantages, although the hitherto unrestricted immigration has had to be limited, largely because of union pressure.

All the members of the Commonwealth, except Canada, belong to the sterling bloc. This no longer has its former importance, yet it makes it possible to convert the national currency into an international legal tender and gives access to the communal gold and dollar reserves. Britain has remained the major purchaser of the products of several former colonies, and grants them a number of preferences. Only Commonwealth governments have access to the British capital market. Borrowed capital accounts for much less than American foreign aid and private investment, but it remains important. In fact, the danger of dollar aid making them dependent on the United States increases their interest in the Commonwealth. What value the Commonwealth nations place in the advantages of a privileged position in the British market has been shown by their resistance to Britain joining the Common Market. With slight exaggeration, one could speak of a recent reversal of fronts: formerly the mother country "begged" the colonies to remain in the Commonwealth when they became independent, now they in turn are asking Britain not to leave them in the lurch!

In the area of foreign policy, the former colonies are discovering numerous advantages of belonging to the Commonwealth. Here the situation has changed fundamentally since the pre-war years. In 1926–1931 the dominions had equal status and full control in their foreign relations; but they accepted their functional inequality and left most foreign policy decisions to London. Since the war, however, the old, and of course particularly the new, members of the Commonwealth have developed their own foreign policy and no longer follow London. The Commonwealth mainly offers "consultation" and "information", which includes Britain's obligation to keep its partners as well-informed as possible of its intentions, but does not allow for intervention or even "joint responsibility". Information in the broader sense is conducted through the Commonwealth Relations Office,[36] the high commissioners, personal communications from the British prime minister and regular conferences of prime ministers. The conferences are an informal and often very personal "exchange of views", which can be very free since there is no strict agenda, no resolutions are made and there is no protocol; the British prime minister acts as host rather than chairman. Without any reduction in their freedom of action, the members of the Commonwealth are here given access to valuable sources of information and the possibility of presenting their own case and making their own demands, which Britain naturally has some interest in reviewing. A forceful stand in London also gives the leaders of smaller states increased prestige in their own internal affairs.

The phrase "independence plus . . ." is sometimes used in order to make clear that membership in the Commonwealth does not entail a restriction of sovereign rights or loss of freedom of decision, but rather an increase in influence and security. The *Economist* put this concisely:

> Strong though the bond of sentiment remains in particular cases, the determining factor in their general agreement not to separate is one of tangible advantage. Their association has become one from which no nation stands to gain by resigning, while each would find that resignation meant a certain loss. For several of them, to resign would amount to becoming isolated in a world full of pressure which their membership helps them to withstand; for all of them, it would amount to enjoying less influence in the world's councils.[37]

Europeans and Americans may see the Commonwealth as no more than the "broken-up" Empire and underestimate its cohesion and effectiveness. In Britain, on the other hand, there is an understandable tendency to stress the ideological basis of this curious organization more than it deserves, to assert that there is a unity of idea and action and to entertain misguided hopes as to its future potential. The Commonwealth is seen as the proof and justification of Britain's claim that it is still a world power. "The necessity of the Commonwealth to Britain's continuing greatness",[38] however, is convincing only in terms of the internal cohesion of the Commonwealth, rather than in the friendly relations of allied partners. London reacted sharply when Dean Acheson, the former secretary of state and adviser to President Kennedy, questioned this cohesion in December 1962 and attacked Britain's attempt to play the role of third power between Europe and the United States.[39] For this was precisely Britain's view of the function of the Commonwealth!

Because it "disposed of" the Commonwealth, it saw itself as standing between America and Russia as a third world power while at the same time remaining outside the continental European bloc. The conservatives especially, who still called themselves the "Party of the Empire" in 1951,[40] wrongly hoped this was so, pointing to the potential of the Commonwealth, which, they said, would surpass even that of America or Russia.[41] A special study group published *The Expanding Commonwealth* programme in 1956, as a reassertion of imperial tradition.[42] But when the party proclaimed in 1949 that "this structure must be fortified by positive acts of statesmanship",[43] this rather time-worn declaration was followed by very little action; the dominions were neither consulted nor informed about the planned Suez actions![44]

The last few years have brought a kind of change of fronts. Besides the Tory wing of the Conservative party, the Labour party also opposed Britain's joining the Common Market and Europe; it blamed the conservatives for betraying the Commonwealth and demanded a programmatic intensification of the economic and political relations with Britain's overseas "partners". Gordon-Walker used nearly the same arguments as the Tories![45] On the other hand, in a much noted article in *The Times*, a conservative cursorily dismissed the Commonwealth as "a gigantic farce"; it was no longer a reality, it tempted Britain to adhere to useless positions and obligations (Aden, defense of Malaysia) and prevented it from adjusting to the remaining possibilities of achieving world power.[46]

It may be true that sentimental ties to imperial tradition and illusions about the cohesion and effectiveness of the Commonwealth prevent Britain from seeing clearly its present status as a secondary power—yet the Commonwealth remains an historic achievement. Britain managed, in a few decades and usually without bloodshed, to complete the transition from the British Empire of the imperialist era to the British Commonwealth of the inter-war years and so to the loose association of today's Multi-racial Commonwealth in which British decolonization has reached its conclusion. Even Asians and Africans have remained in the "club" and keep up fairly close relations with the former colonial power. The concept and reality of the Commonwealth changed and were readjusted, which made it possible for Asian and African states to become members in the Empire's "successor organization"; this in turn allowed Britain, the imperial power *par excellence,* to make decolonization a smoother and psychologically more tolerable process. The Commonwealth concealed Britain's loss of world power, for the grant of self-government and dominion status appeared not as a break or secession but as a long-planned change of status within the Empire. It could easily be interpreted as such and this enabled the British national consciousness and sense of mission to adjust to the world-wide process of decolonization and to step into the post-colonial era.

II. France

LA PLUS GRANDE FRANCE AND ECONOMIC DEVELOPMENT

The colonial idea to which French opinion had remained more or less indifferent before the war has been taking root and growing day by day in the public mind since the re-establishment of peace. We are becoming more and more clearly aware of the additional force and prestige which our country gains from the immense and magnificent domain acquired through the prophetic act of faith of a few inspired men, long misunderstood and formerly almost disavowed. We are beginning, as England did two centuries before us, to "think imperially".

A fortunate development; but too slow and too incomplete. France has not yet become sufficiently conscious of the extent to which its colonies offer possibilities of prestige, elements of power and prosperity for its material recovery and opportunities to diffuse and display the splendor of its spirit. None of our national preoccupations is as important as that one. They all, whether they concern our security, our financial recovery, problems of population or of the reinforcement of our influence in the universal concord of people, they all have their full significance and precise implications only if viewed from this aspect. In fact, on reflection one may rightly say: France will be a great colonizing power, or it will cease to be France.[1]

With these words the radical socialist Léon Archimbaud introduced his report on the 1930 colonial budget. They were by no means original. Similar phrases occurred in any number of newspapers, books on colonial questions and speeches in parliament. With wearying insistence it was repeated that France had become aware of the importance of its colonial Empire during the First World War. "During this war France has learnt that it has colonies."[2] Before 1914, it was said, the mother country had taken little notice of its overseas territories; colonial policy—conquest, pacification, administration and economic development—was the affair of a small circle of private individuals and a few directly interested groups, not of the people as a whole. But hundreds of thousands of colonial soldiers had helped them win the war and France had become aware of a "new factor of French power; the black forces".[3] The colonies had also supplied France with immense amounts of raw materials and food, and ensured the provisioning of the severely threatened metroplis.

Political writers studiously avoided mentioning the many disturbances in the colonies during the war and applauded the alleged loyalty of the colonial subjects, which, they said, bore witness to France's civilizing achievement and had produced a feeling of solidarity with the mother country. Both parties had become aware of this community of interests and were proud of belonging to a greater whole.

> The idea, the image of a new entity, had gradually taken shape in men's minds where the continental Fatherland and the Frances of overseas are, if not indissolubly merged, at least closely linked and compose the real force of a Greater France whose security no longer relies on 40 million but on 100 million human beings and which can demand all the nourishment for its life from the whole of a domain twenty times the size of the mother country.[4]

Many similar phrases appeared in political writings and became commonplace: "France of the five parts of the world", or "France of a hundred million inhabitants". We will have to start here, since these phrases are evidence of a specific state of mind. The theory that the general public had become aware of the colonies' importance only during the war was found, as we have seen, in Britain too, but it is difficult to determine whether the theory was valid. Britain was primarily thinking of the dominions, which had self-government, "voluntarily" associated themselves with the mother country and formed a loose imperial league. France, by contrast, stressed the concepts of "France" and *patrie* and included the colonial peoples too. It postulated the unity of a Greater France which also embraced the colonies. Britain fixed its policy on the basis of self-governing colonies, closer to the mother country by accepting their claims to autonomy and basing the Commonwealth on a loose partnership. France, on the other hand, started from a supra-national concept of "the French" which embraced both the citizens of the metropolis and the colonial subjects; it aimed at an integrated total population of a hundred million inhabitants of the national territory, which extended to the colonies and formed, or was to form, an indissoluble unity. After the war, both Britain and France asserted that their future colonial policy would be the gradual grant of freedom; but they had different concepts of freedom. In the British Empire it referred to the territories and political communities that were to obtain self-government; according to the French concept "freedom" could only mean individual freedom within *la plus grande France*, i.e. equal status for the colonial inhabitants and those of the metropolis.

The term "Empire" occurs in France around 1930,[5] and people even claimed that there was a French brand of imperialism. By that time, the English scarcely ever used this term—which had become pejorative—and tended more and more to replace "Empire" by "Commonwealth". But French political writers thought that the term was an effective way to show the indissoluble unity of the mother country and the colonies, as well as the economic and political importance of the overseas territories. In 1934, under the patronage of the "Société de Géographie commerciale et d'études coloniales", a "Ligue de la République Impériale Française" was formed. Its aim was to disseminate a "collective imperial mystique" and to demonstrate the need for economic development in accordance with the idea of a "total France".[6] The fact that when a "young radical-socialist deputy" like Pierre Mendès-France published two articles on the "Empire Français", the term "Empire" did not cause offence is evidence of the growing sense of Empire in France.[7] The colonial economic conference in 1934 in fact popularized terms such as "Empire" and "imperial policy" and made them acceptable to the moderate Left, which wanted to overcome the depression in France by economic development of the colonies and demanded that the metropolis should increase its engagement overseas in the interests of the colonial peoples. Representatives of the young nationalist Right influenced by Maurras also took up the demand for an imperialist policy; however, they also criticized the fact that Republican educational methods stimulated the natives' desire for emancipation.[8]

Like England, France hoped its colonial Empire would justify its claim to world power. The war had resulted in the formation of power blocs and it was thought France could counter this situation only through its overseas territories. "In the face of such giants as the United States, the British Commonwealth of Nations, the reorganized Russia of tomorrow, European France would count for little . . . but there is a Greater France."[9] Even in Europe, France with its forty million inhabitants was faced by Germany's sixty-five millions; moreover it was potentially threatened by the falling birth rate. The idea of "security" was bound up with the colonial Empire, in so far as the Empire increased French power and had enabled France to recruit soldiers in the mandated territories too, in spite of the resistance of Wilson and Lloyd George. Ostensibly this was for defence purposes only, but in fact France had permission to use the colonial troops in Europe.[10] Germany, and Britain and America too, were later to object to this obvious misuse of the mandate principle. But France was proud of its *Force Noire*, which had already been propagated in 1910 by General Mangin, and strengthened it. It stationed the *tirailleurs sénégalais*, who by no means came only from Senegal, in Algeria, Morocco, Syria, the Rhineland and the Ruhr. A favourite French argument was that, thanks to its colonial forces, the mother country could curtail military service and devote itself to reconstruction work.

National service for French citizens was indeed reduced to eighteen months in 1922, while the colonial "subjects" had to serve three years. "Yesterday, France needed colonial contingents for the war. Tomorrow it will need them in order to refashion its military instrument. Henceforth its security will be a tributary of its colonies."[11] This obvious exaggeration of the function of the colonial forces may have served a purpose in that it helped to justify the *Force Noire* as such; but at the same time it revealed the typical ambivalence in national claims throughout the twenties. The insistent nationalism and claim to great power were curiously associated with an inner lack of security and a rarely admitted sense of weakness. The British imperialists hoped that their demand for more attention to the Empire would ensure Britain's position of world power at sea, which was jeopardized by the rise of the United States. But France thought it needed colonial troops for its own security so that, in spite of its defeat and the Treaty of Versailles, it could face its potentially stronger German neighbour with some hope of victory. The slogan of a "France of a hundred million" helped the French overcome their oppressive feeling of inferiority and to feel that France, too, could be the leading continental power in the future.

It is striking that the inadvisability of using colonial troops was rarely seen or acknowledged in France. In countless newspaper articles and books, patriotic writers reported on the courageous deeds of the colonial soldiers and the medals they had won, and spoke of the great sacrifices the colonial inhabitants had made to defend the *mère patrie* during the war. That these soldiers had been recruited by dubious methods and sometimes under compulsion, and that the much-praised governor-general of West Africa, Van Vollenhoven, had resigned because of this was seldom confessed.[12] The theory of the hundred million French was an ideological attempt to justify the conscription and use of colonial troops in Europe; they were alleged to be serving the common "patrie"—but that the African soldiers were not citizens but merely "subjects" and that these same Africans had been denied a national consciousness was also left unsaid. The radical socialist Sarraut interpreted German criticism of the stationing of "blacks" in the Rhineland as German racialism: France, he asserted, recognized its African soldiers as "brothers" and thus gave proof of French superiority.[13] The economic, social and psychological effects of the recruitment, which suddenly confronted young Africans with an entirely new environment and subjected them to an unaccustomed climate and dangerous illnesses, were rarely described. In addition this recruitment made the latent scarcity of labour in Africa more acute and economic progress more difficult. The critical objections often stemmed from different motives. A recognized expert on Africa such as Delafosse was concerned with the future well-being of the Africans,[14] whereas the "colonialists" were worried about the immediate economic losses and the danger that the recruitment of "coloured" troops would foster the emancipation movement and increase the subjects' "obstinate attitude".[15]

Economically too, so it was said, France was dependent on the colonies. Since the war there had been a deficit in foreign trade, and currency was weak; the overseas territories could supply the mother country with the raw materials and foods which it could otherwise purchase only by foreign exchange while at the same time they could provide a great consumer market, which could help France regain its economic independence. The colonies enabled France to "no longer be the victim of the appetite for money of foreign producers".[16] This statement was chiefly directed at the United States on whom Europe had become dependent during the war. Again and again political writers give evidence of this anti-Americanism. The desire to concentrate on the colonial possessions and the tendency to autarchy in France corresponded to Britain's hopes of overcoming the effects of the First World War through its colonies and ensuring itself the freedom of action generally accorded to a world power. Like that of the *Force Noire*, the economic potential of the Empire was greatly exaggerated: "without it there will be catastrophe one day."[17] The economic development of the colonies seemed a safety line, the only means of preventing the loss of power, of compensating for the unconfessed sense of weakness. It was more than mere rhetorical exaggeration or an attempt to rally readers and listeners to the great cause when even the experts drew an almost grotesquely false picture of the colonies' economic potential.[18] This can be understood properly only if one sees it as the expression of the profound wound the war had dealt to the French national consciousness.

Many of the treatises on economic development were inspired by *La mise en valeur des colonies* which Albert Sarraut published in 1922–1923. Sarraut was one of the most influential politicians of the pre-war Radical Socialist party; from 1911 to 1914 and again from 1916 to 1919 he had been a successful governor-general of Indochina, and from 1920 to 1924 colonial minister. In later years he intervened again and again in the colonial discussion. In a sense one can compare his book to Lord Lugard's *Dual Mandate* which appeared at the same time. Sarraut, it is true, was concerned more with the economic development of the colonies than with methods of administration; but both Sarraut and Lugard saw these issues as a unit and tried to find a new basis for future colonial policy and a concept which complied both with the economic interests of the mother country and the interests of the natives. Both created a compendium which served as a kind of guide to the ministries and the colonial administration, as well as to political writers and members of parliament; they both had a lasting influence on colonial theory and the discussion of colonial issues.

Sarraut justified colonial rule with arguments very similar to those of the *Dual Mandate*.[19] He approached the situation from the point of view of the colonies' importance to the mother country. France, he said, needed colonial forces for its security and needed the colonies' economic potential for its financial recovery:

> Can France, which knows the perils of its financial situation, hope to improve it if it condemns itself to remaining dependent on abroad for the acquisition of the raw materials, the commodities or goods which are the mainstay of its industrial and commercial life? Now, our colonies produce or can supply the cotton, wool, silk, rubber, wood, fats and minerals which the French market buys annually from foreign depots for thousands of millions of francs. Our overseas territories overflow with resources which it is up to us to use methodically, increasing the present production. Is it known that, in its present state of development, the external domain of France involves business concerns whose total value exceeds 12 thousand million francs? A considerable figure, certainly, but it is one which will seem low in a few years when, if we but try, colonial production will have been tripled by the utilization of the great economic machinery for which this book offers the public the general outline and the programme. But there is better to come. The incorporation of the colonial action in our national life will then seem to be only the preface and the preparation for the essential role that France can and must play in solving the grave problems which the evolution of mankind will impose on the preoccupations of the world tomorrow.[20]

National recovery required a large-scale development of the "national territory", for which the colonial territories offered almost unlimited potential, Sarraut said.[21] Once again it becomes clear how the economic difficulties after the First World War were bound up with a national claim to power and how salvation was expected from a projected development of the colonies. Similar theories can be found in the British discussion, but they were not central to it and the expectations were more modest. It is striking that France arbitrarily included the colonies in its "national territory"—an integration on which the British imperialists never presumed. In Britain, "national" referred to the United Kingdom and not to the Dependent Empire, while in France "Empire" stood for an extended nation including the colonies.

The economic development postulated by Sarraut gave precedence to the needs of the mother country—"to supply, without any delay, to the needs of our national life the increased amount of primary products that it demands, this is the aim".[22] Consequently he does not discuss industrialization in his large-scale programme of investment, but at most talks of refining local raw materials such as sugar. In compliance with the general situation after the World War, Sarraut wanted to guard this intensified policy of economic development against the nineteenth-century "exploitation"; even the term *mise en valeur* (economic development) indicates an innovation, i.e. a systematic development which is to profit both the mother country and the colonial inhabitants. "Accordingly the

French colonial operation, planned for the profit of both parties, is no longer exploitation of one race by another, but on the contrary association, according to the apt formula which has become the motto of our colonial policy."[23] Here too, the similarities to Lord Lugard's theories are striking. By postulating a complementary relationship and a community of interests between the mother country and the colonies, France thought it had avoided the problem of economic development directed only at the needs of the metropolis.[24] The question of the economic and social effects of this compulsory development of certain export products, whether it might eventually destroy existing structures and harm the individual colonies in their economic development, was not asked nor was it an acute issue as yet. By asserting that the colonies were not just markets, but were "living entities", whom France was attempting to civilize, Sarraut considered he had broken with pre-war policy and laid the foundations of a policy of reform.

Sarraut asserted that this new policy of economic development, unlike mere exploitation, paid a great deal of attention to the civilizing mission and would make funds available for improving hygiene, schooling, research, etc. Sarraut included this in his analysis. Nor did he fail to mention that French Equatorial Africa had been hopelessly neglected, so that in Brazzaville, for instance, there was only one hospital with beds for sixteen Europeans and forty-four natives.[25] His basically utilitarian arguments were characteristic of the 1920s, alternating between exploitation and a modern "policy of development". Native policy was primarily a function of economic development: "A question of labour force: this is the master key to the economic edifice we must build." The improvement of the infrastructure, long-term planning and the cultivation of new crops for export depended on a sufficiently large labour force, "hence the necessity of organizing ... an energetic battle against disease".[26] For the time being he even wanted the educational system to be based directly on economic utility, since schooling, he thought, had the purpose "of greatly improving the value of colonial production ... it is necessary first to consider the economic utility of educating the masses".[27]

So the economic development of the colonies should be systematically pursued in order to utilize their "immense" potential and put it at the service of the home economy. This was the purpose of Sarraut's work, and the main part of the book is a detailed inventory of the individual colonies and their future potential. On 27 February 1920 the author gave a detailed exposé to the Senate, and in April 1921 he proposed a law "in order to establish a general programme of economic development for the French colonies".[28] The fifteen-year programme included extensive public works and the improvement of social services; it was to be financed by state subventions, loans and private capital. The motion aroused some attention and was referred to the appropriate commission, but then it disappeared from the parliamentary programme and was never really brought up for discussion.

In the following years political writers and parliamentary deputies repeatedly quoted Sarraut's book. Everyone interested in the colonies spoke of economic development and urged its realization.[29] Sarraut's detailed documentation was widely admired and cited again and again as an example of the kind of in-depth study that was so badly needed at the time. Unfortunately the French Government would not listen to Sarraut's admonitions and had no intention of promoting economic development with state funds or generous loans.

In the inter-war years, France's colonial economic policy continued to be determined by the traditional "colonial pact"; France treated the overseas territories as the mother country's "possessions" and its policy was addressed to the economy of the metropolis which it tried to guarantee against outside competition. Tariff policy complied with this attitude and was clearly distinct from the British system of free trade. The new tariff ruling in 1928 was based on that of 1892 and confirmed extensive economic "assimilation" on the one hand, and on the other, dissociation from the outside: the *vieilles colonies*—i.e. above all the West Indies— and Algeria, together with Madagascar and Indochina, were equated with the mother country in so far as they enjoyed free trade with the metropolis from the outside: the *vieilles colonies*—i.e. above all the West Indies— had its own tariffs, but gave preferences to the mother country; Tunisia was tied to France by a restricted tariff union, while Morocco and the mandated territories, as a result of international agreements, had no special status. So the colonies had the advantage of free access to the French market but were also largely dependent on imports from the mother country for ready-made goods. Imports from abroad were not forbidden and did greatly increase after the war, but they were subject to a high tariff. This was intended to "protect" the colonial power.[30]

As in the British Empire, production for export rose rapidly between 1919 and 1929: groundnuts in Senegal and the Sudan (from about 200,000 to 6,000,000 tons), coffee and cocoa on the Ivory Coast, rubber in French Equatorial Africa, rice and minerals in Indochina, wheat and phosphate in Morocco, wine in Algeria and Tunisia, etc. But this was not followed by industrialization.[31] During the depression, markets and prices crashed and production fell equally, while the mother country's ready-made goods were priced above the world-market level.[32] Moreover, the mother country was faced with competition from the colonies: sugar from the Antilles competed with the sugar beet from Northern France, corn and wine from North Africa competed with that of the French farmers. Both colonial and home interest groups demanded some kind of protection from Paris: French agriculture needed fixed quotas and tariffs, while the colonies—settlers, importers and administration— pointed to the need for a consumer market, stressed the precarious financial situation and prophesied social unrest.[33] The Algerian and Tunisian colonists even threatened to secede,[34] and in their turn attacked the colonial pact! Finally France introduced a system of fixed quotas and financial loans to the colonial producers in order to create some kind of settlement.

After 1930 the colonies and the mother country became even more interdependent. While the colonies had lost their foreign markets because of excessive prices and import restrictions, the mother country's exports to the continent had shrunk so that France was more than ever interested in its overseas market. Consequently the colonies' involvement in French foreign trade rose sharply[35]; in 1932 Algeria was the most important market for French products.[36]

After 1931, the growing importance of the colonial market and the conflict between diverging interest groups set in motion a movement for coordination within the Empire, aiming to distribute and regulate production, to stabilize prices and to regulate competition. Its model was the British imperial conference in Ottawa. In 1934–1935 a "Conférence économique de la France métropolitaine et d'outre-mer" was laboriously set up and much discussed in the press; its aim was to mediate the claims of the various economic groups and to step up the production of raw materials required by the mother country.[37] Again there was talk of a generous investment programme, to the sum of 11.2 thousand millions distributed over fifteen years; a "Fonds National pour l'outillage public des colonies" was proposed for which the state was to advance 150 million from its budget funds within seven years. This proposal was modelled on the British Colonial Development Fund of 1929. But the French plan was not implemented, although the state contribution stipulated was small and the sugar-beet industry alone required four times the proposed amount.[38] In spite of high-sounding phrases[39] and a great deal of propaganda, internal political considerations, the lack of understanding of colonial affairs and the increasing needs of the metropolis won the day.

The Eurafrican programme can be seen as a variant of these plans for closer economic coordination within the Empire. In 1904 Onésime Reclus had already coined the phrase "let us leave Asia, let us take Africa". While the nationalist emancipation movement had begun in Asia where it was ousting the European rulers, in Africa there was still abundant opportunity for colonization. Albert Sarraut was chiefly interested in Africa, as was Georges Valois who spoke in 1931, after a journey there, of "Africa, the watershed of Europe". In July, under the auspices of the "Comité national pour l'organisation française", he submitted a ten-year plan for opening up Africa, and the so-called Eurafrica Society was founded.[40] These ideas found some sympathy in 1933 when Eugène Guernier, then president of the Moroccan chamber of commerce and a representative of economic circles interested in the colonies,[41] published a book called *L'Afrique, champ d'expansion de l'Europe* (Africa, field of expansion for Europe). His arguments are representative. Europe, plagued by overproduction and unemployment, was seeking markets and room for emigration. A large-scale development of Africa could provide both: for a century [!] Europe would be able to send its excess population there—he counted on some fifteen to twenty million persons. In Asia, Europe was already embarrassed by the forces of nationalism and at a disadvantage because of American protectionism. But Africa might make it possible for Europe "to feed its industries, and even more, to sustain them".[42] Guernier reckoned that France's financial requirements amounted to 100 thousand millions, which would be spent mainly on the infrastructure. What about the African inhabitants? France would improve their civilization, said Guernier, referring back to Sarraut. He spoke of maintaining existing social structures and alleged that he was concerned with the "condition of the native". Colonial development would enable Europe "in its turn to create an Africa in its image".[43]

Guernier underrated the problems of large-scale investment, mass immigration and mass colonization and, astonishingly, took as his principal example Lyautey, who had tried to restrict European immigration into Morocco! His book clearly shows the false sense of "generosity" which a leading representative of the colonial economy and an eager propagandist of French imperialism brought to his dealings with African affairs. It is hardly surprising, then, that Guernier defended Italy's Abyssinia policy while at the same time wanting France to have a part in the "development" of that country by means of a League of Nations mandate.[44] Between 1933 and 1935 plans for a Eurafrica played a substantial role in French colonial policy and one which seems curious today. Guernier's book received an award from the Académie Française[45] and was frequently cited in the colonial discussion. Various "committees" were formed, and Joseph Caillaux, usually a sceptical man and well-versed in economic affairs, found it necessary to describe the exploitation of Africa's allegedly immense potential as Europe's duty, speaking at the International Economic Conference held in London in 1934.[46] Like the economic development of France's own colonies in the past, a common European development now seemed to promise recovery from the economic crisis; this was also, clearly, an attempt to confront the power blocs of America and Russia with a unified European economic front extended to include Africa. It is true that France showed particular interest in this project because it had extensive thinly settled and underdeveloped territories in Africa and a European engagement would therefore be to its considerable advantage. It is tempting here to recall France's successful attempt after the Second World War to use the European economic community and its development fund for appropriating extensive sums for its own or former territories.

There was little talk of the African inhabitants in the Eurafrica projects. Perhaps this was partly due to the fact that the planners came from "colonialist" circles who saw the native question only as a problem of labour force, and partly to the fact that people took for granted the complementary relationship between the mother country and the colonies and consequently assumed that the opening up of Africa would also benefit the native population. It is not surprising that the experienced administrator and expert on Africa, Robert Delavignette, felt it necessary to oppose these rather far-fetched projects. He said it was paradoxical that Europe should suddenly expect help from Africa now, and that the real situation was being entirely distorted. Africa was poor and not suited for colonization. The small settler communities which were being planned would be an unmistakable threat to native rights and this was irreconcilable with France's civilizing mission.[47] However, not much came of the Eurafrica projects—as little, in fact, as of the much-discussed Sahara railway plan and Sarraut's development fund.

After the First World War, colonialist political writers and members of parliament engaged in active propagandizing in order to familiarize the French public with the need for economic development in the Empire and the importance of the colonies, but basically everyone knew that the sense of imperialism they postulated was still very weak. As in England, there was criticism of the schools because the textbooks hardly mentioned the colonies. Education and propaganda were also themes of the colonial exhibitions held in Marseilles in 1922 and in Paris in 1931. Marshal Lyautey was persuaded to act as honorary president of the world colonial exhibition and with great pomp and rhetoric praised the splendid achievements of France's "civilizing genius". The apparent success of this exhibition—for instance the number of books sold—was counted as evidence of interest in the colonies. The delegate-general of the 1931 world exhibition, Olivier, governor of Madagascar, described as the purpose of the exhibition "to show the true face of colonization to those who do not know it".[48] He urged an awareness of the situation in world politics: while the European states were in conflict with one another, 1200 million non-white people were preparing the counter-attack; Europe, which had lost prestige since the war, relied on non-European raw materials and must try to bring the different races closer together; in six months, thanks to the exhibition, the "colonial idea" had gained more ground than in the past fifty years. And yet the question of whether France had an "imperial sense"—by comparison with Britain— is always answered in the negative.[49] Two years later Lyautey had to admit with some disappointment that the exhibition "has in no way changed the attitude of mind of mature thinkers, nor of the people on the spot who were not convinced beforehand".[50]

Nevertheless a small élite of younger Frenchmen was available for the administration, the colonial army and the missions, and in Paris countless societies and committees represented the interests of the colonies.[51] There is no doubt that the colonial firms and financial institutes associated with them exerted a considerable influence on the government, parliament and the parties. But the general public showed little interest in colonial issues in spite of all the propaganda. As in England, parliamentary debates on the colonies were rare and always poorly attended. The colonial budget was the only subject that gave rise to short discussions, but the colonial members of parliament and the party specialists discussed it more or less among themselves. There were frequent critical references to the fact that obviously only military operations—as in Morocco and Syria—or riots roused the interest of the parliamentarians and the press, produced excited debates and made headlines. But no one took much notice of economic development or concrete issues affecting the native inhabitants. The same applied to the political parties: colonial policy was ignored or only incidentally debated in their annual conferences. One of the results of this was that it was either the deputies of the overseas sections or the representatives of the colonial economy who determined, or at any rate exerted a strong influence on, the course and attitude of the parties.

This lack of interest among the parliamentarians was to some extent a result of the government's optimistic pronouncements. For instance, during the great Indochina debate in January 1930, the colonial minister declared: "To tell the truth, the political state of our colonial domain is, on the whole, excellent."[52] A few months later the parliamentary reporter Albert Lebrun, later president of the Republic, again praised the civilizing achievements of France in the sphere of public works, schooling and sanitary services, without even going into the real problems.[53] In the debate on Indochina on 13 June 1930, the colonial minister, answering a criticism by the socialist Moutet, said he considered the existing political representative bodies quite sufficient. "The representative assemblies are presently functioning in all the protectorates. These assemblies pronounce on almost all sections of the budget, particularly on those concerning public works and the living conditions of the natives. In Cochin China, the colonial council meets at least once a year [!]. . . ."[54]

But this does not mean that colonial policy lay outside party politics. Experts on parliamentary practice have pointed out how important decisions were delayed in the interests of the always somewhat unstable government majority and that the appointments or dismissals of governors-general were a question of party politics.[55] Lyautey's recall by the syndicate government in 1925 may well have been justified, but the manner in which it was done and the poor reception given to this celebrated proconsul in Marseilles were shameful. In 1934 the prefect of police of Paris, Chiappe, who was disliked for his close connections with right-wing radicals, was removed and appointed resident-general of

Morocco, although he had no colonial experience and this "punitive transfer" necessarily compromised the higher colonial administrative posts! On the other hand the members of parliament showed such interest in obtaining government offices that they had to be checked by a special law.[56] Typical of this incongruity between postulates and reality is André Tardieu's attack on the régime of the Third Republic between the wars: "We have the Empire, where is our conscience?" and his resigned realization that: "we could, to expand ourselves, see ourselves as 100 million, which we are. We prefer to remain 40 million and to mutually devour each other. It is more worth-while . . .". France, thought Tardieu, had neglected an empire which could have served as a source of moral revival and become an economic and political force.[57] These ideas were entirely in line with Albert Sarraut's colonial ideology; but they were in curious contrast to the fact that neither as a member of parliament nor as president did Tardieu demonstrate his sense of Empire by doing much about the colonies.

So it is not surprising that all attempts to reform the central colonial administration, and especially the many attempts to subordinate all the non-European territories to a single and suitable colonial ministry, failed. In 1920 a reform of the colonial ministry produced, as in England, a departmental reorganization into sections instead of the former geographic system, and parliament set up a special department for the affairs of Algeria, the protectorates and the colonies. At the same time, a commission formed on Sarraut's persuasion proposed a ministry "of external France", but this proposal was not pursued, largely because of the opposition of the French Algerians.[58] During the formation of the cabinet in January 1934, Daladier considered forming an overseas ministry under Henry de Jouvenel with a secretary of state for North Africa (Algeria, Tunisia and Morocco); but under pressure from the French Algerians he had to abandon the project and content himself with the ministry of the interior.[59] Paul Reynaud revived it in the name of the finance commission in 1935, but without success.[60] Neither the reorganized "Conseil supérieur des Colonies" nor the "Haut Comité Mediterranéen" created by Flandin in 1935, which was meant to coordinate policy in North Africa and the Levant, became effective. However, the coordination conference for North Africa under Albert Sarraut finally managed to play a role in 1937–1938.[61] This imperial conference criticized the inadequacy of the colonial ministry: there were not enough special departments, statistics or documentation and the staff was even smaller than it had been in 1894. The colonies had provided additional staff for Paris and sometimes even paid it themselves; this, as Paul Reynaud stressed, was an unsatisfactory state of affairs. The central colonial administration of Belgium was better developed than the French.[62]

Although after 1919 the slogan "Greater France" proclaimed a unity between the mother country and the colonies, on the strength of which France justified its claim to be a great power, and although economic development seemed a way out of the economic difficulties, the colonies continued to be left to their own devices and hardly received any economic or financial support from the metropolis. Much the same applied in Britain; but British policy rested on a deliberate decentralization of the Empire, to which British free trade corresponded, whereas France saw its overseas possessions as part of the national territory and administered them centrally from Paris. The contrast between French claims and reality was proportionally great. In the political sphere this led to immobilism, since the concept of Greater France did not correspond to a policy of reform or a view of the future that seriously considered the implications inherent in it; nor was France prepared gradually to pursue the *rattachement* of the colonies to the mother country postulated by this concept.

ASSIMILATION OR ASSOCIATION?

We propose to preface our main theme, namely, the discussion within France on colonial policy and the future of the colonies between the wars, by a brief outline of the administrative structure.[1]

The distinction between the dominions and the colonies in the British Empire—apart from the case of India with its special status—resided chiefly in the difference between colonial settlements and territories with non-British populations, which were constitutionally recognized as areas of self-government and as such lay under colonial control. In the French colonial Empire, however, the curious difference of status among the individual territories was determined by history. British Crown Colonies could become dominions, but no change of status occurred or was foreseen in the French colonies. From 1925 on the British dominions and colonies were clearly subordinated to two different ministries, whereas in Paris the subordination remained arbitrary and ineffective: the *vieilles colonies* (Antilles, Guiana, Réunion, agencies in India) and Algeria, which was added in 1830, were organized into departments; their administrative structure was similar to that of the metropolis and they were governed from the ministry of the interior; the colonial ministry formed in 1894 was responsible for the territories in Black Africa conquered in the late nineteenth century (French West Africa, 1904;

French Equatorial Africa, 1910), Madagascar and Indochina; Tunisia and Morocco, where French rule was formally based on protectorate agreements and the fiction of independent states was maintained, were under the foreign ministry. The same applied to the League of Nations mandates in the Levant, but not to Togo and Cameroun, which were administered by the colonial ministry. There were similar distinctions even within a compact area such as Indochina. The Indochinese Federation created in 1887 embraced the older, directly administered colony of Cochin China, the Annam Empire and the kingdoms of Laos and Cambodia, which were theoretically ruled by the traditional authorities but in fact by the governor-general. Tonkin also had a special status; it belonged to Annam but was largely ruled directly.

The territories under the ministry of the interior and the foreign ministry legally formed part of the national territories of the *République une et indivisible* and their inhabitants accordingly had French nationality. The protectorates of North Africa, on the other hand, remained "foreign states", whose citizens had the status of *protégés*. French nationality did not necessarily imply French citizenship, and a clear distinction was made between *sujets* and *citoyens*. Apart from the French colonials, those natives who had either been naturalized *in globo* or who had obtained citizenship by an administrative decree, were full citizens. Besides the old-established Algerian Jews, who had become citizens in 1870 by special decree, all the inhabitants of the *vieilles colonies* and the Four Communes in Senegal (Gorée, Saint-Louis, Dakar and Rufisque) had been naturalized in 1916. The African citizens in Senegal were granted permission to keep their special status in private law. Individual naturalization was theoretically open to every native, but it had to be requested from the administration and was subject to a number of conditions: knowledge of the French language, conclusion of military service, etc. Above all it meant the renunciation of the applicant's personal status and his subordination to French law, i.e. exit from his former community and native origins, religion and law, and transfer to the French community.[2]

Apart from the native inhabitants of the *vieilles colonies* and the Senegalese communities, who were integrated and "assimilated" in administrative terms and were citizens, the majority of natives had the status of "subjects". This applied not only in the colonies, but even in Algeria, which was constitutionally integrated and not a colony.[3] The subjects did not enjoy the political rights and personal liberties guaranteed by citizenship and were not, therefore, entitled to vote in French parliamentary elections. They were under a special ruling in questions of taxation, military service and jurisdiction, in addition to forced labour for public works. They were also subjected to the *indigénat*, a special system of administrative justice which made a more rapid procedure possible but also allowed imprisonment, confiscation and collective punishments.

The distinction between citizens and subjects within the Republic, which was further underlined by the *indigénat*, ensured the special status of the European minorities, particularly in Algeria, and safeguarded the colonial power.

The contrast with the British Empire is obvious. True, in the British Empire, all subjects of the Crown had the status of "British subject", which could be compared to French nationality, and the "native" was subject to a special ruling; but the native could never obtain the narrowly circumscribed citizenship of the mother country, i.e. of the United Kingdom; for this would have seemed absurd to a Briton. The concept of native "citizenship" in the French colonies reflects the specific French concept of assimilation and the problems inherent in French colonial policy between the wars. We will return to this later. Citizenship meant voting rights. Unlike Britain, which did not admit colonial representation in Parliament, some French colonies could elect representatives to the Parliament of Paris: these were the *vieilles colonies* and Indian agencies, the Four Communes in Senegal, Cochin China and Algeria. Algeria elected eight deputies and three senators. The racial composition of the citizens determined a colony's parliamentary representation. The *vieilles colonies* and Senegal also sent native deputies, such as Gaston Monnerville from Guiana, later president of the Conseil de la République, and Blaise Diagne, the native mayor of Dakar, whereas the deputies from Cochin China and Algeria were Europeans who chiefly represented the interests of the French colonials.[4]

As in metropolitan France, the administrative structure of the colonies was centralist. The governor-general or governor controlled the administration, the police and the armed forces, but had no control over jurisdiction or the *indigénat*. Legislation, however, was vested in the parliament of Paris, which could decree special colonial laws or pronounce by an additional declaration that laws of the mother country were also valid for the overseas territories. This "specification" of legislative power was necessary in practice, but it was also an expression of colonial domination and revealed the discrepancy between the postulated "one and indivisible Republic" and the true situation. The president of the Republic, i.e. the colonial ministry, was responsible for legislation by decree, and the governor had the right to make regulations. So most of the legislation was done in the bureaux and was not under parliamentary control. The prefects of metropolitan France could be transferred from one province to another at will, and similarly the upper- and lower-grade colonial officials could change their sphere of activity: specialization in a particular field or even promotion in place was not usual, unlike British practice. The administrative cadre was frequently moved elsewhere, sometimes even from Black Africa to Indochina, or from Algeria to Morocco and the reverse. Control of the administration by colonial inspectors who travelled to the colonies from Paris was also centralist.

In Tunisia and Morocco the situation was slightly different. There France, as the protectorate power, was represented by a resident-general and formally had only an advisory function. But we shall show how in Morocco this "indirect system" lost its original character and was replaced by direct administration.

The governor-general was assisted by the *Conseil de Gouvernement*, consisting of the most important officials and several appointed members representing the people: it had consultative powers only and was comparable to the British executive council.

More important were the general, i.e. colonial councils in the *vieilles colonies*, Algeria and Cochin China, which had a budget right comparable to the *conseils généraux* of the departments. In Cochin China, for instance, this council also had members who were representatives of the subjects; but in practice it was above all a local representation of the French colonials and their economic interests.[5] It was the same for Algeria's financial delegations, which served as models for analogous bodies in Indochina, Madagascar, Tunisia and Morocco. They represented the French citizens, interest groups, and the subjects in two or three sections, but their powers were restricted to budget affairs and economic issues. This division into sections, the numerical preponderance of the colonials and the indirect appointment of native representation ensured the dominance of the French colonials.[6]

These bodies were quite different from the legislative councils in the British colonies, both in composition and in responsibility. Perhaps the legislative councils did not have a very great importance in the Crown Colonies because of the official majority, but they were spokesmen for the administration rather than representatives of interest groups like the analogous French institutions. The distinction between Britons and natives was largely a result of the division into official members and elected members, and not a question of citizenship, i.e. voting rights, or separate advisory sections. The conflicts that arose were due to the transition to representative government and the differences between the colonial administration and the elected natives. In the French territories, by contrast, the governor or resident was faced by a representative body which did indeed assume parliamentary responsibilities but represented the French colonials, not the natives. The depoliticization of the British colonials together with the increasing politicization of the natives in the British colonies corresponded, in the French territories, to a politicization of the French colonials together with wide-scale elimination of native elements. But France prided itself on its policy of naturalization, which made it possible for the natives to acquire civil rights and, in principle at least, provided access to political representation.

The question of future developments arose here. In the British system, the future was to a certain extent preordained as a gradual transition from the official majority of the Crown Colony to representative government; in the French territories various roads were open. Either France could pursue an active policy of naturalization, in order to "wean" the emancipated élite and integrate it into the community of French colonials, or it could convert the representative bodies so as to favour the native elements, so that in time they would form a kind of local parliament. Both roads had obstacles. In each case France could count on resistance from the French colonials, who feared that "liberalization" meant they would be outvoted by the natives and that they would lose their control in the representation of interest groups. This situation led to a certain parallel with British policy in East Africa. It also threatened, even after the reforms in the years after the First World War, to arrest any further development. In other words, just as London, once it had given the settlers a voice in the legislative council in the East African colonies, later had difficulty in granting the natives political rights because of the resistance of the European minority (unlike the case in West Africa and Asia), so Paris too was faced by obstinate resistance from the different interest groups; although they had only consultative powers, they defended their *situations acquises*, gained support at home from groups interested in the colonies, and managed to prevent reforms benefitting the natives.

In the French territories there was the additional difficulty of mapping out a possible road towards a colonial parliament. The representative bodies had deliberately obtained no legislative power, for within Greater France, i.e. a one and indivisible Republic extended overseas, legislative power could lie only with the parliament of Paris. To grant more than the representation of interests with consultative powers, or administrative decentralization, would have presented a threat to the unity of the whole and contradicted France's centralist tradition. Between the wars this difficulty was evaded by sheer immobilism: after the establishment of representative bodies, the last in Indochina in 1928, the "constitutions" were not altered, or at least only in minor details, even though the emancipation movement in Indochina and North Africa was growing rapidly and clamouring for active reforms.

The difference between the British and French Empires becomes even clearer here. Around 1920 the two situations could still bear comparison as analogous stages of development, in spite of the divergence of fundamental concepts; this was no longer true in 1939. While London was taking the step towards semi-responsible government in India, Burma and Ceylon, Paris adhered to the 1928 Grand Conseil in Indochina; while Egypt and Iraq formally obtained independence, France maintained the protectorate status in Tunisia and Morocco and even strengthened "direct" rule.

We are chiefly interested in the question of how Paris envisaged the future and in its attitude towards the emancipation movements. What "method" did France try to employ, and what was its aim? Was there a programme of decolonization comparable to the British "gradual grant of self-government", and if so, on what concepts was it based?

Unlike the British political writers, who either were reluctant to enter into theoretical discussions or cursorily applied the concepts of trusteeship and self-government, the French liked to differentiate between various possible methods of colonial policy: *refoulement* or *assujettissement, autonomie, assimilation,* and finally *association.*

These terms must be briefly outlined, since they concern our discussion and the different policies were always based on one or another of these "models".

Refoulement and *assujettissement* were mainly used to refer to the past. They served to bring out the contrast between current "positive" methods and the former simple use of force. *Refoulement* meant the persecution or gradual suppression of the original settlers, as allegedly practised by England in the North American colonies, Australia and New Zealand. This allegation was often linked with polemics against the United States and Great Britain: it was cheap hypocrisy to postulate sovereign rights or even to take an anti-colonial attitude once the problem —the existence of a foreign people at a primitive stage of civilization— had been solved by *refoulement.* France, it was said, had never employed such methods; for instance in Algeria in the nineteenth century France had neither eliminated nor persecuted the Muslim inhabitants but had recognized their claims. So, unlike America and certain dominions, it was now faced by the problems of a multi-racial society. In any case, such procedure was obsolete and out of the question.

In the same way *assujettissement,* subjection, was considered a simple rule by power, which admittedly did not seek to eliminate or persecute the natives, but nevertheless oppressed them and exploited their labour, suppressed riots by bloodshed and ignored the civilizing mission. Perhaps this was true of European methods in the late nineteenth century, but it hardly applied now, they said, and in any case it was irreconcilable with France's "generous spirit". So discussion centred on the concepts of autonomy, assimilation and association.

By "autonomy" French political writers meant self-government rather than administrative decentralization and a certain self-sufficiency in the colony. The "policy of autonomy" aimed above all at dissociation and eventual independence. The colonial power satisfied itself with a minimum of administration, granted political rights and parliamentary institutions at an early date and made no attempt to assimilate the natives. Naturally, this idea was proclaimed with an eye to Great Britain, which had already granted its colonial settlements political independence in the nineteenth century and was now allegedly engaged in extending this method to non-British territories. France, of course, was chiefly thinking of India here, but Egypt and Iraq were also mentioned and later West Africa. It is characteristic of the French attitude that the political writers actively opposed the British procedure and deliberately distinguished their own doctrine from the British one.

In fact, knowledge of the British territories was scant; the French discussion usually cited only that the dominions were a special case, concerning settlers of British origin who had previously driven out or eliminated the usually rather small native populations and who even after obtaining independence, had remained tied to the mother country in a number of ways. Or it was simply said that autonomy was equal to independence or led to secession and was therefore irreconcilable with the concept of Greater France. The aim of French policy was a permanent and if possible even closer association between the colonies and the mother country. The French political writers believed that their rejection of a "policy of autonomy" was justified by the crises in the British Empire after the First World War. They alleged that the unrest in India and in Egypt was in crass contrast to the good relations that existed between colonial power and natives in Indochina, Tunisia and Morocco and proved that British colonial policy was a failure. We shall see how this view changed over the next few years, as the criticism gave way to a friendly recognition of British policy as a possible model in the final phase of decolonization. But between the wars France was still proud of its own conception of future colonial policy, a policy which would not lead to autonomy or secession.

Here we come upon the concept of "assimilation". In its general sense it was interpreted to mean integration of the colonies into the national territory. The colonies were potential overseas "provinces" which would obtain an administrative structure similar to that of the mother country and be subject to the same laws. The natives were therefore potential Frenchmen, who would be integrated into the supra-national French civilization irrespective of colour, religion or cultural traditions. They would be granted civil rights and be governed democratically from Paris through their own parliamentary representation. There would be no self-government on the local level, as there was none in the departments. In effect, assimilation defined decolonization as total integration and equality of status.

In retrospect it would be possible to show evidence of assimilatory tendencies in French colonial policy at the time of the ancien régime. Since such tendencies were also apparent in Spain and Portugal, political writers have spoken of them as a characteristic of the Latin powers or the Latin race and have made comparisons with ancient Rome. A more important factor was the French Revolution. The planters on the Antilles had obtained autonomy and sent representatives to the States-General; the constituent assembly included colonists, representatives of colonial trade and reformers. The decisive break had occurred, for the colonies elected their representatives in Paris. Subsequently the revolutionary convention not only abolished slavery and declared that all citizens of the colonies, irrespective of race, were French citizens with full civil rights, but also declared the colonies to be "integrated parts of the Republic ... subject to the same constitutional law", in Article 6 of the 1795 constitution. So the question of how the existence of the colonies could be reconciled with the revolutionary slogans of liberty and equality was resolved, not by granting political autonomy or even independence, but by integration and assimilation. The old monarchy's centralist tradition, which was taken over by the Revolution and is reflected in the phrase "the one and indivisible Republic", was associated with the enlightened belief in the unity of mankind and the universal rights of man. France saw itself as the purveyor of a humanitarian and republican creed, a civilization that was not dependent on nationalist concepts but was potentially universally valid and assimilated races of different origins by means of education, laws and cultural influences and integrated them into the supra-national community.

Henceforth assimilation seemed a liberal and progressive policy—just as the grant of local self-government with a view to ultimate full self-government constituted the liberal view in nineteenth-century Britain. In 1839–1848 British radicals and reformers had risked taking the decisive step towards responsible government; similarly, after 1848 the Republic followed in the steps of the Revolution. It finally freed the West Indian slaves and re-established parliamentary representation (Guadeloupe was represented by a native deputy) in the Four Communes and in Senegal as well. Algeria was divided into departments and *arrondissements* and obtained parliamentary representation, although franchise was restricted to the French settlers. After the interlude of the Second Empire, the Third Republic readopted the policy of the Second, and it was predictable that soon after the final victory of the republicans in 1879 the administration of Algeria would be directly subordinated to the respective ministries in Paris. But this *rattachement* (1881) also demonstrated the ambiguity of the term "assimilation". It implied political and administrative integration of the colony into the national territory, with parliamentary representation and transfer of the colony to the mother country's legal system; it also implied cultural assimilation of the natives with equal status in law and full civil rights. In the *vieilles colonies* and Senegal the two facets were not distinguished, while in Algeria administrative integration was not linked with an assimilative native policy.

We shall have to ask: who wanted assimilation, what purpose did it serve, and who was to be assimilated? Again there are certain parallels with the British concept of self-government, since the question of who should obtain self-government, the settlers or the population as a whole, resembles the French dilemma: to whom should assimilation apply, to the French colonials only or to the natives as well?

Critical discussion of the policy of assimilation began around 1890. In 1892 the idea of Algerian *rattachement* was abandoned in favour of a combination of parliamentary representation and local autonomy. The Algerian administration was by no means popular and people warned against transferring it to the newly won Tunisia. Governors and colonial officers such as Lanessan, Galliéni and Lyautey became aware that the "pacification" of large, closely-settled areas with well-established cultural patterns needed new methods and that French rule could be established more smoothly if one tried to win the co-operation of the inhabitants, built on existing institutions and applied civilizing pressures slowly and "indirectly". Under the influence of the natural sciences, new theories were becoming current that made clear the fundamental differences between races, civilizations and mentalities and rejected assimilation as deluded nonsense. In any case there was still the question of whether a policy that was perhaps valid and likely to succeed in the *vieilles colonies* whose old-established mixed population had no indigenous civilization could also be valid for the new colonies in Indochina and North Africa. In fact assimilation seemed to show signs of dangerous effects; for instance, it was alleged that in India Western education had destroyed the old society and a semi-educated class had emerged which was already turning against the colonial power.[7]

So even before 1914 the concept of assimilation was superseded by that of association. The meaning of "association" is best understood in Jules Harmand's *Domination et Colonisation*, published in 1910, which continued to influence the colonial discussion between the wars. Harmand used the terms in their original sense: "colonies" are simply areas of settlement, while "domination" means a foreign civilization ruling over the natives. Colonies of this kind are founded on force, and can be justified only by the superior civilization of the colonial power to which the colonies must defer, economically, militarily and politically. The native population is unassimilable and will never fully accept the foreign power. On these grounds Harmand opposed administrative integration and over-hasty assimilation. He thought the colonies should have their own organizations, with statutory rights and their own tariffs. Representatives in parliament, he said, could benefit only the European minority and forcibly preserved special interests and abuses, since the colonial deputies always demanded "assimilation in terms of profits but autonomy in terms of power".[8]

Harmand outlined the policy of association as follows:

> Yet it always teaches tolerance and liberalism in autocracy; everywhere it prescribes scrupulous respect for customs, habits and religions; everywhere it substitutes mutual aid for the pure and simple exploitation of the native labour forces and the usurpation of their goods and their land. It promotes their intellectual development. By trying to make their work more personal and more profitable it tends to make it more productive. By seeking to draw them together and to unite them by bringing their interests closer, it makes submission easier.

> But a realistic and wise policy of association resolutely and firmly reserves all the rights of domination and takes all its exigencies into account. It in no way wants to prepare or realize an equality which is always impossible, but rather wants to establish a certain equivalence or compensation of reciprocal services. Far from enfeebling the rule, it wants to reinforce it by reducing the frictions and hatred.[9]

Instead of transferring the mother country's institutions, and instead of cultural association, Harmand wanted to maintain existing administrative and social structures, to inspire respect for native customs and religions, set down a careful land policy and prevent crass exploitation. These ideas are reminiscent of Lugard's indirect rule and of Lyautey's concept of the protectorate. In what was to be a characteristic change of position, the maintenance of existing institutions and the traditional way of life came to sound a liberal note beside the assimilatory attempt to impose one's own civilization on a foreign people. Association could be viewed as a form of "co-operation" between the colonial power and the natives.

The pragmatic nature of the new concept is clear: the maintenance of existing structures was to make foreign rule more tolerable. For the primary task of the colonial power is to guarantee and consolidate its domination: "everything that has the effect of consolidating and guaranteeing it is good, everything that can weaken and compromise it is bad." The instruments of power must not be surrendered; the "subjects" should not be naturalized on a large scale and should neither obtain franchise in the local assemblies nor be able to take over the administration's authority.

Since Harmand was writing before 1914 he could still state the case of the rulers very clearly. But after the war this was no longer possible; liberal and reformist aspects had to be stressed even if the basic intention was the same. Harmand could also still assume that the domination would be permanent—at least for the foreseeable future. So it remained an open question whether association would eventually result in integration and assimilation or whether on the contrary it would lead to a political autonomy resembling the British self-government.

Between the wars it was impossible to avoid discussing the future. Since this is of particular interest to us, we now propose to outline the terms used in the colonial discussion and to try to explain their fundamental ambivalence.

After 1919 there was little open support for a policy of assimilation. Pre-war criticism, the difficulties of implementation, as well as the extension of the political horizon and development of the modern sciences of sociology and ethnology had compromised the term. But those who still openly used it, and we must stress this, included the native deputies of the *vieilles colonies* and Black Africa. It was they who believed in integration and assimilation and described France as their fatherland. For instance, in the cabinet debate on 21 December 1922, the deputy from Guadeloupe, Boisneuf, pointed out that he owed his parliamentary mandate to assimilation: "I only say that assimilation must be the aim of French colonization . . . colonization consists in making the native evolve from his civilization towards French civilization. . . . This is the aim and the justification of colonization." Blaise Diagne, the deputy mayor of Dakar, supported him: "This is true for the blacks, for we do not have the same past as the yellow races. . . . Either you will gradually give all these great domains certain liberties, so that one day you will have created for them their own individual and self-centered personality [!], which is colonization in the manner of the English . . . or, starting from the decolonization which is based on reason and in the heart . . . you must gradually manage to create an attraction towards the central hearth."[10]

In the same year, in an open letter to the American Marcus Garvey, Diagne dissociated himself from the latter's theses of African nationalism and contrasted them with the idea of emancipation within France—as Frenchmen.[11] Some years later, in January 1930, when the former governor-general of Indochina, the socialist Varenne, demanded in parliament that the Annamites should gradually be granted autonomy, Blaise Diagne protested: "Indeed no, we must tell them that we have a common fatherland . . . we must not let any hopes survive that by the fact of creating another fatherland, a new fatherland, this [a distinction between Annamite and French youth] could happen one day. There are not two fatherlands. There is but one." So while the French socialist wanted to accede to the claim for emancipation of the Indochinese élite and condemned the former methods of cultural assimilation, the African defended them—even for the Far Eastern territories. This was a remarkable reversal of positions! However, the ambivalence of the term "fatherland" became clear. When the colonial minister spoke of France's desire to bring the natives closer to the "duties of French citizens", and thereby tacitly supported assimilation—quoting Diagne as evidence of the native's agreement—the latter replied that by "fatherland" he did not mean metropolitan France but Greater France. "And that France is not necessarily in Europe but can be found wherever France is."[12]

We are not concerned here with how far the not unopposed Diagne, a citizen of one of the privileged Four Communes and a successful deputy, was recognized by the young Senegalese and African élite as a representative spokesman. We could quote similar words not only from the *vieilles colonies* and Black Africa but also from Algeria (i.e. Ferhat Abbas), and even Indochina, although there the demand for naturalization and full citizenship often disguised a desire for autonomy or independence. More important, I believe, is that the desire for assimilation, which Boisneuf and Diagne formulated so strikingly, did in fact give evidence of the effectiveness and influence of French education and of the success of the civilizing mission. But at the same time it represented an appeal to metropolitan France to accomplish this mission which it had noisily proclaimed and to accept its implications. Diagne, and he was not alone, was prepared to renounce a *personnalité propre* in the sense of African nationalism or territorial self-government, if the policy of assimilation remained convincing and opened a path to emancipation not just for him but for the entire colonial population. France was taken at its word and people demanded the realization of Greater France aiming not just at a final integration of the colonies into the national territory and an extended metropolitan France, but at an effective "national" community; apart from providing cultural aid and economic development, this also meant that France should slowly yet continuously and consistently extend the grant of civil rights to the native peoples who were becoming emancipated.

This did not occur, or at least France did nothing in the inter-war years to promote the concept or to make it effective in political and institutional terms. The number of naturalizations remained very low in Indochina and Algeria as well as in Black Africa. The process was lengthy and the administration did not facilitate it, but on the contrary made it more difficult. In 1936 there were less than 2500 native citizens among the 15,000,000 inhabitants of French West Africa outside the Four Communes! The renunciation of personal status continued to be the essential precondition for acquiring citizenship, although there had been a precedent in Senegal in 1916. This precedent was described as a mistake by arguing, for example, that in legal terms it was contradictory and untenable that voters and deputies could have a say in the laws concerning family and inheritance by which they themselves were not bound. A generous policy of naturalization, and the inclusion of educated natives in the colonial administration, could perhaps have tied the emancipated élite in Algeria and Black Africa to the mother country in the name of Greater France, and emancipation could perhaps have been achieved by means of assimilation. It is significant that important national leaders did not become nationalists or form national parties until after the disappointment of their expectations; this was the case with Ferhat Abbas after the Blum-Viollette reforms and in Black Africa after the Second World War.

But we are not doing justice to France if we explain its hesitant policy of naturalization only in terms of the conservative attitude of the administration and the influence of "colonialist" interests. Since the war the liberals and reformers had also rejected assimilation and, in the name of association, had constantly pointed out the differences in the indigenous civilizations. We shall see that even the Socialist party wavered between assimilation and autonomy. Paradoxically this produced a pro-native attitude among those who were against any form of emancipation and who were interested in maintaining the *status quo*. As a result, hardly anyone—except in the Algerian question and even then cautiously—actively supported assimilatory naturalization with all that it implied in the field of administration and law. So the lack of real alternatives produced a situation in 1939 not unlike that in 1919.

We have already pointed to the ambivalence of the French concepts. It is necessary here to distinguish between administrative integration and equality under the law for the French colonials on the one hand and a native policy of assimilation on the other. The latter had the support of the native deputies and the socialists. But a man like Arthur Girault, in the inter-war period a specialist on colonial law, was concerned only with the question of how to prevent the secession of the colonies under the leadership of the French colonials. In his *Principes de Colonisation et de Législation coloniale*, which appeared in a fifth edition in 1927, Girault supported assimilation, which he considered characteristic of the Latin race. He thought it could be readily adapted to the differences among the peoples, their geographic locations, etc. and required an "eclectic" method. Colonies, he thought, must not become caricatures of the mother country. Girault often referred to the case of Corsica: it had a special status and yet belonged to the national territory and sent representatives to parliament. Parodying a famous saying, he wrote that "a little thought takes one away from assimilation, but a lot of thought takes one back to it".[13]

We should like to quote here two rather long passages as examples of a form of argument that seems symptomatic:

> But if one reflects at length, one sees profound resemblances beneath the apparent differences. In the colonies, as in Europe, we are dealing with men who have human passions and who must be governed by human methods. These passions are violent among the colonists, given the ordinary ardour of their temperament, and no one has the power to make them nonexistent. During the first years of a colony, these colonists, absorbed in the pursuit of wealth, generally take little interest in political liberties. But later there will be some among the men born in the colony who turn their efforts towards winning popularity and power. They become party leaders and have a programme. Now, the Metropolitan Government, which is concerned with keeping its colony, must try to prevent the birth of a programme of separatism and to obtain the personal approval of the inhabitants. In order to achieve this, it must treat the inhabitants of the colonies with justice, giving them the means of defending their interests and safeguarding their legitimate self-respect. The policy of assimilation is the safety valve which prevents the rupture: To the man whom we prevent from being prime minister in his own country because his country is a colony, we must offer in exchange the possibility of being prime minister of France. The people whom we forbid local patriotism must be inspired with

love for the common fatherland, the cult of the Empire. The imperialist policy, by which English statesmen are currently trying to strengthen the ties which unite the different parts of the British Empire, has revived, under another name and on the other side of the Channel, our old policy of assimilation which we are now trying to avoid. Basically, this is still the policy whose ideal is a state of affairs in which there would no longer be a *metropolis* and *colonies*, but simply the *Nation*, as revolutionary France used to call it, the *Empire*, as the Anglo-Saxons say today. "I do not like this word *colonies*," said Kipling, "the Empire is all of us".

In fact, we are giving up the policy of assimilation because we are only just getting to know our colonies; we shall come back to it when we know them better. Whereas formerly we thought that we could attain at one bound the distant ideal towards which the patient nations are slowly travelling now, discouraged, we are temporarily turning our back on it.[14]

The policy of assimilation, freed in this way from the exaggerations which compromise it but for which it cannot be held responsible, appears both very patriotic and very lofty. It sacrifices neither the interest of the colonies nor that of the mother country. On the contrary, it not only sees to material needs and advantages but also, what is far more important, to the dignity and the legitimate susceptibilities of the parties concerned. Assimilation is a big enough formula to satisfy the aspirations of everyone. A policy of patriotic concord and wide fraternity, it unites the hearts and uplifts them.

Assimilation is the only possible ideal when autonomy is impracticable or dangerous, but it can be pursued everywhere. Tempered by large-scale decentralization extending if necessary as far as federalism [symptomatically understood here as administrative decentralization], it procures all the advantages of autonomy but also has an incontestable moral superiority in that instead of dividing it unites: this unique Parliament, composed of men who all speak the same language in spite of their different origins, who have come from all the parts of the world where the same flag flies to discuss the general interests of their common fatherland, is the eloquent and evident manifestation of this. Here is the salvation for the future. If in the eighteenth century England had followed the advice of Adam Smith and given the right of representation in Parliament to its colonies in America, it would probably have kept them. The establishment of a federal Parliament is perhaps the only means it has left today of keeping Canada and Australia. Except for communal representation there is, indeed, no choice except forced or amicable separation, except subjection, which provokes a colony that is already mature to rebel, or autonomy, whose ideal is emancipation.[15]

It is clear which variant of assimilation Girault is describing. For him, assimilation was the only alternative to "autonomy" in the sense of the autonomy of the British dominions; the phrase about "keeping Canada" is an exaggerated and biased interpretation of the attempts at federation within the Commonwealth. Girault judged British imperial policy negatively, as secession and dissolution, in contrast to his idea of a "single parliament" as an expression of a completed assimilation. Girault was clearly attempting to placate the French colonists, who naturally demanded their political rights and had to be satisfied: "there is therefore in fact no reason for differentiating and refusing to the colonies the benefits of the legislation judged good for the metropolis."[16] And the natives? The analogy with the British dominions was obviously inept, since the settlers in the French colonies—for not only Algeria is meant—formed only a dwindling minority in a population with a very strong civilization of its own.

In native policy, Girault prophesied that with the rapid population growth in the colonies, at the end of the twentieth century France would have to govern a hundred million persons. So he defined assimilation, in the sense of a rapid adoption of French civilization, as an "old delusion"; traditional customs must be respected, but always with an "iron grip beneath a velvet glove. . . . Any attempt at resistance must be immediately and completely suppressed".[17] In spite of the protectorate, he thought, French goods and ideas would penetrate, and economic development (Girault refers back to Albert Sarrault) would bring about a civilization resembling that of Europe.[18] "We shall try to raise the natives up to our civilization."[19] Thanks to the "collaboration of the natives"—which is obviously taken for granted—"we shall be able to transform completely, in the course of the twentieth century, the countries that we have decided to civilize".[20] It is not clear whether, in spite of the refusal to embark on rash assimilation, this native policy does not turn out to be the same thing. For Girault laid great stress on the aspect of domination, promising integration, parliamentary representation and equality under the law only to the French colonials and paying little attention to the natives. Since the natives could hardly ever be really assimilated, submission and resignation were all that was left to them: the colonial power would attempt to "oblige the natives to live in peace under French rule, and try to make them appreciate its practical advantages and improve their material conditions".[21]

This conclusion is astonishing, even if we take into account that Girault's *Principes* first appeared in 1894 and therefore still bear the stamp of the pre-war era. But although Girault revised his *manuel* and taught colonial law, he still managed to avoid these decisive questions or buried them under clichés in his three-volume work. In terms of economic issues and population, he was presumably planning for decades ahead, which was why he spoke of a "complete transformation" of the colonial social structure; but then he stopped short at "collaboration", by-passing the need for a deeper discussion of native policy and more details of its ultimate aim.

Albert Duchêne's arguments were not unlike Girault's. Duchêne spent many years as director for political affairs in the colonial ministry. He did not, however, use the term "assimilation" directly. He described General Mangin's phrase about the "nation of a hundred million" as "apt, almost classic," since it implied a "common fatherland".[22] France, he said, could not have friendly relations with "delicate federations" like the British dominions. He dismissed the fundamental legal distinctions between the status of citizen, subject and protégé with the remark that these were "merely Christian names, and French is the surname". Even the sovereigns in the protectorates had acquired "a French mentality, a French soul". The emperor of Annam, for instance, had been educated in France. Assimilation was in line with French tradition, but did not mean a crude approximation of the mother country: rather it opened the way "towards autonomy, a special autonomy which cannot be compared to the self-government of the British dominions but is none the less important. It is chiefly an administrative and budgetary autonomy".[23] French jurisdiction was becoming increasingly important, since in the long run two different systems could not exist side by side. Duchêne's view of the future encompassed a degree of decentralization within a common fatherland. His concept remained assimilatory, although he said no more about representation in parliament and ignored the native question to such an extent that it is not clear whether he meant to promote assimilation or was content to maintain permanent rule by the French colonials and the administration. This influential colonial bureaucrat gave very few details, yet it becomes apparent that Duchêne, like Girault, saw assimilation quite differently from the native deputies and the reformers.

The arguments against assimilation date from the pre-war era and we have described them earlier: France was no longer dealing with only a few small islands and coastal positions which had long been under French administration and had few indigenous traditions. It was nonsense to speak of assimilation for the peoples of Indochina, Northern Africa or even Black Africa; one had to accept their traditions and be cautious about transferring French institutions and laws. Any precipitate action was dangerous and would have unfortunate effects. For us it is important to note that even the anti-assimilation arguments are no more than ambivalent attempts to justify divergent positions.

One of the most severe critics of assimilation was Louis Vignon, professor at the École coloniale. In his comprehensive work *Un programme de politique coloniale, les questions indigènes*, published in 1919, he attacked this "French stupidity" with scientific thoroughness. Vignon was influenced by the socio-ethnological treatises of Le Bon and Saussure and began his analyis with Negro, Berber-Arab and yellow nations and communities integrated by race, religion, environment and history. He said the natives were not "backward", but were simply "other men". To want to make them into Frenchmen was ridiculous and presumptuous;

assimilation would disintegrate their traditional structures. Vignon described the methods of conquest with surprising frankness. The occupying power, he said, had encountered resistance which it broke by means of repression and destruction. The colonizers had introduced alcohol and disease and had recklessly exploited the natives. In Algeria they had expropriated land and property, and the concessions in the Congo had had catastrophic results; European industrial goods and processes were destroying indigenous crafts.[24] Apart from the Marxist writers, Vignon was one of the only Frenchmen to describe the effects of imperialist policy and of assimilation in this manner!

Vignon did not oppose assimilation by association, for he thought the latter merely disguised a tendency to assimilation. Instead he contrasted it with the concept of the protectorate, which he saw as the "art" of governing the native inhabitants through their own institutions and authorities and slowly leading them towards "a better social, political, economic state . . . which, however, will not cease to comply with their mentality, which will remain in conformity to the evolutionary faculties of their intelligence".[25] The traditional rulers, chiefs and notables were to be given power in order to provide an administrative framework, while the colonial power would chiefly be concerned with practical issues: modernization of agriculture, construction of irrigation works, etc. It would be better to reform the taxation system and the prejudice against the natives than to speak of franchise and similar Western "achievements". Here Vignon was obviously thinking of Lyautey's protectorate in Morocco, and perhaps also of Lugard's theories of indirect rule. The conservative accent is plain, for Vignon counted on very long periods of transition, and, like Lyautey and Lugard, was sharply opposed to the *évolués*, the emancipated class of semi-educated natives. So Vignon merely wanted to promote technical training and warned against "encouraging French travel for the young natives".[26] He did not consider questions of future developments. Like Harmand, he was against relaxing the system of government or admitting natives into the higher colonial service: "never appoint them to the office of administrator or judge, for these are essentially offices of sovereignty, of domination, reserved solely to the Whites to ensure their political power."[27] Yet he criticized the excessive number of minor white officials: in Indochina for example, they had prevented the Annamites from gaining access to administrative posts. Vignon hoped the protectorate system and material and cultural aid would rally the traditional authorities to the French cause; however, he counted on some latent conflict. In fact, he betrayed his scepticism when, referring to Indochina, he wrote: "perhaps . . . they will become reconciled, in some lustra [!] to our presence."[28] At another point he even contemplated the possibility of secession, saying that France would have to take care that the day when, obeying a law of nature, they claim their freedom, this should happen gradually and amicably; and again, that at the moment when they are sufficiently evolved, mature and stable, they will be able, on the departure of their tutors, to "make it" alone, without cries or revolutions.[29]

Here Vignon went beyond Harmand, by accepting at least the possibility of decolonization; given this, the concept of the protectorate could lead only to self-government and independence. But he still saw this as only a vague possibility for the distant future.

Vignon was strongly influenced by the racial theories of the late nineteenth century; his views are those of the ruler and social conservative. Yet his attacks on assimilation are worthy of note. He wanted to formulate a "positive" native policy which would eliminate as far as possible the exploitation, abuses and social disintegration resulting from the colonial conquest and protect the original character of the native communities. Perhaps his concept of the protectorate was no longer relevant to the situation in Indochina and especially to the problem of Algeria (where he actively opposed the reform law of 1918–1919),[30] but in Lyautey's Morocco it had produced positive results. At any rate, Vignon's criticism of assimilation implied a policy of reform.

The rejection of assimilation sometimes sounded a very "colonialist" note and provided useful arguments against political reforms, particularly in the question of naturalization and citizenship. This is particularly true in the case of Algeria. By asserting that the race, religion and social structures of the Muslims precluded a "premature" policy of assimilation, the colonists and their associated societies in the mother country could oppose naturalization *in globo* and extension of the qualifications for citizenship. The French colonials claimed French law and parliamentary representation, but described its extension to the natives as "premature". Naturalization, they thought, should apply only to the individual as a "reward" for services rendered to the colonial power; the administration would see to it that this "generous gesture" would be made only to "safe" candidates and in exceptional cases.

We shall describe the attitude of the French Algerians later. Here, however, we should mention Jean Runner's *Droits politiques des indigènes*, published in 1927. Runner declared his sympathy with the violent resistance of colonial circles that protested against what was in fact a rather modest naturalization law. His thesis was that "a sovereign nation, that seeks to conserve its rank, must always maintain control of the access to the quality of citizen and must not let this title be prostituted".[31] However, the natives might obtain representation in the local assemblies, since these had only consultative powers. But franchise was dangerous and unsuitable for the colonies, i.e. for the natives, since it was a European principle. Runner considered British policy in India and West Africa just as mistaken as the creation of a people's council in the Dutch Indies[32] and declared that "the participation of the natives of Indochina in the government of their colony is therefore assured".[33] His criticism of assimilation led him to object both to naturalization and to the British system of granting representative organs. In effect, then, he was approving the *status quo* in the "colonialist" sense and trying to prevent the political emancipation of the natives.

Most of the political writers preferred the concept of association to assimilation. Albert Sarraut, in his *Mise en valeur*, again provides the decisive clues[34] for an understanding of how the methods outlined by Jules Harmand in 1910 were interpreted between the wars. Although he categorically gave precedence to the political and economic interest of the colonial power,[35] Sarraut also strove to create a modern and "liberal" colonial doctrine which would take into account the emancipation of the natives. Economic development would bear fruit only under a policy of association, of collaboration between the mother country and the colonial inhabitants. But, on what would this collaboration be based? French colonial policy, said Sarraut, was guided by the concept of justice—one of the many rhetorical phrases of these years. But Sarraut set himself apart from those who assumed there was an unbridgeable gap between the black and the white races and who at best wanted an authoritarian paternalistic form of government. He said French policy was based on the declaration of human rights and it was the duty of the colonial power to overcome the backwardness of the non-white peoples. The value of an individual did not lie in the colour of his skin; if an individual was capable of higher things—higher obviously meaning in terms of Franco-European civilization—then France must not fail to help him raise himself up and take advantage of his rise. "On this juridicial and moral basis rests our legislation of French naturalization for the natives."[36]

The chief differences between the British doctrine and Vignon's theories become apparent here: although Sarraut did not urge assimilation and stressed the natives' different character and traditions, his efforts at liberalism and desire for reform led him to conclusions which bear a clear assimilatory stamp and, in terms of civilization and politics, aimed at a "common Fatherland".[37] This tendency is also apparent in his comments on educational policy. He sharply opposed using standard teaching methods because they took no account of the different native civilizations and he emphasized—although this was nothing new—the need for practical training. The schools should concentrate on training for the lower grades of the administration, the colonial army and the economy. The French language should be compulsory in all grades; there was no mention of teaching in the local language. Sarraut wanted to give those who were capable access to all grades of education; it was wrong to "assign a limit to their intellectual ascent, a barrier, the obstacle of a veto" or to tell them "you shall go no further, you shall know no more".³⁸ (Belgium followed this policy in the Congo until after the Second World War!)

These few comments characterize French educational doctrine between the wars. The education of the masses was to be of a practical nature; it was to train a useful administrative cadre—which would be cheaper than white labour; meanwhile a small élite would have access to French university education and these few natives would be subjected to civilizing and cultural influences and permanently bound to the mother country. Naturalization became a privilege of the élite, for France "deliberately opens, for whoever of her protégés deserves to enter, the gates of the French city".³⁹ But Sarraut, as he himself said, rejected any pseudo-liberal system of naturalization and urged only a slight relaxation of existing rules. Renunciation of personal status remained a *sine qua non*. He considered it more important to give the "French non-citizen" more political rights in his "native city" than to pursue a misunderstood policy of assimilation. Sarraut's explanations leave much unsaid; but it is clear that he was far from approving a native policy on the lines of a protectorate system or indirect rule, and saw the native cadre as no more than an auxiliary. His reference to the "native city" is odd, since he wanted the young élite to be naturalized and taken out of traditional society.

Sarraut thought native representation in the local assemblies was still inadequate. He wanted to extend the native electoral body and make it truly representative. But the "representative institutions" were to remain advisory boards and not develop into legislative bodies of the British kind. The inclusion of natives in the consultative institutions, and native access to the administration, which he alleged already existed, seemed sufficient answer to their demands.⁴⁰ Sarraut was emphatically opposed to giving up any sovereign rights.⁴¹ He visualized the colonies as organisms with a life of their own, and wanted to make the colonial administration and legislation more flexible; but he explicitly stated that "autonomy" meant only administrative decentralization, which did not lead to independence but created even closer ties with the mother country. A "close political dependence" should remain, together with the "fundamental concept of national unity".

Indeed how could the "family tie" be relaxed in an era when the colonies' economic development and defense against the outside world made aid from the mother country necessary? Sarraut found it ridiculous to speak of independence, since the colonial inhabitants still lacked a "national consciousness" and it would only result in chaos. The natives, he said, were aware of this, and "the idea of independence, far from tempting them, terrifies them". In Indochina this had been very much the case, in spite of the country's great historical past, and the élite considered the idea of independence "a pure absurdity". And if administrative autonomy should nevertheless one day inspire the desire for independence, this was a problem that would only concern our grandchildren.[42] Sarraut admitted that Britain granted generous constitutions and initiated reforms, but he thought this was only a form of "verbal liberalism", pointing to British racial discrimination. France did not need to fear separatism since the colonies were bound to the mother country by "ties of gratitude".

So the doctrine of association was to be a "middle road" between assimilation and political autonomy. It was distinct from the policy of integration and citizenship that had been pursued in the *vieilles colonies* and the Four Communes of Senegal in 1916. Given the existence of a large population with its own civilization, Sarraut thought their social structures and cultural traditions should be accepted: but at the same time he believed that even in the future, political emancipation could be avoided or prevented. There were two points on which one could give in to the natives' demand for independence: the élite trained and influenced by France could be granted naturalization and civil, i.e. voting rights; or a certain amount of native representation in the colonial advisory boards could be permitted. By "combining" the two concepts, France hoped to avoid both assimilation and autonomy and yet ensure lasting ties between the mother country and the colonies. The assimilatory elements of this "association" cannot be overlooked, however, either in the cultural or the political and legal spheres: the colonies were to remain parts of Greater France, and the seat of political decision-making would be Paris; at most the colonies could be granted a certain decentralization and representation of their interests. Since native representatives would remain a minority both in parliament and in the colonial bodies, there was no danger to the existing power of the mother country and the association would remain one of unequal partners. The precondition for the existence and durability of association as a form of decolonization was the assumption that the emancipated élite would remain content with naturalization and that its political demands would be satisfied by the grant of franchise in parliamentary elections; as a result, the élite would be willing to give up any claims to effective political participation in colonial decision-making, to nationhood—except for the French one—and to independence, as "pure absurdity".

This assumption may still have been valid around 1920 in North Africa and Indochina, in spite of the activity of several nationalist organizations and movements, and in Black Africa it could even be said to be valid until the Second World War. But it no longer applied to the situation around 1931, when Sarraut, in his equally respected book *Grandeur et servitude coloniales*, again discussed colonial policy. He drew a good outline of the dangerous position Europe found itself in at the time, especially in Asia, and of the emerging colonial emancipation movements. He also described the effects of the First World War and subsequent changes in economic structure, and urged his countrymen to acknowledge the vital importance of the colonies to France and acknowledge the challenge they provided. But, curiously, his attitude to the national movements and to the possibility of the colonies seceding had not changed since 1923 and he used the same dubious formulas: the colonial peoples did not want independence, and even if they did, this would only concern future generations. It is still incredible how an apparently logical Frenchman could make such deductions from his own premises—obviously he did not dare to draw the logical conclusions and clung to the theory of an existing or at least potential "association" between the mother country and the colonies.

In concrete questions too Albert Sarraut remained one of the older generation; he continued to enjoy great respect throughout the 1930s and was appointed to coordinate policy for North Africa in 1937,[43] but he still stood by the positions of 1923. For instance he wanted to grant university education only to those "who are least likely to stumble and fall; university education can be vouchsafed only to those who are capable of receiving and absorbing it".[44] This sounds legitimate, but in practice it meant that university education was subject to control and that the candidates would be tested on their loyalty. However, Sarraut admitted that the French-schooled natives must be used in the administration more frequently than before. This demand was often raised in political writing and in parliament, but it was never realized because of the *esprit de corps* of the colonial services and the pressure exerted by officials. Sarraut also considered admitting natives to administrative "offices of authority", i.e. senior posts in the colonial administration, and around 1931 he was forced to accept this possibility in principle. Jules Harmand and Louis Vignon, to name two representative examples, were strongly opposed. Sarraut did not want to enter into the legal question of whether these senior posts could be open only to Frenchmen and naturalized natives, nor did he want to draw a strict line between them. But he did help clarify the situation somewhat, declaring that access to these offices would be possible only

> when the intellectual and moral gulf which still separates us from the natives has been bridged. This cannot be achieved overnight by a certificate of naturalization. In principle, objectively speaking, I see no obstacle to appointing natives to offices of authority in a colony. In fact, they already occupy the lower grades; but positive applications to the upper grades of the hierarchy cannot be granted until we have subjects available who have long since accepted our moral guidance and who have willingly integrated themselves heart and soul into the French nation. These aspirations to the senior offices of authority will be satisfied at a definite future time, but the date is not yet settled.[45]

These sentences seem to be characteristic of the French colonial concept between the wars. Sarraut wanted to show his willingness to reform, and actually did go a step further than Harmand, but he laid down conditions that were essentially assimilatory in nature, thereby relegating effective access to offices of authority to an indefinite future. Clearly the ultimate aim behind association was assimilation; in other words, because he started from the assumption of Greater France and an integrated national unity, Sarraut had to stipulate that only the native who had really become a Frenchman could anticipate rising to a senior post. A non-Frenchman would be a threat to this unity and could become the instrument of a national secession movement. Sarraut failed to recognize that at the time when he was making vague references to the future, there were already natives who were French "at heart" and should now be admitted to offices of authority. Either he was not sure of their existence, or he was hesitant to take the decisive step. But if in 1931 there was still no assimilated élite, how could Sarraut assume that it would emerge in the future, especially since he had explicitly referred to colonial emancipation movements? Once again it becomes clear that Paris indulged in false hopes, and tended to avoid making a decision by repeating phrases.

The difference from British policy is evident. Britain, too, laid down conditions—"civilization", "education", "maturity"—and British conservatives and liberals also argued about the date when concessions would have to be granted. But no British political writer would stipulate integration "heart and soul", for the issue of native access to the higher administrative service took on a different meaning in the British concept. It referred to self-government and was designed to satisfy an élite and to guide national emancipation into the right channels. However, a certain loyalty, in the sense of collaboration with the colonial power, was presumed; accordingly the number of Indians, Burmese and Ceylonese in "offices of authority" greatly increased in the inter-war years, while in Indochina, for instance, it remained small.

Sarraut proved equally conservative in the question of representative bodies. He was in favour of increasing their powers in the field of finance, but was strongly opposed to extending them into "parliaments" and granting a constitution. Demands of this kind would come from a few intellectuals, he thought, but not from the masses. Here again Sarraut referred the problem to the future.[46] In effect he was approving a policy of *status quo* dominated by the French colonials which, for the time being, contented itself with advisory bodies.[47] It is not clear whether Sarraut, who definitely considered himself liberal and yet found that his —modest—proposals for reform were turned down by the colonials for being excessive, wanted to conciliate the emancipation movement. He obviously believed that France had now achieved all that was possible in the political sphere and should concentrate on economic development, on raising the standard of living of the masses, and on its civilizing mission. Perhaps we can put it as follows: because the concept of association implied neither an explicit and consistent policy of naturalization in the sense of assimilation, nor the gradual grant of effective political responsibility, as was Britain's aim,[48] the result was necessarily a tendency to depoliticize, even to make the mistaken assumption that further political rights need not be granted until later, without specifying what the nature of these rights would be.

The idea of association, as Albert Sarraut tried to formulate it, dominated French colonial discussion between the wars. A brief reference to other, perhaps equally representative political writings, will clarify what we have said and illustrate some variants.

Typical of countless similar publications and newspaper articles are the *Commentaires sur la colonisation* by the economic writer Robert Doucet, published in 1926. He thought the tendency to secession in the colonial world applied only to the British Empire: India, Egypt, etc. In fact, he said, Britain had not known how to implement its policy of "collaboration". (Here the anglophobe Doucet equated British rule in India with old-style exploitation.) The colonial peoples profited from Europe, but "do they understand? This is the whole question . . . we are advancing towards the unknown".[49] In the French colonies there were no open rebellions, "nor even serious misunderstandings" between the metropolis and the natives! Since Doucet was opposed to granting civil and voting rights, alleging that the doubtful electoral methods were well-known, there remained only association, which was realistic and consisted in "not having principles". Colonial policy must be based on economic considerations and its task was economic development. The natives should become good workers, which was why one should satisfy their "legitimate needs" as far as possible—i.e. security, sufficient food, hospitals and schools. It was quite inconceivable, he said, that Congolese or Sudanese could govern themselves—Doucet does not mention North Africa or Indochina. For the rest, one might give a small élite access "to the French family through the door of naturalization".[50] Naturalization, it appears, was regarded as a means of delaying political emancipation, by continually neutralizing the élite. Doucet, like many other political writers, was in favour of an intensified programme of colonization, and he saw the settlers as instruments for spreading French culture who therefore occupied an important place within Greater France.[51] It is not surprising then that Doucet contemplated representation in parliament for all the colonies, and even the protectorates, but with franchise restricted to the French. Naturalization, he thought, had been pursued too rapidly. [!] He also thought a colonial parliament was conceivable, with about fifty representatives of the French colonials "to whom one could perhaps [!] later join some representatives of the native population appointed by a small élite of notables".[52] The number of restrictions here is worthy of note! The "colonialist" accent of Doucet's book is plain, but even more striking is how, in the name of association, he postulated the integration of the colonies and arbitrarily surrendered the native inhabitants to the settlers' rule—presumably under the assumption that even in the future there would be no emancipation movements.

Georges Hardy deserves special mention here. He was director of education in Morocco from 1919 to 1926, director of the École coloniale from 1926 to 1932 and rector of the Academy of Algiers from 1932 to 1937. His book *Nos grands problèmes coloniaux*, which appeared in 1933 as part of the Colin series, became widely known. Like Sarraut in 1931, Hardy started out from the threatening situation in the colonies, but then reversed himself and declared that the national movements were not dangerous.[53] Only on this assumption could he formulate a colonial policy that would not lead to dissociation! In the chapters on economic and social questions, he combined criticism of the existing state of affairs with practical proposals for reform that prove his great experience and reflect the objective judgment of a scholar. He thought one had to start from the traditional institutions and authorities, but instead of simply trying to maintain them, as the conservatives advocated, one should renew, modernize and emancipate them. Hardy stressed the importance of agricultural training, the setting up of model stations and the struggle against the "exploitation of native by native" (e.g. the tenant system in Cochin China, the *corvée* for chiefs and feudal princes) and against profiteering; on the other hand, he accepted forced labour for improving the culture of certain products. The traditional system of collective property should be abolished gradually.

Hardy realized the difficulty of colonization: "The whole difficulty therefore consists in promoting the European colonist without injuring the native: these are propositions which have sometimes seemed antinomic."[54] The state must intervene to control land rights and land purchase, work contracts, concessions, etc. Hardy also criticized the racial arrogance of many of the whites who described the natives as *bicots*.

His views on political questions and the ultimate aim of French colonial policy are less clear. Hardy saw no contradiction between respect for existing social structures and traditions, and gradual assimilation.[55] He was obviously thinking of Algeria when he said that the settlers were ready for such a policy provided that assimilation was spread over a sufficiently long period of time. It was an optimistic assumption, and it raised the question of whether the Muslims were prepared to wait for the date set by the colonists. For the rest, Hardy was in favour of association based on a solidarity of interests between two societies "that will leave to each its own personality, institutions and customs". It was not at all certain yet, he thought, that all the colonies would follow the example of the British colonial settlements and dominions and that all colonial domination would lead to "schisms"; instead the lengthy period of colonial occupation could produce a *rapprochement* and a "desire for communal life". One could easily imagine systems

> equally distinct from subjection and from independence, capable of protecting the weak or the late arrivals without impairing their development of their true liberty: and it is probably in such symbioses that those colonizing nations who are equal to their task will see the formulas for the future. [56]

At least Hardy was concerned with the future. It is characteristic of the French attitude that he resisted the idea of eventual dissociation and sought a different way out of the dilemma. And we may consider it symptomatic that even such an expert on colonial affairs was able to tell us little about this "symbiosis".[57] He considered the transition to parliamentary assemblies premature and did not say how he envisaged native representation or the institutional ties between the metropolis and the colonies. But these were the decisive questions! Since Hardy was not aiming at self-government and was willing to give political consideration even to the French colonials outside Algeria and wanted to reserve legislative power to the parliament of Paris, he in effect went no further than defending the *status quo*—or at best proposing a few reforms. None of this could hide the fact that his views on the future of association, in spite of phrases like "collaboration" and "communal life", were unclear—perhaps necessarily so.

We should refer here in somewhat more detail to Léon Archimbaud's *La plus grande France*, published in 1928. Today, rightly perhaps, it is forgotten; but it is an extremely striking catalogue of the clichés and rhetorical phrases that appeared in political writing and parliamentary discussions during those years. It is all the more representative in that Archimbaud was a well-known radical socialist deputy, who spent many years as a reporter on the colonial budget and had demonstrated his interest in the overseas territories as publisher of the *Revue de Pacifique* (1922-1936). The book is an apologia for Greater France and an attempt to propagate an "imperial mentality". He criticized French education for paying too little attention to the colonies and, by contrast, praised the committees that were organized around colonial issues. No other nation was "as capable as ours of making itself accepted by the natives, i.e. loved by them".[58] There followed, of course, the usual attacks on the Anglo-Saxons who had driven the natives out—in Australia they were allegedly still doing this in the nineteenth century. France, on the other hand, had proclaimed equality at the time of the Revolution.[59] France was free of racial discrimination and, unlike Britain, was not solely concerned with economic profit. "In colonial affairs we have clean hands. Not every colonizing nation can say the same."[60] Such phrases were common among right-wing colonials, but sound curious coming from a Radical Socialist who liked to stress his "revolutionary" views. Naturally Archimbaud referred to Sarraut's *Mise en valeur;* he thought the need for economic development had become urgent since the war, since the financial situation in France did not make it possible "to buy in the great world markets at any price".[61] France must become as autarchic as possible and establish a market of "a hundred millions".[62]

He criticized the colonial administration's habit of transferring officials from one department to another, the inadequate ministerial cadre and the paper war. . . . The natives caused little trouble, especially in Indochina:

> As for an internal peril, may I be allowed to say that it does not exist . . . the native question has never become an issue there as it has, for instance, in British India, and it is certain [!] that it will never become an issue of that kind. Apart from a few brainless young people whose opinion is of no value, the Annamites have never demanded that France should evacuate Indochina.[63]

"Generosity" had been carried too far, and assimilation had been a mistake: but it had now given way to the "healthy formula of association" which Archimbaud, however, did not manage to explain fully. France must develop the natives within their own traditions, he said, protecting them from exploitation: that is to say, "one cannot too much stress the need for prudence in native affairs". He fully supported political rights for the French settlers, who—except in Algeria—were being denied the right to vote: "the colon, who is in fact a *sur-français*, is also a *sous-français*, a second-class citizen, denied the indefeasible rights allowed to the French of the mother country". The governors spoke only of the rights of the natives, he asserted, and not of those of the settlers. "Under a system of this kind, we will soon come to the paradoxical result that the natives will have more rights than the French and that the latter will be in part ruled by the natives" [!].[64] Consequently, Archimbaud demanded representation in parliament for all the colonies, a demand that conformed to the assimilatory and centralist tradition of the Radical Socialists and which was accepted in a party resolution of the 1927 annual conference.[65] The commission's request that the Algerian natives should be granted three deputies was opposed by the party delegate from Algeria![66] Archimbaud was not in favour of generous naturalization: "our aim is not to make the native into a metropolitan Frenchman, but into a colonial Frenchman, and we must make him able, not to participate in the government of France, but to collaborate in the administration of his country".[67] He too considered that the political rights of the natives were sufficiently guaranteed by native representation on the advisory boards.

The fact that the Radical Socialists' colonial expert adopted the clichés of the right wing throws a curious light on the attitudes of a party that proudly asserted its loyalty to the Left. Even more remarkable is that Archimbaud, in his final chapter, said almost the opposite of what he had asserted before, as though he were finally trying to put forward a progressive Radical Socialist programme after all. Now he not only said that France had had no real colonial doctrine since 1870, but even added that "nowhere do the natives have a serious part in the government of their country" and that to speak of "collaboration" or "association" was a "bad joke". There were, it was true, advisory bodies, but "their role is usually pure facade"; most of the members were appointed and their votes had no significance—"such a parody of popular representation is not worthy of France".[68] The policy of association would lead to autonomy and this was the ultimate aim of French colonial policy—even if it took a hundred or two hundred years. For him autonomy meant local government: the settlers of all the colonies should be represented in parliament, but he dismissed as "premature" the question of whether the natives should also have a corresponding representation. The number of French colonials must be raised; the emigration of 100,000 Frenchmen would not harm the mother country: "native policy, which is the great issue today, would be made much easier" [!] then, for it was the small white colonist who showed the native the meaning of the French family and who fulfilled the civilizing function. We might, perhaps, interpret Archimbaud as follows: the stronger the French minority, the sooner one can allow native representation in local government and perhaps even in parliament.[69]

So the Radical Socialist Archimbaud supported the concept of Greater France and a lasting association with the colonies. At first he used the notion of association as a means of restricting representation in parliament to the French colonials and of relegating the natives to local assemblies. The settlers appeared to be instruments of cultural assimilation, but this assimilation did not have to entail the grant of political rights. He did not consider the native question topical; nationalist rhetoric emphasized the "generosity" of France and this strengthened the hope that the natives would willingly accept French domination in the future too.[70] Archimbaud carefully avoided any embarrassing questions.

Archimbaud may be said to be representative of the majority of his party and of the many deputies of the moderate Left who took little interest in the colonies and whose notions of progress were closely bound up with their national sense of mission. The concept of Greater France and its civilizing mission allowed them to avoid paying critical attention to the details of colonial affairs. In a similar way the British slogans of "trusteeship" and "gradual grant of self-government" set the conscience of both the "man in the street" and the parliamentary representative at rest.

We do not dispute that a few outsiders were more seriously preoccupied with colonial problems and were prepared to accept the implications of a Left-oriented policy, as is evident from a discussion within the influential Ligue des Droits de l'Homme.[71] The socialist Félicien Challaye demanded a resolution against colonialism as such, which, he said, was like war because it could not be reformed but could only be abolished. The League must stand by the sovereign rights of the colonial peoples. Assimilation was the expression of a racial arrogance that sought to impose its own civilization on other peoples. Challaye demanded freedom of the press and the right to form political and union organizations: these reforms, he thought, would be preparation for the future independence of the colonies. By contrast, Maurice Viollette, deputy of a socialist splinter group and governor of Algeria from 1925 to 1927, proposed assimilation. Viollette, well known by his efforts to form a reform-oriented, popular front government in the colony, wanted to see more attention devoted to the positive aspects of colonization and warned against premature retreat. He sharply attacked capitalist exploitation and the untenable situation in Indochina in which Annamite scientists, after their training in Paris, were relegated to insignificant positions in the colonial administration. At the same time, the North Africans, for instance, wanted "to be French, not in the fashion of the French Algerians", but "in the fashion of the Frenchmen of France". This meant doing away with discrimination, giving equal status under the law and recognizing the élite! Albert Bayet, an important writer in the Radical Socialist press, demanded large-scale representation for the natives in the "representative assemblies", saying that the colonial peoples must be allowed to decide of their own free will "whether or not they wish to remain our associates". A representative of the Hanoi section attacked assimilation, saying it was nonsense to keep repeating that France would remain in Indochina for ever. Another speaker defended assimilation and demanded native representation in the French parliament: "We believe in the assimilatory force of our race, in the force of aspiration of French civilization. We believe that the peoples colonized by us will evolve much more rapidly towards independence, towards liberty, that they will more rapidly become free men in a free country, if they seek to be annexed to France." Here independence was interpreted as full emancipation and claimed to be a form of assimilation!

This discussion within the Ligue des Droits de l'Homme makes clear the divergence of opinion within the French Left and shows two different notions of decolonization: national emancipation and the future grant of independence, or assimilation within Greater France. We shall see that even the Socialist party was divided on this question. But in general the moderate Left tended to avoid choosing one or other of these fairly consistent solutions and was content with association. So it is not surprising that even the resolution that resulted from this discussion remained vague. It did speak of "free peoples", but did not specify whether this meant individual emancipation within France or national independence.[72]

Towards 1930 the notion of federalism also entered the French discussion, in connection with Briand's Europe project. The Count de Fels, who claimed to have coined the phrase, described the idea of a United French States as "the crown of French imperialism".[73] Perhaps Africans such as Blaise Diagne would accept integration and assimilation, but not so the Asians of Indochina whose national consciousness aimed at sovereignty. Only federalism could calm the tensions and turn the colonies into parts of "a fatherland of which France would be the nucleus". De Fels, in a new departure, was considering a loose association of autonomous members. But he did not discuss institutional questions, nor did he say whether the French parliament should remain in charge of foreign policy, defence, etc. or whether a "colonial parliament" should be formed to give the colonies a voice in issues of general concern. Pierre Lyautey, the son of Marshal Lyautey and an ardent politician, also proclaimed the idea of a French United States, and asked the remarkable question: "When shall we say of a president of Indochina or Tunisia, as is said in the Anglo-Saxon world, 'that man is one of the best men of the Empire'?"[74]

Is this comparison with Britain justified? Apparently Lyautey saw the dominions and the French colonies as parallels and wrongly judged the Commonwealth as a model for federation. At any rate, the French federalists were certainly not prepared to grant Indochina or Tunisia and Morocco dominions status; they adhered to the idea of federal institutions in order to assure the pre-eminence of metropolitan France. It is worth noting that Lyautey again recalled ancient Rome, which had granted the viceroys in Egypt and Syria almost complete independence and yet had introduced Roman law; the threat to the Empire had come only with the over-hasty assimilation of the barbarians.[75] Lyautey did not describe the federal institutions, although the question of how to reconcile the national claims of the natives with leadership by the metropolis is a central one and was to recur in 1946 when federation again came under discussion. Nor did he say that the Commonwealth, although it had British settlers, was not a federation—precisely because it had proved impossible to be fair to both partners in terms of institutions. France did not want a solution that depended overmuch on imponderables, and therefore held fast to an institutionally fixed framework. Moreover, France mistakenly saw federalism as a developed and extended form of local autonomy. It did not want to equate the metropolis and the colonies nor to transfer its sovereign powers to a supra-national body; France preferred to preserve the Paris parliament's power of decision and to give the colonies only an apparent share in overall political decision-making. This anticipates the problems of the French Union and federalist plans after the Second World War.

It seems appropriate here to give a brief sketch of the Catholic attitude. *Le Droit de Colonisation* (1930) by Joseph Folliet, a recognized specialist on colonial affairs in Catholic circles who often intervened in the discussion even after the Second World War, exemplifies the Catholic view. Folliet's theories were adopted or confirmed by the Parti Démocrate Populaire,[76] by a number of politicians and by the *Semaine Sociale* of 1930 which was devoted to the colonies.[77] Even the left-wing Catholic journal *Esprit* published[78] an article by Folliet in which he wrote: "this work . . . is born of an anguish."[79] Folliet had been familiar with the colonial situation since his youth and was proud of French achievements, but he was also only too well aware of the discriminatory attitude of the French soldiers and the contempt felt by many whites for the natives. It was painful, he thought, "to be a helpless witness to the injustices and abuses, some of which are odious and others stupid"; the French people must consider themselves responsible as a whole, and "France would be in a state of extremity, as Péguy said, if it deliberately stopped its ears and eyes". However, the Catholics only rarely raised their voices in protest against these abuses.[80] After the Rif revolt, in which the Communists had openly supported the rebels, the socialists had remained silent and the Right had used cheap arguments, it was difficult for him, he said, to offer a convincing defence of colonial policy.

Folliet consulted Catholic teachings and remarked that in recent years the Catholics had scarcely ever shown concern with the colonial problem and that only since the war had a few treatises and articles appeared. In broad historical lines, he traced the Catholic attitude from Las Casas, Francisco de Vitoria and papal pronouncements. He rejected racial and economic arguments and adopted the theories of a Spanish international lawyer, according to which the resources of this earth are available to all mankind and colonial domination is legitimate as long as the natives are unable to take over the exploitation of these resources themselves. We referred earlier on to the similarity between the Catholic arguments and Lord Lugard's *Dual Mandate*.

Folliet went on to discuss intervention "in the name of charity" and "civilizing action", which he justified by claiming that "the civilization of the world is a Christian civilization". For the Catholic, this answered the question of the indigenous value of native civilization and the function of the colonial power, whose job it was to act as missionary and civilizing influence.

With respect to Georges Hardy, Folliet rejected assimilation as he did "complete autonomy", since this would preclude any civilizing influence. There remained "adaptation", which more or less corresponded to association. "In the native civilization, we will destroy or reform that which, in terms of economics, is not viable and that which, in moral terms, contradicts natural law or philosophic or religious truth; we will preserve all the rest."[81] Folliet recalled Vignon and supported the concept of the protectorate; but he did not make it clear how the willingness to accept and tolerate a foreign civilization with all its institutions and beliefs could be reconciled with the exclusive claim to truth of the Christian Catholic world. Any attempt to form a unity of religion, law and morals in a Muslim society would presumably lead to many contradictions of "religious truth"!

In his practical proposals Folliet proved to be a reformer. He criticized existing agrarian laws, objected to forced labour (with reference specifically to the Gold Coast and its economic successes), and demanded the extension of education and that the workers have the right to form trade unions. He considered the medical services quite inadequate. Folliet took the notion of "tutelage" seriously and believed that at a given moment dissociation would necessarily take place, whether peacefully or by force. Here he pointed to an important problem: "The difficulty lies in fixing the moments when the colonizing powers must hand over the reins to their possessions; the educator will always have the tendency to continue to judge his pupil still too inexperienced."[82] But what are the criteria of "maturity"? Were Folliet's aims confined to the economic situation and would he be satisfied with the existence of an educated élite able to take over the reins of government, or was successful Christianization a precondition? In the latter case, obviously, dissociation would have been inconceivable, at least in the most highly developed territories in North Africa and Indochina.

Folliet's arguments are representative of Catholic doctrine between the wars and were broad enough to satisfy both the Right and the Left of political Catholicism. One side found itself confirmed in its Catholic paternalism, the other was gratified by the frank exposure of certain "abuses" and the demand for reform. After the Second World War, the newly founded Mouvement Républicain Populaire could pick up the thread and, on the basis of Folliet's theories, formulate a modern colonial policy.

THE SOCIALIST PARTY

We have not paid much attention to the political affiliations of the individual political writers, nor have we spoken much of party doctrine. Obviously there were connections between colonialist circles and the bourgeois Right; but the parties themselves were so little organized that they provide no suitable basis for discussion. Albert Sarraut and Léon Archimbaud were, it is true, important radical socialists and were to a certain extent representative of their party, but one can hardly speak of a

Radical Socialist colonial doctrine. For the Socialist party itself (SFIO), however, the point of departure does lie in the party, for it tried to formulate a programme, demanded fractional discipline and deliberately set itself apart from the bourgeois Right and Centre.

When the Socialist party was founded in 1905, Paul Louis, an influential member, tried to guide it into doctrinaire Marxist course. In his book *Le Colonialisme*, Louis explained colonial expansion in exclusively economic terms; the capitalist system had hoped, he said, to find a market for its products in the underdeveloped countries and tried to delay its inherent crisis temporarily by taking the profits of colonial exploitation. Colonial domination was gained at the price of the mother country's workers; it drove the subjected territories into political seclusion and made international tensions more acute. The "civilizing mission" was merely an ideological superstructure designed to harness public opinion and to gain parliamentary support. There could be no compromise and no "socialist colonial policy", since exploitation would not come to an end until there was revolution and until production was in the hands of the proletariat.

Yet reform tendencies appeared even before 1914. The party might protest military engagements and denounce the methods of economic exploitation, but it also had to ask itself whether it was still possible for the colonial powers to make a rapid retreat without condemning the colonies to refeudalization. Socialists warned against "premature surrender" and were prepared to accept the mother country as protector and educator.[1] Jaurès, who was primarily concerned with reducing international tensions, approved the 1911 Morocco agreement, which brought him a little closer to the position of the British Labour party.

Immediately after the First World War the Socialists were faced with the question—in colonial affairs and in general—of whether to break with the Communists. At the Congress of Tours in 1920, which led to the split in the party, the majority group under Léon Blum refused to identify the emancipation of the European proletariat with the movement for liberation of the colonial peoples, i.e. to openly support Lenin's concept of national opposition and take part in subversion against the mother country.[2] They wanted above all to give economic and social aid to the colonial peoples and to prepare them for gradual political emancipation. This put the Socialists in a difficult position. The Communists accused them of compromising, while the bourgeois parties and the colonial press attacked their allegedly doctrinaire anti-colonialism on the grounds that it was hardly any different from that of the Communists and only served to undermine French overseas positions. In order to refute this, the socialist Nouelle declared in parliament in 1929: "We are not anti-colonials!"[3]

This question became acute during the Abd-el-Krim rebellion in Morocco. The Communists and affiliated organizations openly supported the rebels and consequently alleged that they were the only champions of colonial emancipation; meanwhile the Socialists had to be diplomatic and even agreed to the necessary war expenditures. Independence, they argued, would be of no advantage to the natives; it was the Socialist party's duty to co-operate with the Moroccan proletariat in order to achieve economic, social and political progress, but not to support a reactionary feudal movement.[4]

The Socialist party did not demand immediate withdrawal, but it did actively voice its disapproval in parliament of colonial abuses, exploitation, administrative errors and dubious repressive measures. The main issue was working conditions in Indochina and Equatorial Africa and the construction of the Brazzaville-Ocean railway provided a good opportunity for criticism. Here they said, Africans were dragged to work and thousands had perished. Villages had been depopulated and others had been burned as punishment for not supplying workers. The administration was either not supervising the concession societies or working with them. In July 1927 *Le Populaire* printed a résumé of André Gide's book on the Congo.[5]

In Indochina too, native labour was being ruthlessly exploited, and Nouelle declared:

> I shall conclude by saying to all the peoples who suffer under our colonial rule that the Socialist party makes their cause its own. It makes its own the cause of the backward peoples of tropical and equatorial Africa who are subjected to the hard law of forced labour. It takes up the cause of the evolved peoples of Asia and Madagascar who rightly demand an ever increasing autonomy. . . . We salute the martyrs of liberty whoever they may be.[6]

The severe repressive measures taken after the 1930 riots were met by protests from the Socialists. In Paris a "Comité d'Amnestie et de Défense des Indochinois et des Peuples colonisés" was formed and counted among its members André Malraux, Marius Moutet, Félicien Challaye, Paul Rivet, Magdaleine Paz, Léon Werth and André Viollis.[7] On 6 September 1933, the party opposed the military actions in Morocco and called on the sections to organize demonstrations "against a policy of colonial conquest".[8] A year later *Le Populaire* turned against the repressive policy of the resident-general of Tunisia, Peyrouton, accusing him of being responsible for provoking the riots and demanding his recall.[9]

More important here is the Socialist party's colonial theory. Was the emancipation they proclaimed to be assimilatory, or did it aim at independence?

Like the British Labour party, the SFIO was also aware in the 1920s of the need to define its position and not to content itself with a general condemnation of imperialism. Pierre Renaudel, an important figure here, demanded the "elaboration of a socialist doctrine" in 1926 in *Vie Socialiste*, while the party set up a commission of enquiry whose report served as a basis of discussion at the 1926 party conference at Clermont-Ferrand. The report rejected colonialism as "a particularly oppressive and exploitative form of capitalism"; at the same time it stressed that simple withdrawal from the colonies was out of the question: the Socialists could not, it said, consent to this kind of "nationalism folded back on itself" since they were concerned with the development of "all the productive forces of the earth".[10] This argument was evidently designed both to refute the right-wing accusation of being "anti-national" as well as the tendency within the party to pay little attention to economic development. The report suggested an international organization whose task it would be to control access to raw materials, economic development and defence, to internationalize the great trade routes and thus to withdraw the colonial question from the sphere of international rivalry. It considered the mandate principle a valuable one, although the League of Nations' system was "a hypocritical imperialist mask". Further points remained vague, however, and it was not apparent whether the mandate system should eventually lead to independence or whether it was merely meant as a form of international control which did not preclude assimilation. In parliament, on 10 June 1927 Léon Blum openly supported decolonization in the sense of eventual independence in answer to a Communist challenge:

> We do not admit that there exists a right of conquest, a right of the first occupant, that benefits the European nations at the cost of the peoples who are not so fortunate as to belong to the white race or the Christian religion. We do not allow colonization by force. We believe that the aim to be pursued for the peoples who at this moment, in effect, find themselves, as is the case of France, in possession of colonial territories, must be to grant them complete independence as soon as possible. We shall have achieved what you call our civilizing mission the day we shall have been able to give the peoples whose territories we occupy liberty and sovereignty. In return, in the given situation for which we are not responsible, which we have always opposed, which we have always obstinately combatted, which we shall combat again at every opportunity, we will not content ourselves with the both over-simple and over-dangerous solution that consists either in preaching insurrection and calling for racial war, or in demanding immediate evacuation with all the perils this would entail both for the colonists and for the natives themselves.[11]

Only a few days later, however, Blum contradicted the African Blaise Diagne when the latter demanded parliamentary representation for the Algerian natives: "In our opinion, it is not in the sense of a wider native representation in the French parliament that we would wish this question to evolve. I say this, if not as party opinion, at least as an opinion shared by most of my comrades; we would like colonial legislation to head more and more clearly towards independence, towards self-government, as it did for the Dominions."[12] This was a clear statement of principle, although the analogy with the British dominions was incorrect, since there it was the settlers and not the natives who had obtained self-government —which is certainly not what Blum intended.

Whether the grant of self-government was the aim of Socialist colonial policy was a particularly vital question in Indochina. We have mentioned in a different context the former governor-general Varenne, who resisted integration and assimilation in 1929–1930. He thought future international political attention would be focussed on the Pacific:

> For Indochina we must perhaps envisage a rather different future than we first imagined. In this tropical valley a vast confederation is forming, an association of peoples, for which France will be a kind of cement, of which it will form the uniting link, for whom our protection will for many years to come, perhaps even for ever, remain indispensable. It is a nation of a new type, which grows, which will demand its place beside France, in the orbit of French policy.[13]

Some months later, again in parliament, Varenne carried these ideas a step further[14]: "I want France to be able to say to these Asians: you have a fatherland, it is in Asia, France is in the process of creating it for you, it is French Indochina." He acknowledged that Moscow was putting its emancipation programme into action, and from India to Korea the colonial peoples were in motion. France had treated these people badly and had not realized the advantages of the protectorate. The Indochinese were being employed only in subordinate positions and were miserably paid; there were no native administrative officers among them as yet. By the prohibition of unions and political organizations, people were being driven into opposition underground. If the élite was not satisfied soon, it would eventually demand full independence. "I see the future of Indochina in a great Indochinese federation, of which France would remain the associate and animating spirit. . . . Only in this way can the Annamites regain the fatherland they think they have lost. We shall help them to gain the greatest autonomy. Total independence? I do not know whether it will come one day. . . ."[15] At any rate, he said, twenty million subjects could not be ruled by force forever. Varenne pointed to British policy in India, and answered an accusation that its experiments had brought Britain no advantages by saying: "Rest assured, they [the English] will come to an agreement with the Hindus sooner than we shall with the Annamites." Varenne proposed a kind of Simon Commission to work out French reforms in Indochina and outlined his proposal for an Indochinese federation associated with the mother country to whom it would leave the control of foreign policy and defence—a concept which was to become the basis of General De Gaulle's post-war policy.

The former governor-general's view of the future is unclear, but he took an energetic stand against the former immobilism and called for a national self-consciousness and the grant of political rights on the local level in the hope of in some way linking the Indochinese nation to France.

In January and again in June, Varenne was supported by Marius Moutet, colonial minister of the Popular Front government in 1946–1947. Moutet considered the accusations against the leaders of the 1930 riots a scandal; repression only drove the élite into opposition. No one was deceived by the native courts, since no one saw the judges as anything more than "creatures of the administration" and all held the colonial administration responsible for the sentences. "We must bring about a complete recovery;" i.e. the Indochinese were to be prepared for self-government.

> Do you have a programme that could lead this country to independence under its own government, by stages which I asked you to fix, and according to a programme followed to its conclusion? It is a particularly difficult task, to lead a people from the Far East towards liberty.[16]

So Socialists such as Blum, Varenne and Moutet maintained that decolonization, at least in the case of Indochina, should proceed not by integration but with a view to future independence or the greatest possible autonomy. Representation in parliament was out of the question —Blum himself explicitly rejected it even for Algeria. When, as party leader, he declared his position, he very wisely did not present it as official party doctrine, thereby personally confirming that there were other opinions within the party. With regard to Algeria, Moutet urged an assimilatory policy of naturalization and parliamentary representation for the natives—in the somewhat compromised form of a special electoral body (cf. p. 326). The North African party sections in particular inclined towards assimilation; their membership was low, it is true, but their delegates carried considerable weight at the party conference, largely because the majority of party representatives showed little interest in colonial issues and left such questions to those who were directly concerned.[17] The sections were composed mainly of Europeans—minor officials, employees and businessmen—who preferred integration because it seemed to combine progressiveness, i.e. the emancipation of the natives, with a guarantee of their own positions. For instance, in 1926 the Tunisian section declared that it was against a "premature evacuation" and defended what it called the positive achievements of colonization. The Europeans in Tunisia were old-established residents and had been of great value in the economic development of the country, "with the result that these Europeans, transplanted, rooted in the colony where they have borne or will bear their children, can with right henceforth consider themselves to be children of the land".[18] This summarized the settlers' problem: the Socialists among them were opposed to withdrawal and therefore aimed at a form of integration. They thought the racial and cultural problem could be turned into a social one and hoped to create a class-conscious proletariat spanning both communities; accordingly the North African congress of socialists also condemned "the movements of xenophobia, of fanaticism and native nationalism".[19]

In accordance with the very divergent opinions within the party, and not least because of the views of the North African sections, the extraordinary party meeting in December 1927 decided in favour of a policy of differentiation. In certain territories, obviously meaning Algeria, the aim should be full assimilation, while other colonies should be prepared for a form of sovereignty; Syria was promised independence.[20] In broad outlines this was the colonial programme of the Popular Front.

In years to come the colonial party sections tried to collaborate with the nationalist groups and upheld their economic and social demands in the press and in local assemblies. In Tunisia, for instance, Bourguiba's nationalist party, the Neo-Destour, had good relations with the newspaper *Tunisie socialiste*.[21] The philosophical successor of Blaise Diagne, Bourguiba was a member of the Socialist party, with the result that the party organization to a certain extent reflected the idea of Greater France and thereby differed from the British Labour party. British socialists sometimes had personal connections with colonial nationalists, who could become party members if they lived in England, but they admitted no overseas organizations. Since the predominantly white sections of the SFIO could support the nationalists' economic demands but could only rarely uphold their political and national demands, the result was a considerable degree of tension: the Socialists concentrated on social emancipation and accused the bourgeois nationalists of premature, and therefore dangerous, nationalism.

In the early 1930s the party as a whole scarcely concerned itself with colonial issues and only after its victory in the 1936 elections did it actively plan a colonial policy. Again the North African delegates proved especially energetic. At the May–June 1936 party congress, the representative of the Tunisian section accused France of relying on the old feudal structures, professedly in the name of the protectorate. The separation of the courts of law and chambers of commerce into French and native sections had resulted in the formation of two blocks "which oppose one another in absolute incomprehension". This had bred a kind of particularism and so it was not surprising that the élite was now becoming nationalist. The Tunisian spokesman opposed this racial and religious nationalism on the grounds that it precluded a union with the European proletariat and awakened false hopes that national liberation would lead to an improvement of the economic situation. In effect, a Tunisian-Arab nationalism would, he said, restrict the SFIO section to the European minority and, therefore, was a threat to integration. The delegate from Constantine, Tahrat, demanded a consistent policy of assimilation. He described "collaboration" as hypocrisy,

> for there can be no loyal collaboration between two peoples who are treated differently. . . . Today the Muslims of Algeria are certainly not aspiring towards the "liberation" of which so much has been said in certain circles. What they demand, above all, is equality, equality between French and Muslims. And I must say that the Algerian Federations are unanimous in demanding the progressive assimilation of the Muslim peoples.[22]

Rejecting the double electoral colleges and a possible special representation of the natives in parliament, Tahrat proposed a single college with gradually increasing franchise. This was the only way to avoid conflict. Naturally, these demands were in complete contradiction to Blum's ideas in 1927.

In order to demonstrate their desire for reform at the moment of coming into office, and in the hope of gaining the co-operation of the nationalists, the Socialist congress addressed a manifesto to the colonial peoples:

> The Socialist Party Congress assures you of its active solidarity. It knows your misery, it desires to put an end to it. With the Popular Front in power, a new era is starting both for the workers of France and for the the peoples whom it includes in its destiny. The hopes raised by the victory of the Popular Front will not be disappointed. . . .

At the same time, the party announced its first practical programme —at least for North Africa. To Algeria it promised repurchase of the great concessions, union rights, the right of assembly and freedom of the press, amnesty, abolition of the *indigénat* and transfer of social legislation from metropolitan France to the colonies; it even promised the abolition of the government-general and the financial delegations. In effect this meant *rattachement* to the mother country, representation in the Paris parliament on the basis of a single college and access for the Muslims to all official posts at equal pay. Tunisia was promised a reform of the Caidat, administrative decentralization, much wider franchise for the Grand Conseil and representation of the French colonials in parliament. For Morocco, a series of social reforms, union rights and freedom of the press was promised.[23] The important Popular Front organization, "Comité de vigilance des intellectuels anti-fascistes", made similar announcements.[24]

What did the party actually achieve? The victory of the Popular Front and Blum's government were greeted with approval by the nationalist organizations in North Africa and Indochina where they raised considerable false hopes; to the French colonials by contrast, the Socialists' fairly generous colonial programme seemed to be the realization of their worst fears.²⁵ The government had unequivocally expressed its desire to introduce a new policy: Marius Moutet, who had always counted as a social reformer and had often criticized the administration and protested against repressive measures, became the colonial minister; Hubert Deschamps, former governor of Madagascar, became head of the Cabinet. Blum appointed Pierre Viénot secretary of state for Tunisian and Moroccan Affairs because his frank nature was likely to win him the trust of the North Africans. Several governors-general were replaced, nationalist leaders were granted amnesty and repressive decrees were suspended. In November Moutet summoned the governors-general to a conference and in his opening address outlined a programme of "altruistic colonization". The policy would be "to let live and give a better life to all of these colonial peoples"; the economic development he demanded was reminiscent of Albert Sarraut's. But he barely touched on political questions or reforms, and one has the impression that Moutet hoped that for the time being economic and social measures would be enough; or perhaps, taking into account the governors' resistance, he was trying to avoid discussion of these matters.²⁶

Several reforms were actually introduced: tax reform and a new labour statute in Indochina, in addition to a decree facilitating naturalization; a ruling on women's and children's labour in French West Africa; in 1937 French West Africa and Madagascar were granted the right to form labour unions and France ratified the convention for the abolishment of forced labour; French social legislation was also transferred to North Africa, but in practice this was only partly effective.²⁷

Politically, the Popular Front government soon encountered stubborn resistance which put a stop to a number of the intended reforms. The agreements with Syria and Lebanon in September and December 1936, modelled on the 1930 British treaty with Iraq, which stipulated independence and entry into the League of Nations but at the same time allowed France military bases and a privileged position, met considerable opposition from the army and the French colonials. In December 1938 when the two reporters of the Senate foreign office department warned against ratifying them, the foreign minister Bonnet abandoned the idea of submitting the agreements to the Senate for discussion and vote.²⁸ In March 1939 Viénot described the French attitude, which was clearly distinct from the British one, as follows:

> For the mass of French opinion, France "possesses" Syria. Its task is to administer it, to safeguard French interests in it. But one does not "negotiate" with colonies, one keeps them. . . . For most Frenchmen, in effect, our mandate in Syria is little more than a fiction. It is our duty to hold what we possess, and a settlement of the kind that we have been led to envisage seems a sort of betrayal.²⁹

The Blum-Viollette reforms for Algeria did not reach parliamentary debate either (cf. p. 332). In Tunisia both the Neo-Destour and the regional Comité du Rassemblement Populaire made demands in line with what the Socialist party had itself announced in its programme; but Viénot was under pressure from the Right, and gave in to it by declaring in November 1936: "The establishment of France in the protectorate countries is of a definitive nature".[30] In spring of the following year, the secretary of state held preliminary talks in Tunis, and in a broadcast on 1 March, he made his position clear. He openly exposed the abuses and urgent need for reforms and promised the Tunisians greater participation in the administration, reform of the Grand Conseil and extension of the educational system. However, these reforms were to occur within the framework of the protectorate agreement to produce an "effective and indissoluble Franco-Tunisian solidarity".[31] While Bourguiba reacted quite favourably, Viénot's statement that "certain private interests of the French in Tunisia do not necessarily coincide with the interests of France", a phrase which seemed to foretell a reassessment of the concession agreements of several large firms, provoked a storm of resentment among the colonists. They protested in the Grand Conseil, called upon their vested rights and asserted that they were the legitimate representatives of French interests in Tunisia.[32] So the Socialists' institutional reforms came to nothing.

The Moroccan nationalists also hoped for French concessions, but the residents-general Peyrouton and Noguès appointed by the Popular Front government supported the settlers and disappointed the Moroccans.[33] When General Franco made his liberal pledges to the Spaniards in Morocco, paradoxically it was the France of the Popular Front government that fell behind. And when the Moroccans increased their demands and tried to assert them forcefully in Paris. Viénot refused to receive a delegation of the "Comité d'action marocaine". The Moroccans expressed their disappointment by demonstrations in Casablanca, to which the resident-general replied by arresting the nationalists. When the Communists in Indochina began to prepare for an "Indochinese congress" designed to work out a programme of reform, the governor-general intervened energetically and prevented the demonstration. With regard to Black Africa, Moutet once again spoke in praise of the full civil rights granted residents of the Four Communes in Senegal and confessed his allegiance to the policy of assimilation pursued there. But he made no move towards extending the policy to the rest of Senegal or even to West Africa.[34] The promised commission of enquiry that was to travel to the colonies and submit proposals was not approved by the Senate until December and had little success.

These few indications must suffice to show that the Popular Front government, like the Labour party in 1924 and 1929, did not manage to implement its announced programme of reforms in spite of its original good intentions and the few small but valuable measures it did take. The government had only a few months in which to act and was fully occupied with economic issues and foreign affairs. An even more important reason for the failure, however, was that the Socialists, occupying a very weak position in the conservative Senate, were dependent on the parliamentary support of the Radical Socialists. The Radical Socialists, however, were not interested in "revolutionary" reforms. Significantly, the Popular Front's electoral programme, unlike that of the Socialist party, had confined itself to promising a commission of enquiry. Incisive reforms in the colonies could only have been carried through in face of the colonists' active resistance and the government did not have the necessary parliamentary support to do this. The revolutionary Left could criticize the half-measures and challenge the government to keep its "promises",[35] but Léon Blum was not prepared to take a revolutionary course, and in any case his influence was small. The results became apparent at once: the moderate nationalists of North Africa and Indochina, who had expected generous reforms from a Popular Front government and would have been ready to collaborate temporarily, were disappointed and found themselves forced to turn to nationalist agitation. Their attacks on the colonial power became increasingly severe and they no longer hesitated to demand independence.

ASSIMILATION IN ALGERIA (1919–1939)

In the *vieilles colonies* France had introduced a policy of integration and assimilation by the time of the French Revolution and in 1946 brought the policy to its conclusion. The territory and its population were small, the former slaves had no indigenous cultural background and the races were very mixed, so there was some hope of successfully assimilating the colony into the distant mother country. Was assimilation also possible in Algeria, France's most clear-cut example of a colonial settlement?

France had "pacified" this extensive territory only after long struggles; it had still had to suppress a revolt of the Kabyles in 1871. The structure of the state was weak—and it was under Turkish domination—but the people stemmed from the Muslim-Arab culture of North Africa, which was entirely different from that of the metropolis; they resisted assimilation from the outset. Yet France attempted to apply a policy of integration. It considered Algeria an extension of the mother country, a part of Greater France suitable for colonization, and Algeria took in a vast stream of settlers. The Democratic Republic of 1848 declared Algeria a part of the national territory, divided it into three departments and, by giving it elected general councils and representation in the French parliament, placed it, ostensibly at least, on an equal footing with the mother country. After Napoleon III's brief reign, the Third Republic continued this policy. In 1881 it even directly subordinated the different branches of the colonial administration to the ministries in Paris. But Algeria remained a special case: the southern territories were administered separately, the Algerian departments were larger than those of the metropolis, and in 1896 the *rattachements* had to be removed again. Henceforth a governor-general under the ministry of the interior was responsible for administration. In 1898 Algeria received its own advisory departments—the financial delegations—and in 1900 it obtained its own budget. Evidently the Parisian bureaucracy was not able to cope with the special political and economic problems of Algeria.

As we have shown earlier, integration and assimilation applied only to French nationals, i.e. to naturalized Europeans and Israelites in Algeria, and not to the autochthonous population. The Muslims were "subjects", not "citizens". The right to vote in parliamentary elections remained restricted to full citizens and so the Algerian deputies represented only the interests of the French Algerians. The "subjects" were also represented in the financial delegations[1] but, in face of the settlers' unified political front, they had only restricted power. A subject could apply for naturalization, but this meant renouncing his personal status, i.e. subordination to French civil law. Few Muslims were prepared to take this step, which meant leaving the traditional community, quite apart from the fact that the administration did nothing to facilitate nauralization.

So the Algerian situation in 1914 was characterized by a certain amount of integration in the administrative field and representation of French citizens in parliament. Though the settlers were in the minority, they disposed of a considerable part of the fertile land and cultivated it with labour under the administrative control of the *indigénat*. This also gave them political control. Land and labour law, educational policy, etc. were applied in the interests of the settlers, and even though the secular Third Republic practised restraint in the religious sphere, its occasional refusal to assimilate the natives was largely a question of expediency and served to ensure the settlers' dominance.

What were the plans for the future? Programmatic assimilation had fallen into disrepute before 1914 and had been replaced by the concept of association. But in the case of Algeria, France asked itself whether any road but assimilation was possible unless it was based on the example of South Africa and "legally" established the predominance of the settler minority for the foreseeable future. Plans of this kind, i.e. attempts to proceed from administrative autonomy to political self-government under white rule, occasionally emerged among the French Algerians, particularly when they wanted to emphasize their opposition to any reform attempts on the part of the mother country by threatening rebellion. But they proceeded no further than defiant threats that did not have much substance for the French Algerian wanted to remain French, and was aware both of his economic and political dependence on the mother country and of his tenuous position as a minority group. As a result, the question of future reforms concentrated on the narrow field between, on the one hand, a defence of the *status quo*, and on the other, gradual assimilation—even if the term "association" was used. Implicitly at least, the concept of the protectorate implied eventual independence or at least a transfer of government power to the natives; this possibility could at least be discussed in Indochina and Black Africa. But in the case of the colonial settlement Algeria—which legally was not a colony at all but a part of France—decolonization seemed possible only within the French state, i.e. it implied inclusion of the Algerian Muslim into the French community, political equality in the administration and parliamentary representation. Logically this would sooner or later lead to parity between the communities, if not to Muslim preponderance. From the start, proposals for reforms consisted of open or tacit attempts at assimilation; consequently they were resisted by the French Algerians who defended their minority rights and were afraid of being "swamped". We shall illustrate this inherent problem of assimilation, which on the whole was a liberal concept of decolonization, in the attempts at reform between the wars.[2]

Discussion of reforms began shortly before the First World War among representatives of the moderate Left; they were also supported by *Le Temps*. Some of the demands made were: equal taxation for French and Algerians, relaxation of the *indigénat*, better native representation in the communal councils of the plenary communes, native representation in Paris either by Muslim members or by the formation of a special council for Algerian and North African affairs.[3] Two questions immediately gave rise to violent debate, since they contained the Algerian problem in a nutshell. Should naturalization without renunciation of personal status be made possible? Should the natives take part in electing the mayor? Now that France, in the name of reform, was prepared to conciliate the Algerian élite—or at least certain groups determined by profession, training, income or military service—the question of naturalization in statute had to be raised. Otherwise there was little hope of increasing the number of "citizens" and giving the Algerians the equal rights they demanded. So integration and assimilation meant that France had to "differentiate" the concept of "assimilation", giving up the idea of complete assimilation under French law and respecting the racial and religious difference of the Algerian Muslims. We have mentioned the undeniable legal difficulties in a different context: was it tenable that within the one and indivisible Republic there should be two different categories of citizens, one with and one without the *code civil?* Was it tenable that Muslim deputies should also decide in parliament on questions of French civil rights? One had to count on a large number of such deputies, for the future at least. The reformers in France could not overlook this argument either, and its retarding influence on the reform policy is difficult to assess.

Attempts at liberal conciliation would also mean an extension of Algerian representation in the financial delegations, in the election of the mayor and in the representation of Muslim interests in Paris. These were the demands of the "Young Algerians", the first loose organization of young Algerians trained in France, who did not aim at national emancipation but at equal rights, conceived in terms of assimilation, in the French community.[4]

The discussion before 1914 had shown the settlers' violent resistance to such reforms and concessions. Naturalization seemed to them a sluice which would give the Muslims access to political emancipation and power, and must under no circumstances be allowed. At first, maybe, it would not be too dangerous, but for the settlers it meant a constant threat to their economic, social and political interests. The same applied to the participation of non-citizens in electing the mayor or the Algerian deputy to the parliament: the one threatened the settlers' dominance in the local sphere, the other the representation of their interests in metropolitan France. Naturally the settlers also employed the legal argument and made renunciation of personal status a condition of any form of naturalization—knowing full well that in this case the number of candidates would remain small. In this way they also defended French sovereignty, which Muslim-Arab nationalism was allegedly already undermining, and played off their own "national" attitude against the treasonable or at least "unrealistic"—i.e. that was not relevant to the situation in Algeria—pseudo-reform policy of certain groups and parties in the mother country.

Resistance among the French Algerians, which the Algerian administration joined to some extent, reached a peak in the February 1919 discussion on the Algerian law. As in Senegal, this law related to the conscription of Algerian soldiers and labourers, which during the war had made reforms seem necessary. In 1912, in spite of the resistance of the French Algerians, France had introduced compulsory military service, conscripted Algerians—officially on a voluntary basis, in fact by force —and in November 1916 had to suppress a revolt in the Aurès Mountains. In order to better assess the numerical potential of the Algerians, the two presidents of the foreign policy commissions of the Senate and the Chamber, Clemenceau and Leygues, sent a letter to Prime Minister

Briand on 25 November 1915 which contained a fairly extensive reform programme: the possibility of legal naturalization, extension of electoral bodies for the natives and greater representation in the financial delegations, participation in the election of the mayor, etc. Ohneck has clearly shown how at first this letter gave rise to a certain amount of discussion, but how it was only Clemenceau's government (in November 1917), to which Leygues also belonged, that took the initiative that finally led to the Algerian law of 4 February 1919. In the meantime, however, the major reforms had been more and more watered down between the government declaration, the department proposal, the government plan and the parliamentary consultation, perhaps because liberal groups in the mother country were also afraid of naturalization, perhaps because the government wanted to conciliate the French Algerians in order to carry the bill in parliament.[5] The 1919 law did in fact facilitate naturalization, since it gave certain "categories" of Muslims access to French civil rights, but it demanded, as before, the renunciation of personal status. The "non-citizens" were reserved a third of the municipal council seats in the plenary communes and were granted an extended franchise to the financial delegations. Henceforth the native municipal councils also took part in electing the mayor. Algerians were to obtain access to some offices, but not to the "offices of authority", which continued to be reserved to full citizens.

The law, which Governor-General Jonnart also approved, was finally accepted by a large majority—though few benches were occupied. *Le Temps* even said: "It [France] has opened them [the Muslims] the gates of the city and has allowed their representatives to sit beside the French citizens, even when their Muslim faith forbids them integral naturalization. And this is only a first step. . . ."[6] So the mouthpiece of the bourgeois Centre openly supported assimilation as the only possible policy in Algeria, but it overestimated both the 1919 reform and the extent to which integration had already been achieved. In the following years France could point to the 1919 reform as proof of its good intentions in order to avoid making new concessions, but in fact it was no real innovation. The number of naturalizations remained low and the settlers continued to predominate in the plenary communes, financial delegations and department councils; Muslims were not represented in parliament and the administration clearly favoured the settlers; most of its staff was recruited in Algeria itself and it excluded "undesirable elements". The assumption of *Le Temps* that this was a first step that would be followed by others proved mistaken, for no important political reforms were made until 1939.

The 1919 law was refused by the French Algerians, even in its adulterated form. Participation of non-citizens in the election of the mayor was still the stumbling block; moreover the settlers were afraid that a strong demand for naturalization would threaten the "security of the colonist". The position of the French Algerians and the rather more moderate attitude of the bourgeois Right in metropolitan France is made clear in an important article in the *Revue des deux mondes*.[7] It called the 1919 law "mistaken sentimentality" on the part of certain circles who understood nothing about Algeria or its "native affairs"; Pan-Islamism was directed, said the article, by Moscow and Berlin and was a threat to the French presence in Algeria. It was ridiculous to accede to the demands of the "Young Algerians", for it was "useless to try to assimilate these men". The author contrasted the small group of *évolués* with the mass of people who, it alleged, did not want political rights but economic and social improvements. Accordingly he dismissed even the moderate reform of 1919 as premature and dangerous. In any case, the *évolués* were "not yet French at heart, and it is premature to consider them such by law". As proof, the author pointed to the lack of interest in naturalization and the demand for instruction in Arabic! The French Algerians "consider themselves injured by the native policy of the metropolis" and had formed a bloc. The article regretted the relaxation of the *indigénat*, postulated restricting freedom of the press and urged an active policy of colonization. The dangerous trend of leasing or selling land to Muslims must be stopped, perhaps by a special tax and restitution of the land that had not yet been allotted.[8] The French Algerians had a legitimate claim to greater autonomy, to the "indispensable liberties":

> Let us give up this ideology which does us so much harm; it has had a certain influence on the birth of the 1919 law, a bad fairy that we have brought to the colony's bedside; more demagogic than liberal, it risks surrendering the native population to the avid tyranny of a few political adventurers who were preparing us, if we were not careful, for a very dark future. In native policy there is a good phrase, spoken by General Laperrine, an old African; why should we not adhere to it: "Do not humiliate or exploit the native; conciliate him by letting him enter, as a sincere collaborator, into an extended France in whose greatness he will participate."[9]

These theses are clear: any reform was going to be considered "premature". However, while the doctrine of assimilation is dismissed as unrealistic, yet the author comes back to it because it was no longer possible to openly support permanent discrimination against the Muslims. The *évolué* was condemned out of fear; he was considered dangerous even if he was assimilated. The French Algerians were not prepared to accept gradual emancipation and inclusion of the élite into the French community. They wanted to maintain the *status quo*. For themselves, however, they demanded greater freedom of decision, in order to protect themselves against interference by the "ideologists" of metropolitan France. The settler as carrier of "sovereignty" was to be promoted both economically and politically. The "good phrase" quoted referred to "collaboration"; but in fact it meant the unrestricted predominance of the settlers, at best tempered by paternalism.

It is not difficult to understand the attitude of the French Algerians, who were represented by their own deputies in the French parliament and supported by the colonial-conservative Right. But the opinions of the Centre parties and of many of the political writers in the mother country were usually couched in such general terms that it is difficult to speak of an actual concept or doctrine. The parties as a whole showed little interest in the Algerian question and left it to "specialists" who were either directly committed or were outsiders in their party.

The views of Albert Sarraut naturally influenced these Centre groups. His concept of association and his assertion that there was a community of interests between the mother country and the colonies was an attempt to go beyond the attitude of mere overlordship and to express his, no doubt seriously meant, desire for reform. Sarraut did not oppose assimilation only in order to prevent emancipation and to describe the grant of political rights to the Muslims as "premature". On the contrary, his opposition was meant to initiate reforms that would preserve traditional customs and would respect them in order, gradually at least, to modernize them by contact with the colonial power. Sarraut did not discuss the Algerian question directly, but one might perhaps interpret his views as follows: The Algerians were to gain easier access to the administration and even to take over "offices of authority"—though only in an indefinite future. Sarraut wanted to improve the educational system but not to overthrow it; naturalization should be facilitated, but not *en masse* and only after cultural assimilation had occurred—certainly the natives could not retain their personal status.

Sarraut's idea of assimilation aimed at a permanent integration of Algeria within Greater France. The same idea recurs in a book by Paul Hutin[10] published in 1933, which explicitly referred to Sarraut, and also to Vignon, Hardy and Pierre Mille.[11] Hutin thought the time had passed "when our duty consisted simply in leading" and that one must aim at an effective community of interests by, among other things, promoting mixed marriages. "Algeria is a land where our race must grow strong roots . . . with the firm desire to assure them [the Algerians] their place, all the place they deserve, that is to say, to welcome our Muslim subjects into the French family."[12] The missions were to serve as instruments of "moral assimilation". Hutin was in favour of granting political rights and facilitating naturalization. This sounds liberal and in effect went beyond current conservative views,[13] but Hutin ignored crucial problems. Although he was a lawyer and his book was entitled *Association des Indigènes et des Français en Algérie*, he did not say whether he supported naturalization in statute or whether he approved equal rights for the two racial communities! In any case neither

Sarraut nor Hutin reveal any tendency to conciliate the small class of *évolués* by making concessions with a view to integration, or to "neutralize" them politically and tie them to France. Perhaps they thought there was no hurry, or they were afraid of the consequences of their own theses, or they feared the reactions of the French Algerians. . . . The Radical Socialists, for their part, also wanted to appear pro-reform. But what little the party evolved in the way of a coherent programme was restricted to representation of non-citizens in parliament. This should be done by a special electoral body which would give the French Algerians, who were well represented in the party, little room for attack and at the same time would conciliate the "Fédération des élus indigènes", the new moderate national organization of Algerian non-citizens led by Dr. Bendjelloul.[14]

We have already described the ambivalence in the Socialist party. Léon Blum and his followers in the party still believed in future self-government in 1927 and opposed native representation in parliament (cf. pp. 312–13). This was a logical attitude in terms of anti-assimilation, but paradoxically it coincided with the settlers' views and was in contradiction with those of Blaise Diagne. By contrast, the Algerian specialist Marius Moutet and the Algerian party section supported gradual assimiliation because they thought it would make it possible to combine sharp criticism of the colonists, the government, the *indigénat* and other exceptional regulations, with France's continued presence in Algeria. Franchise should be granted to an increasingly wider élite, thought Moutet, and he began rather modestly by considering a double electoral college.[15] It was not until 1936 that the party went as far as demanding full integration with naturalization in statue and a single college.

It is characteristic considering the internal insecurity of the Socialist party and the lack of interest in Algeria within it that the Left's Algeria programme, which was later applied by the Popular Front government, was formulated not by the SFIO as a whole nor by any member of the party but by Maurice Viollette, a deputy of the small Parti Républicain-socialiste, which was closer to the left-wing bourgeois camp of Radical Socialism.[16] Viollette was the deputy of Eure-et-Loire from 1902 to 1928, senator until 1940 and deputy again from 1945 to 1955. He had already taken part in the discussion during the First World War when he proposed assimilation; in 1925 after the victory of the Cartel des Gauches, he became governor-general of Algeria. He actively combatted Communist agitation and at the same time won the trust of Algerian Muslims. Viollette's attempts at social reform came to an end, however, when the settlers forced him to resign on 9 November 1927.

In 1928, in the name of the coming centenary celebrations, he made notable proposals for reform, suggesting that the mother country should allow Algeria a special credit for education, irrigation works and trade-unions, introduce social security, abolish the *indigénat*, equate the natives with the citizens in military service and have four deputies nominated to parliament in a special electoral body (one deputy per department and one Kabyle). The president of the plenary assembly of the financial delegations should be elected, instead of simply coinciding with the office of chairman of the settlers' delegation.

In 1931 Viollette published *L'Algérie vivra-t-elle*, a book which critically illustrated the Algerian situation. Viollette claimed that the expropriation of the Muslims' land and property was continuing and their living conditions were so deplorable that not even compensation could do much good. The colonists complained about an inadequate labour force but they paid very low wages and sabotaged even modest attempts at social legislation. Medical care and education were quite inadequate, although in 1930 the French Algerians had refused a credit from the mother country on the rather dubious grounds that it would be a threat to Algerian autonomy. The metropolis exerted control in theory only, since the financial delegations, led by the colonists, were developing into a parliament and were trying to create a kind of "dominion" that would sanction minority rule. Viollette criticized the colonists' contemptuous attitude towards the *évolués* and warned: "If France commits the impardonable crime of not understanding and not listening to them [the *évolués*], they will be reduced to an exasperated nationalism as in Indochina."[17] The administration, he said, was preventing the grant of civil rights and even those who were naturalized were not fully accepted. Any questions of franchise were dismissed by the settlers.

On the other hand, Viollette argued strongly for French colonization: he meant, however, only for small land-holders, because they were more hard-working, required less capital to establish themselves and, above all, because "our irrefragable establishment" could occur only through the medium of "the French house", and close contact with the natives would lead to "a renewal of the native mentality". This thesis sounds curious today, but it was not inconsistent with a concept of assimilation.

On 3 July 1931, Viollette proposed reforming the Senate. He reiterated the demands of 1928 and proposed a new system of franchise and representation, in order to give equal rights to Frenchmen and natives. Qualified groups of Muslims should be naturalized and retain their personal status, and they should vote in parliament on an equal basis with the full citizens. A new fourth section should be set up in the financial delegations embracing certain professions (doctors, lawyers, etc.). It should not be formed on a racial basis but according to the census, thereby helping to reduce the friction between Muslims and Europeans. This liberal proposal—which did not imply universal franchise, however—was fairly conciliatory to the French Algerians and in no way threatened their predominance: it also ensured that the élite would have equal rights and an effective say in political decision-making. Moreover it checked discrimination and promised "reconciliation" with a view to progressive assimilation,[18] all the more so as the former governor-general demanded naturalization in statute.

Naturally the French Algerians flatly rejected this project and did not stop short of hurling personal invective at Viollette. Once again they interpreted the concept of assimilation according to their own ideas and asserted that naturalization in statute was in contradiction to the sacrosanct principle of "equality before the law".[19] More important in our context, and characteristic of the French Algerian policy of those years, is that the proposals were not discussed in the Senate, nor did they arouse interest among political writers or in the political parties. The mother country still lay under the spell of the "centenary" which had propagated the idea of *Algérie française* in speeches, demonstrations and widespread publicity so that any public criticism was pushed into the background. People spoke of a pacified, "quiet" Algeria in which a spirit of co-operation and mutual understanding between Muslims and Europeans would reign; at the same time, as a useful contrast, they stressed the Pan-Islamic sentiments and Communist infiltration which were infecting the *évolués* and threatening the "quiet development" of the country.

In effect there was considerable tension. Both the Fédération des élus and the Association of Ulémas founded in 1931, and even Ferhat Abbas had welcomed Viollette's proposals, either because they themselves were in favour of assimilation or because the project seemed acceptable as a temporary reform measure. Yet the supporters of national emancipation were increasing in number. The *Étoile nord-africaine* of Messali Hadj, which at times came close to the Communists' position, organized the Algerian workers in the mother country and soon demanded independence, supported Islam and the idea of "*Algérie notre patrie*", as did the Ulémas. The years 1933–1934 brought the first street demonstrations and strikes and the provocative anti-Jewish riots in Constantine, which led to repressive measures both by the French Algerians and by the government, now entrenched in their respective positions. At the same time the French Algerians and the mother country were involved in a violent economic dispute. The wine growers of Algeria and those of the mother country were in competition and the wine growers of Southern France demanded that the large landowners of Algeria restrict their cultures, while the colonists called upon their supposedly equal rights and threatened autonomy or even secession.

Viollette did not resume his efforts to institute a liberal reform policy until March 1935. In the Senate he called on the minister of the interior, Régnier, to tell him how the government intended to keep the promises it had made to the Algerian Muslims on the occasion of the centenary. He also drew a dark picture of the economic situation: famine in places, usury and lack of agrarian credits, failure to enforce social legislation, inadequate medical assistance. Again he warned the Senate that the administration and the financial delegations were aiming at autonomy and he criticized the administration's interventions in the elections, its awkward action against the Ulémas, etc. At present, naturalization in statute of qualified Muslims applied to only a few hundred voters: yet this was evidence that France was granting equal rights. If France wanted to be and to remain a Muslim power—which in fact it had always claimed to be, partly in order to attack Great Britain—then it must accept citizens with personal status. Viollette formulated the attitude of the French Algerians and the dilemma of the mother country in striking terms:

> ... when they [the natives] protest against the abuses they find, you are indignant; when they applaud, you are suspicious, and when they are silent, you are afraid. ... We cannot abandon our six million Muslims, ten million soon; we must attach them to ourselves, we must show them that the French fatherland is their fatherland, belonging to them as it does to us. These men say to us, "We do not have a fatherland, we want the French fatherland. We want it, we request it of you."[20]

In the debate in the Senate the Algerian senators put forward the usual arguments: much was being done for the native Algerians, the masses were not yet interested in political rights, the *évolués* on the other hand were by no means pro-French: "we must burst this abscess of propaganda for citizenship with personal status. We must empty it from the root. ..."[21] Even the minister of the interior, Régnier, gave considerable support to the French Algerians, evaded the issue of economic aid and declared that France had already done its utmost with the 1919 reforms:

> You must not ask us to go further, because it is impossible ... I found Algeria very beautiful, very healthy, very strong, slightly restless on the surface, naturally. ... Because of this, authority must be respected ... if necessary [France] will use force.[22]

The "Décret Régnier" followed some days later. It stated that anyone who incited the natives to demonstration or resistance against French sovereignty would be subject to stern punishment. Viollette gained scant support in the Senate, even from the Socialists, and had to withdraw his agenda. A few well-meaning articles appeared in bourgeois papers,[23] but *Le Temps* refused to support him and even the radical *Revue politique et parlemantaire* took the position of the settlers.[24]

With the victory of the Popular Front, there seemed a chance for reform. We mentioned earlier the Socialist party congress in May–June 1936 and their programme. It went even further than Viollette and not only demanded naturalization in statute and a single electoral college for parliamentary elections, but even wanted to abolish the governor-general and the financial delegations; i.e. it demanded complete integration. The Popular Front parties achieved an astonishing success in Algeria and won three of the ten deputies' seats. Léon Blum appointed Viollette minister of state in his government, thereby demonstrating his desire for serious reforms. Spokesmen for the Algerians also indulged great hopes; in June 1936 they assembled for a Muslim congress and decided on a *Charte revendicative*, demanding the abolition of all laws and economic and social measures of "exception" and asking for "pure and simple attachment to France", the removal of the financial delegations, a common electoral body and civil rights in statute. This meant that the national groups had adopted the demands of the Socialist party programme—although the demand for universal franchise went beyond the party programme—and showed that they were in favour of assimilation and integration, evidently because at the time it seemed the only way of taking the new government at its word and carrying the cause of emancipation and equal rights a step forward. Internal differences of opinion remained, however; apart from the Élus, who were prepared to accept integration (Ferhat Abbas still openly denied the existence of an Algerian nation in 1936[25]), the demand for an Algerian state clearly was winning increasing support.

The new course became obvious at once. A delegation from the Muslim congress travelled to Paris and talked with Blum, Viollette and Jules Moch. Minor reforms were made: freedom to travel for Algerians, amnesty, transfer to Algeria of the new French social legislation (forty-hour week, paid holidays, etc. for the urban workers), election by the plenary assembly of the chairman of the financial delegations, demand to the administration to generously grant applications for civil rights, Muslim access to all civil and military offices, including the offices of authority. The success or failure of these measures was necessarily a question of politics. In October the government announced that it would very soon introduce a law "extending the right to vote to certain categories of Algerian natives", and on 30 December, the famous Blum-Viollette motion was put forward.[26] Certain categories of the Muslim population were to obtain French civil rights and retain their personal status. This meant, essentially, that a French élite and a Muslim middle class, rather than the Algerian masses, were to be accepted into the circle of French Algerians and to take part in parliamentary elections in a common electoral body. For "one can no longer treat as subjects, without essential political rights, the French natives who have fully assimilated French thought but who, because of family reasons or religious motives, cannot abandon their personal status". Other issues such as the reform of the financial delegations and communal authorities, the position of the governor-general, and full integration in the sense of *rattachement*, which were postulated by the Socialist party, were left out for the time being.

The Blum-Viollette bill adopted the most important of Viollette's proposals in 1931 and 1935 and implemented them as government reforms. Paris reckoned on some twenty thousand Muslim voters who, since they would continue to be a minority group among the full citizens, would scarcely constitute a threat to the settlers' predominance at the present time. So at first the proposal was more a question of principle —emancipation of the Muslim Algerians by the grant of civil rights in a statute. Nevertheless, naturalization of this kind, and only of this kind,[27] would in due course increase the number of Muslim citizens and electors and was therefore a potential threat to the position of the French settlers. Moreover, it was conceivable that electoral coalitions between the French left-wing parties and Muslim voters would come into being in the near future, and create an entirely new constellation of power. Eventually this coalition might even break down the division according to racial communities, so that full integration and political assimilation, together with respect for Muslim civilization in the private sphere might become a reality.

The French Algerians immediately began to resist the Blum-Viollete bill with all their might. Just after the elections, a *Rassemblement National* had formed; it was an anti–Popular Front committee, led by the mayor of Oran, Abbé Lambert, which took up radical positions. It raised protests in the financial delegations, in the Algerian press, in parliament and in the colonialist organs of the mother country, so that this issue became a kind of test of power after the almost unanimous decisions of the congress of mayors in January 1937 and the "mayors' strike" in March 1938, which was designed to prevent a parliamentary resolution. Very few new arguments emerged. The projected law, it was said, contradicted French law, was a threat to French colonizing work in Algeria and surrendered the European minority into the hands of the Muslim masses; the natives would very soon dominate the communes. The Popular Front project, they said, had been inspired by the Communists and was "anti-French"; it was a plot against the settlers. The political radicalization of the French Algerians was reflected in their relatively strong membership in the *Parti socialiste français* and the *Parti populaire français* with their fascist and anti-semitic tendencies.[28]

The agitation was successful, for neither Léon Blum's government nor its successor was able to carry the reform bill through parliament. In effect the bill first went to the franchise department of the Chamber, which —finally—agreed to a first section on 4 March 1938, but it got stuck in the parliamentary machine and never really reached debate. The Radical Socialists were chiefly to blame for this failure, for the bill could not be carried in parliament without their support. Opposition was not unanimous, but the party on the whole tended to oppose it. Although the undersecretary of state in the ministry of the interior, Auband, who was in charge of Algerian affairs, supported the law and Albert Sarraut also exercised his considerable influence, there was no great conviction in the support. For instance, Sarraut also referred to the concept of an "Algerian State" which, he said, would extend Muslim rights and representation within an autonomous state; this concept was in contradiction to the Blum-Viollette bill.[29] The Radical Socialists in Algeria, and above all, Senator Cuttoli, dissociated themselves from the ideas of the radical Right, yet they defended the settlers' position in this decisive issue. Deputy Guastavino skilfully pointed out to the franchise commission that the parliamentary representation of Algeria would go to the Socialists.[30] The party had been driven to the right in its overall political position; it remained "national" in its Jacobine tradition and turned towards the metropolis. In 1946, no less than Édouard Herriot warned of the consequences of full integration of the colonies. France, he declared, did not want to become a colony of its own colonies! The nationalists in Algeria launched protest actions and the French Algerians called on the defence of French sovereignty and the presence of France in Algeria. So the programmatically progressive but in fact very moderate Radical Socialists were only too willing to abandon the Blum-Viollette bill, and even to take repressive action against the nationalists.

Prime Minister Léon Blum did not want to jeopardize the coalition and did not urge a parliamentary decision, since he was hard pressed in both foreign and internal policy. The party paper *Le Populaire*, however, openly supported the bill and on 17 January described it as the "great reform". It was high time, it said, that France tried to achieve a lasting "reconciliation" of the Muslim people by a policy of "total and progressive assimilation": "We must decide whether or not we want to keep a French Algeria. French Algeria will not remain French unless France manages to retain the allegiance of the Muslim populations."[31] During the party congress in July 1937 the government was urged to take action both by the Algerian delegates and by the reporter on colonial affairs, Maurice Paz. Not even the Régnier decree or the Chautemps circular had been annulled, they said, and the Algerian administration must be cleaned up. Again full integration was demanded. The government, however, refused to reply to these reproaches from the "militants". It is not surprising that the other bourgeois parties and their papers such as *Le Temps* or the *Revue des deux mondes* did not support the reforms either.

In 1939 the French colonial system was still the same as it was in 1919, although there had been great changes in the economic and social fields and although the Algerian Muslim emancipation movement had made itself felt in a number of organizations. Reforms were urgently necessary. The efforts during the First World War had at least led to the law of 1919; but attempts to reform between the wars were defeated by the resistance of the French Algerians and bourgeois right-wing circles in metropolitan France. Their victory had been all the easier because the general public in the mother country paid little attention to Algeria and even the left-wing parties' reform policy lacked conviction. Although France took pride in its presence in North Africa, it took that presence for granted and willingly overlooked the gathering crisis. In the late 1930s there were a few critical articles in the press warning against the danger of neglecting the economic, social and political problems in Algeria, but they did not crystallize into a general desire for reform, nor did they take effect in parliament. In 1936, after long delays and confusion, the Socialist party finally committed itself and proposed a coherent programme of assimilation, but it was not able to put it into practice.

In general there was hesitation to openly support assimilation or to accept its implications. People preferred to speak of association, although in the special case of Algeria it was not a useful concept and could easily deteriorate into a mere defence of the *status quo*. The terms remained ambiguous. We have shown earlier how the French Algerians manipulated assimilation, claiming it when they wanted to defend their own rights or to oppose naturalization in statute and rejecting it when they wanted to show that the Muslims could not be assimilated or to underline that Algeria was a special case. Many of the reformers came into similar difficulties, when they demanded a liberal attitude towards the native civilization in Algeria and at the same time said that they could see no possibility of reform except along the lines of eventual integration. Naturalization in statute was meant to be a solution to this dilemma, but in fact it posed legal difficulties and offered its opponents a strong argument.

The notion of "autonomy" also caused difficulties. The institutional structure of the country was a good basis for such a policy and autonomy complied with a practical need, since it was difficult to administer Algeria from Paris. At times the French Algerians used the demand for autonomy as a means of obtaining a free hand from Paris, threatening secession if it was not given. At the same time, Algerian autonomy seemed to comply with a concept of association that abandoned the notion of full franchise, *rattachement*, and a single electoral college and offered to conciliate the Muslims' desire for emancipation by increasing their voice in local affairs. Yet autonomy remained a theory; a pro-reform policy of autonomy could not have solved the problem of the European minority and moreover it was hardly possible to make any practical proposals how decolonization should proceed from this basis. What remained was vague hints and at best a kind of compromise which consisted of continuing to treat Algeria as an integral part of the national territory, tolerating Algerian representation in parliament and granting no more than extensive administrative decentralization. France tried to take this road in 1947 with the Organic Statute for Algeria—but the inherent problems of this colonial settlement remained unsolved.

In effect France now had no choice in Algeria but to follow the path of integration and assimilation. This had become evident between the wars when reform proposals were based on the concept of assimilation, and even those who opposed assimilation were forced to agree that Algeria was a special case. Of course, it is impossible to say whether it would have been possible on this basis to satisfy the Muslim Algerians, not only momentarily but for the future too, as had happened in the *vieilles colonies*. It is worth noting that until well into the Second World War there was a pro-integration feeling among educated Algerians; if the Blum-Viollette proposals had been accepted it might have been possible to "neutralize" national demands and perhaps to reduce the desire for emancipation to a minority movement. Admittedly, reforms in naturalization and the franchise without supplementary reforms in Algeria itself and without a change of attitude among the settlers would have been insufficient. But the settlers would have continued resisting even if the bill had been passed. It is equally certain that the failure of the Popular Front government was a great disappointment to the Algerian élite; it drove those who were in favour of integration into the nationalist camp and opened the way for the demand for an "Algerian Republic" during the Second War.

It is important to note that although France was evidently unable to do other than to postulate the reforms that seemed necessary within a concept of integration and assimilation, it was not in fact prepared to do even this. A consistent policy of integration would have meant not delaying naturalization but granting it generously, perhaps even making it compulsory, as Ferhat Abbas demanded at times. Moreover, it would have meant a gradual extension of the franchise and a ready inclusion of Algerians into the administration, the army and perhaps even the government, as had happened in the case of Diagne and was to become practice after 1945. In the final analysis, France would have had to decide to give Algeria parliamentary representation corresponding to its population and to expect a large number of Muslim deputies. This view of the future was not yet possible between the wars, quite apart from the resistance of the French Algerians; curiously enough—or characteristically—it was not even discussed much.

Finally we would like to make an apparently obvious comparison. France's Algeria policy, based on the concept of assimilation, cannot simply be contrasted to the British colonial policy that aimed at self-government. Comparisons must refer to similar situations and only in the case of Kenya can a meaningful comparison be made between the French policy and the British. In Algeria, as in Kenya, there was a small minority of settlers who had confiscated or otherwise appropriated a part of the land following the conquest of the country in the nineteenth century. They had opened up the country economically with the help of native labour, considered themselves natives of the country and were therefore resolved to defend at all costs their minority rule against the emergent emancipation movements. Any concession to the natives obviously seemed a threat to their own existence, since it risked leading to further concessions and to "swamping" the minority. The demand for a majority in the financial delegations, for franchise restricted to French citizens and correspondingly restricted representation in the metropolitan parliament corresponded to the fight for representative and responsible government in Kenya. In both cases it was the logical consequence of the basic concepts and traditions. Both in Algeria and in Kenya the settlers had to refuse native franchise and representation on principle, whether in the parliament of the mother country or in the legislative council of the colony. They did so in order to avoid creating a precedent or opening a road that would one day lead to full equal rights for the two communities under the motto of "one man one vote".

It would be easy to show how similar were the attitudes and arguments in the two cases. In both, resistance between the wars was at first directed less against the still weak national movements than against reform tendencies and certain groups of reformers in the mother country. At the same time, for reasons of expediency, the settlers expected economic aid from the metropolis and at the same time demanded autonomy in order to defend themselves against intervention "from outside" and to ensure that they had sole control over questions regarding the natives. Since they were aware of their economic and political weakness, they could do little more than threaten secession. Yet, by their resistance, they did succeed in making the mother country abandon any idea of granting concessions to the non-European inhabitants; in spite of all criticism and declarations to the contrary, the mother country did not seek to impair the settlers' domination. But neither in Kenya nor in Algeria did the metropolis surrender its final authority; it could, therefore, reserve itself control in the future—in 1960, over the heads of the settlers, France granted the Algerian Muslims, i.e. the Africans, independence. Between the wars Britain was just as unable to carry out the policy of "development to self-government" in Kenya as France was with its policy of consistent assimilation in Algeria. Both political concepts were meant to be liberal and aimed at a form of decolonization, but in the special cases of colonial settlements they would have led to "coloured majorities", which neither mother country was prepared to accept. They sought ways out and compromises in association or partnership between the two racial communities, but such concepts were largely "on paper" and proved unworkable. In order to be effective they would have required a complete change of attitude towards the natives. Except for a small minority, the settlers who had moved to the colonies and had fought for economic and social progress with the help, and at the price, of the natives, were aware of their perilous position as a minority group. So this very necessary change in attitude could not be expected, nor was it psychologically possible.

DIRECT ADMINISTRATION IN WEST AFRICA

Earlier on we outlined Lord Lugard's policy of indirect rule on which the British administration in West Africa was based. The system was carried over to other territories between the wars and elaborated into a coherent doctrine, which met with increasing criticism in the 1930s and tended more and more after the Second World War to be replaced by a less conservative modern local administration. We now propose to describe how France administered its West African colonies, what was its attitude to the traditional authorities and what was the meaning of ideas such as assimilation and association with respect to France's colonial and political intentions in West Africa.

The structure of the French administration, as we know, was centralist and the governor-general of French West Africa in Dakar, to whom the governors of the individual territories were subordinated, had considerable authority over the administration and army, finance, taxation and the legal system. While legislative power was vested in Paris, however, the governor-general did have the right to issue decrees which gave him considerable freedom of decision. Except in the Four Communes in Senegal, the natives had the status of "subjects". The Conseil Colonial, which represented not only the Four Communes but the whole of Senegal after 1920, had little importance. The territory was divided into *cercles* headed by a *commandant du cercle* who was not, as his title may imply, a military officer but a civil administrator in the higher colonial service. His position corresponded to that of the district commissioner in the British colonies. The *commandant* had authority over the local administration and "ruled" over vast areas and a great number of natives far from Dakar. Robert Delavignette has described these administrators as the "true chiefs of the Empire" and has shown their difficult position, the great variety of their duties and also the fascination of this post.[1]

The *chefferie*, that is the traditional system of rule in its many forms varying from clan and village communities to tribal rule and to actual kingdoms, had an important function in the French system, though it cannot be compared with the great emirates in Northern Nigeria or with the native authorities in general.[2] But the basis for an analogous development existed: the conquest and possession of the African backlands in the 1880s took a similar form to the British conquest, with military expeditions, pacts with native rulers and the establishment of a system of "internal protectorates". New struggles, the extension of the administration and economic interests soon removed the last vestiges of autonomy from the traditional authorities; in the kingdom of Samory in the Sudan the dynasty was a foreign one—as with the Fulahs in Northern Nigeria—so France could justify its action as the liberation of subjected peoples or, as in the case of the kingdom of Dahomey, as part of its civilizing mission. Some dynasties remained, but they were usually in thinly settled and economically unimportant regions. For the rest, the larger kingdoms were destroyed, arbitrarily dismembered and to a great extent replaced by direct administrations. Even when the heirs to ancient dynasties were employed as *chefs de canton*, they had no personal authority but were "civil servants" of the colonial power.[3] After the First World War there were still individual cases in which France arbitrarily appointed no heirs or where ancient, large *chefferies* were divided up into *cantons* for reasons of administrative expediency.[4]

In the villages the administration had to rely on the chiefs and village heads, since there was not sufficient French staff to fill the entire administration. The village chiefs were grouped together and subordinated to the *chefs de canton*.[5] The *chefferie* was built into the system of direct administration and became a part of it. The *chef* served the *commandant* as executive organ in the fields of public health, road building, etc. He collected taxes and handed them over to the *cercle*, keeping a portion as wages. But, unlike the native authority, the *chefferie* obtained no treasury of its own and thus did not have power over any specific field of local administration. Nor did the *chef* have any juridical power. So what was characteristic of indirect rule—a native treasury and a specific sphere of native jurisdiction—was lacking in the French system. Delavignette commented on this: "We do not hesitate to raise a black man to the office of magistrate in our own law. But we do hesitate to devote a black to the exercise of his own Custom and we prefer to create artificial jurisdictions which are native in nothing but name."[6] The tendency towards bureaucratization was also apparent in the manner of appointment. On the whole the administration was willing to appoint the candidate whom custom named as chief, as long as he seemed trustworthy and relatively educated and receptive. But it did not try very hard to find the legitimate *chef* and to acknowledge him alone. *Chefs* were appointed or deposed rather arbitrarily; administrative employment was often considered proof of competence, but graduates of the army, post-office employees, translators and even servants served as *chefs de canton*. They received special training, less devoted to African law, ethnology, etc. than to French law and administrative methods,[7] and after spending a term with a *commandant*, they could be appointed even to the villages and *cantons* of other tribes.

So the *chef* had little in common with the traditional chief of the

British native authority. He had to forfeit his religious sanction as chief and was no longer the embodiment of a community integrated by the unity of the dead and the living; instead he became the confidant of the colonial power and represented not so much the interests of the community, as the administration's attitude to the "subjects". As a result, the natives often did not obey him but a "hidden" legitimate chief. That the chiefs were not true spokesmen for the natives was also proved by the fact that they always supported the administration in the councils. In Senegal this led to latent tensions between them and the elected representatives of the African "citizens".

There was no lack of efforts towards "Africanizing" the institution of the *chefferie,* relaxing the direct administration and anchoring the chief more firmly in African society. The legendary Van Vollenhoven (who had been governor-general of Indochina for thirty-seven years and took over French West Africa in 1917, resigning his post in protest against compulsory conscription and against the appointment of Diagne as high commissioner, and finally falling at the front) made the administration aware of the importance of African society in his much quoted circular of 15 August 1917:

> Before destroying the framework of the autochthonous society, we must build. . . . the hour has passed, in Africa as in the other continents of the world, when a command can be imposed or maintained against the will of the peoples.[8]

In the search for a suitable middleman, nine times out of ten the administration encountered "the traditionally obeyed chief". "One can define these chiefs as functionaries who exist even when they have no attributions and whose authority is acknowledged even when there has been neither investiture nor delegation of powers." In the argument about whether to appoint the traditional and legitimate or the most educated and open-minded candidate, Van Vollenhoven decided for the former—obviously in contradiction to current practice—for he thought that only the former had real authority and would be accepted by the people: "It must not be he who pleases the administrator most but he who pleases the people most." The chief would remain the "intermediary", however, a "functionary", though of a special kind, and not the sole bearer of local power:

> . . . The rule which determines the attributions of the native chief must be as follows: they have no power of their own of any kind, for there are not two authorities in the *cercle,* French authority and native authority; there is but one!
>
> The *commandant de cercle* is the only commander: only he is responsible. The native chief is only an instrument, an auxiliary. It is true

> that this auxiliary is not just an agent who transmits and that he puts at the service of the *commandant de cercle* not only his activity and his devotion but also his knowledge of the country and the real influence which he may have over the inhabitants of this country. The native chief never speaks, never acts in his own name, but always in the name of the *commandant de cercle* and by formal or tacit delegation from the latter. I think that this absolute principle has been stated sufficiently clearly to prevent it . . . from being in any way equivocal. . . . I have set out the reasons which incited us to have recourse to the concourse of chiefs. These reasons are not inspired by the interests of the chiefs. They are not ancient sovereigns whose kingdoms we want to take over; the kingdoms either did not exist or have been overthrown by us and will never be re-established. These reasons are solely inspired by the interests of the peoples under our authority. Between us and these peoples there must be a medium: it is the chief who is this medium; not because it is imposed upon us but because we have chosen it so, and we have chosen it because it is the best course.

These words, which are intended to define the position of the chief, make the differences between the French system and indirect rule quite plain. Although the chief and the native authority were an integral part of the administration in the British system too, they were not just delegates and executive organs but independent authorities, and as such were not created by the colonial power but only recognized and employed. France had little sympathy with such a concept, since it contradicted the French centralist view of the state and the "indivisibility" of French sovereignty.

In 1929 Governor-General Jules G. Carde again criticized the frequent practice of replacing traditional chiefs by *évolués* and stressed the usefulness of the *conseils de notables* formed in 1919 which had even [!] developed initiatives of their own.[9] Carde's successor Brévié stressed the need for a native policy based on African societies and in conformity with the special function of the chief even more forcefully in his opening address before the *Conseil de Gouvernement* and in his circulars of September 1932.[10] He said the "native cadres" were inadequate, because France was indulging in the illusion of indirect administration even though "educational action" was impossible as long as a single European was confronted by thousands of natives. The chiefs should not just be the "mandatories of an administration" but should also be accepted as "representatives of ethnic collectivities" who would voice the concerns of the village. The village was the "native social cell" and was personified in the chief, who was by no means only a simple autocrat. Like Van Vollenhoven, Brévié stressed that the chiefs remained "executors of orders, informers, advisors". This meant that, implicitly at least, he was dissociating himself from indirect rule and native authorities.

Between the wars the governors-general clearly tried hard to do justice to recent ethnological research, to understand the chief as the embodiment of the African social structure and to rely more heavily on traditional institutions and African customs.[11] The question was, however, whether the chief could really be the representative of his community if he was only an executive organ. He would necessarily make himself disliked as an instrument of the colonial administration because of his difficult position "between hammer and anvil". (He was responsible for collection of taxes, compulsory vaccination, requisition of labour for public works, etc.) In any case he remained a quasi-functionary in the service of the direct administration. In line with this was the new statute for Senegal in January 1935 which listed the "administrative attributions" of the chief.[12] The instructions were only partly obeyed in practice, since they were continually renewed until the decrees of Eboué in 1941 (cf. p. 362). So between the wars there was a certain similarity between the British and the French administrations, but the criticisms and decrees took different forms. The British warned against dogmatization and overestimating the value of indirect rule and criticized the administration's neglect of the *évolués*, while the French demanded a reduction in the influence of the functionaries in the direct administration and had more sympathy for the inherent values of traditional African society.

For the most part, the colonial administration and most of the specialists on Africa did not consider the future. Native policy interested them with regard to practical tasks, but not as a question of the ultimate aim of French colonial policy. Economic development, social services, overcoming the depression after 1930, improving medical care and the educational system, were more urgent than the discussion of possible decolonization. Unlike the case in Indochina and North Africa, there was no "national" resistance as yet in Black Africa to challenge the colonial power. British slogans and principles such as trusteeship, indirect rule and self-government contained the idea of decolonization, programmatically if no more, and seemed to forecast eventual withdrawal; but the French discussion on Africa centred on the image of Greater France and openly or tacitly aimed at integration and assimilation.

As an example of French policy we might note Marcel Olivier, governor of Madagascar from 1924 to 1931, director of the World Colonial Exhibition in 1931 and author of the much noted book *Six ans de politique sociale à Madagascar* (1931), with a foreword by Albert Sarraut. Olivier started with the land issue and described his efforts to create order and stability in the complex question of landownership. He staunchly supported European colonization because it had helped to develop the thinly settled island economically by supplying export products, on whose income Madagascar depended. He thought European and native agriculture were complementary and both deserved to be promoted by the administration. So Olivier wanted larger agrarian credits and better agricultural training facilities for the natives, but also a land tax and administrative aid in order to supply native labour for the settlers; without "pressure" from the administration, nine-tenths of the European farms would have to be abandoned! Olivier believed in a "natural" process of selection. The hard-working native farmers would be able to survive in spite of high taxation, while the "incompetent and the lazy" would automatically become agricultural labourers at the disposal of the large concerns! Olivier admitted that the wages paid after the war were far too low, but went on to defend the 1926 decree that had been violently criticized in France, which stated that natives who had been recruited for military service but not called up could be obliged to work in "the public interest".

We shall not go into further detail here. What is important in our context is that a governor who on the whole was pro-reform openly demanded stronger European colonization. Comparison with Britain's West Africa policy makes the differences apparent at once. Even in Kenya the immigration of settlers was encouraged after the war. But Britain soon became aware of the problems this entailed and henceforth anyone who defended the settlers or attempted to increase their numbers—in the interests of a white man's country—was *eo facto* proved "colonialist". France, by contrast, was not confronted with the problem of self-government in a plural society and based its policy on the idea of Greater France and integrated colonies. Consequently the settlers seemed an important means of achieving cultural assimilation. As long as there was enough land, France could hope for an "association" of the racial communities.

Olivier also wanted reforms in educational policy. He was in favour of taking steps to improve native schooling and the use of the local language in the lower grades. His views contradicted the popular dogma, particularly widespread in Africa, of instruction exclusively in French, and the reform was undertaken in 1929. Olivier also opposed the "chimera" of assimilation: "to say assimilation is to say destruction". Attempts to artificially revive traditional institutions and authorities were pointless, however, since the colonial power had destroyed them and had filled even the lower administrative posts with European officials. The principle still applied that no native could rise higher than the lowest European official; this obviously drove the *évolués* into opposition. He had, said Olivier, attempted to form a special cadre of native officials when he was governor in 1930, and he had given them access to certain posts hitherto reserved for Europeans. But even this rather modest reform was strongly opposed!

In the more narrow political sphere Olivier was content to keep the *status quo*. Although he was willing to change the electoral methods of native representation in the *Délégations économiques* and to give more attention to the urban *évolués*, yet he firmly objected to any attempts to transform the delegations into *Assemblées délibératives*. This, he thought, would mean politicization, which must be avoided.[13] In fact,

Olivier was in favour of depoliticization, and he clearly stressed that economic and social questions took precedence over political ones.[14] This tendency was all the more remarkable in that Madagascar already had its own administration before the French occupation and was certainly far more highly developed than Black Africa. Moreover, in British West Africa legislative councils had long since been established, while Olivier still considered them "premature" for Madagascar in 1931. *Assemblées délibératives*, he thought, corresponded to the concept of self-government. This, it seems, was irreconcilable with a policy based on the integral unity of the national territory, a policy which granted no more than a degree of decentralization and representation and aimed at eventual assimilation. Although Olivier described this policy as destructive, because it tried over-hastily to recast traditional institutions and customs according to the French model, he was eventually forced to accept it and present it as the ultimate aim of French colonial policy. "Assimilation is but a distant aim"[15]; "it is designed not to provoke an evolution but to mark its end".[16] Olivier's example makes it clear that the reformist-minded opposition, which still accepted assimilation and did not replace it by self-government, almost necessarily led to institutional immoblism and depoliticization.[17]

The outstanding expert on Africa, Henri Labouret, sought a solution. In his essays *A la recherche d'une politique indigène dans l'ouest Africain* of 1930–1931,[18] he elaborated Brévié's theses, leaving out the direct political issues. But in 1935 he opposed assimilation and suggested his own concept of federalism to replace it.[19] He was one of the few writers of the inter-war period who managed to point out the logical conclusion of an assimilative policy of naturalization. One day the former natives would outnumber the European French in the electoral bodies and the French parliament and the sovereign rights of Greater France "would pass into the hands of the new civilized men". Naturalization in statute was also problematic. As a way of giving the natives political emancipation "while at the same time maintaining them in an extended French community", he proposed instead a federal solution. The "subjects" could gradually obtain equal rights in their respective colonies and then administer the country together with the French. Here Labouret referred to the British dominions, overlooking the fact that one could not speak of an "association" between the protectorate power and the natives in the dominions. He had an equally mistaken view of the Commonwealth, which he saw as a federation. Labouret suggested a "progressive federalism of France and its possessions" within an "Empire which must remain 'one and indivisible'". It is remarkable that this recognized Africanist and specialist on colonial questions, who supported the political Right, admitted that the formula a "nation of a hundred million inhabitants" was in fact questionable and implied results which France could never accept. Yet, he thought, France should be accommodating towards the aspirations of the *évolués,* since otherwise "trouble will break out and they will contemplate violent separation". This contradicted the countless statements in colonialist circles which asserted that all was "quiet" in the colonial Empire, apart from an insignificant minority of "agitators"! By contrast with assimilation or a mere adherence to the *status quo,* federalism seemed to take local autonomy seriously and offered the natives a sphere of influence of their own. Federalism would not, as had happened in the Commonwealth which he mistakenly used as an example, break up the institutional unity of the whole. After the Second World War, France tried to take this road, but it encountered obstacles in the attempt to create an institutional structure that reconciled colonial efforts at emancipation with the maintenance of French sovereignty. It was easy to speak of federalism because one could content oneself with general theories!

Another attempt to solve the dilemma between secession and self-government on the one hand and integration and assimilation on the other, was made by Robert Delavignette. Delavignette represented a number of younger administrators and experts on Africa who, fascinated by their duties and tacitly feeling sympathy for the natives, concerned themselves with Black Africa and the Africans as human beings. His book *Les paysans noirs,* published in 1913, was intended to be programmatic. Delavignette thought the issue was not so much how to raise export production as how to produce enough food to raise the local standard of living. "It frightens me when people speak of a land without taking into account the men of this land", was his apt phrase.[20] Delavignette was influenced by Emmanuel Mounier's theory of personalism and was concerned with *"l'Homme",* Man inside his natural environment. African society with its inherent values must be brought into fruitful contact with the modern world, in order to build a "New African World". He developed these ideas further in later books, *Soudan-Paris-Bourgogne* (1935) and *Les vrais chefs de l'empire.* Abstractions like assimilation and association, direct or indirect rule, were of little use, he thought. Much as Delavignette stressed the sacramental function of the *chef* and described the characteristic features of African law and religion, yet he warned against the danger of merely restoring the *chefferie.* The colonial power's task was not to renew or to support an old feudal system. "What we must do is not to restore them, but to install them. Not to restore them in a feudal system that is dying, but to install them in an emergent modern Africa."[21]

"This New World is not an ideological edifice but a living reality, the result of an experimental native policy. . . . We are creating the New African World. In the name of what ideology should this experiment be arrested: in the name of what pretense at realism should our achievements be dismissed?"[22] Delavignette addressed himself to Senghor, the first *agrégé* from French West Africa and the representative of a new Africa that was in the process of being born with French aid.²³

Delavignette did not put forward a political programme, nor does he appear to have considered this urgent. Just as he dismissed assimilation and association as abstractions, he did not think much of discussions on an institutional settlement of the relationship between mother country and colonies. He knew how important it was to give the European-educated élite the means to rise on the social scale, but for the time being he gave precedence to economic and financial aid. Credits from the metropolis were urgently needed after the deflation and economy measures imposed by the world financial crisis.²⁴ He did not envisage future independent African states, but neither did he support crude integration. Instead he foresaw an as yet unspecified form of autonomy within a greater whole. "Fortunately there is another method of 'Gallicizing' [!] Africa than this division into well-ordered departments around Paris."²⁵ After 1945 Senghor and Delavignette both sought a Franco-African community of this kind: "Fraternity in spite of differences, is this so difficult to understand?"²⁶ Perhaps, we may add, not to understand, but to institutionalize!

The educational system had a special place in France's Africa policy, since the "civilizing mission" was to be accomplished primarily through assimilation and integration, and also the federal solution envisaged by Labouret and Delavignette presumed an élite stamped by France. The colonial school system was centralized like that of metropolitan France and organized from Paris. State schools dominated, unlike in Great Britain and Belgium, and instruction was left to the missions while the mother country merely gave financial support. The teachers came primarily from the mother country, and the curriculum was also largely the same as in France, giving rise to much ridicule and criticism. Instruction was almost exclusively in French—except in Indochina and Madagascar—allegedly because there were too many local tongues and access to the modern world was best gained by knowledge of the French language. In fact, the French language was designed to be an instrument of integration and assimilation. In 1919 the governor-general of French West Africa openly said:

> We must not, in fact, forget that a sovereign nation does not definitively fix the nationality of the peoples whom it allows into its family [!] until it has taught them to speak its language, to think in its language. [And again, a year later:] It is only when they are able to speak our language that they will learn to think in French and will have been definitively acquired into our culture.²⁷

This was plain enough. Instruction in the French language was to make the Africans into Frenchmen. Frenchmen, it is true, with black skins, but nevertheless stamped by French culture and therefore prepared to consider themselves French citizens and to be loyal to France. Just as a Breton, a Celt or an Alsatian could use his mother tongue in the local sphere but nonetheless was and wanted to be French, so too the African was to become French by virtue of the formative influence of the "civilization" administered by the French language and to achieve his intellectual and political emancipation within Greater France. Georges Hardy, director of the École coloniale and a specialist in colonial education, held the same views, although he laid greater stress on the instrumental value of French instruction. It would "ensure the cohesion of our Empire" and train the natives to be "loyal and grateful subjects".[28]

Naturally this intensive cultural process had to be restricted to a minority. Governor-General Carde coined a popular formula: "instruct the mass and free the élite". Although the masses should acquire an elementary knowledge of French, on the whole they should be instructed in a more practical sense, while those who were best qualified should be "separated" from the mass and "Gallicized" with a view to forming an élite. This process could take them from the *lycée* to the metropolitan universities. Here there was no discrimination and no segregation, black and white students attended the same schools and had to pass the same examinations. University education gave access to the *Concours*, to the liberal professions and even to a political career in metropolitan France. In the mother country—though not in the colonies themselves—educated Frenchmen with black skins encountered hardly any social discrimination and were accepted as equals.

The differences between French and British policy are obvious. Unlike Belgium and Holland, Britain did not overlook the possibilities for intellectually and politically influencing the subjects of the Empire. Convinced of the superiority of its institutions, Britain carried them over to successive colonies, and British law continues to apply in some independent states today. British educational methods and even school curricula were often adopted too. The ideal of the "gentleman" as an expression of the British way of life and British character proved comparable to the image of "French civilization" in the French colonies. But the intentions were different. Britain did not want to "wean" an élite of Asians and Africans from their society and "make" them into Englishmen in the sense of potential British citizens. Instead the élite was to gradually take over the leadership of its own country and form the basis of a new government. The 1925 memorandum *Education in British Tropical Africa*, which served as a directive for educational policy between the wars, stated that "education should be adapted to the mentality of the various peoples . . . training . . . the people in the management of their own affairs . . . it must include the raising up of capable, trustworthy, public-spirited leaders of the people, belonging to their own race".[29] Accordingly instruction was to begin in the local tongue and did not aim to forcibly create Englishmen. The vernacular seemed the most suitable language for local communication, for learning to read and write and for the first encounter with modern civilization. No Englishman would have said that the student must learn to think in English in order to become a member of the British "family". In the higher grades, instruction was naturally in English, but this was conceived less as Anglicization or as an instrument of assimilation than as a way of establishing contact with the rest of the world, emerging from local isolation, and coming to terms with modern civilization.[30]

The advantages and disadvantages of the two educational systems need not be discussed further here. There is no doubt that France was very successful both in culturally imprinting an élite and binding it politically. At the same time, it can be said that France did not make full use of its given possibilities—especially in Black Africa, although not only there. The percentage of children at school remained small,[31] and until 1946 the teaching staff and financial resources were inadequate. France should have had great interest in devoting special attention to education, although this would have presupposed enough jobs and opportunities for the educated in the administration and in private firms. The absence of local representative bodies and the extensive depoliticization should have coincided with the entry of the educated natives into the economy and the state,[32] but this happened even less than in the British territories. Blaise Diagne might have been a deputy and even under-secretary of state, but by and large the administrative cadre remained European. This lack of opportunities for the *évolués*, together with racial discrimination, not only produced anger—which was to work to the advantage of the national opposition—and turned frustration into resentment; it also gave conservative circles in metropolitan France a good argument for slowing down educational improvement.[33]

In the same way, as we have shown, naturalization should have been granted generously if France wanted its efforts at integration and gradual assimilation to seem convincing. But the experts on Africa and the reformers joined the French colonials and colonialist interest groups in opposing assimilation and its consequences such as naturalization, franchise, access to the administration, more *communes de plein exercice* (self-governing municipalities), etc. In addition the creation of local "parliaments" was considered out of the question, because they seemed to contradict the notion of integration into Greater France. The result, we repeat, was a definite tendency towards depoliticization and immobilism.[34]

LYAUTEY AND THE PROTECTORATE IN MOROCCO

The protectorate was an instrument of French colonial policy fundamentally opposed, even in contradiction, to integration and assimilation, and it is inseparable from the person and influence of Marshal Lyautey, the most important of the French proconsuls.[1] For thirteen years, from 1912 to 1925, Lyautey "ruled" in Morocco, put his experiences and ideas on paper, attracted a circle of disciples and tried to force the metropolis to accept and continue his work. Lyautey accepted the legal basis of the protectorate and based his ideas on a number of earlier models. We can dismiss Dupleix's methods in India in the eighteenth century, the protectorate over Tahiti in 1843 and also the dubious pacts with African chiefs in the years after 1880, which have been described as "internal protectorates" by the lawyers but were of a rather theoretical nature and usually soon turned into normal colonial administrations with a tendency towards direct rule. More important models were the protectorate agreements with Madagascar, Indochina (e.g. the emperor of Annam and the rulers of Cambodia and Laos) and Tunisia, which began by recognizing the territories' nationhood, and established French control only in order to secure them from attack by foreign powers and give them the possibility of economic improvement. Since this procedure demanded less military and financial resources than would have been required by occupation or annexation, it seemed the most suitable way of extending French domination in the competition for the "partition of the world". This method was all the more suitable in that it gave the great powers little occasion to intervene and also enabled France to deceive its own public, which had little interest in colonial conquest, or at least to make it accept the *fait accompli*.[2]

These early protectorates very soon changed in nature. When the queen of Madagascar protested against the agreements, and after the rebellion which made a lengthy process of "pacification" necessary, Galliéni deposed the queen and made the island a colony in 1896. In Indochina, the protectorates over Annam, Cambodia and Laos formally remained, but in 1887 they were largely neutralized in the Union Indochinoise and their administrative structure, especially in the Annamite Empire, became French. The term "protectorate" could now be used only in a legalistic sense, particularly since the administration of Indochina was also turned over to the colonial ministry. From then on, the traditional authorities were almost all disbanded and the emperor of Annam rarely appeared in any political capacity. The status of protectorate was not reinvoked until 1945–1946, when France attempted to incorporate Indochina, Tunisia and Morocco into the French Union as associated states. Tunisia, however, remained a protectorate in a more specific sense, although the treaty of La Marsa on 8 June 1883 gave France very extensive powers[3] which could hardly be reconciled with the idea of a protectorate, and although Tunisian authorities and institutions were soon replaced by French ones or bypassed. Characteristically, in the 1890s protectorate status was conceived as a transitional solution leading to eventual annexation.[4]

Lyautey was also much influenced by the discussion of assimilation which we have described earlier. Around the turn of the century this influence was reflected in his sharp criticism of the Algerian administration, in the attempt not to "Algerianize" Tunisia and in the new methods of "pacification" employed in Indochina and Madagascar: Military action was to be supplemented by attempts to persuade the native inhabitants to collaborate, by the utilization of existing institutions and authorities and by restraint in applying civilizing pressures. The important writings of Governor-General Lanessan exerted a strong influence on his disciples, Galliéni and Lyautey.

French rule in Morocco was based on the Fez agreement of 30 March 1912, which was the result of economic and consular intervention, military action and diplomatic negotiations. It spoke of an "accord" between the two states by which France granted the sultan protection of his person and his throne and promised to guarantee "the religious position, the traditional respect and prestige of the sultan". The sultan for his part declared himself ready "to institute a new régime in Morocco consisting of the administrative, judiciary, educational, economic, financial and military reforms which the French Government considers it useful to introduce in the Moroccan territory" (Art. I). These reforms were to be based on proposals by the French Government, but decreed in the name of the sultan. Morocco was thus recognized as a state outside the "national French territory". However much the lawyers discussed Morocco's position in international law and its implications,[5] in fact it had now been firmly established that France would not only control foreign policy, diplomatic representation and defence, but could also, as in the case of Tunisia, determine the internal structure of the country, apart from religious affairs, as it saw fit. The concept of the protectorate was interpreted very broadly, giving the mother country extensive powers. Lyautey's view of French policy in Morocco was as follows:

> The concept of the Protectorate is that of a country that keeps its institutions, governs and administers itself with its own organs, under the simple control of a European power which, substituted for it in foreign

representation, generally takes over the administration of its Army and its Finances, and directs its economic development. What dominates and characterizes this conception is the formula control, as opposed to the formula direct administration.[6]

So the French protectorate was characterized by "control" as opposed to direct rule. The resemblance to indirect rule is apparent, although in the case of Morocco the concept was applied to an entire country which was allegedly to continue ruling itself and was subject only to foreign control and influence. Indirect rule, by contrast, referred to local administration only and incorporated the native authorities into the machinery of colonial rule. It is important to note that in principle Lyautey wanted the old institutions and authorities to remain and to continue to serve as instruments of administration, while France merely issued "directives" and exerted control, without replacing the autochthonous order by its own machinery or legal system. In both cases, respect for the existing order was combined with considerations of expediency, for "no régime offers greater opportunities of using the local organisms to our advantage and developing their resources".[7] The colonial power acted only "indirectly"; when it "inspired" reforms, i.e. in practice when it issued orders, it did not come into direct contact with the inhabitants but gave these orders in the name of the existing authorities and had them executed by its organs. This system could function only on condition of maintaining the authority and the prestige of the sultan, the pasha and the elders. Like Lugard and his successors in Nigeria, Lyautey tried to do this in Morocco. He paid the sultan all due respect, strengthened his representative position, respected his religious position too and kept up personal contacts with Moroccan leaders.

This attitude reflected Lyautey's own background and beliefs. He came from a conservative Catholic family from Lorraine and remained a monarchist all his life: with his highly developed sense of authority, hierarchy and loyalty, he was attracted to the "feudal" structure of Morocco. He saw it as his "mission" to modernize and "develop" this country, whose strangeness he loved and whose antiquities, architecture and art he took the trouble to preserve under French guidance. What better proof of France's greatness than rule of this kind? He demanded from his colleagues a sense of responsibility, activity, the ability to make decisions and the desire to "realize" them, and—what for him was the essence of all colonial activity—an understanding of the land and the people, knowledge of the foreign language and the desire to protect and promote the prestige and dignity of the ancient order and its representatives. Most of his colleagues were of noble French families and, like their leader, were opposed to the Republic and its parliamentary structure and prepared to serve not the régime but France itself. Lyautey's aim was to "bring them [the Moroccans] to feel the benefits of foreign rule and to accept rather than submit to it".[8] Accordingly, native policy in a protectorate meant

> the desire and the ability to study the natives, to understand them, to penetrate their institutions and their sentiments, their motives and their ambitions; next, the wish and the ability to free oneself of European prejudice. Native policy is based on the principle that a people holds to its customs and its institutions, good or bad, and that it will consider ours, even if they are better, odious if we tried to force it to respect or even practise them; similarly, that our civilization, so perfect in our view, astonishes or shocks it [the people] and that, convinced as we are that it is in its interests to abandon its civilization for ours, it is necessary to bring it to this decision slowly, with patience and skill.[9]

Lyautey particularly admired Great Britain for its adaptability, its loose administrative structure and its small need of British-born staff.[10] He wanted to set up an administration that conformed to the nature of the protectorate and the Fez agreement; it should be quite distinct from direct administration with its tendencies towards integration. The sultan remained the formal head of the autocratic and theocratic government, held court, resided in his palace and exercised his religious functions. Laws (*dahirs*) and sentences were pronounced in his name. He appointed the ministers and officials, including the French ones. French law was not applicable, unless transformed into Moroccan *dahirs*. Admittedly, effective power was vested in France, in the person of the resident-general, who "directs all the administrative services", as was stated laconically in the decree of 11 June 1912 establishing the position of the French Government representative. A high French official served as middleman between the sultan and the maghzen and supervised the Moroccan ministers (*vizirs*); in the local sphere French *contrôleurs* backed and assisted the pashas and caids. The colonial power had legislative power and the appointment of local officials was based on its proposals! Even more important was that, apart from the vizirs who were relegated to the conduct of religious affairs, there appeared the so-called *Services neo-chérifiens*, which were technically ministries for agriculture, public works, finance, public health and post and communications. In theory they were Moroccan offices, but in fact they were entirely occupied by Frenchmen; their directors formed a *Conseil des directeurs* which governed and had only very loose connections with the sultan and the maghzen. The situation in Tunisia was similar.

The chief difficulty of the protectorate lay in the fact that it had obvious tendencies towards becoming simply direct administration. For if the traditional feudal institutions and authorities were not capable of taking over certain of the duties of a modern administration, the controllers had to intervene and administer more or less directly. While Great Britain exercised restraint here and largely restricted itself to the functions of law and order, Lyautey pressed for action and demanded "incessant control".[11] But how could one ensure the prestige and authority of the Moroccan notables under this kind of control? Would not the protectorate become a mere fiction and the attempt to maintain the traditional authorities mere expediency which would eventually achieve the reverse, resulting not in modernization and democratization of the traditional administration, but in refeudalization,[12] confirmation of privileges and a defensive reaction to innovations? If the colonial power did not intervene but at the same time supported the traditional ruling class, the result might be the firm establishment of pre-colonial abuses. This was the case against indirect rule. The effects of such a policy were clearly evident in Morocco in the domains of the great caids in the south, particularly the pasha of Marrakesh, El-Glaoui. Even Lyautey had protected this pasha from criticism because the latter had acceded entirely to French wishes, created a certain counter-force to the sultan and allowed France to economize on military and administrative staff.[13]

It should have been in the nature of a protectorate to actively try to modernize the class of notables and to give a French-educated élite access to the administration. But although Lyautey spoke of the need to train a Moroccan élite, he restricted secondary and university education to the sons of families of notables, intentionally kept their numbers small, and tried to develop this élite within the Muslim tradition. Access to the French *lycées* was not to be a rule, the final examination of the Collèges musulmans was not of the same standard as the *baccalauréat*, and the Institut des Hautes Études Marocaines was less a university than a research institute, mainly serving the administration. Study in France was restricted as much as possible.[14] The few Moroccans who had passed the French final examinations were unable to bring about a "Moroccanization" of the administration, especially since the notables of the maghzen were just as suspicious of the educated élite as were the French officials, whose resistance Lyautey had already encountered.[15]

The opposition to cultural assimilation—which led to segregated schools —the assumption that a separate Moroccan-Muslim educational system could be set up, which would be modernized from within and able to cope with modern tasks, and a decided preference for the class of notables, together with the open distrust for the French élite who had risen from the middle classes, all succeeded in slowing down the process of modernization. This complied with Lyautey's conservative views and his sense of tradition, but it also jeopardized the success of the whole system. Morocco was becoming modernized and economically developed and yet in the 1930s it still had no modern administrative staff of its own and only a few scholars; under these circumstances the trend towards direct administration became even stronger.

A similar ambivalence characterized the question of French colonization and the political representation of the colonies. Lyautey achieved much in the economic development of Morocco, particularly in building towns and ports, extending communications and developing raw materials. Moreover, much to the annoyance of the settler and colonialist economic circles in the metropolis, he did not leave exploitation of the phosphate mines to private enterprise but put it under state supervision, thus ensuring important revenues to the Moroccan state. Lyautey was convinced that without French settlers, Moroccan agriculture could not be economically developed and modernized. However, he did not want to create a second Algeria under any circumstances and he attacked the settlers' "Algerian mentality"[16]; he also stressed that a policy based on the old-style alienation of land was out of the question now,[17] and tried to slow down the immigration of lower-class whites as settlers and officials. Nevertheless, he strongly believed that colonists were necessary in their capacity of modern agronomists; consequently he had to create a legal basis for European acquisition of land. He did this with the land laws of April 1919.[18] The effects of these laws were rather questionable and in any case it is doubtful whether European colonization could even have been reconciled with Lyautey's concept of the protectorate. At any rate, it was almost inevitable that the colonists and businessmen that emerged as a class should make political claims and demand representative bodies to defend their own interests, as became clear after the First World War. Quite apart from this, there was the difficulty of introducing a European system of landownership, the imposition on the natives and the latters' inadequate protection by the administration. Although Lyautey invoked the initiative and diligence of his fellow-countrymen, he also pointed out that the status of protectorate did not permit representative bodies. The 1919 Conseil de Gouvernement, consisting of the directors of the administration and the presidents of the chambers of commerce and agriculture, was restricted to technical and economic coordination, had no political character and naturally had no legislative powers.[19] The French Moroccans violently criticized these restrictions, since they had neither parliamentary representation nor a legislative council, but the situation complied with Lyautey's concept of the protectorate and with his authoritarian and anti-parliamentarian views. Moreover, since Lyautey maintained the authoritarian character of pre-colonial Morocco and did not try to create a constitutional monarchy, there could be no representative bodies for the Moroccans either.

Lyautey's view of the future is difficult to establish from available evidence. Certainly he was vehemently opposed to those who saw the protectorate merely as a transitional step towards direct administration or integration on the pattern of Algeria. He was only too well aware that the mother country, especially the parliament and the ministerial bureaucracy, was suspicious of his concept and did not really accept it.[20] Lyautey went very far in his defense of Morocco, asserting that it was not suitable ground for an "Algerian policy". He waxed so enthusiastic about the former sovereign state, with its embassies in Paris, London and St. Petersburg, with its rich merchants, its educated class and even its flourishing agriculture [!] that one is tempted to ask how France could justify its rule in Morocco at all.[21] In defence of his policy, Lyautey asserted that the protectorate functioned well and was not just a façade.[22] However, he was highly critical of the internal administrative organs. In his magnificent exposé of 18 November 1920[23] he contrasted theory and practice, asserting that in actual fact neither the sultan nor the vizirs had any power and did not even have an advisory say in the government; the relationship between maghzen and colonial administration was only a formal one, of no political significance. Even in local affairs, the collaboration of the Moroccans was usually a mere fiction; "in effect, we are drawing closer and closer to direct administration". Lyautey emphatically warned against this. The world war, he said, had created a new situation, since thousands of Moroccans had fought or worked in Europe, sovereign rights had been proclaimed, and in Russia, Egypt, Tunisia and Algeria revolutionary resistance had begun that was echoing in Morocco too.[24] The young generation was sensitive to its exclusion from public affairs:

> they suffer from it and they speak about it. It is only a step from there to becoming receptive, when the day comes, to suggestions about regaining their rights and to hostile aspirations. They will become more and more aware of their value and their strength . . . [the Berbers] have nothing of the habitual inertia of the Eastern Muslims. They are a laborious, active people, avid for instruction, open to new ideas . . . [Morocco would soon be over-populated and the Europeans would become a diminishing minority]. So we will have only a very fragile dam with which to oppose the tidal wave. There would be no greater danger than allowing European immigrants to commit imprudences for which they will have to pay dearly, than allowing the seeds of discontentment and unease to grow among this people.

Lyautey wanted to inspire his subordinates with loyalty to the idea of the protectorate and asked them to behave accordingly. They should be prepared to collaborate with the sultan and the maghzen and to train young Moroccans for government offices so they could gradually replace the French.[25] For if the élite was not able to collaborate, it would be driven into opposition. France must play its role as tutor and "big brother",

> benefitting in this way from having to deal not with dust but with a nation whose emancipation will take place under our tutelage, under our direction, to our profit, whereas it would be a dangerous illusion if we were to imagine that we shall control it indefinitely with our thin and fragile pellicle of occupation.

These phrases show astonishing far-sightedness on the part of the proconsul, even if one takes into account that he was primarily concerned with the class of notables, whom he saw as the future élite, and scarcely paid any attention to the more bourgeois heralds of national emancipation. It was this unrest and these nationalist currents in Asia and the Middle East, now beginning to affect North Africa, that led him to expect national emancipation in Morocco too after the First World War. Until then he had evidently been convinced that the protectorate policy of "economic and social penetration" would develop into "close collaboration", and that the Moroccans would continue to accept France as their protector.[26] But around 1920 he was willing to admit the temporary nature of the protectorate and in 1926 he is alleged to have said to a friend: "It will be necessary within ten years to reconsider Moroccan independence."[27] We have no precise details as to how he expected dissociation to take place. No doubt Lyautey trusted in the existence of economic and spiritual ties between Morocco and France and counted on bilateral agreements that would give the former colonial power a privileged position. The question was not yet topical for him, and he said no more about it in later years. What we must note here is that Lyautey of all people—and one can compare him to Lord Milner in this respect—warned against illusions in face of the Arab emancipation movement and accepted the implications of his concepts. Since he set off the protectorate against annexation, putting no trust in the vague notion of association, he had to be prepared to set a term to Morocco's dependency and to accept the possibility of future self-government.

But were the mother country and Lyautey's successors prepared to do this? In 1920 Lyautey himself had had to confess the partial failure of his policy and in the following years it was only with difficulty that he managed to impose it in the face of the pressures brought against him. He was obliged to admit with great disappointment that the French had direct administration "under their skin".[28] No Moroccan staff was available to replace the French officials. Perhaps the metropolis was proud of the achievements of the great proconsul, yet people either did not understand his aims or interpreted them as a conservative anti-republican policy which would eventually be "normalized" and replaced by the more "progressive" policy of integration. A change in this direction began immediately after the marshal's retirement. His successor, Steeg, a Radical Socialist politician appointed by the Cartel des Gauches, had been governor-general of Algeria and carried Algerian methods of administration to Morocco. For instance, he appointed an official from Algeria who had no experience in Morocco as the new director for native affairs and quickly replaced Lyautey's team.[29] Moreover, Steeg was a man who made decisions at his desk and, unlike Lyautey, neither associated with the natives nor established contacts with Moroccan authorities. The number of French officials in the country grew rapidly and by the end of 1928 there were 14,412, whereas Britain managed with 4888 in India![30] No doubt the French officials accomplished a great deal in economically developing the land, but they were a burden on the budget and prevented the Moroccans from gaining access to the administration. Education was not modernized, as would have complied with a Radical Socialist colonial policy, and Steeg did not train an administrative or technical and economic Moroccan cadre. In addition, Steeg, unlike Lyautey, deliberately encouraged colonization[31]; in June 1926 he declared to the Rabat chamber of commerce: "We must ensure the growth of the French people by a methodical development of colonization."[32] As in Algeria, he gave special support to the small settlers.[33] A law in 1927 made expropriation of property easier,[34] while the administration gave the settlers financial support and tax privileges.[35] This benefited the Moroccan economy, since the modern factories concentrated on export production, but the discrepancy between the European and the native sector became even more distinct. When the Europeans experienced difficulties after the depression, the Moroccan state had to intervene to give financial aid from its budget resources, which largely came from taxation of the Muslim inhabitants.

The French Moroccans also were granted a greater political voice. In 1927 Steeg created a third college in the government council, consisting of elected representatives of the French citizens. The council became increasingly political in nature, assumed parliamentary functions and made insistent demands.[36] The settlers' demands had a decidedly colonialist accent: they wanted administrative support and economic aid, attacked even modest attempts at social legislation for the Moroccans,[37] criticized the "soft" policy of the resident, demanded stricter "control" of the caids and reintroduction of collective punishment, etc.[38] Similarly in 1934 *L'Afrique Française* demanded the prohibition of the journal *Maghreb*, published by young socialists in Paris, and wanted the protectorate power to take complete control of criminal cases:

> It is clear that our native policy requires serious reform. We must restore order in the street and above all in men's minds. If we are not firmly resolved to have France represented by its own representatives, to suppress any attacks against French authority without hesitation, we shall have to abandon our colonial policy and overseas expansion.[39]

The French Moroccans took a strong stand against the resident-general, Ponsot, formed a committee of coordination and demanded legislative powers for the government council.[40]

In our context it is particularly important to note that the writers on colonial policy either openly rejected the protectorate concept—and demanded direct administration[41]—or reinterpreted it, until it became meaningless. André Colliez, for instance, who distinguished three forms of protectorate in his detailed work *Notre protectorat marocain 1912–1930*, counted Morocco as a "protectorate of administration", in which the protector power

> holds all the strings, controls all the machinery; the governing bodies of the country have no more than the appearance of authority, everything they do has been suggested to them, imposed sometimes, but it is they who do it. They alone act.[42]

Colliez did not intend this to be a criticism of the existing situation, but rather an affirmation of French colonial policy! Similarly, the well-known specialist on colonial law, Arthur Girault, had no sympathy at all with Lyautey's aims, and welcomed the change from protectorate to colonial status, adding: "What does it matter whether this protectorate is or is not transformed into annexation later? The essential is to have not the appearance but the reality of power."[43] In 1926 Doucet, in his *Commentaires*, did in fact call Lyautey "the master of masters", but continued by demanding both more intensive colonization and representation of the protectorate in the French parliament (naturally only the French would vote).[44] A series of articles in *Correspondant* once again attacked the general public's lack of interest in questions of empire and praised the success of the Rif revolt; but it also demanded a strong pro-Berber policy and wanted to transform the Moroccan into "a true Frenchman". Small-scale colonization was being neglected, although this alone could provide a "solid armature". The aim of a French maghreb policy should be

> to ensure for our race a field of expansion which supplements that of Algeria and to maintain before the world our traditions, our language and our culture, against the competition of the immense domains of the yellow, Anglo-Saxon and Spanish worlds.[45]

So the French explicitly or tacitly considered the Morocco protectorate similar to Algeria. Although there were constant references to Lyautey, his concepts were no longer understood. Morocco and Tunisia were treated not as states but as colonies, as potentially integral parts of Greater France that should be administered accordingly. It was openly admitted that Moroccan institutions and authorities were nothing more than façades, and people were actually proud of the fact that they had made the protectorate serve their own ends so well and that in spite of earlier fictions they had set up a more or less direct administration. They did not, it is true, go so far as to demand annexation and integration, and the question of the future was left open. But at the same time, there was no word to the effect that the protectorate might one day come to an end: France was in Morocco and would remain in Morocco!

The nationalist movement in Morocco was supported both by the class of notables and by the young intelligentsia. Finding good grounds for protest in the Berber *dahir* of 1930,[46] it was nevertheless either not taken seriously or repressed. The "Comité d'action marocaine" began by agitating for a "return to the protectorate". It demanded less direct administration, the replacement of the French directors by Moroccan ministers, an elected national council, a Moroccan university and economic and social reforms, but it did not yet demand independence. Its 1934 *Plan de réformes* was rejected by the resident-general, Ponsot.[47] The nationalists' demands were perhaps hardly realizable at the time, but they could at least have formed a basis for negotiations. Yet France was unwilling to "compromise" and defended the status quo. Here again the result was depoliticization, for the Moroccan élite was neither employed in the administration of its own country nor did it have a representative body through which it could have gained political influence and made its demands heard.

Berque[48] rightly saw a parallel between the Ferhat Abbas campaign for naturalization in statute in Algeria, and the Moroccan call for a return to the protectorate. In both cases the issue was emancipation, and the Muslim élite demanded equal rights and liberty. One might add that France was challenged to put into practice the policy it had been proclaiming for so long, and to accept its implications: legal and political equality in Algeria (in the name of integration and assimilation), but in Morocco a true protectorate, i.e. internal autonomy and administrative positions in government for the Moroccans. But in both cases France refused to recognize the consequences of its own proclamations. Just as the assimilative reforms failed in Algeria, in Morocco no attempt was made to return to the protectorate. In the political writings of the 1930s there were, it is true, a few critical articles on France's Moroccan and Tunisian policy,[49] but not even the Popular Front government was able to bring about a change of course. General Noguès tried to make certain liberal reforms and reopened talks with the sultan, but he soon found himself obliged to take repressive measures and to arrest the nationalist leaders. At any rate, authoritarian rule, beneath the façade of a protectorate, survived until the beginning of the war.

France was proud of Lyautey's achievements in Morocco. His work was praised because it seemed to justify France's claims to colonial power. The critics of assimilation thought the marshal's concept of the protectorate was a more up-to-date and generous method of maintaining and stimulating Muslim society. But it was inevitable that the protectorate should become more and more of a façade, since France was not content with the policy of laissez-faire as pursued by Britain in the Indian and Malayan princely states, but instead aimed at economic development. It was difficult to reconcile this development with the slow modernization and restoration of the country's "medieval" social and administrative structure demanded under the protectorate without the help of the French civil service. Moreover, France could not repudiate its centrist and bureaucratic traditions and so, consciously or unconsciously, it applied Algerian administrative methods in the protectorates and eventually pursued a form of colonization that was hardly reconcilable with indirect rule.[50]

Morocco and Tunisia were considered part of Greater France—not institutionally but in the French mind. Although this did not prevent France from repealing the protectorate agreement and eventually granting independence, it did make such a procedure seem like "surrender", which France wanted to avoid at all costs. There were no views on the future of the protectorate in the colonial discussion between the wars, and it is symptomatic that even those writers who criticized the actual situation and were in favour of various reforms said nothing about the future of French policy. Self-government or independence, which would basically have been in line with the protectorate concept, were unmentionable. People spoke of association or collaboration but were unable to offer any practical details. Not until after the Second World War was there any attempt to give "association" an institutional basis, in the form of states that were autonomous in internal affairs but whose foreign policy and defence were under the control of the French Union. But the "association" agreement never took effect, for Morocco and Tunisia now demanded independence or at least the recognition of their right to independence, which France refused. Until the end, France tried to maintain the institutional ties. When decolonization eventually took place it did not entail a re-examination and repeal of earlier agreements, which would have complied with the concept of the protectorate and had been done by Great Britain between the wars, but it happened in a roundabout fashion, giving rise to new terms such as "co-sovereignty" and "interdependence". The only result, however, was what Lyautey had already foreseen in 1920.

COLONIAL POLITICS DURING THE SECOND WORLD WAR

After the fall of France in 1940 the colonies had to take a position for or against the exile government of General Charles de Gaulle. At first de Gaulle seems to have intended to join Noguès in Morocco or Puaux in Syria,[1] but on 27 June he summoned the governors and military leaders of the Empire "to become a part of the council of defense of overseas France whose aim it is to organize and to co-ordinate all the elements of French resistance in the Empire and in England".[2] Free France was to organize itself in the colonial Empire and to continue its resistance there. The colonies, which had previously been merely an appendage to the mother country, gained new importance in the mind of General de Gaulle and his colleagues, since they gave Free France its first territorial basis from which to reconquer metropolitan France.

The summons of 27 June was largely unheard. General Catroux, governor-general of Indochina, would have been willing to join de Gaulle, but he had been replaced on 25 June by Admiral Decoux. Puaux in Syria, Peyrouton in Tunisia and Noguès in Morocco, after some hesitation, chose Vichy. The fear that if they joined London they would be more or less open to attack by the German and Italian armies played as great a part in their decision as the conservative attitude of the high military and colonial officials, their traditional anglophobia—which was renewed after the French naval defeat at Mers-el-Kebir—or the fact that Marshal Pétain, the hero of Verdun, was now head of state. In Black Africa, Cayla in Madagascar and Boisson, governor-general of French West Africa who had been appointed high commissioner for the whole of Africa south of the Sahara, supported Vichy. At first Boisson had hesitated, but on 4 July he gave the order to adhere to the armistice and forbade all attempts "to constitute on this territory any illegal representative organs", i.e. to take up contacts with Free France.[3] But in Lagos General de Gaulle managed, by means of a special mission under Plévan and Larminat, to win over Cameroun and Equatorial Africa. The Guianese governor of Tchad, Eboué, whom Georges Mandel had transferred from Guadeloupe to Africa in November 1938, played a laudable role, for he decided in favour of de Gaulle early on and thus made it easier for Free France to gain a foothold in Africa. Soon after, he was appointed governor-general and in years to come he was, no doubt rightly, celebrated as the representative of a successful French policy of assimilation.[4]

We do not propose to describe in detail the reconquest of the colonial Empire. The first action, the attempt to rally French West Africa by a British naval attack on Dakar, failed owing to Boisson's resistance, and he was able to hold the seat of his office. The occupation of Syria and Lebanon by British and French troops followed in June 1941, and General Catroux took over the administration in the name of Free France. In May 1942 Britain attacked Madagascar, followed in November by the Allied landing in North Africa. Indochina, however, remained under Japanese control until 1945.

At the same time that Free France was relying heavily on the colonial Empire for support in its attempts to regain the metropolis, nationalist aspirations in the colonies were becoming more pronounced. The collapse of the ruling power without a struggle, combined with the barrage of anti-colonial propaganda launched by the enemy as well as by the Allies, served to undermine its authority. Economic problems in the colonies made it easier for the nationalist organizations to rally the masses and the time seemed ripe for presenting their demands, or even imposing them by force. France had ceased for the most part to be a consumer and supplier of goods and it was becoming increasingly more difficult to find a market for colonial products. Prices were rising and there was the problem of the black market. In the areas that had been recovered by Great Britain, a market for colonial products could be guaranteed only if prices were lowered—French prices before the war had been above the world market level. The reduction of prices would affect colonial producers. Forced production, sometimes by authoritarian measures, and the lack of import goods created additional problems.[5] The nationalist movements tried to exploit this situation and, instead of assimilative reforms such as easier naturalization, freedom of the press, franchise or equal social legislation, or better native representation in the administration, leaders in Syria and Indochina, in the North African protectorates, and even in Algeria raised a unanimous and resolute demand for independence. Ferhat Abbas' Algerian Manifesto of February 1943 exemplifies this trend.

Was General de Gaulle's Free France willing to meet these extensive demands? How did it envisage the future?

Before going into this, we should make a few comments on the Vichy Government's colonial policy. To this day it is still overshadowed by the general discussion and has not yet been appraised objectively. It is too easy to characterize Vichy policy as one of racial discrimination and ruthless exploitation of native labour in contrast to Free France's policy of generous reforms. It is undeniable that the colonial policy was dominated by the conservative tendencies that characterized the Vichy system as a whole and that there were no real innovations. The Vichy régime, however, was under pressure from Allied propaganda, had few means of asserting itself and was therefore forced to make some concessions. In April 1941 General Dentz promised the Syrian nationalists, who had organized strikes and demonstrations, independence after the war and granted them a cabinet with a prime minister and consultative assemblies. In Indochina the much-abused Admiral Decoux skilfully managed to maintain a semblance of French authority although Japanese troops had already entered and the Japanese embassy and secret police had established contact with the nationalists and were agitating against France. On the one hand Decoux supervised and persecuted the nationalists, but on the other he also promoted "local patriotism", tried to ensure the prestige of Emperor Bao Dai and accepted an increased number of Annamites into the administration.[6] In Algeria, by contrast, the administration surrendered to the traditional anti-semitism of the settlers and repealed the Loi Creminaux of 1870 which nationalized Algerian Jews; nationalist opposition was suppressed and bided its time. In Black Africa racial discrimination also increased, as demonstrated by the dissolution of the colonial council and the elected municipal councils of the Four Communes.[7] On the other hand, in August 1941 High Commissioner Boisson issued administrative orders which resembled similar pronouncements between the wars and can be compared to those of Eboué.[8]

Little political writing appeared at the time. Marshal Pétain wrote a foreword, in the form of a letter, to *L'Empire français de demain*, published in 1943,[9] of which the dominant accents are anti-semitism and polemics against foreigners in the colonies and against the Popular Front government.[10] Naturally Pétain objected to assimilation because it would either reduce the metropolitan French colonists to a minority, or would at least result in breaking the promises that had been made to them. The term "French citizen" could apply only to a Frenchman, not to an African or Asian, he said. The book considered establishing a system of imperial civil rights to be granted individually to a loyal élite that would also obtain wider representation in "mixed bodies" in the respective colonies. The author concentrated on Africa believing, like Guernier, that the continent was destined "to become the chief field of exploitation and expansion in Europe".[11]

René Maunier deserves further mention. A member of the Colonial Academy and of the international Colonial Institute, he published his *L'Empire français, propos et projets* in 1943.[12] In it he mentioned the colonial peoples' desire for emancipation, but dismissed it as "a dream . . . for tomorrow".[13] He was not concerned with conciliating or channelling national aspirations by means of concessions or reforms. To his mind "Empire" meant the extended French nation, a French state of a hundred million inhabitants, "citizens or subjects, but all French by law". With this empty phrase he put aside the old dispute about naturalization and the problem of the demarcation between "citizen" and "subject".[14] Maunier also described the Empire as "a community, a collective organism, a living being", which already existed in fact and should now be given a legal framework. He considered it necessary to "declare the unity of the French Empire by publicly and solemnly proclaiming in the Constitution that the national territory, and hence the French State, is the French Empire, apart from the protectorates".[15] Civil rights, taxation, mining and land rights should be centralized. This was not, he said, a question of assimilation and it was ridiculous to create "grotesque caricatures" of French conditions and to organize elections on the French pattern. Maunier agreed to certain reforms, including a relaxation of the *indigénat*, and wanted to make naturalization possible but only on condition "that they should fully understand that to be Frenchmen is to live as Frenchmen, to adopt our customs and to obey our laws". Instead of domination this would lead to an association of which the natives would approve, "acquiring a taste for it and accepting it deliberately". Like Paillard, Maunier had a "vision of a Eurafrica", a more or less autarchic large-scale economy. There was no lack of references to Dr Wagemann, Dr Funk and Dr Ley![16]

Paillard and Maunier adopted and elaborated the theses of the conservative and colonialist political writers between the wars. The integration of the colonies that they postulated did not correspond to political assimilation of the natives, which meant that integration would primarily benefit the French colonials and would facilitate the economic exploitation of Africa. They did not contemplate liberal reforms and clearly supported the Vichy rulers' attitude. The only fairly new idea was that the integration of the colonies should be reflected in their constitutions. This was done in a draft constitution proposed by the Vichy régime; but basically it merely "legalized" the existing situation.[17]

While Vichy largely succeeded in avoiding losing the French colonies to the Axis powers and superficially at least ensured the continuity of its rule, Brazzaville became the capital of Free France. Here, on 27 October 1940, de Gaulle personally announced the formation of a "Conseil de Défense de l'Empire". Since Vichy was collaborating with the enemy, de Gaulle said he was the legitimate government of France and would negotiate questions regarding overseas France with the foreign powers. Members of the council included Catroux, Muselier, Larminat, Eboué, d'Argenlieu and Leclerc. De Gaulle created a high commission for the colonies which he entrusted first to Leclerc, then to Larminat. The new governor-general of French Equatorial Africa, Eboué, was given the task of issuing directives for the administration, thus creating the basis for a Free French colonial doctrine.

In November 1941 Eboué summoned a conference of fifty governors, administrators, missionaries and specialists and presented his report, *La nouvelle politique indigène pour l'Afrique équatoriale française*. After three days' debate the report was accepted in its essentials and went to the colonial administration as a circular.[18] It is worth noting that the unrest among the *évolués*, who were claiming full civil rights and no longer paying their taxes, was at least one of the motives for the conference and for Eboué's pronouncements, which were to be of importance for the future.[19] In line with Free France's at least verbally expressed desire for reform, Eboué used the term "revolution" in his opening address. French Equatorial Africa, he said, was fighting for its life: there was a lack of trained staff and necessary material and the native peoples were in a state of crisis; in certain areas the native population was actually decreasing, partly as a result of the economic policy and the migratory movements, partly because African society had lost its traditional cadre and was "disintegrating and dispersing". Economic development was not possible, however, without a strong and healthy population;

if necessary one should even consider the importation of foreign labour! Eboué took a strong stand against assimilation and direct administration:

> to make or remake a society, if not in our image, at least according to our habits of mind, is to proceed towards certain defeat. The native has customs, laws, a fatherland [!] which are not ours. We will not make him happy either on the principles of the French Revolution or by substituting our officials for his chiefs, for our officials will think for him but not in him.[20]

Traditional African society with its indigenous institutions held and formed the native. His land and his tribe were his "fatherland", without which he could not flourish or develop. African common law should be applied as far as possible, and in questions of civil law the natives should also decide for themselves: "They will do so much better than us." On the basis of his experiences in Ubangi, Eboué rejected the thesis that intervention in African practices was necessary to prevent abuses in legal practice, etc. These abuses were not so very reprehensible and there were counter-forces at work. So: "We shall remain extremely discreet legislators . . . Africa must keep, and perfect, an African law."[21] Chiefs were still being arbitrarily appointed and deposed, although there was no great choice available, for "the chief pre-exists"! The traditional authorities should not be treated as officials but as an aristocracy that deserved respect; "so I condemn any tendency to standardize the chiefs".

Eboué's actions and instructions were striking but not really original. They followed a line leading from Van Vollenhoven to Boisson and showed the influence of British indirect rule, although Eboué did not want to give the native chiefs their own treasuries and was less concerned with tribal and state structures than with the individual African. His theses also had a decidedly conservative accent in curious contrast to the British discussion taking place at the same time. Eboué wanted an administration that would function with the help of the chiefs and notables, even propagating this as a "revolutionary" new departure, at a time when Britain was already turning away from indirect rule and had resolved to rely more on the *évolués*.[22] Eboué was aware of the fact that the traditional authorities alone were no longer adequate and that a class of natives was emerging, particularly in the towns, that stood outside the tribal order and was heavily influenced by the colonial power. He accused the Europeans of distrusting the *évolués* instead of accepting them and training them to become self-sufficient. He wanted to overcome the citizen-subject alternative and to turn the attention of the native to the affairs of his own country:

> Instead of the vague and misconceived conceptions which appear to associate certain natives to the Government of the whole of France or the

whole of the Empire, we will take pains, without demagogy and with the certainty of doing right, to transform them first into excellent citizens of their own country.[23]

This aim was to be achieved by a "political statute of the *évolués*" by which the administration of the towns that stood outside native law could be transferred to Africans. Belgian policy in the neighbouring Congo no doubt influenced these ideas.

Eboué tried to put his theses into practice. Apart from setting up schools and a labour bureau, he created the new legal status of the *notable évolué* (29 July 1942) and the first "native communes".[24] But Eboué did not concern himself with the political future—which admittedly was not really the affair of the governor. Although he himself was a product of this policy of assimilation, he did not consider naturalization, in the sense of the acquisition of full civil rights and franchise to the French parliament, urgent, and was more concerned with cultural and political emancipation in the local sphere, including a rapid improvement of the educational system. Evidently Eboué was aiming at autonomous African territories within a greater French whole, although he did not go into further details. Nevertheless, the Guianese governor-general's circular had considerable effect and influenced preparations for the constitution of the French Union in 1946.

The invasion of North Africa in November 1942 and the formation in Algiers on 3 June 1943 of the "Comite National Français de la Libération Nationale" seemed to make it possible, if not necessary, to establish guide-lines for a post-war colonial policy. The *évolués* had begun to agitate, while at the same time the United States was urging that the colonies should be put under international control and was directing its anti-colonialist attacks with particular vehemence against France. In this rather critical situation, Free France tried to demonstrate the integral unity of the "Empire", to assert itself as a great power and to refute these attacks announcing reforms.[25] General de Gaulle realized the need for such reforms, and in autumn 1943 he instructed the commissioner for colonies, René Pleven, to set up a commission; at the same time the overseas committee of the consultative assembly of the Socialists summoned P. O. Lapie to submit a report. On 13 January 1944 the assembly briefly debated and then accepted the report.[26] Lapie had previously acted as governor of Tchad and had put Eboué's directives into effect in his administrative instructions; de Gaulle read these and is said to have been impressed by Lapie's plans for federation.[27]

Two weeks later the second colonial conference met in Brazzaville (30 January to 8 February 1944). Under the chairmanship of Pleven, eighteen governors, technical experts, advisers from Tunisia and Morocco and deputies of the "parliament" took part. General de Gaulle underlined the representative nature of the conference by flying via Dakar to

Brazzaville in several stages with "deliberate solemnity".[28] In his opening statement he spoke of the "immense events which are overwhelming the world", recalled France's civilizing mission and stressed the need to "establish on new bases the conditions for the economic development of our Africa" and the "imperial power's" duty to settle its relationships anew with the overseas territories. The natives should participate in the administration of their territory, and the territories should be "integrated into the French community".[29] Here de Gaulle brought into play the notion of the "Community" and indicated, though in very vague terms, his own colonial concept: a certain autonomy within Greater France.

Here we shall devote our attention only to the conclusions reached by the conference, beginning with its economic, social and political recommendations. The governors assembled in Brazzaville naturally referred to Eboué's circular, but paid more attention to the dynamic element than their African colleagues had done. The younger generation, so they said, was in opposition to the older one and must be attended to, for "it is they whom we must not disappoint because they represent the positive element, the chief motivating element".[30] In contrast to Eboué, the conference stressed the need to modernize and regularize African common law in certain critical questions—the position of women, the dowry, polygamy. It also recommended "constant intervention by the Administration" in the administration of justice. A uniform penal code was to be prepared for the whole of French Africa. Particular attention was paid to the improvement of the educational system, which was to be based on large-scale planning, the building of schools and a scheme for rapidly training teachers. An academy of medicine was to be created in Africa on the model of that of Hanoi, but there were still no plans for an African university. The racial reforms envisaged sound rather modest; as a result of the war effort, the large-scale exploitation of African resources and labour took precedence over all else. The *indigénat* was to be gradually abolished; forced labour would remain until after the war. The conference even recommended that compulsory labour be substituted for compulsory military service, on the controversial model of Madagascar! It supported industrialization, but rather hesitantly. Tariff rates were to be brought more closely in line with the interests of the individual colonies, but the primary aim was to be an imperial economic policy directed from Paris and primarily addressed to the requirements of the mother country. Unlike Eboué, or perhaps in spite of Eboué, the majority of governors were pro-assimilation. This was evident in the emphatic demand that teaching should be conducted entirely in the French tongue and the use of the vernacular should be "absolutely" forbidden. It was also evident in the general aims of native policy:

> So the main problem consisted in seeking the surest methods of promoting the evolution of these native masses in the sense of an assimilation

conforming more and more closely to the principles that constitute the common basis of French civilization.³¹

Once again tradition proved stronger than all opposing tendencies, and again the fundamental distinctions between the French and British concepts became clear! Even in its political recommendations and ideas, the Brazzaville conference remained in the "imperial tradition" of the inter-war years, wanting to integrate the colonies "definitively" into the French state by means of a comprehensive general ruling. The question was not of future secession but rather the opposite—decolonization and integration. What de Gaulle had already indicated by the term "Community" was elaborated by Pleven in his opening speech:

> From time to time we read that this war must end by what is called a liberation of the colonial peoples [another reference to the anti-colonialism of the United States]. In the great colonial France there are no peoples to liberate and there is no racial discrimination to abolish [!]. There are people who feel French and who want to take and whom France wants to give a greater and greater part in the life and democratic institutions of the French community. There are people whom we intend to lead, step by step, towards the acquisition of their own personality, in the case of the more mature populations, towards political franchises, but who do not want to know of any other independence than the independence of France.³²

These words contained both the practical recommendations of the conference and the general programme and problems of French colonial policy immediately after the Second World War. France felt it necessary to reply to anti-colonial pronouncements and, unlike before 1939, to prove its desire for decolonization. At the same time, it was hypocritically declaring that there were no people under French rule who had to be liberated or wanted to be liberated, because they all felt French and wanted to remain French.³³ Although the demand for independence could be heard everywhere, national aspirations were not taken seriously—Pleven's words recall Sarraut's phrase that "independence terrifies them". The demand for emancipation was ascribed to individuals alone; there were no people who wanted to be liberated, at most there were certain individuals who claimed equal rights and liberties. But France, thought Pleven, either had already granted this kind of liberty or would eventually concede it within the French Community and thus bring decolonization to a conclusion. Liberty, in the sense of national liberty, i.e. liberty outside France and with sovereign rights, was out of the question. Only France as a whole could be independent, i.e. the possessor of sovereignty. A decisive and much-quoted passage, which became the basis of all further political proposals for reform, was unusually frank:

> The aims of the civilizing work accomplished by France in the colonies are distinct from any idea of autonomy, any possibility of evolution outside the bloc of the French Empire: the eventual, or even ultimate [!] constitution of self-government in the colonies must be avoided.[34]

The rare use of the English word "self-government" in French political writing shows, characteristically, that there was no equivalent term in French and that the Brazzaville conference expressly dissociated itself from the British policy.[35] Whatever reforms or political liberties France conceded could be granted only within the framework of the French state extended overseas! So colonial autonomy and native participation were not meant as a preliminary step towards full self-government in the British sense, but merely as an extended form of administrative decentralization.

> We want the political power of France to be exercised with precision and rigour in all the territories of its Empire. We also want the colonies to enjoy great administrative and economic freedom. We also want the colonial peoples to feel this freedom themselves and want their sense of responsibility gradually to be formed and trained so that they shall become associated in the administration of the common weal in their country.[36]

This "great administrative freedom" also applied to the colony proper, although the governors were thinking of an extension of their own sphere of influence rather than "African autonomy". The Africans would, so to speak, indirectly enjoy their "freedom" and "responsibility"; they were only "associated" in the administration of their territory.

> The attributions ... of the Assemblies would be deliberative, for the budget vote and the establishment of programmes for new works, consultative in all matters pertaining to legislative powers or rulings vested in the governor.[37]

This administrative autonomy was to be settled on an entirely new basis, by the creation of "representative assemblies" in the respective territories, with a very wide franchise for the Africans but separate electoral colleges for French and natives.

The African deputies were to obtain a voice in budgetary matters and an effective share in the administration. But legislative powers remained vested in Paris, and the governor would continue to have exclusive executive powers. The natives were to be guaranteed greater access to official posts—we recall this demand from the inter-war years—although at the same time it was stressed that "the cadres of command and direction can only admit French citizens".[38] This did not exclude the Africans—as long as they were naturalized and gave up their personal status—but it made it clear that France was not willing to surrender any of its powers and in fact granted little more than administrative decentralization in the departments. This small degree of political self-government corresponded to colonial representation in the parliament of the mother country, in accordance with the liberal French conception. What was the Brazzaville conference's view of this issue?

First the conference recommended colonial representation in the constitutional assembly. The new constitution, unlike the pre-1875 one, would have to include overseas France, which added to the desire to prove the indivisible unity of Greater France and led to the demand for the representation of all the colonies in the constitutional assembly. For the first time it was established that the colonies would have a part in deciding the constitution of the mother country—and not only French citizens, but the native population too! This representation should be "adequate to the importance of the colonies in the French community", a phrase which sounded "liberal" but in fact meant that the number of overseas deputies was fixed arbitrarily and was not in proportion to the population, as was the case in the metropolis. This led to problems which were to seriously affect the resulting 1946 constitution.

Opinions were divided as to whether this new interpretation also meant colonial representation in the French parliament. The final resolution of the conference made it clear that a mere rise in the number of deputies was not a satisfactory solution; it was better to have a "colonial parliament, or preferably a federal assembly". The duty of this assembly would be to reconcile the indivisible unity of the "French world" with the "local liberty of each of the territories". The very important issue of the distribution of authority between the Paris parliament, the federal assembly and the territories themselves was left until later. Colonial federalism appeared here for the first time in an "official" document, but not all the members of the conference were in favour of it; one of the governors remarked that in a one and indivisible Republic only an increased representation in parliament was admissible.[39] Laurentie, the future director of political affairs in the overseas ministry, opposed this integrationist view by saying, with some right, that the colonies would obtain only minority representation in the future parliament—only forty to fifty deputies had been mentioned for a constituency of some five hundred—and added that this would disappoint them. Proportional representation, which would lead to a shift in the balance of power and perhaps even to metropolitan France being outvoted, was out of the question. In the past the issue had been more or less ignored and France had not realized the consequences of a consistent policy of integration and assimilation. But now, when more far-reaching reforms were under discussion, the problem could no longer be avoided.

"Federal representation" appeared to present some kind of a solution to the growing dilemma. But was this really federalism? The Brazzaville conference took it for granted that the federal assemblies would be consultative only.[40] The characteristic vagueness of the French about the meaning of federalism is apparent in the vote of a governor who described assimilation as a specifically French concept and urged a "policy of assimilation", although of a weaker and less uniform kind, "tending towards the idea of federation"! In practical terms he postulated administrative decentralization, which he presented as federalism.[41] But true federation would have had to consist of a distribution of sovereignty between the federation and its members and equal rights for the metropolis and the colonies within a super-ordinate Whole—which would take charge of foreign policy, defence, currency and overall economic policy. Such a concept would have had far-reaching consequences that were irreconcilable with the one and indivisible Republic and could hardly hope to settle the relations between mother country and colonies.

The main tendencies of the Brazzaville recommendations were clear: a genuine desire to re-establish ties between the mother country and the colonies, but no grant of self-government, not even as an ultimate aim; administrative autonomy for each territory, the introduction of franchise for the natives, representation in the constituent assembly and, on the other hand, the creation of an assembly for overseas France. This anticipated the constitutional decisions of the Fourth Republic on Black Africa. It also predicted future problems, specifically the question of the importance of the federal element. Could the territories have a "political personality" if their authority was restricted to a vague budget right and basically extended no further than administrative decentralization? Was France really prepared to give up its former policy of depoliticization and to surrender to the natives a part of the political decision-making? Where would the evolution of the actual constitution lead? Either the local assemblies would remain ineffectual, in which case the *évolués* would not be satisfied, or they would gain political power and would become a basis for future parliaments, in which case conflict with the indivisible Republic and with the mother country, which reserved itself sovereign rights, would become inevitable.

It is worth noting that the natives had no part in this important conference. Governors, parliamentary deputies and experts tried to lay down a post-war policy and to prepare reforms, but without negotiating with spokesmen for the natives or even consulting them. The difference with the British attitude is striking and was based on the divergence of basic concepts. London worked through commissions in which the natives collaborated, and even if the colonial administration had the ultimate power of decision, it attempted to make decisions by consensus and avoided merely dictating. Characteristically Brazzaville repeatedly praised the glorious French colonial tradition and recalled the names of Brazza, Galliéni and Lyautey. The Brazzaville conference was chiefly concerned with the constitution of the mother country, while analogous conferences or commissions in Britain prepared reforms for the individual colonies. The British colonies had their own constitutions which led gradually towards self-government, while the legal status of the French territories or colonies derived from the French constitution.

No great attention was paid to the rather important question of whether the native élite agreed to the plans for its future that were being prepared in Brazzaville and whether it would be satisfied with administrative decentralization and a voice in budget affairs. Nevertheless the new order that was being discussed was intended not as a transitional solution, but a more or less final ruling which did not provide for any further development. Even in issues regarding Black Africa the consent of the *évolués* was taken for granted and in any case not considered decisive. In fact the *évolués* greeted the Brazzaville conference as a hopeful beginning to decolonization, and even among the natives there was some approval of integration into Greater France and even cultural assimilation.[42] Among the opposition was Fily Dabo Sissoko, himself a product of assimilation and an outstanding authority on French cultural history. In the report he presented to the conference; Sissoko stated that while integration and assimilation had been right for the *vieilles colonies*, this policy was impossible for Africa; the number of natives alone was an obstacle and a legally ratified policy of assimilation would constitute a "peril for the colonizer". In addition he thought the differences in the levels of civilization too great and stressed the danger that this policy would separate the élite from the masses.[43]

Sissoko said nothing about political issues, but presumably tacitly at least he was against the Brazzaville recommendations, particularly the proposal that school instruction should be exclusively in French. The same applies to Senghor, who had been an officer in the French army and a prisoner-of-war in Germany. Even before Brazzaville Senghor had expressed his views in a contribution to a book with the informative title *Communauté impériale française*.[44] He outlined the ambivalence of assimilation and association and tried to transcend this antinomy with his much-quoted formula "to assimilate, not to be assimilated". He thought cultural contact with the colonial occupation should be viewed as an opportunity for the autochthonous civilization to assimilate what it found most useful. Senghor objected to proportional representation in the French parliament because he realized the impossibility of "drowning [!] the representatives of metropolitan France in some Bourbon palace under the waves of colonial deputies who would be supported by seventy million individuals". Instead he suggested a form of imperial citizenship, which would make it possible on the one hand to set up legislative bodies in the individual colonial territories (Antilles, French West Africa, North Africa, etc.) and on the other hand to elect representatives to a "federal parliament" responsible for foreign policy, defence, etc. This would ensure the "unity of the Empire" within a community that had its own spiritual content and yet embraced the different civilizations.[45] This system outlined by Senghor bore some resemblance to the Brazzaville proposals but went beyond them: the individual colonies were to receive both administrative decentralization and political autonomy, while the "imperial parliament" would have both an advisory function and sovereign powers. We shall see that France was not prepared for this kind of federalism.

We do not want to deny the importance of the Brazzaville conference in any way, for it did prove Free France's desire for reforms and established the basic guide-lines for French colonial discussion between 1944 and 1946.

Although Black Africa's war effort had been forcibly encouraged in every possible way in order to strengthen France's position among the Allies, putting the African inhabitants under a great strain, a series of new laws gave evidence of Brazzaville's reforming influence. On 1 April 1944 the *corvée* and taxation in kind were abolished throughout Black Africa; in July a uniform penal code was established; and in August France authorized the formation of professional unions. A conference in Dakar was also engaged in working out a large-scale educational programme which planned fifty thousand primary schools, two hundred upper primary schools and seventy-five *écoles normales*, in order to train fifty thousand teachers.[46]

The Brazzaville conference was intended to be a general colonial conference but it devoted its main attention to Black Africa and dealt neither with the problems of North Africa nor with those of Indochina. We should now examine, what were Free France's and General de Gaulle's reactions to the emancipation movements in the Arab and Far Eastern territories and the plans for the new relationship between the colonies and the mother country after the war.

As we have shown, Vichy had already promised Syria and Lebanon independence after the war. On the entry of British-French troops in June 1941 Catroux declared:

> I have just put an end to the régime of the mandate and proclaimed you free and independent. Henceforth you shall therefore be sovereign and independent peoples . . . your independence and your sovereign status will be guaranteed by a treaty which will define our mutual relations.[47]

Free France gave in to British pressure and proclaimed the independence of both countries in September and November; yet in the treaty it tried to restrict the meaning of independence and to gain a privileged position for France. In August 1943, after the electoral victory of the national candidates, the Lebanese Government demanded full sovereignty and independently altered its constitution, whereupon the French high commissioner repealed it and arrested the government. French hopes of negotiating treaties on the model of the 1930 British-Iraqi agreement proved deceptive, largely because of the opposition of the Allies and the Arab movement. The opportunity missed before 1939 could no longer be made up in 1944, it proved too late to repeal an independence that had already been proclaimed and France lost the chance of making use of the strong sympathy and cultural ties between the mother country and the Syrian and Lebanese upper classes.

Provisions for independence were not yet under discussion in North Africa.[48] After the occupation of Tunisia in May 1943 the bey was arrested and then deposed, admittedly at the instigation of General Giraud. More important than the accusation of collaboration with the Axis powers seems to have been the charge that during the Vichy régime [!] Moncef Bey had presumed to set up the Chénik cabinet without the consent of the resident-general! On his arrival in Tunis on 27 June 1943, de Gaulle declared:

> We must organize in the empire, on a larger and more fair basis, a collaboration between the sovereign power and the loyal millions whom it is its duty to guide.[49]

What this was supposed to mean was unclear, especially since the direct administration was being substantiated by means of decrees (July 1943 to March 1944) which transferred the bey's powers to the French administration. In September 1945 France replied to the Tunisian nationalists led by Bourguiba and the union leader Ferhat Hached by instituting a few minor reforms. In August 1946 the members of a national congress in Tunis, whose motto was independence, were arrested. The result was a three-day general strike. A few reforms in the economic and social sphere naturally did not satisfy the nationalists.

In Morocco the appointment of Gabriel Puaux as resident-general was sufficient indication of the conservative course. On 11 January 1944 the Istiqlal ("Independence") party handed the sultan, the representative of France and the Allied authorities, a manifesto which became very important for the future. It refused the protectorate and demanded independence. Morocco, it said, was indeed dependent on French aid in administration, economy, and defence, but the "collaboration" must be on the basis of independence. Puaux preferred repression to collaboration and he arrested the political leaders. The social and economic reforms of 1944, which as in Tunisia showed a tendency to depoliticization, did not accomplish their aim of neutralizing the opposition.

The Algerian situation was more complex. Shortly after the Allied landing on 22 December 1942, Ferhat Abbas addressed a message to the "responsible authority", i.e. to the Americans and French, requesting a conference on political reforms. When he received no reply he published the famous *Manifeste du peuple algérien* on 10 February 1943.

In it Ferhat Abbas did not repudiate French culture or the French tradition of liberty, but attacked assimilation. "Applied automatically to some and refused to others [it] has reduced Muslim society to the most complete servitude." Land had been confiscated and every kind of discrimination was practised against the Arabs. Administration, army and press were in the hands of the European minority. Now the oppressed majority was demanding its "place in the sun". A new policy had become urgently necessary, for "the time has passed when a Muslim Algerian will demand anything but to be a Muslim Algerian". This demand implied self-determination and an Algerian constitution on the basis of universal franchise. A slightly milder addition to the manifesto spoke of Algeria's political autonomy "as a sovereign nation", but did not prevent France from retaining a degree of control, to be determined later. Today we can see how the Algerian manifesto led to later conflict, for Ferhat Abbas, who until the war had supported a more moderate policy of assimilation, now began to speak of an "Algerian nation".[50] This was a new development in the question of relations between the Arab majority and the European minority and it meant that the idea of Algeria as an integral part of the national territory had come into dispute. This "national" claim made it impossible for Catroux, who on the whole was ready to institute reform, to accept the manifesto as a basis for discussion. On 22 September 1943, the elected Muslims in the financial delegations refused to take part in its sessions, provoking Catroux to dissolve the Muslim section and to arrest its president, Ferhat Abbas.

The unrest in Algeria required some kind of initiative from France. Following the advice of Catroux, on 22 September 1943 General de Gaulle spoke in Constantine of the need for reforms and announced the conferment of civil rights on certain categories of Muslims, without renunciation of their personal status. An ordinance on 7 May confirmed this promise: all the other "Muslim Frenchmen" would receive equal rights with Frenchmen without becoming "citizens".[51] Special taxation, the *indigénat*, etc. were abolished. Universal franchise was introduced, though in a restricted form, with the establishment of separate electoral colleges: in the one, the new Muslim citizens (some 60,000, mainly notables, officials, decorated veterans, etc.) would vote together with the c. 450,000 non-Muslims; in the other, the remaining c. 1,600,000 Algerians. The second electoral college obtained a right to two-fifths of the seats in the financial delegations and the communal bodies. In comparison to the pre-war policy and considering the violent resistance on the part of the French Algerians, these were very extensive reforms. France had finally accepted naturalization with personal status, thus opening the road to a great increase in the number of full Muslim citizens. In effect, this was simply a realization of the Blum-Viollette bill. And even though all the Algerians had equal rights under the administration and obtained franchise, the additional resolution on separate electoral colleges ensured the continued predominance of the French Algerians. They had a majority in the first college, could "neutralize" the Muslim citizens and retained control of the financial delegations.

Moreover, the March 1944 reforms were still based on the concept of assimilation, making it possible to continue on the basis of liberal projects begun in the inter-war years. At the same time, the difficulties and limitations of assimilation became obvious, for if pursued consistently it would jeopardize the position of the settlers and have very far-reaching results, particularly with regard to the parliament in Paris. For quite understandable reasons France was not prepared to accept the consequences of its policy, which was why it took refuge in special resolutions that engendered distrust and opposition among the Muslims.

In any case the nationalists had already made claims that went beyond assimilation and demanded internal autonomy, if not independence. Ferhat Abbas had good contacts with the other nationalist organizations, including Massali Hadj. In March 1944 he formed the new party "Les Amis du Manifeste et de la Liberté," which demanded a "republic federated to the French Republic, renovated, anti-colonial and anti-imperialist". In short, the reforms introduced by General de Gaulle and the demands of Ferhat Abbas were based on entirely different premises and had opposite aims!

The events in Sétif contributed to alienating Algeria from France. During the victory celebrations on 8 May 1945, in an atmosphere of increasing tension between Muslims and Europeans, the forces of law and order took measures to suppress a nationalist demonstration. The Algerians, who were in any case restless due to their economic difficulties, retaliated with bloody reprisals against the French settlers.[52] The administration took military action which resulted in several thousand dead, and then dissolved the new party and arrested Ferhat Abbas. The French Algerians welcomed the repression and the temporary elimination of the opposition, the mother country considered the severe action necessary and even the Communists approved of the brutal measures to quell the alleged "fascist plot".

These brief indications are intended to recall the situation in North Africa between 1942 and 1946. General de Gaulle's Free France wanted to appear ready for reform, but in fact it developed no clear programme for a post-war policy. Nor is there any evidence of previous discussion or planning. France was on the defensive *vis-à-vis* its allies and the Arab nationalist movement. Its reform policy was hampered by the need to maintain its imperial positions and to defend the integrity of the national territory. Neither before nor shortly after the Allied landing in North Africa was there any programmatic declaration to calm the nationalists and create a basis of trust for negotiations. The speech in Constantine was, it must not be forgotten, an answer to the Algerian manifesto and the nationalist demonstrations. The reforms that were introduced continued along the lines of pre-war efforts or avoided the economic and social spheres. Even in the protectorates of Tunisia and Morocco, French policy aimed neither at internal autonomy nor at self-government, not to mention independence. Here too it remained based on the idea of "indissoluble ties" with France, which led to conflicts with the national emancipation movement. Since the nationalists now, as opposed to before the war, openly demanded independence or at least the right to independence, they obviously appeared as secessionists and agitators and were forcibly repressed.

While at Brazzaville Free France was discussing the future of Africa and the position of the colonies within a new constitution and trying to deal with these problems after the Allied landing in North Africa by announcing a "reconstruction of the Empire", the Resistance organizations in the metropolis concerned themselves remarkably little with the future of the colonies. This was not due to lack of time or opportunity, for there was intensive discussion of institutional, economic, social and political issues. But unlike Free France in London and Algiers, which gained support in the Empire from the outset and could not avoid practical colonial questions, the internal Resistance concentrated on reconstruction of the mother country.[53] Although the left wing dominated in the Resistance and there was much talk of structural reforms, any comments on future colonial policy had a traditional and national accent. People stressed the civilizational achievements of the past and the "loyalty" of the natives in the moment of crisis; they attacked Vichy's policy of "surrender"—with regard to Indochina!—and stressed the importance of the overseas possessions for France's position as a world power. In the name of a "France of a hundred million inhabitants" they supported intensive settlement, even in Tunisia and Morocco! Politically, they supported integration, native access to the administration, social reforms and a certain local autonomy, but all within Greater France. Colonial representation in parliament was to be extended, which seemed to be a "progressive" attitude. Like the Brazzaville conference, the Resistance utterly rejected the concept of self-government or even national self-determination, without asking itself whether this integration could have a satisfactory constitutional solution and would satisfy the colonial peoples' desire for emancipation.

There was lively discussion in the political writings of Free France and liberated France between 1944 and 1945 on future institutional ties between the mother country and the colonies. But the consultative assembly in Algeria scarcely devoted any time to the question. Its debate on 13 January 1944, shortly before Brazzaville, was decidedly inadequate. The federal plans that emerged in this discussion concern us more here. We have already mentioned the Socialist P. O. Lapie, who in his report to the consultative assembly and in articles in the press[54] was one of the first to actively support federal decolonization. A self-confessed "disciple" of Eboué's, Lapie abandoned assimilation and considered it the duty of France "to create a Fatherland for the natives which will one day take its place in the concert of nations".[55] He was, it seems, the only French speaker to accept the right to self-determination and the possibility of future dissociation. As a basis for this, and also in order to create an acceptable relationship between the colonies and France, he suggested federation. According to his proposals this federation was to embrace colonies and protectorates alike and to have its own parliament and its own government. He added, however, that France would "rule", since France would have sovereign powers within the federation in such matters as foreign policy, defence, high court justice, etc.[56] Here lay the difficulty of the French concept of federalism. For how could France continue to exercise certain sovereign rights within a federation? And how could one speak of federation if the mother country did not want to "merge" in the great union and would not or could not surrender its decisive powers?

We have seen how the federal plan was discussed in Brazzaville and was accepted in the final resolution. René Pleven had already spoken of federation in the consultative assembly when on 13 January he declared emphatically: "The hour has come to expose, to probe in depth the federal concept." Yet, obviously unaware of any contradiction, he openly supported integration and assimilation at the Brazzaville conference! General de Gaulle also used the federal formula at a press conference in Washington on 10 July 1944: "I believe that each territory under the French flag must be represented within a system of a federal kind of which the metropolis shall be a part and where the interests of each individual shall be heard."[57] The federal thesis was also a way of countering American criticism and of announcing a programme of decolonization without giving up the concept of Greater France. But in practical terms it proved impossible to square the circle: either the federation was "genuine" and the metropolis "merged" in it, or France insisted on its position as leader and the federation would become more or less a fiction.

Paul Emile Viard's "Essai d'une organisation constitutionelle de la communauté française"[58] serves to illustrate this dilemma. Viard was dean of the faculty of law of Algiers and later an influential (Mouvement Républicain Populaire) deputy to the constituent assembly. His use of the term *Communaute,* taken from de Gaulle, was to show both the variety of colonies, protectorates and mandates with their different legal statutes, and to express the unity of the whole. The future constitution was to be based on the concept of "France as a whole", not just restricted to Metropolitan France. It was necessary now to "set up the sovereign organism of the whole of France". Comparing this with Great Britain's policy, Viard showed himself fully aware, unlike other French speakers between the wars, that in the future dominion status would also apply to those colonies that were not so by settlement. But he stressed that political independence "would seem inadmissible to the French mind", for it was based on imponderables which "our excessively logical minds would have difficulty in grasping". France, he thought, was not psychologically prepared to accept central power based anywhere but in Paris, and must remain the sovereign power. Like Pleven in Brazzaville, Viard asserted, without even mentioning the situation in North Africa and Indochina, that the natives were not even thinking of

> creating for themselves a political life independent of that of the mother country. We have no indications [!] of this kind, and I can even say that we find no serious trace of a desire to set up a system comparable to that of the dominion. . . .

Representation in parliament was an innate French concept, but complete integration, meaning equal political rights, was impossible because if the power of decision remained with the French parliament, which Viard took for granted, the imperial parliament would simply become a meaningless colonial council.

So Viard suggested an interim solution. The colonies should have a part in exercising sovereignty and be represented in the Senate. If a quarter or a third of all the seats were reserved to them it would produce a "happy equilibrium"! The colonies could participate in electing the president of the Republic, and a similar solution would be found for the protectorates and mandated territories. Extensive decentralization was also necessary, and this could be done by freeing the governor-general from the allegedly strict control of the Paris bureaucracy and allowing him to act directly as representative of the president of the Republic. But the colonial assemblies were to obtain no legislative power, and foreign policy, army, justice, higher education and the major "public services" remained with the metropolis.

This rather important "Essai" sounds a similar note to the Brazzaville proposals and anticipates certain elements of the 1946 constitution. It did not aim at a federal "Community", for in spite of granting statutory rights to the colonies, it adhered to the sovereignty of the French parliament so that the idea of colonial representation in the Senate was rather deceptive. The "fairly free local life" demanded by Viard was equally dubious, since the territories were conceded only minor powers. There was no word of franchise for the natives and their representatives; as a French Algerian, Viard was chiefly concerned with satisfying the French settlers.

Two Frenchmen who had emigrated to America outlined plans for a "genuine" federation in spring 1945.[59] On the model of the United States they proposed a "Federal Union of the French nations" consisting of five federations (of which metropolitan France would be one!), six provinces and two territories—geographically associated colonies. It would have two chambers patterned on the Senate and the House of Representatives, which would set up a federal government with its own prime minister and could decide on foreign policy, police, trade, etc. The federal language would be French. Each inhabitant would obtain two citizenships, that of his own federation and that of the Union. The authors thought that to accept the concepts of autonomy and self-government, in the sense of eventual dissociation, was to reduce France to the status of a mere European mother country, "it is to accept old age, death tomorrow". This makes it clear once again how the projects for federation were linked with the national aspirations of Free France and its claim to world power. Federation seemed to answer the need for reform and the emancipation movements without impairing the French claim to leadership. But since the authors supported complete parity for the member states, they were obliged to transfer the sovereign rights of the French parliament to the new federal chambers, in which metropolitan France would no longer have a majority. Naturally France objected, so it became necessary to seek a compromise, which would *eo ipso* have a quasi-federal character.

The federation discussion gained impetus from events in Indochina. In spite of the Japanese occupation troops and the anti-French propaganda, the French administration under Admiral Decoux managed to hold its own. The colonial power lost prestige and was undermined, but the rural population still did not really question it. Nationalist forces, however, were organizing themselves on Chinese soil under Communist leadership. In May 1941 the Independence Front of Vietnam, the Viet Minh, came into being, asserted itself as a collective national movement and proclaimed war against the French and Japanese "fascists".[60] In summer 1944 the Viet Minh began to strengthen its positions by guerrilla action in the more remote regions of Tonkin. On 9 March 1945 Japan took power after Decoux had refused an ultimatum. The following day Vietnamese independence was proclaimed; Emperor Bao Dai disavowed the 1885 protectorate agreement and began to collaborate with the Japanese. The French administration collapsed, and anti-French demonstrations, looting and persecution began. All reminders of the colonial power were removed. The Viet Minh, for their part, continued to fortify their positions, organized a liberation army, and on 13 August, two days before the Japanese capitulation, called for a general uprising. On 25 August Bao Dai abdicated, on 29 August Ho Chi Minh formed a provisional government in Hanoi and proclaimed Vietnamese independence on 2 September. The same day 200,000 Indochinese demonstrated in Saigon in the name of independence.

On 8 December 1943 General de Gaulle had declared in Algiers:

> To these peoples who have managed to affirm their national consciousness and their sense of political responsibility, France intends to give a new

political status in the heart of the French community where, in the framework of the Indochinese federal organization, the freedom of the different countries of the Union will be extended and consecrated.[61]

By this declaration Free France announced its willingness to settle the constitutional position of Indochina anew after the war and to grant the individual territories some autonomy. But for the rest the declaration, in accordance with de Gaulle's views, was fairly vague and gave no details on sovereign or native rights. Neither Algiers nor Paris concerned itself with the future status of Indochina. The problems of Black Africa and North Africa seemed more urgent at the time and in any case negotiations with the Allies and preparations for military reconquest took precedence, although no attempt was made to anticipate events by a programmatic declaration. Not until 24 March 1945 did the French government announce, in reply to the Japanese take-over and in preparation for Allied action, that

> the Indochinese federation will form, together with France and the other territories of the Community, a French Union, whose interests abroad will be represented by France. At the heart of this Union, Indochina will enjoy its own freedom.

The constituent assembly would decide on the federal organs of the Union. At the head of the Indochinese federation would stand a governor-general with French and Indochinese ministers. A council of state would obtain budget rights and be able to advise on legislation.[62]

This was the first expression of the concept of the French Union.[63] The Union would incorporate Indochina together with the metropolis and other territories of the Empire, i.e. Tunisia and Morocco. Two declarations made it clear, however, that France would remain responsible for foreign policy in the Union. Indochina's "own freedom" obviously meant a wide degree of autonomy, but the reference to the governor-general, French ministers, and the mere advisory legislative power of the council of state greatly limited this autonomy. In fact it meant clear control for the colonial power. The declaration of 24 March thus had a significance similar to the Brazzaville resolution, in as far as it was more than a general announcement. In effect, it was an attempt to provide some kind of answer to the question of Indochina's future status and its relations with France. There was to be greater autonomy in Indochina than in the colonial territories, yet the close institutional ties with France were to remain, both within the Union whose seat was in Paris and in the administration.

Again we can draw a comparison with British policy in India, Burma and Ceylon. Britain had aimed at semi-responsible government before the war, promised dominion status and was even on the point of establishing it in 1945. French concessions to Indochina sound modest by comparison, especially since they were not balanced by participation, in a form yet to be decided, in the French Union. For France was envisaging neither self-government and independence, nor true internal autonomy. The latter would have had a great effect in Indochina and might have provided a real basis for negotiations. But the declaration of 24 March lagged behind events: independence had already been announced in Hanoi on 11 March and Vietnam had been proclaimed a republic.[64]

The declaration evoked great response at home. The French pointed with satisfaction to American comments in the press stressing France's desire for decolonization but misinterpreting the March declaration.[65] The danger of trusteeship in Indochina seemed to have been averted.[66] Henri Laurentie, the former high commissioner of Equatorial Africa and current director of political affairs in the overseas ministry, spoke of a "fundamental act which decisively and in one blow transformed all the notions of French colonial justice".[67] The colonial inhabitants were in the throes of a revolution that compelled the European powers "to be resolutely anti-colonialist".[68] It required imagination to break through the former immobilism and the French Union was an acceptable concept because it opened the way both to autonomy (*particularisme*) and to complete assimilation.[69] Laurentie was very eager to institute reforms, but he presupposed collaboration from the Indochinese and consequently turned his attention chiefly to economic and social questions.[70] The director of the École coloniale and liberal expert on Africa, Robert Delavignette, adopted a similar attitude, though it led him to different conclusions. In his essay "L'Union française", in which he also referred to earlier pronouncements, he distinguished French policy from the British and spoke of an "entirely new course very different from the British Dominion". The French concept, he said, was based on the idea of civil rights, which France now granted without loss of personal status. Colonies in the old sense of the term no longer existed since the projected French Union would be a "common organism": "Tomorrow we shall all be natives of the same French Union."[71] It was an organic union that would make it possible in the future to make the loose union into a "unity".[72] Delavignette did not say how this future integration was to take place.

The political parties were also beginning to concern themselves with the French Union. The Socialist André Philip suggested a second chamber, a *Conseil supérieur de la communauté française*, with half the seats for metropolitan France and half for the colonies, that would have the power of decision in questions regarding the Union.[73] The MRP deputy François de Menthon spoke of federal representation in similar terms. He suggested a Union council that would have consultative powers and be the first step towards the "integration of the Empire into a French Union".⁷⁴ The deputy Aujoulat, a doctor from Cameroun, reported on the MRP party congress in 1945. Starting with Brazzaville and the theses of his party colleague Viard, he demanded colonial parliamentary representation combined with local assemblies. He did not question French sovereignty and described the whole as a "French community".⁷⁵

We have attempted to show how Algiers and then Paris began to concern themselves with future colonial policy between 1944 and 1945 and how they tried to establish the relationship between the mother country and the colonies on a new basis. France had become aware that pre-war institutions, concepts and attitudes could no longer put a stop to Asian and African emancipation movements. The anti-imperialist attitudes of America and Russia also forced it to re-examine its positions. But at the same time France hoped to give proof of its greatness in and through the colonial Empire and to assert its claim to world power. On 15 May 1945, a few days before the capitulation of Germany, no less than Gaston Monnerville, the native deputy from Guiana and future president of the Council of the Republic, declared in the consultative assembly: "Without the Empire France would be no more than a liberated country today. Thanks to its Empire, France is a victorious country."⁷⁶ This shows the importance that Equatorial Africa's support of General de Gaulle's Free France acquired in the newly won national consciousness.

The old dispute about assimilation or association lost its relevance now, to be replaced by new concepts such as Community, French Union, and Federation, which became the leitmotivs of French decolonization. France did not want to follow the English course and gradually grant its colonies independence, but sought a solution compatible with its traditions and aspirations. Colonialism was to be overcome by promoting the subjects to the status of full citizens and by creating political entities that would be incorporated into the new constitution of France. France proved flexible enough to try to find an order for the *vieilles colonies*, Black Africa, the North African protectorates and Indochina that suited their respective conditions, but remained within an institutionalized whole. Greater France, which hitherto had been only a postulate and an ideological view of the colonies' relations to the mother country, was now to become a reality. France would integrate the individual parts of its colonial Empire into Greater France in the name of decolonization —a form of decolonization which was allegedly based not on dependence but on equal rights and which therefore offered some hope of a solution for the future.

New problems emerged, however. A consistent policy of integration and genuine "federalism" threatened to shift the balance of power from the metropolis to the colonies, which the mother country neither could nor would accept. The result was a variety of compromise and interim solutions. And in the end it was by no means certain whether the colonial peoples, whose emancipation had been given such impetus by the Second World War, were at all willing to be incorporated into a French Union, to give up their claims to an independent state.

THE UNION FRANÇAISE

The Brazzaville conference resolved the question of colonial participation in the constituent assembly and it was not discussed further. In September 1945 the government appointed sixty-three deputies to represent the colonies. Except in the *vieilles colonies*, the representatives were elected in two colleges—citizens and non-citizens.[1] Of the sixty-three, thirty-eight were autochthonous. These thirty-eight usually adhered to the left-wing parties in the mother country, while the Algerians were represented by moderate nationalists such as Dr Bendjelloul and two Communists (Ferhat Abbas and his friends were in prison). Although the number of representatives was by no means proportional to the population, this colonial representation did emphasize liberated France's new policies. In the future the mother country and the colonies, except for Indochina, which did not take part in the assembly, were to form a unit on a parity basis. The "subjects" collaborated in working out a constitution which would eventually establish the status of the colonies too. Muslims also had a voice in the decision on "French civil status". Deschamps has compared the decision of September 1945 with that of 4 August 1789 which put an end to the feudal rule of the ancien régime.[2]

We shall not describe in detail the operation of the constituent assembly. We merely point out that the constitutional commission heard a ruling by the overseas committee under Marius Moutet in which the autochthonous deputies were strongly represented. The parties also worked out their own proposals. In addition, on 11 April 1946 the Senegalese Senghor reported to the National Assembly on those sections of the draft constitution that affected the French Union. The assembly accepted them on 19 April after lengthy discussion.[3]

From the outset it proved necessary to establish a compromise between assimilatory and federal tendencies; between legal equality of rights and strong parliamentary representation on the one hand, and a combination of local autonomy and "federal institutions" on the other. France continued to distrust genuine federation as a step towards dissociation.[4] Senghor considered the compromise successful but international lawyers pointed to its internal contradictions. France was eager to abolish the status of "subject" and to proclaim equal rights. Article 44 of the draft constitution accordingly stated: "All the nationals and French dependents of the metropolis and the overseas territories enjoy the rights of citizenship."[5] This was a significant step beyond the pre-war situation, particularly since there was now no question of the natives giving up their personal status and the policy announced in the Algeria decree of 7 March 1944 was extended to all subjects—excluding the protectorates of North Africa and Indochina, of course. This step was clearly of an assimilatory nature and consequently the assembly gave due emphasis to the conferment of citizenship: France would really become a nation of a hundred million inhabitants, it was abolishing all racial discrimination (Marius Moutet) as well as colonial imperialism. "The main effect, the capital effect of the 1946 Constitution will be the recognition of the Rights of Man and citizenship", Senghor stressed.[6] But he did not fail to point out that such a statement of principles must be linked to concrete constitutional decisions and living reality![7]

Article 41 also proclaimed the end of colonial rule: "France, together with the overseas territories on the one hand and the associated states on the other, forms a union based on free consent." The territories consisted of the colonies in Black Africa and Madagascar, while the *vieilles colonies* and Algeria counted as "overseas departments" of the metropolis. "Associated states" meant Tunisia, Morocco and Indochina. This differentiation was intended to account for the difference in legal status and the relationship of the respective territories to the mother country. The departments were integral parts of the mother country and were henceforth considered overseas provinces, the territories obtained a certain autonomy, while the protectorates were accepted as loosely associated states. Article 41 also established the principle of association by "free consent", i.e. of two partners with equal rights who joined to form a "Union". The consent of the overseas departments and the territories was tacitly taken for granted![8] Article 114 stated that "the one and indivisible French Republic [!] recognizes the existence of territorial collectivities . . . the communes, the departments, the overseas territories and federations". By contrast with Article 41, this declared that the overseas territories were integral parts of France, of a "one and indivisible Republic"; in fact it arbitrarily integrated them!

Consequently the local autonomy of the overseas territories was restricted to administrative decentralization. They obtained elected assemblies and budget rights, but no legislative power. Legislation continued to be reserved to the parliament. And yet France thought it had opened the way to the acquisition of that "political personality" of which the Brazzaville conference had spoken. In accordance with Senghor's motto "to assimilate, not to be assimilated", thought France, the African people would now be able to develop on the basis of their own civilization and tradition. Senghor accepted the idea of the overseas territories as parts of the Republic, although he still tried to uphold their right to decide either for full integration or for autonomy and association at a given time: "The peoples of the Union will be able to develop freely: they will have the possibility of proceeding, according to their wishes and their special character, either towards assimilation and integration or towards association and federation . . . the door to the future remains open."[9] This was a rather generous interpretation. A change of status for the African territories would necessarily have entailed a change in the constitution—and this became a source of misunderstanding.

Parliamentary representation also became, necessarily, a source of future conflict. France agreed to it in principle, unlike the Brazzaville conference, but the manner of execution was left to future legislation; in fact it involved such decisive questions as the number of deputies, franchise, separate electoral rolls, etc. France was aware that proportional representation was impossible, and even native deputies such as Senghor realized it. "To compensate for this inequality we shall give them local liberties."[10] Under-representation in parliament was to be compensated by an extension of local autonomy—a natural and apparently sensible compromise. But were these "local liberties" possible within an indivisible Republic? Would the Africans accept under-representation if they obtained no legislative power and no real executive power either in the local sphere? This was to become the main source of criticism in the future: under-representation was discrimination, said the critics, and even in the local sphere the Africans were not acquiring a "political personality".

The question of the formation and powers of the "Council of the French Union", which was to serve the overseas territories as an additional representative body, provoked violent discussion. But this question rested on a completely false premise; the discussions on the institutions of the French Union concealed a more general issue that was of decisive importance for the first constituent assembly: a one-chamber system or a two-chamber system? In the name of its traditional "revolutionary republicanism", the Left supported a one-chamber system, while the bourgeois Centre and Right favoured a second chamber as a counter-force and delaying factor. This overlapping of two problems of very different kinds gave rise to the paradoxical situation that the left-wing parties and the native deputies were those who wanted to provide the council with only minor powers. Senghor referred back to the 1795 constitution and opposed the idea of a "reactionary second chamber", while Aimé Césaire, the Communist poet and deputy from Martinique, asserted that the colonial deputies were chiefly interested in a mother country that was strong and democratic, i.e. left wing. As a new senate, the Union council would become a reactionary instrument, thought Césaire, which must be prevented.[11] The Communist proposal was based on the principle of democracy and local autonomy and was an integrational concept, which, however, did not preclude the possibility of later reinterpretation in the sense of the right to self-determination. At any rate the Communists wanted the Union council to obtain only consultative powers.[12]

The Socialists' attitude was extremely ambivalent. The deputy P. O. Lapie again formulated his concept of federation: within the French Union "all the peoples and all the collectivities have a right to independence and to the flowering of their civilization and their language, their culture and their spiritual life". He wanted to create socialist republics freely associated with France in the name of liberty, equality and fraternity and forming a kind of commonwealth.[13] Although the French Socialist party referred to the principle of federation in its draft constitution, it did not want federalist institutions until later—evidently because at that particular time the left-wing party could not yet accept a Union council with legislative powers![14] By contrast the spokesmen to the MRP, such as the French Algerian Viard, who had also warned against integration in the constitutional commission and had supported an integrationist solution, considered the powers of the Union council inadequate. The council should at least participate in electing the president of the Republic and obtain a hearing in parliament for its report,[15] they said. Similarly René Pleven of the democratic opposition tried to revalue the second chamber by introducing a federative concept of the French Union. The proposed council was no more than a caricature, he said, which certainly did not come up to the hopes of Brazzaville, and it must obtain certain legislative powers. Moreover the draft constitution would prevent a viable development, for "we are living in a century of nationalism".[16]

The final decision fell to the left-wing parties: the Union council would obtain only consultative powers and would not necessarily obtain a hearing. Like the Communists, the left wing and the overseas deputies thought that acceptance of their draft constitution meant they could proclaim the end of colonialism, even though they did not allow the French Union to obtain legislative powers by virtue of which it could immediately have begun to evolve as a federal court. The French refused the draft constitution in the referendum of 5 May 1946; the French natives overseas had agreed to it, while the majority of French colonials said "No".

Although the first assembly did not succeed in carrying its draft constitution, it did make several important legislative decisions:

On 12 March 1946 the integration of the *vieilles colonies* came to an end under pressure from the natives led by Césaire, existing inequalities and special rulings were abolished and the new social laws were henceforth also applied to the overseas departments. A month later, on 11 April, the assembly abolished forced labour and created an investment fund for its overseas territories (FIDES) from the mother country's public funds, which made it possible to actively promote both economic and social development in years to come.

But most important of all was that on 7 May 1946 the assembly passed a bill by the Senegalese Lamine-Guèye proposing to grant all "subjects" full French citizenship. This put an end to the uncertainty that had arisen after the rejection of the first draft constitution. The "Loi Lamine-Guèye", which naturally abolished the *indigénat* and assured civil rights and liberties to the former subjects, can be described as the *Lex Caracalla* of France. Even the "primitive" African in the bush obtained full French citizenship. However much the law was the product of circumstance in May 1946, it still represented the culmination of a long process of development and proved the strength of the French policy of integration and assimilation immediately after the Second World War.

Before and during the second constituent assembly the national emancipation movements became increasingly more important and penetrated the awareness of the mother country. The Algerian amnesty freed Ferhat Abbas and enabled his party to gain an overwhelming victory in the elections to the second assembly. Of the fifteen deputies to the Muslim electoral college, thirteen belonged to the Amis du Manifeste. They protested the twofold electoral college and demanded an "Algerian state" federally associated with France—which meant that the nationalists had also adopted a federal programme. In Madagascar too the native leaders were raising the banner of "independence", although within a French Union, in their election propaganda. This heralded the 1947 uprising. Black Africa was faced with difficulties in economic and social adjustment, partly as a result of the abolishment of forced labour and the *indigénat*, which expressed themselves in the form of strikes. Here too, the nationalists gained ground and the colonial French saw their plantations and business concerns, as well as their personal positions, jeopardized. In 1946 the "Rassemblement Démocratique Africain" (RDA), which became an important super-regional organization, was formed. The native deputies had also been disappointed by the French colonials' refusal of the first draft constitution and had become suspicious. The election to the second assembly on 2 June produced no significant changes in the colonies, apart from Algeria. The overall result was that the MRP moved to the forefront to become the strongest party while the Communists and Socialists lost their hold. The thirteen deputies of the Amis du Manifeste played a decisive role here; the Algerian deputies even succeeded in bringing about the rejection of a proposal for "freedom of instruction". Many of the deputies from the Right and Centre saw in this a warning against consistent, i.e. proportional, colonial representation in parliament. The events in Indochina in spring and summer 1946 (cf. pp. 397–98) contributed to dampening the desire for reforms and gave impetus to the parties of the Right.

Consequently the autochthonous deputies found themselves forced onto the defensive. In July they formed an "Inter-groupe", an inter-fractional group under Lamine-Guèye, the Senegalese vice-president of the commission for the overseas territories. The proposals worked out by the Intergroupe were adopted by the commission and even accepted in a slightly modified form by a weak majority in the constitutional committee, thanks to the support of the Socialists and Communists. These proposals throw some light on the attitude of the African politicians at the time.[17] They severely condemned colonialism as such and any unilateral action that tried to force a constitutional solution upon the former colonies without consulting the natives. By contrast, they proclaimed the right to self-government! The federal French Union, they said, must be formed of "nations and peoples" who voluntarily associated themselves to the metropolis; the African territories could not be unquestioningly taken in as parts of the Republic, but should be partners in the Union. In addition, the overseas inhabitants should obtain the right to decide themselves on their status within the next twenty years: "The peoples of the French Union will have the opportunity to choose, within the framework of this Union, either the status of free State associated to France by international treaty, or complete integration into the Republic." The transition to the status of associated state which was envisaged for the protectorates and for Indochina was also to be open to Black Africa and Algeria. For the rest, they denied that the assembly was responsible for establishing relations between the former colony and the mother country. The institutions both of the Union and of the territories must be decided by a special constitutional assembly in which the overseas territories had a majority.

The trend of these proposals is clear. The native deputies refused to have a constitution imposed upon them by the mother country and did not want to make the final decision on their future status yet. They wanted to reserve themselves the right to change their status, as an expression of the recognition of their sovereign rights. They took seriously the principle of free consent and postulated a more or less loose federation of equal partners.[18] These theses reflect Sissoko's and Senghor's proposals in 1944–1945, Ferhat Abbas' concept of an Algerian state and the demands of the Madagascar nationalists. They also show how Senghor gradually moved from the concept of a federal republic to that of confederation.

This proposal by the constitutional commission is unfortunately almost forgotten today. It had its own inherent logic, and at a moment when the nationalists were demanding independence but protesting the charge that they were aiming at dissociation, it offered a programme for decolonization capable of reconciling the demands for autonomy with the interests of the mother country. Above all it would have permitted a flexible adaptation to the rapidly changing situation. It is tempting to draw a comparison with British policy after 1945. Britain was as reluctant as France to foresee African self-government or independence in the near future, yet it was prepared to accept self-government as a justified aim. Dominion status and Commonwealth roughly correspond to the status of associated state and to the French Union in the Inter-groupe's proposal: similarly the willingness of the Africans to accept this territorial status, together with the possibilities of a later change, could have created a parallel with the British concept of a transitional régime.

Almost at the same time as the deputies of the Inter-groupe, the colonialist groups intensified their activities. Their attitude is apparent in the petitions of the "Comité de L'Empire" addressed to the government[19] and in the newspaper *Marchés Coloniaux* which took over from *L'Afrique Française*. On 12 March 1945, for instance, the committee proposed an imperial consultative council, whose composition would not have threatened the predominance of metropolitan France and which would have given the French colonials a decisive role. Representatives of the mother country, representatives of the French colonials and natives were to be in a proportion of 2:2:1![20] In July of the same year the committee took a stand against the projected representation of the colonies in the constituent assembly: only French citizens should vote, it said, for

> the intrusion of non-citizen native elements, replacing the colonists who have founded and developed the empire, and replacing the natives, who by their merit or their degree of evolution have risen to citizenship, would be a shock to the whole imperial edifice which constitutes the force and the pride of France.[21]

The native deputies aimed at independence and threatened French sovereignty. The idea of a single college was particularly untenable since it would lead to outvoting the settlers. These were the French colonials' main tenets. The motto "to uphold the Empire"[22] served as a protest against a policy of "surrender" such as was heralded by the grant of independence to Syria or the negotiations with Ho Chi Minh:

> France can only be reborn if it rejects once and for all the masochistic rubbish with which it persists in weakening itself since its temporary defeat in 1940.[23]

Naturally the French colonials defended the existing economic structures against *étatisme*, warned against "over-rapid" industrialization and objected to trusteeship for Cameroun and Togo.[24] *Marchés Coloniaux* abandoned the notion of a France of a hundred million inhabitants i.e. assimilation with citizenship, and supported administrative decentralization, but without urging effective native participation in the local administration. In fact it supported a colonialist anti-assimilation policy![25] Naturally *Marchés Coloniaux* criticized the first draft constitution and called on every "colonial" to vote "No" in the referendum on 5 May 1946.[26]

The arguments were clever: under-representation for the colonies was a hypocrisy that could not survive long, while proportional representation would result in an overseas majority and "we would have committed suicide. Thank you". The inter-party quarrels in the metropolis echoed in Sudan and Laos, said the paper. . . . It wanted a "federal chamber" responsible for imperial affairs. This meant that the colonial Right was also adopting federalism and further increasing the existing confusion in the use of this term. "We must readjust the entire structure of the French Union on a federal basis."[27] Reduced franchise and a double electoral college in the local sphere as well as for elections to the federal chamber could guarantee the French colonials' interests. The paper even demanded an immediate repeal of the civil rights law of 7 May 1946 and wanted to restrict parliamentary representation to French citizens, as it had been before, i.e. including loss of personal status![28]

A manifesto prepared by several colonial associations also attacked this law and the idea of a single college, asserting that the natives only wanted law and order and were completely unconcerned with franchise and parliamentary representation.[29] It took a severe view of the Inter-groupe's proposed constitution, calling its originators a "shameful syndicate of separatists"[30]:

> Metropolitan predominance would disappear; the empire would be pulverized within twenty years. It would comply with the separatism dear to certain representatives who want to prevail with their programme of total emancipation.[31]

"Separatism" became a slogan with which to compromise the nationalists and to discredit any attempts to conciliate the natives as a policy of "surrender" under Communist influence. Corresponding demands were also made by the "États généraux de la colonisation française", which met in Paris in August 1946.[32] Here one can speak of a real counter-offensive of an altogether provocative kind. The formula about a "federal French Union" cannot conceal that its adherents were defending pre-war positions.

The government felt obliged to take account of right-wing resistance to the text accepted by the constitutional committee. The MRP deputy Coste-Floret supported the proposed constitution, but after intervention by Édouard Herriot, the Socialist overseas minister, Moutet requested that the assembly put aside for the time being the part of the constitution concerning the French Union and wait for a government motion. Only by a highly unusual government intervention could the proposals from the Left be delayed at the last moment and the Empire be "saved"! Naturally the native deputies, supported by the Communists, protested. But since the Socialists were shifting to the right and coming closer to the MRP, the Left was weakened and had to make concessions. On 29 September 1946 the second meeting of the National Assembly accepted the new text, which was essentially based on the government bill, by 440 votes to 106. The Right and the Radical Socialists rejected it while the MRP, the Socialists and even the Communists, as well as the African deputies, approved it. Ferhat Abbas' party and the deputies from Madagascar abstained.[33]

We can discuss in brief a few points from the lively discussion in the second assembly. First we must mention Herriot's famous vote of 27 August with which he applied "emergency brakes" to the proposals of the constitutional committee.[34] Herriot was the embodiment of the Third Republic: progressive and liberal in programme, restrained in execution, patriotic in the old sense. In addition the Radical Socialist party had strong internal links with colonialist circles and had shifted to the right since 1945. Accordingly, Herriot began by defending the colonial past in striking terms. He thought reforms in the colonies were indeed necessary, but the project of the constitutional commission with its "acephalous and anarchic federalism" was untenable. The Brazzaville conference, he said, had envisaged a much stronger central executive (typical interruption: "The Brazzaville conference is outdated!"). The interests of the mother country were being neglected, he asserted, and there was not a word about national defence: France could never give up Dakar and other strategic positions. The import of raw materials and food from the colonies was necessary to France's survival; after all, in 1938 the colonies' contribution to French export had been 28 percent. The close association in education must not be dissolved. The committee's proposal practically stipulated a right to secession, since it stated that the territories could freely decide their status at a given moment. The metropolis was granting its provinces a right to secession! The conferment of full citizenship upon all the subjects together with representation in parliament was a problem that had unacceptable implications:

> How many citizens will there be in the overseas territories? According to many there will be more than in the territories of the metropolis. As one of my friends once said in a manner both pleasant and profound, France would thus become the colony of its former colonies.[35]

It was obvious what Herriot, speaking for the Centre and the Right, and perhaps also for the entire French population, had in mind: the overseas departments and territories were integral parts of the national territory which could not be granted the right to self-government either now or in the future; the new constitution should establish integration once and for all to prevent any chance of the national unity "breaking up". Consistent integration also jeopardized the predominance of metropolitan France. What was left was an alleged federation which ensured both the predominance of the mother country and the position of French colonials overseas. Its institutions had to be "manipulated" in such a way that the final power of decision remained with the mother country!

This colonialist interpretation of federation emerges even more clearly in the arguments of the right-wing deputies. They thought that the "French minorities" must be guaranteed a voice in the territories; but a single college would lead to elimination of the whites. French citizenship implied certain obligations which could hardly be reconciled with the retention of personal status. So what was necessary was a special citizenship of the Union, "with the possibility of acquiring total [!] French citizenship as the law actually prescribes if certain conditions are fulfilled". Since citizens alone could be represented in the parliament, they would create an assembly of the French Union. Malbrant, the white deputy from Tchad, claimed to be aiming "at a fully federal formula which must consist of the final stage of the territorial and political evolution of the French world".[36] The federal formula allowed Malbrant to exclude natives from the French parliament and to relegate them to a Union council which might obtain some further powers later but would never question French sovereignty.

The new project proposed by the commission, which was inserted with few changes into the text of the constitution, took account of these objections from the Right. As a result, "federalism" acquired a colonialist accent, the États généraux de la colonisation française and the discussion in parliament had, as it were, compromised the federative solution. The native deputies who had been forced onto the defensive now demanded integration and equal legal status. Since they could not impose the kind of federalism proposed by the Inter-groupe, they now aimed at integration.[37] However, the Algerians led by Ferhat Abbas and the deputies from Madagascar, who demanded nationhood within the French Union, adhered to their original positions. Senghor thought conditions were not yet suitable for genuine federalism. The metropolis and the colonies should strive towards "assimilation" in order to create together "a new civilization whose centre will be Paris".[38] Similar arguments came from the Communist Angeletti[39] and the fellow-traveller Pierre Cot.[40] Confessions of loyalty to France were made—by Ferhat Abbas too[41]; no one in Africa was aiming at secession. What they demanded was equal rights under a policy of integration. "To begrudge us the integration into the French family which we demand, is a concept which shocks and revolts us."[42] Senghor described Herriot's intervention as "racism" and discrimination.[43] One could not, he said, declare the African territories parts of the one and indivisible Republic and then to try to avoid the implications of this by making further provisions. The people were not even demanding proportional representation; at any rate there had been no differentiation between first- and second-class Frenchmen during the war.

The double electoral college, which had hardly been questioned by the first constituent assembly, was now subjected to sharp criticism: it was discrimination to give the same importance to several hundred Europeans as to hundreds of thousands of natives. The attackers pointed to the États généraux de la colonisation française as evidence of resistance and efforts to turn back the clock. The dispute about the double college almost led to a split[44] and forced the metropolis to compromise: there was to be a single college for appointments to the local assemblies in Senegal. This second constituent assembly also gave more emphasis than the first, in line with the Inter-groupe's proposals, to the temporary character of the constitutional provisions and thus to the possibility of a future change of status, particularly, of course, to a transition to the status of associated state. The French Union must appear a free association, it said.[45] There was no lack of references to the U.N. charter.

A brief reference to the text of the constitution of the Fourth Republic is necessary here. A passage from the preamble concerns us most:

> France, together with the overseas peoples, forms a Union founded on the equality of rights and obligations, without distinction of race or religion. The French Union is composed of nations and peoples who pool or coordinate their resources and their efforts in order to develop their respective civilizations, to increase their well-being and to assure their security.
>
> Faithful to its traditional mission, France aims to lead the peoples in its charge to the freedom of administering themselves and conducting their own affairs democratically: avoiding any system of colonization founded on arbitrary principles, it guarantees everyone equal access to public offices and to the individual or collective exercise of the rights and liberties proclaimed or confirmed above.[46]

These words were largely based on the Inter-groupe's draft constitution but, significantly, limited it. France announced the end of colonialism—but only of colonialism based on arbitrary principles, which naturally allowed various interpretations. The constitution confirmed the conferment of citizenship and thus put an end to individual emancipation. The mother country took over the task of leading the colonial peoples "to the freedom of administering themselves", but failed to say whether this meant full integration or nationhood. Certainly there was no longer any question of sovereignty.

An inherent contradiction has been pointed out in the preamble. While the third paragraph is directed to the future, the first two mention the "nations and peoples" who form a community with France. As postulated by the Inter-groupe, the colonies are to become partners allegedly freely associated with France. This became a source of dispute. For while the metropolis pointed to the third paragraph and stressed France's leadership role, the colonial deputies wanted to be considered "decolonized" and free to decide their own destiny.[47]

For the time being both the overseas departments and the territories were considered parts of the French Republic which, together with the former League of Nations mandates and the associated states, formed the French Union. Article 60 states: The French Union is formed on the one hand of the French Republic which embraces metropolitan France, the departments (*vieilles colonies* and Algeria) and overseas territories (Black Africa and Madagascar), and on the other hand of the territories (Togo and Cameroun) and the associated states (Morocco, Tunisia, Vietnam, Laos, Cambodia). Naturally the constitution gave no details about the internal structure of the associated states; however, the territories were to obtain their own statute and elected assemblies; the question of franchise was left to a special law. The legislative power in the territories was to remain with the parliament, the executive with the governor.

Article 75 clears the way for a change of status: "The status of the respective members of the Republic and of the French Union is capable of evolution;" so the transition to associated state was possible. This was a concession to the native deputies. But since such a change required a parliamentary resolution, the decision remained not with the members but with the parliament.

The Union as a whole consists of three units: the president (identical with the president of the Republic), the high council, and the assembly. The high council is composed of delegates of the French Government (the territories are not separated here) and the delegates of the associated states. By contrast the assembly consists of an equal number of deputies from metropolitan France and from the overseas departments, territories and associated states. Suddenly the one and indivisible Republic is split apart here, and even the assimilated departments are counted as overseas territories—in order to underline the importance of the metropolis!

The powers of the assembly (Article 71) are purely consultative and restricted to a minimum: the assembly has neither legislative powers for questions concerning overseas territories nor obligatory consultation. The parliament and the government decide on what to present to the assembly: the latter can present proposals, but the parliament is in no way bound by them and is not even obliged to take a stand. All attempts from either side to give the Union assembly further powers and to create the elements of a federation failed.[48]

The overseas territories, however, continued to be represented in parliament. Here colonialist demands, as represented by the États généraux de la colonisation française, did not succeed. The number of deputies and the manner of election remained reserved to future legislation. The constitution does not decide between a single or double electoral college, but neither does it preclude one or the other possibility. We have already mentioned that some concessions had to be made to the native deputies in this much disputed question.

How could one judge the constitutional provisions of 1946? Henri Culman wrote: "The French Union is the French solution of the twentieth century."[49] In historical perspective one must formulate this a little more cautiously: the French Union was an attempt at decolonization corresponding to the French state and colonial tradition. From the conference of governors in Brazzaville the road led via the discussion in Algiers and Paris in 1944–1945 to the two constituent assemblies in 1946. In the atmosphere of reform France was willing to conciliate the emancipation movements and international anti-colonialism. Decolonization was proclaimed and initiated.

But decolonization was not conceived as gradually letting the colonies obtain independence or as the recognition of their claims to nationhood, but rather as an emancipation within an institutionalized whole that was maintained by France and remained oriented towards France. The old idea of Greater France still survived and was designed to legitimate the French claim to world power. The Empire became the French Union, the "natives" became "autochthons". While the Third Republic had kept the colonies outside the constitution, the 1946 constitution applied to the metropolis and the overseas territories. The colonies were granted by the constitution a special status within the whole and even became, like the African territories, integral parts of the Republic. Since the colonies were represented in the constituent assembly by their own deputies and the citizens accepted the text of the constitution by referendum, France could proclaim the end of colonial rule. In addition it was granting all its subjects full French citizenship, and French law became generally valid in the overseas territories. In parliament, the former subjects were represented by elected deputies.

At the same time the limitations of this integration became clear. The French in the mother country did not want to become a colony of the former colonies and consequently could not concede proportional representation even as a future goal. In the local sphere universal franchise in a single college jeopardized the French minority. The immediate application of certain laws seemed senseless and likely to cost an impossible price. And finally there was the question whether the "autochthons" approved of assimilation and integration at all or wanted it. Some territories were certainly willing, but in others spokesmen were already demanding sovereignty, political autonomy and nationhood. The discrepancy between what France planned or considered as a natural precondition for any negotiations, and what the emancipation movement maintained as the aim of its agitation, was particularly great in Algeria: while the constitution presented the Algerian departments as parts of the

Republic, Ferhat Abbas' party demanded an autonomous "Algerian state"!

The result was necessarily a compromise; in principle decolonization had been proclaimed, but in fact the provisions for its execution upheld the dominant position of the metropolis. The clearest example of this was the franchise, which was restricted in spite of general conferment of citizenship. The overseas territories were granted elected assemblies but with severely limited powers and they continued to be largely ruled from Paris. The former protectorates were recognized as states, but only on condition that the Union, and thus the mother country, retained sovereignty. The overseas deputies were a minority in parliament, and this was not compensated by a transferral of important powers to the central organs of the Union. The traditional policy of depoliticization was relaxed a little, but not to the extent indicated by the pronouncements of the mother country.

The attempt to present as "federalization" the conversion of the Empire into a French Union was unconvincing and led to a "Babylonic confusion" (Ansprenger). The French Union was not a genuine federation and decolonization largely proceeded by way of integration. Assimilatory tradition rather than federalism prevailed.

One can interpret the constitutional resolutions of the Fourth Republic as an attempt to avoid the inherent consequences of both methods of decolonization and to reconcile them. France neither pursued complete integration with its apparently untenable implications, nor recognized the territories' sovereign rights, because this might have included the right of dissociation from the French Union. Article 75 provided for a change of status, but characteristically it was seldom taken seriously by French thinkers and in the following years more or less dropped into oblivion. The integration of the overseas territories and departments was considered final, and any changes of status seemed to threaten secession, which jeopardized "French presence in the world".

If the mother country thought it had found in the 1946 constitution a more or less permanent solution to the colonial problem, the overseas deputies who spoke for the emancipating movements considered the compromise no more than a preliminary, transitional step leading either to full integration or to genuine federation, or even confederation. As a result they agitated on both levels, in conformity with the nature of the compromise.

How far was the French Union, or rather the mother country, able to accede to these partially overlapping demands, and how far did it prove able to adjust, in order to bring the decolonization it had initiated to a smooth conclusion?

INDOCHINA, TUNISIA AND MOROCCO

In spite of anti-French agitation in Saigon after the Japanese surrender, British and French troops managed to win back Cochin China in the autumn of 1945, restore the administration and begin "pacification". But supporters of the Viet Minh continued to terrorize "collaborators", i.e. Indochinese who co-operated with France. The educated class, particularly the young intellectuals, began to withdraw from such "compromising" and marked time. Only a very generous policy of reform would have offered some hope of creating the necessary basis of trust. One way or another the final decision now lay with Tonkin.

In this phase of administrative disorganization, when even Chinese troops marched in as "liberators", the Viet Minh managed to build up its position. "The entire population was taking part in the new mystique of *Coc Lap*" (independence).[1] Although the Viet Minh alleged it was a collective movement of all the national forces, around the turn of 1945–1946 Communist and anti-Communist groups were at odds in Hanoi. Ho Chi Minh, who found himself isolated in his foreign policy and hard pressed in economic and financial affairs, agreed to negotiate. On 6 March 1946 he and Sainteny, representing Leclerc, signed an agreement by which France recognized "the Republic of Vietnam as a free State, with its own Government, its Parliament, its army and its finances, forming a part of the Indochinese Federation and of the French Union". This was a great concession. France had not promised independence in the full sense of the term yet it granted autonomy, together with a Vietnamese army and the recognition of Ho Chi Minh as head of government. For his part Ho renounced his claim as spokesman for the whole of Indochina and agreed to the entry of French troops into Hanoi. No doubt he considered the agreement of 6 March no more than a temporary solution. French opinion was divided. While Leclerc and Sainteny were prepared to co-operate with the Viet Minh in face of the Asian emancipation movements and the weakness of their own forces, the administration in Saigon under Admiral d'Argenlieu viewed the agreement as a concession imposed by the critical situation; it should be revoked or by-passed as soon as possible and under no circumstances should it prevent the restoration of effective French control. An atmosphere of distrust already pervaded the conference of Dalat [Indochina] held between 17 April and 11 May 1946. This conference was primarily concerned with the federation of Indochina and the question of whether Cochin China belonged to it or whether this colony should remain under French rule for the present. France tried to transfer wide powers to the federation—with a high commissioner as head of the executive—and held a dominant position in the French Union, while Ho Chi Minh started from the assumption that Vietnam had already achieved independence, demanded diplomatic representation in Paris and considered the federation no more than a vehicle of economic co-ordination.

Ho was invited to the Paris negotiations on the Indochinese-French community. President Bidault himself officially received him with great ceremony. Meanwhile, however, after careful preparation but without the consent of the Paris government, d'Argenlieu took the initiative. On 1 June in an attempt to isolate the Viet Minh in Tonkin and Annam he proclaimed the Republic of Cochin China. Ho naturally protested violently against this dubious manoeuvre which strained the lengthy negotiations taking place in Fontainebleau. Each side entrenched itself in its positions. The Communist leaders of the Vietnamese Republic hoped to negotiate a bilateral agreement between two independent states, while France adhered to the French Union idea and was prepared only to give Vietnam the position of associated state within the Union. "Our conception of the French Union is not that of an alliance but that of states closely united by common organs",[2] said a French representative. At the second conference in Dalat, d'Argenlieu intervened again to try to establish the position of Cambodia, Laos and Cochin China in the federation of Indochina, but did not invite the Viet Minh to the conference. The Fontainebleau conference came to nothing. Ho Chi Minh and the Socialist overseas minister, Marius Moutet, signed a *modus vivendi* agreement on 14 September, which did not touch on decisive points such as "independence" and the position of Cochin China. Meanwhile, in Hanoi, radical elements led by Vice-President Giap gained ground and tried by means of sabotage, boycotts and terrorism against French civilians and the military, as well as against anti-Communist Tonkinese, to prevent any agreement with France. As a result non-Communist nationalist groups were gradually driven out. Saigon resolved to "teach them a severe lesson" and bombed the harbour of Haiphong on 23 November, provoking the Viet Minh attack on Hanoi on 19 December. The Indochinese war began.

Perhaps it would have been possible to negotiate with Ho Chi Minh after France's first military victories in Tonkin and to form a coalition government for the whole of Vietnam. It is impossible to tell whether this might have neutralized the Communists, and admittedly it would have presupposed abandoning the Cochin China experiment and recognizing the Republic of Vietnam. General Leclerc seems to have made moves in this direction, partly because he was aware of the immense difficulties of jungle warfare.³ The Socialist presidents Blum and Ramadier also showed interest in such a "solution". But Admiral d'Argenlieu and the Centre and right-wing parties in the mother country rejected it, alleging that the attack on Hanoi had permanently discredited the Viet Minh and that negotiations would appear to betray France's legitimate interests. The result was a compromise. D'Argenlieu was replaced by the Radical Socialist Bollaert who was entrusted with persuading the Indochinese states to accept the constitutional status of associated states and with initiating negotiations with "possible partners". But when Ho Chi Minh again proved willing to negotiate in March and April 1947 (Mao had not yet come to power in China), the French practically stipulated capitulation and their conditions were therefore rejected. Meanwhile, with the ousting of the Communist party from the government, French policy had moved to the right. On 15 May Bollaert declared: "France will remain in Indochina and Indochina in the heart of the French Union." So the Viet Minh could no longer be the sole partner in the negotiations. The "Bao Dai experiment" finally seemed to offer a way out.

We shall not describe the Indochinese war in detail. On the French side it was waged with modern weapons and crack troops, on the Viet Minh side with the methods of "revolutionary" warfare on the Chinese example. Gradually it developed into a struggle between the Western world and the Communist bloc. It ended, after the spectacular defeat of France at Dienbienphu, with the Geneva conference in July 1954 which agreed on the temporary partition of Vietnam.

The war in Indochina remained a focal point of French party politics and ideological discussion for years. While the Left demanded negotiations with Ho Chi Minh, the Right refused to embark on a policy of "surrender" (cf. pp. 419–20). The unstable governments were unable to pursue a united policy and left the decision to the Saigon administration. The army was not given sufficient backing and France did not grant the assistance of regular troops. On several occasions it was declared that the war had been won. Intrigues, betrayal and corruption in Paris and Saigon turned the bloody conflict in Asia into a "rotten war" which gnawed at the strength of the mother country and had to be ended one way or another. This feeling was particularly strong because France had not succeeded in gaining sufficient Vietnamese support to successfully combat Communist infiltration and jungle warfare.

We must briefly outline the French attitude during the war and the policy towards non-Communist Vietnam. As we said earlier, France tried to base its policy on the 1946 constitution, which envisaged the status of associated members within the French Union for the states of Indochina, i.e. internal autonomy but no sovereignty in foreign affairs. Foreign policy and defence were the responsibility of the Union, which

France dominated. Accordingly, Bollaert described the French Union on 15 May 1947 as

> a harmonious whole formed of territories who, aware of their solidarity, agree in their own interests to adhere to a greater community. . . . France wishes the restrictions of their sovereignty to be as minimal as possible. Although it intends to reserve its place on the federal plane, it no longer wants to intervene in the internal administration of the States.

Some time later he added: "The French Union can have but one army as it can have but one diplomacy."[4] But France had already conceded Ho Chi Minh his own army on 6 March 1946. Was it possible to wage war against the Viet Minh, who had raised the banner of independence and liberation, without giving one's partners this same independence? Emperor Bao Dai, who had occasionally collaborated both with the Japanese and with the Viet Minh in 1945, managed to exploit his strong position. Moreover, for Bao Dai, whom his opponents described as a "puppet of the colonial power", it was a point of honour to persuade France to accept the "magic" word "independence". The French Government wanted to avoid this, with regard to North Africa and in the fear that it would be an obstacle to the French Union, but it finally had to give in. On 5 June 1948 after laborious negotiation, France solemnly recognized

> the independence of Vietnam, which is responsible for freely realizing its unity. For its part, Vietnam proclaims its adherence to the French Union in the form of State associated to France. The independence of Vietnam has no limits other than those imposed on it by its membership of the French Union.[5]

Now even the concept of independence was surrounded by "Babylonic confusion"!

The French Government, under pressure from the Right, continued to reserve to itself powers of diplomatic representation and foreign policy and refused to give in on the question of Cochin China. Months passed before France conceded Vietnam its own army and diplomatic representation as well as full legislative and juridical power, by the Auriol–Bao Dai agreement of 8 March 1949. But Vietnam still remained within the French Union. Now France believed it had made the final decision, and on 3 January 1951 President Auriol declared: "The struggle for the independence of Vietnam no longer has a *raison d'être*, this independence has been achieved."[6] Indochina thought otherwise and pressed for "full independence". Cambodia demanded bilateral negotiations on the model of the Commonwealth, and in October 1953 a nationalist congress, with active co-operation from Bao Dai, declared in

Saigon: "An independent Vietnam could not participate in the French Union in its present form." The first negotiations had to be postponed, owing to the stubborn resistance of the right-wing dominated parliament. In January 1954, High Commissioner Dejean promised new talks on the preamble of the constitution, but until April Paris was not prepared to contemplate bilateral relations or to recognize the "total independence of Vietnam and its full and entire sovereignty". In June (after Dienbienphu and the Geneva conference!), an association agreement was finally accepted. It provided for common boards, but operated on the basis of full equality of the partners, thereby placing Vietnam outside the French Union. The later conventions were bilateral agreements.

Decolonization of Indochina was imposed on France by armed force; it was not part of a policy planned and gradually put into effect. France thought that the declaration of 24 March 1945 provided a generous formula, but it had underestimated the strength of the desire for emancipation after the Japanese occupation. Perhaps the concept of the French Union could have remained valid, at least for a few years, if Paris had accepted the full autonomy of Indochina—or rather of the three states Vietnam, Laos and Cambodia—from the outset, and if it had not revoked or avoided by its plans for federation the concessions that had been forced from it in the agreement with Ho Chi Minh. However, to do justice to French policy, one must remember the political and psychological difficulty of having to negotiate with a Republic of Vietnam under Communist leadership. In this sense the situation in Indochina was fundamentally different from that in Burma or Indonesia. Any readiness for concession, as shown by Leclerc and left-wing circles in metropolitan France, was attacked from the start; both the administration in Saigon and conservatives in France had good arguments with which to sabotage further negotiations with the Viet Minh and they tried to reach a solution by brute force. This produced a paradoxical situation in that France had to grant Bao Dai what it had refused Ho Chi Minh in 1946. France let itself in for a bloody war in order to uphold "French presence" and because it did not want to recognize the Viet Minh's claim to independence; yet it was forced to grant this same independence during the war to non-Communist Indochina. This concession was made only after many months of difficult negotiation, and it was made reluctantly—under American pressure—destroying all chances of winning the support of the masses and the non-Communist nationalist élite and giving the Viet Minh no real alternative. In the end, France had no choice but to reinterpret what had been a colonial war as an anti-Communist crusade.

Meanwhile, France also had to come to terms with the emancipation movements in Tunisia and Morocco. There the discussion did not reach its peak until some time after the Geneva agreement. The existing situation and French policy were similar in the two territories. Their legal basis was still the protectorate agreement with its fiction of a Tunisian and a Moroccan state. Here the problem was the relatively strong resident settler minority, whom the mother country could not simply "sacrifice". Moreover the settlers were influential both in local administration and in Paris and tried to undermine any proposed reforms. The Muslim nationalist movement was rapidly expanding, supported by the Arab states of the Middle East. Since the Second World War the nationalists had been pressing for independence or at least full internal autonomy. They demanded annulment of the protectorate agreement and recognition of Tunisian and Moroccan sovereignty, in addition to a bilateral agreement which took French interests into account. But France adhered to the protectorate and only conceded a few internal reforms, which did not satisfy the nationalists and were sabotaged by at least some of the settlers at first. Attempts were then made to establish a kind of co-sovereignty and to give the French colonials a direct part in the parliament and the government of both states. In fact, at a time when a trend towards self-government was becoming apparent, France tried to guarantee the privileged position of the settlers in a new way, or better, by a new detour. Naturally, these all too transparent efforts, which could hardly be reconciled with the concept of the protectorate, were strongly opposed and finally came to nothing.[7]

In February 1947 France replied to a wave of agitation in Tunisia the previous summer by appointing a new resident-general, and by making some modest reforms: the Tunisians and the French were granted parity representation in the Cabinet, under the chairmanship of a Tunisian. In fact policy-making and administration remained in the hands of France. In 1949 Bourguiba was allowed to return to Tunis, and in April 1950 he stated his demands in Paris; a homogeneous Tunisian government and the abolition of the offices of resident-general and his administration; the election of a constituent assembly on the basis of universal franchise. The "legitimate interests" of France were to be settled by agreement.

Robert Schuman, the foreign minister responsible for the protectorates, wanted to be conciliatory. On 11 June 1950 he declared in Thionville that the new resident-general's mission was "to lead Tunisia ... to that independence which is the ultimate objective for all the territories in the heart of the French Union". This objective could only be achieved by degrees, he said, but it must begin by a reduction of direct administration.[8] As in Indochina, this was the first time the word "independence" had been used officially, although this independence was to apply only within the French Union and remained rather vague. Nevertheless the reaction of the Tunisian press was positive and Bourguiba also showed signs of approval. Even the Neo-Destour party secretary participated in Chénik's new government, which was to open negotiations with France. The reform of February 1951 did not go very far, however: the French "advisers" to the Tunisian ministers were recalled. Now the Tunisians pressed for the next stage, homogeneous government.

This provoked the full force of the settlers' opposition. They openly withdrew their allegiance from the resident-general and threatened rebellion. The resident-general of Morocco, Juin, the governor-general of Algeria, Naegelen, and the right-wing minister in the French Government, Martinaud-Déplat, also objected.[9] The French Government, supported by the Right after the elimination of the SFIO, capitulated. Once again it was Robert Schuman who made known the change of policy. In a letter dated 15 December he wrote that Paris refused

> to end their [the settlers'] participation in the functioning of the political institutions. The government is strongly attached to this principle which appears the only one capable of ensuring, by a fruitful Franco-Tunisian association, the harmonious development of these institutions.[10]

This meant co-sovereignty. The French in Tunisia were to obtain franchise and to be represented in the government, thus becoming co-bearers of sovereignty. In order to emphasize the new course, the resident-general De Hautecloque arrived on board a destroyer! The more conservative historian Le Tourneau has rightly compared this situation to that of 1936–1938 when the settlers blocked the reform policy and imposed their wishes on the government in Paris. No less than Robert Schuman himself revealed in a sensational newspaper article how he, the responsible foreign minister, had lost any real power of decision: since the residents and the civil service identified with the settlers, while the government had to compromise with the parliamentary Right, the hierarchical power of command in the protectorates had been lost.[11] This heralded the functional crisis in the Fourth Republic, which was to come to grief over the Algerian question.

The Tunisians tried to bring their quarrel with France before the United Nations. Since the bey refused to dissolve the Chénik cabinet, Bourguiba and other Neo-Destour leaders were arrested on 18 January 1952, and Chénik in March—without the knowledge of Schuman![12] In all likelihood it was French counter-terrorists who murdered Ferhat Hached, the Tunisian union leader, in December. But De Hautecloque asserted that "the nationalists know the game has been played out and they have lost. The Tunisians, who forget easily, have already forgotten the name of Bourguiba".[13]

There was another reform attempt in 1954, but it did no more than maintain parliamentary representation in the Tunisian assemblies. Although even such paltry concessions went too far for the settlers, who accused Paris of a policy of "surrender", the Neo-Destour now spoke of the "perpetual dupery of the régime of co-sovereignty".[14] Sabotage, assassinations and *fellagha* [guerrilla] attacks began.

It was left to Mendès-France to prevent the outbreak of a bloody conflict. On 31 July he resolutely set out for Tunis, visited the bey and declared:

> The internal autonomy of the Tunisian state is recognized and proclaimed without reservations by the French Government . . . this is why we are ready to transfer to Tunisian persons and institutions the internal exercise of sovereignty.[15]

There was no question of co-sovereignty now, and Paris was willing to transfer internal administration to the Tunisians, reserving itself sovereign rights in foreign policy alone. But Mendès-France, who had hoped to introduce a generous decolonization coupled with economic aid, was prematurely thrown out of office.[16] His successor Edgar Faure negotiated with Bourguiba (who had been brought out of exile and taken directly to Paris) the conventions of 3 June 1955, according to which Tunisia obtained internal autonomy. But since France had already granted Morocco full independence on 5 November, the Tunisians increased their agitation: on 20 March 1956, in spite of the resistance of Socialist president Guy Mollet,[17] they became independent.

Unlike the bey of Tunis, who remained in the political background, the sultan of Morocco took an active part in the emancipation movement. He made a provocative speech in Tangier on 10 April 1947 which challenged the protectorate power, described Morocco as an Arab country, and welcomed the Arab League, without even mentioning France. Paris replied to the challenge by appointing Juin resident-general. Marshal Juin, from Algeria, whose specialty was certainly not diplomacy and who preferred more practical measures, was to introduce reforms with a view to internal autonomy. If the sultan resisted, he could be deposed![18] Juin tried to by-pass the Istiqlal and to find other support. In October 1950 the sultan presented his demands. Today they seem very moderate and they would doubtless have created a basis for negotiation, but Paris held back. In the following year Juin and the sultan came into conflict when the resident-general demanded an open disavowal of the Istiqlal and brought in Berber tribes to exert pressure on the sultan; on 25 February he forced him to capitulate. The nationalist agitators became more insistent. The resident-general showed little desire for reforms and still hoped to eliminate the Istiqlal.[19] Once again the sultan made known his desire to come to an agreement with France but he did not get a hearing in Paris; the refusal was not given until months later.[20] The murder of Hached in Tunisia provoked strikes and demonstrations in Casablanca which resulted in considerable loss of life. Hundreds of nationalists were arrested, liberal settlers were exiled. The nationalists and the administration mutually accused one another of provocation, and vehement discussion began in the mother country. While the Left supported the nationalists and sharply protested the administration's repressive measures, the Right demanded energetic action and opposed "premature" concessions. Both Paris and Parisian legal circles now introduced the "Action el Glaoui" in the hope of finding a way out of a situation that was completely out of control. In spite of an explicit counter-demand by the government [!], the pasha of Marrakesh, a traditional rival, was not prevented from addressing a real ultimatum to the sultan and marching in Berber tribes. On 19 August 1953 the sultan was deposed and deported.

His successor proved more adaptable and signed the decrees laid before him; but he found little popular support. The relaxation of tension in Morocco for which France had so fervently hoped did not take place. Instead the deposed sultan became a martyr and a symbol of the new emancipation movement. The throne question blocked all negotiations with France, and terrorism and counter-terrorism reigned. . . .

After unsuccessful attempts to reach a compromise the French Government had to agree in October 1955 to the return of the exiled sultan and, as with Bourguiba, negotiated with him personally. In an agreement with the foreign minister Pinay on 6 November, the sultan declared himself willing to set up a new government and introduce democratic reforms, "and to conduct negotiations with France destined to make Morocco accede to the status of independent State united with France by the permanent ties of a freely accepted and defined independence".[21] Without a murmur France had had to abandon its stubborn resolution to grant internal autonomy but never independence and to defend its "permanent interests" in Morocco under any circumstances.

A new concept now emerged, that of "interdependence". The term appeared in the declaration of independence for Morocco of 2 March 1956 and in the Tunisian protocol on 20 March which stated:

> In respect of their sovereignty, France and Tunisia agree to define or to complete the modalities of a freely realized interdependence between the two states, and to co-operate in the domains where they have common interests, particularly in matters of defence and foreign relations.[22]

France signed very detailed conventions with Tunisia and Morocco concerning military and economic matters and the rights of the French settlers. But what was interdependence? It was meant to make the dissociation seem more attractive to the French public, while giving the impression that it was establishing a novel yet lasting association with Tunisia and Morocco. In fact France revoked the reluctantly granted independence. The concept of interdependence therefore becomes symptomatic of France's general attitude towards its North African protectorates after the Second World War.

Between the wars, as we have seen, the concept of the protectorate was rather vague, and its future validity was seldom seriously disputed. Few people realized that one day the "protectorate relationship" could come to an end. They preferred to operate with terms such as association, collaboration, community of French and Muslim interests, etc. which indicated permanent and indissoluble ties between the mother country and the protectorates and underlined the French claim to power. Even the mandated territories in the East were considered "legitimate possessions" which France could not surrender without surrendering its own power. For Great Britain, the status of protectorate or mandated territory served as a means of granting states such as Egypt and Iraq formal independence, and Britain confined itself to bilateral agreements which guaranteed it military bases, control of foreign policy and a certain amount of indirect influence on internal policy. France, by contrast, always rejected this type of imperial rule. But the French arguments were never very convincing. France pointed to the relatively large groups of settlers in Tunisia and Morocco—though not in Syria and Lebanon— and asserted that this was a different situation and one that required establishing much closer relations with the mother country. In fact economic interests and strategic questions had just as much if not more importance for London as for Paris. The difference in attitude had deeper roots: to the French public the word "independence" remained taboo, even for the protectorates. The prevailing image was that of a larger union, based on institutions and secured by them, a greater whole under French leadership.

The French Union which France created after the Second World War provided the special status of associated state for the protectorates; they were to have internal autonomy while foreign policy, defence, etc. were left to superordinate boards of the Union. France thought this gave it a chance to remain a world power overseas for decades to come. Even the left-wing experts on Africa believed in the possibility of such an institutionalized union. For instance in 1948 Robert Montagne hoped that Morocco would enter the French Union,[23] while C. A. Julien, a Socialist, considered that a federal solution would create such close ties between France and the protectorates that the latter would give up their demand for independence.[24] François Mitterand still held this opinion in 1954.[25] We can certainly not maintain that such a solution was an illusion from the start, for both Bourguiba and the sultan were basically francophile and interested in obtaining technical and economic aid from the mother country. For it to have been successful, however, France would have had to concede relatively rapid and far-reaching reforms and to agree to a revision of the protectorate agreements. But France adhered to the protectorate agreements and took no pains to make the status of associated state seem attractive to Tunisia and Morocco. Manoeuvres such as co-sovereignty and the removal of the sultan led to a hardening of fronts and ultimately to terrorism and counter-terrorism. It is characteristic that even liberal political writers were willing to adopt the cliché "interdependence" and that even at this late stage they continued to hope for the creation of institutional ties between the mother country and the former protectorates.[26] By comparing the French Union with the Commonwealth they gave the impression that France had long been aiming at a goal very similar to Britain's—namely a kind of compromise between full independence and federal institutions.[27] We shall enter into greater detail about French discussion on the French Union and the colonial problems in the years 1946–1955 in the following chapter.

THE REVISION OF THE UNION FRANÇAISE AND THE POST-WAR DISCUSSION, 1946–1955

The French Union cannot be said to have achieved what the constitution of 1946 intended. The aim had been to convert the colonial Empire into an institutionalized Union which would reconcile the emancipation movements with the "permanent interests" of the colonial power. The reasons for the failure are many. The increase in pace and scope of activity of the emancipation movements made all compromise unacceptable and the nationalists' demands for independence were made more and more resolutely. "Independence" became their rallying cry and served as an integrational factor for the not yet stabilized social structures. The East-West conflict also provided support for efforts at social revolution within the nationalist organizations, and moderate leaders were forced to increase their demands under pressure from the Left. The U.N. also played an important role, taking an anti-colonialist stance and giving small and weak independent states a chance to act on the "world political stage". But it would be wrong to see outside pressure as the only reason for the Union's failure. France did little to make the institutions of the Union acceptable or to give the overseas member states the feeling that they had a part in general policy-making, or that they could successfully represent their claims before the mother country. Paris was too preoccupied with other matters, and both the general public and most of parliament continued to show little interest in overseas affairs. It seemed easier to adhere to the established order than to gradually accede to former subjects' escalating demands, whether within the institution of the French Union, or by a generous interpretation or even revision of the constitution. This would have been the only way of giving the alleged partners a sense of entering into a true union with the mother country, which would have compensated for the surrender of the status of formally independent state or even made this surrender seem advantageous.

The "Union" between the French Republic and the associated states got no further than the preliminary stages. After laborious negotiations France did come to agreements with Cambodia, Laos and Bao Dai's Republic of Vietnam, by promising "independence within the framework of the French Union", but France had to shift its position again during the 1953-1954 agreements, conceding the states their own foreign policy and army, and contenting itself with bilateral arrangements. The North African protectorates never became members of the Union. French lawyers might discuss whether the protectorate agreements even allowed for automatic entry into the Union as associated states—this question was answered in the affirmative at first but later in the negative —yet one way or another France would have had to agree on the active participation of member states in the institutions of the Union. Agreements of this kind were not even discussed, for neither the protectorates nor the metropolis showed much interest in entering the French Union! The nationalists saw the status of associated state as meaning the renunciation of their demanded independence. While in principle the protectorate was a temporary solution, the French Union was intended to be a permanent arrangement and the constitution did not provide for exit from the Union. Moreover, the nationalists saw the Union as an order imposed and created by France which was not based on the parity of the partners. Rather than entry into an existing Union, the nationalists therefore wanted round-table negotiations.[1] France, however, considered that the existence of the protectorates confirmed its claim to power and therefore did not press for the association agreements foreseen by the constitution. Neither the government nor the residents-general welcomed active participation by Indochinese and North African politicians; since the status of associated state had proved no more than a transitional step towards full independence in Indochina, they were aware and afraid of the "danger of infection" for North Africa. When the sultan of Morocco evinced interest in the French Union during a visit to Paris, some circles are said to have considered this an added reason for deposing him![2]

Accordingly, the Union's high council met only three times—the first time, characteristically, not until 1951! Gonidec wrote: "The French Government shows no eagerness for the 'assistance' of this organ."[3] The efforts of the Indochinese to make the council function as an advisory organ in decisions on overseas policy were rejected. The devaluation of the piastre in May 1943 was decided without consulting the associated states and this precipitated the crisis in the Union.⁴

The two other organs of the French Union, the presidency and the assembly, were similarly ineffectual. President Auriol did not take full advantage of his opportunities and, for instance, made no journeys to the former colonial Empire. The Assemblée de l'Union française met regularly and no doubt did some positive work, but government and parliament tried to restrict its role as far as possible. This assembly, which in fact was fully qualified, was not given an adequate role in the legislation and administration of the overseas territories and its proposals were ignored by parliament. The powers of the assembly, which were small in any case, were not extended.⁵ The native deputies' disappointment is understandable. They now shifted their activity to the Paris parliament and the local assemblies in the hope of participating in the "exercise of sovereignty" after the extension of their territorial autonomy.⁶

There was much criticism of the French Union and talk of revising it, but no positive steps were taken. Meanwhile decolonization was continuing and eventually proceeded outside the 1946 constitution. In July 1953 the Gaullist deputy Dronne introduced a motion to revise the constitution in the name of the RFP (Rassemblement du Peuple Français).⁷ The Union, he stated, existed only on paper. The president was not elected by the Union, the assembly had no effective power and the high council did not act. The Union should obtain its own ministers with special powers, and the associated states should participate in the election of the president. In short, the Union should acquire a "federal character". In 1955 the "Indépendants d'Outre-mer" launched a new attack, led by Senghor.⁸ The agreements in Indochina, they said, had already shattered the framework of the Union and similar developments were apparent in North Africa. Article 75 provided for a change of status for the African territories, but this was a "hypocritical formula" so long as government and parliament refused even minor reforms. Black Africa was not demanding the status of associated state, which had proved a failure in Indochina, but the status of "state integrated—by degrees—into a Federal French Republic". The one and indivisible Republic of 1789 no longer conformed to the situation in 1955. Integration by assimilation could not be reconciled with the African demand for self-realization and in any case it was unfeasible in practical terms. On the other hand, they said, the natives realized that independence in the full sense of the term was inconceivable for the small and economically weak African units: "interdependence" was the motto of the twentieth century. They wanted a revised constitution which would create a confederation with the associated states and convert the republic into a federation, with federal boards responsible for foreign policy, defence and economic planning, while the territories obtained their own internal governments. Senghor explained his proposals again in an essay in *La Nef*.[9] These proposals are striking and coherent: the recognition of independence and sovereignty in Indochina and North Africa must be the precondition for a new association with France; only then could France be given a privileged military and economic position. Black Africa was striving for internal autonomy together with participation on the federal boards. This would mean the achievement of equal rights and yet avoid "Balkanization".

Was the mother country prepared for such an incisive revision of the constitution? The Assemblée de l'Union française discussed the report of deputy Alfred Bour from March until July 1955, while after some discussion parliament resolved, on 24 March, to revise Title VIII of the constitution. But a year passed before Paul Coste-Floret (MRP) submitted his report on 5 July 1956, and it took the "Commission du suffrage universel" several months longer to come to a decision. It submitted its report on 26 March 1957, but the resolution was never passed by parliament. . . .

We cannot describe the countless proposals, reports and essays individually here, so we will limit ourselves to a few general observations.[10]

Today the legalistic character of the discussion seems curious and perhaps specifically French. The conversion or reconstruction of the institutions of the Union was debated in legal terms, as was the distribution of power between the Union and the territories and between the Union and the parliament, in an attempt to balance the divergent interests in a compromise. What was not discussed was the possibility that independent states might one day also emerge in Black Africa.[11]

Assimilation and consistent integration no longer formed the point of departure for a progressive reform policy. To increase the number of overseas deputies in parliament was no longer suggested either, perhaps because the metropolis had become aware of the implications of such an increase, perhaps because the African spokesmen now pursued other aims. In addition the Right pointed out the social and financial effects of the 1946 assimilatory laws and hoped that the grant of autonomy would clear the way for special territorial rulings in social legislation, wage and taxation policy.

Some demanded constitutional changes, others were content with readjustments in order to avoid the laborious and time-consuming process of revision. In characteristic terms they demanded the transfer of effective consultative powers or even of the power of decision in certain questions to the Assemblée de l'Union and an extension of the responsibilities of the territorial assemblies. But it proved difficult to concede legislative powers and their own governments to the territories, since this would destroy the framework of administrative decentralization. This problem anticipates the 1956 *Loi Cadre*.

Naturally there was much talk of federalism again, with supporters on both the Left and the Right. Their interests and attitudes were different, but their desire for a federal solution always had the same goal: to prevent the emergence of independent African states. But there were still many different interpretations of the term. We have described the proposal for "genuine" federalism of the Indépendants d'Outre-mer. Their primary aim was to remove the responsibility in questions of foreign policy, defence, economic planning, etc. from the French parliament and to transfer it to Union boards in which the overseas territories would be strongly, if not proportionally, represented. Special ministers would be responsible to the Union parliament. The Socialist Oreste Rosenfeld supported this proposal,[12] but characteristically his own party did not back him.[13] The mother country was not prepared for such extensive reforms, fearing that they would produce results similar to complete integration—namely reducing French freedom of decision and shifting the balance in favour of courts in which the native deputies would form a strong minority or even a majority! Instead France sought a compromise, as in 1946, which was of questionable legality. Indeed, if the parliament in France was to retain the ultimate power of decision in colonial affairs, a genuine federation could never come into being. It is proof of the difficult situation in which France found itself, and of the lack of understanding of federalism as such, that in many cases the fashionable term "federalism" was inadmissibly used in the sense of administrative decentralization. Even Pierre-Henri Teitgen, an MRP Socialist who specialized in constitutional questions and the French Union and was pro-reform, used the term to indicate "a wide autonomy of the territories within the unity of the Republic, the political achievement of administrative decentralization".[14] This interpretation might be valid for the *Loi Cadre* prepared by Coste-Floret, but it had little to do with federalism.

George Scelle,[15] an influential lawyer and specialist on federation, cursorily qualified the 1946 attempt to discover a federal structure in the constitution of the metropolis as "imperialist hypocrisy". It would be just as ridiculous, he said, to declare Madagascar or Dahomey a "French territory" as to make the Union assembly responsible only for overseas questions and not for Union questions as such; the French Union was by no means a "federal parliament". For political reasons Scelle also wanted to reserve real policy-making to the mother country and to grant the assembly only consultative powers. All parliaments, he alleged, had started as mere consultative boards! Scelle also tried to demonstrate legally that the concept of federalism did not imply "equality of competences", by referring to the Pan-American Union and the Commonwealth. The Commonwealth could be an example only if France was prepared to give up the idea of institutional ties and to rely on the Union members acknowledging French leadership. This was precisely what France did not want; in fact federalist plans were designed to prevent just such a true independence. Spokesmen for Indochina and Bourguiba might postulate a conversion of the French Union into a Commonwealth,[16] but France was not content with informal or bilateral agreements and strove for an institutional solution.[17] Some writers tried to evade the dilemma by describing the long overdue reform of the Union as a temporary one, since "genuine" federation could not be realized until later. Consequently "genuine" federation was once again dismissed and the entire discussion was no more than an alibi.

It is difficult, and would require considerable research, to describe in detail the attitudes of the French political parties to the colonial question after the Second World War. There was certainly no unity of position within the parties themselves. Even in the disciplined MRP there was a left and a right wing, and even Georges Bidault finally came into such conflict with his party that he was expelled from it. It was often the case that the policy espoused by party members who were ministers in the government was criticized by influential deputies in the same party. Because of this striking inconsistency, we shall confine ourselves to a few general observations and outline only the main features of the discussion within France.

The position of the Communist party is not of great interest in the context of this discussion. After the liberation, the party at first became a member of the government and, in the interests of eventually coming to power, did not support the colonial emancipation movements over-vehemently. Instead it described the nationalists as feudal bourgeois reactionaries or, during the Sétif uprising in 1945, as fascists, and pressed for a settlement between the interests of the mother country and those of the colonies. The party accepted the Indochina declaration of 24 March and tried to persuade the Viet Minh to modify their demands, arguing that the right to self-determination must not necessarily lead to dissociation and did not preclude certain forms of collaboration. Although the Communist party always supported the native deputies in the constituent assemblies, it eventually accepted the French Union.[18] After its exclusion from Ramadier's government, however, in 1947, it threw caution to the winds and supported the nationalist parties, openly urging the immediate grant of independence. It now "unmasked" any efforts at compromise and any transitional solutions as imperialist attempts to suppress the emancipation movements in the interests of French "monopoly capital" and of the American allies in order to continue the old policy of exploitation in a new form. Now the party backed Ho Chi Minh, protested against the war in Indochina and openly called for desertion and sabotage.[19]

Naturally the party strongly opposed the bloody repression of the 1947 revolt in Madagascar, the severe reprisals against the RDA in 1949, the North Africa policy, and above all the deposing of the sultan of

Morocco, and tried to exploit these actions as propaganda. The war in Algeria gave the Communists a chance to agitate too; however, they had to restrain themselves a little owing to the rather ambivalent attitude of the workers and the electorate and they were not quite able to come up to the expectations of the Algerian nationalists.

More interesting and more problematic was the attitude of the Socialist party. As a responsible government party or coalition partner of the left Centre it could afford even less to ignore "national" issues. It found its supporters less among the proletariat than in petit bourgeois rural circles, who were interested in economic and social reforms and supported a "progressive" programme, but rejected any policy of "surrender". In addition, since the party had to make concessions to its coalition partners, it often had to sanction a policy which contradicted its own doctrine. At first the Socialist party adhered to pre-war concepts. The party, it was alleged, was combatting exploitative colonialism and stood for the right to self-determination and emancipation. But conditions were generally not yet ripe for immediate independence and premature withdrawal would only clear the way for the old feudal or new bourgeois capitalist forces to oppress the masses. It was even possible that a different colonial power would simply step in to replace France.[20] As before 1939, the party therefore justified the temporary maintenance of French control by stressing France's civilizing achievements:

> The detention of territories formerly colonized is only admissible now in so far as the colonizing function resolves itself into a civilizing and educative function. It cannot be pursued against the wishes of the colonized people. It aims at guiding it [the people] to the ability to govern itself freely. It is then, it is when it ceases to be, that it retroactively finds its political and moral justification.[21]

As early as 1946 Léon Blum felt entitled to say with regard to Indochina: "The old colonial system . . . is today a changed matter!"[22] Even though this old party leader aimed at true independence, as he had done between the wars,[23] other Socialists pointed out that the French Union would make it possible for the former colonies to remain within Greater France. Their favourite argument was that independence had become an obsolete concept and did not correspond to present-day trends towards association. Senghor himself said in the party's national council: "The reality of today is not independence but interdependence."[24] In this way the demand for independence could be condemned as "separatism". The Socialist creed was curiously merged with nationalist arguments here. Alduy presents an example:

> This is the whole problem: to reconcile the principle of the right of the peoples to govern themselves with the actual condemnation of separatism . . . secession, lethal for France, illusion for the territories.[25]

Federation seemed a way out, and Alduy was one of its most eager exponents in 1947–1949.[26] In accordance with the preamble of the constitution, the French Union, as a "continuous creation", must be accommodating to all efforts at autonomy and must realize the principle of full equal rights for Union partners. Sovereignty was vested in the entire Union and therefore also extended to the metropolis.[27] As we mentioned earlier, Oreste Rosenfeld took up the concept of "genuine" federation again in 1955, but the party as such was against it. When it spoke of federalism in its resolutions, it meant only the French Union of the 1946 constitution; the term was dropped after 1950![28] Now the demands for revision ran as follows: recognition of "sovereignty and independence within the framework of the French Union" for the associated states—although the party did not enter into details about the meaning of this contradictory formula; a change of status for the trusteeship territories and for Madagascar, which would become associated states in accordance with Article 75; a single electoral college and an increase of the mixed communes in the African territories; better distribution of power between the territorial assemblies and the Union assembly.[29] But in 1956 the Socialists added that the sovereignty of parliament must not be affected and that France must not introduce a policy of "surrender". For the rest, the Socialist theses were rather vague and conventional; the party had veered to the right and wanted to prevent the discrepancy between its programmes and its effective policy as a government party from becoming too apparent.

The difficulty of establishing a Socialist policy became very clear in the Indochina question. In 1946 the party reached an agreement with Ho Chi Minh; but could it in fact accede to Ho's demands for full independence? It was difficult for the ageing and not very energetic Moutet to impose his wishes in face of the agitation staged in Paris and Saigon and its backing by Prime Minister Bidault. Even a Cabinet crisis would have had little success. Shortly before Léon Blum came to power he had urged an agreement with the Viet Minh "on the basis of independence"; but as early as 23 December events in Hanoi had put him in an awkward position from which it was difficult to find a way out that would gain parliamentary support. The right-wing Socialist Ramadier was to make liberal declarations when he became prime minister, yet he countered Ho Chi Minh's offer to negotiate by stipulating impossible conditions. Although the "militants" and *Le Populaire* had reservations about the "Bao Dai experiment",[30] the party had to give parliamentary protection to the policy of a government to which it belonged itself. Even if it continued to be in favour of negotiating with the Viet Minh, it could not oppose the demand for increased military action. With regard to Tunisian and Moroccan policy, the Socialists soon called for autonomy and subsequently for the right to independence with additional bilateral agreements. But they did not stipulate the acceptance of their theses as a condition for their participation in the government.[31] It was left to the Radical Socialists Mendès-France and Edgar Faure to introduce a change of course!

Undisturbed by government responsibility, parliamentary possibilities and the mood of the electorate, the left-wing intellectuals openly expressed their views on colonial policy and vehemently attacked the immobilism of the Fourth Republic. Sartre's *Les Temps modernes*, Claude Bourdet's *France Observateur*, the left-wing Catholic *Esprit* and later the *Express* had very different attitudes, yet they formed a common anti-capitalist and anti-colonialist front in their unconcern with party politics and in their attacks on the "system" of the Fourth Republic and its adherence to the *status quo* in overseas questions. *Les Temps modernes*, and *France Observateur* often came very close to Communist theses: France, they said, was supporting and defending a policy of capitalist exploitation; interested economic groups in the colonies, in the administration and in parliament had carried the day and were sabotaging reforms. In his much respected essay "Les Maîtres de l'Afrique du Nord", Claude Bourdet tried to demonstrate the close connections between the colonists, industry and the banks, and to show the political influence of certain prominent personages.[32] It was they who were chiefly to blame, he thought, for the critical situation in Madagascar, for the failure of the talks with Ho Chi Minh and for the delaying tactics in North Africa. His conclusions are obvious: a consistent and complete change of course, socialist reforms, the recognition of the right to autonomy and independence, negotiations with the nationalists before it was too late and while they were willing.

L'Esprit put forward somewhat more moderate demands. France was refusing, said J.-M. Domenach, to accept the world political situation. It must negotiate with Ho Chi Minh and convert the protectorates and Madagascar into associated states. He criticized

> this reflex of inferiority and fear that mark our policy in questions concerning the French Union. Fearing secession at every turn, we tighten the ropes until they threaten to break.[33]

L'Esprit wanted to work out a "progressive plan for emancipation" with the spokesmen for the nationalist movement. Accordingly Domenach supported a federal solution which was similar to what Alduy had proposed.[34] It was important, he said, to note the "transitory régime" of the French Union, which provided for a change of status for African territories too and would gradually come to resemble the Commonwealth. The Commonwealth had demonstrated in advance how independence could be reconciled with political, economic and cultural co-operation. "Our only chance of great power is to accede to this in our turn."[35] A generous policy of decolonization, based on a desire for internal renovation, offered the only real alternative to the hesitant attitude of the Fourth Republic which would either lead to colonial war or compel France to capitulate.

The Radical Socialists stood to the right in the Fourth Republic, although under Mendès-France the "progressive revolutionary" tradition broke through once again and temporarily influenced party policy. But a conservative if not reactionary course prevailed, particularly in colonial policy. The party hardly had any part in deciding the constitution of the French Union and rejected the proposals of both constituent assemblies. It was the Radical Socialist Herriot who finally managed to have the proposal of the constitutional department rejected, thereby ensuring the interests of the metropolis. In so doing he also disavowed Gaston Monnerville, who had supported the Inter-groupe's federal proposals. Strong economic interests came into play within the party and gave it a "colonialist" stamp: Luc Druand-Reville was senator from Gabon, member of the Académie des Sciences Coloniales and the party "expert" on Africa and the French Union: in addition he was a member of several colonial societies and a major exponent of "overseas capitalism". René Mayer, deputy from Constantine, who was president in 1953, and had connections with the Rothschilds and in "big business", took up the case of the French Algerians. Henri Borgeaud, who represented Algeria in the Senate from 1946 to 1959, was for a long time the head of the RGR faction. Deputy Georges Blanchette was one of the richest and most influential men in Algeria. Martinaud Déplat, the administrative president of the party from 1948 to 1955, had commitments in Tunisia and belonged to the right wing. Senator Antoine Colonna counts as the most important spokesman for the large number of French colonists in Tunisia.

It is not surprising, therefore, that Druand-Reville set forth colonialist and conservative proposals at the Radical Socialist party congress in 1949 as the reporter for overseas France.[36] His report began with the usual praise of France's colonial past[37] and he quoted Jules Ferry, reiterating the latter's arguments. A few abuses could not invalidate the great French achievement. France continued to rely on the colonies for its raw materials and export market. Since 1945 there had been a certain amount of confusion and anti-colonialism had become fashionable, but this ideology was dangerous, "above all because of the spirit of surrender which permeates it". This cliché was used to compromise all attempts at reform. Naturally there was no lack of attacks on Russia and the United States, while British colonial policy continued to seem "less specifically human" than French policy and oriented solely towards exploitation. The colonial nationalists, it was asserted, were small minorities of évolués whose status the Brazzaville conference had wrongly raised, and who were now directing their "native racism" against France. Examples of this trend were the revolt in Madagascar and the Vietnamese nationalist activities led by Ho Chi Minh. "Take care, surrender on a single point would lead to general ruin." Without its overseas possessions France would be a power of the rank of Poland or Portugal. "The Radical party, which has a fundamental notion of the greatness of France, set itself on the road to demolishing French sovereignty once before, with President Herriot" (a reference to Herriot's "emergency break"). Druand-Reville praised the Radical Socialist Bollaert, "inventor of the solution to the agonizing question of Indochina", i.e. of Bao Dai, and attacked assimilation—earlier Radical Socialists had considered it a liberal and progressive policy. It had been nonsense, he said, to give the "autochthons" political rights and parliamentary representation in 1946, since the *évolués* were already demanding new rights, autonomy and even independence. Equality had been interpreted in such a way, he asserted, that it jeopardized the domination of the mother country; an example was the single electoral college in the African territories. Labour legislation had led to a decrease in production, while other projects had been "hair-raising" and had been avoided only by timely Radical Socialist intervention. In effect, Druand-Reville had a personal part in the successful delaying tactics, and the Code Moutet of 1947 could not be enforced until 1952.[38]

The party congresses in the following years moved along the same lines, although the general statements had a more traditional "Radical Socialist" tone. Opposition to a policy of "surrender" remained strong:

> Our country depends bodily on the Overseas peoples. . . . North Africa is the last chance for France . . . without these three countries . . . we would have lost our rank of great power . . . for us this is a question of life and death. . . . It must be made quite clear, in Africa as abroad, that we will abandon none of our essential rights. . . . We shall remain.[39]

While Morocco would long be dependent on France, France itself had "acquired imprescriptible rights". A minimum [!] of "auto-determination" was necessary, but without questioning the protectorate treaties.[40] Roche made the ingenious proposal of a Moroccan federation based on national and ethnic factors. Apart from the maghzen, which was responsible for Moroccan affairs, the French Community should be under a high commissioner. Above him should be a governor-general appointed by the president of the French Union, who would represent France in the Union and on the international boards.[41] This so-called reform proposal in 1953 was in fact a variant of co-sovereignty, designed to bind Morocco closely to the mother country and ensure, at least indirectly, that the settlers remained in a dominant position. There was not a word about the sultan! How far Roche was implicated in the removal of the sultan remains an open question, but in any case the party backed his manoeuvre and congratulated him on his influence in Morocco.[42] The major opposition to Mendè's-France's Tunisian policy came from Borgeaud, Colonna and Martinaud Déplat; Déplat sharply opposed Bourguiba and the idea of negotiations in parliament on 10 August 1954, in order to torpedo the Carthage speech.[43] René Mayer dissociated himself from Mendès-France's policy and managed to overthrow him in February 1955. However, it was the Radical Socialist Edgar Faure who continued Mendès-France's policy in Tunisia and Morocco and brought it to its conclusion, i.e. granting the full independence which had been considered out of the question two years before.[44] It is characteristic of the internal state of the Radical Socialist party that Martinaud Déplat took a stand against Faure, the president of his own party, in the fight over the conventions with Morocco on 8 October 1955![45]

Albert Sarraut served as president of the Union Assembly and reiterated his old proposals at the 1951 party congress. Everyone had a right to exploit mineral resources in the undeveloped areas, and colonization was justified as an "agent of civilization".[46] France's mission lay, he said a year later, in the "integration of Africa into Europe". This was a convenient phrase which meant little but corresponded to Radical Socialist ideas.[47] France had acted too hastily in Black Africa and had given the Africans rights which they did not understand.[48] This was followed by talk of "the primordiality of social and economic questions over politics".[49] After 1952 the Radical Socialists also felt it necessary to urge a reform of the Union by granting further powers to the local and Union assemblies. But the party developed no original ideas of its own and devoted no special attention to this reform. The Radical Socialist party's general attitude towards the colonial debate in these years was based on the economic interests of its members or on the familiar pre-war theses which now led to immobilism and checked any timely reforms.

It would be interesting to discuss the role of Mendès-France in greater detail, but here we must be content with a few observations on François Mitterand, who belonged to the democratic opposition but adhered to Mendès-France's ideas. In his 1953 book *Aux frontières de l'Union française*, with a foreword by Mendès France, Mitterand attacked French overseas policy. He was in favour of negotiating with Ho Chi Minh and pointed out the contradiction of granting independence to Laos, Cambodia and Bao Dai and even promoting Indochinese nationalism against the Viet Minh while refusing these same concessions to Tunisia and Morocco and repressing nationalism there. This would only drive North African nationalists into the arms of the Communists and would spoil any chances of reaching an agreement with a man like Bourguiba. Mitterand wanted to concede "sovereignty" to Tunisia, in the sense of internal autonomy, and postulated a dual nationality which would give the French Tunisians voting rights and ensure them representation in the Tunisian parliament. The Republic of Tunisia would continue to belong to the French Union, "even if it does not adhere to it explicitly". Mitterand described the "federal structure" as the "only obstacle to the excessive development of the aspirations towards integral independence and to the encroachments of increasing tutelage", but he did not define this federal structure more clearly. The protectorates, however, should not be converted into associated states, as provided for in the constitution, for "the example of Vietnam would be annoyingly contagious. All that has been done in Saigon is in direct opposition to the French Union".[50] Mitterand preferred bilateral negotiations with formal retention of the protectorate treaties; he wanted to grant internal autonomy but to reserve foreign policy, defence, etc. to France or to common boards. In 1953 he protested that even Bourguiba did not ask for more. As we briefly mentioned, Mendès-France had tried to introduce a similar policy in 1954 in his Carthage speech. But while Bourguiba considered internal autonomy only a transitional solution, Mitterand and Mendès-France wanted it as a more or less permanent arrangement. Characteristically Mitterand contemplated a "Eurafrican France":

> From the Congo to the Rhine, the third continent-nation will be balanced around our metropolis[51] ... to make the united republic flexible [with regard to the African territories], to prevent the creation of associated states, to federate the protectorate states [Tunisia and Morocco], this is the task to be accomplished, the task which will lead eighty million men to their destiny.[52]

Generous concessions were to become the basis of a new form of "Greater France". Influential spokesmen of the left-wing bourgeois opposition still believed in 1954–1955 that they could avoid opening the road to independence for Tunisia and Morocco and maintain institutional ties with the mother country. This proves how much the traditional concept of Greater France affected French discussion of decolonization and stood in the way of any agreement on eventual dissociation. It is not surprising either that Mitterand misunderstood British policy and drew false conclusions from it. He compared the grant of self-government to Nkrumah in 1951 with the North Africa policy he had conceived, on the grounds that three British ministers also remained in the cabinet in the Gold Coast to ensure imperial control. In fact, while London knew that this could only be an interim solution on the way to full dominion status, Mitterand viewed it as evidence of permanent ties, such as he wanted to establish in slightly different form in Tunisia and Morocco! His assumption proved an illusion and laid politicians such as Mitterand and Mendès-France open to the reproach that they were either playing a double game or were entertaining false hopes by supporting a policy of unnecessary renunciation and "surrender".

The Right could take this as a basis for criticism. Its arguments are self-evident and we can summarize them briefly, particularly since we intend to speak of General de Gaulle and his supporters in a later connection. The right-wing policy heralded in 1946 by the États généraux de la colonisation française and by the activity of the Comité de l'Empire, was pursued after the enforcement of the constitution with a readjustment of aims to combat any policy of concession and to defend the "French presence". The stock phrase about "surrender" informed the whole discussion and served as a strong argument. The Right asserted that with their allegedly liberal reform policies the government, the left-wing parties and the intellectuals were destroying the former mighty colonial Empire piece by piece because of their weakness, their party interests or their ideological confusion, and accused them of making concessions to the "secessionist" nationalists and of committing high treason with their policy of "surrender". To refute this accusation the Centre and Left tried to present their reform policy as the only remaining chance of preventing precisely such a "surrender". It is hard to tell if, or how far, the Right was acting on behalf of concrete economic interests, whether it was reflecting a general conservative and reactionary attitude in colonial questions or whether traditional nationalism was the decisive factor. In party politics the Right was chiefly represented by the "indépendants et Paysans"; but we must note that it was more of a collective movement, and that for instance a supporter of the national Right such as Paul Reynaud spoke out of turn on several occasions, both when he supported European union and in his colonial policy. *France Outre-mer* and *Marchés coloniaux* were the chief public organs representing colonial interests.

With tiresome repetition, the Right recalled France's historic achievement in civilizing its overseas territories and in leading them to prosperity. This task was not yet concluded, it asserted, and France still had a "civilizing mission". The colonial French played a key role, asserted the Right, and their field of action must be defended for only thus could France remain a great power in political, economic and cultural affairs. A stereotyped anti-Americanism linked the political Right with the left-wing intellectuals, although some of their arguments were different. The Americans had impeded the reconquest of Indochina, were supporting the national opposition both directly and indirectly, and wanted to take possession of the economic positions abandoned by France. At the same time, the Right dismissed colonial emancipation as the work of only a small number of treacherous agitators who were neither representative of the masses nor capable of bearing responsibility. It was quite mistaken to want to make concessions to this pseudo-élite, for this would only be taken as a sign of weakness and provoke new demands. The mother country, particularly the left-wing parties of course, was disrupting the generally good relations between natives and Europeans and thereby preparing the way for "surrender". From the outset the Right had distrusted the agreement with Ho Chi Minh, approved the action of the administration in Saigon and held the Viet Minh solely responsible for the failure of the talks in Fontainebleau and the outbreak of the bloody conflict.

It wanted to wage war against the "traitors" with full force; negotiations with the Viet Minh were pointless; Emperor Bao Dai must guarantee French presence and French interests. France was defending not just itself but the whole of Western civilization in Indochina.

The entire armoury of arguments emerged in Frédéric Dupont's *Mission de la France en Asie*, published in 1956. Dupont, a former president of the Paris municipal council, minister for the associated states and reporter on the military budget, belonged among the most influential members of the Right in colonial questions.[53] He had written his book, he said himself, in order to protect the French army in North Africa against the same fate as had befallen it in Indochina, namely lack of support, contempt and betrayal—and by so doing he more or less anticipated and justified the problematic attitude of the army in the Algerian war. He revealed the lack of national unity, the parliamentary intrigues, the tensions within the Cabinet and the weakness of the government, and accused Communists, Socialists and the left-wing intellectuals of prevarication, treason and "cowardice". He blamed the Socialists specifically for having demanded negotiations with the Viet Minh, delaying the Bao Dai experiment and rousing anti-French suspicion. The army, he said, had been systematically slandered. The report on tortures in Indochina, which Paul Mus had published in *Témoignage chrétien* in 1950, appeared to Dupont to be an example of the "masochism of certain degenerate intellectuals".[54] The Geneva agreement and the policy of Mendès-France were expressions of this reprehensible defeatism, which even *Le Monde* had backed. The Bandung conference, at which slave-holding states were indicting France, was ridiculous and it was equally shameful that the Americans "who have exterminated the Indians . . . call us colonialists". The right wing also attacked the English who were letting Indians starve, while French engineers were building factories [!] and roads in Indochina with the savings of the mother country, and they took an equally vehement stand in the Tunisia and Morocco question, particularly when Paris abandoned the concept of sovereignty in 1954 and opened the way for internal autonomy and independence. A resolution of the first party meeting of the Indépendants in December 1954 stated.

> North Africa is the extension of France. France cannot conceive of itself without it. . . . The Congress asks the deputies to oppose the present Government policy in North Africa, because, under cover of reforms which draw their apparent audacity from equivocation, this policy will finally result in nothing but despair and abandon.[55]

Roger Duchet, the secretary-general and the Indépendants' most influential parliamentarian, managed to assert this policy of "France interdépendante" (the title of the party organ) in parliament and to see to it that it went further than mere programmatic statements.[56] The former resident-general of Morocco, Gabriel Puaux, not only wanted to adhere to "co-administration" in 1954, but even asserted that the majority of the inhabitants approved of a solution which ensured French interests and that "only the paranoiacs will remain irreducible."[57] Among these paranoiacs he naturally counted Bourguiba! In effect what Puaux's proposals meant was that France should take a strong position, in the dubious supposition that this would silence the nationalist opposition and put an end to the growing terrorism. Another example of this policy is the parliamentary debate of 6–7 October 1955, during which the Right tried to block Edgar Faure's Morocco policy. One deputy attacked the president: "Your directives? Discussion with the Istiqlal, pressure on our friends, softness and cowardice towards our adversaries, negotiation, concessions, retrocessions, surrender, continuous incapacity which will one day enable the French people to wake up parked in the metropolis." The government was preparing for a withdrawal "à l'anglaise" [!]: "You are ... in favour of surrender. ... Do you not think you have had enough now, that the hour for resistance is come ... and that you must put an end to French powerlessness after the defeat of Indochina."[58] Another deputy mocked the slogan "one-way independence" which prepared the road for "secession", although nine-tenths of the French in Morocco considered this policy wrong. The deposed sultan had refused reforms, while the new sultan was willing "to constitute a government in which the French would participate, thus creating a true Franco-Moroccan community", i.e. co-sovereignty with French ascendancy.[59] The United States and Russia, the Arab League and even Great Britain were a threat to France's strategic interests. Arab nationalism was just "fanaticism", whereas El-Glaoui was a good friend to France. The government, by contrast, was negotiating with "a handful of assassins". Frédéric Dupont again attacked *Témoignage chrétien* and François Mauriac and spoke of the "desertion of a part of the French intellectual élite".[60]

It appears in retrospect that an almost pathological chauvinism threatened to bar any realistic view. Influential spokesmen of the bourgeois Right, not to mention the extreme Right, were fascinated by the idea of "la France Seule" (France alone), whose greatness and power seemed jeopardized because the whole world was plotting against it. Admittedly their interest in their fellow citizens in Tunisia and Morocco, who could not simply be sacrificed, was understandable, and it was only natural to defend them and to repress anti-French agitation. But how could serious politicians entertain the illusion, at a time when Britain had already renounced a major part of its imperial positions and Arab nationalism was reaching ever more threatening proportions, that they could calm the tensions in Tunisia and Morocco, whose protectorate structure was based on eventual independence, without extensive reforms—or that they could effect the solemnly invoked "Franco-Muslim collaboration" by means of repression? Neither economic interests nor the actions of the French colonials in or outside of the French parliament provide an adequate explanation of this attitude. The situation was a direct result of the fact that France lacked the kind of effective concept of decolonization that would have seen withdrawal as the meaningful conclusion of a policy of expansion. The image of a Greater France, which survived in such vague notions as association and collaboration and which France wanted to institutionalize in the French Union, made the recognition of sovereignty, even in the protectorates, appear to be a loss of power and prestige and of national territory, as well as the dissolution of Greater France. The traditional nationalism that informed wide sections of the French public vehemently resisted this.

To conclude we must touch briefly on the attitude of Catholic France, although neither the pronouncements of the clergy nor the attitude of the parliamentary deputies makes it fully clear. In contrast to pre-war years, after 1946 Catholic discussion on the colonial question was extremely lively and ranged through all the variants from Right to Left. In 1945 the Mouvement Républicain Populaire appeared on the scene as the first Catholic party with mass support. This party, with its demand for social reforms, formed the coalition government of "tripartism" together with Communists and Socialists. The party gradually shifted to the Right, found its constituency among the bourgeoisie, and was forced to form a Cabinet with the right wing. Tendencies towards the Left survived, however, even though they were scarcely visible on the surface because of fractional discipline. We have already mentioned the deputy of Cameroun, Dr Aujoulat, who was responsible for the report on colonial policy at the 1945 party congress, where he attacked colonialist exploitation and demanded reforms. The MRP had an active part in working out the constitution and the sections regarding the French Union, and in following years it strongly supported conversion of the Union along federalist lines. The assembly should be granted further powers and later become a "deliberative assembly". The high council should finally begin to act, and the French ministers of foreign affairs and defense would obtain the status of ministers of the Union—so wrote the overseas minister, Coste-Floret, in 1948.[61] The party congress of the same year supported decentralization in Africa and universal franchise in two ballots, but with a single electoral college.[62] One party committee wanted to leave the decisions on becoming associated states and on full integration to the territories themselves, as provided for in Article 75 of the constitution.[63] A number of these proposals were chiefly addressed to the militants and were designed to demonstrate the party's pro-reform attitude; in fact they said little that was new and were often rather conformist.

In 1953 Georges Le Brun-Kéris, who had been in charge of African questions in the party's secretariat-general from 1951 to 1958, published a book entitled *Mort des colonies?* It exposed the "mandate character" and temporary nature of colonial rule, yet described a rapid withdrawal and the grant of independence as "premature". The author supported this thesis by dubious references to the economic development of India and Pakistan since 1947 and to "Muslim obscurantism". He considered the formula "independence within the framework of the French Union" particularly likely to reconcile national emancipation with French interests, but rejected any solution for Tunisia that did not ensure "French presence"; Morocco, he thought, would also require French control for a long time to come.[64] Naturally Le Brun-Kéris proposed a federal solution for Africa, but offered no practical details. The only point on which he appears resolute is the rejection of a pan-African union and the Grand Counseil![65] On the other hand it must be pointed out that Dr. Aujoulat, the secretary of state in the overseas ministry from 1948 to 1952, was responsible for the labour legislation.[66] The MRP also managed to enter into an *apparentement* (alliance) with Senghor's Indépendants d'Outre-mer and in 1954–1955 it actively supported, through Aujoulat, their demand for a major reform of Title VIII of the constitution, with a view to genuine autonomy for the territories with their own governments.[67] The 1956 *Loi Cadre* was prepared by the overseas minister Teitgen.[68] But in the MRP too there was a discrepancy between declarations and effective action as a government party. We have mentioned the foreign minister Robert Schuman, who in face of the general taboo spoke of independence for Tunisia in 1950 but then gave in to right-wing pressure and adopted the concept of co-sovereignty (cf. pp. 401–2). In similar fashion the party congress in 1953 proposed replacing the protectorate with an association agreement,[69] but the party ministers had neither the desire nor the opportunity to support this resolution. The MRP did not protest the deposing of the sultan of Morocco, but later it supported the North Africa policy of Mendès-France and Edgar Faure.

The extra-party colonial debate was very tense, and every point of view, from the left-wing intellectual anti-colonialism of *Témoignage chrétien* and *Esprit*, via *La Croix*, to the conservative conformist patriotism of *La France catholique*, came to light.[70] One could even speak of a questioning of conscience, which was not confined to a theoretical discussion of the right to colonize but rather strove to determine attitude towards the events in Indochina, Tunisia, Morocco and later Algeria. Behind this lay a significant change of policy in Rome and in the religious orders responsible for the missions. The Catholic Church wanted to dissociate itself from the colonial powers and to appear to be a universal institution, not necessarily confined to European civilization alone. It greeted desires for emancipation with benevolence if not support, and tried to keep in touch with the Catholic educated élite.[71] This policy was reflected in the encyclical *Evangelii Praecones* of 2 June 1953. Pope Pius XII had already spoken of "your fatherland" and "your country" in a message to the Catholics in Madagascar in 1951. Subsequently the declaration of the apostolic vicars of Madagascar in November 1953 attracted considerable attention by stating, among other things. "We recognize the legitimacy of the aspiration towards independence as well as any constructive efforts to achieve it". This pronouncement, which Rome did not refute, was welcomed by the Left, condemned by the French administration and dismissed by Catholic conservative circles as irresponsible demagogy.[72] In 1957 a book appeared in a Protestant publishing house with the expressive title *Le Vatican contre la France d'Outre Mer?* which reproached the Catholic Church with playing emancipation as a trump card and systematically undermining French overseas positions. Books such as the Jesuit Father Michel's *Le devoir de decolonisation* (1954) or Robert de Montvalon's *Ces pays qu'on n'appellera plus colonies*, can only be named here.

It was not only the left-wing intellectuals from *Témoignage chrétien* who used sharp words in this discussion. Joseph Folliet, whom we mentioned earlier as the Catholic colonial specialist of the inter-war years (cf. pp. 307–8), declared himself in 1946 to be "humiliated as a Frenchman and as a Christian" and urged negotiations with Ho Chi Minh. In *Témoignage chrétien*, on 2 August 1949, in the aforementioned article "Non, pas ça", Paul Mus protested the tortures in Indochina and the entirely one-sided information supplied by the French press—for which Mus was accused by the Right of high treason. After the unrest and repressions in Casablanca in 1952, François Mauriac intervened in the discussion, first in *Le Figaro*, then regularly in his "bloc-notes" in *L'Express*. Mauriac also presided over the "Comité France Maghreb", which included such well-known Catholic personalities as Coste-Floret, Folliet, Delavignette, Madaule and Domenach, as well as the Senegalese Diop. He wanted the protectorate agreements revoked and efforts made towards negotiating with the nationalists; the deposing of the sultan was a scandal. French North Africa policy required complete reorientation, free from the pressure of economic interests and the French colonials, so that one could begin "fraternal collaboration" with the former colonies. This Catholic intellectual thought the former rather complacent attitude and the acknowledgement of abuses were not a convincing argument. Mauriac saw himself caught in a moral conflict—in the Indochinese war and above all in the Algerian question—between the basic concepts of Christian life: belief versus politics, church versus state, individual versus nation.

BLACK AFRICA AND THE *LOI CADRE* (1946–1956)

The 1946 constitution integrated Black Africa, but it gave the territories a special status rather than a departmental structure, as in the *vieilles colonies*. This was to ensure administrative decentralization and to give the former natives a voice in the elected territorial assemblies. In fact it provided a kind of compromise between full assimilation and proportional parliamentary representation—which did not seem possible or suitable—on the one hand, and autonomy on the other—which seemed like a preliminary step towards "secession" and contradicted the concept of Greater France.

Compromises also had to be made within the territories at first, quite apart from the fact that the status provided for in the constitution did not come into effect [!] and the institutions were established by means of decree. Franchise was restricted to certain categories of inhabitants[1]; this seemed necessary with regard to the Africans' vastly differing levels of education, although it was difficult to reconcile with the principle not all subjects were to enjoy full civil rights. The same applied to the double electoral college, which separated citizens with French nationality from citizens with local nationality and gave the small minority of French colonials a privileged position.[2] The economic and social importance of this minority may have partly justified their privileges, but naturally the African élite saw it as discrimination and as an attempt to maintain colonial rule. In fact, the two colleges co-operated very well in the territorial assemblies.

But the assemblies had very little power. Legislation remained entirely reserved to parliament and even in local affairs the local assemblies had neither legislative nor executive power; this was reserved to the overseas ministry and to the governor as the sole head of the executive. Since the whole civil service was under the governor, there was only a limited degree of "local administration". The assemblies had the right to vote on the budget and thus obtained some share in determining the utilization of funds, but a major part of the expenditure was fixed in advance, often making discussion on the budget a mere illusion.[3]

Moreover, although the constitution proclaimed full equal rights in the occupation of offices, the administration managed to check any "Africanization" and to reserve most of the "offices of authority" to the French.

France was justifiably proud that Africans sat in the French Parliament, were represented in the U.N. delegation and even could and did become ministers. But this cannot hide the fact that the colonial administration changed very slowly and scarcely differed from pre-war times. In private concerns, "Africanization" was equally hesitant.[4]

This is not to deny that the territorial assemblies fulfilled an important function. Franchise was introduced in French Black Africa, the number of voters rose in 1951 from 1.25 to 5 million[5] and the proportion of Africans among them continued to increased. Although the administration intervened in the elections and even tampered with the votes on occasion,[6] the assemblies managed to exert some control and presented demands which the administration could not simply ignore. African politicians became familiar with parliamentary procedure and were confronted with the complex questions of modern administration. In addition, the Africans could assert their interests in the Paris parliament. Black Africa was still definitely under-represented,[7] but the parties in the mother country took pains to conciliate the overseas deputies and tried to gain their support when they had a weak majority. The elections to parliament and to the territorial assemblies gave the Africans another, hitherto unknown, field of activity.[8]

If before and immediately after the Second World War African politicians usually joined the metropolitan French parties, particularly the Socialist party, now they formed indigenous African parties. It is sufficient here to name the "Rassemblement Démocratique" founded in Bamako in 1946 and the "Bloc Démocratique Sénégalais" (which split from the SFIO in 1948). The RDA, led by Houphouet-Boigny, which was the first extra-territorial party with mass support, joined the Communists in parliament at first, but separated from them after the uprisings on the Ivory Coast in 1949 and joined the coalition government. In 1956 Houphouet-Boigny became minister. Gradually his political programme shifted from the demand for extensive autonomy to integration in the Republic; meanwhile the BDS led by Senghor largely took the opposite position, first accepting integration, then demanding federation and finally supporting confederation. At any rate the constitution of the Fourth Republic offered no more than a temporary "solution" to decolonization and African politicians soon demanded increased responsibilities in the territories. Independence was not yet under discussion, but they spoke of obtaining genuine self-government and effective participation in political and administrative decisions. The colonial administration and the mother country showed little interest in meeting these fairly understandable demands. Paris was prepared to grant economic aid, but decided to adhere to administrative decentralization and hesitated to transfer legislative power and government control to the territories. In April 1954, when Senghor and Aujoulat (MRP) asked the government to grant the territories legislative powers by instituting reform of the French Union, the overseas minister evaded the issues saying that Title VIII of the constitution could perhaps be supplemented, but that "it is a question of conserving the integrity of the central organization of the Republic while at the same time allowing the territories to settle affairs of local interest themselves",[9] i.e. the unity of the Republic and the dominance of parliament and the central administration remained a *sine qua non*. This obviously could not satisfy even the moderate Indépendants d'Outre-mer. The government was also under pressure from the Right.[10] But the long-overdue reform did not come into effect until 1956 and the *Loi Cadre*.

While the 1946 constitution once again settled the relations of the mother country and its African colonies, granted civil rights and introduced a process of democratization, the modernization of the local administration advanced very slowly. "Contrary to the British, the French have constructed the superstructures before the base."[11] Even in the British colonies conversion of the native authorities into a local government after 1945 lagged behind political development at the head. Since France refused to give the territories legislative power and referred the African politicians to parliament, it would have been natural for it to promote the administration of the communes and to give the Africans direct administrative powers. In fact this would have meant a rapid increase of the plenary communes (Dakar, Saint Louis and Rufisque), i.e. the grant of French communal rights with general franchise and an elected mayor. A corresponding law, increasing the number of full communes to twenty-six in French West Africa and six in Equatorial Africa, was proposed as early as 1948, but was not passed until 1955 [!]. Like their colleagues in the mother country, African politicians and deputies took possession of the offices of mayor and thus strengthened their positions.[12]

It was difficult to reconcile the tradition *chefferie* with the conferment of citizenship, franchise, territorial assemblies and plenary communes. Eboué's 1941 circular requesting that the administration seek out the authentic chiefs and persuade them to collaborate, soon proved outdated, for the emancipated élite was by then replacing the chiefs in leadership positions. The 1946 constitution did not mention chiefs, and the chiefs had no representation of their own in the territorial assemblies, unlike in the British Empire. No attempts were made to incorporate the chiefs and notables into the new electoral and representative system. In Senegal a general election for the appointment of the village chief was introduced in 1947 which ultimately resulted in the elimination of the notables and the loss of the specific character of the African chiefs.[13] Several chiefs no doubt adapted themselves to the new situation, but on the whole they became the representatives of a conservative if not reactionary course and came into conflict with the *évolués*; the nationalist press described them as "lackeys of the colonialist administration".[14] Chiefs even formed unions to represent their demands—and their wages

—more forcefully! On the other hand, African politicians thought it necessary to take the traditional authorities into account and had to try to obtain at least passive collaboration from the chiefs. According to a 1949 bill, which the chiefs had a part in working out, chiefs were to be elected according to law and the administration would merely confirm the election; "any attack on the legitimate authority of the customary chief will be punished". He was to obtain higher wages, and in return learn to read and write in French or Arabic.[15] The African politicians were eager to reduce the power of the bureaucracy and to make the chief the true "intermediary" between the people and the administration. Prescriptive law and general franchise must be reconciled, said Senghor: "There are no more customary chiefs in the true sense of the term, but autochthonous chiefs, semi-functionaries. This is the reality of which we must speak if we wish to reorganize the *chefferie* on healthy bases, i.e. both legal and effective." This bill was not passed in parliament either, and we must ask whether the fact that Senghor acted as reporter was sufficient cause for the administration and the right-wing parties to reject it. New statutes were decreed only after the *Loi Cadre* had transferred the responsibility of deciding on the *chefferie* to the territories. Sékou Touré abolished *chefferies* in Guinea in December 1957, while interim and transitional solutions were in effect in the other territories. In regions that are both far from the coast and economically weak, the chiefs still have considerable importance today.

Labour laws naturally stood in the forefront of social questions. We have already mentioned the first measures applied: unionization rights and controlled labour in 1944, and the abolition of forced labour on 11 April 1946. The Code Moutet of October 1947, which established the principle of equal wages for equal work in the mother country and overseas, was suspended by Moutet's successor because of massive pressure, particularly from the *Comité de l'Empire français*. The employers pointed to the low productivity of the African workers, to foreign competition and to the allegedly demoralizing effects of massive wage increases, and prophesied a sharp fall in production.[16] The administration appears to have backed these proposals, although the wages of African workers were minimal and there was still discrimination. As we have seen, it was Dr. Aujoulat who helped to carry the 1952 Code du Travail through parliament. The code proposed union rights, the interdiction of forced labour, "equal wages for equal work", and in addition a forty-hour week, obligatory Sunday rest, paid holidays, etc. The provisions for its execution allowed time for adaptation to African circumstances. This remarkable labour law largely corresponded to the one in force in the mother country and was a consequence of the extension of citizenship to all subjects. Ansprenger has described it as the "last monument to the policy of assimilation"—assimilation in the liberal progressive sense.[17]

Great improvements were also made after 1945 in the African educational system. The Brazzaville conference had demanded this, the French Union and the conferment of citizenship made it urgent. Primary schooling was rapidly extended, the number of *lycées* and *collèges* was quickly multiplied.[18] Through FIDES, the mother country made funds available for building schools. But instruction, except in Madagascar, remained exclusively in French. Here too France followed the Brazzaville directives and confirmed the trend towards assimilation of the 1946 constitution. But African politicians themselves expressed little desire for change and even retained French as the official language after independence. In spite of "Negritude" and the call for "Africanization" they were deeply impregnated by French schooling and culture, quite apart from the practical difficulties which giving up French would have entailed.

In 1950 the Institut des Hautes Études was founded in Dakar, and in 1957 it was expanded to become the first real university in French Black Africa. By comparison with British West Africa, the transition to higher education was late, for France preferred to train the African élite in the metropolitan universities, although the danger of alienating the students from their indigenous civilization was repeatedly stressed, particularly by the conservatives. Significantly, it was Senghor who criticized the foundation of Dakar University, seeing it only as a gesture of prestige on the part of mother country.

We must add a few observations on economic policy. Here too we can start from the constitution, whose preamble postulated a co-ordination of economic efforts and envisaged a large-scale economy; this would comply with the traditional concept of Greater France and it received new impetus after the Second World War. The "great whole" constituted by the tariff union and tariff preferences, currency convertibility, bills of exchange, and stabilization agreements for certain products was intended to ensure a secure market, but also and above all to help compensate for the lack of dollars and to give France a certain economic independence from the United States.[19] As had already happened in France after the First World War and in Britain in 1945, the Fourth Republic strove to promote overseas economic development on a vast scale in order to compensate for its weakened economic position in Europe. This time however, France did not let it rest at programmatic declarations. In spite of the need for investment in the metropolis, post-war France raised vast funds for the development of Africa, primarily from its public resources. In each territory a ten-year plan was to apply; FIDES would provide the capital and examine the granting of credits. However, these plans were largely prepared in Paris and presented to the local assemblies only for consultation, few native experts from the territories were represented even in the directorate of FIDES. The centralist concept of a "great whole" directed from Paris was also obvious in economic planning. The British procedure, which was based on similar considerations but largely let the individual territories work out their own plans for development, was therefore less open to the reproach that the object of the plan was to supply the needs of the mother country.

Investment credits were used primarily to improve the infrastructure. Impressive achievements occurred in the construction of ports, streets, airports, railway lines, dams and electricity works over a very short time. Also, FIDES granted resources for the construction of schools, hospitals and research institutes.[20] In subsequent years the emphasis was shifted to agriculture and industrial production. For 1955, Moussa calculated that the entire French "aid to development" came to 171 thousand million francs, of which 72.5 thousand million went to the overseas territories, i.e. about one-fifth of all public investment![21] In private investment, apart from intensive building schemes in towns such as Dakar and Abidjan, mining and traditional export production was in the forefront; the production and export of groundnuts, cocoa, coffee, rubber, wood and bananas increased tremendously in a very short time. The main trade was with the metropolis, which paid prices above the world market level but also forced the territories to buy French imports at equally inflated prices. This gave rise to criticism on both sides but was characteristic of a specifically French situation which survived even after independence in some places.[22]

There was still little effort at industrialization, even for refining local raw materials. "The resistance of the French economy to the industrialization of the overseas territories appears an established fact."[23] Primarily the overseas territories were to supply raw materials and food, buying their industrial goods from the mother country. There was little possibility of promoting their own production by a similar tariff policy. Not without justice, African politicians and left-wing political writers repeatedly accused France of maintaining the *pacte colonial* and not granting public investment funds in accord with the real needs of the African territories, with the result that the already widely monopolized trade and capital companies gained additional profits.[24] Yet the comprehensive scheme of developmental aid was greeted with much praise from Africans too and doubtless contributed towards relieving political tensions. It also made African leaders realize that they continued to depend on French aid and must not provoke a premature break with the mother country. But the metropolis was beginning to ask itself whether this large-scale and costly investment of public funds was still a sensible and responsible policy at a time when France had to begin to withdraw in the political field!

There was no revision of the French Union, but events marched on and a decision had to be made. If France wanted to avoid conflict in Black Africa it had to accede in one way or another to the growing demands of the overseas deputies. This realization seems to have penetrated government circles and the parties around 1955. Now that the decolonization of Indochina, Tunisia and Morocco, which had been of foremost interest until then, had been "solved", Black Africa became the focus of discussion. Here at least France was more willing to make concessions in the interest of avoiding bloody conflict and secession. British policy in West Africa, especially the Gold Coast, made it necessary for France to take the initiative. In 1951–1952 Nkrumah became the first leading African nationalist to become prime minister of a colony! French Africa had in the past paid little attention to the British territories and African politicians certainly did not consider the British concept of self-government a model worth emulating; language difficulties, education in Paris, representation in parliament, quite apart from bad communications along the coast, resulted in a predominantly pro-French viewpoint. But developments in the Gold Coast just before independence had the effect of a signal which was not ignored in French Africa. Now the party leaders could point to the Gold Coast as an example; in addition they were under pressure from the Left to increase their demands and Paris had to try to make up for previous delays. The French answer to this challenge was different from the British one, but it had to sound equally attractive if it was to survive and demonstrate the "liberal" character of French policy. The overseas minister, Defferre, referred to this challenge during the parliamentary debate on the *Loi Cadre*.[25]

Concessions were particularly urgent in Togo. As a former League of Nations mandate, Togo was under U.N. trusteeship and had a special status as "associated territory". There was danger that the rapid developments in the Gold Coast would provide an example for Togo and finally inspire a desire for union. Moreover, the U.N. was exerting pressure on France; if France wanted to save face or even withdraw Togo from the influence of the Trusteeship Council, it had to grant autonomy relatively soon. In April 1955 the powers of the territorial assemblies were extended and a cabinet was formed with African politicians. At last the decisive step had been taken. In August 1956, Togo became an "autonomous Republic", and its independent powers were extended again in March 1957. France began to negotiate the abolition of trusteeship and granted Togo full internal autonomy in February 1958. Sylvanus Olympic, the leader of the nationalist party, became president. Thus, even before the end of the Fourth Republic, Togo obtained the status that General de Gaulle was to envisage for it in the Community! Naturally the African deputies took the opportunity to remark on the political and psychological effects of the reforms in Togo: "It is a question . . . of not proving right those who think that they gain more from being outside the Republic than in the heart of the Republic."[26]

It is likely that France would have been too late to take the decisive step of decolonizing Black Africa had the coalition of the Left not won the parliamentary elections in January 1956. It was Guy Mollet's government that finally broke through the traditional "immobilism". The energetic Defferre of the French Socialist party (SFIO) whipped the motion prepared by the previous government through Cabinet, committee and parliament in a surprisingly short time, supported and advised by Houphouet-Biogny, the "ministre délégué à la Présidence du Conseil." Defferre rightly said: "By acting quickly, we will not be at the mercy of events. There exists presently in the overseas territories a certain unease, and it is necessary to dissipate it by efficacious action to restore a climate of confidence."[27] It was a question of regaining the initiative so that the reform would not appear to be a victory for the opposition and thus seem insincere. The government managed to do this to a considerable extent.

The innovations of the *Loi Cadre* of 23 June 1956 and the executive decrees in spring 1957 can be summarized in brief: universal franchise and a single college for all elections. This clearly reduced the representation of French colonial interests, both in Paris and in the territorial assemblies, although individual Frenchmen managed to be placed on "autochthonous lists". Political decision-making was effectively transferred to the Africans. The territorial assemblies obtained wider powers and could make final decisions. The chief innovation was the introduction of a ministerial council, elected by the assembly and equipped with executive power; although not directly responsible to the assembly, it depended on its approval. The governor was chairman of the ministerial council and remained directly subordinated to Paris; only the vice-president was African.[28] This was a major step towards a parliamentary system. It was predictable that the position of the governor would become merely a formal one, while the vice-president would rise to become the responsible president of the territory, particularly since he would be at the head of the strongest party.[29]

The attempt to give the territories a certain amount of genuine autonomy was matched by the distinction between *services d'état* (state services) and *matières locales* (local affairs). The territories were now to have their own civil service which would be controlled by them and not by the Paris administration. However, the state services, for which the governor was responsible, had rather broad powers, including not only foreign policy, the army, general security, currency and tariff questions, but also economic planning and supra-territorial communications, higher education and radio stations (also propaganda). So one can speak of full internal autonomy only in a limited sense, particularly since the Paris administration indirectly reserved itself further powers.

We must also mention here the efforts made to hasten the "Africanization of the cadre" which, as we established earlier, did not progress much in spite of the 1946 constitution. The former principle of equal access under equal conditions (*concours* system) in effect had led to discrimination, as had happened in the Indian Civil Service, since the candidates from the mother country had the advantage in language and better educational facilities. So the 1956–1957 reforms gave an advantage to the Africans and Madagascans. The École Nationale de la France d'Outre-Mer quickly developed into a training centre for the African civil service.

On the whole the *Loi Cadre* remained within the constitution and put into practice what had long been proclaimed the French policy. The transition to semi-autonomy with African parliaments and governments was now completed and the effective power of the autochtonous politicians also extended to the territories. The future development of the territories remained open, however, at least in principle. France had not yet decided whether the *Loi Cadre* was a preliminary step towards a federal republic or towards full independence and confederation.

Again we can draw a parallel with British policy in West Africa. The Gold Coast and Nigeria were on the road to independence, but for the time being London kept the controls in its hand: British ministers sat in the cabinet and the governor had reserved rights. In historical terms, this corresponded to the "state services" of the *Loi Cadre*. But sovereignty was restricted in an entirely different way in the British territories: in African government and in the position of the governor. France, by contrast, starting out from the idea of a one and indivisible Republic, granted a certain political autonomy to the territories that basically still belonged to the national territory, but reserved sovereignty to the parliament as before. There is a further parallel: the *Loi Cadre* created a situation within the territories that can be compared to the representative government in the British colonies, namely an elected legislative assembly, in place of an appointed governor and a government that had no parliamentary responsibility. In both cases this was to produce conflicts which resulted in efforts to create a parliamentary system.

A comparison of British and French policy makes it clear that one aspect of the *Loi Cadre*, which is much discussed and still very relevant today, was particularly important. This is the so-called "Balkanization" of French Black Africa. From Brazzaville in 1944 to the 1946 constitution and thence to the reform of 1956–1957, the efforts towards decentralization and autonomy primarily benefitted the territories themselves. The great administrative units, French West Africa and Equatorial Africa, survived and remained responsible for important tasks of a supraterritorial nature, but they declined steadily in importance. The *Loi-Cadre* was mainly directed at the territories and intended to strengthen their "political personality". It was even explicitly stated that the position of the governors-general must be modified, "with a view to transforming them into organs of co-ordination". Consequently the powers of the Grand Conseil were not extended and there was no cabinet council in Dakar or in Brazzaville. The former administrative duties were either transferred to the territories or directly subordinated to the administration in Paris; state services were also placed under the control of the overseas ministry. The territories now became administratively and politically important, and the federations "degenerated" into mere areas of co-ordination.

This disintegration of the large administrative units was criticized with particular vehemence in Senegal. Senghor, for that matter, coined the term "Balkanization" of Black Africa. On 29 January 1957 he moved a vote of protest in parliament,[30] pointing to the unanimous stand of the Grand Conseil of French West Africa, of a number of territorial assemblies and of the African trades-union. This was an "Oudinot operation", he alleged, i.e. an attempt on the part of the colonial administration to reserve all administrative responsibilities to itself and, in a reference to the "state services", to give something to the territories with one hand only to take it back with the other. He could see no reason why such services as post, radio, education, etc. should be transferred to Paris instead of being left to the federations. And why had the federations not been granted a cabinet council? Senghor emphatically warned against taking a step which was not only contrary to African interests but also called into question "Franco-African" community.[31]

Senghor's "Balkanization" theory was characteristic of his overall conception. This culturally and politically assimilated intellectual, who had become aware of his "Negritude", was not pursuing an anti-French policy; while he wanted political and cultural self-determination for Africa, he also wanted to maintain close ties to the former mother country. The concept of this association might vary gradually from integration into the one and indivisible Republic, to confederation—as long as the principle of equal rights was upheld. But, said Senghor, this principle would be negated if the metropolis was faced with a variety of small and economically weak African territories. Only larger units, embracing several territories, could function as true partners.[32] Senghor's concept did not preclude the possibility that Senegal had a concrete interest in the maintenance of French West Africa, or at least a part of it. Dakar was its natural centre and had long also been the administrative and economic hub of a large area; so Balkanization would obviously be a blow to Senegal. The opposition of the Ivory Coast was equally understandable, since it had its own centre in Abidjan, disposed of a large indigenous import market and had different interests in terms of transport and communications.

On 29 January Gabriel Lisette approved the *Loi Cadre* in the name of the RDA, partly in view of French West African decrees.[33] The "vast wholes", he said, must be based on "realities"; it should remain for the territories to decide on eventual union. By contrast Houphouet-Boigny strongly opposed the large units (within the French Equatorial Africa the coastal and economically very rich Gabon took the same attitude), and demanded direct "association" with France, in the not unfounded assumption that this would save Gabon from serving as "milch cow" to the poorer territories of the African backlands. Senghor's federation thesis gained sympathy within the RDA, however, and it was adopted by Sékou-Touré in Guinea and confirmed by a party congress in Bamako in September 1957. In winter 1958 the Ivory Coast finally broke off relations with Dakar. . . .[34]

But we are chiefly concerned with the attitude of France. It is debatable whether Paris promoted Balkanization in order to have to deal not with large African units but with a multiplicity of territories that would remain financially dependent on the mother country and could perhaps even be played off against each other. Unfortunately it is not possible to give a simple answer to this.[35] When Guy Mollet took Houphouet-Boigny, the leader of what was then the strongest African party, into the cabinet, this anticipated a non-federative solution, particularly since the African socialists under the Senegalese Lamine-Guèye showed little interest in federal government.[36] During the preparation for the *Loi Cadre*, before Defferre's time, opinions are said to have been divided in the administration. Cornut-Gentille, the governor-general in Dakar, is said to have spoken against the retention of French West Africa and Equatorial Africa, Chauvet in favour.[37] Pierre-Henri Teitgen (MRP), who had a major part in working out the motion and acted as parliamentary reporter in January 1957, declared as early as 20 March 1956 that a reform must be introduced in the territory and not at federation level: "The territory must be the political and administrative unity"; only thus was it possible "to engage [all the population] in the great enterprise of local democracy". It was becoming urgent to dissolve the federations.[38] The colonialist Right turned against Senghor, asserting that large units would make secession easier.[39] Paris even contemplated dividing up the island of Madagascar into individual territories with their own parliaments and governments, but the Madagascan politicians managed to prevent this. The advocates of federation were also the propagators of Pan-Africanism, and they considered Balkanization a good way of preventing the formation of blocs, of directly associating the autonomous territories to France and persuading them to renounce certain sovereign rights such as foreign policy and defense. Either Paris cannot have realized the disadvantages of Balkanization, or maybe it hoped that the survival of superordinate institutions controlled by the mother country could prevent it.[40]

Here French policy differed decisively from the British. Before and particularly after the Second World War, London was anxious to establish larger federative units in its colonial territories: in the West Indies, Malaya and East Africa. In West Africa, Nigeria was gradually converted from an administrative unit into a genuine federation. Britain may have hoped that with the help of the conservative North it could postpone the grant of self-government for a while, yet it actively opposed Balkanization and granted Nigeria—where it would have been particularly easy to dissolve the colonial unit into autonomous territories—its independence as a single, large state. Admittedly London granted self-government to the regions first, but at the same time it promoted the central courts and only "released" the colony after the federation had been established. Since Great Britain had accepted eventual independence, it was obviously interested in establishing independent states that could stand on their own feet economically. It is not surprising then that it was the small and economically weak colonies that posed particular problems in Britain's decolonization policy and that were always neglected in British discussions. Britain assumed that these colonies, which could neither be federated nor attached to a larger unit, would content themselves with self-government and voluntarily transfer control of their foreign relations to the former colonial power. When this assumption proved false, there was no choice but to grant the small units full independence too. . . . By contrast, France did not strive for federative associations, since it based its policy on the institutionalized unity of the French Union, in which the small territories held a special position. The smaller and weaker the units, the more chance there was of preventing the distintegration of Greater France. If today we try to explain the Balkanization of former French West Africa in terms of tribal loyalty and the African politicians' claim to power, we must not forget that France certainly did not try to check this process and in fact even promoted it.

On the whole, African party leaders and deputies—even Sékou Touré! —approved of the *Loi Cadre*.[41] They proposed certain additions during the parliamentary consultation and perhaps held different views on individual points, but even the critical Senghor approved of the inclusion of the "state services", on the whole.[42] They were glad that parliament did not accede to the conservative and colonialist proposals to postpone the decision or give in to the vehement attacks on the single college and cabinet council in the territories.[43] Once again the Africans demonstrated their allegiance to France. But they also pointed out quite clearly that the *Loi Cadre* could only be a preliminary step towards further autonomy, and not a permanent settlement. Senghor spoke of the "second stage towards the autonomy of the overseas territories". Each territory, he said, needed a "constitutional statute", i.e. its own constitution and recognition as a state. The *Loi Cadre* had been imposed, he said, by a parliament that was under-represented overseas. Title VIII of the constitution must be revised, for "the *Loi Cadre* will very soon be superseded by events". The object to be aimed at was a "confederal Union, composed of freely associated independent states".[44] Although the Africans often used the term "Federal Republic", the discussion increasingly centred on independence. In the aforementioned resolution of the party congress at Bamako in September 1957, the *Loi Cadre* appeared "an irreversible step on the road towards the emancipation of the African populations". Independence was an "inalienable right" and France spoke of a "freely consented association" in the name of independence. African politicians spoke of a federal state with its own parliament and government,[45] but it is unlikely that they still seriously expected France to surrender its control of foreign policy, defense, etc. Senghor, who did not want to provoke a break with France, acknowledged the difficulty and declared himself ready to renounce participation in foreign policy, as long as internal autonomy was extended and effective collaboration made possible in economic questions. However, he viewed this as no more than a transitional solution.[46] At the moment, he said, the "equality" of the partners and the recognition of the right to self-determination and independence were the decisive factors.

That the Africans were particularly concerned with independence became more and more clear to France. The parliamentary discussion on the *Loi Cadre* spoke of the need for a future extension of autonomy but not of self-government or even of possible exit from the French Union.[47] It was not even decided whether, in accordance with Article 75 of the constitution, a change of status for the territories should be considered in order to make them associated states. Borella quite rightly said that the *Loi Cadre* was partly designed as a means of avoiding a far-reaching reform.[48]

Some thought this law had "solved" the African problem for a long time to come, since it granted African leaders what they had long been demanding.[49] In the administration pessimists are even said to have counted on a "period of indulgence" of at least three years.[50] But by 1957 it became apparent that attitudes were changing. For instance, Maurice Duverger declared in *Le Monde* on 6 February 1957 that the policy introduced with the *Loi Cadre* had already virtually converted France into a federation, and that the public must be deceived no longer.[51] People still spoke of federation,[52] but they had become aware of the vagueness of the term[53] and tended more and more to replace it by that of "Franco-African Community". France had carefully avoided the word "independence", but the Africans' demands as expressed in Bamako, and the independence of Ghana now forced it to proclaim the right to independence, since it was the only means of relieving the distrust.[54] France slowly began to realize that legalistic attempts to prematurely pin down a movement that was still in flux had proved a mistake and must be given up. A loose confederation now seemed the only possibility. Oreste Rosenfeld (SFIO), for instance, deliberately abandoned his concept of federation because, as he said, there were no "federative organs". Public opinion, he added, was against surrendering sovereignty, but since Bamako the Africans were no longer satisfied with a subordinate position. The new order must be more of a confederation; but this threatened the institutions with the same fate as the French Union unless France began by negotiating at a round table with all those concerned.[55]

The British Commonwealth entered the discussion here in the rather unexpected role of example. France envisaged a "commonwealth *á la française*", i.e. it did not want to content itself with mere informal ties, but wanted to furnish the "Franco-African Community" with institutions too.[56] In parliament on 3 February 1958 François Mitterand proposed that the government summon a conference "with a view to creating a Franco-African community and determining its fundamental institutions".[57] This future community was to be worked out on the basis of recognition of the right to independence and full "equality" for all partners. France was prepared to grant full autonomy and confined itself to proposing confederation, yet obviously it still hoped it would be possible to create a greater unit in which France would continue to act as leader. This anticipated General de Gaulle's concept of the Community and the fall of the government in May 1958 made it feasible!

Discussions on Africa during the last months of the Fourth Republic made it clear that the colonialist Right was also giving up its hopes of federalism and adapting to new formulas such as independence, Franco-African Community, French Commonwealth, etc. For instance, the newspaper *France Outre-mer* wrote:

> What is envisaged here is the affirmation of the principle of equality in the situation of the contractants, whose agreement, entirely free, must form the base of the future community. This is to say that we consider it desirable, with regard to the solidity of the construction, that by a decision prior to the vote on the final dispositions, each of the partners might consider himself independent from the moment he engages his future.[58]

It seems to have become clear to the Right that resistance to decolonization had become pointless and that unilateral solutions would always be distrusted by the Africans and furthermore would not stabilize the situation. Now that the *Loi Cadre* had transferred political decision-making to the African politicians, it was necessary to adapt quickly and to negotiate bilateral agreements. Only in this way could a new legal basis be established and France's economic interests possibly be secured.

It is worth examining, however, whether these interests were indeed as important as France had hitherto believed. Even with increasing autonomy France had to continue to support the economic development of the African territories. Was this expense worth-while when France's own industrial expansion required immense investment capital, and especially when it had to hand over its power and control in Africa in any case? This argument was the basis of what is called "Cartierism", or the "anti-colonialism of the Right".

The question of whether the great military and administrative expenses incurred by the ruling power in the colonies were balanced by any profit, was by no means new. The liberal national economists of the early nineteenth century, Hobson in his critique of imperialism and Grover Clark in his 1936 study *Balance Sheets of Imperialism*, had asked this question and replied in the negative. The right-wing bourgeois parties, however, had countered these economic arguments and dismissed them as anti-national. Without a colonial empire, they argued, France could not be a great power. Economically France needed an overseas export market since its industrial goods were priced above the world market level and were hardly able to compete. Since the depression, this dependence on a market with tariff protection had become even stronger and after the Second World War the scarcity of dollars and the difficulties in the French balance of trade had provided additional support for the argument that the colonies were economically necessary to France's survival.

The grant of independence to Tunisia and Morocco raised the first doubts. Admittedly colonists and businessmen were streaming back to the metropolis, voluntarily or compelled by circumstance, and it was proving impossible to maintain profitable positions. But trade relations had by no means been broken off, in fact they were expanding thanks to the foreign credits that the independent states were obtaining. The loss of these colonies was perhaps a heavy blow to directly interested economic circles, but it was to the national advantage. It saved considerable state expenditure, and moreover the capital that had hitherto flowed into the colonies now became available for economic expansion at home. Had not the example of the Netherlands proved former theses wrong? The economic journal *L'Entreprise* examined the situation in an article with the significant title "Une economie prospère sans colonies: les Pays Bas" ("An economy prospers without colonies: the Netherlands"). Indeed, since 1948, the Netherlands, whose prosperity had seemed to rest on the exploitation of Indonesia's immense riches, had experienced a sensational boom and real wages had leapt up in spite of the population increase. The loss of its colonial Empire had not spelled disaster, as had been predicted, but had confronted the country with a "question of survival" and forced it to speed up industrialization. Capital was not flowing out, as before, but was at the disposal of the mother country. The article also pointed out that as a colonial power the Netherlands would have been obliged to pay compensation for war damages and to raise the natives standard of living by means of comprehensive investment and assistance schemes, while an independent Indonesia "can no longer exact economic aid. The relations between the former metropolis and the young Republic are no longer based on gifts: they are based on contracts". Political relations were extremely tense, it was true, but the large companies continued to prosper. The Netherlands' share of Indonesia's national income had perhaps fallen, but "this is a net revenue". So the example of the Netherlands showed that without colonies it was not only possible to survive economically, but actually to hasten domestic development.

The well-known journalist Raymond Cartier contributed to the unusual popularity of these theories with a series of essays entitled "En

France noire" published in the journal *Match* in August and September 1956.[59]

These articles, in the form of a travel journal and full of striking examples, emphatically supported a clear-cut theory. French Africa was poor, said Cartier, of little use and cost immense sums. What little Africa produced, such as coffee on the Ivory Coast, France had to buy at an artificially adjusted price; "the poor territories are costly because they produce nothing and the rich Ivory Coast is costly because it produces something." France also had to pay for the administration, the armed forces, the airports and radio stations, and made investment resources available through FIDES. Naturally Cartier did not fail to name the numerous false investments in the aid schemes (bridges without street connections, concrete market halls which were not used, etc.). In addition, he said, the political rewards for this aid were small. The Africans expected the aid and laughed at it, and most of the recruits to the Communist party came from highly developed areas. The result: "We have a moderate need of Africa. It has an immense need of us." Would it not be more advantageous to invest the millions in the metropolis rather than in remote regions that were politically insecure and wanted to secede from France anyway? "The precedent of Morocco is a striking example: so many towns, mines, public works drawn from French resources and lost!" Overseas investments since 1946 could have served to modernize the metropolis; a number of French provincial towns were in greater need of a new *lycée* than of a small central African market! Cartier also pointed to the Netherlands, Switzerland and the German Federal Republic, and warned the Africans: "Are you absolutely sure that it is in the interests of France to keep you at all costs?" One might grant Africa autonomy, but it was quixotic that France should pay for dissociation. France had an interest in remaining in Africa, but not "at any price". It was asking for blackmail, he said, to give the impression that the economic future of France depended on its remaining in Africa. France should continue to grant developmental aid, but only after stern negotiations and never without first securing certain political advantages.

This illustrated journal with its high readership, and not inconsiderable political influence, popularized a current theory and prepared the way for a "re-evaluation of values". During the Indochinese war, the same Cartier had supported the traditional theory of the economic and political necessity of having colonies, also in *Match*. He changed his views at the moment when economic aid took the place of the former colonial policy of predominantly private investment; now the funds came from the national budget and offered France little direct gain. Since France had fixed a time-limit to its stay in the colonies, he thought it would be to the "national" advantage to accept decolonization and even to promote it. The former colonies also depended on financial aid after independence, so there was some likelihood that France could withdraw from its obligations while at the same time exploiting its aid in political terms.

Cartier's theories gave rise to lively discussion. The former inspector of finances in French West Africa, Jean Ehrhard, confirmed them in his much noted book *Les destins du colonialisme*, published in 1957. A purely economic examination led him to the conclusion that "far from leading to a spreading-out of resources, an egoistic pursuit of purely metropolitan economic interests would inspire a concentration. Thus, one often affirms that without the overseas territories France would be no more than a Spain. From a strictly economic point of view it would be more correct to say that France could have become a Switzerland, a Sweden, a Norway or a Germany, countries in which for the last ten years the per capita income has exceeded or attained the level reached by France."[60] With these arguments the author could attack the anti-colonialism of the left-wing intellectuals and assuage the French conscience by pointing to the actual aid being given, while at the same time destroying the hitherto sacrosanct theories of the colonialist Right. Politically Ehrhard was in favour of a loose federal structure as outlined by Senghor, which would "compel" extensive autonomy in the territories, while also providing a serviceable policy of development. Ehrhard gave interesting details on the nature of this structure in the second part of his discussion.

Ehrhard's book made some impression in the Paris ministries.[61] It found its counterpart in Pierre Moussa's *Les Chances économiques de la Communauté franco-africaine*, which tried to show, with very detailed statistical material, the economic advantages of the overseas territories. Moussa considered the budget expenditure bearable and urged a "dynamic concept of the French whole".[62]

This worried the Africans, of course, and they sharply attacked "the defeatism of Raymond Cartier". Now it was they who, by a paradoxical reversal of position, reminded France of its responsibilities overseas. Relations between the metropolis and Africa must not, they said, be based solely on economic considerations. As French citizens the former subjects deserved a better fate than to be thrown into independence the moment colonial rule became unprofitable.[63] Senghor even took up the slogans of the "colonialists": "The calling of France is not the calling of Holland . . . I am appalled at the idea that France could withdraw from Africa!"[64] In effect Cartier made it clear to the Africans that in the future they would have to depend more on France rather than less.

The influence of Cartierism and its right-wing anti-colonialism on the French public is difficult to assess. Left-wing politicians, unionists and intellectuals were attracted by the theory that the mother country urgently needed the investment credits which were flowing into Africa with such doubtful results,[65] but it proved difficult to say this openly, for refusal to grant economic aid and withdrawal for reasons of profit could be interpreted as "colonialism", and could compromise the traditional anti-colonialism of the Left. André Blanchet, the liberal-minded correspondent on Africa for *Le Monde*, published an article entitled "Condamnés à l'Indépendance":

> Lively as the temptation may in fact be to "condemn" the African countries to independence, it would be unworthy of a great nation even apparently to impose on its former colonies a choice between a definite political statute and the renunciation of all material aid.[66]

Like Senghor, Blanchet too was using the "national" argument! There can be little doubt that Cartierism made a certain impression on the French bourgeoisie and even on circles without direct economic interests. Perhaps Cartierism also helps to explain the surprisingly weak opposition to General de Gaulle's Africa policy. However, when in spite of the failure of the Communauté, de Gaulle continued to make very wide-scale financial and developmental aid available in the interest of French influence in Black Africa, public unease and dissatisfaction grew. Raymond Cartier gave expression to this mood too, in his articles "Attention, la France dilapie son argent".[67] The economic situation in France, he wrote, was showing signs of weakness. Many people felt that France was "shouldering responsibilities that were too heavy for it", and was jeopardizing its future at the cost of a small gain in prestige. The German economic miracle was continuing; even the U.S. was tending to cut back its numerous aid schemes, although this formed only 4 percent of its budget in 1962 as opposed to almost 9 percent in France. Moreover the resources were drawn from investment capital, of which only a limited amount was available; meanwhile half of France was "underdeveloped". Cartier wanted to reduce aid to development to 1 percent of the national budget. These articles again generated discussion, since they responded to a widespread unease and at the same time put into words the problems in the national mind. By contrast with General de Gaulle, who tried to maintain or expand French influence and power overseas by the traditional methods of economic aid, Cartier was in favour of a withdrawal to the "hexagon" of the metropolis. Since the metropolis urgently needed funds for development during this phase of economic and social upheaval, France should first establish the internal preconditions for assuming a modern leadership role.

THE COMMUNAUTÉ

The Communauté was the last stage in the decolonization of French Black Africa. Although it was partly predetermined by circumstance, it is so much the personal achievement of General de Gaulle that it seems in order here to recall his attitude on the colonial question. First we must return to the Brazzaville conference. In his opening address on 30 January 1944 de Gaulle stressed the importance of imperial power and the imperial mission, and also announced a reform of the existing power structure. In the future the African territories were to collaborate in working out their own affairs and to form a "French Community" together with the metropolis. A few months later in the Indochina declaration (24 March 1945) he spoke of a federation. De Gaulle remained true to this concept in the years that followed; here, however, only its general outlines are apparent. After his resignation as president of the provisional government, when he founded the Rassemblement du Peuple Français (RPF), he gave further details in a speech at Bayeux (16 June 1946):

> The future of the 110 million men and women who live under our flag lies in an organization of a federative type, to which time will gradually give a firmer form. But even our new constitution must make a start in this direction and guide the coming development into the right channels.[1]

A "Great Council of the French Union" would be formed of representatives of the economic unions and similar organizations, and representatives of the African territories, which would be empowered to advise on all matters concerning the Union: budget, foreign relations, internal problems, national defence, economy, transport, communications. The federal structure would be incorporated in a strong head of state standing above the parties, who would also act as president of the French Union and in whose election the overseas territories would take part. From here one can trace a direct line to the 1958 constitution and the Communauté: the electoral *modus* of the president meant that the former colonial dependency had been abolished, but without France having to surrender its powers of decision. The mother country even had a majority in the consultative body of the Union.

In this context we can mention Professor René Capitant, who belonged to the intimate circle around de Gaulle at the time and proposed a draft for a "federal constitution" in 1946.[2]

At a press conference on 24 April 1947 de Gaulle reiterated his Bayeux theses. The overseas territories were a "vital question" for France and therefore the mother country must assume sovereign powers. More important than representation in parliament were the Union assemblies with advisory powers and the common president who united the Republic and the Union.[3] The Gaullists' objections to the 1946 constitution and the parties responsible for it are particularly clear in a 1950 RPF report in which they attacked the conferment of citizenship and the reduced franchise of the Africans. The rural population, said the report, could be represented only by general franchise, although on two levels, while a "double college" secured the interests of the French colonials and the metropolis. Obviously this general but indirect franchise was intended to oust the évolués and the African politicians! The territories would obtain a statute of their own, "within the framework of French sovereignty", with a view to a future federal Union. But they warned against acting too hastily. The legislative body of the federation, as de Gaulle had said in his Bayeux speech, would consist of two chambers: the parliament with deputies from the overseas territories and a Union assembly of which the territories would appoint the third section. As the executive body he envisaged a high council which would be composed of French ministers and delegates from the associated states. But they were only to "assist"; the true power would remain with the president.[4]

The Gaullists wanted by their federalist concept to distinguish themselves from the Fourth Republic. We have mentioned the deputy Dronne, who requested a corresponding revision of Title VIII on 10 July 1953 (cf. p. 408). Jacques Soustelle also spoke in 1954 of a "French bloc whose federal structure will be a supreme guarantee for all".[5] The combination of local decentralization and concentration on the president to guarantee the unity of the whole, was presented as a federal solution. But polemics against the "system" which continued to pursue an assimilatory policy and ignored the desire of the overseas peoples for emancipation could not hide the fact that the Gaullists too paid homage to a "verbal federalism", which was neither based on a true "equality" of the partners nor was prepared to accept independence in any form.

The Gaullist movement might have been split into a right and a left wing, but it was nevertheless undeniably nationalist. A party leaflet of the "Action Républicaine et Sociale" (ARS), the successor to the RPF whose members included such notable personages as Debré, Soustelle and Chaban-Delmas, shows this very clearly.[6] Its motto was "France will not leave". Foreign powers—this was aimed at the United States—and the U.N. were interfering in the affairs of Indochina and North Africa, they said, and trying to drive France from its overseas positions.

But without these positions, French power would be threatened; it was only by virtue of its support in the French Union that France would be able to join European or Atlantic unification movements.

> By integrating the French Union more firmly, France will have less fear that the European and Atlantic integrations can do it harm. It will be able to assert its rank there and an influence conforming to its past and its potential. . . . The ARS believes that the government should not hesitate to put an end to the attacks of our enemies and to the doubts which have taken hold of our friends, by making it known with the greatest firmness that France is resolved, come what may, to remain in all the countries and all the positions of the French Union.

The actual proposals for revision remained vague, however. "Federalism with discernment" clearly meant integration, since the ties were said to remain indissoluble and the Republic remained "one and indivisible in its essence". The association of the protectorates was in no circumstances to lead to independence or to bilateral conventions, but was intended to insert the protectorates into a framework determined by France.

The attitude of the Gaullists to the colonial question in 1950–1958 was one of ruthless opposition to the governments of the Fourth Republic because they had not pursued the Indochinese war with full force and were proceeding from concession to concession in North Africa. On 23 February 1952 the Conseil National of the ARS demanded "a war in Indochina conducted with all available means and all necessary firmness".[7] In North Africa de Gaulle built on his personal relations with the sultan of Morocco, but Gaullist politicians were sharply opposed to recalling the sultan. The negotiations with Tunisia, they said in January 1955, should "end by tracing the framework of institutions which would indissolubly establish an organic link between France and Tunisia".[8] Senator Debré considered bilateral conventions a mistake; "since we do not know exactly of what kind the new French Union should be, the projects of Franco-Tunisian convention risk leading to the secession of Tunisia, risk ruining the position of France in Morocco".[9] By making vague references to a renovated French Union that would establish indissoluble ties with the mother country and French control of foreign policy, defence, etc. the Gaullists opposed the decolonization which Edgar Faure had already brought to a conclusion in the critical cases of Tunisia and Morocco.

Michel Debré's foreword to a book published in 1957 by the former vice-president of the Comité national de la Résistance, M. Blocq Mascard, was a renewed attack on the idea of European integration which, said Debré, would deliver France into the hands of Germany, and on the Fourth Republic, whose only "achievements" were the "surrender of overseas France". The French nation would not resign itself to this, he asserted; it would rebel, with the help of the army and the overseas French under the leadership of General de Gaulle![10] Blocq himself took up a project for federation worked out by the other side between 1954 and 1956, according to which both the metropolis and the overseas territories should be represented in a federal senate in the proportion of 34 to 21. Executive power would rest with a president elected by a wider electoral college but not responsible to the senate. The territories, as a group, would obtain their own governments with corresponding responsibilities. This not uninteresting proposal, which was obviously adapted from de Gaulle's, contradicted the unitarian tradition of the metropolis too plainly to have any chance of being taken seriously. In any case, since the overseas territories were to remain under-represented in the federal senate and in the electoral college which appointed the president, the old problem remained unsolved: the metropolis justifiably insisted on its political and economic preponderance and demanded over-representation, while the Africans rightly reproached it with allowing only an "unreal" federalism and aiming at "colonialist" domination.

The excessive sensibilities of the Gaullist nationalists, who saw any willingness to make concessions as evidence of "surrender" and adhered to the idea of "indissoluble" ties, i.e. the maintenance of the greatest possible control by the mother country, seemed to offer little hope for a "liberal" overseas policy after the Fourth Republic was overthrown in May 1958. Yet it soon became apparent that de Gaulle shared the extremist views of his supporters only to a limited extent; he proved flexible enough to steer a course adapted to the decolonization process which was already under way and to carry it "to a happy end". He came back to the theory of a "community" which he had supported several times since 1944, and was able to capitalize upon his enormous prestige in Africa, which paved the way for the co-operation of African politicians. The latter had used the constitutional crisis to announce further demands and to create *faits accomplis*. On 2 May a congress of party leaders from Madagascar had demanded a "republican state associated to France", while Sékou Touré outlined a plan on 7 June which would confer "complete internal autonomy" on the African territories. Senghor's newly-founded "Rassemblement Africain" made similar demands, namely a

> federal republic uniting France, the groups of territories and the non-grouped territories on the basis of free co-operation, absolute equality and the right to independence, the groups of territories and non-grouped territories being endowed with a central autonomous government, responsible before the legislative Assembly and having all the attributes of internal sovereignty, excepting control of diplomatic relations, defence, currency, higher education and the magistrature, which are reserved to the government of the federal republic.[11]

In a memorandum on 9 July 1958, Senghor and Dia pointed out that the term "federative republic" had come to possess almost "magic powers" in Africa; the constitution of the Fifth Republic must therefore form a federal republic, although this federation should be "light and dynamic". The executive organ, besides the president, should be not a federal parliament but a kind of "contact assembly", which would exercise only minor legislative powers and serve as a means of "cohesion". In addition, the constitution should recognize the territories' right to self-determination, i.e. give them constituent power and the right to independence.[12] So Senghor had passed from federation to confederation; he was ready to leave external sovereignty to the French president without renouncing the right to independence and to decide whether to break this final tie with France at a given moment. The recognition of the right to independence, which he said Africa had no intention of claiming immediately since it was aware of its economic weakness and dependence, became a *sine qua non*, since it was the only way of breaking away from the colonial status and satisfying the principle of equal rights.[13]

In a sense Senghor anticipated the future Communauté. But for the time being de Gaulle evidently had a different image of the "vast and free community" which he had announced in a "friendly message" on 13 July. He spoke of "a great political, economic and cultural whole". It would give the African territories greater internal autonomy but be of a permanent nature, so as to ensure France's position as a world power for the future too.[14] The government proposal published on 30 July and submitted to the advisory constitutional committee corresponded to this concept.[15] It adhered to overseas representation in the Senate of the mother country and did not recognize the members of the federation as states. In addition it confronted the Africans with a definite choice; since the government proposal did not mention the right to independence it implied the possibility of a change of status. The Communauté, in its very vague form at the time, applied only to the former associated states.[16]

The government's intentions "leaked" prematurely and provoked disappointment, protests and further demands from the Africans. On 27 July Senghor's party, going beyond his own position, accepted "immediate independence" in its final resolution at a congress in Cotonou.[17] Tsiranana, head of the government of Madagascar, demanded an "independent Republic, which would voluntarily federate with France",[18] while Sékou Touré demanded recognition of the right to independence and refused African representation in the French parliament.[19] In *Le Monde* on 31 July, Senghor pointed out, with some right, that the government's newly proposed constitution was a step backwards since Article 75 of the 1946 constitution had at least provided for the possibility of a change of status to associated state. "It is a retreat without equivocation. One would think that everything is being done to provoke a break."[20]

A special study group within the advisory constitutional committee tried to conciliate the Africans. With active assistance from the MRP deputies Teitgen and Coste-Floret, it suggested a special article which would allow the territories to choose the status of independent state within a confederation.[21] But de Gaulle intervened personally on 9 August and vetoed the proposal: independence was out of the question. A referendum would present the Africans with the choice of secession, with all its grave consequences—particularly economic—or federation in the proposed form! So de Gaulle wanted both to create much firmer and more lasting ties with France and to force a solution by referring to the consequences of choosing independence. The Africans had understandably hoped to avoid just this choice and did not want to bar the way to independence by association agreements—and bar the way to economic aid! Coste-Floret confessed: "It is a difficult situation, in that the overseas territories can only obtain independence if they vote 'No' in the referendum. It would be better to give them this opportunity with a 'Yes' vote too".[22]

The constitutional committee sought a settlement. In order to avoid making a choice between federation and confederation it adopted the notion of the Communauté, which had originally been proposed for the associated states. It proposed that the members of the Communauté would be described as states, and their authorities more closely defined. Although the committee wanted to admit the African states' right to a change of status after five years, including that of independent state, the government partly revoked this concession, laconically asserting that the moment an African member state declared independence it would have to leave the Communauté. This meant, of course, that it would forfeit French economic aid![23]

We need not go into the details of de Gaulle's journey to Africa.[24] In spite of the brusque behaviour of Sékou Touré and opposition in Senegal, it was a spectacular success. De Gaulle addressed the Africans as "partners" and outlined in striking rhetorical terms the great future of the Communauté; he also reminded them of "all the consequences" which a "No" in the referendum would entail![25] The result is well-known: except for Guinea, all the African territories and Madagascar assented to the constitution of the Fifth Republic and thereby chose entry into the Communauté.

The road leading from the preliminary government proposal to acceptance of the constitution shows how difficult Gaullist France found it to accept the African territories' right to self-determination or the possibility of their leaving the French association of states. At first the referendum was primarily a skilful move, proclaiming the "voluntary" nature of entry into the Communauté and at the same time exerting massive pressure for permanent integration. France only reluctantly admitted the possibility of a change of status. Criticism of the French Union, attempts at revising it, the *Loi Cadre* and the discussion during 1957–1958, had paved the way to the Communauté, but it was the 1958 *coup d'état* that gave France the real opportunity to revise the constitution in such a way that the African nationalists also agreed to it. De Gaulle's enormous prestige in Africa was an important factor in this agreement.

Title XII of the new constitution and the decree of 19 December established the institutional bases of the Communauté.[26] The territorial assemblies must first decide on their status (department, territory in the accepted sense, or member state); as was to be expected, they decided in favour of the third. Subsequently they could work out their own constitutions and withdraw from the legislative sphere of the metropolis. Internal autonomy was now total, the overseas ministry vanished, the former "state services" were transferred to the Communauté, at the head of which stood the president of the Republic, General de Gaulle. He had the role of "arbiter" in a community of equal members. A senate (180 representatives for the metropolis and Algeria, 114 for overseas) served as the legislature, but had only advisory powers, while the presidents of the member states formed the executive council. The metropolitan ministers also acted as ministers of the Communauté, but they were responsible to the French parliament.

In effect the Communauté was "more than a federation, less than a federal state".[27] It proclaimed the principle of equal rights and postulated a common policy in the responsibilities "delegated" to it by the African member states. The African states now had full internal autonomy, but the metropolis still decided—in practice if not legally—on foreign policy, defence, economic planning, raw materials policy, etc. This inequality of the partners was inevitable because France, for understandable reasons, was not prepared to surrender its control of foreign policy by transferring it to a body such as the executive council—quite apart from the fact that the president of the Communauté was, after all, General de Gaulle!

France interpreted the positive results of the referendum as a permanent settlement. The new institutionalized Community appeared to be based on the free assent of the member states; at the same time the financial aid it granted gave Paris a tool for making secession movements seem unfeasible. The senate never really obtained any influence of its own, but the executive council met several times in 1959 and made some remarkable decisions: French became the accepted official language, the *Marseillaise* became the national anthem and the tricolour was declared the flag of all the member states. It created a "Nationality of the French Republic and the Communauté" and prepared a common budget. The diplomatic service and the army were to be reorganized under the control of the Communauté, and a secretariat-general was to serve as coordinating board.[28] Now the lawyers could begin to interpret the articles of the constitution!

Once again the old difficulty of allegedly federal institutions arose. The metropolis would not surrender its sovereignty, while the African states strove for a share in overall policy-making and felt slighted. For instance, now, unlike in the Fourth Republic, no Africans sat in the French Cabinet, although French ministers could act as executive organs of the Communauté! The administration remained on the defensive, and no genuine Franco-African diplomatic service ever came into being. The organs of economic aid, like the individual French ministers, communicated directly with the African states, thereby increasing the impression that they continued to be directed from Paris.

Other factors also spoke against the permanence of the Communautè. Paris replied to Guinea's choice of independence by immediately withdrawing its administrative organs and cancelling its financial aid; this step was meant to dissuade other states from following Sékou Touré and was taken in the expectation that the small, weak country would prove unable to survive.[29] Instead Guinea received help from other quarters and managed to cope: the fact that Sékou Touré could appear before the U.N. and was officially received by the president of the United States was a direct challenge to other African leaders. On 1 January 1960 de Gaulle had to grant the trusteeship territories Togo and Cameroun full independence without suspending technical and financial aid. So the special position in international law of the former League of Nations mandated state created a precedent that speeded up the disintegration of the Communauté.

The Senegalese were particularly eager to follow the new road. On 1 October 1958 Senghor had described the Communauté as merely a preliminary stage on the way to full independence. The British Commonwealth had become a model for the desired combination of external sovereignty and close collaboration.[30] The initiative came from the newly-founded Mali Federation (Senegal and Sudan). In autumn 1959, these two member states requested full independence but without, as Article 86 of the constitution decreed, leaving the Communauté. Paris made its disappointment plain, but de Gaulle proved willing to adjust to the new situation. The desire for independence had become too strong and must be taken into account as a psychological factor, he declared at a press conference on 10 November 1959. He let it be seen that France was willing to continue granting aid, thereby dissociating himself both from the conservatives who, he asserted, would not recognize the signs of the times, and from the theories of the Cartierists, who, he said, were prepared to promote the secession of the former colonies.[31] At a meeting of the executive council in Saint-Louis, de Gaulle declared himself prepared to negotiate, to the great surprise of many African and French politicians.[32] In Dakar on 13 December he stressed Mali's right to "international sovereignty", which it would attain "with the agreement and the aid of France".[33] Now de Gaulle had granted what Sékou Touré had demanded in vain a year before, avoiding the terms of the constitution which did not provide for independence within the Communauté—precisely because de Gaulle himself had managed to prevent any such resolutions![34] The treaties between France and Mali were signed in April 1960. These were now bilateral agreements between two sovereign states who agreed to "voluntary co-operation". The president of the Republic was recognized as head of the "renovated Community"; the heads of state were to meet for periodic consultation. So France had practically arrived at the status of Commonwealth.

It was predictable that other states would follow Mali's example. In 1960, Madagascar and the four states of former French Equatorial Africa became independent, and members of the U.N. Houphouet-Boigny, president of the Ivory Coast and Senghor's opponent, was irritated by de Gaulle's compliance and now proclaimed his desire for independence, forcing Paris into bilateral "co-operation agreements" which did not even mention the Communauté. The "renovated Community," proved to be a chimera in institutional terms. All that remained was "co-operation", i.e. the extensive technical and financial aid which France was and still is prepared to continue granting to the now independent states, in contradiction to earlier declarations. Financial aid proved ineffectual in preventing decolonization, but served to maintain French presence in Africa in the post-colonial era.

Like Great Britain, France also managed to accept concept of decolonization once it had taken place and incorporate into it the national consciousness. The peaceful withdrawal from Black Africa was now interpreted as evidence of the liberal attitude that had always characterized French colonial policy. In fact decolonization had by no means proceeded according to original plans. The "Commonwealth" was inherent in the British concept, but not in the French. To the last, Paris had refused to accept the British procedure as a model. France was resolved to go its own way and not even to agree to gradual self-government or to the possibility of future independence. It was prepared to relax and reorganize the structure of colonial rule, but not to shatter the institutional framework embracing the metropolis and the former colonies. This attitude was at the root of the Brazzaville conference and the 1946 constitution, of the *Loi Cadre* and of the 1958 Communauté. One could describe it as the "connecting thread" running through French decolonization. The old image of a "France of a hundred million inhabitants" remained alive until the end. Decolonization was to be made possible without breaking up the whole. The grant of administrative autonomy, together with citizenship, franchise and representation in parliament, indicates a kind of compromise which was meant to answer both the nationalists' desire for emancipation and the "vital" interests of the mother country.

In effect the *Loi Cadre* and the Communauté meant that France had finally given up the idea of integration, but not the hope of creating an institutional unit out of the former Empire. The concept of association current before 1939 was replaced by that of federation after the Second World War, in order to postulate a lasting association between metropolis and overseas territories. But it soon became clear that France could tolerate only an "unreal" federation; the inequality of the partners was all too obvious, and even more important, "genuine" federation would have meant transferring sovereignty to the common councils and thus the failure of precisely what France hoped to achieve. So although the French Union and the Communauté had some value as transitional solutions, neither could be a final reply to the demand of the former colonial peoples. Paris closed its mind to this insight to the last; nevertheless the institutional ties were gradually loosened in such a way that the transition to an "informal Commonwealth" could take place without leading to a break. This process had not been proclaimed as the aim of French colonial policy, as it had in the British case, or as the conclusion of a laborious process of emancipation planned in advance by the metropolis, and France continued to hope it could check it or guide it into other channels. Those African states that are as yet scarcely capable of surviving alone continue to have close ties with France, French civilization continues to be the "cultural home" of many *évolués* and the attempts at assimilation of earlier decades continue to bear fruit; yet it would be futile to search for a sense of unity as it is found in the concept of the Commonwealth. This lack of unity made it easier for France to adapt to the international political situation of the post-colonial era and not be tempted to take positions based on sentiment; but it is paradoxical, although explicable, that France continued to the last to cling to the "indissoluble unity" of the metropolis and the overseas territories.

FROM ALGÉRIE FRANÇAISE TO THE RÉPUBLIQUE ALGÉRIENNE

We have already seen the problems of decolonization in Algeria. The country had long belonged to the national territory of France in more than merely legal terms; it was not a colony, it was governed by the ministry of the interior, and it was felt to be an integral part of the mother country. In such a country gradual integration and assimilation at first seemed the only possible path—in the sense of giving political equality to the Muslim inhabitants within France. The attempts at reform between the wars, and especially the Blum-Viollette project, had aimed in this direction, but had not come to anything. Free France under de Gaulle adopted the same policy and by the decree of 7 March 1944 granted certain categories of Muslims full French citizenship without renunciation of their personal status.

In the meantime, however, the Algerian emancipation movement had finally dissociated itself from all ideas of assimilation or integration and demanded self-government. Surprisingly enough it was Ferhat Abbas, who in the 1930s had still counted as spokesman for the Algerian *évolués*' readiness to accept assimilation, who was the author of the Algerian manifesto of February 1943. The manifesto resolutely opposed integration and demanded the formation of an Algerian state that would be associated with France but would have internal autonomy and rest on the sovereign rights of the Algerian people. This threatened the predominance of the French settlers, for an Algerian state, whether based on consistent integration or autonomous and based on democratic franchise, would mean that the minority of French Algerians would be "swamped" by the Muslim population and would obviously lose its privileged position. So from the start, Paris was caught between the totally unreconcilable demands of the nationalists and settlers. This became clear after the decree of 7 March was rejected by the French Algerians as a threat to the "French element" and a dangerous concession,[1] and by the Muslims as an inadequate and integrationist reform which was not related to the demand for nationhood. In the following years no solution was found to this dilemma and the Fourth Republic finally came to grief over the struggle.

Since the new institutional order of Algeria was the responsibility of the National Assembly, the provisional government had to begin by confining itself to social, economic and administrative reforms.[2] Governor-General Chataigneau, who had worked on the Blum-Viollette plan, made active efforts to promote Muslim agriculture, raised the wages of the Algerian workers and initiated a programme of industrialization. He devoted particular attention to education, which was still quite inadequate.[3] In September 1945 the financial delegations were replaced by the financial assemblies (twenty-two Europeans and fifteen Muslims), and Algerians were appointed senior officials. The governor-general was aiming at an Algerian assembly without a double electoral college in which, by a gradually extended franchise, the balance of power could slowly shift from the Europeans to the Muslims.[4] This was a challenge to the French Algerians and in February 1948, with the help of René

Mayer, the Radical Socialist deputy from Constantine and later prime minister, Chataigneau was removed.

The constituent assemblies paid only incidental attention to Algeria. Earlier on (cf. p. 382) we contrasted the attitude of the Muslim deputies who belonged to the "Élus" group under Dr Bendjelloul in the first constituent assembly, with Ferhat Abbas' Amis du Manifeste et de la liberté in the second. Correspondingly, their demands were diametrically opposed. Bendjelloul aimed at assimilation and full equal rights for the Algerians: citizenship with personal status, a single college for all elections, abolition of discriminatory rules, removal of the governor-general and the mixed communes, approximation of the Algerian administration to that of the mother country.[5] In striking contrast to this, Ferhat Abbas and the second assembly followed the Algerian manifesto and the slogan "neither assimilation, nor new masters, nor separatism", demanding an autonomous Algerian republic with its own parliament, its own government and even its own flag.[6] Although Ferhat Abbas promised loyalty to France and, at first at least, agreed to remain within the French Union, this claim to sovereignty and allegiance to Algeria as the "fatherland" of the Muslims outside France provoked a storm of resentment and opened the Algerian deputies to the suspicion of "separatism" and high treason. In fact the theses of Bendjelloul and Ferhat Abbas, although mutually opposed, corresponded to the only two methods of decolonization that would have been in line with the concept of the French Union: either full integration on the model of the vieilles colonies, and consequently equal civil rights for Europeans and Muslims, or recognition of the sovereignty of the "colony" as had happened with the North African protectorates and Indochina, together with a federal alliance as associated states. Because they had to a certain extent taken France at its word, the two wings of the Algerian national movement presented a grave alternative: either Algeria was an integral part of the Republic, or, with regard to its Muslim people, it was a special territory which could not be fully integrated like the *vieilles colonies*—in which case the category of associated the state seemed to apply.

But in 1946 France was not prepared to accept either of these inherently logical "solutions" both of which, in fact, were bound up with very grave implications. Full integration with proportional representation in parliament would have turned the metropolis into "a colony of its colonies" and the recognition of an autonomous Algerian state would have opened the way to secession. Each alternative threatened both the power of the settlers and, directly or indirectly, "French sovereignty". Naturally it was not only the French Algerians but also the colonialist Right in the mother country that opposed the Algerian demands. For instance, on 14 February 1946 the "Comité de l'Empire français" addressed a letter to the government pointing to the "anxiety" of the French population in Algeria which was threatened, as a minority, with being "fatally submerged by the successive waves of new electors" and had the feeling "of being abandoned by metropolitan opinion".[7] On 30 March René Moreux, chief editor of *Marchés coloniaux*, turned against Bendjelloul's demands for integration[8] and on 13 July he opposed Ferhat Abbas, saying that general franchise without a double electoral college in an Algerian parliament would put the seventeen European deputies at the mercy of the 137 Muslims: "this we shall *never* accept, even as a distant possibility. There must be no doubt on this."[9] The Left dissociated itself from these colonialist views and gave some support to the demands of the Algerian deputies, but it could not but realize the complexity of the situation and was by no means prepared to encourage a consistent process of decolonization. For this would not only drive the French inhabitants into a difficult position, but beyond this would also place before the mother country the grave decision of either being "governed" by Muslim deputies or having to agree to the future secession of a part of the national territory.

We cannot describe in detail here the origins of the 1947 Algerian statute.[10] Since both Ferhat Abbas' party and Bendjelloul's Fédération des élus were now striving for an autonomous Algeria, even the Socialists began to give up their previous assimilatory policy. Algeria was now to receive its own body of laws and a kind of parliament, but without forfeiting its representation in the National Assembly. The laws of the mother country were to continue to be valid for Algeria under certain conditions; double electoral colleges were foreseen.[11] The government project followed the Socialist proposals and was even changed in the Socialists' favour by a department of the interior that had a small majority of Communist, Socialist and Muslim deputies. Naturally the French Algerians and the parties of the Right opposed it. A remarkable shift of fronts occurred, for now it was the French Algerians who wanted as little autonomy as possible. They not only rejected the concept of a "statute" as such but even wanted to restrict the powers of the Algerian assembly to mere deliberation on the budget, thereby largely depoliticizing it. Obviously they assumed that even with parity representation the settlers would no longer be able to assert their interests and that it would therefore be better to hand over responsibility to the mother country's parliament! For the rest, they were chiefly interested in the constitution of the electoral colleges. Now only Europeans were to be permitted to vote in the first electoral college in order to prevent a gradual "invasion" and coalition of the Muslims in both colleges; in addition the Right demanded a two-thirds majority in the Algerian assembly, which would give the settlers a kind of veto. The Ramadier government, which had to rely on the support of the radicals after the elimination of the Communists, had to give in on this in order to make it at all possible to carry through and to accept the two-thirds majority clause. The statute was approved on 27 August by 320 to 88 votes (including deputies from the bourgeois Right such as Pinay, Laniel, Reynaud) with 186 abstentions (including the Communists) and came into force on 20 September.

The Algerian statute was intended to be a compromise between full integration and genuine autonomy; in fact it was not very different from the existing order. Algeria, as a group of overseas departments, remained a part of the one and indivisible Republic and could therefore have neither legislative power nor its own government. The governor-general appointed by Paris exercised executive power. The Algerian assembly was superficially different from the financial delegations but it had equally small powers. The settlers were allowed the double electoral college, parity representation and the two-thirds majority clause. Nor did the much disputed statute fulfil its expected role, for Governor-general Naegelen began to systematically influence the elections and openly tampered with the votes after the nationalists gained a clear victory in the communal elections and launched a campaign of intimidation in the elections to the Algerian assembly. The Muslim electoral college thus gained a considerable majority but lost representational power, so the nationalists had even more incentive to embark on "extra-parliamentary" opposition. The administration and the settlers showed little interest in the assembly, which developed few initiatives of its own and either did not fulfil the duties delegated to it by the statute, such as settling the difficulties between religious observance and the state, the organization of instruction in Arabic, abolishment of the mixed communes, etc. or else delayed in doing so.

Yet France thought it had come up with a reformist policy for Algeria and began to turn to other questions. In the following years overseas issues were dominated by the discussion on Indochina. France contented itself with "realization of the statute" and postulated a community of interests between European and Muslim inhabitants which was coming into being if not already in existence. During the years 1948–1954 the Fourth Republic had no clear concept of Algeria. Meanwhile a dangerous polarization of political forces was becoming apparent; the French Algerians and Messali Hadj's MTLD (Mouvement du Triomphe des Libertés Démocratiques) became more and more radically opposed. A rapid increase in population also contributed to hastening proletarianization or *Clochardization* (Germaine Tillon) in the towns and in the country, while the still small but rapidly growing class of educated Muslims had little chance of gaining access to the administration or the economy and therefore became increasingly responsive to extremist slogans. On 1 November 1954 a small secret organization that had split from the MTLD instigated the rebellion.

We shall not describe here the actual fighting or the different Algerian policies of the rapid succession of governments. The Algerian war visibly aggravated the crisis in the Fourth Republic and the latter, due to its lack of stable and active minorities, was condemned to immobilism.[12] Instead, we shall turn to a few aspects of the discussion within France, in which all the parties took part with increasing intensity, leading to comparison with the Dreyfus affair.

The attitude of the bourgeois Right was relatively unanimous and clear. In 1949 Roger Duchet had assembled the numerous groups of "moderates" into a disciplined fraction of the "Indépendants et Paysans" whose hundred or so deputies occupied an important position in the parliamentary power structure. Duchet's *Pour le Salut public* once again reflects the almost unchanged nationalism of the traditional Right which, now driven onto the defensive, opposed any policy of "surrender". After the defeat in Indochina and the secession of Tunisia and Morocco, France was playing out its last card as an overseas power in Algeria; any concessions would be equivalent to a "decline of France". The world seemed to be in league against France: Nasser and international Communism, as well as Britain and the U.S. were trying, thought Duchet, to drive France out of the maghreb. Behind Algeria lay the Sahara, "swollen with riches . . . which will make us, tomorrow, a great modern power".[13] With its back to the wall, France must now fight the Algerian war to the very end, while at the same time taking energetic measures to combat the treacherous Communist party and the growing defeatism at home. The head of this "party of defeat" and representative of the "intelligentsia of the Left" was once again said to be Mendès-France, who was "always there when the fatherland is being humiliated".[14] Duchet interpreted Prime Minister Mollet's tumultuous reception in Algeria on 6 February 1956 as an "upsurge of patriotism"; the call for an emergency government and a "strong man" became louder.

The attitude of the Communist party was also relatively clear.[15] Between 1944 and 1947 it had to be cautious, but in 1954 it could express its solidarity with the NLF (National Liberation Front), protest the Algerian war and demand immediate negotiations with the "authentic representatives of the Algerian nation". Its internal political structure, quite apart from considerations of Soviet foreign policy, forced the Communist party to be rather restrained, however. Since they did not want to be completely isolated and did want to promote the popular front movement, the Communists did not at first refuse to support Mollet's government; in March 1956 they even acknowledged its authority. There remained, however, a certain distrust of the Pan-Arabism of the NLF leaders, and the Communists did not adopt the slogan of "independence" until rather late. In addition, the party had to act cautiously because of the patriotism of the French workers, particularly since relations between Algerian and French workers remained tense and the violent quarrel between the NLF and Messali Hadj's rival party made it difficult to adopt a positive attitude towards the Algerian rebels. So although the Communist party supported the NLF, it was careful not to gamble with the unity and security of its own organization.

By contrast, the left-wing intellectuals committed themselves resolutely. The "Algerian people" were rising against its capitalist exploiters, they said. Slogans such as assimilation and integration had proved to be systematic deceptions; "to this violence the only reply could be violence, and Algerians have taken up arms".[16] The existence of a million Frenchmen on Algerian soil did not have to be taken into account; since those colonialists were identified with the system of exploitation it seemed justified to employ revolutionary measures to overthrow them. Colonial methods of repression, particularly the use of torture, naturally played a very important psychological role in the discussion; apart from effects on the left wing, these methods also provoked a more general examination of conscience, reflected in a flood of reports and discussions on the problems of violence and terrorism. By contrast the terrorism of the NLF was either glossed over or legitimized as a weapon in the revolution of the oppressed. Jean Paul Sartre openly admitted his approval of terrorism on the part of the rebels.

It was difficult for the Radical Socialists and the Socialists to give a satisfactory answer to the challenge presented by the Algerian war. Former positions proved outdated and the Socialists were accused of betraying the proletariat and serving as a tool of the fascists. Both parties were seeking a compromise, hesitated, and were finally weakened by internal disputes.

When the rebellion broke out Mendès-France was prime minister, François Mitterand minister of the interior. Their first reactions are well-known. On 5 November Mitterand distinguished between the North African protectorates and Algeria, saying that one could and must negotiate with the Tunisian and Moroccan nationalists, but with the rebels in Algeria "the only negotiation is war. Algeria is France; from Flanders to the Congo [there is] only one law, only one nation, only one Parliament".[17] Mendès-France spoke equally plainly on 12 November:

> One does not compromise when it is a question of defending the internal peace of the nation, the unity and the integrity of the Republic. The departments of Algeria form a part of the French Republic. They have been French since long ago and in an irrevocable manner. . . . Never will France, or any French Government or Parliament, whatever their other particular tendencies, give way on this fundamental principle.[18]

This was unmistakable. By confirming that Algeria had the status of an indivisible part of the national territory and by denying the existence of Algerian nationalism (which provoked the North Africa specialist C. A. Julien to protest),[19] he excluded the possibility of negotiating with the rebels and adopted a policy of suppression. As reformers, Mendès-France and Mitterand were concerned with "winning back" the Muslim inhabitants by other means. They had already postulated various measures before 1 November, such as free elections according to the Algeria statute, Muslim access to the civil service, numerous administrative reforms, energetic measures in the economic and social field.[20] It seemed vital to bring about a change in the mentality of the mother country if former promises were to sound convincing. *L'Express,* which stood close to Mendès-France, wrote on 13 November:

> There is still some chance of making the European and Muslim peoples in Algeria into a French community. If one proclaims "French Algeria", one must not treat the French Muslims as Muslims when it is a question of their rights and as Frenchmen when it is a question of their duties. . . . Either one will give its whole content to the title of French citizen granted to the natives and will facilitate their access to political responsibilities and public offices. Or they will seek independence. . . .[21]

Unlike the French Algerians and the right-wing parties in the mother country which were mainly concerned with the restoration of "order", Mendès-France thought it necessary to introduce military, political and economic reforms at the same time, and he proclaimed integration as the aim of the reform policy. People had in fact become aware of the vagueness of this concept, and later a special committee was even set up to define it [!],[22] but obviously no other was available if one excluded the possibility of an autonomous Algerian state. Administrative decentralization could be granted as promised in the statute, but the primary concern had to be to follow a consistent policy of assimilating the two communities, which did not preclude helping the Muslims in education, the use of the Arabic language, etc. Such a policy, if at all possible, could bear fruit very slowly at best. Was it still possible after the outbreak of rebellion and in face of the open or tacit resistance of the French Algerians?

Jacques Soustelle, whom Mendès-France had appointed governor-general in January 1955, became the chief exponent of integration, Soustelle had belonged to the intellectual Left between the wars, joined de Gaulle in 1940 and after 1946 became the leader of the Gaullist party; he is difficult to classify according to the traditional categories of Right and Left and should perhaps be considered primarily a nationalist. He had violently attacked government inactivity in *L'Express* and had supported reforms, thus inciting the settlers' distrust.[23] In a memorandum on 7 January, towards the end of his tenure of office, he described the integration, which Mendès-France's successor Edgar Faure declared as the government programme.[24] He wanted Algeria to keep its originality, but only as a province of France. The governor-general should be removed and the Algerian assembly dissolved. Universal and equal franchise, and particularly the single college, would equate the Muslim people with the Europeans and ensure a strong representation in parliament.[25] In effect, this was a more consistent form of integration than had ever been postulated by the Left, since it abolished the former privileged position of the Europeans and equated the Algerian Muslims with the metropolitan French. Moreover, this version of French Algeria reconciled Soustelle's nationalism with his reformism and made it possible both to oppose the adherents of the *status quo* and to combat any policy of "surrender".

Initially the French Algerians resisted Soustelle's reform plans. "The announcement of reforms gives the greatest hopes to the agitators", declared General Aumeran, the deputy of Algiers. At the same time, however, the governor-general was confronted with "Algerian reality" and under pressure of the NLF massacres he had to undertake repressive measures. Since even the moderate Algerian nationalists, again influenced by NLF terrorism, rejected integration, Soustelle with his policy of "French Algeria" tended more and more to become a spokesman for the settlers, who now also took up the slogan of integration as an alternative to negotiation. Meanwhile the paths of Mendès-France and Soustelle had split. Supporters of Mendès-France, particularly *L'Express*, gave up the concept of integration and gradually steered towards a policy of negotiation. They thought a "valid interlocutor" must appear after free elections, even at the risk that nationalists would be elected. With this spokesman France should negotiate further procedure and the new order of Algeria within an as yet undefined statute of autonomy.[26] "To regain the lost confidence" was also the main theme of a *Note sur L'Algerie* in February 1956.[27] Mendès-France suggested amnesty, freedom of the press, cleaning up the official machinery, expropriation of large landholdings, increase of Muslim wages and the grant of financial aid, in order to document the solidarity of interests and to gain the "reciprocally necessary co-operation". However, the decisive question—whether to negotiate with the NLF—remained unanswered. What would happen if the Algerians sabotaged the elections and continued to demand recognition of an independent Algerian state as a *sine qua non*? Was Mendès-France prepared to go beyond the federative plan proposed in 1956?[28]

This also outlines the problems of the Socialists' policy. The Front Républicain had won the elections of 2 January 1956 with proposals that coincided with those of the Mendèsists. The party wanted to end the "stupid and inconclusive war" (Guy Mollet) and was supported in this by *Témoignage chrétien* and *France Observateur*, yet it was not prepared to ally itself with the extreme Left, fearing lest it then appear a "party of surrender". The SFIO neither accepted the right to secession and the NLF as the sole spokesman for the Muslims, nor integration in Soustelle's sense. The Socialists continued along the lines of their interwar policy, evaded economic and social problems and referred—on the whole with some justification—to the difficulty of independence, for even independence would not manage to solve Algeria's problems. Mollet declared at the 1957 party congress:

> Independence resolves nothing either for the Europeans swept aside by a religious state or for the Muslims who would fall under the direction of a feudal dictatorship [!] . . . It is not true that the Socialists have proclaimed a so-called right of the peoples to decide their own fate without reservation. . . . The rights of the Algerian people exist in the measure [meaning the French settlers]. . . . The only problem to be resolved in Algeria is that of enabling two peoples of different origins to coexist without tearing each other apart.[29] [Similarly, Mollet said in his investiture speech 31 January 1956:] It means maintaining and reinforcing the indissoluble unity between Algeria and metropolitan France. . . . It means at the same time recognizing and respecting the Algerian personality and realizing the total political equality of all the inhabitants of Algeria.[30]

Like Mendès-France, Mollet demanded really free elections with a single college, together with administrative reforms and economic aid, in order to prepare the way for "discussion" on the future status of Algeria. His aim was democratization; the country was to receive extended autonomy, with legislative and executive powers in order to safeguard the "Algerian personality", i.e. the Muslim inhabitants, without driving out the settlers.

Mollet's policy after 6 February and the attitude of his minister for Algeria, Lacoste, met violent criticism within the Front Républicain and within the Socialist party. Mendès-France left the government and found support among a group of influential Socialist politicians (Daniel Mayer, André Philip, Gaston Defferre) who proposed special resolutions at the party congresses and tried to force the prime minister of their own party to change his views. Yet they were unable to really shake Mollet's leadership and were eventually excluded from the party's leading bodies.[31] The dispute, which was reflected in the *Revue socialiste*,[32] was in fact less concerned with ultimate aims[33] than with the actual and much more important question of the ways and means of bringing the bloody war to a rapid end. When and with whom should one negotiate? While the internal party opposition demanded the immediate opening of negotiations, hoping that this would persuade representative groups of Algerian nationalists, if not the militarily weakened NLF, to change course and make it possible to find a compromise solution, Mollet and Lacoste insisted on armistice, in fact on the capitulation of the NLF, before beginning political negotiations. In addition, on 6 February Mollet had himself experienced the French Algerians' resolute attitude and therefore thought it would be necessary to act cautiously and leave the army a more or less free hand in order to prevent a putsch. The subsequent governments, who had to rely on the support of the Right in parliament, worked on similar considerations. Paris became more and more dependent on Algeria and ultimately found itself unable to prevent the disaster after all.

France's attempt to decolonize its overseas territory within its own association of states no doubt had its justification in the case of Algeria. For with respect to the settlers no other way seemed conceivable, nor was any other way discussed except by the Communists and a few left-wing intellectuals—and even they slowly adopted different positions. But if the demand for independence and statehood was and had to remain taboo, the only alternative was full integration, which was conceived in its most consistent form by Soustelle. The Socialists, for instance, tried to find a compromise by proposing an Algerian autonomy which as such was fully democratic but would let Algeria remain within the French association of states. It is impossible to say whether one of these "solutions" would have managed, if applied in time, to check Algerian nationalism. One way or another the European minority would have felt threatened. In 1957–1958 France was finally faced with the uncomfortable alternative of either continuing the war with full force and great losses, with little expectation of a real "victory" and very vague if not false hopes of saving French Algeria, or of accepting the possibility of an independent Algeria in the no less vague hope, which later proved equally false, that it could then assure the interests of the French settlers by means of bilateral negotiations. The one alternative stood at the centre of the discussion and had the support of the administration, the French Algerians and the army. The other was supported by the group round Mendès-France and a few dissident Socialists, but also by two of the most influential French political writers: Maurice Duverger and Raymond Aron. Neither can be classified in traditional party terminology and both made efforts to see the question outside its mere French perspective and to set it within an international framework.

In a much-noted article in *Le Monde* on 25 January 1957 Duverger began with the example of England, which had not recognized in time the emancipation movements in its American colonies in the eighteenth century but had then taken this lesson to heart and in future years had granted independence within the framework of the Commonwealth. Indochina could be a similar lesson to France:

> The question is not of knowing whether one is for or against French Algeria . . . it is a question of knowing whether this form of French Algeria is viable. That question has been settled. The movement for national liberation which is agitating Africa and Asia is irrevocable. The old colonies will sooner or later turn into national States . . . the only real question is that of the ties which these new States will maintain with the ex-metropoles.

France, he said, had to decide whether to maintain outdated structures for a few more years, or to erect new ones "within the framework of a French Commonwealth". Public opinion was not yet up to the challenge of "decolonization" and preferred, he said, to make Russia, Britain, Egypt, etc., into scapegoats for its own difficulties. Numerous disappointments had produced an inferiority complex which was now expressing itself in rigid nationalism. Duverger gave no further details of his "solution" and turned out to be excessively optimistic, but he analysed French reactions correctly. He pressed his fellow-countrymen to become aware of the world-wide phenomenon of colonial emancipation which now made all former theories obsolete. The well-known national economist of the Mendès-France circle, Alfred Sauvy, employed similar arguments.[34]

Much more important was the publication in June 1957 of *La tragédie algérienne* by Raymond Aron. With characteristic brilliance Aron questioned the taboos, theories and alleged alternatives of the former Algerian policy. He believed France must come to terms with the idea of an Algerian state. In demographic terms alone integration was impossible, since the Muslim population was increasing rapidly and proportional representation in parliament would destroy the already weak régime— quite apart from economic and social problems. "Independence" had become a magic word. The government thesis (truce first, then free elections) might sound liberal, but it by-passed the real problem, for these elections would probably give the nationalists a majority. Elections or direct negotiations, autonomy or some other compromise—one way or another they would all lead to independence since no other way out was conceivable now that Tunisia and Morocco had established a precedent. "The ties with Algeria are not indissoluble. By recognizing the Algerian personality, one ceases to exclude an Algerian State."[35] The economic argument was not convincing, he pointed out, for France could get over the eventual loss of the Algerian market and the investment funds could be used inside the metropolis. The Netherlands had provided an example of this kind of economic adaptation. Naturally Aron was aware that the real problem was the French Algerians. He believed that a certain amount could be achieved by negotiation, but that if worst came to worst one would have to resettle the European inhabitants at state costs. Aron did not consider Algeria necessary to France's position as a great power:

> as for great power, France no longer has it, can no longer have it. . . . It is by refusing to recognize the conditions of future wealth, of future greatness, that the French risk precipitating their decline.[36]

The importance of this book lay in logic with which Aron shattered earlier taboos, and above all in the fact that Aron, who was not a committed left-wing intellectual but a self-confessed anti-Communist, a sociologist and political scientist concerned with factual arguments, renounced the idea of "indissoluble ties" with Algeria and considered the recognition of an independent Algerian state inevitable—not out of sympathy for the NLF or in the name of a revolutionary ideology but as a logical if painful result of the international political situation. Aron managed to make the idea of "surrender" admissible, so to speak, even in the camp of the Right, as "Cartierism" had similarly done in the case of Black Africa.

A "Report of high officials", which reached the public in January 1958, also showed how, over the years, the government's repeated promises that military pacification was in its final stages, lost conviction and independence was seen as the only alternative.[37] The report said that the NLF should not be excluded from negotiations; only an agreement signed by this extreme radical group had some hope of survival. France should recognize an Algerian state and the "call of independence" and perhaps even set up an interim government of Muslims, French Algerians and representatives of France. The Europeans in Algeria and the Algerians in France should be granted dual nationality, while a common defence organization could guarantee primary French interests. A number of professors held a similar attitude.[38]

Such theses necessarily appeared defeatist and treacherous to the French Algerians and to exponents of French Algeria in the mother country. Jacques Soustelle replied to Aron in an article, "Le drame Algérien et la décadence française", whose title alone indicates the nature of the attack.[39] Aron was pretending to be objective, he said, but was completely mistaking the Algerian problem. It was dubious and morally untenable to want to give up a province when it cost the nation more than it paid it, or to agree to a transfer of the inhabitants and to want to compensate them with money for the loss of their homes. How could one speak of colonialism when all the inhabitants were French citizens? What should happen to the numerous Muslims who had fought on the side of France? Aron was obviously surrendering, without batting an eye, to the terrorism of the NLF; "he dares to present this as wisdom and even as courage."[40] National interests were the decisive ones for Soustelle and he vehemently attacked Aron's idea of a continental France limited to the "European hexagon". The Sahara, he asserted, offered new opportunities for France to free itself from dependence on America and the Arab world. After the loss of Indochina, Tunisia and Morocco, France must keep Algeria, for

> to go beyond a certain point is to risk death . . . to abandon Algeria is to condemn France to decadence; to save Algeria is to put an end to the ghastly process of degradation, to give back to our country, to its people, to its youth, their chances and their future.[41]

Aron's and Soustelle's theses clearly reflect two quite different temperaments and two opposite views of Algerian policy, formulated without consideration of parliamentary possibilities. They also represent the characteristic divergences in French national consciousness after 1945, which became very marked in the Algerian question. For France, wounded by the defeat in 1940, was working at its recovery and introducing a process of modernization; at the same time it was seeking to restore its "greatness" and political power. But what did greatness mean after the Second World War? Could a France that was aware of its "humiliating" dependence on the United States simply give up its colonial possessions and even allow terrorist nationalists to wrest from it a "province", an old integrated part of the national territory? Was not agreement to such a loss proof of political and moral decadence? Or "greatness" and national interests would have to be reinterpreted. Aron and Duverger saw France's only chance in showing its willingness to free itself from the narrow national attitude of sovereignty and to adapt itself to the interdependence of the modern world. This would mean accepting decolonization, promoting economic and social progress and seeking new forms of French "greatness" and "presence in the world".

The Fourth Republic came to grief over the Algerian question, but General de Gaulle fought his way back to power with the help of the army and the Algiers putschists. To "solve" the Algerian question became his most urgent and difficult task. De Gaulle had attacked the immobilism of the "system" and promised a revival of France, but he had hardly ever taken a definite stand on the future of Algeria or formulated his own concepts. The general's attitude between 1958 and 1961, with which we are concerned here, is not easy to establish, since it is difficult to distinguish between his true intentions and political manoeuvres. De Gaulle made numerous and long speeches, but was "sibylline" in his decisive pronouncements, so that the formulas he used were open to different interpretations.[42]

His first pronouncements after taking power sound an integrationist note and are reminiscent of Soustelle's theses. In a speech in Algiers on 4 June de Gaulle spoke of the *Français à part entière*; henceforth there were only Frenchmen in Algeria with equal rights and duties who would all have franchise in the promised constitutional referendum, "in a single and same college". With the deputies elected in this way, "we shall see how to do the rest".[43] At the same time he described Algeria as "organically a French territory today and forever".[44] So its inhabitants, unlike those of the African territories, could not choose independence in the referendum; "Yes" was to mean willingness for renovation "within the French framework" while the possibility of "No" was not considered at all.[45] The voting, supervised by the army, and the results of elections to the national assembly on 13 December were in France's favour in spite of the NLF[46] and gave de Gaulle a point of departure for further measures.

So for the time being the general really did act consistently with his proclaimed intentions: full franchise for the Muslims without change of personal status, a single college, strong parliamentary representation (sixty deputies!) with a Muslim majority. De Gaulle went far beyond the 1947 Algerian statute and in a certain sense caught up on what the weak Fourth Republic had neglected to do or had not succeeded in doing in face of resistance from the French Algerians! These reforms appeared to aim at integration according to Soustelle's interpretation, but in fact they were much closer to the Socialist concepts. For in spite of much persuasion, de Gaulle deliberately avoided adopting the slogan of "French Algeria"[47] and openly supporting integration—which led to increased friction between him and the French Algerians. Obviously he wanted to hold open another door. His aim was not simply the integration of Algeria into the mother country, but a different, new Algerian statute: full equal rights and democratization as precondition for an autonomy which would ensure the Muslims their share in government without prejudicing French interests or separating Algeria from the "French framework".

In order to create the basis for this solution, General de Gaulle, to the great surprise and annoyance of both French Algerians and the army, described the struggle of the rebels as "courageous".[48] Although he was stepping up the military action, he did not want to bar the way to reconciliation and truce, in the hope of being able to reduce the NLF to a minority or even to silence it. At the same time he clearly dissociated himself from the "Comité du salut public", began to clean up the administration and in December replaced his delegate, General Salan, by a civilian. His "Plan de Constantine" for economically developing Algeria, announced on 3 October 1958, had the same aim of making good on previous promises and creating a new basis of trust with the Muslims.

In his directives for the elections de Gaulle stressed the freedom of the parties and the need for "true competition", for only this could fill the political vacuum and allow effective political forces to appear.[49] The head of state was prepared to enable the nationalist organizations —perhaps not the NLF—to participate in the elections. On 23 October he welcomed Ferhat Abbas' willingness for an armistice, which the latter had announced a few days earlier, and coined the sensationally effective formula of a "peace of the brave" which the rebels could obtain by laying down their arms.[50] De Gaulle did not, however, want to begin negotiations yet. Instead he spoke of the Algerian "personality" which could advance towards a new future in "close association" with France.[51] These phrases met violent opposition from the French Algerians because they diverged from the policy of integration and no longer even stipulated that Algeria was a "French territory". Algeria was now clearly distinguished from the metropolis.[52] In striking contrast to these phrases, which remained vague and seemed to incline towards the status of "associated state", Prime Minister Michel Debré did not give up his demand for integration.[53]

In 1959 de Gaulle continued the "pacification", tried to rally the army to his policy and then took the decisive step towards a solution of the Algerian problem in his declaration of 16 September.[54] He said a community had now been set up with the African states, but the Algerian question was still awaiting an answer; the slogans used hitherto had proved sterile and a solution could be expected only "by the free choices that the Algerians themselves choose to make as to their future. . . . Taking into account all the Algerian facts, national and international, I consider it necessary that this recourse to self-determination be proclaimed as from today". In four years at the latest the Algerians could decide their own fate by a referendum in which they would have to choose either secession, full integration, or the third possibility, a "government of Algerians by the Algerians . . . backed by aid from France and in close union with France in matters of economy, instruction, defence, foreign relations". With this declaration France recognized for the first time the sovereign rights of the Algerians and their right to secession. No other than de Gaulle himself had thus given up the traditional premise, hitherto considered indisputable, that Algeria was an indivisible part of the national territory! He was serious about the "Algerian personality" and the liquidation of "Papa's Algeria",[55] saying that Algeria could not be compared with any other French province and must develop independently.

So Algeria, if not Tunisia and Morocco, was to be confronted with the same choice offered to the African territories: in the future, Algeria was to be able to decide on its relations with France on the basis of the right to self-determination. As in the case of Black Africa in 1958, de Gaulle also warned Algeria of the consequences of secession: independence was possible, but it would mean the withdrawal of the French and would therefore lead to "a miserable, dreadful and horrible political chaos". Association with France, by contrast, would mean French aid during the period of recovery and the transfer or "communal" exercise of certain sovereign rights. Thus the Communauté was extended to Algeria, a fact which has not received sufficient attention. For the rest de Gaulle made several restrictions: the decision by referendum would be made only after a transitional period, at the conclusion of the military "pacification", in order to give France time to check the extreme nationalists and to create a pro-French attitude by means of economic aid. The Sahara should remain reserved to France, but in case of secession he foresaw a "regrouping" of the French Algerians, i.e. partition of the country, or repatriating the European settlers in the mother country.

Such was General de Gaulle's position. He accepted the right to self-determination, because the existing system of elections obviously had no hope of solving any problems and the international implications of the Algerian problem made such a step seem necessary. De Gaulle stressed the Algerian desire for emancipation and the international phenomenon of decolonization, which France could not evade. He also pointed out, with some right, that although in military terms the battle had been won, the methods and slogans used hitherto would not provide a permanent political settlement, prevent a new rebellion or even suppress new acts of terrorism or sabotage. So further concessions were indicated. At first, the negotiations were only to result in an armistice, i.e. in the capitulation of the NLF, and not in a political agreement. The NLF was not yet accepted as the only or even the main spokesman for the Algerian people. But the talks in Melun at the end of June 1960, in which France laid down conditions but did not "negotiate", came to nothing and de Gaulle had to change course. In Évian-les-Bains the French recognition of the NLF could barely be disguised by setting up a provisional government. After "Algerian Algeria", the counterpart to "French Algeria", came the "Algerian Republic"[56]; and from an autonomous Algeria "federatively tied to France" without external sovereignty, the road eventually led to a sovereign and independent state[57] that promised to guarantee the rights of the French settlers bilaterally. The tone and arguments changed correspondingly. If France had hitherto insisted on its rights and interests, it now stressed the vital importance of French aid to an independent Algeria. In analogy to its warning to Black Africa, France now said: Algeria relied more on France than France on Algeria; only France could supply Algeria with the comprehensive financial aid it would need in the future.[58] In an effort to persuade the NLF to give in, France threatened the expulsion of Algerian workers in the metropolis.[59] But it proved necessary to give up a few of its former hopes, for even the Sahara—which Paris wanted to keep for itself—eventually had to be recognized as a part of the Algerian territory. The threat of a "regrouping" and partition of the country made little impression. Nor could France maintain the thesis that a certain period must elapse between the armistice and the referendum, but had to accept the "préalable" of the NLF, i.e. the right to independence.

It has been asserted in different quarters that General de Gaulle wanted an independent Algeria from the start or at least accepted it as inevitable. This is largely based on unconfirmed statements in 1957 which are supposed to have referred to future independence.[60] According to different points of view, these statements could be interpreted as the far-sightedness of a statesman or as proof of treacherous opportunism in regard to his friends and the army. But I am inclined to think that de Gaulle's Algerian policy evolved gradually and was continually affected by the internal and external balance of power. Originally he obviously envisaged a statute of autonomy within the French association of states which would be liberal enough to gain the approval of a majority of the Muslim inhabitants; but then the undeniable desire for emancipation[61] persuaded him to shift to self-determination, hoping to create an Algerian state which, like Black Africa, would at least remain in the French sphere of influence in foreign policy, defence and general economic policy. Only in the final phase did de Gaulle fully accept independence and try to protect immediate national interests, above all in the Sahara, by the "blackmail" of technical and financial aid. What part was played here by his irritation at the attitude of the French Algerians, their demonstrations and attempts at a putsch and finally the terrorism of the SAO (Secret Army Organization), is hard to say. Doubtless one can attribute considerable importance to the desire to end the Algerian war, even at the price of great sacrifices. In terms of the above-mentioned discussion between Soustelle and Aron, de Gaulle gradually turned away from Soustelle and adopted Aron's theses. The "greatness" of France did not lie in Algeria and the continuance of an ultimately ineffectual resistance, but in a consistent process of decolonization—even at the price of the French Algerians—which would correspond to the international balance of power and at the same time give France a free hand to engage in an activated and "independent" foreign policy.

III. Towards a Comparison

THE DECOLONIZATION OF AN ANTI-COLONIAL POWER: THE UNITED STATES IN THE PHILIPPINES

The Americans have always regarded themselves as an anti-colonial power. As a former colony that won its independence in a lengthy struggle against a European colonial power, the United States had always distrusted the colonial expansion of Europe and took the part of colonial peoples who were fighting for their emancipation.

In historical terms, however, a certain parallel might be drawn between European expansion overseas and the occupation of the North American continent. This occupation was based on a continuous movement of settlement and technological advance, but it was also accompanied by conquest and did not come to an "official" end until 1893 with the closing of the legendary "frontier". The Northwest Ordinance of 1787, which can be judged in terms of a "doctrine of decolonization", provided for administering the newly-acquired territories "colonially" at first, and then gradually incorporating them into the Union with full equal rights. Congress reserved to itself the decision on admitting a Territory to statehood and on the conclusion of decolonization; moreover the American legislators discussed the "ripeness" of the people in very much the same way as the British, and the Territories occasionally complained that Washington was treating them as colonies. American expansionism had an integrationist and assimilative character, as is particularly apparent in the conferment of statehood on Alaska and Hawaii in 1959 and 1960. Yet no real colonialist mentality ever evolved in America and the process of territorial expansion was not understood as colonial expansion.

With the Spanish-American war, the stated goal of which was to be the liberation of Cuba, the United States became a colonial power in the accepted sense of the term. In conquering and annexing Pacific islands thousands of miles away whose numerous inhabitants were of different races and culturally independent, America entered into competition with the great European and Asian powers. It was even more contradictory that a colonial rebellion against the tyranny of Spain, whose adherents welcomed the Americans as liberators, had to be defeated before the new colonial power could impose its rule! But for the fact that it was an influential group of imperialists that energetically and pointedly pursued conquest and annexation, one would be tempted to say that the United States, in a fit of "absence of mind" (as Seeley called it) established itself as an Asian colonial power.[1]

The strong resistance to annexation, particularly in the Senate, is well-known. The new self-assurance of the new great power, which suddenly burst out of the narrow sphere of the Western Hemisphere into world politics, the hopes in business circles (which ultimately proved to be unfounded) that the Philippines would provide access to trade with China and the sense of having a civilizing mission (Rudyard Kipling wrote his famous poem "The White Man's Burden" in February 1899 for the Americans!) only barely managed to carry the day. Imperialist interests in America ran parallel to the European ones. The difference lay only in the strength of traditional resistance to colonial expansion and the dislike of leading politicians such as McKinley and Taft for annexation. One could say that the United States assumed colonial power with a bad conscience. It was no accident that in the following years America was unwilling to describe itself as a colonial power and preferred to use expressions such as "dependencies", "dependent territories", etc. for its overseas possessions.

The need to make concessions to the anti-imperialist forces in Congress became clear in the first pronouncements on Philippines policy. On 14 February 1899 the Senate accepted a resolution whereby the Philippine Islands should not be annexed as an integral part of the national territory and would not, therefore, be able to obtain statehood in the future. The population was to be prepared for local autonomy and at a given time would be granted a voice on its own destiny.[2] Taft, the first governor-general, said in January 1900 that the Philippines "might be developed into a self-governing people".[3] Elihu Root's well-known instructions on 7 April 1900 to a commission which was to prepare for the transition from military to civil administration and for the institutional improvement of the colony, stated that a foreign centralized bureaucracy should be avoided and the Islands should be given franchise and a broad local government on the American pattern with the greatest possible inclusion of the native populations. American institutions should form the basis of a "just and effective government" and guarantee individual rights and liberties. These instructions said nothing, however, about the future status of the colony. Yet they may be considered liberal. The Democratic party under Bryan even decided on a resolutely anti-imperialist course and in the presidential campaign of 1900 Bryan demanded immediate independence for the Philippines. This would certainly have been impossible in Europe at the time.

Taft described the aim of the Republican administration between 1900 and 1912 in a report to President Theodore Roosevelt:

> ... the national policy is to govern the Philippine Islands for the benefit and welfare and uplifting of the people of the Islands and gradually to extend to them, as soon as they shall show themselves fit to exercise it, a greater measure of popular self-government. ... What should be emphasized in the statement of our national policy is that we wish to prepare the Filipinos for *popular* self-government. This is plain from Mr. McKinley's letter of instructions and all of his utterances. It was not at all within his purpose or that of Congress which made his letter a part of the law of the land that we were merely to await the organization of a Philippine oligarchy or aristocracy competent to administer the government and then turn the Islands over to it. ... Another logical deduction from the main proposition is that when the Filipino people as a whole show themselves reasonably fit to conduct a popular self-government, maintaining law and order and offering equal protection of the laws and civil rights to rich and poor, and desire complete independence of the United States, they shall be given it.[4]

This declaration is important. It demonstrates that the United States felt obliged very early on to accept the principle of independence for the Philippines and to justify its own domination in this manner. The natives, however, must first reach a certain degree of maturity and show themselves "fit" for self-government; naturally it would be up to America to decide when this had occurred and when the numerous conditions for self-government had been fulfilled.[5] The American arguments here are not basically different from the British ones and are dangerously close to being hypocritical. The possibility of independence was "generously" accepted, but at the same time America stipulated almost impossible conditions which could be interpreted at will, thus taking back with its right hand what the left had granted! The reference to "popular government" makes this even clearer. Paradoxically, or perhaps characteristically, it was the Republicans who stipulated democratic procedure in the Philippines as a precondition for further steps towards self-government. Superficially this sounded liberal; in practice it meant that the emancipation movement was delayed and self-government was relegated to the distant future. For the time being it still remained an open question whether the colonial power for its part promoted the process of democratization it demanded or whether it prevented it, either deliberately or by simply fixing a certain social structure. We shall see that this particular aspect of American colonial policy deserves close attention in the case of the Philippines.

America was sincere in its declaration that it would introduce elections early on and include Filipinos in the administration. As early as 1907, after a test as to their cultural qualifications, there were elections to an assembly which obtained certain legislative powers and provided a platform for the new nationalist party. The executive naturally remained in the hands of the Americans. The governor-general not only had a veto right but also appointed the members of a commission which had part legislative and part executive duties. But four of the five commission members were Filipinos. The United States proceeded to politicize its colony early, so that it differed considerably from the British, Dutch and French colonies in South-East Asia.

Under the Democratic administration the differences became even greater. Since 1900 the new government party had asked for an early declaration of independence,[6] and in March 1912 the Philippines committee introduced a proposal for a law that would immediately give the Islands internal autonomy and promised full independence by 1921.[7] This heralded the "timetable" policy, i.e. setting a deadline when the promise of self-government would have to be fulfilled. The United States was the only colonial power to actually hold to its promise, unlike England which discussed the question of timetables but repeatedly refused to set them. However, the proposal was never discussed, for in spite of anti-imperialist pronouncements President Woodrow Wilson was not prepared to support independence. But on 6 October 1913 the new governor, Harrison, read a declaration by Wilson which explicitly declared that the "ultimative independence of the Islands" was the aim of American policy. Similarly the preamble of the 1916 Jones Act, first proposed in 1914, stated: "It is, as it has been, the purpose of the people of the U.S. to withdraw their sovereignty over the Philippine Islands and to recognize their independence as soon as a stable government can be established therein." It is worth noting that the Democrats confined themselves to the term "stable government"! But the American attitude in the Philippines issue coincided with the party's political platform only in a limited sense. The attitude towards foreign policy as such and thereby also towards isolationism always played an important and specifically American role. For instance, Senator Lodge, a friend of Roosevelt and an influential nationalist and interventionist, described the renunciation of the Philippines as irreconcilable with national dignity, while the no less nationalist but isolationist Senator Borah pleaded for withdrawal![8]

The Jones Act itself brought decisive reforms. Both houses of the legislature were now elected on a wider franchise; the governor obtained a veto right and in case of conflict the American president had the ultimate power of decision. The appointment even of senior officials required the assent of the Philippine Senate—a concession on the American model but which was very unusual in a colony and decisively restricted the power of the governor. An innovation was the state council consisting of the heads of the administrative departments. Historically this "constitution" can be compared with the British reforms in India in 1918–1919. The Philippines were to obtain a high degree of self-government without America surrendering its control. As in the American constitution, the assembly had considerable legislative power, but at the same time the position of the governor-general was strengthened by a division of powers. He appointed the department heads, i.e. the ministers, and obtained the right, or rather the duty, to supervise the administration. So the American presidential system was carried over to a colony, offering a remarkable parallel with America's own period as a colony. But even in the British era, i.e. in the colonial situation, the system had not worked satisfactorily. This was because the governor was not elected by the people and supported by his party but was appointed by the colonial power, and his was therefore an alien office. Conflicts between the Philippine legislature, the executive, which was not responsible to it, and the governor were inherent in the system.

Harrison, however, evaded this conflict by being conciliatory and implemented the Jones Act according to the preamble rather than according to the directives received. He actively encouraged the appointment of Filipinos in the administration, discussed legislative measures in advance with Filipino leaders, particularly wth Osmenā, the spokesman for the assembly, and largely refused to exercise his rights. Since the nationalist party controlled the legislature, exercised patronage and thus exerted an indirect control over the administration, around 1920 the Islands enjoyed extensive autonomy, while at the same time the "presidential" régime took on parliamentary features.

But this laissez-faire attitude had its darker aspects: dissension and corruption in the administration, a deficit in the budget, the threat of a collapse of the national bank, the railway and state industries. Harrison considered that these were merely transitional features of the transfer of government responsibility to the Filipinos. Self-government, he said, was necessarily bound up with a certain amount of inefficiency. In reply to a Philippine mission which had demanded the recognition of national self-determination, President Wilson declared before Congress in December 1920 that the Philippines had reached the desirable "stable government" and that it was now the duty of the U.S. to hold to its earlier promises.[9] This step complied with the anti-colonialism of his party and with the attitude Wilson had taken at Versailles, but had few parallels in contemporary European colonial policy, even if one takes into account that Wilson no longer had a majority in Congress and had no hope of such resolutions being accepted!

The Republicans Harding and Coolidge did not continue Wilson's Philippines policy. For them isolationism in foreign policy and "back to normalcy" did not mean granting independence to the colonies. General Wood, a former governor of Puerto Rico, introduced the new policy. He was an administrative expert on a scale comparable to the great British governors-general. Although externally he adhered to the Jones Act, Wood claimed reserved rights and full executive power and cleaned up the administration. Even the Filipino politicians acknowledged his accomplishments in this respect. The conflict inherent in the constitution could, however, no longer be evaded. Friction occurred repeatedly between the assembly and the government, the nationalist leader and the governor-general. In 1923 the Filipinos left the state council. Neither General Wood nor President Coolidge proved willing to accede to the demands for autonomy or to begin to liberalize the régime. They said the conditions for independence had not yet been fulfilled, either in the sphere of foreign policy and economy or with regard to a democratic form of government. The schoolmasterly tone in which these criteria were enunciated could hardly hide their claim to domination.[10] Finally, in 1928–1929, it was Henry Stimson who managed to reopen talks with Filipino politicians and to persuade them to re-enter the state council. He took the nationalist party into consideration when he appointed ministers and came close to setting up a responsible government by avoiding American intervention in the administration where possible and confining himself to certain sovereign rights and powers of control.[11]

The discussion among political writers inclined in the same direction. Admittedly only a few writers supported an early grant of independence, yet equally few were in favour of a repressive course. The latter naturally included the Manila Americans.[12] The liberals recalled the numerous promises and criticized the criteria by which the "fitness" of the colony for independence was measured. They said the standard of, for instance, the South American states had certainly been reached, and the small European states were not prepared to defend themselves against a major attack either. The national movement was authentic and involved more than a minority! They proposed an autonomy statute with a later plebiscite on independence. This willingness to reform went beyond what we have seen in the European sphere and prepared the ground for the discussion in 1930–1934.[13]

The American system can be compared neither with British indirect rule nor with French methods. The conditions for indirect rule were lacking, for there had been no native rulers with their own administration since Spanish times. The class of notables, however, had not yet been destroyed or replaced by a new administration. The social structure was a result of the cultural "assimilation" the Spanish administration imposed on the Malayan inhabitants and it had certain similarities with South America. Instead of the loose clan and village structure with its subsistence farming characteristic of the pre-Spanish era, there was now "feudal" aristocracy of large landowners. These were the well-known "caciques" who controlled the dependent tenant farmers and agricultural labourers and maintained their domination by direct pressure, threats and credit grants at exorbitant interest rates. The Americans made no attempt at agrarian reform. Some few credit aids, protection laws and unions were introduced, but they were of little benefit. With the rapid expansion of cash crops, particularly sugar, the capital investment companies' large landownership even expanded to reach the traditional rice areas.[14] Agrarian unrest was a part of the picture in the Philippines from Spanish times to the Huk revolt!

Some aspects of American colonial policy deserve particular mention. By largely leaving local administration to the caciques and creating a legislative assembly early on, the administration further increased the caciques' power. The landowners acted as bosses of the nationalist parties, manipulated the elections and managed to violently oppose any measures that contradicted their interests. Perhaps self-government was granted too soon, particularly since the great mass of farmers, tenants and labourers remained excluded from the franchise. A certain parallel with the British West Indies comes to mind (cf. p. 110). The inherent liberalism of American policy reached its limit in the Philippines and it is worth asking whether the paternalist system of the Dutch, in its intentions at least, did not achieve more for the farmers in Indonesia than the American refusal to interfere with social structure in the Pacific islands. The colonial power and the Filipino upper classes had many practical interests in common and were both concerned with maintaining the *status quo*. The nationalists might demand independence and strongly oppose the U.S., but they were recruited from the upper class of landowners and stayed clear of any social revolutionary or even democratic mass movement. In 1934–1935 the Sakdal movement of tenant farmers and day labourers was bloodily suppressed. This was a very different case from the national movements in India and particularly in Indochina and Indonesia, which did not disappear even with independence.

The problems of social structure are particularly important in our context because it was the Americans who stipulated a democratic procedure as a condition for independence. But how could such a condition be fulfilled while the colonial power was supporting the feudal, bourgeois-capitalist upper class?

On the other hand the Americans extended the educational system, the instrument of social emancipation, very quickly and very actively; in this respect they were very different from the European colonial powers. Conditions were favourable, since the colonial power found an existing Spanish-speaking élite and could build on the Spanish administration. Between the wars a relatively high number of children entered schools, in 1938 20 percent of national and local expenditure flowed into education. In Manila there were technical schools and a university, and a considerable number of Filipinos studied in the U.S.[15] Instruction, however, was exclusively in English, since there were not enough Spanish-speaking teachers and moreover the Americans were convinced that the English language opened the door to modern civilization. Here America proved considerably less adaptable than Britain. Yet America did not aim at cultural assimilation in the sense that France did but instead disrupted the Malayan-Spanish culture and forced it to adopt some dubious elements of the American way of life. For the rest, the use of a foreign language made it more difficult to teach the rural population, so indirectly this once again benefitted the ruling class. American educational policy in the Philippines, as opposed to British and French policy, was to have a definite political character and aimed to train the Filipinos for political responsibility and to provide them with a national consciousness. Pictures of national heroes hung in the classrooms and the national anthem was taught. This was clearly a specifically American attitude!

It is also worth noting the early and consistently encouraged occupation of the administrative cadre by Filipinos. In 1914 the number of American officials was still 24 percent, mainly teachers, but in 1932 it was reduced to 2 percent. Practically the entire administration, up to the secretaries-of-state and the chief ministers, was occupied by Filipinos. A Filipino even presided over the high court.[16] Here the United States certainly went further than the European colonial powers.

The tariff and economic policy, by contrast, were strictly "colonialist". The colony was to produce foodstuffs and raw materials and also to serve as a market for export goods. The Americans invested in the production of sugar, tobacco, cocoanut, copra and hemp for export, and controlled trade, banking and shipping, but they were not interested in industrialization.[17] Per capita income was higher than in the other areas of South-East Asia, but public investment for development purposes was lower.[18] Since the America-Philippines trade had been tariff free since 1909–1913, Philippine production was one-sidedly directed at the U.S. In 1930, 79 percent of goods exported went to the United States, in 1933 it was 87 percent. The production of sugar rose from 356,000 tons in 1921 to 1,000,000 tons in 1932, and 94 percent went to America; 60 percent of the state revenue came from taxes on sugar. Food production, by contrast, remained stationary. The tenant farmers were often even forbidden to cultivate food.

It is obvious that with tariff-free import it was scarcely possible for the Philippines to develop its own industry. The tariff policy was originally intended to help Philippine production and to serve as evidence of American goodwill—and it met with resistance from American producers[19]—but in later years it was in crass contradiction to the alleged aim of preparing the Philippines for self-government. How was independence or even internal autonomy to be possible if economically the Philippines continued to be dependent on the American market? The Filipino members of the legislature recognized this dilemma and sharply opposed the tariff policy![20]

American tariff policy bore a certain resemblance to the French. The imperial concept which saw the colonies as parts of the national territory and continually tried to create closer ties with the mother country considered free trade "logical" and inherent in the system, though not in the American system—quite apart from the fact that the U.S. professed to be the expert on the open-door policy and violently protested British, Dutch and French attempts between the wars to prejudice America in their own colonies by tariff and investment legislation. While the colonial power aimed at political self-government, it created at the same time a very extensive economic dependence.[21] The argument that economically the Philippines were still not self-sufficient enough and therefore not yet "ripe" for independence was hardly convincing, for America had created this system of dependence itself and even in the 1920s it had made no efforts to even gradually adapt the Philippine economy to the international market.

This curious discrepancy between self-government in the political field and a kind of assimilation in the economic, a discrepancy that was also apparent between ideology and political aims on the one hand and the economic structure on the other, resulted in the confusing movement which led in 1934 to the statute of autonomy and to independence. Several economic groups already felt threatened by the competition of Philippine imports in the 1920s, and they therefore urged the abolition of free trade. They were the American sugar producers in Cuba and on the continent, certain organizations of farmers, and the rope industry. The unions, which had in any case always supported independence, joined them, in order to put a check on the immigration of Filipino labour to California. But a tariff wall could be erected only if the Philippines became a foreign country, i.e. obtained independence! So it was said that

> they [the Philippines] are hanging like a millstone about the necks of the cotton producers and the peanut, bean and corn producers of the U.S. Let us give them their independence and get rid of the Philippine Islands now . . . and hereafter when their cheap and inferior stuff comes in to swamp our American farmers we can put a tariff on it and preserve the home market for our American home people.[22]

Since any radical solution had to mean economic disaster for the Philippines, a paradoxical reversal of positions began to occur. While purely economic interests could ally themselves with traditional anti-colonialism and isolationist tendencies, the conservative imperialists had to oppose the nationalist argument and came closer to the pro-Philippine liberals who supported independence but did not simply want to abandon the colony to its economic fate. Stimson wrote in January 1929:

> what I would fear was that when the dilemma was presented between tariff against the Philippines on one side and independence on the other, the American Congress remembering the long continued demands for

immediate independence by the Filipinos would at the behest of the American special interest give the Filipinos immediate independence and disregard the real harm and cruelty which this could do to them.[23]

The Timberland resolution of February 1928, which was to limit tariff-free sugar imports to 500,000 tons, was rejected; but after the outbreak of crisis the movement could no longer be halted—in spite of the opposing interests of the Manila Americans, the American export industry and the administration! The economic arguments stood on shaky ground, for Philippine trade had practically no importance in relation to overall American trade. President Hoover even vetoed the Hawes-Cutting Act of January 1933 because the interim periods were too short and the Filipinos would not achieve economic independence. The motives were egoistic, he said, the act did not bring freedom but "new and enlarged angers to liberty and freedom itself".[24] But Hoover was outvoted by a coalition of Democrats and Republicans from the farming areas. Not only Hoover and Stimson rejected the proposal, even the Philippine assembly did so, because the relatively early removal of their tariff advantages appeared economically intolerable. This produced the perhaps unique situation that an act passed by the legislative body of the mother country for the grant of independence—although with interim periods and reserved rights—was rejected by the nationalists!

In rejecting the Hawes-Cutting Act, the Filipinos were speculating on the presidency of Franklin D. Roosevelt, hoping for far-reaching concessions from a Democrat. Roosevelt had, it is true, developed from an imperialist and interventionist in Caribbean matters into an anti-imperialist and supporter of the "good neighbour" policy. But he had still supported Wood in 1922 and in his 1932 presidential campaign rejected Philippine independence "for many years to come"[25]; although he spoke in indefinite terms, he returned to the traditional positions of the Democratic party.[26] In 1935 the president called the signing of the Independence Bill "one of the happiest events in my office"[27] and during the Second World War he liked to present American policy as a model for the European colonial powers. But in 1934 he conceded the Philippines only a minimal alteration of the proposed act and "benevolent consideration" of economic questions that would arise later.[28] So the Philippines approved the Act as a compromise between measures.

It seems appropriate here to make a few comments on the discussion in Congress and in the press.[29] The economic arguments are self-evident. The farmers' organizations and the unions urged immediate independence and short transitional periods, minimal import and immigration quotas and an early abolition of free trade; meanwhile the Manila Americans and export associations pointed to their investments in the Philippines, and demanded, clearly in an attempt to delay independence *ad calendas Graecas*, interm periods of twenty to thirty years.[30] It is characteristic of the American attitude that hardly anyone in Congress openly dared to oppose the grant of independence, unlike in Europe where the very word "independence" was still taboo!

Naturally, and this too is typically American, the groups interested in independence and the anti-colonial Democrats both used moral arguments, appealed to the anti-colonial tradition of America and urged honouring earlier promises. Senator King declared in the Senate: "The declaration of Independence is the basis of our political institutions, and it is the lodestar by which our political policies must be concerned."[31] His colleague, Broussard, added: "There is no place in this Republic for a dependent colony. We repudiated the colonial idea when we separated from the British Empire. . . . We have no legal or moral right to hold the Filipinos as dependent people. Not being an integral part of the Nation and our country not an Empire with dependent colonies."[32] If the supporters considered that the conditions for independence had been fulfilled, the opposition, mainly drawn from the Republican camp, continued to describe it as premature. The Philippines still had too little administrative practice and too many illiterates, they said. Only a minority wanted dissociation. These arguments were not essentially different from the European ones.

It is also important to note the "get rid of the Philippines" mood, whose motives seem to have been less pro-Filipino than isolationist. Why should America worry about the Filipinos if they wanted independence? America had enough problems of its own and the Philippines cost more than they contributed.[33] Opponents of the Independence Act pointed to American interests in the Pacific. The independence of the Philippines, they said, would produce a power vacuum that might tempt Japan to attack; the American general staff had an interest in maintaining the military bases. The opposition also discussed neutralizing the islands by means of a unilateral protection agreement, but then rejected this.[34] The other side proved stronger. They said the Philippines were a burden to American security because they could involve America in a Pacific war against Japan. They recalled that Theodore Roosevelt had described the Philippines as the Achilles' heel of America, so "the sooner we clear out of the Philippines the better"[35] The isolationists trusted in the Japanese desire for peace or simply left the defence of the archipelago to other, allegedly more interested, colonial powers.[36]

Stimson, an opponent of the Independence Act, must be mentioned here. He sharply attacked the "selfish interests which want to get rid of the Philippines" and saw the Islands as an important strategic and political outpost which must not be laid open to Japanese attack.[37] He thought he had found a solution with "dominion status", which would grant the Philippines full autonomy and American tariff concessions, while it reserved foreign policy and defence to the United States. Quezon even seems to have given his verbal assent to this.[38] But the idea found little support in America since it complied neither with American economic interests nor with the attitude of the isolationists and would therefore have destroyed the "unnatural coalition".[39] The same applied to Senator Vandenberg's proposal to grant independence at once with a ten-year transitional period for economic adjustment.[40]

A further aspect of the discussion is of interest. In the Senate committee Nicholas Roosevelt prophesied that Philippine independence would have retroactive effects on the European colonial territories. It would stimulate the emancipation movements and could provoke unrest, for instance in the Dutch Indies.[41] This argument against independence was resolutely dismissed however, and the report of the committee stated:

> To give weight to such a theory would be to recognize an unsound philosophy or policy repugnant to the very best traditions of our Nation. . . . The finest pages of our history are those recording the conflicts that have followed our own departure from colonial dependency. . . .[42]

On the contrary, America should not give up its solidarity with the colonial peoples and should not deny its own traditions—particularly for the sake of American prestige in Asia: "There are in Asia 600 million peoples who believe in the altruism and fairness of America. . . . They are watching with confidence but with earnestness America's promise to help the Philippine people."[43] Harrison had already defended his and Wilson's policy with the argument that America must have "clean hands" at the moment when Asia became involved in anti-colonial and anti-European agitation.[44] During the Second World War, the United States under Franklin Delano Roosevelt tried to use this anti-colonialism in its own interests and resolutely dissociated itself from the European colonial powers. Between 1930 and 1932 even the opponents of the Independence Act adopted this argument. They said that America must remain in the Philippines and bring its work to an end there because of its responsibilities of democratization and liberation in Asia.[45]

During the phase of imperialist expansion in Europe the United States also began to expand and to become a colonial power. But the national consciousness did not identify itself with the concept of a colonial empire and America's "bad conscience" here led it to create the fiction of transitory rule; decolonization, to judge by the pronouncements at least, was conceived as an element of the American concept from the very start. We have seen how the establishment of representative institutions, the "Filipinization" of the administration and the educational system were promoted to a far greater extent than in Indonesia or Indochina. The American Philippine policy was not paternalistic—indeed it granted the semi-feudal upper class extensive participation and thus created new problems,[46] quite apart from the problem of economic dependence. The Americans tried to present the Independence Act of 1934 as evidence of their anti-colonialism and to surround themselves with the aura of liberator. "I trust they [the Filipinos] will see in it the fulfilment of a magnanimous policy untainted by selfishness", wrote Senator Hawes![47] In fact decolonization succeeded only under pressure from economic interest groups who took scant interest in the future of the liberated Philippine people. Although traditional American anti-colonialism played a not inconsiderable role, it must not be forgotten that the decolonization of 1934 had a rather "colonialist character". We may say with Malcolm that "paradoxically it was America that declared its independence from the Philippines and not the Philippines that had obtained their independence".[48]

The 1934 act gave the Philippines independence, but only after a transitional period of ten years. The constitution[49] was worked out by a constituent assembly and approved by the Philippine electors in a referendum. Foreign policy and defence remained controlled by the U.S., the Philippines continued to be under the American flag and the officials still swore allegiance to the American president. The United States could intervene and had a veto right in parliament, and the American Congress retained its legislative powers in questions of trade and tariffs. The transitional régime was called a "Commonwealth" in memory of the self-government of the British dominions,[50] but the restricted Philippine autonomy is not really comparable. Yet the constitution provided to surprisingly smooth collaboration between the colonial power and the nationalists; no doubt this was in large measure due to the fact that the date for independence had been set.

The Independence Act also provided for a transitional period in tariff policy. For the time being trade was to remain free, although with fixed quotas for Philippine products, and later there was to be a gradual increase in the export duty until all tariff preferences were abolished in 1946. In the interests of American exporters, imports into the Philippines remained free, however, even in the second half of the transitional period! Here Great Britain went further, for in 1921 it had already granted a certain tariff sovereignty, which was a heavy blow to the British textile industry. The American secretary of agriculture Wallace also fixed sugar quotas in June 1934 which were far below the Philippine level of production, resulting in serious market difficulties. The same applied to cocoanut exports. The *New York Herald Tribune* criticized this as follows:

> The iniquity of this act lies not only in its injustice, but in its cynicism. The ink was scarcely dry on the signature of the new independence bill, which specially safeguards the Filipinos against the arbitrary closing of the American markets for Philippine products, when the Senate passes this measure which violates the basic principle underlying the independence

bill.... With one hand Congress offered independence in a form not desired by the Filipinos and with the other it destines them to ruin.[51]

Since only 6 percent of the sugar quota could be imported in its refined state, opportunities for industrialization were limited. The Americans were critical of the Philippine Government's attempts to allot public funds for industrialization, partly becuse they wanted to introduce the principle of "free enterprise" into the developing country, partly in the interests of their own export economy. Tariff protection also seemed impracticable.[52] These measures, which showed little evidence of goodwill, largely prevented the Philippine economy from being able to adapt on time and therefore crudely contradicted the purpose of the transitional period! Accordingly, the question soon arose of whether the 1946 deadline could be kept, and pro-Philippine writers proposed a prolongation of the period of economic adaptation.[53] In 1938 a Philippine-American commission envisaged postponing it to 1960, thus reopening the possibility rejected in 1930-1932 of a combination of independence and retention of preferences.[54] On the other hand the Philippines' dependence on the American market also provided America with an argument for going back on the promise of independence. In a broadcast on 14 May 1939 High Commissioner McNutt demanded a "realistic re-examination" of the entire complex; foreign policy, tariffs, immigration, currency, etc. should remain under American control, while the Philippines should obtain preferences—though the quota system should be maintained and American producers given consideration![55]

The curious discrepancy between the ideology of freedom, political far-sightedness and the network of economic interests re-emerged during the final phase of decolonization. On 4 July 1946 President Truman proclaimed the independence of the Philippines, thereby keeping the promise of 1934 which had on several occasions been confirmed during the war. Yet the liberated colony obtained the vitally necessary credits for reconstruction (400 million dollars) only under fairly damaging conditions. The Trade Act of 1946 (Bell Bill) extended the end of the period of adaptation from 1946 to 1974 and limited the quotas of Philippine exports to the U.S., while imports from America remained tariff and quota free (until 1954). The result was excessive imports in luxury consumer goods, a loss of state revenue and a delay in industrialization. Even worse, the pre-war exporters, predominantly Americans, were privileged and moreover the Americans were legally equated with Philippine citizens, making it easier for them to mine raw materials. The privilege had actually required an amendment to the Philippine constitution![56] Although representatives of the administration and Secretary of State Byrnes made it clear that the United States itself was responsible for Philippine dependence on the American market and that America was interested in a healthy development of the Islands, Congress insisted on its conditions.[57] Naturally this trade agreement met decisive opposition in the Philippines and was interpreted as neo-imperialism, i.e. as an attempt to counter political independence with economic ties. A large part of the goodwill which the 1946 proclamation had won for the Americans was lost again. It was the same in the military field. America did not agree to the Philippines' request for military aid against the Communist-controlled Huks until the Philippines placed military bases at the disposal of the U.S. in March 1947 under conditions which could not but irritate national sensibilities.[58]

Not until after 1955 were economic relations and military agreements settled on a more or less bilateral basis. The United States now had to conciliate the anti-Communist governments and reduce all traces of former colonial status because of the Bandung conference and the Chinese challenge. At the risk of exaggeration it could be said that America did not bring decolonization to an end until 1955, several years after the British, Dutch, and French withdrawal from the vast area of South-East Asia!

THE UNSUCCESSFUL COMMONWEALTH: THE NETHERLANDS IN INDONESIA

The Dutch position in South-East Asia is comparable to Belgium's position in Africa: a small Western European state without international aspirations controlled a large colonial territory of great economic potential and concentrated its efforts on systematic exploitation. The economic benefits of this policy are undeniable, and administrative control was more intensive than in the British or the French Empire. The Dutch administration in Indonesia and the Belgian in the Congo were admired by English and French specialists and certain aspects of the native policy also seemed worth emulating, especially social policy in the Katanga mines and Dutch attempts to prevent the disintegration of the Indonesian village structure and to make technical advice and cash credits available to the native farmers. Both the Dutch Indies and the Belgian Congo seemed to be spared emancipation movements; until the outbreak of the Second World War the Netherlands could feel absolutely secure in Indonesia, like Belgium in the Congo until the 1950s. In both these colonial empires decolonization was unsuccessful, however, because economic exploitation and social paternalism completely overshadowed political questions and the colonial powers neither envisaged nor prepared for gradual dissociation. Finally there is a parallel in the fact that the Dutch and Belgian colonial administrations, which were long considered exemplary, are now judged very negatively.

The size discrepancy between the tiny Netherlands and the Indonesian archipelago, whose population had reached seventy million in 1940, explains why special forms of indirect rule were provided for in the Dutch administration and formed a part of the colonial concept from the start. It was only natural to try to economize on administrative staff and to utilize existing institutions and authorities. In the eighteenth century the East India Company had signed protectorate agreements with Indonesian princes and forced them to supply certain products. In the nineteenth, Van den Bosch's infamous "culture system" employed local regents and the village aristocracy as organs of repression. In the "ethical policy" after 1900, by contrast, the village structure was to be maintained and encouraged, while on the other hand the former loose control over island life was to be tightened. Like Great Britain with its protectorate in Malaya, the Netherlands operated on a "short contract" in the Outer Provinces.

Article 118 of the basic law of the Dutch Indies stated that "in so far as the circumstances admit it, the native population will be left under the immediate leadership of its own heads, appointed or recognized by the Government".[1] This principle brought the Dutch system close to the British one. Indirect rule was practised on two levels. On the "government level", Indonesia was divided into government land and native states; of these four were in Java, the other 265 in the Outer Provinces. They were mostly smaller territories of several tens of thousands of inhabitants. Unlike the protected states in British Malaya, which remained legally independent, the Indonesian native states were part of the Dutch territory. Formally the administration was conducted by native authorities, but in fact the Dutch officials "ruled".[2] The very closely settled government land of Java (93 percent of the island) was divided into districts whose seventy-six appointed regents were mostly drawn from the local aristocracy and formed "a hereditary colonial officialdom".[3] Beside the regent stood the Dutch resident, in analogy to the British district officer. However, the colonial expert Furnivall has made clear a distinct difference: the British colonial officer was primarily a magistrate who supervised the application of the law and collected taxes but avoided intervening directly as far as possible, whereas the Dutch resident administered directly, wanted to act "positively" and treated the natives in a paternalistic fashion.[4]

Control was relaxed in the 1920s and indirect rule was democratized by means of regents' councils, in which the regent acted as chairman. This reduced his prestige without giving the Europeans access to his office. In any case it no longer proved possible to cope with the challenges of a modern administration and a crisis began to emerge in indirect rule, with tensions increasing between the traditional upper classes and the young Western-trained élite, as had happened in West Africa. The lower level of indirect rule concerned the village, which was to be cared for by a welfare policy. Hygiene measures, road building, improvement of agriculture, establishment of elementary schools, etc., was to take place within the traditional village structure and with its aid, by using the village leader's powers of compulsion to carry through reforms. Under Dutch paternalism, "light compulsion" seemed legitimate and forced labour survived within the villages. We referred above to Furnivall, a British official in Burma, who compared British and Dutch methods. Britain in Burma, particularly in Lower Burma, he said, confined itself to maintaining law and order and made allowances for the rather unique money market and production, which had led to a disastrous disintegration of the native social structure. On the other hand, Dutch paternalism with its dubiously legal "light compulsion" had made social adaptation easier and had done positive work for the Indonesian farmers.[5] By contrast, Emerson in 1937 was more critical of the system. He thought the authority of the local leader was questionable and corruption frequent.[6] An official report in 1941 described the village head as "almost exclusively an instrument of the government".[7] In fact it was true that within the colonial system the traditional leaders took on an authoritarian character and lost their credibility with the population and could therefore hardly serve as instruments of "democratization".

The economic situation was equally ambivalent. The acquisition of landed property was forbidden to non-Indonesians, and to a certain extent this managed to limit the advance of the Europeans and the Chinese. Farm production was increased by the "light compulsion",[8] but the European plantations, which had sufficient capital and technical power, produced the lion's share (the plantation was usually on leased government land or property leased from Indonesians) and utilized the system of compulsion in the villages for their own ends.[9] The Indonesian farmers' indebtedness to Chinese financiers and the degradation of becoming a tenant on one's own property was inevitable, largely because the population was increasing by leaps and bounds—from 37.7 million in 1905 to 60.7 million in 1930! The standard of living did not, therefore, rise, even in the period of prosperity before 1930[10] and the world-wide depression had catastrophic effects. Indonesia's dependence on the world market, and the dominating position which the Europeans and Chinese occupied in economic life, aroused a sense of frustration among the Indonesian intelligentsia who began to feel that anti-capitalism was their only protection against this "alienation".

Indirect rule and paternalistic measures were combined with elements of force in cultural policy too. The Dutch made little attempt at cultural assimilation, for they believed in the different character and independence of Indonesian culture and civilization. Native law, *adat*, was submitted to intensive research, codified, taught to trainee colonial officials in Leiden and applied in Indonesia. There was a great deal of religious tolerance and the missions were not very active; Islam enjoyed freedom of movement and the Dutch attitude to it was favorable; however, the attempt to separate religion from politics failed.[11] The Dutch language was not used as an instrument of cultural influence, a restraint which characteristically seemed incomprehensible to a French observer.[12] The language, apart from the vernaculars and Dutch, was a "Bazaar Malayan", which made communication easier but had no cultural function. Whether this served the Dutch colonials as a means of dissociating themselves from the Indonesians and thus made it more difficult for the latter to rise in the social scale is an open question.

The Dutch did not try to Westernize the natives and attempted to keep the number of Western-trained élite, who would be the future nationalists, as small as possible. It paid no great attention to education, and in 1940 the number of illiterates was still said to be 93.6 percent. There was a technical college (1919), a college of law (1924) and a medical college (1926), yet the number of Indonesian students remained relatively low.[13] Since the secondary schools and colleges demanded high fees, access was granted primarily to Europeans and Chinese. Professional opportunities for Western-trained Indonesians were also bad, for natives were admitted only to the lower ranks of the administration in the plantations, trade and industry, while public administration remained reserved to the local dignitaries or to the Dutch. Moreover the anti-nationalist Eurasians enjoyed an extensive monopoly in the army and the police. In October 1940 only 221 of the 3039 senior officials were Indonesians.[14] This produced the frustrating situation that while the number of Western-trained Indonesians was small, most of them still could not find suitable positions. This frustration also contributed to the rise of nationalism.[15]

The development of representative bodies began during the First World War. The impulse, as in the local councils in the 1903 decentralization law, came from the Dutch colonists who demanded a certain administrative autonomy and greater freedom from the mother country. In 1918 a peoples' council (*volksraad*) with consultative powers was formed; of the thirty-nine members, fifteen were Indonesians, some elected, some appointed. The new Dutch constitution of 1922 deleted the words "colonies and possessions in other parts of the world" and declared that the Dutch Indies were an integral part of the kingdom—a step which Great Britain never took and which is more reminiscent of France. So the Indonesians were Dutch citizens with franchise in their domicile. Just as the Dutch colonials were represented in the peoples' council, so an Indonesian Communist was a member of the Dutch parliament between 1933 and 1940.[16] The new basic law for Indonesia in 1925 established the autonomy of the colony, restricted the reserved rights of the Crown, and transferred budget and legislative powers to the peoples' council. It is characteristic of the colony, restricted the reserved rights of the Crown, and transferred behind the proposals made by a commission of experts on Indonesia and that the second chamber managed to exert a delaying influence.[17]

The new *volksraad* of 1927 had sixty members, thirty-eight elected and twenty-two appointed. Of the elected members twenty were Indonesians. The local councils served as electoral colleges, which in turn largely consisted of officials.[18] But unlike Britain, the Netherlands left its officials a great deal of freedom of political opinion and even tolerated open criticism of the government. But the government, naturally, had means of influence and "guidance". The local councils also represented rural Indonesia, while the town councils, particularly the one in Batavia, effectively privileged the Dutch and "governed" on the Dutch pattern.[19] The small but important urban middle class and the European-trained intelligentsia were therefore under-represented and could not assert themselves effectively in the council. The government was aware of this discrepancy and occasionally appointed nationalist leaders members of the *volksraad*.

The powers of the *volksraad*, apart from the governor's veto and the fact that the chairman of the council was appointed by the government, were legislative. The executive, however, remained Dutch and directly responsible to The Hague. Only one field, education, was directed by Indonesians. We find the well-known problem of representative government recurring: although the council could criticize openly, it could not assume government responsibility, while at the same time the national opposition found in it a forum for propaganda. One could compare the *volksraad* with the French colonies' financial delegations, in so far as the Dutch colonials obtained control of the budget and a voice in economic policy. The common roll was even abolished in favour of radically segregated electoral bodies. At the moment when a European-trained middle class which fulfilled the census qualifications was emerging, the colonial power introduced separate representation, which the Indonesians naturally saw as discrimination in the interests of the rulers; this gave impetus to an anti-Dutch campaign.

What were the Netherlands' views of the future? How did the Dutch intend to treat the nationalist movement? Was the tendency towards future self-government or towards closer association with the mother country?

Little attention was evidently devoted to these questions in the mother country. The pragmatic Dutch were not interested in problems that did not yet seem acute. What is probably more important is that the Netherlands developed no real imperial concept or ideology and therefore did not feel obliged to consider the possibility of decolonization. Whereas Britain justified its domination by development towards self-government and France prided itself on its civilizing mission and strove for a lasting association between the mother country and the overseas territories, the Netherlands stayed put.

At the beginning of the century the great Islamist Snouk Hurgronje had prophesied a progressive Westernization of Indonesia in the spirit of liberal reformism; on the basis of this he envisaged a close and lasting association between the Netherlands and Indonesia which would come into being by promoting education, including natives in the administration and political autonomy.[20] But after the First World War the belief in association or assimilation weakened. Van Vollenhoven, who trained the administrative élite in Leiden, started out from the assumption that there were clearly two different civilizations. Alhough in 1922 he supported liberal reforms, and Dutch officials intensified the "reintegration of Indonesian life" in the local sphere,[21] this policy had no practical purpose and bore a definite conservative accent, since the much-praised indirect rule was played off against the new nationalism and the bureaucratic machinery was designed to guarantee future Dutch domination.[22]

The question of the future aroused comparably little interest among political writers. Much was said about future autonomy, but little distinction was made between administrative autonomy under Dutch leadership and political autonomy as a first step towards Indonesian self-government.[23] Kat Angelino spoke in his comprehensive work of a "Greater Netherlands Commonwealth", a community of peoples of different civilizations, but without giving more details or discussing institutional issues.[24] Hendrik Colijn, leader of the "anti-revolutionary" (i.e. conservative) party in the mother country and prime minister from 1933 to 1939, was highly critical of the institution of the *volksraad*. He thought that since Indonesia was a unit only in a geographic sense, it must therefore be given a federal structure. Since responsible government or even the inclusion of Indonesians in the executive was inconceivable or at least impracticable, the *volksraad* could be nothing more than a stage for polemic. Colijn proposed setting up two autonomous provinces, Java and Sumatra, which would each be divided into territories. The Indonesians would receive political rights and direct responsibility in the provincial administration; general issues outside provincial responsibilities should remain reserved to Dutch control.[25]

No doubt much could be said in favour of a federal structure in the archipelago, and a wide area of responsibility for the local institutions of self-government would have been very useful. Colijn, however, was not thinking in terms of self-government, starting from the provinces, as the British did in India, but believed that the emancipation movements could be driven out into the provinces and thereby maintain colonial rule in the centre for an indefinite period.[26] To what extent the efforts at administrative decentralization during the 1930s were aimed at this is difficult to assess.

In Indonesia itself the journal *De Stuw* became the mouthpiece of a small group of intellectuals who explicitly dissociated themselves from official policy and demanded an autonomous republic which would have only loose ties with the mother country—presumably on the lines of the British Commonwealth. Such theories, however, seemed too radical in the 1930s and encountered little sympathy. More important was a collective movement of conservative forces, the "Vaderlandische Club" (fatherland club), which was founded in 1929 in reaction to the agitation in 1926–1927. It was a typical colonial European organization, which openly supported repression of the nationalist "agitators" and proclaimed that there were indissoluble ties between Indonesia and Holland. One of the leaders of the club declared in the *volksraad* in 1939 that the "ethical policy" was outdated; Indonesian society could never become economically self-sufficient and required strict Dutch guidance within an imperial economy.[27] Colijn's conservative government also supported these theses, so that Governor-General de Jonge (1931–1936), a former director of the Royal Dutch, could declare: "We have ruled here for three hundred years with the whip and the club, and we shall still be doing it in another three hundred years."[28] Anyone who wanted "independence" could be accused of treason.[29] In the *volksraad* in 1936 very moderate Indonesians passed a motion calling for a conference which would discuss a kind of ten-year plan for self-government—within the Dutch constitution. This would have made it possible to obtain some collaboration from the nationalists, but the Dutch Government was not prepared before World War II to consider self-government and sternly rejected the proposal in 1938; it would be better, it said, to promote administrative decentralization than to introduce a fundamental reform of the political structure.[30]

We should recall here that Ceylon had had semi-responsible government since 1931 and Burma since 1935–1937, each with its own government responsible to an elected legislative council. In 1934 the Philippines obtained a deadline for independence. But the Netherlands would not contemplate dissociation. Indonesia "belonged" to the mother country, was a part of the national territory and a source of Dutch wealth. The Dutch colonial concept stood between that of England and that of France, with the exception that there was no provision made for future decolonization. Vague references were made to an association between two autonomous areas under the Dutch Crown, but in effect the Dutch simply defended the *status quo* and tried to evade the question of the future. The paternalistic policy had some positive achievements to boast, but the nationalists naturally saw it as a form of ruthless colonialism which offered no hope of reform and therefore provoked radical attitudes.

Even after the outbreak of the Second World War and the Japanese invasion the government did not feel impelled to adopt a more flexible attitude. A new Indonesian proposal in the *volksraad* (the Wihowo resolution of February 1940) asked for an imperial conference to prepare for a responsible parliamentary system; it was rejected, after the invasion, on the grounds that the responsibility for such a conference lay with the Dutch parliament which, however, could not take action at the moment.[31] Even the modest proposal of replacing the official description "Inlander" by "Indonesian" and "Dutch Indies" by "Indonesia" was rejected. It is understandable that the Indonesians reacted sharply to this tactical error![32] A commission was set up in September 1940 under the chairmanship of Visman but it only submitted its report in December 1941. It said Indonesians and Europeans should have full equal rights but the archipelago should obtain autonomy, with an imperial council as superordinate body.[33] But these proposals were too vague and came too late to have any effect. Many Indonesians welcomed the Japanese as liberators and a large part of the nationalist opposition proved willing to collaborate with the occupying forces.

At first the Dutch government-in-exile in London continued to pursue its former policy. After the war, it said, a conference with representatives from the mother country, Indonesia and Surinam would meet to discuss the future—no decision could be made until then. In October 1942 in an article in *Foreign Affairs* the foreign minister, Van Kleffens, sharply attacked American anti-colonialism and the Americans' phrases about democracy, independence and self-determination, "as if these were constant values for all times and for all circumstances . . . we still are blind to what the world really needs".[34] In South-East Asia the requirements for independence were non-existent, and in any case the *volksraad* had legislative power "for practically all Indian affairs". Dutch colonial policy adhered to the Atlantic Charter, asserted the foreign minister, although he also stressed that the Indonesian archipelago would remain "part of the Kingdom of the Netherlands" and that only the constitution of Indonesia and its position within the Dutch kingdom were open to discussion.

Shortly afterwards, on 6 December, the Dutch government in-exile found itself obliged, probably under American pressure, to take a stand on post-war policy. A declaration by Queen Wilhelmina stated:

> I am convinced, and history as well as reports from the occupied territories confirm me in this, that after the war it will be possible to reconstruct the Kingdom on the solid foundation of complete partnership, which will mean the consummation of all that has been developed in the past. I know that no political unity nor national cohesion can continue to exist which is not supported by the voluntary acceptance and the faith of the great majority of the citizens. I know that the Netherlands more than ever feels its responsibility for the vigorous growth of the Overseas Territories and the Indonesians recognize in the ever increasing collaboration the best guarantee for the recovery of their peace and happiness. The war years have proved that both peoples possess the will and the ability for harmonious and voluntary co-operation. . . . I visualize, without anticipating the recommendations of the future conference, that

they will be directed towards a Commonwealth in which the Netherlands, Indonesia, Surinam and Curaçao will participate, with complete self-reliance and freedom of conduct for each part regarding its internal affairs, but with the readiness to render mutual assistance. . . .

It is my opinion that such a combination of independence and collaboration can give the Kingdom and its parts the strength to carry fully their responsibility, both internally and externally. This would leave no room for discrimination according to race or nationality; only the ability of the individual citizens and the needs of the various groups of the population will determine the policy of the government.[35]

This declaration, which followed on the heels of a number of proposals between the wars and then became the basis of the Indonesia policy after 1945, stated the Dutch concept of decolonization. It shows how the terminology had changed during the war. Anti-imperialist statements now seemed necessary and the declaration spoke of partnership; the term "Commonwealth" was used to express the association of independence and collaboration. It did not imply the British system, however, but a form of federation in which the individual parts of the Empire would have internal autonomy while foreign policy, defence, and also tariff and currency questions were decided by superordinate imperial bodies. The Dutch concept is actually more comparable to the French Union with its associated states. The December 1942 declaration did not describe the federal structure in detail but left this to later conferences, raising the question of whether the Dutch were really prepared to transfer external sovereignty to federal bodies. What kind of autonomy was Indonesia to have? Did the Dutch intend to accept an Indonesian Government, or did they believe they would be able to guarantee their influence by means of a veto right and special powers for the governor?

It would be wrong to judge the queen's declaration and similar pronouncements[36] only by their lack of success in implementation. In contrast to the rigidly conservative pre-war attitude, they at least proclaimed the principle and guide-lines of a generous reform policy which complied with the demands of the moderate nationalists and seemed to promise better relations. And we must not forget that Van Mook, who had a part in formulating the declaration of 6 December and played a very important role in the following years, was a member of the Stuw movement and a proponent of a liberal policy.[37] Under "normal" circumstances and if Indonesia had remained under Dutch rule during the war, there would surely have been some chance of gradually pursuing emancipation and improving relations with the former colonial power by negotiation.

The Japanese occupation created an entirely new situation whose effects were either not recognized or not taken sufficiently into account by the Dutch government-in-exile.[38] As in Indochina, Japan not only removed the colonial administration and dealt a severe blow to the

European power, but also disseminated systematic anti-Dutch propaganda and managed to enlist the Indonesian nationalists in its own purposes. The Japanese released nationalist leaders from prison, formed a representative council under Sukarno, set up an Indonesian army and created youth associations. In October 1944, Japan promised independence and set up a constitutional commission which prepared the Republic of Indonesia, which was proclaimed on 17 August 1945, a few days before the Japanese capitulation, by Sukarno and Hatta. A constitution was approved on short notice and a cabinet set up. Japanese weapons were used to arm at least rudimentary forces. Much like the French in Indochina, the Dutch now found themselves, at the moment when they wanted to resume their pre-war position, faced with the *fait accompli* of a proclaimed republic controlled by the young and radical generation of nationalists who had refused to collaborate with the colonial power before the war and had spent several years in exile.

Van Mook had counted on a strong national movement but not on finding an already established republic. Like the French Government, the Dutch now asked itself whether it should recognize this republic and in what form. The returning colonial power had few troops at its disposal and was dependent on Allied help. But Lord Mountbatten, the high commander on this front, was, as Dutch historians all too willingly overlook, the representative of a distinctly liberal policy and he showed much goodwill to the nationalists in Burma. So it is understandable that he would not install strong military forces in Indonesia or engage in open battle with the Republic. The English even recognized the Republic *de facto* and called on the Dutch to begin negotiations. But the Dutch saw the Republic as a régime set up by Japan, and wanted to arrest the members of the government as collaborators and traitors rather than consider them legitimate partners. In November 1945 Van Mook made a declaration to this effect: the Netherlands recognized Indonesian aspirations to nationhood and was prepared for friendly co-operation within the "Commonwealth"; Indonesians would obtain a considerable majority in the *volksraad* and could form a ministerial council under the governor-general.[39] This declaration reaffirmed that of 6 December and indicated a decisive step forward by comparison with pre-war times; but by 1945 it was overtaken by events. For there was no talk of accepting a Republic of Indonesia, and the Dutch officially ignored its existence. Van Mook, who represented the mother country in Indonesia, was still under pressure from his own conservative government.[40]

We have no space here to outline the subsequent laborious negotiations, the numerous proposals and counterproposals, the ineffectual arguments, the intervention of the United Nations and two Dutch "police actions". We shall confine ourselves to a few comments on Dutch policy.

The Netherlands had to start negotiating with the Republic and accept Indonesia's right to decide its destiny, i.e. to agree to the planned association with the mother country or to choose independence. The Dutch claimed that for the time being they still held the only sovereign power in the archipelago while the Republic pointed out that it existed *de facto* and demanded bilateral negotiations. Only after France, on 6 March 1946, had accepted Ho Chi Minh's republic as part of the federation of Indochina did the Dutch accept the Indonesian Republic. Indonesia for its part agreed to this and, for the time being at least, gave up its claim to represent the entire archipelago as a sovereign republic.

At the conference of Manilo in Celebes, the Dutch tried to gain control of the Outer Provinces that were not in the Republic and to install autonomous governments which were to have equal rights within the federation. For this manoeuvre the Dutch exploited the traditional distrust of Java and the local sense of patriotism in order to exaggerate the opposition to the Republic and to deny its claim to leadership. In this way they hoped to assume a decisive role in the federation of Indonesia and the proposed Union. This is a striking parallel to the situation in Indochina and the attempts of the French Government to neutralize the republic of Ho Chi Minh! But the agreement of Linggadjali (27 March 1947) forced the Dutch to recognize the *de facto* authority of the Republic over Java and Sumatra, who for their part declared themselves willing to enter into a federation with two other republics, which would then associate itself with the mother country. However, the Dutch did not manage to create a basis of trust and each of the two "partners" tried to build up positions of power in the territory of the other. The Dutch began an economic blockade and after the Catholic party came to power it embarked on its first "police action", which started on 21 July 1947 and ended with the armistice on 17 January 1948. On 9 March 1948 an interim federal government was unilaterally announced, consisting of the governor-general and a majority of Dutch department heads; the Republic had to accept the conditions laid down by the colonial power before the real government of the "United States of Indonesia" was formed. In addition the Dutch wanted to incorporate the Republic with the other autonomous territories on a parity basis only and wanted, as far as possible, to totally "liquidate" it in the transitional period.

The Republic saw through this manoeuvre and stressed that the complete preponderance this would give Java utterly excluded parity representation; it dismissed the other territories as products of Dutch "neo-colonialism". A short-term ultimatum was finally followed, on 19 December 1948, by the second Dutch "police action". But although the police occupied the most important towns of Java and Sumatra it did not manage to put an end to the guerrilla warfare. At this point the United Nations intervened and the United States, which had hitherto tried to mediate, openly attacked Dutch actions. On 1 August 1949 a cease-fire was agreed and on 2 November, afer a round-table conference, an agreement was signed in The Hague by which the Netherlands pledged itself to transfer its entire Indonesian Empire, with the exception of West New Guinea, to the United States of Indonesia, which was to consist of the Republic together with fifteen other autonomous states and would be a partner in a Dutch-Indonesia Union. The "partners" were independent sovereign states, although they recognized the Dutch queen as head of the union. So, instead of the federation proclaimed on 6 December 1942 a kind of Commonwealth had now come into being. But this non-British Commonwealth did not prove viable and was terminated by Indonesia in 1954. After the withdrawal of the Dutch, the Republic had, as expected, very quickly managed to assert its claim to leadership.

Great Britain had promised autonomy to India, Burma and Ceylon during the war and full self-government after the war. This was the decisive reason why a surprisingly smooth decolonization had been possible after 1945 in spite of severe tensions and numerous clashes. The Labour government had curtailed the transitional periods and by changing course on time had created a basis of trust which made possible an orderly transfer of power and made it seem advantageous to the former colonies to remain within the Commonwealth. Even in Burma in the early post-colonial era there was a considerable amount of collaboration with the mother country. France and the Netherlands, by contrast, also forced during the Second World War to formulate a decolonization programme, did not feel obliged to acknowledge demands for independence and contented themselves with very vague promises of autonomy within a federated whole, in which their own political and economic influence would remain secure. In a sense France and the Netherlands had the misfortune of having their colonial empires occupied by Japan, for this destroyed the preconditions for the realization of their programmes. The claim to independence and power of the revolutionary, nationalist republics, which the two colonial powers found on their return, could not be reconciled with a federal system which conceded some autonomy but no external sovereignty. It was relatively easy for Britain to give in to Burma, although it did so hesitantly by force of circumstances, because it had long since accepted the principle of independence and only the ways and means of transferring power now came under discussion; but it was more natural for France and the Netherlands to manoeuvre in an attempt to neutralize the forces that were insisting on independence. To negotiate with the revolutionary nationalists seemed to the Dutch to compromise their purpose from the start and to imply the renunciation of the former colony. In retrospect it has become clear that a gradual transfer of power that complied with the interests of the colonial power would have been possible only if a timely agreement had been reached. Like Mountbatten in Burma and Leclerc in Tonkin,

Van Mook and the Socialist overseas minister Logemann seem to have come to this conclusion after their initial reluctance:

> There is only one realistic approach from our side, alongside of which all else is pure fantasy; and that is that if we wish to solve this problem in a way which will stand the criticism of world history, then we must, with all the earnestness and sincerity that is in us . . . aim at co-operation with the nationalistic group of Sjahrir and therewith to reach agreement. There is no other way.[41]

But neither Leclerc nor Van Mook and Logemann managed to convince their own governments, whereas England had the good fortune to have a Labour government during the critical transitional period. Unlike in India and Burma, it was impossible to create a basis of trust in Indochina and Indonesia. Both sides distrusted each other, tried to outmanoeuvre each other, and finally turned to sabotage, terrorism and military action. The Dutch would no doubt have succeeded in conquering Indonesia by force, but they could hardly hope to really pacify or stabilize it. As in Indochina, the Japanese occupation had destroyed the nimbus of undefeatable colonial power and had roused revolutionary national voices which could not easily be silenced again. France took the Indochinese war upon itself; the Netherlands, by contrast, "capitulated" under pressure from the United Nations. In both cases the transfer of power was unilaterally forced on the colonial power, which thus lost most of its political and economic position.

BELGIAN PATERNALISM IN THE CONGO

The former Belgian Congo is located between British West Africa and British East Africa. While the western part has access to the Atlantic via Leopoldville and has an economic structure similar to the former French Congo, Katanga, a mining area chiefly producing copper, gold, diamonds and uranium, directly borders on Northern Rhodesia in the east. This intermediate position had a strong effect on Belgian colonial policy, which can be said to have stood "between" France and Great Britain. The "originality" of Belgian colonial policy, as of Dutch, resided primarily in the fact that it was guided neither by the concept of integration nor by the gradual grant of self-government; Belgium hoped that a policy of paternalism would enable it to avoid decolonization and that the empiricism upon which it prided itself would prevent it from having to enter into any "irrelevant" discussion on methods or ultimate aims.

It is well-known how Belgium became a colonial power more or less against its wishes. A self-willed king took part as a "private person" in the partition of Africa, acquired a colony and acted as ruler over "his" Congo Free State. It was only in 1908, when the ruthless exploitation provoked a wave of international protest which compromised Belgium, that it was forced to take over the royal heritage. Soon, however, Belgium came to terms with its position as an important colonial power. It was proud of is kingdom and actively embarked on the economic development of the Congo with its wealth of raw materials. Belgium, which had no overseas commercial tradition like the Netherlands and France, also had no concept of Empire or sense of mission. Instead, it was an industrial nation interested in economic development and responsive to social issues. The pragmatic and in some respects dubious combination of a capitalist industrial society and a Catholic mission in the most "primitive" and culturally backward area of Africa stamped the character of Belgium's Congo policy.

A few comments will suffice to outline economic and social policy.[1] Like France, during the First and again in the Second World War, Belgium became aware of the importance of its colony—not, it is true, as a potential area of recruitment for soldiers and labour, but as a source of wealth and a supplier of foreign exchange.[2] The colonial minister Louis Franck (1919–1924) hastened the economic development and placed major emphasis on the mining provinces of Katanga and Kasai. There, owing to the heritage of the Free State, the mining concerns' great need of capital and the development of communications, a few large concerns (Société générale, Union Minière, Brufina, Forminière, etc.) controlled the economy. The Belgian state was directly involved in these societies, and was interested in obtaining high rates of profit, since between 40 and 50 percent of the state revenues consisted of taxes from these concerns.[3] Naturally these large corporations in Belgium as in Leopoldville, took part in formulating colonial policy, but the extent of their influence will have to be assessed by future historians. The Second World War presented a great opportunity for development by giving added impetus to mining, which, thanks to the great American need for raw materials, continued after the war. Belgium began at an early date to establish and to encourage local industries and in 1949–1950 it began a ten-year plan with the aim of improving communications and supplying energy, but which also made resources available for building towns, for native settlements and for education.

The Congo distributed several large concessions for plantations. Leverhulme, later Unilever, had already addressed requests to this effect to the colonial administration of British West Africa but had been refused because London was resolved to concentrate on the African producers and considered plantations incompatible with indirect rule. But Belgium had no such reluctance.[4] In fact, however, its settlers policy was very modest. In 1955 colonists represented only 10 percent of the approximately 190,000 Europeans, and they were concentrated in the provinces of Kivu and Katanga. After the Second World War the administration was more careful about giving land to settlers in order to avoid a clash with the Africans, as had happened in East Africa, and to prevent the establishment of settlers' reservations and political claims.[5] The natives supplied cotton for export, but concentrated on food for local consumption.

The coal, iron and steel industries, the construction and communications and the plantations needed a high quota of labour. In Katanga alone in 1924, eighty thousand workers were engaged in production. But the Congo was thinly settled and since, moreover, production was still concentrated in only a few regions, the local labour supply was inadequate. So the need for labour became a focal point of the discussion in the 1920s.[6] Africans were hired in remote districts by recruitment agencies with the "help" of the administration, often by very dubious methods. This had the usual social effects: while the villages emptied and social life disintegrated, the workers who were torn out of their tribal order and unprepared for industrial life settled in the mining areas. The administration attempted to intervene: only a set percentage of natives should migrate and recruitment was to be allowed only under certain circumstances; the distribution of new concessions was to be made dependent on the availability of labour. The Union Minière tried to counteract fluctuations in the labour force by building settlements and instituting social welfare, and much was achieved by this society during the Second World War—as is acknowledged by even the most critical observers.[7] The contrast with the miserable conditions in Rhodesia at the time was striking. It is clear that the rapid expansion and high profits with low wages made this social policy easier to pursue. Its paternalist character is equally evident: while the society built settlements, schools and hospitals, it did not allow any real unions, thus effectively controlling the social and political activity of African labour.

The Congo Government followed the example set by the mining societies. In the 1950s it initiated a respectable programme for building "Cités Africaines", particularly in the outskirts of Leopoldville, and improved medical and social care.[8] It could not, however, keep pace with the rapid increase in population in the towns.[9] Yet there is no doubt that the Belgian administration achieved outstanding results in this field and was in advance of the other colonial powers in several respects.

The Belgians liked, and still like, to stress that unlike in British East Africa, there was no colour bar in the Congo. It is true that no job was reserved to whites, and unlike in Rhodesia the mining societies began early to train qualified labour. The same applied to the administration. Opportunities for advancement were limited, however, on the one hand by the training facilities, and on the other by what was in effect a real colour bar. For it remained unwritten law that all important posts were occupied by Europeans. There was strict social segregation, partly legalized by regulations, in the residential quarters, in transport, in cafés, and of course in social intercourse. The difference between Brazzaville and the Congo would strike any traveller: there, there were "French citizens", while in the Congo there were modern towns and progressive welfare measures but a strict division according to colour.[10] It was not until 1954 that colonial ministers, governors-general and finally King Baudouin began to reject segregation and to call on their fellow-countrymen to "collaborate" with the Africans. Regulations were altered, schools integrated, etc.[11] So the relaxing of discrimination began rather late; it met with resistance from the whites and contrasted with the rapid formation of an African middle class, which assumed an organizational form in 1954 with the administratively promoted "Association des Classes Moyennes Africaines".

Educational policy also went its special way in the Belgian Congo. Like Britain, Belgium left education largely to the missions. By 1946 the Congo had a school attendance rate of 56 percent, in 1958 the percentage was 77.5, as opposed to only 34.8 in the French territories.[12] Yet education remained largely restricted to the lowest grades,[13] for its purpose was to train labour and a lower cadre for the economy and the administration. At the top stood the numerous medical and agrarian assistants, who could not, however, rise to become doctors or agronomists. University education in Europe was prevented as far as possible and the Congo only obtained its two universities in 1954 and 1956. One hundred and ten students were registered in 1957–1958. Here the contrast with British and French policy becomes particularly striking; they tried to train an élite and provided access to university education at an early date. France based its policy on cultural assimilation and England on the idea of self-government, while Belgium concentrated instead on economic development which, for social reasons, required a broad basis of "civilized Africans" before Belgium could grant access to university education. Belgian political writers therefore very frequently attacked the semi-literacy, the "arrogance of the intellectuals" and the danger of disintegration in African society. But the frequent emphasis on the difference between African and European civilization and the backwardness of the Congo was in curious contradiction to the situation in French Equatorial Africa and above all to the fact that the Belgian missions trained African priests at an early date and that Rome appointed an autochthonous bishop: so the Congolese were capable of completing Catholic theological training (some in Rome), but not of becoming doctors, agronomists or engineers.

The political aims of this much-praised Belgian educational policy are self-evident! Africans were needed as an industrial and administrative cadre, but must not jeopardize colonial domination. A Western-trained élite was always the nucleus of nationalist opposition and therefore was a threat. In 1955 Henri Depage, in a treatise published by the colonial academy, took note of the quiet in the Congo, and asked whether Belgium had not simply postponed the "possibility of defeat" and "whether we must not fear a terrible awakening"; but he still limited university education to teaching natural sciences, medicine and agronomy, for

> it is not desirable either to teach Law in a country where the law has not yet taken shape [!] or to immediately give natives a profession—that of lawyer—of which one can say that it sometimes lives only on the retributions of others [!]; and with regard to the applied sciences (engineering), to give natives a profession which must normally place them in a position of command over a considerable number of black workers whom their work condemns to live together in close agglomerations.[14]

So the Congolese should not be trained as lawyers or engineers, although Leopoldville and Elisabethville had now developed into modern towns and an industrial society was taking shape in some regions. The Africans were to be kept out of precisely those two professions which chiefly supplied the upper cadre of the economy, administration and politics! Later, when the Congolese became politically active and claimed a part of the leadership, their demand was rejected on the grounds that such cadres did not yet exist. The fact that Belgium promoted economic development, the educational system and even the training of lower technical cadres more than the other colonial powers while at the same time it arbitrarily limited opportunities for cultural and thereby social advancement in the hope that this would ensure better and more lasting law and order in the Congo than in the neighbouring territories plagued by "agitators"—this was a paradox of which Belgium did not become aware until 1959–1960, i.e. when it granted independence.[15]

The administration itself was also in a sense intermediate between that of France and Britain. The 1908 colonial charter had declared that the Congo was part of the national territory, yet the colony remained subject to special legislation. This was enforced by royal decree and thus lay within the jurisdiction of the colonial ministry. The governor-general could issue an ordinance, but it had to be confirmed by decree within six months. These strong centralist tendencies were also reflected in the fact that the Belgian Parliament was responsible for conferring concessions and offering subscriptions for loans and had to grant its approval of the annual Congolese budget—a regulation unknown in both France and England. In addition, while an annual report was submitted to the parliament, it was hardly discussed.[16] The Belgian parliamentarians showed just as little interest in colonial policy as their British and French colleagues.

Beside the governor-general stood the "Conseil de Gouvernement", which after its reorganization in 1947 included the heads of the administration, sixteen representatives of economic groups (chamber of commerce, settlers, employees, etc.), some appointed notables and eight representatives of African interests. The African representatives were exclusively Congolese from 1951 onwards. This council, which to a certain extent represented the interests of the Europeans, met annually but only for a few days and was purely consultative. The same applied to the six provincial councils. These institutions are comparable to the institutions in French Africa rather than to the legislative assemblies in British Africa. But in the French system the less important colonial assemblies were at least sustained by franchise and parliamentary representation of white and black citizens; in the Congo, by contrast, not even the Belgians had franchise. Evidently the colonial administration did not want to lay itself open to pressure from the settlers and the mining societies and at the same time wanted to avoid being accused of discriminating against the Africans. Until the Second World War the contrast with the situation in the British and French Empires was, perhaps, not so great; but after 1945 when France and England made structural reforms which gave Africans some political responsibility, Belgium contented itself with secondary measures which finally resulted in the failure of decolonization in 1960.

The higher administrative service was closed to the Africans until the 1950s.[17] On 1 January 1960 there were only thirty-three African higher officials in Katanga, of whom seventeen were employed in the department of agriculture and seven in the health service. In Leopoldville three cabinet attachés and a few mayors of suburban communities were African and there were ten African adjutants in the Force publique, but no black officers. Even in comparison with French Equatorial Africa the difference is striking.

After the First World War Belgium adopted the methods of indirect rule in native administration. Until then, the chiefs had perhaps been recognized as supporters of the administration, but Belgium had evolved no systematic native policy. Rebellious tribes were dissolved, while others were split by dividing up the province, or fragmented when Belgium appointed clan leaders as chiefs—quite apart from the decimation due to forced labour, migration, etc. In 1917 the number of tribal units had risen to 6095, resulting in a state of near anarchy.[18] Louis Franck was particularly concerned after the war with appointing the "right" chief, establishing new borders, clarifying juridical power and with levying taxes to pay for village expenses.[19] Units that were too small were amalgamated into a *secteur* with a council of chiefs; each sector was to have its own law court, school and sanitary service. Outside the industrial centres this resulted in a certain amount of stability. But it would be wrong to draw a comparison with Northern Nigeria, for there were only larger and more closely organized tribal states in the mandated territory of Ruanda-Urundi. Many of the same problems emerged in the Congo as in Southern Nigeria and the French territories; many of the units were too small and the chiefs too "primitive" to satisfy the requirements of a modern administration. Attempts to educate the sons of chiefs met resistance from the missions.[20] No attempts were made until 1957 to convert the *chefferie* into a modernized local government which would also take account of the European-trained African, which was ten years later than in the French and British territories. Once again it becomes apparent how late the criticism of traditional policy began; but then the former, allegedly so successful, methods were denounced as a total failure.[21]

In 1931 Belgium made an interesting attempt to set up *centres extra-coutumiers* (extra-customary centres) which were to give a new solidarity to the masses torn from their tribal order. They seem to have functioned rather well, with a council of appointed representatives of the different tribes and an appointed chief; but in the 1950s they were replaced by the Cités africaines. The 1957 "Statut des villes" separated the European and African quarters of the towns; the first elections for the post of African mayor in the Cités africaines were held in December.

After all that, it is hardly surprising to find no evidence of a Belgian doctrine of decolonization until long after the Second World War. Decolonization was scarcely even mentioned in colonial political writings or official pronouncements, and it is tempting here to speak of a deliberate depoliticization of colonial policy. It seemed ridiculous to envisage a possible end to Belgian rule, for Belgium assumed that the immense Congo with its backward African inhabitants would need European administration for decades to come. Belgium thought it was pursuing economic development and fulfilling its civilizing task in an exemplary fashion since it had long since replaced the former policy of exploitation by a paternalistic native policy which accomplished its purpose and justified Belgian rule. In the name of indirect rule Louis Franck, a representative spokesman of the early 1920s, rejected assimilation: he said the question was one of the protection and development of existing institutions and the training of "better Africans", not of the dubious transplanting of elements of European civilization.[22] As in the British Empire, the vernacular was used in the lower grades in the schools, and the overall educational system was not based on the idea of an assimilated African élite; the Congo was a part of the national territory, but it had no institution of naturalization and the colour bar maintained racial segregation. On the other hand, there was no question of its being a white man's country like East Africa, or of self-government either. Indirect rule was not so much a means of future self-government as a tool for the protection of the autochthonous society which largely remained a-political.[23] On 25 July 1933, no less than the Duke of Brabant, later King Leopold III, stood before the senate and accused the Belgian colonial system of treating the native inhabitants as a "tool of production". The real interests of the colony demanded

> the moral and material advancement of the native. Let us establish contact with him. Let us try to know him. Let us meet him resolutely on the human plane where our solidarities can assert themselves and our interests merge.

At the same time the duke demanded an intensive promotion of native agriculture,[24] which his son, King Baudouin, followed up in 1955.

Governor-General Pierre Ryckmans (1934–1947) can be taken as representative of the official Belgian "colonial doctrine" in the 1930s. In his highly respected book *Dominer pour servir* (1931), in which he coined the slogan "to make the Blacks known (*faire connaître les Noirs*), he described different features of African society and tried to gain sympathy and support from readers at home for the plight of the colony after the depression. He said it was a paradoxical misconception of the situation to want to further increase taxation in order to obtain the necessary funds for economic development. Loans would also burden the future development of the Congo. The Belgian state should take over the so-called expenses of sovereignty, for "the Force publique does not defend the Congo; it defends the Empire of Belgium in the Congo"![25] Since Ryckmans did not expect direct help from budget funds, he hoped this method would give access to more money for investment and civilizing tasks. In 1956 the reformer Van Bilsen reiterated this demand.[26]

In 1934 Ryckmans clearly opposed the settlers' demands and criticized the all-too frequent change of colonial minister and the lack of understanding exhibited by many of the colonial officials for the complex and difficult position of the chiefs. He advocated actively promoting education and countered the current attacks on the alleged arrogance of the *évolués*.[27] Ryckmans' position in Belgium is comparable to that of Albert Sarraut in France. Characteristically, he did not refer to the future or to the possibility of representative institutions, but contented himself with calling on his country to fulfil its ruling mission in the sense of this being the white man's burden.[28]

Unlike in Britain and France, the Second World War did not inspire any serious colonial discussion in Belgium.[29] The Congo experienced a phase of prosperity, largely thanks to the uranium discovery which made it possible to build the American atom bomb; there was no national African opposition as yet. From 1945 to 1947 the colonial minister, Godding, actively carried out social reforms (establishment of works councils,

Fonds du Bien-être Indigène, Cités africaines, calls on the Congolese to form their own groups and clubs and to create an African press).[30] In July 1946 Governor-General Ryckmans said: "The mass of natives is badly housed, badly nourished, illiterate; destined to sickness and premature death". These were words which his deputy Leo Petillon reiterated, in an attempt to make known Belgium's great tasks; but they encountered opposition from colonialist circles.[31] Ryckmans believed emancipation must begin at the base and only when the masses were civilized could the Congolese obtain political responsibility. In other words, he left the problems to be faced by the next generation. He did not question the ruling structure, and Belgian colonial policy remained depoliticized.[32] "The political problem is not yet raised", said Ryckmans in 1948, clearly setting the Congo apart from the British and French colonial Empires.[33]

In 1948 a "Charte de mérite civique" was introduced, which conferred a special status between that of native and European on the rapidly increasing number of *évolués*. In 1952 an immatriculation law also gave the *évolués* the opportunity to be legally equated with the Belgians. These measures were of an assimilative kind, reminiscent of the statute of the *évolués* in French Equatorial Africa in 1942 and of French naturalization legislation in general. As in the case of French naturalization, the immatriculation law required the African to make an application which the administration would examine as to the standard of civilization —with the result that the number of legally assimilated Africans remained small in the Congo too. Unlike in French Black Africa, immatriculation was not associated with political rights in the Congo since not even the Belgians had franchise.

The Congo discussion between 1950 and 1955, in which the colonial minister, Pierre Wigny (initiator of the ten-year plan), administrators and university teachers and also Governor-General Petillon and even the king (cf. his speech in Leopoldville on 17 May 1955) took part, led to the following theses[34]:

The much-praised and allegedly specifically Belgian attitude of "patient empiricism"[35] no longer seemed sufficient to some writers. They said Belgium needed a "doctrine"; the administration must have an aim and must offer the Congolese élite a future, "a hope". "Where have we got in the Congo? Let us have the honesty to admit that we have got practically nowhere."[36] By comparison with France and England, Belgium was some ten years behind.

The political emancipation of the Congo—"in the measure of its capacity"—now emerged as a topic of discussion. It was to begin in local affairs. It had been a mistake, it was now asserted, to appoint Africans to the government council and the provincial councils while they had no part in local administration.[37] The 1957 Statut des Villes was to contribute towards correcting this.

Belgium still felt obliged to reject the political demands of the Belgian settlers; *they* were restless, it was alleged, not the natives![38] This is reminiscent of the situation in British East Africa in the 1920s. Indeed, Belgium liked to compare the Congo with Rhodesia or Kenya, rather than with West Africa, describing an autocratic colonial administration as the right means of ensuring the natives' interests.

The "official" efforts to remove the colour bar were mentioned earlier. Even the king and the governor-general challenged the whites to change their attitude. This was followed by administrative measures, which forced colonialist circles to prove that they were progressive and ready to "collaborate".[39]

The vague idea of a "Belgo-Congolese community" of a somewhat "integrated" nature was discussed.[40] Its protagonists were obviously thinking in terms of the French overseas territories that had obtained a degree of administrative autonomy in 1946, without this having impaired France's sovereignty. Governor-General Petillon was a prominent exponent of this thesis, which was then taken over by Colonial Minister Buisseret, although in October 1954 the latter had still warned against "precipitous not fully prepared measures" and had wanted to concentrate on economic development, for "the rest will come".[41] Pierre Wigny considered dissociation possible but not inevitable; just as Flemings and Walloons lived together in Belgium, he said, so there could be a community of Belgians and Congolese. Wigny wanted to give one Congolese Belgian civil rights, which, he said, did not preclude extensive autonomy or a temporary renunciation of franchise. Children, he added, had no franchise either! Even Wigny still thought of Congolese elections and a Congolese legislature as only remote possibilities,[42] although the Africans in neighbouring Brazzaville had had their own territorial assembly for years and elected deputies to the parliament.

The Belgian Socialist party, which had hitherto paid little attention to the Congo, formulated its doctrine at an extraordinary party congress in the summer of 1956. The aim of its policy was "autonomous government", which would be achieved by means of gradual democratization, a single college, and the abolition of discrimination. The Socialists spoke of a "future federation", but even for them this did not yet seem a matter of concern.[43]

But did the Congo have time to prepare for autonomy from below? Pierre Ryckmans asked: "Will thirty years of peaceful progress be given to us?" "We are no longer quite free," he said, "to set the pace of progress according to reason only. Yet I am full of hope".[44] But Ryckmans was an exception; other writers did not raise this question and seemed to have either overlooked or made light of the "African revolution" outside the Congo.[45] Belgium was convinced that it stood outside the general trend towards decolonization and that it could continue to pursue its allegedly successful policies in the Congo. "Our charter of 1908 contains all that San Francisco proposes. The English and French colonial policies are chiefly remarkable for their violent and grave failures"[46]; this appears to have been the popular view. Colonial Minister Buisseret said to an American journalist on 2 November 1954:

> We have temporarily postponed political reforms, as we believe that economic expansion and efforts to improve the social structure should come first. We believe that this policy is bound to create the fundamental conditions for peaceful coexistence in the framework of economic and social progress.[47]

In December 1955 and February 1956, however, a lecturer at the colonial institute in Antwerp, J. J. Van Bilsen, outlined a well-defined reform programme.[48] He called attention to the international situation and the emancipation movements in Africa, saying that Belgium could not ignore them. Traditional paternalism was no longer adequate and Belgium must keep in touch with new developments. This required not only political institutions, even at the centre, but also planning for the future and above all "élite planning". Instead of clinging to the assertion that the Congo was not yet ripe for political emancipation, one should create a basis for it and try to hasten the process. Instead thousands of Africans were being barred from access to university education and from positions of authority. Van Bilsen demanded a special fund to make university education in Belgium available to capable Congolese. He also realized that in comparison to France, Belgium exerted little assimilative attraction, but he still hoped for a Congolese federation that would establish loose ties with the mother country. This was the first time the principle of a future independent Congo had been voiced; Van Bilsen thought that a process of decolonization spread over thirty years with the help of time-limits would create the conditions for an orderly transfer of power; it would also show the authenticity of Belgian efforts and might thereby gain the co-operation of the Congolese. This was a real diversion from the traditional paternalism and the programme outlined a policy of development in accordance with the Congo's special situation.

Van Bilsen's essay, which represents a decisive break-through in Belgium's Congo policy, encountered violent resistance in colonialist circles. The influential *Revue coloniale belge* tried to ignore it,[49] while at the same time attacking the "horrifying idea of fixing a delay of thirty years to the political emancipation of the colony".[50] *L'écho du Katanga* spoke of "insane propositions" which demonstrated a willingness "to welcome the grave-diggers".[51] Even the colonial minister, Buisseret, classed Van Bilsen among the irresponsible strategists who fixed dates. Thirty years seemed much too short a transition period for the emancipation which Belgium so earnestly claimed to be initiating—an attitude which is all the more surprising in that Ryckmans had also spoken of a thirty-year period and had even asked whether Belgium could expect such a long "period of indulgence" at all.

Van Bilsen's "Plan de trente ans" also incited the Congolese to take a stand. In July and August 1965 the *Manifeste de Conscience Africaine* (Iléo) and the counter-manifesto of the Abako (Kasavubu) appeared, demanding parliamentary institutions with legislative responsibilities and a plan for emancipation; the Congolese themselves found a period of thirty years acceptable.[52]

This might have been the right moment to begin talks with the first organizations of *évolués* and to determine the framework for a gradual emancipation; Lumumba was prepared to do so at the time.[53] But the colonial minister and the governor-general ignored the manifesto and developed no initiatives of their own. The administration saw no need for urgency.

In spite of all these efforts even the progressive proposals and time-limits suggested by Van Bilsen soon proved unsatisfactory. In 1956 the French parliament passed the *Loi Cadre* which established an African government in Brazzaville. Ghana became independent a year later. In 1958 several hundred Congolese visited the world exhibition in Brussels —an event which played a considerable part in the creation of a rudimentary Congolese "national consciousness". On 24 August General de Gaulle gave the Africans on the other side of the Congo River the choice between loose ties with France and full independence. Finally, in December, the Pan-African conference met in Accra and Lumumba attended it as representative of the Mouvement National Congolais. The era when the Congo stood outside the revolutionary movement was clearly drawing to an end, and Belgium was becoming aware of this.[54]

However, the new Christian Socialist government did not set up a commission for the preparation of political reforms until after the 1958 parliamentary elections. The commission submitted its report in December. Petillon, who had become colonial minister, realized the urgency of making a new beginning and even spoke of "decolonization", but he had to retreat under the influence of conservative and colonialist circles. The hopes that the government would issue a declaration and promise future independence on 18 October (for the fiftieth anniversary of the Belgian Congo), which would become a basis for talks with the Congolese, proved unfounded.[55] The declaration was planned for 13 January. Meanwhile there were the riots of 4–7 January 1959. Europeans were attacked in the African suburbs of Leopoldville, houses were looted, schools and mission buildings set on fire. The Force publique and Belgian troops intervened and Congolese leaders were arrested.

The riots in Leopoldville, which had economic, social and political sources, can be compared to those in the Gold Coast in 1948 and the Ivory Coast in 1949. Like the British and French at the time, the Belgian administration was taken by surprise and showed astonishment at the extent of the pent-up resentment and anti-European feelings which had now broken loose. The revolt was an indication that the time had come for a change of course and resulted in the introduction of decolonization. But whereas Britain and France still had time to grant autonomy and independence in stages and to "control" developments, Belgium was now pressed and believed that it would have to take great steps to catch up.

A week after the riots, on 13 January, the king made the promised declaration which stated, among other things: ". . . it is our firm resolve today to conduct, without disastrous delays, but without ill-considered precipitation, the Congolese peoples towards independence in prosperity and peace".[56] The government also announced a reform programme, based on the report of experts[57]:

> Belgium intends to organize a democracy in the Congo capable of exercising the prerogatives of sovereignty and of deciding on its independence. . . . The realization of the ultimate objective will be pursued without trouble and with the collaboration of all the inhabitants of the Congo. The power of decision will gradually be left in their hands in more and more vast fields and in democratic forms, in step with the transformation of the institutions which will take place in a progressive but accelerated manner. . . . At the end of this evolution it is desirable, in the interests of the two countries, that associative ties should be maintained between the Congo and Belgium who will freely decide on them at that moment.[58]

The existing councils were to gradually obtain legislative powers; the future transfer of executive power, however, was only vaguely hinted at.

The two declarations of 13 January 1959 proclaimed independence as the aim of Belgium's Congo policy. Doubtless this meant that a decision had been made. However, they made no mention of transitional periods, provoking critical comments from Van Bilsen.[59] For the rest, Belgium was hoping for a form of association comparable perhaps to the French Community. It was clear that at present the Congo was not yet fit to take over government power and that the years of delay would have to be made up rather quickly. But would the African revolution give Belgium—and the Congo—a chance to catch up on what had been missed and accomplish the transfer of power in an orderly fashion?

Belgian reactions were twofold. While the Socialists applauded and the Société générale, representing economic interests in the Congo, bided its time, the settler organizations announced that they had reservations.[60] Colonial circles also pointed out that there was no African cadre yet, so there was no cause for concern.[61] Similarly Minister Van Hemelryk stressed at a press conference "that Belgium will not give up its power except in so far as the new Congolese institutions should be capable of respecting public and private commitments".[62] And this would not be the case for many years! On the other hand, there was now evidence of a sudden strong tendency to self-criticism, particularly with respect to the former policy of depoliticization.[63]

In the euphoria of its former successes and borne along by a rapidly expanding movement, Kasavubu's Abako and Lumumba's Mouvement National Congolais quickly increased their demands. They spoke in terms of independence for 1960 or 1961. Belgium gave in to the growing pressure, either because it had lost faith in its former policy or because it wanted to avoid new revolts which would compel it to use force.[64] This was indeed the only hope of guaranteeing Belgian economic interests in an independent Congo and maintaining an orderly administration. So the projected periods and dates were shortened in rapid succession.

On 16 October 1959 the colonial minister announced the early election of both legislative chambers and the formation of a government—not yet envisaged in January—under the governor-general. The parliament would work out the constitution while at the same time it would determine the "communal institutions" between the Congo and Belgium.[65] Yet at the conference in January and February 1960 the intended four-year period of transition had to be given up.[66] Superficially the decision to declare independence as early as 30 June was based on a compromise with even more radical Congolese demands, but in fact it meant that Belgium had capitulated. The government was interested in creating a favourable atmosphere, trusted in the goodwill of the Congolese, and wanted to prevent the breaking off of relations. Moreover, the Socialist party had already taken a stand against installing troops. Now Brussels wanted to proclaim independence too soon rather than too late, in the hope that the elections would bring in a relatively moderate government with whom it could work out the problems of the transfer of power; Belgium also believed this was the only way of maintaining its economic position. A detailed protocol with countless resolutions was painstakingly worked out in order to facilitate the transition and to ensure Belgian interests.[67] But as it was, a Congolese Government installed itself— just before 30 June—without preparation, without experience or an adequate cadre and was immediately confronted with the mutiny of the Force publique. If the Belgians had not categorically rejected Kasavubu's demand to form a provisional government, this essentially not very grave event would not have had such decisive importance and would perhaps not have led to the collapse of order and the failure of Belgian decolonization.

The term "paternalism" is frequently misused, but in this case it accurately describes Belgian policy. Belgian paternalism no doubt had positive results, but it did not prove to be a viable policy in the arena of decolonization. Belgium thought it could afford to do without a "doctrine" of its own and content itself by believing that its economic and civilizing achievements would prevent it from having to make political reforms or to hand over responsibility to the *évolués* in the foreseeable future. The colonial statute of the Congo may have complied with the pre-war situation, but after 1945 it was definitely a form of depoliticization. For Belgium confined itself to establishing a few consultative bodies that had no effective importance, did not hold elections and was very restrained in giving the Congolese responsible posts in the administration, even though Africans already sat in the French parliament and even acted as ministers, and the transition to responsible government had been completed in the British territories. There is another discrepancy if we remember that the Congo does not belong to West Africa but to Equatorial Africa, which is much less developed and has close relations with East Africa. The size of the Congo, the artificiality of its borders and the corresponding lack of a sense of solidarity among its numberous tribes may have justified slow action and posed particular problems; but on the other hand the Congo was particularly advanced economically and socially, for it was in the middle of a kind of industrial revolution and unlike most other African states had a broad class of resident workers and lower technical cadres in industry and the administration.[68] In this respect conditions were more conducive to successful decolonization than in other parts of Africa. Looking back, it seems paradoxical that it should have been precisely here that the development of and access to higher education was deliberately restricted and Africans scarcely had a chance to gain experience in the administration.

Belgian policy, which refused to take cognizance of African emancipation movements, was about ten years behind Great Britain and France. The situation in West Africa, and British and French efforts and aspirations around 1946, are comparable to those of Belgium in the Congo in 1956.[69] The two trends clashed in about 1958 when Ghana had become independent and General de Gaulle proclaimed the French Community, while the first local elections had only just taken place in the Congo and there was no legislative assembly at all yet. Belgium did not manage to make up its delay rapidly or even, as originally hoped, to complete the dissociation in stages. The transfer of power failed because it was not adequately prepared.

DOCTRINE VS. REALITY OF ASSIMILATION: PORTUGAL IN AFRICA

Belgium, which became a colonial power rather late, was a highly industrial Western European state; it developed the Congo economically and hoped to be able to avoid decolonization by means of a policy of paternalism. By contrast, Portugal in bordering Angola considered itself the oldest imperial power, with long experience and its own imperial consciousness; it thought it had created lasting ties with its overseas territories and escaped the effects of the Asian and African emancipation movements. But was this in fact the case? As early as the sixteenth century the great Camões had sung of the Empire and Catholic Portugal's idea of a universal civilization, although he had himself experienced the brutal reality of colonial rule.

Today Portuguese colonial policy is an integral part of Salazar's Estado and must be evaluated in connection with the national fascist revolutions of the twentieth century.[1] In the last century there was little interest in the colonies, and Portugal, because of its political instability and economic weakness, would not have been able to compete with the great imperialist powers. Its traditional closeness to England, however, made it possible for Portugal to establish itself in the remaining parts of Britain's former eastern Asiatic Empire (Goa, Timor and Macao) and to take part in the trade with the Far East, while its African possessions (São Tomé, Angola, Mozambique) declined in importance with the end of the slave trade. In the 1890s Portugal drew the hinterland under its rule and began to exploit African labour. But, as in Leopold II's Congo, world attention was drawn to conditions in the colonies and Portuguese colonial policy became the object of sharp criticism, particularly from British colonial reformers.[2] Its African possessions even became the object of plans for partition between the great powers.

The Republic (1910–1926) was highly conscious of its colonies, appointed a series of prominent governors and tried to liberalize native policy.[3] However, it did not achieve much. Forced labour survived in the guise of contract labour which served both the public sector and private enterprise. A number of the badly selected and inadequately paid officials were corrupt and took part in exploiting the Africans. Belgian and British capital served to build relatively large networks of railways and ports, but these mainly served Congolese, Rhodesian and South African exports. Since there was a lack of Portuguese private capital, the colonies were forced to solicit loans in the years of relative prosperity and came to the border of bankruptcy during the depression. In administrative terms the Republic promoted decentralization and transferred fairly extensive powers to the governors. Under the new financial autonomy, momentary surpluses could be reserved for future development instead of being paid back to the mother country or to deficient neighbouring colonies as before. Whether this policy of administrative decentralization and autonomy could have eventually led to political reforms with a view to self-government is hard to say. But the problem of the racial communities would inevitably have emerged.

At the end of the Republic in 1926 Salazar's authoritarian régime introduced a new policy. The "national revolution" made Portuguese nationalism the focus of its ideology. The Estado Novo (New State) attacked democratic parliamentary fragmentation, demanded national unity and tried to build up mass movements supporting the régime by means of a national union. The state was idealized and the régime oriented towards the executive. The colonial territories acquired particular importance, for Portugal's various territories scattered throughout the world helped it to present itself as a great power—"o país dos quatro Impérios . . . com províncias em quatro partes do mundo" (the land of the four Empires . . . with provinces in the four parts of the world). So it was said:

> We must keep alive in the Portuguese people the dream of an overseas, the consciousness and the pride of the Empire. Africa is more than a country for exploitation . . . for us Africa is a moral justification and our *raison d'être* as a power; without it we would be a small nation, with it we are a great country.[4]

Portugal saw itself as the civilizing nation par excellence. Portuguese men had made the great discoveries and had opened up and colonized vast territories; above all they had civilized and Christianized them. Portugal did not go overseas to seek raw materials but to bring light into the darkness of the heathen world. Camões' people did not exploit their overseas possessions as the other powers did, but civilized them, "o imperio português—projeção no mundo da latinidade e da cristandade" (the Portuguese Empire—projection into the world of latin civilization and Christianity).[5] Salazar's régime appealed and continues to appeal to this tradition and encouraged imperialism in order to justify and affirm its rule.

The Portuguese Empire was to be distinct from all other colonial empires. The overseas possessions were not—it was and still is said—colonies in the usual sense of the word, but integral parts of Portugal

—or better, parts of a Pan-Lusitanian community that embraced continental and overseas Portugal. Instead of the usual decentralization and colonial administrative autonomy, Salazar's régime aimed at centralization and integration. This new concept was reflected in the 1930 colonial act—when Salazar himself was colonial minister!—which in turn was adopted in the new constitution of 1933. Article 2 states:

> It is the true duty of the Portuguese nation to fulfil its historical function, to possess and colonize overseas areas, to civilize the native inhabitants and to exert its moral influence in accordance with the *Padroado* in the east.

Like continental Portugal, the Portuguese possessions in Africa and Asia together with the islands of Madeira and the Azores are a part of the Portuguese territory and constitute "the Portuguese colonial Empire" (Article 3).

In spite of the policy of legal integration the term "colony" was curiously retained and, symptomatically, expressed the combination of a postulated imperial unity and a relationship of domination. The structure of the administration had a correspondingly authoritarian accent.[6] The colonial minister "ruled" by means of decrees and a strictly hierarchical bureaucracy. The imperial council, i.e. the council for overseas provinces in Lisbon, as well as the councils in the colonies with their ex officio appointed members, had only advisory powers and carried little weight. The authoritarian system had in any case eliminated all organized opposition, which left little room for discussion; overseas trade was strictly supervised and colonial reality, unlike in all the other colonies, was as far as possible hidden from the critical eyes of foreign journalists.

The Second World War altered this centralist and authoritarian structure only slightly. The régime managed to survive and to adapt to the new international situation in foreign policy, and the challenge presented by the Second World War to other colonial territories was successfully kept away from Portuguese Africa. In 1950–1951 the term "colony" was replaced by "overseas province", which legally at least brought the process of integration to its conclusion. Henceforth, as was said in official pronouncements and political writings, Portugal formed an indissoluble unit in which the overseas provinces were fully equated with those of the mother country. The path France had tried to follow in Algeria and in its African colonies, although in a more flexible manner, was carried by Portugal to its logical conclusion. With a stroke of the pen it changed the constitution and eliminated the colonial statute, thereby allegedly anticipating the process of decolonization by a policy of integration and assimilation. Henceforth there were no official "colonial" problems for Portugal! Intervention by the U.N. could be rejected on the grounds that this body had no right to concern itself with the internal affairs of a member state. In 1955 Portugal refused to recognize its overseas possessions as "non-self-governing territories" or to report to the Trusteeship Council, and protested discussion in the Security Council or in the General Assembly. An example:

> The fact remains that my country does not practise any type whatever of colonialism within the Portuguese nation. Portugal has been for centuries a unitary nation, and it has always been recognized as such by the international community. We are a multiracial nation, as many other nations; our land and our people are dispersed over several continents, as is also the case with other nations, but we comprise only one unit, completely independent and solid—politically, juridically and socially—one country with the same strong national feeling.[7]

Decolonization by integration failed in the French colonies, except in the *vieilles colonies*, because it would have meant the cultural assimilation of millions of Africans whom France would have had to give full political rights and proportional representation in parliament. This would have led to the transfer of administrative control to the former subjects and changed the balance of power within Greater France, which the metropolis was not prepared to accept. By granting territorial autonomy, double electoral colleges and under-representation in parliament, France tried to escape the consequences of its policy of integration, but it was soon forced to admit that this kind of compromise would satisfy the overseas citizens for only a short time and would eventually create conflict. How did Portugal act here? It is obvious that the authoritarian régime concealed the problem. Since the political rights of the citizens in the mother country were restricted, the parliament had no power of political decision and the overseas provinces had only advisory bodies, it was relatively easy for Portugal to proclaim the equal status of all its "subjects". Opposition at home was suppressed in the same way as the African emancipation movement! As long as the political rights of the Portuguese were confined to a pseudo-election of the president of the Republic and appointments to parliament—without any alternative solution—it would on the whole have been conceivable to give full franchise to all African citizens without essentially changing the existing system.

Until recently at least Portugal has not taken this path but has found its own solution by distinguishing between legally "civilized" and "uncivilized" Portuguese. The criterion was naturally the Portuguese and Christian European way of life, which meant that *eo ipso* all whites and a large number of mulattoes could be recognized as "civilized" and "of age". The natives, by contrast, with their special legal position of *indígenas*, counted as "minors" and had to prove their standard of civilization before they could obtain full rights as *assimilados* and be equated with the white Portuguese. According to a 1954 decree, the candidate for assimilation had to be at least eighteen years old, speak fluent Portuguese, have finished his military service, be able to support his family, have adopted the European way of life and given up his tribal rights. If his application was accepted, the assimilated native was no longer subject to native taxation and forced labour but paid the same taxes as the white man, obtained franchise and access to positions of authority. This system had features in common with the French distinction between "citizens" and "subjects" and the procedure of naturalization; and like the French, the Portuguese administration made the act of assimilation difficult.[8]

Even more than the French, the Portuguese were proud of their differentiation between *indígenas* and *assimilados*. Portugal claimed to have rejected any form of racial discrimination, since it possessed or was constructing a multi-racial community, and this was alleged to fundamentally distinguish it from all the other colonial powers, particularly the Anglo-Saxons. The Portuguese colonizer had never practised racial discrimination; he did not distinguish according to race but according to level of civilization. Portugal had brought Christian civilization to Asia and Africa, thus building a bridge between racially different peoples. Portugal liked to point to Brazil, and also to Goa and Macao with their multi-racial societies, asserting that it had the same objective in Africa.

> A multi-racial society is therefore possible, be it Portuguese-American as in Brazil, or of Portuguese-Asiatic stock as in Goa, or still, as we find in Angola and Mozambique, based on Portuguese-African nationalism.[9]

As a result, even if miscegenation was not officially encouraged it was accepted, for the mulattoes seemed particularly good instruments for penetrating the hinterland and establishing a link between African and European civilization.

As an example of this form of argument we can cite the then undersecretary of state in the overseas ministry and former director of the colonial institute, Adriano Moreira, who tried to give an historico-sociologico-philosophical justification of Portuguese policy in Africa.[10] He attacked the theories of men like Spengler and Toynbee, which were based on the idea of the equal validity and legality of different cultures and would result in racial discrimination; they produced a political conflict and would lead to the withdrawal of Europe from Africa. Portugal by contrast, he said, was convinced of the need for racial and cultural influence and based its policy on the same premises as the declaration of human rights, since it rejected certain aspects of foreign civilizations as contradicting humanity. The civilizing work of the Catholic Church was not aggressive and destructive but a preparation for a universal culture, which, it was implied, would bear a Christian European Catholic character. The Portuguese policy of assimilation is a policy of cultural integration and cultural inter-penetration, and not the aggressive expansion of the dominant group. Where the policy of assimilation does imply the substitution of one set of cultural patterns for another, it is merely in those fields in which maintenance of human dignity demands a degree of intervention that [it] is now being proclaimed in universal declarations of the rights of man as the common duty of mankind.

Portugal's policy of multi-racial communities, Moreira claimed, anticipated the world state and was the only up-to-date and progressive doctrine. No other colonial power identified itself with assimilation to the extent that Portugal did, or used it to justify its claim to power.[11] In its role of Latin sister nation France occasionally openly supported assimilation and even in later years it could not deny that it had assimilatory hopes; but since the First World War at least it had given this up and confined itself to an "association" of autonomous units with inhabitants of different races within Greater France—this was largely because it had recognized the difficulties inherent in the notion of assimilation and doubted the possibility of putting it into practice. So one may ask, what did Portugal achieve in Africa? What was the real situation?

There was no legal colour bar or visible segregation, as even the most critical observers had to admit. An entirely different atmosphere reigned in Portuguese Africa from that in the British colonies or the Belgian Congo. The situation was roughly comparable to that in East and Central Africa since the number of whites, above all settlers and businessmen, was relatively large and posed the problem of a multi-racial society. Public facilities were equally open to both communities. Mulattoes were legally and socially recognized and even the *assimilados* were widely accepted. Africans obtained posts in the administration, assimilated natives from the Cape Verde Islands could rise to senior posts. With some right Portugal could speak of a cultural bar, fundamentally different from the colour bar in the other colonies.

But this cannot disguise the fact that the *assimilados*, i.e. the Africans legally equated with the whites, were a dwindling minority.[12] Statistics show an entirely different picture from official pronouncements and from the assertions of the political writers. The *assimilados* scarcely had any influence and even after the Second World War, in spite of the activity of the missions and the schools, the pace of assimilation did not really increase, largely because the administration, as we have shown, in no way encouraged it. The Portuguese called on their hundreds of years of activity as missionaries and carriers of civilization, but the result was scanty! Moreover the assimilated natives were concentrated in the towns which had grown at an immense rate and in any case had a Portuguese character, since they were dominated by the white population. If black and white mixed much more easily than in other parts of Africa, at the same time the difference between town and hinterland became more clear and accentuated a problem that existed throughout Africa. Assimilation "absorbed" the small upwardly-mobile class, satisfied it by giving it access to the civil service and separated it from the majority of the African population. Legal assimilation served as a safely valve. If Portugal had allowed a large and rapidly growing number of *assimilados*, they would soon have gained an important influence and sooner or later jeopardized the rule of the whites.

The doctrine of assimilation could have led one to expect that Portugal, in spite of its undoubtedly small financial resources, would take active measures to promote education in order to realize as soon as possible the multi-racial community it proclaimed.[13] But this was not the case and even in 1955 illiteracy stood at 98 percent, i.e. considerably higher than in the other colonial territories. The lower grades were segregated; the children of non-assimilated Africans were to obtain rudimentary education in an *Ensino de adaptação* and above all to learn the Portuguese language; instruction was left to the missions and was conducted with the help of numerous African teachers. The state elementary school, by contrast, was reserved to whites, mulattoes and *assimilados*, so that the children of non-assimilated natives could be educated only in a European-style mission school. Since this required school fees it was available to few. The secondary and high schools also laid down difficult requirements, such as an upper age limit which was prohibitive for many young Africans. So it is no wonder that in 1960 there were only thirty Africans among the thousand pupils in the Liceu Salazar in Lourenço Marques.[14] University education took place in Portugal, but in 1961 there were only some forty African students.

This educational system bears some resemblance to the French, in that instruction according to the curriculum used in the mother country made full education possible to the European colonials while at the same time culturally assimilating a small African élite. The assimilated class remained to some extent immune from national emancipation movements for a long time. But the French example had shown that at a given moment no amount of cultural indoctrination by the mother country would prevent the rise of African nationalism.

The thesis of a multi-racial community in a state of construction in no way prevented the exploitation of African labour or the maintenance of forced labour. The overwhelming majority of Africans remained abandoned to the authoritarian control of the administration. Allegedly there was no racial discrimination and there were no reservations; instead Portugal "civilized". And since regular work belonged to European civilization the Africans were compelled to do "civilizing labour": "Natives are encouraged to work, idleness being considered the worst social evil."[15] Unless he could prove that he had spent enough time cultivating his land or had a firm work contract or had paid his taxes, the African could be recruited for public works or forced to do allegedly voluntary contract work. This characterized Portugal's economic system; the activity of the recruiting agents, the open or only thinly disguised compulsion, low wages and heavy penalties for breach of contract were crass exploitation of African labour. France did not abolish forced labour until 1946, but the *corvée* had long since applied only for public works and had lost much of its importance; the English relied upon a head tax to force the Africans to accept paid labour. But Portugal went much further.[16] Contract labour was made available to private enterprise and to the plantations, and the administration also supplied labour—on contract—to the Union of South Africa, for which it received ten shillings per head. Needless to say, the "civilizing" value of this system was dubious! Portugal tried to justify itself by stressing the shortage of available labour; but at the same time there was mass emigration to neighbouring mining centres that paid higher wages and where the African workers were better treated in spite of segregation.

In spite of all affirmations to the contrary, no positive native policy could be built on this basis. The chiefs remained tools of the administration and were incorporated into the system of forced labour. For the rest, the statute of *indigena* made the colonial situation only too clear: restricted freedom of movement, identification cards, administrative justice, corporal punishment, forced cultivation of cotton, etc. This can be compared to the French *indigénat*, but the latter was certainly less rigid and was abolished in 1946, while Portugal renewed the native statute in 1954.

Censorship imposed by the Salazar régime makes it difficult to establish the degree to which colonial policy was criticized within Portugal. It is known, however, that Henrique Galvão, an inspector in the colonial administration, violently criticized forced and contract labour in a 1947 report.[17] Little is known of opposition colonial concepts. Civil disturbances in March 1961 resembling those in Leopoldville, shocked Portugal and turned the eyes of the outside world to the Portuguese colonies. The popular image of "an oasis of peace where normalcy reigns as opposed to the rest of Africa"[18] could no longer be maintained, although bloody repression managed to restore law and order; border controls and censorship were strengthened and the government alleged that the disturbances had been provoked from outside, by Ghana and by Communist intervention.

At the same time that it was engaging in repression and the continuing battle against terrorist infiltration in the northern border areas, Portugal initiated a few reforms. On 30 June 1960 the special penalties for breach of contract were abolished, on 2 May 1961 the compulsory cultivation of cotton was abolished and on 12 June a new municipal law was decreed. The abolition of the 1954 native statute on 6 September 1961 removed the distinctions between "civilized" and "uncivilized" inhabitants and Portugal proclaimed the legal equality of Europeans and Africans in

Portuguese Africa. In some respects this is reminiscent of France's conferment of civil rights on her colonial subjects in 1946. Portugal could counter critical world opinion by saying that it had fully realized a multi-racial society. But the actual validity of this constitutional change remains doubtful, for labour and economic structures cannot suddenly be altered; newer industrial concerns appear, however, to have adapted to freely recruited labour in a short time.[19] The new order established in 1961 is, moreover, essentially a reaction to the wave of anti-Portuguese opinion abroad and the U.N. "inquisition".

Portugal intends to keep its African possessions and sees no need for a change of policy. Officially it has completely decolonized its territories and protects its provinces against attack from without and against internal revolutionary activity. It contrasts its multi-racial community both with the apartheid of South Africa and with the grant of self-government and independence in the English and French territories. African nationalism is considered nonsense, since, according to the usual arguments, the borders are artificial, there is no national self-consciousness and self-determination would only lead to new tribal wars.[20] According to Salazar, self-determination is "the brilliant principle of political chaos in human societies".[21] Since the catastrophe in the Congo, Portugal naturally considers its prognoses confirmed. While the other colonial powers had weakly and opportunistically given in to the "winds that blow in Africa", he alleged, Portugal remained true to its historical calling and was defending European Christian civilization, "which the West seems to have forgotten".[22]

The Portuguese administration is increasing its resistance to change by actively encouraging immigration and new forms of settlement policy. The European population in Angola and Mozambique has risen sharply in the last years; in Angola alone there were 44,083 inhabitants in 1940, 78,826 in 1950, 109,568 in 1955 and c. 175,000 in 1961.[23] The state tries actively to attract settlers and in 1961 established special settlement agencies: "We proclaim the high priority of settlement by people from continental Portugal."[24] This was, so to speak, the Portuguese reply to the challenge of African nationalism and terrorist infiltration. The administration worked out a several-year plan and triggered a decided economic boom with the help of state funds, altering the face of the towns very quickly. European settlement is also designed to strengthen the forces of resistance in case of attack from abroad. But immigration has brought with it racial tensions. The immigrants feel alien in the colonial atmosphere, they live more or less cut off in predominantly white sections of the urban centres and compete with Africans for semi-professional opportunities (taxi drivers, hotel staff, lesser-grade civil service). The administration has had to warn against these tendencies which all too clearly contradict the *raison d'être* of the multi-racial society. Since the riots, a small minority has been driven onto the defensive, particularly as Portugal is under strong pressure in foreign policy and obtains little support now from its former allies, Britain and America. If this should lead to an open or tacit conflict, it is inevitable that Portugal will shift closer to South Africa and Southern Rhodesia.

We shall not answer the question of whether Portugal will manage to implement the idea of a multi-racial community in time to gain the support of the African inhabitants and to bring its assimilatory decolonization to a successful end, or whether the *New York Times* will have the last word. On 11 February 1961 it wrote:

> Governments cannot stop clocks or turn them back. This is 1961, not 1861 or 1561. Portuguese policy has been based on the belief that African nationalism would stop at the border of Angola and Mozambique, or be stopped. King Canute had as much chance of stopping the tide from coming in.[25]

CONCLUSION

Historical and political research has begun to include within the scope of its enquiry the many facets of the process of decolonization. In this work we have concentrated on an aspect of decolonization of particular interest to the historian. The object was to trace the European discussion on the future of the colonies since the First World War and to show the concepts, theses and hopes on which the colonial powers based their ideas of the future. If one considers colonialism as a system of domination and superimposition, then decolonization does not mean just the withdrawal of the colonial power, but the establishment of new relations between the colonial power and the former colony on the basis of equal status and self-determination. In place of a relationship of power we then have equality and freedom. But these two concepts allow for different interpretations. Either one begins with the individual and sees decolonization as the emancipation of the individual within the body of the state and the society which embraces the mother country and the former colonies, or one starts from the communities and interprets emancipation as the attainment of sovereignty and independence. Integration and assimilation contradict national liberation; the former subjects are either accepted as citizens with equal rights and agree to this form of emancipation, or they form an independent state.

The colonial policies of Britain and France reflect the differences between these two concepts. The divergence can be traced back to the national self-consciousness that evolved in the seventeenth and eighteenth centuries and that found itself confronted with colonial emancipation movements beginning with the secession of the British colonies in America and the French Revolution. How can colonial domination be reconciled with the colonial power's own concept of freedom? The British concept was based on corporate freedom and aimed at a legally secured free state on the one hand, at representation and a part in policy- and decision-making on the other. The liberty and equality proclaimed by the French Revolution was based on a centralist state and its object was the voluntary incorporation of the individual into the national community represented by the parliament. At the time of the ancien régime England had already granted its colonies a high degree of autonomy; in the nineteenth century it met colonial demands for emancipation with the "gradual grant of self-government". In the twentieth century this form of decolonization, which was first tried out on the colonial settlements, was extended to the Asian and African territories and came to its "logical" conclusion in the loose, non-institutionalized structure of the Commonwealth. France, by contrast, started from the concept of Greater France and thought it could satisfy demands for emancipation with cultural assimilation, administrative coordination and the grant of citizenship and representation in the Paris parliament. The integration of the *vieilles colonies* served as the model. French hopes of creating an institutionalized whole that would cause the colonial peoples to renounce their claims to national emancipation remained alive until the final phase of decolonization.

It would be a mistake, however, to try to establish an early willingness to decolonize and a purposeful and ethical policy of decolonization among the intentions of the colonial powers. We have tried to show how a definite constellation of events forced the respective colonial powers to reply to a challenge that either had an international source or stemmed from the agitation of national emancipation movements. Concessions and reforms were often granted reluctantly but, deliberate or involuntary, they followed certain definite principles and tended towards a corresponding conversion of the imperial structure. Rhetorical formulas alone could not solve the real problems in the individual territories. Variants had to be accepted and compromises made. We have also shown how the basic concepts of decolonization were by no means as unequivocal as the political statements would lead one to believe and that the colonial powers hesitated for a long time to accept the implications of their own theses. For instance, Great Britain long believed that its much-proclaimed policy of self-government, in the sense of responsible government and dominion status, could be confined to the colonial settlements and that it could restrict itself to granting internal autonomy in Asia and Africa. France, by contrast, shrank before the grave consequences of consistent integration, yet still hoped that it could avoid dissociation and safeguard a Greater France by institutional means.

The lesser colonial powers could go their own way in administrative methods, yet they too had to decide for one or the other policy of decolonization. The United States very soon chose integration in some cases, particularly that of the Philippines, and the grant of self-government in others. Portugal, on the contrary, believed it could solve the problem of decolonization by consistent assimilation. Holland and Belgium remained convinced for many years that they could confine themselves to economic development. Here they achieved much that was good, but they were in danger of missing the right moment for gradual adaptation to the process of emancipation; they jeopardized their own achievements by their lack of administrative and political preparation at the moment when dissociation could no longer be prevented.

We have outlined and compared these different policies of decolonization, but without attempting to systematize them or even to evaluate which concepts and methods proved most successful. What indeed would be the criteria for such an evaluation? It is tempting to trace the policy of the new states and the thought patterns of their ruling classes back to their colonial heritage, but it is easy to overlook the fact that the effective influence and imprint of the colonial régime varied according to the territory. In general terms, one may say that the European colonial powers began to prepare too late for withdrawal and only reluctantly gave up their paternalistic and autocratic structures. They wanted to prevent politicization and were reluctant to include the natives in administration or the policy-making. Even the liberal colonial reformers thought there was "still time" and counted on much longer periods of transition. The extraordinary increase in the pace of decolonization due to the Second World War and the subsequent East-West conflict was not predictable. References to the desirable "maturity" or "fitness" for independence helped to delay the withdrawal of the colonial power, but in the last phase of decolonization this led to problems, since the colonial powers had to grant independence before the colonies had the necessary administrative cadre. This does not, however, mean that decolonization came "too soon"; most of the colonial powers no longer had any excuse to stay, for their continued presence could only result in a further increase of tensions, which would have made successful decolonization even more unlikely.

Decolonization was hastened by many different factors; but its source lay in the process of modernization instigated by the colonial powers. This process in turn was simply a part of current world technological revolution and the spiritual and social changes that accompany it. Colonial conquest itself stimulated the forces which would one day lead to emancipation. The theme of this work has been how Europe adapted to the process of emancipation after the First World War and replied to the challenge it presented. We hope to have contributed towards an understanding of this fascinating process.

Notes

INTRODUCTION: INTERNATIONAL ASPECTS

1. Cf. my article, "Die USA and die Kolonialfrage (1917–1945)", *Vierteljahresschrift für Zeitgeschichte* (1965), p. 1.
2. David Hunter Miller, "Der Ursprung des Mandatssystems" (The Drafting of the Covenant), *Europische Gespräche*, VL (1928); Henry R. Winkler, *The League of Nation Movement in Great Britain 1914–1919* (1952), ch. VIII; H. Duncan Hall, *Mandates, Dependencies and Trusteeship* (1948).
3. Quoted by G. Fischer, *Un Cas de decolonisation. Les États-Unis et les Philippines* (1960), p. 50.
4. H. Duncan Hall, *op. cit.*, pp. 32, 49. See also comments by Lord Lugard, for many years the British representative, in "Das Mandatssystem und die britischen Mandate", *Europische Gespräche* (1924).
5. H. Duncan Hall, *op. cit.*, p. 171. Lugard believed that this was in fact a question of conflicting loyalties: Margery Perham, *Lugard, The Years of Authority 1898–1945*, II (1960), 651.
6. The early colonial expansion of the sixteenth to eighteenth centuries is given as an example of a "primitive accumulation" of capital. *Capital*, Bk. 1, ch. 24.
7. K. D. Erdmann, "Die asiatische Welt im Denken von Karl Marx und Friedrich Engels" in *Historische Forschungen und Probleme, Festschrift für Peter Rassow*, ed. K. E. Born (1961).
8. Tibor Mende, *Gespräche mit Nehru* (1956), pp. 15 f.
9. The Second Congress of the Communist International, transcript of the proceedings (1921), p. 224. See also Lenin's theses in his *Selected Works*, 2 vols., II (1947), 770 f. Excerpts in Walter Grottian, *Lenins Anleitung zum Handeln. Theorie und Praxis sowjetischer Aussenpolitik* (1962), pp. 166 f.
10. Essays by Stalin in *Werke*, SED ed., IV (1951), 143 f. *Fragen des Leninismus*, 3rd ed. (1951).
11. A detailed discussion in D. Boersner, *The Bolsheviks and the National and Colonial Question (1917–1928)* (1957). There is no corresponding account of Stalin's times.
12. For Lenin, cf. Grottian's excerpt from a speech to the Second Congress (1920), pp. 173 f. Stalin at the 6th Congress of the Communist International (1928): "In the imperialist countries the Communist parties must give systematic aid to the revolutionary movements for liberation in the colonies and to the movements of oppressed peoples as such. First of all, very active aid is the duty of the workers of the land on which the oppressed nation is dependent in financial, economic or political terms. The Communist parties must openly recognize the right to secession of the colonies and develop propaganda for this purpose, i.e. propaganda for the independence

of the colonies from the imperialist state. They must recognize the right of the colonies to armed resistance against imperialism (i.e. to rebellion and revolutionary war), propagate this resistance and support it actively with all the means at their disposal. The Communist parties must pursue the same policy with respect to all oppressed peoples.

"In the colonial and semi-colonial lands themselves, the Communist parties must engage in a bold and consistent struggle against foreign imperialism and unceasingly try to rally them to the idea of association with the proletariat of the imperialist countries and of union with them; they must openly put forward, propagate and put into effect the solution of agrarian revolution, in order to call upon the broad masses of the peasants to throw off the feudal yoke; they must declare war upon the reactionary, medieval influence of the church, the mission, etc." Transcript . . . , IV, 95 f.

13. *Das Flammenzeichen vom Palais Egmont.* Official transcript of the Congress . . . (1927).

14. "Neubau des Deutschen Reiches", in *Politische Schriften* (1933), sec. 8, "Zur Weltlage", pp. 286 f. France's power and claims are completely overestimated and misjudged. It said that with its "army of black millions" France could become "mistress of Africa" and that a new Faschoda was on the way. While France was setting Africa in motion and Russia was dynamizing Asia, British dominance was threatened.

15. Oswald Spengler, *Jahre der Entscheidung* (*The Hour of Decision*) (1934), p. 42.

16. *Ibid.,* p. 58.

17. *Ibid.,* p. 210: "It was not Germany that lost the World War; the West lost it when it lost the respect of the coloured races.

"The importance of this shift of the political centre of gravity was first realized in Moscow. In Western Europe it is still not realized. The white ruling nations have abdicated their former rank. They negotiate today where yesterday they would have commanded, and tomorrow they will have to flatter if they are even to negotiate. They have lost the feeling of the self-evidence of their power and are not even aware that they have lost it."

18. Paul Valéry, "La crise de l'esprit", in *Variété* (1924), pp. 11 f. Cf. also the preface to *Regards sur le monde actuel et autres essais* (1945).

19. Maurice Muret, *Le crépuscule des nations blanches* (1926), p. 232.

20. "We are warned that civilization is endangered by the rising tide of colour. . . ." J. W. Gregory, *The Menace of Colour,* 2nd ed. (1925), p. 1. Lothrop Stoddard, *Clashing Tides of Colour* (1935).

21. Heinz Gollwitzer, "Die Gelbe Gefahr. Geschichte eines Schlagwortes", in *Studien zum imperialistischen Denken* (1962).

22. Harold Nicolson, *Nachkriegsdiplomatie* (*Postwar Diplomacy*), p. 158. Curzon, *The Last Phase 1919–1925. A Study of Post-War Diplomacy* (1934), p. 159.

23. The text was intended as introduction to the *Survey of International Affairs,* edited by Toynbee, but appeared separately as a book. Besides Toynbee's *A Study of History* (especially Vols. VIII and XII), his most important works since the war are *Civilisation on Trial* (1948) and *The World and the West* (1953).

24. There are remarkably few points of reference either in William Ashworth, *A Short History of the International Economy since 1850,* 2nd ed. (1962), pp. 218 f., or in Louis Pommery, *Aperçu d'histoire économique contemporaine,* I (1952).

25. L. S. Amery, *National and Imperial Economies,* 2nd ed. (1924), pp. 57 f.

26. Ashworth, p. 234.

27. In 1915 Lancashire had a two-thirds share in the Indian cotton import which constituted 40 percent of the British export; only one-third of the demand was supplied by Indian manufacturers. In 1932 it was already 80 percent, of which 10 percent came from Japan and only 10 percent from England. Hans Schlie, *Die britische Handelspolitik seit Ottawa und ihre weltwirtschaftlichen Auswirkungen* (1937), p. 49. British iron and steel exports to India also fell from 896,000 tons in 1913 to 658,000 tons in 1929, 194,000 in 1932 and 301,000 tons in 1935; p. 43.

28. Prices in January 1933 by comparison with January 1929 (gold price index): rice, 41 percent; cotton, 34 percent; coffee, 41 percent; sugar, 50 percent; rubber, 13 percent; copper, 29 percent; tin, 47 percent. *New Cambridge Modern History*, XII (1960), 33.

29. *Op. cit.*, p. 34. "It is worth noting that in the Indian case and for all primary-production countries, the terms of trade worsen during a depression, and improve during a boom, thus exaggerating the effects of the trade cycle. For industrial countries, such as Great Britain, the reverse happens: i.e. changes in the terms of trade tend to moderate the effects of the trade cycle." Vera Anstey, *The Economic Development of India*, 4th ed. (1952), p. 502.

30. The most important points have already been mentioned in *Das Schicksal des deutschen Kapitalismus* (1926), 2nd ed. (1930). Bonn took up the theme again in a much respected essay, "The Age of Countercolonization", *International Affairs*, Vol. XIII (1934), and developed it further in 1938 in his book *The Crumbling of Empire. The Disintegration of World Economy*. Bonn had already been interested in colonial politics before 1914; cf. *So macht man Geschichte* (1953), pp. 137 f.

31. "All over the world a period of countercolonization began, and decolonization is rapidly proceeding." Art. "Imperialism", in the *Encyclopedia of the Social Sciences* (1932), p. 613. "I called this process decolonization" (*International Affairs*, p. 845; Bonn's translation of the word "Antikolonisierung" from *Schicksal des deutschen Kapitalismus*, p. 41). In 1938 he wrote: "A decolonization movement is sweeping over the continents", *Crumbling of Empire*, p. 101. In the 1937 Chatham House publication, *The Colonial Problem*, the term is used with reference to Bonn, p. 228, and with regard to India, p. 237.

32. *Crumbling of Empire*, p. 37. In 1943, Bonn reminded the Americans of Russian imperialism and warned them against unilateral anti-colonialism. "The Future of Imperialism", *Annals of the American Academy of Political and Social Science*, CCXXVIII (1943), 76.

33. *International Affairs*, p. 845.

34. *Crumbling of Empire*, p. 423.

35. After completing this work we came across W. Schmokel, *Dream of Empire: German Colonialism 1919–1945* (1964).

36. *Die Gegenvorschläge der Deutschen Regierung zu den Friedensbedingungen* (1919), pp. 45 f. Graf Brockdorff-Rantzau, *Dokumente und Gedanken um Versailles* (1963), pp. 49, 149. Hans Poeschel, *Die Kolonialfrage im Frieden von Versailles* (1920).

37. In 1929 at the Industrie- und Handelstag, E. J. Jakob, *Kolonialisches Quellenheft* (1935), p. 93. Also Dr. Schnee (DVP) on 24 June at the Reichstag: "It is obvious [!] that it would be a great relief to our currency policy if we received a considerable part of these overseas raw materials from our own colonial territories. . . ." *Stenographische Berichte*, CDXXV, 2839.

38. Reichstag 14 March 1921, *Stenogr. Berichte*, CCCXLVIII, 2894, 2899a; 3–4 March 1922, CCCLIII, 6135 f. Jakob, *Quellenheft*, p. 50.

39. Cf. the questionnaire composed by the *Europäischen Gespräche*: "Soll Deutschland Kolonialpolitik treiben?" (Should Germany pursue a colonial policy?) Those who replied in the negative included M. J. Bonn, Albert Einstein, Franz Carl Endres, F. Friedensburg, Thomas Mann. XII (1927), 609 ff. Those in favour included Lord Mayor Dr. Konrad Adenauer: "The German Empire must without fail strive to acquire colonies. There is too little space in the Empire itself for the large population . . . ," p. 611.

40. Some examples in Jakob, *Quellenheft*, p. 51. Breitscheid in the Reichstag 17 March 1931, *Stenogr. Berichte*, CDXLV, 1653.

41. Cf. *Koloniale Rundschau* VIII (1925), p. 253: the board consisted of Dr. Bell (vice-president of the Reichstag), Centre; Dr. Dernburg, Democratic party; Dr. Quessel for the Social Democrats; Sachs, DNVP; and Dr. Schnee, DVP.

42. Stresemann's position can be seen in his *Vermächtnis*, II (1932), 22, 172, 213, 251, 283, 296, 333 ff. In the letter to the crown prince, the colonies are not counted among the great tasks of the near future ("grossen Aufgaben für die nächste absehbare Zeit", II, 553). A general work on the diplomacy of the Weimar Republic in Kordt's memoirs: "In the Wilhelmstrasse in the '20s there was also a colonial section in a remote corner. That even many members of the Foreign Office were unaware of its existence could not be attributed to the fact that they wanted to hide it. But in fact the colonial section seemed more like a place of liquidation, in which three or four gentleman from the former colonial office were at work. The colonial questions were also dealt with from time to time by the economic department in connection with questions of the supply of raw materials. On the whole the discussion remained rather academic until the time of the Third Reich." Erich Kordt, *Nicht aus den Akten* (Stuttgart, 1950), pp. 42 f.

43. Cf. diary entries of Generaloberst Halder on 30 June 1941, quoted in H. A. Jacobsen, *Der Zweite Weltkrieg in Dokumenten* (1959), p. 225. Henry Picker, *Hitler's Tischgespräche im Führerhauptquartier 1941–1942* (1951), pp. 50, 123. Günter Moltmann, "Weltherrschaftsideen Hitlers", in *Europa und Übersee, Festschrift für Egmont Zechlin* (1961), pp. 213 f.

44. Gerhard L. Weinberg, "German Colonial Plans and Policies 1938–1942", in *Geschichte und Geschichtsbewusstsein, Festschrift für Hans Rothfels* (1963). More detailed is Schmokel, ch. 4.

45. Particularly in Währhold Drascher, *Die Vorherrschaft der Weissen Rasse* (1936). Corresponding criticism of British, and especially French, native policy followed, e.g. in Paul Rohrbach, *Deutschlands koloniale Forderung* (1935), pp. 123, 130 f.

46. A speech by Goebbels in Berlin on 17 January 1936 was the prelude (Schulthess' Europ. Geschichtskalender, LXXVII, 8) and immediately provoked sharp reaction abroad: cf. House of Commons, Debates 1936, CCCVIII, 934. Also Ribbentrop in Leipzig on 1 March 1936, *Dokumente der deutschen Politik* V, 202; Schmokel, pp. 97 f.

47. Report of the talk between Halifax and Hitler on 19 October 1937 on the Obersalzberg (*Akten zur deutschen auswärtigen Politik 1918–45*, I [1950], 51).

48. Neville Henderson, *Fehlschlag einer Mission* (n.d.), p. 102. Winston Churchill, *The Second World War*, I (1949), 200. For the point of view of the Eastern Zone, see Horst Kähne, "Zur Kolonialpolitik des faschistischen deutschen imperialismus", *Zeitschrift fur Geschichtswissenschaft* (1961), p. 3.

NOTES 533

49. The reply of a government representative, House of Commons, Debates 15 February 1937, CCCXX, 815. Prime Minister Baldwin on 22 March 1937, *Keesing's Contemporary Archives*, p. 2993c.

50. "Germany's colonial demands", in *Foreign Affairs*, January 1937. Schacht concludes: "The German colonial problem is not a problem of imperialism. It is not a mere problem of prestige. It is simply and solely a problem of economic existence. Precisely for that reason the future of a European peace depends upon it!", p. 234. Andre François-Poncet asserts that Schacht had wanted to turn Hitler's aspiration away from Eastern Europe. *As Ambassador in Berlin* (1947), p. 268. Also Schacht's evidence at Nuremberg, IMT, XII, 470.

51. A report published by Chatham House summarized these aspects: *The Colonial Problem. A Report by a Study Group of Members of the RIIA* (1937); also a long section in *The British Empire* (RIIA, 1937).

52. E.g. Sir Arthur Salter in the House of Commons on 5 February 1936, House of Commons, CCCVI, 219; the *Economist* of 19 October 1935, etc. Cf. also O. Louwers, *Le problème coloniale du point de vue international* (1936), pp. 82 f.

53. Louwers, *op. cit.*, p. 102.

54. Speech in Hamburg on 3 March 1936, in *Hamburger Monatshefte für Auswärtige Politik*, March 1936. Letter to *The Times* signed by Vernon Bartlett, Gilbert Murray, Noel-Buxton, Arnold Toynbee, on 7 October 1937; by contrast, Amery in a letter to *The Times, Monatshefte*, p. 774, and Toynbee's reply, pp. 784 f.

55. *Keesing's Contemporary Archives*, 8 March 1938, p. 3970 G.

56. P. J. Noel-Baker in a speech before the Labour party in the House of Commons. Also the party brochure: *The Demand for Colonial Territories and Equality of Economic Opportunity* (1936).

57. Halifax's visit to Berlin in November 1937 and to the Obersalzberg, cf. *Akten zur deutschen auswartigen Politik 1918–45*, I, 44 f. Keith Feiling, *The Life of Neville Chamberlain* (1946), p. 333.

58. Bullitt to the secretary of state on 20 February 1937 on a talk with Delbos, in *Foreign Relations*, I (1937), 46. Again, Bullitt on 6 November 1937, p. 153; 22 November 1937, p. 158; 1 December 1937, p. 181.

59. For the talks between Henderson and Ribbentrop and Hitler, *Akten zur deutschen auswärtigen Politik*, I (1938), 186, 196 f., 201 f. *Fehlschlag einer Mission*, p. 70, 133. Cf. also Halifax to Henderson on 4 April 1938: "There are two kinds of difficulty: British public aversion to giving back colonies to the Nazis at all; and giving them back without a quid pro quo". In *Documents on British Foreign Policy 1919–1939*, I, 622.

60. E.g. M. J. Bonn and Chancellor Hermann Müller in their replies to the questionnaire of 1927, in *Europäische Gespräche*, XII (1927), 616.

61. Paul Mus, *Viet-Nam, sociologie d'une guerre* (1952), p. 33.

62. Evidence for this paragraph in my article: *Die USA und die Kolonialfrage*, pp. 10 f.

63. House of Commons, CCCLXXIV, 68 (9 September 1941).

64. Summer Welles, *The Time of Decision* (1944), p. 383.

65. Vernon McKay, "The Impact of the UN in Africa", in *Africa Today*, ed. C. Grove Haines (1955). Richard J. Kozicki, "The UN and Colonialism", in *The Idea of Colonialism*, ed. Robert Strausz-Hupé and Harry W. Hazard (1958). J. W. Brügel, "Das Treuhandschaftssystem der Vereinten Nationen", in *Europa-Archiv* (1960), p. 22. James N. Murray, *The United Nations Trusteeship System* (1957).

66. Cf. the attitude of the former colonial governor and British represent-

ative in the Trusteeship Council of 1947–1956, Sir Alan Burns, *In Defence of Colonies* (1957), ch. 5.
67. McKay, *op. cit.*, p. 374.
68. Cf. my article and Bibliography.
69. J. H. Brimmel, *Communism in South-East Asia* (1959), p. 172.
70. G. H. Becker, *The Disposition of the Italian Colonies 1941–51* (1952), pp. 77, 81.
71. Cf. pp. 411–12.
72. Selected bibliography in German: Boris Meissner, *Die marxistisch-leninistische Lehre vom "Staat der nationalen Demokratie"*; and Richard Loewenthal, "Kommunismus und nationale Revolution", *Aus Politik und Zeitgeschehen*, appendix to *Parlament*, X, 6 March 1963. Fritz Schatten, "Nationalismus und Kommunismus in Afrika", *Ostprobleme* (1962), p. 16. Lazar Pistrak, "Die Strategie der Sowjets in Afrika", *Aussenpolitik* (1962), p. 1. Soviet policy in Africa in *Neue Zürcher Zeitung*, 20 April 1962.
73. Khrushchev at the Twentieth Party Conference of the CP of the Soviet Union. The demand of the developing countries to complete their economic development with the help of private capital was now accepted; cf. *Grundlagen des Marxismus und Leninismus*, pamphlet (1960), pp. 482, 490 f.

I. GREAT BRITAIN

THE THIRD BRITISH EMPIRE

1. *The Third British Empire*, 2nd ed. (1927).
2. *Op. cit.*, p. 14.
3. *Op. cit.*, p. 155.
4. Unfortunately there is no enquiry into imperialist and anti-imperialist trends before 1914. For references to this, cf. Elizabeth Monroe, *Britain's Moment in the Middle East 1914–1956* (1963), pp. 136 f., and A. P. Thornton, *The Imperial Idea and Its Enemies, a Study in British Power* (1959).
5. "The Cement of Empire", 25 May 1914 in *Subjects of the Day*, p. 19.
6. House of Lords, *Debates*, XXXII, 162.
7. Henry R. Winkler, *The League of Nation Movement in Great Britain 1914–1919* (1952).
8. *Documents and Statements Relating to Peace Proposals and War Aims, Dec. 1916–Nov. 1918*, ed. Dickinson (1919). Going beyond Wilson, Lloyd George declared: "The general principle of national self-determination is therefore as applicable in their cases [natives of the German colonies] as in those of occupied European territories", p. 114.
9. Lloyd George, *War Memoirs*, I (1933), 118, 123, except for South-West Africa and the Pacific Islands.
10. *My Political Life*, II (1953), 104, 160 f.
11. P. H. Kerr, "Political Relations between Advanced and Backward Peoples", in *An Introduction to the Study of International Relations*, ed. A. J. Grant (1916). Also "Commonwealth and Empire" in *The Empire and the Future* (1916).
12. "Intervention is also the only method of providing for the orderly progress towards self-government", particularly for areas with their own civilization such as India; *Commonwealth and Empire*, p. 80.
13. *Op. cit.*, p. 87.
14. *Political Relations . . .* , p. 143.
15. *Round Table*, September 1919. J. R. M. Butler and Lord Lothian assert (*Philip Kerr, 1882–1940* [1960], p. 323) that Kerr was the author of the unsigned article.
16. *Op. cit.*, p. 668. Similarly T. E. Lawrence, "The Outlook in the Middle East", *Round Table*, December 1919. He also speaks of a "genuine nationalism" in Egypt, of the difficulties of the British occupation of Mesopotamia and the necessity of granting the nationalists self-government in order to win them as partners in the Commonwealth. An "Oriental Dominion" would be a major "achievement", since it seemed the alternative

to a possible conflict between the British Commonwealth and the "Oriental World", p. 97.

17. Butler, *op. cit.*, p. 69.

18. "The extent of this work after the war, sometimes known as the white man's burden, will never be so vast that it will never be accomplished at all unless it is shared in proportions equal to their strength by the four allies now united in fighting the German", p. 69.

19. Letter of October 1918, quoted in Butler, *op. cit.*, p. 68. Urged by Kerr, Curtis wrote the important article "Windows of Freedom", in *Round Table*, December 1918, in which he stressed the role of the U.S. but rejected the American concept of a league of nations in charge of colonial administration. Only when such a league had become an institutional world government could it take over such grave tasks.

20. *Op. cit.*, p. 663.

21. Cf. the essay "Windows of Freedom". Neither the U.S. nor Great Britain could retire into an isolation "which was never splendid". Nationalism and the balance of power had led to the war, and Britain had "outlived its time". In so far as the League of Nations really fulfilled its task the Commonwealth could only gain "by using its naval power as the agent of the League to check aggression". "The British Commonwealth is a genuine League of Nations, and a good deal more. It is a League and more than a League, a State and less than a State" (p. 17).

22. Cf. p. 17.

23. Vladimir Halperin, *Lord Milner et l'évolution de l'imperialisme britannique* (1950), pp. 192 f. Milner himself wrote: "Those who, in their enthusiasm for a wider world-embracing League, are indifferent to the maintenance of the League of British Nations, run the risk of throwing away the substance for the shadow". *Questions of the Hour*, 2nd ed. (1925), p. 200.

24. Appendix to *Questions of the Hour*. Also speech given as colonial minister, 10 April 1919, "The British League of Nations", in *United Empire* (1919-20), pp. 223 f.

25. See article "The Aftermath of War" in *Questions of the Hour*.

26. George E. Kirk, *Kurze Geschichte des Nahen Ostens*, (n.d., 1958), pp. 160 f. Elizabeth Monroe, *Britain's Moment in the Middle East, 1914-1956* (1963), pp. 55 f. Elie Kedouri, "Sa'-ad Zaghloul and the British", *Middle Eastern Affairs*, No. 2, ed. A. Hourani, *St Antony's Papers*, No. 11 (1961).

27. Details on a draft constitution by the protectorate authorities; cf. Kirk, *op. cit.*, p. 161.

28. Lord Lloyd, *Egypt since Cromer*, I (1933), 293. Balfour in the House of Commons on 17 November 1919: "British supremacy exists, British supremacy is going to be maintained, and let nobody either in Egypt nor out of Egypt make any mistake upon this cardinal principle of HMG." In *House of Commons*, CXXI, 771.

29. Cf. Milner's letter to Lloyd George on 28 December 1919, quoted in A. M. Gollin, *Proconsul in Politics* (1964), p. 590.

30. Report of the Special Mission to Egypt. *Commonwealth Documents* 1131 (1921). Also Milner in the House of Lords on 4 November 1920, XLII, 212 f.: "My intimate conviction is that, while there is undoubtedly an element of Egyptian nationalism which is anti-British, the better and stronger elements of it are not anti-British but simply pro-Egyptian, that between the honest pro-Egyptian nationalist and a British imperialist statesman there can be a good and permanent alliance, and that here is no permanent conflict of interests."

31. Cf. the diaries of Duff Cooper, a young employee in the Egyptian department of the Colonial Office, *Old Men Forget* (1954), pp. 102 f.
32. Besides Duff Cooper, also Halperin, *Milner*, pp. 63 f. Nicolson mentions a memorandum by Curzon on October 11, 1920 in which Curzon agreed to Milner's proposal, *Nachkriegsdiplomatie, op. cit.* p. 176.
33. *The Egyptian Problem* (1920), pp. 302 f.
34. "Egypt a Nation", *Round Table*, X (1920), 43. *Economist*, 28 August 1920. Similarly W. Ormsby-Gore (under-secretary of state for colonies, 1922–1929), "Egypt and the Milner Proposals", *Nineteenth Century*, December 1920.
35. Duff Cooper, *op. cit.*, p. 103.
36. *House of Lords*, 4 November 1920, XLII, 180, 190.
37. *Egypt since Cromer*, I, 312 f., 560 f.; II, Introduction. Lord Salisbury uses the same arguments; cf. *House of Lords*, 4 November 1920, XLII, 183.
38. *Op. cit.*, Introduction, pp. 4 f. He continues: "In all these countries the real problem has been administrative, and we have chosen to regard it as political. What was the reason? Was it simply the hypnotism exercised over us by the disastrous cry of 'self-determination'? or were we also the victims of a growing indifference to responsibilities which did not appear to concern our purely material welfare?"
39. *Op. cit.*, p. 8.
40. Kedouri, *Sa'-ad Zaghloul*, p. 154.
41. Annoyed that even Curzon had given in, Churchill passed him a note over the table during the Cabinet meeting reading: "Surely you cannot realise how very seriously an Egyptian surrender will be attached to your own great reputation in the British Empire. It leaves me absolutely baffled to comprehend why you should be in this side or why you should have insisted on keeping Egyptian affairs in your hands, only to lead us to this melancholic conclusion. It grieves me to see what is unfolding." Quoted in Leonhard Mosley, *The Glorious Fault, The Life of Lord Curzon* (1960), pp. 247 f. For Curzon's attitude in 1921–1922 cf. Nicolson, *op. cit.*, pp. 177 f.
42. Quoted in Elie Kedouri, *England and the Middle East. The Destruction of the Ottoman Empire 1914–1921* (1956), p. 189. Similarly the former liberal prime minister, Asquith, in the House of Commons on 23 June 1920: "Whatever may be its possibilities of resurrection, reconstruction or revitalisation, it is certainly not a duty which is incumbent upon us to take upon our already overburdened shoulders", CXXX, 2236.

THE BRITISH COMMONWEALTH OF NATIONS

1. Halperin, *Lord Milner*, pp. 189 f.
2. Quoted in Butler, *Lord Lothian*, p. 40, note.
3. Cf. Butler, *op. cit.* ch. III. Kerr, for instance, thought that Curtis' Organic Union would drive Canada to secession; letter in November 1909, p. 39. Carroll Quigley, "The Round Table Groups in Canada, 1908–1938", *The Canadian Historical Review*, September 1962.
4. J. D. B. Miller, *Richard Jebb and the Problem of Empire* (1956).
5. W. K. Hancock, *Survey of British Commonwealth Affairs*, I (1937), 41.
6. *Selected Speeches and Documents on British Colonial Policy 1763–1917*, ed. A. B. Keith (ed. 1953), pp. 247 ff.
7. *Op. cit.*, p. 358.
8. "The Dominions and the Settlement", in *Round Table*, V, 325.
9. Hans E. Bärtschi, *Die Entwicklung vom imperialistischen Reichsge-*

danken zur modernen Idee des Commonwealth im Lebenswerk Lord Balfours (1957), p. 135.

10. "It will then be plain that the liberties which have been saved cannot be secured for the future, unless the burden involved is recognized as a first charge on the revenues, not of one, but of all the free communities of the Commonwealth in peace as well as in war." *The Problem of the Commonwealth* (1916), p. 7.

11. Hancock, *op. cit.*, I, 52 f. S. A. de Smith, *The Vocabulary of Commonwealth Relations*, 1954. Nicholas Mansergh, *The Name and Nature of the British Commonwealth*, 1955. Alfred Zimmern had also published his famous *The Greek Commonwealth* in 1911.

12. Earl of Cromer, "Imperial Federation", in Cromer, Haldane, Marshall, et al., *After-War Problems*, ed. W. H. Dawson (1917).

13. "The Growing Necessity of Constitutional Reform", in *Round Table*, 7 December 1916.

14. Bärtschi, *op. cit.*, p. 137.

15. "The Organisation of the Empire, a Suggestion", *The Nineteenth Century*, March 1917.

16. John Bowle, *Viscount Samuel, a Biography* (1957), p. 153.

17. Bärtschi, *op. cit.*, p. 140.

18. *Round Table*, December 1920, p. 12, note 2, explicitly dissociates itself from Curtis.

19. *Imperial Unity and the Dominions* (1916). *Letters on Imperial Relations* (1935).

20. *Imperial Unity*, p. 7.

21. *Op. cit.*, p. 24.

22. *Op. cit.*, p. 25.

23. *Op. cit.*, p. 510.

24. *Selected Speeches and Documents*, p. 376.

25. *Op. cit.*, p. 379.

26. *Op. cit.*, p. 391.

27. *Op. cit.*, p. 397.

28. "We are not a State but a community of States and nations. We are far greater than any Empire which has ever existed, and by using this ancient expression we really disguise the main fact that our whole position is different, and that we are not one State or nation or Empire, but a whole world by ourselves, consisting of many nations, of many States, and all sorts of communities, under one flag.... We are a system of States and not a stationary but a dynamic and evolving system, always going forward to new destinies." Speech before the British Parliament on 15 May 1917, quoted in W. K. Hancock, *Smuts, The Sanguine Years*, Vol. I, 1870–1919 (1962), p. 431.

29. Patrick Gordon-Walker, *The Commonwealth* (1962), p. 98.

30. R. MacGregor Dawson, *The Development of Dominion Status 1900–1936* (1937). E. A. Walker, *The British Empire, Its Structure and Spirit*, 2nd ed. (1953), pp. 150 f. Gordon-Walker, *op. cit.*, pp. 98 f. *Speeches and Documents on the British Dominions 1918–1931*, ed. A. B. Keith (1932).

31. J. D. B. Miller, *The Commonwealth in the World* (1958), p. 42.

32. E. A. Walker, *op. cit.*, p. 152.

33. *Speeches and Documents on the British Dominions 1918–1931*, pp. 161 f. H. Duncan Hall, "The Genesis of the Balfour Declaration of 1926", *Journal of Commonwealth Studies*, I (1962), 3. Hall also shows how memoranda by Smuts and L. S. Amery prepared for the 1926 formula and how Hertzog finally made concessions after all, amongst others giving up the word

"independence", because Mackenzie King (Canada) could only see this as meaning secession. For Balfour cf. also Bärtschi, *op. cit.*

34. Prime Minister Baldwin called the Crown "the last link of Empire that is left"; quoted in N. Mansergh, "The Commonwealth at the Queen's Accession", *International Affairs*, July 1953, p. 279.

35. As an example we can take Lord Lloyd, Chairman of the Navy League and the Empire Economic Union, who declared in an interview with an Australian newspaper: "The United States of America, following a policy of mutual economic co-operation over a vast and rich territory, have built up a position as the dominating power in the economic world. In Europe, farseeing men realise that the day of small economic units is passing away, and our former allies and enemies are being forced to consider some sort of closer economic union for a continent. In the coming realignment of world economic forces the nations of the Empire cannot afford to remain isolated economic units. They will be compelled, unless they are to fall behind in the whole progress of world-development to combine to make the Empire one economic unit. I do not admit that the problem is one incapable of solution. The British Empire, so largely peopled by men of common origin and common tradition, naturally dependent on one another for food, raw materials, and manufactured goods, should be able to find ways and means for promoting the greater interchange of their products. This is surely within the capacity of men of knowledge, ability, and goodwill, meeting in conference together." Quoted in Colin Forbes Adam, *Life of Lord Lloyd* (1948), p. 247. Similarly Robert Hadfield, "Economic Organisation and Development of Empire", *Contemporary Review*, November 1929, p. 575; Robert Stokes, *New Imperial Ideals* (1930), p. 49. L. S. Amery in *The Empire in the New Era* (1948), p. 10, writes: "We are face to face with the gradual emergence of a new type of greater unity, economic and political, in the world's affairs."

36. Besides a number of articles in the *Round Table*, cf. also Viscount Sandon, "The Problem of the British Empire", *Nineteenth Century*, October 1920.

37. *House of Commons*, CCLIX, 1188 f.

38. "The League of Nations is the deus ex machina of the British Commonwealth. That Commonwealth, if it is to survive, must survive as a League within a larger League, a society within that larger society." *Third British Empire*, p. 71. Ireland had joined in the British sanctions in 1935 against Italy, not in order to support Britain, but because of its obligation to the League of Nations. Lord Elton, *Imperial Commonwealth* (1945), p. 488.

39. Cf. p. 55.

40. Cf. among others, *My Political Life*, II, 163 f.; Edward Grigg, *The Faith of an Englishman* (1936), p. 326: "easy pretext . . . to shirk its real responsibilities for common defence".

41. Amery's diary: "It is true it leaves the way equally clear to dissolution. That is a risk we have got to run, and if the will to unity is there we shall overcome it." *My Political Life*, II, 394. On Amery, W. F. Gutteridge, "L. S. Amery and the Commonwealth", *Political Science* (New Zealand), VIII (1956), 2. For Kerr's attitude, cf. Butler, *Lord Lothian*, p. 108.

42. *Empire in the New Era* (1928), p. 2.

43. Ernest Barker, *Ideas and Ideals of the British Empire*, p. 83.

44. E.g. the Balfour declaration: "They [the dominions] are autonomous Communities *within* the British Empire."

45. ". . . we have since [1926] tended to use Commonwealth for the whole, whenever the emphasis has been on the steady extension of self-govern-

ment, and Empire when emphasizing its complex variety or the great tradition of the past." Amery, *My Political Life*, II, 389 f.

46. "The creation of that Commonwealth of many nations, many races, and many colours, of which we have dreamed." "Harvest of Victory", *Round Table*, September 1919, p. 668.

47. "Extension ultimately to the rest of the Empire with its 370 millions of coloured peoples ... will gradually assimilate the position of the dependencies to that of the United Kingdom and of the Dominions." *The Government of the British Commonwealth of Nations* (1921), p. 10.

48. J. Coatman, *Magna Britannia* (1936), p. 62.

49. *The Letters of T. E. Lawrence*, ed. D. Garnett (1938), p. 308. Great Britain should withdraw its troops from Iraq and transfer the administration to the Arabs: "we should hold of Mesopotamia exactly as much (or as little) as we hold of South Africa or Canada. I believe the Arabs in these conditions would be as loyal as anyone in the Empire, and they would not cost us a cent." In 1928, however, Lawrence was in favour of bilateral agreements, which would give Britain a privileged position in defence; p. 578.

50. *Empire in These Days* (1935), p. 179.

51. Amery tells how the drafters of the Balfour declaration deliberately attempted to dissociate the dominions from the rest of the Empire and did not consider gradually extending it. *My Political Life*, II, 389. Cf. also N. Mansergh, *Name and Nature*, p. 5.

THE QUESTION OF DOMINION STATUS FOR INDIA (1917–1939)

1. The best-known is the declaration by Sir Thomas Munro, the governor of Madras, in 1824, when he said that England must rule India until the Indians had "abandoned most of their superstitions and prejudices, and become sufficiently enlightened to frame a regular government for themselves, and to conduct and preserve it. Whenever such a time shall arrive, it will probably be best for both countries that the British control over India should be gradually withdrawn". *The Concept of Empire*, ed. G. Bennett (1953), p. 70. In 1883 Macaulay called the day when British-Western civilization would have led India to independence "the proudest day in English history", *op. cit.*, p. 74. Cf. also George D. Bearce, *British Attitudes towards India 1784–1858* (1961).

2. Cf. *The Expansion of England* (1883), p. 227.

3. "It is vain, however, to pretend that India can be granted self-government on the colonial lines. It would mean ruin to India and treason to our trust. The Empire cannot apply the same policy to the Colonies and to India. ... Were India to be lost, she herself would reel back into chaos, and the British Empire, at any rate in Asia, would perish. ..." *Concept of Empire*, pp. 355 f.

4. J. D. B. Miller, *Richard Jebb and the Problem of Empire* (1956), p. 33.

5. M. N. Das, *India under Morley and Minto. Politics behind Revolution, Repression and Reforms* (1964), particularly ch. VI. For this and the following, cf. Dietmar Rothermund, *Die politische Willensbildung in Indien, 1900–1960* (1965), p. 50.

6. E.g. letter to Morley on 28 May 1906, Das, p. 66. Before the Imperial Legislative Council on 25 January 1910 he said: "We have distinctly maintained that the representative Government in its western sense is totally inapplicable to the Indian Empire and would be uncongenial to the traditions

of Eastern peoples—that Indian conditions do not admit of popular representation—that the safety and welfare of this country must depend on the supremacy of British Administration. . . . We have aimed at the reform and enlargement of our Councils but not at the creation of parliaments." Quoted in Marquess of Zetland, "Self-Government for India", *Foreign Affairs*, October 1930, p. 2.

7. Above all Morley's well-known statement in the House of Lords on 17 December 1908: "If I were attempting to set up a Parliamentary system in India, or if it could be said that this chapter of reforms led directly or necessarily up to the establishment of a Parliamentary system in India, I, for one, would have nothing at all to do with it. . . . If my existence, either officially or corporeally were prolonged twenty times longer than either of them is likely to be, a Parliamentary system in India is not the goal to which I for one moment would aspire." *House of Lords*, CXCVIII, 1983 f., quoted in *The Evolution of India and Pakistan 1858–1947*, ed. C. H. Philips (1962), p. 85.

8. For this and the following see the excellent article by S. R. Mehrotra, "The Politics behind the Montagu Declaration of 1917", in *Politics and Society and India*, ed. C. H. Philips (1963), p. 72. Also the interesting letter quoted by Das, pp. 66 f., and the remark to Minto: "As times go on, Indian discontent or alienation . . . will be sure to run into the same channels of violence as Italian, Russian, Irish discontent." 8 July 1919, Das, p. 21.

9. *Evolution of India*, p. 162.
10. Mehrotra, p. 77.
11. *House of Lords*, 24 June 1912, p. 156.
12. *House of Lords*, 29 July 1912, p. 745.
13. Milner, *The Nation and the Empire*, 1913. Also Lord Bryce, the famous author of *The American Commonwealth*, who thought, in 1914: "Everyone admits in his heart that it is impossible to ignore the differences which make one group of races unfit for the institutions which have given energy and contentment to another more favourably placed," quoted in Hugh Tinker, *Ballot Box and Bayonnet* (1964), pp. 10 f.
14. Cf. the evidence in Mehrotra, p. 77.
15. Memorandum quoted by Mehrotra, p. 76.
16. "S. R. Mehrotra, Imperial Federation and India 1868–1917", *Journal of Commonwealth Political Studies*, I (1961), 38.
17. Presidential address by Sinha at the Bombay congress in 1915, quoted in Mehrotra, "The Politics . . .", p. 81.
18. Text in *Evolution of India*, pp. 171 f. The English king is requested "to issue a proclamation that it is the aim and intention of British policy to confer self-government on India at an early date".
19. Quoted in Smith, *Oxford History of India* (1961), p. 780.
20. Again I follow Mehrotra, pp. 82 f.
21. Chamberlain to Chelmsford in spring 1917: the aim of British policy must be "free institutions with a view to ultimate self-government within the Empire", quoted in Sir Charles Petrie, *The Life and Letters of the Right Honorable Sir Austin Chamberlain*, II (1940), 76.
22. Among others, *Evolution of India*, p. 264.
23. The 1916 Hindu-Muslim draft constitution did not provide for responsible government but contemplated a different kind of relationship between the legislative and the executive council; Rothermund, p. 75.
24. Ronaldshay (later Lord Zetland), *The Life of Lord Curzon*, III (1928), 164. Mehrotra, p. 95. It is not certain what Curzon expected from this change and on what ideas and concepts he was working.

25. "If you analyse the term 'full Dominion Self-Government', you will see that it is of somewhat wider extent, conveying that not only will the Executive be responsible to the Legislature, but the Legislature will in itself have the full powers which are typical of the modern Dominion. I say there is some difference of substance, because responsible government is not necessarily incompatible with a Legislature with limited or restricted powers. It may be that full Dominion self-government is the logical outcome of responsible government, but it is a further and a final step." *Speeches and Documents on the Indian Constitution 1921–1947*, ed. Gwyer and Appadorai, I (1957), 220.

26. *House of Commons*, 6 August 1918, CIX, 1147.

27. "Report on Indian Constitutional Reforms", *Commonwealth Documents*, Vol. 9109 (1918), Art. 180.

28. In the "Letters to the people of India on Responsible Government" in 1918 Curzon described the 1917 declaration as "in substance the most important ever made on the place of India in the British Commonwealth. . . . The Pronouncement is binding on the Secretary of State in all its terms", p. 13.

29. Cf. *Speeches and Documents on the Indian Constitution 1921–1947*, Gwyer and Appadorai, I, 1.

30. E.g. Lord Meston, "Quo Vadis in India", *Contemporary Review*, October 1920. Valentine Chirol, *India Old and New* (1921).

31. *The Indian Annual Register*, ed. Mitra (1919), p. 16. Sydenham had rejected the reforms of 1919 while Foreign Minister Lord Curzon defended them. *House of Lords*, 12 December 1919, XXXVII, 993 f.

32. Hancock, *Survey of Commonwealth Affairs*, I, 170 f. Robert Blake, *The Unknown Prime Minister. The Life and Times of Andrew Bonar Law 1858–1923* (1952), p. 421.

33. *The Crumbling of an Empire. September 1916–March 1922, a Chronological Statement of the Decline of British Authority in India* (1922).

34. *House of Lords*, 7 February 1922, XLIX, 33.

35. *The Lost Dominion* (1924). A. Carthill is a pseudonym for Bennett Christian Huntington Calcraft Kennedy.

36. *House of Lords*, 7 July 1925, LXI, 1092.

37. Birkenhead, reports his son, was critical of the Montagu-Chelmsford reforms from the start, for India was "not capable of Dominion Status for centuries. . . . All the conferences in the world cannot bridge the unbridgeable", p. 506 f. "It does not do to take these people too seriously; indeed I find it increasingly difficult to take any Indian politician very seriously." *The Life of F. E. Smith, First Earl of Birkenhead*, by his son (1960), p. 149.

38. *Retrospect. The Memoirs of Viscount Simon* (1952), pp. 144 f.

39. Birkenhead, p. 512.

40. Even a liberal Indian politician like Sapru had to dissociate himself from this on 27 December 1927: ". . . if our patriotism is a prejudice and if the patriotism of the seven Members of Parliament is to be treated as impartial justice, then we Liberals feel justified in telling the Government here and in England: You may do anything you like in the assertion of your rights as supreme power, but we are not going to acquiesce in this method of dealing with us. Neither our self-respect nor our sense of duty to our country can permit us to go near the Commission." Gwyer and Appadorai, p. 210.

41. Text in Gwyer-Appadorai, pp. 225 f., or *Evolution of India*, p. 286. The origin of the declaration is still not certain. It was based on talks between MacDonald, Benn and Irwin, while Baldwin is said to have given the assent

of the Conservative party on condition that Simon was asked first. He was not asked, however. Cf. Simon, *Retrospect*, pp. 150 f.

42. Irwin says, in retrospect: "Indian opinion professed itself greatly outraged by what in several quarters was described as a denial of India's right to Self-Government, and the reaction in nationalist circles was sharp. While there were of course many responsible and wise persons in India, as in this country, who did not at all like the straightforward declaration I proposed to make, to me and, I think, to most people in India the case for it appeared overwhelming, since the dilemma seemed inescapable. It was surely hard to say what the 'progressive realisation of responsible government' could mean except the ultimate achievement of status equivalent to that enjoyed by the Dominions, to which they had moved by precisely the same road as that now marked out for India. Moreover the Governor-General's Instrument of Instructions used a language that could hardly bear any other interpretation. 'For above all things it is Our will and pleasure that the plans laid by Our Parliament for the progressive realisation of responsible government in British India as an integral part of Our Empire may come to fruition to the end that British India may attain its due place among Our Dominions.' But if the words 'progressive realisation of responsible government' could or did mean something less than this, then it was not strange that Indians should recoil from the idea of second-class membership in a graded Imperial society, and turn their thoughts, as they were beginning to do, in the direction of independence. To anyone at the Indian end this seemed the great danger which had to be forestalled, and which indeed could probably be forestalled without too much difficulty, if quite groundless suspicions and misunderstandings could be removed." Lord Halifax, *Fullness of Days* (1957), p. 120.

43. Gopal quoted a remark of Gandhi's: "I can wait for the Dominion Status constitution, if I can get the real Dominion Status in action, if today there is a real change of heart". *The Viceroyalty of Lord Irwin 1926–1931*, pp. 51, 110.

44. Samuel Hoare, *Nine Troubled Years* (1954), p. 90.

45. There is an amusing report by Lord Stamfordham, the political confidant of King George V. On 2 September 1929 he wrote to the viceroy: "Oh! what a hubbub about your statement about 'equal Dominion status' and how much talk in both Houses of Parliament! I listened to Reading, Birkenhead, Parmoor and Passfield. Poor old Parmoor—he got so mixed, referred to Ramsay MacDonald as 'Lord MacDonald', and more than once spoke of 'Her Majesty's Government', which rather touched me, as I fancied his mind was like mine, often wandering back to the much despised Victorian period!" Harold Nicolson, *King George the Fifth* (1952), p. 505.

46. My student, Dietrich Klauthke, is preparing a thesis on British India policy and the parties between 1927 and 1947. I am indebted to him for much information.

47. Samuel Hoare, *Nine Troubled Years*, pp. 45 f.

48. John Evelyn Wrench, *Geoffrey Dawson and Our Times* (1955), pp. 266 f. *History of the Times*, II (1952), 872 f.

49. Butler, *Lord Lothian*, pp. 179 f.

50. In a conversation with Thomas Jones, in *A Diary with Letters 1931–1950* (1954), p. 29. In a speech to the Conservative party on 4 December 1934 Baldwin said: "You must remember that in many parts of the Empire there is sympathy with the ideals of India. . . . It is my considered judgment in all the changes and chances of this wide world to-day that you have a good chance of keeping the whole of that sub-continent of India in the Empire for ever. You have a chance, and a good chance, but I say to you that if you refuse

her this opportunity, if you refuse it to her, you will infallibly lose India, whatever you do, before two generations are passed. That, to my mind, is the choice. Believing that, I can do no other than give you the advice I do . . . so convinced am I that I am right in this matter—as convinced as some of my friends are that I am wrong—that if I stood alone I would put these views before you. . . ." He reviewed the whole Indian question again over the radio on 5 February 1935, and reminded the critics of the bill that if they argued, as they did, that parliamentary government was not suited to the East, then the conclusion must be "that for a hundred years we have been on the wrong track in our Indian policy; that we should now reverse our steps and set out again in the direction of autocracy and despotism. Those who use this argument cannot pretend that they stand by the pledge we gave in the Preamble of the Act of 1919. . . . In accordance with our historic policy and with the object of keeping our Empire together, we have given India certain pledges. Those pledges must be fulfilled." From A. W. Baldwin, *My Father: The True Story*, pp. 176 f. Similarly the Marquess of Zetland (governor of Bengal 1917–1922 and biographer of Curzon) wrote in "Self-government for India", *Foreign Affairs*, October 1930: "But whether the extreme nationalist come to London in October or whether they do not, matters cannot rest where they are. Great Britain is pledged to go forward with an experiment fraught with momentous consequences, whether for better or for worse, to peoples numbering not less than one fifth of the human race; and she cannot now withdraw from the furrow which she has set forth to plough", p. 12. See also, "After the India Conference", *Foreign Affairs*, April 1932.

51. "The Indian Tragedy", 19 April 1930. Gandhi "is a supreme symbol of the relentless urge for unimpeded self-expression, which is the strength and force of awakened India". The Indians were expecting a rapid fulfilment of the 1917 promise and were rightly suspicious.

52. "The proceedings of the Round-Table Conference have awakened people in this country to the dominating fact that, with whatever transitional safeguards you please, real responsibility in the Central Government, as in the Provinces, is demanded by all shades of 'moderate' Indian opinion, without distinction of race, faith or caste, and is also supported by the rulers of the States. It is a demand which the great majority of British citizens both in this country and in the Commonwealth as a whole are disposed to recognise as just in principle. We have no interest, moral or material, in India which would warrantably lead us to contemplate, as an alternative to co-operating in the realization of that demand, the intolerable prospect of repression and revolution which refusal of it would inevitably entail. With all respect to Mr. Churchill, who has suggested that 'it is not yet too late. . . . The key to Indian government is still in our hands', we venture to assert that there can be no going back. This country has heard the case stated in the capital of the Empire by India's spokesmen, and the opinion of the country has conceded the essential principles for which they asked. The rest is for the lawyer or the expert. The Indian Empire is ended, the day of the Indian Federated Commonwealth has begun. It is useless for Mr. Churchill to moan for the past." "The Conference of the Future", 24 January 1931, No. 4561, p. 155.

53. Speech broadcast on 1 January 1935 in *Evolution in India*, p. 316.

54. Typically British is Philip Kerr's letter to Dawson: "To take responsibility of government which converts every Radical into more or less a Conservative. . .". Butler, *Lord Lothian*, p. 182.

55. *House of Commons*, 7 November 1929, CCXXXI, 1312 f.

56. *House of Commons*, 11 February 1935, CCXCVII, 1719–22. Similarly

Amery wrote: "Undoubtedly the conditions of India are not such as to make equal status possible to-day . . ." but ". . . recognition of equality in co-operation within the British Empire as between Asia and Europe may mean a great deal not only to the British Empire, but to the world". 5 June 1935, quoted in *My Political Life*, III, 108.

57. In a speech before the European Association in Calcutta he said: "However emphatically we condemn the civil disobedience movement . . . whatever powers we find necessary to take to combat it, so long as it persists we should . . . make a profound mistake if we under-estimate the genuine and powerful feeling of nationalism that is to-day animating much of Indian thought. And for this no simple, complete, or permanent cure has ever been or can be found in strong action by the Government." From *The Times*, weekly ed., 1 January 1931.

58. E.g. Lord Meston, *Nationhood for India* (lectures in the U.S.) (1931).

59. E.g. the report from India in *Round Table*, XII (1922).

60. Rothermund, p. 157.

61. Hoare, *Nine Troubled Years*, p. 87; Nicolson, *King George the Fifth*, p. 509.

62. Das, *India under Morley and Minto*, p. 70.

63. P. vi.

64. A memorandum of the European Association states, among other things, that the ministry for the police must not be transferred to Indians until "local European opinion considers this safe" [!], p. 249.

65. "If these 300 millions had been really determined against British rule, they would never have accepted it," p. 259.

66. To treat India the same as the white dominions would be "absurd, and nothing of the kind has ever promised. . . . Dominions are bound by those loyalties of blood, language, religion, history and literature to the mother country", pp. 283, 285.

67. P. 319.

68. Cf. also the reader's letter of another retired ICS man in reply to the article "The Indian Tragedy" in the *Spectator* (cf. note 51, pp. 68–69), 3 May 1930. The younger and more active members of the Indian Civil Service were no doubt more progressive. Of their position, difficulties and attitude there is an excellent description in Philip Woodruff (Philip Mason), *The Men who Ruled India*, II, 220, 244 f.

69. Birkenhead, p. 518. Lord Winterton (conservative under-secretary of state for India 1922–1929) took a similar position in a letter to *The Times*: it was important to distinguish between responsible government and dominion status, as Southern Rhodesia had shown: "As a result of the Imperial Conference of 1926 Dominion-status has attained a very special meaning which is inapplicable in all particulars to India. Dominion-status obviously confers on the countries within the Empire which possess it both the right and the obligation to undertake their own military defence. Should India, as a result of the amendment of the Government of India Act receive Dominion Status, it will involve the withdrawal of the British Army; if, on the other hand, Parliament decided to grant a further or full measure of Responsible Government, the British Army can remain in India. . . . Before the advent of the present administration the phrase 'Dominion Status' was carefully avoided when reiterated promises were made that the British goal in India was Responsible Government within the Empire." *The Times*, weekly ed., 24 July 1930, p. 120.

70. *House of Lords*, 5 November 1929, LXXV, 404 f.

71. "To me it has been a matter of deep regret that the term has ever

been used in relation to India.... There is no accepted definition of Dominion status.... I should have preferred to put it in this way, that the goal that we have in view as the ultimate state of things in India is one by which all Indian affairs should, so far as is compatible with the continuance of British India as part of the British Empire, be managed by Indians in India with the very minimum of interference by Parliament here.... The existence of Indian States and Indian Princes creates a state of affairs so entirely different from that which obtains in any part of the Empire." *House of Lords,* 5 November 1929, LXXV, 410.

72. "Take the hackneyed phrase 'Dominion Status'. During the Great War India obtained Dominion-status so far as rank, honour and ceremony were concerned. The representatives of the Government of India attended the Imperial War Conference, they attended the Peace Conference, and they are included among the British Dominions who serve on the League of Nations ... but I did not contemplate India having the same constitutional rights and system as Canada in any period which we could foresee. ... I do not admit that the sense in which the expression 'Dominion Status' was used 10 or 15 years ago implied Dominion structure or Dominion rights ... I do not admit that it means structure or rights. The word 'status' means rank—not necessarily rights or structure." *House of Commons,* 3 December 1931, CCLX, 1287–88.

73. "... the moment you set up responsible Government at the Centre, you begin to make effective the transfer of sovereignty." *House of Commons,* 11 February 1935, CCXCVII, 1655.

74. *India Speeches* (1931), p. 40.
75. *House of Commons, op. cit.,* p. 1653.
76. *House of Commons, op. cit.,* p. 1651.
77. *India Speeches,* pp. 87 f.
78. *Op. cit.,* p. 47.
79. *Annual Conference* (1918), pp. 64 f.
80. "The conference therefore demands the full and frank application of this principle [democratic self-determination] in the reorganisation of the Government of India that is now in progress, in such a way as to satisfy all the legitimate aspirations of the Indian people; it asks that corresponding measures may be taken in Burma, Ceylon, and other parts of the British Empire in which Self-Government is demanded. It emphatically protests against the militarist and repressive methods adopted by the present British Government, and expresses its sympathy with the peoples now held in subjection. It denies the right of any Government to govern a country against the will of the majority; and while expressing the hope that all the peoples of the British Empire will prefer to remain as parts of that Empire so soon as their aspirations have been dealt with in a thoroughly conciliatory manner by the granting of adequate measures of autonomy, it declares that the final decision must rest with those people themselves." *Annual Conference* (1920), p. 156.

81. E.g. *Annual Conference* (1927): "We reaffirm the right of the Indian peoples to full self-government and self-determination, and therefore the policy of the British Government should be one of continuous cooperation with the Indian people, with the object of establishing India, in the earliest moment, and by her consent, as an equal partner with the other members of the British Commonwealth of Nations." Cf. also the party programme, *Labour and the Nation* (1928), pp. 157 f.

82. *House of Commons,* 5 December 1919, CXXII, 817.
83. *House of Commons,* 22 May 1919, CXVI, 671. *Annual Conference* (1920), pp. 157 f.

84. "I would dearly like to be able to withdraw the English tissue from Bengal and give the Swarajists Swaraj there just for the fun of seeing results." Priests (Gandhi) and lawyers could not rule! Letter to H. G. Wells on 25 April 1925, *Letters and Selected Writings*, ed. M. Olivier (1948), p. 157.

85. Letter to Holmes on 1 July 1924, from *Holmes-Laski Letters, 1916–1935*, ed. M. de Wolfe Howe (1953), p. 628.

86. Secretary of State Wedgwood Benn: "We are entering upon a new era, we are attempting to enter what may be the greatest chapter in the history of the British Commonwealth, namely a free and voluntary association of a great self-respecting nation in partnership with the British Commonwealth for the promotion of the good of the world. We have tried to prove the sincerity of our faith when we say that we desire to see India reach Dominion Status . . .". *House of Commons*, 18 December 1929, CCXXXIII, 1555–58.

87. Mrs. Besant protested that the 1919 reforms did not provide for responsible government. Philip Snowden (minister of finance, 1924) was speaking of hunger in Eastern Europe, she said, not of India: ". . . give them freedom and their people would not starve", *Annual Conference* (1920), p. 152.

88. In June 1917 he already wrote to an Indian nationalist: "The British Government should lay it down that Colonial Home Rule is the end they have in view, though it may take even fifty years to complete the process. They should lay down the stages and the dates. . . ." Josiah C. Wedgwood, *Memoirs of a Fighting Life* (1940), p. 130.

89. The *Socialist Review* described the Labour government's India policy as "the one great failure of the Labour government". Richard W. Lyman, *The First Labour Government*, (1924; n.d. [1957]), p. 215. A rather Communist note is sounded in John Beauchamp, *British Imperialism in India*, prepared by the Labour Research Department (1934), which describes Gandhi and the other nationalist leaders as collaborators with the bourgeoisie and traitors.

90. *Annual Conference* (1930), p. 216.

91. *Op. cit.*, p. 218.

92. *Holmes-Laski Letters*, pp. 1261, 1264. See also Beatrice Webb, *Diaries 1924–1932*, ed. M. Cole (1956), p. 266: "For Dominion Status has been promised to India over and over again during and after the Great War. But in how near or how distant a future? Next year or fifty years hence? And how can any one kind of uniform status be given to the whole of India, broken up as it is, into native states and British India, with different races, languages, castes and religions. The problem seems to be to put the several ruling native cliques and communities into the position of refusing instead of claiming powers from the British Government; to make those who claim to govern India on behalf of the people of India distrust their capacity to combine in order to do it so as to delay Self-Government until some sort of common will has been evolved".

93. Cf. *Annual Conference* (1932), p. 95; Landsbury's resolution, pp. 178 f.; and *Annual Conference* (1933), p. 79. But at the party congress of 1934, when Krishna Menon demanded a resolution in favour of "immediate" responsible government and a constitutional assembly, Henderson decidedly refused it and pointed to the 1933 resolution. The Labour attitude is very clear in the article "The Future of India" by Attlee in *New Statesman and Nation*, 25 March 1933, pp. 377 f., and "The India Report", *op. cit.*, 24 November 1934, pp. 744 f. Similarly Jones Morgan M.P., *Whither India?*, Labour party pamphlet, February 1935.

94. House of Commons, 6 February 1935, CCXCVII, 1167 f.; 4 June 1935, CCCII, 1824 f.
95. P. 245 f. Also *As It Happened* (1954), pp. 64 f.
96. Cf. the very remarkable correspondence between Lord Lothian and Nehru, 31 December 1935 to 17 January 1936, in *Nehru, a Bunch of Old Letters* (1958), pp. 217 ff.
97. Besides what we have mentioned earlier, it is worth noting R. Coupland, who described the 1935 Indian constitution as the "penultimate stage" before full dominion status and drew a parallel with Canada in 1868 and South Africa in 1910, pp. 115, 157. India as a dominion "would mean that its circumference has been extended beyond the world of European race and civilization to embrace a part of Asia—that all the gulf which nature set between them and all that has been done to deepen it has not prevented their final in a common cause". *The Empire in These Days* (1935), p. 135. Also, "The British Empire", *Royal Institute of International Affairs* (1937), p. 132.

TRUSTEESHIP AND SELF-GOVERNMENT IN THE COLONIES

1. *House of Commons*, CXVIII, 2174.
2. Ernest Barker, *The Ideas and Ideals of the British Empire* (1941), pp. 64 f. Also a detailed study by Robert Schneebeli, *Die Zweifache Treuhänderschaft. Eine Studie über die Konzeption der britischen Kolonialherrschaft* (1958), 25 f.
3. Barker, *op. cit.*, pp. 66.
4. Excerpts printed in *The Concept of Empire, Burke to Attlee, 1774–1947*, ed. George Bennett (1953), pp. 210–13.
5. Hobson, *Imperialism* (ed. 1905), pp. 210–13.
6. Amery in the aforementioned speech in the House of Commons on 30 July 1919. Zimmern, *Third Empire*, p. 89. A further example: "The standards of administration so imposed are no higher than those which His Majesty's Government have imposed upon themselves. . . . The declarations of HMG have made it clear that the fundamental principles of policy laid down for both the British dependencies and the mandated area are the same." "Report of the Commission on Closer Union in Eastern and Central Africa", *Commonwealth Documents* 3234 (1929), pp. 34 f.
7. Lugard summarizing this Lugard cf., "The White Man's Task in Tropical Africa", *Foreign Affairs*, October 1926. For Lugard, cf. Schneebeli, *op. cit.*, and the large-scale biography by Margery Perham, *Lugard*, 2 vols. (1960).
8. Lugard, *op. cit.*, pp. 60 f.
9. *Op. cit.*, p. 60.
10. E.g. Sir Edward Grigg (later Lord Altringham), governor of Kenya 1925–1931: ". . . the supply of raw materials is even now a subject of acute anxiety to many civilised Powers. The growth of markets is equally important to all". If there was no market or raw material prices rose, real wages would fall. So "where a native people cannot clear the jungle and develop the talent confided to them in the wealth of their soil, the task shall be undertaken for them by the civilised Powers". An area that had been opened up must not become jungle again. These were the limits of the principle of self-determination. It could not be applied everywhere. "These are peoples to whom self-determination is nothing better than a means of rapid suicide." *The Greatest Experiment in History* (1924), pp. 196 f.

11. "Evolution and progress are a law of nature, and since the necessities of his existence compel civilised men to share the produce of the tropics, let us see to it that the progress is accompanied by as much benefit and as little injury to the natives as may be." *Op. cit.*, p. 91.

12. *Op. cit.*, p. 617.

13. In this context we may note the remarkably realistic views of J. H. Oldham, for many years very active as secretary of the International Council of Missionaires: "Two cautions are perhaps in place if in the discussion of the principle of trusteeship exaggeration and unreality are to be avoided. The first is that it must not be supposed that the government of subject peoples is undertaken, or in existing circumstances can be expected to be undertaken, from purely philanthropic motives. There is no such thing as a missionary nation. Individuals may become missionaries, but the day is far distant when this may be expected from a nation. The European Powers are in Africa primarily from economic, not humanitarian motives. Their object is the development of their own industries and trade, but the benefit may be reciprocal. All that need be insisted on is that the advantage should always be mutual; and that if and when interests conflict, the issue should be decided not through the arbitrary and selfish exercise of superior power, but on the basis of impartial justice. And this, as we have seen, is not the quixotic demand of an impossible idealism, but the declared aim of responsible statesmen. It is a policy to which the governments of the leading Powers are publicly committed." *Christianity and the Race Problem* (1924), quoted in Lord Altringham, *Kenya's Opportunity* (1955), p. 37.

14. *The Future of Colonial Peoples* (1943), p. 16.

15. *Pan-Africanism or Communism?* (1956), p. 228.

16. Quoted in Martin Wight, *The Development of the Legislative Council (1606–1945)* (1946), p. 146.

17. *Ideas and Ideals, op. cit.*, p. 66.

18. *House of Commons*, CXVIII, 2176.

19. *Appendices to the Summary of Proceedings*, Ottawa, 1927, p. 92.

20. *House of Commons*, 7 December 1938, CCCXLII, 1246 f. Similarly in Oxford in 1939 before 180 colonial officials, quoted in Charles R. Buxton, "The Government of Crown Colonies", *Political Quarterly* (1939), p. 516.

21. James T. Shotwell, *At the Peace Conference* (1937), p. 171.

22. "From Empire to Commonwealth", *Foreign Affairs*, II (1922), 97.

23. 1938 ed., p. 1639.

24. "The Case for Imperialism", *Spectator*, 13 October 1939, p. 497.

25. 10 May 1927, quoted in Wight, *The Development of the Legislative Council*, p. 2.

26. Cf. the relatively legalistic book by Wight.

27. The former governor of Jamaica, Olivier, describes the difficulties of this situation: "What is the use, they protest, of our coming here to talk and to urge what we, as representative men of the Colony, know to be expedient and just for our constituents when the Governor has made up his mind beforehand or the Colonial Office has given him his orders? The official automatons of the mechanical majority do not even take the trouble to attend to what we are saying but sits silent, bored and yawning till the times comes for them to vote, not as they may think, but as they are bid." Lord Olivier, "Crown Government", *The Crown Colonist*, April 1932, p. 205.

28. *Letters to the People of India on Responsible Government* (1918), pp. 18, 23, 32.

29. Wight, *op. cit.*, pp. 79, 92.
30. "Report of the special commission on the Constitution," *Commonwealth Documents* 3131 (1928). Also Lennox A. Mills, *Ceylon under British Rule 1795–1932* (1933). S. Namasivayan, *The Legislatures of Ceylon 1928–1948* (1951).
31. *Op. cit.*, p. 18.
32. *Op. cit.*, p. 21.
33. *Op. cit.*, p. 32.
34. A general work is: "Problems of Parliamentary Government in Colonies", special number of *Parliamentary Affairs*, Vol. VI, No. 1 (1952–53), pp. 55 f. Wight, *op. cit.*, pp. 87 f.
35. Great Britain also had a special representation of the Europeans, but in the form of corporate representation. "Interests", such as banks, trade, shipping, etc., were reserved to unofficial mandate; this was so to a relatively small degree in India, particularly so in Hong Kong and the Straits Settlements, Nigeria in 1922, Gold Coast in 1925. It disappeared gradually in the upper "grades" of self-government; Wight, *op. cit.*, pp. 85 f.
36. Among others he writes: "In surveying the situation in Ceylon we have come hesitatingly to the conclusion that communal representation is, as it were, a cancer on the body politic, eating deeper and deeper into the vital energies of the people, breeding self-interest, suspicion and animosity, poisoning the new growth of political consciousness, and effectively preventing the development of a national or corporate spirit", p. 39.
37. Lead article in *The Times*, weekly ed., 19 December 1929.
38. *Round Table*, XVIII (1928), 711 f.
39. "The Ceylon Report", Round Table, XIX (1928).
40. *Manchester Guardian*, 23 February 1928: "There would appear to be no place in our Eastern possessions where the experiment of responsible Government may be tried with greater safety than in Ceylon."
41. Colonel Wedgwood spoke of "the most courageous Report which I should never had dreamed of expecting from a Conservative Government. That Report shows that England is acting honestly when she says she is anxious to put subject races in a position to govern themselves, and that we really do desire to keep all of these free peoples within our Empire". *House of Commons*, 30 April 1929, CCXXVII, 1475.
42. *Op. cit.*, p. 45.
43. *Op. cit.*, p. 95.

COLONIAL DEVELOPMENT, 1929–1940

1. This is made clear in the important book *The British Empire* (RIIA, 1937), whose economic section deals almost exclusively with the dominions.
2. André Siegfried, *Die englische Krise* (1931), is still notable.
3. Lord Lugard, "The Crown Colonies and the British War Debt", *Contemporary Review*, 1920. Cf. also Schneebeli, pp. 117 f.
4. Sir George V. Fiddes, *The Dominions and Colonial Offices* (1926), p. 69. In 1926 grants-in-aid only amounted to £684,000 (Cyprus, St. Helena, Somaliland, Nyasaland, Tanganyika and Northern Rhodesia).
5. Cf. Amery's report in Parliament, 1929, *House of Commons*, CCXXVII, 1409.
6. F. M. Bourret, *Ghana. The Road to Independence 1919–1957* (1960), pp. 22 f.

NOTES

7. W. M. Macmillan stresses this in *African Emergent* (1949), p. 208.
8. F. V. Meyer, *Britain's Colonies in World Trade* (1948), p. 126.
9. Bourret, *op. cit.*, p. 66. "Report of the Commission on the Marketing of West African Cocoa", September 1938, *Commonwealth Documents* 5845 (1938).
10. "The Future of Colonial Trusteeship", *Round Table*, September 1934, reprinted in *Empire in These Days* (1935), pp. 256 f.
11. *Questions of the Hour*, 2nd ed. (1925), p. 181.
12. "Report of the East Africa Commission", *Commonwealth Documents* 2387 (1925).
13. *Op. cit.*, p. 182.
14. *Op. cit.*, pp. 190 f. Also Linfield, "Empire Development", *Contemporary Review*, March 1926, p. 321.
15. Roland Olivier and I. D. Fage, *A Short History of Africa* (1962), p. 211.
16. *The Times*, weekly ed., 25 April 1929; cf. also *Gleanings and Memoranda* (organ of the Conservative party), June 1929.
17. *Opt. cit.*, 16 May 1929.
18. *Op. cit.*, 16 May 1929 and 23 May 1929.
19. "Colonial Development", *Commonwealth Documents* 3357, House of Commons 12 July 1929, CCXXIX, 1255.
20. Under-secretary of State Lunn said on 17 July: "It will no doubt mean a good deal in prosperity to some industries at home", CCXXX, 475.
21. This is also emphasized by Charles Jeffries, *The Colonial Office* (1950), p. 150.
22. *House of Commons*, 19 July 1929, CCXXX, 871 f. Similarly in the *Manchester Guardian*, 13 July 1929.
23. *Op. cit.*, p. 706.
24. Macmillan quotes a report by the Colonial Development Committee in 1934, *op. cit.*, p. 209. Similarly Sir Bernard Bourdillon, "Colonial Development and Welfare", *International Affairs*, XX (1944). Bourdillon mentions the position taken by the Committee on National Expenditure in 1931, which stressed the need to create employment and is said to have had an influence on the policy of the Colonial Development Fund. Under the 1929 act 8 million pounds were spent, of which 3.2 million were in loans and 5.6 million in grants. Thirty percent went in transport, 10 percent in irrigation, 16 percent in public health. Creech-Jones in *Fabian Colonial Essays* (1945), pp. 72 f.
25. Macmillan, *op. cit.*, p. 210.
26. 26 April 1930, p. 939.
27. *House of Commons*, 17 July 1929, CCXXX, 491.
28. Perham, *Lugard*, *op. cit.*, II, 662.
29. Sir Charles Jeffries, *The Colonial Office* (1956), pp. 42, 110 f. Also Fiddes, "Dominions and Colonial Offices", *op. cit.*; Sir Cosmo Parkinson, *The Colonial Office from Within 1909–1945* (1945); Amery, *My Political Life*, II, 340; Kenneth Robinson, *The Dilemmas of Trusteeship* (1965), pp. 29 ff.
30. "Education Policy in British Tropical Africa", *Commonwealth Documents* 2374 (1925); Perham, *Lugard*, II, 657 f.
31. J. I. Roper, *Labour Problems in West Africa* (1958), p. 59.
32. Fiddes, *op. cit.*, p. 33.
33. Butler, *Lord Lothian*, p. 138, Survey, preface.
34. *Contemporary Review*, CLV, (1939), 140.
35. "The Hailey Survey", *Africa*, January 1939, pp. 6 f.
36. P. xxiv.

37. Lord Hailey, "Some Problems Dealt With in the *African Survey*", *International Affairs*, March 1939, p. 201.
38. Told to the author verbally.
39. Annette Baker Fox, *Freedom and Welfare in the Caribbean, a Colonial Dilemma* (1949).
40. "Imperial Responsibilities in the West Indies, by a Correspondent", *Round Table* (1938), p. 643.
41. *House of Commons*, 14 June 1938, CCCXXXVII, 79 f.; 23 February 1939, CCCXLIV, 635 f.
42. "The Truth about the West Indies", *Nineteenth Century*, CXXIV (1938). "The Scandal of West Indian Labour Conditions", *Contemporary Review*, CLIII (1938).
43. "Imperial Responsibilities", *op. cit.* The biographer Stafford Cripps tells how during a visit to Jamaica in summer 1938 he learnt of the critical situation in the West Indies. Colin Crooke, *The Life of Richard Stafford Cripps* (1957), pp. 200 f.
44. *Op. cit.*, pp. 170–72.
45. *Op. cit.*, p. 172.
46. Preface to the 1938 ed., p. 6.
47. *Op. cit.*, p. 13.
48. "West Indian Royal Commission Report", *Commonwealth Documents* 6607 (1945). In case it provided material for German war propaganda the report was not published until 1945.
49. "West India Royal Commission 1938–1939. Recommendations", *Commonwealth Documents* 6174 (1940), p. 25.
50. *Commonwealth Documents* 6607, p. 249.
51. "Africa's Need", *Economist*, 12 November 1938, pp. 312 f.
52. "Statement of Policy on Colonial Development and Welfare", *Commonwealth Documents* 6175, February 1940, p. 4.
53. *House of Commons*, 21 May 1940, CCCLXI, 47.
54. "Statement of Policy", p. 4.
55. *Op. cit.*, p. 45. In the name of the government Lord Lloyd declared in the House of Lords on 2 July: "The Bill embodies new principles which constitute a landmark in colonial policy. . . . I am bound personally to say that I have always felt that there was a degree of truth in the reproaches directed at us by our rivals that, whilst we controlled so vast a colonial empire, we did mightily little to develop it". *House of Lords*, CXVI, 725 f.

THE COLONIAL DOCTRINE OF THE LABOUR PARTY

1. *Fabianism and the Empire*; cf. Bernard Semmel, *Imperialism and Social Reform* (1960). Also, Tingfu Tsiang, *Labour and Empire* (1923).
2. In August 1917 the Labour party executive still supported the idea of an international administration, while the Independent Labour party was against it. The Inter-Allied Labour and Socialist Conference in London in February 1918 took up the ideas of the ILP. Henry R. Winkler, cf. *The League of Nations Movement in Great Britain 1914–1919* (1952), pp. 200 f. Leonard Woolf also later rejected the idea of international administration under the influence of Lord Lugard; cf. Perham, *Lugard*, II, 643.
3. E.g. the report *Colonial Empire* (1933), p. 6.
4. Party programme, *Labour and the New Social Order*, quoted in Rita Hinden, *Empire and After* (1949), p. 115.

NOTES

5. Woolf's essay "Economic Imperialism" (1920) is a summary of *Empire and Commerce in Africa*.
6. *Op. cit.*, p. 352.
7. "It is true that for Europe to withdraw to-day from Africa and to leave these non-adult races to manage their own affairs is impossible . . . no change for the better would be brought about by the European State withdrawing its control", p. 357.
8. *Op. cit.*, p. 364.
9. *Op. cit.*, p. 367.
10. *Annual Report* (1920), p. 113.
11. E.g. *Annual Report* (1923), pp. 239 f.
12. "They had either to be whole-hearted Imperialist or else give the whole thing up." *Annual Report* (1926), p. 253.
13. "The job of their Party for the moment was to watch over the interests of their fellow subjects in all parts of the Empire", said Clyness, M.P., in the name of the party executive. *Annual Report* (1925), p. 321; and (1939), p. 312.
14. Despatch to High Commissioner Allenby, 7 October 1925, quoted in Monroe, *Middle East*, p. 142. More details on MacDonald in B. J. Sacks, *J. Ramsay MacDonald in Thought and Action* (1952), pp. 444 f.
15. Cf. Robert G. Gregory, *Sidney Webb and East Africa. Labour's Experiment with the Doctrine of Native Paramountcy* (1962), p. 84.
16. *The Empire in Africa. The Labour's Policy* (1926). Rita Hinden overlooks the fact that the text largely coincides with the memorandum of 1919–1920, *op. cit.*, p. 119.
17. *Report of the Proceedings of the 57th Annual Trade Union Congress* (1925), pp. 553 f.
18. There is an individual characterization of this personage in Gregory, *op. cit.*, pp. 88 f.
19. Gregory, p. 87.
20. "Presidential Address", *Annual Report* (1922), p. 170. Left-wing resolution (1925), p. 232; (1926), p. 252.
21. *House of Commons*, "Debate on the Address", 3 July 1929, CCXXIX, 194 f.
22. "I think that governors will agree that since we came into office we have not issued any revolutionary edicts or urged any extreme reversal of local policy. . . . We realize it would not be wise—even if it were possible or desired—to have the lines of policy in our overseas territories changed about in response to political changes at home." *The Times*, weekly ed., 17 July 1930.
23. Colonial Office Conference 1930, text in *Documentation coloniale comparée*, III (1930), 35 f.
24. *Sydney Olivier*, ed. Margaret Olivier (1948), pp. 166, 177, 182.
25. "So he has to pick his way warily to some compromise which would safeguard native interests as far as they can be safeguarded with the white settlers in possession of land and capital. Anyway he will be denounced by idealists and no one will be satisfied." *Beatrice Webb's Diaries 1924–1932*, ed. Margaret Cole (1956), pp. 223 f. Lugard in *Webb*, *op. cit.*, pp. 214 f. "The left wing is in revolt—determined to have the blood of the settlers to make them feel that they are beaten", p. 229. Cf. also preface, p. xiii.
26. *New Statesman and Nation*, 16 March 1929, 27 September 1930. "Lord Passfield is pursuing a sound policy in his efforts to solve it." 15 November 1930, p. 165.
27. "The transfer of responsibility must be made to a democratic com-

munity, and not to one controlled by vested interests or with a restricted franchise." P. 4.

28. Cf. his article "If I Were Foreign Secretary", *World Review of Reviews*, June 1936, quoted in Eric Estorick, *Stafford Cripps, Prophetic Rebel* (1941), pp. 266 f. Also, "We all realise that Empire, like his blood brother capitalism, is built upon the exploitation of a depressed class, and can only thrive so long as that exploitation and suppression can continue". 13 July 1938.

29. *Problems of a Socialist Government* (1933).
30. *Op. cit.*, p. 281.
31. *Op. cit.*, p. 283.
32. "The Colonial Civil Service", *The Political Quarterly*, IX, April 1938 (special number on the Empire), 541.
33. *Op. cit.*, p. 551.
34. "The Government of Crown Colonies. The Development of Self-Government", *op. cit.*, p. 525.
35. In very stereotyped terms, though directed against the left wing, he writes, for instance: "Simple surrender of all ill-gotten gains was undesirable and unpractical", p. 229; "in large areas the peoples are not ready", p. 241.
36. "I am no imperialist but an Empire exists in the world . . . let us begin on firm grounds." But a resolution for Empire Free Trade was refused by 1.8 against 1.4 million votes, *TUC Report* (1930), p. 257. The 1929 presidential address already recalled that "the British Empire has a greater potential home consumption than the US". *TUC Report* (1929), p. 64.
37. *TUC Report* (1935), p. 178.
38. The 1929 resolution; cf. also appendix to the *Annual Report* of the Labour party (1922), p. 5.
39. *Empire*, July 1938, p. 15.
40. Allan Bullock, *The Life and Times of Ernest Bevin* I (1960), 435.
41. In his presidential address in 1937 Bevin said: "News is coming through that all is not well regarding Labour matters in our colonies . . .", and referred to the unrest in the West Indies. *TUC Report* (1937), p. 74. A similar resolution in *TUC Report* (1938), p. 433.
42. Bullock, *op. cit.*, p. 632.

INDIRECT RULE IN WEST AFRICA

1. Compare with p. 112. Also important is Margery Perham, *Native Administration in Nigeria* (1937). A good summary in Lucy Mair, *Native Policy in Africa*. A recent study is D. A. Low, R. C. Pratt, *Buganda and British Overrule 1900–1955* (1960), pp. 163 f., 118 f.
2. Quoted in Margery Perham, *Lugard*, II, 469.
3. Compare the well-known "definition" of Donald Cameron: "The system of native administration generally adopted in the Protectorate of Nigeria is known as 'Indirect Administration' and, based on several principles, is designed to adapt for the purpose of local government the tribal institutions which the native peoples have evolved for themselves, so that the latter may develop in a constitutional manner from their own past, guided and restrained by the traditions and sanctions which they have inherited, moulded or modified as they may be on the advice of British Officers and by general control of those officers. It is an essential feature of the system that, within the limitations and in the manner which will be discussed below, the British Government rules through these native institutions which

are regarded as an integral part of the machinery of government". *Principles of Native Administration and Their Application* (1934), p. 1.

4. *Op. cit.*, p. 4. "We endeavour to purge the native system of its abuses, to graft our higher civilisation upon the soundly rooted native stock", p. 5.

5. The most important, he said, was "the allegiance of a people to a tribal head freely given and without external cause", *op. cit.*, preface, pp. 3, 9.

6. *Op. cit.*, p. 17.

7. *Op. cit.*, p. 28. He stresses that "there are not two sets of rulers— British and native—working either separately or in co-operation, but a single government . . .", *Dual Mandate*, p. 203.

8. "The White Man's Task in Tropical Africa", *Foreign Affairs*, October 1926, p. 64.

9. Perham, *Native Administration*, p. 120.

10. *Dual Mandate*, pp. 196, 226.

11. Cf. Bourret, *op. cit.*, pp. 36–81.

12. "The formation of the Provincial Councils provides the people with the machinery for the preservation and development of their national institutions." The government "whose policy it has been always to maintain native institutions" would support the chiefs against opposition by the educated élite. Sir Gordon Guggisberg, *The Gold Coast. A Review of the Events of 1920–1926 and the Prospects of 1927–1928* (1927), pp. 4, 18. Also, David E. Apter, *The Gold Coast in Transition* (1955), p. 133.

13. Besides Bourret and Apter, cf. also J. D. Fage, *Ghana, a Historical Interpretation* (1959), p. 80; and David Kimble, *A Political History of Ghana. The Rise of Gold Coast Nationalism 1850 to 1928* (1963), pp. 440 f., 493 f.

14. Sir Donald Cameron, *My Tanganyika Service and Some Nigeria* (1939). Mair, *Native Policies*, pp. 138 f. Hailey, *African Survey* (1938), pp. 435 f.

15. Lord Altrincham, *Kenya's Opportunity* (1955), p. 224.

16. Cf. Mary Bull, "Indirect Rule in Northern Nigeria 1906–1911", in *Essays in Imperial Government, Presented to Margery Perham* (1963).

17. *Op. cit.*, p. 50.

18. *Op. cit.*, p. 67.

19. "The policy which I have outlined certainly does not admit of the institution of schools where young natives are to be taught to read and write English, and as a natural corollary European habits and customs. Nothing could be more subservient of the policy than this. . . . I hotly oppose the extension of the system of European education to the great majority of natives who are still untouched." Pp. 219–21.

20. *Op. cit.*, p. 54.

21. Perham, *Lugard*, II, 464 f., also admits this. Five hundred native authorities of thirteen different types had been constituted, she said, and "find the chief" had all too often turned into "make the chief". Moreover, the small units in the south-east had been unsuited to their new functions.

22. Quoted in Perham, *Native Administration*, pp. 331–32.

23. *Principles*, p. 8.

24. *Tanganyika Service*, p. 99.

25. "I doubt sometimes whether we have done a great deal to impress on the minds of the Native Authorities concerned that the amelioration of the social and economic conditions of a people is one of the primary duties of an Administration", *op. cit.*, p. 332.

26. *Principles*, p. 16.

27. A brilliant discussion and criticism is Margery Perham's "A Re-state-

ment of Indirect Rule", *Africa*, VII (1934). Also, Perham, "Some Problems of Indirect Rule in Africa" in appendix to *Journal of the African Society*, XXXIV, (1935). *Native Administration*, pp. 350 f.

28. *Nigeria, a Critique of British Colonial Administration* (1936).

29. "Indirect Rule became a formula as hieratic and as dead of reactive development as an outworn theology", p. 215. In 1926 a memorandum presented by the small Nigerian Democratic party to the under-secretary of state, Ormsby-Gore, already said that indirect rule "has practically been elevated to the sacrosanct heights of an administrative fetish, the criticism of which implied official excommunication", in *West Africa*, 10 April 1926, p. 417.

30. Cf. the lively diary by Crocker, e.g. on 16 March 1934: "The so-called financial autonomy is pure pretence."

31. A. Victor Murray, *The School in the Bush* (1929). Similarly, "Education under Indirect Rule", *Journal of the African Society*, April 1935. Sir James Currie, "The Educational Experiment in the Anglo-Egyptian Sudan 1900–1933", *Journal of the African Society*, January 1935.

32. R. S. Rattray, "Present Tendencies of African Colonial Government", *Journal of the African Society*, January 1934. By contrast also Richmond Palmer, "Some Observations on Capt. R. S. Rattray's paper", *ibid.*; Northern Nigeria was developing well, he said. . . . In 1924 Lord Raglan criticized this: the emirs of Northern Nigeria had become autocratic and were corrupt; they extracted money from their subjects without the administration being able to intervene or wanting to intervene, *House of Lords*, 17 December 1924, Vol. LX. Lord Olivier took up the defence with a reference to the successes of Lugard and Clifford.

33. Murray, *School in the Bush*, p. 278.

34. E.g. Tracy Philipps, "The New Africa", *Nineteenth Century*, CXXII (1937), 575 f.

35. The Ghanaian sociologist K. A. Busia confirmed this in critical retrospect. A former official of the Nigerian administration, H. Cooper also pointed to the tendency to treat the chiefs primarily as executive organs and "to measure a chief's usefulness by his devotion to British rule and his belief in British infallibility. The true yardstick—his willingness to speak out frankly and in the interests of his people, even if this meant opposing official policy—tended to get lost in an eager exchange of courtesies". "The Gold Coast and Nigeria on the Road to Self-Government", *Africa To-day*, ed. Haines (1955), pp. 293, 307 f. Perham also speaks of the danger of autocratization, *Restatement*, p. 327.

36. E.g. Colonel Wedgwood in the House of Commons on 7 June 1939: "There is another matter which everyone interested in colonial politics has always before his mind, and that is the question of direct or indirect rule. I wonder what the goal, or the pole star as it has been called, of the Colonial Office is about direct or indirect rule in our Colonial Empire. I and all my friends on these benches wish for direct rule as a natural step towards responsible Government. Indirect rule is the bolstering up of landlord and aristocrat domination in these countries. Their own chiefs have become landlords. Expropriation takes place as it took place long ago in this country. The chief is becoming the owner of the land, just as the land of the highlands became the property of the clan chiefs." *House of Commons*, CCCXLVIII, 527.

37. Murray, *Education under Indirect Rule*, p. 229.

38. Perham, *Lugard*, II, 420. "The Europeanised African is indeed separated from the rest of the people by a gulf which no radical affinity can

NOTES 557

bridge. He must be treated as though he were of a different race." *Dual Mandate*, p. 81.

39. *Dual Mandate*, pp. 86 f. "There is abundant opportunity for the educated African."

40. In 1939 Cameron believed that one could include the educated Africans in the native authorities. "Room must be left for the gradual introduction of educated Africans as members of the Chief's customary Council of Advisers, although they may not occupy any office which by native custom entitles them to a seat." *Tanganyika Service*, p. 99.

41. Busia, in *Africa To-day, op. cit.*, p. 293.

42. *Empire in These Days* (1935), p. 170.

43. *Op. cit.*, p. 147. Similarly in the volume *The Colonial Problem* (1937), p. 259, published by the RIIA.

44. *Re-statement*, p. 324.

45. *Op. cit.*, p. 361.

46. *African Survey* (1938), p. 1648.

47. "Indirect Rule from a Native's Point of View" (August 1936) in *Negro Year Book* (1937), p. 376; talks with Africans in Perham, *Some Problems*, pp. 19 f.; a very radical view, of course, in George Padmore, *How Britain Rules Africa* (1936), pp. 322 f.

48. Bourret, *op. cit.*, pp. 38, 49, 76.

49. Quoted in J. S. Coleman, *Nigeria, Background to Nationalism* (1960), p. 165.

50. "The Growth of Empire", speech before the Royal Colonial Council, in *United Empire* (1922), p. 743.

51. Perham, *Lugard*, II, 416.

52. *Op. cit.*

53. Lugard, "The Growth of Empire", in *United Empire* (1922), p. 743.

54. *Dual Mandate*, p. 205.

55. "The danger of going too fast with native races is even more likely to lead to disappointment, if not to disaster, than the danger of not going fast enough", p. 198.

56. "Election by secret ballot, government by debate and decisions by majority votes, is not a form of government which, so far as we know has ever been evolved by coloured races, nor has it proved very successful in Europe. . . . With the spread of education they will learn the system adopted by Europe and America and, if suitable, they can adopt them. But let us not forget how many centuries were needed to evolve this system in Europe." Lugard, 1933, quoted in Robert Schneebeli, *Die zweifache Treuhänderschaft* (1958), p. 217, note 95.

57. Cf. above, p. 86.

58. *Native Races*, p. 78.

59. *Op. cit.*, p. 23.

60. *Op. cit.*, p. 78.

61. Fairly long excerpts in Coleman, *op. cit.*, pp. 192–94.

62. *Principles*, p. 4. Lugard had still deliberately distinguished between north and south and even doubled a number of departments. Perham, *Lugard*, II, 416.

63. Kalu Ezera, *Constitutional Development in Nigeria* (1960), pp. 27 f.

64. "Nationhood, which the opponents of the Provincial Councils have taken as their slogan and which they accuse us of deliberately retarding, will surely be the more rapidly achieved by uniting the chiefs, and through them their people. . . . Provincial Councils" were "breakwaters defending our native constitutions and customs against the disintegrating waves of

western civilisation. They are the chief means by which the nationality of the Africans of the Gold Coast will be built up out of the many scattered tribes", Sir Guggisberg, A *Review of Events*, pp. 21–24.

65. *Tanganyika Service*, p. 107.
66. *Op. cit.*, p. 86.
67. Philip Mitchell, Cameron's secretary for Native Affairs, in 1924–1934 had similar ideas. In a letter to a critic of indirect rule he considers it as a form of local government which must be modernized and "civilized"; above all, the sons of chiefs must be carefully educated. Then the councils of chiefs could be amalgamated into provincial councils. "Ultimately we may have a dual legislature for a generation or so; and then some arrangement which will allow the people of all races who live in Tanganyika to govern themselves through common institutions. But all this is a long way off." Quoted in *African Afterthoughts* (1954), p. 131.

Cameron wanted to leave the decision on whether to introduce representative institutions to the Africans themselves. "As far as I am concerned I would leave that to their genius. I would not force it upon them. . . . Whether the native . . . will turn to western systems of government with the vote and the ballot I do not know. Again I say that that must be left to his own genius." Speech before the Joint Select Committee on Closer Union in East Africa, 1931, quoted in Low-Pratt, p. 168.

68. *Re-statement*, p. 334.
69. *Native Administration*, p. 363.
70. "Among the many doubts and uncertainties, however, one thing is certain, that it is both our duty and our interest to assist the Africans of Nigeria to build a sound united state." *Native Administration*, p. 363.
71. "There is, however, one branch into which I believe Africans should not enter, that is the Administrative Service. This should aim at being increasingly advisory in its functions." *Op. cit.*, p. 361.
72. *Op. cit.*, p. 360.
73. "This depreciation of the Legislative Council is directed towards its unsuitability as the future focus of political development, and not to its conduct of affairs hitherto", p. 360. Margery Perham also tried to refute the reproach of being "sentimental"; in the long run the Africans of Northern Nigeria and Tanganyika would be better prepared than the currently more educated masses in South Africa. This was directed against Philip Kerr, who was critical of indirect rule and considered it unsuitable as a method of involving the Africans in modern life. Cf. Butler, *Lord Lothian*, pp. 140 f.
74. "Some Problems Dealt With in the African Survey", *International Affairs*, March 1939, pp. 210 f.
75. "The Government of Crown Colonies, The Development of Self-Government", *Political Quarterly* (1938), pp. 521 f.
76. E.g. D. Westermann, *Der Afrikaner heute und morgen* (1937), pp. 193 f.
77. Perham, *Re-statement*, p. 331.
78. Sir Andrew Cohen, *British Policy in Changing Africa* (1959), p. 25.
79. Coleman, *op. cit.*, pp. 153 f.
80. "Some Problems . . .", p. 204.

EAST AFRICA: KENYA AND CLOSER UNION

1. Elspeth Huxley, *White man's Country. Lord Delamere and the Making of Kenya*, 2 vols. (1935; 2nd ed., 1953). An excellent study is George Bennett's *Kenya, a Political History* (1963).

NOTES

2. Text in appendix to Lord Altringham, *Kenya's Opportunity* (1955), p. 246. For the differences of opinion between settlers and the Colonial Office in questions of land and work, see Bennett, pp. 12 f.

3. "In every direction the sphere of the Indian in this country is not complemental but competitive with those of the European and the African. . . ." The Indians were unclean, of doubtful morality and incited the Africans to commit crimes. The Indians in Africa were "quite obviously inimical to the moral and physical welfare and the economic advancement of the native". London must decide between "the vital interest of the African and the ambition of India". Quoted in Huxley, *op. cit.*, pp. 113 f.

4. Huxley, *op. cit.*, pp. 130 f.

5. Ed. Wood (later viceroy in India, as Lord Irwin) represented the British government as under-secretary of state for colonies, Lord Winterton the Indian government. Text in "Indians in Kenya", memorandum, *Commonwealth Documents 1922* (1923), p. 7.

6. "Indians in Kenya", pp. 10, 11 (our emphasis).

7. Robert G. Gregory, *Sidney Webb and East Africa. Labour's Experiment with the Doctrine of Native Paramountcy* (1962), pp. 22 f.

8. Roland Oliver, *The Missionary Factor in East Africa*, 2nd ed. (1963), pp. 253 f.

9. "Kenya belongs, as already stated, to tropical Africa. The existence of this White island has made complex what would otherwise have been a simple situation. . . . The welfare of the native African, the original inhabitant of the country, must come first. This, then is the paramount principle. In its light difficulties do not disappear, but things fall more naturally into their place. . . . It is, however, our trust here in Great Britain. We cannot hand it over to ten thousand white colonists or to 22,000 Indians, or to the two together. . . ." "Kenya", *Round Table*, XIII (1923), 523.

10. Nicholas Mansergh, *South Africa 1906–1961. The Price of Magnanimity* (1962).

11. E.g. E. D. Morel, "Two African Policies", *Contemporary Review*, September 1923, contrasts West and East Africa. He thought the 1923 declaration had been very urgent, since "the practices which have been allowed to grow up in Kenya during the past fifteen years are both repugnant to natural justice and a grave reflection upon our recent Tropical African record", p. 310. Similarly, John H. Harris, "British Justice and Native races", *op. cit.*, October 1924.

12. Leys, pp. 67, 144. In 1934, 2027 settlers owned over 5.1 million acres, i.e. about one thousand hectares each. Hailey, *African Survey*, p. 821. Only a little over 10 percent was under cultivation!

13. Ross, *op. cit.*, pp. 145 f.

14. Criticism of the tax policy in the House of Commons, 1925, *House of Commons*, CLXXXVII, 132.

15. "That heartcry of Kenya's leading statesman, worthy to be inscribed in letters of brass on a tablet of mud in the Council-House: 'If the policy was to be continued that every native was to be a landowner of a sufficient area on which to establish himself, then the question of obtaining a sufficient labour supply would never be settled'." Olivier, "The European Problem in Africa", *Contemporary Review*, October 1928, p. 458. "If the natives are induced to go in for cotton growing in the reserves on a large scale, what is going to be the labour position in the European areas where millions of capital have been sunk? Our present labour difficulties will be intensified to such an extent that we should be ruined, as you may be sure that once

the native had tasted comparative luxury from his cotton growing he would not be prepared to come back to work on our farms at the present rate of wages when the boom was over and cotton was no longer what it is to-day." From a settler's electoral speech, April 1924, quoted by Leys, p. 380.

16. Arguments in Huxley, pp. 288 f.

17. "Nothing should be done or said to hurt the feelings of those white men who go out to these countries and extend the bounds of our Empire, or that would tend to hamper in any way their devotion to this country." Royce in the House of Commons on 25 February 1924. *House of Commons*, CLXX, 210.

18. All these arguments recur, after the Second World War, in the correspondence between two notable experts: Elsbeth Huxley and Margery Perham, *Race and Politics in Kenya* (1944; 2nd expanded ed., 1956).

19. "Report of the East Africa Commission," *Commonwealth Documents* 2387 (1925).

20. *Op. cit.*, p. 21.

21. *Commonwealth Documents* 2904.

22. "For these reasons (thin settlement, etc.) East Africa has already been committed to what is known as the Dual Policy—that is, to a combination of non-native and native production." Governors' conference in Nairobi in 1926, quoted in Gregory, *op. cit.*, p. 59. "The Dual policy of increasing the quality and quantity of production on the native lands pari passu with the development of European cultivation is accordingly necessary", "East Africa Report," p. 181.

23. *Commonwealth Documents* 2904, p. 5.

24. "I do not wish to exaggerate the dangers latent in one association [Kikuyu Central Association] of this kind; they are not serious, at present. But the existence of this tendency amongst the younger men shows that any promise of political advancement and influence outside the normal lines of tribal development is bound to prove a strong attraction and certain to increase the difficulties by which progress on tribal lines is already beset. Amongst the counter-attractions nothing can be more potent than the promise of adding native voters to a common electoral roll. It means that the abler young men will endeavour to qualify as voters and politicians under our institutions rather than the leaders of their tribes under the institutions which are natural to them. It means, that the influence of our institutions will permeate the tribal reserves or finally destroy all hope for evolution under the tribal system. Instead of educating the Africans to a better Africa, as we are now striving to do, it will turn all its natural leaders into inferior Europeans, with most of our faults and few of our virtues, a danger to themselves and all other communities." From Grigg's dispatch to Lord Passfield on 11 September 1930 in "Papers Relating to the Closer Union of Kenya, Uganda and the Tanganyika Territory", (1931), *Colonial*, No. 57, p. 14.

25. "Although in some places it may be many years before the native can take a direct part in the central Legislature . . .", *Commonwealth Documents* 1904, p. 5. "Bringing the African people, when fit for it, into the central Legislature of the Colony through their own institutions and in harmony with them rather than outside their own institutions and in conflict with them . . .", Grigg's dispatch, p. 15. So in the remote future perhaps a few chiefs or indirectly appointed representatives of the Native Councils could enter the legislature council of Kenya, in which the settlers had long since had a majority!

26. "While these responsibilities for trusteeship must for some considerable

time rest mainly [!] on the agents of the Imperial Government, HMG desires to associate more closely in this high and honourable task those who as colonists or residents have identified their interests with the prosperity of the country." *Commonwealth Documents* 2904, p. 7. These words were plainly a criticism of the "alone" in the 1923 declaration!

27. Here we must note Amery's definition: "By the Dual policy is meant a policy which recognizes our trusteeship towards the native population, whom we found on the spot and whom it is our duty to bring forward and develop in every possible way—but also our trusteeship to humanity at large for the fullest development of these territories and towards those in particular [!] of our own race who have undertaken the task of helping forward that development." Quoted in Huxley, p. 193.

28. "It needs more consideration than it has received." Grigg's dispatch, p. 17. "The first is that the white population should be either steadily reinforced or else removed and compensated" [!] Grigg, *The Constitutional Problem of Kenya* (1933), p. 17; *House of Commons*, 25 July 1935, CCCIV, 2081.

29. Amery himself gave the goal as responsible government, "on the basis of Rhodes' principle . . .", "Problem and Development in Africa", *Journal of the African Society*, July 1929, p. 332; similarly Lord Lothian, "The New Problem of Africa", *Round Table*, June 1927; Butler, *Lord Lothian*, pp. 133 f.

30. Altrincham, *Kenya's Opportunity*, p. 191. Grigg spoke of Rhodes' and Milner's ideals, p. 214.

31. *My Political Life*, II, 360.

32. Quoted in Huxley, p. 220.

33. In December 1926 a manifesto already had said: "Consideration of any such scheme [closer union] is conditional on an elected majority having been granted and that the following essential safeguards are included . . .", Huxley, p. 215; "It is a vital necessity to any scheme of co-ordination based on the radiation of civilization from Kenya that we should have a free Council here." The constitution of Southern Rhodesia appeared to be the model, since the British reservations had not proved effective in native policy. Delamere's speech on the 1927 Kenya constitution in the appendix to Altrincham *Kenya's Opportunity*, pp. 258 f.; Delamere before the Hilton-Young Commission, Huxley, pp. 226 f.

34. The first thing, that we started to do, was to try and help to kill the spread of the West Coast policy in the East." Quoted in Huxley, p. 206.

35. *Tanganyika Service*, pp. 225 f.; Altrincham, pp. 211 f.

36. Perham, *Lugard*, II, 679.

37. Altrincham, pp. 211 f.

38. "Report of the Commission on Closer Union of the Dependencies in Eastern and Central Africa", *Commonwealth Documents* 3234 (1929); also, Gregory, pp. 69 f; Bennett, pp. 67 f.

39. E.g. Lord Scott's (second man in Kenya) letter to *The Times*, in which he writes, among other things: "One thing must however, be clear, and that is that the Government of each country must be responsible for the administration of the native affairs in its own territory. This cannot be taken out of their hands, or else Government would be impossible." *The Times*, 14 November 1929; also, Altrincham, appendix F, pp. 271 f.; Gregory, p. 73.

40. Altrincham, p. 217.

41. Philip Mitchell, Cameron's secretary for Native Affairs, spoke of a "privy conspiracy", *African Afterthoughts* (1954), p. 117.

42. *House of Commons*, 13 March 1929, LXXIII, 458 f.
43. *The Times*, weekly ed., 31 October 1929.
44. The lead article, "The Future of East Africa", essentially agrees with the Hilton-Young Report and stresses: "The power to define and interpret the term of trust—the principles of native policy—must remain with the Imperial Government." Such vague concepts as trusteeship and Dual Mandate must be defined. In East Africa, as in Ceylon, it was a question of finding a system of government for multi-racial communities. *The Times*, weekly ed., 24 January 1929; on 1 August 1929: "There is a particular need for taking great care that the protection of essential native interests is not handed over, in the interests of immediate harmony, to any hands but those of the Imperial Government."
45. On 26 January 1929 the *Economist* published an article, "The Future of East Africa," that spoke of the "constructive proposals for dealing with the problem of two intermingled communities differing greatly . . .". The British Empire was on the way, as the Ceylon commission had shown, to find a corresponding solution, after its "invention" of dominion status. On 2 March 1929 Lugard's summons for a Joint Select Committee was welcomed by *The Times*, and it praised Lugard as a "detached observer" after his speech in the House of Lords. On 25 October 1930 it wrote: "It is as natural for the settlers to cherish this desire [to change the Kenya constitution] as it is impossible for the Imperial Government to satisfy it".
46. The settlers' distrust was justified, the common roll should be refused. "East Africa", *Round Table*, XIX, (1928–1929), 506.
47. "Report of Sir Samuel Wilson on his Visit to East Africa, 1929", Commonwealth Documents 3378 (1929); also Gregory, pp. 105 f.
48. "Statement of the Conclusions of HMG as Regards Closer Union in East Africa", *Commonwealth Documents* 3574 (1930).
49. *Commonwealth Documents* 3573 (1930).
50. *Op. cit.*, p. 6.
51. A telegram from Delamere to the colonial minister gives a good picture of the concepts, arguments and demands of the settlers: "Attitude of Imperial Government as now expressed involves breach of previous pledges. East African colonists stand on principle that the white race is the only people which has proved its capacity to govern mixed races.
"We must challenge the doctrine of political and economic paramountcy of natives as interpreted in these documents, and claim the closer association in trusteeship foreshadowed in the 1927 white paper.
"White settlers permanently domiciled in East Africa cannot accept designation 'immigrant community', as applied to themselves, or the right of Indian immigrants to participate on same basis as Europeans in the government of East Africa. They regard Indian representation on local legislatures desirable only as a convenient method of enabling Indian sectional views to be voiced. They also consider it imperative that closer union should be accompanied by an unofficial majority in at least one territory.
"The principles of a common electoral roll and a racially mixed federal council cannot be accepted. Although closer union involving constitutional changes is still considered desirable the conference regrets that the retrogressive spirit of the new proposals has definitely antagonised European opinion". Quoted in Huxley, pp. 279–80.
52. "Papers Relating . . .", p. 11. Sharp words also in the legislative council, Bennett, p. 73.
53. Quoted in Gregory, p. 121.
54. Details on the opinions and theories presented, Gregory, pp. 127 f.

55. Curiously, Gregory overlooks this.
56. "... the Committee's recommendations are conservative in the good sense and not in the bad. While they leave the door open for economic co-operation, within the limits that are at present practicable, between the several territories under British administration or control in East Africa, they do close the door—and this presumably for a long time to come—upon a very dangerous political vision. This vision was the prospect of a United East Africa enjoying dominion status as a 'White man's Country'. Those who dreamed this dream cherished the hope that, if East Africa were once united, the white settlers in the highlands of Kenya Colony would leaven the lump. The result would have been a latter-day reproduction of 'the South' of the United States as it was before the American Civil War. Indeed, it would have been far worse; for even if the white settlers were to succeed in occupying the Highlands in Tanganyika as well as in Kenya, they would remain an infinitesimal minority in the total population of British East Africa; and to hand the government of this great region over to this dominant caste would have been equivalent to handing India over to a brahman raj. This possibility, which has never (we believe) come within the range of practical politics has been finally ruled out by the combined effect of common sense at Westminster and financial stringency in East Africa." "Common Sense on East Africa", 7 November 1931, p. 854.
57. Bennett, pp. 77 f.
58. Cf. also Wilhelm E. Mühlmann, *Chiliasmus und Nativismus* (1961), pp. 118 f.
59. Quoted in Huxley, p. 115.
60. Letter from Wilson to Grigg on 18 February 1930, quoted in Perham, *Lugard*, II, 691.
61. Eric A. Walker, *The British Empire*, 2nd ed. (1953), p. 194.

THE DISCUSSION DURING THE SECOND WORLD WAR

1. Lord Elton, *Imperial Commonwealth* (1945), p. 516.
2. The discussion was provoked by a *Times* report from Batavia on 18 February 1942 about the last days of Singapore and a commentary on them. The left-wing liberal *News Chronicle* thought on 19 February: "What does this mean? It means that for 100 years the British administration in Singapore sat there as an occupying force. It never attempted . . . identifying itself with the Asiatic population, still less with encouraging their active loyalty and support. Our failure has been largely due to the attitude of complacent superiority towards coloured peoples that has marked British colonial administration in the East, and for which we are now paying the price. . . . If this last chance is not seized history may write of British rule in the East that it received the fate it deserved." On 28 February it pointed to MacArthur's resistance in Bataan, which, unlike the British in Malaya, had been backed by the natives! Cf. also Rita Hinden, *Empire and After*, p. 144.
3. For Burma, cf. the report and commentary in Michael Collis, *Last and First in Burma 1941–1948*, (1958).
4. *Economist*, 21 March 1942, pp. 386 f.
5. Capt. L. D. Gammans, "A Creed for the Colonies. The Imperial Outlook and the New Deal", *The Times*, 15 March 1943.
6. "The Position of Colonies in a British Commonwealth of Nations."

Romanes Lecture, 1941. *The Future of Colonial Peoples* (RIIA, 1943). *World Thought on the Colonial Question* (1946).
7. *House of Lords*, 20 May 1942, CXXII, 1095.
8. "The future", p. 52.
9. "The Position," p. 11.
10. "The Future", p. 24.
11. *Op. cit.*, p. 25.
12. "They [the colonies] will know that social advance can in the long run be secured only by a material development sufficient to provide the funds which the social services require, and that the possibility of achieving this depends as much on the introduction of foreign capital as on the more systematic organization of native production. Looking at the present conditions in some of the colonies, they might feel called upon to remind their colleagues that, in building up a political future the stunted body is no less an obstacle than the dwarfed mind, and they might not unreasonably express a hope that we should not give our native population cause to complain that when they ask for bread, we had offered them a vote." "The Position". pp. 40 f.
13. "The Position", p. 32.
14. "Real test lies in our readiness to appoint natives of the country to the Administrative Service." *House of Lords*, 6 May 1942, CXXII, 914.
15. *World Thought*, p. 11.
16. Speech before the Royal African Society on 12 April 1943, *Journal of the Royal African Society*, July 1943, p. 116.
17. "The Position", pp. 36 f.
18. "The prospect of admission to membership of that Commonwealth of free peoples should afford to the British colonial peoples an ideal which should inspire them to create for themselves the conditions which justify the grant of independence; it should no less serve to guide them in the use which they may determine to make of the independence they have achieved." *The Future*, p. 63.
19. "I do not see how it is possible that we can ever expect these units, situated as they are, small in resources, and with little political balance, really to attain to responsible Government or eventually to the position of a Dominion. I ask myself how I could see Sierra Leone with a responsible Government or as a Dominion." *House of Lords*, 6 May 1942, CXXII, 194; "The Position", p. 33.
20. E.g. "The International Interests in Colonies", *Round Table*, XXXV (1944–1945).
21. Cf. also Smuts' famous speech before the Empire Parliamentary Society on 25 November 1943, *Documents and Speeches on British Commonwealth Affairs 1931–1952*, ed. Mansergh, I, 573 f.
22. *Argument of Empire* (1943).
23. P. 87; but the words are still rather vague.
24. P. 230.
25. *Democratise the Empire, a Policy of Colonial Reform* (The Democratic Order No. 6), (1941).
26. P. 46.
27. P. 42. "Having lost faith in democracy ourselves we did, more or less consciously, design this system as an escape from the complications and dangers of popular government. Because of that arrière pensée Indirect Rule has failed to be the constructive force it might have been if it had really formed a training ground where all young and able men might be learning in their own locality the practice of politics and civil administration. The

Victorian axiom was not overtly repudiated, only out of fashion, but by our own backsliding we left our subjects with no clear prospect of ever attaining an effective voice in control of the government that still effectively enough controls their new Native Authorities."

28. P. 64.
29. P. 64.
30. Vol. 33, No. 129.
31. "More effective intervention on our part to promote their development than the traditions of a previous generation had contemplated."
32. *Op. cit.*, p. 15.
33. *From the British Empire to the British Commonwealth* (1941), p. 50.
34. "The Ideas and Ideals of the British Empire" (1942), p. 83.
35. *The Framework of the Future* (1944), pp. 10, 25.
36. *Forward from Victory* . . . , by four young conservatives (1944), p. 67.
37. "Had been marked by slowness, reluctance and indecision." Elton, p. 516.
38. *House of Lords*, 20 May 1942, CXXII, 1096.
39. One of the exceptions was W. B. Mumford, who proposed "a definite 20-40-60-years plan, leading ultimately even in the more backward areas to Dominion Status". "The Future of the Colonies. Independent Member-states in a Greater Commonwealth", *Time and Tide*, 10 February 1940, p. 133. It is worth noting the steps demanded by this "liberally" intended programme!
40. Speech on 10 November 1942, *The Times*, 11 November 1942.
41. Cf. p. 32.
42. As a further example we may take an article in *The Times* by Margery Perham on p. 2, 21 November 1942 entitled "America and the Empire. The Aftermath of Mr. Willkie's Broadcast". Although Perham dissociated herself from the American criticism, she did ask for understanding: "Taken broadly and at best, the American challenge to us to hasten the work of deimperializing the Empire can only lead to good".
43. "We mean to hold our own" was, he said, a Tory argument. "Labour does not think of the British Commonwealth in terms of 'Empire' . . . [it] is not the sort of phrase the British public would choose as an accurate expression of its post-war aims." *Daily Herald*, 11 November 1942.
44. *War and Empire*, 14 November 1942, pp. 597 f.
45. *House of Lords*, 3 December 1942, CXXV, 388.
46. *House of Commons*, 24 June 1942, CCCLXXX, 2017.
47. *Op. cit.*, p. 2121.
48. *Op. cit.*, p. 2019.
49. *House of Lords*, CXXV, 415 f.
50. This is very clear in the commentary by the conservative *Daily Telegraph* on 3 December 1942.
51. During the debate a speaker said that this was the first time the government was speaking of partnership. But Harold Macmillan had done so earlier.
52. *House of Commons*, CCCXCI, 48.
53. *Britain Looks Ahead*, II (1943), 72, quoted in Coleman, *Nigeria*, p. 238.
54. The comparison with the trust in private law was not accurate, he said, since this referred only to the protective function and not to the obligation to supply any lack in the income of the person entrusted out of one's own pocket. Stanley in a speech in Oxford, 5 March 1943, quoted in *Concept of Empire*, ed. Bennett (1953), p. 414.

55. *Op. cit.*, p. 415. Also, e.g. "throughout the greater part of the colonial Empire, it is, for the present, at any rate, the British presence alone which prevents a disastrous disintegration and British withdrawal today would mean for millions a descent from nascent nationhood into the turmoil of warring sects". Stanley before the Foreign Policy Association in New York on 19 January 1945, quoted in Coleman, *Nigeria*, p. 238.

56. Characteristic of the British terminology is Stanley's comment on the American address: the aim for the entire colonial Empire was to attain a maximum of self-government as soon as possible within the framework of the Empire. Self-government, not independence, was in the real interests both of these territories and of the whole world. But there could be no self-government as long as the economic and social conditions did not improve and as long as there was financial dependence. *Keesing's Contemporary Archives*, 20 March 1945.

57. There is a general study with details in the report published by the administration: "The Colonial Empire (1939–1947)", (1947), *Commonwealth Documents* 7167.

58. West India Royal Commission 1938–1939. Recommendations (1940), *Commonwealth Documents* 6174. Also Annette Baker Fox, *Freedom and Welfare in the Caribbean, a Colonial Dilemma* (1949); J. H. Parry and P. H. Sherlock, *A Short History of the West Indies* (1960). "New Era in the West Indies", *Round Table*, XXXIV (1943–1944).

59. Parry and Sherlock, *op. cit.*, p. 282.

60. There is a good outline in Chales H. Archibald, "The Failure of the West Indies Federation", *The World To-day*, June 1962.

61. A good general outline in Helmut Peets, "Die Rolle des Erziehungswesens in der englischen Kolonialpolitik in Nigeria", in *Erziehung und Politik in Nigeria*, ed. H. N. Weiler (1964).

62. "Asquith Report" (1945), *Commonwealth Documents* 6647. "Elliot Report" (1945), *Commonwealth Documents* 6655. Haily, *African Survey* (1956 ed.), pp. 1180 f.

63. "Dispatch from the Secretary of State for the Colonies to the Colonial Governments Regarding Aspects of Colonial Policy in War-time", 5 June 1941 (1941), *Commonwealth Documents* 6299.

64. "Colonial Development and Welfare," dispatch from the secretary of state to the colonial powers (1945), *Commonwealth Documents* 6713. Discussion in the House of Commons on 7 February 1945, *House of Commons*, CDVII, 2092 f.

65. The Crown Colonies for instance only appear in 14 percent of the conservative and 9 percent of the labour declarations, while India only appears in 2 percent of the conservative and 9 percent of the labour declarations. Moreover these declarations usually contained only a few commonplaces. R. B. MacCallum and Alison Readman, *The British General Election of 1945* (1947), pp. 98 f., 112. The results of an enquiry in 1948 sound almost incredible: 51 percent could not name one colony, 77 percent believed that the colonies paid taxes to Britain. *U.K. Social Survey, Public Opinion on Colonial Affairs* (1948), quoted in S. A. Haqe Haqqi, *The Colonial Policy of the Labour Government (1945–1951)* (1960), p. 5, note 7.

THE LABOUR PARTY DURING AND AFTER THE SECOND WORLD WAR

1. *House of Commons*, CCCLXXX, 2027.
2. Vote in the House of Lords, cf. above, p. 228.
3. *House of Commons*, CCCLXXX, 2046.
4. Margaret Cole, *The Story of Fabian Socialism* (1961), pp. 267 f.
5. Julian Huxley, for instance, was not a member of the Labour party but the liberals' colonial expert.
6. "This Conference considers that the time has arrived for a restatement of the principles of the Labour party as applied to the government of the colonies and to the status of colonial peoples.

"This should be a charter of freedom for colonial peoples abolishing all forms of imperialist exploitation and embodying the following main principles:

1. All persons who are citizens of the colonial commonwealth should be considered to possess and be allowed to enjoy equality of political, economic, and social rights in the same way as the citizens of Great Britain.
2. The status of colony should be abolished and there should be substituted for this that of States named according to the country in which they are situated and having an equal status with the other nations of the Commonwealth.
3. In all colonial areas there should be organized a system of democratic government, using the forms of indigenous institutions in order to enable the mass of the people to enter upon self-government by the modification of existing forms of colonial administration in conformity with these principles.
4. In all colonial areas, in Africa and elsewhere, where the primitive systems of communal land tenure exist, these systems should be maintained and land should be declared inalienable by private sale or purchase. All natural resources should be declared public property and be developed under public ownership.
5. A commonwealth council of colonial peoples should be set up on which each former colonial state should be represented in accordance with the number of its population, but giving also special attention to the representation of national groups within each state." *Annual Conference*, (1942), p. 155.

7. *Annual Conference* (1943), p. 207.
8. *The Colonies. The Labour Party's Post-War Policy for the African and Pacific Colonies* (1943). The report follows that of 1933.
9. *Plan for Africa*, p. 29. "We cannot escape the charge of neglect and indifference." Creech-Jones in *Colonial Essays*, p. 69.
10. Preface to Creech-Jones, *op. cit.*, p. 11.
11. *Op. cit.*, p. 10.
12. "Often their natural leaders are ignored. There seems indifference in high places to the popular movements. Our replies to their offers are often half-hearted and disdainful": Creech-Jones, *House of Commons*, 24 June 1942, CCCLXXX, 2044. "Colonial peoples are also in a critical mood. They want action"; *House of Commons*, 13 July 1943, CCCXCI, 72.
13. Creech-Jones, 26 June 1942, *op. cit.*, p. 2045.
14. *Op. cit.*, p. 2044.
15. In the name of the National Executive Committee Noel-Baker sup-

ported the resolution, *Annual Congress* (1943), p. 208. Cf. also *International Action in the Colonies, Report of a Committee of the Fabian Research Bureau*, September 1943.

16. "Control of Dependent Territories", *New Commonwealth*, 2 March 1953, pp. 214 f. The "Statement of policy on colonial affairs" of 1954 accordingly says no more about the U.N. Appendix VIII to *Annual Conference* (1954), p. 199.

17. Creech-Jones, *House of Commons*, 24 June 1942, *op. cit.*, p. 2044: "A supplementary charter". Again, on 13 July 1943, CCCXCI, 72.

18. There are a few details on the possible contents of such a charter in J. Huxley and P. Deane, *Future of the Colonies. Target for Tomorrow*, No. 8 (1944). Lord Hailey, *The Colonies and the Atlantic Charter* (speech before the Royal Central Asian Society) (1943), p. 242.

19. *Annual Conference* (1943) (Freeman), p. 207. Brailsford in *Colonial Essays*, p. 24.

20. "Everywhere the goal should be political self-government, but attainment of that goal in many instances cannot be near at hand." *Annual Conference* (1943), p. 4. "It would be ignorant, dangerous nonsense to talk about grants for full self-government to many of the dependent territories for some time to come." Herbert Morrison on 10 January 1943, *The times*, 11 January 1943.

21. "Socialist at the same time because of their dislike of imperialism and control of one people by another, they cannot stop their ears to the claims of the colonial peoples and renounce responsibility towards British territories because of some sentimental inclination to 'liberalism' or international administration. To throw off the colonial Empire in this way, would be to betray the peoples and our trust." Creech-Jones in the preface to *Colonial Essays*, p. 13.

22. Leonard Woolf in *Fabian Colonial Essays*, p. 92.

23. *Op. cit.*, p. 98.

24. *Kenya: White Man's Country?* Report to the Fabian Colonial Bureau, January 1944.

25. "British Colonial Policy with Particular Reference to Africa", Speech in Chatham House, 30 November 1950, *International Affairs* (1951), p. 180.

26. Speech on 10 January 1943. *The Times* printed the text on 11 January 1943 and supported it!

27. Cf. Annual Conferences, *New Fabian Colonial Essays* (1959).

28. *Op. cit.*, p. 184. One could not know, he said, which way things would go and whether the situation would really be favourable.

29. E.g. Under-Secretary of State Ivor Thomas on 29 July 1947: twenty constitutions were being worked out at the time, *House of Commons*, CDXLI, 370. Further details in the report "The Colonial Empire (1947–1948)", *Commonwealth Documents*, 7433. Creech-Jones in *New Essays*, pp. 51 f. References to the work of the Colonial Office also in Cohen, *Changing . . . ,* p. 84.

30. E.g. Creech-Jones in the House of Commons on 29 July 1947, *House of Commons*, CDXLI, 270; *Commonwealth Documents* 7433, p. 9.

31. Bennett, pp. 99 f.

32. Dr. Morgan, 9 July 1946, *House of Commons*, CDXXV, 287. Guest, 29 July 1947, CDXLI, 301.

33. *New Statesman and Nation*, 19 January 1946, p. 46. Letter from Horriban as chairman, and Rita Hinden, Secretary of the Fabian Colonial Bureau.

34. *Empire*, May–June 1946, p. 2; July 1946, p. 2. Also criticism of the party's lack of interest: "The Party itself does not maintain a single official to deal with colonial affairs, its members show only the most cursory interest in them and spare only a few minutes to discuss them at its Annual Conference". August 1946, p. 2.

35. "Britain without Empire, II," in *The Nation*, 12 April 1947: "No one seriously supposes that any one of our African colonies is ripe for self-government, or can be permitted to embark upon it", p. 416.

36. Fenner Brockway, *Outside the Right* (1963), pp. 168 f.

37. E.g. R. Palme Dutt, *Britain's Crisis of Empire* (1950).

38. *Commonwealth Documents*, 7433, p. 6.

39. Quoted in Richard Gray, *The Two Nations. Aspects of the Development of Race Relations in the Rhodesias and Nyassaland* (1960), p. 198. Very similarly the future prime minister Harold Wilson, then president of the Board of Trade: "It is in the future development of the Colonies that so many of us pin our hopes of a great contribution towards a long-term balance between the Sterling Area and the rest of the world". Quoted in Don Taylor, *The Year of Challenge* (1960), p. 100.

40. The Colonial Office introduces the report on the year 1947–1948 with the question: "What contribution had the Colonies to make to the problem of dollar shortage? What new enterprise could be introduced"? "The Colonial Empire", *Commonwealth Documents* 7433, p. 1.

41. *House of Commons*, 21 February 1946, CDXIX, 1365. Again on May 16, 1947: "HMG must maintain a continuing interest in the area if only because our economic and financial interests in the Middle East were of vast importance to us. . . . If these interests were lost to us, the effect on the life of this country would be a considerable reduction in the standard of living". *House of Commons*, CDXXXVII, 1964.

42. "More Dollars from Africa", *Sunday Times*, 16 May 1948.

43. *Commonwealth Documents* 7433, p. 1.

44. The Labour government declared: "The purposes of colonial development are complementary with those of European recovery", quoted in Taylor, *op. cit.*

45. "A plan for the mechanized production of groundnuts in East and Central Africa", *Commonwealth Documents* 7030.

46. The Overseas Food Corporation "was established to undertake schemes for the production of foodstuffs to meet UK needs [!]", "The Colonial Empire (1947–1948)", *Commonwealth Documents* 7433 (1948), p. 64.

47. *House of Commons*, 16 February 1945, CDVIII, 541 f.

INDIA ON THE ROAD TO INDEPENDENCE, 1939–1947

1. Apart from general studies of Indian history we may note R. Coupland, *Indian Politics 1936–1942* (1943); R. P. Masani, *Britain in India* (1960); V. P. Menon, *The Transfer of Power in India* (1957); Leonhard Mosley, *The Last Days of the British Raj* (1961); Dietmar Rothermund, *Die politische Willensbildung in Indien 1900–1960* (1965), pp. 183 ff.

2. *Commonwealth Documents* 6121 (1939); *Speeches and Documents on the Indian Constitution 1921–1947*, ed. M. Gwyer and A. Appadorai, II (1957), 490 f.

3. The viceroy in Bombay on 10 January 1940, quoted in K. P. Bhagat, *A Decade of Indo-British Relations 1937–1947* (1959) (documents), p. 90.

4. *Commonwealth Documents* 6219 (1940); Gwyer and Appadorai, p. 504.
5. The secretary of state for India, L. S. Amery, said very clearly: "There can be no agreement on a Government responsible to the Legislature until there is agreement on the nature of the Legislature, and upon the whole structure of the Constitution". *House of Commons*, 14 August 1940, CCCLXIV, 875.
6. *House of Commons*, 26 August 1939, CCCLII, 1666.
7. *House of Commons*, 14 August 1940, CCCLXIV, 904.
8. *Annual Conference* (1941), p. 171. Again the left-wing opposition in *Annual Conference* (1942), p. 161.
9. As Lord Privy Seal Attlee answered Harold Laski, who had evidently criticized Secretary of State Amery, on 16 November 1940: "Thanks for your letter on Nehru. The position is very difficult. It is no use assuming that the fault is all on one side. Amery did his best to try to get Indian leaders to make a fresh start, but there was no response. Gandhi has entered on a policy of deliberately courting arrest of his followers which puts the Government of India in a dilemma. They could not ignore Nehru's activities . . . ." (We are indebted to Mrs. Laski for kindly bringing this letter to our attention.)
10. *House of Commons*, 26 October 1939, CCCLII, 1637.
11. Speech on 21 November 1940, in *India and Freedom* (1942), p. 27.
12. Speech in Manchester on 19 November 1941, *op. cit.*, p. 45; and *House of Commons*, 14 August 1940, *op. cit.*, p. 68.
13. There is a good description of the position of Congress and the Muslim League in Coupland, *The Future of India* (1943), pp. 32 f.
14. *Commonwealth Documents* 6350 (1942); Gwyer and Appadorai, p. 520. Also, Coupland, *The Cripps Mission* (1942); Colin Cooke, *The Life of Richard Stafford Cripps* (1957). Winston Churchill, *The Second World War*, IV, 12.
15. In the House of Commons Amery explained that the aim of British policy was Indian unity, "but we would sooner see India divided and free than keep the various elements for ever chatting against us and against each other under a sense of impotent frustration". *House of Commons*, 28 April 1942, CCCLXXX, 908.
16. Churchill himself indirectly confirmed this on 16 May 1946 when he declared: "These proposals were made by us at a moment when the danger of Japanese invasion threatened India in a terrible manner and I personally, was induced to agree to them by the all-compelling war interest, as it seemed, of trying to rally all the forces in India to the defence of their soil against Japanese aggression and all the horrors that would follow therefrom". *House of Commons*, CDXXII, 2121.
17. Gandhi's words are well-known: leave India to the hand of God, or in modern terms, to anarchy, quoted in Caspar Schrenk-Notzing, *Hundert Jahre Indien* (1961), p. 90. This sentence provided grist for the conservatives' mill, since they naturally did not forget to present it as evidence of the Congress party leaders' irresponsibility.
18. *House of Commons*, 10 September 1942, CCCLXXXIII, 302.
19. *House of Commons*, 30 March 1943, CCCLXXXVIII, 81.
20. *Annual Conference* (1943), p. 40. The 1944 conference criticized the attitude of the party leaders: the Atlantic Charter must be taken seriously, and dominion status must be proclaimed at once. Speaking before the party executive committee, Gordon-Walker defended the members of the government (Attlee, Bevin, Morrison), pp. 186, 189.
21. "The British Government would not overrule any decision taken by

India not to remain in the British Commonwealth after the war if the people of India had established an agreed constitution." Bhagat, p. 253.
22. Gwyer and Appadorai, pp. 557 f.
23. *House of Commons*, 15 August 1945, CDXIII, 57.
24. This also becomes clear in Wavell's declaration after his return from India: "... to promote the *early* realisation of self-government in India ... to convene *as soon as possible*, a constitution-making body ..., bringing India to Self-Government at the *earliest possible date* ...", Bhagat, p. 324.
25. *House of Commons*, CDXX, 1421 f.
26. Cf. also Cooke, *Cripps*, pp. 342 f.
27. Mosley, pp. 22 f.
28. Gwyer and Appadorai, pp. 577 f.
29. Gandhi: "it is the best document the British could have produced in the circumstances", quoted in Bhagat, p. 356.
30. Even the usually pro-Nehru Michael Brecher is critical in his well-known biography of Nehru. Azad is also critical, *India Wins Freedom* (1959), p. 160.
31. The secretary of state for India in the Labour government, Lord Pethick-Lawrence, in the House of Lords on 25 February 1947, CXLV, 944.
32. Gwyer and Appadorai, p. 667.
33. Writers have not noted the fact that the *New Statesman* had already demanded a "time limit" on 8 February—in answer to the boycott of the constitutional assembly by the Muslim League. Similarly, the old, left-wing expert on India, H. W. Brailsford on 15 February: "It is to announce at once that we shall complete our withdrawal from India by a specified date, not more than twelve months hence. That said, we should call on Pandit Nehru to form a re-modelled Interim Government, to which full powers will be granted to act in the new circumstances. We should add to our announcement the recommendation that before the Viceroy leaves New Delhi the Constituent Assembly shall appoint a provisional President of the Indian Union to take his place. Such an announcement would transform Indian politics. As troopship followed troopship homewards and one barracks after another was emptied, Indian doubts in our sincerity would vanish, and the Muslim League would have to revise its tactics. How quickly it would adjust itself one cannot say. What is reasonably certain is that it could not for very long maintain its refusal to negotiate directly with Congress, or to enter the Constituent Assembly. The same considerations apply to the Princes. The key to a peaceful settlement is to treat the Constituent Assembly as the legitimate fountain of power. What solution Congress and League will hammer out, when they face each other without the presence of a foreign power, we need not try to guess. Conceivably, they may adopt the Mission's compromise with a few modifications. So soon as Hindus and Muslims realise that it lies with them alone to determine how they shall live as neighbours in their own land, their instinct of self-preservation will bring them together. The best service we can render to peace is to leave them with the friendliest of farewells, alone", pp. 127 f.
34. "We took the view that the fixing of a definite term ... should provide the strongest inducement to them to sink their differences and to act together." *House of Commons*, 5 March 1947, CDXXXIV, 506. "The fixing of an early date is designed to impress on the Indian parties, first of all, the complete sincerity of HMG in their promise to transfer power and authority, and secondly, a sense of the urgency of finding solutions to their outstanding difficulties, themselves, without the assistance and control of

this country." Lord Pethick-Lawrence in *House of Lords*, 25 February 1947, CXLV, 949. Similarly, Lord Listowel, p. 985. Attlee said in retrospect: "they would talk and talk and talk, and as long as they could put the responsibility on us they would continue to quarrel among themselves. Therefore I concluded the thing to do was to bring them right up against it and make them see they'd got to face the situation themselves". Francis Williams, *A Prime Minister Remembers* (1961), p. 208.

35. The Labour minister Dalton summarized the situation, writing, in retrospect: "If you are in a place where you are not wanted and where you have not got the force, or perhaps the will, to squash those who don't want you, the only thing to do, is to come out". Hugh Dalton, *High Life and After. Memoirs 1945–1960* (1962), p. 211.

36. Williams, p. 209; Dalton, p. 211.

37. Attlee indirectly admitted that he was obeying Churchill; Williams, p. 209.

38. *House of Lords*, 25 February 1947, CXLV, 935.

39. *House of Commons*, 6 March 1947, CDXXXIV, 678.

40. *House of Lords, op. cit.*, p. 968.

41. *House of Lords, op. cit.*, p. 1048.

42. *House of Lords*, 26 February 1947, CXLV, 1016 f.

43. Williams, p. 202. Another letter of congratulations from Edward Cadogan, conservative member of the Simon commission, *op. cit.*, p. 203.

44. The pointed picture, given by Mosley as a direct attack on Lord Mountbatten, certainly does not do justice to the difficult question.

45. "I shall give you complete assurance. I shall see to it that there is no bloodshed and riot. I am a soldier, not a civilian. Once partition is accepted in principle, I shall issue orders to see that there are no communal disturbances anywhere in the country. . . ." Azad, *India Wins Freedom*, p. 190.

46. Bhagat, p. 419.

BURMA AND CEYLON

1. Note the long general study by John F. Cady, *A History of Burma* (1958). For the agrarian problem cf. M. Zinkin, *Asien und der Westen* (1953), p. 127.

2. J. S. Furnivall, "Twilight in Burma; Reconquest and Crisis", *Pacific Affairs*, XXII, 1 March 1949. For Furnivall's views cf. also his basic work, *Colonial Policy and Practice. A Comparative Study of Burma and Netherlands India* (1948–1956).

3. Maung Maung, *Burma's Constitution*, 2nd ed. (1961), p. 32.

4. The Indian nationalist K. M. Panikkar expressed the following views in 1943: ". . . while still subject to British control [Burma] was no longer a colony, and practically governed itself". *The Future of South-East Asia, An Indian View* (1943), p. 13.

5. Nicholas Mansergh, *Survey of British Commonwealth Affairs. Problems of Wartime Co-operation and Post-War Change 1939–1952* (1958), p. 241.

6. Important for what follows: Maurice Collis, *Last and First in Burma (1941–1948)* (1958), pp. 26 f. Cady, pp. 430 f.

7. Collis, p. 35.

8. U Saw told of his talk with Churchill: "Churchill said, closely studying my face: Tell me, Mr. Prime Minister, are not the Burmese happier under British rule than under Thibaw?" U Saw answered by comparing England

under German rule, to which Churchill "did not reply at once but got up in anger and paced the room for a few minutes without further speech. He then said in sorrow rather than in anger: I do not know what has come over you young people nowadays". Quoted in Maung Maung, A Trail in Burma (1962), pp. 7 f. We cannot vouch for the authenticity of this report, but it sounds genuine.

9. "It is to that high position of Dominion status . . . that we wish to help Burma to attain as fully and completely as may be possible under certain contingencies immediately after the victorious conclusion of the war." Quoted in Cady, p. 431.

10. Collis, p. 189.
11. Quoted in Cady, p. 491.
12. Collis, p. 210.
13. Cady, p. 494.
14. Blue Print for Burma, ed. National Union of Conservative and Unionist Associations, November 1944.
15. The Times, 15 November 1944.
16. "But economic development must proceed, even at the risk of slowing down the process, on lines which appeal to national sentiment and tradition. Nothing else will give reality to the pledges which Britain must honour."
17. Readers' letters in The Times, 24 November and 2 December 1944.
18. House of Commons, CDVI, 1078 f.
19. P. 1099. For the preparations within the Labour party, cf. e.g. E. E. Dodd, "Reconstruction in Burma and Malaya", in Four Colonial Questions, ed. Fabian Colonial Bureau, December 1944. But it speaks only vaguely of future dominion status!
20. ". . . unwise at this stage to commit ourselves to publicly announced programmes." Secretary of State Amery, House of Commons, CDVI, 1127.
21. Printed in Documents and Speeches of the British Commonwealth, ed. Mansergh (1953), pp. 760 f.
22. House of Commons, CDXI, 495.
23. P. 403.
24. The Times, 2 June 1945.
25. In December Collis had written in the Observer that even acceptance of the Blue Print proposals hardly sufficed now: "Our Burmese critics, let us hope, will be indulgent, be slow to distrust us, be patient and co-operate. But my own frank opinion is that chance of a happy issue in Burma remains faint", p. 230.
26. "The Future of Burma", Pacific Affairs (1945), pp. 158 f.
27. Furnivall, Twilight, op. cit.
28. Collis, pp. 257, 262.
29. "It is very difficult to see how anything short of handing over complete power to a provisional Government could ease it." Collis, p. 277.
30. The Times, 6 April 1946, "Tension in Burma". Again on 6 June 1946: among the young Burmese there was a feeling of frustration, and their reconstruction required co-operation: "Burmese want their country reconstructed in their own way, and not in ours." On 5 August it stressed again that one must accept their right to dissociation!
31. Cady, p. 539.
32. House of Commons, 20 December 1946, CDXXXI, 2342 f.
33. House of Commons, CDXXXI, 2343, 2350.
34. Cf. Attlee's report in "As It Happened" (1954), p. 188. Also the commentary in the New Statesman: "The political life of Asia no longer

moves at a leisurely tempo. The Western Powers, after a century or more of imperialist rule, now face politically minded people who, in many cases, helped to win the war against Japan, and now demand their independence. Nothing can stem the tide of their conscious maturity; the real problem is whether we, the French and the Dutch, are willing to move peacefully in the same stream of history. . . . The delegation, expected in London this week, includes some of the ablest of Burmese statesmen. It will be warmly welcome, and it will meet many friends here who have the highest respect and affections for the Burmans, and who fully accept the case for Burmese independence. If the Burmans can believe this and overcome suspicions, often unhappily justified in the past, they will find the Government willing to meet their demands and to rebuild Burmese-British relations on a new foundation of friendship", 11 January 1947, p. 23.

35. Cady, p. 572.
36. Cf. the biography by Sir John Kotelawala, An Asian Prime Minister's Story (1956).
37. Generally the decision was negative. E.g. Lennox A. Mills, "Government and Social Services in Ceylon", Far Eastern Survey, 25 August 1943; "Soulbury Report", Commonwealth Documents 6677 (1945), p. 22; "The Soulbury Report", Round Table, XXXVI (1945–1946), 57; Ivor Jennings, The Dominion of Ceylon (1952), pp. 40 f. The judgement was positive in the judgement of Ceylonese writer S. Namasivayam, The Legislatures of Ceylon, 1928–1948 (1951), pp. 29 f. He pointed to the rapid Ceylonization of the administration, the extension of social services, etc.
38. Namasivayam, p. 120.
39. For this and what follows, cf. Sir Ivor Jennings, The Constitution of Ceylon (1949), pp. 3 f.
40. The declaration of 26 May 1943 in Documents and Speeches, pp. 714 ff.
41. Documents and Speeches, pp. 719 f.
42. "Statement of Policy on Constitutional Reform", Commonwealth Documents 6690; excerpts in Documents and Speeches, pp. 721 f. Cf. also Ivor Jennings, "Peaceful Island in a Troubled Ocean", the Listener, 5 May 1949.
43. Op. cit., pp. 723 f.
44. Sir Charles Jeffries, Ceylon, The Path to Independence (1962), pp. 113 f. Jeffries played a decisive part in the negotiations.
45. Documents and Speeches, p. 748.
46. Op. cit., pp. 749 f.
47. Op. cit., pp. 756 f.

FROM LEGISLATIVE COUNCIL TO INDEPENDENCE: THE GOLD COAST AND NIGERIA

1. Coleman, Nigeria, p. 240; cf. also Awolowo, Path to Nigerian Freedom (1947), p. 30.
2. Lord Swinton, I Remember (1948). Also M. Forbes. "The Impact of the War on British West Africa", International Affairs (1945), pp. 206 f.: Coleman, p. 251; Bourret, Gold Coast, pp. 142 f.
3. The number of unions in Nigeria rose from nine in 1941 to ninety-one at the end of the war; the number of union members rose from thirty thousand in 1944 to ninety-one thousand in 1948. J. I. Roper, Labor Problems in West Africa (1958), pp. 61, 107.

4. *Africans and British Rule* (1941).
5. "Education for Self-government", *Foreign Affairs*, October 1945.
6. P. 16. Similarly, the preface to Martin Wight, *The Development of the Legislative Council* (1946), pp. 9 f.
7. *On Governing Colonies* (1947) (the book appears to have been written around 1945).
8. P. 109.
9. "Many of our troubles in India arose from the fact that though the goal of self-governing was for long the common place of political declaration they were made with too many mental reservations. . . ." "Native Administration in Africa", *International Affairs* (1947), p. 339.
10. Quoted in L. Gray Cowan, *Local Government in West Africa* (1958), p. 62.
11. Dispatch on 25 February 1947. Cf. also Cowan, p. 63 Creech-Jones in the House of Commons: "A growth of local government and municipal life, an adaptation of native administration to carry increasing burdens of services", 29 July 1947, *House of Commons*, CDXLI, 270. The Labour party's interest in questions of local administration is also evident in *Local Government and the Colonies*, ed. Rita Hinden (A Report to the Fabian Colonial Bureau) (1950).
12. Cowan, pp. 63 f.
13. Earl of Listowel, "The Modern Conception of Government in British Africa", *Journal of African Administration*, I (1949), 104.
14. Bryan Keith Lucas, "The Dilemma of Local Government in Africa", in *Essays in Imperial Government*, presented to M. Perham (1963), p. 200.
15. Cowan, pp. 66 f.
16. *Op. cit.*, pp. 77 f.
17. Bourret, p. 158; Rita Hinden, *Local Government*, pp. 96 f. 112 f.
18. Bourret, p. 181.
19. Philip Garigue, "Changing Political Leadership in West Africa", *Africa* (1954), p. 3.
20. Cf. the essay by Lucas, *op. cit.*
21. The Ghanaian K. A. Busia spoke of a "culpable neglect of the development of local Councils". London and the nationalist leaders had directed too much attention to the Legislative council in the Centre, so that the Gold Coast had attained self-government "without a single local authority mature enough to be able to perform all the functions expected of a modern government authority". "The Prospects for Parliamentary Democracy in the Gold Coast", *Parliamentary Affairs*, Vol. V, No. 4 (1952), pp. 440 f.
22. Bourret, pp. 162 f.; Apter, pp. 143 f.
23. "Proposals for the Revision of the Constitution of Nigeria", *Commonwealth Documents* 6599 (1945), introductory note.
24. *Op. cit.*, p. 5 (dispatch of 6 December 1944).
25. Coleman, p. 273.
26. Governor Macpherson several times appealed to the Nigerians for unity, and in 1950 the colonial minister James Griffiths declared: "any tendency to break up Nigeria into separate parts would in the view of HMG be contrary to the interests of the peoples of all three Regions and of Nigeria as a whole." Coleman, p. 469, note 5. Azikiwe and the NCNC were in favour of a "federal Commonwealth of Nigeria". Coleman, p. 324.
27. Awolowo in 1947: "Since the amalgamation [i.e. since 1914] all the efforts of the British Government have been devoted to developing the country into a unitary state. . . . This is patently impossible". Quoted

in Coleman, p. 324. "Nigeria is not a nation. It is a mere geographic expression. There are no 'Nigerians' in the same sense as there are 'English', 'Welsh' or 'French'. The word 'Nigeria' is merely a distinctive appellation to distinguish those who live within the boundaries of Nigeria from those who do not." *Path to Nigerian Freedom*, p. 47. Balewa in 1948: "Since 1914 the British Government has been trying to make Nigeria into one country, but the Nigerian people themselves are historically different in their backgrounds, in their religious beliefs and customs and do not show themselves any sign of willingness to unite. . . . Nigerian unity is only a British intention for the country". Quoted in Coleman, p. 320.

28. E.g. Awolowo's critique in *Path to Nigerian Freedom*, p. 119.

29. Cf. the critique of Harold Cooper (an Englishman who had served in the colonies for twenty years), "Political Preparedness for Self-Government", *Annals of the American Academy of Political and Social Science*, July 1956, p. 73.

30. Thus B. Richard for instance, had proposed a nine-year transitional phase after which the constitutional situation could be re-examined; *Proposals*, p. 13.

31. Bourret, pp. 165 f. And particularly Dennis Austin, *Politics in Ghana 1946–1960* (1964), pp. 58 f.

32. Rather exaggeratedly, Cooper, *op. cit.*, p. 72. Even the *New Statesman*, on 24 February 1951, declared in retrospect: "Officials [i.e. also the Labour government] have repeatedly under-estimated this pace of African development", p. 208.

33. "Report of the Commission of Enquiry into Disturbances in the Gold Coast" (1948), *Colonial*, No. 231 (1948).

34. "Statement by HMG on the Report. . .", *Colonial*, No. 232 (1948).

35. "Gold Coast. Report to His Excellency the Governor by the Committee on Constitutional Reform" (1949), *Colonial*, No. 248 (1949). It emphasizes "the complexity and stress of modern life, the desire for change and the progressive outlook, which are now pervading even the remote village . . .", p. 9; "There is a popular cry throughout the country for universal adult suffrage", p. 10. The composition of the commission explains why it demanded more consideration of the chiefs.

36. "Statement by HMG on the Report . . .", *Colonial*, No. 250 (1949). "The desire of Africans to bear responsibility for the initiation and execution of policy has the fullest sympathy of HMG", p. 8.

37. Austin shows this clearly, pp. 51 f. Also, Hans N. Weiler, "Legislative Council and Indirect Rule. An examination of British Colonial Policy on the Gold Coast", in *Kultur im Umbruch, Studien zur Problematik und Analyse des Kulturwandels in Entwicklungsländern*, ed. G. K. Kindermann (1962). Weiler sees a kind of break in the elimination of former directly and indirectly elected Africans, which contradicted the picture of a continuous constitutional development.

38. Sir Charles Arden-Clarke, "Eight Years of Transition in Ghana", *African Affairs* (1958), p. 36.

39. Nkrumah and the governor have given a short but informative description of their first encounter at the moment of their release from prison and commission to form a cabinet: Nkrumah, *Autobiography of Kwame Nkrumah* (1957), pp. 137 f. Arden-Clarke, "Gold Coast into Ghana", *International Affairs*, January 1958.

40. I am chiefly following Coleman, ch. 14 and 18. Also, Kalu Ezera, *Constitutional Developments in Nigeria* (1960).

41. The grants-in-aid for education rose from £281,000 in 1944–1945 to £520,000 in 1946–1947 and £1,300,000 in 1948–1949; Ezera, p. 48.
42. E.g. Barbara Ward Jackson (on the staff of the *Economist*), "The Gold Coast. An Experiment in Partnership", *Foreign Affairs* (1954). Arden-Clarke, *Eight Years* . . . , p. 36.
43. "The British Problem in Africa", *Foreign Affairs*, July 1951, p. 637.
44. Margery Perham, "The Colonial Dilemma", the *Listener*, 14 July 1949. Everything pointed to the need for rapid economic and political development in Africa. But were conditions suitable? "Political development is in danger of outrunning economic development", p. 52. Similarly Kenneth Bradley, "Political Leadership and Devolution": "Above all, there is so little time. In the political as well as in the economic and social development of these backward peoples we are always up against the perhaps quite insoluble problem of trying to do the work of a thousand years in one generation. If we succeed, even partially, it will be one of the finest achievements in the history of mankind; and if we fail, the attempt itself will, I think, have been our vindication". The *Listener*, 4 August 1949, p. 180.
45. In retrospect both Sir Charles Arden-Clarke, *op. cit.*, p. 35, and Margery Perham, *The Colonial Reckoning* (1962), confirmed this.
46. "I hope this committee will not go wild and go all native and suggest immediate Self-government." *House of Commons*, CDLXVII, 2889.
47. *House of Commons*, 12 July 1950, CDLXXVII, 1478; also Duncan-Sandys to *The Times*, 7 August 1948.
48. *Op. cit.*, p. 1456.
49. "Indirect Rule in West Africa. Is Democracy Safe for the Negro World?", *Round Table*, XXXIX (1948–1949), 129 f.
50. "Self-government in the Gold Coast. Progress of a Constitutional Experiment", *Round Table*, XLII (1951–1952), 332.
51. Another essay on the Gold Coast three years later takes the same tone. It said the 1954 elections were a last step towards "full Self-government". The new constitution worked "with the maximum of consent", the Africanization had progressed and Nkrumah's government had made progress, particularly in the grave issue of the diseased cocoa plants. The problem of the Ashanti was not yet solved, but it was an illusion to believe in the possibility of a "two-thirds" dominion status. "A Nascent Dominion. African Self-Government in the Gold Coast", *Round Table*, XLV (1954–1955), 154.
52. "African Independence and After. Some Reflections on Self-government", *Round Table*, XLVI (1955–1956).

PARTNERSHIP IN THE RHODESIAN FEDERATION?

1. Cf. p. 223.
2. In detail, Richard Gray, *The Two Nations, Aspects and Development of Race Relations in the Rhodesias and Nyasaland* (1960), pp. 43 f.
3. In 1952 only 3.8 percent of the land in Nyasaland was privately owned. Gray, p. 83.
4. Pp. 103 f.
5. Pp. 41 f. For this and the following cf. also Robert I. Rotberg, "The Federation Movement in British East and Central Africa 1889–1953", *Journal of Commonwealth Political Studies*, Vol. II, No. 2 (1964), pp. 151 f.
6. Gray, p. 182.

7. *A New Deal in Central Africa*, ed. Colin Leys and Cranford Pratt (1960), p. 9.

8. "Report of the Rhodesia and Nyasaland Royal Commission", *Commonwealth Documents* 5949 (1939).

9. 31 July 1939, Gray, p. 193.

10. The ambivalence of the British attitude is very clear in the declaration of the secretary of state in the House of Lords: "If there is one thing which trusteeship involves . . . it is the right of the Africans to have a free chance . . . to learn a skilled trade and to operate that skilled trade"; but without the administration trying to intervene in the gentleman's agreement between the unions and the mining concerns. Lord Bledisloe had to admit on the same day: "The trusteeship of the UK is ideal in theory and on paper, but the state of Northern Rhodesia and Nyasaland illustrates in somewhat glaring colours the extreme difficulty of exercising that trusteeship efficiently 'longa manu' at a distance of 6000 miles." 31 July 1939, quoted in Gray, p. 185. Thus Bledisloe practically admitted that London largely neglected its function as trustee and left the decision to the settlers!

11. Quoted in Harry Franklin, *The Failure of the Central African Federation* (1963), p. 28. There is a good report in Welensky, *4000 Days. The Life and Death of the Federation of Rhodesia and Nyasaland* (1964).

12. The attitude of the *Round Table* is typical: "The British Government may have to sacrifice, as trustee, some measure of ultimate African self-rule [!] in return for greater security and prosperity. The Europeans of Southern Rhodesia on the other hand, will have to yield some measure of their resolve to confine the development of each race in separate channels. A mixed assembly is part of the price they would have to pay for federation." "Greater Rhodesia", *Round Table*, XXXIX (1948–1949), 233.

13. Quoted in *House of Lords*, 6 July 1953, CLXXXIII, 230.

14. "Once the Imperial Government have granted this constitution they have lost all control—don't forget that." 16 July 1951, quoted in Leys and Pratt, p. 28.

15. It is impossible to assess here how far the left wing of the party influenced the Labour government and, for instance, put pressure on the moderate and pro-settler minister Gordon-Walker. Cf. e.g. *New Statesman and Nation*, 15 September 1951: "It is difficult to see how Mr. Griffiths [Creech-Jones' successor as colonial minister] and Mr. Gordon-Walker can do other than conclude against federation at this time. For otherwise they will cast away not only every principle of colonial policy for which the Labour Policy has stood, but also the friendship for Britain of many million Africans", p. 273. Details on the conference in Franklin, ch. 4–6. The conference had "degenerated into a Native Benefit Society", said Huggins; Leys and Pratt, p. 32.

16. Leys and Pratt, p. 33; Franklin, pp. 67 f.

17. Leys and Pratt, p. 39. Excerpts from the constitution in *Documents and Speeches on Commonwealth Affairs 1952–1962*, ed. Mansergh (1963), pp. 115 f.

18. House of Commons, 27 July 1953, DXVIII, 900 f.; 16 December 1953, DXXII, 413 f.

19. "I will accept that the beneficiaries do not agree with it. That does not take away from the trustee the obligation to carry out his responsibility, and we are the trustees at the present time." Sir I. Fraser, 4 May 1953, *House of Commons*, DXV, 117.

20. Baldwin in the House of Commons on 4 May 1953, DXV, 99. Lord

Altrincham (formerly Sir E. Grigg, governor of Kenya): "I regard African opinion as negligible." *House of Lords*, 7 July 1953, CLXXXIII, 278.

21. *House of Commons*, 24 March 1953, DXIII, 675.

22. *House of Commons*, 27 July 1953, DXVIII, 943.

23. In 1949 Minister of State Lord Listowel gave in to conservative pressure and recognized the settlers as a community with equal rights: "What we want is a partnership between all who have made their homes in these Territories." *House of Lords*, 30 November 1949, CLXV, 118. Similarly the governor of Northern Rhodesia. Leys and Pratt, p. 9.

24. *House of Commons*, CDLXXXII, 1168 f.

25. Quoted in Franklin, p. 53.

26. E.g. Baldwin: "It is not for us in this House to say what is meant by partnership. The people who have to work the partnership are those in Central Africa. . . . Partnership does not necessarily mean advancement in the political field [!]. . . . I suggest that Southern Rhodesia have done more to further partnership than has been done in any of the Colonial Territories." *House of Commons*, 27 July 1953, DXVIII, 931. Accordingly Baldwin expressed his trust in Huggins.

27. Text in *Parliamentary Affairs*, Vol. VI, No. 1 (1952), p. 133. Leys and Pratt, p. 37.

28. "The Government both here and in England must accept the fact that millions of Africans will consider themselves abandoned and their trust unjustified, and that this fact will not be forgotten." Quoted in Franklin, p. 81.

29. Above all the former colonial minister Griffiths in the House of Commons on 27 July 1953, *House of Commons*, DXVIII, 921; 4 May 1953, DXV, 47; 16 December 1953, DXXII, 406 f.

30. "Power must eventually pass into the hands of the immense African majority." Letter to *The Times*, 1 March 1953, quoted in Leys and Pratt, p. 45.

31. "I would define partnership as . . . first, a settled purpose to do everything possible with mutual good will for the progressive social, intellectual and moral advancement of the African peoples . . . secondly . . . , the proportionate place held by Europeans will steadily diminish, and the place occupied by Africans will steadily increase." *House of Lords*, 2 April 1953, CLXXXI, 600.

32. Franklin, then colonial official in Northern Rhodesia, p. 57.

33. "Full democracy . . . no less valid in the plural societies than in any other type of society . . . by universal adult suffrage, on the principle of one person one vote." *Labour's Colonial Policy. The Plural Society* (Labour Research Dept.), July 1956, pp. 30 f. Also Griffiths in the House of Commons on 4 June 1957, *House of Commons*, DLXXI, 1190 f. Gaitskell, 27 July 1959, DCIX, 1292. The party's National Executive Committee demanded, in March 1958, "an unequivocal statement that the objective of the Federation is complete democracy and equal rights for every citizen". Quoted in Leys and Pratt, p. 172.

34. Cf. Franklin, pp. 105 f., 160 f.

35. Cf. the report by Anthony St. John Woods, *Northern Rhodesia, the Human Background* (1961). For many years Wood was colonial official in Nigeria, and even when he reached retirement age, he had himself sent to Northern Rhodesia. He points out the difficulties of colonial service in a settlers' territory and sharply criticized the Europeans' practised discrimination. Also, Kenneth Kaunda, *Zambia Shall Be Free, an Autobiography* (1962).

36. Franklin, p. 14.

37. For example, on 2 March 1956 Welensky said: "We Europeans have no intention of handing over the Federation to anyone, because we have no intention of getting out. We believe that the African should be given more say in the running of his country, as and when he shows his ability to contribute more to the general good, but we must make it clear that even when that day comes, in a hundred or two hundred years' time, he can never hope to dominate the partnership. He can achieve equal standing, but not beyond it." Similarly, Lord Malvern (formerly Sir Huggins), the first prime minister of the Federation: "In the distant future Africans may earn the right to become equal partners, which means that they could have a half share in the partnership but never more than that." Quoted in Philip Mason, *Year of Decision. Rhodesia and Nyasaland 1960* (1960), p. 69.

38. In 1948 his proposal was approved by the election results, but he did not put it into practice for fear of giving the opposition to the Federation additional arguments. Meanwhile, in March 1948, of the 47,000 registered voters only 258 were Africans. Sir Huggins' commentary on the electoral law was typical: it would come to "almost as much as closing the Roll for fifteen years", Gray, p. 309.

39. Travel report by Eric Mettler in *Neue Zürcher Zeitung*, 5 March 1960.

40. Parliament numbered fifty-nine deputies, of which forty-four were elected by the Europeans; nine Africans were elected in boroughs with European majorities and therefore had to be acceptable to the United Federal party! Four indirectly elected Africans represented Northern Rhodesia and Nyasaland, two Europeans were appointed. Mason, p. 86. In 1961 the population of the Federation was 8.2 million Africans and some three hundred thousand whites (population proportion in 1961: in Southern Rhodesia: 1:33, Northern Rhodesia, 1:42, Nyasaland, 1:588). Of 19,767 registered voters, 1165 were Africans. Patrick Keatley, *The Politics of Partnership* (1963), p. 223.

41. "Report of the Nyasaland Commission of Inquiry", *Commonwealth Documents* 814 (1959). The *Neue Zürcher Zeitung* commented on 25 July 1959: "There are still judges in England!" Cf. also Mason, pp. 203 f.

42. Cf. the exciting report by Sir Michael Blundell, a respected leader of the liberals in Kenya, *So Rough a Wind* (1964), pp. 267 f.

43. C. E. Carrington, "Mr. Macmillan in Africa", *The World To-day*, March 1960.

44. E.g. "Your University College of Salisbury is giving a first-class education to men and women of all races. I look forward to the day when the same spirit will inspire your technical colleges and your secondary schools [!]." Quoted in Mason, p. 234.

45. A fairly long excerpt in *Documents and Speeches on Commonwealth Affairs 1952–1962*, ed. N. Mansergh (1963), pp. 347–51.

46. On 3 December 1959 the *Neue Zürcher Zeitung* reported that in the course of the year the mining concerns had begun to stop their financial aid to the United Federal party. This change of policy primarily affected the Rhodesian Selection Trust, in which American capital played an important role.

47. "Report of the Advisory Commission on the Review of the Constitution of Rhodesia and Nyasaland", *Commonwealth Documents* 1148 (1960). Macmillan had acceded to several of Welensky's demands concerning the composition of the commission and the extent of its obligations. Keatley,

pp. 443 f.; cf. also "Some Reflections on the Monckton Report", *The World To-day*, December 1960; Mason, pp. 231 f.

48. Unlawful Organization Bill, Preventive Detention Bill, etc. By February 1959 the African National Congress founded in 1957 had been banned and five hundred leading Africans were arrested.

49. E.g. *Matters of Moment*, 28 January 1960. Similarly on 25 February 1960.

50. 22 November 1960, p. 255. "It ought, however, to be clearly understood that the Europeans of Southern Rhodesia will on no account submit to the fate inflicted upon Kenya by a defeatist Government in the UK", 8 November 1962, p. 213.

51. *House of Lords*, 28 March 1960, CCXXII 360.

52. Cf. Keatly, pp. 446 f.

53. Report on the party conference in the *Neue Zürcher Zeitung*, 13 October 1960.

54. *Wind of Change. The Challenge of the Commonwealth. By a Conservative Group*, ed. Lord Colyton (1960). Cf. also *East Africa and Rhodesia*, 5 May 1960, 26 May 1960.

55. Another example: "The truth is that democracy and multi-racialism are incompatible." Worsthoren, "Perils of Premature Democracy in Africa," a series of articles in the *Daily Telegraph*, excerpts in *East Africa and Rhodesia*, 7 April 1960, pp. 752 f.

56. "By the disappearance of race differences as the predominant feature of politics." Similar arguments were used by the former governor of Nigeria and under-secretary of state for colonies, Sir John Macpherson, in a speech before the Royal Commonwealth Society, in *East Africa and Rhodesia*, 5 May 1960, pp. 832 f.

57. The slogan "too far and too fast" was also advanced by Lord de la Warr before the Joint East and Central Africa Board, in *East Africa and Rhodesia*, 5 May 1960, p. 909.

58. Keatly, p. 459.

59. *Op. cit.*, p. 456.

60. Franklin, pp. 210 f. On the disputed plans for an imperial state, cf. Welensky, pp. 200 f.

61. On 8 February 1962 the *Neue Zürcher Zeitung* reported new disputes in the party.

62. *The Times*, 4 February 1960.

63. *The Times*, 23 March 1960.

64. *The Times*, 5 December 1960.

65. Lord Salisbury, 14 February 1961; Lord Robins, 21 February 1961; and Lord Selborne, director of a British company with connections in Katanga, on 22 February 1961.

66. The *Economist*, 3 December 1960, pp. 999 f.

67. Cf. The *Economist*, 18 February 1961: the accepted phrases and formulas must finally be re-examined. It was not sensible to speak of "multiracialism" when, as in Northern Rhodesia, 250 Africans were paired against only 8 Europeans.

68. A short general summary, among others, in J. J. B. Somerville, "The Central African Federation", *International Affairs*, July 1963.

69. *Keesing's Contemporary Archives*, 7 November 1964, p. 11520. Cf. also the reports in the *Neue Zürcher Zeitung*, 27 and 29 October 1964.

FROM THE BRITISH COMMONWEALTH OF NATIONS TO THE MULTI-RACIAL COMMONWEALTH

1. Gordon-Walker, *The Commonwealth*, p. 114.
2. Nicholas Mansergh, *Survey of British Commonwealth Affairs. Problems of Wartime Co-operation and Post-War Change 1939–1952* (1958), pp. 90 f. Francis Williams, *A Prime Minister Remembers* (Attlee) (1961), p. 54.
3. *Documents and Speeches on British Commonwealth Affairs, 1931–1952*, ed. N. Mansergh, I (1953), 562 f.; *Survey*, p. 165 f.
4. *Documents*, pp. 568 f.; *Survey*, pp. 173 f.
5. *Documents*, pp. 575 f.; *Survey*, pp. 176 f.
6. E.g. speech before Parliament on 31 January 1944, *Documents*, pp. 579 f.; similarly on 11 May 1944, *Documents*, pp. 587 f.
7. The communiqué of 23 May 1944 states: "The existing methods of consultation have proved their worth . . . they are peculiarly appropriate to the character of the British Commonwealth. . . . it is a creed that the methods now practised are preferable to any rigid centralized machinery." *Documents*, p. 596.
8. *Documents*, p. 597.
9. P. 7.
10. "The British Commonwealth, Its Place and Service of the World" (1942). *Britische Aussenpolitik* (1945).
11. "The British Commonwealth and the World", in *India and Freedom* (1942); *The Framework of the Future* (1944); *Thoughts on the Constitution* (1947); "The British Commonwealth", in *World Affairs* (1948).
12. Grigg, *British Foreign Policy* (1944), p. 147.
13. Amery, *Thoughts on the Constitution*, p. 146.
14. Amery, *Framework . . .*, p. 16.
15. *India and Freedom*, p. 115; *Framework . . .*, p. 25.
16. "Many of us would, I think, depreciate the idea that the political evolution of the colonies should take the form of Dominion status, such as has recently been held out to Ceylon. We find it difficult to believe that this form of relationship, involving as it does an independent sovereign status, would be appropriate to the majority of the colonies as we know them, or would be to the benefit either of the colonies themselves or the empire or indeed the world." "British Colonial Administration", in *Colonial Administration by European Powers* (RIIA, 1947), p. 91 (text of a conference held in late 1946).
17. Very clear in *The British Commonwealth and World Society. Proceedings of the Third Unofficial Conference on British Commonwealth Relations*, London, 17 February–3 March 1945, ed. R. Frost (1947).
18. *Survey*, p. 249. An excellent summary in Mansergh, *Commonwealth Perspectives* (1958), p. 24.
19. Gordon-Walker, p. 136.
20. *Ibid.*, p. 138.
21. Quoted in Mansergh, *Perspectives*, p. 28.
22. P. 30. On 2 March 1949 Attlee reported to the king how he sought and gained the agreement of Churchill and other conservatives to make it possible for India to remain in the Commonwealth by accepting the republic. At the meeting of prime ministers, the dominions also agreed to this. Peter Fraser from New Zealand is said to have made a particularly strong

impression on Nehru here. Williams, *A Prime Minister Remembers*, pp. 218 f.

23. M. S. Rajan, *The Post War Transformations of the Commonwealth, Reflection on the Asian-African Contribution* (1963), p. 10.

24. From a speech before the Royal Empire Society on 12 October 1950, *Documents* . . . , pp. 1217 f.

25. *The Commonwealth*, p. 382. Also, "Policy for the Commonwealth", in *Fabian International Essays* (1956–1957).

26. Equally clear in John Strachey (War Minister in the Labour government), *The End of Empire* (1959), pp. 253, 262.

27. On 29 April 1960 *The Times* wrote that as long as South Africa "continue in their present extremist rigour then the Commonwealth partnership will suffer still greater shock and disillusionment"; on 10 May: "In the long run the Commonwealth must rest upon truth and not on fiction. It is a multi-racial Commonwealth." On 8 October *The Times* attacked the "clique" in the South African Government, but was against excluding it from the Commonwealth. But after the final decision, it wrote, on 16 March, that without the withdrawal of South Africa, "the unity of the Commonwealth would have been gravely threatened. . . . We can now see the Commonwealth without equivocal reservation as being firmed on a secure multiracial basis".

28. Gordon-Walker, *The Commonwealth*, p. 188 f.; Martin Reiser, *Das Commonwealth of Nations. Begriff, Rechtsnatur, Wesen* (1961), p. 2.

29. *India and Freedom*, p. 108. Sir Ivor Jennings, *The British Commonwealth* (1948; 4th ed., 1961), p. 13. Hodson: "The British Commonwealth, then includes both independent and dependent countries . . . it is the rightful name of the whole British Empire", p. 154.

30. An attack on the concept of "dominions" also in Hodson, pp. 152 f.

31. Pp. 158 f.

32. K. M. Panikkar, *The Future of South-East Asia* (1943), pp. 49, 55: "When that is given effect, a fourth British Empire will have come to existence . . . an Indo-British partnership which creates such a non-racial conception of freedom will in itself constitute the justification of Britain's history in the East!"

33. Frank H. Underhill, *The British Commonwealth, an Experiment in Co-operation among Nations* (1956), p. xxi and a special chapter.

34. N. Mansergh, *The Name and Nature of the British Commonwealth* (1955), p. 6.

35. Gordon-Walker, Pt. III; Miller, pp. 58 f.; P. F. Gonidec, "Metamorphose du commonwealth", *Revue juridique et politique de l'Union française* (1950–1952), pp. 232 f.

36. For example the number of telegrams sent out from the office rose from 5600 in 1938 to 26,000 in 1955.

37. "Commonwealth Fallacies," 14 July 1956, p. 108.

38. Oliver S. Franks (former British ambassador in Washington), *Britain and the Tide of World Affairs*, Reith Lectures (1954), p. 14.

39. Speech before the West Point Military Academy on 5 December 1962: Britain had lost an Empire and had not yet found its place in world politics; the Commonwealth was not a political unit and was not suited to give Great Britain an intermediate position between Europe and the U.S. Prime Minister Macmillan replied sharply on 7 December: Acheson seemed to misunderstand the role of the Commonwealth in world politics completely; *Keesing's Contemporary Archives* (1962), pp. 10287–88.

40. 1951 party programme: *Britain Strong and Free*, p. 11.

41. "It is the most successful experiment in international relations which the world has ever known. We believe that if the British Empire were to break up Britain would become a third-class power, unable to feed or defend herself. The same fate would quite certainly befall every other country of this family of nations, one by one, and thus would crumble to ruin the world's greatest bulwark of Liberty and Democracy." ". . . its role as a leader of free peoples against the encroachments of world communism. . . . It is sometimes forgotten that the potential strength of the British Empire and Commonwealth is greater than that of either the United States of America or the USSR." *Imperial Policy, a Statement of Conservative Policy for the British Empire and Commonwealth* (1949), pp. 1, 8, 9.

42. "It has only to develop its resources to match the power of the US of America or the USSR. If the Commonwealth ceases to expand then will mankind be in danger of ultimate catastrophe. Millions throughout the world look to the Commonwealth for leadership and the Commonwealth looks to London." *The Expanding Commonwealth* (1956), pp. 3, 23.

43. *The Right Road for Britain*, party programme (1949), p. 56.

44. James F. Tierney, "Britain and the Commonwealth: Attitudes in Parliament and Press in the UK since 1951", *Political Studies*, VI (1958), 228 f.

45. Gordon-Walker spoke of a "real force in the world", an "economic entity" and even of a "considerable approach to a Commonwealth strategic pattern", and sketched out the defence question in the Pacific and the system of treaties, without even mentioning the special role of the U.S.! *The Commonwealth*, pp. 324 f.

46. "A Party in Search of a Pattern, II. Patriotism Based on Reality Not on Dream", by a Conservative, *The Times*, 2 April 1964, p. 13.

II. FRANCE

LA PLUS GRANDE FRANCE AND ECONOMIC DEVELOPMENT

1. 31 July 1929, *Journal Officiel*, [henceforth J. O.] *Chambre des Députés, Documents parlementaries* (1929), Annexe 2262, p. 526.
2. Joseph Cailley, "L'avenir de nos colonies", *Revue des Sciences Politiques* (1917), p. 215.
3. Alfred Guignod, "Les troupes noires pendant la guerre", *Revue des deux mondes*, 15 June 1919, p. 878. 518,638 soldiers and 183,928 workers are mentioned, René La Bruyère, "Le problème de la mobilisation d'Outre-Mer" in *Revue des deux mondes*, 1 May 1933, p. 173.
4. Albert Sarraut, *La mise en valeur des colonies françaises* (1922), p. 17.
5. E.g. *L'Empire colonial français*, several editors, with a foreword by Gabriel Hanotaux (1929). Pierre Lyautey, *L'Empire colonial français* (1931), is a general outline with detailed information.
6. *Revue Économique française*, published by the Société de la Géographie commerciale et d'études coloniales (1935), pp. 262 f. The term "France totale" also occurs in the opening address of the colonial minister Louis Rollin at the imperial conference, cf. *L'Afrique française* (1934), p. 699.
7. These were two articles in *Le Capital*, August 1934.
8. Robert Francis, Thierry Maulnier, Jean-Pierre Maxence, *Demain la France* (1934); cf. Karl Epting, *Das französische Sendungsbewusstsein in 19. und 20. Jahrhundert* (1952), pp. 94 f.
9. Henri Hauser (economic historian at the Sorbonne), "Greater France", *Foreign Affairs*, December 1923, p. 211. Pierre Lyautey, *op. cit.*, p. 521. "A nation without imperialism . . . is condemned to decadence. . . . The twentieth century seems to be that of the triumph of empires, of five or six empires which will share the world", Jean Vidailhet, "La démocratie française et son impérialisme", *Révue Économique française*, April 1935, pp. 346, 551.
10. R. St. Baker, Wilson, *Dokumente*, I, 335 f.
11. Sarraut, *op. cit.*, p. 17. "The evolution and methodical organization of the native premium are the necessary preface to the new statute to be envisaged for the French army", p. 62.
12. An exception is the conservative professor at the École Coloniale, Louis Vignon, who mentioned the "silent hostility", the frequent riots, which often made a state of siege necessary. *Un programme de politique coloniale* (1919), p. 246.
13. *Mise en valeur des colonies* (1923), p. 100.

14. M. Delafosse, "Les points sombres de l'horizon en Afrique occidentale", *Afrique française* (1922), p. 276.
15. E.g. the attitude of the Ligue Maritime et Coloniale, in *Afrique française* (1922), p. 109.
16. Sarraut, p. 75.
17. Albert Sarraut, "Nationalisons l'idée coloniale" in *L'Europe nouvelle*, 1 May 1926.
18. "The intensive economic development of our overseas resources dominates the whole problem of our material life tomorrow. This alone [!] will certainly cure our financial situation . . . this alone will lower the high cost of living, will forearm our industries against the lack of raw materials and their workers against the miseries of unemployment", *op. cit.*, p. 580. The reporter on the colonial budget, Leon Archimbaud, said in the Chamber of Deputies on 4 December 1931: "Our colonies can provide us with all the materials we need [!]. They are the reservoir and the outlet for our national industries. No aspect of our activity can afford to remain apart from the great currents of exchanges which mutually activate the gains of the metropolis and of its distant possessions." *Documentation coloniale comparée*, II (1931), 6.
19. E.g. "France, who colonizes, does not only work for itself; its profit is one with the profit of the world . . .", p. 18.
20. Pp. 17 f.
21. P. 27, "means that are more or less limitless. . . ."
22. Sarraut, *op. cit.*, p. 339.
23. *Ibid.*, p. 19.
24. The term "complementary" is also found in Henri Lorin, "Ce que doivent être nos colonies", *Revue des deux mondes*, 15 September 1919, p. 432.
25. Sarraut, *op. cit.*, p. 433.
26. *Ibid.*, p. 94. Sarraut himself stressed the utilitarian aspect: "If, in effect, one analyses the main elements that constitute what one calls our native policy, for instance medical care and education, one is struck by the essentially traditional utilitarian tradition of each of them", p. 93.
A clearly colonialist accent is apparent in the vote of the deputy Marcel Habert: the colonies should be developed for the profit of France in order to supply the products which would otherwise have to come from abroad, ". . . we have just shown you how we must turn an affectionate eye on the natives in order to ensure ourselves their aid . . . having secured the material life of these natives, we must give them education. Which education? . . . Let us not waste our time by giving them primary education, which is no use to them, let us not give these children, whom we need as workers, courses in history or literature, let us give them technical education . . .". J. O. Chambre, 29 June 1920, p. 2561.
27. Quoted in P. F. Gonidec, *Droit d'outre-mer*, I (1959), 225.
28. J. O., Doc. parl., Annexe 2449 (1921), pp. 1571–1665.
29. An Englishman commented in polemic, and not unjustified tones: "Journalists and politicians become lyrical when they write about the magnificence of this discovery." Denis Gwyan, "France and her Colonial Resources", *Contemporary Review*, September 1923, p. 340.
30. The reporter on the colonial budget in the Senate, Senator Albert Lebrun (later president of the Republic) gave a positive view: "For the colonial producers it constitutes a precious guarantee for the sale of their production to France. Similarly, thanks to it, French industry is assured of finding the

protection and aid it needs in the assimilated colonies" [!], *Documentation coloniale comparée*, II (1930), 17.

On the other hand, the honorary governor, Camille Guy, was very criticial: French tariff policy was still that of the colonial pact, for instance, parliament regulated the production of rum in favour of the metropolis; the governors were all against an assimilatory tariff policy. Indochina, for example, produced 1.7 million tons of rice, but France only bought 150,000 tons. But how could Indochina export to other countries when the imports from these countries were subject to high duties? Assimilation "condemned the colonies to stagnation or even regression". "La politique coloniale de la France", *La politique coloniale de la France. Conférences organisées par la Société des Anciens Élèves de l'École libre des Sciences Politiques* (1934), p. 260.

31. Cf. e.g. the "official" attitude of Louis Mérat (director of economic affairs in the Colonial Ministry): "The simplest and most effective temporary remedy against the industrialization of our colonies consists in prolonging, as far as possible, by a policy of support and by commercial agreements, the era of agricultural, pastoral, production, forestry and mining. Our colonies have the incontestable right to industrialize themselves for their own needs or in order to conquer foreign markets, because for them this is a means of wealth which, besides, cannot on the whole, harm French industry. The case *is different when it is a question of overthrowing the metropolitan market*, i.e. certain colonial markets." "La loi douanière coloniale de 1928 et l'évolution économique des colonies" in *Revue politique et parlementaire*, CLXXII (1937), 466.

32. Paul Reynaud gives an impressive report on the state and problems of the colonial economy after the depression: many products were priced above the world market level, but not imports from France. Either one must guarantee the colonies better prices for production, or enable them to import from other areas, *Documentation coloniale comparée*, I (1935), 46.

33. The French, among others, pointed to the allegedly low production prices in North Africa, or they argued that colonial production replaced the agricultural production of the metropolis, bananas instead of fruit, rice for cereal, coffee for wine. René Hoffherr, a recognized specialist on economic problems in the colonies, attacked these theories in "Comment organiser une économie française d'Empire?", *Politique étrangère*, III (1938), 185 f. On the other hand, Pierre Mille, "La Conférence impériale", *Le Temps*, 2-3 January 1935: "let us repeat for the thousandth time that the native can only buy if he has also sold". "The Position of the Colonial French" by E. Guernier, *Pour une Politique d'Empire* (1938).

34. The resolution to unite the Tunisian settlers in 1934, cf. Hoffherr, p. 185.

35. 1913: 12.5 percent; 1927: 13 percent; 1932: 25 percent; 1937: 26 percent; C. J. Gignoux, *L'économie française entre les deux guerres, 1919 à 1939* (1942), p. 188.

36. Gignoux, *op. cit.*, p. 189.

37. J. H. Priestley, *France Overseas* (1938), pp. 428 f.

38. Louis Pichat, "L'outillage public de la France d'outre-mer", *Revue politique et parlementaire*, CLXIII (1935), 279. Pierre Mille, "Démonstration par l'absurde", *Le Temps*, 10 November 1937.

39. Speeches by the president of the Republic, Lebrun, and the colonial minister, Rollin, in *L'Afrique française* (1934), pp. 696 f.

40. Gérard Barget, "Le problème de la redistribution, ses modalités", *Esprit* (1935), p. 423.

41. Cf. details in *Marchés coloniaux*, 8 April 1950, p. 743.
42. P. 156. Similarly Vidailhet in the aforementioned essay: "Indeed, we are not unaware that in Asia and America we will not find what we seek. But Africa is at our gates: it is a new continent which offers many hopes and of which France alone possesses a third of the land. . . . We must integrate Africa into Europe, gradually . . .", "La democratie française et son imperialisme", *Revue economique française*, April 1935, p. 444.
43. P. 5.
44. "Pour une politique d'Empire" (1938) (articles in Moroccan newspapers, 1934–1935), pp. 57 f.
45. *Marchés coloniaux, op. cit.*
46. *Esprit* (1935), p. 425.
47. "Idées blanches sur l'Afrique noire" in *L'Afrique française* (1935), pp. 13 f. "Action colonisatrice et Paysannat indigène", *L'Afrique française* (1935), p. 526. Both articles give further references to Eurafrican essays and committees.
48. "Les origines et les buts de l'exposition coloniale", *Revue des deux mondes*, 1 May 1931, p. 54.
49. "Philosophie de l'exposition coloniale", *op. cit.*, 15 November 1931, pp. 283 f.
50. "Après l'exposition coloniale", *op. cit.*, 1 January (or 1 April) 1933, p. 53.
51. We list the directors of the political department of the colonial ministry without giving details of the individual organizations. The names clearly show a combination of representatives of national conservatism and economic representatives, as in England.
"One can cite the French Union, the Institut français, the Academy of Colonial Sciences. The aim of the colonial Union is to group the commercial interests of our possessions; its successive presidents have been MM. Mercet and le Neven. Created after the war, the Institut colonial proposes to defend the general interests of colonization; its presidents have been MM. de Rouvre and Admiral Lacaze; its secretary-general is M. Gheerbrandt. Finally, in the five years or so of its existence, the Academy of Colonial Sciences, whose public usefulness is recognized, has gained the same prestige as its corresponding institutions. Its successive presidents have been MM. Gabriel Hanotaux, Marshal Franchet d'Espéry, Paul Doumer and Lacroix; its permanent secretary is M. Paul Bourdarie, and members are recruited by co-optation. Nor must it be forgotten, taking a more specialized aspect, that the Comité de l'Afrique française, has taken fruitful action; its successive presidents have been Prince d'Arenberg, MM. Jonnart and Roume; M. Terrier, assisted by M. Ladreit de Lacharriere, has been its devoted secretary-general for more than thirty years. The Comité de l'Asie française and that of Océanie française, where the parts played by MM. Senart, Robert de Caix and Froment-Guieysse have so often been both judicious and percipient, deserve just as much praise." Albert Duchêne, *La politique coloniale de la France* (1928), p. 314.
52. *J. O., Chambre*, 31 January 1930.
53. *Ibid.*, 25 March 1930.
54. *Ibid.*, 13 June 1930.
55. E.g. the replacement of Weygand by Sarrail in Syria in 1924, ed. Bonnefous, *Histoire politique de la troisième République*, IV (1960), 87.
56. The absence-on-leave of a parliamentary deputy was restricted to six months, which did not prevent him from taking a governor's post, but did make it more difficult, since the deputy then had to give up his mandate. J.

Paul-Boncour, *Entre deux guerres, Souvenirs sur la IIIe. République*, II (1945), 408.

57. "There are two notions to create or restore: the notion of the Empire and the notion of the State. First, the Empire; it is made up of territories, but also of the real or virtual means which the European and overseas territories contain; even more it is made up of the collective conscience of those who live there; the Empire is a material notion and a moral notion, which, having been conceived and exploited, can be the most fruitful guarantee of a positive policy of organized peace. Next, the State; it is an expression of that conscience put into action; it is the eternal centre of the history of France; a superior force—because it translates the whole and acts in its service—to the individual forces which, great as they may be, divide. France has neglected the Empire since 1918; drunk with the desire to safeguard the metropolitan soil. Faithful to the destiny of its life and to the spirit of the times, Clemenceau has passionately lived in the service of European peace without pressing hard on the exigencies of our imperial life. But it is this that would save us in case of danger whether in 1935 when our national forces will be weakened by the injuries of war, or whether in a potential hypothesis of international solitude. The imperial conscience must be born. It would be a source of self-assurance, not of imperialist psychosis; for this latter state is a disease of the mind, which plain reality suffices to prevent." *L'épreuve du pouvoir* (1931), p. xviii.

58. Robert Raynaud, "Un ministère de la France extérieure", *Revue politique et parlementaire*, CXXXVII (1928), 421 f.

59. Robert Montagne, "Comment organiser politiquement l'Empire français" in *Politique étrangère*, Vol. III (1938).

60. J. O., 28 June 1935 (Annexe No. 5601).

61. Montagne, *op. cit.*

62. Annexe No. 5601. It was asserted that one of the buildings of the colonial ministry had been built at the cost of the Indochinese budget, under the pretext of a visit by the emperor of Annam. *Réalités coloniales* (1934), p. 50. The author also attacked the colonial exhibitions, on the grounds that the few available resources of the ministry could be better spent on other tasks.

ASSIMILATION OR ASSOCIATION?

1. Among the comprehensive literature we might mention Arthur Girault, *Principes de Colonisation et de Législation coloniale*, 4th ed. (1921). Louis Rolland, Pierre Lampué, *Précis de droit des pays d'outre-mer* (1949), P. F. Gonidec, *Droit d'outre-mer*, Vol. I (1959).

2. Auguste-Raynold Werner, *Essai sur la réglementation de la nationalisté dans le droit colonial français* (1936).

3. There is a complete list of the number of "French citizens" (not separated according to citizens of European origins and naturalized natives) and of the entire population in 1938 in Michel Devèze, *La France d'outre-mer* (1948), p. 16. A few examples: Guadeloupe, 247,000 – 247,000; Martinique, 304,000 – 304,000; French Indies, 323,000 – 323,000; Algeria, 7,200,000 – 988,000; French West Africa, 14,900,000 – 90,000 (including of course the inhabitants of the Four Communes!); French Equatorial Africa, 3,400,000 – 5,000; Madagascar, 3,700,000 – 31,000; Indochina, 25,000,000 – 42,000.

4. R. A. Winnacker, "Elections in Algeria and the French Colonies under the Third Republic" in *American Political Science Review*, XXXII (1938). Winnacker points out that the important Wallon Amendment of 1875, which was passed by only one vote, was approved by twelve of the fifteen colonial deputies; the hotly disputed credits for Tonkin in 1885 enjoyed a similar fate: the parliament accepted it by 273 to 263 votes, but fifteen of the sixteen deputies from the colonies were in favour: p. 265.

5. Note how right-wing, bourgeois Paul Reynaud judged the Assemblées Indochinoises on 28 June 1935 as reporter on the colonial budget:

"There is little one can say about them except that they represent absolutely nothing, neither by their mode of designation nor in the competence of their members.

"Their mode of designation is a deceit which gives rise to the most dire consequences. How can one allow the Annamite councillors of the Conseil colonial of Cochin China to really represent the mass of their compatriots (four million) when it is known that they are elected by an electoral college of 1200 to 1800 electors!

"As for the French elements, experience shows that things are so serious that the few balanced and conservative elements want nothing to do with them (besides, would they be elected?). But a colonist who has not succeeded has time to present himself before a chamber of agriculture or of commerce in order to acquire a title which will enable him to defend his interests more effectively. We know what that means." *Documentation coloniale comparée*, II (1935).

6. The Grand Conseil des intérêts économiques et financiers of Indochina, founded in 1928, numbered fifty-four members, for instance; of these thirty-one were French, i.e. citizens, eleven elected and twenty representatives appointed by the chambers of economics; the twenty-three natives were appointed by the local assemblies in the individual states, so they were usually notables. In the Tunisian Grand Conseil there were two separate sections in 1922 with forty-one Tunisians as opposed to fifty-seven Frenchmen, i.e. citizens.

7. For the discussion before 1914 cf. Raymond F. Betts, *Assimilation and Association in French Colonial Theory 1890–1914* (1961). Martin Deming Lewis, "One Hundred Million Frenchmen: The 'Assimilation' Theory in French Colonial Policy", in *Comparative Studies in Society and History*, IV (1962), 2.

8. J. Harmand, *Domination et Colonisation* (1910), p. 348.

9. Harmand, *op. cit.*, p. 160.

10. *J. O., Chambre*, 21 December 1922, p. 4408.

11. "We, black Frenchmen, we are in favour of remaining Frenchmen, since France has given us all its rights and we are merged without reservation with its own European children. None of us aspires to seeing French Africa exclusively delivered up to the Africans, as the American Blacks, at whose head you place yourself, are demanding—without authority, incidentally.

"No propaganda, no Black or White pressure will remove the feeling that France alone is able to work generously to advance the Black race. The French Black élite, which has responsibility for the natives in our colonies, could not allow, without renouncing its new duty, the theories of separatism and revolutionary emancipation, to which your name is ascribed, to cause trouble or disorder where calm and order are the indispensable factors of the security of us all.

"Having said this, we willingly acknowledge that the social conditions imposed on the Blacks in America are odious and that we protest in solidarity with you, as do besides all white Frenchmen, who do not understand the injustice of the white Americans to the Blacks." Letter dated 3 July 1922, in *Revue Indigène* (1922), p. 275, quoted in R. L. Buell, *The Native Problem in Africa* (1928), p. 81.

12. *J. O.*, 28–30 January 1930, p. 293.
13. I, 108, note 1.
14. I, 109.
15. I, 105–06.
16. I, 74.
17. I, 430.
18. I, 432.
19. I, 6.
20. P. 431.
21. IV (Algeria), 5th ed., 81.
22. *La politique coloniale de la France* (1928), p. 314.
23. "Organisation coloniale", in *La politique coloniale de la France* (Conférences organisées par la Société des Anciens Élèves de l'École libre des Sciences Politiques, 1934), p. 167.
24. Pp. 170 f.
25. P. 212.
26. P. 495.
27. P. 268.
28. P. 314.
29. P. 218.
30. P. 537, note 1.
31. This was a government motion on 24 November 1924, for a law that would have removed naturalization from the sphere of administrative appraisement and automatically granted it to all those natives who, giving up their personal status, had mastered the French language and could show a diploma, the legion of honour or a military distinction. Cf. Runner, "This demagogic project, which largely aims at fulfilling the claims of a few native agitators, has provoked lively discussions and a volume of criticism, particularly on the part of M. Sambuc in a report presented to the 'Comité des jurisconsultes de l'Union coloniale.' M. Sambuc denounces the dangers of this right to naturalization accorded to natives and which would be mainly used by those whose purpose is not disinterested, and he adds: 'We believe that the grant of French citizenship to our subjects and protégés must remain a favour, an exceptional reward, subject to the free and sovereign appreciation of the superior authority, and that the latter is responsible for showing itself more or less liberal in the conferment of such a reward, according to the conditions and the organization and the development of each colony.' In the colonial chronicle of the Societé d'Études et d'Informations économiques, an article on this motion criticized it primarily for being too much marked by favour and reward. The author of the article adds: 'The main reproach against this motion is that it classifies the titles of the natives according to our notions and not theirs . . . , except in very rare cases, these automatically naturalized persons will never be more than second-class Frenchmen; this is of interest neither to them, nor to us'", p. 40.
32. Pp. 136, 141 f.
33. P. 92.
34. This is summarized, in similar terms, in "L'oeuvre coloniale de la

France", in *Études de Colonisation comparée*, ed. Louis Franck (1924), Vol. I.

35. "I repeat and I emphasize, it is a necessity of political and of economic power for the metropolis which is at the source of this expansion." *J. O., Sénat*, 27 February 1920.

36. *La Mise en valeur*, p. 101.

37. ". . . Considering as younger brothers the races which are under its tutelage, France takes them by the hand to lead them to a new future; it shares with them, not only the benefits, the fruits and the benefices, but also the moral obligations by means of which they become aware of their duties vis-à-vis us for the safety and communal defence of their common inheritance", *J. O., Chambre*, 2 July 1920, p. 2666.

38. P. 98.

39. P. 101.

40. Sarraut complacently stresses what has already been achieved: "We have largely [!] opened the administrative cadres, the public offices, to native workers. We have increased the representative organs in which the people can make themselves heard through their delegates and join with us in administering their common inheritance". *L'oeuvre coloniale*, p. 23.

41. *J. O., Sénat*, 27 February 1920.

42. P. 126.

43. Cf. p. 277.

44. Sarraut, *Grandeur et servitude coloniales* (1931), p. 153.

45. Sarraut, *op. cit.*, p. 163.

46. "The various representative assemblies which we have spontaneously instituted have rendered the services we expected of them. They have played an educative role from a political point of view. At present, it is true, none of them is an assembly of legislative power. But they have not yet reached the end of an evolution which is itself dependent upon progress in the political education of our subjects and protégés.

"Can one fix this moment?

"I distrust greatly certain noisy individuals who, in the Latin Quarter, or, beyond our frontiers, in the international congresses, claim for their compatriots the full exercise of political rights leading to regular representation and [who demand] for their country, a constitution. In fact they represent no more than tiny minorities: the mass of natives is indifferent to their agitation and does not feel the hour has come for an overthrow recommended by chiefs without parties. But if the hour of colonial parliaments has not yet sounded, on the other hand, it is my formal opinion that the local representative assemblies must rapidly develop into a more liberal statute, particularly from a financial point of view." Sarraut, *op. cit.*, pp. 164 f.

47. Sarraut wrote in similar terms on the Radical Socialist party congress of 1931. He was concerned with making clear to the party representatives the importance and topicality of colonial questions, and here too he spoke of the "counter-offensive of the native forces awakened by European dynamism . . . rumbles of thunder rise from the multitude of colonized races". *Compte-rendu*, p. 356.

A liberal policy was necessary, and the colonies were not simply export markets but "living entities . . . solitary parts of the national territory which we must . . . lead forward to the same destiny as all the parts of the civilizing continent". This demonstrates his integrationist tendencies. For the natives, Sarraut demanded access to the administration and membership on representative boards, but also warned against curiously "premature" reforms: "We do not have the right to give, head over heels, certain powers and rights to certain native races which they would not know how to use", p. 364. As though in 1931 there was any "danger" of granting excessive concessions.

48. Sarraut himself wrote: "I reject the systems of naturalization en masse, like the systems of self-government or universal suffrage collectively conferred on native peoples." *Grandeur et servitude coloniale*, p. 167.

49. Robert Doucet, *Commentaires sur la colonisation* (1926), p. 15.

50. *Ibid.*, p. 54.

51. "... to implant on these lands a French population as large as possible, to strongly impregnate our native subjects with our ideas, our sentiments and our culture", p. 11. "Tunisia is not becoming Gallicized because our compatriots are in the minority there", p. 23.

52. P. 71.

53. Georges Hardy, *Nos grands problèmes coloniaux* (1933), pp. 15, 146.

54. Hardy, *op. cit.*, p. 178.

55. "This conception of progress in the original framework can therefore agree very well with assimilation. What most of the colonials condemn today is sudden and total assimilation, assimilation en masse. But they easily [!] accept assimilation according to qualifications—for those individuals who have risen to the level of culture and morality of the Europeans; they also accept assimilation as the ultimate aim of colonization after a series of stages which it is in the interests of all of us not to disrupt. It seems that, given this, one could come to an agreement and conciliate everybody's aspirations, those of the tutors and those of the pupils, of the colonizers and the colonized." P. 51.

56. P. 210.

57. Hardy expresses himself similarly in his well-known historical work published in 1937: *La politique coloniale et le partage de la terre au XIXe et XXe siècle. (Évolution de l'humanité)*. There were in effect "pupil societies" which had become aware of their respective personalities—for instance India, the Philippines, Iraq—and demanded independence. But usually the demands for independence remained on the surface, even for example in Tunisia and Morocco. The serious disturbances in Indochina and the Dutch Indies are described by Hardy as "serious troubles, but without import for the future which have remained without a future"! Basically it was a question of "crises of growth and mutual accommodation" and not "signs of a break; there is no lack, in our European countries, of provinces which have for long rebelled against annexation and which have ended by merging perfectly into the national unity". In consequence, "... circumstances in no way show that contemporary colonization, in the possessions where the native population dominates, feels that the ground is giving way beneath its feet. Admittedly European authority is contested and disputed in places and at certain times; but everything points to the fact that, catastrophes apart, this authority is far from having exhausted all its resources of permanence. To keep strictly to the colonial sphere of action, it is, therefore, difficult to contend seriously that there is a 'twilight of Europe' or a 'decline of the white race'", pp. 464 f.

58. Léon Archimbaud, *La plus grande France* (1928), p. 10.

59. The parallel between the French colonial Empire and the Commonwealth is striking again: England had six votes in the League of Nations, France only one—"what an inequality", p. 35.

Archimbaud compared the situation of the natives in the French colonies with that in the dominions (Indians, Maoris, etc.) but did not point out the differences between French and British West Africa, Indochina and Malaya, etc.

60. *Ibid.*, p. 23. "The absence of any spirit of avarice which reigned over the acquisition of our colonies . . . our colonial wars were not inspired by a desire for gain, by the will to impose on the natives our cottons or our brandies. . . . Our expeditions have always [!] been motivated either by massacre . . .", p. 22.

61. P. 161.

62. "I would also say without hesitation that France must draw the greatest possible yields from its colonies . . . [then] our industries would be less vulnerable to the sudden fluctuations of the world economy", p. 167. The Radical Socialist party congress held in Marseilles in November 1922 proposed a resolution demanding that Sarraut's motion should come before parliament, "considering that the economic and financial state of France requires that we should free ourselves as far as it is possible from the duty we pay abroad for our raw materials". *Compte-rendu*, p. 229.

63. *La plus grande France*, p. 48.

64. P. 91.

65. Paris, October 1927, *Compte-rendu*, pp. 306 f.

66. Lombarde, the secretary-general of the Algiers party organization, requested a reconsideration by the commission, for which he naturally used the argument about personal status allowing the Muslim deputies a voice in French marriage laws. The commission reporter retorted: during the war one had not questioned the religion of the natives either.

Similarly again in Angers in 1928: the party commission wanted to give the natives better representation on the local councils: "The native who is the principal supplier of taxes must be allowed to inspect the use of the taxes", pp. 300 f. The Algerian delegate Weynn replied: "We should be swamped. . . . Remember that the Muslim natives, after a century of occupation, still have no education [interruption: whose fault?], no political education".

67. P. 112.

68. P. 186.

69. A few years later Archimbaud, as a good Radical Socialist, could proclaim rhetorically: "We should like to see in the Chamber, seated at our side, yellow deputies and a greater number of black deputies; on that day we would have honorably continued the policy of 1793 and of 1848." *J. O.*, 31 January 1930, p. 324.

70. Cf. also Archimbaud as reporter on 22 December 1924: "You cannot impose supplementary expenses on the colonies. You can only do so when the colonies have deliberative chambers, when they can vote to control their expenditure. We remain within the democratic French tradition. When we arrived in Indochina, we found men under the yoke of the Chinese and exploited by their own mandarins. These men have experienced French peace. . . . We consider them, we republicans, as minor brothers, and tomorrow, when they have reached the same stage of civilization as we, it will be our duty to emancipate them. Here is the tradition of the French Revolution. The day, I repeat, when they have arrived at the same stage of civilization as we, when they have deliberative assemblies which will vote on the budget, they can impose whatever charges they wish." *J. O., Chambre*, 22 December 1924, pp. 4712 f.

71. Congrès National, 23–25 May 1931. *Compte-Rendu sténographique* (1931), pp. 287–427: "La Colonisation et les Droits de l'Homme". Cf.

also T. Ruyssen, member of the central committee, "La Colonisation et le Droit", in *Les Cahiers des Droits de l'Homme* (1925), pp. 489 f.
72. Congrès National, p. 427.
73. "Les États-Unis français", *Revue de Paris*, 1 June 1930, p. 482.
74. *L'Empire colonial français* (1931), p. 525.
75. The same applies for E. du Vivier de Steel, "Avant la conférence franco-coloniale", *Revue des deux mondes*, 1 September 1933. Here too there is a comparison with the United States and with Brazil and the author says that each colony "must become a different State in the confederation", but "it is subordinated to the Gallicization of the native spirit, to the establishment, in our possessions, of a greater proportion of Frenchmen", p. 162.
76. Ernest Pezet in the name of the fraction in the Indochina debate on 27 June 1930, *J. O., Chambre*, pp. 2751 f.
77. *Semaine Sociale de France* (Marseilles, 1930). *Compte-rendu des cours et conférernces*.
78. Joseph Folliet, "Coup de bagarre", *Esprit*, December 1935 (special issue on colonization).
79. *Le Droit de Colonisation*, p. 7.
80. There is an outstanding short essay by Émile Dermenghem, "Les catholiques et les abus coloniaux", in *Vie intellectuelle*, November 1928. People in the metropolis would blush with shame if they knew how things really stood; the Catholic newspapers did not report on the abuses.
81. P. 322.
82. P. 343.

THE SOCIALIST PARTY

1. R. Thomas, *Politique socialiste et problème colonial. Essai sur l'évolution de la politique coloniale du Parti Socialiste (SFIO) de 1905 à nos jours*. Memoir of the Institut des Hautes Études d'Outre-Mer (1950) (manuscript); also, "La politique socialiste et le problème coloniale de 1905 à 1920", *Revue française d'Histoire d'Outre-Mer*, CLXVII (1961), 213 f.
2. The motion of the "Comité dit de Résistance Socialiste," signed among others by Léon Blum, anticipated the attitude of the party in the years to come: "It will not cease from acting as it has always done, for the benefit of the native peoples whom the capitalist system abandons to conquest, exploitation and slavery. But it refuses to confuse the movement of revolt of the oppressed peoples with the work of liberating the proletariat; it cannot accept propaganda which would tend to falsify the class war and to unleash a war of races that is equally opposed to its principles of fraternity and its desire for peace." Congrès National, 25–30 December 1920, *Compte-rendu*, p. 589.
3. *J. O., Chambre*, 25 June 1929, p. 2184.
4. In August 1925 the SFIO proposed a resolution to this effect and declared itself the "adversary of evacuation". The party congress in May 1926 confirmed this, *Compte-rendu*, p. 21.
The Morocco discussion in parliament on 21 June 1929 can be seen as an example of the difference of positions. Speaking on behalf of the Communists, Marcel Cachin declared: "It is 25 years since French imperialism decided to seize Morocco. After 25 years it has still not achieved the overall submission of the country...". The "dissidents" numbered more than 100,000 men and they "resist and protect their independence against any attempt at

foreign rule, arms in hand". A real war was being fought against the free Berbers. "The Banque de Paris et des Pays-Bas" dominated in Morocco. . . . "We say that we have no business in Morocco, that we must withdraw, that you are only there to serve the large-scale interests of capitalism . . . to help the peoples regain their liberty, their independence", *J. O., Chambre*, pp. 2134 f.

The socialist Riviere protested the inadequacy of reports in the press and the regiment general in Morocco: "In my position as a socialist I am against all colonial enterprises. . . . Also, there can be no question of accepting the oversimplified formula that has been developed: 'evacuate purely and simply'. I can also affirm, in the name of many natives whom we have asked, that they consider themselves happier than before, that our rule, however little it does, is still preferable to that of the maghzen, the sheiks and certain caids. We are far from ruling with justice and equality, but in the regions that we have visited brutal expropriation no longer exists. . . . We have also brought to this country a little security and a lot of hygiene. . . . Believe me, there can be but one method of rapid penetration. We must bring them all that is good in our civilization. We must build . . .", pp. 2139 f.

5. *Voyage au Congo* (1927).
6. *J. O., Chambre*, 14 June 1929, p. 2099, also 28 January 1930.
7. Leon Werth is the author of *Cochinchine* (1926); André Viollis, of *Indochine* (S.O.S., 1931).
8. Alfred Grosser, *La IVe République et sa politique extérieure* (1961), p. 112.
9. *Le Populaire*, 7 September 1934, 12 September and following.
10. Excerpt in *Le Populaire*, 1 May 1926.
11. *J. O., Chambre*, pp. 1841 f.
12. *J. O., Chambre*, 11 July 1927, p. 2528.
13. *J. O., Chambre*, 14 June 1929, p. 2066.
14. Debates from 28–30 January 1930 and 26 June 1930.
15. *J. O., Chambre*, 20 June 1930, p. 2603.
16. *J. O., Chambre*, 27 June 1930, p. 2768.
17. Thomas, p. 76.
18. *Renseignements coloniaux* (1926), No. 2 bis, p. 104.
19. *Renseignements coloniaux* (1926), No. 5 bis, p. 242.
20. "It does not demand the pure and simple evacuation of the colonies which France presently occupies. Peace would gain nothing from this and it could even be threatened by the sudden explosion of revolts or greed. But our colonial policy must be adapted to the diversity of the types of colonies. Thus, for some, it must aim at complete assimilation, for others at the institution of mandates exercised under the effective control of the SDN oriented towards the constitution of societies of native States capable of self-sufficiency. Independence with, as corollary, the most prompt evacuation possible of the colonies is the target one must assign to the progress of colonization . . . [the party] declares itself in favour of the recognition of the independence and the unity of Syria, constituted as a free State, admitted to the Society of Nations, freed from all military occupation or tutelage." *Le Programme d'action immédiate du Parti Socialiste, voté au Congrès National extraordinaire de Paris* (December 1927), (1928), pp. 47 f. Gonidec on p. 90 quotes obviously from Doriot, *Le PC et les colonies*, a resolution taken from the party conference of 1927, but we have not been able to discover its location.
21. Jacques Berque, *Le Maghreb entre duex guerres* (1962), p. 350.
22. *Compte-rendu*, pp. 100 f.

23. *Compte-rendu*, pp. 234 f. Cf. also *Le Populaire*, 4 November 1936. The party congress of July 1937 in Marseilles reiterated this demand.

24. Its members included Paul Rivet, Paul Langevin, Alain. At first the congress sharply attacked past colonial expansion. Syria and Lebanon should become independent, while the other territories should obtain a "true native representation" by means of greatly extended franchise, with the deliberate aim of "taking away from the French minority its privilege of having a stronger representation than the native mass". *La France en face du Problème colonial* (1936), p. 55.

25. E.g. the article "Demain?" in *L'Afrique française*, May 1936, pp. 250 f. One could expect a government based on abstract theories and that mistook the facts; the mass of the natives, by contrast, wanted only security, justice and well-being.

26. Text of the speech in the *Revue de Pacifique*, May 1936, pp. 615 f. Also *Le Populaire*, 11 December 1936. Paz wrote about Moutet in an article, "Les problemes coloniaux": "he has made the main focus of his doctrine economic well-being, this guarantee of the colonial peoples' political satisfaction." *Le Populaire*, 11 December 1936.

The tendency to exclude political reforms, at first at least, is also apparent in Moutet's stand in parliament: "Colonization, to us, means the development of the masses who live in the colonies, by raising their material, social, economic, intellectual and cultural level." (The political is missing!) This requires enormous resources. The tariff policy raised the prices of consumer goods in the colonies and created dissatisfaction, but yet Moutet wanted to adhere to the established practice; the principle "that the colonies should be, to a large extent, a privileged market for the metropolis, is a necessity [!]". He wanted to conciliate the *évolués* and supported giving them equal rights in the administration, but said nothing about reforming the local assemblies. *J. O., Chambre*, 15 December 1936.

27. P. F. Gonidec, *Droit de Travail des territoires d'Outre-Mer* (1958).

28. A. H. Hourani, *Syria and Lebanon, a Political Essay* (1946), pp. 219 f. Stephan H. Longrigg, *Syria and Lebanon under French Mandate* (1958), p. 218. Viénot's widow in *Le Monde*, 7 March 1958.

29. Quoted in Grosser, *op. cit.*, p. 27.

30. Quoted in Jean Lacouture, *Cinq hommes et la France* (1961), p. 124. For North Africa, cf. above all C. A. Julien, *L'Afrique du Nord en marche*, 2nd ed. (1952), pp. 84 f.; 156 f. Roger le Tourneau, *Évolution politique de l'Afrique du Nord musulmane, 1920–1961* (1962), pp. 79 f., 145 f.

31. Speech, excerpt in *Le Populaire*, 2 March 1937.

32. Berque, p. 294. In 1937 *L'Afrique française* wrote: "In effect Tunisia represents a large department" [!], p. 169.

33. Cf. J. Ladreit de Lacharrère, "L'arrivée de M. Peyrouton", *L'Afrique française*, June 1936, pp. 359 f. The resident general had found agreement, not least because he declared, on his arrival: "I am a colonial . . . there are articles of an intellectual nature which are not export articles"—thus dissociating himself from the Popular Front government. There followed exaggerated praise for General Noguès in *L'Afrique française*, October 1936, pp. 508 f.

34. Cf. interview with Moutet in *Le Populaire*, 20 October 1936.

35. E.g. Daniel Guérin, *Au service des colonisés 1930–1953* (1954) (articles from these years). Guérin belonged to the Trotskyist "revolutionary left" which was banned from the party in spring 1938.

ASSIMILATION IN ALGERIA (1919-1939)

1. The first two delegations, with twenty-four members each (colonists and non-colonists), were elected by the French citizens only. The third, that of the natives, numbered only twenty-one members (fifteen Arabs and six Kabyles); of the fifteen Arabs six were appointed and nine elected on a restricted franchise. The delegations deliberated separately.

2. I refer to the work of one of my pupils, Wolfgang Ohneck, *Die französische Algerienpolitik 1919–1939*, thesis, Heidelberg (1964), to which I owe important points.

3. Charles Robert Ageron, "Une politique algérienne libérale sous la troisième République (1912–1919)", *Revue d'Histoire moderne et contemporaine* VI (1959), April–June.

4. Their 1912 programme proposed, among other things, an extension of the franchise for the Algerian assemblies, representation in parliament, election of the mayor, naturalization with retention of personal status. Cf. Charles Robert Ageron, "Le Mouvement 'Jeune Algérien' de 1900 à 1923", *Études Maghrebines* (Mélanges Charles André Julien, 1964).

5. Ohneck, ch. B, I b–d.

6. Quoted in Ohneck, *op. cit.*, p. 73; *Le Temps*, 3 February 1919.

7. H. de la Martinière, "Avant le voyage du président. La question indigène au lendemain de la guerre", *Revue des deux mondes*, 15 March and 1 April 1922.
Very similarly Dr. J. Gasser, senator from Oran and member of the Académie des Sciences Coloniale, *Le rôle social de la France dans l'Afrique du Nord* (1924); a criticism of the government and parliament because they had instituted the Algerian reforms; the French Algerians had been against the conscriptions because of the political consequences; very anti-assimilatory polemics against the Jeunes Algériens, praise of the military administration, etc.

8. These demands were met in 1924 and 1926, on the one hand by stipulating a period of residence of twenty years before the land could become legally owned (this made it more difficult to sell to Muslims); on the other hand it was made easier to divide up the commercially owned land. Cf. Robert Favier, "L'évolution de la propriété rurale européenne en Algérie", *Revue politique et parlementaire*, CLXIII (1935).

9. De la Martinière, *op. cit.*, p. 682.

10. *La doctrine de l'Association des Indigènes et des Français en Algérie* (1933).

11. A colonial publicist of the left Centre, on the staff of *Le Temps*.

12. P. 221.

13. "By raising them up to our level, we shall be able to give them liberty within the framework of our laws and our institutions while also respecting their own", quoted in François Marsal, *Le domaine colonial français* (1929), p. 348.

14. Ohneck, *op. cit.*, pp. 115 f.

15. Ohneck, *op. cit.*, pp. 121 f.

16. A detailed study in Ohneck, pp. 134, 150 f.

17. *L'Algérie vivra-t-elle?*, p. 424.

18. "We believe that the differentiation between natives and non-natives is dangerous; we must try to remove it with care and deliberation, so we must amalgamate, assimilate, and not divide", quoted in Ohneck, p. 200.

19. Viard, professor of law at the University of Algiers and deputy of the MRP after 1945 declared: "to grant citizenship in statute, is to definitively break with the principle of assimilation which is the basis of our native policy in Algeria", quoted in Ohneck, p. 204.

20. *J. O., Sénat*, Debates, 22 March 1935, p. 381.

21. Roux-Freissireng, senator from Oran, quoted in Ohneck, p. 225.

22. Quoted in André Nouschi, *La naissance du nationalisme algérien 1914–1954* (1962), p. 76.

23. E.g. "L'Algérie et ses problèmes" in *Revue des deux mondes* (1935). The governor-general was under pressure from the government and the Algerian deputies and "could not think of starting the least reform of any depth"; the financial delegations represented only the settlers and the Muslim delegates felt isolated. The *évolués* were suffering from a psychosis of political equality and despaired of the future, and yet the French Algerians had no sympathy for this and reproached them with ingratitude. The administration was Algerianized and narrow-minded; the élite was perhaps small, but "one would have to be blind or without faith to treat it as a negligible quantity and to see it as nothing but a handful of vulgar ambitious men and déclassés". The author refused naturalization, however, and thus adhered to the *status quo* in political terms.

24. Octave Dupont, "Les troubles en Afrique du Nord et les franchises indigènes en Algérie", *Revue politique et parlementaire*, CLXIV (1935). Even the 1918 reforms had been too extensive and it would be ridiculous to extend the franchise; what was necessary, by contrast, was to re-establish effective authority and to suppress the agitators. A follower of Viollette, on the other hand, was Gaston Bouthoul, "Le 'Malaise' algérien", in the bourgeois *Revue de Paris*, Vol. XLII, April 1935.

25. The much quoted words and the opposition between Ben Badi and the Ulémas in Julien, pp. 110 f. Nouschi, p. 89.

26. *J. O., Chambre, Doc. parl.* (1936), Annexe 1596.

27. People were aware of this: e.g. E. F. Gautier, "Menaces sur l'Afrique" in *Revue de Paris* (1934–1935): "They [the Muslims] solicit it [naturalization] and obtain it eventually. But this movement is not of great consequence. The Muslim who applies for naturalization by the same token accepts the civil law. Horrible blasphemy, since he thus denies the Koran, the only divine civil law of the Muslim . . .", p. 47.

28. Philippe Machefer, "Autour du problème algérien en 1936–38: La doctrine algérienne du PSF. Le PSF et le projet Blum-Viollette" in *Revue d'histoire moderne et contemporaine*, X (1963), April–June; Paul Guitard, *SOS Afrique du Nord* (PPF), (1938).

29. Details again in Ohneck, *op. cit.*, pp. 283 f. The party's colonial commission proposed at the October 1936 party congress to promote integration and remove the financial delegations, while on the other hand proposing compulsory naturalization in statute for certain categories of Muslims.

30. Machefer, *op. cit.*, p. 148.

31. *Le Populaire*, 7 January 1937, interview with Viollette.

DIRECT ADMINISTRATION IN WEST AFRICA

1. *Les vrais chefs de l'empire* (1939), new ed. (1946) under the title *Service Africain*, and English translation *Freedom and Authority in French West Africa* (1950). The Marxist view, by contrast, in Jean Suret-Canale, *Afrique noire*, Vol. II, *L'ère coloniale 1900–1945* (1964), pp. 398–413.

2. *Le problème des chefferies en Afrique noire française*, Notes et Études documentaires, February 1959, No. 2508. R. Cornevin, "L'évolution des chefferies traditionelles dans l'Afrique noire d'expression française", in *Recueil Penant*, (1961), pp. 235 f., 379 f.

3. "He is not the continuer of the ancient native kinglet.... Even when the person is identical, there is nothing now in common between the old state of affairs and the new one. The *chef de canton*, even if he is the descendant of the king with whom we have negotiated, has no power of his own. Appointed by us, according to a selection on discretionary principles, he is only our assistant." Report of a colonial inspector on 5 October 1950, quoted in Cornevin, p. 380.

4. R. L. Buell, *The Native Problem in Africa* (1928), p. 988.

5. In 1939 in French West Africa there were 15,000,000 inhabitants in 118 *cercles*, 2200 *chefs de canton*, and 48,000 *chefs de villages*.

6. Delavignette, *Chefs de l'Empire*, p. 153.

7. Cf. Buell, *op. cit.*, p. 993.

8. *Une âme de chef* (1920), reproduces the circular, pp. 38–50. Excerpts in Notes et Études, p. 18.

9. 30 November 1929, *Documentation coloniale comparée*, II (1929), 248.

10. "Discours d'Ouverture", 1 December 1930. *Documentation*, II (1930), 350. *Circulaires su la Politique et l'Administration indigènes* (Gorée, 1932), excerpts in Notes et Études, pp. 19 f.

11. An example: Yves Peson, "Soixante ans d'évolution en pays kissi", *Cahiers d'études africaines*, Vol. 1 (1960).

12. Notes et Études, p. 15.

13. P. 258. He calls the proposal "a bit too fast on the draw". Cf. also a declaration on 18 May 1926, quoted in Jean Runner, *Les droits politiques des indigènes des colonies* (1927), p. 70.

14. P. 269.

15. Cf. *Documentation coloniale comparée*, II (1930), 478 f.

16. *Six ans*, p. 270.

17. This same tendency is apparent in the speech by the governor-general *ad interim* of Madagascar, Berthier, given before the economic and financial delegations on 16 October 1929: "Whatever some delayed partisans of the theories of assimilation in favour in the last century, but condemned since then both by experience and doctrine, might say on the subject, your assembly complies with and satisfies the present needs of the Grande Île. Certainly, its constitution is not perfect, but, in the true interests of that country, it must evolve within its present framework, taking care not to prematurely introduce political elements who could not, in my opinion, but do harm to the harmonious development of Madagascar and even compromise the civilizing work which France has taken upon itself. Moreover, a number of mature thinkers now admit that the political institutions of ancient Europe, attacked by some, criticized by others, do not comply with the needs of modern colonization." *Documentation coloniale comparée*, II (1929), 339.

18. In *L'Afrique française* (1930–1931). Published as a special edition by the Comité de l'Afrique française (1931).

19. "L'Accession des Indigènes à la Citoyenneté française", *L'Afrique française* (1935), pp. 721 f.

20. "Pour le paysan noir, pour l'esprit africain", *Esprit*, No. 39 (1935), p. 384. Cf. also "Sénégal at Niger", *L'Afrique française*, August 1932, p. 481.

21. *Les vrais chefs de l'Empire*, p. 141.
22. P. 250.
23. For his part Senghor dedicated his contribution to *La Communauté impériale française* (1945), p. 57, to Delavignette.
24. Cf. his criticism of the efforts made hitherto: "villages without wells, without watering places, in front of the lorry route, this is metropolitan phariseeism", *Esprit*, p. 382.
25. *Les vrais chefs de l'Empire*, p. 90.
26. P. 260.
27. *L'Afrique française* (1920). *Renseignements coloniaux*, p. 32, and *ibid.* (1921), p. 100. Governor-General Carde again in 1929: "Let us, therefore, teach French in the lower grades; let us teach the children to speak and write in good French, so that they may think in good French." *Documentation coloniale comparée*, II (1929), 251.
28. Quoted in L. P. Mair, *Native Policies in Africa* (1936), p. 213.
29. *Commonwealth Documents* 2374 (1925), p. 4.
30. As an example of the British attitude we can take the famous, although dating from 1904, report of the commission appointed by the Government of India to enquire into the condition and prospects of the University of Calcutta. The English language was described as a "pathway leading into a rich intellectual life", although the native language remained of greater importance. "A man's native speech is almost like his shadow, inseparable from his personality . . . it is through our vernacular, through our folk-speech, whether actually uttered or harboured in our unspoken thoughts, that the most of us attain to the characteristic expression of our nature and of what our nature allows us to be or to discern. . . ."
31. In 1939, 80,000 children were in elementary schools—whereas 2,700,000 were of school age. Michel Devèze, *La France d'Outre-Mer* (1948), p. 61.
32. Unfortunately there are as yet no studies of the Africanization of the cadre.
33. As an example we can take *L'Afrique française* (1934), p. 720: "During the academic year 1933–34, the William Ponty School has supplied 57 new teachers on the secondary level, 24 pupils at the École de Médecine, and 5 at the École Vétérinaire. It has also recruited 80 new pupils by means of the *concours*. The École des Pupilles Mécaniciens de la Marine has counted 45 pupils, of which 22 of the third year have obtained the baccalauréat.

"The École de Médecine de Dakar has recruited 22 medical students, 2 pharmacy students, 15 midwifery students, 15 visiting hospital nurses.

"The École Vétérinaire of Bamako has recruited 5 veterinary students.

"These various establishments provide technical training. Below them there exist the Enseignements Primaires et Professionnels, in the major towns of the colonies. In 1934 the eight higher primary schools were attended by 930 pupils as opposed to 974 in 1933. By careful measures which one cannot praise too highly the attendance was deliberately reduced this year to avoid that the young people, without jobs on leaving because of the decrease of openings now in commerce, industry and the administration, should be dismissed."

34. Robert Delavignette, *L'Afrique noire française et son destin* (1962), p. 99.

LYAUTEY AND THE PROTECTORATE IN MOROCCO

1. The comprehensive literature on Lyautey includes Jean Dresch, "Lyautey", in *Les techniciens de la colonisation*, ed. C. A. Julien (1947); and General Catroux, *Lyautey le Marocain* (1955).
2. This can be shown very clearly in the case of Tunisia, cf. J. Ganiage, *Les origines du protectorat français en Tunisie (1868–1881)* (1959). Also the comments by Henri Brunschwig in *Mythes et Réalités de l'Imperialisme colonial français, 1871–1914* (1960), pp. 53 f.
3. Article 1: In order to facilitate the exercise of its Protectorate for the French Government, S. A. Le Bey pledges himself to embark on administrative, judiciary and financial reforms which the French Government considers useful.
4. Several quotations in Gonidec, p. 216.
5. E.g. Gonidec, pp. 208 f.
6. *Lyautey l'Africain, textes et lettres du Maréchal Lyautey*, ed. Pierre Lyautey, Vol. IV, 1919–1925 (1957), p. 28.
7. Lyautey, *Paroles d'action (1900–1926)*, 3rd ed. (1938), p. 172.
8. Cf. the impressive meeting between Hugo von Hofmannsthal and Lyautey: "I have also grown to love the new France which I perceived here. The old marshal Lyautey met me with great warmth. He came, in fact ran, across the great hall to me, took my hand in his and said: 'Monsieur, you are at home—you are in your own house, and this is why: I command here, I am a Lorrain, your emperors are my dukes, and I consider the destruction of Austria a most deplorable crime.' Then, with extreme graciousness, he introduced me to his young gentlemen. I am very happy to see him and all these officials—an elite of young officers and officials with whom I already made friends on the ship—in Rabat again." Letter from Marrakesh, 15 March 1924, correspondence with Carl J. Burckhardt (1956), p. 182.
9. *Paroles d'action*, p. 469.
10. *Op. cit.*, p. 7. Also speech in London before the African Society, *Journal des Débats*, 6 December 1928.
11. *Textes et lettres*, I (1953), 220.
12. But at the same time feudalism loses its original meaning and becomes confused with the methods of nepotism, blackmail and mere economic exploitation. Cf. Berque, *Le Maghreb entre deux guerres* (1962), p. 42.
13. IV, 14 f., 157 f. Robert Montagne, *Révolution au Maroc* (1953), p. 143.
14. Cf. e.g. the 1922 document which Hardy published in *Afrique française*, August 1934.
15. On 20 May 1921: "From the outset I had given notice of my intention to see the best qualified spend a time in the various residential services after their studies. I have come back to this on several occasions, but I have encountered inertia, not to say repugnance, so that nothing has been done", IV, 131.
16. The colonists were "imbued with the Algerian mentality", had no understanding of the pride and the privileges of the land. Lyautey referred critically to the words of the president of the chamber of agriculture of Casablanca, IV, 19.
17. 5 December 1923, *Paroles d'action*, p. 397.
18. The collective property of the tribes and villages was legalized, but at the same time this made it possible to hand over a part of it to the state

for the purpose of colonization. On the other hand, a majority decision could divide up the collective property into private property, in which case the state reserved itself a certain part.

19. On 24 November 1919: one consequence of the protectorate was "that the French political institutions have no place in Morocco. Our nationals can have bodies and professional representation there, but can have no political representation. The demands and polemics on this subject do not therefore represent any more than washed ink and wasted time". *Paroles d'action*, p. 300. Again in a farewell address before the Conseil de Gouvernement on 5 October 1925, p. 428.

20. In a letter to Prime Minister Millerand in July 1920 Lyautey accordingly protested against certain terms of the parliamentary report, which spoke, among other things, of a "normal regime". "What else do they want? Does not the term 'normal regime' simply mean the electoral regime of the French departments is envisaged? May I therefore be allowed to say that, far from being a normal regime for Morocco, this would be the most abnormal of regimes". IV, 48; cf. also *Paroles d'action*, p. 389.

21. Pp. 172f., 373, 398; IV, 26.

22. We quote a fairly long text of 1916, since it also shows Lyautey's concept of the protectorate: "Morocco is a protectorate. But this word, although it stands for a great and simple colonial doctrine, is usually regarded as a form of etiquette and not a reality: people see in it, if not a lie, at least a theoretical formula, a transitional formula, destined to disappear after successive modalities. And this feeling is so strong that in Morocco, as elsewhere before the war, it was difficult, and almost seemed pointless, to resist the impulse which many believed fatal towards direct government, towards annexation *de facto* preceding legal annexation. The war has made it an absolute political necessity to change course; and this new experience, begun in a sense of prudence, has fully succeeded. The protectorate thus appears not a theoretical transitional formula, not even a formula at all, but a permanent fact: the economic and moral penetration of a race, *not* by subjecting it to our might or even to our liberties, but by a close association in which we administer it in peace through its own organs of government according to its own customs and liberties.

"It is in this direction that our policy is frankly and definitively oriented. First we have tried to raise the personal prestige of the sultan, by reviving around him the ancient traditions and ceremonies of his court, to scrupulously guarantee the autonomy of his religious power, to enforce his trust and his authority by including him in our projects and by requesting his ideas and his opinions. The maghzen has been more closely associated to our daily government. Before the war his role had decreased imperceptibly by the force of our administrative habits to a simple right to veto projects which were communicated to him. Today, in effect, he has a real right of examination and his initiative is even solicited in many cases. The Conseil de Vizirs has become a living institution, a regular organ of the Administration. All our projects are submitted there and explained as to content and tendency and aim. The administration of Habou goods is similarly exercised under the effective control of a council. . . .

"Finally, everywhere, in the provinces, we have tried to give the natives not just the semblance of power, but an effective share in the administration and true authority in order to guarantee their customs and their liberties." *Rapport général sur la situation du Protectorat au Maroc, 31 July 1914* (1916), p. xiii f.

23. IV, 25 f.
24. Cf. also report dated 21 December 1920, pp. 102 f.
25. Again on 20 May 1921, pp. 131 f.
26. III (1918), 68.
27. Quoted in André de Peretti, "L'indépendance et la France", *Esprit*, IV (1947), 571. In 1961, the conservative magazine *Paris Match* reinterpreted this in praise of Lyautey: photos showing Lyautey's statue being taken down in Casablanca were captioned: "Lyautey had foreseen the independence of Morocco and it is thanks to his 'French Peace' that royal authority is now undisputed there, outside ancient tribal quarrels". 19 April, No. 629, p. 148.
28. "We have direct administration under our skin, we functionaries from France, officials from Algeria." IV, 30.
29. Rom Landau, *Moroccan Drama, 1900–1955* (1956), p. 133.
30. André Colliez, *Notre protectorat Marocain 1912–1930* (1930), p. 187.
31. So for instance Lyautey pointed on 5 December 1923 to the thousand settlers with 400,000 hectares, "It is really worth something and these figures increase every day"—he had to defend himself against the reproach that he was not promoting colonization. But he immediately added: "I chiefly count on the Moroccan population itself" and spoke of the "vast, well-cultivated domains" he had found in 1908—words obviously directed against the French colonials and their arguments; *Paroles d'action*, p. 398.
32. *La Paix française en Afrique du Nord* (1926), p. 210.
33. Landau, p. 135; in 1935, 840,000 hectares in 3822 factories were in European hands; Albert Ayache, *Le Maroc* (1956), p. 154. Cf. also M. M. Knight, *Morocco as a French Economic Venture* (1937), p. 66; Berque, pp. 244, 249.
34. Knight, pp. 58, 67. Text of an official brochure of 1928, quoted in Ayache, pp. 151 f. No less than Georges Hardy, the close colleague of Lyautey, wrote in 1937: "We took care to forbid the native collectives to directly alienate their property and place them under the protection of guardianship councils. But in practice, usury, the ploys of the speculators, the tenacity of the colonists, have overcome all the precautions, and one may ask if, from a humanitarian point of view, it would not have been more expedient to play honestly and once and for all to separate the domain of colonization and the land reserved to native collectives." *La politique coloniale et le partage de la terre aux XIXe et XXe siècles*, p. 380.
35. Concerns with modern methods of cultivation obtained tax relief—which did not prevent the settlers from demanding full tax exemption! Cf. also Louis Le Barbier, *Le Maroc agricole* (1927), pp. 147, 111.
36. M. Flory, "La notion du protectorat et son évolution en Afrique du Nord", *Revue juridique et politique de L'Union française* (1954), p. 473.
37. Colliez, p. 320, note; similarly for Tunisia, Robert Raynaud, "Socialisme et colonies", *Revue politique et parlementaire* (1925).
38. For example: "The Chamber of Agriculture of Rabat, 5 November 1927; the Association des Agriculteurs et Éleveurs de Tadla and Oued-Zem, 15 December 1927; the Association des Colons of Sidi-Sliman, 5 September 1928; the colonists of the Nord du Maroc, 29 September, have protested vigorously against the current policy; finally, the Union des Associations du Maroc, including 30 groups, adopted, on 2 November 1928, the following order of the day: VOEU considering:
"That for some years there has been a marked increase in thefts and crimes committed to the prejudice of the Europeans and about all the natives;

"That the general causes of this disquieting situation can be attributed:

"1. To the influence of certain propaganda practised in Arab circles;
"2. To the inadequate surveillance of the tribes by the caids and chiefs;
"3. To the bad education of the native chiefs and the inadequate action in certain cases, of the civil controllers;
"4. To the use of a system of justice unsuited to the mentality of the delinquents and to the absence of methods of repression;
"5. To the premature institution, in this country, of social reforms whose character has been wrongly interpreted by the primitive populations of the Bled and which are the cause of excessive abuses;
"6. Finally, perhaps also due to the absence of a rational and co-ordinated native policy, that the multiplicity of thefts, armed thefts or of crimes would soon cause this country to fall back into the anarchy it has been in for centuries. That a feeling of latent revolt and of *coup de main* is still strongly rooted in the customs of the tribes in the interior and that they must therefore be governed;

"That the security of property and person constitutes a primordial means of pacification, work and progress.

"The Union des Associations Agricoles du Maroc demands that the means used to remedy this state of affairs should include return to collective tribal responsibility, extension of the power of the caids to solve the pasture-land offences and settle the quarrels concerning work contracts, agricultural associations, etc. . . . , reinforcement of the authority of the civil controls, which should have better control of the native chiefs.

"And notifies that it is essential to arrive at the complete pacification of Morocco, that there is a need to undertake immediate measures for the military and administrative reorganization of the regions called insecure." Quoted in Colliez, pp. 318–19.

39. P. 262.

40. René Thomasset, "Les problèmes marocains", *Revue politique et parlementaire*, Vol. CLXVII (1936). For the settlers' protests in 1934, cf. Berque, pp. 265 f.

41. E.g. *Réalités coloniales* (1934), pp. 15: "The Frenchman . . . is above all and mainly a man of direct administration. That is his natural course, the one that best suits his temperament, his character, his destiny."

42. P. 166. One must not promote the prestige of the sultan too much, since he could one day turn against France; p. 498.

43. *Principes de colonisation et de législation coloniale*, I (1927, 5th ed.), 431.

44. P. 50.

45. Roger Labonne, "Grandeur et Servitude marocaines", *Le Correspondant*, 25 December 1928, 10 January 1929.

46. Cf. among others, Landau, pp. 142 f.

47. C. A. Julien, *L'Afrique du Nord en marche* (1952), pp. 151 f. R. Le Tourneau, *Évolution de la politique de l'Afrique du Nord Musulmane 1920–1961* (1962), pp. 189 f. The old Lyautey, by contrast, retorted during a banquet, "I must say: there is something justified in the plan for Moroccan reforms", Catroux, *Lyautey*, p. 299.

48. P. 83.

49. E.g. Thomasset, *op. cit.*, who criticized the policy of the "great caids", and the neglect of education, and demanded more consideration of the educated élite in the administration. Similarly, "Les progrès du Nationalisme marocain en milieu berbère", *Revue politique et parlementaire*,

Vol. CLXXVI (1938). Robert Montagne, "Comment organiser politiquement l'Empire français", *Politique étrangère*, III (1938), 176 f. For Tunisia, cf. Frédéric de Richement, "L'avenir de la Tunisie", *Revue politique et parlementaire*, CLXXIII (1937), and "L'Islam et la nationalité française", CLXXIII (1937).

50. We have seen that everyone demanded increased colonization. Even F. Charles-Roux, who knew Lyautey and celebrated him, wrote: "The field open to French colonization is vast." "Le maréchal Lyautey et le Maroc français", *Revue politique et Parlementaire*, CXXIII (1925), 407.

COLONIAL POLITICS DURING THE SECOND WORLD WAR

1. Telegrams to Noguès on 19 and 24 July: "Everyone here thinks that you are about to become the grand chief of the French resistance." G. Vaucel, *Documents: La France d'outre-mer dans la guerre* (1948), p. 135. On 25 June, to Puaux and Mittelhauser: "I myself am at your service", Jacques Soustelle, *Envers et contre Tous* (1947), p. 56.
2. De Gaulle, *Mémoires de guerre*, Vol. I, "Appel", 1940–1942 (1954), p. 274.
3. Soustelle, p. 100.
4. Cf. among others de Gaulle, pp. 90 f. Edgar de Larminat, *Chroniques irrévérencieuses* (1962), pp. 121 f. Jean de la Roche, *Le Gouverneur général Félix Eboué 1884–1944* (1957).
5. Michel Devèze, *La France d'outre-mer* (1948), pp. 170 f.
6. Paul Isoart, *Le phénomène national vietnamien* (1961), p. 310. Admiral Decoux, *A la barre d'Indochine* (1949).
7. J. Richard-Molard, *Afrique occidentale française* (1952). Philip Neres, *French-speaking West Africa* (1962), p. 23. Jean Suret-Canale, *Afrique noire*, Vol. II, 1900–1945 (1964).
8. Three directives of African colonization. Among other things they state: "To colonize is essentially to advance the native societies in the paths which we have chosen for them.... It is both the élites and the masses who must follow us." For the rest, measures in the sphere of food, residential building, education, agrarian policy and industrialization took precedence. Deschamps, *Méthodes et doctrines*, pp. 177 f. We did not see the original text.
9. Jean Paillard, *L'Empire français de demain* (1943).
10. The anti-semitic, anti-democratic and anti-British attitude of the author became clear in two earlier writings: *La fin des Français en Afrique noire* (1936) (referring to the immigration of Syrians and Lebanese) and *Faut-il faire de de l'Algérie un Dominion?* (1938).
11. P. 153.
12. Maunier also used some identical words in his collective work *L'Empire et ses ressources*, ed. Centre d'information interprofessionnel (1942). The 1943 book thus has a representative, if not official, character.
13. *L'Empire et ses ressources*, p. 17.
14. P. 5. "The colonies are dependent, integrated into the state which forms part of the national territory", p. 16.
15. *Propos et projets*, p. 59.
16. P. 139. The text speaks of a certain Dr. Funke, but probably means the NS minister of economic affairs, Walter Funk.
17. Title VI. The government of the Empire. Article 41.

1. The overseas territories, over which the French State exercises its sovereignty or to whom it extends its protection, from the Empire.
2. In the Empire, the government exercises its authority through the intermediary of senior officials who are responsible for the internal and external security of the areas administered or controlled by them.
3. The Empire is governed by special legislation.
Article 42.
1. A Conseil de l'Empire will be set up by the president of the Republic with the purpose of making recommendations in questions concerning the French overseas territories.
2. In the parts of the Empire where the social development and security permit it, a consultative council will stand beside the representative of the head of state.
3. The conditions under which the traditional co-operation of certain colonies in the national representation will take place will be determined by law.
Quoted in Ansprenger, appendix, pp. 453–54.
18. I am using the Rufisque edition of 1948.
19. De la Roche, p. 137.
20. P. 7.
21. P. 27.
22. Note also the following passage: "Instead of allowing a crowd of proletarians more or less badly dressed, more or less speaking French, to form contact with us, we shall do well to create an élite of chiefs and notables", p. 11. This largely corresponded with the British attitude in 1920!
23. P. 17.
24. Devèze, p. 180. Suret-Canale, p. 586.
25. In his opening address in Brazzaville Pleven made it clear that the conference must mainly document "the affirmation of our faith in the mission of France in Africa . . . the affirmation of our desire to take upon ourselves, above all without sharing them with any anonymous institution, the immense but exalting responsibilities that are ours, vis-à-vis the races who live under our flag", *Conférence africaine française*, ed. Ministère des Colonies (1945), p. 21.
26. J. O., *Assemblée consultative Algers*, 13 January 1944, p. 13.
27. From a talk with P. O. Lapie. For the plans, cf. below pp. 375–76.
28. *Mémoires*, II, 184.
29. Text of the speech in *Mémoires*, II, 555 f.
30. Governor Saller, who was supported by the influential Laurentie, Conference, p. 85.
31. P. 39.
32. P. 22.
33. Pleven wrote very similarly a few months later in the preface to a special number of the journal *Renaissances*, October 1944: "The French colonies, like the other provinces of France, [!] want to help rebuild the French house. They wish, and their hope will not be disappointed, that the plans of the architects of the Constituent will give them a place in it where they will be at ease", p. 8.
34. P. 32.
35. Pleven even explicitly stressed that the French did not want to copy the British concepts in Brazzaville; "the word Commonwealth in particular has deliberately been kept out", p. 80.

36. P. 32.
37. P. 35.
38. P. 37.
39. P. 82.
40. Pp. 73, 79.
41. He demanded the transformation of the French Empire into a federal State, but "the political domain" must remain with France, and he too started from the idea of a one and indivisible Republic! P. 77.
42. P. 91.
43. Pp. 100 f. Sissoko's contribution was reprinted in *Renaissances*, October 1944 (Sissoko was *chef de canton* in French West Africa).
44. Robert Lemaignen, Léopold Sédar Senghor, Prince Sisowath Youtévong, *La Communauté Impériale Française* (1945).
45. Pp. 84 f.
46. Ansprenger, pp. 63 f. Devèze, p. 185.
47. Gonidec, pp. 242 f. Also, A. Layton Funk, *Charles de Gaulle, The Crucial Years 1943-1944* (1959), p. 196.
48. For the events in North Africa the above-mentioned books by Julien and Le Tourneau give summaries. We give no details.
49. *Mémoires*, II, 95.
50. An excellent study of Ferhat Abbas in Jean Lacouture, "Ferhat Abbas ou la recherche d'une patrie", in *Cinq hommes et la France* (1961), pp. 284 f.
51. Text of the Constantine speech in *Mémoires*, II, 548 f., the Ordonnace, II, 557 f. Cf. also General Catroux, *Dans la bataille de la méditerranée 1940-1944* (1949), pp. 434 f.
52. An attempt at an objective description of these events in Robert Aron, et al., *Les origines de la guerre d'Algerie* (1962), pp. 91-151.
53. Henri Michel, *Les courants de pensée de la Résistance* (1962), pp. 407 f.
54. Cf. p. 364.
55. "Pour une Politique coloniale nouvelle", *Renaissances*, November 1943.
56. 13 January 1944 in the consultative assembly; also in *Les deserts de l'action* (1946), p. 251.
"The new French colonial policy is this: a clearer realization than ever before that the colonizing nation's sole aim is to transform the colonized areas into states which will some day be its own equals. . . . All French colonies must some day be freed from their link to France, if such is their wish. . . ." In order to make this link "pleasant", he had proposed the federal solution. "The New Colonial Policy of France", *Foreign Affairs*, October 1944, p. 105.
57. Charles de Gaulle, *Discours et Messages 1940-1946* (1946), p. 454.
58. In *Renaissances*, October 1944.
59. De la Roche, Jean Gottmann, *La fédération française* (1945; Montreal, 1945) (the manuscript was completed on 6 March 1945 in New York).
60. Cf. P. Devilliers, *Histoire du Viet-Nam de 1940 à 1952*, 3rd ed. (1952); Isoart, *op. cit.*, pp. 318 f.
61. Quoted in Isoart, p. 321.
62. Text of the declaration in Ali Maatern, *Colonialisme, Trusteeship, Indépendance* (1946), pp. 224 f.
63. Paul Mus told how he had proposed this concept in order to transform the relationship of colonial dependence into a "parity association"

and how Laurentie, the political director in the overseas ministry, had eventually agreed; *Le Destin de l'Union française* (1954), pp. 83 f.

64. Note the paternalistic accent and extremely vague content of de Gaulle's message to Indochina on 15 August 1945: "The enemy has capitulated. In this decisive hour the mother country turns to its children in the Indochinese Union, in order to assure them of its pleasure, sympathy and recognition. By their attitude toward the enemies and by their loyalty to France the sons of France [!] have shown that they are worthy of a greater and freer national existence. At the moment when France has found Indochina again it solemnly declares itself prepared to implement the provisions it has determined to the general good. Long live the Indochinese Union; long live France." *Keesing's Contemporary Archives* (1945), p. 373.

65. Quoted in E. de Curton, "Vers une union fédérale française", in *Renaissances* (1945), No. 10. The *Washington Post* commented that Indochina would be the first dominion of the Union, i.e. it equated the postulated French Union with the Commonwealth!

66. Jacques Ponchelet, "Union française ou Trusteeship", *op. cit.*, pp. 57 f.

67. "L'Union française", *Renaissances* (1945), No. 10, p. 54. Cf. also "Notes sur une philosphie de la politique coloniale française", *Renaissances*, October 1944, p. 14.

68. "Les colonies françaises devant le monde nouveau", *Renaissances*, October 1945, No. 15, p. 4.

69. "These two examples, Indochina and the Antilles, clearly show what could be, depending on their choice, the destiny of the other parts of the Union. Some will no doubt evolve towards particularism without losing solidarity with the mother country, while others will tend rather to become assimilated. Either solution is open: the near future will indicate in what direction the respective colonies are tending", *L'Union française*, p. 55. Similar passages also in "Anniversaire de Brazzaville", *Renaissances* (1945), No. 9, p. 112.

70. Cf. "Précisions sur la politique coloniale" in *Marchés coloniaux*, 29 December 1945.

71. "L'Union française" in *Esprit*, July 1945, p. 232.

72. "L'Union française et le problème constitutionnel", *Politique* (1945), No. 19, p. 420.

73. "Thèses pour servir à une discussion sur la future Constitution", *Cahiers politiques*, August 1954.

74. "Vers la Constitution de la IVe République", *op. cit.*

75. Report of Dr Aujoulat on colonial policy, printed as a brochure (1945).

76. Quoted in Alfred Grosser, *La IVe République et sa politique extérieure* (1961), p. 27.

THE UNION FRANÇAISE

1. The franchise was, understandably, still subject to certain restrictions; in French West Africa there were 117,000 voters in population of 17,000,000.

2. Franz Ansprenger, *Politik im schwarzen Afrika* (1961), p. 65. Hubert Deschamps, *Méthodes et Doctrines coloniales de la France* (1953), p. 186.

3. Of the comprehensive literature on the subject we cite only Pierre Lampué, *L'Union française d'après la Constitution* (1947); François Borella, *L'évolution politique et juridique de l'Union française depuis 1940* (1958).

4. The influential deputy for overseas affairs, Boisdon, said in the constitutional commission: "The aim must be to avoid a federalism that could lead to dissociation from the Empire. A federal chamber would draw us into unknown and perhaps dangerous paths", quoted in Henri Culman, *Union française* (1950), p. 79.

5. In judicial terms it was not yet clear what sort of citizenship this was; cf. Lampué, p. 11; Borella, p. 40.

6. *J. O.*, 11 April 1946, p. 1713.

7. Cf. also Senghor's essay "Défense de l'Afrique noire" (completed 1 May 1945) in *Esprit*, July 1945. In spite of Brazzaville, he said, little had really changed. Africa demanded more for its territories than a mere consultative assembly; it also wanted equal rights in the appointment of officials, removal of the *indigénat* and forced labour. The constituent assembly conceded most of these demands!

8. A representative of Madagascar criticized this: "There can be no question of a freely consented union without previous fulfilment of the conditions necessary for a free and enlightened adhesion", *J. O.*, 11 April, p. 1718.

9. Senghor as reporter, p. 1714.

10. Preliminary notes by the constitutional commission, Annexe 885, p. 851.

11. *J. O.*, 11 April, p. 1719.

12. Article 50 of the Communist draft: "The French Republic solemnly proclaims that only the consistent application of the principles of democracy to the peoples and races of the overseas territories will create conditions favourable to the rapid development of these peoples and races towards a régime of liberty, in fruitful friendship with the French nation." Annexe 20. The term "liberty" is typically ambivalent here!

13. *J. O.*, 20 March 1946, pp. 932 f.

14. "We do not conceal our desire to see this council of the French community gradually evolve into a federal organism in so far as the different territorial assemblies become more solid. One day will come when the representation of the overseas territories [in parliament] . . . can be suppressed, and functions that are no longer consultative but deliberative can be given to the council of the French Union. This does not seem possible to us at the moment . . .", *Documents* (1945–1946), Annexe No. 444 pp. 59 f. With some right Pleven could refer to Lapie as a member of the SFIO and to the Communist Mercier, who had demanded a real federal assembly in Algiers. *J. O.*, 11 April, p. 1721.

15. *J. O.*, 19 April 1946, pp. 2065 f. Coste-Floret had also stressed the two-chamber system strongly on 15 April, p. 1846.

16. *J. O.*, 19 April 1946, p. 2062.

17. Text in Daniel Boisdon, *Les institutions de l'Union française* (1949), pp. 41–42; in part also in Borella, p. 14.

18. The reporter Coste-Floret (MRP) also stressed, with reference to the possibility of a change of status, that the draft "is much more clearly inspired by the federalist concept", *Documents*, II, 295, 350.

19. *L'Action du Comité de l'Empire français. Principales interventions auprès des pouvoirs publics* (October 1944 to March 1946).

20. P. 40.

21. 16 July 1945, p. 54.
22. Lead article by editor-in-chief René Moreux in the first issue of 17 November 1945.
23. 25 January 1946, p. 101; headed "La France ne traitera en Indochine qu'avec des interlocuteurs lyaux".
24. 26 January 1946, p. 75.
25. Claude Vion, "Politique impériale et décentralisation", in *Marchés coloniaux*, 26 January 1946, p. 77.
26. René Moreux on 27 April 1946, p. 389.
27. *Ibid. Refaire la Constitution de l'Empire*, 4 May 1946, p. 411. *Repenser toute notre politique coloniale et refaire la Constitution de l'Empire*, 25 May 1946, pp. 493 f.
28. "Pour un statut de l'Union française", 13 July 1946, p. 689.
29. In the issue on 1 June 1946. The manifesto is signed by the Académie des Sciences coloniales, Comité de l'Afrique française, Comité de l'Empire française, Comité de l'Océanie française, Journal de la Marine marchande, Ligue maritime et coloniale, *Marchés coloniaux*.
30. 14 September 1946, p. 944.
31. "Les partis et l'Union française", 10 August 1946. Cf. also a submission by the Comité de l'Empire française to Overseas Minister Moutet on 12 March 1946, in *L'action* . . . , pp. 87 f. "The project would, in effect, lead to excluding the French from the local sovereign assemblies [!] and to introducing the natives to the exercise of French sovereignty." This is followed by a ridiculous comparison with the Commonwealth!
32. Cf. Ansprenger, pp. 69 f. The content of the resolution of the "States-General" in Devèze, p. 266. It states, among other things: "The accession to French citizenship could not be a measure of a collective order, obligatorily extending rights to all the inhabitants of the Empire, most of whom would not understand either their meaning, or their grandeur, or which some would even deliberately transgress, but is an individual fact largely open to all those who are capable of grasping its moral, social and political implications. . . . The agitations provoked by a few autonomist *évolués* considered by some irony of fate as the authentic representatives of the overseas peoples, whereas in fact they are generally nothing but the expression of the feudalism of the past or the tyranny of tomorrow, must not let us forget the aspiration of the mass of natives to French peace in order and work." The States-General "therefore expresses the wish that the French Government, whose essential mission it is to guarantee the endurance of the superior interests of the country and of civilization in the territories of the French [!] Empire, should maintain there, beyond the parties, beyond local or temporary contingencies, the sacred principle of French sovereignty."
33. A good description of these rather complex events in Boisdon, pp. 33 f.
34. Ansprenger, p. 71.
35. *J. O.*, 27 August 1946, p. 334.
36. *J. O.*, 18 September 1946, p. 3793.
37. This shift is made clear in Deschamps, *Méthodes et doctrines*, p. 195.
38. 18 September 1946, p. 3791.
39. P. 3787.
40. P. 3817.
41. "I have nowhere felt the sweetness of life more than in France.

... No one asks France to leave. We need France. ... No one thinks of betraying the interests of France", p. 3820.

42. Yacine Diallo from Guinea, p. 3814. Diallo's theses go very far: "One must hope that the French Union will be realized and that the territories of overseas France will one day become French provinces. This is what we dream of." Similarly, Sissoko, p. 3820.

43. 27 August 1946, p. 3334.

44. Cf. the interview of Ansprenger with Lamine-Guèye, Ansprenger, p. 72.

45. Particularly the Communist Angeletti on 18 September, p. 3787; and Césaire, p. 3797. Houphouet-Boigny on 19 September, p. 3849.

46. Text in "Von der Dritten fur Vierten Republik", *Berner Quellen zur neueren Geschichte*, XIV, XV (1950), 130.

47. The internal contradictions are sharply emphasized in Borella, pp. 51 f. Lampué sees the whole preamble as a program for the future, p. 17.

48. As a reporter Coste-Floret tried to stress the federalist elements and spoke of "a draft for a federal assembly" and an "embryo of federal government", 18 September, p. 3786. By contrast Gaston Monnerville, who was elected president of the council of the Republic shortly after, warned against making promises and then not keeping them. He said it was a question of "a façade rather than reality".

"Excuse me for saying that we have already submitted to the trial of a consultative assembly and that we have no desire to do so again. One experience has sufficed for us not to want to give the appearance of an 'ersatz' assembly to an assembly which ought to appear as a definitive organism to the metropolis and to the people as the first step towards the realization of the reforms that are so much desired and have been so much promised.

"Send metropolitan delegates to the Assemblée de l'Union, under conditions which an organic law or a constitutional law will determine; give these assemblies the power to discuss these questions, but truly give it the political and deliberative power that it needs, for if not, we know what will happen. Your assembly will issue instructions which will be followed or not followed. It will have a tribune which make it possible for the overseas delegates to pose questions.

"Believe me, ladies and gentlemen, that if, after these questions have been discussed at the Assemblée de l'Union, and after deliberations have been taken and then transmitted to the sovereign assembly, the latter does not follow the Assemblée de l'Union and leaves the texts in green cartons, it will create unease. This will become aggravated. Once more people will say—an unjust thought but one which is, alas, verifiable in the facts: 'France has again promised and not kept its promise'.

"Do not allow people to say this. This, in my opinion, is what seems most serious about the project that has been submitted." (Applause from various benches of the Left and extreme Left.) *J. O.*, 18 September, p. 3809. This is exactly what was to happen! Yet Lampué asserted: "Everything indicated that the constituent intended to teach this assembly a lesson of great importance", p. 33.

49. *L'Union française* (1950), p. 5.

INDOCHINA, TUNISIA AND MOROCCO

1. Devilliers, *Histoire du Viet-Nam*, p. 177. We are not citing the comprehensive memoirs and literature on the war. Also important are Isoart, *op. cit.*; Ellen I. Hammer, *The Struggle for Indochina* (1954); and Borella, *op. cit.*
2. Devilliers, p. 296.
3. Cf. the documents in J. R. Tournoux, *Secrets d'État* (1962), pp. 453-57.
4. Quoted in Borella, p. 356.
5. Quoted in Borella, p. 358.
6. Quoted in Borella, p. 360.
7. Again we refer to Julien, *op. cit.*; Le Tourneau, *op. cit.*; Borella, *op. cit.*; also "Maroc et Tunisie", special issue of *La Nef*, March 1953.
8. Le Tourneau, p. 119. On 19 July Schuman stressed before the council of the Republic: "We cannot maintain indefinitely the direct administration exercised by the French. This is precisely the object of our reforms." Quoted in *La Nef*, p. 160.
9. Jean Lacouture, *Cinq hommes et la France* (1962), p. 148.
10. Le Tourneau, p. 122.
11. In the highly respected foreword to "Maroc et Tunisie", *La Nef*, pp. 7 f.
12. Asserted by Jacques Fauvet, in *La IVe République* (1959), p. 208.
13. Quoted in Borella, p. 412.
14. Quoted in Gonidec, p. 276.
15. Quoted in Le Tourneau, p. 134.
16. During a secret meeting with Bourguiba, Mendès-France is said to have spoken more or less as follows: "We are determined to make Tunisia the field of an experiment—as a forerunner to friendly decolonization. On the institutional plan as on that of financial aid, we want to help you to show that emancipation can take place with co-operation. Also you will remain at 'the head of the group' which will gradually include Morocco, the countries of Black Africa, even Algeria . . .", quoted in Lacouture, p. 162.
17. Lacouture, p. 167.
18. A. Juin, *Le Maghreb en feu* (1957), p. 72.
19. Note the directives which Boyer gave to Latour, Juin's first colleague, on 8 March 1951: "general aim . . . to create first local assemblies . . . to reach, after a longer [!] period of time, to the summit of the pyramid of a deliberative assembly". It is also worth noting the following comments: a generation had not been enough to create a Moroccan élite. Or, "nationalism becomes intolerable as soon as it becomes anti-French" [!], *Vérité sur l'Afrique du Nord* (1956), pp. 12 f. De Latour nevertheless began by speaking of the "stupid conservatism" among senior officials at the residence-general, p. 141.
20. Le Tourneau, p. 232; good summary in Fauvet, *La IVe République*, pp. 217 f., 293 f.
21. Quoted in Le Tourneau, p. 247.
22. Quoted in Gonidec, p. 278.
23. "Morocco between East and West", *Foreign Affairs*, January 1948, p. 360.
24. "Crisis and Reform in French North Africa", *Foreign Affairs*, April

1951, p. 455. Julien considered the government's demand to discuss only within the protectorate as dubious, since even Libya was now independent.

25. Cf. also the declaration by minister Pierre July on the new Morocco policy: France wanted to create a "lasting Union between France and Morocco" and give the latter the status of "sovereign state", but stipulated as a basis for negotiations "permanent French presence . . . equal representation of its interests and complete maintenance of France's responsibility in the sphere of defence and foreign affairs". *Keesing's Contemporary Archives*, 1 October 1955.

26. E.g. G. P. Johannot, "Les conditions d'une durable 'présence française' au Maroc", *Revue politique et parlementaire* (1955), No. 217. One must proceed with courage, in the sense of the preamble of the constitution, and show the way to independence, p. 219.

27. Ives G. Brissonière, "La notion d'interdépendance", *Revue de défense nationale*, July 1956, pp. 847 f. He interpreted the notion and believed he could show its "precise meaning". The "features of a France-Tunisia-Morocco association are becoming clear . . . a concerted diplomacy and common defence, these are the two pillars and the two tests of interdependence".

THE REVISION OF THE UNION FRANÇAISE AND THE POST-WAR DISCUSSION, 1946–1955

1. Cf. Borella, pp. 395 f.
2. Borella, p. 400.
3. P. 381.
4. Borella, p. 370.
5. E.g. Georges Boussenot, former deputy of Réunion and Madagascar, "L'Assemblée de l'Union française: son rôle l'élargissement de ses pouvoirs", *Revue politique et parlementaire*, January 1953, p. 29. Lamine-Guèye, *Étapes et perspectives de l'Union française* (1955), p. 65.
6. Georges Boussenot, "Un danger pour l'Assemblée de l'Union française": "The native élites have a tendency to prefer local assemblies with restricted but effective powers to it—because it only has consultative powers." In *Marchés coloniaux*, 15 March 1952.
7. J. O., *Assemblée Nationale* (1953), Documents Annexe 6506.
8. J. O., *Assemblée Nationale* (1955), Documents Annexe 10,398.
9. "Pour une solution fédéraliste", *La Nef*, IX (1955). "Against the centrifugal current of the associated state there is but one solution: The French Republic . . . it is because we do not want to remain in the French city but in our own quarter with our church and our school that we prefer, as the ultimate end of our evolution, the state integrated into the French Republic to the associated state". In *Marchés coloniaux*, 4 April 1953, p. 1006. "Le Fédéralisme est la vérité du XXe siècle et l'avenir de l'Union française", *Marchés coloniaux*, 17 September, 1955.
10. A general survey in Alain Coret, "Le problème de la réforme du titre VIII de la constitution de 1946" *Revue juridique et politique de l'Union française* (1956), No. 1, pp. 87–142. Also a series of proposals in the appendix to Bour's report, "Assemblée de l'Union française" (1955), Annexe 104. Besides Borella, p. 315, cf. also P. Lampué, "Pour une réforme de l'Union française", *Cahiers de la République* (1959), p. 7.
11. As an example we can again cite Boussenot, who had full sympathy

with the desire for autonomy of the native élite and demanded reforms of the Union, but at the same time started out from the thesis: "Overseas France constitutes the necessary complement to continental France"—economically and militarily! Without the overseas territories, France would one day become a secondary power like Spain. "And it is precisely because overseas France does not want to remain indefinitely [!] soldered to metropolitan France that it is right to demand only the impression but also the assurance that it will never become the poor relation to whose recital of grievances and aspirations Paris will listen only intermittently and with half an ear." "L'Assemblée de l'Union française, son rôle, l'élargissement de ses pouvoirs", *Revue politique et parlementaire*, January 1953, p. 35.

12. *Cahiers de la République* (1940), No. 10, pp. 35 f.

13. Cf. p. 663.

14. J. O., *Assemblée de l'Union française*, July 1955, p. 678. Cf. also the essay by René Galbrun (inspector of overseas France) in *Revue politique et parlementaire* (1956), No. 1, p. 70. Or a journalist's comment: it was a question "of finding the form of federal cooperation which would, in each territory, bring with it a degree of autonomy or of variable integration and which must create the indivisible unity of the great French Republic"; Pierre Paraf, "Nouveaux rendez-vous africains" in *Revue politique et parlementaire*, 1955, No. 217, p. 140.

15. "Le Fédéralisme et l'Union française" in *Revue politique et parlementaire* (1948), No. 14.

16. The Vietnamese Bun Kinh declared before the Assemblée de l'Union française on 7 July 1955: "We do not think that the French Union can evolve, in the future, towards a Confederation", since the general hatred of supra-national institutions was much too great; they did not want to give up their freedom of decision to certain councils in Paris; Gonidec, p. 355. King Norodom Sihanouk of Cambodia accordingly postulated a transformation of the French Union into a Commonwealth; *Dokumente*, Bour, p. 11. On 12 March 1954, Bourguiba declared: "The French Union must proceed little by little towards the formula of the British Commonwealth, i.e. to the union of states endowed with sovereignty." Quoted in Coret, p. 108.

17. The contrast with the British situation was asserted with dubious arguments. For instance, an important article stated: "It would be dangerous to simply draw a line of demarcation with the United Kingdom which, thanks to stronger economic ties than ours [!?], an indirect administration which has more respect for the local cadres, has been able to pursue a policy tending towards the establishment of independent African states in West Africa." René Servoise, "Introduction aux problèmes de la politique française", *Politique étrangère* (1954), No. 4 (special issue on the problems of overseas France). This assertion by the experienced economist is obviously inapposite—particularly since Servoise stresses that France still adhered to the Pacte colonial; even if it did, this thesis would be more convincing in the opposite sense!

18. Alfred Rieber, *Stalin and the French Communist Party 1941–1947* (1962), pp. 314 f. For Indochina, cf. also Hammer, *Struggle for Indochina*, p. 201.

19. As an example we can take the declaration by Mme. J. Vermeersch (Thorez's companion) in parliament on 27 January 1950: "We are continuing our fight against the war in Vietnam. We shall fight for the complete independence of the Vietnamese people, we shall fight for the return of

the expeditionary force. We shall continue, with all the people, the battle against sending troops and war materials. . . . The armed fight of the Vietnamese people against French imperialism is a considerable help to the workers and the democratic movement in France. The victory of the Vietnamese people over the aggressor will be the victory of the people of France." Quoted in Isoart, pp. 382 f.

20. E.g. E. Cohen-Hadria, "Le fait colonial", *Revue socialiste* (1947), No. 14, p. 307. If France would leave Tunisia—this in 1947!—who would take control in Bizerte?

21. Léon Blum in *Le Populaire*, 5 December 1949.

22. Ministerial declaration on 23 December 1946, in *Année politique* (1946), p. 545.

23. Cf. his Indochina declaration on 10 December 1946, two days before his investiture as prime minister, *Le Populaire*, 10 December 1946, quoted in Isoart, p. 372.

24. Conseil National, 19–22 March 1947. *Le Populaire*, 20 March 1947. Cf. also the party congress resolution in July 1948: "Socialism has always adopted an attitude of understanding and sympathy with regard to the aspirations of the overseas peoples towards the realization of their independence. However, it feels that in a world placed under the sign of interdependence, only the realization of a federal-type political system will safeguard the essential rights of the collectivities. . . . Interdependence without a federal organization must normally put into play the traditional forces of aggression or autochthonous neo-capitalism. . . ." *Le Populaire*, 6 July 1948.

25. Paul Alduy, "L'Union française, mission de la France", *Revue socialiste*, No. 299 (1948), p. 21.

26. Apart from the above-mentioned essay, cf. "Le problème colonial à la lumière du socialisme", *Revue socialiste*, No. 7 (1947). "Pour une structure politique de l'Union française", *Esprit* (special issue) (1949), No. 7. Alduy at the 1949 Party Congress, *Le Populaire*, 18 July 1949.

27. The local assemblies and the Assemblée de l'Union française were to obtain legislative powers, while the Union should also have its own executive; *L'Union française*, p. 86.

28. At the party congress, Guy Mollet openly rejected the term "fédération": "The term association would be greatly preferred". *Le Populaire*, 5 July 1955.

29. Conseil National du Parti socialiste, ayant pouvoir de congrès, 24–25 January 1953, Annexe II, Bour, p. 27. The June 1956 congress accepted the following resolution: "At the same time that we extend the powers of the territorial assemblies it is necessary to put into effect a better legislative organization, particularly by giving the Assemblée de l'Union française extended powers, . . . but without calling into question the sovereignty of parliament. Opposed to any policy of 'surrender', the Socialist party proclaims that a policy of evolution must be pursued on all levels . . .", *Le Populaire*, 2 July 1956.

30. *Le Populaire*, 6 June 1948, 29 October 1948; O. Rosenfeld in *Le Populaire*, 21 January 1949. The 1950 party congress: "The SFIO has indicated special reservations. Bao Dai cannot be considered the qualified representative of the Vietnamese people". *Le Populaire*, 13 July 1950; Isoart, p. 384.

The May 1950 party congress unanimously demanded "that without delay negotiations should begin between the Government of the Republic [the Socialists were involved in this government!] and the qualified representatives of the Tunisian Nation in order to fix the date for suppression of the protectorate and the successive stages for the accession of Tunisia to the status of a sovereign and independent State . . . and simultaneously to sign a treaty of association between the French Republic and Tunisia to co-ordinate action on the basis of equality, on the national defense plan, foreign policy and economic and cultural relations". Text in the 1951 report. In July 1953 there is mention of the "internal autonomy of a Tunisian State", *Rapports*, p. 103. A year later Julien rejected the idea of co-sovereignty, because the Moroccans demanded internal sovereignty. "We must say clearly that Morocco has a right to its sovereignty and its independence." *Le Populaire*, 5 July 1954.

31. Grosser, p. 115.
32. In *Temps modernes*, June 1952.
33. Grosser, p. 115. "De l'Empire à la Communauté des Peuples", *Esprit* (1949), No. 7, p. 1085.
34. In *Temps modernes*, June 1952. In the same issue, Claude Gérard, "Pacte colonial et démocratique." He wanted a federal assembly as a "federal senate", loose ties with the associated states in the sense of a confederation with a high council and a deputy prime minister as head of the executive.
35. P. 1093. In the same issue, Jean Lequiller, "L'exemple anglais": "Independence against or with us, united with or without us: this is the question", wrote Bertrand d'Astray with reference to the Viet Minh in 1947. "Pour un Lyautey socialiste", *Esprit*, February 1947. "We must create a happy precedent for our desire for a French Union". André de Peretti, "L'Indépendance marocaine et la France", *Esprit* (1947), No. 4, p. 571.
36. Report of the 1949 party congress, "La politique de l'Union française".
37. Druand-Reville in July 1953 before the Académie des Sciences morales et politiques: "Can one without injustice accuse France of colonialism when all its colonial actions prove that . . . it has never intervened overseas in order to subject, or to dominate, but rather to pacify, to liberate, to promote. . . ." Quoted in Robert de Montvalon, *Ces pays qu'on n'appelle plus colonies* (1956), p. 10.
38. Gonidec, *Droit de travail*, pp. 47 f.
39. 1950 congress, Paul Devinat, *Rapport de l'Union française*, pp. 6, 15.
40. 1953 congress, report by Henri Caillaret, *Afrique du Nord et Union française*.
41. *Le rencontre est possible*, pp. 128–37. In more detail, *Perspectives marocaines* (1953).
42. Grosser, p. 132.
43. *J. O., Assemblée Nationale*, p. 4047.
44. "Quelques réflexions sur le problème du protectorat", *La Nef*, p. 224.
45. *J. O., Assemblée Nationale*, p. 4977.
46. 1951 congress, Albert Sarraut, *La doctrine radicale et l'Union française*, p. 2.
47. E.g. "We shall thus constitute a Europe-Africa entity, a French Republic which would be both European and African." André Marie, former prime minister, "La structure de l'Union française ne peut être que fédérale," in *Marchés coloniaux*, 23 July 1956, p. 1682.
48. 1950 congress, p. 17.
49. 1952 congress.
50. "Conditions d'une negotiation", in "Morocco and Tunisia", *La Nef* (1953), p. 216.

51. *Aux frontières*, p. 35.
52. "Paradoxes et promesses de l'Union française", *La Nef* (1955), p. 231. An attitude similar to Mitterand's is taken by General Catroux, "L'Union française, son concept, son état, ses perspectives", *Politique étrangère*, (1953), p. 3.
53. These arguments have already appeared in "Faut-il rester en Indochine?", in *Revue politique et parlementaire* (1950).
54. P. 350.
55. Quoted in Grosser, p. 134.
56. Cf. "Pour le salut public, Tribune libre, no. 32, July 1958" (Article in *France indépendante*), e.g. on 5 June 1956 against Mollet's government: "But besides him [Lacoste in Algeria], in Tunisia and in Morocco, M. Savary has pursued a policy of surrender. The contradiction is flagrant. It cannot last. M. Savary's achievements can be judged by their results. They are disastrous. The joint Franco-Moroccan declaration of 2 March has conceded independence, in defiance of the principles sought and proclaimed last October by the government and the Assembly, in defiance of the treaties for which respect had been affirmed, in defiance of the position and the rights of the French community in Morocco, in defiance of the honour and the interests of France. The recent independence agreement is a hateful comedy. . . . M. Savary's policy destroys North Africa. It also destroys France. It continues the policy practised by M. Mendès-France, whose loyal colleague he was before and during the Geneva negotiations", p. 33.
57. "Essai de psychanalyse des protectorats nord-africains", *Politique étrangère* (1954), No. 1, p. 27. Cf. also "Deux aspects des mouvements politiques en Afrique du Nord" in *Marchés coloniaux*, 7 April 1951. The protectorate was outdated, new forms must be sought. "But the necessary evolution must not take place under the direction of the Destourians, old or new. It will be the work of the Tunisians educated at our school, fed on our spirit, of those who are blinded neither by egoistic ambition nor by cynical appetites, and who cannot conceive the future of their country without French presence." As though the nationalists, particularly Bourguiba, had not attended French schools and were not impregnated by French culture! Moreover, it was easy to arbitrarily describe anyone who did not accept French presence in the desirable sense as egoistic or a cynic.
58. J. O., *Assemblée Nationale*, 6 October, p. 4814.
59. J. O., 7 October, p. 4876.
60. J. O., 8 October, p. 4930.
61. *Construire l'Union française* (1948), p. 26.
62. P. 35. Cf. also Coste-Floret, p. 27.
63. Dr. Aujoulat, *La vie et l'avenir de l'Union française* (1947), p. 19 (report of a party commission).
64. Pp. 120, 124.
65. P. 103.
66. Ansprenger, p. 90.
67. J. O., *Assemblée National*, 8 April 1954, pp. 1925–27.
68. Ansprenger, p. 91.
69. Grosser, p. 124.
70. I have taken a few details from Claude Francescani, *L'opinion catholique et la décolonisation depuis la fin de la deuxième guerre mondiale*, diploma, Faculté des Lettres (Paris, 1959), manuscript.

71. Numerous documents and details in François Méjan, *Le Vatican contre la France d'Outre-Mer* (1957).

72. Méjan, p. 163. From the reaction of the French press in Tananarive: "The French in this country do not tolerate that anyone should endanger the position of France in Madagascar, be it by temporal demagogy or by spiritual demagogy."

BLACK AFRICA AND THE *LOI CADRE* (1946–1956)

1. Borella, p. 185, lists: officials, military, people with a driving license, *évolué* notables. In each case the precondition was the ability to read either French or Arabic, which gave the administration considerable political control.

2. The double electoral college did not apply in Senegal.

3. Teitgen (MRP) pointed out in parliament on 20 March 1956 that in the past year Senegal had had a budget of 6 thousand millions, of which 5.5 were already allotted. *J. O., Assemblée Nationale*, p. 1074.

4. African deputies constantly complained that, in spite of excellent training, their fellow-countrymen found it difficult to find employment in private concerns. E.g. Senghor: "But the tragedy is that our engineers are not employed. It took me three years to find a job in Africa for two engineers from my area who had left the école supérieure d'électricité, whose standard of excellence is well known." *J. O., Assemblée Nationale*, 22 March 1956, p. 1193.

5. Kenneth Robinson, "French Africa and the French Union", *Africa Today*, ed. Haines (1955), p. 325.

6. Ansprenger, p. 101. Claude Bourdet, "Les élections Outre-Mer", *Temps modernes*, August 1951.

7. Forty-three deputies represented a population of 30,000,000: one deputy overseas represented 520,000 inhabitants, in the metropolis it was one for 79,000. The overseas representation (including Algeria and the whites) constituted 13 percent of the parliament. Proportional representation would have given Algeria 100, and the rest of the overseas territories 400 deputies. Borella, pp. 187 f.

8. Ansprenger, pp. 115 f.

9. *J. O., Assemblée Nationale*, 9 April 1954, p. 2027.

10. During the debate, the minister of the interior Martinaud-Déplat (cf. pp. 416–17) called on the one and indivisible Republic and declared: "The government therefore intends to proclaim solemnly [!] that any attack on any one of the elements of the French Republic would call into question the very principles of its national sovereignty and that it could not, under any circumstances, agree to discuss it", p. 2017.

11. Hubert Deschamps, *L'éveil politique africain* (1952), p. 92. The high commissioner of Madagascar, Chevigne, is said to have referred to the lack of a "municipal life" already in a speech in 1947. While Africans were being sent to Paris as deputies, they remained barred from local affairs. Henri Labouret, *Colonisation, Colonialisme, Décolonisation* (1952), p. 119.

12. Ansprenger, pp. 241 ff. L. Gray Cowan, *Local Government in West Africa* (1955), pp. 112 f.

13. "Le probléme des chefferies en Afrique Noire française", *Notes et Études documentaires* (1959), No. 2508, p. 16.

14. Deschamps, *L'éveil*, p. 97. Labouret, *Colonisation*, pp. 184 f.
15. Deschamps, p. 99. Ansprenger, p. 120.
16. "There are cases when one must fight to the death. The application of these texts which in Africa will raise prices that are already exorbitant entails the risk of irreparable consequences. Tomorrow we shall have to fight in parliament . . . against the extension of new social measures that may seem generous but which would ruin the country." Jean Foulon, "Les français sont un peu fous", *Climats*, 28 April 1952.
17. Ansprenger, p. 236.
18. Ansprenger, pp. 108 ff., Hailey, *African Survey* (1956), pp. 1193 f., Deschamps, p. 87.
19. The economic importance of the overseas territories to the metropolis was in fact great. The overseas saved France 250–300 million dollars a year, said Moussa. In 1954, 26 percent of all imports came from overseas (excluding Indochina), while 31 percent of exports went there. Pierre Moussa, *Les Chances économiques de la communauté franco-africaine* (1957), pp. 27, 34.
20. Ansprenger, p. 105, gives a chart of the period 1947–1957 (no. =thousand million French francs):

	French West Africa	French Equatorial Africa
Infra structure	109.82	47.89
Social investments	40.85	16.13
Productive investments	59.59	18.28

21. Moussa, pp. 125 f.
22. The sub-commission Intégration métropole Outre-Mer pointed out to the commissariat-general in a report du Plan that the import of African products at exaggerated prices had in 1952 brought in 12.5 thousand millions. On the other hand, the French president of the Grand Conseil of French West Africa remarked in 1953 that imports from France were 40 percent above the world market prices—so how could French West Africa compete with African and Asian imports? "The loyalty of the AOF [French West Africa] is threatened only by high French prices." *Le Monde*, 29 April 1954, quoted in René Servoise, "Introduction aux problèmes de la République française", *Politique étrangère* (1954), No. 4, pp. 394, 403. Moussa assessed the burden on the overseas countries at 20 thousand millions, p. 83.
23. Moussa, p. 123. In 1957 the AOF and Togoland are said to have imported tinned tomatoes [!] for 940 thousand millions, but only 230 thousand millions worth of machines; Robert de Montvalon in *Dokumente* (1958), No. 14, p. 367.
24. E.g. Senghor in the *Assemblée nationale* on 8 April 1954, p. 1913. The left-wing publicist Marcel Willemns, "Un bilan de la colonisation française: L'économie de l'Afrique noire", *Temps modernes* (1955), p. 10. J. Dresch (professor at the Sorbonne), "Questions Ouest-Africaines", *Revue politique et parlementaire*, No. 199 (1949).
25. *J. O.*, *Assemblée nationale*, 21 March 1956, pp. 1108 f.
26. *J. O.*, *Assemblée nationale*, 29 January 1957, p. 367; similarly Mamdou Dia (Senegal) on 30 January 1957, p. 423.
27. On 1 March 1956, quoted in Borella, p. 268, "Do not let us give credit to the false idea that our parliament pays attention to the overseas peoples only when blood is flowing. Let us prove that we know how to act differently under the present circumstances". Defferre on 21 March, *J. O.*, p. 1108. It is pointed out again, however, that very few deputies were interested in overseas affairs; 20 March 1956, p. 1079.

28. This strange solution was based on a compromise between the government draft, which provided for the appointment of half the members by the governor, and the Africans' demands for a responsible cabinet. Africanus, *L'Afrique noire devant l'indépendance* (1958), pp. 13–18. An example of African criticism of the government proposal also in Apithy, *Combat*, 29 January 1957.

29. Marice Duverger, in *Le Monde*, 6 February 1957.

30. In the same way Mamadou Dia (the future prime minister of Senegal): "Federations already exist (AOF, AFF). We simply ask that these facts be taken into account and that these federations are not dismantled." *J. O.*, 30 January 1957, p. 398.

31. *J. O.*, 29 January 1959, pp. 372 f. "The one and indivisible Republic, in the sense of a unified and centralized State—it is with this that I shall end—was in the nineteenth century a national need: It was the force of France and the volunteers were right to go to battle at Valmy crying: long live the nation!

"But today we are in 1957, in the twentieth century, at a time when the strongest states and empires have a federal structure: USA, USSR, India, Canada, Brazil, Western Germany, Yugoslavia, and closer at hand, England, which will give independence to the Gold Coast in the heart of the Commonwealth, which has ceased to be British.

"To federate frightens some members of the Assembly. But, my dear colleagues, to federate is not to separate. To federate, in the etymological sense of the word, is to tie, but without suffocating, as is too often forgotten.

"To cling to the myth of the 'one and indivisible Republic', for it is a myth, otherwise there would be three hundred black and Arab Berber deputies in this Assembly (very good! very good, from the centre), to cling to this myth is, I fear, to work towards the degradation of France. It is to practise the most sterile immobilism.

"I tell you that France is a living tree: it is not dead wood destined for the axe. When you have dismembered the federations of Black Africa, you may well fear that the territories will turn, some towards Lagos, others towards Accra. . . .

"M. Sourou-Migan Apithy, reporter: But no!

"M. Léopold Sédar Senghor: My dear colleague, I am listening. . . . Take care, I say, lest if you Balkanize the federations of Black Africa, the territories do not turn, some towards Lagos, others towards Accra, others towards Rabat.

"Dakar and Brazzaville, admit it, are after all more French, since it is France you are worried about. When the children have grown up, at least in Black Africa, they leave their parents' house and build a house, their own house beside it, but in the same square.

"The square of France, believe me, we do not want to leave it. We have grown up there and it is good to live there. We simply want, M. Minister, my dear colleagues, to build our own houses there, which will at the same time extend and fortify the family square, or rather the hexagon of France." (Applause on several benches at the centre.)

32. In an interview Senghor said: "We believe that to extol the autonomy of the territories is not to want this autonomy. In effect, the 'Europeans' believe that forty-three million Frenchmen cannot resolve the great political and economic problems that have arisen in 1957. How could three million Sudanese or simply six hundred thousand Mauritanians do so? In the framework of a federal French Republic, an AOF of twenty million inhabitants along with the metropolis can constitute a balanced whole and its personality

can flourish. An Ivory Coast or a Senegal of two million inhabitants cannot do so. This is why we consider that the *Loi Cadre* is a regression in as far as it Balkanizes the federations of Black Africa. Yet this *Loi Cadre* can be an instrument of emancipation if the Africans wish it." *Le Monde*, 2 February 1957. Cf. also André Blanchet, "L'itinéraire de partis Africains depuis Bamako", *Tribune libre* (1958), No. 31, p. 86. "A certain equilibrium must reign in the federal French Republic; however, in face of a metropolis of forty-four million men, an AOF of twenty million and an Algeria of ten million inhabitants, it is still too weak." Also the conversation between Senghor and Teitgen, "Ce que veulent les Africains", *France-Forum*, December 1957, pp. 16 f.

33. *J. O.*, p. 371. Also Diawadou Barry (deputy from Guinea), who spoke of the "useless general governments and their organs of reinforcement, i.e. the grand conseils. The first should long since have disappeared, have been no more than simple organs of co-ordination". *J. O.*, 20 March 1956, p. 1071. Barry thus anticipated the concept of co-ordination!

34. More details in Blanchet, "L'itinéraire", pp. 82 ff.

35. The well-informed Africanus reported: "Everything, or almost everything, urged this: the territorial assemblies who act as interpreters of all the ancestral or recent particularities; the politicians, the governors and the heads of local services, impelled by the desire for action and responsibilities or by the simply vanity of being 'the first in the province rather than second in Rome'; the representatives of private interests who believed, not without reasons, that this more easily assured them of a power closer to them and more easy to implement; finally, the minister of overseas France, who, feeling his existence threatened, sought consolation in the multiplication of his children . . .", p. 76.

36. Blanchet, pp. 95 f.

37. P. 85.

38. *J. O.*, 20 March 1956, p. 1075.

39. The Right applauded the comments directed against Senghor, *J. O.*, 30 January 1957. A representative of the right-wing parties, such as Roger Duchet, described Bamako's "federalism" as the "most certain way of breaking up the French Union and losing France", Blanchet, p. 131.

40. A commission of the Assemblée de l'Union française sharply criticized the concept of federation late in 1956: neither historical, ethnic nor economic reasons condoned such a thing. The dangers of Balkanization were dismissed, since the institutions of the Republic "together guarantee the territories the exercise of their own affairs and their participation in the life of a great power", quoted in Colin Newbury, "The Government General and Political Change in French West Africa", *African Affairs*, No. 1; *St. Antony's Papers*, No. 10, ed. K. Kirkwood (1961), p. 56.

41. Ansprenger, p. 249. The only critics were the radical student organizations (FEANF), which dismissed the *Loi Cadre* as "a decoy", Blanchet, p. 120.

42. Senghor, however, commented that the radio had been declared a "state service"; the argument about state monopoly was not watertight, he said, and France wanted to reserve itself an instrument of propaganda; 31 January 1957. The University of Dakar had been built only for reasons of prestige. "We should prefer our students to be sent to France, to French universities." [!] January 1957, *J. O.*, p. 445.

43. For instance René Malbrant, a white deputy from Tchad, attacked the idea of a single college; the capital investments were threatened; for-

tunately no one yet was speaking of giving up parity representation in Algeria too. *J. O.*, 20 March 1956, p. 1080. Another reference to Algeria on 30 January 1957. André Roger Sanglier (French colonial from Madagascar) also attacked the single college: how did the government think it would protect itself against subversive propaganda? Was it ready for such a thing, or was it considering hara-kiri?

44. Senghor, "Pour une communauté franco-africaine", in *Cahiers de la République* (1957), p. 7.

45. Text of the resolution in appendix to Blanchet, p. 187. A similar statement by Lisette, vice-president of the RDA, "Après Bamako", in *Cahiers de la République* (1957), No. 10, p. 33.

46. In the aforementioned conversation between Senghor and Teitgen, "Ce que veulent les Africains", *France-Forum*, December 1957. The metropolis should not accept genuine federalism on the model of the U.S. or Switzerland as long as it bore the financial burden not only of the whole but also of their territories.

47. *J. O.*, 30 January 1957, p. 408.

48. P. 270.

49. P. Lampué, "Pour une réforme de l'Union française", in *Cahiers de la République* (1957), p. 7.

50. Blanchet, p. 126.

51. "La peur des mots", *Le Monde*, 6 February 1957.

52. E.g. Senator Léon Hamon (MRP), "Sur le pont d'Abidjan" in *Revue politique et parlementaire* (1958), p. 224. One should create a clear-cut situation and let the former vice-president take over as head of the territorial government; moreover, a "federal orientation" was necessary, for otherwise "we would let the mystiques [!] turn elsewhere—towards independence and the example of Ghana: the incapacity of the French Parliament to implement this reform of Title VIII of which it has spoken for years can, moreover, only have a deplorable result", p. 329. *Ibid.*, "La mise en place des pouvoirs politiques en Afrique noire" in *Cahiers de la République* (1957), p. 7. Also, Maurice H. Lenormand, "La loi cadre et la réforme constitutionelle vues à travers quelques structures fédérales contemporaines", *Revue politique et parlementaire* (1957), No. 223.

53. E.g. Teitgen refers to this in *France-Forum*, p. 20.

54. E.g. Georges Chaffard in *Le Monde*, 30 January 1957. He rejected Senghor and Houphouet-Boigny's theses and postulated open recognition of the "right to independence"; only then could one prepare "on the basis of equality . . . a final solution of a very broad confederal nature". Also the aforementioned book by Africanus. The well-informed writer analysed French difficulty in deciding what to do about the independence of the African territories: "Two mistakes mislead a good part of French opinion here. The first is to confuse independence and secession; the second is to believe that it is possible to stop and to delay for a long time, by legal artifice, what our own principles and the nature of things command us not only to accept but also to pursue with intelligence and decision to the end", p. 57. This barrier must be overcome before anything new could be created which did not rely fundamentally on technical aid and mutual interest. The *Loi Cadre* had been a frightened concession and it would have been better to start with the status of Togoland. A loose federation could still be formed. "Seen in this way, the political independence of the overseas territories is in no way opposed to the constitution of a vast French world, organized as a living association of different peoples all enjoying self-determination and tied one

with the other less by the constricting force of laws or treaties than by the clear conscience of the advantages of their community", p. 61.
55. "Problèmes constitutionnels", in Cahiers de la République (1957), No. 10, p. 39.
56. Besides the abovementioned Africanus and Chaffard, cf. also Blanchet, pp. 138, 156. Ibid., "Commonwealth et Union française", Marchés tropicaux (new title of Marchés coloniaux), 31 August 1957. R. de Lacharrière, "Revision constitutionnelle et fédérale. Théories et illusions", Le Monde, 25 October 1957.
57. Blanchet, p. 141. The Senegalese d'Arboussier, president of the Grand Conseil of the AOF, referred back to Mitterand's "round table"; a federal state of the Franco-African Community could come into being "on a parity level", Le Monde, 12 April 1958.
58. Quoted in Blanchet, p. 139. In the same sense a leader in Marchés tropicaux: "Vers une Communauté franco-africaine," 16 November 1957.
59. In the issues of 11 August; 18 August and 1 September.
60. 3rd ed. (1958), p. 53.
61. This is asserted by the well-informed Blanchet, L'itinéraire des partis africains depuis Bamako (1958), p. 176.
62. Cahiers de la Fondation Nationale des Sciences Politiques (1957).
63. Among others, the influential deputy Lisette at the Bamako Congress, Blanchet, p. 178.
64. 30 August 1958, quoted in Ansprenger, p. 259.
65. Blanchet mentioned a union leader, p. 176. The Socialist opposing view in J. Ries, "L'heure de la lucidité IV, conséquences de la colonisation pour les métropoles", Revue socialiste (1957), pp. 261 f.
66. Ansprenger, p. 259.
67. Paris-Match, 19 February and 7 March 1964.

THE COMMUNAUTÉ

1. Gilbert Ziebura, Die V. Republik, Frankreich's neues Regierungs system (1960), p. 35.
2. Pour un constitution fédérale, (1946).
3. Charles de Gaulle, Le RPF, Conférence de presse, 24 April 1947. Reprinted as a brochure.
4. L'Union française, problèmes politiques, économiques et sociaux relatifs à l'Union française. Rapport approuvé par les assises nationales du Peuple français, June 1950.
5. "De l'Empire à la République fédérale," in Jours de France, 16 December 1954.
6. "Eléments d'un programme de l'ARS," Bour, Annexe V, Autumn 1952, pp. 37 f.
7. Quoted in Grosser, La politique extérieure, p. 140.
8. Government and parliament should "determine, before any convention, the institutions of the French Union that are necessary to the establishment of definitive organic ties, not only between France and Tunisia, but also between France and the other states and territories of the French Union", quoted in "Eléments d'un programme," p. 14.
9. "Les idées, les faits", May 1955. In the debate on the ratification of the Franco-Tunisian conventions Dronne proposed a "prejudicial motion" which aimed at "the institution of federal ties between Tunisia and France

NOTES 625

in the framework of a renovated French Union", quoted in Coret, "Le problème de la réforme du titre VIII de la constitution de 1946", *Revue juridique et politique de l'Union française* (1956), No. 1, p. 114.

10. "La prochaine république sera-t-elle républicaine?" in *Tribune libre* (1948), No. 23. Text of the draft constitution in the appendix. For its origins cf. Blanchet, *Itinéraire*, pp. 133 f.

11. Gonidec, pp. 323 f.

12. Ziebura, p. 252.

13. For this and what follows, cf. above all Ansprenger, pp. 261 ff.

14. André Passeron, *De Gaulle parle* (1962) (excerpts from speeches 1958–1962), p. 450.

15. For its origins, cf. besides the author and Ansprenger and Gonidec, pp. 323 f., also Gilles Néra, *La Communauté* (1960), pp. 9 f.; Marcel Merlé, "La Constitution et les problèmes d'outre-mer", *Revue française de Science politique*, March 1959; Victor Silvera, "Passé de l'Union française et avenir de la Communauté", *Revue juridique et politique de l'Union française* (1958); Antoine Azar, *Genèse de la Constitution du 4.10.1958* (1961).

16. This also applies for the intervention of de Gaulle on 9 August: "federal whole" with the African territories, "a more vast Community" with the "other States", Passeron, p. 451.

17. Quoted in Ziebura, p. 256. He postulated negotiations with France on the basis of a multi-national confederation of free and equal peoples". More detail in Ansprenger, p. 330.

18. *Le Monde*, 23 July 1958.

19. *Le Monde*, 24 July 1958.

20. Excerpt in Ziebura, p. 257: "I note that a choice has been overlooked: the choice for independence in the form of associated states. Nowhere is there mention of the right to self-determination". More detail in "Fédération et Confédération", *Marchés tropicaux*, 30 August 1958.

21. In *Le Monde* on 23 July the well-known lawyer Georges Vedel also spoke in favour of the recognition of independence on principle and freely consented negotiations with the African governments. Similarly, Marcel Merle in *Le Monde*, 14 August.

22. Ansprenger, pp. 271 f.

23. Articles 86, 87 of the constitution; Ziebura, p. 132; Ansprenger, pp. 269 f. Michel Debré also considered treaties of association only for the states of Asia or white Africa, in a remarkable speech on 27 August on the draft constitution, Ziebura, p. 109. I cannot agree with Ansprenger when he asserts, pp. 272 f., that de Gaulle had accepted the concept of a "Community capable of development" under the influence of Boganda in Brazzaville.

24. Ansprenger, pp. 271 f.

25. Passeron, p. 457.

26. Ziebura quoted the text, pp. 115, 262 f. Cf. also C. Massa, "Die französische Verfassung vom 5.10.1958. und die überseeischen Gebiete" in *Europa-Archiv* (1959), No. 4.

27. Marcel Prélot, quoted in Ansprenger, p. 270.

28. A good outline of the history of the Community in Yves Guéna, *Historique de la Communauté* (1962), pp. 88 f.

29. It is characteristic that de Gaulle spoke mockingly of Guinea; it remained to be seen whether "it happens that a State really comes into being", press conference, 23 October 1958, Passeron, p. 462.

30. *Le Monde*, 1 October 1958; similarly, "Vers l'indépendance dans l'amitié", in *Cahiers de la République* (1958), No. 16, pp. 52 f., and

"Indépendance nominale, terme ultime de notre évolution dans le cadre de la Communauté", *Marchés tropicaux*, 23 May 1959. Dia on 7 July 1959.
31. Passeron, p. 465.
32. Walter Schütze, "Bilanz and Perspektiven der franfösischafrikanischen Gemeinschaft", *Europa-Archiv* (1960), No. 5, p. 163.
33. Passeron, p. 469.
34. Néra's attempt to bring this independence movement into accord with the Community and to interpret it so that it fitted into the text of the constitution is not convincing; pp. 85 f.
"What we want is a progressive but rapid transformation of the Community into a multi-national confederation." Ziebura, p. 277. President Tsiranana of Madagascar in November 1959: "The Community must be a very elastic whole tending to become a kind of Commonwealth in which each country will be independent, although bound to the others." Quoted in Guéna, p. 138.

FROM ALGÉRIE FRANÇAISE TO THE RÉPUBLIQUE ALGÉRIENNE

1. The Sorbonne professor Bernard Lavergne can be taken as an example of a colonialist polemicist in the mother country. He wrote, in retrospect: "Thus the die had been cast. The unexpected had been posed, without any previous consultation with the country, an entirely new principle in our policy, which had been rejected by our public opinion and by the parliament and which was to compromise, to overthrow even, our whole Algerian policy, and lay as a heavy mortgage on the colonial policy of France" (1948), p. 130. Lavergne's book runs through the whole register of French-Algerian arguments: assimilation was impossible, the Algerian manifesto was a challenge, there was no Algerian nationalism, the colonists paid good wages, etc.
2. Of the comprehensive literature on Algeria we note only the following general works: Thomas Oppermann, *Die algerische Frage* (1959) (with a bibliography); M. K. Clark, *Algeria in Turmoil. A History of the Rebellion* (1960); Thankmar Münchhausen, *Ziele and Widerstände der französischen Algerienpolitik von 1945–1958* (Heidelberg, 1962), manuscript.
3. In 1945 only 100,000 out of 1,200,000 school-age Muslim children went to school, as opposed to 200,000 children from European families; Münchhausen, p. 94.
4. Münchhausen, pp. 97–100.
5. *Documents de l'Assemblée Nationale* (1946), Annexe No. 376: "Muslim Algeria, which for so long has claimed its rights to live and to its definitive integration into the metropolis . . . Algeria will have the same departmental and communal administration and the same administrative cadres as those of France", p. 374. Dr. Bendjelloul on 8 March in the Assemblée Nationale, *J. O.*, p. 646.
6. Gabriel Esquer, *Histoire de l'Algérie (1830–1957)* (1957), pp. 84 f.
7. "L'action du Comté de l'Empire français", p. 86.
8. "Un nouvel édit de Caracalla ne résoudrait rien", *Marchés coloniaux*, 20 March 1946, p. 293.
9. "Notre Algérie", *Marchés coloniaux*, 13 July 1946, p. 691.
10. Pierre Lampué, "Le Statut de l'Algérie", *Revue juridique et politique de l'Union française* (1947).
11. Assemblée Nationale, Annexe of 6 February 1947.

12. Münchhausen gives the best study. An excellent outline in Jacques Fauvet, *La IVe République* (1959), ch. 5.
13. *Tribune libre*, No. 32, July 1958 (essays from *France-Indépendante*), pp. 81, 110.
14. P. 135.
15. Rieber, pp. 320 f.
16. "L'Algérie n'est pas la France", *Temps modernes*, November 1955, p. 577.
17. *Le Monde*, 6 November 1954.
18. *J. O.*, *Assemblée Nationale*, p. 4961.
19. "It is time to contemplate some simple and effective measures. M. Mitterand is wrong to affirm that there must be no Algerian nationalism. Nationalism is the concentrated form of patriotism. The moment frontiers exist, it is impossible for the aspirations towards liberty and equality not to become translated into a national form." *Témoignage chrétien*, 12 November 1954, quoted in Claude Extier, *La Gauche hebdomadaire, 1914–1962* (Kiosque series) (1962), p. 209.
20. Münchhausen, pp. 149 f.
21. Quoted in *La Gauche hebdomadaire*, p. 210.
22. Münchhausen, pp. 182, 185.
23. Cf. Soustelle's own report: *Aimée et souffrante Algérie* (1956).
24. "It is our aim to attain a complete integration of Algeria as soon as possible, an integration which will respect its own originality and personality in areas such as language and religion, but which will acknowledge to all inhabitants without discrimination the rights and duties, the opportunities and obligations which go with being French citizens", *Keesing's Contemporary Archives*, 1 October 1955.
25. *Aimée et souffrante Algérie*, pp. 36, 93 f., 108 f., 246.
26. At the Radical Socialists' party congress in November 1955. *Programme d'action, Algérie, Exposé de PFM*, 3–6 November 1955.
27. *Cahiers de la République* (1956), p. 1.
28. *Sauver l'Algérie française. Le dossier du parti radical 1955–1957*, published by the party, pp. 24 f.
29. Report in *Le Populaire*, 1 July 1957. The secretary of the railways union (CGT-FO) answered an Algerian unionist that it was wrong to "pretend that Algeria's struggle for national independence is intimately tied to the liberation of the Algerian people". The French workers would stand by Algeria's side when they "became aware that in giving independence to Algeria, the Algerian people would enjoy a better life. . . . But the desire that the French workers feel is not to see the Algerian worker free himself from certain masters only to fall under the yoke of native feudalism" (1956), quoted in Georges Fischer, "Syndicats et décolonisation", *Présence africaine*, October 1960, p. 32.
30. Quoted in Münchhausen, p. 241.
31. Daniel Ligou, *Histoire du Socialisme en France 1871–1961* (1962), pp. 616 ff.
32. Jean Ries, secretary of the federation of Tunisia, uses almost all the arguments of the colonial Right in his 1957 essay "L'Heure de la lucidité I, Perspectives socialistes en Afrique du Nord II"! In 1958, several writers contradicted this, cf. Ries again (1958).
33. E.g. Defferre: "He proposes negotiation accompanied by a change in methods and even objectives. The former must be an elaboration of a statute of very broad autonomy instituting an Algerian government and

parliament.... Everyone, in principle, is against surrender.... The true policy of French presence is that which allows one, thanks to reforms instituted in time, to restore fraternity between the natives and the Europeans.... The independence of Algeria does not correspond to the particular circumstances in this country. Nor does it comply with the true interest of the inhabitants." Report on the party congress in *Le Populaire*, 29 June 1957.

34. "Au sud rien de nouveau", *Le Monde*, 11 and 14 May 1957. "The emancipation of the peoples who could not be adequately assimilated is part of a definite line of history and simply follows the process of liberation at the head of which we placed ourselves in 1789." The slogan "to lose Africa" represented a Malthusian attitude, and did not comply with the idea of a France that renewed itself. "One form of dominating the peoples is dead, as much for economic as for political reasons. The revolt of certain countries is no more than the result of our delay in understanding a new situation".

35. P. 32.
36. P. 72.
37. Oppermann, pp. 123 f. Münchhausen, p. 328.
38. Report in *Le Monde* on 20 March 1958. After the opportunity for full integration had been missed and Morocco and Tunisia were already independent, it was a delusion to contemplate anything but the future independence of Algeria. Either France would grant this independence through negotiation or Algeria would gain it by force and without France. ... As a basis for negotiation one must therefore accept the right to independence and also the recognition of the NLF as an important spokesman for the Muslims. On this basis even the nationalists would agree to guarantee the rights and interests and above all the fair treatment of the settlers. The document is signed by several professors from the Collège de France and the Sorbonne.
39. *Tribune libre*, 6 August 1957. Then again Aron, with "L'Algérie et la République", *Tribune libre*, No. 33, July 1958.
40. P. 45.
41. Pp. 68 f.
42. Besides Münchhausen, Thomas Oppermann, "Die Endphase des Algerienkonfliktes 1929–1962", *Zeitschrift für ausländisches öffentliches Recht und Völkerrecht*, XXIII, (1963), 1. Louis Terrenoire, *De Gaulle et l'Algérie* (1964). Robert Buron, *Carnets politiques de la guerre d'Algérie* (1965).
43. André Passeron, *De Gaulle parle* (1962), pp. 150 f.
44. 6 June, Passeron, p. 154.
45. 29 August, Passeron, pp. 164 f.
46. P. 167; 80 percent of the registered voters voted, of whom 90 percent voted yes.
47. He used "long live French Algeria" exceptionally, Passeron, p. 156.
48. As early as the first speech on 4 June: "a fight which I myself acknowledge to be courageous", p. 152.
49. Passeron, p. 173.
50. P. 175.
51. "I believe that future solutions will be based on the courageous personality of Algeria and its close association with the French metropolis." Passeron, p. 176.
52. December 1958, p. 180.
53. Several quotations in Alain Savary, "Nationalisme algérien et grandeur française", *Tribune libre*, January 1960, No. 54, pp. 137 f.

54. Passeron, pp. 201 f.
55. P. 194.
56. For the first time in September 1960, Passeron, p. 266.
57. Press conference on 11 April 1961, Passeron, p. 287.
58. "They will determine an Algerian destiny which will be united with the destiny of France. This is indeed useful to France, but it is necessary to Algeria. France is prepared to give fraternal aid." July 1960, Passeron, p. 243. Cf. also the speech before the officers on 10 December 1960, Terrenoire, p. 209.
59. Passeron, pp. 250 f. Again on 11 April 1961: "If the Algerian inhabitants wish, in fact, to be tempted to break with France, to the degree that we should no longer have any part in their destiny, we would not oppose it. Naturally we would immediately stop investing our resources, our men, our money, in an enterprise which would henceforth be hopeless. We would advise those of our countrymen who were there to leave the territories concerned since they would really run too much of a risk. Inversely we should send home those Algerians who live in France and who would cease to be French", p. 291.
60. Le Monde, 9 September, 1957, quoted in Oppermann, Die algerische Frage, p. 123.
61. In a speech to officers in December 1960 de Gaulle said: "Precisely because of the rebellion, the inhabitants of this Algeria which is in a very great majority Muslim, because this rebellion, and everything connected with it, is taking place in a new world, in a world which does not at all resemble the world I have known myself, when I was young. There is, as you well know, this concept of liberation which extends from one end of the world to the other, which has spread to our Black Africa, which has spread over all that was formerly empire, without exception, and which cannot fail to have considerable consequences here." Passeron, p. 273.

III. TOWARDS A COMPARISON

THE DECOLONIZATION OF AN ANTI-COLONIAL POWER: THE UNITED STATES IN THE PHILIPPINES

1. We only point out the most recent general surveys: Garel A. Grunder and William E. Livezey, *The Philippines and the United States* (1951). Georges Fischer, *Un cas de décolonisation, les États-Unis et les Philippines* (1960). Whitney T. Perkins, *Denial of Empire. The U.S. and Its Dependencies* (1962).
2. Perkins, p. 198. It is also worth noting that they did not want to exercise their imperial rule by non-colonial methods. Thus the first Philippines commission under Schurman praised the British concept of the Crown Colony, but then referred to the American territorial system as "non-colonial", without making the differences clear.
3. Grunder and Livezey, p. 63.
4. Grunder and Livezey, p. 85.
5. For the practical conditions made by Governor Forbes, Wilson and Taft, cf. Perkins, p. 218.
6. However, the party changed its attitude noticeably. While in 1905 and 1908 it started out from the example of Cuba, in 1912 it stated: "We favor an immediate declaration of the nation's purpose to recognize the independence of the Philippine Islands as soon as a stable government can be established." Party platform in the appendix to W. Cameron Forbes, *The Philippine Islands* (1928), p. 569.
7. Perkins, p. 221.
8. Perkins, pp. 225 f.
9. "Allow me to call your attention to the fact that the people of the Philippine Islands have succeeded in maintaining a stable government. . . . I respectfully submit that this condition precedent having fulfilled, it is now our liberty and our duty to keep our promise to the people of the Philippine Islands by granting them the independence they so honorably covet." Quoted in G. Kirk, *Philippine Independence* (1936), p. 48. Cf. also Francis Burton Harrison, *The Cornerstone of Philippine Independence* (1922), pp. 287 f.
10. Coolidge's two letters in February 1924 and April 1927 in the appendix to Forbes, pp. 548 f., 557 f.
11. Henry L. Stimson, "On Active Service in Peace and War, 1948. Future Philippine Policy under the Jones Act", *Foreign Affairs*, April 1927. E. E. Morison, *Turmoil and Tradition. A Study of the Life and Times of Henry L. Stimson* (1960), ch. 17. Maximo M. Kalow (a Filipino),

"Governor Stimson in the Philippines", *Foreign Affairs*, April 1929. Quezon also praised Stimson highly in *The Good Fight* (1946), p. 140.

12. Nicholas Roosevelt, *The Philippines. A Treasure and a Problem* (1926). Theme: "a thankless burden" which America could not, however, give up. Forbes (1928), pp. 418 f. The secretary of the American chamber of commerce in the Philippines took a "colonialist" attitude: the "solution ... is a very simple one. First, the stability of the Government which existed ... has been destroyed by Filipino administration, so that independence not only can with entire honor be postponed indefinitely, but ought to be postponed. Second a brief act should follow, nullifying all local laws that infringe upon the power of the Governor General and that link legislative and executive authority mischievously together". Walter Robb, *Current History*, XIX (1923–1924), 287.

13. E.g. Raymond Leslie Buell, "What about the Philippines", *Atlantic Monthly* (1924). C. C. Batchelder, "Philippine Independence", *Foreign Affairs* (1924), No. 3. Stephan P. Duggan, "The Future of the Philippines", *Foreign Affairs*, October 1926.

14. James S. Allen, "Agrarian Tendencies in the Philippines", *Pacific Affairs*, March 1938. Leopold T. Ruiz, "Farm Tendency and Cooperation in the Philippines", *Far Eastern Quarterly*, February 1945. Felix M. Kessing, "Cultural Trends in the Philippines", *ibid*.

15. Pauline Crumb Smith, "A Basic Problem in Philippine Education", *Far Eastern Quarterly*, February 1945. A critique also in Jose A. Lansang, "The Philippine-American Experiment: A Philippine View", *Pacific Affairs* (1952), Fischer, pp. 23 f.

16. Fischer, pp. 41 f.
17. Good general outline in Kirk, pp. 55 f.
18. Fischer, p. 21.
19. Perkins, p. 213.
20. Kirk, p. 59.
21. Paul V. McNutt, American high commissioner and first U.S. ambassador in the Philippines, described the situation: "In the Philippines before the war the national economy was geared entirely to export trade. And 95% of that export trade was with the U.S. Except for rice and fish which are locally consumed, 98% of all other products in the Philippines, amounting to 260 million dollars in 1941, is produced for export. ... And I might and should say here and now that we, the U.S. managed it that way. We are responsible for the dependency of the Philippines on the American market. Our businessmen and our statesmen in past years allowed the Philippines to become a complete economic dependency of the U.S. to a greater degree than any single State of the Union is economically dependent on the rest of the U.S." In *Hearings*, 15 February 1946, quoted in Shirley Jenkins, "Philippines", in *The Development of Self-Rule and Independence in Burma, Malaya and the Philippines*, ed. J. Cady (1948), p. 98.

22. Senator Heflin on 9 October 1929, quoted in Kirk, p. 96. Also other examples in Kirk.

23. *On Active Service*, p. 147.

24. Text of the veto in appendix to Kirk pp. 227 f. Hoover *Memoirs*, III (1952), 332–33.

25. F. R. Dulles, "The Anti-Colonial Policy of F. D. Roosevelt", *Political Science Quarterly* (1955), pp. 2 f.

26. In Salt Lake City on 17 September 1932: "The American people

are interested in Philippine independence, which the Democratic platform endorses." Quoted in Kirk, p. 117.

27. *Public Papers*, ed. Rosemann, IV, 494.

28. *Op. cit.*, III, 119.

29. All the views became directly or indirectly apparent in the Hearings held by both houses of Congress, 1930 and 1932.

30. The Philippine-American chamber of commerce sent propaganda material to firms and newspaper editors "asking them to oppose Philippine Independence", Senate Hearings (1930), pp. 180 f.

31. 72nd Congress, 2nd Session, pp. 311, 341.

32. 71st Congress, 1st Session, pp. 4326, 4587.

33. E.g. Tucker, "A Balance Sheet of the Philippines", *Harvard Business Review* (1929).

34. Nicholas Roosevelt, "Philippine Independence and Peace in the Pacific", *Foreign Affairs*, April 1930.

35. Senate Hearings (1930), pp. 64 f.; (1932), p. 52.

36. A strange combination of conservative colonialist views and isolationism is apparent in Henry Cabot Lodge: it was ridiculous, he said, how the U.S. treated the Philippines as "our equals", imposed the English language and American law, and gave power to the mulattoes; only a genius like General Wood was capable of exercising the system of "responsibility without authority". "We are doing the Filipinos more harm than good . . . the Philippines at present do us more harm than good. . . ." The American capitalists invested little and strategically the islands were "the weakest link in our chain of national defense". As alternative there was only "govern or get out"—and since America did not want to rule, withdrawal was the only solution. The European colonial powers already had enough possessions, to sell to Russia or Japan was not diplomatically possible—so there remained only to give them to Germany: "Another Teutonic Power in the Far East would probably be a pacifying factor". "Our Failure in the Philippines, Shall We Govern or Get Out," *Harper's Magazine*, January 1930.

The Englishman Sir Frederick White opposed the proposals for naturalization in *Pacific Affairs* in 1934: "The Philippine as a Pawn in the Game". Japan would find opportunities for slow intervention; when would America intervene? The well-known international lawyer Quincy Wright replied to White: "A Pawn Approaches the Eighth Square", *op. cit.*, September 1934, with typically isolationist arguments: The Philippines and Guam "are not now assets to America's Far Eastern diplomacy" but were "serious liabilities". Without the Philippines the U.S. would not risk Japanese attack, since the Aleutians and Hawaii were too far away. Great Britain and France must take over the defence of the Philippines in the their own interests.

37. *On Active Service* (diary entries on 10 February 1932), p. 149.

38. *Op. cit.* (6 January 1929), pp. 147, 149.

39. Theodore Roosevelt, son of the president, former governor of Puerto Rico and the Philippines, supported this concept in his book *Colonial Policy* (1937), pp. 187 f.

40. 73rd Congress, 2nd session, pp. 5097 f.

41. Senate Hearings (1930), p. 347.

42. Quoted in H. B. Hawes, *Philippine Uncertainty, an American Problem* (1932), p. 208.

43. House of Representatives, Hearings (1932), pp. 123 f., 163.

44. *Cornerstone*, p. 343.

45. Senate Hearings (1930), pp. 283, 407.

46. The report of the Bell commission of 1951, which was to determine the conditions for American economic aid, not only demanded a fight against corruption and nepotism but also fiscal and agrarian reform, minimum wages for agricultural workers, etc. This has a rather hypocritical tone, since it now demanded from an independent state and in a relatively short time what America had not been able or had not attempted to do as a colonial power. Fischer, p. 317.

47. Senator Hawes, "The Philippines Independence Act", *Annals of the American Academy of Political and Social Science*, CLXVIII (1933), 154.

48. G. Malcolm, *The Commonwealth of the Philippines* (1936), p. 100.

49. Text in appendix to Malcolm, pp. 435 f.

50. Malcolm, p. 134.

51. Quoted in Kirk, pp. 134 f.

52. Fischer, pp. 218 f.

53. Kirk, pp. 214 f. Ralston Hayden, "The Philippines, in Transition", *Foreign Affairs*, July 1936.

54. Fischer, p. 148.

55. Fischer, p. 164. Paul V. McNutt, "The Philippines: Asset or Liability", *Annals*, CCXV (1941).

56. In the Constitution the exploitation of natural resources (wood, water, oil, minerals) was only foreseen for Philippine citizens or capital investment companies with at least 60 percent Philippine participation. The amendment equated the American citizen with the Filipinos and removed all conditions for the companies!

57. In exaggerated and one-sided terms Senator Tydings, chairman of the Senate commission for Philippine affairs, said: "The truth of the matter is that most of the people, outside the Filipinos, who favor this bill are fundamentally opposed to Philippine independence. Many of them have told me so. . . . Their whole philosophy is to keep the Philippines economically, even though we lose them politically . . .", quoted in Abraham Chapman, "American Policy in the Philippines", *Far Eastern Survey*, 5 June 1946, p. 168. Jenkins found that "in spite of this recognition of the short-sightedness of past economic policy, the legislation adopted by the U. S. Congress in 1946 to regulate trade with the Philippine Republic simply sought to perpetuate the previous relationship. This represented a real victory for the economic interests with holdings in the Philippines—a reversal of the situation at the time of passage of the Independence Act, when these American groups fearing competition from Philippine products were wielding more influence." *Op. cit.*, Cady, pp. 98 f.

58. Fischer, p. 173; Chapman, p. 169.

THE UNSUCCESSFUL COMMONWEALTH: THE NETHERLANDS IN INDONESIA

1. Rupert Emerson, *Malaysia, A Study in Direct and Indirect Rule* (1937), p. 412.

2. Cf. in general Emerson.

3. Harry J. Benda, "Tradition und Wandel in Indonesien", *Geschichte in Wissenschaft und Unterricht*, I (1963), 48.

4. J. S. Furnivall, *Netherlands India. A Study of Plural Economy* (1939), p. 260. G. H. Bousquet, *La politique musulmane et coloniale des Pays-Bas* (1939), p. 95.

5. Furnivall, pp. 381 f., 467.
6. Emerson, pp. 433 f.
7. George McTurnan Kahin, *Nationalism and Revolution in Indonesia* (1952, 1959), p. 16.
8. Furnivall, pp. 319, 322.
9. Bousquet, p. 93.
10. "They were rather worse off in 1930 than in 1913", Furnivall, p. 401.
11. Besides Bousquet, cf. Harry J. Benda, *The Crescent and the Rising Sun* (1958).
12. Bousquet, p. 129.
13. In 1935–1936, 516 out of 1020 students were Indonesian; Bousquet, p. 137. For a general study, Furnivall, pp. 364 f.
14. Kahin, p. 34.
15. Furnivall, pp. 250 f. Kahin, p. 33. J. M. van der Kroef, "Economic Origins of Indonesian Nationalism", in *South Asia in the World Today*, ed. P. Talbot (1950).
16. A. Vandenbosch, "Indonesia", in *The New World of South East Asia*, ed. Lennox Mills (1949), p. 87.
17. E. Moresco (former vice-president of the India Council), "The New Constitution of the Netherlands Indies", *Asiatic Review*, April 1927. Moresco also asserted that in 1925 the colonial ministry had wanted to give half the seats in the peoples' council to the natives, but that parliament had refused this; p. 221.
18. Alexandre von Arx, *L'évolution politique en Indonésie de 1900 à 1942* (1949), p. 322, gives a few statistics: in 1939, 1000 out of 2288 voters [!] were appointed; of the 1452 Indonesians 515 were official or appointed voters.
19. Thanks to a high tax census and the Dutch language as an electoral qualification, almost no-one but the Dutch could vote. Batavia with its 530,000 inhabitants had only 12,749 voters in 1948, of whom 8563 were Dutch, 3469 Indonesian and 718 Asians; Vandenbosch, Mills, *op. cit.*, p. 90.
20. Benda, *The Crescent and the Rising Sun*, pp. 26 f.
21. Robert van Niehl, *The Emergence of the Modern Indonesian Elite* (1960), pp. 248 f.
22. Benda, pp. 36, 65, 69.
23. Bousquet, p. 147.
24. A. D. A. De Kat Angelino, *Colonial Policy*, Vol. II, "The Dutch East Indies" (1931), pp. 651 f.
25. Bousquet, pp. 133 f. A. Arthur Schiller, *The Formation of Federal Indonesia 1945-49* (1955), pp. 15 f.
26. Bousquet welcomed the plans for federation as a policy of "divide et impera". The Dutch, by contrast, refused this interpretation or, like Van Vollenhoven, opposed a federal structure; Schiller, pp. 17 f.
27. Justus M. van der Kroef, "Colonial Indonesia: Conservatism Reconsidered", *Journal of East Asiatic Studies*, January 1957, p. 39. A further example of the conservative attitude of the former Dutch minister of finance, Treub, "Dutch Rule in East Indies", *Foreign Affairs*, January 1930.
28. Quoted in Leslie H. Palmer, *Indonesia and the Dutch* (1962), p. 35.
29. Bernard H. M. Vlekke, *Nusantara, a History of Indonesia*, 5th ed. (1959), p. 391. The Visman Commission accordingly decided that no-one demanded independence in the Hearings!

30. Vlekke, p. 395; von Arx, p. 332.
31. Vandenbosch, Mills, p. 97; J. M. Pluvier, "Dutch-Indonesian Relations 1940/1941", *Journal of Southeast Asian History*, March 1965.
32. *Op. cit.*
33. Jan O. M. Broeck, "Indonesia and the Netherlands", *Pacific Affairs*, September 1943.
34. E. N. van Kleffens, "The Democratic Future of the Netherlands Indies", *Foreign Affairs*, October 1942, p. 87.
35. Quoted in Van Mook (among others), *The Stakes of Democracy in Southeast Asia* (1950), pp. 180 f.
36. E.g. George H. C. Hart (chairman of the economic and financial commission), "The Netherlands Indies and Her Neighbours", *Pacific Affairs*, March 1943: "a nation of Indonesian, Dutch and Chinese citizens is emerging . . . full partnership in fact, no more and no less . . . strong Indonesian nation", pp. 21 f. H. van Mook, *Past and Future in the Netherlands Indies*, speech before the Institute of Pacific Relations, 18 May 1945. The acting governor-general spoke of a cabinet under the governor-general, p. 15. American criticism of the declaration in Raymond Kennedy, "Dutch Charter for the Indies", *Pacific Affairs*, June 1943.
37. David Wehl, *The Birth of Indonesia* (1948), p. 29.
38. For what follows, besides Kahin, Wehl, Van Mook and Palmer, cf. also Alastair M. Taylor, *Indonesian Independence and the United Nations* (1960).
39. *Keesing's Contemporary Archives*, 5 November 1945; Palmer, p. 49.
40. Visman, chairman of the 1940 commission, mentioned the Japanese propaganda, but then spoke derogatorily of the "so-called Republic Indonesia" which was in no way representative, "pure nationalism is safe in the hands of the Dutch". *The Situation in Java* (speech in New York, November 1945), p. 11. The conservative attitude is even clearer in the report on Indonesia, 1950, by the Dutch prime-minister-in-exile (1940–1945), P. S. Gerbrandy. According to him the Republic was "only a form of words . . . had no following among the population". Even before the war "a free State had existed in the Indies", pp. 135 f. Gerbrandy hotly opposed Van Mook, Van der Plas and Logemann, who had come from the Struw movement and were responsible for the policy of surrender after 1945. For the negotiations between England, Van Mook and Indonesia, cf. also Idrus Nasir, Diajadiningrat. *The Beginnings of the Indonesian-Dutch Negotiations and the Hage-Veluwe Talks* (1958).
41. 2 May 1946, quoted in Wolf, p. 38.

BELGIAN PATERNALISM IN THE CONGO

1. Of the general literature we note here Alan P. Merriam, *Congo; Background of Conflict* (1961). Georges Brausch, *Belgian Administration in the Congo* (1961). Ruth Slade, *The Belgian Congo. Some Recent Changes* (1960). Travel book by Basil Davidson, *The African Awakening* (1957). Michel Merlier, *Le Congo de la colonisation belge à l'indépendance* (1962) (very "left wing"). René Cornevin, *Histoire du Congo (Léopoldville)* (1963).
2. E.g. "The War had torn away 'the veil of mystery in Africa'. The Congo has revealed itself in all its great national significance. . . . Did we have no more territories, ports, treasures? Indeed! yes, since, there,

[we have] incalculable riches, ten million blacks [note the order of listing], a vast, rich and fertile terrain, ports in one of the most beautiful anchorages in the world . . . that it is the flesh of our flesh and that henceforth, whatever one did, it would be impossible for Belgium to live without its great equatorial possession." Jacques Crokaert (secretary of the Congrès Colonial Belge), "Le développement économique du Congo belge pendant la guerre", in *Colonisations comparées* (1926), p. 207.

3. Merriam, p. 37.
4. Naturally the British were and are proud that they refused the applications for concessions and thus justified their trusteeship.
5. Hailey, *Survey* (1956), p. 45.
6. Buell, *Native Policy*, II, 534. The official reports admit the abuses: it was necessary to "repeople the menaced communities". "Inadmissible waste . . . abuses exist in the employment of non-adults . . . dreadful mortality". Chiefs were paid for their help in recruiting, which led to abuses. *Documentation colonial comparée* (1929), No. 1, pp. 15, 19, 45. During the crisis the unemployed were sent home, "an arrogant attitude. They were immediately subjected to close surveillance", 1932 report, *Documentation coloniale* (1933), No. 1, p. 14. For criticism of the outdated methods with their wear and tear on labour forces, cf. also Governor General Ryckmans, *Documentation coloniale* (1936), No. 1, p. 15.
7. E.g. W. M. Macmillan, *Africa Emergent*, p. 174. Basil Davidson, *op. cit.*; *ibid.*, "Enlightened Colonialism: the Belgian Congo", *The Reporter*, 27 January 1955; John Gunther, *Inside Africa* (1953), p. 672.
8. Brausch, p. 7.
9. Leopoldville had 40,000 inhabitants in 1939, 100,000 in 1945, 300,000 in 1955, and 400,000 in 1960.
10. Cf. for example the report by a Dutch journalist in *African Affairs* (1949–1950), p. 120.
11. A good general picture in Brausch, p. 19. The decisive measures were not taken until between January and August 1959.
12. Brausch, p. 10.
13. Merriam, p. 44.
14. Henri Depage, *Contribution à l'élaboration d'une doctrine visant à la promotion des indigènes du Congo belge*, ed. Académie Royale des Sciences Coloniales, N.S.V., II (1955), 19.
15. E.g. Francis Moheim, "Le problème des cadres au Congo", *La Revue générale belge*, April 1960.
16. Marzorati on the development of the constitution in *L'évolution politique du Congo belge* (1952), p. 19.
17. Brausch, p. 30.
18. Buell, II, 482; Hailey, *Survey* (1956), p. 222.
19. "Quelques aspects de notre politique indigène au Congo", in *Études de Colonisation comparée*, I (1924), 94 f.
20. Brausch, pp. 52 f.
21. In 1952 Governor-General Petillon said in the government council: "Our old conception of indirect administration . . . timid and mitigated as it was at the beginning, has not ceased weakening. Under the pressure of economic circumstance and the state of war, with the praiseworthy desire to proceed faster and better, we have tried to undertake everything and to lead the Congolese masses, for good or evil, to a happiness conforming to our concepts." Quoted in Hailey, p. 223. "We have asked everything of the native chiefs without giving them the means, and we have taken away

their prestige and authority by putting educated clerks before the illiterate chiefs. . . ." The annual reports in 1949 and 1951 had underlined that a large number of the chiefs could no longer cope with their duties—"we have lost 30 years". G. Moulaert, "Notre politique indigène", in the conservative colonial *Revue coloniale belge*, 1 February 1954, pp. 81 f.

22. *Op. cit.*, p. 85, "to develop an African civilization in the Congo", p. 129.

23. In a handbook for the administration he, Louis Franck, had asked: "What are we doing in the Congo? And I replied: 'We are following a dual aim: to spread civilization and to develop the markets and the economic affairs of Belgium'." *Op. cit.*, p. 87.

24. Quoted in Georges Hardy, *La politique coloniale et le partage de la terre aux XIXe et XXe siècles* (1937), p. 347.

25. P. 223.

26. "A propos des budgets coloniaux" (1956), reprinted in *Vers l'indépendance du Congo et du Ruanda-Urundi* (1958), pp. 63 f.

27. "In the colony, the white is the strong one and the black the weak one", *La politique coloniale* (1934), p. 17.

28. Similarly Alfred Moeller, "La politique indigène de la Belgique au Congo", *Journal of the Royal African Society*, July 1936.

29. E.g. Van der Kerken, *La politique coloniale belge* (1943), is confined to criticism of the administrative structure, economic and financial policy. Also Van der Linder, *L'évolution du Congo belge* (1940–1947) (Académie des sciences coloniales, 1948).

30. Brausch, p. 66.

31. R. Brasseur, "Situation des Indigènes", *La Revue coloniale belge*, 15 December 1949, p. 742.

32. Robert Godding, "Developments in the Administration of the Belgian Congo", in *Colonial Administration by European Powers* (RIIA, 1947): "The main principle has been, from the beginning, material and spiritual improvement of native conditions of life", p. 47. Broad outlines of economic and social questions follow, but there is very little on the political problems. Rvckmans, when he retired as governor-general, addressed his colleagues: "If I had had to leave a final message, I would say to you that the function of the State is to make and guarantee the happiness of man and that the prosperity of a country is the prosperity of its inhabitants, and that Belgium will have succeeded in its colonial work when the natives live happily under our flag." Quoted in *Principles and Methods of Colonial Administration*, Colston Papers (1950), p. 49. Brausch, p. 64, referred to a Senate commission in 1947 which reported in detail on economic, social and cultural questions, but scarcely touched on political questions. Similarly, Pierre Wigny, *Que ferons-nous au Congo?* Société belge d'Études et d'Expansion, December 1947.

33. Revised edition of *Dominer est Servir* (1948), p. 74.

34. Several publications and essays: "L'évolution politique du Congo belge", *Études coloniales*, Fasc. 1. Institut de Sociologie Solvay. *Compte rendu des Journées Interuniversitaires d'Études Coloniales*, 29–30 December 1952 (various representative writers). Antoine Rubbens, "L'apprentissage de la démocratie au Congo belge", *Revue politique*, December 1953. G. Marzorati (governor of Ruanda-Urundi, 1926), "The Political Organization and the Evolution of African Society in the Belgian Congo", *African Affairs*, LIII, (1954). Pierre Ryckmans, "Belgian Colonialism", *Foreign Affairs*, October 1955.

Pierre Wigny, "L'avenir politique du Congo", *Revue générale belge*, June 1951. "Methods of Government in the Belgian Congo", *African Affairs*, L (1951). "Le destin politique du Congo belge", *Revue générale belge*, 15 March 1955.

35. Used on several occasions, e.g. by Guy Malengreau (Lyons University), in *Africa To-day*, ed. Haines, pp. 337, 354.

36. Malengreau, "La participation des indigènes à la vie politique", in *L'évolution* . . ., p. 27. "I doubt very much whether we have any principles." Wigny, *Methods*, p. 310. "Le problème est à peine abordé", Wigny, *Le destin*, p. 747.

37. The chefferies were greatly in need of reform, but "the doors of the Conseils superieurs of the colony are being opened wide [!]", Pierre Deschamps, "L'éducation démocratique d'un peuple", *Revue générale belge*, 15 March 1955, p. 785.

38. E.g. Marzorati, *The Political Organization* . . ., p. 111.

39. As of 1 January 1957 the *Revue coloniale belge* was renamed *Belgique d'Outre-Mer*. Photographs of well-dressed Congolese and meetings between white and black were deliberately used.

40. On 17 June at the opening of the Conseil de Gouvernement, Petillon said: "This Belgo-Congolese community . . . everyone hopes for it today. . . . It is not only a question of assimilating into our institutions and our life an increasing number of elite individuals . . . we must offer, by organizing things in such a way that they will accept it with enthusiasm, the possibility of association." *Revue coloniale belge*, July 1955, p. 528. And again: "we must, every day and with care, continue to fashion the fraternal community we want, a community of Belgians of Africa and Belgians of the Empire . . . this would imply great psychological transformations . . . the old and fertile paternalism will no longer be suitable". Quoted in *Revue coloniale belge*, 1 September 1956, p. 656. Marzorati: "to prepare for a Belgian Union", of two communities with internal autonomy and beyond this, a Union with its own institutions, *L'évolution* . . ., p. 14.

41. Quoted in Van Bilsen, *Vers l'indépendance* (1958), p. 275.

42. "There will come a day [!] when the blacks of Africa vote", *Revue générale belge* (1955), p. 760. "Are the younger generations mature enough to sit in the deliberative assemblies as of now? . . . We must know how to take our time." *Belgique d'Outre-Mer*, April 1957, p. 288. Georges Hostelet, in *L'oeuvre civilisatrice de la Belgique au Congo de 1885–1953* (1954), is very restrained in the question of political reforms and made only vague demands for a few councils, particularly on the local level; pp. 369 f.

43. *Congo. Positions socialistes (1885–1960)* (1961). Parti socialiste belge. Congrès extraordinaire, 30 June–1 July 1956. Programme pour le Congo et le Ruanda-Urundi.

44. *Belgian "Colonialism"*, p. 101.

45. It was evidently the intentional policy of the *Revue coloniale belge* to report as little as possible on the rest of Africa. So for example in 1956–1957 it reported only on the content of the *Loi Cadre* and said little on the independence celebrations in Ghana; in 1958 it did not report on de Gaulle's visit! In the October 1956 issue Harold Ingrams of the British Colonial Office sketched constitutional developments in the British territories; but an editorial preface completely changed the sense of his article by giving the impression that Ingrams was only speaking of areas with a relatively old culture, i.e. not of Africa.

46. G. Mouaert, "Une politique congolaise nouvelle", *Revue coloniale belge*,

1 October 1956, p. 746. It made the usual reference to the failures of the British groundnut project in Tanganyika and the French Office du Niger. The professor at the colonial institute in Brussels, Maurice Verstaete, thought the *Loi Cadre* was "extremely bold . . . it suddenly instals a political democracy". For the Congo French methods were "perhaps pernicious". "Nouvelle orientation de la politique française d'Outre-Mer", in *Problème d'Afrique Centrale* (1956), No. 32, p. 84.

47. Quoted in Brausch, introduction, p. 2.

48. "Un plan de trente ans pour l'émancipation politique de l'Afrique belge", first printed in Dossiers de l'Action Sociale Catholique. We are using the reprint in Vers *l'indépendance* (1958), pp. 163 f. Cf. also the essay, "Des bourses pour Africains", which points out that at the time only two dozen Africans from the Congo and Ruanda-Urundi were studying in Belgium, as opposed to thirteen hundred from French West Africa in France.

49. On 15 April 1956 it gives only a brief summary of the contents, without giving an opinion, p. 265. In very small print there is a report of a meeting in Brussels under the chairmanship of Wigny at which Van Bilsen expressed his views, p. 273.

50. G. Moulaert, *Une politique congolaise nouvelle*, 1 October 1956, p. 745. This article, however, referred to Van Bilsen's proposals for taking over the "expenses of sovereignty".

51. Quoted in *Revue coloniale belge*, November 1956, pp. 863 f.

52. The manifesto printed as Document I in the collection of documents *La Crise Congolaise*, 1 January 1959–15 August 1960, Chronique de politique étrangère XIII, July–November 1960, pp. 439 f.

53. Cf. Patrice Lumumba, *Le Congo, terre d'avenir, est-il menacé?* (1961). (The MS was completed at the end of 1956.) He makes concrete proposals, unlike the vague comments of Belgian writers. Also Lumumba's letter to Brausch, *op. cit.*, p. 78.

54. However, on 17 December 1958, two weeks before the riots in Leopoldville, *Le Soir* wrote: "But what does the Mouvement National Congolais represent? Nothing and nothing again. Only, in certain urban centres of the Congo there exist a few handfuls of intellectual *évolués*, of clerks, who believe they have something to say. . . . Is this bad? They are serving their apprenticeship". Quoted in *Belgique d'Outre-Mer*, January 1959, p. 7.

55. Van Bilsen, *L'indépendance du Congo* (1962) (essays, 1958–1961), p. 40.

56. The declaration continues: "In a civilized world, independence is a status that unites and guarantees liberty, order, progress. It can only conceive of itself in terms of solid and well-balanced institutions. Well-tried administrative cadres, a social, economic, financial organization that is well assured, in the hands of experienced technicians, an intellectual and moral formation of the people without which a democratic régime would be no more than derisive, a delusion and tyranny. It is the realization of these basic conditions that we are striving for and to which we intend to devote ourselves . . .", *La crise congolaise*, p. 453.

57. "Le Rapport du Groupe de travail", *Belgique d'Outre-Mer*, February 1959, pp. 79 f. Autonomy is mentioned several times, but on the other hand—as with General de Gaulle—there was also talk of the possibility of later choosing between independence and association. A "true executive council" is foreseen for a later stage, like the second chamber, which is not possible "for many years".

58. *La crise congolaise*, pp. 454 f.

59. Van Bilsen wanted a "solemn engagement and timing", "La Belgique devant le problème du Congo", *Revue générale belge*, February 1959, p. 83.
60. Cf. the point of view of Fedalcol on 17 January 1959, in *Congo 1959, Documents belges et africains* (1960), pp. 26 f. The settlers threatened resistance, p. 29.
61. E.g. "no date has been fixed . . . the term independence has not been determined". The king "puts the Congolese on their guard against a precipitancy which could provoke disorder, poverty and tyranny. . . . At present the Congo has neither the economic structure nor the industrial and equipment or public resources, or social cadres, or the administrative machinery essential to assure independence, even in the sense in which it is understood today. . . . There is nothing in the country so far which would contribute towards autonomy . . .", Daniel Ryelandt, "Souveraineté et indépendance", *Belgique d'Outre-Mer*, February 1959, pp. 75 f.
62. Quoted in *Belgique d'Outre-Mer*, April 1959, p. 238.
63. "We have systematically [!] kept away from political problems because we were certain that this policy . . . would be more inclined to be a cause of disorder than a factor of emancipation." Louis Ameye, "Le temps de la conscience", *Belgique d'Outre-Mer*, February 1959. "The troubles at Leo have awakened Belgium, which was too sure of itself and of the excellence of its Congolese policy." Étienne de la Vallée Poussin, "La Belgique en présence de ses responsabilités", *Belgique d'Outre-Mer*, March 1959, p. 145.
64. It is worth noting that the acting governor warned in August against an "untenable position" in the Lower Congo and demanded a clear stand on the question and a shortening of the time limits; *Congo 1959*, p. 149.
65. *Chronique congolaise*, pp. 456 f. *Congo 1959*, pp. 168 f.
66. Text of the talks in Georges H. Dumont, *La Table ronde belgo-congolaise, January–February 1960* (1961).
67. A positive view of the Table ronde, in *Belgique d'Outre-Mer*, March 1960, or L. Moyersaen, vice-president of the Chamber, "La Table Ronde et l'avenir d'un grand État indépendant au centre de l'Afrique", *Revue générale belge*, April 1960, p. 8: "a well-considered plan . . . the crowning of a constructive achievement".
68. Davidson, pp. 132 f., 149 f.
69. One could quote examples: the extension of university education and the incipient Africanization of the cadres. Conversion of indirect rule into modernized local administration. Autonomy but not yet independence. On the African side, the formation of national parties and organizations.

DOCTRINE VS. REALITY OF ASSIMILATION: PORTUGAL IN AFRICA

1. Because of our lack of adequate knowledge of the language we have chiefly relied on non-Portuguese literature, although aware that most of this sharply attacks Portugal: James Duffy, *Portuguese Africa* (1959) (abbrev. Duffy I); *ibid., Portugal in Africa* (1962) (abbrev. Duffy II); Thomas Okuma, *Angola in Ferment, the Background and Prospects of Angolan Nationalism* (1962); *Angola, a Symposium, Views of Revolt* (1962). A pro-Portuguese study, F. C. C. Egerton, *Angola in Perspective* (1957). Also, Eduardo Mondlane, "Mozambique", in *Africa in the Modern World*, ed. Stillman

(1955). Hermann Jung, "Schwarz oder Weiss in Angola?", in *Aussenpolitik*, VIII (1961).
2. Duffy II, pp. 134 f.
3. Duffy I, pp. 246 f.
4. Lead article in *O mundo português*, quoted in Duffy I, p. 276. Cf. also *O pensamento do Ministro das Colónias Dr. Armindo Monteiro* (1934).
5. The overseas minister Moreira asserted that Portugal had never used force [!] in acquiring its overseas territories, except to defend its natural rights—which he sees in the case of Vittoria as the legitimate claim to travel in any country, to reside there and to practise one's trade! *Portugal's Stand in Africa* (1962), p. 156.
6. This is stressed by Armindo Monteiro (then ambassador in London), "Portugal in Africa", *Royal African Society Journal*, XXXVIII (1939), 265 f.
7. Dr. Vasco Vieira Garin, Portuguese representative at the U.N., in January 1961, quoted in Okuma, p. 108.
8. This is confirmed by Egerton, p. 253. The certificate cost the applicant a considerable sum. Duffy II, p. 165. The 1954 decree seems to have restricted rather than extended the qualification: Hailey, *Survey*, p. 233.
9. Salazar in parliament on 30 November 1960, in *Portugal* (1960), p. 359.
10. Lecture in Coimbra, 18 March 1960, English translation in *African Affairs* LIX (1960). Reprinted under the title "Political Unity and the Status of Peoples" in *Portugal's Stand in Africa*, (1962).
11. As an example we can point out the national economist A. J. Cardoso, who wrote in *Angola Your Neighbour* (Johannesburg, 1950): "It is a fact commented upon by everybody that in the Portuguese colonies, whether localized in Africa, Asia or Australasia, a peaceful atmosphere has prevailed now for centuries, in startling contrast to the state of affairs at present observed in the same continents, in territories governed by other nations.

"This fact is the outcome of our policy of assimilation of native peoples, markedly realistic and based upon an experience of long centuries of civilizing action by means of which we are gradually raising them to our level so that in time we will make them all as Portuguese as the Portuguese of the Mother-Country distinct from these only in their colour . . .", from *The Imperialism Reader*, ed. L. Snyder (1962), p. 497.

12.

1950	Total Population	Civilized	White	Mulattos	Indians	Black
Angola	4,145,000	135,355	78,826	26,335		30,039
Mozambique	5,782,000	92,619	48,813	25,165	12,673	4,353

From Hailey, *Survey* (1956), p. 232.
13. Besides Duffy I and II, cf. a good general study by the same author, "Portuguese Africa (Angola and Mozambique): Some Crucial Problems and the Role of Education in Their Resolution," *Journal of Negro Education* (1961), No. 3.
14. Duffy II, p. 176.
15. José de Almada, "Portuguese Colonial Administration", in *Colonial Administration by European Powers*, ed. RIIA (1946), p. 80.
16. Lively description in Davidson, pp. 250 f.
17. Duffy II, pp. 15, 186. Galvão was arrested in his attempt to build up an anti-Salazar organization in December 1952, but escaped to South America in 1959 and came to world attention during the Santa Maria affair.
18. Dr. Fernandes, chairman of the executive committee of the National Union in a speech in Laurenço Marques on 28 October 1960 in *Portugal* (1961), No. 1, p. 23.

19. Davidson stressed the role of American enterprise.
20. "Africa cannot purely and simply transform colonial territories into independent states. Africa cannot from its tribes construct a mosaic of small republics without means of independent life and each incapable of living with the others around it." Fernandez, "The Presence of Portugal in Africa", *Portugal* (1960), No. 4, p. 258.
21. On 30 June 1960 in *Portugal* (1961), No. 3, p. 129. The colonial minister Moreira described the riots in 1961 as "a plan intended to destroy in months a multi-cultural and multi-racial achievement that has endured for centuries". *Portugal's Stand*, p. 171.
22. Augusto de Castro, editor-in-chief of *Diário de Notícias, Portugal*, 1961, No. 4, pp. 216 f.
23. Okuma, p. 7.
24. From a speech by Moreira on 28 August 1961. *Portugal's Stand*, p. 185.
25. Quoted in Okuma, p. 116.

Bibliography

Action, l'-, du Comité de l'Empire français. *Principales interventions auprès des pouvoirs publics (oct. 1944–mars 1946)*.
Adam, Colin Forbes. *Life of Lord Lloyd*. 1948.
Africanus. *L'Afrique noire devant l'indépendance*. 1958.
Ageron, Charles Robert. "Le mouvement 'jeune algérien' de 1900 à 1923". In *Études Maghrébines, Mélanges Charles André Julien*, 1964.
———. "Une politique algérienne libérale sous la troisième République (1912–1919)". In *Revue d'Histoire moderne et contemporaine*, VI, 1959.
Akten, zur deutschen auswärtigen Politik, I. 1950.
Albertini, Rudolf von. "Die USA und die Kolonialfrage (1917–1945)", In *Vierteljahreshefte für Zeitgeschichte*, 1965.
———. "The Impact of Two World Wars on the Decline of Colonialism". In *Journal of Contemporary History*, 1969.
Alduy, Paul. "Le problème colonial à la lumière du socialisme". In *Revue socialiste*, 1947.
———. "L'union française, mission de la France". In *Revue socialiste*, 1948.
Allen, James S. "Agrarian Tendencies in the Philippines". In *Pacific Affairs*, March 1938.
Almada, José de. "Portuguese Colonial Administration". In *Colonial Administration by European Powers*, ed. RIIA, 1946.
Altrincham, Lord (Grigg, Sir Edward). *Kenya's Opportunity*. 1955.
Amery, L. S. *My Political Life*. 1953.
———. *National and Imperial Economies*. 2nd ed. 1924.
———. "The British Commonwealth and the World". In *India and Freedom*, 1942.
———. "The British Commonwealth". In *World Affairs*, 1948.
———. *The Empire in the New Era*. 1948.
———. *The Framework of the Future*. 1944.
———. *Thoughts on the Constitution*. 1947.
Angelino, Kat. *Colonial Policy*, Vol. II. *The Dutch East Indies*. 1931.
Angola, a Symposium. Views of Revolt. 1962.
Année politique. 1946.
Ansprenger, Franz. *Auflösung der Kolonialreiche*. München Dtv, 1966.
———. *Politik im schwarzen Afrika*. 1961.
Anstey, Vera. *The Economic Development of India*. 4th ed. 1952.
Apter, David E. *The Gold Coast in Transition*. 1955.
Archimbaud, Léon. *La plus grande France*. 1928.
Arden-Clarke, Charles. "Eight Years of Transition in Ghana". In *African Affairs*, 1958.
Aron, Raymond. *La tragédie algérienne*. 1957.
———. *Les origines de la guerre d'Algérie*. 1962.

Arx, Alexandre von. *L'évolution politique en Indonésie de 1900 à 1942.* 1949.
Ashworth, William. *A Short History of the International Economy since 1850.* 2nd ed. 1962.
Asquith—Report. 1945. Cmd. 6647.
Attlee, Clement R. *As it Happened.* 1954.
———. *The Labour Party.* 1937.
Auguste-Raynold, Werner. *Essai sur la réglementation de la nationalité dans le droit colonial français.* 1936.
Aujoulat, Louis. *La vie et l'avenir de l'Union française.* 1947.
Austin, Dennis. *Politics in Ghana 1946–1960.* 1964.
Awolowo, Obafemi. *Path to Nigerian Freedom.* 1947.
Ayache, Albert. *Le Maroc.* 1956.
Azad, Maulana Abul Kalam. *India Wins Freedom.* 1959.
Azar, Antoine. *Genèse de la Constitution du 4.10.1958.* 1961.
Baker-Fox, Annette. *Freedom and Welfare in the Caribbean, a Colonial Dilemma.* 1949.
Baldwin, A. W. *My Father: The True Story.* 1955.
Barker, Ernest. *Ideen und Ideale des britischen Weltreiches.* German ed. 1941.
Bärtschi, Hans E. *Die Entwicklung vom imperialistischen Reichsgedanken zur modernen Idee des Commonwealth im Lebenswerk Lord Balfours.* 1957.
Bearce, George D. *British Attitudes towards India 1784–1858.* 1961.
Beauchamps, John. *British Imperialism in India,* prepared of the Labour Research Department. 1934.
Becker, G. H. *The Disposition of the Italian Colonies 1941–1951.* 1952.
Benda, Harry J. *The Crescent and the Rising Sun.* 1958.
———. "Tradition und Wandel in Indonesien". In *Geschichte im Wissenshaft und Unterricht.* 1963.
Bennett, George. *Kenya, a Political History.* 1963.
Berque, Jacques. *Le Maghreb entre deux guerres.* 1962.
Betts, Raymond F. *Assimilation and Association in French Colonial Theory 1890–1914.* 1961.
Bhagat, K. P. *A Decade of Indo-British Relations 1937–1947.* 1959. (Documents.)
Bilsen, Josef van. *L'indépendance du Congo.* 1962. (Essays of the years 1958–1961.)
———. *Vers l'indépendance.* 1958.
Birkenhead, (Earl of). *The Life of F. E. Smith, First Earl of Birkenhead, by His Son.* 1960.
Blake, Robert. *The Unknown Prime Minister. The Life and Times of Andrew Bonar Law 1858–1923.* 1952.
Blue Print for Burma. ed. National Union of Conservative and Unionist Associations. 1944.
Blundell, Michael. *So Rough a Wind.* 1964.
Boersner, D. *The Bolsheviks and the National and Colonial Question (1917–1928).* 1957.
Boisdon, Daniel. *Les institutions de l'Union française.* 1949.
Bonn, M. J. *Das Schicksal des deutschen Kapitalismus.* 1926. (2nd ed., 1930.)
———. *So macht man Geschichte.* 1953.
———. "The Age of Counter-Colonization". In *International Affairs,* XIII, 1934.

———. *The Crumbling of Empire. The disintegration of World Economy.* 1938.
———. "The Future of Imperialism". In *Annals of the American Academy of Political and Social Science*, CCXXVIII, 1943.
Bonnefous, Ed. *Histoire politique de la troisième République.* 1960.
Borella, François. *L'évolution politique et juridique de l'Union française depuis 1940.* 1958.
Bourdet, Claude. "Les maîtres de l'Afrique du Nord". In *Temps modernes,* June 1952.
———. "Les élections outre-mer". In *Temps modernes,* Aug. 1951.
Bourdillon, Sir Bernard. "Colonial Development and Welfare". In *International Affairs,* XX, 1944.
Bourret, F. M. *Ghana. The Road to Independence 1919–1957.* 1960.
Bousquet, G. H. *La politique musulmane et coloniale des Pays-Bas.* 1939.
Bouthoul, Gaston. "Le Malaise algérien". In *Revue de Paris,* XLII/4, 1935.
Bowle, John. *Viscount Samuel, a Biography.* 1957.
Brausch, Georges. *Belgian Administration in the Congo.* 1961.
Brecher, Michael. *Nehru.* German translation. 1963.
Brimmel, J. H. *Communism in South-East Asia.* 1959.
Brissonière, Yves G. "La notion d'interdépendance". In *Revue de défense nationale,* July 1956.
Britain Strong and Free. 1951. (Programme of the Conservative party.)
British Commonwealth, The, and World Society. Proceedings of the third unofficial conference on British Commonwealth Relations. London 17.2.–3.3.45. Ed. R. Frost. 1947.
British, Empire, The. Ed. RIIA. 1937.
Brockdorff-Rantzau, (Graf). *Dokumente und Gedanken um Versailles.* 1925.
Brockway, Fenner. *Outside the Right.* 1963.
Brügel, Johann W. "Das Treuhandschaftssystem der Vereinten Nationen". In *Europa-Archiv,* XXII, 1960.
Brunschwig, Henri. *Mythes et Réalités de l'impérialisme colonial français 1871–1914.* 1960.
Buell, R. L. *The Native Problem in Africa.* 1928.
Bull, Mary. "Indirect Rule in Northern Nigeria 1906–1011". In *Essays in Imperial Government, Presented to Margery Perham.* 1963.
Bullock, Allan. *The Life and Times of Ernest Bevin.* I. 1960.
Burns, Alan. *In defence of Colonies.* 1957.
Buron, Robert. *Carnets politiques de la Guerre d'Algérie.* 1965.
Busia, Kafi A. "The Prospects for Parliamentary Democracy in the Gold Coast". In *Parliamentary Affairs.* V/4. 1952.
Butler, J. R. M. *Lord Lothian (Philip Kerr) 1882–1940.* 1960.
Buxton, Charles R. "The Government of Crown Colonies". In *Political Quarterly,* 1939.
Cady, John F. *A History of Burma.* 1958.
Cailley, Joseph. "L'avenir de nos colonies". In *Revue des sciences politiques,* 1917.
Cameron, Donald. *My Tanganyika Service and Some Nigeria.* 1939.
———. *Principles of Native Administration and Their Application.* 1934.
Capitant, René. *Pour une constitution fédérale.* 1946.
Cardoso, A. J. *Angola Your Neighbour.* Johannesburg, 1950.
Carthill, A. *Verlorene Herrschaft.* German translation, 1924. With a Foreword by K. Houshofer.

Catroux, Georges. *Dans la bataille de la méditerranée 1940–1944.* 1949.
———. "L'union française, son concept, son état, ses perspectives". In *Politique étrangère,* 3, 1953.
———. *Lyautey le Marocain.* 1955.
Chapman, Abraham: "American Policy in the Philippines". In *Far Eastern Survey,* 5/6, 1946.
Chirol, Valentine. *India Old and New.* 1921.
Churchill, Winston. *The Second World War.* I, IV. 1949.
Clark, M. K. *Algeria in Turmoil. A History of the Rebellion.* 1960.
Coatman, John. *Magna Britannia.* 1936.
Cohen, Andrew. *British policy in Changing Africa.* 1959.
Cohen-Hadria, E. "Le fait colonial". In *Revue socialiste,* 1947.
Cole, Margaret. *The Story of Fabian Socialism,* 1961.
Coleman, J. S. *Nigeria, Background to Nationalism.* 1960.
Colliez, André. *Notre protectorat marocain 1912–1930.* 1930.
Collis, Maurice. *Last and First in Burma (1941–1948).* 1958.
Colonial Development and Welfare. 1945. Cmd. 6713.
Colonial Empire (1939–1947), The. 1947. Cmd. 7167.
Colonial Empire (1947–1948), The. Cmd. 7433.
Colonial Problem, The. Ed. RIIA. 1937.
Colonies, The. The Labour Party's Post-War Policy for the African and Pacific Colonies. 1943.
Concept of Empire, The. Burke to Attlee, 1774–1947. Ed. George Bennett. 1953.
Conférence Africaine française. Ed. Ministère des colonies. 1945.
Congo 1959. Documents belges et africains. 1960.
Congo 1959. Positions socialistes (1885–1960). 1961.
Cooke, Colin. *The Life of Richard Stafford Cripps.* 1957.
Cooper, Duff. *Old Men Forget.* 1954.
Cooper, Harold. "Political Preparedness for Self-Government". In *Annals of the American Academy of Political and Social Science,* July 1956.
Coret, Alain. "Le problème de la réforme du titre VIII de la constitution de 1946". In *Revue juridique et politique de l'Union française,* 1956, 1.
Cornevin, René. *Histoire du Congo (Léopoldville).* 1963.
———. "L'évolution des Chefferies traditionelles dans l'Afrique noire d'expression française". In *Recueil Penant,* 1961.
Coste-Floret, Paul. *Construire l'Union française.* 1948.
Coupland, Reginald. *Empire in These Days.* 1935.
———. *Indian Politics 1936–1942.* 1943.
———. *The Cripps Mission.* 1942.
———. *The Future of India.* 1943.
Cowan, L. Gray. *Local Government in West-Africa.* 1955.
Craddock, Sir Reginald. *The Dilemma in India.* 1929.
Creech-Jones. Arthur. "British Colonial Policy with Particular Reference to Africa". In *International Affairs,* 1951.
Crise, Congolaise, la. (1.1.1959–15.8.1960). Chronique de politique étrangère XIII, July–November 1960.
Crocker, Walter R. *Nigeria. A Critique of British Colonial Administration.* 1936.
———. *On Governing Colonies.* 1947.
Crokaert, Jacques. "Le développement économique du Congo belge pendant la guerre". In *Colonisations Comparées,* 1926.
Cromer, (Earl of). "Imperial Federation". In Cromer, Haldane, Marshall et al., *After War Problems.* Ed. W. H. Dawson. 1917.

Crumbling, the, of an Empire. Sept. 1916–March 1922. A Chronological Statement of the Decline of British Authority in India. 1922. Ed. Indo-British Association.
Culman, Henri. *Union française.* 1950.
Currie, Sir James. "The Educational Experiment in the Anglo-Egyptian Sudan 1900–1933". In *Journal of the African Society*, Jan. 1935.
Curtis, Lionel. *The Problem of the Commonwealth.* 1916.
Curzon, (Lord). *Subjects of the Day.* 1915.
Dalton, Hugh. *High Life and After. Memoirs 1945–1960.* 1962.
Das, M. N. *India under Morley and Minto. Politics behind Revolution, Repression and Reforms.* 1964.
Davidson, Basil. *Erwachen des Afrika.* 1957.
Dawson, Robert MacGregor. *The Development of Dominion Status 1900–1936.* 1937/65.
Decoux, Admiral. *A la barre d'Indochine.* 1949.
Delavignette, Robert. *L'Afrique noire française et son destin.* 1962.
———. *Les vrais chefs de l'empire.* 1939. New edition: Service Africain 1946. English translation: *Freedom and Authority in French West Africa.* 1950.
Depage, Henri. *Contribution à l'élaboration d'une doctrine visant à la promotion des indigènes du Congo belge.* Ed. Académie Royale des Sciences Coloniales N.S.V. 2, 1955.
Dermenghem, Émile. "Les catholiques et les abus coloniaux". In *Vie intellectuelle*, Nov. 1928.
Deschamps, Hubert. *Les Méthodes et les doctrines coloniales de la France.* Paris, 1953.
———. *L'éveil politique africain.* 1952.
Devèze, Michel. *La France d'outre-mer.* 1948.
Devilliers, Philip. *Histoire du Viet-Nam de 1940 à 1952.* 3rd ed., 1952.
Dispatch from the Secretary of State for the Colonies to the Colonial Governments regarding Aspects of Colonial policy in War-time. 1941. Cmd. 6299.
Documentation coloniale comparée, 1929–1936.
Documents and Speeches of the British Commonwealth. Ed. Mansergh. 1953.
Documents and Speeches on Commonwealth Affairs 1952–1962. Ed. Mansergh. 1963.
Documents and Statements relating to Peace Proposals and War Aims, Dec. 1916–Nov. 1918. Ed. Dickinson. 1919.
Documents on British Foreign Policy 1919–1939.
Dodd, E. E. "Reconstruction in Burma and Malaya". In *Four Colonial Questions.* Published by Fabian Colonial Bureau, Dec. 1944.
Doucet, Robert. *Commentaires sur la colonisation.* 1926.
Drascher, Währhold. *Die Vorherrschaft der Weissen Rasse.* 1936.
Dresch, Jean. "Lyautey". In *Les techniciens de la colonisation.* Ed. Ch. A. Julien. 1947.
Duchêne, Albert. *La Politique coloniale de la France.* 1928.
Duffy, James. *Portugal in Afrika.* 1962.
———. *Portuguese Africa.* 1959.
———. "Portuguese Africa: Some Crucial Problems and the Role of Education in Their Resolution". In *Journal of Negro Education*, 3, 1961.
Dulles, F. R. "The Anti-Colonial Policy of F. R. Roosevelt". In *Political Science Quarterly*, 1955.

Dumont, Georges H. *La Table ronde belgo-congolais, Jan.–Feb. 1960.* 1961.
Dutt, R. Palme. *Britain's Crisis of Empire.* 1950.
Eboué, Félix. *La nouvelle politique indigène pour l'Afrique équatoriale française.* 1941.
Education Policy in British Tropical Africa. Cmd. 2374. 1925.
Egerton, F. C. C. *Angola in Perspective.* 1957.
Ehrhard, Jean. *Les destins du colonialisme.* 1957. 3rd impression, 1958.
Elliot—Report, 1945. Cmd. 6655.
Elton, (Lord). *Imperial Commonwealth.* 1945.
Emerson, Rupert. *Malaysia, a Study in Direct and Indirect Rule.* 1937.
Empire, The, and the Future. 1916.
Empire, L'-, colonial français. 1929.
Empire, L'-, et ses ressources. Ed. Centre d'information interprofessionel. 1942.
Epting, Karl. *Das französische Sendungsbewusstsein im 19. und 20. Jahrhundert.* 1952.
Erdmann, Karl D. "Die asiatische Welt im Denken von Karl Marx und Friedrich Engels". In *Historische Forschungen und Probleme, Festschrift für Peter Rassow.* Published by K. E. Born. 1961.
Esquer, Gabriel. *Histoire de l'Algérie (1930–1957).* 1957.
Estorick, Eric. *Stafford Cripps, Prophetic Rebel.* 1941.
Etudes, de Colonisation comparée. Ed. Louis Franck. 1924.
Evolution, The, of India and Pakistan 1858–1947. Ed. C. H. Philips. 1962.
Évolution, L', politique du Congo belge. Études coloniales Fasc. 1. Institut de Sociologie Solvay. Compte rendu des Journées Interuniversitaires d'Études Coloniales, 29–30. Dec. 1952.
Expanding, The, Commonwealth. 1956.
Extier, Claude. *La Gauche hebdomadaire 1914–1962.* 1962.
Ezera, Kalu. *Constitutional Development in Nigeria.* 1960.
Fabian Colonial Essays, 1945.
Fabianism, and the Empire. Fabian Society 1900.
Fage, J. D. *Ghana. A Historical Interpretation.* 1959.
Fauvet, Jacques. *La IVe République.* 1959.
Feiling, Keith. *The Life of Neville Chamberlain.* 1946.
Fels, Christian Edmond de. "Les États-Unis français". In *Revue de Paris,* 1.6.1930.
Fiddes, George V. *The Dominions and Colonial Offices.* 1926.
Fischer, Georges. "Syndicats et décolonisation". In *Présence africaine,* Oct. 1960.
———. *Un cas de décolonisation. Les États-Unis et les Philippines.* 1960.
Flammenzeichen, das, vom Palais Egmont. Offizielles Protokoll des Kongresses gegen koloniale Unterdrückung und Imperialismus, Brüssel 10.2–15.2.1927. Published by the "Liga gegen Imperialismus". Berlin, 1927.
Flory, M. "La notion de protectorat et son évolution en Afrique du Nord". In *Revue juridique et politique de l'Union française,* 1954.
Folliet, Joseph. "Coup de bagarre". In *Esprit,* Dec. 1935. (Special number on Colonization.)
Forbes, M. "The Impact of the War on British West Africa". In *International Affairs,* 1945.
Forbes, W. Cameron. *The Philippine Islands.* 1928.
Francescani, Claude. *L'opinion catholique et la décolonisation depuis la fin de la deuxième guerre mondiale.* Diplôme d'études, Fac. des Lettres. Paris, 1959. (Manuscript.)

Franklin, Harry. *Unholy Wedlock. The Failure of the Central African Federation.* 1963.
Franks, Oliver, S. *Britain and the Tide of World Affairs.* Reith Lectures, 1954.
Funk, A. Layton. *Charles de Gaulle. The Crucial Years 1943–1944.* 1959.
Furnivall, J. S. *Colonial Policy and Practice. A Comparative Study of Burma and Netherlands India.* 1948–1956.
———. *Netherlands India. A Study of Plural Economy.* 1939.
———. "The Future of Burma". In *Pacific Affairs,* 1945.
———. "Twilight in Burma. Reconquest and Crisis". In *Pacific Affairs,* 1949.
Ganiage, J. *Les origines du protectorat français en Tunisie (1868–1881).* 1959.
Garigue, Philip. "Changing Political Leadership in West Africa". In *Africa,* 1953.
Gasser, J. *Le rôle de la France dans l'Afrique du Nord.* 1924.
Gaulle, Charles, de. *Discours et Messages 1940–1946.* 1946.
——— *Le RPF. Conférence de presse 24.4.1947.* (Printed as a pamphlet.)
———. *Mémoires de guerre. L'Appel 1940–1942.* 1954.
Gautier, E. F. "Menaces sur l'Afrique". In *Revue de Paris,* 1934–1935.
George, Lloyd. *War Memoirs,* I. 1933.
Gide, André. *Voyage au Congo.* 1927.
Gignoux, C. J. *L'économie française entre les deux guerres, 1919 à 1939.* 1942.
Girault, Arthur. *Principes de Colonisation et de Législation coloniale.* 4th ed., 1921; 5th ed., 1927.
Godding, Robert. "Developments in the Administration of the Belgian Congo". In *Colonial Administration by European Powers.* RIIA, 1947.
"Gold Coast, The, and Nigeria on the Road to Self-Government". In *Africa To-Day.* Ed. Haines. 1955.
Gold Coast, The. Report to His Excellency the Governor by the Committee on Constitutional Reform. 1949, Colonial No. 248.
Gollin, A. M. *Proconsul in Politics.* 1964.
Gollwitzer, Heinz. *Die Gelbe Gefahr. Geschichte eines Schlagwortes. Studien zum imperialistischen Denken.* 1962.
Gonidec. P. F. *Droit d'outre-mer,* I. 1959.
———. *Droit de Travail des territoires d'Outre-Mer.* 1958.
———. "Métamorphose du Commonwealth". In *Revue juridique et politique de l'Union française,* 1950–1952.
Gopal, S. *The Viceroyalty of Lord Irwin 1926–1931.* 1957.
Gordon-Walker, Patrick. *The Commonwealth.* 1962.
Gray, Richard. *The Two Nations. Aspects and Development of Race Relations in the Rhodesias and Nyasaland.* 1960.
Gregory, Robert G. *Sidney Webb and East Africa. Labour's Experiment with the Doctrine of Native Paramountcy.* 1962.
Gregory, J. W. *The Menace of Colour.* 2nd ed. 1925.
Grigg, Sir Edward. *Britische Aussenpolitik.* 1945.
———. *The British Commonwealth, Its Place in the Service of the World.* 1942.
———. *The Faith of an Englishman.* 1936.
———. *The Greatest Experiment in History.* 1924.
Grosser, Alfred. *La IVe République et sa politique extérieure.* 1961.
Grottian, Walter. *Lenins Anleitung zum Handeln. Theorie und Praxis sowjetischer Aussenpolitik.* 1962.

Grunder, Garel A.; Livezey, William E. *The Philippines and the United States.* 1951.
Grundlagen des Marxismus und Leninismus. Lehrbuch, 1960.
Guéna, Yves. *Historique de la Communauté.* 1962.
Guérin, Daniel. *Au service des colonisés 1930–1953.* 1954.
Guernier, Eugène. *Pour une Politique d'Empire.* 1938.
Guèye, Lamine. *Étapes et perspectives de l'union française.* 1955.
Guggisberg, F. Gordon. *The Gold Coast. A Review of the Events of 1920–1926 and the Prospects of 1927–1928.* 1927.
Gunther, John. *Inside Africa.* 1953.
Gutteridge, W. F. "L. S. Amery and the Commonwealth". In *Political Science* (New Zealand), VIII, 1956.
Guy, Camille. "La politique coloniale de la France". In *La politique coloniale de la France.* Conférences organisés par la société des Anciens Élèves de l'École libre des Sciences Politiques. 1934.
Hailey, (Lord). *African Survey.* 1938. (1956 edition.)
―――. "British Colonial Administration". In *Colonial Administration by European Powers.* RIIA, 1947.
―――. "Native Administration in Africa". In *International Affairs.* 1947.
―――. "Some Problems Dealt With in the "African Survey". In *International Affairs.* March 1939.
―――. *The Colonies and the Atlantic Charter.* 1943.
Halifax, (Lord). *The Future of the Colonial Peoples.* 1943.
―――. *Fullness of Days.* 1957.
Hall, H. Duncan. *Mandates, Dependencies and Trusteeship.* 1948.
―――. "The Genesis of the Balfour Declaration of 1926". In *Journal of Commonwealth Political Studies.* I, 3, 1962.
―――. *The Government of the British Commonwealth of Nations.* 1921.
Halperin, Vladimir. *Lord Milner et l'évolution de l'impérialisme britannique.* 1950.
Hammer, Ellen I. *The Struggle for Indochina.* 1954.
Hancock, W. K. *Argument of Empire.* 1943. German translation: *Für und Wider das Weltreich.* 1946.
―――. *Smuts. The Sanguine Years.* Vol. I, 1870–1919. 1962.
―――. *Survey of British Commonwealth Affairs.* Vol. I. 1937.
Haqqi, S. A. Haqe. *The Colonial Policy of the Labour Government, 1945–1951.* 1960.
Hardy, Georges. *La politique coloniale et le partage de la terre au XIXe et XXe siècle.* (*Évolution de l'Humanité*). 1937.
―――. *Nos grands problèmes coloniaux.* 1933.
Harmand, Jules. *Domination et Colonisation.* 1910.
Harrison, Francis Burton. *The Cornerstone of Philippine Independence.* 1922.
Hart, Georges H. C. "The Netherlands Indies and Her Neighbours". In *Pacific Affairs*, March 1943.
Hawes, H. B. (Senator) *Philippine Uncertainty, an American Problem.* 1932.
―――. "The Philippine Independence Act". In *Annals of the American Academy of Political and Social Science,* CLXVIII, 1933.
Henderson, Neville. *Fehlschlag einer Mission.* N.d.
Hinden, Rita. *Empire and After.* 1949.
Hoare, Samuel. *Neun bewegte Jahre.* German translation, 1955.
Hobson, J. A. *Imperialism.* 1902.

Hoffherr, René. "Comment organiser une économie française d'Empire?" In *Politique étrangère*, 1938, 3.
Hofmannsthal, Hugo von. *Briefwechsel mit Carl J. Burckhardt*. 1956.
Holmes-Laski, *Lettres*, 1916–1935. Ed. M. de Wolfe Howe. 1953.
Hoover, Herbert. *Memoiren*. 1952.
Horriban, J. F. *Problems of a Socialist Government*. 1933.
Hostelet, Georges. *L'oeuvre civilisatrice de la Belgique au Congo de 1885–1953*. 1954.
Hourani, A. H. *Syria and Lebanon. A Political Essay*. 1946.
House of Commons, Debates.
House of Lords, Debates.
Hutin, Paul. *La doctrine de l'Association des Indigènes et des Français en Algérie*. 1933.
Huxley, Elspeth. *White Man's Country. Lord Delamere and the Making of Kenya*. 2 vols. 1935.
Huxley, Elspeth; Perham, Margery. *Race and Politics in Kenya*. 1944. 2nd, enlarged impression, 1956.
Huxley, Julian; Deane, Ph. *Future of the Colonies. Target for Tomorrow*. Nr. 8, 1944.
Imperial Policy, A Statement of Conservative Policy for the British Empire and Commonwealth. 1949.
Imperialism, The. Reader. Ed. L. Snyder. 1962.
Indian, The. Annual Register. Ed. Mitra. 1919.
Indians in Kenya. Memorandum Cmd. 1922 (23).
"Indirect Rule from a Native's Point of View (Aug. 1936)". In *Negro Year Book*. 1937.
International Action in the Colonies. Report of a Committee of the Fabian Research Bureau. Sept. 1943.
Isoart, Paul. *Le phénomène national vietnamien*. 1961.
Jacobsen, Hans-Adolf. *Der Zweite Weltkrieg in Dokumenten*. 1959.
Jakob, E. J. *Kolonialpolitisches Quellenheft*. 1935.
Jeffries, Charles. *Ceylon, the Path to Independence*. 1962.
———. *The Colonial Office*. 1956.
Jenkins, Shirley, "Philippines". In *The Development of Self-Rule and Independence in Burma, Malaya and the Philippines*. Ed. J. Cady. 1948.
Jennings, Ivor. *The British Commonwealth*. 1948. 4th ed. 1961.
———. *The Constitution of Ceylon*. 1949.
———. *The Dominion of Ceylon*. 1952.
Jones, Thomas. *A Diary with Letters 1931–1950*. 1954.
Journal officiel. Assemblé de l'Union française.
Journal officiel. de la République Française. Chambre des Députés, Débats parlementaires.
Journal officiel. de la République Française. Chambre des Députés, Documents parlementaires.
Journal officiel. de la République Française. Sénat, Débats.
Juin, Alphonse. *Le Maghreb en feu*. 1957.
Julien, Charles André. *L'Afrique du Nord en marche*. 2nd ed. 1952.
Jung, Hermann. "Schwarz oder Weiss in Angola?" In *Aussenpolitik* 8, 1961.
Kahin, George McTurnan, *Nationalism and Revolution in Indonesia*, 1952.
Kähne, Horst. "Zur Kolonialpolitik des faschistischen deutschen Imperialismus". In *Zeitschrift für Geschichtswissenschaft*, 1961, 3.
Kaunda, Kenneth. *Zambia Shall Be Free. An Autobiography*. 1962.
Keatley, Patrick. *The Politics of Partnership*. 1963.

Kedouri, Elie. *England and the Middle East. The Destruction of the Ottoman Empire 1914–1921.* 1956.
———. "Sa'-ad Zaghloul and the British". In *Middle Eastern Affairs,* No. 2. Ed. A Hourani, St. Antony's Papers. No. 11. 1961.
Keesing's Contemporary Archives.
Keith, Arthur B. *Imperial Unity and the Dominions.* 1916.
———. *Letters on Imperial Relations.* 1935.
Kennedy, Raymond. "Dutch Charter for the Indies". In *Pacific Affairs,* June 1943.
Kenya: White Man's Country? Report to the Fabian Colonial Bureau. Jan. 1944.
Kerr, Philip H. "Political Relations between Advanced and Backward Peoples". In *An Introduction to the Study of International Relations.* Ed. A. J. Grant. 1916.
Kessing, Felix M. "Cultural Trends in the Philippines". In *Far Eastern Quarterly,* Feb. 1945.
Kimble, David. *A Political History of Ghana. The Rise of Gold Coast Nationalism 1850 to 1928.* 1963.
Kirk, G. *Philippine Independence.* 1936.
Kirk, George E. *Kurze Geschichte des Nahen Ostens.* N.d. (1958).
Knight, M. M. *Morocco as a French Economic Venture.* 1937
Kongress, Der 2., der kommunistischen Internationale. Protokoll der Verhandlungen. 1921.
Kordt, Erich. *Nicht aus den Akten.* Stuttgart. 1950.
Kotelawala, Sir John. *An Asian Prime Minister's Story.* 1956.
Kozicki, Richard J. "The UN and Colonialism". In *The Idea of Colonialism.* Ed. Robert Strausz-Hupé and Harry C. Hazard. 1958.
Labour Party, Reports on Annual Conference.
Labouret, Henri. *Colonisation, Colonialisme, Décolonisation.* 1952.
Labour's Colonial Policy. The Plural Society (Labour Research Dep.). July 1956.
Lacouture, Jean. *Cinq hommes et la France.* 1961.
Lampué, Pierre. "Le statut de l'Algérie". In *Revue juridique et politique de l'Union française,* 1947.
———. *L'Union française d'après la Constitution.* 1947.
———. "Pour une réforme de l'Union française". In *Cahiers de la République,* 1959, 7.
Landau, Rom. *Moroccan Drama, 1900–1955.* 1956.
Lansang, Jose A. "The Philippine-American Experiment: A Philippine View". In *Pacific Affairs,* 1952.
Larminat, Edgard de. *Chroniques irrévérencieuses.* 1962.
La Roche, Jean de. *Le Gouverneur Général Félix Eboué 1884–1944.* 1957.
Latour, Boyer de. *Vérité sur l'Afrique du Nord.* 1956.
Lavergne, Bernhard. *Une révolution dans la politique coloniale de la France.* 1948.
Le-Barbier, Louis. *Le Maroc agricole.* 1927.
Lemaignen, Robert; Senghor, Léopold Sédar; Youtévong, Prince Sisowath. *La communauté Impériale Française.* 1945.
Letters, The, of T. E. Lawrence. Ed. D. Garnett. 1938.
Letters to the People of India on Responsible Government. 1918.
Lewis, Martin Deming. "One Hundred Million Frenchmen: The "Assimilation" Theory in French Colonial Policy". In *Comparative Studies in Society and History,* IV, 1962, 2.

Ligou, Daniel. *Histoire du socialisme en France 1871–1951*. 1962.
Ligue des Droits de l'Homme Congrès National 23.–25.5.1931. Compte-Rendu sténographique. 1931.
Lisette, Gabriel. "Après Bamako". In *Cahiers de la République*, 1957, 10.
Listowel, (Earl of). "The Modern Conception of Government in British Africa". In *Journal of African Administration*, Vol. I, 1949.
Lloyd, (Lord). *Egypt since Cromer*. Vol. I, 1933.
Local Government and the Colonies. Ed. Rita Hinden. A Report to the Fabian Bureau. 1950.
Loewenthal, Richard. "Kommunismus und nationale Revolution". In *Aus Politik und Zeitgeschehen, Beiträge zum "Parlament"*, Vol. X, 6.3.1963.
Longrigg, H. *Syria and Lebanon under French Mandate*. 1958.
Louis, Paul. *Le Colonialisme*. 1905.
Louwers, O. *Le problème coloniale du point de vue international*. 1936.
Low, D. A.; Pratt, R. C. *Buganda and British Overrule 1900–1955*. 1960.
Lucas, Bryan Keith. "The Dilemma of Local Government in Africa". In *Essays in Imperial Government, presented to M. Perham*. 1963.
———. *The Dual Mandate in British Tropical Africa*. 1922.
Lumumba, Patrice. *Le Congo, terre d'avenir, est-il menace?* 1961.
Lyautey l'Africain, textes et lettres du Maréchal Lyautey. Ed. Pierre Lyautey, 1919–1925. 1957.
Lyautey, *Paroles d'Action* (1900–1925). ed. 1938.
Lyautey, Pierre. *L'Empire colonial français*. 1931.
Lyman, Richard. W. *The First Labour Government 1924*. (1957).
Maaem, Ali. *Colonialisme, Trusteeship, Indépendance*. 1946.
MacCallum, R. B.; Readman, Alison. *The British General Elections of 1945*. 1947.
Machefer, Philippe. "Autour du problème algérien en 1936–38. La doctrine algérienne du PSF. Le PSF et le projet Blum-Violette". In *Revue d'histoire moderne et contemporaine*, X, 1963.
Macmillan, William Miller. *Africa Emergent*. Pelican Books. 1949.
———. *Democratise the Empire. A Policy of Colonial Reform* (The Democratic Order No. 6). 1941.
———. *Warning from the West Indies*. 1938.
McKay, Vernon. "The Impact of the UN in Africa". In *Africa Today*. Ed. C. Grove Haines. 1955.
McNutt, Paul V. "The Philippines: Asset or Liability". In *Annals of the American Academy of Political and Social Science*. CCXV, 1941.
Mair, L. P. *Native Policies in Africa*. 1936.
Malcolm, G. *The Commonwealth of the Philippines*. 1936.
Mansergh, Nicholas. *Commonwealth Perspectives*. 1958.
———. *South Africa 1906–1961. The Price of Magnanimity*. 1962.
———. *Survey of British Commonwealth Affairs. Problems of Wartime Co-operation and Post-War Change 1939–1952*. 1958.
———. "The Commonwealth at the Queen's Accession". In *International Affairs*, July 1953.
———. *The Name and Nature of the British Commonwealth*. 1955.
Maroc et Tunisie, Sondernummer von La Nef. March 1953.
Marsal, François. *Le domaine colonial français*. 1929.
Marzorati, G. *L'évolution politique du Congo belge*. 1952.
Masani, R. P. *Britain in India*. 1960.
Mason, Philip. *Year of Decision. Rhodesia and Nyasaland*. 1960.

Massa, Ch. "Die französische Verfassung vom 5.10.1958 und die überseeischen Gebiete". In *Europa-Archiv*, 1959, 4.
Maung, Maung. *A Trail in Burma*. 1962.
———. *Burma's Constitution*. 2nd ed. 1961.
Maunier, René. *L'Empire français, propos et projets*. 1943.
Mehrotra, S. R. "Imperial Federation and India 1868–1917". In *Journal of Commonwealth Political Studies* 1961, 1.
———. "The Politics behind the Mantagu Declaration of 1917". In *Politics and Society in India*. Ed. C. H. Philips. 1963.
Meissner, Boris. "Die marxistisch-leninistische Lehre vom 'Staat der nationalen Demokratie'". In *Aus Politik und Zeitgeschehen, Beilage zum "Parlament"*, Vol. 10, 6.3.1963.
Méjan, François. *Le Vatican contre la France d'Outre-Mer*. 1957.
Mende, Tibor. *Gespräche mit Nehru*. 1956.
Menon, V. P. *The Transfer of Power in India*. 1957.
Merlier, Michel. *Le Congo de la colonisation belge à l'indépendance*. 1962.
Merriam, Alan P. *Congo; Background of Conflict*. 1961.
Meston, (Lord). *Nationhood for India* (delivered in the U.S.). 1931.
Meyer, F. V. *Britain's Colonies in World Trade*. 1948.
Michel, Henri. *Les courants de pensée de la Résistance*. 1962.
Miller, J. D. B. *Richard Jebb and the Problem of Empire*. 1956.
———. *The Commonwealth in the World*. 1958.
Mills, Lennox A. *Ceylon under British Rule 1795–1932*. 1933.
———. "Government and Social Services in Ceylon". In *Far Eastern Survey*, 25.8.1943.
Milner, (Lord). *Questions of the Hour*. 1923.
———. *The Nation and the Empire*. 1913.
Mitchell, Philip. *African Afterthoughts*. 1954.
Mitterand, François. *Aux frontieres de l'Union française*. 1953.
Moltmann, Günter. "Weltherrschaftsideen Hitlers". In *Europa und Uebersee, Festschrift für Egmont Zechlin*. 1961.
Mondlane, Eduardo. "Mozambique". In *Africa in the Modern World*. Ed. Stillman. 1955.
Monroe, Elizabeth. *Britain's Moment in the Middle East 1914–1956*. 1963.
Montagne, Robert. "Comment organiser politiquement l'Empire français". In *Politique étrangère*, 3, 1938.
———. *Révolution au Maroc*. 1953.
Montvalon, Robert de. *Ces pays qu'on n'appellera plus colonies*. 1956.
———. *Dokumente*, 1958, 14.
Mook, H. van. *Past and Future in the Netherlands Indies*. Speech before the Institute of Pacific Relations, 18.5.1945.
———. *The Stakes of Democracy in Southwest Asia*. 1950.
Moreira, Adriano José Alves. *Portugal's Stand in Africa*. 1962.
Moresco, E. "The New Constitution of the Netherlands Indies". In *Asiatic Review*, April 1927.
Morgan, Jones (M.P.). *Whither India?* Labour party pamphlet. 1935.
Morison, E. E. *Turmoil and Tradition. A Study of the Life and Times of Henry L. Stimson*. 1960.
Mosley, Leonhard. *The Glorious Fault, The Life of Lord Curzon*. 1960.
———. *The Last Days of the British Raj*. 1961.
Moussa, Pierre Louis. *Les Chances économiques de la Communauté franco-africaine*. 1957.
Mühlmann, Wilhelm E. *Chiliasmus and Nativismus*. 1961.

Münchhausen, Thankmar. *Ziele und Widerstände der frz. Algerienpolitik von 1945–1958.* Diss. Heidelberg, 1962. Manuscript.
Murray, A. Victor. "Education under Indirect Rule". In *Journal of the African Society,* April 1935.
———. *The School in the Bush.* 1929.
Murray, James N. *The United Nations Trusteeship System.* 1957.
Mus, Paul. *Le destin de l'Union française.* 1954.
———. *Viet-Nam. Sociologie d'une Guerre.* 1952.
Namasivayan, S. *The Legislatures of Ceylon 1928–1948.* 1951.
Nasir, Idrus. *Diajadiningrat, The Beginnings of the Indonesian-Dutch Negotiations and the Hage-Veluwe Talks.* 1958.
Nehru, Jawaharlal. *A Bunch of Old Letters.* 1958.
Néra, Gilles. *La Communauté.* 1960.
Neres, Philip. *French-Speaking West Africa.* 1962.
Newbury, Colin. "The Government General and Political Change in French West Africa". In *African Affairs,* No. I. St. Anthony's Papers No. 10. Ed. K. Kirkwood. 1951.
New Cambridge Modern History. Vol. XII, 1960.
New Deal, A, in Central Africa. Ed. Colin Leys and Cranford Pratt. 1960.
New Fabian Colonial Essays. 1959.
Nicolson, Harold. *Georg V.* German translation, 1954.
———. *Nachkriegsdiplomatie.* German edition, 1934.
Niehl, Robert van. *The Emergence of the Modern Indonesian Elite.* 1960.
Noel-Baker, P. J. *The Demand for Colonial Territories and Equality of Economic Opportunity.* 1936.
Nouschi, André. *La naissance du nationalisme algérien 1914–1954.* 1962.
Ohneck, Wolfgang. *Die französische Algerienpolitik 1919–1939* (Diss. Heidelberg. 1964) 1967.
Okuma, Thomas. *Angola in Ferment. The Background and Prospects of Angolan Nationalism.* 1962.
Oliver, Roland; Fage, I. D. *A Short History of Africa.* 1962.
———. *The Missionary Factor in East Africa.* 2. ed., 1963.
Olivier, Marcel. *Six ans de politique sociale à Madagascar.* 1931.
Olivier, Sydney. *Letters and Selected Writings,* Ed. M. Olivier. 1948.
Oppermann, Thomas. *Die algerische Frage.* 1959.
———. "Die Endphase des Algerienkonflikts 1959–1962". In *Zeitschrift für ausländisches öffentliches Recht und Völkerrecht,* Vol. XXIII, 1963, 1.
———. *Oxford History of India.* 1961.
Padmore, George. *How Britain Rules Africa.* 1936.
———. *Pan-Africanism or Communism.* 1956.
Paillard, Jean. *Faut-il faire de l'Algérie un Dominion.* 1938.
———. *La fin des français en Afrique noire.* 1936.
———. *L'Empire français de demain.* 1943.
Palmer, Leslie. H. *Indonesia and the Dutch.* 1962.
Palmer, Richmond. "Some Observations on Capt. R. S. Rattray's Paper". In *Journal of the African Society,* Jan. 1934.
Panikkar, Kavalam M. *The Future of South-East Asia. An Indian View.* 1943.
Papers Relating to the Closer Union of Kenya, Uganda and the Tanganyika Territory. 1931 (Colonial No. 57).
Parkinson, Cosmo. *The Colonial Office from Within 1909–1945.* 1945.
Parry, J. H.; Sherlock, P. H. *A Short History of the West Indies.* 1960.
Parti radical-socialiste. Compte-Rendus des Congrès.
Parti socialiste (SFIO). Compte-Rendus des Congrès.

Parti socialiste belge. Congrès extraordinaire 30.6–1.7.1956. Programme pour le Congo et le Ruanda-Urundi.
Passeron, André. *De Gaulle parle.* 1962. (Extracts from speeches, 1958–1962.)
Paul-Boncour, J. *Entre deux guerres. Souvenirs sur la IIIe République.* 1945.
Peets, Helmut. "Die Rolle des Erziehungswesens in der englischen Kolonialpolitik in Nigeria". In *Erziehung und Politik in Nigeria.* Published by H. N. Weiler. 1964.
Perham, Margery. *Africans and British Rule.* 1941.
——. "A Re-statement of Indirect Rule". In *Africa,* VII, 1934.
——. *Lugard.* 2 vols. 1960.
——. *Native Administration in Nigeria.* 1937.
——. "Some Problems of Indirect Rule in Africa". In *Supplement to Journal of the African Society,* Vol. XXXIV, 1935.
——. "The Colonial Dilemma". In the *Listener,* 14.7.1949.
Perkins, Whitney T. *Denial of Empire. The U.S. and Its Dependencies.* 1962.
Person, Yves. "Soixante ans d'évolution en pays Kissi". In *Cahiers d'études africaines,* 1960, 1.
Petrie, Sir Charles. *The Life and Letters of the Right Honorable Sir Austin Chamberlain.* 1940.
Philip, André. "Thèses pour servir à une discussion sur la future Constitution". In *Cahiers politiques,* Aug. 1954.
Picker, Henry. *Hitlers Tischgespräche im Führerhauptquartier 1941–1942.* 1951.
Pistrak, Lazar. "Die Strategie der Sowjets in Afrika". In *Aussenpolitik,* 1962, 1.
Plan, A, for the Mechanized Production of Groundnuts in East and Central Africa. Cmd. 7030.
Pluvier, J. M. "Dutch-Indonesian Relations 1940–1941". In *Journal Southeast Asian History,* March 1965.
Poeschel, Hans. *Die Kolonialfrage im Frieden von Versailles.* 1920.
Political Quarterly, The, IX, 4, 1938. (Empire special edition.)
Pommery, Louis. *Aperçu d'histoire économique contemporaine.* Vol. I, 1952.
Priestley, H. J. *France Overseas.* 1938.
Principles and Methods of Colonial Administration. Colston Papers. 1950.
Problème, Le, des cheffries en Afrique Noire française. Notes et Études documentaires. No. 2508. 1959.
Problems of Parliamentary Affairs, VI, 1, 1952–53.
Programme, Le, d'action immédiate du Parti Socialiste, voté au Congrès National extraordinaire de Paris (Dec. 1927). 1928.
Proposals for the Revision of the Constitution of Nigeria. Cmd. 6599. 1945.
Puaux, Gabriel. "Essai de psychanalyse des protectorats nord-africains". In *Politique étrangère,* 1954. 1.
Quigley, Carrol. "The Round Table Groups in Canada, 1908–1938". In *Canadian Historical Review,* Sept. 1962.
Rajan, M. S. *The Post War Transformations of the Commonwealth. Reflection on the Asian-African Contribution.* 1963.
Rapport du Docteur Aujoulat sur la politique coloniale. Printed as a pamphlet. 1945.
Rapport général sur la situation du Portectorat au Marco vom 31.7.1914.
Rattray, R. S. "Present Tendencies of African Colonial Government". In *Journal of the African Society,* Jan. 1934.

Reiser, Martin. *The Commonwealth of Nations*. Begriff, Rechtsnatur, Wesen. 1961.
Report, Colonial Empire. 1933.
Report of Proceedings of the 57th Annual Trade Union Congress. 1925.
Report of Sir Samuel Wilson on His Visit to East Africa. 1929. Cmd. 3378.
Report of the Advisory Commission on the Review of the Constitution of Rhodesia and Nyasaland. Cmd. 1148. 1960.
Report of the Commission Appointed by the Government of India to Inquire into the Condition and Prospects of the University of Calcutta. 1904.
Report of the Commission of Enquiry into Disturbances in the Gold Coast. 1948. Colonial No. 231.
Report of the Commission on Closer Union of the Dependencies in Eastern and Central Africa. Cmd. 3234. 1929.
Report of the Commission on the Marketing of West African Cocoa. Sept. 1938. Cmd. 5845. 1938.
Report of the East Africa Commission. Cmd. 2387. 1925.
Report of the Nyasaland Commission of Inquiry. Cmd. 814. 1959.
Report of the Rhodesia and Nyasaland Royal Commission. Cmd. 5949. 1939.
Report of the Special Commission on the Constitution. Cmd. 3131. 1928.
Report of the Special Mission to Egypt. Cmd. 1131. 1921.
Report on Indian Constitutional Reforms. Cmd. 9109 (1918).
Richard-Molard, J. *Afrique occidentale française*. 1952.
Rieber, Alfred. *Stalin and the French Communist Party 1941–1947*. 1962.
Ries, J. "L'heure de la lucidité IV, conséquences de la colonisation pour les métropoles". In *Revue socialiste*, 1957.
Right Road, The, for Britain. Conservative party programme. 1949.
Robinson, Kenneth. "French Africa and the French Union". In *Africa to-day*. Ed. Haines, 1955.
———. *The Dilemmas of Trusteeship*. 1965.
Rohrbach, Paul. *Deutschlands koloniale Forderung*. 1935.
Rolland, Louis; Lampué, Pierre. *Précis de droit des pays d'outre-mer*. 1949.
Roosevelt, Nicholas. *The Philippines. A Treasure and a Problem*. 1926.
Roosevelt, Theodore. *Colonial Policy*. 1937.
Roper, J. I. *Labour Problems in West Africa*. 1958.
Rosenfeld, Oreste. "Problèmes constitutionnels". In *Cahiers de la République*, 1957, 10.
Rotberg, Robert I. "The Federation Movement in British East and Central Africa 1889–1953". In *Journal of Commonwealth Political Studies*, Vol. II, No. 2, 1964.
Rothermund, Dietmar. *Die politische Willensbildung in Indien 1900–1960*. 1965.
Rubbens, Antoine. "L'apprentissage de la démocratie au Congo belge". In *Revue politique*, Dec. 1953.
Ruiz, Leopold T. "Farm Tendency and Cooperation in the Philippines". In *Far Eastern Quarterly*, Feb. 1945.
Runner, Jean. *Les droits politiques des indigènes des colonies*. 1927.
Ruyssen, Th. "La Colonisation et le Droit". In *Les Cahiers des Droits de l'Homme*. 1925.
Ryckmans, Pierre. *Dominer pour servir*. 1931.
———. *La politique coloniale*. 1934.
Sacks, B. J.; *J. Ramsey MacDonald in Thought and Action*. 1952.
Sarraut, Albert. *Grandeur et servitude coloniales*. 1931.
———. *La mise en valeur des colonies françaises*. 1922.

———. "Nationalisons l'idée coloniale". In *L'Europe nouvelle*, 1.5.1926.
Sauver l'Algérie française. Le dossier du parti radical 1955–1957. Published by the party.
Schatten, Fritz. "Nationalismus und Kommunismus in Afrika". In *Ostprobleme*, 1962.
Schiller, A. Arthur. *The Formation of Federal Indonesia 1945–1949.* 1955.
Schlie, Hans. *Die britische Handelspolitik seit Ottawa und ihre weltwirtschaftlichen Auswirkungen.* 1937.
Schmokel, W. *Dream of Empire. German Colonialism 1919–1945.* 1964.
Schneebeli, Robert. *Die zweifache Treuhänderschaft. Eine Studie über die Konzeption der britischen Kolonialherrschaft.* 1958.
Schrenck-Notzing, Caspar. *Hundert Jahre Indien.* 1961.
Schütze, Walter. "Bilanz und Perspektiven der frz.-afrikanischen Gemeinschaft". In *Europa-Archiv*, 1960, 5.
Seeley, John Robert. *Die Ausbreitung Englands.* German edition. 1954.
Semaine Sociale de France, Marseille 1930. Compte-rendu des cours et conférences.
Semmel, Bernard. *Imperialism and Social Reform.* 1960.
Senghor, Léopold. "Ce que veulent les africains". In *France-Forum*, Dec. 1957.
———. "Pour une communauté franco-africaine". In *Cahiers de la République*, 1957, 7.
Servoise, René. Introduction aux problèmes de la politique française". In *Politique étrangère*, 1954, 4. (Special edition on the problems of overseas France.)
Shotwell, James T. *At the Peace Conference.* 1937.
Siegfried, André. *Die englische Krise.* 1931.
Simon, John. *Retrospect. The Memoirs of Viscount Simon.* 1952.
Slade, Ruth. *The Belgian Congo. Some Recent Changes.* 1960.
Smith, Pauline Crumb. "A Basic Problem in Philippine Education". In *Far Eastern Quarterly*, Feb. 1945.
Smith, S. A. de. *The Vocabulary of Commonwealth Relations.* 1954.
Somerville, J. J. B. "The Central African Federation". In *International Affairs*, July 1963.
Soulbury Report. Cmd. 6677. 1945.
Soustelle, Jacques. *Aimée et souffrante Algérie.* 1956.
———. *Envers et contre Tout.* 1947.
Speeches, Selected, and Documents on British Colonial Policy 1763–1917. Ed. A. B. Keith. 1953.
Speeches and Documents on the British Dominions 1918–1931. Ed. A. B. Keith. 1932.
Speeches and Documents on the Indian Constitution 1921–1947. Ed. Gwyer and Appadorai. 1957.
Spengler, Oswald. *Jahre der Entscheidung.* 1933.
———. "Neubau des Deutschen Reiches". In *Politische Schriften*, 1933.
Stalins Werke. SED-Ausgabe. 1951, Vol. IV.
Statement by HMG on the Report to His Excellency the Governor by the Committee on Constitutional Reform. Colonial No. 250. 1949.
Statement by HMG on the Report of the Commission of Enquiry into Disturbances in the Gold Coast. Colonial No. 232. 1948.
Statement of Policy on Colonial Development and Welfare. Cmd. 6175. Feb. 1940.
Statement of the Conclusions of HMG as Regard Closer Union in East Africa. Cmd. 3574. 1930.

Steeg, Théodore. *La paix française en Afrique du Nord.* 1926.
Stimson, Henry L. *On Active Service in Peace and War.* 1948.
Stoddard, Lothrop. *Clashing Tides of Colour.* 1935.
Stokes, Robert. *New Imperial Ideals.* 1930.
Strachey, John. *The End of Empire.* 1959.
Suret-Canale, Jean. *Afrique noire.* Vol. II. *L'ère coloniale 1900–1945.* 1964.
Swinton, (Lord). *I Remember.* 1948.
Tardieu, André. *L'épreuve du pouvoir.* 1931.
Taylor, Alastair M. *Indonesian Independence and the United Nations.* 1960.
Taylor, Dan. *The Year of Challenge.* 1960.
Temple, Sir C. L. *Native Races and Their Rulers.* 1918.
Terrenoire, Louis. *De Gaulle et l'Algérie.* 1964.
Thomas, R. "La politique socialiste et le problème de 1905 à 1920". In *Revue française d'Histoire d'Outre-Mer*, CLXVII, 1961.
———. *Politique socialiste et problème colonial. Essai sur l'évolution de la politique coloniale du Parti Socialiste de 1905 à nos jours.* Mémoires de l'Institut des Hautes-Études d'Outre-Mer. 1950 (manuscript).
Thornton, A. P. *The Imperial Idea and Its Enemies. A Study in British Power.* 1959.
Tierney, James F. "Britain and the Commonwealth. Attitudes in Parliament and Press in the UK since 1951". In *Political Studies*, 6, 1958.
Tinker, Hugh. *Ballot Box and Bayonnet.* 1964.
Tourneau, Roger le. *Évolution politique de l'Afrique du Nord musulmane 1920–1961.* 1962.
Tournoux, J. R. *Secrets d'État.* 1962.
Toynbee, Arnold. *A Study of History* (Vols. VIII and XII).
———. *Civilisation on Trial.* 1948.
———. *The World after the Peace Conference.* 1925.
———. *The World and the West.* 1953.
Tsiang, Tingfu. *Labour and Empire.* 1923.
Trade Union Congress. Reports.
Underhill, Frank H. *The British Commonwealth. An Experiment in Co-operation among Nations.* 1956.
Union, L'-, française. *Problèmes politiques, économiques et sociaux relatifs à l'Union française. Rapport approuvé par les assises nationales du Peuple français.* June 1950.
Valéry, Paul. "La crise de l'esprit". In *Variété*, 1924.
Vandenbosch, A. "Indonesia". In *The New World of South East Asia.* Ed. Lennox Mills. 1949.
Van der Kerken. *La politique coloniale belge.* 1943.
Van der Kroef, J. M. "Economic Origins of Indonesian Nationalism". In *South Asia in the World Today.* Ed. Ph. Talbot. 1950.
Van der Linden, *L'évolution du Congo belge (1940–1947).* Académie des Sciences coloniales. 1948.
Vaudel, G. *Documents: La France d'Outre-Mer dans la guerre.* 1948.
Verstaete, Maurice. "Nouvelle orientation de la politique française d'Outre-Mer". In *Problème d'Afrique Centrale.* No. 32. 1956.
Vidailhet, Jean. "La démocratic française et son impérialisme". In *Revue économique française*, April 1935.
Vignon, Louis. *Un programme de politique coloniale.* 1919.
Viollette, Maurice. *L'Algérie vivra-t-elle.* 1931.
Viollis, André. *Indochine. S.O.S.* 1931.
Vlekke, Bernard. H. M. *Nusantara. A History of Indonesia.* 5th impression. 1959.

Walker, E. A. *The British Empire, Its Structure and Spirit.* 2nd ed. 1953.
Webb, Beatrice. *Diaries 1924–1932* Ed. M. Cole. 1956.
Wedgwood, Josiah C. *Memoirs of a Fighting Life.* 1940.
Wehl, David. *The Birth of Indonesia.* 1948.
Weiler, Hans N. "Legislative Council and Indirect Rule. Eine Unterschung zur brit. Kolonialpolitik an der Goldküste". In *Kulturen im Umbruch, Studien zur Problematik und Analyse des Kulturwandels in Entwicklungsländern.* Published by G. K. Kindermann, 1962.
Weinberg, Gerhard L. "German Colonial Plans and Policies 1938–1942". In *Geschichte und Geschichtsbewusstsein. Festschrift für Hans Rothfels.* 1963.
Welensky, Roy. *Welensky's 4000 Days. The Life and Death of the Federation of Rhodesia and Nyasaland.* 1964.
Welles, Summer. *The Time of Decision.* 1944.
Westermann, D. *Der Afrikaner heute und morgen.* 1937.
Westindia Royal Commission 1938–1939. Recommendations. Cmd. 6174. 1940.
Westindia Royal Commission. Report. Cmd. 6607. 1945.
Wight, Martin. *The Development of the Legislative Council (1606–1945).* 1946.
Wigny, Pierre. *Que ferons-nous en Congo?* Société belge d'Études et d'Expansion. Dec. 1947.
Williams, Francis. *A Prime Minister Remembers.* 1961.
Wilson, Woodrow. *Memoiren und Dokumente.* I, 1923.
Wind of Change, The Challenge of the Commonwealth. By a Conservative Group. Ed. Lord Colyton. 1960.
Winkler, Henry R. *The League of Nations Movement in Great Britain 1914–1919.* 1952.
Winnacker, R. A. "Elections in Algeria and the French Colonies under the Third Republic". In *American Political Science Review*, XXXII, 1938.
Wood, Anthony St. John. *Northern Rhodesia, the Human Background.* 1961.
Woodruff, Philipp (Philip Mason). *The Men Who Ruled India.* Vol. II. 1954.
Woolf, Leonard. *Economic Imperialism.* 1920.
———. *Empire and Commerce in Africa.* 1920.
Wrench, John Evelyn. *Geoffrey Dawson and Our Times.* 1955.
Zetland, (Lord) (Ronaldshay). *The Life of Lord Curzon.* 1928.
Ziebura, Gilbert. *Die V. Republik. Frankreichs neues Regierungs system.* 1960.
Zimmern, Alfred. *From the British Empire to the British Commonwealth.* 1941.
———. *The Third British Empire.* 2nd ed. 1927.
Zinkin, M. *Asien und der Westen.* 1953.

Also, articles from:

African Affairs
Afrique Française, Renseignements coloniaux
Belgique d'Outre-Mer
Le Capital
Combat
Contemporary Review
The Crown Colonist
Daily Herald
Daily Telegraph
Economist

Esprit
Europäische Gespräche
Foreign Affairs
Marchés coloniaux (subsequently: *Marchés tropicaux*)
Le Monde
The Nation
Neue Zürcher Zeitung
New Statesman and Nation
Nineteenth Century
Observer
Paris-Match
Le Populaire
Portugal
Renaissances
The Reporter
Revue des deux mondes
Revue politique et parlementaire
Round Table
Socialist Review
Spectator
Le Temps
Time and Tide
The Times
The World To-day

Index

INDEX

Abbas, Ferhat, 20, 288, 289, 328, 330, 334, 357, 360, 372-74, 387, 390, 391; imprisoned and freed, 382, 386
Abd-el-Krim, 9, 310-11
Abidjan, Ivory Coast, 430, 434
Abyssinia, 122-23
Accra, Ghana, 222, 223
Acheson, Dean, 261-62, 583
Addison, Lord, 211
Aden, 78
Adenauer, Konrad, 532
Afghanistan (Afghans), 9, 12, 36, 38, 44
Africa(ns), Belgium and, 499-513. See also Belgian Congo
Africa(ns), France (the French) and, 265ff., 278-309, 347-58, 396-406ff.; Algerian independence and, 319ff., 452-69 (see also Algeria); assimilation or association, 278-309, 319-35; colonial administration, 278-309ff., 336ff. (see also specific aspects, countries, events, issues); Community and, 376-82, 437-38, 442, 443-52; decolonization and, 5ff., 21ff., 358-82ff., 400ff., 406-24 passim, 425ff., 443-52ff., 523-25 (see also specific aspects, countries, events, issues); direct administration in West Africa, 336-46; and economic development of colonies, 265-78; First World War and decolonization, 5ff., 21ff. (see also under First World War); and French Union, 382-95, 406-24 passim, 425; Loi Cadre (1946-1956), 425-42; nationalist movements and (see Nationalism; specific countries); post-Second World War colonialism and decolonization (1946-1955), 406-24; Second World War and decolonization, 21ff., 358-82ff.; SFIO and colonialism, 309-19; Socialist Party and colonialism, 309-19
Africa(ns), Great Britain (the British) and, 5ff., 21ff., 35, 47, 48ff., 78ff., 91ff. (see also Great Britain; specific aspects, countries, events, issues); colonial development (1929-1940), 99-115; and federation, 164, 173, 225, 230-50; First World War and decolonization, 5ff. (see also under First World War); Indirect Rule and, 124-41; Labour Party and colonial doctrine, 115-23; nationalist movements and (see Nationalism; specific aspects, countries); Second World War and decolonization, 21ff., 158-75, 212ff. (see also under Second World War); transition from British Commonwealth to multi-racial Commonwealth, 252-62; and trusteeship and self-government, 78ff., 91ff., 99-115, 212-29, 230ff. (see also Mandate system; Self-government; Trusteeship; specific countries); white settlers and, 142-58, 162, 165, 178, 180, 230ff. (see also specific countries)
Africa(ns), Portugal and, 514-23. See also specific countries by name
African Survey (Hailey), 86, 106-7, 112, 113, 160, 164
Africanus, 622, 624
Afrique, champ d'expansion de l'Europe, L' (Guernier), 274
Ageron, Charles R., 598
À la recherche d'un politique indigène dans l'ouest Africain (Labouret), 342

Alaska, 473
Alduy, Paul, 412-13, 414, 616
Algeria, France and, 10, 25, 26, 28, 146, 267, 272-73, 277, 294, 319-35, 360-61, 372-75, 394-95, 420; and assimilation (1919-1939), 319-35; and colonial administration, 279-81, 283, 285-86, 288, 295, 303, 304, 306, 316, 319-35, 354, 356, 357; decolonization and independence, 452-69; Élus, 328, 455; Étoile-nord africaine, 10, 328; and French Community, 449, 452ff.; French Socialists and, 314-15, 316, 318, 326ff.; and French Union, 382, 386, 387, 390, 391, 393, 411, 415, 423, 424; Jews in, 279, 321; MTLD, 456, 457ff.; Muslim-Arabs, 316, 319-35, 452ff.; nationalism, 360-61, 373ff., 452; NLF, 28, 457ff., 464-68; Organic Statute (1947), 333; reforms, 321ff., 465ff.; SAO, 469; settlers and, 146, 277, 279-80, 295, 304, 319-35, 352, 372-74, 377, 452ff.; Ulemas, 328-29; war (1954), 456ff.
Algérie vivra-t-elle, L' (Voillette), 327
Algiers, formation of "Comité National Français de la Libération Nationale (1943) in, 364ff., 375, 381, 394
Allenby, Lord, 43, 44, 45
Altringham (Altrincham), Lord. See Grigg, Edward (later Lord Altringham)
American Revolution, 3
Amery, Julian, 236
Amery, L. S., 14, 19, 37, 38, 42, 51, 55-56, 57, 68, 120, 166, 236, 538, 539, 540, 545, 548, 561; and Burma's independence, 198-99, 202, 573; and Commonwealth of Nations concept, 253-54, 259; and India's independence, 186, 187, 188, 189, 194, 570; and Kenya, 150-55, 231
Amritsar (India) outbreak (1919), 65, 75, 77
Angelino, Kat, 492, 634
Angell, Norman, 37
Anglo-Indian Society, 65
Angola, 514, 518, 522-23, 641
Annam Empire (Annamites), 279, 288, 293, 294, 306, 313, 347-48, 360-61. See also Indochina
Ansprenger, Franz, 428, 611, 612, 619, 620, 625
Antilles, 278, 284-85, 370. See also West Indies
Anti-Semitism, 20, 328, 360-61
Arabia, 230. See also Arabs; Middle East; specific countries by name
Arab League, 403, 421
Arabs (and Moslems: nationalism and nationalist movements and), 4, 5, 38, 39, 40-46, 315-16, 319-35, 351, 355, 364, 372, 373-74, 382, 386, 401-6, 421-22, 452ff., 491. See also Middle East; specific countries, events, people
Archimbaud, Léon, 265, 303-5, 309, 586, 593-94
Arden-Clarke, Charles, 223, 229
Argenlieu, Admiral Georges T. d', 362, 396, 397, 398
Argument of Empire (Hancock), 164-65
Aron, Raymond, 462, 463-65, 628
Ashanti people, 127, 136, 173, 219, 224, 226
Asia, 4, 11-12, 17, 45, 523-25 (see also specific countries, events, individuals); "Asia for the Asians," 197ff.; autonomy,

668 INDEX

523–25; Burma and Ceylon, Second World War and independence, 196ff.; decolonization, 184ff., 196–212, 358ff., 396–400, 406–24 *passim;* Dutch in Indonesia, 487–99; Europe and "awakening" of, 11–13; French and, 278, 279, 298–99, 307, 313, 354, 358ff., 382ff., 396ff., 406–24 *passim* (*see also* specific countries); India and independence, 184–96; Portugal and, 514ff.; Second World War and decolonization, 184ff., 196–212, 358ff., and transition to multi-racial Commonwealth, 250–62; U.S. and Philippines, 473–87
Asquith, Herbert Henry, 50, 62, 537
Asquith, Judge, 173
Assimilation, French colonialism and principle of, 283, 284–86ff., 319ff., 386, 409, 416, 454ff., 523ff.: in Algeria, 319–35, 373ff., 454ff.; in Equatorial Africa, 425ff.; French Union and, 384, 386, 416; in Morocco, 348ff.; Second World War and, 359, 361ff., 380, 386; in West Africa, 336ff., 341ff., 372–74
Assimilation, Portuguese in Africa and, 514–23
Association, French colonialism and principle of, 283, 286ff., 325ff., 342, 358, 405–6, 452; French Union and, 383–84, 393, 397, 398, 405–6, 407ff., 434–35ff., 445, 452; Second World War and, 362ff.
Association des Indigènes et des Français en Algérie (Hutin), 325–26
Astray, Bertrand d', 617
Atlantic Charter, 22–23, 25, 159, 168, 170, 177, 212, 497
Attlee, Clement R., 66, 75, 76, 122, 180; and Burma's independence, 204–8, 255–56, 573; and India's independence, 186, 188, 189, 190–91, 192–95, 570, 572, 582
Auband, and Algerian reform bill, 331–32
Aug San, 197–98, 201, 203–8
Aujoulat, Louis, 381, 422, 423, 426, 428
Aumeran, Adolphe, 460
Auriol, Vincent, 399, 408
Australia, 6, 48, 77, 143, 170, 250, 251, 252–53, 259–60
Autonomy, 137, 147, 523–25 (*see also* Freedom; Nationalism; Self-government; specific aspects, countries, events); Algeria, 452–69; Equatorial Africa (1946–1956), 425ff.; French colonialism and, 283–84, 287, 291–92, 297–98, 313, 333, 343, 344, 364ff., 367–70ff.; Indochina, Tunisia and Morocco, 396–406; Indonesia, 490–99; Philippines, 474; Second World War and, 364–82 (*see also* Second World War)
Awolowo, O., 27, 213, 214, 221, 575, 576
Azad, M. A. K., 190, 191, 571
Azikwe, N., 27, 213, 221
Azores, 516

Baku, Second Comintern and "Congress of the Peoples of the East" at, 10
Balance Sheet of Imperialism (Clark), 438–39
Baldwin, Stanley, 68, 69–70, 103, 539, 542, 543, 544–45, 578, 579; and India, 68, 69–70
Balewa, A. A. T., 225, 576
Balfour, Lord, 42, 51, 54–55, 536
Balfour Declaration, 56, 57, 63, 66
Bamako, 426, 435, 436, 437
Banda, H., 240, 242, 245, 246
Bandung Conference (1955), 27, 420
Bao Dai, Emperor, 360, 378, 398, 399, 400, 407, 413, 416, 417, 420, 616; abdication of, 378
Barbados, 89, 110–11, 173
Barker, Ernest, 59, 79, 84, 153

Barnes, Leonard, 121–22
Barotseland, 162
Barry, Diawadou, 622
Baudouin I, King of Belgium, 502, 506, 511
Bayet, Albert, 306
Beaverbrook, Lord, 19, 55, 68, 99
Bechuanaland, 180
Belgian Congo, 82, 83, 87, 141, 242, 297, 364, 525; Abako, 510, 512; Belgium and paternalism in, 499–513, 514, 525; Charte de mérite civique, 507; *chefferie,* 504–5; Cités Africaines, 501, 505, 507; Congo Free State, 500; economic development, 499–506ff., education in, 502–3; and independence, 500, 503–13; Mouvement National Congolais, 510; Statut des Villes, 507; Union Minière, 500
Belgium, 19, 24–25, 297, 364, 497–513, 525; and paternalism in the Congo, 499–513, 514, 525 (*see also* Belgian Congo)
Bell, C. Jasper (and Bell Bill), 486, 633
Bell, Gertrude, 46
Benda, Harry J., 633, 634
Bendjelloul, M. S., 326, 382, 454, 455
Benn, Wedgwood, 186, 542, 547
Benue (Northern Nigerian emirate), 124–25, 129–32, 135, 136
Berque, Jacques, 357
Berthier (Madagascar governor-general), 600
Besant, Annie, 75, 547
Bevin, Ernest, 122–23, 182, 554
Bidault, Georges, 394, 411, 413
Bilsen, J. J. van, 506, 509–10, 511, 638
Birkenhead, Lord, 66, 68, 72–73, 542, 545
Blanchet, André, 442, 622, 623, 624
Blanchette, Georges, 415
Bledisloe, Lord, 169, 232, 578
Blocq-Mascard, M., 445–46
Blue Print for Burma, 199–200, 201–2
Blum, Léon, 289, 310, 316–17, 318–19, 326, 373, 398, 595, 616; and Algeria, 312–13, 314, 330–34, 373; and Indochina, 412, 413
Blundell, Michael, 580
Boers, 50, 53, 58, 142, 143. *See also* Boer War
Boer War, 4, 34–35
Boisdon, Daniel, 610
Boisneuf, René A., 288–89
Boisson, Pierre, 359, 361, 363
Bollaert, E., 398, 399, 416
Bonn, M. J., 16–17, 531, 532, 533
Borah, William E., 476
Borden, Robert, 33, 53
Borgeaud, Henri, 415, 416
Borneo, 78, 158, 159
Bour, Alfred, 409
Bourdet, Claude, 414
Bourdillon, Bernard, 221–22, 552
Bourguiba, Habib, 20, 315, 318, 372, 401–5, 411, 416, 418, 421, 613, 615, 618
Bousquet, G. H., 634
Boussenot, Georges, 614–15
Bouthoul, Gaston, 599
Brabant, Duke of (*later* King Leopold III of Belgium), 506
Brailsford, Henry W., 37, 121, 571
Brausch, Georges, 635, 636, 637, 639
Brazil, 518
Brazza, Pierre S. de, 369
Brazzaville, 22, 271, 311, 433, 502; conferences, 362–63, 364–71ff., 375, 379; French Union and, 382, 383, 384, 385, 394, 415, 429, 443, 451, 510
Brévié, Jules, 339, 342
Briand, Aristide, 307, 323
British Commonwealth. *See* Commonwealth of Nations (British Commonwealth)
British Commonwealth, The (Smuts), 53–54

INDEX 669

British Empire, 132
British Guiana, 89, 173, 178
Brockway, Fenner, 75, 121, 123, 181
Broussard (U. S. Senator), 483
Bruce, Lord, 252–53
Bryan, William Jennings, 474–75
Bryce, Lord, 51, 541
Buganda, 162
Buisseret, A., 508, 509
Bullitt, William C., 533
Bun Kinh, 615
Burke, Edmund, 79
Burns, Alan, 219–20, 222, 534
Busia, K. A., 173, 556, 575
Butler, R. A., 67, 167, 193, 248
Buxton, Charles R., 80, 118, 119, 120, 122, 139, 153
Byrnes, James F. 486

Cachin, Marcel, 595
Caillaux, Joseph, 274
Calabar, Nigeria, 136, 141
Caldecott, Andrew, 208–9
Cambodia, 279, 393, 399–400, 407, 417
Cameron, Donald, 7, 128–32, 136–37, 152–53, 554, 555, 557, 558
Cameroon (Cameroun), 24, 279, 359, 388, 393, 422, 450
Camoes, Luis Vaz de, 514, 515
Canada, 48–49, 50, 52, 53, 54, 55, 56, 58, 90, 137, 170, 242, 247, 291; and British Commonwealth of Nations, 250–51, 252, 259–60
Cape-Cairo line, 36
Cape Colony, 145
Capital Investment in Africa (Frankel), 107–8
Capitant, René, 443–44
Capricorn African Society, 239
Carde, Jules G., 339, 345
Cardoso, A. J., 641
Cartier (Raymond) and Cartierism, 439–42
Casablanca, 403–4
Catholic Church (*see also* Missionaries): and Belgian missionaries, 500, 502; and French colonialism, 307–9, 414, 422–24; and Portuguese Africa, 514, 518
Catroux, Georges, 359, 362, 363, 371, 618
Cayla, Léon, 359
Cecil, Lord, 37, 153
Central Africa (*see also* specific countries by name): effect of Second World War on, 20; federation as post-Second World War issue and, 230–50; and transition from British Commonwealth of Nations to multiracial Commonwealth, 252ff.
Césaire, Aimé, 384–85
Ces pays qu'on n'appellera plus colonies (Montvalon), 424
Ceylon, 15, 16, 21, 25, 27, 40, 58, 78, 89, 90–98, 101, 118, 119, 493; and British Commonwealth of Nations, 254, 255, 256; constitution and, 157, 172, 209–12; decolonization and, 173, 177, 196, 208–12, 300; and Second World War, 163, 165, 172
Chaban-Delmas, Jacques, 444
Chafford, Georges, 623
Challaye, Félicien, 306, 311
Chamberlain, Austen, 44, 62, 68
Chamberlain, Joseph, 34, 35, 41, 42, 49, 55, 79, 81, 103, 182
Chamberlain, Neville, 19, 155
Chances économiques de la Communauté franco-africaine, Les (Moussa), 441
Charles-Roux, F., 606
Chataigneau, General, 453–54
Chautemps, Camille, 332

Chauvet, and retention of French West Africa, 435
Chelmsford, Lord, 62, 64, 94
Chénik, M., 401, 402
China, 4, 6, 9, 10, 12, 17, 23, 26, 35, 474
Chirol, Valentine, 44
Church, the. *See* Catholic Church; Missionaries (missions)
Churchill, Winston S., 22–23, 36, 44, 45, 46, 56, 68, 69, 73–74, 145, 537, 544; and Burma, 198–99, 201, 205–6, 572–73; and Commonwealth of Nations, 251, 258–59; and India's independence, 188–90, 192, 193, 195–96, 570, 582; and Rhodesia, 235; and Second World War and decolonization, 159, 168, 169, 177, 182, 188–90, 192, 193, 195–96, 198–99, 201, 205–6
Clark, Grover, 438–39
Clemenceau, Georges, 322–23
Clifford, Hugh, 135–36
Coatman, John, 57–58
Cochin China, 276, 279, 280, 281, 302, 396, 397, 399
Cold War, 22, 25, 28; East West conflict and decolonization, 525
Colijn, Hendrik, 492, 493
Colliez, André, 356, 604, 605
Collis, Maurice, 202–3, 573
Colonial Empire, The, 120
Colonialisme, Le (Louis), 310
Colonial Policy and Practice (Furnivall), 83
Colonies, The (Fabian Society pamphlet), 176
Colonna, Antoine, 415, 416
Color ("coloreds"; racial discrimination and segregation), 11, 22–29, 41, 84ff., 96ff., 180 (*see also* specific aspects, countries, individuals); Belgian Congo and, 501–2, 508; British and, 33ff., 57ff., 78ff., 99–115, 134, 231–50; French use of colored troops in First World War, 266–69ff.; Portuguese Africa and, 518–20
Colyton, Lord (H. L. Hopkinson), 234, 244
Commentaires sur la colonisation (Doucet), 301–2, 356
Common Market, 253, 260, 262
Commonwealth, French and, 437–38, 451, 462
Commonwealth of Nations (British Commonwealth), 33–47, 48–58, 99, 195–96, 214, 220, 223, 225–29, 241ff., 246; Burma and, 201–8; Ceylon and, 208–12; and Conference of Westminster (1930), 55; Empire Free Trade and, 55, 56; First World War and, 48ff.; Imperial War Cabinet (First World War) and, 53, 62; India and, 59–78, 188ff., 194–96; and Parliament of Westminster, 49, 51, 52, 55; Second World War and, 48ff.; and Statute of Westminster (1931), 55, 56; transition to multi-racial Commonwealth, 250–62; use of "Commonwealth" term, 51, 53, 57, 253ff.
Communauté impériale française (Senghor), 370–71
Communism (Communists), 17, 116, 229 (*see also* Cold War; Marxism; specific aspects, countries, individuals); Algeria and, 455, 456, 457, 462; Burma and, 208; Cold War (East-West conflict), 22, 25, 28, 525; and First World War anti-colonialism, 8–11, 529–30; and French colonialism, 310–11, 318, 326, 328, 392, 521; and French Union, 382, 384–85, 387, 389, 390, 396–400, 411–12, 414, 417, 426, 440; Indochina, 318, 396–400; Indonesia, 490; and Second World War decolonization, 22, 23, 25; Vietnam, 396–400
"Community," French concept of, 376–82, 392, 416, 437–38, 442, 443–52

"Condamnés à l'Indépendance" (Blanchet), 422
Congo, 15, 25, 28, 35, 82, 83, 242, 246, 499–513, 514, 522. *See also* Belgian Congo; French Equatorial Africa
Congress Against Colonial Oppression (1927), 10
"Congress of Peoples of the East" (1920), 10
Constitutions (constitutional development): Algeria, 330; British colonialism and, 86, 91–98, 119, 154, 173, 180, 196ff., 212ff., 219ff., 224ff., 236ff., 242ff., 247ff., 425ff., 432ff., 436, 437, 443–44; Burma and Ceylon, 196–212; Equatorial Africa and, 425ff., 432ff., 436, 437, 443–44; Burma and Ceylon, 330, 368–70, 372, 376, 382–95, 409, 413; India, 185, 188; Indonesia, 490; Philippines, 476; West Africa, 212ff., 219ff., 224ff. (*see also* West Africa, British; West Africa, French)
Coolidge, Calvin, 477–78, 630
Cooper, Duff, 537
Cooper, H., 556, 576
Cooper, John, 227
Cornut-Gentille (Dakar governor-general), 435
Corsica, 290
Coste-Floret, Paul, 389, 409, 410, 422, 424, 448, 610, 612
"Counter-colonization," M. J. Bonn's theory of, 16–17
Coupland, Reginald, 58, 101, 105, 107, 132, 153, 548
Coussey, J. H., 223, 227–29
Cox, Percy, 46
Craddock, Reginald, 71–72
Cranborne, Lord, 170–71, 193
Creech-Jones, Arthur, 123, 175, 176, 177, 178, 181, 183–84, 567, 568, 575; and Burma, 200, 202; and Gold Coast, 223, 227
Crépuscule des nations blanches (Muret), 12
Crewe, Lord, 46, 60, 62
Cripps, Stafford, 121, 182, 552; and Burma's independence, 202, 205; and India's independence, 186, 188, 189, 190, 193, 195, 205, 209
Crise de l'esprit, La (Valéry), 11–12
Crocker, W. R., 130, 215, 556
Crokaert, Jacques, 636
Cromer, Lord, 35, 42, 44, 45, 84
Cromer, Lord (son), 44
Cuba, 473, 481
Culman, Henri, 394
Cunliffe-Lister, Philip (Lord Swinton), 106, 213
Curaçao, 495
Curtin, John, 251, 252
Curtis, Lionel, 38, 40, 49, 64, 536; and introduction of "Commonwealth" concept, 51–52, 53, 56, 57; and self-government in India, 61, 62, 64, 91
Curzon, Lord, 12, 60, 62–63, 65, 84, 537, 542; imperialist policies of, 35, 36–37, 60, 84; on unity of British Empire, 35, 36–37
Cuttoli, Maurice, 332
Cyprus, 78, 84, 89, 94, 101, 177, 244

Dahomey, 337, 410
Dakar, Senegal, 279, 280, 288, 336, 359, 371, 390, 427, 429–30, 433, 434, 435, 451; University, 429
Daladier, Édouard, 277
Dalat (Indochina) Conference, 396–97
Dalton, Hugh, 572
Danquah, J., 213, 222, 228
Dawson, Geoffrey, 38, 68, 544
Debré, Michel, 444, 445–46, 467, 625
De Chair, Somerset, 202
Decline of the West (Spengler), 11
Decolonization: analysis of process of, 523–25; Hailey and early use of term, 163ff.; M. J. Bonn's introduction of term, 16–17
Decoux, Jean, 359, 360, 378
Defferre, Gaston, 431–32, 435, 461, 627–28
De Gaulle, Charles. *See* Gaulle, Charles de
Dejean, Maurice, 400
Delafosse, Maurice, 268
Delamere, Lord, 143, 145, 147, 152, 153, 561, 562
Delavignette, Robert, 275, 336–37, 343–45, 380, 424
Delbos (French foreign minister), and Cameroun, 19
Democracy (democratization), 88, 94ff., 112, 165, 187, 202, 217, 385, 427, 435. *See also* Autonomy; Constitutions (constitutional development); Elections; Freedom; Nationalism (national emancipation movements); Self-government; specific aspects, countries by name
Denmark, 158
Dentz, Pierre, 360
Depage, Henri, 503
Dermenghen, Émile, 595
Deschamps, Hubert, 317, 382, 619, 620
Destins du colonialisme, Les (Ehrhard), 441
Devlin, Lord, 240
Devoir de colonisation, Le, 424
Devonshire, Lord (and Devonshire declaration), 82, 146–47, 148, 152, 155–56
Dia, Mamadou, 621
Diagne, Blaise, 280, 288–89, 312, 326, 334, 338, 346
Diallo, Yacine, 612
Dienbienphu, 398
Dilemma in Inda, The (Craddock), 71–72
Diop (Senegalese member of "Comité France Maghreb"), 424
Domenach, J.-M., 414–15, 424
Domination et Colonisation (Harmand), 286–87
Dominer pour servir (Ryckmans), 506
"Dominion" ("Dominion status"), use of term by British, 48ff., 179. *See also* Commonwealth of Nations (British Commonwealth); specific countries by name
Donoughmore (Lord) and Donoughmore Commission and Report, 91–92, 95–97, 119
Dorman-Smith, Reginald, 197, 198–99, 201, 202, 203–4
Doucet, Robert, 301–2, 356
"Drame Algérien et la décadence française, Le" (Soustelle), 464–65
Droit de Colonisation, Le (Folliet), 307–9
Droits politiques des indigènes (Runner), 295–96
Dronne, Raymond, 408, 444, 624–25
Druand-Reville, Luc, 515–16, 617
Dual Mandate in Tropical Africa (Lugard), 80–83, 126, 269, 271, 308
Duchêne, Albert, 292–93
Duchet, Roger, 420, 457, 622
Duncan Hall, H., 57
Dupleix, and India, 347
Dupont, Frédéric, 420, 421
Durham, Lord, 48; Durham Report, 57, 60, 64, 90, 147, 148, 157
Dutch, the. *See* Netherlands
Dutch East Indies, 488, 494. *See also* Indonesia; Netherlands
Duverger, Maurice, 437, 462–63, 465
Dyer, General, 65, 75

East Africa, British and, 7, 15, 78, 82, 87, 89, 94, 98, 102ff., 117, 119, 142–58 (*see also* specific countries, individuals, people); "Black Papers," 155; "dual policy," 150ff.;

INDEX 671

Indirect Rule, 128, 141, 142ff., 165, 166; Kenya and Closer Union, 142–58; Parliamentary Commission, 150; partnership in the Rhodesian Federation, 230–50; Second World War and decolonization, 164, 178, 180, 181–82; settlers and conflict, 142ff., 166, 167, 169
East Africa and Rhodesia, 243
Eboué, Félix, 340, 359, 361–64, 365, 376, 427
Education in British Tropical Africa, 345–46
Egypt, 5, 9, 10, 12, 15, 20, 21, 27, 84, 98, 117–18, 119, 283–84, 307, 536, 537; British Commonwealth status and independence and, 38, 39, 40, 41–46
Ehrhard, Jean, 441
Einstein, Albert, 532
Elections (franchise; voting): Algeria, 329, 330, 333, 335, 373, 455, 456, 465; British in West Africa and, 136, 139, 141, 218, 224ff.; Burma and Ceylon, 204ff.; East Africa, 238, 239, 240, 242ff., 249–50, 425ff., 432, 444; French colonialism and, 304, 316, 382, 425ff., 432, 444; French Union and, 382, 388; India, 186, 187, 188, 196; Jamaica, 173; Kenya, 144, 145, 240; Philippines, 475–76; Second World War and, 369, 373
Elgin, Lord, 143, 144
El-Glaoui. See Glaoui (Pasha El-Glaoui)
Elisabethville, 503. See also Congo
Elliot, Walter, 173
Emancipation movements. See Autonomy; Nationalism (nationalist emancipation movements); Self-government; specific aspects, countries, individuals, issues
Emerson, Rupert, 489
"Empire," British use of term, 53–54ff.
Empire and After (Hinden), 179–80
Empire and Commerce in Africa (Woolf), 117
Empire français, propos et projets, L' (Maunier), 361–62
Empire français de demain, L' (Pétain), 361
Empire in Africa: Labour's Policy, The, 117
Empire in These Days (Coupland), 58
Empire or Democracy, A Study of the Colonial Question (Barnes), 121–22
Endres, Franz Carl, 532
"En France noire" (Cartier), 439–42
England. See Great Britain
Epp, Ritter von, 18
Equatorial Africa, French. See French Equatorial Africa
Esprit, L', 414, 423
"Essai d'une organisation constitutionelle de la communauté française" (Viard), 376–77
Ethiopia, 20
Eurafrican programs, France and, 273–78, 362, 418
Eurafrica Society, 273–74
Evangelii Praecones (encyclical of Pius XII), 423
Expanding Commonwealth, The, 262

Fabian Colonial Essays, 176
Fabian Society, 115, 176–77
Facing Mount Kenya (Kenyatta), 156
Far East, 20, 22, 38, 39, 158ff., 202, 314, 371–72, 514. See also specific countries by name
Faure, Edgar, 403, 414, 417, 421, 423, 445, 459–60
Federation (federalism), 307, 342–43, 364–70ff., 375ff., 381ff., 387, 388, 390–91, 409–11, 413, 434–36ff., 441, 444ff. See also specific countries by name
Fels, Christian E. de, 307

Ferry, Jules, 415
Fez agreement (1912), 310, 348, 350
Field, Winston, 239, 247, 248, 249
Fiji Islands, 94
First World War, 3ff. *(see also* specific aspects, pects, countries, events, individuals); Belgian Congo and, 500; British Commonwealth of Nations and, 48ff., 61ff.; and British trusteeship and self-government in colonies, 78ff., 98ff.; and decolonization, 3–11, 12–13, 14, 20ff., 29, 34, 35, 36–47, 143, 523, 525 *(see also* specific countries by name); economic importance to non-European countries of, 14–17; French colonialism and, 265ff., 299, 332–33, 352, 353–54; Indonesia and, 490; Versailles Treaty, 18
Flandin, Pierre E., 277
Folliet, Joseph, 307–9, 424, 595
Forbes, W. Cameron, 630
Foreign Affairs, 19
Foulon, Jean, 620
Four Communes. See Senegal; specific Communes by name
Fourteen Points, Wilson and, 6
France, 3, 8, 10–12, 17, 20, 59, 64, 81, 82, 87–88, 90, 94, 99, 110, 273, 523–25; and administration of colonies, 278–309ff., 347ff. *(see also* specific colonies by name); and Algerian independence, 452–69 *(see also* Algeria); ARS party, 444ff.; assimilation in Algeria (1919–1939), 319–35; assimilation principle, 283, 284–86ff., 319–35, 336ff., 341ff., 348, 361ff., 425ff., 523ff.; association principle, 283, 286ff., 325ff., 342, 358, 362ff., 405–6; autonomy concept, 283–84; and "Balkanization" of Africa, 434–36; BDS party, 426; Belgian colonialism and, 499, 502, 503–4, 508–9, 510–11, 513; and British colonialism compared *(see under* Great Britain); and colonial ideology, 265–78ff.; and colonial policy during Second World War, 358–82; and Communists and colonialism, 382, 384–85, 387, 389, 390, 396–400, 411–12, 414, 417, 426; and decolonization, 266ff., 282ff., 333–35, 394–95, 396–406ff., 425, 523–25 *(see also* specific aspects, concepts, countries, individuals, issues); Dutch colonialism and, 493, 498–99; education in colonies and, 289, 296–97, 299, 300, 309, 344–46, 351, 365, 371, 428–29; and "Empire," 267, 270ff., 278ff., 361ff.; and Equatorial Africa (1946–1956), 425–42ff. *(see also* French Equatorial Africa); and Eurafrican program, 273–78, 362, 418; and "fatherland" concept, 288, 293, 296; and federalism concept, 307, 342–43, 364–70ff., 375ff., 381–82ff., 385, 387; FIDES and, 385–86, 429–30, 440; First World War and colonialism, 5ff., 23, 24, 26, 27–28, 265ff., Force Noire, 267–69; French Community, 365ff., 376–82, 392, 396, 416, 437–38, 442ff., 467; French Revolution, 3, 284–85, 319; French Union, 307, 348, 364, 378–80, 381, 382–95, 396–406ff., 425ff., 443ff., 454, revision and post-war discussion (1946–1955), 406–24ff.; "gratitude ties," 298; "Greater France," 266, 267, 277–78, 282ff., 288, 298, 300, 301, 320, 325, 342, 346, 356–58, 370ff., 376ff., 385, 394, 412, 418, 422, 425, 524; and "interdependence" concept, 404–6, 408–9; Intergroupe, 387–88, 389–93; Ligue des Droits de l'Homme, 306–7; *Loi Cadre,* 409, 423, 425–42, 449, 451–52; and Morocco protectorate, 347–58 *(see also* Morocco); Mouvement Républicain Populaire

(MRP), 309, 376, 385, 386, 389-90, 410, 411, 422-23, 426, 448; and naturalization of colonials, 281, 289-90, 295, 296, 297, 298, 301-2, 320, 322, 323ff., 342, 346, 357, 364, 367-68; Portugal and, 517-18; and "protectorate" concept, 287, 294ff., 308, 321, 347-58, 405-6; Radical Socialists and colonialism, 303-7, 319, 326ff., 390, 414ff., 458, 460; RDA party, 426, 434; right-wing colonial policy, 419ff., 439ff., 457; RPF, 443-44; Socialists (SFIO) and colonialism, 116, 309-19, 326ff., 385, 387-90, 397, 398, 402, 412-15, 426, 431ff., 451, 460-61, 462; U.S. colonial policy compared with, 479-81; and West Africa, direct administration in, 336-46 (see also West Africa, French)
France Observateur, 414, 460
Francescani, Claude, 618
Franck, Louis, 500, 504, 637
Franco, Francisco, 318
François-Poncet, André, 553
Frankel, S. H., 107-8
Franks, Oliver S., 583
Fraser, I., 578
Fraser, Peter, 582-83
Freedom (see also Autonomy): French and British concepts compared, 266ff., 283-84, 523ff.
Freetown, 165
French Equatorial Africa, 22, 24, 124, 126-27, 136-37, 271, 272, 279ff., 311, 359, 362ff., 502, 510, 513 (see also Congo); "Balkanization" and, 434-36; chefferie, 427-28; "Community" concept, 443-52; decolonization, 425-42, 443-52; France and Loi Cadre (1946-1956), 425-42; French Union and, 386ff., 393ff., 409ff.; Second World War and, 359, 362ff.
French Guiana, 278, 280, 281
French Guinea. See Guinea, French
French Indochina. See Indochina
French West Africa. See West Africa, French
Freyer, Hans, 4
Friedensburg, F., 532
Funk, Walter, 362, 606
Furnivall, J. S., 83, 94, 202-3, 488, 489
"Future of the Colonies" (article in Round Table), 166
Future Policy in Regard to Eastern Africa (Amery), 150-51

Gabon, 415, 434-35
Galbrun, René, 615
Galliéni, Joseph, 286, 347, 348, 369
Galvão, Henrique, 641
Gambia, 78, 101
Gammans, L. D., 159
Gandhi, Mohandas K., 20, 27, 70, 75, 76, 77; civil disobedience and arrest (1930), 67; and independence for India (1939-1947), 61, 64, 65, 66, 184, 186, 188, 544, 547, 570, 571
Garvey, Marcus, 288
Gasser, J., 598
Gaulle, Charles de, 22, 313, 358-60, 362, 364-66, 371, 373, 374, 376, 377-78, 381, 418, 443-52, 510, 609, 625, 629; African policy, 438, 442, 443-52, 465-69; Bayeux speech (1946), 443, 444; "Community" concept and, 438, 442, 443-52, 467
Gautier, E. F., 599
Geneva conferences, 27, 56, 398, 420
George V, King, 70
Gérard, Claude, 617
Gerbrandy, P. S., 635
Germany, 35, 36, 49; First World War and colonialism, 6, 7, 36, 128, 152, 267-68; Hitler and National Socialism, 17-20; Second World War and the British, 184ff., 250ff.; Weimar Republic, 18, 20
Ghana, 173, 223-29, 437, 510, 521. See also Gold Coast
Giap, Vo Nguyen, 397
Gibraltar, 78
Gide, André, 311
Giraud, General Henri H., 372
Girault, Arthur, 290-92, 293, 356
Glaoui (Pasha El-Glaoui), 351, 404
Goa, 514, 518
Godding, Robert, 506-7, 637
Goebbels, Paul J., 532
Gokhale, G. K., 60
Gold Coast, British and, 78, 89, 98, 99, 100-1, 165, 173, 212-29, 309, 430 (see also Ghana); Achimota College, 100; "Gold Coast Disturbances," 222, 229, 510; independence, 212-29; Indirect Rule in, 127-28, 139, 165; Second World War and reforms, 173, 182
Gordon-Walker, P. O., 257-58, 262, 570, 578, 582, 584
Grandeur et servitude coloniales (Sarraut), 298-301
Great Britain, 33-47, 48-58, 59-78ff., 99-115ff., 124-41, 142-58ff., 212-29, 230-50ff.; African Students Union (in London), 123; anti-imperialism (anti-imperialists) in, 37ff.; Belgian colonial policy compared with, 499, 500-1, 502, 503-4, 508-9, 510-11, 513; and "benevolent despotism," 61, 71; and Burma and Ceylon, 196-212 (see also Burma; Ceylon); and "Closer Union" issue, 142-58; and colonial development (1929-1940), 99-115ff.; Colonial Development and Welfare Bill and Fund, 103-5, 109-10ff., 113, 162, 169, 173-74, 178, 182-84, 216-17; and colonial doctrine of Labour Party, 115-23; and "Colonial Empire," 78-98, 99-115ff., 175ff., 250-62; colonialism and Second World War, 23, 25-29, 86, 132, 158-75ff., 212-29, 230-50 (see also under Second World War); colonial policy compared to French, 46-47, 171, 173, 184, 266, 267, 270, 278, 280, 281-84, 287, 291-92, 295-96, 300-1, 303, 307, 310, 334, 337, 339, 340, 341, 342, 344, 345-46, 350-51, 363, 366, 387-88, 405-6, 429-30, 431, 433, 435-36, 437-38 (see also specific aspects, colonies); and Commonwealth, 33-47, 48-58 (see also Commonwealth of Nations; specific countries by name); and decolonization, 33-47, 48ff., 196-212, 523-25 (see also specific aspects, countries); and Dominion status for India (1917-1939), 59-78, Dutch colonial policy compared with, 488, 489, 493, 496, 498-99; and economic development in colonies, 99-115, 162, 169, 173-74, 178, 182-84, 212ff.; and Egypt, 38, 39, 40, 41-46; and Empire Free Trade policy, 81, 83, 99, 122; and federation concept, 164, 173, 230-50; First World War and, 5-8, 34, 35, 36ff., 48ff., 78ff., 98ff. (see also under First World War); and independence for India (1939-1947), 184-96 (see also India); and Indirect Rule in West Africa, 124-41, 142ff., 212ff.; and Kenya (East Africa) and Closer Union, 142-58, 230-50; First World War, 175-84; Labour Party policy and colonialism during and after the Second World War, 175-84; Labour Party policy and India, 66ff., 78; and "paramountcy" concept, 154-58, 236ff., 247; and partnership in Rhodesian Federation, 230-50; and

INDEX

regional commissions and councils, 164; and Second World War, 17, 18–25, 26, 27, 28, 158–75ff., 184ff., 196ff., 212ff., 230ff. (*see also under* Second World War); "Third British Empire," 33–47, 48ff.; and Trade Union Congress (TUC), 122–23; and transition from Commonwealth of Nations to multi-racial Commonwealth, 250–62; and trusteeship and self-government in colonies, 78–98, 99–115ff., 124ff., 142ff., 158ff., 175ff., 184ff., 196–212ff., 230ff. (*see also* Trusteeship; specific aspects, countries); U.S., colonial policy compared with, 479–81
Gregory, Robert G., 146–47
Griffiths, James, 104, 575, 578, 579
Grigg, Edward (*later* Lord Altringham), 128, 548, 559, 560, 561, 579; and "Commonwealth" concept, 253–54; and "dual policy," 150–55; and India, 68; and Kenya, 120, 150–55; and League of Nations, 56
Grousset, René, 12
Guadeloupe, 285, 288
Guastavino, Jean, 332
Guérin, Daniel, 597
Guernier, Eugène, 273–74, 361
Guggisberg, Frederick Gordon, 100, 127–28, 139, 555, 558
Guiana. *See* British Guiana; French Guiana
Guinea, France and, 428, 435, 448, 450–51. *See also* Sékou Touré
Guy, Camille, 587

Hached, Ferhat, 372, 402, 403–4
Hadj, Messali, 328, 456, 457
Hailey, Lord, 63, 67, 82, 86, 106–7, 110, 112, 114, 122, 215–16, 636; and African emancipation, 215–16, 221; and first use of term, "decolonization," 163; and Indirect Rule, 133, 138, 139, 141, 215–16; and Second World War decolonization, 160–64, 165, 166, 167, 170, 175–76, 177
Haiphong, 397
Halifax, Lord (*formerly* Lord Irwin), 66–67, 68, 70, 72–73, 75, 77; and Commonwealth of Nations, 252–53; and independence of India, 189–90, 193–94
Hamon, Léon, 623
Hancock, W. K., 164–65, 238
Hanoi, 378, 380, 396, 397–98
Harding, Warren G., 477
Hardinge, Viscount, 62
Hardy, Georges, 308, 325, 593, 602, 604, 637; his views on France and colonization, 302–3, 345
Harlow, Vincent, 238
Harmand, Jules, 286–87, 294, 295, 296, 299–300
Harris, John, 106
Harrison, Francis B., 476, 477, 484
Hart, George H. C., 635
Harvest of Victory (Kerr), 39–40
Hatta, Mohammed, 496
Hautecloque, Jean de, 402
Hawaii, 473
Hawes-Cutting Act, 482–85
Hemelriyk, Maurice van, 511
Henderson, Arthur, 19
Herriot, Edouard, 332, 389, 390–91, 415, 416
Hertzog, J. B. M., 54, 250
Hilton-Young, Edward, 153, 154
Hinden, Rita, 176, 179–80, 553
Hindustan, 188
Hitler, Adolf, 18–19
Hoare, Samuel (*later* Lord Templewood), 67, 69, 70, 186–87, 193, 194
Hobson, John A., 4, 35, 37, 79–80, 117, 121, 438–39

Ho Chi Minh, 388, 397, 398, 399, 400, 411, 413, 414, 415, 417, 419, 424, 497; forms provisional government in Hanoi and proclaims Vietnamese independence on abdication of Bao Dai, 378; recognized by French as head of government, 396
Hodson, H. V., 253, 259
Hoffherr, René, 587
Hofmannsthal, Hugo von, 602
Holland. *See* Netherlands
Hong Kong, 78, 158, 165, 177
Hoover, Herbert, 482
Hopkinson, H. L., (Lord Colyton), 234, 244
Horriban, J. F., 121, 568
Hostelet, Georges, 638
Houphouet-Boigny, Félix, 27–28, 426, 434, 435, 451, 623
Hour of Decision, The (Spengler), 11
Huggins, Godfrey (Lord Malvern), 233–36, 239–40, 244, 580
Hurgronje, Snouk, 492
Hutin, Paul, 325–26
Huxley, Elsbeth, 560
Huxley, Julian, 176, 567, 568

Ibo tribes, 130
Ideas and Ideals of the British Empire, The (Parker), 166
Imperial Colonial League (Germany, 1933–1936), 18
Imperialism (Lenin), 8–9
"Imperialism" ("imperialist"), British use of terms, 7, 35ff., 38ff., 57, 86
India, 4, 5, 8, 9, 10, 14, 15–16, 21, 22, 25, 26, 27, 54, 57, 58, 65, 84, 90, 94, 98, 99, 105; Amritsar outbreak, 65, 75, 77; and Burma, 196, 198; Caliphate Protest movement, 65; and Commonwealth of Nations, 33–40 *passim*, 44, 47, 78, 163, 166, 168, 173, 175, 177, 181, 184ff., 253, 254, 255–57; Congress Party, 61ff., 64, 65, 66–67, 69ff., 141, 184ff., 255, 256–57; and Dominion status question (1917–1939), 59–78, 117–18; and "Draft Declaration," 188–90; and First World War, 61ff.; French Agencies in, 278, 280, 283–84; Gandhi and civil disobedience (*see* Gandhi, Mohandas K.); Home Rule, 60; Independence Act (1947), 195–96; independence for (1939–1947), 184–96; India Act (1935), 185; Muslim League, 62, 70, 184ff.; Mutiny, 8, 59; partition of, 194–95; Second settlers from, in Kenya, 143ff.; Simla Conference, 190–91; *swaraj*, 67, 255
Indian Empire Society, 68
Indian Ocean, 36
Indochina, 4, 10, 15, 20, 21, 25, 26, 64, 77, 159, 184, 195, 208, 272, 276, 298, 340, 440, 444, 445; French colonial administration in, 280, 281, 282, 286, 288–89, 293–96, 306–18 *passim*; and French Union, 382, 383, 386, 387, 396–400, 407–8, 411, 412, 416, 417, 424, 444, 445; nationalism and decolonization in, 306–21 *passim*, 378–80, 386, 396–400, 407–8, 411, 413, 415–16, 424, 430; Second World War and decolonization of, 297–98, 340, 359, 360, 377, 378; Vietnamese independence, 278–80, 388, 396–400, 407–8, 411, 412, 413, 417 (*see also* Ho Chi Minh; Vietnam)
Indonesia, Netherlands and, 4, 10, 15, 21, 25, 26, 64, 77, 83, 87, 195, 208, 375, 439; decolonization of, 487–99; education in, 490, 491, 492; and independence, 498–99; *volksraad*, 490ff., 496
Industrialization, 61 (*see also* Westernization);

French colonialism and, 270, 272ff., 388, 430, 439, 453; U.S. colonialism and, 486
Ingrams, Harold, 638
"Interdependence" concept, French colonialism and, 404–6, 408–9
Iraq, 10, 36, 47, 119, 283
Ireland, 38, 54, 251, 287, 539
Irwin, Lord. *See* Halifax, Lord (*formerly* Lord Irwin)
Italy, 17, 20, 24, 27
Ivory Coast, 272, 434, 440, 451

Jamaica, British West Indies, 78, 89, 109, 172–73, 177
Japan, 4, 12, 14, 16, 17, 20, 21, 26, 39; and Burma and Ceylon, 197–98, 199, 200, 203, 205, 206, 207, 208; and Dutch in Indonesia, 493–96; and Second World War and British and French colonialism, 20, 158–59, 166, 170, 205, 206, 207, 208, 251, 360, 378, 379, 396; and U.S. in Philippines, 483–84
Jaurès, Jean, 310
Java, 488, 492, 497
Jebb, Richard, 49–50, 52, 60
Jennings, Ivor, 209
Jews, 279, 321. *See also* Anti-Semitism
Jinnah, M. A., 188
Jones Act, U.S. in Philippines and, 476–77
Jonge (Dutch governor-general in Indonesia, 1931–1936), 493
Jonnart, Charles C., 323
Jouvenal, Henri de, 277
Juin, Alphonse, 402, 403, 613
Julien, C. A., 405, 458, 605, 614, 617
July, Pierre, 614
Jyengar, S., 72

Kabyles, 319, 327
Kaduna (Northern Nigerian emirate), 124–25, 129–32, 135, 136
Kano (Northern Nigerian emirate), 124–25, 129–32, 135, 136
Kariba Dam, 239
Kasai, 500
Kasavubu, Joseph, 510, 512
Katanga, 487, 499, 500, 501, 504, 509
Kaunda, K., 242, 246, 248, 579
Keith, A. B., 52–53
Kemal, Mustapha, 9, 13
Kennedy, John F., 261
Kenya, British and, 47, 56, 78, 82, 89, 94, 99, 102, 117, 120, 128, 142–58, 563; and Closer Union, 142–58, 230–31; comparison of French colonialism with, 334–35, 341; Devonshire declaration and "Paramountcy of Native Interests," 82, 146–47, 148, 151, 155–56; Indirect Rule in, 142ff., 230ff.; Masai, 149; Mau Mau rebellion (1954), 156, 240–41, 243; Second World War and decolonization, 178, 180, 230–31, 240–41, 243–45, 247, 248; white and Indian settlers' conflict, 142–58, 165, 178, 230–31, 240–41, 243–45, 248
Kenya (Leys), 149
Kenya from Within (Ross), 149
Kenyatta, Jomo, 28, 156, 243, 248
Kerr, Philip (*later* Lord Lothian), 68, 106, 544, 548, 558; and changing concept of "British Empire," 38–40, 41, 49, 51, 56, 61, 86; and India, 61, 68, 86, 548; and self-government, 86
Key to My Position (Milner), 41
Khama, Seretse, 180
Khrushchev, Nikita S., 27, 534
King (U. S. Senator), and Philippine independence, 438

King, W. L. Mackenzie, 252
Kingsley, Mary, 115
Kipling, Rudyard, 291, 474
Kitchener, Lord, 13, 36, 45
Kivu, 501
Kleffens, E. N. van, 494, 635

Labour and the Empire, 118
Labouret, Henri, 342–43, 344
Labour Party in Perspective, The (Atlee), 76, 122
Lacoste, Robert, 461
Lagos, Nigeria, 125, 131, 134, 136, 141, 165, 359
La Marsa, treaty of (1883), 348
Lambert, 331
Lamine-Guèye, A., 386, 387, 435
Lampué, Pierre, 612, 623, 626
Lanessan, Jean Marie de, 286, 348
Laniel, Joseph, 456
Lansbury, George, 10
Laos, 279, 347, 388, 393, 400, 407, 417
Laperrine, General, 324
Lapie, P. O., 364, 375–76, 385, 607
Larminat, René de, 359, 362
Las Cas, Bartolomé de, 308
Laski, Harold J., 75, 76, 121, 122, 123, 176, 181, 570
Latour, Boyer de, 613
Laurentie, Henri, 369, 380
Laurier, Wilfrid, 50, 259
Lavergne, Bernard, 626
Law, Andrew Bonar, 44, 51
Lawrence, T. E., 46, 58, 535, 540
League of Nations, 6–8, 19, 34, 37, 40, 54, 56–57, 63, 80, 317; Advisory Council, 7; mandate system, 6–8, 18, 19, 23–24, 80, 83, 115–16, 118, 128, 177; Permanent Mandate Commission, 7–8
Lebanon, 21, 47, 317, 359, 371–72
Le Bon, Gustave, 293
Lebrun, Albert, 276, 586
Le Brun-Kéris, Georges, 422–23
Leclerc, General, 362, 396, 397–98, 400, 498–99
Lenin, N., 8–9, 10, 13, 310; *Imperialism* by, 8–9, 27, 28; Twelve Points of, 9
Lennox-Boyd, Lord, 227, 239–40
Lenormand, Maurice H., 623
Leopold II, King of Belgium, 500
Leopold III, King of Belgium, 506
Leopoldville, 499, 503, 504, 510–11
Le Tourneau (French historian), 402
Levant, French, 277, 279. *See also* Middle East; specific countries by name
Leverhulme, 1st Viscount, 500–1
Ley, Dr., 362
Leygues, Georges, 322–23
Leys, Norman, 120, 149, 560
Liberia, 15
Linfield, F. C., 103
Linggadjali agreement (1947), 497
Linlithgow, Lord, 184
Lisette, Gabriel, 434, 623, 624
Listowel, Lord, 579
Lloyd, Lord, 44–45, 55, 68, 539, 552
Lloyd, Selwyn, 227
Lloyd George of Dwyfor, David Lloyd George, 1st Earl, 37, 44, 45–49, 54, 68, 103, 267, 535
Locke, John, 79
Lodge, Henry Cabot, 476, 632
Logemann, Johann H. A., 499, 635
Loi Cadre, 409, 423, 425–42, 449, 451–52, 510
Lost Dominion, The, 65–66
Lothian, Lord. *See* Kerr, Philip (*later* Lord Lothian)

INDEX

Louis, Paul, 310
Lourenço Marques, 520
Lugard, Frederick (*later* Lord Lugard), 80–83, 99, 115, 147, 548, 557, 561; and Indirect Rule theory in British Africa, 124–27, 130–40 *passim*, 153–54, 215, 287, 294; and Kenya, 147, 153–54; and trusteeship ("dual mandate") concept, 80–83, 86, 99, 269, 271, 308
Lumumba, Patrice, and Mouvement National Congolais, 510, 512, 639
Lyautey, Marshal L. Hubert G., 102, 274, 275, 276, 286, 369; background and beliefs, 347–58; and Morocco protectorate, 102, 274, 276, 347–50; and "protectorate" concept of French colonialism, 287, 294, 295, 307
Lyttelton, Oliver, 235–36

Macao, 514, 518
Macdonald, Captain, 175
MacDonald, Gordon, 186
MacDonald, James R., 75, 76, 118, 120, 583
MacDonald, Malcolm John, 85, 108, 113–14
McKinley, William, 474
MacLeod, J. N., 240–41, 243–44, 245–46, 247
Macmillan, Harold, 169–70, 176, 182, 240, 241–42, 243, 244–46, 583; colonial reforms and self-government in British Africa and, 169–70, 176, 240, 241–42, 243, 244–46
Macmillan, William M., 104, 109–12, 114, 122, 139, 176, 551, 636; criticism of Indirect Rule theory by, 165–66; *Warning from the West Indies, a Tract for the Empire* by, 109–12
McNutt, Paul V., 486, 631, 633
Macpherson, John, 224, 581
Madagascar, France and, 272, 275; colonial administration, 279, 281, 317, 340–42, 344, 347, 348; and decolonization and independence, 423–24, 433, 435, 446ff.; and French Union, 383, 386, 387, 390, 393, 410, 413, 414, 415, 423–24, 433, 435, 446ff.; Second World War and, 359, 365
Madaule, Pierre, 424
Madeira, 516
Magna Carta (Coatman), 57–58
Maîtres de L'Afrique du Nord, Les (Bourdet), 414
Malaya, British and, 15, 21, 78, 94, 99, 101, 124, 256, 488, 489; Federation and Commonwealth and, 256, 257; Second World War and, 158–59, 162, 166, 178
Malaysia, 27. *See also* Malaya
Malbrant, René, 391, 622–29
Malcolm, G., 485
Malengreau, Guy, 638
Mali Federation, 450–52. *See also* Sudan, French colonialism and
Malinowski, Bronislaw, 105
Malraux, André, 311
Malta, 78, 84, 89, 94, 165, 177
Malvern, Lord (Godfrey Huggins), 233–36, 239–40, 244, 580
Mandate system, 6–8, 18, 19, 23–24, 80ff., 83, 115–16, 118, 128, 177, 267, 272. *See also* Trusteeship; specific aspects, countries, individuals, issues
Mandel, Georges, 359
Mangin, Charles, 268, 293
Manifeste du peuple algérien (Abbas), 371–72
Manila Conference, 497
Mann, Thomas, 532
Mao Tse-tung, 25, 398
Marrakesh, 351, 404
Martinaud Déplat, Leon, 415, 416–17, 619
Martinique, 384

Marxism (Marxists), and nationalist movements, 21, 160. *See also* Communism (Communists); specific countries and individuals by name
Marzorati, G., 636, 637, 638
Massey, William F., 53
Mau Mau uprising (1954), 156, 240–41, 243
Maunier, René, 361–62, 606
Mauriac, François, 421, 424
Mauritius, 101
Maurras, Charles, 267
Mayer, Daniel, 461
Mayer, René, 415, 417, 453–54
Mboya, Tom, 243
Mehrotra, S. R., 541
Mein Kampf, 18
Memorandum on Native Policy (Passfield), 154–55, 231–32
Mendès-France, Pierre, 267, 403, 414, 415, 416–17, 418, 420, 613; and Algerian independence, 457–63
Menon, Krishna, 547
Menthon, François de, 380–81
Mérat, Louis, 587
Merlé, Marcel, 625
Mesopotamia, 5, 38, 46, 61
Meston, James, 61
Michel, Father, 424
Middle East, 4, 5, 9–10, 15, 21–22, 38, 39–46. *See also* Arabs (and Moslems . . .); specific countries by name
Mille, Pierre, 325, 587
Milner, Lord, 40–42, 55, 85–86, 102, 135, 536, 541; an exponent of imperialism, 36, 37, 38, 40–42, 45, 51, 57, 168; and Kenya, 102, 103, 143, 145, 151; *Key to My Position* by, 41–42; and Middle East (Egypt), 43–44; "Round Table" group and, 35, 38, 44, 51, 57, 68, 74; and "Two Empires" theory, 61
Minto, Lord, 35, 60, 91, 541
Mise en valeur des colonies, La (Sarraut), 269–72, 296, 304
Missionaries (missions), 130, 142, 147, 156; Belgian Congo and, 500, 502
Mission de la France en Asie (Dupont), 420
Mitchell, Philip, 180, 558, 561
Mitterand, François, 405, 417–18, 458–59, 627
Moffat, John, 237, 248
Mollet, Guy, 403, 431, 435, 457, 460, 461, 616
Moncef Bey, 372
Monckton (Lord) Commission and Report, 242, 246
Monnerville, Gaston, 280, 381, 415, 612
Montagu, Edwin S., 5, 44, 58, 60, 62–64, 65–66, 67, 71, 94
Montagne, Robert, 405
Monteiro, Armindo, 641
Montvalon, Robert de, 424, 620
Mook, H. van, 496, 499, 635
Moreira, Adriano, 518–19, 641, 642
Morel, Edmund D., 35, 37, 80, 115, 559
Moresco, E., 634
Moreux, René, 455, 611
Morley, John, 35, 60, 62, 91, 540, 541
Morocco, France and, 6, 9, 25, 28, 102, 267, 272, 273–74, 276, 277, 347–58, 445; Abd-el-Krim rebellion, 310–11; colonial administration, 279, 280, 281, 282, 284, 295, 307, 316, 317, 347–58; Fez agreement, 130, 348, 350; French Socialists and, 310–11, 316, 317, 318, 413, 416–17; French Union and, 393, 400–6, 412, 413, 414, 416–23; and independence, 400–6, 413, 418, 420–23, 430, 439, 440, 445; Lyautey and protectorate, 347–58ff.; and Moslems, 351, 355; and Sec-

ond World War and nationalism, 358, 359, 364ff., 372, 375, 379
Morrison, Herbert, 179, 181, 568
Mort des colonies? (Le Brun-Kéris), 422–23
Moslems. *See* Arabs (and Moslems . . .); Middle East; specific people, places
Mounier, Emanuel, 343
Mountbatten, Lord: and Burma, 180, 201–2, 203–4, 207, 496, 498–99; and India, 191, 192, 194–95, 256
Moussa, Pierre L., 430, 441, 620
Moutet, Marius, 318, 389, 597; and Algeria, 326, 383; becomes colonial minister, 317; and Indochina, 276, 311, 314, 317, 382, 383, 397, 413, 416
Movement for Colonial Freedom (Great Britain, 1950s), 181
Mozambique, 514, 518, 522–23, 641
Müller, Hermann, 533
Multi-racial Commonwealth, transition of British Commonwealth of Nations to, 250–62
"Multi-racial communities," British colonialism and, 245–50ff.
Multi-racial societies, Portugal and, 518ff.
Mumford, W. B., 565
Munro, Sir Thomas, 540
Muret, Maurice, 12
Murray, Gilbert, 37
Mus, Paul, 21, 420, 424, 608
Muselier, Emile, 362
Muslim League (India), 62, 70, 184ff.
Muslims. *See* Arabs (and Moslems . . .); Middle East; specific countries by name

Naegelen, Marcel, 402, 456
Namasivavam, S., 574
Napoleon III, 320
Nasser, Gamal Abdel, 27, 457
Nationalism (nationalist emancipation movements), 4ff., 24ff., 523–25 (*see also* Autonomy; Self-government; specific aspects, countries, events, individuals, organizations, issues); Africa and (*see* Africa; specific countries); Algeria and, 319–35, 452–69; Asia and, 196ff., 206ff. (*see also* Asia; specific countries); British colonialism and, 39ff., 48ff., 59–78, 123, 135–36 (*see also* specific aspects, countries, events, individuals, issues); Burma and Ceylon and, 196–212; First World War and, 4ff. (*see also* First World War; specific countries); French colonialism and, 282ff., 289ff., 298ff., 302ff., 310ff., 382–95, 406–24 (*see also* specific aspects, countries, events, individuals, issues); India and, 59–78, 184–96; Indochina, Tunisia and Morocco, 353–58, 396–406, 444ff. (*see also* Indochina; Morocco; Tunisia); Indonesia and, 487–99; Philippines and, 478–87; post-Second World War and, 406–24, 425ff., 443ff.; Rhodesia and, 230–50; Second World War and, 21ff., 161ff., 175ff., 196ff., 358–82ff. (*see also* Second World War; specific countries); West Africa and, 212–29 (*see also* specific countries)
National Socialism, Germany and, 17–20
Native Races and Their Rulers (Temple), 129
NATO (North Atlantic Treaty Organization), 159
Nehru, Jawaharlal, 20, 67, 76; and British Commonwealth of Nations, 256; and Communism, 9, 10, 27; and constitution for India (Report, 1928), 67, 98, 548; and independence for India (1939–1947), 184, 186, 190, 191, 194, 570, 571, 583
Nehru, Motilal, 72
Nerá, Gilles, 625, 626

Netherlands, 10, 16, 21, 25, 83, 87, 439, 440, 463; and Dutch Indies and Indonesia, 159, 184, 484, 487–99 (*see also* Indonesia); and Second World War, 158, 159; U.S. foreign policy and, 481, 484
New Imperial Ideas (Stokes), 56
New Zealand, 48, 50, 53, 77, 143, 147–48, 170, 250, 251, 259–60
Nicolson, Harold, 12–13
Nigeria, British and, 27–28, 58, 78, 80, 89, 98, 99, 101, 106, 120, 212–29; and decolonization and independence, 173, 181, 212–29, 433, 435; and Indirect Rule, 124, 125–27, 128–41; Trade Union Congress and, 212; and unity, 220–21, 225
Nkomo, J., 246, 249
Nkrumah, Kwame, 27, 82, 173, 213, 218, 222–24, 228, 431, 576
Noel-Baker, P. J., 533, 567
Noel-Buxton, Edward, 19
Noguès, Charles, 318, 357, 358, 359, 606
Norodom Sihanouk, 615
North Africa, 10, 16, 17, 20, 21, 272–78, 309 (*see also* specific countries by name); Algerian independence, 452–69 (*see also* Algeria); assimilation in Algeria (1919–1939), French and, 319–35; decolonization, 20, 358ff., 370ff., 400–6, 407, 408, 411–24 *passim*, 444, 445, 452–69 (*see also* specific aspects, countries, individuals, issues); French and, 10, 16, 21, 278ff., 286ff., 293, 298, 299, 306, 307ff., 314–19ff. (*see also under* France; specific countries by name); French Union and, 382–95, 407, 408, 411–24 *passim*, 444, 445; Great Britain and (*see under* Great Britain; specific countries by name); Lyautey and Morocco protectorate, 347–58; Russia and, 10, 17; Second World War and emancipation movements, 20, 350ff., 370ff. (*see also* Nationalism; Second World War; specific countries by name)
North American colonies, British and, 3, 4, 524
Northern Nigeria, 126–27, 129–41. See also Nigeria
Northern Rhodesia, British and, 78, 89, 99, 100–1, 120, 230–50, 499 (*see also* Rhodesia); and Commonwealth of Nations, 257; Copperbelt of, 231, 232, 233, 244; Indirect Rule and, 124; partnership and federation, 230–50
Northey, Edward, 147, 156
Nos grands problèmes coloniaux (Hardy), 302–3
Notre protectorat marocain 1912–1930 (Colliez), 356
Nouelle, Georges, 310, 311
Nouvelle politique indigène pour l'Afrique équatoriale française, La (Eboué), 362–64, 365
Nu, U, 27, 206
Nyasaland, 78; and Rhodesian Federation, 230–50

Ohneck, Wolfgang, 598
Oldham, Joseph H., 120, 147, 153, 549
Old World and the New Society, The, 176
Olivier, Marcel, 275, 340–42
Olivier, Sydney (Lord Olivier), 35, 80, 115, 118–19, 153, 556; and India, 75; and West Indies, British and, 108–9, 120, 549
Olympio, Sylvanus, 431
Ormsby-Gore, William, 102, 106, 150, 556
Osmeña, Sergio, 477
Ottoman Empire. *See* Turkey (Ottoman Empire)
Ottawa Agreements (1932), 55, 99

INDEX 677

Overseas Food Corporation, Great Britain and, 183

Padmore, George, 82–83
Pahlevi. *See* Reza Khan Pahlevi, Shah
Paillard, Jean, 362
Pakistan, 188, 189, 191, 194–95, 253, 254, 255, 256
Palestine, 36, 112, 165
Panikkar, K. M., 259, 572, 583
Parker, Ernest, 166
"Partnership," British colonialism and, 230ff., 245
Passfield, Lord (Sidney Webb), 154–55, 231–32, 553, 560. *See also* Webb, Sidney (*later* Lord Passfield)
Patel, V., 190
Paternalism: Belgium in the Congo and, 499–513; Dutch in Indonesia and, 488; U.S. in the Philippines and, 484–85
Path to Nigerian Freedom (Awolowo), 214
Paysans noirs, Les (Delavignette), 343
Paz, Magdaleine, 311
Paz, Maurice, 332, 597
Péguy, Charles, 308
Perham, Margery, 105, 108, 176, 560, 565; and East Africa (Rhodesia), 238, 560; and Indirect Rule in British colonies, 132–33, 137–39, 555–56; and West African colonialism, 137–39, 214–15, 216, 225–26
Persia, 9, 10, 38, 44
Pétain, Marshal Philippe, 359, 361
Pethick-Lawrence, Lord, 190, 572
Petillon, Leo, 507, 508, 510, 636, 638
Peyrouton, Marcel, 311, 318, 359, 597
Pezet, Ernest, 595
Philip, André, 380, 461
Philippines, U.S. and, 180, 214, 483–87; decolonization and, 473–87, 525; Hawes-Cutting Act, 482; Huks, 479, 487; Independence Act, 482–86; Jones Act, 476–77; Sakdal movement, 479; tariff and economic policy, 479–82, 485–87; Timberland Resolution, 482; Trade Act (Bell Bill), 486
Pichat, Louis, 587
Pinay, Antoine, 404, 456
Pius XII, Pope, 423
Plan for Africa (Hinden), 176
Plévan, René, 359, 364, 607, 610; and federation, 376, 377, 385; and French "Community," 366–67
Plus grande France, La (Archimbaud), 303–5
Political Quarterly, The, Buxton on British trusteeship in, 122
Ponsot, Henri, 355, 357
Portugal, and colonialism, 19, 25, 28, 284 (*see also* specific Portuguese colonies by name); and African colonialism, 19, 25, 28, 284, 514–23, 525; and Asian colonialism, 514ff.; and colonial economic system, 520–21, 524; and colonial education system, 520; Estado Novo, 514, 515ff.
Potsdam Conference, 26
Principes de Colonisation et de Législation coloniale (Girault), 290–92
Principles of Native Administration and Their Application (Cameron), 129–30
Problem of the Commonwealth (Curtis), 51–52
Programme de politique coloniale . . . , Un (Vignon), 293–95
Protectorates, French colonialism and concept of, 287, 294ff., 308, 321, 347–58, 405–6; in Indochina, 378; in Morocco and Tunisia, 347ff., 372, 375, 405–6 (*see also* Morocco; Tunisia)

Puaux, Gabriel, 358, 359, 372, 421
Puerto Rico, 214, 477

Quezon, Manuel L., 483

Racism (racist policy; segregation), British colonialism in Africa and, 231–50. *See also under* Color; specific aspects, countries
Raglan, Lord, 556
Ramadier, Paul, 398, 455–56
Rance, Hubert, 204
Rattray, R. S., 127, 556
Reading, Lord, 68, 153
Reclus, Onésime, 273
Refoulement (assujettissement), French colonialism and principles of, 283
Régnier, Marcel, 328–29, 332
Renaudel, Pierre, 311–12
Report on Nutrition in the Colonial Empire, 108
Réunion, 278
Reveil de l'Asie (Grousset), 12
Reynaud, Paul, 277, 419, 456, 587, 590
Reza Khan Pahlevi, Shah, 9
Rhineland, 267, 268
Rhodes, Cecil, 34, 143, 145, 151, 236
Rhodesia, British and, 15, 178, 230–50, 501 (*see also* Northern Rhodesia; Southern Rhodesia); African National Congress, 233, 240; federation, 180, 230–50
Richard, B., 576
Richards, E. C., 220–21
Ries, Jean, 627
Rivet, Paul, 34, 597
Riviere, on France and the French in Morocco, 596
Robins, Lord, 244
Roosevelt, Franklin D.: and U.S. and Philippines, 482, 484; Second World War and anti-colonialism of, 22–25, 159, 168
Roosevelt, Nicholas, 484, 631, 632
Roosevelt, Theodore, 475, 476, 483, 632
Root, Elihu, 474
Rosebery, Lord, 49, 51
Rosenfeld, Oreste, 410, 413
Ross, W. McGregor, 120, 149
Rothermere, Lord, 19, 68
Round Table (British periodical), 35, 38, 40, 44, 49, 50–52, 61, 62, 95, 109, 147, 153, 166, 227–29
Rowlett Acts, 65
Roy, M. N., 9
Ruanda-Urundi, 25, 505, 637, 639
Rufisque (Senegal commune), 427. *See also* Senegal
Runciman, Walter, 101
Runner, Jean, 295–96
Russell, Bertrand, 37
Russia, 4, 17, 35 (*see also* Cold War; Communism; Marxism; Soviet Union); Bolshevik Revolution and Communist theory of imperialism, 8–11; and British, 35, 36, 39, 40; and Japan, 4; and Second Comintern (1920), 9, 10
Ryckmans, Pierre, 506–7, 508–10, 636, 637

Sadauna of Sokoto, 219, 225
Sahara, 457, 464, 467
Saigon, 396, 398, 400, 419
Sainteney, Jean, 396
Saint Louis (Senegal commune), 427, 450. *See also* Senegal
Salan, General, 466
Salazar, António de Oliviera, and Portuguese colonialism, 514, 515–16, 521–22, 641
Salisbury, Lord, 44, 68, 193, 235; and Kenya

constitution, 243–44; and Northern Rhodesian constitution, 245–46
Samory kingdom (Sudan), 337
Samuel, Herbert, 51, 104–5, 169
San Francisco Conference (1945), 251
Sanglier, André Roger, 623
Sankey, Lord, 76
São Tomé, 514
Sapru, quoted on British in India, 542
Sarrail, Maurice, 8
Sarraut, Albert, 274, 275, 277, 317, 325–26, 331–32, 366, 585, 586, 592–93, 617; and colonial association and assimilation, 292, 296–301, 302, 304, 309, 317, 592–93; and colonial development by French, 269–72, 273, 275, 417; and French use of black troops, 268
Sartre, Jean Paul, 414, 458
Saussure, Felix G. de, 293
Sauvy, Alfred, 463, 618
Scelle, Georges, 410–11
Schacht, Hjalmar, 18, 19, 533
Schnee, Dr., 531, 532
Schuman, Robert, 401, 402, 423, 613
Scott, Lord, 561
Second World War, 8, 11, 18ff., 158ff. (see also specific aspects, countries, events, individuals, issues); and acceleration of political change and decolonization, 20ff., 86, 158–75ff., 184ff., 525 (see also specific aspects, countries); and African political emancipation, 132, 133, 212ff., 230ff. (see also specific aspects, countries, individuals); Belgium in the Congo and, 500, 504, 505, 506; British and decolonization, 18ff., 23, 25–29, 86, 132, 158–75ff., 184ff., 196ff., 212ff., 230ff., 525 (see also specific countries); Dutch in Indonesia and, 487, 493–96; French colonial policy during, 358–82 (see also under France); and French decolonization, 298–99, 334, 358–82ff., 406–24, 425ff. (see also under France); Portugal in Africa and, 516; and transition of British Commonwealth of Nations to multi-racial Commonwealth, 250ff.; U.S. in the Philippines and, 483–85
Seeley, John R., 59, 474
Sékou Touré, 435, 436, 446, 447, 448, 450, 451; and abolishment of chefferies in Guinea, 428; and Loi Cadre, 436
Selborne, Lord, 44, 193
Self-government, Belgium in the Congo and, 505–6ff. See also Belgian Congo
Self-government, British colonialism and, 48–58ff., 98, 99ff., 115–23; Burma and Ceylon, 196–212; Canada, 48–49; Commonwealth of Nations and, 48–55, 59ff.; East Africa and, 142–58, 230ff.; India, 59ff., 184–96 (see also India); Indirect Rule in Africa and, 142–58, 230ff. (see also specific colonies); Indirect Rule in West Africa and (see also specific colonies); Rhodesia and, 230–50; Second World War and, 160–75ff. (see also under Second World War); transition from British Commonwealth of Nations to multi-racial Commonwealth, 250–62; and trusteeship, 88–98; and West Africa, 124–41, 143
Self-government, Dutch in Indonesia and, 492–97. See also Indonesia
Self-government, French colonialism and, 281ff., 313ff., 319ff., 336ff., 367–70ff., 387ff. (see also Nationalism; specific aspects, concepts, countries, individuals, issues); Algeria, 452–69 (see also Algeria); French Union and, 382–95, 406–24, 425ff.; Indochina, Tunisia and Morocco, 396–406 (see also Indochina; Morocco; Tunisia); post-Second World War, 406–24, 425ff.; Second World War and, 298–99, 334, 358–82ff., 406–24, 425ff. (see also specific colonies by name)
Self-government, U.S. in the Philippines and, 474–87
Senanayake, D., 210
Senegal, France and, 267 (see also Senghor, Léopold S.); colonial administration, 279, 285, 288, 289, 298, 318, 322, 336, 338, 339, 361; Four Communes, 279, 280, 285, 288 (see also specific Communes by name); and French Community, 446–48, 450–52; and French Union, 383–84, 386, 387, 391–92, 426, 427, 434–35ff., 448; and independence, 450–52; and Loi Cadre, 427ff., 434
Senghor, Léopold S., 20, 343–44, 370–71, 382–83, 387, 391, 408–9, 423, 429, 441, 442, 609, 610, 619, 620, 621–22, 623; and "Balkanization" of Africa, 434–35, 436, 621; and BDS party, 426, 428; and French Community, 446–48, 450, 451
Seretse Khama, 180
Servoise, René, 615
Sétif (Algeria) uprising, 26, 28, 374, 411
Shan States, Burma, 201
Shaw, Bernard, 115
Shotwell, James, 85
Sierra Leone, 78, 89, 101
Sihanouk. See Norodom Sihanouk
Simla (India) conference, 198
Simon, John, 19, 66, 188, 193; and Simon Commission, 66, 68, 75
Singapore, Second World War and fall of, 21, 158–59, 167, 211
Sinha, S. P., 541
Sissoko, Fily Dabo, 370, 387, 608
Six ans de politique sociale à Madagascar (Olivier), 340–42
Smith, Adam, 291
Smith, Ian, 249–50
Smuts, Jan Christian, 164, 538, 564; and British Commonwealth of Nations, 33, 50, 54, 251, 252, 258; and British "Empire," 53; Rhodes Lectures and Black Africa (1929), 106
Snowden, Philip, 103, 547
Sokoto (Northern Nigerian emirate), 124–25, 129–32, 135, 136
Somaliland, 24
Sorensen, Reginald, 186
Soudan-Paris-Bourgogne (Dalavignette), 343
Soulbury, Lord, 209
Soustelle, Jacques, 444, 459–60, 462, 464–65, 466, 627
South Africa, 6, 21–22, 25, 35, 37, 38, 50, 54, 148, 164, 170, 234, 236, 241, 250–51, 252, 320; and Boer (South African) War, 4, 34–35, 142; and British Commonwealth of Nations, 250–51, 252, 258; and Kenya, 142, 144, 145, 158; and racism, 231, 233, 234, 236, 239, 241, 242
South America, 8, 13, 24. See also specific countries
South-East Asia, 10 (see also specific countries by name); British and decolonization, 201–12 (see also under Great Britain; specific countries by name); Dutch in Indonesia, 487–99; U.S. and, 476
Southern Nigeria, 125, 505
Southern Rhodesia, 28, 78, 146, 148, 157–58, 230–50 (see also Northern Rhodesia; Rhodesia); declaration of independence by, 250; and federation, 230–50
Soviet Union, 9, 17, 18, 122, 253, 256, 261–62

(*see also* Cold War; Communism; Russia); and decolonization, 22, 23, 25, 26–29, 160, 313; and French colonialism, 274, 381, 421
Spain, 3, 284, 318, 473–74, 478–80
Spanish-American War, 473–74
Spengler, Oswald, 11, 518
Stalin, J. V., 9, 26–27, 28
Stanley, Colonel Oliver F. G., and British trusteeship and colonial self-government, 171–72, 216–17, 565, 566
Steeg, T., 354–55
Sterling bloc nations, 260
Stimson, Henry L., 478, 481–82, 483, 630
Stockdale, Frank, 172
Stokes, Robert, 56
Straits Settlements, 94
Stresemann, Gustav, 18, 532
Studies in Colonial Nationalism (Jebb), 49–50
Sudan, British colonialism and, 13, 15, 35, 46, 78, 98, 229
Sudan, French colonialism and, 272, 337, 388 (*see also* Mali); and independence, 450–52
Suez Canal, 42, 43, 46, 59, 118, 244, 262
Sukarno, Japanese in Indonesia and formation of representative council under, 496
Sumatra, 492, 497
Surinam, 494, 495
Survey of British Commonwealth Affairs (Hancock), 164
Swaraj, 67, 255
Swinton, Lord (Philip Cunliffe-Lister), 106, 213
Sydenham, Lord, 65
Syria, France and, 8, 47, 267, 276, 307, 358, 359, 360; French Socialists and, 315, 317; independence of, 12–13, 21, 315, 317, 371–72, 388

Taft, William Howard, 474, 475
Tahrat, on assimilation for Moslems in Algeria, 316
Tanganyika, 7, 19, 78, 101, 102–3, 128, 137, 149, 151, 152, 563; groundnut scheme, 183; independence and, 240, 247, 248
Tardieu, André, 277
Tchad, 359, 390
Teitgen, Pierre-Henri, 410, 423, 435, 448, 619, 622
Témoignage chrétien (Mus), 420, 421, 423, 424, 460, 627
Temple, Charles L., 129, 130, 135, 136
Templewood, Lord (Samuel Hoare), 186–87, 193, 194
Temps modernes, Les (Sartre), 414
Third Empire (Zimmern), 37, 57, 85, 166
"Third World," East-West conflict and competition for influence in, 28
Thomas, Ivor, 568
Thomas, J. H., 118
Thomasset, René, 605
Thorez, Maurice, 26, 615
Thoughts on the Constitution (Amery), 254
Tilak, B., 65
Tillon, Germaine, 456
Timor, 514
Todd, Reginald, 239
Togo, 279, 388, 393, 450
Togoland, 24
Tonkin, 279, 378, 397, 498
Touré. *See* Sékou Touré
Toynbee, Arnold, 13, 19, 40, 518, 530, 533; *World after the Peace Conference* essay by, 13
Tragédie algérienne, La (Aron), 463–65
Tredgold, Robert, 243
Trinidad, 108, 109, 173
Tripolitania, 26
Truman, Harry S., 486
Trusteeship, British colonialism and (*see also* Mandate system; specific aspects, countries; individuals, issues): Burma and Ceylon, 196–212; and Closer Union in East Africa, 142–58; colonial development (1929–1940) and, 99–115; colonial doctrine of British Labour Party and, 115–23, 175–84ff.; Indirect Rule in East Africa and, 142–58; Indirect Rule in West Africa and, 124–41, 142, 212ff.; Rhodesia and, 230–50; Second World War and, 160–75ff., 212ff.; and self-government, 78–98 (*see also* Self-government, British colonialism and); use of terms "trustee" and "trusteeship," 79ff., 160
Tsiranana, P., 447, 626
Tunisia, French colonialism and, 10, 25, 28, 272–73, 278, 359, 364, 372, 375, 379, 445; colonial administration and, 281, 282, 286, 307, 311, 316, 318, 347, 348, 356–58; French Socialists and, 314–16, 317, 318; and French Union, 383, 393, 400–6, 413, 415, 416–18, 420–23, 445; and independence, 400–6, 413, 416–18, 420, 421–23, 430, 439, 445; Moslems (Arabs), 315–16; Neo-Destour party, 401–3
Turkey (Ottoman Empire), and colonialism, 5, 7, 36, 37, 38, 42. *See also* specific countries by name
Turton (member of British Parliament), and constitutional changes in Northern Rhodesia, 245–46
Twentieth Century Empire, The (Hodson), 253
Tydings, M. E., 633

Ubangi, 363
Uganda, British colonialism and, 78, 124, 143, 149; cotton in, 15, 99; elections and, 240; and federation, 151; and independence, 240, 247, 248
U.N. *See* United Nations
Underhill, on "Second Commonwealth," 259
Union Française, L' (Delavignette), 380
Union of Democratic Control, British, 37
Union of South Africa. *See* South Africa
United Africa Company, British, 183
United Nations: Committee on Information from Non-self-governing Territories, 24; and decolonization, 23–25, 26, 28, 160, 164, 170, 242, 244, 247, 252, 253, 392, 402, 406, 444, 450, 451, 496, 497, 499; and Dutch in Indonesia, 496, 497, 499; General Assembly, 25; and Portuguese colonialism, 516–17, 522; Security Council of, 25; Trusteeship Council of, 23–25, 177
United States, 429, 473; Belgium in the Congo and, 500, 506; British and colonial period in, 3, 4, 48; British in Canada and, 48, 54, 55, 56; and British colonialism, 159–60, 164–65, 168, 177, 179, 183, 202, 211, 214, 242, 247; and British Commonwealth of Nations in Second World War, 251, 253, 260, 261–62; and Dutch in Indonesia, 497; expansionism, colonialism, and decolonization, 473ff., 525; First World War and anti-colonialism, 5–7, 8, 11, 12, 13, 14, 15, 17; and French colonialism, 267, 269, 274, 364, 381, 419, 420, 421, 444; and Philippines, 167, 180, 473–87, 525; Second World War and decolonization, 22–23, 25–27, 159–60, 164–65, 168, 177, 179, 183, 202, 211, 214, 242, 247

U Nu, 27, 206
Urbanization, effect of First World War on, 5
U Saw, 197, 572–73
U.S.S.R. *See* Russia; Soviet Union

Valéry, Paul, 11
Valois, Georges, 273
Vandenberg, Arthur H., 484
Van den Bosch, and "culture system" in Dutch East Indies, 488
Varenne, A., 218, 313–14
Vatican contre la France d'Outre Mer?, 424
Vedel, Georges, 625
Vermeersch, J., 615–16
Versailles Treaty, 18, 54, 62, 268
Verstaete, Maurice, 639
Viard, Paul Emile, 376–77, 381, 385, 599
Victoria Falls conferences, 232, 235
Vidailhet, Jean, 588
Viénot, Pierre, 317–18
Vieira Garin, Vasco, 641
Viet Minh, 25, 378, 396–400, 411, 413, 417, 419–20
Vietnam, 378–80, 388, 393, 396–400, 407, 411, 413, 415–16, 417, 419–20. *See also* Indochina
Vignon, Louis, 293–95, 296, 299, 308, 325, 585
Viollette, Maurice, 289, 306, 318, 326–34, 373
Viollis, André, 311
Vion, Claude, 611
Vischer, Hans, 106
Visman (Visman Commission), and Indonesian autonomy, 494, 634, 635
Vitoria, Francisco de, 81, 308
Vollenhoven, C. van, 268, 338, 339, 363, 492, 634
Vrais chefs de l'empire, Les (Delavignette), 343

Wagemann, Dr., 362
Wallace, Henry A., 485
Ward, Joseph, 50
Warning from the West Indies (Macmillan), 109–12, 165
Watson, A. K., 222, 223, 227–29
Wavell, Lord, 190, 191, 571
Webb, Sidney (*later* Lord Passfield), 115, 116, 117, 118, 119–20, 154–55, 231–32, 553, 560; and affirmation of British Empire, 116; *Memorandum on Native Policy* (1930), 231–32
Wedgwood, Colonel Josiah C., 75, 104, 118–19, 550
Welensky, Roy, 233, 234, 243, 244, 245–46, 247–48; and Rhodesian Federation, 239–40, 244, 245–46, 247–48, 580
Werth, Léon, 311, 596
West Africa, British, 15, 16, 21, 27, 78, 89, 97, 98, 117, 119, 142, 162, 230, 236, 241 (*see also* specific colonies by name); and French West African colonialism compared, 336, 339, 340, 341, 343, 345–46; and Indirect Rule in, 121, 124–41, 142, 143, 148, 162, 165, 212ff.; and Second World War and decolonization, 162, 165, 180, 182, 212–29, 230ff.
West Africa, French, 15, 16, 21, 24, 28, 136–37, 219, 268, 278, 283, 289, 317, 431 (*see also* specific colonies by name); and British colonialism compared (*see under* West Africa, British); *chefferie* system of rule in, 336ff., 427–28; direct administration in, 336–46; and *Loi Cadre*, 427, 433ff.; Second World War and nationalist movements, 359ff., 370ff. (*see also* specific countries, individuals, people)
West Africa, Portugal and. *See* Portugal; specific colonies by name
West African National Conference, 135–36
Westernization (*see also* Industrialization; Urbanization; specific aspects, countries); British colonialism and, 59, 93, 101, 131ff., 134, 138, 139, 140; Dutch in Indonesia and, 489, 490; French colonialism and, 218, 222, 228, 344, 351
Western Sudan, British and, 124
West Indies, British, 15, 78, 80, 89, 94, 101ff., 108–12, 118, 120, 123, 168 (*see also* specific islands by name); and federation, 164, 173; Second World War and decolonization, 161, 164, 167, 173, 177
West Indies (Antilles), French, 272, 278, 284–85
Westminster, Parliament and Statute of, 49, 51, 52, 55, 56
White, Frederick, 632
Whitehead, Edgar, 239, 247–48
"White man's burden": Kerr on British and, 40; Kipling on U.S. and, 474
"White Man's Burden, The" (Kipling), 474
"White man's country," British and partnership in Rhodesian Federation and, 230ff.
"White supremacy," Zimmern on British imperialism and concept of, 34
Wight, Martin, 96
Wigny, Pierre, 507, 508, 637, 638, 639
Wilhelmina, Queen, 494–95
Willemns, Marcel, 620
Willingdon, Lord, 67
Willkie, Wendell L., 23
Wilson, Harold, 569
Wilson, Samuel H., 106, 154
Wilson, Woodrow, 6, 8, 12, 13, 37, 80, 267; anti-colonialism of, 6, 8, 12, 13, 484; and mandates, 80, 267; and Philippines, 476, 477, 484
Wingate, Reginald, 42–43
Winnacker, R. A., 590
Winterton, Lord, 146, 545
Wood, Leonard, 118, 146, 477–78, 482, 632
Woolf, Leonard Sidney, 117, 176, 552, 553, 568
World after the Peace Conference, The (Toynbee), 13
World Wars I and II. *See* First World War; Second World War
Wright, Quincy, 632

Yalta Conference, 23
"Yellow peril," Europe and pre-1914 warnings of, 12
Yorubas (Nigerian tribes), 136
"Young Turk" revolution (Middle East, 1908), 4

Zaghlul, Saad, 42–43, 46
Zanzibar, 248
Zimmern, Alfred, 33–34, 36, 47, 56, 57, 63–64, 85, 165, 166; and India, 33–34; and reforms, 32–34, 36; *Third Empire* by, 33, 57, 85, 166